THE OXFORD HANDBOOK OF

JUDAISM AND ECONOMICS

THE OXFORD HANDBOOK OF

JUDAISM AND ECONOMICS

Edited by

AARON LEVINE

2010

OXFORD
UNIVERSITY PRESS

Oxford University Press, Inc., publishes works that further
Oxford University's objective of excellence
in research, scholarship, and education.

Oxford New York
Auckland Cape Town Dar es Salaam Hong Kong Karachi
Kuala Lumpur Madrid Melbourne Mexico City Nairobi
New Delhi Shanghai Taipei Toronto

With offices in
Argentina Austria Brazil Chile Czech Republic France Greece
Guatemala Hungary Italy Japan Poland Portugal Singapore
South Korea Switzerland Thailand Turkey Ukraine Vietnam

Published by Oxford University Press, Inc.
198 Madison Avenue, New York, New York 10016
www.oup.com
Oxford is a registered trademark of Oxford University Press

Library of Congress Cataloging-in-Publication Data
The Oxford handbook of Judaism and economics / edited by Aaron Levine.
p. cm.
Includes bibliographical references and index.
ISBN 978-0-19-539862-5 (cloth : alk. paper)
1. Economics in the Bible. 2. Money—Biblical teaching. 3. Economics—Religious
aspects—Judaism. 4. Bible. O.T.—Criticism, interpretation, etc. 5. Rabbinical
literature—History and criticism. 6. Jews—Economic conditions.
7. Jewish law. 8. Jewish ethics.
BS1199.E35O94 2010
296.3′83—dc22 2010038237

1 3 5 7 9 8 6 4 2
Printed in the United States of America
on acid-free paper

Contents

Contributors ix

Prologue xix

Acknowledgments xxi

Introduction 3
Aaron Levine

I. Economic Theory in the Bible

1. The Right to Return: The Biblical Law of Theft 29
Eliakim Katz and Jacob Rosenberg

2. Eliezer the Matchmaker: Ethical Considerations and Modern Negotiation Theory 42
Aaron Levine

3. Land Concentration, Efficiency, Slavery, and the Jubilee 74
Jacob Rosenberg and Avi Weiss

II. Economic Theory in the Talmud

4. Risk and Incentives in the *Iska* Contract 91
Jeffrey L. Callen

5. Externalities and Public Goods in the Talmud 107
Ephraim Kleiman

6. An Extended Talmudic Search Model 127
Yehoshua Liebermann

7. Optimal Precautions and the Law of Fire Damages 146
Jacob Rosenberg

8. Valuation in Jewish Law 168
Keith Sharfman

9. Could What You Don't Know Hurt You? Information Asymmetry in Land Markets in Late Antiquity 182
P.V. (Meylekh) Viswanath and Michael Szenberg

III. Jewish Law, Ethics, and the Modern Society

10. Hetter Iska, the Permissible Venture: A Device to Avoid the Prohibition Against Interest-Bearing Loans 197
J. David Bleich

11. Ethical Demands on Creditors in Jewish Tradition 221
Yoel Domb

12. The Jewish Prohibition of Interest: Themes, Scopes, and Contemporary Applications 239
Daniel Z. Feldman

13. Interloping Behavior in the Marketplace in Jewish Law 255
Howard Jachter

14. Principles of Ethical and Communal Investment in Judaism: A Jewish Law Approach 269
Asher Meir

15. The Art of Moral Criticism: Rebuke in the Jewish Tradition and Beyond 295
Moses L. Pava

16. "Know Before Whom You Stand": Trust, the Marketplace, and Judaism 307
Jonas Prager

17. Payment for Organ Donation in Jewish Law 324
Fred Rosner and Edward Reichman

18. The Theory of "Efficient Breach": A Jewish Law Perspective 340
Ronald Warburg

IV. Economic Public Policy and Jewish Law

19. Public and Private International Law From the Perspective of Jewish Law 363
Michael J. Broyde

20. Jewish Environmental Ethics 388
Yehuda L. Klein and Jonathan Weiser

21. The Global Recession of 2007–2009: The Moral Factor and Jewish Law 404
Aaron Levine

22. The Employee Free Choice Act, Unions, and Unionizing in Jewish Law 429
Dani Rapp

23. Rabbinic Responses to Rapid Inflation in Israel, 1973–1985 445
Daniel Schiffman

24. Jewish Ethics, the State, and Economic Freedom 468
Meir Tamari

V. Comparative Law Studies Relating to Economic Issues

25. Economic Substance and the Laws of Interest: A Comparison of Jewish and U.S. Federal Tax Law 479
Adam Chodorow

26. Transfer of Ownership in E-Commerce Transactions from the Perspective of Jewish Law: In Light of Israeli and American Law 499
Ron S. Kleinman and Amal Jabareen

27. The Jewish Guarantor and Secular Law: Stumbling Blocks and Their Removal 523
Roger Lister

VI. Judaism and Economic History

28. Babylonian Jews at the Intersection of the Iranian Economy and Sasanian law 545
Yaakov Elman

29. Coins and Money in Jewish Law and Literature: A Basic Introduction and Selective Survey 564
Laurence J. Rabinovich

30. Economics and Law as Reflected in Hebrew Contracts 584
Yosef Rivlin

31. Talmudic Monetary Theory: Currency in Rabbinic Halakhah 605
Lawrence H. Schiffman

VII. The Economics of Judaism

32. The Economic Progress of American Jewry: From Eighteenth-Century Merchants to Twenty-First-Century Professionals 625
Barry R. Chiswick

33. How Economics Helped Shape American Judaism 646
Carmel Ullman Chiswick

Glossary 663

List of Abbreviations 673

Name Index 675

Subject Index 685

Contributors

J. David Bleich is Herbert and Florence Tenzer Professor of Jewish Law and Ethics at the Cardozo Law School of Yeshiva University. Rabbi Bleich is also Professor of Talmud (Rosh Yeshiva) at Rabbi Isaac Elchanan Theological Seminary, an affiliate of Yeshiva University, and is head of its postgraduate institute for the study of Talmudic jurisprudence and family law. Among his published works are: *Jewish Bioethics; With Perfect Faith: Foundations of Jewish Belief; Contemporary Halakhic Problems* (five volumes); *Time of Death in Jewish Law; Judaism and Healing*; and *Bioethical Dilemmas: A Jewish Perspective* (two volumes), as well as the Hebrew-language *Be-Netivot ha-Halakhah.* He was a Woodrow Wilson Fellow and a postdoctoral fellow at the Hastings Center. He is a fellow of the Academy of Jewish Philosophy and a member of the Governor's Commission on Life and the Law.

Michael J. Broyde is professor of law at Emory University School of Law and the Academic Director of the Law and Religion Program at Emory University. His primary areas of interest are law and religion, Jewish law and ethics, and comparative religious law. Professor Broyde received ordination (*yoreh yoreh v'yadin yadin*) from the Rabbi Isaac Elchanan Theological Seminary, an affiliate of Yeshiva University, and is a member (*dayyan* and *haver*) of the Beth Din of America, the largest Jewish law court in America. He is also the Founding Rabbi of the Young Israel Congregation in Atlanta. Professor Broyde's books include: *the Pursuit of Justice* (Yeshiva University Press); *Human Rights and Judaism* (Aronson Publishing House); and *Marriage, Divorce and the Abandoned Wife in Jewish Law: A Conceptual Understanding of the Aguna Problem in America* (Ktav), and he has written more than 70 articles on matters of Jewish law.

Jeffrey L. Callen is the former Charles I Rosen Chair of Business Administration, the Hebrew University, a former Research Professor of Accounting, New York University, and currently the Joseph L. Rotman Chair of Accounting, University of Toronto. He is also the former editor-in-chief of the *Journal of Accounting, Auditing and Finance.* He has published extensively in economics, finance and accounting journals including the *American Economic Review*, the *Journal of Law and Economics*, the *Journal of Finance*, the *Journal of Financial Economics*, the *Accounting Review*, the *Journal of Accounting Research* and the *History of Political Economy.*

Barry R. Chiswick is Distinguished Professor in the Department of Economics at the University of Illinois at Chicago and Program Director for Migration Studies,

IZA - Institute for the Study of Labor, Bonn, Germany. He received his PhD in Economics with Distinction from Columbia University and an Honorary Ph.D. from Lund University, Sweden. Professor Chiswick received the 2007 Marshall Sklare Award from the Association for the Social Scientific Study of Jewry (ASSJ) and delivered the Sklare Lecture on "The Rise and Fall of the American Jewish PhD." He is a member of the UIC Jewish Studies Committee and serves on the Editorial Board of *Contemporary Jewry.*

Carmel U. Chiswick is Professor Emerita in the Department of Economics at the University of Illinois at Chicago. She received her Ph.D. from Columbia University in the City of New York. In addition to her work on the economics of religion, her research includes studies of household work, family formation, immigration, employment education, and economic development. Professor Chiswick was a longtime member of the UIC Jewish Studies Committee, served on the National Technical Advisory Committee for NJPS 2000/01 (the National Jewish Population Survey), and is currently on the Editorial Board of *Contemporary Jewry.* She is the author of *The Economics of American Judaism* (Routledge 2008), a collection of selected papers from her research on the economics of Judaism.

Adam Chodorow teaches tax law at the Sandra Day O'Connor College of Law at Arizona State University, where he is also a faculty fellow of the Center for the Study of Law, Science and Technology. Professor Chodorow writes on a wide range of tax issues—from the propriety of taxing virtual income to the appropriate way to value businesses for estate tax purposes. Professor Chodorow has also written extensively on Biblical tax systems, exploring the similarities and differences between the U.S. Federal income tax and such systems. In particular, he focuses on the ways in which the culture and context of the different systems help shape the law. His works in this area include: "*Biblical Tax Systems and the Case for Progressive Taxation,*" 23 *Journal of Law & Religion* 53 (2008), "Maaser Kesafim and the Development of Tax Law," 8 *Fla. Tax Review* 153 (2007), and "*Agricultural Tithing and (Flat) Tax Complexity,*" 68 *U. Pitt. L. Rev.* 267 (2006).

Yoel Domb, a graduate of Jerusalem College of Technology's Business School as well as an ordained rabbi of the Israeli Chief Rabbinate, has been teaching Jewish business ethics for the last ten years at the Jerusalem College of Technology, as well as researching the subject at the Jerusalem Center of Business Ethics (BEC) and Keter - The Center for Halacha and Economics. He has published many articles on the subject, some of which are available on the BEC website www.besr.org in addition to working on two books, one addressing the issue of tax evasion in Jewish law and the other relating to ethical aspects of loans. Both books are due for publication in the coming year (in Hebrew). Other articles of his have appeared in English, such as "A Torah Approach to Paying Taxes" and "The Ethics of Grabbing" (*Mishpacha* magazine, 2008).

Yaakov Elman is Professor of Jewish Studies at Yeshiva University, where he teaches courses in Bible and Talmud. He received his M.A. in Assyriology from Columbia University and his Ph.D. in Rabbinic Talmud from New York University. Professor Elman is the author of *Authority and Tradition: Toseftan Braitot in Talmudic Babylonia*; and is the co-editor of *Transmitting Jewish Traditions: Orality, Textuality, and Cultural Diffusion*. Prof. Elman has published widely in the field of *Talmud*, and his research interests include rabbinic theology, unfolding systems of rabbinic legal exegesis, the cultural context of classical rabbinic texts, and Rabbinic and Sasanian intellectual history. He is also an associate of the Harvard Center for Jewish Studies.

Daniel Z. Feldman received ordination (*Yoreh Yoreh v'Yadin Yadin*) from the Rabbi Isaac Elchanan Theological Seminary, an affiliate of Yeshiva University. A former associate of the Bella and Harry Wexner *Kollel Elyon* (post-ordination institute of higher learning), Rabbi Feldman is currently on the staff of Yeshiva University's Stone Beit Midrash Program and serves as Director of Rabbinic Research for Yeshiva University's Center for the Jewish Future. Rabbi Feldman is the rabbi of Etz Chaim of Teaneck, NJ. His area of research is Talmudic and rabbinic law and theory. Rabbi Feldman's major publications include *The Right and the Good: Halakhah and Human Relations* (Jason Aronson, 1999) and *Divine Footsteps: Chesed and the Jewish Soul* (Yeshiva University Press, 2008), as well as three Hebrew volume of Talmudic essays.

Amal Jabareen received his Ph.D. from Bar-Ilan University. He has been a full-time member of Ono Academic College Faculty of Law since 2004. Professor Jabareen's research interest is in intellectual property law, electronic commerce and property law. He has published in these areas. Professor Jabareen is a member of the Israel Bar Association.

Howard Jachter, Rabbinic Judge, Rabbinic Court of Elizabeth, New Jersey, is Professor of Bible and Jewish Law, Torah Academy of Bergen County, New Jersey. He is the author, *Gray Matter*, volumes one, two, and three. He received his B.A. from Yeshiva College, his M.S. from Bernard Revel Graduate School, Yeshiva University, and his Rabbinic Ordination as a Rabbinic Judge (*Yadin Yadin)* from Rabbi Isaac Elchanan Theological Seminary, Yeshiva University. He holds a Certification to Serve as a Jewish Divorce Administrator from Israel's Chief Rabbinate.

Eliakim Katz has a Ph.D. in economics from London University. He is currently professor and former chair of the economics department at Northern Illinois University. He has published over one hundred papers in economics journals, including *American Economic Review, Journal of Political Economy, Journal of Economic Theory, Journal of Public Economics, Economic Journal, European Economic Review, Economica*, and others.

Yehuda L. Klein (A.B., Political Science, Cornell University, 1972; Ph.D., Economics, University of California, Berkeley, 1985) is an associate professor of Economics at Brooklyn College of the City University of New York and the Executive Officer of the Doctoral Program in Earth and Environmental Sciences at the Graduate Center of the City University of New York. His current research projects address issues of urban sustainability, environmental justice and adaptation to climate change. He has published in the Journal of Public Economics, the Atlantic Economic Journal, Southern Economic Journal, Resources and Energy, and Jewish Law.

Ephraim Kleiman is Don Patinkin Emeritus Professor of Economics at the Hebrew University of Jerusalem. He is a graduate of the Hebrew University of Jerusalem and holds a Ph.D. from the London School of Economics. After serving briefly with the Israel Finance Ministry, he joined the Economics Department of the Hebrew University in 1963. A long-time student of the Palestinian economy and of its relationships with Israel, he also served as the senior economic advisor to the Israeli delegation at the Israel-PLO economic negotiations in Paris in 1993–1994. Dr. Kleiman's research interests over the years have included international trade, public finance, and history of economic thought, with special reference to economic thought in the Talmud, as well as the role of wage and financial indexation under inflation. His articles on these and other topics have been published in *The Review of Economic Studies*, *Review of Economics and Statistics*, *The Economic Journal*, *The Quarterly Journal of Economics*, *Kyklos*, and *History of Political Economy*.

Ron S. Kleinman is a senior lecturer at the Ono Academic College Faculty of Law in Israel, where he teaches Jewish Law and Torts. He received his Ph.D. from Bar Ilan University and rabbinical ordination from the Chief Rabbinate in Israel. Dr. Kleinman's research is focused mainly on merchant customs relating to methods of acquisition and customs pertaining to monetary laws, and how these laws pertain to Jewish law and the law of the State. Dr. Kleinman has published numerous articles in refereed academic journals in both Hebrew and English on these topics and on other issues. Dr. Kleinman is chairman of the Israeli Committee of the Jewish Law Association, and a member of the editorial boards of *Health Law and Bioethics* (Hebrew), the Journal of the Center for Health Law and Bioethics, Ono Academic College, and of *Magal* (Hebrew), the Law Review of the Institute for Advanced Torah Studies, Bar Ilan University.

Aaron Levine, editor of this volume, is the Samson and Halina Bitensky Professor of Economics at Yeshiva University. A Phi Beta Kappa at Brooklyn College, he earned his Ph.D. at New York University, and was ordained in Jewish civil and ritual law at the Rabbi Jacob Joseph School and is the spiritual leader of Brooklyn's Young Israel of Ave. J. Professor Levine's research specialty is the interaction between economics and *halakhah*, especially as it relates to public policy and modern business practices. He has published widely on these issues, including five books and numerous monographs. His books include *Free Enterprise and Jewish Law* (1980); *Economics and Jewish Law* (1987); *Economic Public Policy and Jewish Law* (1993); *Case Studies in Jewish Business Ethics* (2000), and *Moral Issues of the Marketplace in Jewish Law* (2005). An associate editor of *Tradition*, Dr. Levine also serves, on an *ad hoc* basis, on the *Bet Din* (rabbinical court) of the Rabbinical Council of America, adjudicating disputes in monetary matters. Dr. Levine is a member of the World Jewish Academy of Science and the recipient of the Irving M. Bunim Prize for Jewish Scholarship. In 1982, he was respondent to Milton Friedman in the Liberty Fund Symposium on the Morality of the Market.

Yehoshua Liebermann is a graduate of Kol-Tora Rabbinical College in Jerusalem and holds a Ph.D. degree from the University of Chicago in Business Administration. He has published numerous scientific articles both in marketing and in economics of Jewish law, in many journals, including *Journal of Marketing*, *Journal of Legal Studies*, and *Journal of Business Ethics*. He is the author of *Business Competition in Jewish Law*, published by Bar-Ilan University Press. Professor Liebermann serves as the Dean of the Undergraduate and Graduate School of Business Administration at Netanya Academic College, Israel. He served formerly as a visiting faculty in the Business Administration Schools of University of Illinois, Chicago Circle, University of Washington in Seattle, and Baruch College, City University of New York.

Roger Lister received his Ph.D. from Oxford University. Currently Professor of Accounting and Finance at the University of Salford, Professor Lister has published more than 60 articles in refereed journals in his field, including a number of articles on Jewish business ethics issues. Professor Lister is a referee for the *Economic Journal*, the *Journal of Business Finance and Accounting*, and *Business History*, and reviews for Blackwell, Holt Rinehart, and Macmillan and ESRC.

Asher Meir received his Ph.D. in Economics from the Massachusetts Institute of Technology and his rabbinical ordination from the Israeli Chief Rabbinate. He is a Senior Lecturer at the Jerusalem College of Technology, and is in charge of the Jewish ethics curriculum in the MBA program at the School. He also serves as Research Director of the Business Ethics Center of Jerusalem. Dr. Meir writes a weekly newspaper column on topics of ethics in business and economics, and a weekly internet column, *The Jewish Ethicist*, examining everyday ethical dilemmas from the standpoint of Jewish tradition. Dr. Meir's books include *The Jewish Ethicist* and *Meaning in Mitzvot*.

Leon M. Metzger, Associate Editor of *Judaism and Economics*, is an adjunct professor and lecturer at Columbia, New York, and Yale Universities, where he teaches alternative investment management courses. He has also taught that course at Cornell and the University of Pennsylvania, and has agreed to teach it at Tel Aviv University. Metzger has also taught economics courses at Yeshiva

University. A *dayyan* (arbitration judge) for the Beth Din of America, expert witness, and consultant on financial services matters, he was associated with Paloma Partners Management Company for 18 years, most recently as its vice chairman and chief administrative officer. Metzger has testified before Congress on capital markets, alternative investments, and operational controls, and has appeared as an expert on valuations and alternative investments before various government agencies. The *New York Times* has profiled his hedge funds course. He holds an MBA from Harvard and a BS in economics from Wharton. Metzger also studied at Kol-Tora Rabbinical College in Jerusalem and Yeshiva R.S.R. Hirsch in New York.

Moses L. Pava is Professor of Accounting and Alvin Einbender Professor of Business Ethics at the Sy Syms School of Business of Yeshiva University, where he has taught for the past 20 years. His research interests include business ethics, the interface between religion and ethics, corporate accountability, and corporate sustainability. He is the author of several books and scores of articles including "*Leading With Meaning: Using Covenantal Leadership to Build Better Organizations.*" He is on the editorial board of *Business Ethics Quarterly* and *Journal of Business Ethics.*

Jonas Prager is an associate professor of economics in the department of economics, faculty of arts and sciences, New York University, New York City. Professor Prager received his Ph.D. from Columbia University in 1964 and his rabbinical ordination from the Rabbi Isaac Elchanan Theological Seminary of Yeshiva University in 5757 (1997). His research interests encompass privatization issues, regulation of financial institutions, and Jewish law. Among his major publications are *Fundamentals of Money, Banking, and Financial Institutions* (1982, 1987) and *Applied Microeconomics: an Intermediate Text* (1993) as well as many scholarly and popular journal articles.

Larry Rabinovich received his law degree from New York University. A partner at the law firm of Schindel, Farman, Lipsius, Gardner & Rabinovich of New York City, his research interest and published scholarship is in the area of economic history as reflected in the *responsa* literature and other Jewish legal writings. Mr. Rabinovich currently serves as Treasurer of the Jewish Law Association.

Dani Rapp is Associate Dean of Undergraduate Jewish Studies and Assistant Professor of Talmud at Yeshiva University. He also serves, on an *ad hoc* basis, on the *Bet Din* (rabbinical court) of the Rabbinical Council of America, adjudicating disputes in monetary matters. Rabbi Rapp received ordination from the Rabbi Isaac Elchanan Theological Seminary, an affiliate of Yeshiva University. He earned his JD from Columbia University's School of Law and is a member of the New York State Bar.

Edward Reichman is Associate Professor of Emergency Medicine and Associate Professor of Philosophy and History of Medicine at the Albert Einstein College of Medicine of Yeshiva University, where he teaches clinical medicine and Jewish medical ethics. He received his rabbinic ordination from the Rabbi Isaac Elchanan Theological Seminary of Yeshiva University and writes and lectures widely in the field of Jewish medical ethics. He is the recipient of a Kornfeld Foundation Fellowship and the Rubinstein Prize in Medical Ethics. He has served on the advisory boards of the New York Organ Donor Network, the Institute for Genetics and Public Policy, and the Halakhic Organ Donor Society. His research is devoted to the interrelationship between medical history and Jewish law.

Yosef Rivlin is Professor of Talmud at Bar-Ilan University. Professor Rivlin has published widely in the areas of Jewish family law; Cairo Geniza legal documents; wills and inheritance; and bills and contracts in Jewish law. The author of five books and more than seventy articles, Professor Rivlin's books include *Jonah* with commentary of Rabbi Elijah of Vilna (Hebrew: *Sefer Yona, Be'ur Ha'gra*), Bnei-Berak, 1986; 1995 (second edition); *Kol Ha'tor* (Hebrew; by R. Hillel Rivlin from Shklov), Bnei-Berak, 1994; *Bills and Contracts from Lucena*, Ramat-Gan, 1995. [Translated into German: *Judentum* 64]; Inheritance *and Wills in Jewish Law*, Ramat-Gan, 1999; and *The Poems of R. Yoshe–Berit Avot Biwsarat Eliyahu*, Jerusalem 2004.

Jacob Rosenberg, former Chair of the Department of Economics at Bar Ilan University and the Rector of the College of Management in Israel, received his D.Sc. in Economics from the Technion, Israel Institute of Technology. His research interests are in the areas of macroeconomics, law and economics, and economics and politics. Professor Rosenberg has published more than fifty articles in refereed journals on these topics. His books include *Introduction to Economics with Examples and Applications from the Israeli Economy* (with S. Eckstein, M. Syrquin, and M. Ungar), Tel-Aviv: University Publications, 1979 (in Hebrew); *Introduction to Macroeconomics,* Tel-Aviv: The Open University, 1980 (in Hebrew), and *Introduction to Macroeconomics, Revised Edition* (with A. Nachmias and G. Ofer), Tel-Aviv: The Open University, 2000 (in Hebrew). Professor Rosenberg was a pioneer in applying the methods and models of economic analysis of law to Jewish law and a significant number of his contributions are in this area.

Fred Rosner, MD, FACP, is director of the Department of Medicine of the Queens Hospital Center in Jamaica, New York, a major teaching campus of New York's Mt. Sinai School of Medicine, where he serves as professor of medicine. He is a Diplomat of the American Board of Internal Medicine and a Fellow of the American College of Physicians. He is also visiting professor of medicine at his alma mater, the Albert Einstein College of Medicine of Yeshiva University. Dr. Rosner is the recipient of the American Medical Association's Isaac Hays, MD and John Bell, MD Award for Leadership in Ethics and Professionalism; the Maimonides Award from the Michael Reese Medical Center and Chicago College of Jewish Studies for

Notable Contributions to the Field of Medicine and Judaica; the Bernard Revel Memorial Award from the Yeshiva College Alumni Association for Distinguished Achievement in the Arts & Sciences; the Maimonides Award of Wisconsin for Distinguished and Extraordinary Service to Learning & Science; a medal from the Ben-Gurion University in Beersheba; and the Lawrence D. Redway Award for Excellence in Medical Writing from the Medical Society of New York. Listed in a number of prestigious Who's Who publications, Dr. Rosner is an international authority and lecturer on medical ethics. He has helped found and serves on a number of bioethics committees; he reviews manuscripts for and serves on the editorial board of a number of professional medical journals. He has published thirty-six books, written chapters by invitation in several dozen books; his bibliography has nearly nine hundred items. He is author of six widely acclaimed books on Jewish medical ethics, including Modern Medicine and Jewish Ethics (Ktav, 1991), Medicine and Jewish Law I and II (Jason Aronson, 1990 and 1993), and Pioneers in Jewish Medical Ethics (Jason Aronson, 1997). Other books include: an English translation of Julius Preuss's classical reference work Biblical and Talmudic Medicine (reprinted in 1993); the Encyclopedia of Medicine in the Bible and the Talmud (Jason Aronson, 1999); and many books on the great Torah authority and physician Moses Maimonides, including a Medical Encyclopedia of Moses Maimonides (Jason Aronson, 1998).

Daniel Schiffman is a lecturer in the Department of Economics and Business Administration at Ariel University Center. He received his B.A. in Economics at New York University, and his M.A. and Ph.D. in Economics at Columbia University. Dr. Schiffman's research interests are history of economic thought and economic history. His publications include "Shattered Rails, Ruined Credit: Financial Fragility and Railroad Operations in the Great Depression" (*Journal of Economic History*, 2003), "The Valuation of Coins in Medieval Jewish Jurisprudence" (*Journal of the History of Economic Thought*, 2005), and "Rabbinical Perspectives on Money in Seventeenth Century Ottoman Egypt" (*European Journal of the History of Economic Thought*, forthcoming 2010).

Lawrence H. Schiffman is Chairman of New York University's Skirball Department of Hebrew and Judaic Studies and serves as Ethel and Irvin A. Edelman Professor of Hebrew and Judaic Studies. He is also a member of the University's Centers for Ancient Studies and Near Eastern Studies. He is a past president of the Association for Jewish Studies. Professor Schiffman received his B.A., M.A., and Ph.D. degrees from the Department of Near Eastern and Judaic Studies at Brandeis University. He is a specialist in the Dead Sea Scrolls, Judaism in Late Antiquity, the history of Jewish law, and Talmudic literature. He served as co-editor-in-chief of the *Oxford Encyclopedia of the Dead Sea Scrolls* (2000). In 1991, he was appointed to the team publishing the scrolls in the Oxford series, *Discoveries in the Judean Desert*. His publications include *The Halakhah at Qumran* (E. J. Brill, 1975); *Sectarian Law in the Dead Sea Scrolls: Courts, Testimony, and the Penal Code* (Scholars Press, 1983);

Who Was a Jew? Rabbinic Perspectives on the Jewish-Christian Schism (Ktav, 1985); *From Text to Tradition: A History of Second Temple and Rabbinic Judaism* (Ktav, 1991); a Hebrew book entitled *Halakhah, Halikhah u-Meshihiyut be-Khat Midbar Yehudah* (Law, Custom, and Messianism in the Dead Sea Sect) (Merkaz Shazar, 1993); the jointly authored monograph, *Hebrew and Aramaic Magical Texts from the Cairo Genizah* (Sheffield, 1992); *Reclaiming the Dead Sea Scrolls* (Jewish Publication Society, 1994; Doubleday paperback, in the Anchor Research Library, 1995);*Texts and Traditions: A Source Reader for the Study of Second Temple and Rabbinic Judaism* (Ktav, 1998); *The Courtyards of the House of the Lord: Studies on the Temple Scroll* (Brill, 2009); and almost 200 articles on the Dead Sea Scrolls and Rabbinic Judaism.

Keith Sharfman is Professor of Law & Associate Director of Bankruptcy Studies at St. John's University School of Law. He has also taught at Cornell Law School and Florida State University College of Law as a visiting professor, and at Marquette University Law School and Rutgers University School of Law as a tenured professor. His teaching and research interests are in antitrust, bankruptcy, contracts, corporate finance, corporate reorganization, Jewish law, law and economics, and legal valuation, and he has published extensively in all of these areas. He also serves as co-advisor to the American Bankruptcy Institute Law Review, as a member of the editorial advisory board of the American Bankruptcy Law Journal, and as Chairman and a member of the executive board of the Association of American Law Schools' Section on Jewish Law.

Michael Szenberg is Distinguished Professor of Economics at the Lubin School of Business, Pace University, Co-editor-in-Chief of the economics series of handbooks by Oxford University Press, and Editor-in-Chief of *The American Economist*. He is author and editor of 13 books including the *Economics of the Israeli Diamond Industry* with an introduction by Milton Friedman, which received the Irving Fisher Monograph Award. He also authored numerous articles and encyclopedia entries.

Meir Tamari, a former Chief Economist in the Office of the Governor of the Bank of Israel and currently an international consultant, has published extensively in the areas of corporate finance, small firms, risk evaluation, and entrepreneurship. His major publication in these areas is *Some International Comparisons of Industrial Financing* (Gloucester, United Kingdom: Technicopy, 1977). A former senior Lecturer in Economics at Bar Ilan University, Tamari pioneered the introduction of a course in Jewish Business Ethics to the curriculum of the University. In 1992, Tamari founded the Center for Business Ethics and Social Responsibility on the campus of the Jerusalem College of Technology. Tamari's major works on Jewish business ethics include: *With All Your Possessions: Jewish Ethics and Economic Life* (Northvale NJ: Jason Aronson, 1987) and *Perspectives on Earning and Spending Money* (Northvale, NJ: Jason Aronson, 1995).

P.V. Viswanath, Professor of Finance at the Lubin School of Business, Pace University in New York, received his Ph.D. from the University of Chicago. He has published numerous articles in the areas of corporate finance and law and economics. Among his more recent publications on the economic aspects of Judaism are "Risk Sharing, Diversification and Moral Hazard in Roman Palestine: Evidence from Agricultural Contract Law," *The International Review of Law and Economics*, November 2000, and (with Prof. Michael Szenberg) "Examining the Biblical Perspective on the Environment in a Costly Contracting Framework," in Carmel Chiswick and Tikva Lehrer (eds.), *Economics of Judaism*, Bar Ilan University Press, 2007.

Ronald Warburg received rabbinic ordination from the Rabbi Isaac Elchanan Theological Seminary (an affiliate of Yeshiva University) and earned his doctorate (SJD) at the Hebrew University Faculty of Law. Widely published in refereed journals in the area of Jewish law, Dr. Warburg is *dayyan* (rabbinical judge) at the Beth Din of America, the largest Jewish law court in America. Dr. Warburg is also a research fellow at the Institute for Jewish Law at the Boston University School of Law and is a member of the editorial boards of *The Jewish Law Annual* and *Tradition*.

Jonathan Weiser (J.D., University of Pennsylvania, 2001; M.A., Education, American University, 1988) is a practicing attorney working in loan markets, high yield investment trading, and related areas. He is the author of *Frumspeak: The First Dictionary of Yeshivish* as well as articles concerning Jewish studies and linguistics in *Ten Daa't*, and *Tradition*. He is currently working on a number of translations as well as on a study of Rashi's use of French.

Avi Weiss earned his Ph.D. from The University of Chicago. He is a faculty member and former chairman of the department of economics at Bar Ilan University, and the former chief economist and deputy general director of the Israel Antitrust Authority. He is Associate Editor of the *Economic Quarterly* and Research Fellow at IZA, Bonn, Germany. He is also a partner in Israel's largest economic consulting firm Giza, Singer and Even Ltd. Professor Weiss' research interests are in the areas of industrial organization, labor and demographic economics, experimental economics and law and economics. Professor Weiss has published more than thirty articles in refereed academic journals in these areas.

PROLOGUE

The Oxford Handbook of Judaism and Economics explores how Judaism as a religion and Jews as a people relate to the economic sphere of life in modern society, and how they did so in past societies.

The intersection of Judaism and economics is multidimensional. To encompass its various aspects, articles for this volume were solicited from the scholarly community that fall into the following areas of study: Jewish Law and Ethics and the Modern Economy; Economic Public Policy and Jewish Law; Comparative Law Studies Relating to Economic Topics; Economic Theory in the Bible and Talmud; Business Ethics and Jewish Law; Judaism and Economic History; and The Economics of Judaism.

Bringing together scholars from such diverse fields as economics, American law, Jewish law, Jewish history, and moral philosophy inevitably entails a clash in styles of writing. To make this volume as cohesive and seamless as possible, a certain degree of uniformity was deemed essential. The uniformity can be found in the way sources are quoted and in the transliteration style.

We recognize that some of the readers of this volume will lack a background in Jewish law. With this in mind the Introduction addresses at length the origin and development of Jewish Law. Treatment of this matter in the Introduction obviates a need for individual authors to provide the necessary background information pertinent for their contributions. Tedious repetition was thus avoided.

Given the interdisciplinary nature of this work, it is recognized that the reader will, at times, desire fuller definitions of terms than what appear in the chapters. The reader should therefore find the Glossary of this work a helpful feature.

Another feature of this work is that each chapter provides a Selected Bibliography. The purpose of the Selected Bibliography is to key in on the most essential sources a future researcher should initially consult with the aim of advancing the research on the particular topic.

Acknowledgments

The Oxford Handbook of Judaism and Economics is the brainchild of Dr. Michael Szenberg, Coeditor of the *Oxford University Press Handbook Series on Economics*. Because economic theory in the *Talmud* is one of his many research interests, Dr. Szenberg proved extremely helpful from the outset in the design of this project. My profound gratitude goes to Dr. Szenberg for his prudent advice on the editorial issues that came up over the project; most of all, however, I am grateful for his enthusiastic encouragement throughout the project.

Putting together *The Oxford Handbook of Judaism and Economics* was a prodigious undertaking. Without very significant assistance, the project would have been beyond reach. I have many to thank.

First, my thanks to my friend Leon M. Metzger. Professor Metzger's expertise in finance and economic issues, his extensive experience as an arbitrator in Jewish courts, and his superior editorial skills were great assets for this project. As associate editor, Professor Metzger put his mark on this volume.

The editorial assistants for this volume, with the exception of Shaul Moshe Seidler-Feller, are all former students of mine at Yeshiva College. Their common denominator is a very strong background in economics and Jewish studies. In scholarship, character, and dedication to the task at hand, this group is representative of Yeshiva College at its best.

David Sidney, chief editorial assistant, has been engaged in this project from its inception. David's primary responsibility was editing and helping in the making of the Glossary. What he actually did was much more. For a number of the chapters, David had penetrating questions and incisive comments for the authors. David's work has brought a number of the ideas presented in this volume to a higher level of precision and organization.

Nathan Hyman assisted in the colossal tasks of copyediting and compiling the indices of this volume. He went considerably beyond these parameters by providing a number of the contributors with suggested improvements in both language and content. When the going got tough, Nathan's alacrity and effusive enthusiasm for the project gave me a much-needed lift.

Daniel Tabak's task was to ensure that the transliterations were put in uniform style. Daniel did much more. He carefully read a number of the chapters and presented the contributors with challenges and calls for clarification.

Shaul Moshe Seidler-Feller was officially involved with transliterations, ensuring uniformity in the presentation of authorities and in sundry stylistic matters. In many ways, Shaul went the "extra mile." He not only completed the task with extradinary speed, but also proved a wizard in spotting missing information and subtle inconsistencies.

Kudos to Uri Westrich for his very capable and meticulous assistance in the preparation of the indices for this book.

A special thanks to my daughter, Aliza, for her editorial suggestions in respect to my own work in this volume. Special thanks also to my son Efraim for his technical assistance.

My thanks to Rabbi Shalom Carmy, Dr. Ephraim Kleiman, Rabbi Dr. Shnayer Z. Leiman and Dr. David Srolovitz for their comments and or advice.

For the past thirty-seven years, I have been employed as a Professor of Economics at Yeshiva University. My profound appreciation to Mr. Richard M. Joel, President of Yeshiva University, for his tireless efforts to create a hospitable environment for scholarship and intellectual growth.

The bulk of the contributions for this volume is aimed at offering direction and even outright prescriptions for marketplace conduct and public policy. These works therefore loosely fall into the branch of Jewish scholarship that is concerned with the application of Jewish law to modern society, popularly called *Mishpat Ivri*—lit. Jewish/Hebrew jurisprudence. The distinctive contribution of the *Mishpat Ivri* chapters of this volume is that economic theory and economic analysis are applied to Jewish law as it relates to modern business practice and public policy. The participation in this volume of scholars of international repute is eloquent testimony that this field and related fields are vibrant academic research areas.

Thirty-seven years ago, when I first began my research into the interface of economics and Jewish law, the application of Jewish law to modern society through the lens of economic analysis and economic theory was a relatively virgin area of research, with few practitioners.[1] My gratitude therefore only increases over time to Rabbi Dr. Norman Lamm, former President and now Chancellor of Yeshiva University and Rosh Yeshiva of Yeshiva's affiliate, the Rabbi Isaac Elchanan Theological Seminary (RIETS), who encouraged my work greatly in those early years. Over the span of twenty years from 1980 to 2000, I published four books in Rabbi Lamm's series, *The Jewish Library of Law and Ethics.*

My debt of gratitude to the Provost of Yeshiva University, Dr. Morton Lowengrub, for the stipend he arranged for the initial stage of this project.

The Oxford Handbook of Judaism and Economics has benefited greatly from the professionalism of the Oxford University Press staff. My gratitude to the

1 In this early period researchers in the field of Economics and the Talmud included Robert Aumann, Barry Gordon, Zvi Ilani, Ephraim Kleiman, Yehoshua Liebermann, Roman A. Ohrenstein, Jacob Rosenberg, Aharon Shapiro, and Meir Tamari.

people who have shepherded this project through the publication process: Executive Editor, Terry Vaughn, Associate Editor, Joe Jackson, Lisa Stallings, Academic Team Leader, and Copy Editor Susan Dodson.

Aaron Levine
Samson and Halina Bitensky
Professor of Economics
Yeshiva University
New York, April 23, 2010

THE OXFORD HANDBOOK OF

JUDAISM AND ECONOMICS

INTRODUCTION

AARON LEVINE

Judaism and Economics explores how Judaism, as a religion, and Jews, as a people, relate to the economic sphere of life in modern society and how they did so in past societies.

Before elaborating on the themes of this volume, some preliminary remarks regarding Jewish law and its development over time are in order.

The Sources of Jewish Law

The sources of Jewish law begin with the *Pentateuch* (i.e., the Five Books of Moses), which, according to Orthodox Jewish tradition, was revealed by G-d to Moses at Mount Sinai (c. 1312 BCE).[1]

The authoritative literary sources dating from after the *Pentateuch* to the beginning of the second Temple period (fifth century BCE) are the Prophets (*Nevi'im*) and the Hagiographia (*Ketuvim*). Since the authors of these books were not primarily concerned with legal matters, the paucity of legal material in these works is not surprising. Nonetheless, the Prophets and Hagiographia provide a basis for various laws and legal institutions not mentioned in the *Pentateuch*.[2]

1 Pinchas Wollman-Tsamir, ed., *The Graphic History of the Jewish Heritage* (New York: Shengold Publishing Inc., 1963), 184. Mattis Cantor *The Jewish Time Line Encyclopedia*, (Northvale New Jersey: Jason Aronson, 1989), p. XIII gives the date for the Sinaic Revelation as 1313 BCE.

2 Menachem Elon, *Jewish Law, History, Sources and Principles, Ha-Mishpat Ha-Ivri*, volume III (Philadelphia: The Jewish Publication Society, 1994), 1,021.

According to Orthodox Jewish tradition, when G-d revealed the *Pentateuch* to Moses at Sinai, He concomitantly revealed to him the Oral *Torah*, which provided a detailed interpretation of the commandments found in the *Pentateuch*. For many centuries, the Oral *Torah* was not committed to writing, but instead it was kept alive by oral transmission from one generation to the next.[3]

Mishnah and the Babylonian and Jerusalem *Talmuds*

Out of fear that the oral tradition would be forgotten, the Oral *Torah* was eventually reduced to writing. This process occurred in two stages: the codification of the *Mishnah,* which took place in the land of Israel (beginning third century CE),[4] and the codification of the *Talmud*, which took place in both Israel (400 CE)[5] and Babylonia (sixth to seventh century CE).[6]

The laws of the *Mishnah* are mostly presented in the form of factual cases rather than through simple statements of the legal principles in abstract form. The authorities cited in the *Mishnah* are designated *tannaim* (from the Aramaic *tenai*—to hand down orally, "study," or "teach").[7]

The basic structure of the Babylonian *Talmud* and the Jerusalem *Talmud* is a commentary on the *Mishnah.* Both *Talmuds*, however, go considerably beyond this description. In that regard, both *Talmuds* include and discuss *Tannaic* sources that were not incorporated in the *Mishnah.* These sources are called *Baraitot.* In addition, the teachings of authorities, called *amoraim* (lit., interpreters), who lived beyond the *Tannaic* period, are discussed. For the Babylonian *Talmud*, these are the teachings of the generations of the third through fifth centuries.[8] For the Jerusalem *Talmud*, the teachings include those of the first three generations of the Babylonian *amoraim* and the five generations of *amoraim* who lived in Palestine. In addition, both *Talmuds* include *aggadic* material, which is biblical exegesis of specific books of the Bible.[9] In terms of literary form, the distinctive feature of both *Talmuds* is dialectic discussion in

3 TB *Berakhot* 5a; TB *Megillah* 19b; Exodus Rabbah 47:1.

4 Stephan G. Wald, "*Mishnah*," Michael Berenbaum and Fred Skolnik, eds., *Encyclopedia Judaica,* vol.14, 2nd ed. (Detroit: Macmillan reference, 2007), 319.

5 Ibid.

6 Stephen G. Wald cites evidence that the redaction of *Talmud Bavli* was an ongoing process that took place over many centuries and in many yeshivot, both prior and subsequent to the time of R. Ashi (d. 427 CE). See Stephen G. Wald, "*Talmud*, Babylonian," *Encyclopedia Judaica*, op. cit., vol. 19, 475.

7 Stephan G. Wald, "*Mishnah*," op. cit., 319.

8 Stephen G. Wald, "*Talmud*, Babylonian," *Encyclopedia Judaica*, op. cit., vol. 19, 470.

9 Louis Isaac Rabinowitz and Stephen G. Wald, "*Talmud* Jerusalem," *Encyclopedia Judaica*, op. cit., vol. 19, 483.

which various *tannaic* and *amoraic* sources are analyzed to elucidate some point of law.[10]

Savoraim

The immediate post-Talmudic period from 500 through 650 CE was called the era of the *savoraim* (lit., the "reasoners"). The preoccupation of the rabbis in this period was completing the redaction of the Babylonian *Talmud* and determining rules for decision in Jewish law.[11]

Geonim

In the next period, called the era of the *geonim* (lit., the "prides" or "geniuses"), religious Jewish life centered around the Babylonian academies of Sura and Pumbedita. Spanning from 650 through 1250 CE, the heads of the academies of Sura and Pumbedita had strong ties with the Jewish communities that had developed in Spain, Portugal, and North Africa.[12] These communities are typically referred to as the Sephardic communities.[13]

Driven by government persecution, Jews in the Geonic time steadily abandoned cultivation of the land and turned toward commerce and the trades. To address the new realities of everyday life, the new economic order proved a catalyst for the *Geonim* to enact innovative ordinances, called *takkanot*.[14]

The middle of the Geonic period corresponded with the early development of Jewish communities in the Rhine valley, typically called Ashkenaz. In this regard, a nascent Jewish community in Mainz can be identified in the middle of the tenth century.[15] Likewise, the existence of a Jewish community in Worms can be identified at the end of the tenth century.[16] Moreover, documentation of the existence of a Jewish community in Speyer in as early as 1084 is evident.[17] The three cities of

10 "*Talmud* Babylonian," op. cit., 470; "*Talmud* Jerusalem," op. cit., 483. For an extensive comparison between the two *Talmuds*, see "*Talmud* Jerusalem," op. cit., 483.

11 Menachem Elon, "*Mishpat Ivri*," *Encyclopedia Judaica*, op. cit., vol. 14, 340.

12 Ibid.

13 Alan D. Corre, Ezer Kahanov, Cecil Roth, Hyman Joseph Campeas, and Yitzhak Kerem, "Sephardim," Encyclopedia Judaica, op. cit., vol. 18, 293.

14 Menachem Elon, "*Takkanot*," *Encyclopedia Judaica*, op. cit., vol. 18, 446.

15 Bernard Dov Sucher Weinryb and Larissa Daemming, "Mainz," *Encyclopedia Judaica*, op. cit., vol. 13, 403.

16 Zvi Avneri, "Worms," *Encyclopedia Judaica*, op. cit., vol. 21, 226.

17 B. Mordechai Ansbacher and Larissa Daemming, "Speyer," *Encyclopedia Judaica*, op. cit., vol. 19, 100.

Mainz, Worms, and Speyer became closely aligned, organized synods, and enacted *takkanot* that were binding on the inhabitants of all three cities.[18]

The most famous of the early Ashkenazi authorities on Jewish law was R. Gershom b. Judah Me'or ha-Golah (Mainz, c. 960–1028). R. Gershom's name is connected with many ancient *takkanot*, most famous of which are his bans against bigamy and the unauthorized reading of private letters.[19]

In the Geonic period, works that distilled Talmudic discussions into practical rulings began to appear. The first work that had a semblance of a codification work was *Sefer ha-She'iltot*, authored by Rav Ahai (Babylonia, first half of the eighth century). The work was arranged according to the weekly portions of the *Pentateuch*. The narrative of a particular portion served as a springboard to discuss the subject matter from the standpoint of *halakhah* (Jewish law). Another early work of this genre, authored at about the same time, was *Halakhot Pesukot* by R. Yehudah b. Nahman Gaon. This work was arranged by subject matter and provided rulings along with a synopsis of the Talmudic sources on which the rulings were based.[20]

At the close of this period, Babylonia ceased to be the dominant center of the Jewish Diaspora. The Jewish communities in North Africa and Europe developed into the new centers of Jewish life.[21]

Rishonim

The next period, called the era of the *rishonim*, spanned from the middle of the eleventh century until the sixteenth century. In this period, three forms of post-Talmudic literary sources flourished. One form was basic commentary on the *Talmud*, without which the *Talmud* would be understandable only to the intellectual elite. Standing out in this regard was the commentary of R. Solomon b. Isaac (*Rashi*, France, 1040–1105) and the novellae of Tosafot (twelfth- through fourteenth-century French commentators). In the area of codification of law, the codes of R. Isaac b. Jacob Alfasi (*Rif*, Algeria, 1012–1103), Maimonides (*Mishneh Torah*, Egypt, 1135–1204), R. Asher b. Jehiel (*Rosh*, Germany, 1250–1327), and R. Jacob b. Asher (Spain, 1270–1340) were exemplary.

Another literary form that flourished in this era was the *responsa* literature. It consisted of the answers that the great authorities in both Sephardic and Ashkenazic countries gave to specific questions in Jewish law that were directed to them. A sampling of the Sephardic authorities were the *responsa Rashba*, authored by R. Solomon b. Abraham Adret (Spain, c. 1235–1310), and the *responsa Ribash*,

18 Alexander Shapiro and B. Mordechai Ansbacher, "Shum," *Encyclopedia Judaica*, op. cit., vol. 18, 532.

19 Shlomo Eidelberg and David Derovan, "Gershon Ben Judah Me'or Ha-Golah," *Encyclopedia Judaica*, op. cit., vol. 7, 551.

20 Menachem Elon, "Codification of Law," *Encyclopedia Judaica*, op. cit., vol. 14, 769.

21 Ibid., 770.

written by R. Isaac b. Sheshet Perfet (Spain, 1325–1408). Representative of the Ashkenazic authorities were the *responsa* of *Maharam of Rothenburg*, authored by R. Meir b. Barukh (Germany, 1215–1293); the *responsa Rosh*, composed by R. Asher b. Jehiel; and the *responsa Maharik*, authored by R. Joseph b. Solomon Colon (Italy, c. 1420–1480).

From this period, there have also come down numerous collections of communal enactments, such as *Pinkas Va'ad Arba Arazot*, *Pinkas Medinat Lita*, and *Takkanot Mehrin*.[22]

Aharonim

The next period of development of Jewish law was the era of the *aharonim* (lit., the later scholars). While scholars differ on when this period begins, the general consensus is that it begins with the appearance of *Shulhan Arukh* by R. Joseph Caro (Ottoman Palestine, 1488–1575) and annotations to the *Shulhan Arukh*, *ha-Mappah*, which is popularly called the *Rema*, by R. Moses Isserles (Poland, 1525 or 1530–1572).[23] In his codification of Jewish law, R. Caro drew heavily on Sephardic authorities, while the *Rema* generally followed the Ashkenazic authorities.[24]

Much of the early work in the *aharonim* period entailed commentary on various parts of the *Shulhan Arukh* and *Rema*. The analyses of these authors often led them to formulate specific rulings. Examples of works of this genre include *Sefer Meirat Einayim* (*Sema*) by R. Joshua b. Alexander ha-Kohen Falk (Poland, 1565–1614), *Siftei Kohen* by R. Shabbetai b. Meir ha-Kohen (Poland, 1621–1662), and *Beit Hillel* to *Shulhan Arukh Yoreh De'ah* and *Even ha-Ezer* by R. Hillel b. Naphtali ha-Levi (Lithuania, 1615–1690).

The period of the *Aharonim* continues to the present day. Throughout this period, *aharonim*, through the medium of *responsa*, have dealt with everyday issues encompassing every sphere of life.[25]

Jewish Law in the State of Israel

When the State of Israel was established in 1948, Jewish law was officially incorporated only in the area of personal status. In a 1953 law, the legislature of the State, the *Knesset*, gave Jewish law exclusive jurisdiction in matters of marriage and divorce.

22 Menachem Elon, "Mishpat Ivri," *Encyclopedia Judaica*, op. cit., 340.
23 Ibid., 340.
24 Menachem Elon, "Codification of Law," op. cit., 770.
25 Menachem Elon, "Mishpat Ivri," op. cit., 340.

In 1950, the Knesset passed the Law of Return. This law granted every Jew the right to come to Israel and automatically become an Israeli citizen upon his or her arrival. An amendment to this law, passed in 1970, defined a Jew for purposes of this law as a person who is considered a Jew under Jewish law.

In a number of matters pertaining to public policy, Israeli law incorporates Jewish law. For example, Israeli law requires that soldiers be provided with kosher food. In addition, a 1962 law prohibits the raising, keeping, or slaughtering of pigs (except in specified areas populated mainly by non-Jews) in Israel.

In the area of civil law, the *Knesset*, in 1952, designated Jewish law as the "main but not the only or binding source for legislation." Several examples of early legislation in the history of the State where civil law is based on Jewish law are the prohibition of delay in the payment of wages and the right of a dismissed employee to severance pay.

In 1979, the Unjust Enrichment Act drew its principles and concepts from Jewish law. In a similar vein, legislation enacted in 1981 established that an offender must be assisted to return to the proper path and not reminded of his criminal past.

Jewish law made further inroads in civil law with the enactment of the Foundations of Law Act of 1980. That law provided that, when the court finds no answer to a legal question under statutory law or case law, or by analogy, it shall decide the issue "in the light of the principles of freedom, justice, equity, and peace of the Jewish heritage." Differing opinions among Israeli jurists about the meaning of this phrase has effectively made it impossible for the court system to apply Jewish law in a blanket manner whenever there are "lacunae" in reaching a decision.

One further inroad was made in 1992 when legislation required the Jewish State to turn to Jewish law as the framework to protect human dignity and freedom.

To be sure, the *Knesset* has enacted legislation in the area of civil law that is contrary to Jewish law. One example of this is the right of a creditor to turn directly to the surety even without initial agreement to this effect.

Finally, in the deliberations of Israeli courts, particularly the Supreme Court, Jewish law has its influence but in no way plays a decisive role in deciding cases.[26]

Subject Matter of Judaism and Economics

The major theme of this volume is to what extent Jewish law accommodates and even enhances commercial practice today and in societies of the past. One aspect of this work is to show the positive contribution Jewish law makes to business ethics and economic public policy. Another facet is to identify the degree to which Jewish

26 Ibid., 354–56.

law accepts and adapts business practices based on the prevailing laws and customs of secular society.

Finally, this work investigates the degree to which Jews as a people have successfully integrated into American economic life, and the related question of how economic forces have played a role in causing the American Jew to assimilate, shedding religious practice and commitment.

Jewish Business Ethics—for Whom?

Many of the chapters of this volume deal with Jewish business ethics and economic public policy. The substance of these chapters describe rules for integrity and prescriptions against hurtful conduct. These rules apply to the Jew in his dealings with Jew and non-Jew alike. To elaborate:

First, according to the principle of *dina d'malkhuta dina* (lit., the law of the kingdom is law),[27] Jews are bound by secular laws relating to social welfare and the marketplace. The binding nature of secular law in these maters applies to interactions with both Jews and non-Jews. Generally, Jewish and secular laws governing such matters as pollution control, workplace safety, and animal welfare are the same. In some instances, however, secular governmental regulation may even extend beyond what Jewish law requires, (e.g., the minimum-wage law).

The application of *dina d'malkhuta dina*, according to R. Joseph Eliyahu Henkin (New York, 1881–1973), has changed over time. In the middle ages, secular governments gave Jews autonomy in matters of civil law. Under this license, Jews established a communal organization, called *kehilah*, and enacted legislation (*takkanot ha-kahal*—lit., ordinances of the community) and penalties for violators. The legal import of *dina d'malkhuta dina* was no more than to conduct oneself as a good citizen vis-à-vis civil laws and regulations of the government. In more-recent times, however, in the absence of the *kehilah* organization, *dina d'malkhuta* may assume the legal character of *takkanot ha-kahal* themselves. Specifically, in democracies where various governmental entities either legislate or have regulatory authority, Jews, who have a say in these matters, effectively cede their *takkanot ha-kahal* function to these governmental bodies. When civil law assumes *takkanot ha-kahal* status, civil law prevails, according to R. Henkin, even when the statute involved varies from Jewish law's position on the matter at hand. Accordingly, as the venue of initial jurisdiction for disputes between Jews, the Jewish court (*Bet Din*) must consider the relevant civil law statute before rendering its decision.[28]

27 Samuel, *Gittin* 10b. The preponderant opinion among halakhic authorities is that *dina d'malkhuta dina* has the force of biblical law. Cf. R. Avraham Duber Kahana Shapira (Poland, 1870–1943), *Devar Avraham* 1:1. A minority position is taken by R. Shemu'el b. Uri Shraga Phoebus (Poland, 1650–1705). In his view, *dina d'malkhuta* operates on the force of rabbinical law (*Beit Shemu'el, Even ha-Ezer* 28, note 3).

28 R. Joseph Eliyahu Henkin, *Kitvei ha-Grye Henkin*, vol. 2, 175–76; *Teshuvot Ivra*, no. 96, sec. 1(4).

The extent of *dina d'malkhuta dina* in commercial relations between Jews and non-Jews is indicated by the fact that the sole jurisdiction in disputes is the secular court.[29] This is in sharp contrast to the procedural rules for adjudicating disputes between Jews, where the venue of original jurisdiction is always the Jewish court. Specifically, neither party is permitted to move the case to secular court unless the Jewish court determines that the special circumstances of the case warrant such a move.[30]

For the ethical person, *dina d'malkhuta* is not just a set of rules and consequences one first discovers in the face of litigation. Instead, these are rules of conduct one must learn *before* interacting with both Jew and non-Jew in the marketplace. Moreover, the ethical person will not exploit the legal system by refusing to satisfy a just and rightful claim until a court, whether Jewish or secular, orders him or her to do so.

Second, while there is substantial overlap between Jewish and secular law in the prohibition of dishonest conduct of various sorts, Jewish law is more expansive. Examples of such expansiveness include Jewish law's notion of "fair competition,"[31] its prohibition against generating false goodwill,[32] and its parameters for permissible whistle blowing.[33] Jewish law prohibits not merely dishonest conduct; it imposes numerous prohibitions against causing someone needless mental anguish (*ona'at devarim*).[34] The question thus becomes whether the Jew's duty to the non-Jew encompasses a moral code beyond the strict requirements of *dina d'malkhuta*. The work of R. Zevi Hirsch Ashkenazi (*Hakham Tzevi*, Germany, 1660–1718) is relevant in this regard. In a diatribe against those claiming that the *Torah*'s prohibitions of dishonest behavior govern only transactions among Jews, R. Ashkenazi advances a powerful argument for nondiscrimination.

Preliminarily, he notes that by dint of *Torah* law, theft (*geneivah*) is prohibited even when the motive of the perpetrator is salutary. Consider the following examples: Suppose thief *T* intends to return his pilferage to the rightful owner and carries out the caper only to teach intended victim *V* to guard his property more carefully. Alternatively, suppose *T* desires to give *V* a gift, but *V* demurs, and so, as a means of accomplishing his objective, *T* steals an item from *V* and makes sure that two witnesses catch him red-handed in the act. The two witnesses will predictably come forward and implicate *T* in the crime. *T* will now finally get his wish to give *V* a gift, as the Jewish court will order *T* to pay *V* the "double indemnity" (*kefel*) payment imposed on a thief.

Salutary motives notwithstanding, the action of the thief in both of these cases is prohibited. R. Ashkenazi concludes that theft is *inherently* an abhorrent act.

29 R. Moses Isserles (Poland, 1525 or 1530–1572), *Rema, Shulhan Arukh, Hoshen Mishpat* 369:11; R. Abraham Isaiah Karelitz (Israel, 1878–1953), *Hazon Ish, Bava Kamma* 10:9, *Likkutim* 16:1.

30 R. Solomon b. Isaac (France, 1040–1105), *Rashi* at Exodus 21:1.

31 For a discussion of this issue from the standpoint of Jewish law, see Aaron Levine, *Moral Issues of the Marketplace in Jewish Law* (New York: Yashar Books, 2005), 93–195.

32 For a discussion of this issue, see *Moral Issues of the Marketplace in Jewish Law*, op. cit., 3–43.

33 For a discussion of this issue, see *Moral Issues of the Marketplace in Jewish Law*, op. cit., 423–83.

34 Leviticus 25:17.

Dishonest conduct sullies the character of the perpetrator and tarnishes his or her soul; hence, dishonest conduct directed at any human being is prohibited, no matter who the victim is.[35] R. Joseph b. Moses Babad (Poland, 1800–1872) writes in the same vein.[36] R. Ashkenazi observes, moreover, that Jews risk a more serious sin when they deal dishonestly with non-Jews than with Jews because, if the non-Jewish victim learns that the perpetrator is Jewish, the offender compounds the sin of theft with the additional offense of disgracing G-d's name (*hilul ha-Shem*). If the victim is Jewish, by contrast, the perpetrator does not commit *hilul ha-Shem.*[37] This distinction is explained by R. Bahya b. Asher (Saragossa, thirteenth century) as follows: If the victim is a gentile, the discovery that the perpetrator is a Jew may incite the non-Jewish victim to disgrace the Jewish religion and brand it a false belief system. When the victim is a Jew, however, discovery that the perpetrator is a fellow Jew presumably does not move the offended party to rail against his own religion as false.[38]

Hakham Tzevi's analysis has much import for the modern marketplace. Jewish law's prohibition of robbery and theft forbids far more than the readily recognizable violations of these transgressions. For instance, the use of leverage to change the terms of a completed deal unilaterally is considered extortion even if the disadvantaged party raises no protest because the change is effected through intimidation.[39] The use of unlawful sales pressure to effect a deal violates the prohibitions of *lo tit'avveh* (do not desire) and *lo tahmod*[40] (do not covet).[41] Misrepresentation (*geneivat da'at*) falls under either the prohibition against falsehood or that against theft.[42] It follows from *Hakham Tzevi*'s latter argument that prohibited dishonesty in relations with non-Jews extends beyond the dictates of *dina d'malkhuta dina* and encompasses the entire gamut of behavior the *Torah* labels dishonest conduct.

Moreover, *Hakham Tzevi*'s basic notion that dishonest behavior debilitates character suggests the wider application of *Torah* prohibitions relating to hurtful, though not technically dishonest, conduct. Representative of this category are the prohibitions against causing needless mental anguish (*ona'at devarim*) and against

35 R. Tzevi Hirsch Ashkenazi, *Hakham Tzevi* 26.

36 R. Joseph b. Moses Babad (Poland, 1800–1872), *Minhat Hinnukh, Mitzvah* 224. The notion that the *Torah* prohibits bad conduct not just on account of the hurtful effect it has on the victim, but also because it sullies the character of the perpetrator, finds expression in the work of Maimonides (*Sefer ha-Mitsvot* 317). Maimonides espouses this principle in connection with the prohibition, "You shall not curse a deaf person. . . ." (Leviticus 19:14). Although the deaf person will not hear the curses, this conduct fosters the character traits of revenge and anger in the perpetrator.

37 *Hakham Tzevi*, op. cit.

38 R. Bahya b. Asher, *Rabbenu Bahya al-ha-Torah*, Leviticus 25:50.

39 For explication of the various violations that may be involved in exercising leverage in commercial and other settings, see *Moral Issues of the Marketplace in Jewish Law*, op. cit., 175–200.

40 Deuteronomy 5:18.

41 Exodus 20:14. For explication of these prohibitions, see *Moral Issues of the Marketplace in Jewish Law*, op. cit., 189–91, 234–44.

42 For sources on the prohibition of *geneivat da'at*, see *Moral Issues of the Marketplace in Jewish Law*, op. cit., 8–9, 266 n. 26.

delivering a true but damaging report about someone (*lashon ha-ra*).[43] In its formulation of these duties of character, the *Torah* describes the target of the hurtful conduct as *ahiv* (his brother) and *amekhah* (your people), respectively. These expressions seem to indicate that the duties apply only in interactions with fellow Jews. Yet, since ill-intentioned, hurtful conduct surely debilitates character, it should be prohibited, at least on a hortatory level, irrespective of the target of the mistreatment.

Third, in the view of the medieval exegete, R. Menahem b. Solomon *Meiri* (*Meiri*, France, c. 1249–1306), Jew-and-non-Jew equality in Jewish law extends considerably beyond the parameters set out by R. Ashkenazi. *Meiri* categorizes all non-Jews who observe the seven Noahide laws[44] as people "disciplined in the ways of religion and civilization," who, as such, have a certain fraternity with the Jewish community. *Meiri* deems such people qualifying beneficiaries of deeds of kindness mandated seemingly only for fellow Jews. A case in point is the duty of a passerby to restore a lost article to its rightful owner (*hashavat aveidah*). Although the *Torah* formulates this obligation as a duty owed "your brother" (*ahikha*),[45] *Meiri* includes a non-Jew "disciplined in the ways of religion and civilization" as a beneficiary of this mandate. *Meiri* rules analogously regarding an income transfer P_1 realizes from P_2 that was not required under the terms of their commercial transaction. In realizing this "windfall," P_1 was not guilty of affirmative deception. Instead, P_1's "windfall" came about because of P_2's error (*ta'ut*). Suppose further that P_1 adjured P_2 to "carefully look into this transaction because I'm relying upon you." If P_2 is an idolater, P_1 may, as a strict matter of law, keep the "windfall." In the opinion of *Meiri*, the error must be rectified, and the "windfall" returned when P_2 is a gentile but not an idolater.[46]

The nineteenth-century halakhic authority, R. Tzevi Chajes (Poland, 1805–1855), quotes *Meiri*'s attitude toward non-Jews approvingly. Both the Christian and Muslim governments of his time, R. Chajes tells us, strenuously enforced the Noahide laws.[47]

43 Leviticus 19:15.

44 The seven Noahide laws consist of six prohibitions and one positive command. The six prohibitions are: (1) murder, (2) incest, (3) robbery, (4) eating the flesh of animals taken from the animal while it was still alive, (5) idolatry, and (6) blasphemy (Maimonides, *Mishneh Torah, Melakhim* 9:1). The seventh law is a matter of dispute. In the opinion of Maimonides, it consists of a duty to set up an administration of justice to enforce the other six laws (*Mishneh Torah*, op. cit., 9:14). Nahmanides (Spain, 1194–1270, *Ramban*, Genesis 34:13), however, expands the ambit of the seventh commandment to include the setting up of civil law and a penal code modeled after the laws of the *Torah* in these matters.

45 "You may not observe your *brother's* ox or his sheep lost and conceal yourself from them; you must surely return them to your *brother*" (Deuteronomy 22:1).

46 R. Menahem b. Solomon *Meiri*, *Beit ha-Behirah*, *Bava Kamma* 113b. For the type of social barrier the rabbis continued to maintain between the Jew and the non-Jew, who is "disciplined in the ways of religion and civilization," see *Beit Behirah*, *Hullin* 13b, B *Avodah Zarah* 6a.

47 R. Tzevi Chajes, *Kol Sifrei Maharats Hayyot*, *Tiferet L'Yisrael*, op. cit., 489—91. *Meiri*'s view has been subject to much discussion and analysis in the scholarly literature. Cf. Mosheh Halbertal, "*Bein Torah Le-Hohkhmah*," (Jerusalem: Hebrew University Magnes Press, 2000), 80–109; Y. Blidstein, "*Meiri*'s Attitude to Gentiles: Between Apologetics and Internalization" (Heb.), *Zion* 51 (1986): 153–66; J. Katz, "More on the Religious Tolerance of *Meiri*" (Heb.), *Zion* 46 (1961): 243–46; E. E. Urbach, "The Origins and Limitations of Tolerance in *Meiri*" (Heb.), in *Jacob Katz Jubilee Volume* (Jerusalem, 1960), 34–44; J. Katz, "Exclusiveness and Tolerance" (Oxford: Oxford University Press, 1986), 185–202.

If a non-Jew "disciplined in the ways of religion and civilization" qualifies as a beneficiary of supererogatory ethical conduct, afflicting this person with hurtful conduct is certainly morally repugnant. According to *Meiri*, the examples of *hashavat aveidah* and the case of *ta'ut* illustrate the general rule that all policies in the workforce and marketplace must apply uniformly to Jews and non-Jews.

Meiri's embracing attitude toward the gentile does not amount to advocacy of equal treatment of Jew and non-Jew. In prohibiting interest payments on a loan, the *Torah* states: "You may not pay interest to your brother—interest on money, interest on food, interest on any matter where it is paid. You may *tashikh* [take][48] from a stranger, but from your brother do not take interest" (Deuteronomy 23:20–21). *Meiri* understands that these verses differentiate between a Jewish and non-Jewish debtor. Given the fraternity *Meiri* saw between the Jews and the gentiles of his time, we would have expected him to say that interest should no longer be charged to gentiles; but he does not. In addition, he states that, in lending money, priority must be given to a Jewish borrower over a non-Jewish borrower. *Meiri*, however, retaining his generally favorable disposition toward gentiles, derives from the phrase, "you *may take* from a stranger," that the non-Jew's livelihood should be our concern: If he requests a loan, although we are not obliged to extend it interest-free, we should at least lend to him on interest, and not turn him away.[49] *Meiri* believes that the fully developed character trait of kindness is manifested partly in the bestowal of kindnesses upon gentiles, but that a higher level of kindness is still due to our own brethren.[50]

Fourth, the Jew's duty to the non-Jew in interpersonal relations is further extended beyond the dictates of *dina d'malkhuta dina* by the principle of *kiddush ha-Shem* (i.e., the duty to sanctify G-d's name). The application of this principle is illustrated by the following story involving R. Shimon b. Shetah (first century BCE):

48 *Meiri*'s interpretation of Deuteronomy 23:21 follows *Sifrei*, which interprets *tashikh* to be the active form (*kal*) of the verb, and, therefore, to mean *take*. Although understanding verse 21 differently than *Meiri*, *Maimonides* (*Mishneh Torah, Malveh* 5:1) also understands the word *tashikh* in that verse to mean take. *Bava Metsi'a* 70b, however, interprets *tashikh* as the causative form (*hiphil*) (i.e. to cause to take and therefore *to pay*). In this interpretation, the entire intent of the verse is just to make us draw an inference: that it is only permissible to cause a non-Jew to pay interest on a loan; however, it is forbidden to cause a Jew to pay interest on a loan. The verse heaps another transgression on top of that already spelled out in verse 20.

49 R. Menahem b. Solomon *Meiri*, *Beit ha-Behirah, Bava Metsi'a* 71a. See, however, Maimonides' interpretation of this verse (*Mishneh Torah, Malveh* 5:1).

50 Another rationale for the differential treatment of Jew and non-Jew in connection with *ribbit* proceeds from the work of Professor Michael Broyde and Rabbi Michael Hecht

In their treatment of the exemption Jewish law calls for in the duty to return lost property when the owner of the property is presumably a gentile, Professor Michael Broyde and Rabbi Michael Hecht invoke the reciprocity principle. This principle states that in a society where the secular law requires one to return lost property, irrespective of whom the owner might be, Jewish law would require this as well. What compels this conduct is the principle of *dina d'malkhuta dina*, discussed earlier. But, if secular law has no such requirement, Jews need not return lost property they find when the owner is presumably a non-Jew. Since, under this system of law Jews would despair from getting back their lost property because the law does not require the finder to return the lost item, the Jew need not be concerned to return the lost property of the non-Jew. The principle here is that the privileges of Jewish law were given only to those who are fully obligated and accepting of Jewish law (Michael Broyde and Michael Hecht, "The Gentile and Returning Lost Property According to Jewish Law: a Theory of Reciprocity," The Jewish Law Annual, vol. XIII, 31–45).

A logical extension of the reciprocity principle is the suspension of the ribbit interdict in connection with loan transactions when one of the parties is a non-Jew.

> It is related of R. Shimon b. Shetah that he once bought a donkey from an Ishmaelite. His disciples came and found a precious stone suspended from its neck. They said to him: "Master, 'The blessing of the Lord will bring riches . . . [Proverbs 10:22].'" R. Shimon b. Shetah replied: "I purchased a donkey, but I have not purchased a precious stone." He then went and returned it to the Ishmaelite, and the latter exclaimed of him, "Blessed be the Lord, G-d of Shimon b. Shetah."[51]

Since the Ishmaelite despaired of ever retrieving his lost precious stone, we can well understand the gratitude he felt toward R. Shimon b. Shetah. But this sentiment should have caused the Ishmaelite to bless R. Shimon b. Shetah. Instead, he blessed the G-d of R. Shimon b. Shetah. R. Jeroham Leibovitz (Poland, 1874–1936) posits that the Ishmaelite was not only filled with a sense of gratitude, but was overwhelmed by R. Shimon b. Shetah's conduct. The Ishmaelite witnessed no ordinary act of kindness, but the type of deed that made the *tzelem Elokim* (image of G-d) evident in the person of R. Shimon b. Shetah. The reaction of the Ishmaelite was in every way akin to the making of a blessing over a fruit before partaking of it. In the blessing over the fruit, we thank G-d for creating the "fruit of the tree." We declare that we see the greatness of the Creator in the fruit we are about to consume. So, too, the Ishmaelite saw the greatness of the Creator in the grand act of kindness of R. Shimon b. Shetah.

The words of R. Shimon b. Shetah, "I purchased a donkey, but I have not purchased a precious stone," cry out against veiled misconduct in the marketplace, whether or not the intended victim is a Jew. Since man is never more vulnerable to the wiles of the Evil Inclination than when given the opportunity for veiled misconduct, overcoming this temptation represents man's greatest triumph. This triumph is magnified when the intended victim is a non-Jew and overcoming the temptation is *kiddush ha-Shem*. Accordingly, the decision to refrain from veiled misconduct in interactions with non-Jews capitalizes on an opportunity for the greatest possible sanctification of G-d's name.[52]

Jewish Business Ethics

Let us now describe briefly the chapters in this volume that deal with business ethics.

Rabbi Yoel Domb demonstrates that Jewish law offers a viable and attractive way to preserve the dignity of the borrower and his business interests, balanced with the interests of his creditor. While Jewish law eschews the ancient idea of placing a debtor at the mercy of his creditor, it allows the use of some methods to protect the creditor's interests. Where the debtor exploits the creditor, Jewish law may even sanction imprisonment or forced labor to induce the debtor to honor his obligation to the creditor.

51 Deuteronomy *Rabbah* 3:3.

52 R. Jeroham Leibovitz, *Da'at Torah*, Parashat Bo, 123–27; Parashat Metsora, 130–33.

As a religion, Judaism generally has no problem with the notion of a competitive marketplace.[53] Nonetheless, Jewish law does not allow a market participant to interfere with transactions in progress in all circumstances. In his contribution to this volume, Rabbi Howard Jachter sets out to define the parameters of prohibited interloping conduct. While the prohibition of interloping conduct is a moral, as opposed to a legal, dictum, it has application to a wide variety of circumstances.

Dr. Asher Meir analyzes the ethical parameters for the investment of charity funds. The principles and sources that Dr. Meir identifies are procedures for accountability and standards of prudence and oversight. In particular, charity funds need to be invested with high regard for sustaining the principal and for adequate liquidity to ensure that the fund's mission is not compromised. Taken together, the Jewish laws regulating individual and communal investment constitute a well-defined religious framework for "socially responsible investment," a framework that can be of use for contemporary Jewish endowment funds.

Perfecting the art of moral rebuke (*tokhahah*) is an essential ingredient for improving the quality and efficiency of human interactions in all spheres of life, including market transactions. In his contribution to this volume, Dr. Moses L. Pava takes up the issue of what is needed to make moral criticism effective. The author presents the thesis that, if moral criticism is to be effective at all, it must always begin as a form of self-criticism. Toward this end Dr. Pava outlines a set of self-examination questions.

In many transactions, one of the parties possesses information unavailable to the other. This phenomenon is referred to as the asymmetric information problem. Unless counteracted, the asymmetric information problem will adversely affect the values of both efficiency and equity. In his chapter, Dr. Jonas Prager demonstrates that Judaism's reaction to the asymmetric information problem is multifaceted. On the one hand, Jewish law launched external enforcement mechanisms that inhibited malfeasance in the first place and punished it when discovered. But more important is Jewish law's insistence that the Jew deal with others with integrity. In this regard, the *Torah* appeals to man's religious instinct, admonishing him that, although he can excuse his conduct toward fellow man, he cannot escape the judgment of the All-knowing G-d. Finally, the "fear of G-d" must be instilled in man from early childhood by parents and the school system.

In their contribution to this volume, Dr. Fred Rosner and Rabbi Dr. Edward Reichman address the issue of organ donation. The primary point the authors make is that the value of human life is supreme in Judaism, as saving human life suspends nearly all biblical and rabbinic prohibitions. Accordingly, the prohibitions against desecrating, deriving benefit from, and delaying burial of the dead, and other prohibitions are all waived for the overriding consideration of saving the organ recipient's life. A related issue is whether financial compensation is permitted for organ donors or their families. The moral issues involved here

53 Cf. Aaron Levine, *Moral Issues of the Marketplace and Jewish Law* (New York: Yashar books, 2005), 128–70.

include the prohibitions against wounding and endangering oneself, the restriction against receiving payment for performance of a mitsvah (a religious deed), and the concept that our bodies are not our own, but rather gifts that the Creator charges us to care for with dignity and holiness. In the opinion of the authors, the preponderant view is that these concerns are all set aside for an organ transplant that saves a life. Therefore, Jewish law permits financial compensation for an organ donor. The principle of *dina d'malkhuta dina* means, however, that secular law must be taken into account. Currently, American law prohibits the sale of organs. Thus, in the United States, Jewish law reinforces secular law in prohibiting financial compensation for organ donation to either the donors or their families.

Dr. Ronald Warburg investigates Jewish law's attitude toward the "efficient breach." The proponents of the theory of "efficient breach," espoused by academicians in the field of Economics and Law, claim that individuals should be allowed to breach a contract and pay damages if they can pursue a more profitable activity. The net result is more wealth for society as a whole. Since the defendants pay damages, the plaintiffs are fully compensated for the injury they have suffered. In his chapter, Dr. Warburg argues that, if we wish to take seriously the moral character of the Jewish law of obligations, we should not encourage efficient breaches. In the context of the issue of trade secrets, Dr. Warburg demonstrates that Jewish law implicitly rejects the theory of "efficient breach" by requiring the violators to disgorge their ill-gotten profits.

Economic Public Policy and Jewish Law

A number of chapters in this volume make public policy proposals rooted in Jewish law.

Professor Michael Broyde addresses the issue of whether Jewish law would support the proposals that would make international law a law for all people and nations. Many in the legal community now contend that the effects of globalization and the diminishing role of national boundaries call for a more expansive system of international law, sometimes referred to as world law. In his chapter, Professor Broyde identifies three principles in Jewish law that might serve as a foundation for establishing international law as the law for all nations and all people. Explored in detail, these principles are treaty law, commercial custom derived from international law, and *dina d'malkhuta dina*.

From the standpoint of Jewish law, Professor Broyde does not see much promise for this proposal to gain any traction. In the Jewish tradition, authority alone does not create law; law must rest on the pillars of justice and fairness as well as on basic right and wrong. Before law can be truly valid, there must be *both* procedural and substantive fairness in the legal system.

Professor Broyde suspects that world law will never meet this dual standard in that it requires the depoliticization of international law, where the wrongs of the mighty are judged by the same standards as the wrongs of the weak and the powerful are held to the same standards of conduct as the powerless.

Another public policy issue that is given treatment in this volume from the standpoint of Jewish law is the joint chapter by Professor Yehuda Klein and Mr. Jonathan Weiser, Esq., that explores the philosophical foundations of sustainable development. The authors discuss the contending worldviews that inform our relationship with the natural world and show how they affect our understanding of the concept of sustainability. In particular, the authors review the ethical assumptions that underlie anthropocentric, ecocentric, and theocentric environmentalisms. Professor Klein and Mr. Weiser demonstrate that Judaism adopts the theocentric worldview. They identify immutable targets toward which to direct practical applications. In Judaism, G-d is the context for all of the potentially conflicting environmental theories. This focus speaks for the need to achieve a synthesis among the various worldviews.

In my chapter, I place the recent global recession in the context of Jewish theological thought. I show that the conduct of the players in the subprime mortgage sector violated specific moral principles. Moreover, no amount of wrongdoing by these players could have spiraled into an international financial meltdown without the financial innovation of the securitization process. I show that Jewish law rejects the legal underpinning of this financial innovation. To prevent the recurrence of the current debacle, Jewish law's *imitatio Dei* principle calls for the restructuring of the incentive system that economic actors face. It consists of replacing the current system of perverse incentives with sticks and carrots designed to tilt economic actors toward virtue and away from wrongdoing.

Since *imitatio Dei* is no more than a guidepost for the form that acts of kindness should take, it does not mandate policies that entail significant per capita expenditure. But *imitatio Dei* applied to the subprime mortgage market is a much more robust principle because implementation of "carrots" and "sticks" in this sector prevents the economy from falling into an abyss. The *imitatio Dei* program hence fulfills the government's antipoverty mandate, which justifies greater expenditure.

Aside from the incentive system, the current malaise indicates we are living in a society of broken promises. Improving the moral climate of society hence entails reinforcing the values of integrity and taking responsibility seriously. Jewish religious thought puts the onus on parents and the educational system to accomplish this.

Rabbi Dani Rapp examines the legal status of unions. He demonstrates that, under Jewish law, workers do not have any power or rights until they agree to unionize. There are two categories of unions: those that represent the entire labor force in a certain area, and those that do not. The former acquires the powers of an agreement among tradesmen. They can coerce new laborers to join the union, restrict members from withdrawing, and are not constrained by laws regarding agreements. When the union does not represent the entire labor force in the local area, the union may not coerce nonunion workers to join, may prevent strikebreaking only among members who originally voted to strike, and is constrained by laws concerning agreements. For both categories of unions, a labor relations board should be established to govern union powers.

For *halakhah* to confer real negotiating power and significant rights upon a union, the union would have to be formed by unanimous agreement. Despite the difficulties involved in forming a halakhically valid union, workers are not totally without protection because the government is entitled to regulate the relationship between labor and management. Any laws they pass are binding and enforceable in Jewish courts.

The Israeli economy experienced rapid inflation between 1973 and 1985, accompanied by an expansion of dollarization and indexation. These developments generated an extensive literature on monetary issues in Jewish law. These issues included the following: Are United States dollar loans permissible, or do they constitute a form of prohibited interest? Is it permissible to index to the dollar or to the Consumer Price Index (CPI)? Is there a fundamental distinction between official devaluation and depreciation? Dr. Daniel Schiffman distills these discussions. He finds that the majority of rabbis allowed dollar and dollar-indexed loans. Indexation to the CPI, however, was far more controversial.

During the same time, Jewish law was applied to the phenomena of black markets in foreign currency, exchange controls, foreign currency trading in globalized markets, the unofficial crawling peg, and the effects of various subsidies on the CPI and on exchange rates. Many of these phenomena had never been discussed in previous rabbinic literature.

The rabbinic analysis of all these new issues, according to Dr. Schiffman, did not lead to significant rabbinic innovations in the realm of Jewish monetary doctrine. Only one doctrinal change had practical implications. That change was the ruling by some rabbis that, under high inflation, debtors who repay late are liable for the opportunity costs that they impose on creditors. For the first time, the Talmudic concept of opportunity cost was applied to problems of monetary instability.

Textual examination of the rabbis' response to the monetary issues of this period suggests, according to Dr. Schiffman, that the rabbis relied on their own intuition in matters of economics, rather than consulting with professional economists. The leading decisors of the late twentieth century are known to have consulted with experts in science, technology, and medicine. Unfortunately, little is known about the extent of professional relationships between rabbis and economists.

Dr. Meir Tamari's chapter investigates the balance between private property and economic freedom needed for wealth formation, on the one hand, and morality and communal justice, on the other. He describes the conceptual framework of the value system Judaism presents for economic activity. The recognition of moral and social responsibilities, both of the individual and of society, requires both moral education and regulation and restrictive legislation to protect weaker members of society.

A constant spiral of "more is better than less" creates a culture of "wants" translated into "needs," of appeals to egoism and selfishness, and of conspicuous consumption. In such a culture, the defenses of morals and ethics inevitably crumble as each individual struggles to find his place at the ever-receding top of the spiral. This creates jealousy, envy, and hatred that inevitably destroy the social fabric of society. Society needs, therefore, to provide both parameters for acceptable standards of living as well as the education toward a pattern of social living that permits enjoyment of the essential and legitimate private property and economic activity. Judaism provides both the moral literature and communal norms essential for such parameters of "enough" that must not be confused with philosophies of poverty or egalitarianism.

Aspects of Jewish Law that Inhibit Accommodation with Prevailing Commercial Practice

In examining the extent to which Jewish law inhibits the Jew from smoothly integrating into the economic life of society, an easily identifiable negative here is its prohibition against interest payments (*ribbit*) in inter-Jewish loan transactions. Recognition that a viable loan market is essential to finance basic research, capital formation, business growth, and the housing market, makes the interest payment prohibition a significant negative factor in excluding Jews from full participation in the functioning of the economic system.

One could argue, however, that the innovation of *hetter iska* (described below) in the sixteenth century goes a long way toward removing the prohibition of *ribbit* as a factor that excludes Jews from full participation in the economic life of society. Basically, *hetter iska* restructures an otherwise loan transaction into a special type of partnership, discussed in the *Talmud*, called *Iska*.[54] In the *iska* partnership, one party supplies the funds, while the other party manages the funds. Most importantly, in the *iska* arrangement, the financier takes on the role of a silent partner with no decision-making or managerial role, while the recipient of the capital conducts business and is the decision maker in respect to the funds he receives. This type of partnership is regulated by *halakhah*. Against this basic structure, *hetter iska* adds various features to make the arrangement attractive from the financier's perspective.

Several chapters in this volume address *ribbit* and *hetter iska*. Rabbi Dr. J. David Bleich's contribution explains the mechanics of *hetter iska* in detail and the limitations of its use. Rabbi Bleich also demonstrates why *hetter iska* should not be regarded as a contrivance. Finally, he addresses the issue of how the secular courts would treat *hetter iska*.

54 TB *Bava Metsi'a* 104b.

In the *hetter iska* described in the *Talmud*, the arrangement calls for the division of profits and losses equally between the financier and the managing partner. Professor Jeffrey L. Callen considers a variation of this basic *iska* model, which was innovated by the Nehardean rabbis of the *Talmud*. Professor Callen analyzes this variant of *iska* both from the standpoint of the prohibition of *ribbit* and the incentive system it sets up. Professor Callen also discusses post-Talmudic rationalizations of the profit-and-loss divisions of *iska* in light of modern Principal-Agent Theory.

Hetter iska does not promote a smooth integration of Jewish law and secular commercial practice because prohibiting interest payments in inter-Jewish loan transactions but allowing interest payments in loan transactions between Jews and non-Jews is discriminatory. Rabbi Daniel Feldman's chapter in this volume addresses this issue. In his chapter, Rabbi Feldman offers a theory of why the *Torah* prohibits *ribbit*. Rabbi Feldman views the prohibition against interest in inter-Jewish loan transactions as a law designed to solidify the familial bond that joins *all* members of the Jewish nation. It does so by requiring a lender to forgo a reasonable profit when lending money to even nonfamily members. Alternatively, the duty to forgo interest on a loan is an expression of the fundamental Jewish value of kindness that all members of the Jewish people are entitled to receive from a coreligionist. If the prohibition of interest is designed to build bonds among Jews and to express a kindness one owes to a coreligionist, the exclusion of non-Jews in the prohibition is understandable as the rarefied responsibility inherent in the law of *ribbit* extends only to those who are extended family, which is the entire Jewish people.

In his contribution to this volume, Professor Roger Lister shows that the Jewish giver or recipient of a guarantee is at risk of transgressing the prohibition of usury if a Jew is lender or borrower or if both lender and borrower are Jews. The danger is particularly significant when an arrangement is ruled by English law. In England, the law of principal and surety is complex and tends not to provide the degree of separation between surety and other parties that is required by Jewish law.

Aspects of Jewish Law that Promote Integration into the Economic Life of Society

Let us now turn to aspects of Jewish law that promote integration into the economic life of society. One principle, explicated above, is *dina d'malkhuta dina* (i.e., the law of the Kingdom is law). Another principle is *kinyan situmta* (lit., acquisition by means of making a mark). This principle says that Jewish law recognizes whatever merchants customarily do to consummate a deal as a valid mode of acquisition even if the particular mode is not mentioned in the *Talmud*.

Dr. Ron S. Kleinman and Dr. Amal Jabareen use these two principles, along with other Jewish law concepts, to identify the moment of transfer of ownership in e-commerce. Of particular concern for them is whether ordering an item online actually effects transfer of ownership or just a contractual duty on the part of the vendor to supply the merchandise to the buyer.

In his study of historical societies, Professor Yaakov Elman shows that the rabbis of the *Talmud* were well-aware of the laws of the land as well as contemporary business practices. The rabbis made these laws and practices work for the benefit of the Jewish community. Areas of everyday life that benefited from this integration included commercial activity, land tenure, and increasing the supply of ritual items.

In his study of Hebrew documents from Ashkenazic communities in the thirteenth to the fifteenth centuries, Professor Yosef Rivlin shows how these documents, operating within the parameters of Jewish law, facilitated economic activity. Of particular interest is how the marriage contract was used to promote family life by innovating incentives to preserve the dowry against loss and erosion. In the commercial sphere, Professor Rivlin shows how a type of reversible sale, called *mashkanta be-nakyata*, did not violate *ribbit* law, while, at the same time, it promoted the mutual interest of the buyer and seller.

Economic Theory in the Bible and Talmud

Economic public policy and guideposts for ethical conduct in the modern societal setting begin for Jewish law by identifying ethical principles and economic theory in both the Bible and the *Talmud*. A number of the chapters of this volume set out to accomplish that goal.

Professor Eliakim Katz and Professor Jacob Rosenberg investigate whether the Biblical law of theft can be explained by economic considerations. The law of theft requires the thief who is caught and found to return the stolen article and pay the owner a fine equal to the value of the article. By admitting to the theft on his own initiative in a court, and returning the stolen article to its owner, the thief, however, is relieved of the fine. The waiver of the fine is at once an incentive for the thief to confess, but it also reduces the penalty for theft. Hence, it is necessary to weigh the net impact of these two opposing effects on the welfare of owners. Professors Katz and Rosenberg use a simple model to consider the conditions under which such pardons increase social welfare.

The absence of effective policing in Biblical and Talmudic times, the difficulties of obtaining a conviction in a Jewish court, and the likely very low probability of apprehension and conviction of a thief all argue for a pardon regime.

I examine the Biblical account of Eliezer's conduct as a matchmaker against Judaism's ethical norms. I demonstrate that, despite the various discrepancies between Abraham's instructions to Eliezer and what happened at the well, on the one hand, and Eliezer's account of them, on the other, Eliezer conducted himself ethically. My chapter also shows that Eliezer's conduct followed the approaches and techniques modern bargaining theory recommends for success, including the use of leverage, creating value, framing, and the understanding of the phenomena of vicious and virtuous cycles.

Professor Jacob Rosenberg and Professor Avi Weiss develop a new approach to the Jubilee laws that can help explain some of the anomalies in the laws. They show that the laws are consistent with two goals. The first is a desire to attain economic efficiency by "spreading the wealth"—limiting the ability of an individual to control resources and thus monopolize markets. The second is to try to avoid the development of slavery within the Jewish nation.

Professor Ephraim Kleiman analyzes a number of cases in the *Talmud* involving the financing of a public good. These cases include the costs of fortifying a town, compensation for goods jettisoned to lighten a ship's burden, and the formula of how to apportion a communal manure heap. Professor Kleiman's analysis leads him to generalize how the rabbis of the *Talmud* from the second and third centuries CE handled the financing of goods involving externalities. Comparison with the corresponding rules of the somewhat-later Theodosian and Justinian Codes underscores the difference in attitudes between the ancient Jewish and Roman legislators.

Professor Yehoshua Liebermann presents a "Talmudic search model" and analyzes it in light of George Steigler's theory of the economics of information. In the economic theory of information, price search is typically conducted before purchase (ex ante). In the Talmudic search model, price search takes place mainly *after* the purchase (ex post). Professor Liebermann buttresses his thesis with his analysis of how a complaint of price fraud (law of *ona'ah*) is treated in the *Talmud.* Of particular importance is the encounter between the merchants of the city of Lydda and R. Tarfon. R. Tarfon raised the overcharge limit from one-sixth to one-third of the market equilibrium price. This change in law made the merchants happy. Their mood quickly changed when R. Tarfon also lengthened to a full day's time the window the buyer had ex post to cancel or modify the transaction on the basis of finding a cheaper alternative. Realizing that R. Tarfon had traded off an extra profit margin for extra ex post search time, the merchants preferred the original, more conservative paradigm of a smaller profit margin along with a considerably shortened ex post search time. Professor Liebermann opines that, for market settings of the Talmudic genre, where a single equilibrium price exists and products are homogeneous, the Jewish law model is more efficient.

Professor Jacob Rosenberg presents an economic approach to understanding fire damages in Jewish law. He demonstrates that the law of strict liability in the case of fire damage to a dwelling above leads to an efficient level of care in the sense that it minimizes the social cost of the fire accident. The same liability rule is not economically efficient, however, in the case of fire damage to a neighboring field. In that case, the negligence rule induces both the damager and the victim to exercise an optimal level of care. This explains why, in the case of fire damage to a neighboring field, the law exempts the damager from liability if he lit the fire at an appropriate distance from the neighbor's field.

Professor Lawrence H. Schiffman investigates the monetary theories that underlie the Talmudic laws that pertain to currency (coinage) and commodities, and the trading of one currency against another or even multiple currencies against each other. The debates recorded in the *Talmud* provide perspectives on the views of the ancient rabbis regarding a number of issues in economic theory. These issues include the nature of currency and commodities, the relationship of the value of currency to price fluctuations, inflation, the use of precious metals to establish monetary standards, and criteria for valuing currency in an international market. Professor Shiffman's chapter examines particular passages in both the Jerusalem and Babylonian *Talmud*s to elucidate those concepts and trace their historical progression. The rabbis are shown to follow a situational, monometallic system allowing for a relativistic determination, whether an object functions as currency or commodity. Despite known evidence to the contrary, Talmudic economic thought assumed that the value of currency remained constant whereas that of commodities changed in response to market conditions.

Professor Keith Sharfman considers from an economic perspective the manner in which Jewish law resolves disputes over the value of legal entitlements. Relative to valuation in other legal systems, Jewish law's most important and distinctive feature is that it tries most valuation disputes before three-judge panels that determine value by majority rule rather than before a single judge or a larger lay jury. Rather than adopt the one-size-fits-all approach of other legal systems, Jewish law instead uses a layered, contextual approach, deploying additional administrative resources, procedural safeguards, and monetary adjustments in situations where economic theory suggests that they are needed. Jewish law's surprising sophistication in this area offers valuable insight to modern legal theorists and policy makers who today are struggling to devise their own solutions to the age-old problem of legal valuation.

Professor P.V. (Meylekh) Viswanath and Professor Michael Szenberg show that markets from antiquity can provide valuable information about the importance of different factors in market pricing of assets. In their chapter, the authors discuss a text from the Babylonian *Talmud* that deals with seasonal prices and trading volume fluctuations in land markets in Roman Palestine. They argue that these fluctuations are probably due to information asymmetry and uncertainty regarding the value of land and the crops growing on it. Modern regulatory authorities might learn from the *Talmud* and work to reduce information asymmetry.

Comparative Law Studies that Relate to Economics

A number of chapters in this volume have addressed issues of comparative law relating to economics. All these papers have already been introduced earlier under various headings, with the exception of Professor Adam Chodorow's essay. Professor Adam Chodorow compares how Jewish law and federal tax law define interest payments. Notwithstanding that both systems define interest payments as a payment for the use of money, the two systems diverge substantially in their holdings regarding a wide range of transactions. Both systems struggle with the question of when to respect the form of a transaction and when to take account of the underlying economic reality, often reaching different conclusions. Comparing the different approaches to the laws of interest reveals how underlying goals, practical constraints, and structure of the legal system affect the development of the law.

Judiasm and Economic History

A number of the historical studies contributed to this volume fit well into the theme of how Jewish economic law fostered participation in the economic life of society. These chapters have already been introduced. The remaining historical paper is described below.

Laurence Rabinovich, Esq., explores aspects of the metrological and monetary systems reflected in Jewish legal writings. The archaeological and numismatic evidence Mr. Rabinovich brings to bear sheds light on the monetary aspects of Abraham's purchase of the Makhpelah cave (Genesis 23), the half-shekel Sanctuary tax, as well as rabbinic interest in topics such as the relationship between gold and silver.

In comparing biblical texts and archaeological evidence from the period of the First Commonwealth (c. 1000 BCE–586 BCE) with other records of the ancient world, it is apparent that weight standards in Judea were modified on at least one occasion. A similar comparison for the Second Commonwealth period (c. 515 BCE–70 CE) establishes yet another change.

The Economics of Judiasm

Last, several chapters deal with the economics of Judaism. Professor Barry R. Chiswick tracks the economic status of American Jewry over the past three centuries. His primary focus is the occupational status of Jewish men and women compared to non-Jews, with additional analyses of earnings, self-employment, and wealth. Taken together, his data suggest that Jews made greater investments in human capital, earned greater returns from these investments, and were more responsive to economic incentives than others.

He draws a number of lessons from the economic experience of American Jewry. First, the Jews sought out niches in the labor market in which they would be subject to less discrimination. Some of these niches were in "socially suspect" occupations, such as in entertainment, including the emerging movie industry in the early decades of the twentieth century. When rewarding sectors opened up, Jews entered them.

Second, the economic experience of American Jewry was the application of entrepreneurial and decision-making skills. From the Colonial Jewish merchants and financiers, to the German Jewish shop owners, to the present managers and professionals, Jews demonstrated a capacity for successful entrepreneurial activity.

Third, the Jews placed high value on learning the skills necessary for advancement, given the time and place.

Professor Carmel Ullman Chiswick discusses the strong impact of economic forces, and changes in the economic environment, on American Jewish observance and American Jewish religious institutions in the twentieth century. Through the opportunity-cost concept, she explains decision making in the realm of religious practice and observance. These decisions relate to time and money spent, including human capital decisions, for both oneself and family. She notes how the orthodox, conservative, and reform branches of Judaism responded to these economic forces.

PART I

ECONOMIC THEORY IN THE BIBLE

CHAPTER 1

THE RIGHT TO RETURN: THE BIBLICAL LAW OF THEFT

ELIAKIM KATZ AND JACOB ROSENBERG

Introduction

According to Jewish Law, a thief who is caught and found guilty must return the stolen article[1] *and, in addition*, pay the owner a fine equal to the value of the article.[2] The thief can avoid this fine by admitting to the theft on his own initiative in a court and returning the stolen article[3] to its owner.[4] In this chapter, we refer to such canceling of a fine as a *pardon*. The pardon is explained in the Talmud by the legal dictum "*Mode BeKnass Patur*" (i.e., "he who confesses in a fine is exempt").

A possible motivation for this pardon may be found in the high threshold required for a conviction in Jewish Law. According to the rules of evidence in Jewish Law, conviction requires two witnesses who observed a crime directly, or who can provide evidence that leaves no doubt whatsoever that the accused individual committed the crime. The stringency of these rules of evidence makes it extremely difficult to obtain a conviction. In view of this, the offer of pardon may be viewed as an incentive to the thief to return the stolen article voluntarily.

1 In this paper we use the term *article* to refer to a good that is, or may be, stolen. This includes both inanimate articles as well as livestock.

2 See Maimonides (Rambam, Egypt, 1,135–1,204), *Mishne Torah Geneivah* 1:4. Also note that in some cases the fine may be greater.

3 Or, in certain cases, its monetary value.

4 *Mishneh Torah, Geneivah*, op. cit., 1:5.

The practice of granting a pardon to (or reducing fines imposed on) those who have committed crimes of property is still current. For example, on more than one occasion, the Israeli army has granted a general pardon to individuals who return stolen military equipment. Under such amnesties, individuals who return stolen equipment are exempt from any punishment. In contrast, if the stolen equipment is returned after the thief is caught, the thief is punished by a fine or a prison sentence.[5]

Granting a complete pardon to a thief in order to induce him to return a stolen article is a special case of a more general incentive mechanism.[6] If the fine imposed on a convicted thief who did not confess voluntarily is $\mathbf{F}$ ($> \mathbf{0}$), then imposing a fine $\mathbf{F} - \boldsymbol{\delta}$ ($\boldsymbol{\delta} > \mathbf{0}$) on a confessed thief constitutes an incentive to confess and return the stolen article. And it is important to note that $\boldsymbol{\delta} > \mathbf{0}$ encompasses $\boldsymbol{\delta} > \mathbf{F}$ (i.e., a reward).[7]

The granting of incentives to thieves in order to motivate them to return stolen articles induces some stolen articles to be returned. On the other hand, since a thief knows that he can avoid penalties associated with theft if he decides, for whatever reason, to return a stolen article, this reduces the risk associated with stealing and encourages more thefts. Hence, it is necessary to weigh the net impact of these two opposing effects of incentives to return on the welfare of owners.[8] This is the purpose of the analysis presented below. The analysis is based on explicit assumptions regarding the behavior of thieves and the difference between the value of the stolen article to the thief and its value to the article's owner.

In our analysis, we assume that the thief does not know the value of the stolen article before the theft takes place. This model permits us to compare situations where (a) fines are imposed on thieves and no pardon is granted, and (b) pardons are granted to thieves who return stolen articles. The model is outlined in the following section and a detailed numerical example is presented in the appendix.

5 Another example, in a different context, is that of amnesties granted to tax evaders. The implications of such amnesties have received considerable attention in the economic literature. See fn. 10.

6 Incentives to self-report infractions have been discussed in the economics literature. For example, there exists an extensive literature that deals with tax amnesties. See, for example, Arun S. Malik and Robert M. Schwab, "The Economics of Tax Amnesties," *Journal of Public Economics* 46 (October 1991): 29–49; Robert Innes, "Remediation and Self-Reporting in Optimal Law Enforcement," *Journal of Public Economics* 72 (June 1999): 379–93; James Andreoni, "The Desirability of a Permanent Tax Amnesty," *Journal of Public Economics* 45, (July 1991): 143–59. Another relevant area in the economics literature is the subject of self-reporting in environmental crimes. See Louis Kaplow and Steven Shavell, "Optimal Law Enforcement with Self-Reporting of Behavior," *Journal of Political Economy* 102 (June 1994): 583–606. These two topics, however, are different from the case studied in this paper, with regard to the nature of the pardon and/or the nature of the crime.

7 The analysis presented in this chapter focuses solely on a pardon. This is because Jewish Law views theft as a religious transgression, so that a reward is not a relevant consideration within this context.

8 Providing thieves with incentives to return stolen articles cannot reduce, and may increase, the welfare of thieves. Hence, by looking solely at the welfare of owners, we are providing a more stringent test of the possible positive effect of such incentives. Moreover, given that Jewish Law disapproves of theft, in theological terms, we ignore the welfare of thieves.

Economic Model

I. No pardon

I (a) *Thieves*

There exist a continuum of stealable articles and a continuum of potential, risk neutral, thieves. To simplify the analysis we assume that each stealable article may be stolen by one specific thief: In other words, thieves do not compete with each other to steal a given article. The mass of stealable articles and the mass of potential thieves are both set at 1.[9]

Stealing requires incurring costs of equipment and time by the thief. These costs are distributed uniformly across the population of potential thieves, and the distribution is defined over the interval [0, 1]. Each thief knows the specific cost, **C**, which he will face if he chooses to engage in a theft.

The value of an article to its owner is 1. This enables us to express all values in terms of the article's value to its owner. In contrast, prior to the act of stealing "his" article, a thief does not know the value[10] of this article (to him). What the thief does know is the distribution of the post-theft value of the article: It is high, $\mathbf{B_H}$, or low, $\mathbf{B_L}$ (> 0), with probabilities **p** and **1 – p**, respectively. Since in general owners attach a greater value to an article than does a thief, we assume that $Bi < 1$ ($i = L, H$). Specifically, $\mathbf{0 < B_L < B_H < 1}$.

After a thief has stolen his article, he will be apprehended with a probability **q**, in which case he has to return the article and pay a fine, **F**. The probability that he is not caught is **1 – q**.

Hence, after the theft has taken place the expected utility of the thief is

$$\mathbf{V_H = (1 - q)\, B_H - qF} \tag{1}$$

if the article transpires to be of the **H** type, and

$$\mathbf{V_L = (1 - q)\, B_L - qF} \tag{2}$$

if the article transpires to be of the **L** type.

In the absence of a pardon, the thief's gross[11] expected utility of theft, $\mathbf{U_N}$, is a weighted average of the two ex post expected utilities.

$$\mathbf{U_N = pV_H + (1 - p)\, V_L} \tag{3}$$

A necessary condition for theft to occur is that $\mathbf{U_N > 0}$,which clearly requires that $\mathbf{V_H > 0}$. Moreover, given that $\mathbf{V_H}$ and $\mathbf{V_L}$ are both smaller than 1, $\mathbf{U_N < 1}$. In this

9 The mass of potential thieves may be smaller than the mass of stealable articles without affecting our results.

10 For example, its resale value in a stolen goods market.

11 Before subtracting the costs the thief incurs in stealing.

connection note that, in Jewish Law, $\mathbf{F = 1}$. Hence, for $\mathbf{V_H}$ to be positive, $\mathbf{B_H}$ must exceed $q / (1 - q)$. This implies that, for any thefts to take place, $\mathbf{q}$ must be significantly smaller than 0.5, (since $\mathbf{B_H} < 1$). Given the stringency of the rules of conviction in Jewish law, $\mathbf{q < 0.5}$ is a reasonable assumption.

In view of the above, all thieves for whom $\mathbf{U_N > C}$ will engage in theft, and all those for whom $\mathbf{U_N \leq C}$ will not. This implies that, in the absence of pardons or rewards, the marginal thief will be characterized by costs $\mathbf{C_N^* = U_N}$. Therefore, the proportion of actual thieves in relation to potential thieves equals $\mathbf{U_N}$.

A simple numerical example will clarify the above. Suppose that the low value of the article to the thief (i.e., $\mathbf{B_L}$) is 0.125 (that is, 12.5 percent of its value to the owner), $\mathbf{B_H = 0.75}$, $\mathbf{q = 0.2}$ and $\mathbf{F = 1}$[12]. Using the above parameter values, the post-theft expected utility of the article to the thief will be $\mathbf{V_L = (0.8)\ 0.125 - (0.2)\ 1 = -0.1}$ with a probability $\mathbf{1 - p}$, and $\mathbf{V_H = (0.8)\ 0.75 - (0.2)\ 1 = 0.4}$, with a probability $\mathbf{p}$. Now, let $\mathbf{p = 0.5}$ (50 percent of the articles are expected to be of the H type). In this case the gross expected utility of the thief (before the theft takes place) under a no pardon regime is:

$$\mathbf{U_N = (0.5)(-0.1) + (0.5)(0.4) = 0.15}$$ [13]

Since $\mathbf{U_N = 0.15}$, all thieves for whom cost is smaller than 0.15 will engage in stealing. But since by assumption costs are distributed uniformly across the potential thieves, this implies that 15 percent of potential thieves will engage in theft, and that 15 percent of stealable articles will be stolen.

I *(b) Owners*

$\mathbf{U_N}$ is the mass of articles that are actually stolen (and their proportion of all stealable articles). The expected utility loss to (the risk neutral) owners is the mass of articles stolen by thieves who are not caught, $\mathbf{(1 - q)\ U_N}$, minus the fines collected from those who are caught, $\mathbf{q(U_N)F}$. Hence, the expected utility loss to an owner in the absence of pardons, $\mathbf{L_N}$, is

$$\mathbf{L_N = (1 - q)\ U_N + q\,(U_N)\ F = U_N\,(1 - q + qF)}$$

Which, substituting for $\mathbf{U_N}$ from (3), yields,

$$\mathbf{L_N = (1 - q - qF)\ (pV_H + [1 - p]V_L)} \qquad (4)$$

II. Pardon

II *(a) Thieves*

If a pardon is offered to thieves who return a stolen article, some stolen articles may be returned. In order to induce a return of at least some articles by the offer

12 As mentioned above, in Jewish Law the fine is equal to the full value of the article to the owner.
13 In other words, 15 percent of the article's value to the owner.

of a pardon, the thief's return of the article must yield a greater utility than the utility derived by keeping it. Since returning the article yields utility of 0, it will be kept only if doing so yields a negative utility. Hence, in order to make a pardon meaningful, we assume $\mathbf{V_L < 0}$. Also, as mentioned above, a necessary condition for theft to occur is that $\mathbf{U_N} > 0$, which clearly requires that $\mathbf{V_H > 0}$. Given a pardon, a thief will return an article of low value and keep an article of high value.

When pardons are granted to thieves who return stolen articles, the thief knows that, if he chances on a low value article, his ex post utility from the theft will be 0. Therefore, given a potential pardon, the gross expected utility before stealing, $\mathbf{U_P}$, is derived from (3) by substituting 0 for $\mathbf{V_L}$.

$$\mathbf{U_P = pV_H}, \tag{5}$$

which is greater than $\mathbf{U_N}$, since $\mathbf{V_L < 0}$.

Hence, the marginal thief is such that $\mathbf{C_P^* = U_P > U_N}$; that is, the availability of a pardon raises the number of thieves.

This is not surprising. The possible pardon makes theft more profitable (less risky), and therefore encourages more individuals to engage in theft. Note that a proportion $\mathbf{(1-p)}$ of stolen articles are returned under the pardon regime, in contrast with the no pardon case, where no article is returned voluntarily.

II *(b) Owners*

The expected utility loss to owners in this case, $\mathbf{L_P}$, equals the expected cost of *unreturned* and uncaught articles, $\mathbf{U_P\,(1-q)p}$, minus the expected fine on caught articles, $\mathbf{(U_P)q\,p\,F}$. From (5) this yields:

$$\mathbf{L_P = (U_P)\,p\,(1-q) - (U_P)p\,q\,F = (1-q-qF)\,p^2\,V_H} \tag{6}$$

III. Comparing Owners' Losses Under Alternative Regimes[14]

We are now in a position to determine the circumstances wherein a pardon increases the welfare of owners.

The difference between $\mathbf{L_P}$ and $\mathbf{L_N}$, which may be referred to as the Loss Gap, is:

$$\begin{aligned}\mathbf{DD = L_P - L_N} &= \mathbf{(1-q-qF)(p^2V_H - (pV_H + [1\text{-}p]\,V_L))} \\ &= \mathbf{(1-q-qF)(1-p)(V_L + pV_H)}\end{aligned} \tag{7}$$

Hence, the sign of **DD** is as the sign of $\mathbf{V_L + p\,V_H}$.

The above condition has an appealing intuitive explanation. The mass of thieves under a no pardon regime is $\mathbf{U_N = p\,V_H + (1-p)\,V_L}$, and the mass of thieves newly induced to steal by the pardon is $\mathbf{U_P - U_N = p\,V_H}$. The introduction of a pardon regime therefore increases losses to owners by $\mathbf{(1-q-qF)p(U_P-U_N)} = \mathbf{(1-q-qF)p^2\,V_H}$ (since $\mathbf{1-p}$ of the stolen articles are returned). At the same time, the pardon induces a $\mathbf{1-p}$ of the original $\mathbf{U_N}$ to return the stolen articles, implying

14 For further elaboration see the appendix.

a reduction in loss to $(1 - q - qF)(1 - p)\, U_N = (1 - q - qF)(1 - p)(pV_H + [1 - p]V_L)$, yielding the above condition.

Interpretation and Implications

Figure 1.1 is a numerical illustration of our results, for the values $B_L = 0.125$; $q = 0.2$; $p = 0.5$; $F = 1$.

In this figure, we plot expected utility losses for different values of B_H, as a result of being exposed to potential thefts under a pardon and under a no pardon regime.

Several points of interest emerge.

First, to ensure that V_H is strictly positive, B_H must be bounded below. Using the parameter values above, B_H must exceed 0.25.[15] This therefore is the starting value of B_H on the horizontal axis.

Second, for values of B_H that are small, defined as sufficiently close to 0.25, the loss to owners under a pardon necessarily exceeds the loss to owners in the absence of a pardon. To see this, consider the expected loss for $0.25 < B_H < 0.38$. For these values of B_H, no thefts take place under a no pardon regime: **For** $B_H < 0.38$, $U_N = pV_H + (1 - p)V_L$ is negative (since $V_L < 0$) so that owners lose nothing. However, within the pardon regime, the ability of thieves to avoid exposure to the negative V_L by returning some stolen articles implies that $U_P > 0$ for $B_H > 0.25$ and thefts do take place. And, while $(1 - p)$ of articles stolen in the pardon regime are returned, the owners still lose a proportion of these.

Third, in both regimes the loss increases with B_H: A higher value of B_H increases the thief's expected utility from stealing, raising the number of articles stolen. However, within a pardon regime, the effect of B_H on (owners') losses is smaller, because some of the articles are returned voluntarily: The effect of B_H on losses within the no pardon regime is multiplied by **p** within the pardon regime.

This is easily seen by noting that,

$$\frac{\partial L_N}{\partial B_H} = p(1-q)(1-q-qf)$$

$$\frac{\partial L_P}{\partial B_H} = p^2(1-q)(1-q-qf)$$

The slope of L_N is therefore greater than that of L_P, and, *above a certain level of* B_H, *the pardon regime is superior.*

A further result concerns the relation between the losses of the owners under the different regimes and the value of **p**. As expected, an increase in **p**, which generates more thefts, raises the expected loss of owners under both regimes. What

15 Because $V_H > 0$ requires that $(1 - q)\, B_H - q\, F > 0$. In this case: $0.8B_H - 0.2 > 0$.

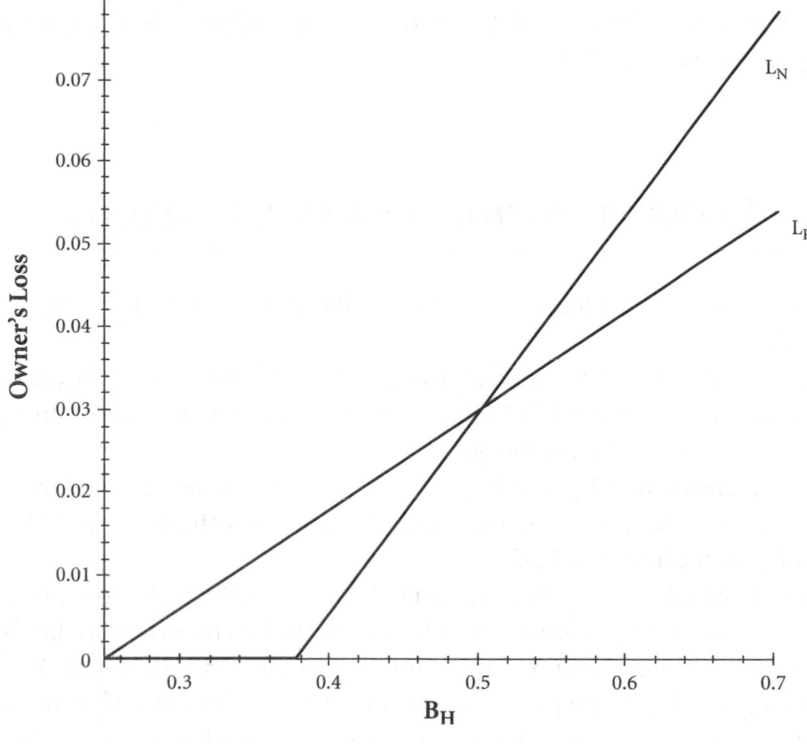

FIGURE 1.1

appears surprising, however, is that, for values of **p** that are not too large, an increases in **p**, which also implies that a smaller proportion, **(1 – p)**, of stolen articles are returned under a pardon regime, reduces the Loss Gap.

This is illustrated in Figure 1.2 for the same numerical values as above (except that $\mathbf{B_H}$ is set equal to 0.5, and **p** is allowed to vary).

Note that, for *all* parameter values, $\mathbf{L_N = L_P}$ at $\mathbf{p = 1}$.[16] This is because, when all articles are **H**, no articles are returned within a pardon regime. Hence, when $\mathbf{p = 1}$, the pardon has no impact, and, trivially, $\mathbf{L_N = L_P}$. Also, note that, for low values of **p**, no thefts take place under both regimes. However, as **p** rises, thefts begin for lower **p** under the pardon regime than under the no pardon regime. This implies that for some low **p** the pardon regime generate a greater owner loss. Hence, if the $\mathbf{L_P}$ curve is to cut the $\mathbf{L_N}$ curve at some **p** below 1, it must cut it from above: At that point the slope of $\mathbf{L_P}$ in **p** is smaller than the slope of $\mathbf{L_N}$ in **p** and for these values of **p** the pardon regime is superior.

In Figure 1.3, we consider the relationship between **p** and $\mathbf{B_H}$. All points on the curve **DD = 0** in Figure 1.3 represent all the combinations of **p** and $\mathbf{B_H}$ for which $\mathbf{DD = L_P - L_N = 0}$. These combinations of **p** and $\mathbf{B_H}$ are such that owners are indifferent between a pardon and a no pardon regime.

16 Recall that $\mathbf{DD = L_P - L_N = (1 - q - qF)(1 - p)\,(V_L + p\,V_H)}$.

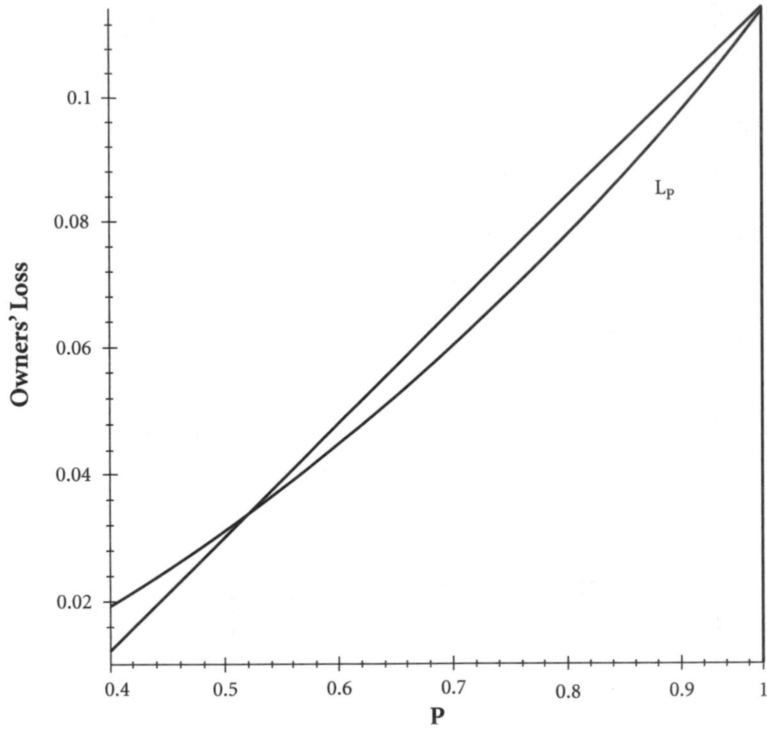

FIGURE 1.2

The slope of the curve **DD** = **o** is negative because, as shown above (Fig. 1.1), an increase in $\mathbf{B_H}$ raises the relative benefit of a pardon regime and reduces the Loss Gap. At the same time, *in the relevant range*, an increase in **p** also decreases the Loss Gap. Consequently, the slope of **DD** = **o**, in the ($\mathbf{B_H}$, **p**), is negative.

All combinations of $\mathbf{B_H}$ and **p** to the right and above the curve **DD** = **o** imply that the pardon regime is superior to the no pardon regime ($\mathbf{L_P} < \mathbf{L_N}$).

The impact of a change in **q** (the probability of apprehension) is reflected by the two **DD** = **o** curves. A lower **q** increases the range for which the pardon regime is superior since the importance of returning stolen articles voluntarily is increased.

Concluding Remarks

According to Jewish Law, a thief who is caught and found guilty must return the stolen article *and, in addition*, pay a fine equal to the value of the article. However, this fine is waived if the stolen article is returned voluntarily. In this chapter we suggest that the waiver of the fine represents recognition by Biblical law of the benefits of incentivize thieves to return stolen articles. It seems likely that there was

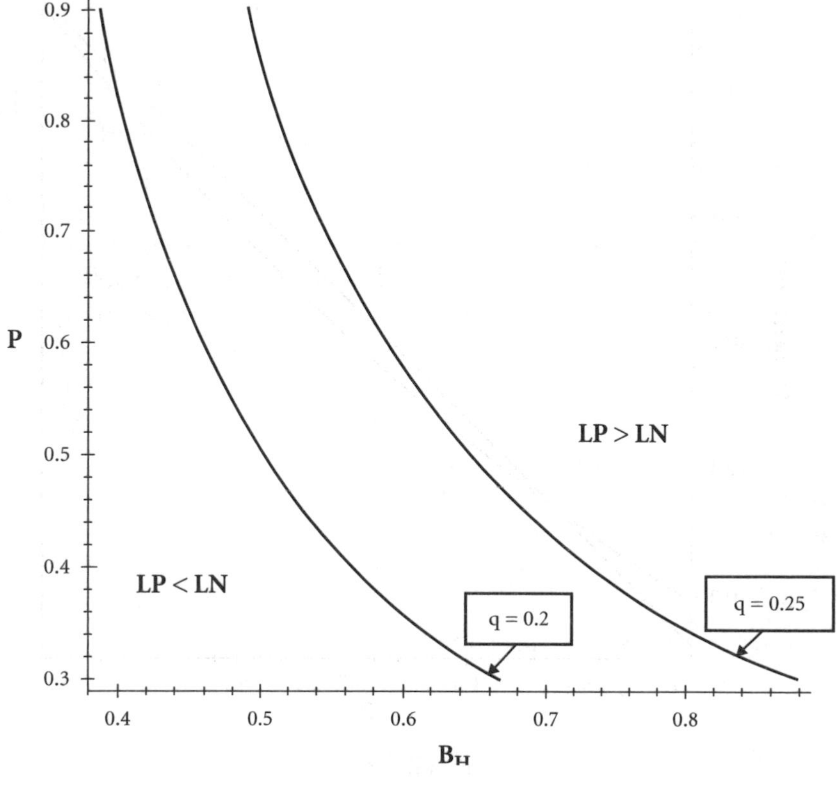

FIGURE 1.3

little in the way of a meaningful policing in Biblical and Talmudic times. In view of this, and in the face of the difficulties of obtaining a conviction in a Jewish court, the probability of apprehension and conviction of a thief must have been very low. In certain circumstances, therefore, it made economic sense to provide an incentive to thieves who discovered they had gotten less than they bargained for to return the stolen articles. It appears that recognizing this, as well as the role of incentives, the Biblical law of theft attempted to provide such an incentive by offering a pardon to thieves who voluntarily returned stolen articles.

APPENDIX: THE ECONOMIC MODEL: A NUMERICAL EXAMPLE

We illustrate our analysis by using a numerical example. The notations used here follow that of the text, and the parameters are as follows:

$\mathbf{B_L}$ = the high value of the stolen article to the thief.
$\mathbf{B_H}$ = the low value of the stolen article to the thief.

F = the fine.
q = the probability of apprehension.
p = the proportion of high-valued articles.

Table A1.1 provides simulated theft data for selected values of the exogenous variables that are indicated in the table's titles, for both the no pardon and the pardon regimes. The calculations are described below.

(a) No pardon regime—First column: There exist one thousand stealable articles and one thousand potential, risk neutral, thieves. Each stealable article may be stolen by one specific thief. The value of an article to its owner is unity. Prior to stealing "his" article, a thief does not know the value[17] of this article to him. He, however, knows that it has one of two possible values: a high value, $\mathbf{B_H = 0.75}$, or low value, $\mathbf{B_L = 0.125}$, with probabilities $\mathbf{p = 0.5}$ and $\mathbf{(1 - p) = 0.5}$, respectively.

After a thief has stolen his article, he will be apprehended with a probability $\mathbf{q = 0.2}$, in which case he has to return the article and pay a fine equal to $\mathbf{F = 1}$. The probability that he is not caught is

$$\mathbf{(1 - q) = 0.8}$$

Hence, *after the theft has taken place* the expected utility of the thief is

$$\mathbf{V_H = (1 - q)\, B_H - qF = (0.8)(0.75) - (0.2)(1) = 0.4} \qquad \text{(A1)}$$

if the article transpires to be of the high value (**H** type), and

$$\mathbf{V_L = (1 - q)\, B_L - qF = (0.8)(0.125) - (0.2)(1) = -0.1} \qquad \text{(A2)}$$

Table A1.1 Theft data for selected levels of p and q

		q = 0.2		**q = 0.2**		**q = 0.12**	
		p = 0.5		**p = 0.25**		**p = 0.25**	
		1	**2**	3	4	5	**6**
		No-pardon regime	**Pardon regime**	No-pardon regime	**Pardon regime**	No-pardon regime	**Pardon regime**
1	Number of thefts	150	***200***	25	***100***	127	***135***
2	Number of articles voluntarily returned	0	***100***	0	***75***	0	***101***
3	Number of thieves caught	30	***20***	5	***5***	15	***4***
4	Fines paid	30	***20***	5	***5***	15	***4***
5	Number of articles lost to their owners	120	***80***	20	***20***	112	***30***
6	Loss to owners	90	***60***	15	***15***	97	***26***

Given: $B_L = 0.125$; $B_H = 0.75$; F = 1; The number of stealable articles = 1,000

17 For example, its resale value in a stolen goods market.

if the article transpires to be of the **L** type.

In the absence of a pardon, the thief's gross[18] expected utility of theft, $\mathbf{U_N}$, is the weighted average of the two ex post expected utilities.

$$\mathbf{U_N = pV_H + (1-p)\,V_L = (0.5)(0.4) + 0.5(-0.1) = 0.15} \quad \text{(A3)}$$

Given our assumption of uniformly distributed costs, the proportion of potential thieves engaging in theft equals $\mathbf{U_N = 15\%}$, implying that the number of thefts is **0.15% of 1,000 = 150**. This is shown in the first column of the first row in Table A1.1.

The number of thieves caught is **150q = 20% of 150 = 30,** and each of these pays a fine of **1** (see first column, third and forth rows).

The number of articles that are lost to their owners is **150 – 30 = 120.** Deducting the fine paid to owners by apprehended thieves, we obtain the average loss to owners (i.e., **120 – 30 = 90**; sixth row).

(b) Pardon Regime—Second column: When pardon is granted to thieves who return stolen articles, the thief knows that, if he chances on a low value article and therefore returns it, his ex post utility from the theft will be 0. Therefore, given a potential pardon, the gross expected utility before stealing, $\mathbf{U_P}$, is derived from (A3) by setting $\mathbf{V_L = 0}$.

$$\mathbf{U_P = p\,V_H + (1-p)(0) = (0.5)(0.4) + 0.5(0) = 0.2} \quad \text{(A4)}$$

The proportion of potential thieves engaged in theft has risen by 5 percent, to $\mathbf{U_P = 20\%}$, and the number of thefts is therefore **20% of 1,000 = 200**. This is shown in the first row of the second column in Table A.1.

After stealing, 50 percent of the thieves (recall that $\mathbf{p = 0.5}$) find that that their stolen articles are of low value and therefore return them. The number of returned articles is, therefore, **50% of 200 = 100** (second row). Of the **100** nonreturned articles, **20** articles are caught and the fine paid is **20** (third and fourth row).

Total owners' loss under pardon regime is, therefore, the nonreturned and noncaught articles (fifth row) minus the fine = **80 – 20 = 60** (sixth row).

The number of theft is generally higher and never lower in the pardon regime, since the expected benefit from stealing is higher in this regime. However, for the parameter values used in the table, the number of voluntarily returned articles overweighs this disadvantage and the pardon regime is superior.

18 Before subtracting the costs the thief incurs in stealing.

(c) A reduction in p—No Pardon Regime—Third column: Suppose that the proportion of high-value articles declines to **p = 0.25**. Since this is the only change we repeat the calculations presented in (a) except that we substitute in (A3) **p = 0.25** and **1 – p = 0.75** to obtain:

$$\mathbf{U_N = p\,V_H + (1-p)\,V_L = (0.25)(0.4) + 0.75(-0.1) = 0.025} \tag{A5}$$

Hence, the proportion of thieves engaged in theft declines to $\mathbf{U_N}$ = **2.5%**, and the number of thefts is **2.5% of 1,000 = 25**. This is shown in the first row of the third column in Table A1.1. The number of thieves caught is **q (25) = 0.2(25) = 5**; each is paying a fine of **1** (third and forth rows). The number of articles that are lost to their owners is **25 – 5 = 20** and, deducting the fines paid by the thieves, we obtain the average loss to owners, **20 – 5 = 15** (sixth row).

(d) A reduction in p—Pardon Regime—Forth column: Repeating the calculation in (**b**), but assuming **p = 0.25** and using (A4), yields

$$\mathbf{U_P = p\,V_H + (1-p)(0) = (0.25)(0.4) + 0.25(0) = 0.1.} \tag{A6}$$

The proportion of thieves engaged in theft equals $\mathbf{U_P}$ **= 10%**, and the number of thefts is **10% of 1,000 = 100.** This is shown in the first row of the second column in Table A1.1.

After stealing, 75 percent of the thieves discover that their stolen articles are of low value, and these articles are returned under the pardon regime. The number of returned articles are **(0.75)(100) = 75** (second row). Of the **25** nonreturned articles, **5** articles are caught and the fine paid is **5** (forth row). Total owners' loss under the pardon regime is: the nonreturned and noncaught articles = 20 (Fifth row) minus the fine = 20 – 5 = 15 (sixth row).

A lower level of **p** reduces the number of theft in both regimes (compare row 1 in columns 3 and 4 to row 1 in columns 1 and 2, respectively). This is a general result since a lower proportion of high-valued articles reduce the expected benefit from stealing. However, the reduction is greater in the no pardon regime than in the pardon regime (compare the reduction of the number of thefts between columns 1 and 3 versus the reduction between columns 2 and 4), leading to a decrease in the advantage of pardon regime. Table A1.1 highlights this result: The lower level of **p** yields that both regimes are identical in terms of owners' loss.

(e) The impact of a change in q—columns five and six: To show the impact of a reduction in the probability of apprehension, **q**, we recalculate the formulas in (**a**) and (**b**) for **p = 0.25** and **q = 0.12**. The results of these calculations are presented in columns 5 and 6, respectively. Comparing columns 5 and 6 to columns 3 and 4 illustrates that, starting from a set of parameters for which both regimes yields an identical loss to owners, a lower **q** yields that the pardon regime is superior to the no pardon regime. A low **q** means that only a small proportion of thieves are caught, so that the voluntary returning of articles, which exists only in the pardon regime, is the main source of reduced owners' costs.

Conclusion

In this appendix we demonstrated that that the waiver of the fine (pardon regime) may represent recognition by Biblical law of the benefits of encouraging thieves to return stolen articles. In certain circumstances—for example, such as presented in column 2 and 6—it makes economic sense to provide an incentive to return the stolen articles. The absence of effective policing in Biblical and Talmudic times, the difficulties of obtaining a conviction in a Jewish court, and the likely very low probability of apprehension and conviction of a thief, **q**, all militate toward a pardon regime. It appears that, recognizing this, the Biblical law of theft attempted to provide such an incentive by offering a pardon to thieves who voluntarily returned stolen articles.

SELECTED BIBLIOGRAPHY

Andreoni, James. "The Desirability of a Permanent Tax Amnesty." *Journal of Public Economics* 45 (July 1991): 143–59.

Innes, Robert. "Remediation and Self-Reporting in Optimal Law Enforcement." *Journal of Public Economics* 72 (June 1999): 379–93.

Kaplow, Louis., and Steven Shavell. "Optimal Law Enforcement with Self-Reporting of Behavior." *Journal of Political Economy* 102 (June 1994): 583–606.

Maimonides, Laws of Theft, 1:4.

Maimonides, Laws of Theft, 1:5.

Malik, Arun S., and Robert M., Schwab. "The Economics of Tax Amnesties." *Journal of Public Economics* 46 (October 1991): 29–49.

CHAPTER 2

ELIEZER THE MATCHMAKER: ETHICAL CONSIDERATIONS AND MODERN NEGOTIATION THEORY

AARON LEVINE

Introduction

In modern society, the dealmaker is one of the most admired economic actors. Through discretion, initiative, creativity, and daring, the dealmaker brings parties together into a mutually advantageous enterprise.

We will focus on the Biblical account of how Eliezer, servant of Abraham, made the matrimonial match between Rebecca and Isaac, described in Genesis 24:1–67. First, we will consider the propriety of the test Eliezer devised in light of the Torah's ethical principles. We will also examine the various discrepancies between Abraham's charge to Eliezer and what happened at the well, on the one hand, and Eliezer's account of them, on the other. Our second concern will be whether the stratagems Eliezer employed as a matchmaker conform to the success formulae recommended by modern theorists in the field of negotiations.

Eliezer's Matchmaking Adventure—Ethical Considerations

Ethical evaluation of Eliezer's conduct perforce begins with the following Midrashic passage:

> Said R. Aha: The table-talk of the servants of the Patriarchs' households is more notable [literally: "beautiful"] than the Torah of their descendants. Eliezer's story is recorded and recapitulated, taking up two to three pages, whereas one of the fundamental rulings of the Torah, that the blood of a creeping thing defiles in the same way as the flesh, is known to us only through the superfluity of one letter in the Scriptures.[1]

R. Aha's dictum apparently puts an imprimatur of ethical propriety on Eliezer's conduct, explaining why the Torah devoted "two to three pages" to record so many moral enigmas regarding his actions. This is implied by R. Abraham Abele b. Hayyim ha-Levi Gombiner (Poland, ca. 1637–1683) in a comment on one of the details of the story. R. Gombiner discusses specifically the protocol that one should not eat before feeding his animals.[2] He opines that this does not apply to drink; one may drink before giving his animals to drink. R. Gombiner derives this from Rebecca's response to Eliezer's request for a drink at the well: "Drink and I will even water your camels."[3] The Torah records this event to teach practical law.[4]

Even as R. Aha's dictum puts the imprimatur of propriety on Eliezer's conduct, we must still set Eliezer's specific actions against the ethical norms of Judaism. Without identifying the underlying principles, it is dangerous to apply lessons learned from Eliezer's conduct to other contexts. Moreover, some of what Abraham said and what Eliezer actually did is subject to dispute.[5] We will therefore take a position on what Eliezer actually did and said, following a representative sampling, if not the great majority, of commentators.

Eliezer's Agency Role

Before analyzing Eliezer's conduct, one must note that Eliezer was acting in the capacity of a *shaliah*, or agent, on behalf of Abraham, his master. Eliezer's commission was to bring home a suitable mate for Isaac.[6] Indeed, Eliezer's first order of

1 *Genesis Rabbah* 60:11.

2 BT *Berakhot* 40a.

3 Genesis 24:26; R. Abraham Abele b. Hayyim ha-Levi Gombiner, *Magen Avraham* to *Shulhan Arukh, Orah Hayyim* 167, note 18.

4 R. Samuel b. Nathan ha-Levi Kolin (Bohemia, 1720–1806), *Mahatsit ha-Shekel* to *Shulhan Arukh, Orah Hayyim*, ad loc.

5 Cf. endnote 79.

6 Genesis 24:2–9; *Moshav Zekenim mi-Ba'alei ha-Tosafot* to Genesis 24:67; *Tosafot* to *Ketubbot* 7b. Some authorities understand Eliezer's agency role as merely to bring home a suitable mate for Isaac.

business and first words of communication with Bethuel and Laban were to identify himself as Abraham's servant.[7] Eliezer then revealed that he was sent to find a wife for his master's son.[8]

Eliezer's *shelihut* status is a critical factor in the analysis of the ethics of his conduct.

One fundamental guidepost for the agent (*A*) in Jewish law is that *A* must conduct all his affairs in accordance with the specific instructions of his principal (*P*). Departing from those instructions violates the agency relationship between *P* and *A* and is grounds for *P* to void the transaction *A* concluded on his behalf. In the absence of specific instruction, *A* may not use his own discretion; instead, he must assess the mindset of *P* and act accordingly. Illustrating this is a law regarding the portion of the crop that the farmer must separate and give to a *kohen* (priest), called *terumah*. If terumah is not given, it is prohibited to consume the crop, and one who violates that prohibition is subject to capital punishment at the hands of heaven.[9] While Torah law allows the terumah obligation to be satisfied with even a single grain, the Sages established standards for giving: A generous person gives one-fortieth; an average person gives one-fiftieth; and a penurious person gives one-sixtieth.[10] Now, suppose *P* appoints *A* his agent in separating *terumah* from his crop but does not specify how much to separate. The rule is as follows:

> If [a person] says to his agent: "Go and separate *terumah* on my behalf," but he gives no instructions as to how much *terumah* he wishes to be taken, [the agent] should separate *terumah* in accordance with the mindset of the owner, and if he does not know the mindset of the owner, he should separate using the intermediate standard, taking one part in fifty as *terumah*. If it turns out that [the

---

Marriage is entered into in two stages. In the first, *eirusin*, the man gives the woman an object of value and recites a standard marriage proposal to her in the presence of two witnesses. While *eirusin* does not permit the couple to live together, it confers marital status on them in most respects, and the woman requires a divorce before she can marry again. The second stage, *nissu'in*, is effected by means of entering a canopy (*huppah*) where a religious ceremony is performed. Only after *huppah* is the couple permitted to live together as man and wife.

Midrash Lekah Tov derives from the narrative that Eliezer effected *eirusin* on behalf of Isaac. The Midrash contrasts the two gifts Eliezer gave Rebecca, saying that the first, which he gave her at the well (Genesis 24:22), was not for *eirusin*, while the second, after Rebecca's family agreed to the match (Genesis 24:51–53), was.

R. Hizkiyah Hizkuni (France, thirteenth century) agrees. Initially, he observes, we find Rebecca's family responding affirmatively and enthusiastically to Eliezer's marriage proposal: "Here, Rebecca is before you; take [her] and go . . ." But in the morning, after Eliezer had given Rebecca the second gifts, the family insists that Rebecca delay her departure: "Her brother and her mother said, 'Let the maiden remain with us days or a set of ten [months]; then she will go'" (Genesis 24:55). Eliezer's second gift, he argues, accounts for their change of attitude. Until then, the family thought the plan was for Eliezer to bring Rebecca to Isaac, who would begin the marriage ceremony with *eirusin*. Eliezer's second gift, however, effected *eirusin* on behalf of Isaac. The family therefore felt that Rebecca could remain at home until the *nissu'in* stage, as was indeed the custom (*Hizkuni* to Genesis 24:53, 55).

Further evidence that Eliezer's mandate was not only to bring home a suitable mate for Isaac, but to effect *eirusin*, and even possibly *nissu'in*, on behalf of Isaac, are the various sources that read into the narrative that, while Eliezer was still in Aram Naharaim, the blessings prescribed for these ceremonies were already recited. See Tractate *Kallah* and *Pirkei de-Rabbi Eliezer*.

7 Genesis 24:33–34.

8 Ibid., 24:37–38.

9 Leviticus 22:14; Maimonides (Rambam, Egypt, 1135–1204), *Mishneh Torah*, *Ma'akhalot Asurot* 10:19.

10 BT *Hullin* 137b.

> agent] subtracted ten parts from the intermediate standard, or added ten to this standard, his actions are not invalidated, and the *terumah* that he separated is accorded the status of *terumah*.[11]

Another guidepost for *A* is that he operates under an implicit mandate from *P*: *le-takkonei shaddartikh ve-lo le-avvotei* (I sent you to improve my situation and not to impair it). The import of this dictum is that the slightest error committed by the agent severs the agency.

Illustrating the *le-takkonei shaddartikh* principal is the following case involving payment of a debt through an agent: *B* owes *L* $1,000. *B* gives $1,000 to *A* and instructs *A* to give *L* the money as payment for his debt. *B* tells *A*, "Pay my debt and retrieve from *L* the deed of indebtedness." *A* gives *L* the $1,000 as payment. But when *A* asks *L* to return the deed of indebtedness, *L* refuses, claiming he took the $1,000 as payment for another debt that *B* owed him. The second debt of $1,000, *L* explains, was the subject of an oral contract and therefore the deed of indebtedness, which evidenced the first loan, remains intact. *L*'s claim that a parallel debt was owed him is believed[12] and *L* has the right to use his document to collect another $1,000 from *B*.[13] Now, had *A* obtained the deed of indebtedness from *L* before paying him the $1,000, *L* would have been unable to claim a second $1,000 from *B*. Notwithstanding that A followed precisely the sequence of actions *B* specified in his instructions (i.e., to pay the debt and retrieve the deed) *A* must deal with *L* in a manner ensuring that *L* does indeed return the document.[14] Accordingly, prudence demands *A* to reverse the sequence of actions *B* mentioned and pay only after retrieving the document from *L*. Since the *le-takkonei shaddartikh* mandate requires *A* not only to carry out his commission in a manner conforming to explicit instruction, but to do so in a manner protecting the interests of his principal, *A* is deemed negligent in first paying and only then asking for return of the document. Consequently, *A* must compensate *B* for his loss.[15]

Further illustrating the *le-takkonei shaddartikh* principle is an aspect of the law of *ona'ah* (price fraud),[16] which prohibits an individual from concluding a transaction at a price more favorable to himself than the competitive norm.[17] A transaction involving *ona'ah* is regarded as a form of theft.[18] Depending on the magnitude of the

11 Mishnah, *Terumah* 4:4.

12 *L*'s claim has credibility on the basis of the principle called *miggo* (lit., "since"), which states that, if a litigant could have won the case with a superior argument and instead advanced a weaker one, even the weaker plea is believed. Since *A* gave *L* the $1,000 without witnesses, *L* could have used the document he had to claim $1,000 from *B* by attesting that he received no money from *A*. Accordingly, *L* retains his right to collect $1,000 from *B* even when *L* concedes that he did indeed receive $1,000 from *A*, but accepted it as payment of a parallel debt *B* owed him that was only orally entered into.

13 BT *Ketubbot* 85a.

14 R. Alexander b. Joshua ha-Kohen Falk (Poland, 1555–1614), *Sema* to *Shulhan Arukh, Hoshen Mishpat* 58, note 4.

15 BT *Ketubbot* 85a; R. Joseph Caro (Safed, 1488–1575), *Shulhan Arukh, Hoshen Mishpat* 58:1.

16 "When you make a sale to your fellow or when you buy from the hand of your fellow, do not victimize one another" (Leviticus 25:14).

17 *Baraita* at BT *Bava Metsi'a* 51a; Rif, ad loc.; *Mishneh Torah, Mekhirah* 12:1; Rosh to *Bava Metsi'a* 4:17; *Tur, Mekhirah* 227:1; *Shulhan Arukh, Mekhirah* 227:1; *Arukh ha-Shulhan, Mekhirah* 227:1.

18 BT *Bava Metsi'a* 61a; *Sema* to *Shulhan Arukh, Hoshen Mishpat* 227, note 1.

price's deviation from the competitive norm, the injured party may have recourse to void or adjust the transaction. The sages identified three degrees of ona'ah. Provided the price discrepancy falls within the margin of error,[19] plaintiffs right to void the transaction is recognized when the difference between the sale price and the reference price was more than a sixth.[20] A differential of exactly one-sixth entitles neither party to void the transaction; the plaintiff is, however, entitled to full restitution of the *ona'ah*.[21] Finally, third-degree *ona'ah* occurs when the sale price differs from the market price by less than one-sixth. In that case, the transaction not only remains binding, but the plaintiff has no legal right to recoup the price differential.[22]

When one or both of the parties to the transaction is an agent, the rules of *ona'ah* are modified. If the plaintiff informed the defendant that he was acting as an agent for a particular person, the occurrence of *any* amount of *ona'ah* allows the principal to invalidate the transaction. This applies even when the transaction falls into an exempt category, where the restitution procedure is either modified or does not apply altogether, as, for example, in real estate transactions. The principal here is *le-takkonei shaddartikh ve-lo le-avvotei*.[23]

This application of *le-takkonei shaddartikh* to the law of *ona'ah* has implications for an agent's risk taking. The agent is a victim of *ona'ah* because he relies on his knowledge of alternative market possibilities and takes the chance that the price he agreed to is indeed the "fair" market price. Had he only engaged in sufficient market research, he would not have overpaid or accepted a below-market price. *Le-takkonei shaddartikh* hence dictates that the agent should not undertake "unnecessary risk" (i.e., risk he could eliminate with sufficient diligence and patience).

We have demonstrated that even when *A*'s action does not directly and explicitly violate *P*'s advance instruction, *P* may still have recourse to invalidate the action. This obtains when either the judgment that produced *A*'s action clearly does not represent *P*'s mindset, or the outcome resulted from *A*'s assumption of unnecessary risk. The flip side is that it is unethical, based on the *hin tsedek* (good faith) imperative, for *A* to intentionally violate the parameters of his authority in the hope that

19 BT *Bava Batra* 78a and Rashi, ad loc.; *Shulhan Arukh*, op. cit. 220:8.

20 *Shulhan Arukh*, op. cit. 227:4, and *Sema*, ad loc., note 6. R. Jonah b. Abraham Gerondi (Spain, ca. 1200–1263), quoted in *Tur*, loc. cit.; in *Rema*, *Shulhan Arukh*, loc. cit.; and in *Arukh ha-Shulhan*, op. cit. 227:4. Ruling in accordance with R. Jonah is R. Asher b. Jehiel, Rosh to *Bava Batra* 5:14. He expresses a minority view that, as long as the plaintiff does not uphold the transaction, the offender, too, is given the prerogative of voiding it. The offender's right proceeds from the magnitude of the price discrimination involved. Because the concluded price diverged more than one-sixth from the market norm, he may insist that the original transaction be treated as an agreement consummated in error (*mekah ta'ut*). Once the transaction is, however, upheld by the plaintiff, the offender loses his right to void the sale, since the offender enjoys no such right when his offense consists of the less severe violation of contracting for a sale price involving second-degree *ona'ah*. Conferring *full* nullification rights on him when his offence is graver seems counter to all canons of equity.

21 BT *Bava Metsi'a* 50b; *Shulhan Arukh*, op. cit. 227:2.

22 Ibid.

In third degree *ona'ah*, plaintiff's claim is denied only when the transaction involved a nonstandardized product. If the product was homogeneous, plaintiff's claim for the differential is honored. (See *Arukh ha-Shulhan*, loc. cit.)

23 BT *Ketubbot* 100a; *Shulhan Arukh*, op. cit. 227: 30. In the event the seller is victimized in a transaction with an agent of the buyer, authorities dispute whether the case is treated as an ordinary *ona'ah* case, or whether the seller is entitled to nullification rights, regardless of the degree of *ona'ah* involved. See *Tur*, op. cit.

P will resign himself to accept the outcome. The *hin tsedek* imperative requires an individual to fully intend to carry out any commitment or offer he makes.[24] It dictates that *A*, upon accepting an agency role from *P*, must fulfill *P*'s reasonable expectations by basing his conduct on an honest assessment of *P*'s mindset and not assuming unnecessary risk.

Eliezer's Test at the Well and the *Le-Takkonei Shaddartikh* Mandate

Two issues require consideration in assessing whether Eliezer acted properly as an agent according to Jewish law: whether Eliezer undertook unnecessary risks, and whether his conduct corresponded to a reasonable assessment of what Abraham himself would have done. Let us begin with the Torah's account of the test Eliezer devised to select a mate for Isaac:

> And he said, "God, God of my master, Abraham, may You so arrange it for me this day, and do kindness with my master, Abraham. See I stand here by the spring of water and the daughters of the townsmen come out to draw water. Let it be that the maiden to whom I shall say, 'Please tip your jug so I may drink,' and who replies, 'Drink, and I will even water your camels,' her will You have chosen for Your servant, for Isaac; and may I know through her that You have done kindness with my master."[25]

R. Jonathan's critique of Eliezer bears directly upon whether his test entailed unnecessary risk:

> R. Samuel b. Nahmani said in the name of R. Jonathan: Three individuals made requests in an improper manner. Two were answered in a proper manner, and one was answered in an improper manner. They are: Eliezer, servant of Abraham, King Saul b. Kish, and Yiftah the Gileadite. Eliezer, servant of Abraham, made an improper request when he sought a wife for his master's son, Isaac, as it is written that Eliezer prayed to God: "Let it be that the maiden to whom I shall say, 'Please tip your jug etc. [so I may drink],' and who replies, 'Drink and I will even water your camels,'[26] let her be the one you have designated for your servant, for Isaac."

24 The prohibition against making an insincere promise is derived by Abbayei (Babylonia, fourth century CE) at BT *Bava Metsi'a* 49a in the following manner:
Regarding the Biblical prohibition against false weights and measures, the Torah writes: "Just (*tsedek*) balances, just weights, a just *efah*, and a just *hin* you shall have" (Leviticus 19:36). Since the *hin* is a measure of smaller capacity than the *efah*, its mention seems superfluous. If accuracy is required in measures of large capacity, it is certainly required in smaller measures. This apparent superfluity leads Abaya to connect *hin* with the Aramaic word for "yes," *hen*, resulting in the following interpretation: Be certain that your "yes" is *tsedek* (sincere) and (by extension) be certain that your "no" is *tsedek* (sincere). If an individual makes a commitment or an offer, he should fully intend to carry it out.

25 Genesis 24:12–14.

26 Ibid., 24:14.

> Now is it possible that he meant to take even a lame or blind girl as a wife for Isaac?[27]

Preliminarily, note that R. Jonathan's purpose is only to highlight the negative side effects of a poorly designed test. Undoubtedly, Eliezer was correct in looking for the trait of kindness. Because compassion,[28] kindness[29] and generosity[30] were the hallmarks of Abraham and his household, only an exemplar of these attributes would be a suitable mate for Isaac.[31]

Why does R. Jonathan find Eliezer's stipulation improper? Surely, if the maiden standing at the well had a physical deformity, Eliezer would not approach her and say, "Please tip your jug so I may drink." Addressing this issue, *Tosafot* posit that R. Jonathan's concern was for a deformity that would not be evident on superficial inspection—such as a wooden leg, or a beautiful, but unseeing, eye.[32]

If R. Jonathan refers to a "hidden" deformity, he objects not to the "please tip your jug" test itself, but rather to Eliezer's reckless stipulation that the girl who passed the test be the bride, without qualification. Eliezer should not have committed himself without first making inquires to ensure that the maiden who passed the test was also free of hidden physical deformities. Now, obtaining trustworthy information in this area is difficult. It would certainly entail making discreet inquiries and obtaining information from multiple sources. It might also entail a considerable financial outlay. But Eliezer was Abraham's agent, and Abraham authorized him to spend whatever was necessary to bring home a bride for Isaac.[33] Accordingly, by neglecting to ensure that Rebecca was free of "hidden defects" before committing himself to the match, Eliezer was in apparent violation of the *le-takkonei shaddartikh* mandate.

However, this is not necessarily so. Investigating to insure against "hidden defects" eliminates "unnecessary risk" only if doing so does not jeopardize the match itself. If it does, Eliezer's stipulation should be characterized as a calculated risk rather than an unnecessary risk. In a calculated risk, the decision maker fully considers the potential costs and benefits of alternative strategies and pursues the course of action that, to his mind, best promotes success.

We suggest that Eliezer assumed a calculated risk rather than an unnecessary risk because alternative plans would have exacerbated the various disadvantages Eliezer was operating under, and they would have considerably weakened, if not altogether nullified, Eliezer's one advantage. We will show that Eliezer's actual stipulation minimized his disadvantages, capitalized on his advantage, and simultaneously created a mesmerizing force that compelled the maiden's family to accept the match.

27 BT *Ta'anit* 4a.

28 BT *Beitsah* 32a.

29 Genesis 18:1–8; *Midrash ha-Gadol* at Genesis 18:1; *Midrash he-Hafets* at Genesis 18:5.

30 BT *Bava Metsi'a* 87a.

31 *Midrash Aggadah* at Genesis 24:14 states explicitly that testing a maiden for her kindness was the proper means of finding a suitable mate for Isaac.

32 *Tosafot* to *Ta'anit* 4a.

33 Genesis 23:2; *Midrash ha-Gadol* at Genesis 24:2; *Tanhuma Yashan, Parashat Va-Yetse* 3.

The first disadvantage confronting Eliezer was his oath not to return Isaac to the land God commanded Abraham to leave.[34] The import of this oath, which Abraham administered, was that Isaac would never leave the Land of Israel,[35] even temporarily.[36] Consequently, the bride would have to depart from Aram Naharaim, travel to join Isaac at Hebron, and never again return to her homeland.

The second obstacle Eliezer faced was his own inferior social status as Abraham's (former)[37] servant, and, in particular, the stereotype that a slave desires a lifestyle of promiscuity.[38] What could be more disadvantageous in convincing Rebecca's family to agree to the match? The plan was for Eliezer to return with Rebecca on a seventeen-day journey from Aram Naharaim to Hebron.[39] In pursuing his mission, Eliezer could not consider himself above the general reputation slaves had at the time. Even in the eyes of Abraham and Isaac, Eliezer was not above suspicion: The Midrash records that Abraham suspected Eliezer of violating Rebecca on the return journey from Aram Naharaim.[40] In another version in the Midrash, it is Isaac who held this suspicion.[41]

Eliezer was himself keenly aware that his status as a slave would handicap his matchmaking efforts: "Perhaps the woman will not wish to follow me to this land."[42] He therefore made it his first order of business to reveal his identity to Bethuel and Laban.[43] Motivating Eliezer's conduct was Rabbah bar Mari's dictum: "[If] you have a fault, bring it up before [anyone else can]."[44]

While Eliezer was operating under a number of disadvantages, Abraham equipped him with one advantage—a document designating Isaac the sole heir of all his possessions, which he instructed Eliezer to show to the maiden's family.[45] Abraham's intention, as R. Solomon b. Isaac (Rashi, France, 1040–1105) says, was "that [people] should jump [i.e., be eager] to send him their daughter."[46]

Let us consider a variant of the plan of action Eliezer chose. Instead of committing himself to the match if the maiden passes the "please tip your jug" test, Eliezer will use the test only to identify a possible candidate. Before showering the maiden with jewelry and approaching the family for consent, Eliezer will make inquiries to ensure that she is free of any hidden physical defects. The information Eliezer seeks relating to "hidden defects" might be nonpublic, and possibly even a well-guarded family secret. To elicit a secret is no small matter. It may well

34 Genesis 24:5–8.

35 Ibid., 24:6; *Midrash Lekah Tov,* ad loc.; Rashi to Genesis 24:8.

36 R. Meir Loeb b. Jehiel Michel Weisser (Malbim, Russia, 1809–1879), *Ha-Torah ve-ha-Mitsvah* to Genesis 24:8.

37 See R. Moses Joshua Judah Leib Diskin (Palestine, 1818–1898), *Maharil Diskin al ha-Torah,* pp. 56–57; R. Abraham Isaac Sorotzkin (New Jersey, b. 1945), *Gevurat Yitshak al ha-Torah,* vol. 1, pp. 50–52.

38 BT *Gittin* 13a.

39 *Pirkei de-Rabbi Eliezer* 16.

40 Ibid.

41 *Midrash Aggadah* at Genesis 24.

42 Genesis 24:5.

43 Ibid., 24:23–24.

44 BT *Bava Kamma* 92b.

45 Genesis 24:10; *Pirkei de-Rabbi Eliezer* 16.

46 Rashi to Genesis 24:16.

require Eliezer to establish an information network to get reliable information from multiple sources. Making these inquires therefore risks publicizing that Eliezer is a marriage broker. Once that is known, Eliezer will inevitably find himself locked in negotiations with the family of the potential bride. The family will surely want to know who he is, who sent him, and much information about the groom. He might then be forced to reveal that the couple would not live in Aram Naharaim, even temporarily. If Eliezer does not blindly commit himself to the match before making inquiries, therefore, he runs the risk of magnifying his disadvantages.

This alternative plan of Eliezer carries another incidental disadvantage: The longer Eliezer stays in Aram Naharaim, the longer he exposes himself to attack by thieves. Note that Eliezer arrived in Aram Naharaim with a conspicuous display of wealth.[47]

Can there be any doubt that Eliezer's stay in Aram Naharaim was fraught with danger? An oft-quoted Midrash records that Rebecca's father, Bethuel, tried to poison Eliezer at the very meeting when Eliezer presented him with the marriage proposal.[48]

In addition to exposing Eliezer to physical harm, a protracted stay in Aram Naharaim would detract from Eliezer's wealth advantage because Eliezer would have to pay handsomely for the information he seeks. Eliezer's conspicuous wealth would invite greed on the part of those who have or pretend to have the nonpublic information Eliezer seeks. Obtaining costly information would force Eliezer to dissipate some of the assets, thereby reducing the effect of showing the maiden's family Abraham's deed that designated Isaac as Abraham's sole heir. Eliezer's "free spending" in Aram Naharaim demonstrates that Eliezer is in control of Abraham's assets while Abraham is still alive. Who can tell what will remain of these assets when Abraham dies? Perhaps Eliezer's "free spending" will leave little for Isaac to inherit. Thus, if Eliezer did not blindly commit himself to the match without investigation, he would compromise his one advantage, that the bride would be marrying a wealthy man.

Let us now analyze how Eliezer's advantages and disadvantages would play out if he blindly accepted the results of the "please tip your jug" test without any investigation to ensure that the maiden was free of hidden faults.

Blind acceptance of the results of the test gives Eliezer the advantage of concealing both his identity and the nature of his mission until he has already committed to the match. Why is this an advantage? Eliezer's social status is more of a handicap if he first comes to the attention of the maiden's family unsure if their daughter is worthy to marry his master's son than if he comes with unqualified and enthusiastic interest in their daughter. Also, if Eliezer proceeds headlong without investigation, it may not occur to the family to discuss where the couple will permanently reside, or whether they should insist that Isaac

47 Genesis 24:10–11.

48 Rashi to Genesis 24:55, quoting *Midrash Rabbah*, ad loc.

visit them before they approve the match. Finally, blind acceptance allows Eliezer the luxury of not having to dissipate the assets of his master, and thus maximizes the impression that the woman who marries Isaac will, indeed, be marrying a wealthy man.

Most importantly, Eliezer's test creates a mesmerizing force that advances the match on an emotional level. By stipulating that the maiden who passes his test is the one God has chosen ("*otah hokhahta*") for Isaac, Eliezer allows himself to argue that God Himself has made the match and both sides must therefore blindly agree to it. This argument carries no weight unless the maiden's family is convinced that Eliezer himself totally relies on the test. Thus, if Eliezer seems unwilling to proceed based on the results of the test itself, and will commit to the match only after ensuring the maiden is free of hidden flaws, Eliezer loses his argument that God made the match. What gives life and dazzle to the presence of a supernatural force demanding the match is Eliezer's willingness to choose the bride entirely because of the test alone, taking his chances that the maiden has no hidden physical flaws.

Another investigation that we would have expected Eliezer to conduct, but that he did not pursue, is an inquiry into the character of Rebecca's brother, Laban, based on Rava's dictum that one who seeks to marry a woman should first examine the character of her brothers.[49] Rava's rationale is that most sons resemble in character the brothers of the mother.[50] Eliezer dispensed with active inquiries into the character of Laban because, we propose, such inquiries would demonstrate to Rebecca's family that, while Eliezer expected them to have blind faith that God Himself made the match, he himself did not.[51]

Another surprise: Why did Eliezer pass up the opportunity to reward Laban for his hospitality, which, according to *Targum* Yerushalmi (not earlier than eighth

49 BT *Bava Batra* 110a.

50 *Baraita*, ibid.

51 A thorough inquiry into Laban's personality would have revealed that he was an idolater and a person of wicked character. Rebecca had two sons: Jacob, who was righteous, and Esau, who was wicked. Eliezer's failure to investigate Laban therefore had the apparently disastrous effect of producing the wicked Esau. Perhaps Eliezer was not remiss in this way. Laban, as the brother of the potential bride, joined into the marriage negotiations and in the process cast himself in a very hospitable light: "For upon seeing the nose ring, and the bracelets on his sister's hands, and upon hearing his sister Rebecca's words, saying 'Thus has the man spoken to me,' he came to the man, and, behold, he was standing over the camels by the spring. He said, 'Come, O blessed of God! Why should you stand outside when I have cleared the house, and place for the camels?' So the man came into the house, and he unfastened the camels; he gave straw and feed for the camels, and water to bathe his feet and the feet of the men who were with him" (Genesis 24:30–32). *Targum Jonathan b. Uzziel* asserts the subject of the hospitable acts in the later verse is also Laban. Also, *Midrash Rabbah* (Genesis 24:31), quoted by Rashi ad loc., understands Laban's remark, "I have cleared the house" to mean, "I have cleared the house of idols." Perhaps Eliezer decided on the basis of these gestures that Rebecca's brother was a man of kindness and, though an idolater, amenable to reform. Then Eliezer's impression of Laban was a sort of examination of his personality, albeit an entirely passive one, and Eliezer did not propose marriage until he fulfilled Rava's dictum. This would explain an anomaly R. Moses Joshua Judah Leib Diskin notices in the Torah's detailed description of Laban's hospitality. The Torah's practice, notes R. Diskin, is to describe the praiseworthy actions of the righteous and the shortcomings of the wicked. Why, then, does the Torah record the wicked Laban's acts of hospitality (*Maharil Diskin al ha-Torah,* Genesis 24:32)? Perhaps to inform us that, in going about his mission to find a mate for Isaac, Eliezer interacted with Laban and reached a favorable impression of him, thus satisfying Rava's dictum.

century CE), consisted not only of preparing quarters for Eliezer and his camels,[52] but also of bringing provisions for the camels and water for Eliezer and his entourage to wash?[53] Rewarding Laban for his "gracious and generous hospitality" would seem a good investment. It might make Laban an ally in promoting the match or, at the very least, neutralize any opposition on his part. The answer, as it appears to this writer, is that rewarding Laban for his hospitality carries with it a serious disadvantage. It decidedly undermines Eliezer's claim that God himself demands acceptance of the match, because if Eliezer really believed this, why would he need to "bribe" Laban in the apparent hope that Laban would prove helpful in promoting the match?

The assertion that God Himself has arranged the match and therefore all parties should blindly accept it is bolstered by an uncanny coincidence. No sooner than Eliezer arrives at the well and makes his stipulation to God does Rebecca also arrive at the well. The very first maiden given the test passes the test with flying colors:

> I had not yet finished speaking to my heart, when behold, Rebecca came out with a jug on her shoulder and descended to the spring and drew water. Then I said to her, "Please give me to drink." She hurried and lowered her jug from upon herself and said, "Drink, and I will even water your camels." So I drank and she watered the camels also.[54]

This coincidence allows Eliezer to assert that only God could have arranged such perfect timing. This argument becomes even more appealing according to the Midrashic exposition that the journey from Hebron to Aram Naharaim usually took seventeen days, but Eliezer made it in three hours.[55] Eliezer was able to prove it, for he could show Laban and Bethuel the date on the deed that made Isaac Abraham's sole heir—the very same date on which Eliezer arrived at Aram Naharaim.[56] One could read into this spectacular coincidence that God "shrank the road" for Eliezer (*ve-nikpetsah ha-derekh alav*) so that he would meet Rebecca no sooner than he had finished stipulating with God his "please tip your jug" test.

The pivotal element in demonstrating that God Himself made the match is Eliezer's deliberate choice to commit himself to the match without first verifying that the maiden was free of hidden physical defects. Without this blind commitment, Eliezer could not show that he himself sees Divine Providence in the whole matter. Once Eliezer's own blind commitment is objectively convincing, the spectacular timing he experiences at the well augments the contention that God Himself made the match, and arguably adds an element of dazzle to his presentation.

52 Genesis 24:31.
53 R. Jonathan b. Uzziel to Genesis 24:32.
54 Genesis 24:46.
55 *Pirkei de-Rabbi Eliezer* 16.
56 Ibid.

The Clinching of the Match and Divine Providence

Rebecca's family's belief that God Himself desired the match is central in motivating their agreement:

> Then Laban and Bethuel answered and said, "The matter stemmed from God! We are unable to speak to you either bad or good. Here, Rebecca is before you: Take [her] and go, and let her be a wife to your master's son, as God has spoken."[57]

Thus, we have demonstrated that Eliezer's stipulation was not an assumption of unnecessary risk. Rather, Eliezer adopted the course of action that he believed had the best chance of succeeding. Eliezer's stipulation was therefore an assumption of a calculated risk, which did not violate his agency role.

Le-Takkonei Shaddartikh and R. Jonathan's Dictum

The above analysis suggests that Eliezer's plan simultaneously satisfies his *le-takkonei shaddartikh* duty to his master, Abraham, but is subject to R. Jonathan's criticism. This is not a contradiction. Competing plans have different advantages and disadvantages. In fulfilling his *le-takkonei shaddartikh* duty, we can expect Eliezer to do no more than what he thinks his principal, Abraham, would regard as the best plan. If all Eliezer's plans have flaws, the most promising plan, despite its flaws, will satisfy the *le-takkonei* mandate. Accordingly, Eliezer is entitled to conjecture that Abraham prefers a plan with an excellent chance of bringing home a maiden who is an exemplar of kindness, while risking that the maiden has a hidden physical defect. The alternative would be a plan ensuring identification of the perfect candidate, but running the significant risk that her family would reject the match.

Having satisfied *le-takkonei shaddartikh* does not, however, justify Eliezer's beseeching of God to arrange a mate for Isaac through the particular plan that Eliezer devised. Since Eliezer knows his chosen plan has a flaw, he should pray for no more than the ultimate success of his mission. Eliezer should be prepared to stay the course and experience setbacks along the way before realizing success. Recall Eliezer's own concluding words to Rebecca's family: "And now, if you intend to do kindness and truth with my master, tell me; and if not, tell me, and I will turn to the right or to the left."[58]

57 Genesis 24:50–51.

58 Ibid., 24:49. One could argue that, even if his plan were not flawed, it would have been improper for Eliezer to beseech God to grant him success through the particular plan he devised. Such an entreaty bespeaks a lack of perfect faith in God's infinite capacity to generate unimagined scenarios and juxtaposition of events to

Eliezer's Conduct and Judaism's Disclosure Duty

Abraham's charge to Eliezer shows that Abraham regarded one aspect of the arrangement as inviolate—that Eliezer not bring Isaac to Aram Naharaim:

> The servant said to him, "Perhaps the woman will not wish to follow me to this land; shall I take your son back from the land from which you departed?" Abraham said to him, "Beware, lest you return my son to there.[59] But if the woman will not wish to follow you, you shall then be absolved of this oath of mine; only, do not return my son to there."[60]

In these verses, Abraham adjures Eliezer twice against bringing Isaac to Aram Naharaim. In the opinion of R. Meir Loeb b. Jehiel Michel Weisser (Malbim, Russia, 1809–1879), the two admonitions refer to distinct matters. In the first, Abraham clarifies that the couple must live in the land God promised him, not where he sent Eliezer to find a bride. The second admonition addresses what Eliezer should do if the woman agrees to leave her country but balks at Eliezer's proposal to bring her to Isaac. It adjures Eliezer to not agree that Isaac will come to Aram Naharaim to escort the bride back to Hebron.[61]

The underlying reason for Abraham's caveat is that Isaac's spiritual development required that he not leave the land God promised Abraham and his progeny. The implication of Abraham's admonition is therefore that Isaac would never leave the country of his residence even temporarily, and thus Rebecca would never return to Aram Naharaim after she left with Eliezer.

In his recapitulation to Bethuel and Laban of Abraham's charge, Eliezer makes no mention of Abraham's stipulation that Isaac neither reside in Aram Naharaim nor even come there to accompany his bride back home. Since requiring Isaac to come to Aram Naharaim is a deal-breaker, should not Eliezer be required to volunteer this information?

In addressing this issue, note that Eliezer's first words to Bethuel and Laban are to identify himself as Abraham's servant. Recall Rabbah bar Mari's rationale for this: Eliezer's identity as a slave is a handicap in convincing Bethuel and Laban to agree to the match. Far better for Eliezer to reveal it immediately, himself, than to have his (former) slave status discovered later through probing by Bethuel and Laban. Since Eliezer is an agent, not a principal, in the negotiations

---

bring about a result. The principle here is, "Is the Hand of God too short? . . ." (Numbers 11:23). There is, however, a big difference between entreating God to grant success to a plan the petitioner knows has a flaw and making the same request for a plan the petitioner sees no fault in. In the latter instance, the petitioner is not guilty of making an improper request. Instead, his failure is an inflated sense of self-worth and excessive self-reliance, reflecting a lack of full appreciation for: "Is the Hand of God too short?"

59 Genesis 24:5–6.

60 Ibid., 24:8.

61 Malbim, *Ha-Torah ve-ha-Mitsvah* to Genesis 24:8.

with Bethuel and Laban, Rabbah bar Mari's dictum is not just a matter of prudent advice, but an absolute requirement, based on Eliezer's *le-takkonei shaddartikh* mandate.

The generalization of Rabbah bar Mari's dictum is that if *P*'s agenda includes items that will predictably be disagreeable to his opposite number, *P*'s agent has a duty to try his best to present the agenda in the order that will cause least harm to *P*'s interests. In Eliezer's situation, we assume that learning of the deal-breaking items would be disconcerting news for Rebecca's family. Accordingly, Eliezer, who is under the *le-takkonei shaddartikh* mandate, should not lend these matters prominence by disclosing them early, thereby very possibly jeopardizing the success of the mission itself. Instead, he should merely inform Rebecca's family of these matters. Imagine for a moment that Eliezer had front-loaded the deal-breaking items, beginning his presentation thusly:

> I am Eliezer, servant of Abraham. At the instruction of my master, I came here to find a bride for his son, Isaac. I am happy to tell you that your daughter, Rebecca, is the bride I have selected. Before I tell the story of how I came about to select her, I feel obligated to inform you that I will be the one accompanying Rebecca to Hebron, where Isaac resides. Under no circumstances will Isaac come here himself to accompany her home. I want it to be absolutely clear to you that the couple will reside in no place other than the land God promised Abraham and his progeny as a heritage. The couple will not come back here even to visit you. Once Rebecca leaves here, she will never come back.

Such an opening just about guarantees that Eliezer's mission will be dead on arrival. If Eliezer does indeed have a duty to disclose the deal-breaking items, he may insert the disclosure into his presentation where it will jeopardize the mission the least.

Eliezer may accordingly be relieved entirely of his disclosure duty, depending on how Rebecca's family responds. At the end of Eliezer's presentation, Bethuel and Laban say:

> The matter stemmed from God! We are unable to speak to you either bad or good. Here, Rebecca is before you, take [her] and go, and let her be a wife to your master's son as *God* has spoken.[62]

If Laban and Bethuel intended merely to acknowledge that God Himself orchestrated events to make the match happen, it would have sufficed for them to say, "The matter stemmed from God." By adding the phrase, "We are unable to speak to you either bad or good," Laban and Bethuel make the stronger and deeper acknowledgment that God demands that they accept the match and not interfere by interjecting deal-breaking conditions. This is suggested in Rashi's comments ad locum:

> "We are unable to speak to you"—to refuse about this matter; "neither by responding with a bad thing"—nor by responding with a proper thing; "for it is

62 Genesis 24:50–51.

> obvious"—that "the matter stemmed from God;" "according to your words"—that He prepared her for you.

If Laban and Bethuel's statement, "We are unable to speak to you bad or good," constitutes an acknowledgment that God Himself demands acceptance of the match and that they will therefore not introduce deal-breaking conditions, their subsequent words, "take [her] and go," conveys the resignation that the couple will reside in Hebron, where Isaac lives, and signal that they will not insist Isaac himself come to Aram Naharaim to bring Rebecca home with him.

Creating a False Impression and the Reasonable Expectation Principle

Suppose Laban and Bethuel had not responded to Eliezer's marriage proposal with their declaration of, "The matter stemmed from God! . . . take [her] and go . . ." Would Eliezer have a duty to inform them that the couple would not live in Aram Naharaim and that Isaac would not come to Aram Naharaim to escort Rebecca home to Hebron? This depends upon the reasonable expectation principle governing the prohibition against creating or failing to correct a false impression. The principle states that *A* is not responsible to disabuse *B* of a false impression that *B* harbors about him unless the false impression is the result of *B*'s reasonable expectations. Otherwise, *B*'s disappointment is considered to result from "self-deception."[63] In the case at hand, based on the facts already on the table, Rebecca's family should deduce that, once Rebecca leaves Aram Naharaim, she would likely never again return. The journey from Aram Naharaim to Hebron takes seventeen days. There are irreconcilable differences between the families on matters of religious belief and lifestyle, which would certainly keep Isaac away. The family cannot presume Rebecca will want to visit them, nor persuade Isaac to come along. Recall that, when Rebecca's family bid her goodbye, they sent her *meineket*, Deborah,[64] to accompany her.[65] *Targum Yerushalm* translates "*meniktah*" to mean a governess. Rebecca left her father's home for Hebron very young, still requiring a governess. In the Rabbis' view, she was only three years old.[66] Since Rebecca had not yet imbibed the culture and mores of her father's country when she left, her family should have recognized the distinct possibility that she would quickly adjust to the lifestyle of her husband, Isaac, and have no desire or inclination to return home.

63 For an explication of this principle with sources, see Aaron Levine, *Moral Issues of the Marketplace in Jewish Law* (Brooklyn, New York: Yashar Books, 2005), 2–42.

64 Genesis 35:8.

65 Ibid., 24:59.

66 Tractate *Soferim* 21.

Accordingly, if the couple's visiting is important to Rebecca's family, the onus is on them to bring up the matter.

Untruths Spoken by Eliezer and Judaism's Ethical Norms

If one contrasts Abraham's charge to Eliezer and the servant's actual experiences against Eliezer's recapitulations to Bethuel and Laban, many discrepancies emerge. Let us examine these discrepancies in *light* of the parameters the Torah sets for truthtelling.

We propose that three of these discrepancies can be explained based on the *darkhei shalom* (lit., "ways of peace") principle, which permits lying to promote peace.[67] Let us begin with these three discrepancies.

1. Eliezer tells Bethuel and Laban:

My master had me take an oath saying, "Do not take a wife for my son from the daughters of the Canaanite in whose land I dwell. Unless you go to my father's house and to my family and take a wife for my son."[68]

Yet Abraham's charge to Eliezer includes no instruction that Eliezer seek a mate for Isaac only from Abraham's father's house and family:

> I will have you swear by God, God of the heavens and God of the earth, that you not take a wife for my son from the daughters of the Canaanite, among whom I dwell. Rather, to my land and to my kindred shall you go and take a wife for my son, for Isaac.[69]

Why did Eliezer misrepresent to Bethuel and Laban that Abraham was interested in marrying Isaac to a girl from Abraham's own family? The *darkhei shalom* principle explains this irregularity. When Abraham heeded God's command to depart from the land of his father, there was much antagonism and hostility toward him. Abraham preached monotheism and battled against idolatry. Adherents to Abraham's ideology were few,[70] and his own family remained idolaters.[71] Besides this ideological divide, Abraham's departure generated resentment and hostility on a very personal level because Abraham left behind his elderly father, Terah, when he departed from Haran. Indeed, the Torah avoids publicizing this fact by recording Terah's death before Abraham's departure from Haran.[72]

67 BT *Yevamot* 65b. For an explication of this principle with sources, see *Moral Issues of the Marketplace in Jewish Law*, op. cit., 43–91.

68 Genesis 24:37–38.

69 Ibid., 24:3–4.

70 *Genesis Rabbah* 42:8.

71 Ibid., 38:13.

72 Ibid., 39:7.

Thus, when Eliezer discovers at the well that Rebecca is the daughter of Bethuel and the granddaughter of Abraham's brother, Nahor, Eliezer should reasonably expect fierce opposition to his marriage proposal. Ideologically, Rebecca's family members are Abraham's enemies; the two families' lifestyles will conflict and perhaps even be repulsive to each other. Moreover, Terah lived for another sixty-five years after Abraham's departure from Haran, dying only five years before Eliezer arrived.[73] The ill feeling against Abraham when he abandoned his elderly father must surely have been rekindled when Eliezer arrived as Abraham's agent to bring home a bride for Isaac.

Since Eliezer should reasonably assume that Abraham's family in Haran is hostile toward his master, a straightforward application of the *darkhei shalom* principle is that he take measures to pacify them. A *darkhei shalom* lie is further justified because relating faithfully Abraham's charge, which did not include any preference for finding a match within Abraham's own family, would probably exacerbate any ill feeling Rebecca's family already harbored against Abraham. But Abraham's sending Eliezer to find a bride for Isaac specifically from his own family is an unequivocal gesture of fondness and reconciliation. Since Eliezer's lie is uttered for the purpose of ending Rebecca's family's ill feeling for Abraham, it qualifies as a *darkhei shalom* lie and is permissible.

This sheds light on other inaccuracies in Eliezer's speech. Preliminarily, we assume that the *darkhei shalom* license applies only if the speaker is reasonably certain that his lie is credible and will not be detected.[74] Accordingly, once Eliezer makes up his mind that a *darkhei shalom* lie is in order, he must ensure that everything he says is consistent with that lie. Let us show how two additional inaccuracies in Eliezer's speech are necessitated by his misrepresentation that Abraham sent him to find a bride for Isaac from Abraham's own family.

2. Eliezer gave Rebecca his gifts of a nose ring and bracelet immediately after she passed his test. Only then did he inquire about her family.[75] But in recounting this story Eliezer reverses the sequence of events.[76]

Noting this discrepancy, Rashi comments:

> He changed the sequence [of events]. For, see, now, that first he gave [the jewelry to Rebecca], and afterwards he questioned [her as to whose daughter she was]. But, in order that they not catch him by his words [thinking that they caught him

73 At the time of his departure from Haran, Abraham was 75 years old (Rashi to Genesis 11:32) and Terah was 145 years old. Twenty-five years passed before Isaac was born, when Abraham was 100 (Genesis 21:8). Another forty years passed before Isaac married Rebecca, as the Torah records that Isaac was 40 when he married (Genesis 25:20). Thus, sixty five years passed from the time Abraham departed Haran to the time he sent Eliezer to find a bride for Isaac. Accordingly, when Eliezer arrived in Haran, Terah had just died five years earlier, at 205 (Genesis 11:32).

74 R. Jacob b. Joseph Reicher (Austria, d. 1733), *Iyyun Ya'akov*, commentary on *Ein Ya'akov* to BT *Yevamot* 63a.

75 Genesis 24:22–23.

76 Ibid., 24:47.

> in a lie] and say, "How could you have given her [the jewelry], when you did not yet know who she was," [he changed the sequence].[77]

The *darkhei shalom* principle adds an ethical subtext to Rashi's comment. Once Eliezer decides to make a *darkhei shalom* lie and represents to Bethuel and Laban that Abraham directed him to find a bride for Isaac from his family, Eliezer must ensure that everything he says is consistent with that lie. Accordingly, Eliezer must misrepresent to Bethuel and Laban that he gave the gifts to Rebecca only after he ascertained her family identity.

3. One more discrepancy apparently necessitated by Eliezer's need for credibility and, thus, consistency with his *darkhei shalom* lie is Eliezer's final entreaty to Bethuel and Laban that they agree to the match: "And now, if you intend to do kindness and truth with my master, tell me; and if not, tell me, and I will turn to the right or to the left."[78]

Rashi explains:

> "To the right"—from the daughters of Ishmael; "or to the left"—from the daughters of Lot, who lived to the left of Abraham.[79]

Since Abraham's charge to Eliezer was that he seek a wife for Isaac from his homeland, we would expect Eliezer to tell Bethuel and Laban only that if they declined the match, he would continue the search elsewhere. Specifying that the search will continue with the other branches of his master's family, namely, Ishmael and Lot, is entirely unnecessary, and an unfaithful rendering of Abraham's charge to him. The *darkhei shalom* principle explains this irregularity. Once Eliezer makes up his mind to speak a *darkhei shalom* lie and represent to Bethuel and Laban that Abraham directed him to find a bride from his family, Eliezer must be alert not only to avoid contradicting the lie, but also not to miss opportunities to reinforce the lie when circumstances warrant it. Otherwise, he will undermine his credibility.

4. A fourth discrepancy in Eliezer's account, which Midrash explicitly rationalizes by invoking *darkhei shalom*, seems unrelated to Eliezer's misrepresentation that Abraham charged him to find a bride from his family.

Abraham blessed Eliezer that he succeed in his mission:

> God, God of the heavens, Who took me from the house of my father and from the land of my birth, and Who spoke for me, and Who swore to me saying, "To your offspring will I give this land;" He will send His angel before you and you will take a wife for my son from there.[80]

77 Rashi to Genesis 24:47. This is also the view of R. Judah b. Betsalel Loew (Maharal, Prague, 1525–1609), *Gur Aryeh*, commentary to Genesis 24:22, and R. Samson Raphael Hirsch (Germany, 1808–1888), commentary ad loc. A contrary view is taken by R. Samuel b. Meir (Rashbam, France, ca. 1085–1158), ad loc.; Nahmanides (Ramban, Spain, 1194–1270), ad loc.; and R. Samuel Eliezer b. Judah ha-Levi Edels (Maharsha, Poland, 1555–1631) to *Ta'anit* 4a.

78 Genesis 24:49.

79 Rashi to Genesis 24:49, quoting *Genesis Rabbah* 60:9.

80 Genesis 24:7.

Eliezer, in his recapitulation, did not report it verbatim, but with a change:

> He said to me, "God, before Whom I have walked, will send His angel with you and make your journey successful, and you will take a wife for my son from my family and my father's house."[81]

Eliezer's recapitulation materially changed what Abraham said. Instead of reporting that Abraham expressed confidence that Eliezer would succeed because God took Abraham out of the land of his father and promised him and his progeny a unique destiny and heritage in the Land of Israel, Eliezer reported that the basis of his master's confidence was that Abraham walked before God (i.e., was obedient and loyal in doing God's Will).

One Midrash explains that Eliezer handled himself with perspicacity, aiming to endear Abraham to Bethuel and Laban. Recounting the blessing verbatim portrays Abraham as proud to leave his family for the unique destiny God set out for him and his progeny. It suggests elitism and would surely antagonize Bethuel and Laban. Because Eliezer's motive was to foster love between the families, his material alteration was permissible; to promote peace, one is permitted to alter the truth.[82]

The foregoing analysis implies an expansive conceptualization of the *darkhei shalom* principle. Why? *Darkhei shalom* provides no blanket license to lie. If ending or preventing discord can be accomplished without resort to falsehood, alternative means must be employed and falsehood is prohibited.[83] Accordingly, to avoid antagonizing Bethuel and Laban, Eliezer should have simply omitted mention of Abraham's blessing. What gave Eliezer the right to report the blessing in a distorted form?

The Midrash propounds here the principle that, when the motive is to end hostility and resentment, a *darkhei shalom* lie is permissible even if it goes beyond ending ill-feeling and is designed to endear one side to the other.[84] Entirely omitting the story about the angel would prevent antagonism. But Eliezer aimed higher: to endear Abraham to Bethuel and Laban. Eliezer hence did not omit the story about the angel, because its upshot is that the angel ensured Rebecca would appear at the well and demonstrate her extraordinary character precisely at the moment that Eliezer made his stipulation with God. The story implies that Abraham's prayer for the success of the mission was fulfilled in Rebecca's appearance at the well. Relating the story hence fosters goodwill toward Abraham.

81 Ibid., 24:40.

82 Midrash quoted by R. Menahem Mendel Kasher (*Torah Shelemah* to Genesis 24:40, *ot* 157). R. Kasher cites *Sefer Hemdat Yamim ha-Teimani* as the source that quotes this Midrash. *Hemdat Yamim ha-Teimani* does not, however, provide the source of this Midrash.

83 R. Israel Meir ha-Kohen Kagan (Radin, 1838–1933), *Hafets Hayyim, Hilkhot Rekhilut* 1:8; R. Nahum Yavruv, *Niv Sefatayim*, 3rd ed., vol. 1, pp. 27–29.

84 Let us take note that R. Menahem b. Solomon Meiri (Perpignan, France, 1249–1316) to *Yevamot* 63a takes the view that a *darkhei shalom* lie is legitimate only to prevent a rift, but not merely to mollify someone or prevent the occurrence of a momentary ruffled feeling. The proposition we offer in the text in no way contradicts Meiri. Once a *darkhei shalom* lie is permitted, the speaker may aim not only to end the hostilities, but to endear the parties to each other.

To see further that the Midrash teaches an innovation in *darkhei shalom*, let us contrast Eliezer's *darkhei shalom* lie in reporting Abraham's desire to establish marital ties with his own family and his *darkhei shalom* lie regarding the blessing Abraham gave him for the success of his mission. The essential difference is whether Eliezer may completely omit the topics pertaining to the lie. The reasonable man would find it odd, if not astonishing, that Abraham sent Eliezer to find a bride for his son, Isaac, in the very land God commanded him to leave. Accordingly, Eliezer must explain to Bethuel and Laban that Abraham foreswore him not to take a bride from the land where his master currently dwelt—Canaan. His options, then, are either to report verbatim to Bethuel and Laban what Abraham said on the matter, or, for the sake of *darkhei shalom*, to alter what Abraham actually said. Since reporting verbatim does nothing to temper Rebecca's family's presumed existing hostility toward Abraham, and may even exacerbate it, *darkhei shalom* compels Eliezer to explain that Abraham sent him to find a bride from Abraham's own family. This approach is designed not only to remove hostility, but to generate goodwill because the alternative leaves hostility intact. In contrast, omitting mention of Abraham's blessing that the mission should succeed compromises nothing. Since Eliezer could have avoided provoking antagonism simply with silence, his mention of the blessing, in distorted form, indicates that *darkhei shalom* licenses falsehood not only to prevent or end discord, but even to enhance relations.

Eliezer need not be concerned that Rebecca and her family will discover the truth—that Abraham charged him to select a bride from the land of his father, not specifically from his own family, and that the plan all along was to convince Rebecca's family to allow him to bring Rebecca home to Isaac. Given the ideological divide on religious grounds between the families and the seventeen-day trip between Aram Naharaim and Hebron, Isaac's location, the reasonable assumption is that Rebecca's family will not opt to accompany Rebecca to Hebron.

In any case, the Torah records Eliezer's first encounter with Isaac on his return to Hebron as follows: "The servant told Isaac *all* the things he had done."[85] The word "all" signifies that Eliezer related not just what transpired, but all the irregularities and missteps that occurred during his mission. If this interpretation is correct, Eliezer set out in his first encounter with Isaac upon his return to ensure that Rebecca and her family would never discover the various discrepancies and inaccuracies he communicated to them. With the secrets protected, *shalom* between the families would be preserved.

5. A fifth discrepancy in Eliezer's speech to Bethuel and Laban concerns his interaction with Rebecca at the well. Initially, Rebecca merely acquiesced to Eliezer's request for a drink. Only after satisfying Eliezer's request did she take the initiative and water Eliezer's camels.[86] Yet in his recapitulation, Eliezer states that Rebecca's

85 Genesis 24:66.
86 Ibid., 24:17–19.

immediate response to his request for a drink was that she would not only give him a drink, but would water his camels also.[87]

Perhaps we can once again invoke the *darkhei shalom* principle as the rationale for this change. Preliminarily, note that the selflessness and nobility of character Rebecca displayed far exceeded the generosity of spirit sought by Eliezer in the test of character he devised. The Sages contrast the righteous and the wicked: "The righteous say [i.e., promise] little and do much; the wicked, on the other hand, say much and perform not even a little."[88] Eliezer's test was designed to find a maiden who would simply promise to give him more than he asked for and, of course, follow through with the promise. Rebecca displayed an even higher righteous level of character refinement by promising little but following through with more than she promised.

Since Rebecca did not just pass Eliezer's test, but passed it with flying colors, Eliezer's report to Bethuel and Laban was not truly a lie. To satisfy the ethical standards of truthfulness, it was sufficient for Eliezer to describe the test he devised at the well and inform Bethuel and Laban that Rebecca had passed.

Why, however, did Eliezer refrain from telling Bethuel and Laban that Rebecca displayed kindness beyond what he was looking for? The answer lies in why person *A*, who promises little, but follows through with much more, displays a more refined character than person *B*, who promises more than he is asked to give and delivers what was promised.

A's actions are superior on at least two counts. First, by not announcing his intention beforehand, *A* draws less attention to the act of kindness than *B*, hence displaying greater modesty. Second, a benefactor should ideally take pains to make the recipient of a kindness feel that he or she owes the benefactor nothing in return.[89]

Since the ideal is that the benefactor take pains to minimize the sense of indebtedness that the recipient naturally feels for the kindness rendered, one should bestow kindness in a manner that makes the recipient feel as little indebted as possible. By suppressing his intention beforehand, *A* avoids verbally communicating to the recipient, "Look what I am going to do for you," hence minimizing the recipient's natural sense that the benefactor expects his indebtedness or reciprocation. Thus, Rebecca's response was also superior to what Eliezer had sought because her kindness was discharged more selflessly than what would have sufficed to pass Eliezer's test.

From Eliezer's perspective, given the lifestyle he observes in his master's household and the ethos he himself personifies, Rebecca's modesty and selfless kindness represent superior character traits. But Eliezer cannot be sure that this judgment will be shared by a culture whose lifestyle is antithetical to Torah values. Instead of viewing Rebecca's conduct as reflecting great magnanimity and selflessness, the culture she lives in may well view her behavior as foolish and naïve. Eliezer was an

87 Ibid., 24:45–46.

88 BT *Bava Metsi'a* 87a.

89 *Midrash Rabbah* at Exodus 2:19.

able-bodied man accompanied by an entourage of ten other men, each riding a camel. We would expect no more than for Rebecca to tell Eliezer to help himself to draw water for his camels. A more than generous response to Eliezer's request would be to physically exert herself to give him a drink. If Rebecca wanted to water Eliezer's camels and avoid being called foolish, she, at the very least, should have drawn Eliezer's attention to what she was doing and indicated that she felt he owed her for this major favor. Rebecca instead put herself in personal service not just for Eliezer but also to water his camels, while drawing minimal attention to her actions and, furthermore, conveying that Eliezer owed her nothing. Reporting to Bethuel and Laban what Rebecca actually did therefore risks her being judged "foolish" for allowing herself to be abused. To prevent this characterization, Eliezer should enjoy a *darkhei shalom* license to misrepresent what actually happened, describing it in a manner that minimizes the likelihood that Rebecca's family will judge her conduct foolish and naïve.

Eliezer enjoys an incidental benefit by using his *darkhei shalom* license to report Rebecca's conduct at the well inaccurately. Recall our assumption that Eliezer expects fierce resistance to his marriage proposal from Rebecca's family. Faithfully carrying out his *le-takkonei shaddartikh* mandate requires Eliezer to advance his cause utilizing every legitimate means. What could be a better means than having Rebecca herself facilitate the clinching of the match? Eliezer anticipates that Rebecca herself may be asked if she agrees to the match. If Eliezer reports verbatim how Rebecca responded to his request for a drink, her family will quite possibly judge her hopelessly foolish, and consequently never say, "Let us call the maiden and ask her decision."

The Ethics of Stretching the Wealth Factor

In sending Eliezer on his mission, Abraham gives Eliezer a document to show the maiden's family in which he designates Isaac as his sole heir. Abraham's intention is to make the match attractive to the maiden's family.

Eliezer goes considerably beyond merely informing Rebecca's family of the deed. Moreover, Eliezer makes use of his authority as manager of Abraham's wealth to advance the match using the wealth factor in ways unrelated to the deed of inheritance.

Eliezer's second statement to Bethuel and Laban, after identifying himself as Abraham's servant, is that Abraham is very wealthy and has made his son, Isaac, his sole heir:

> God has greatly blessed my master, and he prospered. He has given him flocks, and cattle, and silver and gold, and slaves and maidservants, and camels and

> donkeys. Sarah, my master's wife, bore my master a son after she had grown old, and he gave him all that he possesses.[90]

Eliezer is not content merely to show Rebecca's family the deed of inheritance. Eliezer also verbally enumerates all of Abraham's assets. Perhaps Eliezer intends to convey that his master's wealth is secure because Abraham held a diversified portfolio.

Eliezer also employs the wealth factor to promote the match by distributing gifts to Rebecca and her family. Rebecca is the main beneficiary. In return for giving drink to Eliezer and his camels, Eliezer showers jewelry upon her.[91] And as soon as Laban and Bethuel agree to the match, Eliezer bestows another set of gifts upon Rebecca. This time, Rebecca's mother and Laban are also beneficiaries of Eliezer's largesse.[92]

Did Eliezer unlawfully distract Rebecca's family from the disadvantages of the match, thereby inveigling them to endorse what they would not otherwise have agreed to?

Relevant here is the Talmudic dictum that it is legitimate for a merchant to embellish new merchandise to charge a higher price. This rule applies only to new merchandise, but not to used items.[93]

The distinction between old and new merchandise, according to Rashi, relates to unlawful distraction. If the merchandise is old, the merchant's enhancements delude the customer into thinking it is new, thereby inveigling him to overpay for it. But when the merchandise is new, the enhancements entail no unlawful distraction. Anyone paying more for the enhancements than their production cost does so with full knowledge.[94]

Rashi's explanation requires further elaboration. One might incorrectly suppose the merchant may sell new merchandise with his added enhancements only where the enhancements are created by the application of a commonly available skill. It would then be reasonable to assume the customer knows, or can easily learn, the cost of creating the improvement. Because the cost of creating the enhancements is standard and readily ascertainable, any premium the consumer pays above the costs of producing the enhancement is made with what amounts to full disclosure. There is then no distraction. This would explain the permissibility of starching

90 Genesis 24:35–36.

91 Ibid., 22:22.

92 Ibid., 24:52–53. *Midrash Lekah Tov* states that Eliezer gave Rebecca the jewelry (Genesis 24:47) as a gift, but the objects of gold and silver and the garments (Genesis 24:53) as a consideration for effecting her betrothal (*eirusin*) to Isaac. Even if Eliezer gave Rebecca the second set of objects not as a gift but to effect her legal marriage to Isaac, the ethical issue we raised in the text still exists because *eirusin* can be effected by giving the woman either a sum of money or an object having the value of a *perutah* (a *perutah* is equal in value to an amount of silver weighing a half-grain of barley; see Maimonides, *Commentary to the Mishnah*, *Kiddushin* 1:1). Since Eliezer could have accomplished *eirusin* by giving Rebecca something of nominal value, but opted instead to give her expensive items, his motive was apparently to make the marriage attractive to Rebecca and her family. Note that other authorities, referred to in note 6, understand that both sets of items were given as gifts.

93 BT *Bava Metsi'a* 60b.

94 Rashi, ad loc.

decorated garments and beating a canvas to make the threads finer—enhancements produced by standard labor and therefore having a definite and easily determinable market value.

This law would then simply be an application of the Sages' view at Mishnah, *Bava Metsi'a* 4:12:

> [The vendor] may not sift crushed beans to sift out the refuse; these are the words of Abba Shaul. But the Sages permit it.[95]
>
> Whose view is identified as that of the Sages? It is the view of R. Aha, as it was taught in a *Baraita*: "R. Aha permits enhancing the appearance of merchandise through something discernible."[96]

Rashi does, in fact, contrast the merchant practices of sifting beans and enhancing new merchandise and explains the dispute between Abba Shaul and the Sages in the following manner: Removing the refuse from crushed beans can be accomplished at a definite cost, which the buyer knows. The dispute between Abba Shaul and the Sages is whether the enhanced appearance of the sifted beans inveigles the customer into paying more for the sifting than warranted. Abba Shaul believes that the enhanced appearance of the beans enables the seller to overcharge the customer by raising their price far beyond the value of the effort involved in sifting. The Sages, however, feel that, since the enhancement is plainly discernible to the customer, the seller does not inveigle him to pay more than warranted for the sifting.[97] Jewish law adopts the opinion of the Sages as normative.[98]

However, while starching a new garment and beating canvas to make the fibers look finer are very much akin to sifting crushed beans, the other examples of enhancement the Talmud cites are not. Artists, whose work is not standardized, paint wicker baskets and arrows on utensils.[99] It will be very difficult and often near-impossible for the customer to quantify the artist's value added.

Nonetheless, if the utensil or garment is new, the seller is not confined to passing along to his customer the cost of the enhancement. According to Rashi's understanding, he is permitted to charge more. The enhancement does not delude the customer into overvaluing the unenhanced garment. The customer accepts with full knowledge any premium he pays above the production cost of the enhancement.

It should be noted, however, that, if the seller's final product is available in very similar form elsewhere in the same marketplace, the seller's pricing policy is constrained by the law of *ona'ah*, which prohibits an individual from concluding a transaction at a price more favorable to himself than the competitive norm.

The seller may thus charge for frills and embellishments he puts into new merchandise even when this value added has no definite price set by the marketplace. He may add more to his price than the expense he incurs in the enhancement

95 Mishnah, *Bava Metsi'a* 4:12.

96 BT *Bava Metsi'a* 60b.

97 Rashi, ad loc.

98 *Shulhan Arukh*, op. cit., 228:17.

99 BT *Bava Metsi'a* 60b.

process. He is entitled to earn a profit on the value added, limited only by the price of similar goods available in the same marketplace.[100] In economic terms, this latitude can be formulated in terms of opportunity cost, the value one foregoes in pursuing a particular course of action. The higher the price the seller charges, the greater the customer's opportunity cost in alternate uses of his money, including savings. The seller's right to turn a "profit" on the value he adds to a new product, even when the value added itself has no definite price, is effectively a right to divert the buyer from using his money in alternative ways by making his product the most attractive use for the buyer's money. If the seller is successful, the buyer cannot claim the seller distracted him from using his money for other purposes.

In Eliezer's case, perhaps the most fundamental application of the principle of lawful distraction is that he had every right to draw attention to the practical benefits of wealth Rebecca would enjoy once married to Isaac. Eliezer's gifts conveyed to Rebecca and her family that Abraham not only possessed much wealth, but that Rebecca would enjoy a high standard of living upon taking up residence in Hebron as Isaac's wife. This impression was in no way misleading. Indeed, once married, Rebecca enjoyed a high standard of living. Isaac stipulated in his marriage contract that Rebecca could take two young goats from his herd every day.[101]

Similarly, Eliezer had every right to place the wealth factor front and center in Rebecca's family's consciousness. Eliezer did not merely carry out Abraham's instruction to show Rebecca's family the deed of inheritance. By enumerating his master's assets, Eliezer emphasized that Abraham's wealth was secure because of his diversified portfolio. One can only surmise that Eliezer introduced these embellishments, beyond Abraham's instruction, with the specific goal of keeping the wealth factor in the forefront of the family's consciousness. If the effect of Eliezer's conduct was to deemphasize the disadvantages of the match, his conduct could still not be regarded as unlawful distraction.

Eliezer's Dealmaking and Bargaining Theory

In this section, we fit Eliezer's tactics into the framework of modern bargaining theory. Until now, we have compared Eliezer's conduct against the ethical standards of the Torah, and we have found Eliezer's conduct proper. But did Eliezer's approach follow the recommended path for successful bargaining? Let us compare Eliezer's conduct as matchmaker with the stratagems G. Richard Shell advocates for successful negotiation.

100 For application of the law of *ona'ah* to the modern marketplace, see Aaron Levine, "*Ona'ah* and the Operation of the Modern Marketplace," *Jewish Law Annual* 14 (2003): 225–58.

101 Rashi to Genesis 27:8, quoting *Genesis Rabbah* 65:14.

Shell identifies the prudent use of leverage as the key to success in negotiation. *Leverage* is, "the power to obtain an agreement 'on your own terms.'"[102] Shell identifies three types of leverage: positive, normative, and negative. We will define these terms and analyze Eliezer's conduct in relation to them.

Normative Leverage

Because of its pivotal role in advancing the match, we will first discuss normative leverage. *Normative leverage* requires identification of a standard or norm that the other side subscribes to. Once that norm is identified, it is possible to argue that the other side should adopt your position because it is consistent with their own standards.[103]

Eliezer shows his greatest mettle and ingenuity in advancing his cause by creating normative leverage, devising his "please tip your jug" test at the well and capitalizing on the circumstance that Rebecca passed it. Eliezer's genius is to recognize that it is within his grasp to make Bethuel and Laban perceive in the coincidence of these events the same Divine Providence he sees. Most critical is that there be no doubt Eliezer himself believes that the events at the well attest that God arranged the match and demands all parties accept it. To prove his own blind belief, Eliezer must forego any inquiry, even discreet, to ensure that Rebecca is free of hidden defect. Likewise, Eliezer must forego any active investigation into the character of Laban, Rebecca's brother, as well as the opportunity to reward Laban for his toil and effort in preparing his lodging, even though this might make Laban enthusiastic about the match, or at least neutralize his opposition. By foregoing all these pursuits, Eliezer demonstrates that God's Will is a mesmerizing force; and to exert efforts to advance the match only casts doubts on his own blind belief that God made the match. Using Shell's terminology, Eliezer creates normative leverage by demonstrating that he himself has perfect belief that God arranged the match and demands that everyone accept it. In the final analysis, this is what makes the match, as amply evidenced by the words Bethuel and Laban utter to signal their approval: "The matter stemmed from God! . . ."[104]

Positive Leverage

Shell defines *positive leverage* as the discovery of what the other side wants that you have, and how badly the other side wants it. Shell finds Donald Trump's definition of leverage very helpful in precisely defining positive leverage: "Leverage is having

102 G. Richard Shell, *Bargaining for Advantage* (New York: Viking, 1999), 90.
103 Ibid., 43–57, 104–14.
104 Genesis 24:50–55.

something the other guy wants. Or better yet needs. Or best of all, simply cannot do without."[105]

Abraham identified his own wealth as something alluring to the prospective bride's family. He therefore instructed Eliezer to show the family the deed in which he made Isaac the sole heir of his estate. Earlier we noted various techniques Eliezer employed to get maximum mileage out of the wealth factor. Here we note still another such technique, which modern scholarship calls *framing*.

Research has shown that framing information in positive or negative terms affects judgment and decisions. Pioneering in this research, Tversky and Kahneman showed that people are more likely to take risks when options focus attention on the chance to avoid losses rather than the chance to realize gains.[106]

Subsequent research demonstrates that what is called *attribute framing* also affects the choice between accepting and rejecting an outcome or event. One study showed that the perception of the quality of ground beef depended on whether it was labeled "75% lean" or "25% fat." Likewise, the likelihood that subjects will accept a medical procedure depends on whether the procedure is described in terms of survival or mortality rates.[107]

Finally, goal framing is a technique to create positive leverage. The desirability of a goal can be enhanced by putting it in either a positive or a negative frame. For example, price differences between cash and credit card purchases can be described as cash discounts or credit card surcharges. Research finds that consumers are less willing to bear the cost of a surcharge than to forego a discount. Accordingly, if a seller wants customers to pay in cash, he should not describe the cash price as a discount from the credit card price, but the credit card price as a surcharge above the cash price.[108]

In all these examples, although exactly the same information is conveyed, judgments and decisions are affected by whether the information is conveyed in a positive or negative frame. It follows that judgments and decisions should certainly be affected by the order in which information is conveyed.

Returning to Eliezer:

> Then the slave took ten of his master's camels, and arose and went to Aram Naharaim . . . He made the camels kneel outside the city at a well of water, at evening time, at the time when the women who draw [water] come out.[109]

By arriving with a display of wealth, Eliezer projects an image of wealth before anyone learns of his mission. Ceteris paribus, this should frame everything Eliezer subsequently says to the family of the prospective bride in a favorable light.

105 Ibid., 102.

106 Daniel Kahneman and Amos Tversky, "Prospect Theory: An Analysis of Decision Under Risk," *Econometria* 47 (March 1979): 263–91.

107 Irwin P. Levin and Gary J. Gaeth, "How Consumers Are Affected by the Framing of Attribute Information Before and After Consuming the Product," *Journal of Consumer Research* 15,3 (December 1988): 374–78.

108 Richard H. Thaler, "Toward a Positive Theory of Consumer Choice," *Journal of Economic Behavior and Organization* 1 (1980): 45.

109 Genesis 24:10–11.

Eliezer preserves his wealth advantage in his skillful management of his disadvantages. Because it is far worse for Rebecca's family to discover on their own that he is a slave, Eliezer discloses that fact first. Eliezer also attempts to neutralize any ill feeling Bethuel and Laban harbor toward Abraham by misrepresenting the instructions Abraham gave him, telling them that Abraham sent him to find a mate for Isaac from his family, when in fact Abraham instructed him only to look for the bride in his homeland. Finally, Eliezer defers mention of two deal-breaking items: that Isaac will not come to Aram Naharaim to accompany Rebecca back to Hebron, and that, once Rebecca leaves Aram Naharaim to marry Isaac, she will never return. Ultimately, Rebecca's family's declaration, "The matter stemmed from God!" obviates any requirement on Eliezer's part to make these disclosures.

Keith G. Allred's work on the norm of reciprocity highlights the importance of Eliezer's *darkhei shalom* lie that Abraham sent him to find a bride from his family. The norm of reciprocity is the human tendency to respond to the action of others with similar action. If we are treated with respect, we tend to respond with respect. If we are treated with suspicion and hostility, we tend to respond in kind. Moreover, a single round of action followed by a reciprocal response can turn into an ongoing cycle. Cooperative action can initiate a virtuous cycle, and hostile interaction, a vicious cycle.[110]

Suppose Eliezer had not begun his marriage proposal with his overture of affection from Abraham, instead saying only that Abraham had sent him to find a bride for Isaac from his homeland. Given Rebecca's family's latent hostility and suspicions, would not this impersonal introduction be a turn-off? In Allred's terminology, this turn-off might very well lead the family to look for "disconfirming evidence" and suspect that the deed of inheritance was a forgery.[111] Moreover, Eliezer was dealing with idolaters and scoundrels.[112] It was therefore no easy task to persuade them that God was orchestrating matters and demanding that that they blindly accept the match. To attune coarse and wicked people to the Divine, Eliezer needed every conceivable edge. Eliezer's gesture of closeness and sociability at the outset was therefore vital in creating an atmosphere conducive to success.

Negative Leverage

Negative leverage is a threat-based strategy founded upon the power to make the other side worse off.[113] Eliezer makes use of negative leverage, though not until his closing words: "And now, if you intend to do kindness and truth with my master, tell me, and if not, tell me, and I will turn to the right or to the left."[114]

110 Keith G. Allred, "The High Cost of Low Trust," in Roy J. Lewicki, Bruce Barry, and David Saunders, *Negotiation, Readings, Exercises, and Cases*, 5th ed. (Boston: McGraw-Hill Irwin, 2007), 267–70.

111 Ibid.

112 Cf. *Midrash ha-Gadol* at Genesis 24:29, 24:58; *Midrash Hemdat Yamim ha-Teimani* at Genesis 24:29; and *Midrash Genesis Rabbah* 60:12.

113 *Bargaining for Advantage*, op. cit., 104.

114 Genesis 24:49.

Eliezer asserts that, if Rebecca's family rejects the match, they will be foregoing the opportunity to do "kindness and truth" with his master, Abraham. What "kindness" and "truth" is Eliezer referring to?

Eliezer's greatest accomplishment was to argue that God Himself orchestrated the match and was demanding that all parties accept it blindly. When Rebecca's family exclaimed, "The matter stemmed from God!" they were experiencing a glorious moment of "truth" in the form of a communication of sorts from God. To accept the match is to preserve this revelation as a cherished and uplifting memory for the rest of their lives. To reject the match is not only to lose this glorious memory, but also to grapple with the guilt and fear of defying God's Will for the rest of their lives. Accordingly, Eliezer's closing words not only entreated the family to accede to the match, but they were an exercise of negative leverage.

In addition, by describing Rebecca's family's agreement to the match as an act of kindness, Eliezer implied that self-interest does not compel their agreement. Why not? An ideological-religious divide existed between Abraham and Isaac, on the one hand, and Rebecca's family, on the other. This divide manifested itself in vastly different lifestyles. On a personal level, Rebecca's family likely harbored resentment and ill feeling toward Abraham. Finally, once Rebecca departed with Eliezer from her hometown, they could not reasonably expect her to return. Agreeing to the match hence entailed their willingness to ignore what was distasteful to them and constituted kindness on their part.

The norm of reciprocity explains why Eliezer's plea for kindness is an exercise of negative leverage. Recall Eliezer's *darkhei shalom* lie to Rebecca's family that Abraham sent him to find a bride for Isaac from his family. Abraham's gesture of closeness and sociability, communicated through Eliezer's *darkhei shalom* lie, should evoke a response in kind from Rebecca's family. If the norm of reciprocity is operative, responding in kind will be regarded by Rebecca's family as something they want to do outside the strict realm of quid pro quo. Refusing the match is therefore not simply rejecting a plea for kindness; it leaves them with the empty feeling of losing something valuable—an unfulfilled need to reciprocate in kind.

Eliezer arrives equipped with no negative leverage to exercise to advance the match. His genius is to create new needs and desires that Rebecca's family did not have before he arrived: the desire to be kind to Abraham, and to preserve the cherished memory that God Himself had communicated to them to accept the match.

Creating Value versus Claiming Value

Setting leverage aside, we may alternatively frame Eliezer's stratagems in terms of creating value, as opposed to claiming value.

Roy J. Lewicki, Bruce Barry, and David M. Saunders use the terms "claiming value" and "creating value" in describing the negotiation process. Negotiations typically feature both a value creating stage and a value claiming stage. In the value creating stage, parties work together to expand the resources under negotiation. In the value claiming stage, the parties decide who gets how much of what. Research shows most negotiators are overly biased toward thinking that negotiation is more about claiming value than creating value. The challenge for negotiators is to balance emphasis on the two stages and the transition from creating to claiming value.[115]

One can discern Eliezer's continual effort to create value for Rebecca and her family to make the match attractive to them. Eliezer does this, as described above, by capitalizing on his advantages. Most importantly, he devises his test and manipulates its results to convince Rebecca's family that God himself demands that the parties accept the match. The greatest evidence of Eliezer's emphasis on creating value is the absence of a bargaining tone in his interaction with Rebecca's family. Eliezer unilaterally and continuously creates ever more value for them before finally requesting their consent to the match.

Even when Eliezer exerts negative leverage, he does not threaten to make Rebecca's family worse off by taking away what the family had before he arrived. Eliezer threatens only that rejecting the match will cause them to lose desires and needs he, himself, created for them; he says they will not satisfy their need to "reciprocate kindness," and implicitly threatens that, rather than cherishing a memory of an encounter with God, they will face the consequences of defying His Will.

Summary and Conclusion

Our study set out to compare the Biblical account of Eliezer's conduct as a matchmaker against Judaism's ethical norms. We also examined whether Eliezer's conduct followed the approaches and techniques modern bargaining theory recommends.

One central finding is that Eliezer's test for kindness at the well, though it risked his bringing home a bride with hidden physical flaws, did not violate his *le-takkonei shaddartikh* mandate as Abraham's agent.

Competing plans will have offsetting advantages and disadvantages. Eliezer's *le-takkonei shaddartikh* mandate entitled him to decide that Abraham would prefer a plan with an excellent chance of bringing home an exemplar of kindness as a

115 Roy J. Lewicki, Bruce Barry, and David M. Saunders, *Negotiation Readings, Exercises, and Cases*, 5th ed. (Boston: McGraw-Hill Irwin, 2007), 488–89.

bride, though risking a hidden physical defect. The alternative would be to ensure identification of the perfect candidate, but run the significant risk of her family's declining the match. Eliezer's plan hence entailed a calculated, not an unnecessary, risk.

From Rebecca's family's perspective, the proposed match with Isaac entailed three drawbacks. One was that, once Rebecca left Aram Naharaim for Hebron, she would never return. A second was that Isaac would not come to Aram Naharaim to accompany Rebecca back to Hebron. Instead, Eliezer, a (former) slave, would accompany Rebecca, despite his inferior social status and, perhaps more significantly, the stereotype of slaves as having loose morals. A likely third disadvantage was Rebecca's family's animosity toward Abraham.

Eliezer was aware of all three. He made no attempt to hide his identity. He first told Rebecca's family he was Abraham's slave. He did not raise the questions of whether Isaac would come to accompany Rebecca to Hebron or whether she could be expected ever to return after departing, but he was not thereby guilty of creating a false impression by dashing Rebecca's family's reasonable expectations. Quite the opposite—Eliezer's *le-takkonei shaddartikh* duty required him not to disclose these matters for as long as possible. Ultimately, Bethuel and Laban accepted fully that God had orchestrated the match and demanded their blind acceptance of it. Their response, "The matter stemmed from God! . . . Here, Rebecca is before you; take [her] and go, and let her be a wife to your master's son, as God has spoken,"[116] obviated any duty to disclose the drawbacks mentioned above.

To overcome Rebecca's family's presumed antagonism toward Abraham, Eliezer engaged in a *darkhei shalom* lie, telling them that Abraham sent him to find a bride from his own family. To ensure his own consistency, Eliezer made a number of other *darkhei shalom* lies. Eliezer also employed a *darkhei shalom* lie to ensure that Rebecca's family would not regard her conduct at the well as foolish and naïve.

We also analyzed Eliezer's conduct in light of modern bargaining theory, demonstrating that he followed the recommended path for success. Eliezer employed various forms of leverage. Most critical was his use of normative leverage after Rebecca passed his test at the well. Eliezer's genius was to show that he himself blindly believed God demanded acceptance of the match, thereby persuading Bethuel and Laban to believe it, too. In the terminology of modern bargaining theory, Eliezer's stratagem can also be described as "creating value" for Bethuel and Laban before requesting that they accept the match. Eliezer also displayed an understanding of how framing, and vicious and virtuous cycles, affect the outcome of a negotiation.

In conclusion, we state our most important finding: Eliezer not only conducted himself ethically but pursued a course of action consistent with a formula for success based on modern negotiation theory.

116 Genesis 24:50–51.

SELECTED BIBLIOGRAPHY

Bible:

Genesis 24.

Genesis Rabbah 24.

Caro, R. Joseph. *Shulhan Arukh, Orah Hayyim*; *Hoshen Mishpat* 58:1, 227:4, 228:17.

Kahneman, Daniel., and Amos Tversky. "Prospect Theory: An Analysis of Decisions Under Risk." *Econometria* 47 (March 1979): 263–91.

Kolin, R. Samuel ha-Levi. *Mahatsit ha-Shekel* to *Shulhan Arukh, Orah Hayyim*.

Levin, Irwin P., and Gary J. Gaeth. "How Consumers Are Affected by the Framing of Attribute Information Before and After Consuming the Product." *Journal of Consumer Research* 15,3 (December 1988): 374–78.

Lewicki, Roy J., Bruce Barry., and David M. Saunders. *Negotiation: Readings, Exercises, and Cases*. 5th ed., 488–89. Boston: McGraw-Hill Irwin, 2007.

Mishnah:

Terumah 4:4.

Shell, G. Richard. *Bargaining for Advantage*. New York: Viking, 1999.

R. Solomon b. Isaac (Rashi) to Genesis 24.

Thaler, Richard H. "Toward a Positive Theory of Consumer Choice." *Journal of Economic Behavior and Organization* 1 (1980): 45.

Talmud (Babylonian):

Bava Batra 78a.

Bava Metsi'a 50b, 61a.

Berakhot 40a.

Beitsah 32a.

Gittin 13a.

Hullin 137b.

Ketubbot 85a, 100a.

Ta'anit 4a.

CHAPTER 3

LAND CONCENTRATION, EFFICIENCY, SLAVERY, AND THE JUBILEE

JACOB ROSENBERG AND AVI WEISS

Introduction: The Need for Reconsideration of the Goals of the Jubilee

The Jubilee, as laid out in the Bible, is generally viewed as a time for celebration—a time during which horns are blown, families reunited, and heirlooms reclaimed. It is a time of freedom, with the release of slaves and the resulting return of their civil liberties, and of social justice, with land sold during the previous fifty years returning to its original owners. Thus, the Jubilee seems to be partially a sociological precept, with its main goal seemingly to achieve a certain degree of equality among people. However, a careful study of the precise decrees raises a number of questions that are difficult to understand when this view of the Jubilee is taken.

The decree that property returns to its original owner is not applied evenly—there are types of property that return and types that do not. If this law is truly sociological, why differentiate? And if economic equality is what is desired, why demand the return of land? Why won't pecuniary compensation do just as well? In fact, from an economic point of view, if the Jubilee decree did not exist the land could be sold for more money, which would at least compensate the original owner for not getting the land back and might in fact leave him better off (since surplus is generally created in all trades).

Given these difficulties, one might look to the rabbinical view of the Jubilee to better understand this institution. In some ways, the rabbinical view is diametrically opposed to the sociological view. According to the rabbis, the Jubilee is not a celebration of our freedom. Quite the opposite—it is a reminder that the world was created by, and thus belongs to, G-d. Since this is so, the division of land to the different tribes should remain as divided by Joshua: Slaves should be freed since we are all slaves to G-d and not slaves to slaves, and the land should be rested during each seventh year, just as the Lord rested on the seventh day of creation.

The Two Goals of the Jubilee Laws—A New Approach

In a symposium dedicated to the study of the Jubilee,[1] and in the ensuing conference volume, we presented a different approach (Rosenberg and Weiss, 1999).[2] We demonstrated that the laws of the Jubilee are concerned with the regulation of productive resources and efficiency, and we suggested that the Jubilee serves the purpose of limiting the concentration of productive resources in the hands of the few.

The current chapter is a substantial extension of the earlier paper. We will show that the laws are consistent with two goals. The first is that discussed above—a desire to attain economic efficiency by "spreading the wealth," thereby limiting the ability of an individual to control resources, and thus monopolize markets. The second goal is to try to avoid the development of slavery within the Jewish nation. This goal also relies on limiting land concentration because too much concentration can lead to a situation in which poor farmers become dependent on loans from rich landowners, which, in the ancient world, often led to widespread slavery. Thus, the two goals are complimentary.

As shall be made clear, our explanation of the Jubilee laws is consistent with the religious explanation. Jewish laws are laid down in a manner that emphasizes the importance of free, mutually beneficial transactions between people with no external intervention. However, as indicated above, intervention exists specifically in this case because of the potential consequences from overly concentrated land ownership—a loss of efficiency and the development of a slavery class. Such intervention is allowable *precisely because* the land belongs to G-d. Thus, our explanation is not at odds with the rabbinical explanation; rather, it helps us understand the circumstances under which G-d's property rights are exercised.

To help make our explanation clear, we will first briefly explain the consequences of factor of production concentration in terms of monopoly theory.

1 "The Jubilee and Its Economic and Social Implications" was held in Jerusalem in May 1998 under the auspices of the Observatiore de la Finance, as part of its "Finance, Cultures and Religions" program.

2 "The Jubilee As Antitrust Legislation," *Finance & Bien Commun/Common Good* Supplement No. 1, Jean-Michel Bonvin ed. *Debt and the Jubilee: Pacing the Economy* (December 1999): 35–39.

We will then show why we believe the Jubilee laws act to prevent inefficiency, and how the Halakha (Jewish law) has dealt with economic problems that may arise from these laws. Only then will we turn to the issue of slavery.

Factor of Production Concentration—the Efficiency Argument

In the ancient world, grain was the most important single commodity produced. As in most markets, control of a large share of the most important factor of production (land) used to produce this good gives those owners "market power" that can be used to raise prices above competitive levels. The ill effects of such a monopoly may extend beyond just high prices and reduced quantities; it can also lead to other inefficiencies, such as underinvestment in research and development and low quality goods. One way to prevent this outcome is by not allowing any individual to gain such market power by limiting resource ownership.

The reason monopolies (and cartels) are undesirable from purely an efficiency point of view is not because the monopolists benefit and consumers lose, nor is it a matter of taking from the rich and giving to the poor; rather, it is because they lead to a misallocation of resources.

To understand this concept, we begin with a perfectly competitive industry. Such an industry is said to exist if there are many producers and buyers, so that no one agent is able to affect the market.[3] When such conditions are met, markets can be shown to be completely "efficient" in that resources (such as land, labor, etc.) are being used in the most beneficial ways, and the most desired products are being produced for those who use them—the consumers. This is the ideal that Adam Smith claimed is attained via the "invisible hand." This is also the benchmark against which all other market outcomes are measured.

The standard monopoly outcome to be avoided is depicted in fig. 3.1.

In this figure we depict and compare two situations—the first with perfect competition in a market and the second with a single producer/monopolist in that market. The outcomes are very different. When competition prevails, the price is lower (P_C) and the quantity greater (Q_C) than when there is a monopoly (when the price and quantity are P_M and Q_M, respectively).

The way this occurs is that the monopolistic producer (or producers in the case of a cartel) realizes that he/she has the ability to affect the market and does so by limiting production and raising prices. He/She benefits by these actions (the profit gained is marked "Monopoly Profits" in the figure) and consumers lose. But the main "evil" from an economist's perspective is that resources are misallocated. Too

3 In addition, goods must be homogeneous, information about prices and the availability of goods must be costless, and there must be no external effects of one entity's actions on another entity (externalities).

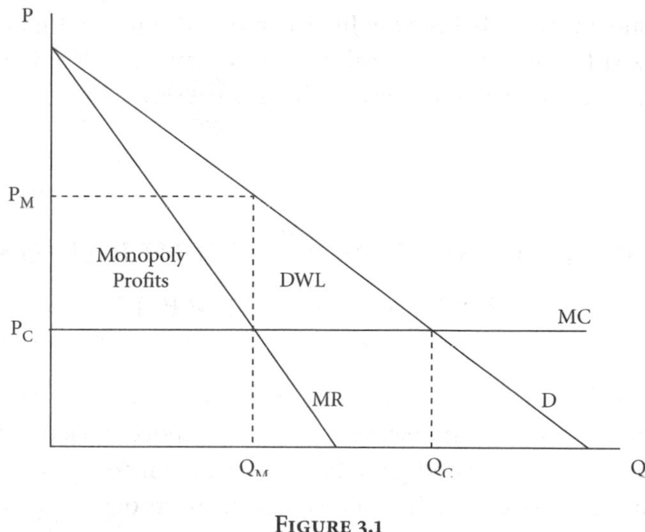

FIGURE 3.1

few of the monopolist's goods are being produced, in that even though consumers are willing to pay the cost of producing these goods they do not receive the goods, because the monopolist artificially limits production and raises prices. As a result, more resources are funneled into other industries, where the goods they produce are less valuable to consumers. Since the consumers' desires are not being met, efficiency is not attained. The efficiency loss is the triangle marked DWL in fig. 3.1.

In an agrarian society, the damage is compounded because most of the population is employed in agriculture. If the agricultural lands are concentrated in the hands of the few, these land owners also have what is known as *monopsony* power over the workers—they can pay the workers unreasonably low wages because the workers have nowhere else to turn for employment. Thus, it is not only consumers that suffer; the workers and their families also suffer. In fact, the feudal systems we are acquainted with from history resulted from monopolistic ownership of land.

Efficiency can be achieved by ensuring that industries are not overly "concentrated," which, in turn, requires that numerous producers carry out production. While this does not guarantee economic efficiency, it increases the likelihood that competition will prevail, and thus limits the ability of a single producer, or a group of producers, to affect prices.

The Jubilee—the Efficiency Aspect

The major biblical decrees pertaining to the Jubilee are:

1. Any agricultural land must be returned to its original owner; even if the land has passed through several hands it is returned to the first owner.

If, however, the land was donated for the use of the sanctuary, it is not returned to its original owner. In addition, if the sanctuary then sold the land, it returns to the sanctuary during the Jubilee.

2. Houses on agricultural land are treated in the same manner as the land. Houses in walled cities, however, are not treated as such; rather, the original owner has one year to redeem his house. If the house is not redeemed within a year, it is not returned to the owner.
3. All Jewish slaves are released.

As discussed above, several questions arise from these rules. Why differentiate between land and houses? Why differentiate between houses in cities and those outside of cities? In fact, why not demand the return of all durable goods sold? Why don't sanctified lands return to their original owners? These questions arise whether we take the sociological view that equality is being sought, or if we take the view that the purpose of returning things to original owners is to remind us that everything belongs to G-d. We believe that if one takes the view that these laws aim to achieve efficiency by preventing too much concentration in the input and output markets, these dilemmas are solved.

The key to this approach lies in the fact that the laws are concentrated around productive resources only—agricultural land (and the houses that service them) and workers (slaves). The purpose of these laws, according to this view, is to keep the resources spread out and to limit the ability of an individual to acquire too much economic power. The reason that houses in walled cities are not included is because these are not used for production, and are thus not subject to these concerns. Similarly, other durables are of no concern since the major factors of production were, at that time, land and labor.

Sanctified lands, on the other hand, are taken out of private hands and given over to the "government." While, from an economic standpoint, private ownership is to be preferred to public ownership, there is little concern that the government will try to "abuse" a monopolistic position. Thus, such lands may remain in government ownership even after the Jubilee.

In other words, economic efficiency is the first goal that we claim the Bible desires. This idea that economic efficiency is being sought is apparent from more than just the laws stated above; it is also evident from some of the finer details of the Jubilee laws. For instance, since agricultural land is to be returned in the Jubilee, it makes economic sense that the price paid for the land would take this fact into account. And, indeed, the Bible specifically states that the price paid should take into account the number of harvests remaining until the Jubilee (note the emphasis on the harvests). In addition, the setting of a specific year as the Jubilee year, and not just stating that the land returns 50 years after it is first sold, also helps attain efficiency, since the cost to second- and third-hand buyers of attaining the pertinent information for setting the price is lower if everyone knows exactly when the land must be returned.

Another sign that efficiency was the major concern is found in the Talmud and in the various codifications of Jewish law that were compiled. One of the problems that can arise as a result of the Jubilee laws is an issue of incentives. Say that market conditions (or land conditions) are such that it is desirable from an economic perspective to make a certain investment—say the planting of trees or the instillation of a new irrigation system. Often the fruits of such investments are reaped over many years, and their economic viability depends on the investor having a sufficiently long time horizon. Under such circumstances, anyone who purchased land from another would refrain from making such an investment once the Jubilee draws near, since he would bear all the costs of the investment but receive little or none of the fruits. As a result, worthy investments would not be made, leading to an inefficiency. To circumvent this potential problem, the Halakha states that, when the land is returned to the original owner during the Jubilee, the receiver must pay to the returner the *value* (and not the cost) of any improvements made on the land. From an economic standpoint this criterion is ideal since it means that the investor's incentives are determined by the value of the investment. The investor will not make investments in order to hurt the original owner, since this will be reflected in his receiving a lower payment. He will also not refrain from undertaking investments that are expected to be profitable, since he will receive the benefit from his toil, either directly from the land while it is still in his possession, or from the original owner to whom the land is returned. With this law, a possible economic inefficiency has been eliminated.

Negation of Slavery as a Social Class

We turn now to the second goal we attribute to the Jubilee laws—that of minimizing the probability of slavery becoming a widespread phenomenon within the Jewish people. To help motivate this idea, we first present evidence on the Torah's negative attitude to slavery.

This attitude is quite evident. It is stated quite clearly in the verse, "For they are my servants . . . they shall not be sold as bondmen."[4] This is restated in the Talmud as, "they are my servants and not the servants of servants," which is, we believe, a negation of slavery as a social class in Jewish society. This negation is not just a social statement about negating the liberty of someone born free; it is first and foremost a religious statement. Fulfillment of the commandments and the decrees of the Torah cannot be completely carried out by a slave with a human owner. Therefore, based on a Torah view, the status of slave is unacceptable.

This attitude is found in a number of places in the Torah. When the Torah mentions G-d's redemption of Israel from Egypt, it denotes Egypt as "the house of bondage." Thus, for instance, in the first of the Ten Commandments it states, "I am the Lord thy G-d, who brought thee out of the land of Egypt, out of the

4 Leviticus 25:42.

house of bondage."[5] This description repeats itself eight more times in Exodus and Deuteronomy.

The expression "house of bondage" is seen to denote a place that creates slavery.[6] It is a symbol of a process that may lead to slavery, as we shall describe below.

There are many other instances in the Torah in which the Children of Israel are reminded that they were freed from slavery, leaving the strong impression that this liberty is something to be treasured, and not reversed. Thus, for example, the Torah tells us, "I am HaShem your G-d, who brought you forth out of the land of Egypt, that ye should not be their bondmen; and I have broken the bars of your yoke, and made you go upright."[7] The implication is clear.

The understanding that the Torah negates slavery is embodied in the Talmud. For example, according to R. Johanan b. Zakkai (Israel, first century CE), the reason for puncturing the ear of a Jewish slave who refuses to leave his owner after six years[8] and states that he loves his master and does not want to go free is that "the ear that heard my voice on Mt. Sinai when I said the people of Israel are my servants,[9] and not the servants of servants, and went and acquired himself an owner, will be punctured."

From the analysis of the Torah decrees it can be deduced that it is the social status that can exist when there is a culture of servitude that the Torah abhors. Thus, the Halakha makes it clear that a worker should not be regarded as a slave, as per the command, "And if thy brother be waxen poor with thee, and sell himself unto thee, *thou shalt not make him to serve as a bondservant. As a hired servant, and as a settler*, he shall be with thee."[10] Rav (Babylonia, third century CE), for instance, says that, because of the desire to make it clear that workers do not have the status as slaves, a worker is free to back out of his commitment to work until half the day has passed, despite being considered like the extended hand of his employer. His source for this ruling is that it is written, "for the children of Israel are my servants—they are my servants and not the servants of servants."[11]

Thus, it seems clear that the Torah negates slavery as a social class. With this, the Torah knows that in the ancient world it was not practical to categorically forbid one from selling oneself into slavery when he fell deeply into debt. The ability of farmers to guarantee their loans was often only through collateralizing their bodies or those of their family members. As we will develop below, what the Torah is addressing in the laws appearing in Leviticus 25 is the concern that slavery will develop as a social class, and therefore it takes steps to avoid this.

5 Exodus 20:2.

6 See R. Bahya b. Asher b. Hlava (Spain, thirteenth century), Exodus 20:2. See also R. Ephraim Solomon b. Aaron of Luntshits's (Poland, 1550–1619) *Keli Yakar*, who explains the use of "the house of bondage" in the first commandment as leading directly to the commandment to release Jewish slaves.

7 Leviticus 26:13.

8 Exodus 21:5–6.

9 Leviticus 25:42.

10 Ibid., 25:39–40.

11 See B *Bava Metsi'a* 10a.

Land Concentration and Slavery

In order to minimize the probability of slavery becoming a widespread phenomenon within the Jewish people, the Torah takes steps to limit land concentration, as discussed above, and legislates the release of all slaves in the Jubilee. The decree to release slaves in the Jubilee appears in Leviticus:

> And if thy brother be waxen poor with thee, and sell himself unto thee, *thou shalt not make him to serve as a bondservant. As a hired servant, and as a settler*, he shall be with thee; he shall serve with thee unto the year of jubilee. Then shall he go out from thee, he and his children with him, and shall return unto his own family, and unto the possession of his fathers shall he return. *For they are My servants, whom I brought forth out of the land of Egypt; they shall not be sold as bondmen.*[12]

Note first that these verses are concerned with situations of economic distress ("if thy brother be waxen poor with you"), and, as we shall describe below, they depict the end of a process. This process includes selling property due to economic distress, borrowing money with interest, and collateralizing any unsold land in order to finance the return of loans and interest. As we will explain, this process can eventually lead to a large part of society returning to a "house of bondage," which is what the Torah wants to avoid.

It is a well-known chain of events in the ancient world that leads to free independent farmers becoming slaves, and to slavery spreading until it becomes a social phenomenon. This can occur when the economy is mostly agrarian and economic conditions are such that a large portion of households find themselves near subsistence levels. For instance, if there is, say, a drought, farmers may be forced to collateralize their lands in order to get loans for food and seed. Obviously, those able to give such loans are the rich landowners. If the drought persists, they will be able to purchase ever-increasing portions of the land because of the existing hardships, with their ability to grant loans and purchase more land increased by the monopoly profits from increased market concentration, as presented above (see the area marked "monopoly profits" in fig. 3.1). If the drought is prolonged, the independent farmers may reach the point where they have to sell their family members and themselves into slavery in order to survive.

Such occurrences at times reached extreme proportions, with a significant portion of the population being enslaved. Just such an occurrence is described in Genesis, where we are told of the seven-year famine in Egypt, during which the farmers first sold their property for food and seed, then their livestock, then their land, and finally themselves as slaves to Pharaoh.[13] This description is universal and matches

12 Leviticus 25:39–42.

13 Mayshar (2007, 25–43) sees the developments in Egypt as part of the laws laid down in Leviticus 25. In the spirit of Biblical scholarship, he suggests that both of these portions were authored by Ezra.

occurrences throughout the ancient world and beyond.[14] Historically, in such situations, we saw instances of declared reforms by rulers in which all slaves were released and their debts forgiven. We will discuss these reforms below.

The Jubilee—The Slavery Aspect

In order to demonstrate that one of the goals of the regulatory rules laid down in Leviticus is to avoid or correct a situation of general subjugation leading to widespread slavery, we adopt Milgrom's (1999) description of the three steps to destitution inherent in the scriptures: (1) someone who has land he can sell; (2) someone who no longer has land and desires assistance from his brethren; and (3) someone who has sold himself into slavery. The sequence described is gradual, eventually leading to bondage of the worker and his family, and to a loss of his family estate.

The First Stage

In the first stage, the worker tries to extract himself from difficulties by selling land:

> If thy brother be waxen poor, and sell some of his possession, then shall his kinsman that is next unto him come, and shall redeem that which his brother hath sold. And if a man have no one to redeem it, and he be waxen rich and find sufficient means to redeem it; then let him count the years of the sale thereof, and restore the overplus unto the man to whom he sold it; and he shall return unto his possession. But if he have not sufficient means to get it back for himself, then that which he hath sold shall remain in the hand of him that hath bought it until the year of jubilee; and in the jubilee it shall go out, and he shall return unto his possession.[15]

The passages refer to someone who is forced to sell some of his land due to economic distress. The last verse guarantees that, if he cannot redeem the land beforehand, it will return to him in the Jubilee, which is described in the Torah before the passages about redemption. However, the Torah does not want him to reach that point and makes it as simple as possible for him to recover his economic independence sooner. Thus, the redemption laws are geared toward reversing the sale of property before the arrival of the Jubilee. The original owner

14 The following example is taken from Mayshar (2007, 47): "Watts (1983) describes the drought which hit one of the villages in Nigeria in 1973-4. He says that at certain times the price increases caused desperate farmers to sell their livestock and property, and began taking loans at exorbitant interest rates (200%). The poorer farmers could not get loans at all except by collateralizing their lands. Some were forced to sell their lands. Watts says that while the poor were selling everything they had, the rich were purchasing property at very low prices, sold grain to farmers for high prices, hired them for next to nothing, and purchased their land for prices they themselves set."

15 Leviticus 25:25–28.

of the land, or one of his close kin, is guaranteed the right to purchase the land back by compensating the owner, but this purchase does not require the agreement of the new owner. The amount to be paid is not set by mutual consent; rather, it is calculated by the land's productive value given the number of years left until the Jubilee. The payment equals the difference between the price paid for the land (which, itself, was determined by the number of productive years until the Jubilee) and the value of the produce in the years that passed since the sale. Given the goal of avoiding long-term collateralization of the land in order to avoid the plausibility of sale of the original owner into servitude, this system of calculation simplifies the redemption process, particularly since there would be a "buyer's market" in times of general economic distress. Therefore, without this system, the land would be sold originally for very cheap and the buyback price would be very dear. Thus, the Bible is trying to return the worker to the status of a landowner who is able to provide for himself and his family, making it less likely that he will become destitute.

The Second Stage

The second stage of distress comes when the person no longer has assets he can sell, and he needs assistance from his peers:

> And if thy brother be waxen poor, and his means fail with thee; then thou shalt uphold him: as a stranger and a settler shall he live with thee. Take thou no interest of him or increase; but fear thy G-d; that thy brother may live with thee. Thou shalt not give him thy money upon interest, nor give him thy victuals for increase.[16]

Here, when a fellow Jew requests financial assistance, the children of Israel are called upon to lend him money without interest. The prohibition against usury in times of distress is of great importance. Interest rates in the ancient world were prohibitively high, reaching twenty to thirty-five percent. In times of widespread economic hardship, when there was much demand for loans, these rates would go even higher. It is, therefore, no surprise that long periods of economic distress would lead to an inability to repay loans and to the rich being unwilling to grant loans unless they were guaranteed exorbitant interest rates. Again, the Bible is trying to keep the worker from reaching the next stage.

The Third Stage

The third stage comes when the person sells himself into slavery for a long period of time. This is far more likely to happen during times of general economic distress, when many are forced to sell themselves or their family members into slavery, and the price received from such a sale is low. Therefore, the return of the

16 Ibid., 25:35–37.

loans taken can be accomplished only with a long period of servitude. In addition, the amount required when the period of distress is lengthened increases, and to guarantee such a large loan could require one to commit to a long period of servitude as collateral.

In this case also the worker may redeem himself at any time before the Jubilee. This is provided for explicitly when the sale is to a "stranger who is a settler," where the Bible makes it a *mitsva* for one of his brethren to redeem him:

> And if a stranger who is a settler with thee be waxen rich, and thy brother be waxen poor beside him, and sell himself unto the stranger who is a settler with thee, or to the offshoot of a stranger's family, After that he is sold he may be redeemed; one of his brethren may redeem him; . . . And he shall reckon with him that bought him from the year that he sold himself to him unto the year of jubilee; and the price of his sale shall be according unto the number of years; according to the time of a hired servant shall he be with him. . . . As a servant hired year by year shall he be with him; he shall not rule with rigour over him in thy sight. And if he be not redeemed by any of these means, then he shall go out in the year of jubilee, he, and his children with him. For unto Me the children of Israel are servants; they are My servants whom I brought forth out of the land of Egypt: I am HaShem your G-d.[17]

The reason the sale to a stranger is singled out is because in this case there is also the fear of assimilation, and so the Torah "suggests" that one of his relatives bail him out as quickly as possible.

The Jubilee—The Last Resort

As presented above, the Bible has tried to make it as easy as possible for one to avoid slavery, to be redeemed from slavery when it cannot be avoided, and to make it as comfortable as possible when one cannot be redeemed. However, the Bible is not satisfied with these steps. At this stage, when all appears lost, along comes the Jubilee and takes a far more direct approach to ending servitude. In the Jubilee, the slave simply goes free unconditionally and his land is returned. This is stated in Leviticus 25:39–41 (quoted above) and is in continuation of the verses on the Jubilee earlier in the chapter:

> In this year of jubilee ye shall return every man unto his possession. And if thou sell aught unto thy neighbour, or buy of thy neighbour's hand, ye shall not wrong one another. According to the number of years after the jubilee thou shalt buy of thy neighbour, and according unto the number of years of the crops he shall sell unto thee.[18]

Release of the slave and the property simultaneously demonstrates the analogy between them; neither the slave nor the land can be sold perpetually. More importantly, from our perspective, since the worker gets his freedom and the

17 Ibid., 25:47–57.
18 Ibid., 25:13–15.

means with which to support himself at the same time, he has the opportunity to turn over a new leaf without being in immediate danger of renewed servitude. The Jubilee is thus the ultimate solution if all the other, less extreme, solutions have failed.

The Jubilee and "Clean Slate" Proclamations

The Jubilee is the most famous of the "clean slate" proclamations that existed in the ancient world. A *clean slate* is a proclamation made by a king, ruler, or general under which any land sold because of economic distress is returned to its original owners, anyone forced into servitude by debts is liberated, and back debts are cancelled. Such laws pre-date the Bible, which, according to the Biblical timetable, was given to Moses in the year 1313 BCE.

According to Hudson (1999), the earliest clean slates were proclaimed over one thousand years earlier. The oldest surviving clean slate was proclaimed by Enmetena, "who ruled the Sumerian city-state of Lagash from about 2404 to 2375 BCE," and about fifty years later, in 2350 BCE, by his successor, Urukagina. In about 2200 BCE another Sumerian ruler, Gudea, also "remitted debts" and returned ancestral land.

One hundred years later, Nammu, the ruler of Ur, issued a clean slate, as did his son, Shulgi. Between 2000 and 1800 BCE clean slates were proclaimed by the Babylonian and Amorite dynasties in Isin and Larsa, and by two Assyrian rulers. Hammurabi proclaimed clean slates in 1792, 1780, 1771, and 1762 BCE, and six consecutive rulers of Hammurabi's dynasty also cancelled debts during the following 166 year period.

These early reforms differed from each other and included private debt forgiveness, tax amnesties, release of slaves and pardon for prisoners, and sometimes the return of lands to their owners. Thus, they included many of the components of the Jubilee.

It has been claimed in some studies that the idea for the Jubilee comes from similar concepts in the Clean Slate proclamations.[19] According to these studies, the reforms were initiated by rulers in order to form public order. The kings and rulers, at least some of them, were concerned with economic and social issues, and in particular with legal and economic assistance for the underprivileged.

However, these same scholars, for instance Weinfeld (1985), note significant differences between the liberty proclaimed by the Torah in the Jubilee and the

19 For example, Weinfeld (1985, 1–19).

proclamations in the ancient East: The Israelites were commanded to proclaim the Jubilee not by decree of a king of flesh and blood, but by decree of G-d; it does not depend on the will of the ruler, but rather occurs every fifty years by a law that also obligates the king. In addition, the impetus for such proclamations in the ancient world was often tied up with the desire of the king to attain popularity among his subjects, and the proclamations were therefore often made when a new ruler rose to power.

And yet, the differences pointed out by Weinfeld and others do not get to the root of the novelty of the Jubilee. According to our approach, the Jubilee represents a negation of the status of slaves and stands at the center of a legal system created by the Torah to avoid the development of a status of slavery, including seeking efficiency by limiting market concentration.[20] The Jubilee, and the other regulations accompanying it, is offered as a built-in solution to the undesired results that can arise from economic distress. Conversely, the other proclamations were more random and dependent on the whims of the ruler, and they did not constitute a well-formulated, consistent policy. In addition, in pronouncing liberty the rulers helped the poor, but the impetus was often to help the ruler by increasing his popularity and portraying him as being just and honest. This was not a challenge to the standing of slaves in society, and it certainly was not designed to negate such a class of citizens. Thus, for instance, the ancient world reforms that included private debt forgiveness and the release of slaves certainly were not considered steps to eliminate slavery.

To summarize, properties at the core of the Jubilee that are absent from the reforms in the ancient world include having the status of a binding law, concern with market concentration in factor of production ownership, negation of the status of slaves, and placement of a dam in the face of sweeping free market forces that lead to slavery. Thus, while there are similarities between the Jubilee and other clean slate proclamations, clearly the differences are quite pivotal.

Conclusion

In summary, we have proposed a new view of the Jubilee laws. We suggest that their objectives include the limitation of economic power in the hands of any individual in order to guarantee healthy competition in markets, and to thereby minimize the probability of widespread slavery. If we are correct, this is an example of an extremely advanced and well-considered set of economic laws, literally millennia ahead of its time.

20 Parts of this argument are also implicit in Mayshar (2007, 19–23).

SELECTED BIBLIOGRAPHY

Bahya b. Asher b. Hlava, Exodus 20:2.

Bible:

Exodus 20:2, 21:5–6.

Leviticus 25:13–57, 26:13.

Ephraim Solomon b. Aaron of Luntshits, *Keli Yakar*, Exodus 20:2.

Hudson, M. "The Economic Roots of the Jubilee." *Bible Review* (February 1999): 26–44.

Mayshar, Joram. *In His Image—The Idea of Equity from Ezra to Nietzsche*, 19–47. Jerusalem: Carmel Publication, 2007.

Milgrom, J. "Some Postulates of the Jubilee: A Pragmatic Solution to Universal Inequities." *Finance & Bien Commun/Common Good* Supplement No. 1, Jean-Michel Bonvin ed. *Debt and the Jubilee: Pacing the Economy* (1999): 15–19.

Rosenberg, J., and Weiss, A. "The Jubilee As Antitrust Legislation." *Finance & Bien Commun/Common Good* Supplement No. 1, Jean-Michel Bonvin ed. *Debt and the Jubilee: Pacing the Economy* (1999): 35–39.

Talmud Bavli:

Bava Metsi'a 10a.

Watts, Michael. *Silent Violence: Food, Famine and Peasantry in Northern Niegeria*. Berkeley: University of California Press, 1983.

Weinfeld, Moshe. *Mishpat u-Tsedaka be-Yisra'el u-Va'ammim*, 1–19. Jerusalem: Magnus Publications, 1985.

PART II

ECONOMIC THEORY IN THE TALMUD

CHAPTER 4

RISK AND INCENTIVES IN THE *ISKA* CONTRACT

JEFFREY L. CALLEN

Introduction

THE purpose of this study is to analyze the conceptual treatment of the *Iska* by the Talmud and medieval post-Talmudic scholars (*Rishonim*), especially as it relates to risk and incentives.[1] It is our contention that the structure of the *Iska* and the profit/loss allocation formulae suggested by the Talmud and the *Rishonim* were at least partially motivated by concerns related to the negative impact of interest prohibitions, risk aversion, and shirking on business opportunities. In addition to R. Solomon b. Isaac's (Rashi, France, 1040–1105) insights regarding shirking, we highlight R. Joseph Caro's (Israel, 1488–1575) insightful analysis of incentives in the context of the tripartite disagreement about *Iska* profit and loss allocations among Maimonides (Rambam, Egypt, 1135–1204), his teachers, and Nahmanides (Ramban, Spain, 1194–1270).

In what follows, we first discuss the Talmudic concepts of Biblical and rabbinic interest, known as *ribbit* and *avak ribbit* (lit. the dust of *ribbit*), respectively, since these are central to the Talmudic formulation of the *Iska*. We proceed to analyze the incentives underlying the *Iska* from the Talmudic perspective. We

1 See Hillel Gamoran, "Investing for Profit: A Study of *Iska* up to the Time of Rabbi Abraham ben David of Posquieres," *Hebrew Union College Annual* 70–71 (1999–2000): 153–65 for a descriptive analysis of the *Iska* in the post-Talmudic response literature. Gamoran argues that R. Abraham ben David (Rabad, France, 1125–1198) of Posquieres' liberal *halakhic* decisions regarding the *Iska* were influenced by business pressures to reduce investor risk. Be as it may, Rabad does not describe the issue in this way nor does he describe the incentive issues underlying the *Iska* structure.

then describe some elements of economic contracting theory and their relevance to the Talmudic and post-Talmudic views of the *Iska*. Finally, we analyze Talmudic and post-Talmudic *Iska* profit and loss allocations and their incentive effects according to R. Joseph Caro.

Biblically Proscribed Interest (*Ribbit*): Time Value and Inflation

Modern economics and finance scholars view interest on a loan as being composed of three components: a component that reflects the real time value of money, a component that reflects (expectations of) inflation, and a component that reflects the credit risk of the loan. By credit risk, we mean the risk that the borrower will not pay back the loan, including accrued interest, to the lender at the contractually specified dates. The latter risk, in turn, is related to the specific contractual features of the loan, such as collateral, the wealth of the borrower, the efficiency of the legal and business system in facilitating and enforcing loan collections, and the risk underlying the project that the loan finances.

Biblical law prohibits the payment of *ribbit* from one Jew to another on both personal and business loans. This stricture made it imperative for the rabbis to define what constitutes *ribbit*. The Talmud, in addition, imposed its own restrictions on the payment of interest in business transactions.

According to the Talmud, three (possibly interrelated) conditions are necessary for *ribbit* to be violated. First, interest must be stipulated explicitly at the time of the loan, to the exclusion of fees paid prior to or after the loan agreement.[2] Fees paid prior to the loan agreement, say to induce the lender to provide financing, or fees paid after the loan is discharged, say to induce the lender to provide further funding at a future date, do not constitute *ribbit*. Second, the interest must accrue to an *explicit* loan (personal or business) and not result from a business transaction. For example, a futures contract in which the buyer contracts with the seller for goods, and immediately pays for the goods at the current market price for delivery at a future date, constitutes a business transaction rather than a loan.[3] Ostensibly, the buyer has lent funds to the seller by the advanced payment for the goods and earns a positive return if the goods appreciate in value by the delivery date. However, from the perspective of the Talmud, the intent to buy goods rather than to finance the transaction per se makes this a business transaction, and the return

2 M *Bava Metsi'a* 75b.

3 M *Bava Metsi'a* 60b. For an analysis of futures contracts in the Talmud, see Hillel Gamoran, "Talmudic Controls on the Purchase of Futures," *Jewish Quarterly Review* New Series, 64 (1 1973): 48–66.

to the buyer is not a *ribbit* violation, although it is a violation of *avak ribbit*.[4] Third, interest must involve the time value of money. To quote: "A general rule of what constitutes *ribbit*: [any transaction involving] the time value of money, declares Rabbi Nahman."[5]

How inflation factors into R. Nahman's dictum is unclear. There is no evidence that Talmudic scholars or *Rishonim* conceptualized interest in terms of inflationary expectations, but there is a discussion in the Talmud regarding the issue of ex post nominal versus real interest. The Talmud considers two hypothetical cases of loans denominated in copper coins where the value of copper coins fluctuates relative to the numeraire currency, a silver coin called a *ma'a*.[6] In the first case, a *ma'a* was worth 100 copper coins at the time of the loan and 120 at the loan discharge. The question in the Talmud is whether payback of the loan (in copper) at the rate of 120 coins involves *ribbit*, given the twenty percent increase in the number of copper coins, or whether there is no *ribbit*, since in terms of the numeraire currency (wealth), the lender has not gained nor the borrower lost.[7] In the second case, one hundred copper coins constitute a numeraire silver coin at the time of the loan, but, in contrast to the first case, the numeraire is worth less than one hundred copper coins at the loan discharge date. The Talmud asks whether paying back the loan at the rate of one hundred constitutes *ribbit* given that the numeraire currency is worth less than one hundred copper coins at the time of the loan discharge.

Interestingly, the Talmud merely poses these two cases without resolving either one. Most *Rishonim* maintain that the first case involves *ribbit*, whereas the second does not, since *ribbit*, according to them, is calculated based on the initial nominal loan amount rather than what the loan is worth at discharge.[8] Thus, a loan of 100 copper coins that requires repayment of 120 copper coins is considered interest despite the fact that neither the lender's nor the borrower's wealth has changed in terms of the numeraire currency. In contrast, a loan of one hundred copper coins to be repaid by one hundred copper coins does not involve *ribbit*, even though the wealth of the parties has changed relative to the numeraire currency. In other words, according to these *Rishonim*, nominal interest rates are usurious and Biblically forbidden by religious sanction even though neither party's wealth is affected in real terms.[9] According to this view, interest includes both the real time value of money and (ex post) compensation for inflation.

4 One could conceptually think of this futures contract as involving two transactions: an initial loan from the buyer to the seller to finance acquisition of the goods, and a sale of the goods from the seller to the buyer at delivery. Nevertheless, since the ultimate intent is a sales transaction rather than a financing transaction, any returns that accrue to the buyer are not considered *ribbit* by the Talmud.

5 B *Bava Metsi'a* 63b. This dictum appears to have been accepted in the Talmud without dissension.

6 B *Bava Metsi'a* 60b.

7 The implicit assumption throughout the discussion is that coins did not change in metal composition through the period in question.

8 So in fact it was decided by R. Joseph Caro in his *Shulhan Arukh, Yoreh De'a* 160:21.

9 B *Bava Metsi'a* 60b.

Risk and *Ribbit*

Strangely, neither the Talmud nor the *Rishonim* acknowledge credit risk as a factor in explaining interest or in defining what constitutes *ribbit.* It is true that there is no bankruptcy concept in Talmudic law and debtors are always required to pay off their loans. Nevertheless, credit risk was clearly an issue. The debtor might simply not have any assets from which the debt could be discharged in a timely manner, if at all. Moreover, until the Gaonic period (sixth–tenth centuries), creditors were not always able to collect the debt from the heirs of the debtor if the heirs had no land from which to discharge the loan.[10] In addition, of course, the debtor might simply skip town with his wealth in hand.

In general, business risk seems to absolve transactions from the stigma of *ribbit.* As noted above, returns derived from business transactions are not deemed to be *ribbit.* The reason seems to be fairly prosaic—namely, that the Bible explicitly prohibits interest on loans, not returns to business transactions.[11] But the issue is not quite so simple. Some *Rishonim* appear to argue that the return on a business transaction is risky, in contradistinction to interest on a loan, which is certain; and it is the riskiness of the business transaction that frees the return from being deemed *ribbit.* R. Yom Tov b. Abraham Ishbili (Ritba, Spain, c. 1250–1330), for one, seems to suggest that it is precisely the riskiness of the business transaction that makes the prohibition of its return non-Biblical. For example, in the case of a joint venture, where goods are financed solely by a silent partner, where the active partner bears the losses (with respect to the sale of the goods), and where profits are split equally, the profit is not deemed to be *ribbit* according to Ritba, because there may not be any profit at all.[12] Similarly, although the futures contract referred to above effectively involves a loan from the buyer to the seller, the risky return to the buyer is not deemed to be *ribbit* because the price of the goods may decrease rather than increase by the delivery date. This is in contrast to a "riskless" Biblically usurious loan with a priori specified interest, which is deemed to be riskless because the debtor is responsible for ensuring payment of principal and interest (and because the Talmud and the *Rishonim* abstract from credit risk).

Avak Ribbit

As onerous as *ribbit* appears to be, the Talmudic rabbis further extended the interest prohibition to business transactions. It is not that the rabbis were unconcerned about the consequences of extending the prohibition to business financing,

10 See Menahem Elon, *Mishpat Ha-Ivri*, 2nd enlarged edition, 2 vols. (Jerusalem: Magnus Press [Hebrew]), 532. The loan portion of an *Iska* is an exception. See B *Bava Metsi'a* 104b.

11 See Rashi, *s.v. le-ribbit de-oraita*, B *Bava Metsi'a* 60b.

12 Ritba, *s.v. en mekabbelim tson u-barzel me-yisrael*, B *Bava Metsi'a* 70b. This is an example of an *Iska*, which we analyze in detail below.

as we shall see. Rather, the Talmudic ethos regarding Biblical prohibitions is to extend these prohibitions to areas not explicitly prohibited by the Bible in order to put a "fence around the Torah."[13] By further extending the prohibition to similar situations not explicitly prohibited by the Bible, the rabbis help to ensure that the Biblical prohibitions are not abrogated.

The negative consequences this extension had on the Jewish business environment throughout the ages are impossible to estimate absent quantitative data, but they must have been considerable. Suffice it to say that much rabbinic ink was spilt, subsequent to the extension of the prohibition against interest to business transactions, in an attempt to mitigate its impact on project financing. Indeed, over time, mechanisms arose, through rabbinic concern and/or economic pressure by businessmen, to minimize the negative impact of these prohibitions on business formation, if not to neutralize them entirely, albeit within the confines of the rabbinic legal thought process.[14] The *Iska* is one such mechanism used in the Talmudic period itself, and in post-Talmudic periods, to mitigate the negative impact of the prohibition of *avak ribbit* on project financing.

Risk and Incentives in the *Iska*

The *Iska* is a joint venture comprising an active partner who manages the project and a silent partner who supplies project financing.[15] According to Rambam, the defining nature of the *Iska*, in contrast to an ordinary partnership, is not the financing aspect but rather that one partner is active and the other inactive. Thus, if both partners provide financing, the partnership is still an *Iska* provided one partner is active and the other silent.[16]

In an ordinary partnership, where both partners are active, both are considered to have equity in the firm and, hence, interest issues do not arise. By contrast, the situation in which one partner supplies nonhuman capital and the other supplies all of the human capital was problematic for the Talmud both from the perspective of *avak ribbit* and out of concern for incentives for business formation. On the one hand, if the financing is in the form of a loan or, equivalently, if the active partner is

13 T.B *Moad Katan* 5a; T.B *Yevamot* 21a.

14 See Haym Soloveitchik, H., "Pawnbroking: A Study in Ribbit and of the Halakah in Exile," *Proceedings of the American Academy for Jewish Research* 38–39 (1970–1971): 203–68; Hillel Gamoran, "Talmudic Usury Law and Business Loans", *Journal for the Study of Judaism* 7(2 1976) 129–42; and Hillel Gamoran (1999-2000). In modern times, the *Hetter Iska* has essentially neutralized the prohibition against *ribbit* even though that was not the original intent.

15 See John H. Pryor, "The Origins of the Commenda Contract," *Speculum* 52(1 1977): 5–37 for a comparison of the *Iska* with similar financing arrangements in Byzantine, medieval Islamic, and European business cultures, such as the Italian Commenda and the Moslem Qirad.

16 Rambam, *Mishne Torah, Sheluhin ve-Shuttafin*, 6:1. The Commenda also appears to be defined similarly. See Pryor (1977). R. Hai b. Sherira Gaon (Babylonia, 939–1038) limited the *Iska* to cases where the active partner did not invest at all. See Gamoran (1999–2000).

solely responsible for all business losses, so that there is no risk to the silent partner, the silent partner is prevented from earning a profit because the profit would be deemed *avak ribbit*. Hence, the silent partner is unlikely to provide funds in the first place because he is prohibited from earning a return on his nonhuman capital. On the other hand, if the silent partner is solely responsible for losses, no interest issues arise, but then the active partner will have little incentive not to shirk or to avoid undue risks, and again the silent partner is unlikely to provide financing.[17]

Clearly concerned that these two options would hamper business investment, the Talmud provided an alternative solution. "The Nehardean rabbis ruled: This *Iska* contract is to be considered half loan and half equity.[18] [By this act], the rabbis promulgated a rule that is to the benefit of the debtor and to the benefit of the creditor."[19] In other words, half of the capital supplied by the silent partner is deemed to be a loan to the active partner, which the active partner then invests in the joint venture, and half is deemed to be the silent partner's equity in the joint venture. Furthermore, in the event of a profit (loss), each partner would end up with half of his capital investment plus (minus) half of the profits (losses), which apparently, according to the rabbis, gives each potential partner sufficient incentive to initiate an *Iska* joint venture "to the benefit of the debtor and to the benefit of the creditor." For example, if the silent partner finances one hundred in the joint venture and there is a gain of forty, the silent partner gets back his fifty of loan and seventy of equity while the active partner ends up with twenty in total. In the event of a loss of forty, the silent partner again gets back his loan of fifty and thirty of his equity investment, so that each partner loses twenty. In the event of a loss of the entire capital of one hundred, the active partner pays back the loan of fifty to the silent partner, so that each loses fifty.

The Talmud still saw a potential interest problem with the fifty/fifty allocation, since the active partner would be working for the silent partner's equity portion in addition to the work undertaken for his own capital input (the loan). Since the only apparent reason that the active partner would be willing to work for the benefit of the silent partner is in recompense for the loan, this would fall under the prohibition of *avak ribbit*. Thus, the rabbis suggested (as one potential solution) that, in addition to the fifty/fifty profit/loss allocation, the active partner should be compensated for his time for each day that he works in the joint venture. In modern economic terms, the Talmud's suggestion is to compensate the active partner with a linear contract involving a fixed salary plus an equal portion of any profits or losses.[20]

17 In contrast, the *Iska* mitigates these disincentives to forming business ventures as emphasized in the next paragraph. Nevertheless, Egyptian Jewish traders often preferred the Moslem Qirad over the *Iska*, according to Genizah documents; and in fact the Qirad absolved the active partner from sharing in the losses. See Abraham L. Udovitch, "At the Origins of the Western Commenda: Islam, Israel, Byzantium?" *Speculum* 37(2 1962), 198–207.

18 The Talmud refers to the silent partner's equity portion as a *pikadon*, a trust, meaning that the silent partner's equity capital is entrusted to the active partner.

19 B *Bava Metsi'a* 104b.

20 M *Bava Metsi'a* 68a. Exactly how this fixed compensation is computed is interesting in its own right but beyond the scope of the current study. For an example of this type of contract in medieval Mediterranean trade, see Shlomo Dov Goiten, "Commercial and Family Partnerships in the Countries of Medieval Islam," *Islamic Studies* 3 (1964): 315–37.

In addition to this linear contract, the *Tosefta* proposes what appears to be a piecewise asymmetric nonlinear solution to the potential interest impropriety of the *Iska* contract.[21] Piecewise asymmetric nonlinear contracts are further discussed more clearly and in more detail by the Talmud in a case in which a deceased man was an active partner in an *Iska* and the contract did not explicitly provide a fixed salary compensation beyond the fifty/fifty allocation. To quote the Talmud: "The sons of R. 'Ilish were faced with a written *Iska* contract in which the allocation was 50 per cent of the gains and 50 per cent of the losses. Rava said: R. 'Ilish was a great man and he who would not have caused others to sin. Therefore, on the one hand, where the contract explicitly states that he receives half of the gain, it is understood (implicitly to mean) that he suffers only one third of the losses. On the other hand, if the contract explicitly states that he suffers half of the losses, it is understood (implicitly to mean) that he benefits two thirds of the gains."[22]

In other words, although he received no salary, Rava presumed that R. 'Ilish, as the active partner, was compensated by an ex ante reduction in the risk of the contract. Otherwise, R. 'Ilish would be causing the silent partner to violate the prohibition against *avak ribbit*, which was unthinkable for a man of R. 'Ilish's probity. Specifically, R. 'Ilish was presumed to have accepted either one of two contracts: (1) 66⅔ percent of any profit and 50 percent of any loss—that is, a third increase in the profit allocation by comparison to an even split; or (2) 50 percent of any profit and 33⅓ percent of any loss—that is, a third decrease in the loss allocation by comparison to a even split.[23]

Interestingly, the Talmudic notion that the active partner should be compensated an additional third in the case of a loss in order to avoid *avak ribbit* finds expression in non-Jewish medieval Commenda contracts. As noted by Pryor (1977), the allocation in which profits were divided fifty/fifty, but the silent partner bears two-third's loss and the active partner one-third loss is archetypical for bilateral sea Commenda contracts at the ports of Genoa, Venice, Amalfi, Marseilles, and Barcelona.[24] Unfortunately, except for the *Tosefta* and the Talmudic story of R. 'Ilish, which document the additional third compensation, no rationale for the one-third is provided by either Jewish or non-Jewish sources.

In addition to the rather terse case of R. 'Ilish, the *Rishonim* based their views regarding the risk reduction properties of these two contractual *Iska* forms on the following Talmudic statement: "The rabbis taught: If the *Iska* contract proportions are near to profit and far from loss (from the perspective of the silent partner) then

21 T *Bava Metsi'a* 4:11 and 4:14. Although opaque, this *Tosefta* seems to suggest that a contract in which the active partner earns two-thirds profit, instead of the customary one-third, solves the *avak ribbit* problem.

22 B *Bava Metsi'a* 68b–69a.

23 See Rashi, *s.v. i palga be-hefsed*, and Ritba, *s.v. mah nafshakh i palga ba-agar*, B *Bava Metsi'a* 69a.

24 The bilateral Commenda is one where the active partner also invests capital, typically one-half of what the silent partner invests. In the case of the unilateral Commenda, where only the silent partner invests capital, the silent partner is normally allocated one-quarter of the profit and is responsible for all losses. In an insightful analysis, Pryor (1977, 29) shows that the unilateral and bilateral Commenda allocations are consistent with the ruling of Rambam's teachers. On the latter's position, see further below.

he (the silent partner) is an evil man; near to loss and far from profit—then he is an especially righteous man; near to both or far from both—this is the measure of an ordinary man."[25] Since the Talmud did not specify exactly what is meant by "near to profit and far from loss," "near to loss and far from profit," "near to both" or "far from both," the *Rishonim* had fairly wide latitude to define these terms. Most interesting are the positions of Ritba, Rambam, and R. Menahem b. Solomon Meiri (Provence, 1249–1316).

Ritba interprets this Talmudic dictum in light of the proportions cited by the Talmud in the case of R. 'Ilish.[26] Where the contract stipulates that the silent partner (lender) incurs half of the losses and takes *more than* one-third of the profits (but less than half), the silent partner is "near to profit and far from loss," and the lender is an evil man. In contrast, a silent partner who incurs half of the losses but is willing to take less than one-third of the profits is considered especially righteous. Finally, a silent partner who incurs half of the losses but is willing to take exactly one-third of the risky profits is "far from both" and an ordinary man. Alternatively, based on the cases of R. 'Ilish, a contract stipulating that the silent partner (lender) incurs two-thirds of the losses and takes half of the profits is a case of "near to both" and characterizes an ordinary man.

Meiri also interprets the Talmudic dictum in light of R. 'Ilish, but he is far more liberal regarding the risks incurred by the silent partner.[27] Initially, Meiri states that the case of the evil man, defined as "near to profit and far from loss," is where the contract stipulates that they divide profits evenly, while the active partner guarantees all losses. In contrast, a silent partner who guarantees all losses but takes half of the risky profits is considered especially righteous. "Close to both" (the ordinary man) covers the linear contact solution and the two cases of R. 'Ilish: a silent partner who takes half of the losses and exactly one-third of the risky profits and a silent partner who takes two-thirds losses and one-half of the profits.[28]

Subsequent to his interpretation of this rabbinic dictum, Meiri, following Rambam, defines a permissible *Iska* much more liberally, as one where the partners' asymmetric profit/loss proportions are such that the proportion of the losses accruing to the silent partner is greater than the proportion of any profits. In other words, as long as the active partner is compensated by some risk reduction beyond the fifty/fifty proportions, the *Iska* is rabbinically permissible. This is in contrast to other *Rishonim*, who maintain that only the two cases mention by R. 'Ilish, one-third profit and one-half loss to the silent partner, or one-half profit and two-thirds loss to the silent partner, are permissible.

25 B *Bava Metsi'a* 70a. See also T *Bava Metsi'a* 4:16.

26 Ritba, *s.v. amar R. Sheshet*, B *Bava Metsi'a* 70a.

27 Meiri, *Bet Ha-Behira*, B *Bava Metsi'a* 70a.

28 Meiri maintains that the case of "far from both" is an empty set. He disagrees with those who interpret "close to both" as a case where the silent partner takes one-third of profits and losses. Irving A. Agis, *Urban Civilization in pre-Crusader Europe*, 2 vols. (Leiden, 1965) provides examples of these standard *Iska* contracts in pre-Crusader Europe.

Incentive Contracts and the *Iska*

Modern economic contract theory deals extensively with the incentive structure of contracts.[29] Two issues are central to the economic analysis of contracts: risk sharing and shirking. The early contract literature assumed that the agency relationship (such as in an *Iska*) involves only the issue of risk sharing, and that the agent (e.g., the active partner) always works in the interest of the principal (e.g., the silent partner). The only factor at issue was how to design a contract that optimized risk sharing among the parties to the agency (e.g., the *Iska*). To the extent that the agent is more risk averse than the principal, it is optimal from the principal's perspective to design a contract that reduces the agent's risk such as, for example, by reducing the agent's proportion in profits *and* in losses in a linear contract with a concomitant increase in fixed salary, or by increasing the proportion of profits or reducing the proportion of losses accruing to the agent in an asymmetric piecewise linear contract.

The more recent contract literature recognizes that the agent's interests are often different from the principal's and, in particular, that agents have a desire to work less (shirk), especially if they are compensated solely by a fixed salary. As a consequence, modern economic contract theory develops the optimal compensation design by trading off the agent's risk aversion against his desire to shirk. Specifically, it is optimal from the principal's perspective to provide the agent with incentives to work hard on behalf of the principal and not to compensate the agent solely through a fixed salary, which is devoid of such incentives. However, incentives imply more risk to the agent and, as a result, the agent will require more compensation to offset the additional risk. The optimal incentive contract from the principal's perspective balances the cost of the additional risk imposed on the agent against the benefit from incentivizing the agent to work in the principal's best interests.

The fifty/fifty linear contract solution of the Nehardean rabbis could be optimal from a pure risk-sharing perspective if, for example, both the active and silent partner have, or are assumed to have, the same degree of risk aversion.[30,31] However, linear contracts are rarely optimal once shirking is a factor. While the Nehardean rabbis did not study modern contract theory, they were likely familiar with human nature and the human condition, and they may have felt that a linear contract provides sufficient incentives from a pure risk-aversion perspective to generate business ventures.

29 See, for example, Patrick Bolton and Mathias Dewatripont, *Contract Theory* (Cambridge: MIT Press, (2005).

30 This can be demonstrated under the assumption that both the principal and agent have constant risk aversion (CARA) utility functions. For example, see Ines Macho-Stadler and J. David Perez-Castrillo, *An Introduction to the Economics of Information: Incentives and Contracts*, 2nd ed. (Oxford: Oxford University Press, 2001, 26–27.

31 However, the solution cited in the previous footnote cannot guarantee that the fixed salary portion is positive. Also, the Nehardean rabbis only suggest a proportional fifty/fifty solution without a fixed salary. Nevertheless, it is likely that they understood the need to impose a fixed salary in order to avoid *avak ribbit*, since this issue was already recognized in the earlier Mishnaic period. See M *Bava Metsi'a* 68a.

The statement of the Nehardean rabbis is too terse for us to judge whether they had risk aversion and/or shirking in mind. Given the nature of their solution, shirking does not seem to be the issue. This surmise is further buttressed by the subsequent Talmudic discussion, where an extreme form of shirking is discussed explicitly, perhaps to contrast with the Nehardean rabbis' putative pure risk-aversion approach.[32] In particular, the Talmud suggests that since, according to the Nehardean rabbis, half of the capital investment in the joint venture is a loan, and loan monies can generally be used for any purpose whatsoever, then surely the active partner can use the loan for any purpose at all, including "drinking it away." The Talmudic sage Rava (d. 352) rejects this possibility, arguing instead that "the reason we call [the business venture] an *Iska* is because the silent partner is [implicitly] saying to the active partner: I gave you the financing in order that you will use it (*le-i'assuke beh*) in the joint venture and not drink it away."[33] The *Rishonim* interpret this implicit directive in two ways. First, by requiring that even the loan portion of the financing be kept in the joint venture, the silent partner can be reasonably confident that a good portion of the capital will not be wasted, and that he will be able to collect this portion of the *Iska* capital when the joint venture ends.[34] More interestingly, Rashi interprets Rava as discussing incentivizing the active partner: "That by using the funds to make profits for himself, that is, for the active partner's own portion, he will be working (*la-'asok*) the joint venture to the best of his abilities (for everyone's benefit)." Equivalently, one can interpret Rashi to be saying that, if the active partner is allowed to use his portion of the financing for personal use, he is likely to shirk rather than work diligently for the benefit of all partners in the business venture.

Of course, Rava's case, wherein the active partner utilizes his portion of the financing for personal use, is an example of an extreme form of shirking (or leads to it), whereas shirking in economic contract theory refers to any action by the active partner that is not in the interest of the silent partner. Generally, when shirking is at issue, the optimal solution will be a nonlinear incentive contract, whereas Rava's incentive contract is the same as the Nehardean rabbis—namely, a linear contract. But, to repeat, a linear contract is almost never optimal with shirking.

As we saw earlier, the story of R. 'Ilish generated a nonlinear contract, of the asymmetric piecewise linear form, wherein the silent partner either receives one-third of the profit and bears one-half of the loss or receives half the profit and bears two-thirds of the loss. Prime facie, the rationale underlying this contractual form is the avoidance of *avak ribbit* rather than the incentivizing of the active partner. Nevertheless, we shall now see that R. Joseph Caro, in his work *Kesef Mishne* (a commentary on Rambam's *Mishne Torah*), insightfully interprets Rambam to say that asymmetric piecewise linear contracts help to provide the appropriate incentive structure for the *Iska*.

32 I am grateful to Dr. Leibl Zoberman for this insight.

33 B *Bava Metsi'a* 104b.

34 See Rashi, *s.v. le-hakhi karu leh iska*, and Tosafot, *s.v. de-lo le-mishtei beh shikhra*, B *Bava Metsi'a* 104b. This is similar to covenants in debt contracts that prevent overly generous cash dividend payments to stockholders, leaving the firm a shell, without assets to cover bondholders' investments. See Jerold B. Warner, "Bankruptcy, Absolute Priority, and the Pricing of Risky Debt Claims," *Journal of Financial Economics* 4(3 1977), 239–76.

Rambam's Position Concerning *Iska* Incentives: The Analysis of *Kesef Mishne*

Rambam deals with the *Iska* in his legal compendium, *Mishne Torah*, primarily in the sixth chapter of *Hilkhot Sheluhin ve-Shuttafin* (the laws of partnerships and agency). Rambam's position is also influenced by the one-third rule, but only if the joint-venture agreement fails to specify a complete profit/loss allocation system. If the *Iska* fails to specify any allocation, Rambam rules that, in the event of a profit, the active partner is to receive his half (the loan portion) of the profit plus an additional one-third of the silent partner's portion in order to compensate for the additional work of being the active partner while avoiding the problem of *avak ribbit.* Thus, the profit allocation is two-thirds for the active partner and one-third for the silent partner. Similarly, if there is a loss, the active partner receives an additional compensation of one-third (of the active partner's portion) to compensate for running the business, yielding an allocation of one-third loss to the active partner and two-thirds loss to the silent partner. In contrast to his teachers, Rambam also maintains that the partners in the joint venture can agree to any allocation, as long as the contract compensates asymmetrically in favor of the active partner in order to compensate the active partner for his additional work. For example, if the contract assigns the active partner one-ninth of any profits but only one-tenth of any loss, then no interest problem arises according to Rambam.

The interesting cases cited by Rambam, from our perspective, involve situations where either the profit or loss allocation is specified, but not both, *and* the allocation is other than fifty/fifty. For example, suppose the contract states that the active partner is to receive three-quarters of the profit and the silent partner one-quarter—thereby, according to Rambam, treating three-quarters of the *Iska* as a loan and one-quarter as equity—and the loss allocation is unspecified. Rambam's teachers maintain that the profit is allocated three-quarters/one-quarter as specified in the contract. However, in the event of a loss, the profit allocation percentage is also utilized to allocate the loss, except that the active partner is compensated for running the business by subtracting from his three-quarter loss, one-third of the *silent partner's* portion. For example, in the event there is a profit of twenty four, the active partner obtains eighteen and the silent partner six, but in the event of a loss of twenty four, the active partner loses only sixteen (three-quarters less one-twelfth) and the silent partner loses eight. Similarly, if the contract specifies the loss allocation but not the profit allocation, then in the event of a loss the contractual allocation specifies the return to each partner. In the event of a profit, the active partner obtains the contractual loss proportion plus one-third of the proportion that should devolve on the silent partner, in order to compensate the active partner for running the business.

Rambam rejects the legal ruling of his teachers because, in his opinion, it leads to a reductio ad absurdum. To see why, suppose the contract specifies that the active partner obtains one-quarter of the profit and the silent partner three-quarters, but there is no mention of the loss allocation. In the event of a loss, the active partner will lose one-quarter less one-third of the silent partner's portion, which is also one-quarter. Thus, the active partner loses nothing and the silent partner bears the entire loss. In fact, suppose the agreement is such that the active partner obtains one-seventh of the profit and the silent partner sixth-sevenths, but there is no mention of the loss allocation. Thus, in the event of a loss, the active partner loses one-seventh less one-third of six-sevenths, or minus one-seventh. Rather than losing, the active partner gains one-seventh and the silent partner bears the entire loss plus the loss of an additional seventh of his capital. Rambam argues that "reason cannot entertain such a solution, and in my opinion it is no more than the words of a dream." In other words, his teachers' solution leads to a reductio ad absurdum where the active partner earns a positive amount despite the overall business venture loss. Moreover, the smaller the active partner's portion, the more he gains in the event of a loss, according to the allocation of Rambam's teachers. Clearly, this is a suboptimal incentive contract.

Instead, Rambam argues that, where the contract specifies only a profit allocation, and there is a loss, the active partner loses two-thirds of *his* profit-based contractual allocation. For example, if the active partner is allocated one-quarter of the profit and the silent partner three-quarters, then in the event of a loss, the active partner loses two-thirds of one-quarter, or one-sixth, and the silent partner loses five-sixths. Where the contract specifies a loss allocation and there is a profit, Rambam maintains that the active partner earns the contractual loss allocation proportion plus one-third of the *silent partner's* allocation. For example, if the contract specifies that in the event of a loss the active partner loses one-quarter and the silent partner three-quarters, then in the event of a profit, the silent partner is allocated one-half: one-quarter from the contractual allocation, plus one-third of the silent partner's allocation. Rambam claims that his allocation will never result in a reductio ad absurdum.

In general, there is very little discussion among the *Rishonim* regarding the incentive issues surrounding the *Iska* contract, despite the fact that *Iska* structure mandated by the Nehardean rabbis—half-loan half-equity—was meant explicitly to benefit both parties and facilitate the growth of business ventures. Rather, the *Rishonim* focus almost exclusively on obviating the problem of *avak ribbit.* Along with Rashi, *Kesef Mishne*, a late *Rishon* or perhaps early *Aharon*, is an exception, although he too was primarily concerned with the interest issue.

Kesef Mishne tries to explain three allocation systems: that of Rambam, that of Rambam's teachers, and an additional allocation system that the students of R. Solomon b. Abraham Adret (Rashba, Spain, c. 1235–c. 1310) attribute to Ramban.[35] *Kesef Mishne* begins his lengthy discussion by noting that, "These words [of Rambam] appear at first blush to be opaque and without reason but G-d has enlightened me to plumb their depths." First, *Kesef Mishne* notes, without explanation, that the differences among these allocation systems are a function of the extra third

35. See *Kesef Mishne, s.v. hodu rabbotai,* to Rambam, op. cit., *Sheluhin ve-Shuttafin* 6:5.

compensation that the active partner is slated to earn in order to avoid *avak ribbit*. He maintains that the allocation system of Rambam's teachers is based on the assumption that the one-third additional allocation received by the active partner as compensation for running the business is solely a function of the *silent partner's* allocated portion, whether the business venture earns a profit or suffers a loss. In contrast, Ramban's system is based on the assumption that the one-third additional allocation received by the active partner is solely a function of the *active partner's* allocated portion, whether the business venture earns a profit or suffers a loss. Second, *Kesef Mishne* goes on to demonstrate that, like Rambam's teachers' allocation, Ramban's allocation also yields absurd results. Finally, *Kesef Mishne* argues that Rambam's system is based on the asymmetric assumption that the one-third additional allocation received by the active partner is a function of the *silent partner's* allocated portion in the event the business venture earns a profit, and of the *active partner's* allocated portion in the event the business venture suffers a loss. According to *Kesef Mishne*, it is the asymmetry in Rambam's allocation system with respect to the additional one-third compensation that prevents a reductio ad absurdum that plagues Rambam's teachers' and Ramban's allocation systems.

More interestingly, although the underlying rationale for these allocations is apparently to avoid *avak ribbit*, *Kesef Mishne* also argues that the asymmetry in Rambam's allocation system provides the best incentives for the business venture to succeed:

> Do not be troubled by Rambam's [asymmetric] position, namely, why if there is a loss we compensate [the active partner] based on the loan portion and if there is a profit we compensate him based on the equity portion. For when there is a profit, it makes sense that if the active partner worked hard on [increasing] the equity portion, [the active partner] should be compensated a lot, and if he worked only a little on [increasing] the equity portion, he should receive a little. Should you say instead that we compensate [the active partner] based on the debt amount, the law is deficient for it may happen that the debt amount is small and the [active partner] will end up working hard on behalf of the equity and yet be recompensed a small amount. . . . But if there is a loss, it should be the opposite, for if [the active partner] is compensated based on the [silent partner's] equity portion, the law is deficient; for there are times when [the silent partner's] equity portion is large, and so the active partner will never lose out [although there is an overall loss], and there are times when the active partner will even take money from the silent partner. Therefore, [in the event of a loss,] we compensate based on the size of the debt, so that the silent partner should help the active partner in bearing [only] a third of the loss that is his due. . . .

In the *Kesef Mishne*'s view all three profit/loss allocation systems solve the interest problem. However, Rambam's asymmetric solution is unique both because the silent partner cannot suboptimally and mechanically profit when the venture as a whole suffers a loss—the reduction ad absurdum argument—and also because the incentives mitigate shirking. Specifically, an overall business venture profit makes it likely that the active partner worked hard to increase the silent partner's portion. Consequently, since the incentive to shirk increases in proportion to the size of the silent partner's portion, an optimal contract should ex ante compensate the active partner more (conditional on there being a profit) the greater the silent partner's equity portion. In contradistinction, an overall business venture loss signals that the active partner did not work sufficiently hard to increase the silent partner's portion. Compensating the active partner based on the silent partner's portion when there is a loss, *Kesef Mishne* argues, could be distortive especially if the silent partner has a large equity portion. Instead, when there is a loss, Rambam compensates the silent partner based on the silent partner's own portion that is at risk, minimizing distortions in the compensation package.

The argument that a piecewise asymmetric nonlinear allocation system provides the appropriate incentives for managing the business venture—in addition, of course, to solving the problem of *avak ribbit*—is unique to *Kesef Mishne*. But, is it also consistent with modern economic contract theory?

As we pointed out above, modern contract theory generally requires a nonlinear contract wherever shirking, in addition to risk aversion, is an issue. Of course, this does not mean that the one-third additional allocation proposed by Rava is optimal, or indeed that any asymmetric piecewise linear contract is necessarily optimal. However, there is a class of contract theory models that rationalizes an asymmetric piecewise linear contract even in a shirking environment, although the optimal contract form does not quite correspond to those proposed by the Talmud. Specifically, Lacker and Weinberg (1989) analyze a model with a risk-neutral principal (silent partner) and risk-averse agent (active partner) who is able to hide his output at some cost to himself. This "state falsification" situation could describe an *Iska* if, for example, the agent is able to falsify the amount earned in the business venture, but suffers a cost if caught cheating—such as the cost of being ostracized by the community. They show that the optimal "no falsification" contract has the property that the silent partner's share increases as a proportion of the business venture's value (above some minimal amount) and is constant for lesser profit or losses. Although not quite the Talmudic asymmetric piecewise linear allocation approach, the Lacker-Weiberg solution is tantalizingly close, suggesting that the *Rabbinic*al allocation format may have optimality properties.[36] We leave this latter conjecture for future research.

It is natural to ask whether the structure of the *Iska* served its purpose in facilitating business project formation as the Nehardean rabbis hoped it would. Although the standard *Iska* allocations of R. ʻIlish appear to provide both a reasonable sharing of risk and sufficient incentives to deter the active partner from excessive shirking, historical evidence suggests that the *Iska* contracts formulated by the Talmud and the *Rishonim* were not in great demand once alternative arrangements became available. In particular, Genizah documents indicate the Egyptian Jewish traders preferred the Moslem Qirad over the *Iska*. Rambam himself was asked to rule on a

36 Jeffrey M. Lacker and John A. Weinberg, "Optimal Contracts under Costly State Falsification," *Journal of Political Economy* 97(6 1989): 1,345–63. The authors show that the "no falsification" contract is generally not optimal and that the optimal contract allows for some lying. They also show that the agent's (consumption) contract with lying will in fact be linear under specific assumptions.

legal issue involving the "Qirad of the Gentiles" entered into by Jewish merchants.[37] Although other allocations were possible, the archtypical Qirad allocated three-quarters of the profit to the silent partner and one-quarter to the active partner but, in contrast to the *Iska*, absolved the active partner from all losses. Clearly, the latter allocation was less likely to deter shirking by the active partner in comparison to the archetypical Talmudic *Iska*. Although it is impossible to state that the *Iska* allocations are superior to the Qirad's, and, in fact, revealed preference suggests otherwise, nevertheless it is hard to believe that the corner solution of the Qirad (no allocation of losses to the active partner) would have dominated the *Iska* except under intense competitive situations. Indeed, one may conjecture that in Egypt of the Genizah period there were many successful traders competing to provide capital and relatively few active traders willing to undertake the risks of medieval trade unless insured completely against losses.

CONCLUSION

Ribbit is conceptualized by the Talmud to include both real and (ex post) inflation interest components but not credit risk. Thus, nominal interest is prohibited even if there is no real return and even if there is a risk that the loan will not be repaid. Nevertheless, in contrast to credit risk, business risk appears to generally remove interest from the realm of *ribbit* and place it into the realm of *avak ribbit*, as in the case of the *Iska*.

Given the likely devastating effect of the rabbinic, a fortiori Biblical, interest prohibition on business project formation, the Nehardean rabbis of the Talmud conceptually restructured the *Iska* contract "to the benefit of the debtor and to the benefit of the creditor," thereby effectively promoting a linear incentive structure both to resolve the *avak ribbit* problem and to provide risk sharing and perhaps even antishirking incentives. Motivated by the *Tosefta*, the Talmud further suggests two asymmetric piecewise linear *Iska* compensation contracts to solve the interest prohibition issue without considering their incentive structures.

With the notable exception of Rashi and the *Kesef Mishne*, medieval post-Talmudic rabbinic analyses focus almost exclusively on the *avak ribbit* aspect of the *Iska*, with little discussion of the incentive effects of the various Talmudic contractual *Iska* forms. Of the exceptions, Rashi recognizes the incentive effects on project success of preventing the active partner from spending his portion of the *Iska* capital on personal use. In his attempt to explain the tripartite disagreement among his teachers and Ramban regarding contractual aspects of the *Iska*, *Kesef Mishne* insightfully analyzes some of the incentive issues of the *Iska* contractual form in addition to interest prohibition issues. Most importantly, *Kesef Mishne* recognizes

37 See Udovich (1962) for a translation of Rambam's responsum.

the differential incentive effects of asymmetric compensation schemes on the active partner's willingness to work on behalf of the silent partner.

SELECTED BIBLIOGRAPHY

Talmud Bavli,
Bava Metsi'a, 60b, 63b, 68a, 69a, 70a, 75b, 104b.
Bolton, Patrick., and Mathias Dewatripont. *Contract Theory*. Cambridge: MIT Press, 2005.
Caro, R. Joseph. *Kesef Mishne, Sheluhin ve-Shuttafin* 6:5.
Ishbili, R. Yom Tov b. Abraham, *Bava Metsi'a* 70a.
Gamoran, Hillel. "Investing for Profit: A Study of *Iska* up to the Time of Rabbi Abraham ben David of Posquieres." *Hebrew Union College Annual* (1999–2000): 70–71.
Lacker, Jeffrey M., and John A. Weinberg. "Optimal Contracts under Costly State Falsification." *Journal of Political Economy* (1989): 97(6).
Maimonides (Rambam), *Mishne Torah, Sheluhin ve-Shuttafin*, Chapter 6.
Meiri, *Bet ha-Behira, Bava Metsi'a* 70a.
Pryor, John H. "The Origins of the Commenda Contract." *Speculum* (1977): 52.

CHAPTER 5

EXTERNALITIES AND PUBLIC GOODS IN THE TALMUD*

EPHRAIM KLEIMAN

INTRODUCTION

INSOFAR as their literary heritage suggests the ancients did not, as a rule, indulge in explicit economic theorizing.[1] But it would be arrogant of us to assume that, where economic phenomena were observed, there haven't been some minds that speculated about their causes and effects. In particular, this may be expected to have been the case when laws were formulated or applied. Unfortunately, unlike the laws or court rulings themselves, such speculations failed, as a rule, to be recorded. The Talmud is probably unique in having preserved much of the deliberations either preceding rulings or else analyzing them.

*This chapter is one of a trio of papers that grew out of a seminar on Economic Concepts in the Talmud, conducted at the Hebrew University in the academic year 1984/1985: E. Kleiman, "Just Price in Talmudic Literature," *History of Political Economy* 19,1 (1987a): 23–45; idem, "Opportunity Cost, Human Capital, and Some Related Economic Concepts in Talmudic Literature," loc. cit. 19,2 (1987b): 261–87; and idem, "Public Finance Criteria in the Talmud," *Working Paper #192*, Department of Economics, The Hebrew University of Jerusalem, 1988. I am indebted to the participants of the seminar for many stimulating discussions, especially to Libby Schwartz, whose supervised seminar paper dealt with the present topic, albeit from a somewhat different angle: L. Schwartz, "The Distribution of the Costs of Public Goods in the Talmud," unpublished seminar paper, Jerusalem, 1984, and idem, "Talmudic Approaches to the Distribution of the Tax Burden," *The Jewish Quarterly Review* 81,1–2 (1990): 75–113. I have also greatly benefited from the comments of Prof. Amadeo Fossati and other participants in the ERMES Paris December 2008 conference, "Public Goods in the History of Economic Thought," on an earlier version of the present chapter.

1 Aristotle was the notable exception. See E. Roll. *A History of Economic Thought*. London: Faber, 1961, 31; also J. A. Schumpeter. *History of Economic Analysis*. (New York: Oxford University Press, 1954), 60–65.

The Talmud does not contain any explicit economic analysis in the modern sense of the word. But many of its rules pertain to economic phenomena and their formulation and discussion required some insight into economic relationships that went beyond the simply commonsensical one. The casuistic discourse in the Talmud often reveals the implicit economic reasoning, or else this can be reconstructed by comparing the rules decreed for closely related yet in some aspect differing cases.[2] The present chapter examines the Talmudic Sages' views of the causes underlying the existence of externalities and of public goods and of the remedies offered for them, which also reveal the taxation principles to which they subscribed.

Practically all the rules and statements examined here are of Tannaite (i.e., Mishnaic) origin, although some of them came down to us through the noncanonic collection of the *Tosefta*, or embedded in the later, Amoraic text of the exegetic *Gemara*, which, together with the *Mishnah*, forms the Talmud.[3] It should also be emphasized that the present investigation is restricted to the economic perceptions of the Talmudic Sages themselves. It does not tackle the much broader questions of how these evolved in the writings of later day Rabbinic scholars or are reflected in today's Jewish religious thought.[4]

Externalities, Torts, and Public Goods

A negative externality occurs when the cost to society as a whole of some activity exceeds that to its pursuers. It constitutes what in legal language is known as a *tort*. The legal system concerns itself with establishing the identity of the parties involved and with estimating the compensation that the perpetrating party should pay the injured one. Correctly assessed, the payment of such compensation also "internalizes" the externality insofar as economic efficiency is concerned: By forcing the perpetrators to account also for the damage they cause to others, compensation brings their private costs to the level of the social ones. It thus makes their action less profitable to them, thereby reducing the extent of the damage to the socially optimal one.

The opposite is true of positive externalities, where the benefits to society as a whole exceed those to their producers. Presumably because the beneficiaries of positive externalities have no cause for complaint, the legal system, whose concern is equity, does not usually provide "remedies" for them. From the point of view of

2 See E. Kleiman, op. cit., 1987a and 1987b, and idem, "Ancient and Medieval Rabbinic Economic Thought: Definitions, Methodology and Illustrations." In B. B. Price (ed.). *Ancient Economic Thought.* London/New York: Routledge, 1997, 78–98.

3 Such Tannaitic text embedded in the *Gemara* is known as a *Baraita*. The authorities of the *Mishnah* are known as Tannaim; those of the Gemara as Amoraim.

4 For an extensive description and analysis of the latter, see A. Levine. *Free Enterprise and Jewish Law.* (New York: Yeshiva University Press, 1980).

economic efficiency, however, this might result in a socially suboptimal level of the activity in question, as its producers will pursue it insofar as it is worth it to them, rather than to society as a whole.

Voluntary market exchange can internalize a positive externality by having those of its beneficiaries who want to enjoy it pay for it, thereby raising the benefit to the provider to the level of that to society as a whole. This, however, hinges on the there being a way to exclude from its benefits those who did not pay for them. As Coase has shown, negative externalities too can be internalized through voluntary market exchange, by the damaged parties "bribing" their perpetrators to desist.[5] This raises the private cost of activities producing negative externalities, for by persisting in them their perpetrators now forego receiving these payments—provided again that those not offering them can be excluded from the damage abatement.

But having the parties suffering the injury pay its inflictor to escape it tends to offend common standards of fairness. Furthermore, the identity of the sufferers of a negative externality, such, as say, a fire set to clear weeds spreading to neighboring cultivated fields, is often unknown until after the event, making the in-advance bribing of its potential inflictor impractical, except perhaps in the case of repeating offenders.[6] Hence the need, even where exclusion is possible, for some rules for dealing with negative externalities, either directly limiting their scope or indirectly by decreeing appropriate compensation.

Where exclusion is unfeasible or else prohibitively expensive, the product or service in question becomes a *public good*, the quantity of which consumed by one member of the public not reducing that available to others.[7] The classic example of the former is the defense of a country from outside enemies, which all its citizens willy-nilly enjoy. An example of the latter is street lighting, which, again, all night passersby enjoy, and where exclusion would necessitate denying access to those who hadn't paid for it. Public goods can also be negative, sometimes referred to as *public bads*, such as, say, the soot spewed by a factory's chimney. As the above examples illustrate, the scope of a good's "publicness" can vary widely, from the national to the urban or the parochial; it can even be global, as in the case of emissions destroying the Earth's ozone layer.

The existence of public goods raises, perforce, the question of how to finance their production, as the impossibility of excluding nonpayers rules out leaving it to a market exchange mechanism. In particular, even if some members of the community were to voluntary contribute toward this purpose, others could be expected to take a "free ride" on them—a behavior that if pursued by everybody would ultimately bring the sum thus collected to zero.[8]

5 This came to be known as the *Coase theorem*. See A. R. Coase, "The Problem of Social Cost." *Journal of Law and Economics* 3 (1960): 1–44.

6 Like that of an ox known to be "an attested danger" (*mu'ad*) (*Mishnah, Bava Kamma* 4:2).

7 P. A. Samuelson. "Diagrammatical Exposition of a Theory of Public Expenditure." *Review of Economics and Statistics* 38,4 (1954): 254–56.

8 It seems that most people do not practice free-riding to the full extent possible. See G. Marwell's and R. E. Ames' aptly titled article, "Economists Free-Ride, Does Anyone Else?" *Journal of Public Economics* 15 (June 1981): 295–310. Attempts to explain why this is so yielded a rich literature in the last two decades (e.g., E. Ostrom. "Collective Action and the Development of Social Norms." *Journal of Economic Perspectives* 14,3 [2000]: 137–58).

Living under Roman or Persian governance, the Talmudic Sages' discussion of the fair apportioning of the burden of providing public goods restricted itself to questions that arose on the local government, municipal level, or even below it.[9] But the principles involved do not differ from those discussed nowadays in the context of much larger, in terms of the number of individuals they concern, projects.

The Talmud's View of Torts and Externalities

The civil law sections of the Talmud deal extensively with torts. The negative externalities considered there are mostly of the garden or backyard variety: a passing camel's load of flax catching fire from a candle put outside a shop; a man slipping on water poured by another in the street; and so on.[10] Insofar as they involved only two identifiable parties, the problem before the courts boiled down to how to determine culpability and to asses the called for restitution. In some cases the damage could be made good in kind, bushel for bushel. Others required pecuniary compensation. As we know, inter alia, from the discussion of bodily harm, the courts were to set it according to market prices.[11]

In ascribing culpability, however, the *Mishnah* tacitly probed the question of how did the externality underlying the tort come into being. This is vividly illustrated by the picturesque case of a jar and a beam carrier going file-wise in the same direction:

> [A] If the man with the beam came first and the man with the jar came after, and the jar broke against the beam, the man with the beam is not culpable. If the man with the beam [suddenly] stopped—he is culpable, but if he said "Stop!" to the man with the jar, he is not. . . . (M. *Bava Kamma* 2:5)[12]

The Gemara associated with the above passage even goes as far as to ask, "What [would be the rule] if a man harms his wife during intercourse?"[13] A succinct general statement sums it all up: "All I am bound to watch over, I render possible the

9 For examples of the provision of local public goods, such as a fire brigade, in antiquity, see Betty Radice (trans.). *Letters of Pliny the Younger.* (London: Penguin Books, 1963), Book Ten, *passim.*

10 *Mishnah, Bava Kamma* 6:6 and 3:1. For citation from the *Mishna* see note 12 below.

11 See Kleiman, op. cit., 1987b.

12 The *Mishnah,* M., is cited by tractate and by chapter and verse. With occasional departures to preserve the style of the original Hebrew or clarify its meaning, the English translation here follows H. Denby. *The Mishnah.* (London: Oxford University Press, 1933).

13 The answer being that, while "the enjoyment is derived by both, it is only he [i.e., the man] to whom the active part can be ascribed" (TB *Bava Kamma* 32a). The Babylonian Talmud is cited by tractate and by number of leaf and its side. The standard English translation is I. Epstein (ed.). *The Babylonian Talmud,* by various translators. (London: Soncino Press, 1935–1952), from which the citations here often depart for the sake of precision or preservation of style.

injury it does." In other words, those who, whether by design or by omission, create an externality are responsible for its consequences.[14]

Although guided by notions of equitableness rather those of output or welfare maximization, the *Mishnah*'s rule, by thus internalizing externalities in the considerations of individuals, brought up the private cost to the level of the social one. Knowing that one will have to pay for the impact of one's actions on others can be expected to make one reduce the level of externality generating activities to below that at which they would have been pursued otherwise—in the case of the beam and jar carriers, by avoiding stopping suddenly and taking care to warn the person behind one if one was about to do so.

It may be worthwhile pointing out here that in a somewhat different context the *Gemara* suggested that the compensation for an injury could be estimated by the sum a person would be ready to pay in order to *avoid* it.[15] It thus seems that its authors would not be taken aback by the equivalence posited by the aforementioned Coase theorem, although they would have rejected its implications on equity grounds.

PUBLIC GOODS AND REGULATION

When the identities of the victims of negative externalities are not known in advance, it is the risk of becoming one, even if they are ultimately bound to affect only a single person, that constitutes a public good, or rather "bad," to which the exclusion principle is inapplicable. In such cases the *Mishnah* tried to prevent, or at least minimize, the generation of such externalities by resorting to legislation reminiscent of today's municipal nuisance prevention ordinances. Thus, for instance, it decreed that, "A man may not keep a dog unless it is bound by a chain," and that operating a shop in a courtyard could be stopped by one of its residents protesting that, "I cannot sleep for the noise of people [i.e., clients] coming and going."[16]

Cases of pure, albeit local, public goods were, where possible, similarly dealt with by the help of the equivalent of today's urban zoning regulations. Thus, it was stated that, "One should not engage in tanning save east of the town." Another opinion held that, "One may engage in it on any side one wishes, except to the west of the town"[17]; for in the Holy Land, as a noncanonical version correctly explains, it is

14 M. *Bava Kamma* 1:2. As will be seen later, this applied also to the benefits ensuing from positive externalities.

15 "They get hold of a man and ask him: 'How much are you willing *not* to have such pain inflicted on you?' And as much as he says they award him [i.e., the injured party]" (TJ *Bava Kamma* 8:1). The Jerusalem Talmud is cited by tractate and numbers of chapter and rule. The English translation is J. Neusner. *The Talmud of the Land of Israel: A Preliminary Translation and Explanation.* Chicago: Chicago University Press, 1982–1991.

16 M. *Bava Kamma* 7:7 and M. *Bava Batra* 2:3, respectively.

17 M. *Bava Batra* 2:9.

the "west (wind) that prevails."[18] A ruling savoring of the classical economics classroom example of the (positive) externalities that orchards and bees exert on one another states that, "One distances . . . mustard (plants) from the bees (hives)."[19] In perfect symmetry with the bees and orchards case, a Tannaite rule embedded in the *Gemara* speaks not only of mustard being harmful to bees, but also of bees being bad for mustard. In fact, the author of this rule goes as far as to leave the matter to negotiation between the two parties: "For [the mustard grower] always can retort: before you tell me to distance my mustard from your bees, remove your bees from my mustards, as they come and devour my mustard's seeds" (TB *Bava Batra* 25b).

Legislation, however, could not be effective when negative externalities originated from without the jurisdiction of the Rabbinic courts, say with a foreign ruler or simply from the elements. These required counter measures that were by themselves nonexclusive (i.e., public goods, the financing of which had then to be found within the affected community itself, raising the question of how the burden should be shared).[20]

Providing for a Town's Security

The first case to be considered here pertains to the apportioning of the costs of maintaining a town's defenses.[21] Because of the scarcity of water sources, as well as for security reasons, rural populations in most Middle East countries could not live on individual homesteads, but had to congregate close to each other (i.e., in "towns"). The reference appears in a tractate devoted almost exclusively to problems arising from the existence of externalities, and states that:

> [B] They compel him (i.e., a resident of a town) to [share in] constructing a town wall, and double gates, and a crossbar. (M. *Bava Batra* 1:5)

The installation of gates and of a crossbar, at least, must have required some specialized work, and could not therefore be effected by a corvée type labor levy on all able-bodied members of the community. As the manner in which this burden should be shared was not stipulated in the *Mishnah*, it became a subject of discussion for later scholars. The *Gemara* quotes two different views, both attributed to

18 *Tosefta, Bava Batra* 1:8. The timelessness of the above passages is underscored by the following recollection, from his service in a rural district north of Jerusalem in the 1920s, of the 2nd Viscount Samuel: "I fought a losing battle to get these manure heaps moved to the eastern edge of the villages (the prevailing wind is from the sea, to the west)." E. Samuel. *A Lifetime in Jerusalem*, (Jerusalem: Israel's Universities Press, 1970), 72.

19 M. *Bava Batra* 2:10.

20 For an up-to-date discussion of externalities, see E. J. Mishan and E. Quah. *Cost-Benefit Analysis*, 5th ed. London: Routledge, 2007, 85–118. R. A. Musgrave. *The Theory of Public Finance*. (New York: McGraw-Hill, 1959), ch. 4–5, probably remains the best both theoretical and practical treatment of alternative approaches to the financing of public goods, provided within a historical framework, accessible to the general reader.

21 For an exhaustive discussion of the Jewish law's, *halakhic*, treatment of this subject, see Levine, op. cit., 136–47.

R. Yohanan (Roman Palestine, first half of the second century CE), one of the foremost Tannaite authorities.[22] The first version runs as follows:

> [C] R. Eleazar [Roman Palestine, mid-second century CE] inquired of R. Yohanan: "When they collect [the impost for the wall], do they collect according to [number of] souls? Or perhaps according to wealth improvement they [should] collect?" He answered: "According to wealth improvement they [should] collect." (TB *Bava Batra* 7b)

However, there survived also another tradition:

> [D] There are those who say [that] R. Eleazar inquired of R. Yohanan: "When they collect, do they collect according to the proximity of houses [to the wall]? Or perhaps according to the wealth improvement they [should] collect?" He answered: "According to the proximity of the houses they [should] collect." (ibid.)

Thus, the two competing traditions of [C] and [D] mention three alternative methods of apportioning the costs of the specific public good—namely protection from marauding bands of robbers, considered here. The first one, which we may designate (C.1), is obviously that of a poll-tax. The second alternative, which appears both as (C.2) and as (D.2), is that of a tax on the resultant economic gain. The term that has been rendered here as "wealth *mammon*, does not posses in the Aramaic of the original the negative connotation with which it was invested in Western culture by the Sermon of the Mount.[23] An alternative reading for "wealth improvement" or "[capital] gain" could be wealth praise, or renown—which could suggest taxation according to means (i.e., an application of what is known in public finance literature as the *ability-to-pay criterion*). However, an examination of other contexts in the Talmud in which the term referred to here appears shows it to have been used always in the sense of betterment or gain.[24]

Finally, in (D.1), the criterion is that of the degree of danger to which residents of different town areas are exposed in the absence of a town wall, and therefore also of the reduction in this risk as a result of the wall having been erected.

Benefit Criteria

All three methods enumerated in [C] and [D] reflect what is known in economics as the *benefit approach* to public finance. This, to use J.S Mill's words, "regard[s] the taxes paid by each member of the community as an equivalent for value received in

22 The textual and linguistic identification of this passage as a *Baraita* points to R. Yohanan "the Cobbler" and his younger colleague R. Eleazar ben Shamua (who is always cited without his patronymic) as the partners to this exchange. It is also consistent with R. Yohanan referring there to his interlocutor as "my son."

23 Thus, "Ye cannot serve God and Mammon" (Matthew 6:24); "the mammon of unrighteousness" (Luke 16:9). Compare this with the Tannaite use of the term "*mammon* laws" to describe all legislation pertaining to civil law, which has carried over also to modern Hebrew (see, e.g., E. Kleiman. "An Early Modern Hebrew Textbook of Economics." *History of Political Economy* 5:2 [1973]: 339–58).

24 See, for example, M. *Bava Kamma* 9:4 and M. *Arakhin* 6:5; also TB *Bava Batra* 135b. The term *wealth improvement* as such is also used to describe an asset being worth more than was originally expected (TB *Kiddushin* 48b–49a).

the shape of service to himself."[25] But they differ in the view of the benefits that the public good in question, namely a town wall, bestows on different individuals. Obviously, a town wall and its appurtenances confer a degree of security on the town's residents. The poll-tax of (C.1) is consistent with assuming that (i) the wall provides protection from danger to life and limb of the inhabitants, and (ii) all of them are equally exposed to this danger.[26] This last assumption is relaxed in (D.1), which assumes instead that, in the absence of a wall, (iii) the risks of exposure to marauding gangs or out of town robbers decrease as one moves away of from the town's perimeter, toward its center. If this is the case, then the benefit from constructing a wall—the risk reduction effected by it—is inversely related to the distance of one's residence from the perimeter (i.e., from the wall). Hence, the suggestion of the "proximity to the wall" as a criterion for the imputation of its benefits and the apportioning of its costs. But the proximity rule of (D.1) does not provide any guidance as to the functional form of the relationship between distance and benefit or cost. It thus leaves unsolved, in contrast to the poll tax of (C.1), the problem of the actual apportioning. This is taken care of in the capital gains criterion of (C.2 = D.2), which rejects both of the assumptions underlying (C.1). Instead of (i), it implies the wall is to provide protection not only to person but also to property. And, instead of either (ii) or (iii), it assumes only that the resultant risk reduction is not uniform; but it does not postulate any specific pattern that this is supposed to follow. Most importantly, from the point of view of economic conceptualization, this last method of distributing the burden resorts to market values to measure the distribution of the ensuing benefits. The use that the Talmud made of changes in market-capitalized values to measure changes in income streams—most notably, in evaluating the economic effects of physical injury—has been pointed out elsewhere.[27] Here we see this use extended to apply also to public goods.

Whether the authorities cited by the Talmud were conscious of it or not, the rule of (C.2) takes into consideration all the direct benefits of the public good in question. For changes in market value of real estate reflect not only the town wall's effect on the safety of the real estate itself and of any property kept there, but also on its desirability as a residence, determined, inter alia, by the physical protection it provides to its tenants.[28] Unlike in our post-Samuelson 1955 world, the Talmud did not inquire about the relationship between the sum total of the additional benefits and the extra outlays of erecting or repairing the wall, to establish the optimal amount of protection.[29] Most probably, it assumed benefits to greatly exceed costs. But by decreeing the taxation required for this purpose to be proportionate to an

25 J. S. Mill. *Principles of Political Economy*, vol. 2. London: John. W. Parker, 1848, 349.

26 Strictly speaking, (b) could be substituted for by a weaker form, in which the risk reduction is the same for all inhabitants.

27 See Kleiman, loc. cit.

28 And probably also the indirect ones, such as increased economic activity, insofar as they were associated with a location, and thus also affected the value of real estate.

29 As Samuelson, op. cit., has shown, the total demand for a public good expresses itself not in the sum total of the quantities individuals wish to consume, but in the sum of the prices they are ready to pay for it.

economic variable, rather than to a physical one like that of (D.1), the present rule enunciated an operational method for the application of the benefit principle to the financing of at least some public goods.

It may be argued, perhaps, that the authorities whose opinions were cited in [C] and in [D] regarded the capital gains generated by the town wall as indicative of ability to pay, rather than of benefits bestowed. That is, indeed, how these passages came to be interpreted in modern times. The Venetian *editio princeps* of the Talmud (1520–1523) omitted the second mention of the word "gain" or "improvement" in [C], and deleted it completely from [D], making the levy proportional to wealth rather than to the wall-induced changes to it.[30] The more reliable of the MSS extant to the contrary, this was followed by most later printed editions.[31] However, as we will now proceed to show, the present interpretation of these passages, as reflecting in all three of their alternatives the benefit approach, is strongly supported by the Talmud's treatment of other instances of public finance.

Sharing the Burden of Billeting

The next reference that we shall consider is found in the same chapter as the one described above. It occurs in the context of a discussion of the rule by which a common of a certain type may be divided among its joint owners. One of the opinions there was that "a courtyard is shared according to [its] entrances" to the structures that it serves.[32] It led by association to the following inquiry:

> [E] Billeting—is it apportioned according to [number of] of people, or according to [number of] entrances it is apportioned? R. Ami [Roman Palestine, third century CE *Amora*] answered him: "According to [number of] people it is apportioned. For it has been taught [to the same effect]: 'Dung in the courtyard is apportioned according to entrances, billeting according to people.' " (TB *Bava Batra* 11b)

With billets assigned by courtyards, rather than by individual households, the sanctions for failing to satisfy the billetees' demands would not distinguish between those households that contributed toward them and those who did not. [E] thus contains two rules: one for the apportioning of the burdens of a public "bad"; the other for that of the benefits of a common.

30 For the sake, apparently, of internal consistency, the standard English translation expunged "improvement" altogether, and rendered (C.2) and (D.2) to read "according to means." See Epstein, op. cit., *Bava Batra*, vol. 1, 31.

31 In restoring the omitted words, we follow the evidence of the Hamburg MS of the Order of *Nezikin*, dating from 1184, and of the Munich Codex Hebraicus 95, the oldest extant MS of the whole Talmud, dating from 1334. Insofar as the passages discussed here are concerned, these two manuscripts differ only slightly from each other, the latter referring to "people" rather than "souls"; but they both differ from the standard printed versions also in that in both [C] and [D] the wealth gain alternative is considered first.

32 TB *Bava Kamma* 11a.

The provisioning of billeted troops, or of traveling government dignitaries, with their horses and pack animals, could be quite demanding. In fact, billeting troops or gendarmerie in a village was still widely practiced in Ottoman, or even British, Palestine as a form of collective punishment. The costs to the reluctant hosts could be so onerous that threat of prolonged billeting was sometimes employed as a tactic to force the extradition of a wanted criminal shielded by the local population.[33] Hence, the need for some rule for their allocation. As in the case of the town wall, one of the rules considered, (E.1) = (C.1), was that of a poll-tax. The other, (E.2), relied on a means test of a sort: In the traditional village architecture of the Middle East, most homes were one-storied structures, with rooms opening straight into the courtyard. The number of such entrances constituted, therefore, an index of the size of the house and ultimately of the household's wealth. Thus, the principal underlying (E.2) was that of the ability to pay. And the logic behind it was the same as that behind any real-estate tax assessed according to some readily observed characteristic, like hearth money, or the window tax still levied in England in Adam Smith's time.[34]

Nevertheless, (E.2) was rejected insofar as sharing the burden of billeting was concerned. The alternative of sharing it on an equal per-capita basis, (E.1), was obviously not preferred on grounds of economic equity, which would have been better served by the "entrances" criterion. Drawing an analogy from the town wall case considered earlier, we hypothesize instead that the failure to provide the food, fodder, and other amenities demanded by the billeted troops could be expected to result either in them being arbitrarily requisitioned, or in the residents being physically abused.[35] Saving them these punishments, the prospect of which was the same for all, may be viewed as the benefit that providing the billeting conferred on them.

Supporting this benefit-approach interpretation of the (E.1) per-capita rule in this case are both circumstances to which it was considered inapplicable, some of which will be considered later, and those for which the alternative one of (E.2) was regarded as the right one. The Tannaite maxim cited in [E] itself provides an example of the latter. The head of this *Baraita* relates to the sharing of animal droppings accumulated in the common courtyard. Dung was valued for its use as fuel, but it could not be traced to any individual animal stabled in the courtyard. It could, however, have been expected to be proportionate to the size of a household's livestock, and therefore to be closely correlated with its wealth. The use, for the present purpose, of a general, easy ascertainable index of wealth, circumvented both the obvious species-standardization problem and that arising from variations over time

33 For a humorous description by a former British police officer of how this tactic was (successfully) applied as recently as the 1930s, see H. Duff. *Sword for Hire.* (London: John Murray, 1934), 295–99.

34 A. Smith. *The Wealth of Nations,* 1776, Bk. 5, ch. 2, ed. E. Cannan. (New-York: The Modern Library, 1937), 797–98.

35 Except for fodder and wine, the requisitioned items would have consisted most probably of foodstuffs in preparation rather than of hoarded stocks, and would not vary very much with the wealth of the household. Billeted troops and officials were forbidden to requisition more than one-third of an occupied house or demand mattresses, firewood, or oil. See *The Theodosian Code.* Trans. C. Pharr. (Princeton: Princeton University Press, 1952) (henceforth, CTh.), 7.8.4, 7.9.2–3.

in the number of beasts and fowl held by individual households. It should be pointed out, however, that here (E.2) represents the benefit approach in its application to the sharing in a positive commons: to each according to their (approximate) input. Hence, the choice of this rule in the case of dung is consistent with its rejection in that of billeting where, because exclusion there is impossible, the use of the same yardstick would have resulted in the application of the ability-to-pay approach.

The Hebrew term translated here as billeting, *akhsanya*, derives from the Greek *ξενια*, meaning originally a mercenary, hence a foreigner (still reflected in today's *xenophobia*). This carried over not only to the billeting of (mercenary) troops but, more generally, to the hosting of any stranger, coming finally to denote not only the act but also its object and its location (i.e., a hostelry).[36] Reading *akhsanya* as a generic for passing strangers, some later day exegetes saw in the parallel drawn in [E] not an irony, equating billeted troops with dung, but a straightforward comparison of two types of commons: domestic dung and dung and chattels left behind by briefly stopping passersby.[37] Under this interpretation, the application of the per-capita rule, (E.1), to the latter would then again be consistent with the benefit approach: The reason for their stopping being, presumably, the safety provided by an enclosure from which their animals would not wander off. It was the mere existence of the courtyard, rather than its size, that mattered, and all its inhabitants could have been assumed to have contributed equally to attracting travelers to stay there.

Warding off Dangers

Three other cases of nonexclusive situations, in two of which the (E.1) per-capita rule is rejected, are considered in another tractate that deals with damages. The context there is that of the recompense, which persons saving the property of others may demand for their efforts. This leads to the discussion of various perils to which property may become exposed. The following Tannaite rule is then cited:

> [F] A caravan that was going through the desert and an armed band came to prey on it—they calculate [shares in buying the raiders off] according to wealth, and do not calculate according to [number of] souls. [On the other hand,] if they hired a guide to go in front of them, they calculate also [shares in his wage] according to [number of] souls. (TB *Bava Kamma* 116b)[38]

36 For the Greek terms, see H. G. Liddell and R. S. Scott. *A Greek English Lexicon*. Rev. by Jones and Mckenzie. (Oxford: Oxford University Press, 1976). For the use of "*akhsanya*" in the Talmud to denote an inn, see, for example, TB *Eruvin* 23b. For its use to describe the billeted troops themselves, see also TJ *Bava Kamma* 3:1.

37 Thus R. Hananel b. Hushiel (N. Africa 990?–1055?), but not the great R. Solomon b. Isaac [Rashi] (France, 1040–1105).

38 This is repeated, in almost the same wording, in TJ *Bava Metsi'a* 6:4 and in *Tosefta*, *Bava Metsi'a* 7:13. A caveat "not to diverge from the custom of the guides" probably refers to calculating the total payment they receive rather than to the way it is shared by members of the caravan. This possibly could also explain the "also" of the text, which otherwise might indicate a double calculation, by both per capita and wealth, without, however, suggesting their relative shares.

In the first of the two scenarios of [F], all members of the caravan share the risk of it being plundered. The resulting material loss will vary, however, with the value of their individual possessions. Raising the required buy-off money according to the shares of individual members in the total wealth carried by the caravan makes the burden of buying the raiders off proportionate to the loss thus averted.[39] It will be shown below, however, that this rule might reflect yet another criterion for sharing the costs of a public good.

The wealth proportionality rule is reversed in the case of paying for the services of a guide. A caravan losing its way in the desert would run various risks, of which by far the most serious one would be that of failing to reach water in time. Hiring a guide lessened, first and foremost, a fatal hazard—that of perishing from thirst—to which all members of the caravan were equally exposed. Hence, the application of the benefit principle required, in this case, that the costs of providing the public good in question be shared on an equal per-capita basis[40].

The benefit approach is, however, abandoned in the last rule to be examined here, that regarding maritime salvage, cited in an analogy to the caravan case:

> [G] A ship which was going by sea, and a gale stood to drown it and they lightened her load—they calculate [shares in the loss] according to the load, and do not calculate according to wealth. (TB *Bava Kamma* 116b)[41]

As the story of the Prophet Jonah, and even more so of St. Paul's journey to Rome, vividly illustrate, jettisoning part of the cargo to restore or increase buoyancy must have been a fairly common practice in the ancient world.[42] Obviously, it could not be pursued but haphazardly, insofar as the identities of either goods or owners were concerned. With the danger over, the question would then inevitably arise as to the manner in which the loss was to be shared.

The application of the benefit principle proper would require that each individual's share in the damage caused by the jettisoning be proportionate to the loss

39 There was no way to ascertain the wealth held by its participants elsewhere. We follow here the commonly accepted traditional interpretation of [F] as referring to the act of buying off robbers. It could be argued, perhaps, that this reflects the benefit approach of the medieval commentators, reasoning backward from the sharing-by-wealth rule. But [F] does not seem to lend itself to any other interpretation.

40 An alternative interpretation of [F] favored by some traditional commentators is that the "guide" referred to here was provided by the armed band itself—along the line of modern day "protection" rackets! But they also tend to explain the per-capita rule as stemming from danger to person. See, for example, M. Tamari, "Medieval Interpretations of the Economic Rules of the Talmud," *Israel Banking Quarterly* 77 (January 1981): 88–99 (in Hebrew).

41 The noncanonical version of the *Tosefta*—"they calculate according to the load and do not calculate according to [number of] souls" (*Tosefta, Bava Metsi'a* 7:13)—seems simply to duplicate the endings of the caravan case of [E], which is also cited there. The Jerusalem Talmud reads: "They calculate according to load and to wealth and not according to [number of] souls" (TJ *Bava Metsi'a* 6:4). This sounds somewhat confused and could, perhaps, be dismissed as a misquotation, were it not for the associated statement in the *Tosefta* that in "letting a boat or a wagon, they calculate according to wealth" (*Tosefta, Bava Metsi'a* 7:14).

42 ". . . There was a mighty tempest in the sea, so that the ship was like to be broken. Then the mariners . . . cast forth the wares that were in the ship into the sea to lighten it of them" (Jonah 1:5); and, "We being exceedingly tossed with a tempest, the next day they lightened the ship; and the third day we cast out with our own hands the tackling of the ship . . . [and ultimately] they lightened the ship and cast out the wheat into the sea" (Acts 27:18–19, 38).

averted by incurring it. This is the loss that he or she would have suffered had the ship foundered. So that, ignoring possible loss of life, it is the individual shipper's share in the cargo's total value that would seem to be the appropriate criterion here.

The principle underlying the rule adopted in [G] becomes clear, however, once it is realized that it refers not to the benefits of the jettison, but to the behavior that made it necessary. The cause of the ship's trouble was overloading (or else jettisoning would have been to no avail). Therefore, an individual's share in the cargo's total weight measured his relative contribution to the creation of the public "bad" concerned. Consequently, compensation money for the owner of the jettisoned goods should be collected from the owners of the rest of the cargo in proportion to their respective shares in the weight of the ship's total load. This manner of sharing the burden of a public "bad" is based ultimately on much the same line of reasoning as underlies the imposition of congestion or pollution taxes in modern societies. It differs from a similarly calculated Pigovian taxation of negative externalities in that the latter is usually imposed ex ante, before the creation of the resulting losses.[43] In the case considered in the Talmud, however, the resultant damage could only be ascertained ex post. Nevertheless, if the rule of [G] was widely known, it would have had the same efficiency effect as an ex ante by weight tax on sea transportation, namely of reducing the tendency to ship cargoes of relatively low value-to-weight ratio.

We may wish to reconsider [F] in light of the present discussion. The criterion decreed there, of the share in the value of the caravan's total cargo, was shown earlier to apportion costs in proportion to the loss averted by buying off the band threatening to rob the caravan. But the value of the cargo was also the cause of the caravan being preyed upon. So that the rule adopted there is also consistent with the cost of the buy-off being shared according to the contribution to the risk that necessitated it. The presentation immediately afterward of [G], where only the latter criterion holds, may have been intended, indeed, to emphasize that this was also the basis of the rule adopted in [F].

Social Justice Origins of the Benefit and the Blame Approaches

In none of the six distinct situations considered in the passages analyzed above does the Talmudic text provide any explicit justification of the rules adopted. But the underlying logic can be inferred from the comparison of the different situations, on one hand, and of the corresponding rules, on the other.

43 A. C. Pigou was the first to suggest taxing activities generating negative externalities and subsidizing those generating positive ones to equalize their private and social marginal costs, thereby restricting the production of the former and expanding that of the latter. See his *The Economics of Welfare*, 4th ed. (London: Macmillan, 1932), II.XI.12.

It can be seen there that, in all but one of the six cases surveyed, two (and once even three) alternative criteria for allocating benefits or burdens are proposed. Altogether, however, only six such criteria are considered, some of them being referred to in more than one situation. Thus, the per-capita rule is considered in four of the six cases: [B], [F(a)], [F(b)] and [E(a)];[44] the ability to pay in three: [F(a)], [F(b)] and [G]; and the "entrances" one in two: [E(a)] and [E(b)]. The three other rules are considered only once each. With the exception of the per-capita one, each of these rules is regarded suitable to only one of the six situations. This is so because under different circumstances the same rule may correspond to a different allocation principle. Thus, the number of entrances constitutes an index of contribution to a common good in the case of a communal dung heap [E(b)], but an index of the ability to pay in that of billeting [E(a)]. Property, or wealth, provides some index of the ability to pay insofar as hiring a caravan guide is concerned [F(b)]; but it may be also an index of the contribution to a common bad in the case of protection money [F(a)], as well as an index of loss averted in both the latter case and that of jettisoning [G]. Its acceptance for buying off robbers, and its rejection in the two other cases, suggests that the basic criterion underlying both this and the previously mentioned rule was that of proportionality to shares in either benefit or culpability.

This impression is further strengthened by examining the three rules considered each in only one of the six. The benefit orientation of the capital gains rule is self-explanatory. The alternative rule or the proximity of dwellings to the city wall is, in this case, clearly intended to provide an index of the benefit that the resultant capital gains measure. Finally, as has already been pointed out, the load, or weight criterion, of the jettison case distributes the burden of a public bad in proportion to the contributions toward its creation.

The present evidence suggests also that the adoption of the benefit and blame or culpability approach stemmed from considerations of social justice, and not of economic efficiency. The discussion is always restricted to problems of distribution among various individuals, and no indication whatsoever is provided as to how the total expenditure on a public good should be determined. The notion that the increments of benefit and of cost should be balanced against each other had to await, of course, the marginalist revolution of the Austrians and of Marshall.[45] But it is revealing of the Talmud's underlying attitude that it ignored the problem altogether. The total outlay on a public good is invariably implied here to be given, though in the case of the city walls, at least, it must have been obvious that more collective security could be purchased by making them, say, higher or thicker.

The conclusion—that these were social justice considerations that led the Talmud toward the benefit/blame approach—is consistent also with what seems to be its abandonment in two of the cases examined here. If our interpretation of them is

44 Successive cases referred to in the same citation are identified by bracketed lower-case letter, in distinction from the numerals used earlier to identify the alternative remedies offered.

45 See, for example, A. Marshall, *Principles of Economics*, 8th ed., 1920, V.II.1 (New York: Macmillan, 1949), 331, with his illustration of this principle by the case of a boy picking blackberries.

correct, than both [F(b)] and [E(a)] involve risk to person, in distinction to that to property only. With efficiency a prime consideration, some recognition should have been given to the different sums of money that individuals of varying wealth would be ready to forgo in exchange for their personal safety. The adoption there of the per-capita rule reflects instead the view that, insofar as protecting it is concerned, all life is equally valuable.[46]

This is not to say that the benefit and blame or culpability approach-based rules adopted by the Talmud were necessarily inconsistent with economic efficiency. On the contrary, the "by-weight" compensation rule of jettison, for one, if taken into account in advance, would have been equivalent to the raising of freight charges, irrespective of the merchandise's worth, thus raising the value-per-weight of sea-borne shipments. The risks of being called upon to share in compensation according to the weight of one's cargo would have deterred merchants from shipping heavy cargoes of low value. As it would have done so by charging them with the expected value of the loss ascribed to their respective cargoes, the "by-weight" rule would have had the same effect as Pigovian taxation of the negative externalities generated by them. The alternative ad valorem rule rejected there, on the other hand, would have had the opposite effect, in that it would have made the shipping of relatively cheap merchandize relatively more attractive.[47]

Comparison with Roman Attitudes

The *Mishnah* and the older portions of the Gemara having been composed in Roman Palestine, their rules invite comparison with those of Roman law. A basic tenet of Roman private law, that "he who suffers the disadvantage of a thing should have also the profits thereof," could have been easily reversed to provide a formulation of the benefit approach.[48] Nevertheless, the two systems differed considerably in this respect.

A straightforward comparison is provided by the rules relating to jettison, where the Romans followed the maritime practice of Rhodes, known as the *Lex Rhodia de iactu,* which still forms the basis of Anglo-Saxon law on the subject.[49] Modern formulations are explicitly consistent with our interpretation of [G] asassuming that

46 Reflected also in the well-known precept that "he who saved a single soul from Israel is deemed as though he saved the whole world" (M. *Sanhedrin* 4:5).

47 In the [F(a)] caravan case, however, it was the ad valorem rule that ensured efficiency—it being the total wealth carried by the caravan that, presumably, provoked the buy-off demands.

48 *The Digest of Justinian*, vol. 2, trans. A. Watson (Philadelphia: University of Pennsylvania Press, 1985), 50.17.10. Paralleled by "according to the pain is the reward" of M. *Avot* 5:23.

49 Justinian's *Digesta* 14.2; and the saying attributed to Antoninus Pius, "I am master of the world, but the law of the sea must be judged by the law of the Rhodians," ibid., 14.2.9; and compare T. G. Carver, *Carriage by Sea*, 13th ed., ed. Raul Colinvaux (London: British Shipping Laws, 1982), 1,346.

only property, but no life, is at stake.[50] Both the Rhodian-Roman and the Talmudic rules make all whose cargo was saved by the jettison compensate the losers. But the former's rule for sharing the burden of compensation is an ad valorem one, in contrast to the "by-weight" rule of the Talmud, which may have preserved elements of the Phoenician maritime law.[51] Unlike the Talmud, the Roman law makes the individual contributions proportionate to the value of the cargoes saved. This benefit not being systematically associated with the cause of the compensated loss, the Roman law's rule did not have the potential efficiency effect of the Talmudic one.

On the other hand, both systems adopted the same rule for sharing the costs of protection money, or ransom paid to robbers. Roman lawmen regarded buying-off pirates as analogous to jettison and extended to it the ad valorem rule applicable to the latter.[52] As we have seen earlier, this is also the Talmud's rule in the corresponding case of the similarly threatened caravan [F(a)]. In both these cases, unlike in that of jettison, the value of the cargo is a measure both of the benefit obtained by buying the robbers or pirates off, and of the contribution toward attracting them, so that a rule based on either the benefit or blame approach is consistent with the attainment of economic efficiency.

Less is known of Roman attitudes regarding situations corresponding to the other cases discussed here. The cities of the Roman Empire collected no regular taxes other than *octroi* duties.[53] Municipal or communal services were procured mainly through compulsory levies, both physical and pecuniary, on their citizens. But the references to such levies, known as *munera*, record mainly exemptions, rather than the rules by which they were imposed. Even the specific duties for which *munera* service was required are only infrequently mentioned.[54] They are known, however, to have included "the maintenance of public roads, buildings, waterworks, river banks, [and providing] means of transportation for public purposes."[55]

Some of these compulsory services must have been levied on all males within a certain age range. But to a considerable extent they seem to have been imposed in a quid pro quo fashion on the holders of state concessions, or in a trade-off against some other imposts. Thus, the upkeep of public baths in the city of Rome fell on the operators of saltpans, while the owners of lands traversed by aqueducts had to look after them in exchange for an exemption from all extraordinary levies.[56]

50 Ibid., 1,444.

51 J. Dauvillier, "Le Droit Maritime Phoenicien," *Revue Internationale des Droits de l'Antiquité*, 3me series (1959): 6, 33–63.

52 Justinian's *Digesta* 14.2.4. This in distinction from goods taken forcibly away by pirates, "which were lost to him to whom it belonged" (ibid.).

53 See J. S. Reid, *The Municipalities of the Roman Empire* (Cambridge: Cambridge University Press, 1913); and F.F. Abbot and A.C Johnson, *Municipal Administration in the Roman Empire* (Princeton: Princeton University Press, 1926).

54 A. H. M. Jones, *The Later Roman Empire, 284–602*, vol. 2 (Oxford: Oxford University Press, 1964), 858.

55 A. Berger, *Encyclopedic Dictionary of Roman Law* (Philadelphia: American Philosophical Society, 1953), 589.

56 CTh. 15.1.53; see also Jones, op. cit., 705.

What the Roman practices and the Talmud had in common was the preferential treatment of scholars. R. Judah the Patriarch (c.135–c.215), the *Ethnarch* (i.e., head) of Palestinian Jewry and editor of the *Mishnah*, is said to have refused successive requests of Jewish plebs that the law-doctors share in the coronation tax imposed on Tiberias, and his grandson was censured for making them contribute toward the building of city walls.[57] To protect their dignity, scholars were excused physical labor on such communal projects as canal digging, even if they had to contribute their share otherwise.[58] For the same reason, rhetoricians and grammarians were under Roman law excused labor levies regarded as demeaning.[59] But under the late Empire, at least, exemptions were also used to provide incentives to certain occupations, as evident from their extension to a long list of professions and trades, running from architects and plasterers, down to coppersmiths, blacksmiths, potters, and plumbers.[60] The Gemara, on the other hand, made it quite clear that participation should be universal:

> [H] Even orphans [contribute] to canal digging, even scholars. . . . For wall supports, and cavalry, and arms—even from orphans (TB *Bava Batra* 8a)

The imposition of compulsory services on selected occupations or on groups associated with the object of these services—as in the aforementioned case of aqueducts—and the wide exemptions from them, suggest that the prime consideration underlying the Roman system was that of administrative expediency. In contrast, the Talmudic principle was quite clearly that of the benefit approach:

> [I] This is the general rule: [for] anything they benefit from—[contributions are collected] even from orphans. (ibid.)

Finally, in a number of instances Roman legislation does specify the manner in which the burden of providing a public good is to be allocated:

> [J] All persons . . . shall be compelled to aid in the construction of walls . . . so that . . . all should be forced to perform these compulsory services in proportion to their landholdings and land tax units. (CTh. 15.1.49)

Given the universality of this levy, the rule stated in [J]—which contrasts sharply with those of [C] and [D] above—is consistent with the ability-to-pay approach. So is the following decree:

> [K] . . . Landlords throughout Bithynia and other provinces shall be compelled to undertake the repair of the public roads and all other such compulsory public services, in proportion to the number of land tax and capitation tax units which they are known to possess. (CTh. 15.3.5)

Although with road maintenance falling apparently only on landholders and the employment of long-established tax assessments, [K] points out again to the importance of administrative ease in Roman considerations.

57 TB *Bava Batra* 8a.

58 Ibid.

59 CTh. 11.16.15 and 18. This ruling of the Theodosian Code, dating by itself from as late as the end of the fourth century, only reaffirmed in this respect what it called an "ancient custom."

60 CTh. 13.4.1–3.

The Roman ability-to-pay attitude to the financing of public goods contrasts sharply with the benefit one of the Talmud. But it seems that the difference between them stemmed ultimately not so much from differences in ethics or in economic comprehension, as from those in the scope of governance. Most of the *Mishnah*, and all the *Gemara*, were formulated under a supremacy of foreign rule—Roman, Byzantine, or Sasanian. Their authors could deal with the economics of public goods in the small scope without giving the slightest consideration to questions of imperial financing or administrative expedience. They could thus pay more attention to both the ethics and the economics of each case than could an imperial administration saddled with ecumenical responsibilities. World government seems to have required greater compromises than the running of a local village.

Summary and Conclusions

An examination of the solutions that the Talmudic Sages offered to certain public goods' situations identified their view of the ensuing benefits and costs, as well as their underlying tax philosophy. Though the immediate, operational standards for allocating the burden of financing public goods varied with the specific circumstances, the ultimate criteria underlying all of them were either those of the benefit approach or of its obverse, the blame or culpability one. The Talmudic authors were aware of the question whether public safety should be viewed as protecting primarily life or property—and their implicit answer to it differed with the nature of the danger averted. They also effected an interesting and original inversion of the benefit principle, in allocating the costs of liquidating a public bad not by the benefit arising from its removal, but by the contribution to its creation in the first instance.

The distributive rules decreed by the Talmud were not the only plausible ones. In all the cases surveyed here, reasonable alternatives were, in fact, considered. We have seen also that the Roman world adopted other solutions to the same problems, occasionally identical with the alternatives rejected in the Talmud. This is clearly evident in the case of jettison, but was probably true of public works as well. In another case, that of billeting, in which the Roman custom cannot be ascertained from the extant legal literature, another interesting alternative is provided by the practice surviving until quite recently in traditional Arab society. [61]

The Talmud approached the problem of financing the provision of public goods from a purely distributive angle. Though its solutions often offered incentives

61 "On the wall [of the guesthouse] was pinned an Arabic list . . . arranged in three columns . . . [which] showed the names of the heads of families—well off, in-between, and poor. . . . If the visitor was a poor man, the family next on the list of poor families would be notified, etc." The visitor's social status was roughly assessed by his dress and means of conveyance (Samuel, op. cit., 70–71).

that had the right sign insofar as economic efficiency was concerned, efficiency seems to have played little, if any, role in determining its attitude to the problem. In sharp contrast to the attitude implied by the Roman practices in these matters, the Talmud also ignored the costs of tax collection and tax compliance.

We have speculated that this neglect of these costs, and possibly also of economic efficiency effects in general, was due to the local finance level of the public goods considered in the Talmud. The plethora of imposts levied by the Roman administration and the iniquities of the tax farmers is much complained of there.[62] But the rules by which these taxes were actually gathered are nowhere discussed.

The silence of the Talmud regarding these aspects of taxation seems to have stemmed from its viewing them as exogenously imposed tributes, succinctly summarized by Jesus' dictum, in response to a query regarding the legitimacy of Roman taxes, to "render unto Caesar the things that are Caesar's."[63] So it dealt with questions of tax rebates or even tax evasion, but not with problems of equity, over which it had no control.[64] But this explanation is not entirely satisfactory. Among Roman taxes there were some that, like the coronation levy referred to earlier, were imposed in a lump-sum fashion on a city or a community as a whole. This left the internal distribution of the burden to the discretion of the municipal council, and the Talmud may have been expected to provide some guidance in the matter. Furthermore, there was also the apostolic contribution, forwarded by Jewish communities throughout the Empire for the support of the Holy Land's Ethnarchy, until the extinction of the latter early in the fifth century.[65] The Exilarch, as head of Mesopotamian Jewry, was probably the beneficiary of a tax levied on Jews living in the Sasanian Empire. Unless these contributions followed the erstwhile Temple tax in taking the form of a poll tax, or else were purely voluntary, questions must have arisen as to the criteria for the distribution of their burden among different members of the community. But the Talmud seems to contain no pronouncements on these matters.

SELECTED BIBLIOGRAPHY

Coase, A. R. "The Problem of Social Cost." *Journal of Law and Economics* 3 (1960): 1–44.

Digest of Justinian. Trans. A. Watson. Philadelphia: University of Pennsylvania Press, 1985. Vol. 2, 14.2.

62 Echoed also in tax farmers being identified with sinners in the roughly contemporaneous Synoptic Gospels of the New Testament. See, for example, Mathew 9:10–11, Mark 2:14–16.

63 Matthew, 12:21.

64 For references to taxes in the Talmud, see J. Dinur, "Taxation System of Roman Palestine as Reflected in Talmudic Literature," unpublished Ph.D. dissertation (Jerusalem: The Hebrew University, 1982) (in Hebrew). For a discussion of tax evasion, see TJ *Bava Kamma* 3:1 and TB *Bava Kamma* 117a.

65 For the extinguishing of the Ethnarchy, and the diversion of the *apostole* to the imperial fiscus, see CTh. 16.8.29, from 429 CE.

Kleiman, E. "Ancient and Medieval Rabbinic Economic Thought: Definitions, Methodology and Illustrations." In B.B. Price (ed.), *Ancient Economic Thought*. London/New York: Routledge, 1997. 78–98.

Levine, A. *Free Enterprise and Jewish Law*. New York: Yeshiva University Press, 1980. Ch. 5, 6, and 9.

Mishan, E. J., and E. Quah. *Cost-Benefit Analysis*. 5th ed. London: Routledge, 2007. Part IV.

Mishnah:

Bava Kamma 1:2, 3:1, 6:6

Bava Batra 1:5

Musgrave, R. A. *The Theory of Public Finance*. New York: McGraw-Hull, 1959. Ch. 4–5.

Pigou, A. C. *The Economics of Welfare*. 4th ed. London: Macmillan, 1932. II.XI.12.

Samuelson, P. A. "Diagrammatical Exposition of a Theory of Public Expenditure." *Review of Economics and Statistics* 37 (1955): 350–56.

Babylonian Talmud:

Bava Kamma 116b

Bava Metsi'a 70a

Bava Batra 7b; 8a; 11b

Jerusalem Talmud:

Bava Kamma 3:1

Bava Metsi'a 6:4

The Theodosian Code. Trans. C. Pharr. Princeton: Princeton University Press, 1952. 7.8.4.

Tosefta:

Bava Metsi'a 7:13

CHAPTER 6

AN EXTENDED TALMUDIC SEARCH MODEL

YEHOSHUA LIEBERMANN

INTRODUCTION

THE search for market information is an essential part of the purchasing process. In many consumer behavior models, the search stage is key to understanding and formulating consumers' response to both internal and external stimuli that motivate buying (e.g., Blackwell, Miniard, and Engel, 2001). Whereas the study of internal search focuses on cognitive resources of the consumer whose cost of utilization is not measurable in typical economic units, external search is associated with a set of more readily measurable economic variables. As a matter of fact, Stigler (1961) in his seminal article on the "economics of information" convincingly introduced the then innovative concept of cost of search.

Originally, Stigler (1961) aimed to test the neoclassical competitive model. This model reaches a theoretically single price equilibrium when three conditions hold: a homogenous product, a market with a large number of both buyers and sellers, and the availability of complete market information to each party. Picking a large metropolitan area (Chicago) accounting for millions of consumers and a large number of dealers, and a certain automobile model as representing a homogeneous product, Stigler (1961) expected a limited price dispersion for the item. Empirical measurements, however, did not support this prediction. This finding led to the conclusion that the complete information assumption did not hold.

The question that naturally arose in consequence was, what was the reason for the incomplete market information? Stigler (1961) attributed the phenomenon to the wider notion of transaction costs, which include all costs a consumer incurs upon initiating a purchasing process, aside from the direct price of the item. Search cost is included in this set. Moreover, it is the cost of seeking market information that limits the amount of search performed by consumers. The limited search generates an inhibited (i.e., less than complete) collection of market information, which in turn is responsible for a price dispersion wider than that theoretically expected.

How does the consumer determine the amount of search he desires? The "economics of information" model suggests the basic principle of weighing marginal cost of search against expected marginal utility of the process. Marginal cost includes such components as value of time, transportation expenses, and energy spent on collecting information. The marginal benefit reflects the potential monetary savings resulting from search. To illustrate, suppose the price a consumer encounters randomly at the first outlet visited is Pn, and a lower price detected by conducting a search is Ps. The marginal gain of search is then the probability, PR, of tracing a still lower price differential (Pn – Ps) times the number of units to be purchased, q, or (PR[Pn – Ps]q). Detecting higher price differentials that account for a higher marginal gain to search requires more time of market search. This in itself increases simultaneously marginal cost to search. Facing both contradicting influences, the consumer selects his or her personal optimal amount of search for each purchasing event.

As with many scientific breakthroughs, the underlying idea of the search model seems unremarkable. Yet it is hard to overestimate its importance. Stiglitz (2000) asserts that the economics of information is the most important development in theoretical economics in the past in the sense of opening up vast research opportunities. By recognizing information as imperfect, many economic and social observations can be better explained. This powerful theory applies to newly introduced personal search technologies like the internet. As Brynjolfsson and Smith (2000) show, the price dispersion of two homogenous products (books and CDs) sold on the internet is narrower than corresponding distributions among conventional retailers, but even on the internet information remains imperfect. Furthermore, Baye and Morgan (2004) show that, on a given price comparison site, price ranges in specific electrical appliance product categories may exhibit about thirty percent difference between the highest and lowest offer for the very same item! These findings may imply that, although search technology has improved dramatically, other considerations play a role—leaving room for a deeper analysis of consumer psychology.

Against this advanced background it is interesting to investigate how search processes for market information were treated by both ancient and more modern Jewish legal authorities. We will demonstrate that the sages of the *Mishnah* already understood that market information is imperfect as well as asymmetric, and we will show how this understanding was articulated into succinct market regulations. This study originates in a previous work of mine that dealt with transaction costs, in general, in Jewish law (Liebermann, 1986). The present study focuses exclusively on the specific case of search for market information.

We provide a brief overview of the nature of Jewish legal writings, for those readers who are not familiar with this genre of legal phrasing. For our purposes it is sufficient to say that Jewish law is composed of several layers of literature. The most basic layers are the *Mishnah* (compiled around 200 CE, in Roman Palestine, in Hebrew) and the Babylonian *Gemara* (compiled around 500 CE, in Babylon, in eastern Aramaic), which together compose the Babylonian Talmud. The Talmud is divided into six volumes that are in turn divided into tractates organized by topic. Tractates are further divided into chapters. The Talmud represents a vast system of laws, regulations, customs, and discussions, all presented in a noncodified form. A typical Talmudic discussion starts with a short passage of *Mishnah* that induces a frequently involved *Gemara* discussion that attempts to clarify the passage, sometimes by comparing it to other sources that may appear to disagree. The outcome might be an expansion or a modification of that specific Mishnaic ruling.

Referring to the Talmud, numerous Jewish legal scholars, from the sixth century to contemporary times, have written comprehensive and authoritative commentaries and *responsa*. In *responsa*, day-to-day practical questions presented to influential decisors by individuals or communities are followed by the decisor's analytic and quite often detailed answer. Some writers integrated the massive literature into formal codes. The most distinct codes were written by Maimonides (Rambam, Egypt, 1135–1204) and R. Joseph Caro (Ottoman Palestine, 1488–1575). The corresponding Hebrew titles of these codes are *Mishneh Torah* and *Shulhan Arukh*.

This study first presents the basic theoretical framework of the Talmudic price search "model," which is based on the legal prohibition of overcharging. We proceed to discuss the economic implications of the basic Talmudic framework. We subsequently turn to the *responsa* literature and depict how a number of practical cases of market information search are handled by Jewish decisors. We relate these *responsa* to some economic notions. We conclude with a brief summary and suggestions of further research directions.

A Talmudic Price Search "Model"

Talmudic law recognizes the cost of search to both buyers and sellers. Two Mishnaic paragraphs bear out the notion of search costs. Both deal with the laws of fraud in sales transactions, based on the biblical verse, "And if thou sell a sale unto thy neighbor, or acquirest aught of they neighbour's hand, ye shall not deceive."[1]

1 Leviticus 25:14. One may wonder how rules governing trade in food and other nondurables find their scriptural origin in a Levitical law governing sale of land. This source reflects the desire to relate as much as possible the "oral" (Talmudic) law to the written (biblical) law.

The first paragraph states:[2]

> Fraud is constituted by [an overcharge of[3]] . . . a sixth of the purchase. (If the vendor overcharged by one sixth, he is considered to have defrauded the vendee, and the overcharge is recoverable; or the sale may be revoked.[4]) Until what time is one permitted to revoke [the sale]? Until he can show [the article] to a merchant or a relative. R. Tarfon ruled in Lydda that fraud is constituted by . . . a third of the purchase, whereat the Lyddan merchants rejoiced. But, said he to them, one may retract the whole day. Then let R. Tarfon leave us in status quo, they requested; and so they reverted to the ruling of the Sages.[5]

From a legal point of view, this *Mishnah* is concerned with the definition of fraud due to an overcharge by sellers. The definition is quite involved and is refined by associated *Gemara* passages. The legal discussion is heavily based on the observation that consumers spend resources to search for a lower price. This specific law of fraud (called *ona'a* in Hebrew) offers protection to consumers whose market information is so incomplete that they are overcharged by more than one-sixth of the market price,[6] by giving them power to revoke the transaction.[7]

The *Mishnah* reports a dispute between the Sages (whose opinion is expressed first in the *Mishnah*), on the one hand, and R. Tarfon, on the other. The Sages' ruling is a normative and vital principle of Jewish business law.

Perhaps some "industrial organization" explanation might be appropriate before going into a more detailed analysis. The law of fraud in sale pertains mostly to food and other nondurables such as clothing and utensils, which probably accounted for the bulk of market transactions. In the early days (first to sixth centuries CE) of agricultural markets, prices might have been set administratively.[8] Yet this hypothesis cannot be said to have been fully proven, although various forms of price intervention and control are documented in Talmudic literature.[9] Regardless of the exact form it took, we must assume a "true market price" existed; otherwise, no overcharge is definable.

Not only does the *Mishnah* take search into account as a market factor, but it also refers to particular characteristics of the search process. The dispute between

2 All quotations from (Babylonian) Talmudic sources are taken from the Soncino English translation of the Babylonian Talmud (Isidore Epstein, ed., 1935).

3 Square brackets contain explanations added by the English editor to the original Hebrew text.

4 Parentheses contain explanations made in footnotes to the main text.

5 B *Bava Metsi'a* 49b.

6 In evaluating the meaning of "one-sixth," two opinions are expressed in the Gemara (ibid. at 296 [49b]). One advocates a measurement based on "the [true] purchase price"; that is, the consumer paid 116.66 percent instead of 100 percent (16.66/100 = 1/6). The other opinion holds that the measurement is based on "the money [actually] paid"; that is, a consumer has a claim for revoking a transaction only after paying at least 120 percent of 100 percent (20/120 = 1/6).

7 "In the case of less than one sixth, the sale is valid" (ibid. at 300 [50b]), since the difference is regarded as having been renounced (ibid., at 296 [49b]), perhaps because of the costs associated with recovering the differential. It may be worthwhile to note that action by the harmed party is conditional on court approval. This procedure did not impose significant transaction costs since for simple civil matters any three (unrelated) men could be regarded as an official court (M Sanhedrin 1:1).

8 Yehoshua Liebermann, *Economic Thought in the Talmud* (unpublished M.A. thesis, Bar-Ilan University, Israel, Department of Economics, 1973,in Hebrew).

9 Aaron Levine, *Free Enterprise and Jewish Law: Aspects of Jewish Business Ethics* (1980).

R. Tarfon and the Sages may perhaps reflect the positive effect of price dispersion on the amount of search. Specifically, the time allowance granted by the Sages to the buyer for consulting an expert (a merchant or a knowledgeable relative) is short and certainly smaller than the full day allowed by R. Tarfon (the commentators unanimously agree on this relationship[10]). According to the Sages, an overcharge of one-sixth entitles the customer to revoke the transaction. R. Tarfon, on the other hand, permits an overcharge of up to one-third before a transaction can be cancelled and allows a full day for ex post consultation. On hearing of R. Tarfon's higher permitted overcharge, Lyddan merchants were happy, since they thought the amount of ex post search allowed for buyers would remain unaltered. However, R. Tarfon was probably aware of the possibility that a higher ceiling for permitted overcharge would result in wider price dispersion in the market.[11] He therefore had to compensate potential buyers by extending their ex post search time. Seemingly, the merchants estimated the expected profits under R. Tarfon's system to be smaller than under the Sages', and therefore refused to adopt the one-third rule. In a sense, the widespread argument that fair trade laws are motivated by the desire to reduce search costs represents a contemporary counterpart to the Talmudic source. It might be added that the overcharge rule does not include transactions of very low monetary values,[12] probably because the costs of rescission are too high. This observation lends additional support to the transaction cost hypothesis.[13]

Search behavior of sellers is discussed as well. In an adjacent paragraph the *Mishnah* refers to merchants who are professional sellers:

> Both the vendee and the vendor can claim for overreaching. Just as the law of overreaching holds good in the case of a layman, so it holds well in the case of a merchant. R. Judah said: "There is no overreaching for a merchant."[14]

10 It might be interesting to mention that, according to a recent Jewish legal scholar, this law of fraud is not binding in the instances in which items are sold for different prices in various outlets. R. Jehiel Michal ha-Levi Epstein (Belarus, 1829–1908), *Arukh ha-Shulhan, Hoshen Mishpat,* 227:7.

11 The shortness of the periods allowed for search might have been, in part, the result of the nature of perishable goods such as fruit, meat, and the like.

12 The explanation offered here as to why Lyddan traders were happy about R. Tarfon's ruling adopts an economic viewpoint. However, alternative explanations based on Jewish legal principles are subtly suggested and analyzed in a comprehensive responsum by R. David b. Solomon ibn Abi Zimra (Radbaz, Egypt, 1479–1573). See *Responsa Radbaz* 794. R. Solomon b. Isaac (Rashi, France, 1040–1105), one of the most authoritative commentaries on the Talmud, explains that Lyddan merchants were initially pleased since "they were knowledgeable in merchandise and selling for high prices." Yet this proposition does not necessarily exclude the possible outcome of wider price dispersion. Many other commentaries offer a variety of explanations of why Lyddan merchants initially believed that R. Tarfon's position would make them better off.

13 "Said R. Kahana: . . . The law of overreaching does not apply *to perutahs* (which are copper coins; i.e., the minimum sum to which it applies in an *issar,* which is a silver coin)" (B *Baba Metsi'a* 55a). Indeed, the Talmud presents an opposing view, but the major codes rule according to R. Kahana (Maimonides, *Mishneh Torah, Mekhira* 12:3; *Shulhan Arukh, Hoshen Mishpat* 227:5).

14 Although the analysis focuses on the cost of search, one may suggest alternative economic explanations of the rule of fraud. The rule of overcharge might have been motivated by the desire either to avoid excessive prices as a result of collusion or to reduce the social cost of haggling. These alternative explanations are not considered in detail since they do not appear related to the logical flow of the Talmudic discussion of the search factor. In addition, the rule of overcharging is directed against price differentials, whereas the prevention of collusion addresses absolute price levels. Haggling is actually also a component of search.

The reason, according to R. Judah, that merchants are not entitled to claim overreaching is explained in the *Gemara*: "There is no overreaching for a merchant because he is an expert."[15] In other words, merchants are fully informed and therefore should not be granted the right to ex post search. However, Jewish law rules against R. Judah, accepting the opinion that merchants are not necessarily fully informed either, and may err, quoting a price that falls considerably short of the market par. To correct for such possible mistakes, professional sellers as well are granted the right to claim for overreaching. Nevertheless, while individual buyers are permitted to revoke transactions only within the time limits specified earlier, "The vendor can always retract. Why? The vendee has the purchase in his hand: wherever he goes he shows it and is told whether he erred or not. But the vendor, who has not the purchase in hand, [must wait] until he comes across an article like his, and only then he can know whether he erred or not."[16] The phrase "until he comes across" suggests a time constraint; it clearly indicates that the phrase "can always retract" should not be taken literally. Indeed, Rambam, in his code, rules:

> Therefore, if the purchased item was a fully homogeneous and standard good, such as peppers and the like, the seller is permitted to retract only as long as is needed to find out the market price.

Clearly, items that tend to spoil will be associated with shorter retraction periods. Also, in markets characterized by frequent price changes, the rule of overreaching is subject to certain modifications.[17]

We can now summarize the basic features of the Talmudic price search model.

1. The laws of overreaching, although traditionally viewed as a legal framework for dealing with price fraud in markets, have economic characteristics that are quite evident.
2. In a sense, the market structure depicted by the *Mishnah* resembles that tested by Stigler (1961). It includes many buyers and many sellers, attesting to the validity of the atomistic assumption of perfect competition. Actually, Schwartz (1993) regards the city of Lydda as the most central interregional agricultural market of its time in Roman Palestine, as well as a center of trade and of industrial capacity. It is reasonable to assume that a considerable part of the trade in Lyddan markets concentrated on standard agricultural products, which are mostly homogeneous. Thus, the homogeneity assumption holds as well. In the *Mishnah*'s market setting, therefore, any possibility of relatively wide price dispersion is the outcome of incomplete information.
3. For standard products there is no information asymmetry between buyers and sellers. Both are potential victims of possible incomplete information. Only for nonstandard items are sellers regarded as having less complete

15 B *Bava Metsi'a* 51a.

16 Ibid.

17 *Mishneh Torah, Mekhira* 12:6 (my free translation).

information in comparison to buyers, for they do not have in hand an item to show to an expert.

4. There exists some partial equilibrium price that serves as a benchmark against which prices paid are calibrated and evaluated. This is the most difficult part of the Talmudic model in the eyes of a professional modern economist. The very fact that the law discusses overcharge beyond a given percentage indicates that prices are dispersed anyway. So, what is the meaning of this supposedly partial equilibrium? Maybe this is the reason underlying the opinion mentioned above that in a modern market setting it is impractical to apply the rules of price overcharge. In the absence of a certain benchmark equilibrium price, there is no way to assess the rate, and possibly even the existence, of overcharge. Acknowledging this observation, the neoclassical competitive equilibrium model gradually shifted from a purely theoretical single equilibrium (price and quantity) to a much more practical concept of a range of equilibrium points reflecting price (and quantity) dispersion.

An alternative way of looking at this ex post search mechanism is in its similarity to modern marketing tools such as refunding or price matching. It is quite common in the retailing industry for consumers to be assured that the price they have paid is the lowest in the market. If they present proof that a competing outlet is charging a lower price for the same item purchased, they are entitled either to cancel the transaction and get their money back or to maintain the transaction and receive a refund covering the price differential. Actually, both alternatives are recognized by Jewish law's overcharge clause. As previously noted, if the overcharge amounts to more than one-sixth of the equilibrium market price, the overcharged party is entitled to call off the transaction. If the discrepancy falls short of one-sixth of the benchmark price, the deceived party is unable legally to revoke the transaction but is entitled to a payback at the value of the price differential. What is perhaps most interesting is the ex post nature of the search process in both instances, which provides some market protection to consumers against greedy high-pricing sellers, but does not generate a foolproof antidote to pricing fraud. As in the case of the Lydda traders, sellers will always try to get away with a hopefully unnoticed above-equilibrium price. They perhaps speculate that, even when noticed, buyers will not necessarily enter into claims and actions intended to revise the transaction terms, because of potential unwarranted transaction costs.

The Talmudic Search Model As Reflected in the *Responsa* Literature

Talmudic discussions are quite often of a more theoretical, even abstract nature. In our specific case, not only theoretical principles, assumptions, and conclusions are put forth. The story of the Lydda merchants vividly depicts a piece of ancient microeconomic history. Imagine the traders in the old Lyddan markets at their vegetable, fruit, meat, or household necessities stores, trying to sell at the highest prices possible, hoping the buyer will not notice the price differential or will not bother to engage in an ex post search process even upon noticing a differential. They presumably developed rather cunning pricing skills so that some overcharge could be sneaked into the price, but not at so outrageous a rate as might alert buyers to their potential loss.

How did R. Tarfon inform them of his ruling? Was he a type of official price regulator in charge of the market? Or was it his students who spread the word? Obviously, this is unknown. What we know, though, is that the new ruling came as welcome news to the entire community of Lydda businessmen, perhaps at an organized meeting. The story continues that R. Tarfon told them about the extended ex post search time allowed by his approach, upon hearing which, the frustrated profit-seeking merchants asked R. Tarfon to leave them alone.

Yet even this detailed documentation of a piece of Lyddan history does not really refocus the student of this portion of the Talmud from theoretical thinking to a more practically oriented discussion. Note that the Talmudic story does not tell about a real case in which some person paid more or charged less than the benchmark price, and then attempted either to cancel the transaction and get his money back, or preserve the transaction and retrieve the price differential paid or charged. At this point the *responsa* literature comes in, frequently documenting specific cases brought to the judgment of an authoritative decisor. These cases are typically more involved than the situations brought up in the Talmudic text. Here we can follow specific arguments raised by parties to the transaction, the way they were analyzed by the decisor, and the conclusions reached thereupon. In this section a modest sampling of *responsa* from varying geographical locations and differing periods is presented, which illustrates how practical market conflicts were handled and decided.

An interesting way of search is described by R. Samuel b. Moses de Medina, (Maharashdam, Greece, 1506–1589).[18] While a price search process is commonly based on some sort of sampling of requested prices in a number of outlets, a different method was practiced by a merchant, Simeon, who was informed that a trader, Reuben (quite often names of parties are disguised and replaced by symbolic representative names), was offering a stock of wool for sale. Instead of searching the market, Simeon approached Reuben and asked him to truthfully disclose the price per unit he paid for the stock. Reuben asserted he paid three and a half *blancos* per unit, and a deal was struck. Later on Simeon discovered that Reuben had actually paid only three *blancos* per unit. Simeon sued Reuben for half a *blanco* times the number of units.

Reuben defended himself by claiming that the overcharge percentage (.5/3.5 = .1428) did not reach the one-sixth (.1666) level that would have provided the legal basis for a refund claim. From a strict legal standpoint, the buyer (seller)

18 *Shulhan Arukh, Hoshen Mishpat* 227:9, and commentators thereon.

who has been overcharged (underpaid) is regarded as if he is ready to forgo a price differential smaller than .1666, which nullifies potential claims on overcharge rates falling short of one-sixth. Nonetheless, Maharashdam strongly rejected this argument and ruled in favor of Simeon. He explained his ruling by stressing the nature of the search process employed by Simeon, which was based on trusting Reuben's word. Once Reuben broke both his religious and moral commitment by lying to Simeon, he was no longer entitled to benefit from the protective aspect of the overcharge law.

From an economic point of view, Maharashdam's ruling expands the scope of efficient search. In accordance with the Talmudic ex post search model, a potential buyer can do an ex ante footwork sampling of the market (traditional search), or show the item purchased to a knowledgeable individual and ask for his assessment of the price paid. Maharashdam adds that, alternatively, he can shorten both ex ante and ex post search time by using the information already available in the market on time, on the word of the seller, without spending any resources on actual search. In behavioral professional language this procedure is termed heuristic—a shortcut set of cognitive steps that facilitates savings in cognitive resources. Simeon perfected the heuristic method by saving not only cognitive resources but time, energy, and possibly out-of-pocket expenses. Obviously, to guarantee the efficiency of the abridged procedure, regulative actions are necessary to make sure that the price information supplied is totally reliable.

As already noted, an overcharge claim is acceptable as long as it is submitted within a given time limit (either that needed to be informed by an expert—as the Sages state—or a full working day, as suggested by R. Tarfon). It so happened that Simeon detected the half-*blanco* price differential after the prescribed time limit. Understandably, since Reuben lied, this becomes the predominant consideration, and the time limit is not as relevant. Had Reuben not falsified the price, he could perhaps have raised the time limit as a legal argument. Preferring the dishonest way of misrepresentation, he could not expect to use the belated filing of the lawsuit to his advantage.

Yet a somewhat similar case was handled by R. Abraham Antebi (Syria, eighteenth century).[19] As reported in the responsum, Reuben and Simeon (once again, proxy names!) had entered into a mixed barter-cash transaction. Reuben handed certain goods and some cash to Simeon, who in turn had to supply to Reuben a specified variety of dye (Nil Puchi—sort of indigo). As it turned out, Simeon had supplied a different variety (Nil Nayeralla). Furthermore, Reuben attested that other buyers paid him twenty-five grossos per unit of the originally stipulated variety (Puchi), whereas the second variety (Nayeralla) sold for only fifteen grossos per unit, although some kinds of the second variety (Nayeralla) could sell for as much as thirty grossos, a per unit price comparable to that of Puchi. Reuben claimed he was deceived by Simeon twice: He neither got the merchandise agreed upon, nor did he pay the usual market price. He therefore demanded compensation. In

19 *Responsa Mor Vaahalot, Hoshen Mishpat*, 21.

addition, Reuben discovered that the information provided by Simeon regarding the price allegedly paid to him by other merchants was false.

Simeon raised two defenses. In the first place, he argued that barter transactions are not subject to the antifraud (*ona'a*) law. In addition, he noted that Reuben had not filed his lawsuit within the legal time limit.

R. Antebi discusses both arguments in depth. He raises several issues in his analysis of the former. First, Talmudic antifraud law refers explicitly to cash transactions only. No direct reference is made to barter transactions. Rambam rules that antifraud law does not apply to barter transactions involving bilaterally nonperishable items like household and work utensils.[20] He states that even an exchange of a needle for armor is valid, for the party that wants the needle is firmly ready to give up the armor for it. However, a bilateral exchange of agricultural produce is fully subject to the antifraud law. Other legal authorities are at odds with Rambam on this point. R. Antebi discusses whether to follow Rambam and, if so, whether the dyes are more similar to agricultural produce or daily utensils.

Second, some Jewish legal scholars argue that, even if antifraud law does not generally apply to barter transactions, it will apply if the items involved in the transaction were explicitly valued in monetary terms. It has to be decided whether the transaction at hand is regarded as barter or, because of a possible valuation, as a cash sale.

Third, R. Antebi addresses whether a mixed barter-cash transaction is regarded as a pure barter or as cash.

R. Antebi analyzes all three issues and concludes that the antifraud law does not apply. He also notes the falsified information presented by Simeon, which, based on the previous case of Maharashdam, would seem to negate Simeon's credibility. Nevertheless, R. Antebi distinguishes between the cases. In the earlier case, the seller had claimed he had personally paid some upwardly biased per-unit price. In R. Antebi's case, however, he said only that some people paid an upwardly biased price. In the first case the buyer relied heavily on the seller's assertion. In the second case the personal credibility of the seller did not have a meaningful effect on the decision of the buyer.

R. Antebi claims that the second argument—that the timing of the lawsuit surpassed the time limits prescribed by the antifraud law—does not relieve Simeon of his responsibility. He raises a few considerations in this regard. First, Reuben is a merchant and bought the merchandise not for his own personal use, but to sell in the marketplace. The problem with the merchandise was discovered when Reuben attempted to offer it to other tradesmen, who tested it and refused to buy what they determined to be items of inferior quality. These events correspond exactly to the Talmudic procedure of showing the purchased merchandise to an expert. The potential buyers who checked the dye and found it unsatisfactory performed exactly the job of an expert the buyer consults. Secondly, this kind of dye could be tested only after the user put it into a barrel for a few days. In other words, its

20 *Mishneh Torah*, *op. cit.*, 13:1.

quality could not be verified without using it first. Finally, Simeon's replacement of the initially promised Nil Puchi with the inferior Nil Nayeralla was not a regular market action where quality variation of some degree is permissible. Replacing the item of significantly higher quality with an inferior substitute did not represent the failure of a quality control measure. It was simply an act of fraud. Note that this analysis invokes not only price search behavior but quality search aspects as well. These will be discussed in more detail shortly.

R. Antebi mentions that his analysis draws on an earlier responsum regarding a similar case, written by R. Simeon b. Zemah Duran (*Tashbets*, Algeria, 1361–1444).[21] In this case again a buyer of dye complained that the merchandise he bought was found, when he tried to resell it, to be rather inferior. The seller claimed that the buyer had tested the merchandise, and that the time limit for showing it to an expert had expired long before the action was brought.

Rashbats states that this specific type of dye (Istis) is known to be characterized by a wide range of variation and is rather easy to fake. Therefore, the buyer had to perform some quality test upon purchasing, to make sure at least that it was not forged. Yet this action did not constitute a real quality test, for real testing could take place only upon actual use (i.e., applying the color, which, naturally, could not be done upon purchase). Rashbats rules that the seller is not entitled to claim exemption on the grounds that the antifraud time limit had elapsed, because no real testing could be carried out before actual use of the dye by end users.

As mentioned above, both latter cases represent an intermingling of price and quality search. The observation that the quality of some items like the dyes in issue cannot be readily assessed brings to mind the well-known product classification by Nelson (1970), further refined by Darby and Karni (1973). Nelson (1970) introduced the distinction between two types of product attributes: search and experience. Search attributes can be evaluated by examining the nature of the product without using it first. An example is the interest rate promised by a bank. A customer does not have to make a deposit and wait for interest to be paid in order to calculate how much interest he got on his deposit. The amount can be calculated beforehand and serves as a criterion in comparing competing bank offers. Unlike search attributes, experience attributes cannot be assessed by consumers a priori and require actual use of the product first. A relevant illustration is taste. It is difficult to describe taste verbally. A consumer buying a can of "spicy pickles" may discover when eating them that they are actually somewhat sweet to his taste. Darby and Karni (1973) added a third classification of attributes: credence. These attributes are not assessable even upon use. Dependability of a car engine repair or sterility of an internal surgery are examples of this category. These attribute types serve as a basis for product (and service) classification by attribute dominance. Thus, Nelson distinguishes between search goods and experience goods, while Darby and Karni add credence goods to the list.

The distinction between search and experience attributes was originally applied to the modeling of advertising. In particular, sellers advertise in an attempt to pro-

21 *Responsa Rashbats*, vol. 4, 1st column, 8.

mote their product. On the consumer side, advertising facilitates search either for quality or for price. The larger the number of advertisers in a given product category, the less footwork the consumer requires to collect a given amount of information. However, advertising efficiency as a market information search saver varies among the three product categories. It may be very efficient for search goods, less efficient for experience goods, and hardly useful for credence goods. This insight has its implications for advertising spending on products in one of the three categories.

In the present context, this threefold classification has its own ramifications. Both Rashbats and R. Antebi agree that the quality of those dyes in question cannot be determined as long as real-life utilization by end users has not taken place. This is a different wording for Nelson's definition of experience goods. In terms of the Talmudic search model, this threefold distinction suggests that the constraint limiting the time allowed for ex post search is not equally applicable to all kinds of goods. To the contrary, search for some types of goods (search) can be readily performed. For others (experience), some difficulties may hamper search speed, and for still others (credence), search may not be practical at all. These differences call for search time spans differentiated by category type, and consequently the time durations during which buyers and sellers are entitled to ask for revocation of seemingly fraudulent transactions—exactly as Rashbats and R. Antebi ruled. The more difficult (i.e., marginally costly) the warranted market information is to obtain, the longer the search time needed (to increase marginally the chance of detecting overcharge or underpayment). In fact, the potential information asymmetry between buyers and sellers and the corresponding times allowed for ex post search, as expressed in Rambam's ruling cited above, also reflect this distinction.

In this regard, it is worthwhile to mention a ruling directly related to the concept of credence attributes and goods. In the major code of Jewish law, the *Shulhan Arukh*, the author, R. Joseph Caro, states that a buyer of land, slave, animal, or any other item, who detects a defect not disclosed by the seller upon sale, may retract even if several years have passed since the transaction took place.[22] Whereas search items are readily assessable at the time of sale or even beforehand, and whereas experience items can be evaluated immediately after purchase through regular usage, this is not the case with credence items, whose assessment is quite burdensome. The discovery of a defect after a long period of time has elapsed actually defines a credence item, which is associated with extremely high search cost, and for which a relatively extended search time is therefore allowed.

An extension to this ruling is provided by R. Vidal Yom Tov of Tolosa (Spain, second half of the fourteenth century) in his famous commentary *Maggid Mishneh* to Rambam's code. He clarifies that, if the defect could have been detected by the buyer either by prior use or through tasting, the buyer is not entitled to ask that the transaction be revoked upon detecting the defect.[23] *Maggid Mishneh* explains that market search is the responsibility of the customer, who may determine the optimal

22 *Shulhan Arukh, Hoshen Mishpat* 232:3.

23 *Magid Mishneh, Mekhirah* 15:3.

amount of it according to his personal balance between marginal cost and marginal utility of search. In contrast to the search for price information, which according to the Talmudic search model can be carried out ex post, the search for quality information with respect to easily detectable defects must be done ex ante. Failing to do so, the buyer is not allowed to shift his responsibility to the seller, unless the seller had made an explicit statement guaranteeing the item to be free of defects.

What is the difference between ex post price search and ex post quality search? Why is a buyer (or seller) entitled to nullify a transaction upon finding out ex post a significant price differential (beyond one-sixth of a benchmark price), although he could have searched the market and detected the differential in advance, and why is a similar right not guaranteed when a physical defect has been spotted ex post, where it could have been identified ex ante?

Apparently the answer is efficiency. What alternative course of action can be recommended instead of ex post search by the buyer when price search is concerned? One option is ex ante search among vendors performed by the seller. Clearly, to shift the responsibility of price search from the buyer to the seller is inefficient. Why would the seller do the job for the buyer? His time cost might be higher than that of the buyer, and, more importantly, he is not interested in a crystal-clear market information setting, as the case of Lyddan traders demonstrates. From the standpoint of sellers, the thicker the information fuzziness in the market, the greater the chance of making extra profits. Every seller will prefer market information ambiguity, for it allows him to intentionally manipulate his customers when he offers them a price. Another option is to limit the buyer himself and allow only ex ante price search. But this option, too, runs contrary to efficiency considerations. It is quite clear that, when a buyer hits randomly the first outlet on his shopping trip and makes his purchase there, he simultaneously samples the price there. In order to complete his ex post search, he has to take just one more sampling step (i.e., visit an expert). If the expert approves his purchase, his total cost of search is minimal; any ex ante procedure will be associated with higher search cost. If the expert detects fraudulent pricing, the buyer may either obtain a refund of the difference and still enjoy the low search cost, or cancel the transaction entirely and get his money back. This latter option will require another round of search associated with another round of potential costs. Nevertheless, it can be shown quantitatively that under some conditions ex post search will still be lower than ex ante search, provided a single equilibrium market price can be measured. To demonstrate this is beyond the scope of the present study.

In the case of quality search, however, these considerations work the other way around. It is unreasonable (inefficient) to impose on the buyer the job of quality search, because the seller is not only much more experienced and knowledgeable in assessing merchandise grade, but also because he has the goods in hand, which in turn means that quality information is much more accessible to him (i.e., less costly to him in comparison to buyers). Interestingly, Moorthy and Srinivasan (1995) develop a model that examines two alternative ways in which vendors can signal quality: money-back guarantees and high price. According to their findings, in a market setting with homogenous consumers, money-back guarantees are essential to signal quality. In a heterogeneous market setting, high price is a reasonable indicator of quality, but a money-back guarantee is still required as a marketing supplement. Note that in the Talmudic "model," ex post search does at least part of the job of money-back guarantees. There are two major differences between the models, though. First, in the management science model, money-back guarantees have the same general effect as high pricing. In the Talmudic "model," they accomplish opposite ends. It is the role of the ex post search (money-back guarantee) to correct for illegally high pricing. This distinction is perhaps an outcome of the underlying presumption of Moorthy and Srinivasan that the vendor aims to signal quality. This is not the case in the Talmudic "model." Second, whereas modern money-back guarantees are voluntarily offered by sellers, the ex post search instituted by Talmudic law is imposed on sellers against their free will. Yet both models acknowledge search cost as a central influence of consumer behavior.

In a similar vein, Kukar-Kinney and colleagues (2007) present empirical evidence of consumers' price fairness perceptions being affected by price-matching refund policies of retailers. Their findings relate fairness perception to refund depth and to product assortment offered by competing outlets. A consumer who made a purchase at a given price in a given outlet and then identified a cheaper price charged by a competitor will perceive greater price fairness in the original outlet the greater their refund and the more unique the product assortment carried by the competitor. Comparison with the Talmudic "model" demonstrates that each model adopts a certain view of the market. Whereas the retailing model is concerned with how to enhance perceived price fairness, the Talmudic "model" imposes price fairness by means of ex post price search. Upon detection of a price offered lower than the price actually charged, the models respond differently. In the retailing model, the retailer is free to choose any refund amount he finds suitable, balancing marketing and service considerations against cash flow and profit and loss considerations. In the Talmudic model, refund depth is not considered by the retailer; it is dictated by the antifraud regulation that requires a full refund and does not allow partial refunds at all. As a concluding remark, it is worthwhile to highlight the similarity of both models in regard to the role of product assortment. In the retailing model, uniqueness of assortments held by competitors is viewed as mitigating the frustration experienced by a customer who identifies a lower price charged by that competitor. Consumers explain to themselves that specializing in a specific assortment enables the retailer to save costs (efficiency!) and thereby charge a lower price. In addition, specialized assortments are not widely distributed and are relatively difficult to find. In other words, they are associated with higher search costs, which may cause the consumer to reduce search and simultaneously the chance of locating a cheaper price of the already purchased item. This same notion underlies Rambam's ruling that a seller who carries a unique assortment and who mistakenly sold an item at a price lower than the market rate is entitled to retract without any time limit, because of transaction costs associated with tracking a similar item in order to present it to an expert and get his professional assessment.

Returning to the *responsa* literature, let us now focus on a responsum that is more price search-oriented, which originates from a very different time and area, written by R. Sholom Mordechai Shvadron (Maharsham, Poland, 1835–1911) of Berezhany. He deals with a complaint filed by two sellers, Reuben (!) and Simeon (!), who sold a certain amount of alcohol to Levi for a 13.5 per unit price. The buyer paid half in cash and the sellers consented to supply the drinks in four installments from December to March, by the twenty-fifth of every month. The rest of the cost had to be paid in four equal monthly installments. Later on, Reuben found out that they had charged Levi a price lower than the market rate, but he did not ask for any legal remedy. Thereafter, Reuben was informed that the price differential exceeded one-sixth—the limit that justified calling off a transaction. He immediately sent a message to his partner, Simeon, letting him know about the price differential and asking him to inform Levi, which Simeon did right away. In the meantime, between the sale and the notification of Levi, eight days had elapsed. The partners ask for permission to supply only half of the quantity agreed upon originally for the price paid. Levi denies the one-week time span and claims he was informed about the supposed price differential only a few weeks later. He also points out that there was no fraud involved, for many merchants had paid the same per-unit price. Levi adds that the transaction has been carried out in a small town—a location associated with higher insurance cost. This exchange represents a classical shift from the abstract Talmudic general structure to fascinating, lively, detailed personal chronicles.

Before Maharsham, the dispute had been brought to the attention of two local rabbinical figures—the rabbi of Yashniza (R. Gelerenter) and the rabbi of Brezov (R. Gabel). The rabbi of Yashniza was inclined to cancel the transaction, using a surprisingly economically oriented reasoning. He explained that Brezov, the town where the transaction occurred, was a very small locality where there was only one dealer able to handle such a large transaction, and where there was no publicly known market rate. In addition, it had taken some time until Reuben realized that the fraud rate had exceeded one-sixth of the price paid. In the meantime Reuben had stayed in a place six miles away, busily harvesting a potato field of his. Once the underpayment rate became clear to him, he immediately informed his partner Simeon by writing, urging him to travel immediately to Levi and let him know about the situation, which Simeon did right away.

Examining R. Gelernter's interpretation of the circumstances of the conflict, two major features stand out. First, the market is small, certainly on the supply side. This implies that competition is far from perfect and that there is no equilibrium price the market will converge to. R. Gelernter describes this setting as a market "without a publicly known rate." Second, Reuben was so busy that he could not allocate time to refine the crude initial information that he and his partner charged Levi, a price lower than customary at some yet unknown rate. Professionally rewording R. Gelerenter's argument, he actually says that Reuben's search cost was prohibitive, and thereby slowed his pace of relevant information collection. Combining both features, a market characterized by imperfect competition and high search cost emerges. No benchmark price exists against which actual price paid or charged can be evaluated. On top of this, search costs are high and thus entitle the victim to a search period longer than usual—up to the point where his marginal expected utility of search is balanced against his marginal cost of search.

R. Gabel, by contrast, maintained that the information presented by R. Gelernter was not fully accurate. In particular, on the specific day the transaction had been signed, a regional market day was held in Brezov, bringing in many out-of-town businesspeople. Other dealers were located on the road from Brezov to Yashniza (Reuben's location). Furthermore, prices and rates were published daily in newspapers. In other words, the market was not as imperfect as R. Gelernter had supposed, and market information sources were plentifully available. R. Gabel rejected the argument attributing to Reuben exceedingly high personal search costs. He claimed that time spans allocated to ex post search are not dependent on personal constraints but rather reflect typical consumer behavior. Personal extraordinary conditions do not entitle one to extra search time.

Presenting these contradictory views, Maharsham adopts R. Gabel's position that, unlike in Talmudic times, information is readily available in modern times. Market information is disseminated not only by newspapers. Reuben, like anyone else, could have found out the market rate by sending a letter or telegram from a nearby post office. Put differently, the alleged prohibitive search cost to Reuben was actually much more moderate, and certainly did not justify the eight days lag before he obtained the desired information.

As evidence supporting his view, Maharsham cites a responsum by R. Abraham b. Moses de Boton (*Lehem Mishneh*, Greece, 1540s–after 1592), who discusses the sale of a rare golden ornament at a price that later proved below market by an unknown rate.[24] *Lehem Mishneh* refers to Rambam's ruling that a seller of a nonhomogeneous item is allowed infinite ex post search time because the seller does not have the item in his possession, and therefore cannot show it to an expert to obtain a price assessment. *Lehem Mishneh* mentions that, in the case of the underpriced ornament, the seller was given time to enable him to search other cities and countries as necessary. Nonetheless, he rules that, if this time limit was not met, he could still call off the transaction at a later date, provided he could show that the price paid fell short of five-sixths of the market price found abroad later. *Lehem Mishneh* attributes the rationale underlying the extended time limitation to the excessive cost associated with market search out of country or even out of town. Thus, as long as the supposedly deceived seller does not end his search efforts, he is not yet ready to forgo the price differential and his legal right to reclaim it. However, in the case of a local search process with normative search costs, exceeding the time limit recognized by the antifraud law is interpreted as forfeiting the legal right to revoking a transaction even in the event of a belated confirmation of the over/undercharge. Based on this distinction, Maharsham concludes that a period of eight days at a time when modern information collection technologies are readily available is not justified by the

24 226.

rationale specified by *Lehem Mishneh*. On these grounds, Reuben and Simeon are not eligible to file a request to cancel the transaction.

But Maharsham raises another point that also reflects economic thinking. Recall that the buyer paid only one-half of the transaction value in cash at the time of sale. The remainder was to be paid in four equal monthly installments. Maharsham asserts that in this instance the sellers would not invest too much in market search, because there was no guarantee that the opened credit account would be paid off in the future. This innovative insight considers uncertainty as inhibiting search. In economic terms, this association is readily explainable. Uncertainty reduces potential marginal utility of search, because the probability of generating a (Pn – Ps) differential is now lower. If the debt is not collected, the differential will not materialize at all. The reduced motivation to search is a legitimate reason not to keep strictly to the predetermined time limits specified by the antifraud law.

This consideration of (financial) uncertainty as inhibiting market search counters that of modern information technology as facilitating search. In evaluating both considerations, Maharsham views the first one (uncertainty) as overriding the latter one (technology). He substantiates this approach through a careful analysis of relevant Jewish legal sources. Consequently, his ruling supported revoking the transaction if the partner sellers could furnish a clear-cut proof that at the time of the sale they could not even have imagined a price differential of the asserted magnitude within the trade boundaries.

Discussion and Conclusions

The present study focuses on market information search processes as reflected in traditional Jewish law, in ancient and more modern sources. The basic Talmudic principle has been termed the Talmudic search "model" and dates back to the second century CE. It is quite surprising to see how considerations underlying the ultra-modern economic theory of information search, for which its founder and developer, George J. Stigler, won the Nobel Prize (1982), are so deeply rooted in ancient Talmudic thinking. Yet, although the Talmud quite clearly acknowledges search costs and the balance between marginal expected utility and marginal cost of search, we place the term "model" in quotation marks because, although the Talmud discusses the associations between economic variables, it is not an economic text that deals with formal models. Economic references made in the legal text of the Talmud are verbal and aimed at regulating market behavior. Their content, though, is invariant notwithstanding language or orientation. They include highly keen economic insights that can be rephrased in modern professional terminology and depict a lively economic market life covered under layers of historical dust.

We started with the concept of Jewish antiprice-fraud law (*ona'a* in Hebrew). It assumes that a single market equilibrium price exists, serving as a benchmark against which prices actually paid can be compared. Though within the economic theory of information price search is typically conducted before purchase (ex ante), price search in Jewish law can be also performed *after* purchase has taken place (ex post). As shown by Aaron Levine, buyers used to search for price information prior to purchase as well. The very fact that overcharge rules are stipulated only for a given range of prices that deviates from a known benchmark market price indicates that both buyers and sellers came into the marketplace with some price information gathered earlier.[25] Nonetheless, the focus of the present study has been directed at the ex post stage of market information search. In a market setting where a single equilibrium price exists and products are homogeneous, this procedure is more efficient.

If the ex post price search reveals that a buyer was overcharged by an amount exceeding one-sixth of the equilibrium market price, this victim of fraud can ask that the transaction be revoked and get a full refund. If the fraud amounts to exactly one-sixth of the equilibrium price, the transaction remains in force, but the victim is entitled to a full refund of the overcharge. When the overcharge is less that one-sixth, the transaction stands and no refund is required. These regulations in favor of the buyer are subject to a time constraint. The procedure cannot take more time than needed to show the merchandise to a knowledgeable relative or an expert trader familiar with the equilibrium price.

The distinct economic feature comes into play with the story of R. Tarfon, who changed the overcharge limit from one-sixth to one-third of the market equilibrium price. This change took place in the ancient city of Lydda, whereupon the merchants there were very pleased. Their positive reaction dissipated quite rapidly when R. Tarfon added another component to his innovative ruling, insisting that a buyer might continue his ex post search the whole day long. Realizing that R. Tarfon had traded off extra margin for extra ex post search time, the merchants preferred the original, more conservative paradigm of a smaller margin along with a considerably shortened ex post search time.

The Talmudic price search "model" was analyzed in light of the classical theory of economics of information (Stigler, 1961). It was then extended to include several cases handled by leading rabbinical authorities and documented in their *responsa*. These cases originate in different periods, geographical areas, and market conditions. They date from the fourteenth to the nineteenth centuries CE, and range over North Africa, Asia, and Europe. They reflect both relatively underdeveloped market settings and more modern market structures.

The *responsa* exhibited do not comprise a representative sample, yet they touch upon real-life personal economic situations that generated business disputes brought for decision by the rabbinical authorities involved. The *responsa* cited refer to both price and quality search processes and were comparatively analyzed in light of theoretical and empirical economic and marketing studies that concentrate on

25 Aaron Levine, "*Ona'ah* and the Operation of the Modern Marketplace," *Jewish Law Annual* (Hebrew University, vol.XIV, 2003): 232.

product classifications and such widely practiced policies as money-back guarantees and price-matching refunds. The *responsa* sources revealed some innovative economic considerations—for example, acknowledging the (negative) effect of information technology improvements on the time allowed for ex post search, or the (positive) effect of financial uncertainty in finalizing a transaction on the very same variable.

We close with two important observations. First, economic theorizing did not start with Alfred Marshal or even Adam Smith. It can be traced to much earlier periods, although admittedly it was not necessarily published in systematic economic writings at those times. Secondly, as this study and other studies included in this volume convincingly show, Jewish legal writings are a rich source of insightful economic thinking. In the case of the present study, expanding the analysis among the many available *responsa* dealing with market information search is likely to yield a better understanding of the extended Talmudic search "model."

SELECTED BIBLIOGRAPHY

Babylonian Talmud:
Bava Metsi'a 49b.
Baye, Michael R., and J. Morgan. "Price Dispersion in the Lab and on the Internet: Theory and Evidence." *RAND Journal of Economics* 35:3 (2004): 449–466.
Bible:
Leviticus 25:14.
Caro, R. Joseph. *Shulhan Arukh, Hoshen Mishpat* 227:9.
Levine, Aaron. "*Ona'ah* and the Operation of the Modern Marketplace." *Jewish Law Annual* (Hebrew University vol.XIV 2003): 225–58.
Liebermann, Y. "Economic Efficiency and Making of the Law: The Case of Transaction Costs in Jewish Law." *Journal of Legal Studies* 15 (1986): 387–404.
Maimonides, *Mishneh Torah, Mekhirah* 12:6.
Stigler, G. J. "The Economics of Information." *Journal of Political Economy* 69:3 (1961): 213–25.
Stiglitz, J. "The Contributions of the Economics of Information to Twentieth Century Economics." *The Quarterly Journal of Economics* 115:4 (2000): 1,441–78.

CHAPTER 7

OPTIMAL PRECAUTIONS AND THE LAW OF FIRE DAMAGES

JACOB ROSENBERG

Introduction

This chapter presents an example of the use of economic analysis to understand Jewish law. The model used is an application of the economic analysis of law,[1] which has become increasingly prominent in the philosophy and study of law. Economic analysis of law deals not only with those aspects of law that are usually regarded as purely "economic," but also with more general categories of law, such as property rights, torts, and family law. Indeed, it can be said to deal with all aspects of civil and criminal law.[2] Following this new approach, the chapter seeks to apply the economic analysis of law to Jewish tort law and, specifically, to laws relating to fire damage.

1 The economic analysis presented here is based primarily on Shavell (1980 and 1987) and Posner (1972) (see also Calabrasi and Hischoff, 1972).

2 The best-known work on this approach is that of Richard Posner in *The Economic Analysis of Law*, first published in 1973. In the introduction to the third edition of the book, Posner writes:

> Perhaps the most important development in legal thought in the last quarter century has been the application of economics to an ever increasing range of legal fields, including those at once so fundamental and apparently non-economic as torts, criminal law, family law, procedure and constitutional law.

Fire Damage in Jewish Law

The economic approach to understanding Jewish law can be illustrated through the economic analysis of three basic laws relating to fire damage:[3]

1. An individual who lights a fire in his field that spreads to a neighboring field is liable if and only if he did not exercise a proper level of care.
2. A damager is exempt from compensating for damage caused by fire to objects *hidden* in a stack of corn in a neighboring field, even when he is liable for damage to the neighboring field, including the stack of corn itself.
3. An individual who lights a fire in the oven in his dwelling that then causes a fire in a dwelling above it is liable for fire damage even if he exercised the proper level of precaution or care.

Three questions can be raised regarding these laws:

1. Why does exercising "proper care" exempt the damager from compensating for fire damage when the fire spread to a neighboring field? After all, the damager was the source of the damage; why should the victim bear the costs?
2. If exercising "proper care" exempts the damager in the case of fire that spreads from one field to the next, why does it not exempt the damager in the case of fire that spreads from his dwelling to one above it?[4]
3. Why is the damager exempt from compensating for damage to objects hidden in a stack of corn, while he is nevertheless liable for damage to the stack of corn itself?

Talmudic commentators and modern researchers of Jewish law have already dealt with the first question. The most widely given answer is, "*force majeure*" (*ones*). More specifically, the damager who has exercised proper care never imagined that the fire would cause harm to someone else's property. Under these circumstances, he is considered "unwillingly compelled" (*anuss*).[5] This answer is based on the understanding that the principle of *force majeure* that appears in the Talmud is derived from the Torah. Hence, it is a basic principle in Jewish law and should therefore apply to Jewish tort law in general and to fire damage in particular.

This answer is typical of the explanations offered by the legal approach to understanding civil law (*dine mamonot*) in the Talmud. This approach attempts to

3 The sources for these laws are cited below.

4 For how the rabbinic literature reconciles the two distancing requirements, see R. Isaac b. Jacob Alfasi (Rif, North Africa, 1013–1103) to B *Bava Kamma 60a*; R. Shabbetai b. Meir ha-Kohen (*Shakh*, Lithuania, 1621–1662), *Siftei Kohen*, *Hoshen Mishpat* 154:1; R. Jacob b. Jacob Moses Lorbeerbaum of Lissa (Poland, c. 1760–1832), *Netivot ha-Mishpat*, *Hoshen Mishpat* 154:1; and R. Avraham Yeshayahu Karelitz (Israel, 1878–1953), *Hazon Ish*, B *Bava Batra* 14:14.

5 Shalom Albeck sees in this claim a general explanation for all laws of damages in the Talmud. See Shalom Albeck, *Pesher Dine Nezikin* (*The Interpretation of the Laws of Damages*) (Tel-Aviv: Dvir, 1990).

find a common principle throughout the casuistic codex of Jewish law. If the search proves successful, scholars who advocate the legal approach will claim to have discovered a legal principle that represents "justice" in Jewish law. Therefore, in order to achieve justice in a manner consistent with the law, we must apply this principle in all cases that come before the court (*bet din*).

The Economics of the Laws of Fire Damages

The economic approach to Jewish civil law, which, as already noted, is an application of economic analysis of law, differs from the legal approach outlined above. According to the economic approach, the origin of a legal principle is not to be found in the collection of cases appearing in the Talmud, but rather in the relevant economic theory that identifies the law that will induce individuals to behave in a socially optimal manner or, in other words, to exhibit what is known as "efficient behavior." More generally, according to the economic approach, the main objective of the law is to provide individuals with an incentive to behave in a specific and desirable manner and to avoid undesirable behavior.[6] Therefore, the "explanation" that an individual who causes damage, even though he took proper precautions, is "compelled" and therefore is exempt from paying damages, is no explanation at all unless we find that this principle induces the relevant parties to adopt socially optimal behavior. The same can be said regarding the concept of a "Torah decree" (*gezerat ha-katuv*). Such a decree is not an explanation in the sense of a statement of cause, and we are therefore permitted to look for an explanation of a Torah decree, at least in the case of civil law.

Efficient behavior in the context of accidents means that both the potential damager and the potential victim take precautions that will minimize the social costs of the accident-prone situation. These include the cost of the accidents themselves and the costs incurred in their prevention.[7] Since the objective of the law is to induce the parties, who take into account the costs of breaking the law, to behave in a socially efficient manner, a formal law is required in situations where, in the absence of such a law, individuals would behave in a socially inefficient manner. When individuals behave in a socially efficient manner even in the absence of such a law, the law need not intervene.

For example, if all fields in which a fire is lit bordered only on fields belonging to the same individual, there would be no need for a law regarding fire damage to

6 According to the Coase Theorem (Coase, 1960), in the absence of transaction costs and well-defined property rights, the parties are able to negotiate an efficient contract without intervention by the law. The economic analysis of law assumes that this is not the case in the common occurrence of accidents (see Calabrasi and Melamed, 1972).

7 A detailed definition of "efficient behavior" is given below.

the fields. It can be safely assumed that the person who lit the fire, being a rational agent, takes full account not only of the benefits of the fire for the purpose of heating, cooking, or burning of waste, but also of its potential damage if it spreads to his other fields. His behavior (i.e., the timing of the fire, the precautions taken against the spread of the fire to adjacent fields, and his supervision of the fire) will be determined by both the benefits of the fire and the potential damage. In other words, his behavior will be efficient. However, the same assumption cannot be made if other individuals own the neighboring fields. In this case, the individual lighting the fire, in the absence of a law, is inclined to invest only minimal resources in watching over it, which is not socially efficient behavior. Therefore, law must be created that will induce the potential damager (and the potential victim) to take the appropriate actions to minimize the costs of an accident.

More specifically, in order to apply the economic approach to explain the laws mentioned above, we must show that individuals will take socially desirable and efficient precautions if the damager is made unconditionally liable for the fire spreading from his dwelling to his neighbor's above it. Moreover, we must show that, if the damager's fire spread from his *field* to his neighbor's *field*, it is socially desirable that he be held liable only if he did not exercise "proper care." We must also show that, even if the damager did not exercise "proper care," it is socially desirable to exempt him from compensation for damage to objects hidden in a stack of corn; this exemption will cause the care taken by the parties to be socially efficient. Toward this end, we must first clarify the concepts of "proper care," "due care," and "efficient care."

Proper Care and Due Care

In Jewish law, the damager's exemption from paying compensation is usually conditional on "proper care," which is synonymous, in the eyes of the court, with "due care" (i.e., the level of care that defines nonnegligent behavior). For example, an individual who lit a fire in his field is exempt from compensating for damage caused to his neighbor's field if he distanced the fire from his neighbor's field by 50 *ammot*.[8] This distance is judged to reflect the level of due care in the case of field-to-field damage; the damager is liable only if he has negligently lit his fire within 50 *ammot*, and hence not exercised due care.

The most salient characteristic of "proper care" is that it is an intermediate level, in the sense that there exist both higher and lower levels of care. It is straightforward to confirm that the sages of the Talmud were acutely aware of the existence

8 *Ammot* is the plural of *amma*, a common measure used in the Torah and the Talmud. It is equivalent to 18 inches according some scholars and to 22.9 inches according to others. The other measures cited in the paper are: *tefakh*—lit. a handbreadth, a measure of length equal to the width of four thumbs—and *bet kor*, an area of a field equivalent to 108 thousand squared meters.

of different levels of care. For example, an individual who lights a fire in his field can choose the distance of the fire from his neighbor's field. The farther he distances the fire, the higher is the level of care and the lower is the likelihood of damage to his neighbor's field. "Proper care," however, requires that he distance the fire only a specified distance from his neighbor's field in order to exempt him from compensation for damage. The *Mishna* states:[9]

> What distance does a fire pass [so that one who lights a fire will be liable for the damage caused by it]? R. Elazar . . . says: We see it [the fire] as if it were in the center of a field that is seeded by a *kur* of seed. R. Eliezer says, 16 *amma*. . . . R. Akiva says, 50 *amma*. R. Shimon says, . . . it depends on the characteristics of the fire.

Clearly, each of the sages of the *Mishna* was aware that the greater the distance of the fire from the neighbor's field, the smaller the risk of its spreading. Nevertheless, each of them exempts the potential damager from exercising a higher level of care than the distance he defines as proper care.

The requirement of an "intermediate" level of care applies in the case of other precautions as well. For example, the higher the wall dividing two fields, the greater the protection from fire damage. Does Jewish law therefore require an extremely high wall? The *Mishna* specifies:[10]

> If [a fire] passed over a fence that is four *ammot* high, or through a public domain, or over a river, the damager is exempt from paying damages.

The fact that "proper care" is an intermediate level of care is clear from the condition that the precautions taken to prevent the spread of a fire need only be effective in the case of an average wind. If an abnormally strong wind comes, which was not present when the fire was lit and could not have been anticipated prior to lighting the fire, then the individual who lit the fire is not liable for damage resulting from the fire's being spread by such a wind. This condition holds even though the sages were aware that it is possible to raise the level of care to prevent the fire from spreading even in the case of an abnormally strong wind. The *Tosefta* states:[11]

> R. Elazar says, [one needs to distance the fire] 16 *amma*; when there is a wind, 30 *amma*. R. Yehuda says, 30 *amma*; when there is a wind, 50 *amma*. R. Akiva says, 50 *amma*; when there is a wind, 300 *ammah*. There was an evening in which a fire spread more than 300 *amma* and caused damage. There was a case in which a fire crossed the Jordan River, because [the fire] was strong.

The end of this passage of the *Tosefta* is not simply a story about an unusual natural event, but rather it is intended to teach that, despite the existence of rare cases in which "proper care," as defined in the first part of the passage, would not have prevented the damage, the law is still satisfied by this level of "proper care." The level of care required in the presence of a wind is greater, but it is still an "intermediate" level of care.

9 B *Bava Kamma* 61b.
10 B *Bava Kamma* 61a.
11 T *Bava Kamma* 6:11.

To summarize, proper care is an intermediate level of care and is a necessary (though not a sufficient) condition in order to exempt the damager from compensating for damage he has caused. Proper care is equivalent to "due care," signifying lack of negligence.

Efficient Care

Efficient care is that level of care that minimizes the *total expected costs* of situations that potentially could lead to an accident.[12] How are "total expected costs" defined?

People light fires in their fields in order to carry out various important tasks, ranging from the disposal of waste to heating and cooking. The lighting of a fire, unfortunately, can easily cause damage in a neighboring field; the probability of this event depends on the level of care exercised by the potential damager, as well as by the person who potentially may suffer damage (the "victim"). A relatively high level of care reduces the risk of damage but is costly to the person taking the precautions. For example, if the damager distances his fire from neighboring fields, the probability of damage is reduced, but this requires additional resources in terms of time and effort, as well as additional costs in acquiring or maintaining tools used to move objects toward the fire. Potential victims of fire damage can also reduce the risk of damage by, for example, building a wall around their fields, but here again costs are incurred in order to reduce the risk of damage. *The higher the level of care, the lower will be the probability of damage, though the cost of care will increase.*

It would be useful at this point to provide an example of the calculation of total accident costs in the case of risk-neutral individuals.[13] Suppose that the damager distanced his fire thirty *ammot*, which cost him ten monetary units. The owner of the neighboring field built a wall around his field, which also cost ten units. These actions reduced the probability of an accident to three percent, meaning that out of one hundred fires to be lit in the damager's field, we expect that three will overcome the precautions taken (i.e., the distancing of the fire from the neighboring field and the building of the wall). Assume that, if an accident does occur, the value of the damage will be one thousand units. "Expected damage" is then calculated by multiplying the probability of damage by its cost ($1{,}000 \times 0.03$), giving a result of thirty units. If we add the cost of precautions taken by the two parties, we obtain that the total cost of the accident-prone situation is $30 + 10 + 10 = 50$ units.

12 The benefit from lighting a fire is assumed to be independent of the level of care. In this case, efficient behavior from society's point of view involves minimizing the total accident costs. Using a more general definition, efficient behavior maximizes the net benefit from the fire (after subtracting total accident costs). In the case of fixed benefits, the definitions are equivalent.

13 We assume that all damagers and victims are risk-neutral in the sense that they care only about expected damages, as defined below.

It is important to emphasize that the *total* accident cost does not necessarily decrease if the damager or the victim increases his level of care. The expected damage will indeed be reduced, but it is possible that the costs of care will increase by a greater amount. For example, suppose that each party increases his level of care such that the combined cost of care increases from twenty to forty, while the probability of damage declines from, say, three to two and a half percent. The expected damage thus decreases from thirty to twenty-five (1,000 × 0.025). Despite the reduction in expected damage, the total cost of the accident-prone situation has increased from fifty to sixty-five since the reduction in expected damage of five units led to an increase in the cost of care of twenty units.

In summary, the total accident cost is the sum of the costs of care of both the damager and the victim, and the expected damage of the accident. Total cost does not necessarily decline when the level of care is increased.

The economic analysis of Jewish law claims that the law in the case of fire damages is formulated so as to induce the parties to choose a level of care and precaution that will minimize the total accident cost. The resulting level of care is socially optimal or "efficient." Any other level of care, whether higher or lower, is not desirable, and therefore a regulation encouraging such a level of care would not find its way into the code of law.

Efficient Care and the Effect of the Law: The Unilateral Care Case

The first law to be considered is the case of fire that spreads from a dwelling to a dwelling above it. We will argue that this is a case of unilateral care in which only the damager is able to take action to reduce expected damage; the victim is unable to take any precautions. The unilateral care model will be introduced using a numerical example that illustrates the relationship between the level of care, the total accident cost, and the impact of the liability rule on the parties involved. It is followed by a graphical illustration in order to show the general validity of the conclusions. The numbers used in the example are arbitrary, though their relative magnitudes are consistent with the relationship between the level of care and total cost assumed in the economic analysis of the law. The efficient level of care will be immediately apparent in the example, and this will enable us to analyze the legal liability rule that induces the damager to choose the socially efficient level of care.

Since the case under consideration is one of unilateral care, the level of care is entirely determined by the damager. Possible examples of such a situation include a bullet that missed its mark, a hole dug near an existing wall that weakens it, and our case of an individual who lights a fire in his oven, which spreads to the dwelling above.

Table 7.1 Expected Damage and Total Cost by Level and Cost of Care

Level and Cost of Care		*Expected Damage of Accident* (**in bold**) *and Total Cost*
Low:	0	**50**
		50
Medium:	10	**30**
		40
High:	20	**28**
		48

Table 7.1 illustrates the relationship between the level of care, expected damage, and total cost. Expected damage (indicated in bold) is calculated as the product of the probability of damage and its cost. Suppose, for example, that the cost of damage is fixed at one thousand units, and that, if the damager chooses a low level of care, the probability of damage is five percent. Therefore, the expected damage for that level of care is fifty (1,000 × 0.05).

If the damager instead chooses a medium level of care, the probability of damage is reduced from five to, say, three percent. Therefore, expected damage is thirty (1,000 × 0.03). Thus, we again find that expected damage declines as the level of care increases.

The *rate of decrease* in expected damage, however, also declines, which is in line with a general principle in the theory of production. Examples of this are common in everyday life. For example, if a lock is installed on the gear shift of a car, the probability of it being stolen is reduced. If, in addition, a lock is installed on the steering wheel, the probability of theft will decline further, but by less than in the case of the first lock. If our example is consistent with this principle, there will always be a level of care beyond which we cannot reduce the expected damage by the full cost of the increase in care.

Table 7.1 illustrates this principle. As the level of care increases, there is a decline in both the expected damage and the total cost of the accident-prone situation, which is calculated as the sum of the expected damage and the cost of care. However, although expected damage continues to decline when we move from a medium to a high level of care, the total cost of the accident-prone situation *increases*. This is a result of a ten-unit increase in the cost of care and a corresponding decrease in the expected damage of only two units.

It is important to reiterate that the present example is one of unilateral care, in which the victim cannot take any action to protect his property from damage, and therefore the cost of care for the victim is not taken into account.

A cursory glance at the table reveals that the efficient level of care is achieved with a total cost of forty at the medium level of care.

Having identified the efficient level of care, we can now determine the law that would induce the damager to choose it. If, for example, the damager faces a no-liability rule, according to which he is exempt from providing compensation without regard to the level of care he has exercised, then he will choose a low level of care. Clearly, he has no incentive to expend any resources on higher levels of care if he has no liability for damage. The other party will, of course, suffer a loss from this low level of care, but this is of no concern to the damager. Since such a no-liability rule, which unconditionally exempts the damager from compensation, would lead to an inefficient level of care, we would not expect it to be the established law in the case under consideration.

Consider, on the other hand, a strict liability rule, according to which the damager is liable regardless of the level of care he has chosen. In this case, the damager bears the entire cost of the accident-prone situation (i.e., both the expected damage and the costs of care). In table 7.1, the total cost, which appears below the numbers in bold, is borne by the damager and depends on the level of care he chooses. The damager will therefore choose the medium level of care, which involves the lowest possible total cost and is precisely the socially efficient level.

We therefore find that strict liability induces a socially efficient level of care in unilateral care cases, where the victim is unable to take action to reduce the likelihood of an accident. As will be shown in the following section, this is the key to understanding the law in the case of damage caused by fire spreading to a dwelling above. It should be emphasized that this does not apply when the victim can also contribute to the prevention of the accident.[14]

A Graphical Illustration of the Unilateral Care Model

In this section, the basic model is illustrated graphically in order to show the general validity of the conclusions derived using the above numerical example. Recall that the model is one of unilateral care, which means that only the damager can invest in costly precautions in order to reduce the likelihood and severity of the damage borne by the victim. We assume that it is beneficial for the damager to be engaged in the risky activity, and that the level of activity and the utility derived from it are constant. We assume further that the parties are risk-neutral or, in other words, care only about expected losses.

We will first use the model to derive the socially efficient level of care (i.e., the level of care that minimizes total accident costs). This outcome will then serve as a benchmark for examining the incentives created by actual laws.

14 The following sections will elaborate on this point.

We make use of the following notation:

x = the amount invested by the damager in means of prevention (i.e., the distance from the damager's fireplace to the ceiling), which also represents the level of care
p(x) = the probability of a fire accident
D = the amount of the potential loss (damage) suffered by the victim

$$TAC = x + p(x)D = \text{total accident cost} \quad (1)$$

We assume that p(x) is decreasing in x, reflecting the fact that greater precaution reduces the probability of an accident, and that D is constant.[15] Thus, expected damages, given by p(x)D, are also decreasing in x. We further assume that p(x) decreases at a decreasing rate. This implies that care has diminishing marginal benefit in terms of reducing accident risk. Intuitively, damagers invest first in the most effective precautions and only later turn to less effective measures.

Social Optimum: As noted in the preceding section, the efficient level of care is the level of care x that minimizes TAC = x + p(x)D.

The graphical solution to the problem is shown in Figure 1, which includes the cost of care x (the linear upward-sloping line X) and the expected damage p(x)D (the downward-sloping convex curve p(x)D).

The total accident cost curve is the vertical sum of the two curves X and p(x) D. (For example, the total cost at point S is the sum a + b.) The summed cost curve TAC is a U-shaped curve that reaches a minimum at the level of care X*, which is the cost-minimizing and therefore socially efficient level. At levels of care below X*, an additional dollar of care reduces the victim's expected damage by more than one dollar, thus reducing total costs. However, beyond X*, an extra dollar of care reduces expected damage by less than one dollar, thus increasing total costs.

Formally, X* is located at the point where the *slope* of the X curve equals (in absolute terms) the slope of the p(x)D curve. The slope of X reflects the *marginal cost of care*, while the slope of p(x)D reflects the *marginal benefit of care* (the reduction in expected damages).[16]

In order to determine the actual choice of x by the damager, we need to introduce a liability rule. First, suppose the damager faces no liability. In this case, the damage to the victim is external to the damager; therefore, he simply minimizes his expenditure on prevention. Thus he chooses x = 0, where his total costs are not minimized. (The damager's private costs correspond to the X line in fig. 7.1, which is minimized at the origin.)

Now suppose that a rule of strict liability is in force, such that the damager is liable for the victim's full costs. In this case, the damager will choose the socially

15 D, the severity of an accident, can be assumed to depend on the level of care i.e., D = D(x). This modification will not change any of the conclusions as long as we assume that D(x) is decreasing in x at a decreasing rate.

16 A formal proof can be found in the appendices of the chapter. However, because of space limitations, the appendices do not appear here and are available from the author: Jacob Rosenberg, Department of Economics, Bar-Ilan University, Ramat Gan, 52900, Israel. Email: rosenby1@mail.biu.ac.il

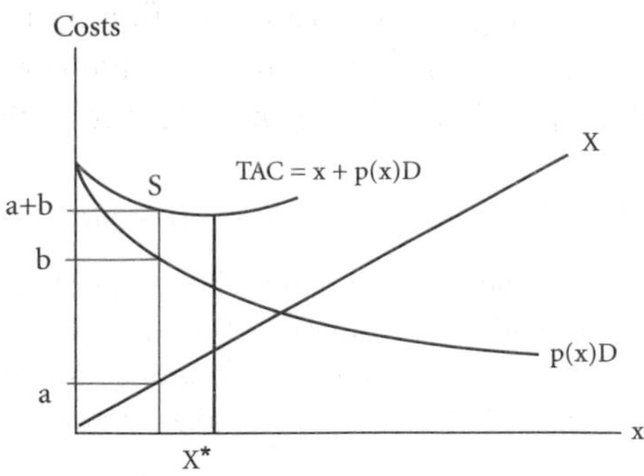

FIGURE 7.1

optimal level X*, since the threat of liability forces him to fully internalize the victim's expected damage. The damager's cost now coincides with the social cost. Therefore, in the case of unilateral care, strict liability motivates the damager to adopt a socially optimal level of care.

The Case of a Fire that Spreads to a Neighbor's Dwelling

The case of a fire that is lit indoors and spreads to a neighbor's dwelling above is, in our opinion, a unilateral care case, in which only the damager can take precautions to reduce the likelihood of an accident. There are virtually no measures that can be taken by the victim to reduce the likelihood that a fire from below will cause serious damage. Therefore, strict (unconditional) liability is efficient from an economic viewpoint; as was demonstrated above, such liability will induce the damager to exercise an efficient level of care.

Following is the text of the law:

> A person shall not set up an oven in his house, unless there is a space above the oven [to the ceiling] of four *amma*. If he sets it up in the upper story, he must leave a clay plaster underneath three *tefakhim* [deep]. In the case of a *kira* [a smaller oven], [the plaster] must be one *tefakh*. *And if he causes damage, he must pay the cost of the damage*. R. Shimon says, the above specifications were only stated so that if he abides by them, he is exempt from payment.[17]

R. Shimon's phrasing indicates that, according to both opinions (that of the first part of the *Mishna*, which is the majority opinion, and his own), the specified distances represent a level of "proper care." The point of contention is whether

17 M *Bava Batra* 2:1.

proper care exempts the damager in this case. The first opinion is that it does not. This means that "proper care" does not constitute due care in this case, because the court holds the damager liable even if he was not negligent—even when he exercised proper care.

Similar rulings can be found in the previous *Mishna*:[18]

> A person shall not dig a pit near the pit of his fellow . . . unless he distances his pit from the side [of the pit of his fellow] three *tefakhim*. . . . The waste of olives and other refuse . . . must be distanced from the wall of one's fellow three *tefakhim*, or the pit in which this refuse is deposited must be plastered with plaster.

In our opinion, these laws share a common feature: They apply in cases of unilateral care, in which the victim cannot take significant precautions to prevent damage from occurring. In these cases, we have seen that strict liability will induce the damager to adopt an efficient level of care. Therefore, in all of these cases, the majority opinion states that, "if he causes damage, he shall pay the cost of the damage." Jewish law adopts the majority opinion.

Fire Damage to a Neighboring Field—A Case of Bilateral Care

In our opinion, the key to understanding the difference in law between the case where a fire spreads from one dwelling to another above it and the case where a fire spreads from one field to another lies in the ability of the victim to take precautions to reduce the probability of an accident. The victim can distance his crops from the border between the two fields, can dig a ditch between the fields, and so forth. In other words, fire damage to a dwelling above is a case of unilateral care while field-to-field fire damage is a case of bilateral care. In the case of bilateral care, if the law considers the damager unconditionally liable (i.e., adopts strict liability), the victim will not have sufficient incentive to adopt an efficient level of care.

We will present a numerical example to help illustrate the case of fire that spreads from one field to the next, prior to our formal analysis. The numerical example, as well as the formal analysis, must now take into consideration the behavior of both parties, since this is a case of bilateral care. The example assumes that each party chooses from three alternative levels of care. The columns in table 7.2 represent the levels of care available to the victim, while the rows represent those available to the damager. As before, the numbers in bold indicate the expected damage and are calculated as the product of the probability of damage and the amount of damage. For example, if the amount of the damage is fixed and equal to one thousand, and if both parties choose a low level of care, the probability of an accident is

18 Ibid.

Table 7.2 Expected Damage (in bold) and Total Cost, According to the Level of Care of Each Party

		Level and the Cost of Care – Victim →		
		Low 0	*Medium* 10	*High* 20
Level and the Cost of Care – Damager ↓				
Low	0	**100** 100	**50** 60	**35** 55
Medium	10	**50** 60	**30** 50	**28** 58
High	20	**35** 55	**28** 58	**22** 62

ten percent. In table 7.2, the upper left-hand cell represents the case in which both parties exercise a low level of care. The expected damage appearing in this cell is one hundred, which is the product of the probability of damage and the amount of the damage when both parties exercise a low level of care (1,000 × 0.10).

Now suppose that the victim, but not the damager, moves up to a medium level of care. The probability of an accident is reduced from ten to five percent and, therefore, the number in bold appearing in the middle cell of the first row is fifty (1,000 × 0.05). If we continue in the same row to the right-hand cell, the expected damage again declines since the victim has moved to a high level of care, and the probability of an accident has declined to three and a half percent. As we move from left to right in the first row, the expected damage decreases since the victim is increasing his level of care. As before, however, there is a decrease in the *rate of change* of the expected damage. That is, expected damage declines by fifty when the victim moves from a low to a medium level of care, while it declines by only fifteen when he moves from a medium to a high level of care. This well-known principle of economics, called the law of diminishing returns, was introduced in the previous case, in which the victim was passive.

Similarly, moving down a given column implies an increasing level of care by the damager, and the expected damage again decreases. For the sake of simplicity, we have assumed symmetry between the damager and the victim with respect to the effects of moving between levels, and therefore each row is identical to the corresponding column (i.e., the top row is identical to the left-hand column; the middle row is identical to the middle column; the bottom row is identical to the right-hand column).

The numbers in bold represent the expected damage for each of the possible combinations of care. We already know, however, that the expected damage is only part of the cost of an accident-prone situation, since the cost of care incurred by the two parties must be added to the expected damage in order to obtain the total cost. The cost of each level of care appears alongside the labels of each row and column. If we add these costs of care to the expected damage, we obtain the total cost of the situation in each cell of the table, which appears below the number in bold. For example, the total cost in the lower right-hand cell is sixty-two, and is the sum of the expected damage (22) and the costs of care incurred by the two parties (22 + 20 + 20 = 62). In the upper left-hand cell, the expected damage equals the total cost, since the cost of care is zero for both parties.

The Parties' Behavior in the Field-to-Field Bilateral Care Case

Recall that the socially desirable behavior of the two parties is that which minimizes total accident cost. The figures in table 7.2 show that the lowest total cost occurs at the intersection of the middle column and the middle row, where minimum total cost is fifty and where both parties choose a medium level of care. This reflects the socially efficient level of care for each party.

There is, however, no assurance that this is the level of care that the two parties will actually choose, since each takes into account only his own costs. Suppose, for example, that the liability rule in this case were the same as in the unilateral care case (i.e., strict liability). The victim would then choose the low level of care, which costs him nothing. The damager would select *his* optimal level of care in light of this fact. In terms of table 7.2, the damager scans only the left-hand column (which corresponds to the level of care chosen by the victim) and chooses the level of care that minimizes his costs. According to the strict liability rule, all costs are borne by him and are minimized (as can be seen from inspection of the first row of the table) when he chooses the high level of care. Meanwhile, the victim will choose the low level. This division of the burden is not efficient, since the total cost of the situation is fifty-five, which is higher than the lowest total cost attainable, fifty, as noted above.

We thus conclude that the law of strict liability does not induce efficient behavior in the bilateral care case of field-to-field fire damage. In contrast, a negligence rule stating that "the damager is exempt from compensation when he exercises the proper level of care" *does* induce efficient behavior. To see this, suppose that the court knows the efficient levels of care for the two parties and defines them as the levels of "proper care." Suppose further that the damager's level of "proper care" is used by the court to define the level of due care in determining the damager's negligence. In our example, the level of due care will then equal the medium level of care. The damager, who is exempt from paying damages if he chooses this level of care, will unhesitatingly do so since he will then bear only his own cost of care (ten), which is less than *his* expected cost if he chooses a different level of care (in which case he must bear the sum of his own cost of care and the expected damage).[19] This is true regardless of whether the victim

19 In table 7.2, 10 is the lowest level of cost appearing in the table.

chooses a low, medium, or high level of care. The victim will also choose a medium level of care since, given the damager's level of care, he thus minimizes his own expected cost, which is equal to forty (his cost of care, ten, plus the expected damage, thirty). To see that this level of care minimizes his expected costs, note that, if the victim chooses a low level of care, his expected cost is the expected damage of fifty, while if he chooses a high level of care his expected cost is forty-eight (20 + 28 = 48). Thus, the victim minimizes *his* expected cost by choosing the medium level of care.

A More General Analysis of the Field-to-Field Bilateral Care Case

In addition to the specific numerical example, a more rigorous presentation of the field-to-field bilateral care case is needed in order to show the generality of our conclusion with respect to field-to-field fire damage.

The unilateral model needs to be only slightly amended in order to describe the bilateral case. This is done by allowing the victim, too, to take precautions in order to reduce the likelihood and severity of an accident. Thus, although x is still defined to be the damager's cost (and level) of care, we now define an equivalent variable for the victim, denoted y.

The probability of an accident depends now on x and on y: $p(x, y)$. As in the unilateral model, we assume that expected damage $p(x, y)D$ decreases in both x and y at a decreasing rate. Total accident cost, TAC, is therefore given by an extended version of equation (1):

$$TAC = x + y + p(x, y)D \qquad (2)$$

Let x^* and y^* denote the levels of care that minimize TAC (both of which are assumed to be positive). Any other levels of care result in a higher total accident cost. Formally:

$$TAC_{min} = TAC(x^*, y^*) = x^* + y^* + p(x^*, y^*)D < TAC(x_j, y_i), \text{ for any pair } (x_j, y_i) \text{ that is not the unique pair } (x^*, y^*) \qquad (3)$$

The unique combination of x^* and y^* represents the socially desirable levels of care.

Let us now consider the actual choices of x and y under a negligence rule. In this case, the damager can avoid liability by choosing the due standard of care x^*, which he does by, for example, lighting the fire a distance of sixteen *ammot* from the neighboring field, in accordance with the opinion of R. Eliezer. If the damager chooses x^*, he avoids liability *regardless of the victim's choice of level of care.* Thus, the cost-minimizing strategy for the damager is to meet the due standard.

Now consider the choice of the victim. Since he rationally anticipates that the damager will meet the due standard, he expects to bear the losses due to any damage incurred. Thus, he chooses his own care level y to minimize his own expected losses: $y + p(x^*, y)D$. This can be achieved only if he chooses y^* (note that this value of y minimizes the victim's cost $y + p[x^*, y]D$, *which is also the value of y that minimizes total cost* $x^* + y + p[x^*, y]D$, since x^* is independent of the choice of y), which, as we already know, is the efficient level of care, given $x = x^*$.

Thus, we have demonstrated that a negligence rule with the due standard of care set at x^* induces both the damager and the victim to choose efficient levels of care and explains why the law coincides with the negligence rule in the case of field-to-field fire damage. In contrast, the law coincides with a rule of strict liability in the case of fire spreading to a dwelling above.

The Field-to-Field Fire Damage Case—Conclusion

We conclude that, since "due care" is determined by the court to be the damager's level of "proper care" (which is the efficient level), it is the rational choice from the viewpoint of the damager, given the negligence rule, and at the same time it is socially efficient. The allocation of the burden of care between the parties minimizes the total cost of the accident-prone situation. Thus, from an economic standpoint, it is desirable that the law exempt a damager who exercises the proper level of care (i.e., due care) from paying damages. From an economic point of view, the distances specified by the *Mishna* in *Bava Kamma* (cited above), which are required to exempt the damager from compensation for fire damage (as they constitute due care), represent the damager's efficient level of care.

Due Care According to R. Shimon

Based on the *Mishna* and the *Tosefta* in B *Bava Kamma* cited above,[20] we are able to present the five opinions regarding the damager's due care under a negligence rule in the case of field-to-field fire damage. The level of due care is expressed in terms of the distance between the fire and the neighboring field and depends on whether a wind was blowing at the time the fire was lit. These opinions are summarized in table 7.3.

R. Shimon's view is that the level of due care should be dependent on the height of the fire, since the probability of a fire accident is an increasing function of the height of the fire. The larger the fire, the higher should be the level of due care.

20 See the section on Proper Care and Due Care above and the citations of the *Mishna* and *Tosefta*.

Table 7.3 Due Care in the Case of Field-to-Field Fire Damage *(Distance measured in ammot)*

	Regular conditions	Windy conditions
Rabbi Eliezer	16	30
Rabbi Yehuda	30	50
Rabbi Akiva	50	300
Rabbi Elazar	75	?
Rabbi Shimon	Dependent on the fire height	

According to the economic analysis, R. Shimon's view is to be preferred, since a single standard will not minimize overall accident costs when expected damages vary for a given level of care. Due care that is dictated by the efficient level of care will mandate a low level of care if the fire consists of a few chips of wood, and a considerably higher level of care if the fire consists of a pile of logs. So how can we explain the view of the other sages who set a single standard for all damagers? The answer lies in administrative costs. Applying R. Shimon's *halakha* would require the *bet din* to investigate the true height of the fire in each particular case, which may not be constant during the time of burning. To do this, the victim must look for witnesses that are able to estimate the height of the fire and the court has to verify their testimony. This is a very high information cost burden on the court and society—a cost that is ordinarily greater than the savings in accident costs that would result from a variable standard.

The above analysis implies that the fundamental point of contention between R. Shimon and the other sages is whether the administrative costs of determining the height of the fire outweigh the savings in accident costs that would result from doing so. R. Shimon is of the opinion that they do not, while the other sages hold the opposite opinion.

The opinion of R. Shimon, that "due care depends on the height of the fire," or, in other words, that due care is determined on a case-by-case basis, is accepted by the Talmud as authoritative.

A mathematical representation of the debate between R. Shimon and the other sages can be found in the appendices (see footnote 16).

Damage to Objects Hidden in a Stack of Corn: The *Tamun* Rule

A damager who lights a fire in his own field is liable only for damages to the stack of corn in his neighbor's field and to the field itself, but he is exempt from compensation for damage to *any* objects hidden in the stack of corn, even if he did not exercise the proper level of care.[21] This is defined as the *tamun* rule, as summarized by Maimonides (Rambam, Egypt, 1135–1204):

> In the case of an individual who lit a fire in his own field, which spread to his neighbor's field, the damager is exempt from damages to all articles hidden in a stack of corn, but pays the value of the volume (of corn) taken up by the articles in the stack of corn; we view the stack as if it were full of corn.[22]

Before attempting to provide an economic explanation of the law, we need to elaborate on the special character of fire damage and to introduce the concept of differential care.

Differential Care

Fire causes damage to a wide variety of objects and types of property. In the case of a dwelling that burns down, all objects in the house are likely to be destroyed, including furniture, clothing, valuables, money, and even the building itself. The case of a field is similar; not only the crop, but also all objects in the field, including tools, border markers, and hidden articles, are lost.

From the discussions in the Talmud that deal with the main categories of damage (*avot nezikin*), it is clear that not all types of damage have the wide range of effects that are characteristic of fire.[23] In the case of fire, the ability to induce variable levels of care according to the value of the potential damage is critical. The greater the potential damage, the higher (and therefore the more costly) is the desired level of care. An individual who differentiates in this manner reduces the total cost of protecting his property from damage; differentiation between objects is therefore efficient. Indeed, examples of this type of behavior are common in everyday life; while one might store valuables in a safe, a door with appropriate locks suffices for protecting electronic appliances in the house.

Before there were safes, banks, and other such means of protection, individuals often hid objects outside their homes—for example, in their fields—in order to prevent theft and reduce the danger of damage due to fire in their dwellings, which was a common occurrence. Of course, if the article is used on a daily basis, hiding it outside the house is not efficient, since the benefit in terms of added protection is

21 This is the majority opinion, according to the interpretation of Rava, at B *Bava Kamma* 61b. R. Yehuda holds that the damager is liable for damages to objects hidden in the stack of corn. Here, again, we will not attempt to explain the disagreement between the sages but will only try to explain the accepted law, which is the majority opinion as explained by Rava.

22 *Mishne Torah, Nizke Mamon,* 14:8–12.

23 For example, a pit in the public domain is likely to cause damage to an animal or person and to articles that the animal or person is carrying. It is less common for a person to fall into a pit since he generally pays attention to where he is walking. In the case of damages caused by the horns of an ox (goring and the like), the damage is usually even more limited and usually occurs—if it occurs at all—between oxen (rather than between oxen and other types of animals or human beings).

offset by the cost in terms of availability. For example, the Talmud (B *Bava Kamma* 62a) states that it is reasonable for a silver chair to be left out in the open in the homes of the wealthy. However, the Talmud is doubtful that pearls would normally be stored in a case used for storing money (an early form of a safe).

We will focus on articles that are hidden outside the house, since clearly they do not need to be readily available. An individual who wishes to hide such an object has two alternatives: either to hide the article in a stack of corn in the field, which is a relatively cheap and reliable method and has the added advantage of easy access, or to bury the object in a pit dug in the field, or in a fireproof vessel, which involves greater bother and less access. The cost in terms of time is higher for the second alternative. Which alternative will the individual choose if there is a real risk of his neighbor's fire causing damage to his field? The answer depends on the law that applies in the case of hidden objects. If the law states that the damager must pay the full cost of damage, then the victim will hide the object in a stack of corn. If, on the other hand, the law states that the damager is exempt from compensation for objects hidden in a stack of corn, then the victim will choose a fireproof hiding place.

The individual's behavior, which is induced by the prevailing law, will affect the total cost of the accident-prone situation. If the damager is liable for hidden objects, then hiding the object in a stack of corn increases the expected damage enormously, since the stack of corn now contains a valuable object that is likely to be destroyed by any fire. Moreover, the damager will exercise a higher level of care given that he is liable not only for the field and the corn but also for the value of an article that may be hidden in the stack of corn. These two cost elements do not exist if the damager has no liability for hidden objects. In this case, the only additional cost is the difference between the cost of a fireproof hiding place and that of a non-fireproof hiding place, which is likely to be smaller than the additional cost of care and the increase in expected damage. Hiding the object in a fireproof hiding place is somewhat more costly in terms of time, but it greatly reduces the expected damage. We will argue that this consideration provides an economic explanation of the *tamun* rule.

The Efficiency of the *Tamun* Rule: A Graphical Analysis

We make use of the unilateral model, in which the damager is exempt from compensation for damage to objects hidden in a stack of corn, in order to illustrate the *tamun* rule. We argue that it will induce people hiding their objects in the field to place them in a fireproof hiding place, which reduces the total cost of the accident-prone situation.

Consider first the situation in which the possibility of hiding objects in the field does not exist, so that total accident cost is given by equation (2) in the case of bilateral care. Assume further that the victim selects the level of care y^*, which cannot be changed once it has been chosen. With y^* fixed, the model is essentially a unilateral care model since, given the victim's level of care y^*, the damager will choose his level of care x^* to minimize his own costs. The total accident cost is obtained by substituting the values x^* and y^* into equation (2):

$$TAC = x^* + y^* + P(x^*, y^*)D \quad (4)$$

Note that D includes only the losses caused by fire damage to the field.

This initial situation is illustrated in fig. 7.2. The downward-sloping solid curve $P(y = y^*)D$ represents the expected loss as a function of x, given $y = y^*$; the solid U-shaped curve $TAC(y = y^*)$ represents the total accident cost as a function of x, given $y = y^*$; and point M represents the minimum value of TAC as defined in equation (4).

Suppose now that the victim decides to hide objects in the field. He cannot change his level of care y^*, but he can decide whether to use a nonfireproof hiding place, which involves no cost, or to use a fireproof hiding place, which involves a small cost h. The damager, however, is allowed to change his level of care, and will do so if this minimizes his costs.

Under the "no liability for hidden objects" rule, the victim chooses to hide the object in a fireproof hiding place. Total accident cost is then

$$TAC = x^* + y^* + h + P(x, y^*)D \quad (5)$$

If h is small and can be ignored, the situation reverts back to the "no hiding" case represented by equation (4). The curve $TAC(y = y^*)$ also represents the case in which a fireproof hiding place is used. The damager will choose x^* (see fig. 7.2) so as to minimize his costs under a strict liability rule (or negligence rule where x^* is determined to be the standard level of due care). These are desired outcomes since x^* (given $y = y^*$) minimizes the total social accident cost, which is represented by the point M.

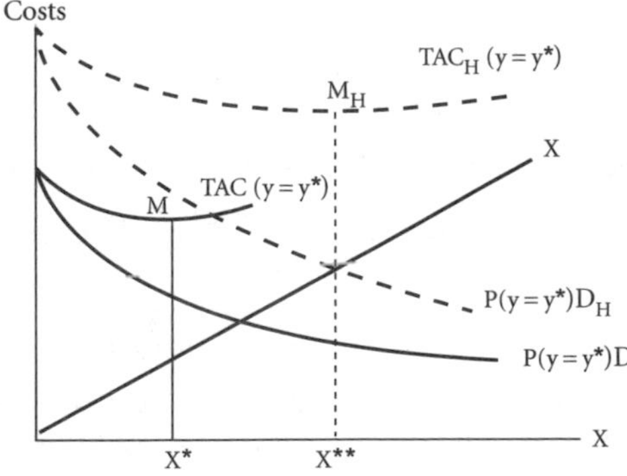

FIGURE 7.2

We will now show that adopting a law that does not follow the *tamun* rule leads to an increase in total accident cost. Given this law, the victim chooses a nonfireproof hiding place and total accident cost is given by

$$x + y^* + P(x, y^*)D_H; D < D_H \quad (6)$$

where D_H is the value of the damage to the field, including the expected damage to the article, and *x* is to be chosen by the damager.

Given that $D_H > D$, expected losses and total costs are higher for any given level of x, as shown by the curves $P(y = y^*)D_H$ and $TAC_H(y = y^*)$, respectively. If strict liability applies to both the field and the hidden article, then the damager will choose the level of care x^{**} (see fig. 7.2) in order to minimize his costs, which are identical to the total accident cost.[24] Figure 7.2 shows that $x^{**} > x^*$ and that the minimum of total accident cost TAC_H (at point M_H) is higher than the minimum of TAC (at point M).[25]

We conclude, therefore, that "no liability for hidden objects" (the *tamun* rule) is to be preferred over "strict liability for hidden objects," since it leads to reduced social accident costs.

In the terms of the preceding section, we can say that the *tamun* rule serves as an incentive to exercise differential care. The rule induces individuals to hide valuable objects that need not be constantly available in a maximally safe manner, while they are not induced to do so for objects that need to be constantly available.

Conclusion

This chapter presented an economic approach to understanding fire damages in Jewish law. It has been shown that the law of strict liability in the case of fire damage to a dwelling above leads to an efficient level of care in the sense that it minimizes the social cost of the fire accident. However, the same liability rule is not economically efficient in the case of fire damage to a neighboring field. In this case, it is the negligence rule that induces both the damager and the victim to exercise an optimal level of care. This explains why the law, in the case of fire damage to a neighboring field, exempts the damager from liability for damage caused by his fire, if he lit it at an appropriate distance from his neighbor's field. In addition, the puzzle of the *tamun* rule was solved by showing that it minimizes the cost of the fire accident, given that people hide precious articles outside the house.

24 If, however, the law is based on the negligence rule, then the court will choose x^{**} as the standard level of due care since x^{**} minimizes the social accident cost if the damager is liable for hidden articles.

25 It can be demonstrated formally that this is a general result: minimum TAC_H (equation [6] at $x = x^{**}$) is higher than minimum TAC (equation [5] at $x = x^*$), given the model's assumptions. The proof can be found in the appendices of the chapter (not included here; see above, footnote 16).

The debate between R. Shimon, who favors variable due care according to fire size, and the other sages, who specify a single level of due care for all damagers regardless of fire size, is also explained in economic terms, if there exist significant administrative costs.

One can therefore claim, at least with regard to the laws studied in this chapter, that their underlying principle is economic efficiency as seen from a social welfare point of view. Does this principle underlie other laws of damages and Jewish civil law in general? The question awaits more comprehensive and intensive research.

SELECTED BIBLIOGRAPHY

Calabrasi, Guido., and J. Hirschoff. "Towards a Test for Strict Liability in Torts." *Yale Law Journal* (1972): 1054-1085.

Calabrasi, Guido., and A. D. Melamed. "Property Rules, Liability Rules and Inabilities: One View of the Cathedral." *Harvard Law Journal* (1972): 1089-1128.

Coase, Ronald. "The Problem of Social Cost." *Journal of Law and Economics* (1960): 1-44.

Maimonides, *Mishne Torah, Nizke Mamon* 14:8–12.

Miceli, J. Thomas. *The Economic Approach to Law*. Stanford University Press, 2004.

Posner, A. Richard. "Theory of Negligence." *Journal of Legal Studies* (1972): 28-96.

Shavell, Steven. "Strict Liability v. Negligence." *Journal of Legal Studies* (1980): 1-25.

Shavell, Steven. *Economic Analysis of Accident Law*. Cambridge, MA: Harvard University Press, 1987.

Talmud Bavli:

Bava Kamma 61a–b.

Bava Batra 17a–20b.

Tosefta: *Bava Kamma*

Bava Kamma 6:11.

CHAPTER 8

VALUATION IN JEWISH LAW

KEITH SHARFMAN*

INTRODUCTION

EVERY legal system needs mechanisms to resolve disputes over the value of legal entitlements,[1] and Jewish law is no exception.[2] Tort damages, restitution for the conversion or theft of property, and the calculation of a redemption price for tithed or consecrated property are just a few of the many cases in Jewish law where a dispute as to the value of a legal entitlement might arise and when, if so, a valuation adjudication becomes necessary.[3] The pervasiveness of such disputes, however, does not always make them easy to resolve.

As in most other legal systems, market value is for Jewish law the guiding principle that governs or at least plays an important role in nearly all valuation disputes.

*Many thanks to Rabbi Dr. Aaron Levine for his invitation to participate in this volume and for his great kindness and courtesy in the editorial process, to Rabbis Ozer Glickman, Chaim Twerski, Shabsai Wolfe, and Dovid Zucker for helpful discussions, and to Deans Joseph Kearney of Marquette University Law School and Andrew Simons of St. John's University School of Law for generous research support.

1 On the problem of legal valuation generally, see Keith Sharfman, "Contractual Valuation Mechanisms and Corporate Law," *Virginia Law & Business Review* 2 (2007): 53–88; Keith Sharfman, "Valuation Averaging: A New Procedure for Resolving Valuation Disputes," *Minnesota Law Review* 88 (2003): 357–83.

2 For studies of valuation in Jewish law, see, for example, Robert. J. Aumann & Michael Maschler, "Game Theoretic Analysis of a Bankruptcy Problem from the Talmud," *Journal of Economic Theory* 36 (1985): 195–213; Jeffrey L. Callen, "Differential Asset Valuation in the Medieval Post-Talmudic Legal Literature," *History of Political Economy* 40 (2008): 183–200.

3 See infra notes 4 through 6 and accompanying text.

Take the simple case of an ox that gores. The owner of the ox is responsible to pay damages, either half or full, depending on whether the goring was habitual or aberrational.[4] But regardless of whether full or half damages are ultimately assessed, the court must in any case calculate the total value of the victim's loss, and that is done with reference to market value (i.e., a comparison of the market value of the victim's damaged property prior to the event with its value ex post).[5] To the extent that market value may be established via an actual market transaction, the market itself is used (e.g., an actual sale transaction can establish the salvage value of the tort victim's damaged property).[6] But part of the calculus inevitably requires an estimate of some value in the absence of an actual market transaction (e.g., an estimate of how much the victim's property hypothetically could have fetched in a sale had it not been damaged). And on such questions, it is often difficult for the parties to predict how the trier of fact will rule, since the selection of a figure (within the bounds of plausibility) is inherently discretionary. As legal valuation is not about searching for a single epistemologically correct value but rather entails the selection of one plausible figure from among many, results cannot be predicted in advance with certainty. And this volatility of outcomes can at times lead to divergent party expectations that impede settlement and thereby cause socially wasteful litigation.

The same market value principles apply in other tort cases, such as an action for damages to compensate for a personal injury to the plaintiff on account of the defendant's negligence. Assuming the defendant was indeed negligent and therefore liable, there remains the issue of damages, the market value of which can be calculated easily in some respects (e.g., the actual cost of plaintiff's medical expenses), still feasibly but with greater difficulty in others (e.g., the plaintiff's lost wages, whose value depends on contestable assumptions as to the appropriate rate with which to discount future earnings to present value), and with near impossibility in others (e.g., the plaintiff's pain and suffering, for which actual market values figures are simply never available).[7] Plaintiffs in such cases press for high damages, defendants press for a low figure, and just where the trier of fact will end up within that range is difficult to predict.[8]

Beyond torts, the same "market value" and "valuation uncertainty" principles still apply, as an example from the law of contracts, the "fair price" doctrines in Jewish law, will show. These doctrines require courts to void sales when the buyer challenges them on the ground that the price charged exceeded market value.[9] Availability to the buyer of the rescission remedy depends critically on the value that the trier of fact attaches to the property in issue. The higher the valuation assessed, the less likely that the price paid will be found to have exceeded market value and hence the less likely

4 Exodus 21:35–36.

5 Maimonides (Egypt, 1135–1204), *Mishneh Torah*, *Nizkei Mamon* 1:2.

6 Exodus 21:36 ("they shall sell the living ox and divide its money, and the carcass, too, shall they divide").

7 Exodus 21:18–19 (requiring tortfeasors to pay the market value of the victim's lost wages and medical expenses in personal injury cases); *Bava Kamma* 84b (applying market value principles to damages for pain and suffering). The same holds true for property damage. See *Bava Kamma* 58b, 59b.

8 This is true not only for Jewish law but for all legal systems. Sharfman, 2 *Virginia Law & Business Review* at 58.

9 On rescission as a remedy for overcharges relative to market value, see Leviticus 25:14; TB *Bava Metsi'a* 74b; Aaron Levine, "Ona'ah and the Operation of the Modern Marketplace," *Jewish Law Annual* 14 (2003): 225.

that the sale will be rescinded. And vice versa—the lower the valuation, the greater the likelihood of rescission. Here too, as with the tort examples, it may well be difficult for the parties to form in advance the same expectations about how the litigation would likely conclude. And with mutual optimism on account of the discretionary nature of legal valuation, the parties may litigate wastefully rather than settle sensibly.

What can legal systems do about this problem? Find ways to make valuation outcomes more predictable. One (substantive) method is to replace market value with something more reliable and predictable, such as liquidated damages clauses that specify a damages figure before a contract is breached, or workers' compensation agreements that determine compensation for work-related injuries in advance of any dispute. Another (procedural) method is to retain market value as the remedial target, but impose procedural mechanisms that improve outcome accuracy and predictability. As it turns out, Jewish law uses both methods.

Substantively, Jewish law at times replaces a market value remedy with a prespecified "fixed value"—that is, a preset figure that may or may not approximate market value in any particular case. For example, Jewish law makes available to would-be donors to the Temple treasury two types of donative vows. One type permits donors to oblige themselves to monetary donations of an amount equal to the market value of a specified asset.[10] A second type of vow allows the donor to pledge the value of a person (either the donor or another) based on a set of fixed values in the final chapter of Leviticus that vary in accordance with the specified person's age and gender but not on the basis of actual market value.[11] The advantage of the latter, so-called "Erekh" vows is that the amount owed on them is never uncertain or in doubt and thus never gives rise to a valuation dispute. Rather than force donors to litigate the valuation question each time they make a vow, the *Erekh* vow provides a mechanism to make binding pledges for specified fixed sums that do not depend on the hard-to-predict assessments of market value that monetary equivalence pledges can often generate.[12]

Jewish law also takes many procedural steps to improve the accuracy and thereby enhance the predictability of litigated valuation outcomes. Some of these are discussed below.

VALUATION PROCEDURES IN JEWISH LAW

Monetary disputes in Jewish law are for the most part heard by three-judge panels[13] whose costs are paid for by the parties.[14] While adjudication by a single "expert" judge is possible, it can occur only if the parties agree to this alternative forum.[15] If

10 See *Mishneh Torah, Arakhin* 8:2.

11 Leviticus 27:1–8.

12 Ibid.

13 *Sanhedrin* 2a.

14 *Mishneh Torah, Sanhedrin* 23:10. By contrast, judges in most other legal systems are paid by the public rather than by the parties.

15 TB *Sanhedrin* 4b–5a; *Mishneh Torah, Sanhedrin* 2:10–11; 5:18.

any party insists, the case must be tried before a panel of three, with each side selecting one panel member and the parties or their designee panelists selecting a third.[16]

Once constituted, the panel must treat valuation questions as issues of fact, as distinct from purely legal questions such as liability or the admissibility of evidence. While Jewish law gives some guidance to panels regarding how valuations are best determined (market value being the main guiding principle,[17] with departures from that principle in a small minority of cases,[18] such as the twenty-percent penalty imposed when tithed or consecrated property is redeemed by its prior owner[19]), much discretion is left to the panel members, who on the basis of the evidence before them must select a resolving value (market-based or otherwise) by simple majority rule.[20]

The size of the valuation panel is expanded from three to ten in cases of complex sacred obligations, such as the redemption of consecrated real property, and the rules governing the types of individuals who may serve, or who must be included, on the panel are relaxed or tightened depending on context.[21]

The Talmudic text quoted below and its accompanying table summarize the basic rules (which are found mainly at the beginning of *Sanhedrin*, the tractate of the Talmud concerning judicial matters) governing the constitution of valuation panels for various types of cases.

> Monetary cases [must be adjudicated] by three judges; cases of larceny and mayhem, by three; claims for full or half damages, the repayment of the double or four- or five-fold restitution [of stolen goods], by three. . . . The fourth year fruit and the second tithe of unknown value are assessed by three. The assessment of consecrated objects for redemption purposes is made by three; valuations of movable property by three. According to R. Judah one of [the assessors] must be a kohen [i.e., a priest]; in the case of real estate, by ten including a kohen; in the case of a person [whose value has been vowed to the Sanctuary], by the same number.[22]

To summarize briefly what is specified in the quoted text and set forth more fully in table 8.1, typical contract and tort cases require a panel of three individuals who meet the ordinary requirements to serve as judges.[23] Strict liability tort cases, in which the plaintiff seeks "half damages" against a defendant who was not at fault (as in the case of damage caused by an ox without a history of goring[24]), require three

16 TB *Sanhedrin* 23a.

17 For example, TB *Bava Mesi'a* 77a (using market value as a benchmark for contract damages). See also the sources cited in note 7, supra.

18 Leviticus 27:31 ("If a man wishes to redeem some of his tithe, he shall add a fifth to it"); TB *Bava Metsi'a* 55b.

19 Ibid.

20 Exodus 23:3 ("after the majority shall they follow"); *Bava Metsi'a* 59b.

21 TB *Sanhedrin* 2a, 14b.

22 See TB *Sanhedrin* 2a.

23 For example, a judge may not be blind. See TB *Niddah* 50a.

24 *Bava Kamma* 33a.

Table 8.1 A Typology of Valuation Panels in Jewish Law*

Type of Case	Composition of Panel	Extra Judicial Requirements or Leniencies	Adjustments to Value
Contracts and Torts (negligence)	3 Judges	None	None
Torts (strict liability)	3 Judges	Only expert judges	–50%
Restitution/Conversion Plus Fines	3 Judges	Only expert judges	+20% or more
Redemption of Second Tithe and Fourth Year Fruit of Unknown Value	3 "Judges"	Only merchant judges; laity, women, and gentiles may qualify	+20%
Assessment of Donative Chattel Vow Obligations and Redemptions of Consecrated Personal Property	3 "Judges"	Only appraisal experts; tribunal must include a priest	None for assessments; +20% for redemptions by prior owner
Assessment of Donative "Person" and Realty Vow Obligations and Redemptions of Consecrated Real Property	10 "Judges"	Only appraisal experts; tribunal must include a priest	None for assessments; +20% for redemptions by prior owner

*This Table follows the scheme set forth in TB *Sanhedrin* 2a as interpreted by TB *Sanhedrin* 14b–15a. See also Maimonides (Egypt, 1135–1204), *Mishneh Torah, Sanhedrin* 5:8 (only "expert judges" may assess fines); *Mishneh Torah, Nizkei Mamon* 2:7 ("half damages" for torts are fines rather than compensatory); and *Mishneh Torah, Arakhin* 8:5 (only "expert" appraisers, one of whom must be a priest, may value donative vows and consecrated property).

"expert" judges, because half damages are a fine rather than compensatory, and only expert judges may award a fine.[25]

Restitution cases, for losses caused by the theft or conversion of property, also require three expert judges. This is so because, like strict liability torts, restitution actions also involve the imposition of fines (twenty percent for armed robbery; one hundred percent for surreptitious theft; and four- or fivefold damages for the sale or slaughter of a stolen ox or sheep) in addition to basic compensatory damages.[26]

Second Tithe produce or fruit grown in a tree's fourth year, which themselves or their proceeds an owner must bring to and consume in Jerusalem at festival time,[27] ordinarily have an indisputable market price and in such cases may be redeemed without assessment by a valuation panel. When, however, their value is uncertain because they lack an apparent market price, as in the cases of spoiled wine or rotten

25 *Mishneh Torah, Sanhedrin* 5:8 (only "expert judges" may assess fines); *Mishneh Torah, Nizkei Mamon* 2:7 ("half damages" for torts are fines rather than compensatory); and *Mishneh Torah, Arakhin* 8:5 (only "expert" appraisers, one of whom must be a priest, may value donative vows and consecrated property).

26 Leviticus 19:23.

27 Leviticus 19:24 ("And in the fourth year all its fruit shall be holy, an offering of praise to the Lord."); TB *Baba Metsi'a* 55b.

produce, a panel of "merchants" must determine their value, with "merchants" defined liberally to include any potential buyer, including gentiles or even the owner's spouse,[28] and the owner must then pay a redemption price equal to the panel's figure plus twenty percent. Diverging from the rule in earlier case categories, the usual requirements for serving as a judge do not apply to those serving as appraisers under what is a more liberalized "merchant" standard, which perhaps explains at least in part why the panel's value figure is somewhat suspect and requires an upward adjustment.

The final categories of cases where valuation panels are required involve sacred vow obligations and redemptions of consecrated property.[29] Here again, the usual rules for serving as a judge do not apply to panel members, who rather must be expert in appraising the type of property or entitlement that is in issue and who must include among them at least one priest. Two additional rules apply in these cases: Twenty percent must be added to the panel's figure in redemption cases, and the expert appraiser panel must be expanded from three to ten for the valuation of real property (whether vowed or to be redeemed) and the assessment of "person" vows (i.e., vows pledging to the Temple treasury a sum equal to the market value of a particular person).

Boiled down to its bare essentials, Jewish law's valuation regime thus consists of seven core features: (1) ordinary three-judge panels that determine value by majority rule; (2) "expert" three-judge panels for the assessment of monetary fines; (3) "merchant" three-appraiser panels to value tithed property of uncertain value for the purpose of establishing its redemption price; (4) "expert" three-appraiser panels to value personal property that was the basis for a donative vow or for the purpose of redemption by the property's original owner; (5) "expert" ten-appraiser panels to assess "person" vows and to value real property that was the basis for a donative vow or for the purpose of redemption by the original owner; (6) mandatory inclusion of a priest on expert appraiser panels; and (7) twenty-percent upward adjustments to panel valuations of tithed or consecrated property when such valuations are used to calculate the owner's redemption price.

These seven features are distinctive to Jewish law. Other legal systems typically allow either a single judge or a larger lay jury to determine valuations.[30] Three judge panels at the trial level are for other legal systems a rarity,[31] and trial panels of ten are (at least to this author's knowledge) unheard of, as are panels of nonjudge appraisers.[32] Other legal systems do not vary the level of judicial resources devoted

28 TB *Sanhedrin* 14b.

29 On sacred vow obligations and redemptions of consecrated property, see generally Leviticus ch. 27 and *Mishneh Torah, Arakhin*.

30 Sharfman, 2 *Virginia Law and Business Review* at 54.

31 For instance, United States law entitles litigants to a "three judge district court" only when specifically required by an act of Congress or in cases involving constitutional challenges to the apportionment of a congressional district or statewide legislative body. See 28 U.S.C. §2284.

32 Use of a binding panel of expert appraisers in bankruptcy valuation disputes has been tentatively suggested as a possibility by Douglas G. Baird and Richard Bernstein, "Absolute Priority, Valuation Uncertainty, and the Reorganization Bargain," *Yale Law Journal* 115 (2006): 1930, 1969. But the suggestion has yet to be taken.

to valuation depending on context. Nor typically do they require participation of a particular interest or group in the valuation process, or apply twenty-percent adjustments to the trier of fact's valuation findings.

Why Jewish law includes these features when other legal systems do not is thus a puzzle. With the help of economics, this puzzle is addressed by the analysis below.

Analysis

Many scholars have written on the subject of legal valuation, concerning both secular and Jewish law.[33] But they have largely done so in specific doctrinal contexts rather than at a higher level of generality.[34] In secular law, much effort has been made to analyze valuation in particular substantive contexts, such as corporate, tax, eminent domain, environmental, and family law, to name just a few specific areas that have attracted particular interest from commentators.[35] But with a handful of notable exceptions,[36] little work has been done on secular legal valuation that generalizes to broader contexts. In Jewish law too, prior valuation research has tended to address specific doctrinal problems, such as Aumann and Maschler's ingenious explication of the Talmud's complex system for valuing competing claims in bankruptcy,[37] or Callen and Liebermann's creative work on the valuation of marriage contracts in mid-term.[38] Though these efforts and others like them have been of high quality, their doctrinal narrowness has foreclosed generalization beyond the immediate categories under discussion.

General consideration of the valuation problem for any legal system as a whole requires an assessment of that system's "interdoctrinal" features—that is,

33 For Jewish law examples, see Aumann and Maschler, supra note 2; Callen, supra note 2; Aaron Levine, "Value Theory in Talmudic Literature," *Tradition* 17 (1978): 23–24; Yehoshua Liebermann, "The Economics of Kethubah Valuation," *History of Political Economy* 15 (1983): 519. For secular examples, see Barry E. Adler and Ian Ayres, "A Dilution Mechanism for Valuing Corporations in Bankruptcy," *Yale Law Journal* 111 (2001): 83; Lucian Arye Bebchuk and Jesse M. Fried, "A New Approach to Valuing Secured Claims in Bankruptcy," *Harvard Law Review* 114 (2001): 2386; James C. Bonbright, *The Valuation of Property: A Treatise on the Appraisal of Property for Different Legal Purposes* (1937); Lee Anne Fennell, "Revealing Options," *Harvard Law Review* 118 (2005): 1399; Saul Levmore, "Self-Assessed Valuation Systems for Tort and Other Law," *Virginia Law Review* 68 (1982): 771.

34 For a discussion of generality and specificity in legal valuation scholarship, see Sharfman, 2 *Virginia Law & Business Review* at 63.

35 For example, Daniel R. Fischel, "Market Evidence in Corporate Law," *University of Chicago Law Review* 69 (2002): 941; Daniel D. Polsby and Martin Zelder, "Risk-Adjusted Valuation of Professional Degrees in Divorce," *Journal of Legal Studies* 23 (1994): 273; John A. Bogdanski, *Federal Tax Valuation Paragraph* 2.01 (Boston: Warren, Gorham and Lamont, 2009); Christopher Serkin, "The Meaning of Value: Assessing Just Compensation for Regulatory Takings," *Northwestern University Law Review* 99 (2005): 677.

36 For example, Bonbright, supra note 33; Bonbright, "The Problem of Judicial Valuation", *Columbia Law Review* 27 (1927): 493; Levmore, supra note 33; Fennell, supra note 33; Sharfman, supra note 1.

37 Aumann and Maschler, supra note 2.

38 Callen, supra note 2; Liebermann, supra note 33.

those aspects that are uniform or substantially shared across doctrinal categories.[39] For most legal systems, such interdoctrinal features include the rules of evidence, jurisdiction, and procedure that apply across doctrinal boundaries, the structure and operation of that system's non-specialized courts of general jurisdiction, and other matters of administration that similarly transcend specific doctrinal areas (such as the manner by which judges are compensated). The seven features of Jewish law identified above meet these interdoctrinal criteria, especially the basic requirement of holding civil trials before multi-member panels that resolve intra-panel differences by majority vote, the interdoctrinal feature to which we shall turn first.

The first thing to note about three-judge trial panels is that they are more costly than trials before a single judge, for the simple reason that paying three judges costs more than paying one. To be sure, three judges sitting together might handle more trials in a year than one judge could. But it is doubtful, given the duplicative efforts that sitting together necessarily entails, that the three judges could handle three or more times as many cases as a single judge. Other things equal, this differential in administrative costs counsels against using multimember panels.

But other things are not equal. Offsetting the higher administrative costs of three-judge panels is the benefit that they are likely to produce by way of more accurate and predictable outcomes. If the benefit of reduced errors exceeds the greater administrative costs associated with three-judge panels, then use of three-judge panels would be cost-justified, as that would be the way to minimize the sum of error and administrative costs, which from an economic efficiency perspective is the central goal of procedural design.[40]

For a number of reasons, we can be confident when parties to valuation disputes utilize three-judge trial panels in accordance with Jewish law that the benefits of this procedure exceed its costs. This is so, first, because in Jewish law it is the parties rather than the public who pay the judges for their time.[41] The parties thus have an incentive to select the cost-minimizing procedure. If shifting from three ordinary judges to a single expert one (an arbitration arrangement to which disputing parties in Jewish law may agree[42]) saves resources on balance in particular cases, we can expect the parties to agree to this shift in cases where they expect it to reduce costs. We may thus also infer, assuming low transaction costs,[43] that three-judge panels are

39 On interdoctrinality, see Edward Rock and Michael Wachter, "Dangerous Liaisons: Corporate Law, Trust Law, and Interdoctrinal Legal Transplants," *Northwestern University Law Review* 96 (2002): 651 (noting a general underappreciation for the interdoctrinal connectedness among legal duties in various doctrinal contexts); Sharfman, 2 *Virginia Law and Business* Review at 62 n.38, and accompanying text.

40 On optimizing the tradeoff between error and administrative costs, see Richard A. Posner, *Economic Analysis of Law*, 7th ed. (New York: Aspen, 2001), 593.

41 Maimonides, *Mishneh Torah, Sanhedrin* 23:5.

42 Maimonides, *Mishneh Torah, Sanhedrin* 2:10.

43 When only two parties are involved with respect to a particular transaction, low transaction costs is usually a reasonable assumption. On transaction costs as an impediment to efficient contracting and on their tendency to be relatively low when the number of affected parties is relatively small, see Ronald H. Coase, "The Problem of Social Cost," *Journal of Law & Economics* 3 (1960): 1; Posner, *Economic Analysis of Law* at 51, 420.

cost-minimizing whenever parties choose to litigate in that way, rather than agree to reduce the panel from three to one.

Private contracting behavior from outside Jewish law also supports this inference. Sophisticated parties to joint ventures who anticipate future valuation disputes tend to agree in their contracts to an appraisal process involving multiple expert appraisers rather than to place their fates in the hands of a single arbitrator.[44] The three-judge panels of Jewish law more closely resemble these multiappraiser valuation mechanisms than do the alternative modes of single-judge or jury adjudication, which is powerful evidence that Jewish law's default use of multimember panels is cost-justified.

Parties to valuation disputes likely prefer three-judge panels because they reduce outcome volatility and thereby make results more predictable and hence settlement more likely.[45] There is both empirical support for this claim,[46] as well as intuitional,[47] which may be seen from a simple numerical example.

Suppose that the members of a three-judge panel all agree that a defendant is liable but disagree as to the extent of liability, each believing that the defendant should pay a different amount. One judge values the claim at one hundred, a second at two hundred, and the third at three hundred. In such circumstances, the principle of majority rule would produce an outcome of two hundred—the maximum (and minimum) liability figure that a majority of the judges would support. The outcome would remain two hundred, irrespective of how much lower (but still above two hundred) the "high" third judge might agree to go, or how much higher (but still below two hundred) the "low" first judge might agree to go. In other words, three-judge panels governed by majority rule always produce the outcome favored by the "median judge" irrespective of the relative extremism or moderation of the median judge's panel colleagues. (This moderating effect is uniquely a feature of valuation disputes, where judgments are rendered along a sliding scale and "splitting the difference" is feasible and often done.[48] For issues on which the judges face a dichotomous choice—guilty or innocent? liable or not liable?—there is no middle ground and thus much less of a moderating effect from three-judge panels.[49])

44 See Sharfman, 88 *Minnesota Law Review* at 364–66 (describing clauses in the joint venture agreements of Merck/Schering-Plough, Verizon/Vodafone, and Cingular Wireless that utilize three-appraiser panels when the parties are far apart on the issue of valuation).

45 Posner, *Economic Analysis of Law* at 598.

46 See evidence from studies of "early offer arbitration" showing that increasing the predictability of outcomes increases the chance of settlement. Amy Farmer and Paul Pecorino, "Bargaining with Voluntary Transmission of Private Information: Does the Use of Final Offer Arbitration Impede Settlement?," *Journal of Law, Economics & Organization* 19 (2003):64.

47 Sharfman, 88 *Minnesota Law Review* at 376 (discussing how reduced outcome volatility leads to a convergence of expectations, which in turn increases the chance of settlement).

48 Sharfman, 88 *Minnesota Law Review* at 359 and n.6; Donald Wittman, "Lay Juries, Professional Arbitrators, and the Arbitrator Selection Hypothesis," *American Law & Economics Review* 5 (2003): 61, 81.

49 Cf. Cass R. Sunstein et al., *Are Judges Political? An Empirical Analysis of the Federal Judiciary* (Washington, DC: Brookings, 2006) (demonstrating the moderating effect of politically divergent panel deliberation).

In the usual case, the median judge will likely be the judge who is jointly selected by the parties or by the parties' designee judges, who are less likely to be partial to either side and are therefore more likely to favor a moderate result. But notice the constraining effect of majority rule: If any judge, including the jointly selected one, comes up with an unexpectedly extreme figure in either direction, that figure will be discarded and have no impact on the final result. Moreover, if one of the party-designated judges is more extreme than the other party-designated judge, the median judge's figure remains the outcome, untainted by any skewing effect reflected in the extremes.

By contrast, there is no such assurance with a single expert judge. A surprising figure (to the parties) from the single expert judge simply becomes the outcome. The disadvantaged party can do nothing about it.[50] Reduced outcome volatility is thus an inherent (and for risk-averse litigants an especially valuable) benefit that is uniquely associated with multimember panels. Single expert judge adjudications, by contrast, involve greater risk of an extreme result,[51] making outcomes on the whole more volatile, party expectations less convergent, and settlements therefore less likely.[52] Perhaps that is why in Jewish law only an expert judge and not simply an ordinary judge may, with the parties' consent, decide a case sitting alone.

Moving beyond the basic requirement of three-member panels, it is possible to justify Jewish law's other procedural requirements on similar efficiency grounds. As discussed above, the optimal level of administrative costs depends on the savings (in the form of reduced error costs) that administrative expenditures can produce.[53] One might think of these costs and savings in terms of averages and then optimize the level of administrative costs on that basis with a set of one-size-fits-all procedures that apply universally. But there may be some particular contexts in which the savings associated with additional administrative expenditures are unusually high relative to cost, such as high-stakes disputes in which the value in controversy is relatively high and thus inaccurate results are especially costly. If such situations are indeed identifiable and segregable, then imposing additional administrative costs only for those narrower contexts may well make sense.

50 It is not clear whether a "high-low" settlement agreement, whereby the parties agree before a case concludes that the defendant will pay no more than X even if the final outcome exceeds X while the plaintiff will receive no less than Y even if the final judgment is for less, would be enforceable as a matter of Jewish law. On such agreements, see Andrea M. Alonso and Kevin G. Faley, High-Low Agreements: You Can Have Your Cake and Eat It, Too," *Brief* 29 (1999): 69.

51 If the probability of a given judge favoring an extreme outcome is x (where x is defined as more than zero and less than 0.5), then the probability of an extreme outcome in the case of a single judge is simply x. The probability of such an outcome with a three-judge panel, however, where at least two judges would need to agree simultaneously on an extreme result, is $2x^2$. Since x is defined as less than 0.5 (i.e., extremism is less likely than not and hence has odds of less than fifty percent), $2x^2$ will always be less than x. The more narrowly one defines extremism, the greater the divergence in risk between the two procedures.

52 Posner, *Economic Analysis of Law* at 598.

53 See ibid. at 593.

Jewish law's contextually required use of expert judges, expert appraisers, and even larger-sized panels all may be understood in this way. Each of these entails additional administrative costs. But each may produce sufficient countervailing savings to justify the additional cost. In addition to reducing the risk of error, which enhancing the size and expertise of panels surely does (at least on average), these requirements also further improve the predictability of outcomes. That said, the additional benefits from these measures likely are small in most cases, given the basic requirement of three-judge panels and the reality of diminishing returns on further investments in administration.[54] It thus seems reasonable to impose these additional requirements with respect to panel size and expertise only in more limited contexts, such as cases involving the imposition of fines, the valuation of real estate, and other high-stakes disputes in which the cost of error is likely to be especially great.

By the same token, relaxation of the general procedural requirements for valuation disputes may be appropriate in cases in which the benefits from those requirements are likely small relative to cost, such as disputes involving low stakes or parties facing high transaction costs. Examples of this might be the redemption of Second Tithe produce and Fourth Year Fruit. The quintessential case of this, one imagines, is a farmer out in the countryside who lacks ready access to judges or courts but wishes to redeem heavy, low-priced, and/or perishable produce for cash so as to avoid the cost of transporting it to Jerusalem and risking that the produce would spoil prior to consumption. Quickly bringing in judges from the closest city (which may be quite far away) to appraise the farmer's produce, if even feasible, would seem to impose a relatively high transaction cost upon the farmer, for what may be produce worth less or little more than what the judges would need to be paid to assess it. There is thus a strong economic case for relaxation of the usual standards (to the extent that they are precautionary and require more than is strictly necessary from a ritual law perspective). In such circumstances, it seems reasonable to permit the farmer to assemble a sort of impromptu panel comprised of "judges" who may lack Jewish law's usual qualifications for judging—they may even be women, gentiles, someone related to the farmer, or (notwithstanding the obvious conflict of interest) the farmer himself![55] The only important criterion is that the panel members have a good sense of how to value the commodity in question.[56]

A somewhat different economic dynamic is likely at work in the case of other redemptions of consecrated property and in the assessment of sacred vow obligations. In these contexts, neither time nor space is of the essence. The property in issue need not be perishable or of little value, and thus there is plenty of time in the usual case for the prospective redeemer or donor to travel to Jerusalem and

54 On the law of diminishing returns, see William J. Baumol and Alan S. Blinder, *Economics: Principles and Policy*, 11th ed. (Mason, Ohio: Cengage Learning, 2008), 143.

55 *Sanhedrin* 14b.

56 But note that it is debatable whether the plain language of *Sanhedrin* 14b explicitly requires even this level of expertise.

assemble a panel there to determine a redemption price or an assessment amount. It is not therefore unreasonable in these circumstances for Jewish law to augment rather than relax the usual standards for judging by requiring that the panel members have expertise in valuation of the specific type of property in issue and that the panel include at least one priest.[57]

As in other contexts, the additional requirements are not administratively costless to obtain. But the added expense (of finding and compensating experts and an expert-priest from a potential panelist pool of reduced size) may still add value on balance here, as elsewhere, if error costs are sufficiently reduced. More expertise and less bias on the panel should produce more accurate results than would obtain from the non-expert and perhaps somewhat biased panel that the (technically unopposed) redeemer or donor would otherwise assemble.[58] The priest requirement reduces bias by giving the Temple treasury's interests (which the priest represents) some influence over the selection of the third "compromise" judge, who in adversarial litigation would be jointly designated by the parties or their designees, as well as a moderating voice in the panel's deliberations once the case is underway. Context-tailored inclusion on the panel of otherwise underrepresented interests, predispositions, and knowledge may thus be expected to improve a panel's accuracy and efficiency in the same way as would increasing the number or quality of judges on the panel—and in some cases, at a lower cost.

Twenty-percent value adjustments for the redemption of consecrated property by its prior owner is a further way to address inaccuracy on account of the underrepresentation of Temple treasury interests. Though we may expect panels in such cases to be somewhat tilted in favor of low valuations given the unopposed nature of the litigation and the underrepresentation of opposing interests on the panel, the twenty-percent premium is a palliative that at least to some extent mitigates those concerns.

A further benefit of the twenty-percent premium is that it adjusts the price uniquely for parties (prior owners) whose subjective valuations are likely to be higher than market value because of the so-called "endowment effect"—the observed economic phenomenon that owners often value property at a higher price once they have owned it than they would pay for the same property on the open market if they had not had any prior connection to it.[59] The redeemer is forced by the twenty-percent rule to compete not only against other auction bidders but also against his own (likely higher) subjective valuation. He cannot simply match the high bid. He must beat it by a wide, twenty-percent margin so that we may be confident that he has paid full value for the Temple property that he has reacquired.

57 TB *Sanhedrin* 14b–15a; *Mishneh Torah*, Arakhin 8:5.

58 Jewish law forbids conscious judicial bias. *Mishneh Torah*, *Sanhedrin* 23:6. But subtle biases unknown even to the judges themselves may be impossible to avoid.

59 On endowment effects, Richard Thaler, "Toward a Positive Theory of Consumer Choice," *Journal of Economic Behavior and Organization* 1 (1980): 39–60.

Lessons and Conclusions

On examination, Jewish law proves quite savvy on the issue of valuation. Using three-judge panels, Jewish law makes valuation outcomes more predictable and thus increases the chance of settlement. Rather than adopt the one-size-fits-all approach of other legal systems, Jewish law instead uses a layered, contextual approach, deploying additional administrative resources, procedural safeguards, and monetary adjustments in situations where economic theory suggests that they are needed. Jewish law's surprising sophistication in this area offers valuable insight to modern legal theorists and policy makers who today are struggling to devise their own solutions to the age-old problem of legal valuation.

The procedures that Jewish law uses to resolve valuation disputes, and the economic insights that they reveal, hold lessons for other legal systems. Just as using three-judge trial panels yields benefits that may justify their costs for valuation disputes in Jewish law, so might three-judge trial panels be cost-justified elsewhere. The use of expert judges, expert appraisers, and even larger-sized panels all have similar predictability effects, though the greater variability and likely smaller average net benefits associated with these measures may justify their use only in more limited contexts, such as high-stakes disputes in which the consequences of error are especially costly.

In disputes in which balanced advocacy or relevant expertise is lacking, as when the value of a legal entitlement is litigated ex parte, the zone of plausible valuation outcomes widens and the benefits from judicial diversity and intrapanel deliberation accordingly increase. Context-tailored inclusion on the panel of otherwise underrepresented interests, predispositions, and knowledge, as with the inclusion of an expert-appraiser priest representing the interests of the Temple treasury, may thus be expected to improve a panel's accuracy and efficiency. Adjusting the valuation figure against unopposed litigants is a further way to address the underrepresentation of countervailing interests and in some contexts may also be a way to account for possible "endowment effects."

While most of these economic insights are not ubiquitously reflected in current law, some are indeed reflected, albeit in an attenuated form, both in current law and in some of the extant proposals for its reform. Consider for instance recent proposals to resolve valuation disputes by averaging a range of values offered by a panel of expert appraisers.[60] Other examples include the requirement to consider the public interest when judicially reviewing the settlement of private antitrust litigation,[61] the routine granting of nonparty motions to file *amicus* ("friend of the court") briefs, such as those often filed by the Solicitor General in U.S. Supreme Court and other appellate litigation,[62]

60 Baird and Bernstein, 115 *Yale Law Journal* at 1969; Sharfman, 88 *Minnesota Law Review* at 370–72.

61 15 U.S.C. §16(e) (the "Tunney Act").

62 For the rules on filing *amicus* briefs in the U.S. Supreme Court and Courts of Appeals, see Sup. Ct. R. 37; Fed.R. App. P. 29.

and the oft-seen requirement or tradition that various administrative and judicial bodies be comprised of politically diverse appointees (such as commissioners at federal agencies like the Federal Trade Commission and judges on bodies like the New Jersey Supreme Court).[63]

Notwithstanding these examples, much more could be done to sensitize current law to the economic concerns that Jewish law addresses. Imagine, for instance, a world where the valuation of bank capital for regulatory purposes is not based simply on self-reported valuation estimates from the banks themselves but rather by appraisal panels comprised at least in part by appraisers in the employ of bank regulatory agencies (these regulatory appraisers being present-day analogs to the nonparty priests who were mandatorily included on valuation panels in ancient times to protect Temple treasury interests). Jewish law's approach to valuation counsels in favor of using a bank capital valuation process whereby countervailing assessments play a role, rather than a process that gives the banks carte blanche to maintain capital reserve levels based on their own self-reported and unopposed valuation figures. Had regulators taken a cue from Jewish law when valuing bank collateral in the past, the financial crisis of 2008 might well have been averted.[64] And if they do so going forward, perhaps the next one will be.

SELECTED BIBLIOGRAPHY

Bible:

Leviticus, ch. 27.

Bonbright, James C. "The Problem of Judicial Valuation." 27 *Columbia Law Review* 493–522 (1927).

Levine, Aaron. *Economics and Jewish Law: Halakhic Perspectives*. Yeshiva University Press, 1987.

Posner, Richard A. *Economic Analysis of Law*, 7th ed. Aspen, 2007.

Sharfman, Keith. "Valuation Averaging: A New Procedure for Resolving Valuation Disputes." 88 *Minnesota Law Review* 357–383 (2003).

Talmud Bavli:

Sanhedrin 2a; 14b–15b.

63 15 U.S.C. § 41 (limiting to three out of five the number of FTC commissioners who may come from the same political party); Deborah T. Poritz, "The New Jersey Supreme Court: A Leadership Court in Individual Rights," *Rutgers Law Review* 60 (2007): 705, 707 (discussing the tradition of partisan balance on the New Jersey Supreme Court).

64 On the failure of bank regulators to value bank capital accurately as a cause of the recent financial crisis, see Richard A. Posner, *A Failure of Capitalism: The Crisis of '08 and the Descent into Depression* (Cambridge, Mass.: Harvard University Press, 2009).

CHAPTER 9

COULD WHAT YOU DON'T KNOW HURT YOU? INFORMATION ASYMMETRY IN LAND MARKETS IN LATE ANTIQUITY*

P.V. (MEYLEKH) VISWANATH AND MICHAEL SZENBERG

Introduction

In the first millennium of the Common Era, the economy of most lands in the Middle East was primarily agricultural. There was a not unimportant export trade in these commodities, and river and ocean transport was sufficiently well-developed to make such trade economically feasible. However, given the cost of transportation, trade occurred primarily in local markets with not insubstantial transactions costs.[1] Examination of evidence regarding these markets could shed light on the impact of transaction costs on trading volume and pricing in modern markets. More important than transactions costs in modern markets, however, are

* We thank Niso Abuaf, Ephraim Kleiman, Daniel Schiffman, and Mark Zitter for helpful comments.

1 See Rosenfeld, Ben-Zion and Joseph Menirav, *Markets and Marketing in Roman Palestine* (Leiden: Brill, 2005) for a thorough study of markets in Roman Palestine.

the costs engendered by information asymmetry. For example, information asymmetry was certainly partially responsible for the recent collapse of mortgage derivatives markets. While agricultural *commodity* markets were probably not characterized by information asymmetry, the market for land probably was. A study of land markets in antiquity could yield lessons for modern markets of financial products, such as IPOs, which are characterized by information asymmetry. On the other hand, consideration of information asymmetry and other economic concepts could shed light on the history of ancient markets, as well.

Description of the Problem and Rashi's Resolution

Jewish legal texts are important sources of information on Middle Eastern economies in the early centuries of the Common Era. In this article, we will focus on the seasonality of land prices, as dealt with in tractate *Bava Kamma* of the Babylonian Talmud. Although the text itself was redacted in Babylonia, it is largely a commentary on the Mishnah, an earlier text redacted in Roman Palestine toward the end of the second century CE.[2] The content and language of the relevant portion of the Talmud indicate that it addresses land located in Palestine, rather than in Babylonia.[3]

The issue of interest for us is found in the tractate *Bava Kamma* on folio 7a–7b. In the course of a discussion, one of the Amoraim[4] says: "In the days of [the month of]

2 The Mishnah is a quasilegal text, based on oral tradition, whose redaction was completed in the second century CE, probably by R. Judah the Prince. It consists of six series of tractates dealing with different subjects. The tractate of relevance to us, BT *Bava Kamma*, is located in the series called *Nezikin*, or "Damages," and deals with various kinds of civil matters, such as agricultural contracts, labor contracts, loan contracts, and so on. BT *Bava Kamma* consists of ten chapters. It deals with damage caused to property and persons and compensation for theft, robbery, and violence. Each chapter of the Mishnah consists of several units, each unit also being called a mishnah (lower case, pl. mishnayot). A Mishnah usually presents a legal ruling that applies to a given situation or a set of related situations.

Jewish law from around the ninth century and onwards is based on two collections of discussions of the Mishnah. Of these, one originates in Babylon and is called the *Talmud Bavli* (Babylonian Talmud); another, originating in Palestine, is called the *Talmud Yerushalmi* (Jerusalem Talmud). Both of these were edited and put in their present form around the sixth century CE. For more details, see Menachem Elon, *Jewish Law: History, Sources, Principles*, vol. 3 (Philadelphia: The Jewish Publication Society, 1994), 1,049 ff.

3 Although the comment regarding the seasonality of land prices is made by an interlocutor in the Babylonian Talmud, it is meant to clarify a *Baraita* (pl. *Baraitot*). *Baraitot* are similar in form and purpose to Mishnayot, but they were not included in the edited collection of Mishnayot. *Baraitot*, which were written in Hebrew (the literary language of Palestine in those days, as opposed to Aramaic, the spoken and literary language of Babylonia), stem from first and second century Palestine. Hebrew may also have been spoken in Palestine in the second century, but this is the subject of an ongoing debate. See David Bivin, *Hebrew as a Spoken Language in First-Century Israel*, 2008, at: http://blog.jerusalemperspective.com/archives/000126.html, viewed December 19, 2008; and Shmuel Safrai, "Spoken and Literary Languages in the Time of Jesus," in *Jesus' Last Week: Jerusalem Studies in the Synoptic Gospels*, vol. 1, ed. R. S. Notley, M. Turnage and B. Becker (Leiden: Brill, 2005).

4 Interlocutors in the Talmud are called Amoraim (sing. Amora), meaning "speaker" in Aramaic. According to Rashi, this Rabbah is Rabbah b. Nahmani (Mesopotamia, c. 270–330 CE), who was head of the academy of Pumbedita in Babylonia.

Nisan, land is dear and in the days of [the month of] Tishrei, land is cheap, and everybody waits until Nisan [to sell]."[5] We see that land prices were higher in Nisan, compared to Tishrei and, furthermore, that the volume of trade in land was higher in Nisan.[6]

R. Solomon b. Isaac (Rashi, France, 1040–1105) explains why prices are higher in the month of Nisan: "Because a purchaser of a field [for cultivation] plows it in the summertime and seeds it in the months of Tishrei and Marheshvan [the first and second months of the Jewish year] . . ." Presumably, Rashi means that land prices are high in Nisan because the fields are ready to be plowed. He adds that "fields are cheaper in the month of Tishrei because there is not enough time at that point to seed them for the coming year." The contemporary Artscroll commentary[7] attributes this to the fact that the field has not been plowed previously, seeming to pick up on Rashi's focus on convenience as the primary determinant of the price.

A Convenience Explanation of Rashi's Resolution

Rashi's explanation for the lower prices of Tishrei is difficult to understand. Why would the landowner not plow it in the summer, whether or not he wanted to sell it? If he wanted to hold on to it, he would, of course, plow it with the intention of seeding it later. If he wanted to sell it in Tishrei, he would still want to plow it in order to get a higher price and also not lose out on an entire growing period! Now, it is of course possible that some individuals would not plow their fields in the summertime, making their fields worth less in Tishrei, but this would not explain why field prices in general would be lower in Tishrei!

It is also significant, as we will see below, that the Talmud considers the lower prices of the months prior to Nisan to be incorrect in some sense. Any explanation of the land price seasonality must explain this as well. In order to proceed further, we

5 The Jewish year consists of twelve months, starting in Tishrei (traditionally around September/October). Nisan is the seventh month and occurs in the springtime. More on this below.

6 While commodity markets, particularly those of perishable commodities, are often seasonal, asset markets are usually not. There may be examples of seasonal asset markets, however. For example, initial public offering (IPO) markets are characterized by dramatic swings in price and volume. The literature (R. Ibbotson and J. Jaffe, "Hot Issue Markets," *Journal of Finance* 30 [1975]: 1,027–42; and J. Ritter, "The Hot Issue Market of 1980," *Journal of Business* 57 [1984]: 215–40) talks of "hot and cold" IPO markets. Jean Helwege and Nellie Liang, "Initial Public Offerings in Hot and Cold Markets," *Journal of Financial and Quantitative Analysis* 39,3 (2004): 541–69 describe their characteristics thus:

> Hot IPO markets have been described as having an unusually high volume of offerings, severe underpricing, frequent oversubscription of offerings, and (at times) concentrations in particular industries. In contrast, cold IPO markets have much lower issuance, less underpricing, and fewer instances of oversubscription.

In that case, as well, there is discussion as to whether the price swings are due to irrationality or to fundamental factors.

7 Schottenstein Edition of the Talmud, Tractate *Bava Kamma* (New York: Artscroll/Mesorah Publications, 2001).

need to understand the context of the Talmud's discussion. The issue at hand is the question of when a person is considered to be entitled to the poor tithe or, in other words, when a person is considered poor.[8] A person with possessions worth two hundred *zuzim*[9] or more is not considered poor.[10] The Amora Abbayei[11] (Babylonia, b. end of third century) raises the unusual case of a person entitled to the poor tithe, but only to a limited extent. This is in contradistinction to an ordinary indigent, who does not have such a limit. Abbayei states that "an owner of houses, fields and vineyards who cannot find a purchaser [is considered needy and] may be given the tithe for the poor up to half the value of his estate."[12] The Talmud asks how such a "fence-straddling" case can exist—either the person is an indigent (he has wealth below two hundred *zuzim*) or he is not! Rabbah[13] clarifies that the person in question has land that would be worth two hundred *zuzim* in Nisan. However, right now (prior to Nisan), the land is worth less, and he could therefore be considered poor. This uncertainty regarding his wealth is sufficient to give him an intermediate status. In other words, the price before Nisan is somehow not a "correct" one to use in valuing the field.

Rashi's "convenience" explanation for why the price in Nisan is higher does not allow us to treat the pre-Nisan price as an incorrect price. Furthermore, for the reasons explained earlier, it is hard to see how his comment regarding the summertime as plowing season explains the general price level for land in Tishrei, even with Artscroll's augmentation.

A "Dividend" Explanation of Rashi's Resolution

Perhaps Rashi means simply that, because the harvest will not be available until the months of Nisan and Iyyar[14] (the next month), we can consider the pre-Nisan price as its "cum-dividend" price, while the post-harvest price is its ex-dividend price (in analogy with the price of a share of stock). Clearly, the "ex-dividend" price would

8 See Deuteronomy 14:28–29.

9 A *zuz* (pl. *zuzim*) was equivalent to a Roman coin, the silver denarium.

10 We know this from the Mishnah in Tractate *Pe'ah*. One who has two hundred *zuzim* may not take from *shikhhah*, *leket*, *pe'ah*, or the poor tithe. *Shikhhah*, *leket*, and *pe'ah* are three different entitlements that poor people had for their own sustenance.

11 Abbaye was a Babylonian Amora, who was born toward the end of the third century CE and taught at Pumbedita. He was a student of his uncle, Rabbah b. Nahmani.

12 Translation from the Soncino edition of the Talmud: http://www.come-and-hear.com/babakamma/babakamma_7.html, viewed March 5, 2009.

13 According to Rashi. This assumption is reasonable, since Rabbah was the teacher of Abbayei, who introduces the initial case of the indigent landowner. The text itself does not name the interlocutor, referring to him simply as *mar*, which means something akin to "sir."

14 Michael Morrison, "Harvest Seasons of Ancient Israel," at: http://www.wcg.org/lit/law/festivals/harvest.htm, viewed December 12, 2008. He uses information from Oded Borowski, *Agriculture in Iron Age Israel* (Winona Lake, IN: Eisenbrauns, 1987), 37. Reprinted with updated bibliography (Boston, MA: American Schools of Oriental Research, 2002).

Table 9.1 Harvesting and ingathering, based on modern agricultural practices in Israel

	March	Apr.	May	June	July	Aug.	Sept.	Oct.	Nov.
Wheat			X						
Barley		X							
Oats			X						
Peas		X	X						
Chick-peas				X					
Lentils		X	X						
Vetch		X	X						
Sesame					X				
Flax					X				
Millet					X	X			
Grapes				X	X	X	X		
Figs						X	X		
Pome-grantes						X	X		
Olives							X	X	X

be lower than the "cum-dividend" price, and the price of the field would, on average, increase over time until the harvest.

While this would explain why the price of a field would peak around Nisan, why would it be lowest in Tishrei? One possibility is that, while the barley harvest occurs in the beginning of Nisan and the wheat harvest occurs toward the end of Iyyar, agricultural land could still be used for other crops, or fruits, which were not harvested until the beginning of Tishrei. Such crops include sesame, flax millet, and fruits such as grapes, pomegranates, figs, and olives. (See table 9.1.)[15] While not all land could be, or was, used for grains as well as fruit, we do have evidence that at least some fields cultivated for grains also had fruit trees planted in them.[16] In any case, Rabbah might have been talking about the overall price for land, and, since some harvests would still not be completed until the beginning of Tishrei, the price of agricultural land, in general, would not reach its nadir until then.

Of course, this is not exactly Rashi's answer, but at least it is consistent with Rabbah's statement, and it does draw on some elements of Rashi's answer. However, this approach does not resolve the issue in an entirely satisfactory manner, since it implies

15 See chap. four in Borowski, *Agriculture in Iron Age Israel*. The table shown here is from page 37 of the 1987 edition.

16 This is evident from the existence of an entire tractate (*Kil'ayim*) dealing with prohibited and permitted cases of raising different kinds of grains and fruit side by side. For example, Mishnah nine in chapter four of the tractate *Kil'ayim* begins: "If one plants two rows [of vines] and there is not between them [at least] eight *amot*, he may not introduce seed there." And again in Mishnah four of chapter six of the same tractate: "One who suspends vines above part of a fruit tree, he is permitted to introduce seed under the other [parts of the tree]." (See http://kodesh.snunit.k12.il/b/h/h14.htm for Hebrew text.)

that the lower price prior to Nisan is an entirely reasonable and correct price. The price of a field is the price of the land plus the crops on it, and ripened crops ready for harvest are more valuable than crops that are not yet ready for harvest! Furthermore, it's entirely reasonable that land with crops on it should sell for more than land without crops! If this is the case, why should the Nisan price be considered more "correct"? Furthermore, why should the volume of trade be higher in Nisan?

Information Asymmetry as an Explanation

We suggest that the answer has to do with information asymmetry regarding the value of agricultural land.[17,18] The quality of unsown land is doubtful. The owner might well have information about the yields of past harvests, but the intending purchaser has much less information. At harvest time, on the other hand, the information regarding the productivity of the field is readily available and visible, and the field's productivity can also be compared to that of other fields in the area. Hence a better public estimate of the "true" value of the field is available in Nisan than before. Prior to Nisan, market prices would be depressed because they would have to factor in the uncertainty; the same reason would inhibit trading.[19] Furthermore, given the fact that the uncertainty is endogenous, and not exogenous, land market liquidity would be further affected. Prices, therefore, could be characterized as being "abnormally" low before Nisan. It thus makes sense to refer to the higher Nisan price as the "true" price.[20] This explains why land prices are higher in Nisan, but we still have to

17 Sandy Bond, "Do Market Perceptions Affect Market Prices? A Case Study of a Remediated Contaminated Site" in Ko Wang and Marvin L. Wolverton (eds.), *Real Estate Valuation Theory* (New York: Springer, 2002) briefly discusses the impact of uncertainty on land valuation. Tzu-Chin Lin and Stephen D. Roach, "The Materialization of Protection of Property Rights through Just Compensation—Experiences from Taiwan and California," Working Paper presented at the Pan Pacific Congress of Real Estate Appraisers, Valuers and Counselors, at: http://www.property.org.nz/AM/pdfs/Pan%20Pacific%20Conference%202008/The%20Materialisation%20of%20Protection%20of%20Property%20Rights%20through%20Just%20Compensation%20-%20 Tzu-Chin%20Lin,%20Stephen%20D.%20Roach.pdf, viewed on March 4, 2009 consider information asymmetry between land owners and the government in the valuation of government-expropriated land.

18 A medieval commentary known as Tosafot comments ad loc. that the prices of houses also exhibited the same seasonality in prices as fields. The answer it gives is that demand for rental houses peaked in Nisan and hence house prices also peaked in Nisan. Tosafot notes that this explanation is not consistent with Rashi's explanation for the seasonality of field prices. However, in an agrarian economy, prices of many consumption goods were probably correlated with prices of agricultural commodities and land, and hence house rental demands may also have peaked in Nisan along with land prices.

Whether, in fact, house prices exhibited seasonality or not is not known; how Tosafot came by this information is not clear.

19 See Keith Brown and Seha Tinic, "Risk Aversion, Uncertain Information, and Market Efficiency," *Journal of Financial Economics* 22 (1980): 355–85 for evidence that prices are depressed during periods of heightened uncertainty.

20 Of course this does not mean that prices would always be higher in Nisan. If the harvest turned out to be bad, the price of land would probably be lower if only because the value of the crop on the land would be low. However, to the extent that the bad harvest implied future bad harvests, the asset value of the land (i.e., the present value of future crops) would be low, as well.

explain why land prices would be lower in Tishrei. Furthermore, what evidence do we have that the harvests occurred in the month of Nisan? Let us look at the evidence a bit more closely.

In Nisan, as we will see, the barley harvest was undertaken and the *omer* offering brought on the second day of Passover. In Leviticus 23:5, we read: "The afternoon of the 14th day of the first month is [the time that you must sacrifice] God's Passover offering." Verse 10 states: "When you come to the land that I am going to give you, and you reap its harvest, you must bring an *omer* of your first reaping to the priest." Josephus (Roman Palestine, 37—c. 100 CE) discusses the procedure and specifies that it is a barley offering:

> On the second day of unleavened bread, that is to say the sixteenth, our people partake of the crops which they have reaped and which have not been touched till then, and esteeming it right first to do homage to God, to whom they owe the abundance of these gifts, they offer to him the first-fruits of the barley in the following way. After parching and crushing the little sheaf of ears and purifying the barley for grinding, they bring to the altar an *issaron*[21] for God, and, having flung a handful thereof on the altar, they leave the rest for the use of the priests. Thereafter all are permitted, publicly or individually, to begin harvest.[22]

At this point, the grain is already standing in the fields, as the verses indicate: "For six [additional] days you shall then eat unleavened bread, with the seventh day as a retreat dedicated to God your Lord, when you may not do any work. Then count seven weeks for yourself. From the time that you first put the sickle to the standing grain, you must count seven weeks."[23] Clearly, at the time of the *omer* offering on the sixteenth of Nisan, the barley crop is standing and visible. There is very little information asymmetry or uncertainty at this point. However, the wheat harvest does not happen until a month later. Since wheat is probably a more important crop than barley,[24] we would expect uncertainty to be lowest at the time of the wheat harvest, toward Iyyar, and not Nisan. Perhaps Rabbah uses Nisan and Tishrei to describe the high and low points because they correspond with two important months in the Jewish calendar—Nisan is the time of Passover and Tishrei is the time of *Rosh ha-Shanah*, the Jewish New Year.[25] Furthermore, prices probably start to peak in Nisan, when complete information about the barley crop and fairly complete information about the wheat crop is available.

21 An *issaron* is a measure that is generally identified as a tenth of an *eifah*. See Exodus 16:36 and William N. Bates, "Archaeological Discussions," *American Journal of Archaeology* 17,4 (1913): 521–68.

22 Josephus, Antiquities 3.250–51, in *Josephus IV Jewish Antiquities Books I-IV*, Loeb Classical Library, (Cambridge: Harvard University Press, 1930), 437–39.

23 Deuteronomy 16:9,10. Translation from: http://bible.ort.org.

24 Wheat is mentioned first before barley in the list of Israelite produce in Deuteronomy 8:8. See Ze'ev Safrai, *The Economy of Roman Palestine* (London: Routledge Press, 1994), 63 for extensive discussion on the importance of wheat relative to barley.

25 Nisan and Tishrei are also the two candidate months accepted in Jewish tradition for the date of Creation. This is first mentioned in the *Seder Olam Rabbah*, which was written in Palestine toward the end of the second century CE.

Table 9.2 Translation of Gezer Calendar Text

1	two months of ingathering (olives) / two months
2	of sowing (cereals)/ two months of late sowing (legumes and vegetables)
3	a month of hoeing weeds (for hay)
4	a month of harvesting barley
5	a month of harvesting (wheat) and measuring (grain)
6	two months of grape harvesting
7	a month of ingathering summer fruit

Table 9.3 Activities over the Agricultural Year According to the Gezer Calendar

Time Period	Activity
Late October to late December	Sowing of cereals (presumably primarily wheat and barley)
Late December to late February	Sowing of legumes
March	Weeding
Passover	Beginning of the harvesting of barley
Spring Equinox to late April	Harvesting of Barley
Late April to late May	Harvesting of Wheat
June and July	Harvesting of Grapes
Late July to late August	Harvesting of other summer fruit
Late August to late October	Harvesting of Olives
Feast of Tabernacles (*Sukkot*)	End of the harvesting season

Aside from the Bible, an important source of information about the agricultural calendar is the Gezer calendar, an inscribed limestone palette discovered in Israel in the early 1900s. The calendar consists of seven lines, outlining eight agricultural chores, and is written in a Northern Israelite dialect. While there is some dispute as to the meaning of the lines, Borowski[26] gives the translation shown in table 9.2. According to him, this corresponds to the activities in table 9.3.

According to this, there were different harvests from Passover until the Feast of Tabernacles, and from the Feast of Tabernacles until Passover, there were no harvests. Thus, late October would be the farthest from the next harvest, and hence the point in time when uncertainty regarding the value of the land would be highest. Although there were fruit harvests after Nisan that continued until late August, they do not seem to have been as important as the grain harvests of the spring and early summer.[27]

26 Borowski, op. cit., 38.

27 In terms of dietary calories, the spring grain harvest was most important. Borowski (1987, op. cit., 57) calls barley and wheat "the main food staple of the ancient Israelite." According to E. P. Sanders, *Judaism: Practice and Belief, 63 BCE–66 CE* (London: SCM; Philadelphia: Trinity Press International, 1992), "Grain constituted over fifty percent of the average person's total caloric intake, followed by legumes (e.g. lentils), olive oil, and fruit, especially dried figs."

Now, if we assume that Tishrei was when the season of ingathering ended and the time for sowing was about to begin, we can explain why prices were lowest at that time. However, in the Jewish calendar of Roman Palestine and Babylonia of late antiquity, late October probably corresponds to a late Tishrei, and maybe even early Marheshvan.[28] Of course, the Gezer calendar refers to late tenth century BCE,[29] and to a location that Borowski identifies as essentially Lod-Ramla, so a difference of a month may not be crucial.[30] On the other hand, modern olive harvesting takes place in Lod-Ramla between mid-September and mid-October,[31] which coincides with the timing given by Borowski. Once again, we might use the same explanation given above as to why Rabbah used the months of Nisan and Tishrei in his explanation, when Iyar and Marheshvan would have been more appropriate. All things considered, the correlation between the seasons and the pattern of land prices is well-explained by information asymmetry.

This interpretation also explains why the volume of trade in land would be lower pre-Nisan and higher post-Nisan. Resolution of the uncertainty and reduction of the information asymmetry would clearly increase incentives to trade.

Although the above discussion has assumed that the information asymmetry is about the value of the land, it may also be about the current crop. As mentioned before, the field could be thought of as a portfolio consisting of the land and the crop that is growing on it. As the stalks grow and the kernels ripen, the quality of the resulting grain becomes more evident. Furthermore, the farmer may have information regarding the quality of the grain that is not immediately apparent by looking at the stalks long before harvest.

Another possibility is that prices of all goods and assets in an economy move together. More money is available at harvest time because produce can be sold at that time.[32] Hence, demand for all goods and assets are greater at that time, leading to higher prices for assets such as fields and houses. While this simple explanation accounts for seasonality in prices and volume, it fails to explain why a lower pre-Nisan price should not be used to estimate a person's wealth. It is possible, though, that the reason for land price and volume seasonality is a combination of all the theories—the funds-availability theory, the convenience and dividend explanations of Rashi, and the uncertainty/information asymmetry hypothesis.

28 This is also consistent with the testimony of Rashi (see above).

29 According to Borowski (1987, op. cit., 32), the date of the inscription has been established from paleographic and orthographic evidence as c. 925 BCE.

30 Borowski, op. cit., 34.

31 Based on information provided in S. Talmon, "Divergences in Calendar-Reckoning in Ephraim and Judah," *Vetus Testamentum* 8 (1958): 48–74.

32 This explanation was suggested by Niso Abuaf in a private conversation.

How Reasonable is the Supposition of Information Asymmetry?

It may be argued that information asymmetry is a reasonable assumption in a firm, where the activities of the managers are not easily observable. It might even be reasonable in the case of land with multiple uses. However, land in Roman Palestine was used almost entirely for agriculture. Furthermore, land was probably unfenced, and work took place in the open. How could there be any element of information asymmetry in such an environment? Indeed, most of the activities involved in cultivating a field are observable, as one of us argued in an earlier work,[33] based on evidence from the Mishnah.[34] Several Mishnayot describe the terms of a rental contract of a field:

> Mishnah 1:
>
> In the case of one who rents a field from his fellow man [he is bound by the following conditions]. In places where it is the custom to harvest with a scythe, he must so harvest. In places where it is the custom to pull up the roots while harvesting, he must so harvest. In places where it is the custom to plough the field after the harvest, he must do so. Everything follows the custom of the land.[35]
>
> Mishnah 4:
>
> In the case of one who rents a field from his fellow man in return for a fixed amount of grain, and does not want to weed. If he says [to the owner], "What does it matter to you, since I have agreed to pay you a fixed amount?," we do not listen to him [the tenant], since he [the owner] can say, "Tomorrow, you will leave this field and it will be covered with weeds!"
>
> Mishnah 5:
>
> One who rents a field from his fellow man, and the field does not yield much of a harvest; if there is enough of the crop to gather a sheaf's worth, he is obliged to attend to it. R. Judah says, "Why set the limit at a sheaf's worth? Rather, if there is as much grain as the amount of seed that he sowed."
>
> Mishnah 8:
>
> One who rents a field from his fellow man in order to plant it with barley, he may not plant it with wheat; [if he rents it in order to plant it with] wheat, he may plant it with barley. R. Simeon b. Gamaliel prohibits it. [If he rents it to plant it with] grain, he may not plant it with beans; [if he rents it in order to plant it with] beans, he may plant it with grain. R. Simeon b. Gamaliel prohibits it.

We see that cultivation involves several activities likely to affect the value of the land, making them relevant conditions in a rental contract. These activities include the method of harvesting, whether or not to weed, what crops to grow there, and to what extent the land lies fallow. A field-owner in a contractual relationship with a

33 P. V. Viswanath, "Risk Sharing, Diversification and Moral Hazard in Roman Palestine: Evidence from Agricultural Contract Law," *The International Review of Law and Economics* 20 (November 2000): 353–69.

34 BT *Bava Metsi'a*, chap. 9.

35 Mishnah 1 continues with a discussion of other situations where custom affects the conditions of rental, but they are not relevant for our purposes.

renter would certainly observe the renter to make sure he complies with the contract. However, the market price of a plot of land is determined by the price that potential buyers are willing to pay. Some of those buyers may have kept a close watch on the seller, gathering information on his farming practices and their impact on the land's value. However, there is no reason to assume that all buyers were sufficiently farsighted to collect such information. In antiquity, there was no "field-rating service," akin to Moody's or Standard and Poor's. Although a neighbor might have this information, it would not be available to all potential buyers. Furthermore, direct observation of the field probably yielded better information on future harvests than second-hand information obtained from neighbors.

The potential market for land was not far-flung, but neither was it tremendously circumscribed. This allows us to assume that not all potential buyers were well-informed about the land. This is supported by the Talmud's requirement that a guardian (*apotrops*) of an orphan's land must advertise for at least thirty days prior to the sale, in order to ensure that the orphans get the highest price possible. As the Mishnah in *Arakhin* states: "Appraisement of orphans' lands is thirty days; that of consecrated things is sixty days, and they cry it out every morning and evening."[36] R. Obadiah Bertinoro (Italy, fifteenth century) explains:

> The judges that go down to the estate of the orphans to sell it for debt appraise it, and cry out for buyers on thirty continuous days. [They do so] day after day: in the morning, when workmen go out to the fields, so that any prospective buyer may direct his employees to look at the field and report. And in the evening, when the workmen come back, so that he who hears the announcement may be reminded of the business in view and obtain the necessary information.[37]

This suggests that the geographical spread of the market was wide enough to benefit from an announcement period as long as an entire month. Furthermore, another Mishnah indicates that there was considerable uncertainty regarding the correct price of land:

> On an appraisement by the judges, when they have gone too low by a sixth, or too high by a sixth, the sale is void [meaning, voidable]. R. Simeon b. Gamaliel says the sale stands—otherwise, wherein lies the power of a court of justice? But if they have made a letter of examination[38] between them—even should they have sold what is worth a *maneh* for two hundred *zuz*, or what is worth two hundred for a *maneh*—the sale stands.

This implies considerable uncertainty as to how to correctly value land, as much as sixteen or twenty percent of the true price.[39] Of course, we have no evidence

36 BT*Arakhin* 6:1. Translation from the Jewish Encyclopedia: http://www.jewishencyclopedia.com/view.jsp?letter=A&artid=1668, viewed March 5, 2009.

37 Translation from the Jewish Encyclopedia: http://www.jewishencyclopedia.com/view.jsp?letter=A&artid=1668#4936, viewed March 6, 2009.

38 The letter of examination, or *iggeret bikkoret*, is a written public notice, synonymous with *hakhrazah*, or advertisement. (Explanation from the Jewish Encyclopedia, op. cit.)

39 If the estimated price was one hundred *zuzim* and the allowable error was 16.66% of that, then the error would be 20% (overestimate) of the true price or 14.29% (underestimate). In point of fact, the Talmud records a disagreement as to whether the allowable error is one-sixth of the estimated price or of the true price. In any case, the error is economically significant.

as to the actual size of errors, only that the law provided for errors of up to twenty percent.

Conclusion

We have explored two approaches to Rashi's explanation of seasonal price and trading volume fluctuations in land markets of Roman Palestine. Neither explanation seems tenable. We suggest that land price fluctuations were due to information asymmetry and uncertainty about the value of land and its crops. Indeed, several sources indicate that information asymmetry was prevalent in ancient land markets.

The evidence of the Talmud, under our hypothesis, indicates that information asymmetry can considerably depress the prices of assets and affect the liquidity of markets. This indicates the importance of attempts to reduce information asymmetry. Future work on market frictions in antiquity might consider other examples of information asymmetry in the agricultural economies discussed in the Babylonian and Jerusalem Talmuds.

SELECTED BIBLIOGRAPHY

Borowski, Oded. *Agriculture in Iron Age Israel.* Winona Lake, IN: Eisenbrauns,1987.

———. *Daily Life in Biblical Times.* Leiden: Brill, 2003.

Elon, Menachem. *Jewish Law: History, Sources, Principles.* 4 vols. Philadelphia, Pa: The Jewish Publication Society, 1994.

Rosenfeld, Ben-Zion., and Joseph Menirav. *Markets and Marketing in Roman Palestine.* Leiden: Brill, 2005.

Safrai, Shmuel. "Spoken and Literary Languages in the Time of Jesus." In R. S. Notley, M. Turnage, and B. Becker (eds.), *Jesus' Last Week: Jerusalem Studies in the Synoptic Gospels, vol. 1.* Leiden: Brill, 2005.

Sanders, E. P. *Judaism: Practice and Belief, 63 BCE–66 CE.* Philadelphia: Trinity Press International, 1992.

Talmon, S. "Divergences in calendar-reckoning in Ephraim and Judah," *Vetus Testamentum* 8 (1958): 48–74.

Viswanath, P. V. "Risk Sharing, Diversification and Moral Hazard in Roman Palestine: Evidence from Agricultural Contract Law." *The International Review of Law and Economics* 20 (November 2000): 353–69.

PART III

JEWISH LAW, ETHICS, AND THE MODERN SOCIETY

CHAPTER 10

HETTER ISKA, THE PERMISSIBLE VENTURE: A DEVICE TO AVOID THE PROHIBITION AGAINST INTEREST-BEARING LOANS

J. DAVID BLEICH

The Problem

Biblical law forbids exaction of interest by a creditor and payment of interest by a debtor in loans between Jews. The underlying considerations are twofold in nature: (a) the obligation to perform charitable deeds includes a responsibility to help the indigent by means of noninterest-bearing provident loans, and (b) interest accepted in return for extending a loan involving neither risk of capital nor personal service is perceived as a form of unjust enrichment.

Although in biblical days the economic structure of society was predominantly agrarian and loans were sought primarily for personal purposes, the strictures against usury apply with equal force to loans extended for commercial purposes. During the Middle Ages, Jews, particularly when they were forbidden to own land, turned to commercial pursuits. Frequently, they became merchants engaged in the buying and selling of goods and produce. Such pursuits required capital investment of sums that few individual Jews possessed. Loans were generally not available unless they were also of financial benefit to the lender. Since interest was not permitted, ways and means had to be found to facilitate commercial endeavors without violation of either the letter or the spirit of Jewish law.

The earliest attempt to overcome this difficulty was that of the sixteenth-century Polish scholar known as R. Mendel Avigdors of Cracow, who composed the earliest version of the *hetter iska*. The *hetter iska* is a document that specifies the terms and conditions under which money is advanced by one individual to another. Its legal purpose is to create a partnership arrangement as distinct from a debtor-creditor relationship.

The issue with which rabbinic thinkers were forced to grapple was the propriety of seizing upon lacunae in the law and fashioning contrivances in order to circumvent the violation. A subterfuge may avoid technical violation of the law but nevertheless thwart the spirit of the law.

Virtually every system of law employs legal fictions for reasons of expediency. A corporation is a legal person and is accorded such status in order to achieve perfectly cogent and moral results. Such "myths" are essentially definitional. The law determines how it wishes to treat certain arrangements and coins a term for use as a type of verbal shorthand in referring to such arrangements. At times, the law, particularly in areas of taxation, provides for options. Determination by a businessman of the beginning and end of his fiscal year is an obvious but relatively trivial example. In such matters, as Judge Learned Hand famously remarked, "Anyone may arrange his affairs so that his taxes shall be as low as possible. . . . Over and over again the Courts have said that there is nothing sinister in so arranging affairs as to keep taxes as low as possible." An individual acting in such a manner is not guilty of moral turpitude.[1]

Jewish law is quite familiar with arrangements designed to avoid the onus of applying the full force of the law. In rabbinic literature there is a term for such an arrangement; it is known as a *ha'aramah*, a term that probably may best be translated literally as "a cleverness." The term "device" probably best captures the flavor of the term without connotation of a moral judgment. Such devices fall into three distinct categories: (a) those that are disdained as inconsistent with the spirit of the law; (b) those that, for one reason or another, are regarded as commendable and actively encouraged; and (c) those with regard to which there is an attitude of complete neutrality.

Perhaps the earliest example of a *ha'aramah* involves regulations pertaining to tithing. Talmudic exegesis establishes that biblical law requires tithing only of produce brought into an abode through the gates of the courtyard. The Gemara, *Berakhot* 35b, bemoans the fact that, "while earlier generations were wont to bring in their produce by way of the front door in order to make it liable to tithing, later generations bring in [the produce] by way of roofs, yards, or enclosures in order to exempt [the produce] from tithing." Clearly, that statement reflects a negative attitude toward the moral legitimacy of the "later generations" who avail themselves of

1 In the case of *Gregory* v. *Helvering* 69 F.2d 809, 810 (2d Cir. 1934), aff'd, 293 U.S. 465, 55 S. Ct. 266, 79 L.Ed. 596 (1935).

such expedients. Indeed, according to some early day authorities, the subterfuge in question was formally banned by rabbinic law.

The reason for the negative view vis-á-vis utilization of such expedients is self-evident. The purpose of the tithe was to provide a livelihood for the Levites who were required to serve in the Temple and who constituted a leisure class charged with providing religious instruction on behalf of the entire populace. Were tithes not to be forthcoming, the Levites would have been compelled to seek employment as artisans or laborers, thereby making it impossible for them to discharge their sacred mission. The spirit of the law would certainly have been thwarted. Thus, this is an example of a disdained *ha'aramah*.

The second category includes devices that are designed actively to promote conformity with the manifold provisions of law. The first-born male offspring of a cow or a sheep belonging to a Jew is sanctified from birth to be brought to the Temple as a sacrificial offering. With the destruction of the Temple, sacrifices are no longer feasible. However, the sanctity of the first-born animal is in no way mitigated. The animal may not be used as a beast of burden; it is forbidden to drink its milk or use its wool. The animal is literally a "sacred cow" that roams virtually at will—as is the case even today in some Hindu communities with regard to animals they regard as sacred—until the animal develops a blemish rendering it unfit as a sacrifice. Unless and until that occurs the animal is a halakhic nuisance in the sense that it is of no benefit to either God or man but poses an ongoing potential for inadvertent sin, "a tort waiting to happen."

The sole remedy is to prevent the animal from achieving sanctified status by transferring ownership of the pregnant animal to a non-Jew before it gives birth. Subsequent to parturition both animals may be reconveyed to the original Jewish owner. Commandments regarding the first-born commemorate the sparing of Jewish first-born in Egypt while the first-born of the Egyptians perished in the last of the ten plagues. Hence, the first-born of an animal belonging to a non-Jew is not sanctified.[2]

No one has ever suggested that it is improper to seek such transfer of title on the grounds that it is a subterfuge designed to frustrate the purpose of the law. Such circumvention of the law represents an instance in which fulfillment of the underlying purpose has become impossible (i.e., the animal cannot be brought as a sacrificial offering because the Temple no longer stands). Despite that factor, the law is not a dead letter; the restrictions governing sanctified animals remain in full force and effect. The only way to avoid transgression and violation of both the letter and spirit of the law lies in obviating its provisions by causing title to become vested in

2 The transfer of ownership, however, must be carried out in accordance with the provisions of Jewish law. Such transfer entails a formal act of *kinyan*, or conveyance. Rules regarding *kinyan* are quite complex. Modes of *kinyan* for transfer of chattel between a Jew and a non-Jew differ from the modes of *kinyan* governing transfer of title between a Jew and a fellow Jew. As a result, one can open virtually any volume of 18th- or 19th-century *responsa* and find a discussion of at least one case in which the efficacy of an act of transfer performed in such a situation is questioned. Those discussions invariably focus upon technicalities, not upon the propriety of the procedure itself.

a non-Jew. That is so even if the calf or lamb and its mother are both subsequently repurchased from the non-Jew. Under such circumstances, employment of a "device" to accomplish that end is worthy of approbation.

The final category is best exemplified by the practice of selling *hamets* (i.e., food products not suitable for consumption during Passover) to a non-Jew. The sale is effected before the advent of the holiday and, typically, the same foodstuffs are repurchased from the non-Jew upon conclusion of the holiday. To some, the transaction has the appearance of a charade since the parties are fully aware ab initio that the effect of the sale will be rescinded at the earliest permissible opportunity.

In point of fact, this arrangement is entirely innocuous. Scripture forbids a Jew to retain any economic interest in *hamets* during the course of the Passover week. A Jew in possession of such foodstuffs on the eve of Passover may avoid the onus of transgression in one of three ways: (a) He may consume such foods in their entirety, a feat beyond human capability if the quantity is gargantuan or inadvisable in the extreme in the case of a copious quantity of alcoholic beverages made from grain; (b) he may totally destroy such items by burning or the like, a procedure that may prove to be cumbersome and is wasteful but, nevertheless, entirely permissible; or (c) he may transfer title to a non-Jew who, since the 613 biblical commandments are binding only upon Jews, is in no way subject to the prohibition. Jewish law does not accord preference to any one of these options over the others. Accordingly, the expedient of sale to a non-Jew is regarded as both halakhically and morally neutral; it is neither encouraged nor discouraged. Choice of that option is generally dictated by considerations of practicality and conservation of wealth. There are no restrictions upon acquiring *hamets* after the holiday, even *hamets* owned by a Jew before Passover, provided that the sale to a non-Jew prior to the advent of the holiday has been properly consummated.[3]

To the extent that there are intimations of criticism in rabbinic literature regarding such sales, the concern is entirely with regard to legal niceties.[4] Proper modes of formal conveyance, or *kinyan*, must be employed in transferring title. More significantly, there can be no valid transfer without a meeting of minds. Both parties must grasp the final and irrevocable nature of the transaction. Neither party may regard it is a pro forma ritual or liturgical act devoid of actionable effect. Small wonder, then, that rabbinic eyebrows were raised on occasion, particularly when the purchaser was an untutored and legally unsophisticated peasant.

In the modern world, loans occur in situations varied and sundry. In antiquity, loans were almost always provident in nature. A farmer's crop failed and as a result he was forced to resort to a loan in order to purchase seed for planting the next year's crop. A person became temporarily incapacitated and was reduced to seeking

3 See R. Moses Sofer, *Teshuvot Hatam Sofer, Orah Hayyim*, no. 102. See also R. Solomon Joseph Zevin, *Ha-Mo'adim be-Halakhah*, 7th ed. (Tel Aviv, 1960), pp. 245–255.

4 Cf., A variant reading of the Tosefta, *Pesahim* 1:6, cited and dismissed by *Bet Yosef, Orah Hayyim* 448. The objection of R. Alexander Schorr, *Tevu'ot Shor, Pesahim* 21a, was limited to selling animals for the purpose of feeding them *hamets* during the course of the holiday. That objection was emphatically dismissed by a plethora of rabbinic scholars. See *Ha-Mo'adim be-Halakhah*, p. 250 and p. 250, note 22.

a loan to put bread on the table. A loan of that nature is described by Scripture as an act of charity "that your brother may live with you" (Leviticus 25:36). Charity assumes many guises. A loan represents a higher form of charity than a gift because the impoverished recipient receives full benefit of the funds advanced without being deprived of dignity. Such loans represent fulfillment of a divine command for which a person dare not demand compensation at the hands of his fellow. Moreover, unlike the majority of commandments with regard to which Scripture does not reveal the underlying rationale, in promulgating the requirement that a loan be interest-free, Scripture is quite explicit with regard to the reasoning: The borrower is in need of funds to sustain himself. The Bible regards profiting from human misery as ignominious; to demand interest is to compound the plight of an already destitute person. In earlier centuries, the Church regarded the taking of interest to be prohibited by natural law; the odiousness of interest-taking was not based upon dogmatic revelation but was regarded as readily apprehensible by the unaided light of moral reason.

In antiquity, all loans were provident in nature. At some point in human history society found it expeditious to rely upon middlemen to transfer commodities from producer to consumer. Tradesmen require at least a modest amount of capital in order to function in that capacity. Only with the advent of the industrial revolution and the construction of factories for the production of consumer goods did the need for vast amounts of capital arise; only in the modern era does capital represent the most prevalent form of generating more capital.

A person is under divine command to come to the assistance of his fellow who is in need. However, he is under no obligation to assist his fellow in amassing wealth. The rationale underlying the prohibition against interest-taking is alleviation of human misery. Yet the law acquires a life of its own. In general, Jewish law regards implementation of the law to be independent of the ends the law is designed to promote. That is the case even when those ends have been revealed to man. For that reason, in the Jewish legal system, policy considerations do not figure prominently in judicial decision making. Hence, the prohibition against giving or taking interest is fully applicable, not only in situations in which societal goals are not advanced thereby, but even in situations in which societal goals may actually be thwarted.

A device that would enable a lender to reap profit from a provident loan would certainly offend the spirit of the law. But a device that restructures the transaction and renders it an investment makes it possible for the individual providing the financing to participate in the profits generated by the investment. Properly crafted so that it does not violate technical strictures, such a device is morally neutral when used in the context of a commercial enterprise.

Many such "devices," although entirely permissible under biblical law, were interdicted by rabbinic decree. Those restrictions were instituted either as a means of constructing a "fence" around the biblical law because of fear that if a particular legitimate practice were to be sanctioned it would rapidly result in other practices violative of biblical law or because the arrangement might be regarded as interest-taking in the eye of an unsophisticated beholder. Practices that have come to be known as Islamic banking include a variety of devices forbidden to Jews by rabbinic decree rather than by biblical law. A repurchase agreement is a case in point: Instead of lending money at interest, a "lender" sells a piece of property and agrees to repurchase it at a specified future date for a higher sum. The transaction is formally structured as a sale coupled with a repurchase agreement but is actually a subterfuge. The funds advanced for the "purchase" of the parcel of real property are really a disguised loan since recovery is guaranteed. The "seller's" sole motivation is use of the funds in the interim; the "purchaser's" sole motivation is the interest he receives in the form of an enhanced repurchase price.

The primary device recognized by Jewish law as an acceptable means of avoiding the prohibition against extending or receiving an interest-bearing loan is known as a *hetter iska*, or "permissible venture."[5] Its function is to substitute some form of profit-sharing representing a return on invested funds for what would otherwise have been structured as an interest-bearing loan.

Promissory Loans

The formula of the original *hetter iska* was based upon a ruling recorded in *Shulhan Arukh, Yoreh De'ah* 167:1, which provides that funds may be advanced on the condition that the recipient use the funds to buy and sell merchandise on behalf of the person advancing the funds until such time as a stipulated profit has been earned; profit over and above that amount then accrues without limit to the recipient. The sum advanced in this manner is termed "half loan, half deposit" in rabbinic literature. During the initial period, the recipient acts solely as a commercial agent on behalf of the principal who advanced the funds; only after the originally stipulated profit has been earned does the deposit revert to the status of a loan and the recipient, who was heretofore considered a bailee, becomes a debtor. Subsequently, no

5 R. Baruch ha-Levi Epstein, *Torah Temimah*, Leviticus 25:36, sec. 192, defends the use of a *hetter iska* during the medieval period:

> At the time the Torah was given, the basis of livelihood and commerce of Jews was agrarian; agriculture was the source and support of their wealth and status for he who had copious produce was considered a rich man. Money was not fundamental or the basis of their activities; and when money was loaned it was not for the purpose of trade and acquisition, but in order to acquire bread and clothing by a person who could not afford such from the yield of his land and work. Accordingly, it is obvious that this poor debtor could not afford to pay interest, while the wealthy lender would suffer no perceivable loss in lending without interest. . . . However, in the Middle Ages, by which time Israel had lost its share and inheritance in working the land and become a nation that sustained itself solely on commerce, the prohibition became onerous, for by then money had become the basis of [the Jews'] life and commerce; it became a business commodity to the lender and to the borrower equally. "That your brother may live with you" applied to both equally. Therefore, our sages saw fit to find a permissive manner to avoid this prohibition considering that, for such purpose, the Torah did not entirely forbid this matter.

profit whatsoever accrues to the lender and hence there is no question of forbidden payment of interest. The text incorporating this formula, which was drawn up by R. Mendel Avigdors for use in lieu of a promissory note, appears in *Nahalat Shiv'ah*, no. 40, and is known as the "*Hetter Iska* of Maharam."

A preeminent eighteenth-century scholar, R. Elijah of Vilna, *Bi'ur ha-Gra, Yoreh De'ah* 167:1, expresses amazement at *Shulhan Arukh*'s ruling that money may be lent in this manner. In the situation that is outlined, the "agent" undertakes to engage in the purchase and sale of merchandise on behalf of the "principal." However, his sole motivation for doing so is the stipulated agreement between the parties to the effect that the sum advanced will subsequently be available for the recipient's own personal use as a loan. Labor or personal services performed on behalf of a creditor as an inducement to extend a loan is a form of interest forbidden by Jewish law. Performance of such services without compensation is, in fact, a disguised interest premium exacted as a precondition demanded for conversion of the funds to a loan. It is for this reason that *Shulhan Arukh* stipulates that the "agent" must be paid for his services, although the payment may be nominal in nature. Such nominal payment to avoid the stricture against usury is analogous to the peppercorn recognized in common law as consideration validating a contract. R. Elijah of Vilna quite evidently regarded token payment as inadequate; forgoing usual compensation was regarded by him as a form of interest-taking.[6]

In terms of making capital available for commercial purposes, an obvious drawback with regard to this arrangement is that the "interest" received by the lender is not tied to the period of time his capital is used by the borrower and does not provide for accrual of interest or sharing of additional profit in the event that repayment is delayed. Subsequently, a modified form of the *hetter iska* was developed by an eighteenth-century authority, R. Abraham Danzig of Vilna, which had the effect of eliminating this difficulty.[7] Under the terms of this modified *hetter iska* the recipient accepts fifty percent of the funds as a deposit and fifty percent as a loan. Any expenditure of a commercial or investment nature is deemed to be a joint venture in which both parties share equally. Thus, technically, half the profits accrue to the "principal" and half to the borrower. The principal may, of course, agree to accept no more than a certain stipulated amount of the profits and the agent may demand that the agreement specify that profits exceeding that amount accrue to the agent as compensation for his services.

Transformation of the *hetter iska* into a transaction in the form of half loan, half deposit is to the advantage of the investor in the sense that only half his funds

6 One way to avoid the problem is to structure the half loan, half deposit so that, although profits are shared equally, the recipient is to bear maximum loss of only one-third of the capital. In effect, the difference between one-half and one-third is "insured" by the financier in return for the services performed by the recipient. That arrangement renders performance of personal services as payment in lieu of a "premium" that might ordinarily be required to insure against loss of the difference between one-third and one-half of the investment. See the *hetter iska* of R. Abraham Brode published in *Noheg ke-Tson Yosef, masa u-matan*, sec. 4. Cf., R. Jacob Isaiah Blau, *Brit Yehudah* 37:4, 40:6, note 12 and 40:1, note 9. This expedient is employed in the *hetter iska* used by Israeli banks.

7 See *Ginat Veradim, Yoreh De'ah, klal* 7, no. 4.

are at even theoretical risk. Another advantage is that it makes accrual of presumed periodic profits possible with the result that procrastination in a repayment results in greater profit to the investor.

It may well be the case that this form of *hetter iska* was also developed, in part, to overcome the objection raised by R. Elijah of Vilna (viz., that mere token consideration in return for personal services is not sufficient to overcome the taint of usury). That objection is grounded in the concern that the recipient expends time and effort on behalf of the financier during the initial period of the arrangement in which the funds are invested solely on behalf of the financier and, clearly, that he is motivated to do so only because he desires that the sum advanced together with the profits generated during that period convert to an interest-free loan as rapidly as possible. However, it may be argued that this is not the case with regard to funds received as a half loan, half deposit. In the latter case, the recipient would expend no less time and effort were he to seek investment opportunities only for the funds he receives as an interest-free loan. No additional time or effort is expended because the investor's funds are commingled with the recipient's borrowed funds. Quite to the contrary, it is more likely than not that any entrepreneur would welcome the opportunity to double the quantity of merchandise he seeks to buy with his own already available funds by acting at the same time as an agent for another individual desirous of acquiring the same type of merchandise or in making a similar investment. Doubling the quantity purchased or the amount of money invested affords the opportunity for taking advantage of economy of scale.

To offer a simple example: Jumbo certificates of deposit require a much higher minimum investment than ordinary certificates of deposit but yield a higher premium. The amount of paper work involved in securing a jumbo certificate of deposit is no different from the amount of paper work required to secure an ordinary certificate of deposit. Assume that A has only $50,000 to invest but that the minimum requirement for a jumbo certificate of deposit is $100,000. Assume also that B has $50,000 available to invest. Under such circumstances, prudence and good business sense would dictate that one of the parties should offer to take custody of the other party's $50,000, commingle the funds, and invest them in a joint certificate of deposit as tenants in common. The motive for doing so is not altruism in helping a friend but self-interest in becoming able to qualify for a higher yield on one's own investment. Similarly, in purchasing merchandise, it is highly likely that, the greater the quantity bargained for, the lower the cost per unit. Hence, it is certainly arguable that in accepting funds in the form of half loan, half deposit, the recipient is motivated solely by self-interest and performs no additional services as compensation for receipt of the loan.[8]

In neither of these formulations is the *hetter iska* a subterfuge or legal fiction. The determining characteristic that distinguishes a loan from a deposit or bailment is that a debtor must always repay the full amount borrowed, regardless of any

8 Cf., *Tosafot, Bava Metsi'a* 104b, s.v. *hai iska*. The arrangement described by *Tosafot* does not seem to involve a potential for economy of scale.

losses he may suffer, while the laws of bailment provide that the bailee need not indemnify the bailor in the event of certain types of losses. Since the *hetter iska* generates a principal-agent relationship, no payment need be made if bona fide losses occur while the borrower functions as a bailee. Under the terms of Maharam's formula there is no obligation whatsoever on the part of the recipient if the loss is sustained during the intial period; according to the modified version such losses are borne equally by the "principal" and the "borrower." The "principal" may, however, set forth certain stipulations to protect himself against loss. He may, for example, stipulate that the agent must bear all losses unless the merchandise purchased is at all times under the latter's personal supervision or unless the agent produces two trustworthy witnesses who testify that he had indeed properly discharged all aspects of his trust.

Although disputed by other authorities, R. Israel Isserlin, *Terumat Ha-Deshen*, no. 302, states that the creditor may even stipulate that only the testimony of the rabbi and the cantor or beadle of the community will be acceptable, despite the fact that such a condition is, in practice, almost impossible to fulfill. The rabbi and cantor are designated as the only acceptable witnesses, not because of their unchallengeable probity, but because they are the two individuals in the community least likely to have personal knowledge of any material fact that would extinguish the recipient's liability.

Conditions such as these serve to protect the capital of the creditor, but do not at all guarantee the payment of "interest" in the event that the debtor denies that he has earned a profit. This drawback was overcome by means of a further stipulation providing that the "principal" may assume that a profit has been earned and that this presumption may be nullified only upon the solemn oath of the "agent" to the contrary. That stipulation has meaningful implications because of a singular socioreligious factor unique to Jews, Quakers, and few others. Pious Jews abjure oaths, even when called upon to swear to matters that are entirely true. Accordingly, the net effect of a stipulation requiring an oath to substantiate an absence of profit is to assure that the creditor will receive "interest" in the form of a guaranteed "profit" even if, in fact, no profit has been earned in any commercial endeavor. Thus, even if no profit has been realized, the stipulated payment is legitimately proffered as a fee for exoneration from the oath that would otherwise be imposed in order to substantiate the absence of profits. The payment is in the nature of an accord and satisfaction.

Whether or not such an oath may be demanded when the "principal" has personal knowledge of the truth of the "agent's" claim that no profit has been earned is a matter of some dispute. Some authorities assert that an oath attesting to facts already known by the party demanding the oath is forbidden as an oath taken "in vain" (i.e., to no purpose). Of course, if an oath cannot be exacted, payment in lieu of the oath cannot be demanded.[9]

9 *Teshurat Shai*, I, no. 3; *Teshuvot Panim Me'irot*, II, no. 3; *Teshuvot Divrei Hayyim*, II, *hashmattot*, no. 16; and R. Moses Feinstein, *Iggerot Mosheh, Yoreh De'ah*, II, nos. 62 and 63, maintain that such an oath cannot be demanded. However, *Teshuvot Maharshag, Yoreh De'ah*, no. 4, disagrees.

In an article published in *Torah she-be-al Peh* (XIX [1967, 100–5], and reprinted in his *Mishkan Shiloh* [Jerusalem, 1995, pp. 281–88]), Rabbi Shiloh Rafael notes that, in our day, an aversion to oath-taking is no longer to be taken for granted. Understandably, there may therefore be a reluctance on the part of some persons to utilize the customary *hetter iska*. The lender may well anticipate a contingency in which the borrower will indeed swear quite truthfully that he has earned no profit. Rabbi Rafael suggests that the requirement for an oath on the part of the debtor be replaced with a stipulation giving the creditor the right to examine the financial records of the debtor and the right to participate in all decisions with regard to the expenditure of the sum advanced. The agreement between the parties would provide that this right be abrogated upon payment of a specified sum or percentage of the capital at the discretion of the debtor.

Nevertheless, in recent years, perhaps because of concern for the qualms expressed by R. Elijah of Vilna, a new form of *hetter iska* has developed among members of the stringently observant community. That agreement is colloquially referred to as the "*hetter iska* of Bnei Brak" because of the locale in which it gained currency.[10] The arrangement is designed to eliminate any possible halakhic pitfall by providing that the funds are advanced in their entirety solely as an investment. Provision is made for payment of a stipulated periodic rate of return as profit upon the investment with any balance in excess of that rate of return to be retained by the recipient. Since there is no loan whatsoever, there can be no taint of interest. All other provisions of such an agreement are identical to those of a standard *hetter iska*. A return even when no profit has been realized is assured by stipulating a presumption of profit rebuttable only by a solemn oath. Capital is protected by stipulating that only the testimony of two halakhicly qualified witnesses is acceptable as proof of loss. The drawback of that arrangement is that, unlike with regard to other forms of *hetter iska*, since no portion is in the form of a loan, the funds advanced are at risk in their entirety.

The *hetter iska* was originally designed to facilitate the lending of capital for commercial purposes. Since the capital was, in fact, invested in mercantile enterprises, and since the creditor assumed a measure of risk, the relationship that was formed was—factually as well as technically—that of partners in a business venture. However, with the passage of time, use of the *hetter iska* became more and more widespread. Greater and greater numbers of Jews earned their livelihood as craftsmen or as hired laborers. The use of a *hetter iska* by a person who is not in any way engaged in a business enterprise appears to be nothing more than a subterfuge. A prominent twentieth-century decisor, Rabbi Moses Feinstein, *Iggerot Mosheh, Yoreh De'ah*, II, no. 62, totally ignoring earlier *responsa* dealing with this problem, strongly implies that a *hetter iska* may by employed only when the borrower is engaged in business ventures. Moreover, declares Rabbi Feinstein, both parties

10 See R. Moses Sternbuch, *Mo'adim u-Zemanim*, VI, no. 41, secs. 1(3) and 1(7). This form of *hetter iska* seems to have been originated by R. Jacob Breisch in Switzerland. See Rabbi Breisch, *Teshuvot Helkat Ya'akov*, III, no. 188, sec. 2, no. 189, sec. 1 and no. 194, sec. 8, s.v. *akhen*.

must know the nature of the commercial venture for which the money is advanced for "[the *hetter iska*] is not an incantation or charm."[11] Rabbi Feinstein adds that the written agreement should state that the money advanced must be used for ventures in which it may reasonably be anticipated that the total profit will be at least twice the amount of the stipulated return. Thus, according to *Iggerot Mosheh*, the *hetter iska* is reserved for use in situations in which the interest paid is, in reality, no more than the actual anticipated profit realized on the portion of the merchandise acquired on behalf of the creditor.

The question of the efficacy of the *hetter iska* in conjunction with noncommercial loans was raised earlier, at approximately the turn of the twentieth century, and discussed in detail by Rabbi Shalom Mordecai Shvadron, *Teshuvot Maharsham*, II, no. 216. Advancing a view contrary to that later espoused by *Iggerot Mosheh*, Rabbi Schwadron justifies the use of a *hetter iska* in conjunction with loans that are entirely of a personal nature. He concedes that, when the funds have not been used for commercial purposes, and no profits have been earned, no interest need be paid. The borrower, however, certainly has the legal and halakhic option of using the money advanced for such purposes; indeed, that is the prima facie purpose of the loan as stated in the written agreement. Under the terms of the agreement the financier may demand a solemn oath that the money has not, in fact, been used to generate profit and that, in fact, no profit has been earned. The amount stipulated as "accord and satisfaction" is then paid by the recipient solely as a means of avoiding the oath that he is otherwise bound to swear.

In the nineteenth century, R. Joseph Saul Nathanson, *Teshuvot Sho'el u-Meshiv, Mahadurah Kamma*, III, no. 160, justified an *iska* arrangement in conjunction with personal loans, for at least some purposes, on entirely different grounds. According to this authority, a loan that makes it possible for an individual to continue practicing his profession or to retain his income-generating employment is to be deemed a commercial enterprise. Therefore, according to *Sho'el u-Meshiv*, a teacher who is burdened by debt or by personal expenses may borrow funds under an *iska* arrangement if failure to receive the loan would force him to abandon his profession and to seek a livelihood in some potentially more lucrative endeavor. Since the loan enables him to continue in his occupation, the loan constitutes a form of *iska* in which the financier becomes a partner. The application of this line of reasoning to student loans designed to enable the student to pursue studies that will qualify him to enter a profession or to make him eligible for higher salaried employment is obvious.

In another responsum, *Sho'el u-Meshiv, Mahadurah Telita'ah*, I, no. 133, Rabbi Nathanson sanctioned an *iska* arrangement in order to enable the recipient to repay a debt and thereby to avert the forced sale of his home. This is categorized as an *iska* by *Sho'el u-Meshiv* by virtue of its service in preventing loss of capital resulting from

11 Similarly, *Mo'adim u-Zemanim*, VI, no. 41, sec. 1(1) writes: "Many err with regard to the intention of Maharam and imagine that [the *hetter iska*] is a chanson (*pizmon*) to render the prohibition against interest inoperative."

the otherwise economically forced sale of the house and/or the opportunity to realize the contemplated appreciated value of the property.

The permissive views of *Sho'el u-Meshiv* were sharply disputed in the early part of the twentieth century by R. Meir Arak, *Teshuvot Imrei Yosher*, I, no. 108. *Imrei Yosher* maintained that the concept of *iska* is limited to profits realized from the investment of capital advanced or from sale of merchandise or goods acquired with such capital. Profits realized from avoidance of loss or from income derived from personal employment do not constitute the fruits of a joint venture and hence, according to *Imrei Yosher*, do not justify use of a *hetter iska*. This latter view is consistent with the position of most authorities including *Ginat Veradim*, *Yoreh De'ah*, *klal* 6, no. 4; *Shulhan Arukh ha-Rav*, *Hilkhot Ribbit*, sec. 42; *Kitsur Shulhan Arukh* 66:10; and *Erekh Shai* 177:7.

A contemporary scholar, Rabbi Moses Sternbuch, *Mo'adim u-Zemanim*, VI, no. 41, sec. 2(7), s.v. *ve-hineh*, points out that with widespread investment in the stock market on the part of small investors there can be no question with regard to the creditor's lack of personal knowledge that no profit has been earned. Indeed, it is not uncommon for individuals who borrow money for personal purposes to use such funds in an attempt to reap short-term profits in the securities market. Since the creditor cannot know that this has not, in fact, occurred, he may, according to all authorities, stipulate that an oath be sworn to that effect.

The *Hetter Iska* in American Law

As explained earlier, the *hetter iska* constitutes a device that is in full conformity with Jewish law. The *hetter iska* has also been recognized by the civil courts as an instrument creating a bona fide partnership interest providing for a limited return upon an investment rather than as a loan instrument requiring payment of interest on borrowed funds. In *Leibovici* v. *Rawicki*, 57 Misc.2d 141, 290 N.Y.S. 2d 997 (Civ. Ct. 1968), the Court upheld the legality of a *hetter iska* that provided a return greater than was permitted by usury laws in effect at that time. In this decision, the Court specifically denied the plea that the agreement was merely a disguised loan and hence constituted a subterfuge to avoid the taint of usury. In a number of cases, the courts have ruled explicitly that payment of a portion of profits in lieu of interest with no guarantee of profit is not usury.[12] In *Leibovici* v. *Rawicki* the Court recognized that a *hetter iska* constitutes an agreement of precisely this nature.

There are, nevertheless, cases in which American courts, primarily New York State courts, have refused to recognize a *hetter iska* as creating a partnership or joint

12 See *Clift* v. *Barrow*, 108 N.Y. 187, 192–94, 15 N.E. 327, 328–30 (1888); and *Mueller* v. *Brennan*, 68 N.Y.S. 2d 517 (Sup. Ct., 1947).

venture. However, in each of those cases either (a) the *hetter iska* issue was irrelevant; (b) the testimony presented to the court with regard to the nature of a *hetter iska* was patently incorrect; or (c) the *hetter iska* was improperly drafted. Those cases underscore the need to draft a *hetter iska* properly and, when testimony is required, to have knowledgeable scholars serve as expert witnesses.

One decision in particular has great relevance with regard to a type of *hetter iska* that has unjustifiably gained currency because of its simplicity. There appears to be a fairly widespread practice within some business circles to use a standard promissory note and to write the words "*al pi hetter iska*" ("in accordance with *hetter iska*"), or to use a rubber stamp bearing those words, above the signatures of the parties. The intent of that legend is to nullify explicit references in the instrument to a loan and interest by declaring actual intent to be a joint venture and shared profit. Read literally and in its entirety, the result is an ambiguity creating doubt with regard to the nature of the instrument and hence the expedient is of dubious efficacy in obviating the prohibition against interest.[13] Moreover, the term *hetter iska* is generic in nature and does not indicate which of the available forumulae or variations thereof is intended. In addition, a significant problem arises in the event that no profits are realized from investment of the funds received. Since there is no specific provision for an oath supporting a claim of the absence of profit, there is no basis for a fee in the form of accord and satisfaction in lieu of such an oath. Accordingly, if the transaction is governed by such a *hetter iska* and no profits have been realized, any sum paid the creditor in excess of principal in the absence of profit is, at best, a "gift" in return for the loan, which is itself a proscribed form of interest.

It is quite likely that the practice of using the formula *al pi hetter iska* evolved from an earlier employed expedient that was not open to these challenges. In earlier times, printed promissory notes were not used. Instead the recipient wrote out a simple declaration in the nature of "I acknowledge receipt of the sum of _______ from _______ in accordance with the *hetter iska* instituted by Maharam Avigdors of Cracow."[14] The instrument (a) contained no contradictory reference to interest, and (b) provided both for profit-sharing and for payment in lieu of an oath by means of incorporation of the provisions of a particular well-known and published *hetter iska* (viz., the *hetter iska* authored by Maharam Avigdors). At times, the slightly shortened formula "*al pi hetter iska shel* [of] *Maharam*" was used on the strength of the common recognition that the only "Maharam" associated with a *hetter iska* instrument is Maharam Avigdors. Use of the formula "*al pi hetter iska shel Maharam*" when the intention is half loan, half deposit is clearly inappropriate.[15]

13 See *Brit Yehudah* 40:8. Cf., R. Shalom Mordecai Shvadron, *Teshuvot Maharsham*, II, no. 252.

14 Cf., the comments of R. Ephraim Zalman Margolies published by R. Aaron Walden in *Shem ha-Gedolim ha-Hadash* (Warsaw, 1865), *Ma'arekhet Gedolim, ot mem*, sec. 51.

15 Cf., *Mo'adim u-Zemanim*, VI, no. 41, sec. 1(2). Cf. also, the comments of R. Ephraim Zalman Margolies, cited *supra*, note 12, in which, although he decries the practice, Rabbi Margolies endeavors to justify its acceptance on the basis of the contention that because the error is so widespread it may be assumed that the party's intention is half loan, half deposit.

A New York trial court found the abbreviated formula to be ambiguous and ordered a trial to determine, inter alia, the nature of the instrument. In *Arnav Industries, Inc.* v. *Westside Realty Assoc.*, 180 A.D.2d 463, 579 N.Y.S.2d 382 (1st Dep't 1992), the Appellate Division found that inclusion of the phrase did not generate a threshold level of ambiguity sufficient to warrant denial of summary judgment on the promissory note. The promissory note that was the subject of dispute in *Arnav* contained a clause specifically stating that "[n]othing herein or in Mortgage is intended to create a joint venture, partnership, tenancy-in-common, or joint tenancy relationship between Borrower and Lender."[16] That clause constitutes an explicit rejection of the relationship a *hetter iska* is designed to create. Absent that clause, the issue of whether references to a loan and to payment of interest are rendered ambiguous by insertion of the phrase "*al pi hetter iska*" remains an open legal question. Nor, if an ambiguity is found to exist, is there any way to predict how a trial court might resolve that ambiguity.

The decision in *Arnav* should serve as a caution against use of an abbreviated *hetter iska* consisting of but a vague and ambiguous phrase. Since that procedure is in any event of dubious halakhic validity, the decision in *Arnav* places no significant burden upon utilization of a *hetter iska*.

Barclay Commerce Corp. v. *Finkelstein*, 11 A.D.2d 327, 205 N.Y.S.2d 551 (1st Dep't. 1960), involved a case in which the plaintiff and the corporate defendant entered into a factoring agreement guaranteeing payment of monies that might become due. The suit was based upon the plaintiff's contention that the accounts receivable that had been assigned were fraudulent. The Appellate Court found that since the alleged fraud was not denied the question of whether or not the *hetter iska* created a partnership was a "phantom" issue.[17]

In *Bollag* v. *Dresdner*, 130 Misc.2d 221, 495 N.Y.S.2d 560 (N.Y. City Civ. Ct. 1985), the parties entered into a properly drafted *hetter iska*. The defendant maintained that (a) the contract was void as usurious, and (b) the transaction constituted an investment by the plaintiff subject to any profits earned or losses sustained. The plaintiff relied upon the *hetter iska* in countering the usury defense but also incongruously alleged that he was entitled to repayment of principal and interest regardless of any profit or loss. Further muddying the waters, the plaintiff's complaint and bill of particulars categorized the instrument as a note and presented an expert witness who testified imprecisely that such forms are employed "when one party is lending money and the other party is borrowing money."[18] The Court also noted discrepancies between the *hetter iska* and testimony regarding liability in the event of absence of profit or of loss of capital. Most damaging was the unequivocal, but patently false, testimony of the expert who "testified emphatically . . . that the agreement did not create a joint venture or partnership."[19] Not

16 *Arnav Industries, Inc.* v. *Westside Realty Assoc.* at 383.

17 *Barclay Commerce Corp.* v. *Finkelstein* at 553.

18 *Bollag* v. *Dresdner* at 562.

19 Ibid., at 562.

only is that statement false, it is absurd, since, if true, it would render the *hetter iska* devoid of purpose. The Court took note of the inherent contradiction in the plaintiff's position in observing, "Yet despite his repeated use of the above-quoted categorization of the transaction it is 'done,' he said, 'specifically not to pay interest.'"[20]

The Court, in this decision, expressly affirmed in principle the validity of a properly drafted *hetter iska* in finding that the *hetter iska* presented to the court "as interpreted by the parties and their witnesses at trial reveals that the transaction was a loan (not an 'investment') and that plaintiff's clear intent was to exact a higher rate of interest than is permitted by law."[21] The Court distinguished the case before it from *Leibovici* v. *Rawicki* on the grounds that in *Leibovici* "the funds were clearly treated as a joint investment."[22]

In *Bollag*, the Court found that the defendant requested the loan that was the subject of litigation for business purposes rather than for personal needs. Accordingly, it found that the policy and reasoning behind the general obligation law §5-521 serve to disallow a usury defense in such circumstances. In doing so, the Court affirmed the *hetter iska* as a valid business contract. However, incongruously, and perhaps cynically, its disallowance of the usury defense notwithstanding, the court refused to allow "interest." The Court found that the plaintiff was prevented from collecting interest by his own pleading. The plaintiff had maintained that the *hetter iska* was entered into specifically to avoid payment of interest. Yet, the plaintiff's own expert witness incorrectly categorized the claim as one to recover "interest." Giving equal credence to both the plaintiff's own statement and the testimony of plaintiff's expert witness the Court declared, "[P]laintiff has made it plain he neither wishes to nor can collect interest. Accordingly, none shall be awarded."[23] The defendant, in effect, was hung from his own petard.

Although recovery of accrued interest was denied, the Court allowed interest on the judgment at the statutory rate from the date of its entry on the ground that there was "no testimony which would bar plaintiff from receiving interest on a judgment (as distinct from interest on a loan)." That finding reflects an erroneous assessment of Jewish law. Recovery of interest on a judgment is indeed precluded by Jewish law. Absence of testimony to that effect is but one more example of the comedy of errors and incompetence on the part of counsel and witnesses reflected in this case.

In an unreported case, *Berger* v. *Moskowitz*, N.Y.L.J 25, (col. 3), vol. 206, no. 85 (October 30, 1991), 25, the Court found that a perfunctory *hetter iska* did not succeed in establishing a partnership agreement because it failed "to identity the nature of the venture let alone the specifics relating to the terms of such venture." The *hetter iska* in question was titled "Business Agreement" and did recite that the sum in

20 Ibid., at 562.
21 Ibid., at 225.
22 Ibid., at 225.
23 Ibid., at 564.

question was advanced "for business and the profit of which agreed on will be ten percent, and the duration [of] the business will be three years from the signing of this agreement." Although inelegantly drafted, the agreement itself would seem to this writer to reflect the intent of the parties that the funds be applied to a business venture and that the ten percent be paid out of profits, the implication being that such profit-sharing was predicated upon actual realization of profits. However, in this case also, the defendant was found liable by virtue of his own admission. The Court declared, "Nor can defendants label this transaction a business venture since MOSKOWITZ wrote a letter to the plaintiffs' attorney stating in part: 'I acknowledge that the unpaid balance of the loan with interest through November 30, 1990, is $268, 200.00.'"

The decision of a U.S. Bankruptcy Court in *In re Stephen Douglas*, 174 B.R. 16 (Bankr. E.D.N.Y. 1994), does not involve any substantive matter pertaining to the legal validity of a *hetter iska*. The issue was whether a certain payment constituted a fraudulent conveyance under applicable statutes. Section 273 of the New York Debtor and Creditor Law denominates as fraudulent any conveyance made by an insolvent for inadequate consideration, without regard to actual intent. The books and records of the debtors reflected no consideration or economic benefit conferred upon Douglas by the defendant. It was also alleged that a promissory note reflecting a loan was executed but was lost. A *hetter iska* was introduced in evidence in support of existence of a loan. That evidence was dismissed on the grounds that it was written on the stationery of a corporation not involved in the proceedings. Since the *hetter iska* was dismissed as irrelevant, the Court found that there was no need to address the legal import of a *hetter iska.*

Heimbinder v. *Berkovitz*, 175 Misc.2d 808, 670 N.Y.S.2d 301 (N.Y.Sup. 1998), involved an action to invalidate various transfers to the defendant corporation that would have otherwise been available to satisfy a judgment against the defendant. The plaintiff sought to hold defendant directors personally liable for breach of fiduciary duty in effecting such transfers. Since a *hetter iska* was employed, the plaintiff also contended that the defendant, in signing the document, personally guaranteed payment of the obligation. The court cited with approval an earlier unpublished decision in *Burger* v. *Baruch Ha'Levi Moskowitz*, Kings County Sup.Ct., Index NO. 15600/91, in which a *hetter iska* constituted the sole contract between two individual parties and was found to establish a valid guarantee. In *Heimbinder*, however, the evidence indicated that the plaintiff's attorney had previously requested a personal guarantee and that the request had been refused by the defendant's attorney. Moreover, the "security agreement" executed by the parties contained a provision for a "guarantee" next to which the word "omit" was entered in handwriting; the defendant's name had been typed beneath the signature line for the guarantor but was crossed out. The plaintiff conceded that there had been a discussion of guarantees but that no agreement was reached; that he had been unaware of the existence of a guarantee provision in the form that was used and that the *hetter iska* was produced by the defendant only after discussions in which he refused a personal guarantee had been concluded; that he could not read Hebrew and relied upon the defendant's categorization of the document; and that the defendant did not portray it as a personal guarantee. Accordingly, the Court found that, in the case before it, the *hetter iska* was not intended to generate a personal guarantee of corporate debt. Nothing in the *Heimbinder* decision casts doubt upon the enforceability of the provisions of the *hetter iska* itself.

Heimbinder, however, serves to establish a significant point of law. A standard *hetter iska* signed by an officer of a corporation in circumstances other than those of *Heimbinder* may well establish a personal obligation even absent explicit indication of such intention. If this is not the desired outcome, the remedy is to indicate explicitly in the document that it is being executed on behalf of the corporation and not in an individual capacity.

Wiesel v. *Rubinstein*, 12 Misc.3d 1168(A) (N.Y.Sup.= 2006), represents a foregone opportunity to seek application of a collateral provision of a *hetter iska*. Kalman Rubinstein signed a series of promissory notes in order to obtain funds to open a kosher pizza shop. The rate of return on each of the notes, most of which were short term in nature, was fourteen percent. Despite an agreement to submit the dispute to a *Bet Din* for resolution, Rubinstein failed to appear before the *Bet Din* to which the parties agreed. The *Bet Din* declined to issue a default judgment. Thereupon, the estates of Sol and Harriet Wiesel sued in New York State Supreme Court. Apparently, the plaintiff made no attempt to have the Supreme Court enforce compliance with the arbitration agreement or to issue a default judgment upon failure to submit to arbitration despite the express agreement between the parties to do so that was incorporated in the *hetter iska*.

Rubinstein seems to have been under the impression that he would prevail in a civil court both because the plaintiffs' claim was barred by the statute of limitations and because the rate of interest was usurious. Nevertheless, he asserted an additional affirmative defense (viz., since "each of the notes contains a notation in Hebrew indicating the notes are subject to *hetter iska* failure of the business absolved him of the obligation to repay the amounts due on the notes").[24]

The Court denied summary judgment based on the statute of limitations on the grounds that the alleged partial payment of the debt had the effect of extending the period within which a suit might be initiated. The Court also interpreted the note as prescribing fourteen percent per annum rather a usurious fourteen percent for a much briefer period. The *hetter iska* defense was ignored in the Court's rejection of the motion for summary judgment, perhaps because it was self-evident that whether or not the business did fail, and whether or not a *hetter iska* provides that such failure cancels the obligation, are triable issues.

In point of fact, a standard *hetter iska* would require a solemn oath to substantiate a claim of nonrealization of profit and testimony of two halakhicly qualified witnesses to establish loss of capital. In this case, an ordinary promissory note seems to have been employed but modified by inclusion of a "notation in Hebrew indicating that the notes are subject to the *hetter iska*." That "notation" was the

24 *Wiesel* v. *Rubinstein* at 1.

incorporation of the earlier discussed phrase "*al pi hetter iska.*" As noted earlier, that phrase may signify only that the term "loan" should be understood as "investment" and that the term "interest" should not be construed as such but as the return of a share of the profits earned by the investment. If so, as discussed earlier, entirely different and much less onerous standards of proof might apply to establishing absence of profit and loss of capital. "Whether or not failure of the business" did indeed absolve the defendant "of the obligation to repay the amounts due on the notes" is a matter to be resolved by a *Bet Din*.

The above notwithstanding, in a Report and Recommendation on Motion to Dismiss in the case of *Edelkind* v. *Fairmont Funding*, 539 F.Supp.2d 449 (D. Mass. 2008), a federal magistrate asserted that in civil courts "*hetter iska* agreements have been interpreted as 'merely a compliance in form with Hebraic law'[25] that does not create a partnership between the parties."[26] In support of that assertion, the Magistrate cited *Arnav Indus. v. Westside Realty Assoc.*, *Barclay Commerce Corp.* and *Heimbinder*. As has been shown, those cases do not serve to establish the Magistrate's conclusion. Quite to the contrary, each of those cases reflects acceptance of the validity of a properly drafted *hetter iska* in creating a partnership between the parties but finds the particular *hetter iska* instruments submitted in those proceedings to be faulty. The *hetter iska* employed in *Edelkind* may also have been defective but that issue was not addressed. These cases serve to underscore the necessity for careful drafting of a halakhicly valid *hetter iska* agreement. A sample text of an English-language *hetter iska* agreement may be found in this writer's *Contemporary Halakhic Problems*, II (New York, 1983, pp. 380–88).

The claim advanced in *Edelkind* was dismissed because Jamie Edelkind was found to have no standing to bring a suit as an alleged third-party beneficiary of a mortgage agreement entered into by his wife. The findings with regard to the *hetter iska*, also apparently signed by the wife, constitute dicta having no bearing upon the merits of the case. Nevertheless, the facts presented in *Edelkind* underscore a serious pitfall based not upon the validity of the *hetter iska* itself, but upon the way it was employed.

It is quite common for a lender to execute a *hetter iska* and immediately thereafter to execute a second, standard mortgage agreement. It is commonly assumed that the lender is better protected legally if he is in possession of a mortgage instrument. Whether or not that is true, there is no gainsaying the fact that the lender feels more secure with a mortgage in his possession. R. Moses Feinstein, *Iggerot Mosheh*, *Hoshen Mishpat*, no. 62, sanctions the practice from the perspective of Jewish law in describing the mortgage instrument as devoid of halakhic validity provided that the *iska* agreement states that it is the governing instrument and the mortgage is designed merely as "*bithonot*," best translated as "reliances"

25 See *Barclay Commerce Corp.* v. *Finkelstein* at 329.
26 *Edelkind* v. *Fairmont Funding* at 454.

or "assurances."[27] Nevertheless, one legal ramification of such practice is evident in *Edelkind*.

In instances such as those described in *Edelkind*, the mortgage agreement is crucial to the enterprise. Fairmont Funding is a mortgage broker. The principals are observant Jews. The firm enters into mortgage agreements in conjunction with the purchase of real property and then sells the mortgage loans to banks. Therein lies the dilemma: The mortgage broker is the lender, both halakhicly and legally; the mortgage broker contracts for interest to be paid to himself. This, as an observant Jew, he may not do. Therefore, he avails himself of a *hetter iska*. The mortgage bankers are non Jews; they do not understand, and would not purchase, a *hetter iska*. Therefore, the mortgage broker, in addition to a *hetter iska*, insists upon a mortgage note that he then sells to the mortgage bank, presumably without informing the bank of the existence of the *hetter iska*.

That was precisely the chain of events reported in *Edelkind v. Fairmont*. The contemplated procedure was recited in detail in the preamble to the *hetter iska* agreement. Jamie Edelkind argued that the *hetter iska* created a partnership in the mortgaged property and, accordingly, Fairmont Funding was not empowered to sell the purported loan without permission or notification of his wife who was thereby denied her option to repurchase Fairmont's investment. Edelkind categorized the mortgage document as a "fiction" and accordingly contended that neither Fairmont nor any subsequent holder of the instrument had any legal rights in the mortgage. Hence, he argued, Fairmont and his wife still own the property jointly as partners and neither Fairmont nor any subsequent holder had any foreclosure rights.

There is merit in Jamie Edelkind's contention but, if so, both he and Fairmont perpetrated a fraud upon subsequent holders of the mortgage. The sole remedy is to insert a clause in the *hetter iska* agreement authorizing the mortgage broker to mortgage the entire property. Indeed, a careful reading of the preamble to the *hetter iska* agreement between Edelkind and Fairmont Funding reveals that this was agreed to by the parties. Clearer language would have prevented Jamie Edelkind from arguing otherwise. In any event, suppression of the *hetter iska* agreement gives rise to an aura of fraud and should not be countenanced. In addition, authorization to assign a mortgage against the entire property should be carefully spelled out in the body of the *hetter iska* agreement.[28]

27 Cf., R. Moses Sofer, *Teshuvot Hatam Sofer, Hoshen Mishpat*, no. 48, who writes that the formula "*al pi hetter Maharam* as was spoken between us" rather than the full text of a *hetter iska* was utilized in order to give full force to the written agreement in civil law as an ordinary loan agreement. The concept seems to be identical to that formulated by *Iggerot Mosheh*. See also the discussion of R. Solomon Kluger, *Teshuvot Tuv Ta'am va-Da'at*, I, no. 208. The basic principle is also accepted by R. Isaac Jacob Weiss, *Teshuvot Minhat Yitshak*, IV, no.16, sec. 2. Rabbi Breisch, *Helkat Ya'akov*, III, no. 195, sec. 6, regards the practice as permissible even if the mortgage is executed prior to the *hetter iska*.

28 There is an additional vague reference to *hetter iska* in a decision of a federal appeals court, *Barclays Discount Bank Limited* v. *Bogharin Bros.*, 743 F.2d 722 (1984) 724. In that case a district court denied a motion for reconsideration on the grounds that the *hetter iska* issue had not been advanced in a timely fashion and further observed that the argument based upon the *hetter iska* contradicted the defendant's own description of the relationship between the parties. In a footnote, the Appellate Court stated, "A *hetter iska* appears to be a religious document purporting to characterize the bank and those to whom the bank charges interest as a 'venture' to avoid violation of religious law." Ibid., at note 2.

Mortgage Loans

Modifying a mortgage note in order to transform it into a halakhicly valid and legally enforceable instrument is a more difficult enterprise. The complexities of both mortgage agreements as well as the particular nature of purchase-money mortgages render adaptation or modification of standard forms virtually impossible. It is therefore necessary to draft an instrument designed to replace a usual mortgage agreement.

A mortgage loan in which the seller accepts a purchase mortgage representing all or part of the purchase price does not lend itself to use of a customary *hetter iska*. Since no cash is actually advanced by the seller to the purchaser, the purchaser has no opportunity to realize a profit from the investment of such funds. Accordingly, the seller has no reason to demand an oath to that effect and no right to accept a stipulated sum in lieu of an oath. Of course, if it may reasonably be anticipated that the market value of the real estate will rise, a partnership agreement might be drafted that would provide for a specified rate of return in lieu of payment of a partnership share of the actual increase in value. However, in the event that the value of the real estate does not rise and no "profit" is realized, acceptance of a stipulated return in lieu of profits poses a halakhic problem. It may be argued that, if real estate values are a matter of common knowledge, there is really no basis to demand an oath to the effect that there has been no increase in value and hence no right to accept monetary payment in lieu of an oath.

There does, however, exist an entirely different and relatively simple expedient that serves to obviate the prohibition against the taking of interest in conjunction with mortgage loans. The procedure is as follows: Title to a portion of the property directly commensurate in value with the principal of the mortgage is vested in the lender. It is then stipulated that the sum that would ordinarily be required as interest be paid to the "lender" as rent for use of the portion of the property that belongs to him. Payments that serve to reduce the principal are deemed to represent payment for acquisition of title to a share in the property in direct proportion to the amount paid. Subsequent payments in lieu of interest are reduced because "rent" is paid only on the diminished portion vested in the lender and the balance of the payment is applied to purchase of an enhanced share of equity.[29]

There is, however, one serious drawback with regard to an arrangement of this nature. Under the terms of a conventional mortgage loan, should the mortgagor default in payment of monthly installments, the property may be foreclosed and seized by the mortgagee. However, the agreement here described creates a situation in which the purchaser and seller share a partnership interest in the property. Hence, if the purchaser should default in his payment of a monthly installment and the property be foreclosed, the proceeds of the foreclosure would perforce be divided in accordance with the respective partnership interests of the purchaser and

29 Cf., *Iggerot Mosheh, Yoreh De'ah*, II, no. 62, sec.2.

the seller. In some situations, division of proceeds in that manner might result in a financial loss to the seller. Such a result would presumably be unacceptable to most persons contemplating the sale of real estate on terms involving deferred payment.

This problem may be remedied by modifying the agreement to provide solely for regular payments of rent for a set period of time. The rental payments would be set at a sum equal to the amount which would represent the periodic payment of both interest and principal in a conventional mortgage loan. The agreement would further provide that, upon expiration of a stipulated time period, title pass to the leaseholder without further payment, or upon payment of a nominal sum, provided that all financial obligations have been satisfied.

In the event of default in payment of the "rent," the mortgagee-lessor would be entitled to terminate the lease as is the case in any landlord-tenant relationship. In this way the mortgagee-lessor would regain title and possession of the entire property.

An arrangement of this nature does, however, give rise to a disadvantage to the purchaser. Upon default, the property is seized by the seller and the purchaser is deprived of the equity that he would have accumulated had he entered into a conventional mortgage. The result might be avoided by including a stipulation providing that, in cases of default and subsequent sale of the property, a portion of the rent be refunded to the lessee. The amount of the refund would depend upon the sum realized upon sale of the property and the time of sale within the leasehold period. A table might be attached providing for the specific amount of such refund depending upon the point within the leasehold period such sale is consummated. The table would provide for a refund equal to the sum reflecting the extent of accrued amortization of capital that would have occurred had the agreement been in the form of a conventional mortgage. It would, further, be specified that such refund be payable only to the extent that the sum realized on resale is in excess of a second specified sum representing what would have been the remaining portion of the unamortized capital as spelled out in such a table.

Should the purchaser further wish to assure himself a portion of appreciated value of the property for which he has been paying "rent," it would be necessary to incorporate a standard *hetter iska* stipulating that a specified portion of the "rent" be invested by the lessor in a profitable commercial joint enterprise and the requisite share of profits be paid to the lessor only in the event of termination of the lease and subsequent sale of the property. The portion of the "rent" to be invested in this manner each month would be specified in the earlier described table and would reflect the amount that would have been applied each month to reduction of principal were the arrangement to have been in the form of a conventional mortgage.

It is readily perceived that, for a variety of legal considerations pertaining to real estate taxes, insurance coverage, and so on, it is desirable that title be vested in the lessee-purchaser, just as, under a standard mortgage agreement, title is vested in the mortgagor. This may be accomplished under the terms of a leasehold agreement as well. It should be emphasized that such a procedure is entirely legal. The lessee-purchaser may be designated as the owner of record even though, in fact, the agreement provides that title is retained by the lessor-seller. The lessee-purchaser is, in effect, the nominee of the lessor-seller and the agreement between the parties to this effect is entirely valid even though it is not reflected in ownership of record.

A further problem that must be addressed is the question of interest deduction for purposes of income-tax liability. Ordinarily, interest payments on leases and mortgages are deductible from income, while rental payments are not. It might seem that under the provisions of an agreement of this nature the purchaser forfeits the income-tax deduction that he would enjoy under the provisions of a mortgage loan. However, on the basis of a number of court decisions as well as Internal Revenue Service regulations presently in effect, it would appear that the purchaser-lessee is fully entitled to deduct any "rental" payment made in lieu of interest that would have been paid under the terms of a conventional mortgage loan.

In an early case, *Dorzbach* v. *Collison*, 195 F.2d 69 (3rd Cir. 1952), bearing directly upon this question, a federal court ruled that a deduction must be allowed for payment of a percentage of net profits in lieu of interest. The proprietor of a clothing store had borrowed money from a bank but, when pressed for payment, was unable to satisfy the debt. The proprietor's wife was substituted as creditor under an agreement that provided that the proprietor would pay his wife twenty-five percent of the net profits of his clothing store business "in lieu of interest" on monies loaned to him. The Court ruled that such payments are deductible as interest.

In another case, *Arthur R. Jones Syndicate* v. *Commissioner of Internal Revenue*, 23 F.2d 833 (7th Cir. 1927), the Circuit Court of Appeals ruled that "interest, regardless of the name by which it is called, may be deducted by the taxpayer from its income."[30] This case involved an arrangement designed to circumvent an Illinois usury statute. Instead of entering into a loan agreement providing for payment of fourteen percent interest, the parties agreed that preferred stock be issued that was to be redeemable at par and that would bear a dividend of fourteen percent per annum regardless of earnings. The Court held that such "dividends" are deductible as interest.

Of even more direct relevance is *Oesterreich* v. *Commissioner of Internal Revenue*, 266 F.2d 798 (9th Cir. 1955), which deals with a different but related matter. In *Oesterreich* the Court held that an agreement providing for payment of "rent" for a stipulated number of years and conveyance of the property thereafter for a nominal sum was in reality a contract for sale of land even though it was entitled a "lease" and, for tax purposes, should be treated as a sale rather than as a lease. In subsequent litigation growing out of the same transaction, *Estate of Hedrick v. Commissioner of Internal Revenue*, 406 F.2d 587 (9th Cir. 1969), this ruling was later reaffirmed.

30 *Arthur R. Jones Syndicate* v. *Commissioner of Internal Revenue* at 835.

These determinations are reflected in I.R.S. Tax Regulations 26 CFR §1.163-1 and §1.483-1, which provide that payments readily construed as interest are to be considered as such even though they are not formally designated as interest.

In order to eliminate any doubt it is advisable to include a section in the preamble to the leasehold agreement stating that the transaction is executed in this manner rather than in the form of a mortgage loan because of a desire to avoid the usury strictures of Jewish law. This should serve to demonstrate beyond cavil that the "rental" payments are indeed "in lieu of interest."

The first option (viz., a leasehold arrangement) is to be preferred because (a) it is simpler to draft; and (b) it more accurately parallels the nature of the situation generated by a conventional mortgage arrangement in which the mortgager acquires proportionately greater amounts of equity with each monthly payment. A sample leasehold agreement may be found in this writer's *Contemporary Halakhic Problems*, II, (pp. 389–96).

There is yet a third expedient that may be employed in lieu of a conventional purchase-money mortgage. The third method is also available for circumventing the problem that is attendant upon other loans that involve no actual transfer of funds between the parties.

The selfsame problem that arises with regard to purchase-money mortgages involving no transfer of cash also arises with regard to loans advanced by brokerage firms for the purchase of stock on margin by educational institutions for payment of tuition and in other situations in which the funds are retained or expended by the lender rather than by the borrower. In such circumstances, when no profit has been realized, the provider of the funds is fully aware of that fact. Hence, payment of the stipulated return in lieu of an oath becomes problematic since many rabbinic authorities maintain that an oath may not properly be demanded when the facts to be confirmed by oath are already known to the person demanding the oath. Such oaths are prohibited as "vain oaths." Hence, it is contended that a fee in lieu of the oath cannot legitimately be demanded. For obvious reasons, the solutions earlier offered with regard to purchase-money mortgages are of no avail with regard to loans of this nature.

There is, however, another remedy that does suggest itself. The parties may enter into an agreement stipulating that the funds credited to the purchase of stock, payment of tuition, or the like, shall constitute an interest-free loan but that the beneficiary assumes the obligation of investing an amount of money equal to the sum credited to him in a commercial venture designed to realize a profit. Fifty percent of that sum would be invested on his own behalf and fifty percent on behalf of the lender of the interest-free loan applied to payment of tuition, purchase of stock, the purchase price of real property, or the like. Since the lender has no knowledge of whether or not such counterpart funds were indeed invested in a profit-making enterprise or whether a profit was actually realized, he is entitled to stipulate that, in the event of a claim that no profit is realized, an oath could be sworn to that effect or that a stipulated sum be paid in lieu of an oath. A sample text of an English language *hetter iska* agreement incorporating these provisions may be found in this writer's *Contemporary Halakhic Problems*, IV (New York, 1995, pp. 380–83).

Summary and Conclusion

Hetter iska instruments can be tailored to reflect the nature of the terms and conditions desired by the parties. Case law indicates that, when properly drafted, civil courts will give effect to the intent of the parties in enforcing the terms of a *hetter iska* agreement. However, as is the case with regard to all legal documents, modifications should be undertaken only by a person possessing the necessary expertise. In order to assure conformity with the requirements of Jewish law and enforceability in a court of competent jurisdiction, the expert preparing such an agreement should be familiar with the provisions of both Jewish and secular law governing the transaction.

SELECTED BIBLIOGRAPHY

Arak, R. Meir. *Teshuvot Imrei Yosher*, I, 108.
Babylonian Talmud
Berakhot 35b
Bleich, R. J. David. *Contemporary Halakhic Problems*, II. New York, 1983, 376–96 and IV. New York, 1995, 378–84.
Bloi, R. Jacob. Isaiah. *Brit Yehudah.*
Breisch, R. Jacob. *Teshuvot Helkat Ya'akov*, III, nos. 188, 189, 194, and 195.
Eisenstadt, R. Meir. *Teshuvot Panim Me'irot*, II, no. 3.
Elijah of Vilna, R. *Bi'ur ha-Gra, Yoreh De'ah* 167:1.
Epstein, R. Baruch ha-Levi. *Torah Temimah*, Leviticus 25:36, sec. 192.
Feinstein, R. Moses. *Iggerot Mosheh, Yoreh De'ah*, II, nos. 62–63.
Ganzfried, R. Solomon. *Kitsur Shulhan Arukh* 66:10.
Grunfeld, R. Simon. *Teshuvot Maharshag, Yoreh De' ah*, no. 4, II, no. 252.
Halberstam, R. Hayyim. *Teshuvot Divrei Hayyim*, II, *hashmattot*, no. 16.
Isserlin, R. Israel. *Terumat ha-Deshen*, no. 302.
Kluger, R. Solomon. *Teshuvot Tuv Ta'am va-Da'at*, I, no. 208.
Nathanson, R. Joseph Saul. *Teshuvot Sho'el u-Meshiv, Mahadurah Kamma*, III, no. 160 and *Mahadurah Telita'ah*, I, no. 133.
Rafael, R. Shiloh. *Mishkan Shiloh*. Jerusalem, 1995, 281–88.
Rafael, R. Shiloh. In *Torah she-be-al Peh*, XIX. 1967, 100–5.
Samuel, B. David., and Moses ha-Levi, R. *Nahalat Shiv'ah*, no. 40.
Schneuer Zalman of Liady, R. *Shulhan Arukh ha-Rav, Hilkhot Ribbit*, sec. 42.
Shvadron, R. Shalom Mordecai. *Teshuvot Maharsham*, II, no. 216.
Sofer, R. Moses. *Teshuvot Hatam Sofer, Orah Hayyim*, no. 102, *Hoshen Mishpat*, no. 48.
Sternbuch, R. Moses. *Mo'adim u-Zemanim*, VI, no. 41.
Tabak, R. Solomon Leib. *Erekh Shai* 177:7, *Teshurat Shai,1 no. 3.*
Teomim, R. Joseph. *Ginat Veradim Yoreh De'ah, Klal* 6, no. 4.
Walden, R. Aaron. *Shem Ha-Gedolim ha-Hadash, Ma'arehkhet Gedolim*, at *ot men*, sec. 51.
Weiss, R. Isaac Jacob. *Teshuvot Minhat Yizhak*, IV, no. 16.
Zevin, R. Solomon Joseph. *Ha-Mo'adim Be-Halakhah*, 7th ed. Jerusalem, 1960), 7th ed.

CHAPTER 11

ETHICAL DEMANDS ON CREDITORS IN JEWISH TRADITION

YOEL DOMB

Introduction

In this article, I will endeavor to demonstrate that Judaism has a unique and valuable ethical contribution to the legal culture that developed over time regarding the recovery of loans.[1] Until recently, other traditions considered borrowers slaves at the mercy of their creditors, and, even today, borrowers in many countries can be imprisoned.[2] However, Judaism from its outset fought to protect the personal rights and freedoms of the borrower. This approach reached its apex in the Talmud, where the lender is enjoined not to make contact with the borrower and to avoid even chance meetings with him if it may cause embarrassment.[3] In medieval times, borrowers' personal rights

1 I should immediately cite as a primary source for this article the seminal work of Professor Menahem Elon, *Freedom of the Debtor's Person in Jewish Law* (Jerusalem: Magnes Press, 1964; Hebrew), where he sets out a detailed description of the various practices used by creditors to retrieve loans in different legal systems. Elon's approach is law-based and I relied on his sources to provide an ethical approach to this topic.

2 In Germany, debt imprisonment was outlawed at the end of the nineteenth century, except in extreme cases, such as a debtor attempting to smuggle assets away. In many American states, too, the practice is illegal. In Israel, however, incarceration is legal and commonly implemented. According to a report submitted to the Knesset Legislative committee in 2006, 2,714 people were arrested in that year for unpaid debts and 192,000 arrest warrants were issued. For a comprehensive analysis of legal trends in Israel regarding debt imprisonment, see Ron Harris, "Legitimizing the Imprisonment of Poor Debtors: Lawyers, Legislators, Judges" in Pnina Lahav, et al. (eds.), *The History of Law in a Multi-Cultural Society: Israel 1917–1967* (Aldershot, UK: Ashgate, 2002).

3 BT *Bava Metsi'a* 75b.

were repeatedly abused, and this led Jewish authorities to search for ways to enable recovery of debts that would not fall afoul of Biblical imperatives. Some even allowed incarceration of borrowers to compel them to pay their debts. I will discuss the moral basis for this transformation and apparent distortion of the original laws concerning borrowers and suggest methods to achieve a fair balance between the creditor's need to retrieve his loan and the borrower's personal dignity and commercial interests.

Ancient Legal Approaches to Debt Retrieval

Ancient legal systems tended to provide a creditor with a wide range of tools for retrieving loans. Some systems allowed taking the borrower himself as forced collateral against the loan. For example, Hammurabian law allowed a creditor who is owed produce or money to take the borrower or his wife, children, and slaves, although he was enjoined not to be cruel to them or cause their death.[4] This method did not always avail the creditor. It did not provide a solution for borrowers who remained recalcitrant even after human collateral was seized, and the financial burden of providing for human collateral often deterred creditors.[5] One alternative provided by the Hammurabian code allowed a borrower to voluntarily sell his family members as slaves for a limited period in order to pay off a loan. The code delineates a maximum period of three years of bondage.[6] Similar provisions were granted in the Assyrian code, which allowed a creditor to treat his collateral as he pleased from the time when a loan was due.[7] In the first tablet of this code, we read:

> If an Assyrian man or woman, who is in the house of the creditor as collateral, be taken [to discharge the debt] . . . he may hit him, tear out his hair, injure him or pierce his ears.[8]

After the debt expires, the human collateral becomes the property of the creditor, and the borrower cedes the right to free his collateral. The only restriction on the debtor is not to be unnecessarily cruel to his new property and not to cause their death.

Human collateral existed in many ancient legal systems, including Eshnunna, Sumerian, Nuzi, and Hittite law.[9] Even when the eighth century BCE Egyptian king Bocchoris abolished creditor enslavement of borrowers, he did not do so for humanitarian reasons,

4 For a detailed description of these laws, see G. R. Driver and H. C. Miles, *The Babylonian Laws* (Oxford: Clarendon Press, 1955).

5 Ibid., 219.

6 Ibid., 209. See also Isaiah 16:14 who sets the official term of a worker at three years.

7 See G. R. Driver and H. C. Miles, *The Assyrian Laws* (Oxford: 1935), 323–28, 271–90.

8 Section 44; see Driver and Miles, ibid., 413.

9 See A. Goetze, "The Laws of Eshnunna," *The Annual of the American Schools of Oriental Research* 31 (1951–52): 69; I. Mendelsohn, *Slavery in the Ancient Near East: A Comparative Study of Slavery in Babylonia, Assyria, Syria, and Palestine from the Middle of the Third Millennium to the End of the First Millennium* (New York: Oxford Univ. Press, 1949), 26–32; J. Nougayrol and Charles Villoreaud, *Le Palais Royal d'Ugarit* (Paris: Imprimerie Nationale, 1957–1970), 103.

but rather because he felt the state had the first right to subjugate its citizens. It would not be in the interest of the state if a soldier about to go to battle was placed in servitude because of an unpaid debt. Thus, the concept of slavery for loans is upheld, with the state having the primary right to its citizen's persons.[10]

We can now begin to understand the Torah's admonition against using a mill and grindstone as collateral, "for he takes a man's life as a pledge."[11] The Torah is referring to the prevalent ancient custom of taking the borrower as collateral for his loan, and it implies that taking away his source of livelihood is equivalent to taking possession of his body. When the Torah stresses "thou shalt not act like a creditor," we now have a clear picture of what is being proscribed.[12]

We can find another Biblical allusion to these practices in the book of Kings, where a woman turns to the prophet Elisha for succor, telling him that "the creditor is coming to take my two sons as slaves to him."[13]

Moreover, the book of Nehemiah describes the plight of some Jews who said:

> "We, our sons, and our daughters, [are] many: therefore we take up corn [for them], that we may eat, and live." [Some] also there were that said, "We have mortgaged our lands, vineyards, and houses, that we might buy corn, because of the dearth." There were also those that said, "We have borrowed money for the king's tribute, [and that upon] our lands and vineyards. Yet now our flesh [is] as the flesh of our brethren, our children as their children: and, lo, we bring into bondage our sons and our daughters to be servants, and [some] of our daughters are brought into bondage [already]: neither [is it] in our power [to redeem them]; for other men have our lands and vineyards."[14]

From the previous description of ancient law, it is clear that the wealthy Jews were mimicking the conduct of creditors in other legal systems who were not constrained by the Torah's dictates regarding loan retrieval. Nehemiah was infuriated by this flagrant violation of the Biblical precepts and succeeded in persuading the creditors to adopt the Jewish practices:

> And I said to them, "We after our ability have redeemed our brethren the Jews, which were sold unto the heathen; and will you even sell your brethren, or shall they be sold unto us? [How can you maintain a double standard of redeeming Jews from Gentile oppression but oppressing them yourselves?] They held they their peace, and found nothing [to answer]." Also I said, "It [is] not good that you do: ought you not to walk in the fear of our God because of the reproach of the heathen our enemies? [At least you should be embarrassed that the heathens will reproach you for leaving the Jewish ways.] I likewise, [and] my brethren, and my servants, might exact of them

10 See C. H. Oldfather (transl.), *Diodurus of Sicily* (London: Heinemann, 1946).

11 Deuteronomy 24:6. See also Onkelos' translation of this verse.

12 Exodus 22:24.

13 II Kings 4:1. According to Josephus (*Antiquities* 9:4), the woman was the wife of Obadiah who had hidden the prophets from Ahab (see I Kings 18:13) and had incurred debts to maintain them, which his wife was now being forced to pay. This does not imply that this form of slavery was legitimate, but that foreign practices influenced the ancient Hebrews as well.

14 Nehemiah 5:1–7.

> money and corn: I pray you, let us leave off this usury". . . . Then said they, "We will restore [them], and will require nothing of them; so will we do as you say."[15]

It is ironic that at the same time that Nehemiah waged his successful battle to protect the personal rights of borrowers, Roman law was developing the most extreme examples of creditor subjugation. According to the Twelve Tables, the earliest version of Roman legal jurisprudence (dating from 451 BCE, around the time of Nehemiah), a borrower who defaulted on his loans received a thirty-day period to pay off his debts, after which he was brought before the praetor (magistrate) and "transferred" to the creditor. He was then chained and brought to the market for three successive market days in order to find a redeemer willing to ransom him. If sixty additional days passed, he was considered the full property of his creditor, who could even have him executed or sold to slavery outside Rome. In a ghoulish addendum, the law states that:

> On the third market day, creditors shall cut pieces (*partis secanto*). Should they have cut more or less than their due, it shall be with impunity [it is not a punishable offence].[16]

The Romans viewed a defaulting borrower as a common criminal who stubbornly refuses to hand over his money. They did not take into account the borrowers' financial situation or his reason for defaulting, and they summarily handed him over to the mercy of his creditors to "cut pieces," which seemingly implies granting them rights to take pieces of the borrower's body.[17]

Centuries later, Shakespeare wrote his epic play, *The Merchant of Venice*, which was based on an Italian novel written some years earlier.[18] He created the character of the Jewish merchant Shylock, who demanded a "pound of flesh" from Antonio if he defaulted on his loan. In casting his merchant as a Jew, Shakespeare distorted the truth, since the Jewish Bible could never countenance such a horrendous practice and indeed fought to protect the rights of the borrower. The Italian novel Shakespeare relied on was based on ancient Roman law, as it appeared in the Twelve Tables. Thus did Shakespeare, who hardly knew Jews, impute them with using legal procedures that they could never have sanctioned.[19]

15 Ibid., 5:8–13.

16 Many authorities were skeptical about interpreting this law in its literal sense. William Blackstone describes it in his "*Commentaries on the Laws of England*," (1765–1769), chap. 31, as a "terrible law, if indeed that law is to be understood in so very butcherly a light, which many have doubted." Other scholars maintained that the law was meant in its literal sense but never actually implemented; see, for example, Gibbon, *Decline and Fall of The Roman Empire*, vol. 8:92.

17 This is synonymous with other Roman laws that ignored intentions and related only to the forms and actions themselves. Later Roman law abolished this practice. See, for example, H. Danker, *Roman Law Pleading: An Outline of its Historical Growth and General Principles* (Indianapolis: W.B. Burford, 1912), 15–18.

18 Fiorentino Giovanni, *Il Pecorone* (Ravenna: Longo, 1974; Italian).

19 Shakespeare was also culpable in depicting Shylock as an inveterate usurer when the Jews were driven to their occupation as money lenders by being prohibited from other occupations.

Restrictions on Creditors in Jewish Law

Besides enslaving a borrower, a creditor has many other options to ensure the retrieval of his loan. He can take collateral or even demand that the courts force the borrower to work for him. He could also agitate the debtor and regularly demand payment from him. Yet, as we shall see, Jewish tradition severely curtails these practices. For example, the Torah demands that a lender return collateral to a borrower at the end of each day if he needs it for his own use:

> If you take your neighbor's raiment as a pledge, you shall deliver it to him by the time the sun goes down. For that [is] his only covering, it [is] his raiment for his skin: what shall he sleep in? And it shall come to pass, when he cries to me, that I will hear; for I [am] gracious.[20]

The lender may not use collateral during the duration of the loan, and, if he does, he must deduct correspondingly from the value of the loan.[21] Moreover, he is prohibited from entering the house of the borrower in order to obtain collateral. In this latter restriction, it is clear that the Torah seeks not only to preserve the freedom of the borrower, but also to maintain his dignity and self-esteem. A person's house is his bastion of security, and to enter and summarily remove collateral pierces that bastion and deprives the borrower of his self-worth. Thus:

> You shall stand outside, and the man to whom you lend shall bring out the pledge to you.[22]

Demanding that the borrower work to repay his debts was a practice endorsed by later Roman Law,[23] but Judaism sees this as close to slavery. Therefore, it was prohibited by many Jewish authorities.[24] Even those who permit it do not *obligate* the borrower to work, out of concern that he might turn from a worker into a slave.[25]

The Talmud adds even more restrictions pertaining to the way that debt can be collected. The creditor cannot approach the borrower in the street, nor can he take collateral outside without going through the courts.[26] The lender should try to avoid unintentional encounters with the borrower, in order not to embarrass him.[27] Presumably, this prohibition would preclude demanding return of the loan when the lender knows the borrower is unable. R. Samson Raphael Hirsch (Germany, 1808–1888) remarks that a borrower commonly searches for ways to evade his

20 Exodus 22:25–26.

21 BT *Bava Metsi'a* 82b; *Mishneh Torah, Malveh ve-Loveh* 3:8.

22 Deuteronomy 24:11.

23 See R. W. Lee, *The Elements of Roman Law* (London: Sweet & Maxwell, 1946), 420, 442.

24 See further development of this point in a later section.

25 R. Jacob b. Asher (Spain, 1270?–1340) implies in the *Tur*, his compendium of Jewish law, that a person may sell himself to pay debts (*Hoshen Mishpat* 97). R. Israel Isser b. Ze'ev Wolf (Venice, 1770–1826) adds that if one would be forced to work it could be akin to slavery and therefore the borrower cannot be obligated to work (*Sha'ar Mishpat, Hoshen Mishpat* 97:3).

26 BT *Bava Metsi'a* 113a.

27 Ibid., 75b.

creditors, but the Torah, in its great sensitivity, requires the exact opposite. Creditors should try to avoid encountering borrowers, in order not to cause them the slightest anguish.[28]

Ethical Underpinnings of the Jewish Approach to Debt

I would like to suggest three possible reasons for the Torah's unique approach to debt retrieval:

1. The Torah's opposition to the institution of forced slavery.
2. The cosmic nature of wealth distribution.
3. The *mitzvah* (commandment) of loaning money.

First, as a nation that was forcibly enslaved for hundreds of years, the Jewish nation has an innate sensitivity toward the institution of slavery. God stresses to the Jewish nation:

> For unto Me the children of Israel are servants; they are My servants whom I brought forth out of the land of Egypt, I am the Lord your God.[29]

Although the Torah does not prohibit slavery, we see that God regards it as an affront to His own covenant with the Jewish people, who are considered His servants in this world. The Torah permits forced slavery only in one extreme case—if a thief is unable to return stolen goods, he must be sold in order to pay for his theft. The Talmud interprets the words "he shall be sold *for his theft*"[30] as implying that he is not to be sold to pay the extra portion required of a thief, but only in order to return the principal. The thirteenth-century authority R. Asher b. Jehiel (Rosh, Germany, c. 1250–1327) takes this Talmudic statement further, deriving from it that no Jew should be sold to pay off his debts.[31]

Second, Jewish tradition sees wealth as a Divine gift, and hence any illicit transfer of money from one individual to another is deemed as interfering with the Divine plan. Even an unpaid loan can cause cosmic ramifications, as it requires Divine intervention to restore the money to the lender.[32] This idea is eloquently stated in the tractate *Avot* (a part of the second-century compendium of the oral law, the Mishnah):

28 R. Samson Raphael Hirsch, *Commentary to the Torah* to Exodus 22:24. R. Hirsch was the leading proponent of Orthodoxy in nineteenth-century Germany and served as the rabbi of Frankfurt starting in 1851.

29 Leviticus 25:55.

30 Exodus 22:2.

31 *Responsa Rosh* 68:10. R. Asher b. Jehiel was a prominent German rabbi until he fled to Toledo, Spain to escape persecution. He authored a treatise on the Talmud as well as numerous *responsa*.

32 This interpretation stands in stark contrast to Kant's rational approach to unpaid loans, which he uses to demonstrate his categorical imperative. Kant saw the moral basis for paying loans in the rational need to fulfill

> R. Simeon said: "One who borrows and does not repay [is following an evil path which should be avoided]. One who borrows from man is akin to one who borrows from God, as it is written: 'The wicked borroweth and payeth not again, but the righteous showeth mercy and giveth.'"[33]

The allusion in this verse is to God (deemed "the righteous") intervening to reimburse the lender when the borrower has defaulted on his loan. Such a serious consequence of loan defaulting should create a more serious approach on the part of the borrower, and this would hopefully make the more extreme measures required to retrieve loans superfluous. This idea is borne out in another Rabbinic source:

> God commanded in the Torah "If you should loan my people (do not be to him like a creditor),"[34] and if he fails to pay you back **it is enough that I call him a wicked man**, as it is written: "The wicked borroweth and payeth not again, but the righteous showeth mercy and giveth."[35]

Specifically, because the Torah sees such consequences issuing from an unpaid loan, it prohibits the lender from using stronger tactics to retrieve his loan.

Third, the Jewish nation was the first to view granting loans as an act of charity and benevolence. Unlike other ancient traditions, it demanded that its adherents disburse part of their wealth as interest-free loans to those in need. Some authorities even view loans as being on a higher level than charity. Thus, we find in the thirteenth-century work *Sefer ha-Hinnukh*:[36]

> This command to lend money is stronger and more obligatory than the command to give charity, since he whose misfortune has been revealed and is known to people . . . is not in such despair and gloom as one who has not yet reached such embarrassment and is in fear of such a situation, and with the little help of a loan may never need handouts.[37]

---

promises, since if people would promise to repay and not repay, the promise itself would be irrational and even futile, as nobody would give it credence (*Grounding for the Metaphysics of Morals*, transl. James W. Ellington [Indianapolis: Hackett Pub. Co., 1993], 422). Kant negates any divine aspect of the loan and indeed does not ascribe any moral significance to the Jewish religion. In his *Religion Within the Limits of Pure Reason*, transl. Theodore M. Greene and Hoyt H. Hudson (Chicago, London: The Open Court Publishing Company, 1934), Kant claims that:

> The Jewish faith was, in its original form, a collection of mere statutory laws upon which was established a political organization; for whatever moral additions were then or later appended to it in no way whatever belong to Judaism as such. (Ch. 3, Part 2)

Yet the Jewish tradition regarding loans seems eminently more moral than its ancient peers, and, as I have shown, its moral underpinnings stem from the Bible and not from "appended" moral additions.

33 Avot 2:9.

34 Exodus 22:24.

35 *Exodus Rabbah* 31.

36 This work has previously been ascribed to R. Aaron b. Joseph ha-Levi (Spain, 1235–1300), a leading rabbi and teacher, but modern scholarship has challenged this assertion.

37 In the 17th century, R. David b. Samuel ha-Levi (Taz, Ukraine, 1586–1667) ruled based on the above logic that one who has the opportunity to either do charity or loan money should preferably loan money to those in need. See his commentary to *Shulhan Arukh, Hoshen Mishpat* 97:25.

Since loans are considered an act of charity, it is no surprise that the lender is adjured to respect the borrower's dignity and not deprive him of his liberty or personal possessions in the event of defaults. Doing so would take away from the purity of the lender's original charitable act.

Based on these principles, we will now set out to explain the sweeping changes that occurred in the laws of debt retrieval during the Middle Ages. We will also attempt to offer an ethical approach to corporate creditor ethics in modern times.

Developments and Changes in Debt Retrieval Law (700–1500 CE)

It was inevitable that such stringent debt retrieval laws would have to be modified. Crooks and con men persuaded innocent individuals to fulfill the religious obligation of granting them a loan and avoided payment until the lender gave up on them. People became more wary of lending money. The shortage of credit also threatened commercial life.

In the Geonic period (c. 700–1000 CE),[38] an enactment was passed enabling creditors to seize assets of borrowers even when unsanctioned by the Talmud.[39] The basis for this enactment was Talmudic legislation passed in order "not to close the door to borrowers."[40] This implies that new regulations can be established in order to enable borrowers to obtain credit from wary lenders.

However, the next enactment met with significant opposition, as it caused severe consequences for borrowers. A borrower who defaulted on a loan had to take an oath that he had no possessions, and he may have even suffered a "limited excommunication."[41] This serious social sanction would have cut off the livelihood of the borrower and deprived him of communal rights for the duration of the excommunication. In a sense, this contradicts the spirit of the Biblical law, as it curtails the liberty and autonomy of the borrower. This enactment seems to have been abolished by the eleventh century, as it is hardly mentioned afterward. However, the concept of taking an oath over unpaid debts remained a part of Jewish law even later.

38 The title "Gaon" was given to the heads of the Babylonian and Palestinian *yeshivot* from the 7th century CE, and therefore this period is known as the Geonic era.

39 According to the Talmud, only immovable assets of widows and orphans may be taken by a creditor. In the time of the Geonim, this ruling was relaxed. Moreover, they allowed creditors to appoint agents to collect their debts so that "a person would not take his friend's money and go off to another country" (Rambam, *Mishneh Torah, Sheluhin ve-Shuttafin* 3:7).

40 See, for example, BT *Sanhedrin* 3a.

41 See S. Asaf, *Tekufat ha-Ge'onim ve-Sifrutah* (Jerusalem: Mosad ha-Rav Kuk, 1955), 62–64. This medium is indeed mentioned in the Talmud regarding a borrower who has property and tries to put off paying his debts, but the Geonim extended it to those who had no assets in the hope that they would reveal their hidden assets.

Some earlier authorities (1000–1500 CE) attempted to relax the Biblical prohibition against entering the house of a borrower. However, Maimonides[42] takes strong issue with those who would abolish these laws:

> Even after this enactment [requiring the borrower to swear that he had no possession], no creditor can enter the house of the borrower, nor even a representative of the courts, as the [Rabbis] did not make an enactment which would uproot the law of the Torah. The borrower himself takes out his possessions and says; this is what I have.[43]

However, R. Isaac b. Jacob Alfasi (Rif, Spain, 1013–1103) maintained that, if the borrower was "aggressive and evil and brazenly refuses to pay his debt, it is permitted to enter his house and find his hidden possessions . . . and thus we act for communal needs."[44] Later on, R. Meir Abulafia (Rama, Spain, 1165–1244) explained that this behavior does not contradict the Torah, as its prohibition only applies if a creditor can locate assets outside the borrowers house. However, if no such assets are available and the borrower is known to be a man of means, the Torah did not intend to prevent creditors from sending court representatives to "find something which could legally serve as payment."[45] Once again, the basis for this interpretation was "not to close the door to [potential] borrowers."[46] Thus, the evolution of legal behavior was embedded in a more innovative interpretation of the Torah.

At the same time as Alfasi and Abulafia were finding new ways to deal with the more obstinate borrowers in Spain, the French school of Tosafists[47] was developing its own ingenious solution to the same problem. R. Jacob b. Meir Tam of Romereux (Rabbeinu Tam, France, 1100–1171)[48] suggested that the Torah only meant to prevent the borrower from taking collateral "to guarantee his money," but not if he intended to retrieve the actual loan. The latter could certainly be done through a court representative.[49] However, these leniencies were eschewed by many other authorities, who adopted the more conservative view of Maimonides.

As for other means of retrieval, imprisoning the borrower or forcing him to work were almost unheard of in the times of early authorities. R. Samuel b. Isaac Sardi (Spain, 1185/90–1255/6) writes: "Similarly, we should not deprive [the borrower] of his liberty, nor does he need to swear or bring proof that he is poor, as these are the

42 R. Moses Maimonides was the most famous leader of medieval Jewry. Forced to flee Spain, he settled in Egypt where he became a renowned rabbi, doctor, and philosopher. Among his works are his *Commentary to the Mishnah*, *Mishneh Torah* (a compendium of the entire oral law), and *Moreh Nevukhim* (a philosophical treatise).

43 Hilchot Malveh Ve'Loveh 2:2.

44 Responsum quoted in *Tur*, *Hoshen Mishpat* 97 and in other sources. R. Alfasi was a leader of Spanish Jewry in the 11th century and composed an abbreviated version of the Talmud with halakhic conclusions emphasized.

45 This precludes basic personal items of the borrower, which cannot serve as collateral.

46 Quoted in *Tur*, ibid. Rama was one of the great Spanish rabbis in the twelfth–thirteenth centuries.

47 A group of prominent French rabbis who developed their own Talmudic schools in the twelfth–thirteenth centuries and added many novellae on each tractate.

48 A grandson of R. Solomon b. Isaac (Rashi, France, 1040–1105), the leader of the French school of Talmudists, Rabbeinu Tam was the undisputed leader of French Jewry in the twelfth century and an author of many of the Tosafot-addenda to the Talmud.

49 Quoted in Rosh, Bava Metsi'a 9:46.

ways of the Gentiles."[50] Apparently, the Gentiles used to incarcerate all defaulting borrowers even when they had no means to pay.

This practice so irked the Jewish authorities that they were willing to countenance a false oath rather than allow a Jew to be thrown into debtor's jail. Maimonides was asked whether a borrower sued by his Jewish neighbor in a Gentile court would be allowed to swear falsely that he owes nothing, since "he is afraid that if he would admit his debt, he would be imprisoned and he has no means to save himself." Maimonides responded that "he can swear that he owes him nothing and think in his heart that indeed he owes him nothing, unless he will have what to give him."[51] In this way the borrower could maintain the Jewish attitude toward debt, even while he stands in a secular courtroom.[52]

Even persuading borrowers to work to pay off debts was proscribed. In France, Rabbeinu Tam took strong exception to this attempt to forcibly retrieve loans, since it seemed akin to slavery. Rosh derived the same ruling from the Torah's permit to obtain collateral from the borrower himself, implying that only material collateral is permitted and not mortgaging the borrower's person for his debt.[53]

However, as circumstances changed and borrowers' evasive tactics became more pronounced, even these more draconian methods of retrieval were cautiously introduced by prominent authorities. R. Alfasi was once again the innovator in this field. He adduced from the Biblical admonition against pressing a borrower for payment in the sabbatical year[54] that in any other year it would be permitted to press the borrower. Since this clearly contradicts the Biblical exhortation against acting like a creditor, Alfasi concludes that the exhortation must not refer to "any profit which the borrower accrues through his own industry, excluding his personal needs and clothing," which can be used to discharge his debt. Thus, he can legally be forced to work in order to pay off his creditors.

Alfasi's words are quoted in a responsum from R. Meir b. Baruch of Rothenburg (Germany, 1215–1293), the leading authority of German Jewry in the thirteenth century.[55] He also brings the comment of R. Judah b. Barzillai al-Bargeloni (Spain, late eleventh–early twelfth centuries) regarding the statement in the book of Proverbs that a borrower is a "slave" of his creditor.[56] Since the Bible expressly forbids slavery, this must refer to the possibility of forced labor to pay off debts, which is similar to slavery but nevertheless permitted. Thus, the very same rationale used by Rabbeinu Tam to prohibit forcing a borrower to work—since he is deemed a slave—serves as the basis for the Spanish rabbis to legitimate such means of retrieval. It is noteworthy

50 *Sefer ha-Terumot*, section 2, part 1, ch. 2.

51 Rambam, responsum no. 299 (Freiman edition), no. 410 (Blau edition).

52 Rambam's approach is based on the Talmudic permit to swear falsely to "robbers, confiscators etc.," if they illegally demand a part of one's produce for the benefit of the king. See BT *Nedarim* 27a.

53 *Responsa Rosh* 78:2.

54 Deuteronomy 15:1.

55 *Responsa Maharam* 146, Cremona edition. R. Meir was an influential rabbi who led German Jewry until he was taken captive by one of the German princes. He refused to be ransomed as this could have led to other kidnappings of prominent figures and he died in jail in 1290.

56 Proverbs 22:7.

that the Ashkenazic R. Meir preferred the view of the Spanish rabbis over his own forbears. Such a departure from tradition, so uncharacteristic of Ashkenazic scholars, could only be justified by a pressing social need—namely borrowers who were too lazy to work and repay their debts. Ironically, Rosh, R. Meir's star pupil, did not accept this ruling of the Spanish scholars, preferring the logic of Rabbeinu Tam to his teacher's ruling.

In the case of debtor imprisonment, the metamorphosis was even more remarkable. In earlier periods, incarcerating a defaulting borrower was deemed a flagrant violation of the Biblical laws. But, as time progressed, more borrowers were using ingenious tactics to evade repaying their debts, and creditors turned to the rabbis for ways to combat the problem. Rosh bemoaned those who "write documents [transferring their property to other's domain] and then take out loans. When these loans become payable, they take out these documents and claim they have no assets, even though all can see that they are holding these assets and doing business with them and they never left the domain [of the borrower]." Rosh invalidated such a document and considered it a sham that could have a deleterious effect on markets. "Since any man could use such a ploy . . . no man would lend money, which could close the door to potential borrowers . . ."[57] Rosh also allowed the courts to pressure a recalcitrant borrower suspected of using sham documents to hide his assets, and he even permitted giving lashes to such a borrower to persuade him to pay. Although he did not allow imprisoning a debtor who owes money to a private party, he permitted it when the debt is owed to the community, such as one who does not pay his communal taxes. He ruled that the lay leaders of a community are not subject to the strictures of the Biblical commands on creditors, which only apply to private debts.[58]

In the fourteenth century, this last protection of a borrower's most inalienable right was gradually eroded. In Germany, one authority found a hint in an obscure Talmudic source that incarceration could be a legally acceptable alternative for borrowers. The Talmud says that R. Abba owed money to the Exilarch, the leader of Babylonian Jewry, whose henchmen were "vexing" R. Abba.[59] From this, R. Alexander Zuslin (Germany, d. 1349) concluded that "if a person has assets and does not pay [debts] he may be jailed."[60] Although the proof is rather weak, as the term "vexing" could have many interpretations, R. Zuslin was obviously searching for a source to justify the imprisonment as a means of pressuring borrowers—already a prevalent practice in his time.

Correspondingly, the Spanish authorities half a century later reached a similar conclusion, although they based it on a different analysis. R. Isaac b. Sheshet Perfet (Rivash, Spain, 1326–1408) argues in a lengthy responsum that, even if the Torah totally negates the concept of borrower imprisonment, there is still room to allow

57 *Responsa Rosh* 78:3.

58 Ibid., 11:7.

59 BT *Yevamot* 121a.

60 *Sefer Agudah* to *Shabbat*, no. 150. R. Zuslin was one of the prominent authorities of his time; he served as the rabbi of a number of famous communities in Germany: Worms, Cologne, Frankfurt am Main, and Erfurt. He died a martyr's death in 1349.

for it as a "communal enactment" to combat duplicitous borrowers, since they deter people from offering credit. Rivash adds that, when he saw judges using these methods, "I wanted to object to this enactment as it contradicts our Torah, and they told me that it was for the benefit of the markets as there are swindlers and this deters creditors [from lending money], and I let them continue this practice."[61]

In the next paragraph, Rivash distinguishes between a borrower who has assets and smuggles them away, who can be forced by various means to pay his debts, and one who is poor and cannot pay his debts—whom it is clearly prohibited to imprison or vex in any other way, since "even passing in front of him to embarrass him is forbidden." The first type of borrower can be prosecuted on the grounds that paying one's debts is a Biblical command, and such commands can be enforced even by corporal punishment. Rivash infers from this that imprisonment would be another legitimate means of forcing the borrower to pay his debts, even though there is no source for such an assumption. He also does not explain how one can practically distinguish between the two types of borrowers. Moreover, it could be argued that there is a third category of borrowers who are not trying to smuggle away assets, but who may be responsible for taking on unnecessary debts that led to their defaulting. Can these borrowers be prosecuted and in what way?

The above analysis reflects an apparent dissipation of the original Biblical concern for borrowers' personal rights. Over a turbulent period of some five hundred years, prominent Jewish authorities seemingly eroded the prohibitions that had been observed over the previous two millennia. It is insufficient to suggest that these changes were merely the result of social upheaval and borrower misbehavior. We need a rationale that can justify these transformations as a continuation of the Biblical spirit and its approach to debt retrieval.

Suggested Paradigm for Changes in Debt Retrieval Law

A close reading of the Biblical text regulating the approach to debt will yield a number of important details that influence the law:

> If you shall lend money to any of My people, even to the poor with you, do not be to him as a creditor; neither shall you lay upon him interest.[62]

First, the obligation to lend money is not described as an imperative, even though the corresponding source in Deuteronomy clearly sees it as such. The allusion to the poor implies that they are the chief target of this command, as they are most likely

61 *Responsa Rivash* 484. Rivash was rabbi of Saragossa, Spain in the late fourteenth century, eventually moving to North Africa.

62 Exodus 22:24.

to need loans for personal use, and thus suffer the consequences of defaulting on them. Moreover, the injunction against acting like a creditor may only apply to the poor borrower mentioned in the verse, who has no means to pay his debt. Indeed, the early Midrashic source *Mekhilta de-Rabbi Yishma'el* interprets, "to the poor with you, do not be a creditor, but to the rich, you may be a creditor." Another source from the same period makes a similar inference from the same words: "Do not act like a creditor—do not pressure him or demand from him when you know he does not have."[63] Even when the Talmud enjoins a lender against deliberately meeting a borrower, it is only when "you know that he does not have [the money]."[64] Some authorities conclude from this that, when the creditor suspects that the borrower has money, it is permitted to demand payment and take action to retrieve the loan.[65] One contemporary authority has even said that the prohibition of "do not be to him as a creditor" does not apply if the borrower has more than the bare necessities that he is entitled to keep for himself.[66]

Thus, the entire Biblical command can be read in an entirely different way. It is not a blanket prohibition against demanding repayment of debts. Rather, it is mandate to show compassion and understanding for those who borrowed with the hope they would able to return, but subsequently found themselves without means to repay their loans. Any other borrower—one who claims poverty even while he maintains a high lifestyle, or one who borrowed recklessly and thoughtlessly—should not be protected from his creditors.[67]

Having established the deeper meaning of the Biblical command, we can now examine the ethical principles upon which it is based. As we stated above, Judaism is very reluctant to legitimate forced slavery. Only when a person has stolen and has no ability to pay can he be sold, with very severe restrictions on the way he is to be treated. If a borrower falsely claims that he cannot repay a loan and evades attempts to retrieve the debt, he is essentially like a thief who cannot return stolen property. When viewed in this fashion, it becomes clear why certain medieval authorities legitimated certain means of debt collection, even though Biblical sources seem to strongly prohibit them. The Bible was referring to people who were deserving of consideration due to their financial stress. However, people who sequester their

63 *Mekhilta de-Rashbi*, quoted by Rashi to Exodus, ibid.

64 BT *Bava Metsi'a* 75b.

65 *Kesef ha-Kodashim, Hoshen Mishpat* 96:1. There is an interesting discussion in the later authorities about why we do not use the rule "*sefeika de-Oraita le-humra*" (i.e., in case of doubt over a Biblical precept one must take the stringent view). The most plausible solution is suggested by R. Moses Schik (Hungary, 1807–1879)—that this rule does not apply where the alternative may enable another to perform a *mitsvah*. In this case, by asking the borrower to pay he would fulfill the *mitsvah* to repay a loan (see BT *Ketubbot* 86a) and therefore, when he may have the ability to pay, one can ask him to fulfill his *mitsvah* without transgressing the Biblical command of oppressing one's borrower.

66 R. Shemaryahu Joseph Nissim Karelitz, *Hut Shani* to *Hoshen Mishpat*.

67 R. Karelitz (ibid. to *Orah Hayyim* 242) posits that one who takes on more debts than he could conceivably repay in a lifetime is deemed a "wicked borrower" as well. Others derive this from the wording of the verse "The wicked borroweth and payeth not again," which implies that some people are deemed wicked from the moment they borrow if it is clear that they will not be able to pay. See the commentary of R. Jonah b. Abraham Gerondi to *Avot* 2:9.

belongings in the hands of others to evade paying debts are effectively stealing the lender's money and could be prosecuted accordingly—even to the point of forced work to repay their debts.[68] In no way does this contradict the spirit of the Bible's prohibition, as even the Bible favors slavery for a thief.

As we saw above, there are other rationales behind the Torah's injunction against acting like a creditor. In a sense, the Torah expects a creditor to place his trust in God and not to aggressively pursue the borrower. However, this does not preclude the courts from acting to retrieve the loan. Although even the courts are enjoined from entering the house and removing the personal belongings of a regular borrower, one who has no intention of paying his debts is deemed "wicked," and the courts can use stronger tactics to prevent him from acting wickedly.[69] Thus, corporal punishment and forced labor are not to be used on standard borrowers, but they could be acceptable when applied to a rogue who deliberately defaults on his debts.

As for the concept of charity applying to all loans and to the creditor's behavior regarding them, a close reading of the Torah suggests otherwise. R. Judah b. Samuel he-Hasid (Germany, c. 1150–1217) is quoted as saying that the Torah's statement "*If* you should lend money" hints that, in many cases, there is no obligation to lend, and it may even be a wrongful act:

> If he knows that even if [the borrower] will have money he will not repay, he is not obligated to lend him, and if he will only repay after arguments or one will have to chase him for months to pay his debt, on such a person it says "do no good for an evil one" and therefore it says: "*If* you shall lend"—as it is not always obligatory.[70]

There are even sources that indicate that a creditor is held responsible for giving his money to untrustworthy characters.[71] It follows, therefore, that the laws protecting borrowers should not apply to such unscrupulous people, and alternative means of retrieval should be available to those who lend to them.

We can therefore state with some certainty that the changes that occurred in debt retrieval law stemmed from an authentic interpretation of the Biblical text. The Torah never intended to protect rogue borrowers from being prosecuted and harassed in order to retrieve loans. In implementing these changes, the authorities were not merely responding to social needs but rather expressing the real intention

68 See R. Meir Auerbach, *Imrei Binah* (New York: Grossman, 1963/4, Rules of Debt Collection, ch. 2), who suggests that one who has intentionally defaulted on his loan should be treated as a thief and should not enjoy the protection that the Torah provides for borrowers. R. Auerbach distinguishes between those who delay paying or do not have the means to pay, who cannot be prosecuted by other means, and those who clearly do not intend to pay their loan at all.

69 The notion that *beit din* can prevent a person from acting wickedly is proposed in the *responsa* of R. Samuel b. Moses De Medina (Maharashdam, Salonika, 1505–1589), *Hoshen Mishpat* 259. Maharashdam dealt with a case of unfair competition where Jewish law deems one competitor a "wicked man," and he affirms that it is the job of *beit din* to prevent a person from acting wickedly, and even coerce him to stop acting in this way.

70 *Sefer Hasidim* 856. R. Judah b. Samuel he-Hasid was a 12th-century German rabbi who founded a movement of pietism and mysticism whose members were known as the "Hasidei Ashkenaz."

71 See BT *Shevu'ot* 39b and Rashi ad loc., where the lender is punished for not being careful to leave his money with an honest person, which ultimately led to his requiring an oath from the borrower.

of the Torah, which was to protect only innocent borrowers who were incapable of repaying their debts.

Corporate Creditor Ethics

On the basis of our previous analysis, we can now examine the Torah's attitude toward corporate debt. Since the Torah's rules are designed to protect individuals from being wrongfully enslaved or personally harassed for a monetary debt, they would not apply to corporate debts, for which there is no personal liability.[72] Thus, it would not be a problem for a borrower to hire debt collectors to seize the assets of a company that has defaulted on a loan.

There would, however, be another vital issue of creditor ethics regarding corporations, which requires a separate discussion. One of the secrets of success in business is the ability to persuade potential investors of a business's long-term financial stability and viability. If a creditor becomes convinced that a borrower will default on his loan, he could theoretically demand repayment before the due date of the loan. However, by doing so he immediately casts suspicion on the business and this may have a damaging effect, since it might cause others to call in their loans, thereby endangering the company's liquidity. Thus, corporate creditor ethics must balance the creditor's need to protect his investment with the borrower's need to maintain his business dealings. The *Shulhan Arukh*—the sixteenth-century codex of Jewish law—discusses this dilemma:

> One who has a bill of debt and comes to court before the debt is due, saying: I have found items belonging to [the borrower] and I am worried that if they will reach his hands, he will stow them away and I will have no way to recover my debt, then if the judge sees some basis for his assertion that he will not be able to recover the debt at the appointed time, the judge should allow him to keep the assets until the debt is due. Similarly, if the borrower took a loan, and before it was due, the creditor saw that the borrower was wasting money and had no immovable assets, or that he was about to leave the country, if the creditor demands his debt or collateral he is entitled to them.[73]

In the above situation, the authorities sided with the lender. As the Geonim pointed out, this is akin to returning lost property to its rightful owner. Alfasi adds that

72 The concept of corporate responsibility can be viewed either as the joint responsibility of those in control of the corporation or as the responsibility of the corporate entity as a whole. Both views are espoused by philosophers and jurists as well as by halakhic authorities. For the first view, see Peter A. French, *Collective and Corporate Responsibility* (New York: Colombia University Press, 1984); Thomas Donaldson, "Moral Agency and Corporations," *Philosophy in Context* 10 (1980). For the second view see John Ladd, "Morality and the Ideal of Rationality in Formal Organizations," *The Monist* 54,4 (1970). Central halakhic sources on this issue include *Minhat Yitshak* 3:1 by Rabbi Yitschak Weiss and *Iggerot Moshe, Yoreh De'ah* 3:41 by Rabbi Moshe Feinstein. The lack of personal liability is a major reason that R. Feinstein adopts the latter view on this issue.

73 R. Joseph Caro (Safed, 1488–1575), *Shulhan Arukh, Hoshen Mishpat* 73:10.

ruling otherwise would discourage potential lenders from investing their money,[74] and Rosh sees this rule as "saving the exploited from the hands of the exploiter."[75] However, it is a later authority who relates this issue to the general topic of creditor ethics. R. Solomon Luria (Maharshal, Lublin, 1510?–1574) sees a moral obligation on the part of the borrower from the moment he takes the loan:

> Even though there is a time mentioned in the bill of debt, the obligation [to protect the lender's investment] begins from the moment the loan is provided, with the proviso that the lender will not demand the debt before it is due . . . and just as it is forbidden for a creditor to harass his borrower, so it is forbidden for the borrower to hold back [fritter away] the creditor's money . . . and therefore it is the law of the Torah to save the one who is being exploited.[76]

According to Maharshal, since the Torah effectively tied the hands of the creditor and prevented him from taking action to recover his money, it is up to the courts to protect his interests and save him from being exploited by the borrower. This is another affirmation of our thesis that the Torah intended to protect only innocent borrowers. Yet how are we to know whether a borrower is acting irresponsibly or is genuinely in need of protection? The above quote from the *Shulhan Arukh* appears to propound two opposing views: One says that it is enough for the judge to see "some basis" in order to justify the lender's seizing property, while the other would require some evidence that the borrower is wasting money or about to flee the country. Maharshal takes the latter view and distinguishes between one who willfully wastes the lender's money and one who has suffered misfortune in his business. The latter cannot be asked to return debts before they are due, even if this endangers the creditor's investment. The implicit understanding is that, when investments go sour, the borrower cannot always be held responsible. However, Maharshal adds another important caveat regarding these loans:

> Now that most of the Jews' livelihood is dependent on credit, and most are businessmen with few assets who take merchandise for a limited period, it is not right for a judge to confiscate his assets, since this will lead to rumors which could hurt his livelihood, and all his creditors will converge on him simultaneously. . . . and I heard of many Jewish and Gentile businessmen who due to rumors spreading about their financial stability suffered grave losses and could not recover their losses afterwards.[77]

Thus, regarding corporate loans, the most important issue is to protect the borrower from unwarranted losses. Going to court to seize assets will invariably cause a ripple effect, and therefore Maharshal suggests that the creditor should secretly make an agreement with the borrower to accept "excommunication or punishment" if he defaults on his debt. The court can also apply pressure to the borrower, but only discreetly, in order not to damage his business interests.

74 *Responsa Rif* 113.

75 Rosh to *Bava Kamma* 1:5.

76 R. Solomon Luria, *Yam shel Shelomoh* to *Bava Kamma* 1:20. A descendant of Rashi and a forceful personality in his own right, Maharshal authored a number of works, including *Yam shel Shelomoh*, in which he discusses numerous Talmudic subjects and their relationship to Halakhah.

77 Ibid.

Conclusion

We have demonstrated that the Torah offers a viable and attractive way of maintaining the dignity of the borrower and his business interests, balanced with the interests of his creditors. While the Torah eschews the ancient idea of placing the borrower at the mercy of his creditors, it allows some methods to be used to protect the creditor's interests. In extreme cases, it may even sanction imprisonment or forced labor to persuade recalcitrant borrowers to pay their debts. This is based on the understanding that there is no ethical basis for protecting those who exploit others' money for their own benefit. They cannot enjoy the protection afforded to honest borrowers genuinely unable to repay their debts.

SELECTED BIBLIOGRAPHY

Asaf, S. *Tekufat ha-Ge'onim ve-Sifrutah: Hartsa'ot ve-Shi'urim*. Jerusalem: Mosad ha-Rav Kuk, 1955, 62–64.

Asher B. Jehiel. *Responsa Rosh* 11:7, 78:2, 78:3.

Auerbach, R. Meir. *Imrei Binah*. New York: Grossman, 1963/4, ch. 2, Rules of Debt Collection.

Bible:

Exodus 22:2, 24–26.

Leviticus 25:55.

Deuteronomy 24:6.

Nehemiah 5:1–13.

Caro, R. Joseph. *Shulhan Arukh, Hoshen Mishpat* 73:10.

Danker, H. *Roman Law Pleading: An Outline of its Historical Growth and General Principles*. Indianapolis: W.B. Burford, 1912, 15–18.

David B. Samuel ha-Levi. *Taz* to *Hoshen Mishpat* 97:25.

Driver, G. R., and J. C. Miles. *The Assyrian Laws*. Oxford: 1935, 271–90, 323–28, 413. *The Babylonian Laws*. Oxford: Clarendon Press, 1955, 219.

Elon, Menahem. *Freedom of the Debtor's Person in Jewish Law*. Jerusalem: Magnes Press, 1964 (Hebrew).

Feinstein, R. Moses. *Iggerot Mosheh, Yoreh De'ah* 3:41.

Giovanni, Fiorentino. *Il Pecorone*. Ravenna: Longo, 1974 (Italian).

Goetze, A. "The Laws of Eshnunna." *The Annual of the American Schools of Oriental Research* 31 (1951–1952): 69.

Harris, Ron. "Legitimizing the Imprisonment of Poor Debtors: Lawyers, Legislators, Judges." In Lahav, Pnina, et al. (eds.). *The History of Law in a Multi-Cultural Society: Israel 1917–1967*. Aldershot, UK: Ashgate, 2002.

Hirsch, R. Samson Raphael. *Commentary on the Torah* to Exodus 22:24.

Jacob B. Asher. *Tur, Hoshen Mishpat* 97.

Josephus, Flavius. *Antiquities* 9:4.

Judah B. Samuel he-Hasid. *Sefer Chasidim* 856.

Kant, Immanuel. *Grounding for the Metaphysics of Morals*. Transl. James W. Ellington. Indianapolis: Hackett Pub. Co., 1993, 422.

———. *The Religion Within the Limits of Pure Reason*. Transl. Theodore M. Greene and Hoyt H. Hudson. Chicago, London: The Open Court Publishing Company, 1934, ch. 3, part 2.

Karelitz, Shemaryahu Joseph Nissim. *Hut Shani*, Vol. 1 *Orah Hayyim* 242.

Lee, R. W. *The Elements of Roman Law*. London: Sweet & Maxwell, 1946, 420, 442.

Maimonides, *Mishneh Torah:*

Malveh ve-Loveh 3:8.

Sheluhin ve-Shuttafin 3:7.

———. *Responsa Rambam*. No. 299 (Freiman edition), No. 410 (Blau edition).

Meir B. Baruch of Rothenburg. *Responsa Maharam* 146. Cremona edition.

Mendelsohn, I. *Slavery in the Ancient Near East: A Comparative Study of Slavery in Babylonia, Assyria, Syria, and Palestine from the Middle of the Third Millennium to the End of the First Millennium*. New York: Oxford Univ. Press, 1949, 26–32.

Medina, R., and Samuel B. Moses de. *Responsa Maharashdam, Hoshen Mishpat* 259.

Perfet, Isaac B. Sheshet. *Responsa Rivash* 484.

Sardi, R. Samuel B. Isaac. *Sefer ha-Terumot*. Section 2, part 1, ch. 2.

Solomon Luria. *Yam shel Shelomoh* to *Bava Kamma* 1:20.

Talmud (Babylonian):

Bava Metsi'a 75b, 82b, 113a.

Shevu'ot 39b.

Wolf, Israel Isser B. Ze'ev,. *Sha'ar Mishpat, Hoshen Mishpat* 97:3.

CHAPTER 12

THE JEWISH PROHIBITION OF INTEREST: THEMES, SCOPES, AND CONTEMPORARY APPLICATIONS

DANIEL Z. FELDMAN

The Prohibitions of Taking and Paying Interest

The prohibition of taking interest, also known as *ribbit*,[1] is one of the most complex areas of Jewish law. The complexity of this realm is multileveled. On one level, it applies in the sense that the concept is one that by its nature is detailed and extensive in scope. The practical implications of the prohibition fill thousands of pages of the codes of Jewish law, monographic treatments, and the *responsa* literature. On another level, the law is also conceptually complex. At first glance, *ribbit* and its basic intent seem simple to comprehend. It appears to address the widely condemned practice of usury, also known as predatory lending, where a lender exploits a borrower's desperate need for assistance by lending at rates of interest that are excessive and often unfeasible. Such a lender understandably earns the condemnation of

1 Referred to by the Torah with the terms "*neshekh*" (biting) and "*tarbit*" (increase), and known since Talmudic times by the term "*ribbit*" (a construct of *tarbit*).

decent society. Many have interpreted the Torah's prohibition in this way—as limiting those who would capitalize on the suffering of the needy and push them further into debt and disadvantage. This is reflected by translations that use the term *usury*, and by later writings, from authors of various faith traditions, that acknowledge the Torah as a source condemning usurious practices.[2] Among traditional Jewish sources, there are indications in this direction as well, starting with the Torah's use of the word *neshekh* (which connotes "biting" into someone). The *Sefer ha-Hinnukh* (anon., thirteenth century) states that interest is forbidden because it eventually deprives a borrower of all his material resources.[3]

However, a close look at the details of the prohibition will reveal that concern for predatory lending is insufficient to explain the Torah's ban against interest. First, an overview of the relevant sources is necessary. The Torah lays out the prohibition against interest in three places:

> If you lend money to any of My people, even to the poor with you, you shall not be to him as a creditor; neither shall you lay upon him interest. (Exodus 22:24)
>
> Take no interest of him or increase; but fear your G-d; that your brother may live with you. You shall not give him your money upon interest, nor give him your victuals for increase. (Leviticus 25:36–37)
>
> You shall not lend upon interest to your brother: interest of money, interest of victuals, interest of any thing that is lent upon interest. Unto a foreigner you may lend upon interest, but unto your brother you shall not lend upon interest, that the Lord your G-d may bless you in all that you put your hand unto, in the land that you go in to possess it. (Deuteronomy 23:20–21)

The Talmud details the rules of the prohibition in the fifth chapter of the tractate *Bava Metsi'a* (60b–75b), where R. Nachman (Babylonia, fourth century) sums up with great brevity the guiding principle involved: *klala de-ribita, kol agar natar leih assur*—"the general principle of *ribbit*, is that all payment for waiting is prohibited."[4]

The Challenge of Categorizing *Ribbit*

How should the prohibition against *ribbit* be categorized? On the one hand, *ribbit* deals with interpersonal monetary transactions, and thus appears to be firmly within the realm of civil law. However, a cursory exposure to the regulations of

2 See, for example, Calvin Elliot, *Usury: A Scriptural, Ethical and Economic View* (Ohio, Anti-Usury League, 1902). Some definitions of the word *usury* do understand the term to be applicable to all interest; many dictionaries list this usage as "archaic." For our purposes, we will use the word to mean predatory lending, in its legal definition of "excessive or illegal interest rate," and distinct from the *halakhic* concept of *ribbit*. See also "The History of Usury" at http://www.affil.org/consumer_rsc/usury.php.

3 *Sefer ha-Hinnukh*, *mitzvah* 68.

4 *Bava Metsi'a* 63b.

ribbit indicates otherwise. First, a borrower is not permitted to waive his rights and volunteer to pay interest. If he does so, he is guilty of transgression.[5] This is not what one would expect from a civil law, and the Talmud itself states that "all conditions are valid" in monetary matters.[6] Both logic and law state that such a mutually accepted arrangement, arrived at without duress or deception, should be unobjectionable. For example, theft ceases to be defined as such when the "victim," with complete freedom of will, offers his property to the taker. Similarly, it is wholly conceivable that a borrower would eagerly and willingly agree to an interest-bearing loan that advances his own goals. Yet his consent does nothing to mitigate the Torah prohibition. Astonishingly, Jewish law views both a buyer who pays interest and his lender as equally culpable of transgression. This is clearly at variance with the totality of civil and criminal law, where holding perpetrator and victim equally culpable is inconceivable.

Another element of the prohibition is also inconsistent with the norms of civil and monetary law. It applies not only to lenders, but also to anyone involved in the transaction, including witnesses and scribes.[7] This expansion gives the prohibition a unique quality of absoluteness. The *ribbit* prohibition contains numerous other expansions of scope. The primary, Biblical model of *ribbit* is *ribbit ketzutzah*—when the interest is set as such from the initial transaction. However, there are numerous other gradations and applications that extend the prohibition further, into categories of descending severity. Many of these, termed *avak ribbit* (the "dust" of *ribbit*), are by rabbinic decree and are thus subject to various leniencies and exceptions. Some of these are discussed below. Furthermore, two of the primary canons of Jewish law, the *Tur*[8] and the *Shulhan Arukh*,[9] codified the laws of *ribbit* in the section dealing with ritual law (*Yoreh De'ah*), and not the section dealing with civil law (*Hoshen Mishpat*).[10]

The proper classification of *ribbit* is actually a subject of debate in the rabbinic literature, as will be discussed further below. Some authorities follow the lead of the *Tur* and the *Shulhan Arukh*, and interpret the prohibition as a ritual one, while others classify it as a civil regulation. The latter possibility requires some explanation, considering the above irregularities and also the fact that the Torah explicitly permits taking interest from a gentile.[11] If taking interest is truly a moral offense, it should be prohibited across the board, and the exception for gentiles is difficult to explain.

It appears, then, that the interpersonal violation is not one of usury, which is a broader moral infraction, but rather an undermining of the familial relationship

5 See *Bava Metsi'a* 61a and *Shulhan Arukh Yoreh De'ah* 160.

6 TB *Ketubbot* 56a.

7 TB *Bava Metsi'a* 75b.

8 R. Jacob ben Asher (Germany and Spain, ca. 1270–1340).

9 R. Joseph Caro (Israel, 1488–1575).

10 It should be noted that the categorization of the *Shulhan Arukh* is of limited significance, as he followed the ordering of the *Tur*.

11 Deuteronomy 23:20. See *Shulhan Arukh, Yoreh De'ah,* 159:1.

expected among members of the Jewish people. This is stated explicitly by Nahmanides (Ramban, Spain, 1194–1270)[12] and his student, R. Solomon b. Abraham Adret (Rashba, Spain, c. 1235–c. 1310)[13]. It is also reflected in the *responsa* of the *rebbe* of Sochatchov, R. Abraham Bornstein (Poland, 1839–1910), entitled *Avnei Nezer*. The section of his *responsa* dealing with *ribbit* is titled *Berit Ahim*. In addition to being an anagram of the Hebrew word "*ribbit*," the word *berit* is significant. The title translates as "The Covenant of Brothers," conveying that the ban against interest constitutes a unique bonding mechanism for the Jewish people.

This explains why even reasonable rates of interest are forbidden. In a general context, they would not be predatory or immoral, but they are out of place among close family members. Thus, the prohibition forms and strengthens a familial connection among the Jewish people. In this manner, the prohibition of *ribbit* would indeed be viewed as an interpersonal regulation, albeit one that is applied differently than other precepts of basic morality.

A Possible Theory of *Ribbit* as Ritual Violation

Nonetheless, as detailed above, the evidence abounds that *ribbit* is not to be categorized as an interpersonal prohibition. One possible theory toward the understanding of *ribbit* as a ritual prohibition may be informed by the fact that the prohibition of taking interest is, in one instance (the source in Leviticus), located in the Torah together with the commandment of the *shemittah* year, when the fields of the Land of Israel must go untended. The *shemittah* directive is often associated with the concept of *emunah*, or faith in G-d. Abstaining from productive agricultural labor for a year, despite the need to eat and provide for one's family, strongly expresses faith in G-d's providence over those who observe His commandments. However, if one were to agree to observe the obligation of *shemittah*, but only on the condition that others guarantee to indemnify him against any possible loss of profit, this might technically fulfill the commandment, but his observance is clearly lacking as an expression of faith.

A similar structure may exist within the prohibition of *ribbit*. The Torah commands the assisting of the needy through loans. Lending money (and objects) to those in need is considered a primary act of *hesed*, or kindness. In his Talmudic commentary, R. Solomon ben Isaac (Rashi, France, 1040–1105) classifies this act as representative of the category of "*hesed* with one's property."[14] Indeed, in much of rabbinic literature, it represents the category of *hesed* as a whole. In his classic work

12 Commentary to Deuteronomy, 23:21.

13 *Responsa Rashba*, Vol. 1, 242.

14 *Sukkah* 49b, s.v. *u-ve-mamono*.

on the principle of *hesed*, [15] Rabbi Yisrael Meir ha-Kohen (Hafetz Hayyim, Poland, 1838–1933) focuses primarily on loaning money and property.

However, *hesed* is only one of the religious accomplishments associated with lending. Several other values may be involved as well. Lending to a poor borrower is also considered an act of *tzedakah* (charity). This is not diminished by the fact that the borrower ultimately returns the loaned object or the funds, as their mere usage has a quantifiable value. In fact, the fact that the item is returned increases the obligation, as no lasting loss is incurred to the lender, who thus cannot so easily exempt himself.

Lending to the poor is a form of charity, but it also constitutes its own separate *mitzvah*. As the Torah states, "If you lend money to any of My people, even to the poor with you, you shall not be to him as a creditor; neither shall you lay upon him interest."[16] Despite the verse's conditional language, the Rabbis taught that, in this context, "if" conveys an obligation.[17] R. Meir Dan Plotzki (Poland, 1867–1928) notes two possible ways of viewing this *mitzvah*: (a) as an obligation to support one's fellow, focused on the result of that support more than on the action itself, and (b) as a method of fortifying one's internal sense of compassion by focusing attention on the financial needs of another.[18] These two approaches can be applied to *hesed* in general.

When the loan prevents the borrower's financial collapse, an additional *mitzvah* is relevant. The Torah restates the prohibition of charging interest with the words, "if your brother become poor, and his means fail with you; then you shall uphold him . . . that your brother may live with you."[19] This phraseology suggests an obligation to be concerned with the ability of others to make a basic living.[20] As R. Avraham Ze'ev Rosner (Israel, contemporary) demonstrates,[21] this is very likely an independent *mitzvah*, with its own rules and formulations.[22] Some assert that this *mitzvah* applies only to a loan that will be used as capital toward an income,[23] while others understand it as applying to any loan that sustains the beneficiary until he finds steady employment.[24]

If the loan is needed to pay for medical expenses or related needs, one accomplishes an additional *mitzvah*. The Torah's commandment to return lost

15 *Ahavat Hesed.*

16 Exodus 22:24.

17 *Mekhilta,* ibid. See R. Yitzchak Kreiser, *Ish Le-Rei'eihu* (on Exodus), 350–52, for theories as to why the obligation would be conveyed in this language.

18 *Keli Hemdah, Deuteronomy* 11:5.

19 Leviticus 25:35–36. See R. Asher Weiss (Israel, contemporary), *Minhat Asher al Ha-Torah,* Exodus, 41.

20 There is a disagreement among the medieval authorities as to whether the phrase "you shall uphold him" represents an obligation of charity (see Maimonides, *Mishneh Torah, Matnot Aniyim,* 10:7) or general life-saving efforts (see Nahmanides, additions to Rambam's *Sefer Ha-Mitzvot,* 16).

21 *Mitzvat ha-Hesed,* 249–53.

22 See *Shulhan Arukh Yoreh De'ah* 249:6 and *Derishah* 249:1. See also R. Dov Rosenthal, *Divrei Yosher* on *Avot, Hiddushim u-Bi'urim,* 2.

23 See R. Yerucham Fishel Perlow, commentary to *Sefer Ha-Mitzvot* of R. Sa'adiah Ga'on, positive commandment 25.

24 See R. Shimon Malkah, *Mishpetei Shimon: ha-Halva'ah Le-Or ha-Halakhah,* 4, fn. 9.

property—"and you shall restore it to him"[25]—is interpreted by the Talmud as implying an obligation to help restore others to health. Failing to assist someone at risk may put one in violation of "neither shall you stand idly by the blood of your neighbor."[26] Of course, this is even more acutely relevant when the loan is necessary for matters of life and death.

The Torah strengthens the positive commandment to extend loans with a negative commandment. In the context of an impending *shemittah* year, the end of which cancels all outstanding loans, the Torah warns, "Beware that there be not a lawless thought in your heart, saying 'The seventh year, the year of release, is at hand,' and your eye be evil against your needy brother, and you refuse to give him, and he will cry unto the Lord against you, and it will be sin upon you."[27]

These multiple sources make it abundantly clear that providing loans when necessary and reasonable is a fundamental interpersonal obligation of the Torah. That being the case, it can be stated that, if one were to declare that he was willing to do so, but only on the condition that he is provided with a signed contract guaranteeing a return on his money comparable to what he would receive from a bank or from an investment, this insistence would be an offense against G-d. It would not necessarily be an interpersonal offense, as the borrower may be more than eager to agree to the arrangement; it would rather be a violation of G-d's command to engage in *hesed* for its own sake.

It is also instructive that the Biblical prohibition against interest only applies when the interest is stipulated at the time of the loan. This indicates that the offense is not the collection of the interest itself, but rather the initial decision to lend on interest. That decision is an affront to the Divine mandate of *hesed*, so fundamentally represented by the act of lending money.

This perspective may illuminate a Talmudic comment that is difficult to comprehend. R. Yose's states that those who lend on interest "deny the G-d of Israel."[28] Even if one assumes the severity of the prohibition, the connection to heresy is unclear. However, based on the above theory, one can suggest that taking interest in particular violates the central mandate of *hesed* that characterizes the Divine charge to the Jewish people. As taking interest is an offense against G-d, rather than the borrower, it is understandable that Maimonides[29] (Rambam, Egypt, 1135–1204) extends this imprecation to the borrower, as he makes this affront possible.[30]

25 Deuteronomy 22:2.

26 Leviticus 19:16.

27 Deuteronomy 15:9. See *Gittin* 36a, and *Torah Temimah*, Deuteronomy 15, no. 29.

28 TB *Bava Metsi'a* 71a. A similar statement appears in the Jerusalem Talmud, *Bava Metsi'a* 5:8.

29 *Mishneh Torah, Matnot Aniyim* 4:7.

30 See also R. Ephraim Solomon of Luntshits (Poland and Bohemia, 1550–1619), *Keli Yakar*, Leviticus 25:36, who asserts that the collection of *ribbit* is an offense to G-d in that it displays a lack of faith that he will supply sustenance. However, it is difficult to see how this is not true of all profit-seeking ventures (or at least those with contractual guarantees, which is the focus in this case), unless one connects the concept directly to the *hesed* obligation, as detailed above. See also R. Aharon Yehudah Grossman (Israel, contemporary), *ve-Darashta ve-Hakarta al ha-Torah,* Vol. 3, 326–30.

A similar position is taken by R. Shimon Pollak (Hungary, 1800s), *Responsa Shem Mi-Shimon*, Vol. 1, *Yoreh De'ah* 15. It is also noteworthy that R. Pollak, in his discussion, considers the implications of the equation of charging

The Talmud states that one who lends money with interest also violates the prohibition against "acting as a creditor."[31] This seemingly separate prohibition enjoins a lender from pressing or appearing to press a borrower for repayment.[32] Ramban explains that the two prohibitions share the common goal of preserving the act of lending money as an act of *hesed.*[33] The prohibition against interest prevents *hesed* from turning into a source of financial profit. Similarly, the prohibition against acting as a creditor prevents the lender from exploiting the loan to gain social standing or honor. In all their interactions, the relationship between lender and borrower must remain as it was before the loan.[34]

The objection might be raised that the above approach is appropriate when the loan is necessary to help the needy in dire financial straits. However, it is clear that the prohibition of *ribbit* applies across the board, forbidding the taking of interest even when the loan is provided to a wealthy businessman investing in a project to further increase his fortune. This need not call the theory into question; it is often the case that the Torah's commandments apply unilaterally, maintaining whether their assumed objective is relevant or not. As such, it is understandable that *ribbit* will be forbidden in all cases. Nonetheless, it is also the case that when the loan is business-related, a mechanism has been provided by the Talmud to allow for profit to come to the lender while still preserving the structure of the prohibition. While a detailed discussion of this mechanism, known as *hetter iska,* is outside the scope of this chapter, mention will be made before the closing section.

Recovering *Ribbit* that has been Paid

A lender who violates the prohibition against interest is obligated to return the interest to the borrower. The Talmud locates this responsibility in the phrase, "that your brother may live with you."[35] The Talmud records a debate between R. Elazar

ribbit with the denial of G-d, to the extent that the prohibition might be considered a crime of idolatry, with the entire stricture that entails. He dismisses that possibility and in this vein discusses the comment of the *Taz* (Poland, 1586–1667) to the ruling of the *Shulhan Arukh* (*Yoreh De'ah* 1:22) that states that one may borrow with interest if it is necessary to do so to save one's life. The *Taz* (160:21) questions the necessity of that statement, as it is clearly established that almost all transgressions may be committed to prevent loss of life. R. Pollak suggests that the necessity for the statement emerges from the comparison to denying G-d. One might have concluded that *ribbit* is equal to idolatry—one of the three offenses that are not suspended to save a life. Thus, the intent is to dispel this notion.

In a different direction, Professor Aaron Kirschenbaum, in his *Equity in Jewish Law* (Ktav Publishing House, 1991, 25–44), after a thorough overview of the themes and rabbinical positions relating to *ribbit*, presents the position that the unique character of *ribbit* is due to it constituting a "legislation of *hesed*" as opposed to being a manifestation of *tzedek* (justice). This view appears to be more consistent with the position that *ribbit* remains an interpersonal principle, albeit an enhanced one. However, the notion that the prohibition is a ritual one, placing an equal burden upon the borrower, would seem to require additional explanation, in the nature of that tendered above.

31 Exodus 22:24.

32 TB *Bava Metsi'a* 75b.

33 Commentary to Exodus 22:24.

34 Leviticus 25:36. See R. Eliyahu Tziyon Sofer, *Sha'arei Tziyon*, Vol. 3, 4:1:4, fn 3.

35 TB *Bava Metsi'a* 61b–62a.

and R. Yochanan as to whether a *beit din* (rabbinical court) will enforce the returning of interest. The *halakhah* follows the view that *ribbit* is recoverable through *beit din*.[36]

R. Israel Zev Gustman[37] (Israel, 1908–1991) posits three ways of understanding *beit din*'s involvement, reflective of different understandings of the prohibition of *ribbit*:

1. *Ribbit* is comparable to theft. Courts ensure the return of stolen property, and the same applies to *ribbit*.[38]
2. *Ribbit* is a ritual law, and not comparable to theft. However, the ritual precept creates an actionable monetary debt.
3. The obligation is not monetary at all. *Beit din's* involvement is comparable to other situations in which they enforce a ritual responsibility (having already established that there is a commandment to return *ribbit* to the borrower).[39]

It is noteworthy that Rambam and Ramban apparently dispute whether returning interest is counted as one of the 613 Biblical *mitzvot* (commandments). In his enumeration of the commandments, Rambam omits any specific reference to it, while Ramban, in his glosses to that work, corrects the omission. In defense of Rambam, the commentary *Megilat Esther* suggests that he felt no need to list this as a commandment, as it is included in the commandment to return stolen money.

In addressing the quandary of classifying *ribbit*, R. Gustman suggests a distinction within the concept of theft (*gezel*). Classical theft, or what he terms "monetary theft," is a civil concept. In addition, there is "ritual theft" (*gezel issuri*)—an act termed theft only because it is deemed so by ritual law. This classification allows the prohibition of *ribbit* to have elements in common with theft while still governed by aspects of ritual law.[40]

The distinction is important for many reasons, among them the fact that monetary law and ritual law are often guided by differing rules. A relevant example is a situation of unresolved doubt (*safek*). In a situation of ritual responsibility mandated by Biblical law, there is a requirement of stringency (*safek de-orayta li-chumra*). However, when the questionable obligation is monetary, the onus of proof falls on the claimant (*ha-motzi mei-chaveiro alav ha-ra'ayah*), effectively absolving one of the responsibility to pay. A related principle allows an individual of whom money is demanded to assert that he subscribes to a minority opinion in his favor (*kim li*) and to exempt himself.[41]

36 *Yoreh De'ah* 161:5.

37 *Kuntreisei Shiurim*, *Bava Metsi'a*, lecture 26.

38 See, for example, *Sefer ha-Hinnukh*, 343, who explicitly formulates the concept in this way.

39 This view is explicit in the commentary of the Rashba. R. Yoav Yehoshua Weingarten wrote an essay refuting this notion in his *Responsa Helkat Yo'av*, Vol. 1, 24.

40 Note also the different innovative approach to the general question taken by R. Hayim Shmuelevitz (Israel, 1902–1978) in his *Sha'arei Hayim* to *Kiddushin*, 14.

41 These questions are discussed at length in R. Gustman's essay, ibid note 37, as well as in R. Shmuel Eliezer Volk, *Sha'arei Tohar*, Vol. 6, 67.

The Effect of the Prohbition on Monetary Regulation

Understanding whether *ribbit* is a ritual or a civil prohibition is relevant to many issues in Jewish law. Under an arrangement of interest, the borrower commits himself to pay an amount of money, and he may indeed hand over this money. As we have seen, both stages of that are prohibited, but, nonetheless, the monetary component of the transaction may be unaffected by the prohibition. Accordingly, it may be that there is a debt imposed upon the borrower, as a consequence of his commitment; however, he is forbidden by ritual law from remitting that debt. Similarly, it is possible that *ribbit*, if paid, becomes the legal property of the lender, despite the fact that he is immediately obligated to return it.

These issues are addressed by a number of authorities on Jewish law. For example, R. Judah Rosannes[42] asserts that,

> *ribbit* is a debt that the borrower has committed himself to, and he is obligated to pay, but that the Torah declared that even though he has obligated himself, he should not pay . . . and even though he is obligated to return the interest, in order to fulfill the declaration of the Torah, we do not say because of that that the borrower was not obligated; rather, even though he was obligated, [the lender] is commanded not to take it.

R. Rosannes states this opinion to explain why a sale that violates the laws of *ribbit* (i.e., the purchaser is charged more for later payment) is still valid.

This position is not unanimously held. R. Abraham Yeshayah Karelitz[43] (Chazon Ish, Israel, 1878–1953) states that, once the Torah prohibits taking interest, this overtakes the presumed civil law and obliterates the debt in all senses. Similarly, R. Isser Zalman Meltzer[44] (Israel, 1870–1953), despite acknowledging some implications of R. Rosannes' approach, maintains that it is a conceptual impossibility for a debt to exist in any sense once the Torah has forbidden its payment.

These issues are also relevant to a lender who dies without returning the ill-gotten interest, passing it on to his inheritors. The Talmud rules that the heirs are not obligated to return the interest,[45] as they would be with stolen goods or other illicit gains. This ruling appears to indicate that the debt is legitimate. However, R. Karelitz notes in support of his opposing position that the heirs are not entitled to collect unpaid interest. If the debt was indeed legitimate, they should have this right, as they are innocent of any ritual prohibition.

42 *Mishneh Li-Melekh*, *Matnot Aniyim* 8:1.

43 *Hazon Ish*, *Nashim*, 42:4.

44 *Even ha-Ezel*, *Malveh ve-Loveh* 6:2.

45 TB *Bava Kamma* 112a, *Bava Metsi'a* 62a. Note, however, the comments of *Tosafot* to *Bava Kamma*, and *Kuntreisei Shiurim*, *Bava Metsi'a* 26:1. Interestingly, many *halakhic* authorities maintain that the inverse is not true: If the borrower dies, the lender remains obligated to make restitution to the heirs of the borrower. See *Responsa Radbaz*, Vol. 3, 604; *Pithei Teshuvah*, *Yoreh De'ah* 161:6; *Darkhei Teshuvah* 161:59; and *ve-Darashta ve-Hakarta al ha-Torah*, Vol. 3, pp. 329–31.

Establishing the ownership status of received interest is important for other purposes as well. In Jewish law, the act of marriage requires the groom to transfer cash or property of value from his possession to the bride's. If he does not own the item of betrothal, the marriage is invalid. The question thus arises if a marriage performed with the proceeds of interest is valid. The discussion is based around a passage in the Talmud[46] that states, "One cannot betroth a woman with [forgiving her] loan[47], but can with [forgiving] the benefit of a loan (lit. *hana'at milveh*)." The latter path, while valid, is, however, forbidden as *ha'aramat ribbit*, or artificial *ribbit*. The Talmud then proceeds to define the term "the benefit of a loan." It cannot mean that there was actual collection of interest, as that would constitute actual *ribbit*, and not *ha'aramat ribbit*.[48] The Talmud concludes that the term refers to extending the time of a loan, to a degree where the extension itself has quantifiable value. This passage never addresses betrothal with actual proceeds of interest, but several medieval authorities maintained, some explicitly[49] and others implicitly,[50] that such a betrothal is indeed valid.[51] R. Aryeh Leib Heller[52] (Galicia, 1745–1813) explains that their view is consistent with that of R. Rosannes, mentioned above. While forbidden ritually, interest is a genuine monetary debt, and, once paid, it becomes the actual property of the owner.

This raises the possibility that unpaid interest might be converted, through forgiveness of the debt, into a value acceptable as a means of betrothal. This would seem to recognize interest-bearing debt as legitimate on some level, despite its prohibited status. R. Israel Jacob Kanievsky (Israel, 1899–1985) discusses the issue,[53] noting that the Talmud's objection to this type of betrothal—that it is "actual *ribbit*"—can be interpreted in two ways, consistent with the two above understandings of *ribbit*: It is forbidden as actual *ribbit*, but nonetheless effective as a means of betrothal; or the fact that it is actual *ribbit* would eliminate the possibility that the technique would be valid.

Further support that interest is legitimately owned by the lender comes from a ruling in some *halakhic* sources[54] that one who buys an item from a seller who obtained it as an interest payment is not obligated to return the item. This is in clear

46 *Kiddushin* 6b.

47 The reasoning for this, as explained by Rashi (s.v. *einah mekudeshet*), is somewhat complex. A betrothal requires that the husband give over something of value to his wife. If he forgives a loan already made to her, he is not giving her anything, as that money is already in her possession, and the expectation is she will spend it (*milveh li-hotza'ah nitnah*). However, as Rashi notes further on (s.v. *lo tzerihah*), it is possible to perform a valid betrothal through forgiving a loan if the identified value is not the money lent but rather a value accorded to the benefit of the forgiving itself (as measured by the sum she would pay to a third party who could convince the husband to forgive the loan).

48 Additionally, as Rashi notes, this method would suffer from the same exclusion as forgiving the principle of the loan.

49 See, for example, R. Yom Tov ben Avraham Ishbili (Spain, 1250–1330), *Hiddushei ha-Ritba* to *Kiddushin*, ibid note 48.

50 See Rashi to *Kiddushin*, ibid note 48. However, note the differing interpretation of R. Ya'akov Orenstein, *Yeshuot Ya'akov*, *Even ha-Ezer* 28:6. See also *Sha'ar Ha-Melekh*, *ishut* no. 16.

51 For an example of an opposing view, see Rabbeinu Yeruham, *Helek Havah*, *Netiv* 22, ch. 1.

52 *Avnei Milluim*, 28:22.

53 *Kehillot Ya'akov*, *Kiddushin*, no. 9 in later editions.

54 See *Knesset ha-Gedolah*, *Hagahot ha-Tur*, *Yoreh De'ah* 161 no. 26, citing *Mahari ha-Levi*, 40.

contrast to the purchase of stolen property, when a buyer must return the item to the victim and then obtain restitution from the seller in *beit din*.[55]

Comparing the Prohbition to Receive Interest and the Obligation to Return Interest

The differing conceptual understandings of *ribbit* may be discerned in a legal dispute between Rambam and the earlier authorities of the Geonic era, concerning returning *ribbit* already collected. In his code, Rambam[56] cites the view of some *Ge'onim* that a borrower who paid interest cannot waive the return of the money. Indeed, as we have seen, payment of interest is assumed to be voluntary, and thus a waiving of one's rights (*mechilah*), and yet this does not mitigate the prohibition. However, Rambam himself differs with the view of the Geonim and allows a fully informed and consenting borrower to waive repayment. The Ra'avad (France, c. 1125–1198), in his glosses, upholds the Geonic view, criticizing Rambam's view as one that would allow the prohibition of *ribbit* to be fully negated in practice. The *Shulhan Arukh*,[57] however, adopts the view of Rambam as authoritative.[58]

In analyzing this dispute, R. Baruch Ber Leibowitz[59] (Kaminetz, 1870–1940) assumes that the question depends on the issue considered above. Is *ribbit* a concept of civil law, in which case voluntary modification is allowed? This is the view of the Rambam. Or is it a ritual law, and hence immutable? This is the view of the Geonim. Clearly, Rambam is aware that *ribbit* is prohibited even when the borrower is willing to pay. However, in this analysis, he would presume that the willingness is artificial, compelled by the borrower's desperate need for funds.[60] However, if after

55 For further discussion of the general topic of ownership of proceeds of interest, see R. Meir Auerbach, *Imrei Binah*, Vol. 1, *Responsa* 2:2 and *Hoshen Mishpat*, *Hilkhot Dayanim*, R. Shimon Shkop, *Sha'arei Yosher*, 5:3.

56 *Mishneh Torah*, *Matnot Aniyim*, 4:13.

57 *Shulhan Arukh*, *Yoreh De'ah* 160:5.

58 This also seems to be the view of Rabbenu Asher (Rosh), *Bava Metsi'a*, 5:2. If it is assumed that waiving the right to have interest returned is effective, it becomes important to clarify what constitutes waiving (*mehilah*). The *Taz* (161:3) asserts that the rule that genuine *ribbit* is returned by force of *beit din* only applies when the borrower demands repayment (based on Rashi, *Bava Metsi'a* 61b). R. Jonathan Eybeschuetz (1690–1764) and R. Jacob Lorbeerbaum of Lissa (Poland, 1760–1832) in their commentaries (respectively, *Tumim* and *Netivot ha-Mishpat*, *Hoshen Mishpat* 9:2) explain this position as based on the assumption that the borrower, by not demanding repayment, is effectively waiving his rights. However, as a point of practical law, this view is a minority view that does not appear to be accepted by later authorities. (See R. Joshua Falk, *Sefer Me'irat Einayim* to *Hoshen Mishpat*).

59 *Birkat Shmuel*, *Bava Metsi'a*, no. 48. A slightly different, oral tradition of R. Leibowitz's analysis is quoted in R. Aryeh Leib Grosnas, *Resp. Lev Aryeh*, Vol. 1, 15.

60 See also *Shittah Mekubetzet*, *Bava Metsi'a* 61a, s.v. *she-kein*, citing Ritva, who also expresses the idea that interest payments by a borrower are considered by the Torah to be nonvoluntary, as they are compelled by the borrower's need for funding. R. Abraham Erlanger (Israel, contemporary), *Birkat Avraham*, *Bava Metsi'a* 278, suggests, within Maimonides' view, that the intent is not that the borrower is actually acting involuntarily, but that the Torah declares it involuntary as a matter of law, regardless of the actual attitude of the borrower.

paying interest a borrower willingly waives his right to restitution, that may be taken at face value.

R. Vidal Yom Tov[61] (Spain, fourteenth century) emphasizes that the point of debate between Rambam and the Geonim is limited to returning *ribbit* that has already been collected. Neither authority would allow *ribbit* to be collected ab initio. His assessment negates the Ra'avad's criticism. R. Aryeh Leib Grosnas[62] (London, twentieth century) notes that the Ra'avad likely understood Rambam's view differently and equated a borrower's waiving his right to returned interest with paying interest ab initio. Thus, he found Rambam's view so objectionable. Accordingly, R. Grosnas identifies three conceptual approaches: the Geonic view, which labels *ribbit* as a ritual prohibition; Rambam per the Ra'avad, which categorizes *ribbit* as civil law; and Rambam per *Maggid Mishneh*, which distinguishes between the collection of *ribbit* (or, perhaps more accurately, the assessment of *ribbit*), which is a ritual prohibition, and the repayment of *ribbit*, which is a moral, interpersonal obligation.

This analysis is consistent with the above theory. As we have delineated, the fundamental ritual offense of *ribbit* takes place when the loan is agreed upon, and it indeed applies even if the interest is never paid. This violation, with its immutable nature, seems to be a ritual precept. On the other hand, to whatever extent *ribbit* is an interpersonal offense, it is in taking and holding onto the borrower's funds. It is thus reasonable that the commandment to return interest, a separate, positive commandment derived from the phrase "that your brother may live with you,"[63] is a wholly interpersonal concept. The ritual violation has already taken place, and returning the money does nothing to address it. Indeed, the ritual violation takes place even if the money is never collected. Returning the money is only conceivable as a means of rectifying an interpersonal injustice.

Working off of his analysis, R. Grosnas considers the question of one who has borrowed $1,000[64] and agrees to pay back $100 a year as interest. After five years, he has paid $500 in interest and none of the principal. At this point, a consideration of his situation yields at least two possibilities:

1. The money he has paid is viewed, as intended, as interest. Even though it is prohibited to charge or to pay interest, as noted above, that may stand independent of the monetary arrangement. Thus, while the lender is obligated to return that money, whether or not he does so, he is entitled to the full repayment of his $1,000.
2. Jewish law does not recognize the payment of interest. Consequently, the money already paid must only be counted toward the principal. As such, the borrower is forbidden to pay anything more than the $500 left to the debt; otherwise, he would violate the prohibition of paying interest.

61 Maggid Mishnah, *Malveh ve-Loveh* 4:13.

62 *Lev Aryeh*, ibid., note 65.

63 Leviticus 25:36.

64 Example is converted to American currency for clarity.

The latter possibility is strengthened by the fact that genuine *ribbit* is actionable in a *beit din*, who would enforce its return to the borrower. Accordingly, it can be argued that the interest, if it remains in the hands of the lender, should be converted to principal.

As R. Grosnas notes, this debate is paralleled in an earlier discussion found in R. Ephraim Navon's (1677–1735) work *Mahaneh Ephraim.*[65] R. Ephraim cites the view of an earlier authority, the Ra'anah, who maintained that a borrower who has already made interest payments but still owes principal cannot justifiably swear that he owes no debt to the lender, with the intent of considering his obligation covered by payments already made. The fact that the lender has a religious obligation to give back the money has, in his view, no relevance, as until he does so, the money is legally his. R. Ephraim himself disagrees, arguing that, since the borrower has the right to seize the illicit payments and retrieve them, he equally has the right to consider them as payment of his principal.

R. Grosnas further notes an important consideration made by R. Akiva Eiger (Hungary, 1761–1837) in his *responsa.*[66] As noted above, heirs are not obligated to return interest collected by their father, and the money is considered theirs. However, posits R. Eiger, perhaps this is only true when the entire principal has already been collected. If, on the other hand, the lender has made only the interest payments, and now wishes to subtract that from his principal obligation, perhaps he is permitted (and consequently obligated) to do so. This consideration assumes that, while the payments become the property of the lender, it is nonetheless true that the obligation to return the money has the effect of, at least, converting it to restitution of preexisting debts, such as the principal. As a practical matter, R. Grosnas concludes that the borrower is forbidden from making payments that exceed the value of his original loan, even if the interest is paid first. The issue of the heirs who inherit *ribbit* is discussed in later literature by R. Chaim Fishel Epstein[67] (1874–1942) and others. R. Epstein concludes the issue is unresolved, and he recommends a settlement between the parties.

Other applications and Extensions of the Prohibition

Once it is established that the prohibition of *ribbit* differs greatly from the crime of usury, and addresses a far greater area of behavior, including that which may otherwise seem innocent, it is appropriate to note some of the effects of this expansion. However, a full treatment of the subject would far exceed the scope of this chapter,

65 *Hilkhot Ribbit*, no. 4.

66 *Responsa R. Akiva Eiger*, Vol. 1, 80.

67 *Responsa Teshuvah Shleimah*, Vol. 1, *Yoreh De'ah* 19.

and thus we must suffice with a brief sampling to serve as a vague illustration of the concept's range. Several excellent works exist, both in Hebrew and in English, addressing these practical applications, and some of these works are listed in the bibliography and have contributed to this outline.

These applications include, but are not in any sense limited to, the following listed below. It should be emphasized that, within these categories, there are often exceptions and exclusions, and this listing is intended only to call attention to these applications, and not in any way to indicate practical *halakhah* regarding them.

1. Not only may one not pay monetary interest, but any favor or service (outside of previously established habit) from the borrower to the lender is forbidden.[68]
2. The prohibition is not limited to cash loans. Commodity loans are subject as well to this prohibition, forbidding one from borrowing a consumable object and returning a larger quantity. Returning the same quantity is potentially problematic as well, as the value of the commodity may go up.[69]
3. Payment of a higher price when payment is accepted at a later date, under many circumstances, may be considered payment of interest.[70]
4. Providing a full refund for an item used for a trial period may constitute a problem, as the buyer "lent" the item to the seller, who received use of the item until the time of return.[71]
5. Brokerage accounts that pay interest without actually purchasing stocks, if owned by Jews, pose a *ribbit* problem (possibly mitigated if the brokerage is a corporation).[72] Similarly, buying stocks on margin through a brokerage poses problems as well.
6. Guaranteeing delivery of a commodity with a fluctuating price at a given rate, in exchange for advance payment, poses a *ribbit* problem.
7. While selling promissory notes at a discount is permissible, the matter is complex and subject to regulation due to the strictures of *ribbit.*
8. Cashing checks at a discount is a highly complicated issue affected greatly by the banking regulations in the relevant country.[73]
9. While the purchase of stocks is not considered a loan, bonds are considered to be interest-paying loans and are subject to *ribbit* restrictions.

68 *Shulhan Arukh, Yoreh De'ah* 160:7.

69 BT *Bava Metsi'a* 60b; *Yoreh De'ah* 160:17.

70 *Shulhan Arukh, Yoreh De'ah* 173:1.

71 See *Shulhan Arukh haRav, Yoreh De'ah,* 173:55; R. Hayim Elazar Schapiro, *Responsa Minhat Elazar,* Vol. 1, 46; R. Jacob Y. Bloi, *Berit Yehudah,* 28:4; R. Yisroel Reisman, *Halikhot Yisrael: The Laws of Ribbis,* 39–41.

72 See *Halikhot Yisrael,* 46. The potential leniency for corporations is a matter of debate and is based largely on a responsum of R. Moshe Feinstein (New York, 1895–1986), *Responsa Iggerot Moshe, Yoreh De'ah,* Vol. 2, 63.

73 See *Halikhot Yisrael,* ch. 12.

A major element of the laws of *ribbit* has been omitted from this discussion, as it is both outside the scope of a brief chapter and also the subject of Chapter 10 in this volume. This is the *hetter iska*, a mechanism, discussed in the Talmud,[74] that enables loans to be made for purposes of business by having the lender share in the risk of the endeavor and also partake of the profit. On the surface, such a technique may seem like an illegitimate subversion of the Torah's commandment. However, as mentioned above, it seems to be inarguably the case that all theories as to the scope of the prohibition are directed toward personal loans, servicing those in need, rather than business-oriented loans. Accordingly, it is understandable that usage of the *hetter iska* has been sanctioned in the latter category, as the prohibition is thus more technical in nature.

Conclusion

We have seen that the Torah's prohibitions against the taking and even paying of interest far exceed in scope that which might be included in a general moral interdict against usury. While the opprobrium of predatory lending and exploiting the desperation of the destitute is self-evident and widely accepted, the Jewish concept adds a broader element not addressed in that anathema. This is indicated in various details of the prohibition, including its inclusion of apparently reasonable business practices, the inability of the borrower to voluntarily pay interest, and the equal condemnation of the "victim" of the offense. We have seen that these details led some analysts and codifiers of Jewish law to categorize *ribbit* not as the civil, interpersonal law that it might seem to be, but rather as a ritual offense, against G-d rather than against man. We have seen possible theories for each categorization. A civil offense may indicate that the Torah is emphasizing the familial bond of the Jewish people (and thus the limitation to the Jewish community, in contrast with broader principles of morality). A ritual categorization may indicate a focus on the obligation of kindness, represented in lending to the needy, and the offensiveness of doing so only when guaranteed a respectable financial return. It was shown how these possibilities affected other issues, such as the legal status of debts and payments of interest, as well as the status of independent obligation of interest, and a brief summary was provided of the effects of the prohibition on a wide range of interactions. In all perspectives, the prohibitions against interest call attention to our obligation to cultivate our more generous instincts, to overcome the focus on our own wants, both legitimate and extravagant, and to strive for a reality where we recognize that we do not live alone, but that our "brother[s] live with" us, as well.

74 BT *Bava Metsi'a* 104b.

SELECTED BIBLIOGRAPHY

Bloi, Rabbi Jacob Y. *Berit Yehudah. Machon Hahoyroa,*Jerusalem, 1979.

Caro, R. Joseph. *Shulhan Arukh*, Yoreh Deah, parts 160–77.

Karelitz, Rabbi Nissim. *Hut Shani: Hilkhot Ribbit*. ed. Hayyim Aryeh Halevi Hochman. Bnei Brak, 2004.

Maimonides, *Mishneh Torah, Malevh v'Loveh* 4:10.

Reisman, Rabbi Yisroel. *Halikhot Yisrael: The Laws of Ribbis*. Brooklyn, NY: Mesorah Publications, 1995.

CHAPTER 13

INTERLOPING BEHAVIOR IN THE MARKETPLACE IN JEWISH LAW

HOWARD JACHTER

Unethical Interference in Jewish Law

Jewish law demands ethical competition in the marketplace. A pillar of Jewish Law is this regard in the Talmud's teaching that "*'ani ha-mehapekh ba-harara nikra rasha*"—"One who intrudes on an impoverished person chasing a crust of bread is regarded as a wicked person."[1] The practical significance of being called a "wicked person" is that the Jewish court will ensure that the culprit is pronounced as such in the public prayer house.[2] Naturally, if the offender wants to avoid the suffering of this humiliation, he need only undo his objectionable action. To be sure, the Jewish court will not order the offender to undo his action.[3] In other words, *'ani ha-mehapekh be-harara* is a moral but not a legal principle.

1 TB *Kiddushin* 59a.

2 R. Shabbetai b. Meir ha Kohen (*Shakh*, Poland 1621–1662), *Siftei Kohen* to *Shulhan Arukh, Hoshen Mishpat* 237:1.

3 Nahmanides, (Ramban, Spain, 1194–1270), *Kiddushin* 59a; R. Solomon Luria (Maharshal, 1510?–1574), *Yam Shel Shelomo, Kiddushin* 59a; R. Jehiel Michal ha-Levi Epstein (Belarus, 1829–1908), *Arukh ha-Shulhan, Hoshen Mishpat* 237:1. A minority view is here expressed by R. Jacob b. Meir Tam (France, 1100–1171, quoted by Nahmanides, *ad loc.*). In his view, the plaintiff gets judicial relief in the *'ani ha-mehapekh be-harara* case. R. Menahem b. Solomon Meiri (France, 1249–1316), *Kiddushin* 59b, rules that "the behavior of a pious and scholarly individual is to return [the item to the victim of the intrusion]." Indeed, R. Moses Feinstein, *Iggerot Moshe, Hoshen Mishpat* 1:60, in a case of intrusion brought to him for adjudication, pressured (but did not compel) the restoration of the status quo prior to the interference.

This desideratum has manifold applications to the contemporary marketplace. For example, intruding on another's attempt to acquire a specific previously owned automobile might be included in this prohibition. Another potential application of prohibited interference is intruding on another's pursuit of a particular plot of land, a case already discussed by the Talmud.[4] R. Moses Feinstein (New York, 1895–1986) extends this prohibition even to intruding on another's pursuit of a spouse.[5]

The Dispute Between Rashi and R. Tam

The precise parameters of this rule are subject to a great deal of debate among Talmudic commentaries and rabbinic authorities throughout the generations. The most fundamental debate regarding this issue is between R. Solomon b. Isaac (Rashi, France, 1040–1105) and R. Jacob b. Meir Tam (France, 1100–1171). Rashi interprets *'ani ha-mehapekh ba-harara* broadly and prohibits interfering with someone acquiring an item even if it is not readily available elsewhere.[6] R. Tam, on the other hand, interprets the law in a far narrower manner, ruling that it applies only to a situation where the item is easily obtainable elsewhere. He believes that only in such a situation is it unethical to interfere with another's pursuit of an item, since one can, after all, obtain it elsewhere.[7]

Rashi's opinion may be based on the Torah's dictum, "Love your neighbor as yourself" (Leviticus 19:18). The Talmud understands this directive as forbidding doing to others that which one would not like done to oneself.[8] R. Abraham Wahrmann (Poland, d. 1841) explains that R. Tam will argue that, even though the Torah commands one to love his neighbor as himself, the Talmud states that one's own interests still enjoy priority above another's.[9] The dictum to avoid doing to others what one would not like done to himself applies only to activities for which one does not sustain a loss. Thus, one may not intrude on another's efforts to obtain an item that he can easily acquire elsewhere for, as R. Tam explains, "Let him go and obtain it elsewhere."[10] However, with regard to an item not readily available

4 BT *Kiddushin* 59a.

5 R. Moses Feinstein, *Responsa Iggerot Moshe, Even ha-'Ezer* 1:91. In this responsum, written in 1956, R. Feinstein permits intruding on a courtship until the couple has formally announced their engagement. However, since 1956 the custom has emerged to refrain from interfering with another's courtship. In a similar vein, R. Jacob Bloi (Israel, contemporary), *Pithe Hoshen, Geneva ve-Ona'a* 9:13, note 30) points out that custom renders it impermissible to move ahead of someone in a line even if that person is waiting for an item that is not readily available elsewhere, and by waiting in line, one will likely miss his opportunity to acquire the desired item—despite the fact that such action may not be proscribed by the *'ani ha-mehapekh ba-harara* principle.

6 TB *Kiddushin* 59a s.v. *'ani.*

7 Cited in *Tosafot* to *Kiddushin* 59a, *s.v. 'ani.*

8 TB *Shabbat* 31a.

9 TB *Bava Metsi'a* 33a.

10 Cited in *Tosafot, Kiddushin* 59a, s.v. *'ani.*

elsewhere, R. Tam explains, "There is no prohibition, for if he [the intruder] does not obtain the specific item, he will not find another one."[11]

Although R. Joseph Caro (Ottoman Palestine, 1488–1575) presents both views,[12] R. Moses Isserles (Rema, Poland, 1530–1572) rules in accordance with the opinion of R. Tam.[13] Later authorities conclude that Jewish law regards R. Tam's opinion as normative. Indeed, R. Solomon Luria (Maharshal, Poland, 1510?–1574) observes that the majority of the Talmudic commentaries subscribe to the approach of R. Tam.[14] Nonetheless, pious individuals are advised to follow the stricter opinion of Rashi.[15]

Although R. Tam's ruling is accepted as normative, authorities place significant limitations on its application. *Tosafot*, (medieval Talmudic glosses, France and Germany, twefth–fourteenth centuries) explain that R. Tam does not permit interference with acquiring an item if the person acquiring the item is doing so in pursuit of his livelihood.[16]

Interestingly, Nahmanides (Ramban, Spain, 1194–1270) writes that even according to *Rashi* one may interfere with another's efforts to acquire an item if that item is made available for all to take. Illustrating this principle are the rules for "fair" competition between qualified indigents to acquire the portion of the crop the Torah gives as an entitlement to the poor, called *pe'ah*. Suppose that P_1 arrives on the field first and pounces on a piece of *pe'ahh*. P_1's action does not legally acquire for him the *pe'ah* as lying on top of the *pe'ahh* is not a valid mode of acquisition. At this juncture P_2 arrives on the scene and manages to make the appropriate *kinyan* (mode of acquisition) and legally acquire the *pe'ahh*. In Ramban's opinion, P_2 is not guilty of interloping action even according to Rashi. This is so because all paupers are entitled to compete for *pe'ah* and P_1's coming on the scene first as well as his efforts to acquire the *pe'ahh* do not make him a *mehapekh* any more than P_2, who arrived on the scene later.[17]

Based on Ramban, R. Aaron Levine (New York, b. 1946) explains why Rashi would not regard a new entrant (C_2) who elicits the same customer base as an established firm (C_1) as guilty of interloping conduct. In this regard, the Talmud records a dispute between R. Huna (Babylon, second half of the third century) and R. Huna b. Joshua (Babylon, fourth century) regarding the parameters of fair competition.[18] Jewish law follows R. Huna b. Joshua and permits the opening of a competing business in an area where someone else already operates a similar establishment.[19]

11 R. Abraham David b. Asher Anschel Wahrmann (Poland, c. 1771–1840), *Kesef ha-Kedoshim, Hoshen Mishpat* 237.

12 R. Joseph Caro, *Shulhan Arukh, Hoshen Mishpat* 237:1.

13 R. Moses Isserles, Rema, *Hoshen Mishpat* 237:1.

14 R. Solomon Luria, quoted in R. Jehiel Michel ha-Levi Epstein (Belarus, 1829–1908), *Arukh ha-Shulhan, Hoshen Mishpat* 237:1.

15 *Shulhan Arukh ha-Rav, Hilkhot Hefker ve-Hasagat Gevul* 10, and *Shut Iggerot Moshe, Even ha-'Ezer* 1:91.

16 BT *Kiddushin* 59a, s.v. *'ani.*

17 BT *Ramban, Bava Batra* 54b.

18 *Bava Batra* 21b.

19 *Shulhan Arukh*, op. cit., 156:5, and *Arukh ha-Shulhan, op. cit.*, 156:6–7.

This ruling, however, seems to contradict Rashi's understanding of *'ani ha-mehapekh*. Consider C_1, who arrived on the competitive scene first, was enjoying the business, and, in some instances, the repeat business, of the same customers C_2 is now competing for. If not for the arrival of C_2, C_1, arguably, would have continued to enjoy the patronage of his customer base. C_2's conduct is, however, not interloping action, according to Rashi. This is so because striving for a legitimate livelihood is such a basic right that the visible striving for a livelihood by an established firm does not entitle that firm to an edge based on being first on the competitive scene. It is therefore not unethical for someone else to pitch for the long-time customers of the established firm because the second entrant is regarded as "invisibly striving" for the same customer base at the same time that the established firm is visibly pitching for their business. "Fair" competition in the marketplace is treated the same way as "fair" competition for the acquisition of *pe'ah*. In both instances the rule is that being on the scene first does not make that person more of a *mehapekh* than other qualified players.[20]

The Stage of the Negotiations

There are several other significant areas of discussion regarding the parameters of the prohibition to interfere with another's acquisition of an item. Authorities differ as to when in the purchasing process the prohibition commences. Rema rules that it starts only when the parties have agreed upon the terms of the deal, and it is only a formal act of acquisition to make the sale legally binding that has yet to be performed.[21] R. Joshua b. Alexander ha-Kohen Falk (Poland, c. 1555–1614) explains that Rema's ruling is intended to protect the interests of the seller. If another buyer were forbidden to interfere even before all terms were settled, the seller would be trapped into accepting the terms of any offer made to him.[22]

R. Falk, however, in his commentary on *Arba'a Turim*, titled *Perishah*, records that the custom has emerged to regard interference as improper even if it occurs at an earlier stage in the negotiations.[23] In this regard, R. Falk says, "When one individual comes to acquire an item from another, and the terms of the purchase are in dispute, and the two parties are in the midst of the negotiations, and had a third party not interfered, the deal would have been completed—this constitutes improper interference."[24] R. Jehiel Michal ha-Levi Epstein (Belarus, 1829–1908) approvingly notes this custom but limits it to a purchase in an organized marketplace, consisting of many buyers and sellers. In respect to transactions conducted

20 Aaron Levine, *Moral Issues of the Marketplace in Jewish Law* (New York: Yashar Books, 2005), 116.

21 Rema, *Shulhan Arukh*, *op. cit.*, 237:1.

22 R. Joshua b. Alexander ha-Kohen Falk, *Sema*, *Hoshen Mishpat* 237:7.

23 *Hoshen Mishpat* 237.

24 R. Joshua b. Alexander ha-Kohen Falk, *Perishah*, *Hoshen Mishpat* 237:1.

outside the organized marketplace, R. Epstein follows Rema's ruling.[25] R. Epstein's view seems to be based on the aforementioned approach of R. Tam, which restricts the prohibition of interference to a situation where there are similar items available. Accordingly, in a marketplace setting, where there are ample opportunities for purchases, there is no legitimate reason to intrude on someone else's negotiation. However, if there is no organized marketplace for the item at hand, another such item might not be available, and thus one may interfere with the negotiation as long as the deal has not been concluded.

Nonetheless, this matter is an unresolved issue in Jewish law, since R. Shneur Zalman of Lyady (Belarus, 1745–1813) does not cite the ruling of R. Falk.[26] To be sure, R. Falk does not record this custom in his commentary (*Sema*) to *Shulhan Arukh, Hoshen Mishpat* 237. As noted above, *Sema* explains (and seems to endorse) the ruling of Rema. In respect to this issue, R. Feinstein adopts varying approaches.[27] Thus, a rabbinic court is not authorized to compel compliance with the custom recorded by Perisha. However, R. Jacob Bloi (Israel, contemporary) writes that proper ethical behavior is to refrain from interfering with ongoing negotiations.[28] R. Bloi rules further that the prohibition to interfere undoubtedly exists if a market price is well-known and not subject to negotiation. The prohibition also applies in a situation where the buyer and seller have agreed to the sale at a price they will determine at a later date.[29]

One wonders as to the propriety of intruding on a negotiation to purchase a house where the parties have reached an agreement to purchase the property but the customary three days for attorney review of the process have not been completed. It seems to this author that Rema would permit such an intrusion, since he forbids an intrusion only when the formal act of transaction is the sole component lacking to complete the deal; here, attorney review is also lacking. Nonetheless, such behavior is not regarded as pious.

A Discounted Item

Rema writes that R. Tam would condone interference with a purchase if the item is available at a discount.[30] The reasoning is that a similar item will not be available elsewhere at so low a price. Maharshal clarifies that the discount must be considerable for this ruling to apply.[31] R. Shabbetai b. Meir haKohen (*Shakh*, Poland 1621–1662) disagrees with Rema, citing Ramban's ruling that no exception is made

25 *Arukh ha-Shulhan*, op. cit. 237:1.
26 *Shulhan Arukh ha-Rav, Hoshen Mishpat* 237:11.
27 Compare Resp. *Iggerot Moshe, Hoshen Mishpat* 1:60, with *Iggerot Moshe Even ha-'Ezer* 1:91.
28 *Pithe Hoshen*, op. cit., 9:16.
29 Ibid., note 37.
30 Rema, op. cit., 237:1.
31 Maharshal, Resp. *Maharshal* n. 36.

if the item is discounted as long as the item is available for purchase elsewhere.[32] *Arukh ha-Shulhan* rules in accordance with *Shakh*, arguing that the Rabbis did not distinguish between sale prices; availability is the sole criterion.[33] Indeed, it is often difficult to establish whether an item is "significantly" discounted, and if Rema's ruling were followed, the prohibition to interfere with a purchase would be eviscerated. Nonetheless, this matter is also left unresolved; *Shulhan Arukh ha-Rav* rules in accordance with Rema,[34] and R. Bloi does not present a conclusive ruling on this matter.[35] Once again, a rabbinic court is not empowered to enforce the ruling of *Ramban*, *Shakh*, and *Arukh ha-Shulhan*, since many dispute their opinion. Nonetheless, following this lenient ruling of Rema is not regarded as pious behavior.[36]

R. Bloi raises the possibility of the permissibility of intruding on a negotiation for a house available for rent or sale during real estate off-seasons (such as winter) when such opportunities are rare. R. Bloi does not issue a definitive ruling regarding this issue.[37] Another issue raised by R. Bloi is a case where the one who intrudes wishes to make a larger purchase (for example, a larger portion of land) than the first potential customer. He considers the possibility of permitting such an intrusion because Jewish law forbids interference only when one interferes in the purchase of the same item. Perhaps the increased size of the potential purchase renders it a different purchase in the eyes of the law, thus placing it outside the scope of the prohibition of improperly competing for the same item. R. Bloi does not present a definitive ruling about this matter either.[38]

Unintentional Intrusion

R. Solomon Zalman Lipschitz (Poland, 1765–1839) writes that it is "obvious" that if one unwittingly interfered with a negotiation he is not classified as an evildoer.[39] *Arukh ha-Shulhan* rules in accordance with *Hemdat Shlomo*.[40] R. Moses Feinstein, however, infers from the absence of such a distinction in the *Shulhan Arukh* that one is considered an evildoer until he rectifies the situation, even if the intrusion was made unintentionally. R. Feinstein argues that even *Hemdat Shlomo* would not excuse someone who had sufficient knowledge of the situation and should have clarified that there were no ongoing negotiations.[41]

32 *Shakh, Hoshen Mishpat* 237:1.
33 *Arukh ha-Shulhan*, op. cit., 237:1.
34 *Shulhan Arukh ha-Rav*, op. cit., 237:10.
35 *Pithe Hoshen*, op. cit., 9:15.
36 Ibid., note 36.
37 Ibid.
38 Ibid., footnote 29.
39 R. Shlomo Zalman Lipschitz, *Resp. Hemdat Shlomo* n. 4.
40 *Arukh ha-Shulhan*, op. cit., 237:2.
41 R. Moses Feinstein, *Iggerot Moshe, Hoshen Mishpat* 1:60.

Intrusion by Another Vendor

The Talmud, its commentaries, and Jewish legal codes speak primarily of an intrusion by another potential buyer. However, R. Bloi notes that *Shulhan Arukh*[42] expands the ambit of *'ani ha-mehapekh* cases to the prohibition for a tutor to offer his services to a father who already has a tutor teaching his child in his home.[43]

Financial Means of the Parties

The Talmud phrases the prohibition in terms of "a poor man" pursuing an item.[44] Accordingly, Rema limits the prohibition to interfering with a poor man's attempt to acquire an item. An exception, Rema notes, is if the item is not available elsewhere. In such a case, one may not intrude even upon a wealthy individual's efforts.[45] *Arukh ha-Shulhan* maintains that the Rema's ruling applies both according to Rashi and R. Tam.[46] However, R. Bloi cites an opinion that regards this comment of Rema to apply only according to Rashi. R. Tam, though, would forbid intrusion on a purchase of an item that is available elsewhere even if the first potential buyer is a wealthy man.[47] Therefore, R. Bloi, in his *Pithe Hoshen*, does not distinguish between a poor or wealthy individual, since R. Tam's opinion is accepted as normative. If one chooses to adopt the stricter opinion of Rashi regarding intrusion on someone acquiring an item that is not available elsewhere, he need do so only regarding interference with a poor individual's efforts.

Seller's Preference

R. Bloi is inclined to believe that a seller is obligated to inform a potential buyer that someone else is in the process of procuring the item. Otherwise, the seller facilitates the second customer's violation of the prohibition to interfere with a sale. However, R. Bloi suggests that, if the new potential customer is willing to offer more than the first customer, the seller may not have an obligation to disclose the existence of the first customer and his efforts. Moreover, R. Bloi outlines circumstances when

42 *Hoshen Mishpat* 237:2.
43 *Pithe Hoshen*, op. cit., 9:15 note 32.
44 BT *Kiddushin* 59a.
45 Rema, op. cit., 237:1.
46 *Arukh ha-Shulhan*, op. cit., 237:3.
47 *Pithe Hoshen*, op. cit., 9:15 note 30.

the seller enjoys the right to prefer the second customer. The example that he cites is a case when an agreement was made (but no formal act of acquisition was performed) to rent a home to a large family and the homeowner subsequently discovered that newlyweds were also interested in renting the home. The newlyweds were far more desirable renters, as they would make less noise and there would be significantly less wear and tear on the house. R. Bloi writes, "It appears from the words of the Jewish legal authorities that the seller enjoys the right to further his own interests."[48]

Similarly, if someone reached an agreement with a customer to purchase a car, and the customer stated he would return the next day to formally seal the deal, the seller might be permitted to sell that car to a customer who arrives and is willing to purchase it immediately. The seller seems to enjoy the right to prefer to sell his wares to a guaranteed customer over a customer whose purchase is uncertain. Moreover, R. Bloi cites an opinion that permits the seller to change his mind if his son wishes to purchase the item he promised to a potential buyer. Nonetheless, there is an ethical (albeit nonenforceable) imperative in Jewish law for a buyer and seller to honor even their verbal commitments.[49]

COMPOUNDED CASE OF 'ANI HA-MEHAPEKH BE-HARARA

'Ani ha-mehapekh cases may involve more than just preempting someone else's anticipated gain. Consider the following case, recorded at *Gittin* 59b. The case entails competition among indigents for the olives left unharvested by a farmer (these olives are the entitlement of the poor). Here, indigent *P1* climbs to the top of an olive tree to retrieve the forgotten olives. *P1* manages to make the olives fall to the ground. Before *P1* can take legal possession of the olives, another indigent, *P2*, pounces upon the olives and takes legal possession of them. Because *P1* was poised to take legal possession of the olives and *P2* snatched away his anticipated gain, *P2*'s interloping action constitutes theft by dint of rabbinical decree (*gezel mi-divrehem*). *P2*'s action is morally repugnant, and he is therefore expected to restore the olives to *P1*.

48 Ibid., note 32.

49 Ibid. In respect to the prohibition to renege on a deal even when the parties have only an oral agreement between them, see *Shulhan Arukh, Hoshen Mishpat* 204:7 and Rema, op. cit., 204:11. In his treatment of this issue, Rema cites an opinion that permits the seller to change his mind if he has an opportunity to sell at a higher fee. However, Rema does not regard this as the accepted opinion in Jewish law. R. Bloi suggests that the case where the second renters would make less noise may be the equivalent of, and perhaps even more compelling than, the case of a higher financial offer—so much so that all opinions might permit the seller to renege on his offer to rent his property to the large family.

Note that in the ordinary case of *'ani ha-mehapekh*, the consequence for the interloper is that he is branded a wicked person, but there exists no duty, even on a voluntary basis, for the interloper to restore what he acquired. To see why *P2*'s interloping action is treated so severely in the case of the olives, we need only recognize that *P2*'s preemptive conduct did not consist of following *P1* up and then down the olive tree and pouncing on the olives before *P1* got a chance to take legal possession of them. Instead, *P2* positioned himself on ground level and sprung into action only after *P1*'s toil and effort dislodged the olives and caused them to fall to the ground. Because *P2* snatches away *P1*'s anticipated gain by free riding on *P1*'s toil and effort, *P2*'s interloping is regarded as *gezel mi-divrehem*.

A modern application of the above case is offered by R. Aaron Levine: Federbush runs a life insurance business. His business plan consists of cold calling teachers who presumably have an employer-given term life insurance policy and convince them to purchase additional coverage in the form of whole life insurance. The argument Federbush foists on the teachers is that, without taking on the additional policy early in their careers when it is relatively low cost, they will be left with no policy at all when their term life policy ends at retirement. Buying life insurance of any kind at retirement age will be prohibitively expensive. Straining their budgets to take on a whole life policy at low fixed recurring payment early in their career would therefore prove well worth it in the long run.

Klapper, an employee at Federbush, quits his job and becomes a freelance whole life insurance salesman. Klapper's business plan is to use Federbush's client list and cold call the teachers on the list. His sales pitch is to inform them right on that he is a freelance whole life insurance sales man and offers to give comparative figures for the various features their policies have. Offering better deals to Federbush's whole life policy holders solicits business from people who own whole life insurance policies only on account of the toil and effort Federbush exerted to convince them that they needed such a policy on top of the very adequate term life insurance coverage they already had. Klapper's solicitations therefore amount to snatching away Federbush's anticipated gain by free riding on the latter's toil and efforts. Such conduct hence violates *gezel me-divrehem*.[50]

Recent Rabbinic Rulings

The following Rabbinic rulings illustrate how *'ani ha-mehapekh ba-harara* is applied to the contemporary marketplace.

1. An individual visited a used automobile dealer, decided to purchase a specific vehicle, and even agreed to the price offered by the dealer. The

50 *Moral Issues of the Marketplace in Jewish Law*, op. cit., 164–65.

customer agreed with the seller to arrange for payment and transportation of the car the next day. However, later that very day another individual became interested in the very same automobile. The dealer offered the same terms of purchase and the customer paid immediately, settled on the terms of transporting the vehicle, and took the automobile. When the original customer arrived the next day, he found that the vehicle he wanted had been sold and he demanded that the car be returned to him.

R. Isaac Oshinsky (Israel, Contemporary) ruled that in principle the situation constituted a violation of the *'ani ha-mehapekh ba-harara* principle. The opportunity to purchase this vehicle was not unique, as others like it were available elsewhere, and thus this situation qualified as one where interference is forbidden even according to R. Tam. R. Oshinsky reasoned that the fact that the first customer was not a poor individual was irrelevant, since in his view the majority opinion in Jewish law does not consider the financial means of the parties involved regarding the application of *'ani ha-mehapekh ba-harara.* R. Oshinsky, however, followed the opinions that this principle does not apply to a situation where the interloper had no knowledge of the original customer. He added that the seller preferred the second customer, who was willing to pay immediately, as opposed to taking the risk that the original customer would not return the next day. Thus, the second customer was not required to give the automobile to the first customer.[51]

2. An Israeli *kibbutz* maintained an automobile for rental to its members at a rate that was significantly lower than the usual costs for car rental. The rules of the *kibbutz* stated that a member wishing to rent the car must write his name on a sign-up sheet with the individual in charge of the car and note the date of the rental. In the case in question, a *kibbutz* member spoke to the person in charge and ordered the car for a particular day. However, he neglected to make a notation on the sign-up sheet. The person in charge forgot about this conversation and, since no name appeared on the sign-up sheet for that specific day, gave the car to a second *kibbutz* member, who wrote his name on the sheet. The original *kibbutz* member demanded compensation for the higher rate he would have to pay for renting a car outside the framework of the *kibbutz.*

   R. Isaac Arama (d. 2002, Israel) ruled that, since other rental cars were available elsewhere, the situation was defined as *'ani ha-mehapekh ba-harara.* The lower price available from the kibbutz does not necessarily exclude this case from this principle. R. Arama noted that *Shakh*, citing Ramban, does not subscribe to the opinion that a lowered price permits intrusion. Moreover, even the opinions that would permit interference do so only when the price differential is highly significant. R. Arama noted that it was not clear whether the difference in this case was that significant.

51 *Tehumin* 22:334–341.

However, R. Arama ruled in accordance with Rema, that one is permitted to interfere until the parties agree on a price. In this case, R. Arama believed that, until a *kibbutz* member formally registered on the sign-up sheet, interference was permitted. Moreover, R. Arama noted that Jewish law recognizes the right of a community to establish rules that govern the interactions among its members.[52] R. Arama understood the *kibbutz* rules to state that formal listing of one's name in writing on the sign-up sheet entitled one to the car. Thus, since the first *kibbutz* member did not comply with the rules of the community, he was not entitled to the automobile. Accordingly, R. Arama ruled that the first *kibbutz* member was not entitled to compensation. R. Arama noted, though, that the second member did not act with good manners. Apparently, the second individual knew of the first individual's efforts to procure the vehicle.[53]

3. An Israeli company was the sole distributor for an Argentine meat company. Every half year, the firms would renew their agreement and the terms of payment. At the end of the term, the Argentine business informed the Israeli establishment that it would no longer serve as its distributor, as it had hired a different Israeli company. The original company sued the second company in the rabbinic court of the *Eretz Hemdah* institute in Jerusalem. The Rabbinic court dismissed the claim of the original company. It noted that Jewish law does not compel violators of *'ani ha-mehapekh ba-harara* to return the item they obtained; the rabbinic court is merely entitled to label the interloper as an "evildoer." Moreover, in this case, the parties had not even commenced negotiations over the next six-month term, and thus interference was permitted according to all opinions in Jewish law.[54]
4. The district rabbinic court of Tel Aviv was presented with a lawsuit regarding *'ani ha-mehapekh ba-harara* between two large nonprofit organizations. The first organization was in the midst of negotiations to purchase a plot of land upon which it would build apartments for its members, when the second organization interfered and offered a larger sum of money for the property and subsequently made the purchase. The first organization argued that the second organization violated *'ani ha-mehapekh ba-harara* and demanded that it relinquish the land in favor of the first group.

   The Rabbinic court argued that, since the second organization could have purchased real estate elsewhere, the case qualified as one of *'ani ha-mehapekh ba-harara.* However, since the negotiations between the seller and the first organization had not been completed, the rabbinic court wrote that it could not classify the second organization as "evil," since

52 Rema, *Hoshen Mishpat* 163:1.

53 *Tehumin* 22:342–344.

54 The opinion appears at http://www.eretzhemdah.org/newsletterArticle.asp?lang=he&pageid=48&cat=1&newsletter=385&article=1428.

many authorities do not forbid interference at that point. Nonetheless, the rabbinic court concluded that, since the second organization's members enjoyed a reputation for being scrupulously observant of Jewish law, it would be proper for them to adopt the stricter opinion in Jewish law and withdraw from their attempt to acquire the lot. It is worth noting that this court did not consider the larger offer to justify the interference in acquiring the land.[55]

5. R. Jehiel Tauber (contemporary, Monsey, New York) was asked whether the following case constitutes a violation of *'ani ha-mehapekh ba-harara.* An individual reached agreement with another party regarding the purchase price of a home. However, a second individual hassled the seller, and thereupon the seller agreed to sell the house to him and abandon the first customer. A third party then wished to interfere and sought to purchase the home. R. Tauber deemed it permissible for the third party to interfere since the second party had violated *'ani ha-mehapekh ba-harara.* One who has violated this rule is not entitled to its protection.[56] R. Tauber based his decision on *Arukh ha-Shulhan*, who cites an opinion that permits interference in such a situation.[57]

   R. Tauber's ruling is somewhat surprising since the *Arukh ha-Shulhhan* does not present this opinion as definitive. Moreover, R. Bloi expresses some reservations about this ruling.[58] Thus, it might have been appropriate for R. Tauber to suggest that, while such behavior is permitted by baseline Jewish law, pious individuals should refrain from such conduct.

6. R. Tauber was also asked whether one is permitted to interfere in a case where the parties have reached agreement on the purchase price of a used automobile but the seller still maintains a "car for sale" sign in its window.

   R. Tauber ruled that it is entirely permissible for another individual to seek to make the purchase. The fact that the seller keeps the "car for sale" sign in his car demonstrates that he is interested in other offers. R. Tauber ruled in accordance with the opinions that forbid interference in a sale only when it is initiated by a buyer, but not when the seller expresses his interest in another buyer.[59] (This principle should help resolve our aforementioned query regarding interference in the purchase of a home when the parties are in the midst of the attorney review stage of negotiations. If the seller still displays his "for sale" sign, it should be permissible for another individual to make a higher offer.)

7. R. Tauber was asked whether it is permissible to intrude on a wealthy individual's attempt to purchase an item that is readily available elsewhere.

55 The decision appears in *Piske Din Rabbaniyyim* 6:202–220.

56 R. Jehiel Tauber, *Meshiv Ba-Halakha*, 190–91.

57 *Arukh ha-Shulhan*, op. cit., 237:2.

58 *Pithe Hoshen*, op. cit., 9:15 note 29.

59 *Meshiv Ba-Halakha*, op. cit., 291.

R. Tauber responded that the predominant opinion in Jewish law regards such behavior as "evil."[60]

8. An agent was sent to purchase a specific item for someone. When he discovered it was on sale, he wished to know if it was permissible for him to purchase it for himself. R. Tauber responded that it is clear from the Talmud[61] that an agent is forbidden to make the purchase for himself, even if the discount is extraordinary. The Talmud brands an agent who betrays the one who sent him "a cheat."[62]
9. R. Tauber was asked if it is permissible to interfere in a case where the parties had concluded a deal, complete with formal transfer of title, to purchase a home at an exceptionally low price, but the contract allowed for both parties to void the deal within a specified amount of time. R. Tauber similarly responded that the Talmud regards one who interferes in a conditional purchase that has been completed as "a cheat."[63]
10. R. Tauber was asked the following: If one purchased an item that, unbeknownst to him, another individual was already pursuing, and then later discovered that another was pursuing it, is he required to sell the item to the original pursuer in order to avoid being labeled as "evil?" R. Tauber noted that this matter is subject to a dispute among rabbinical authorities, and he concludes that pious behavior would be to return the item.[64]
11. R. Tauber was asked if it is permissible to interfere with a purchase that is in the midst of negotiation. He responded that baseline Jewish law permits such interference, but that the custom has emerged not to interfere in such circumstances.[65] We note that this response is at variance with the Tel Aviv Rabbinic court decision, which deemed it pious behavior to refrain from intervening at that stage but stopped short of concluding that there is a custom to abstain from interference even at that stage.
12. R. Samuel Wosner (Israel, contemporary) was asked about the following situation: A seller offered his product for $1,800 and the customer did not agree to this price. He resolved not to make the purchase, since he thought the seller would not budge from his asking price. In the meantime, the seller hired an agent to find another buyer and found someone who was willing to pay $1,800 but wanted a few days to consider the deal. Subsequently, the original customer returned and stated he was willing to purchase the item for $1,600, which was the last offer the buyer had earlier made to the seller.

    R. Wosner ruled that the seller could choose either customer, since neither had reached the point where all that was missing was the formal transfer of title. The first customer did not have a valid claim on the item,

60 Ibid., p. 293.
61 BT *Kiddushin* 59a.
62 *Meshiv BaHalakha*, op. cit., 287.
63 Ibid.
64 Ibid., 294.
65 Ibid., 289.

since he had resolved not to purchase it, even though he claimed that this resolution resulted from his mistaken assumption that the seller did not seriously consider his offer to buy the item for $1,600. The second customer also lacked a valid claim, since he requested a few days to contemplate the deal. It seems, then, that even those who forbid interfering with a negotiation would permit intrusion in this case, since the buyer and seller were not in the midst of a negotiation.[66]

Conclusion

Jewish law seeks to strike a balance between a free marketplace and ethical behavior on the part of market participants. Talmudic commentaries and legal authorities throughout the generations have limited the full application of the prohibition of unjust interference. In doing so, the goal of maximizing marketplace freedom is achieved. Nonetheless, there is a plethora of ethical gray areas in which Jewish law leaves the ultimate decision in the hands of the parties themselves. There is a baseline standard, and anyone who violates it is regarded as evil; there is also a higher standard, which is regarded as pious behavior. The individual is allowed to choose whether to follow the baseline or the pious standard. Thus, while Jewish law forbids interference in a purchase in many situations, in many others the decision is left to the ethical sensitivities of the individual to achieve a balance between the Torah's noble ethical goals and the practical necessities of life.

SELECTED BIBLIOGRAPHY

Bloi, R. Jacob. *Pithe Hoshen, Geneva ve-Ona'a*, 12–16.

Caro, R. Joseph. *Shulhan Arukh, Hoshen Mishpat* 237, with commentaries of *Siftei Kohen, Sema* and *Pithe Teshuva.*

Epstein, R. Jehiel. *Arukh ha-Shulhan, Hoshen Mishpat* 237.

Feinstein, R. Moses. *Shut Iggerot Moshe, Even ha-Ezer* 1:91 and *Hoshen Mishpat* 1:60.

Talmud Bavli:

Kiddushin 59a, with commentaries of Rashi, *Tosafot* and Ran.

66 R. Samuel Wosner, *Teshuvot Shevet ha-Levi* 4:212.

CHAPTER 14

PRINCIPLES OF ETHICAL AND COMMUNAL INVESTMENT IN JUDAISM: A JEWISH LAW APPROACH

ASHER MEIR*

GENERAL INTRODUCTION: FINANCIAL GOVERNANCE IN JEWISH TRADITION

JEWISH tradition recognizes that communal institutions cannot function without financing: "If there is no flour, there is no Torah."[1] It is equally true that financing cannot be effective without proper governance. Thus, it devotes significant attention to the topic of appropriate financial management of public funds. Wherever we find discussion of the functioning of any communal institution, we find also discussion of the appropriate principles of its financial management.

For example, in ancient times, the center of Jewish worship was the Temple in Jerusalem. The Temple was not only a place of worship, but also the original example and paradigm for a Jewish communal organization. In the innumerable accounts of the workings of the Temple in the Bible and the Talmud, we naturally find a description of the role of the *kohanim*, the priests who carried out the Temple service, and the details of their rituals. But we also find dozens of mentions of the

*The author would like to acknowledge the support of the Shoresh Charitable Trust. I would like to thank R. Mark Goldsmith and R. Dr. Aaron Levine for their many helpful comments.

1 M *Avot* 3:17.

gizbar, the treasurer of the Temple, and the details of his management of the complex finances of this huge organization. The book of Kings (II 12:10–17) describes how a special chest was made to collect donations; then "the king's scribe and the high priest bound and counted the money that was found in the Lord's house. And they gave the money that was weighed out to the workers appointed in the house of the Lord, who then distributed it to the carpenters and the builders who worked in the House of the Lord."

Alongside worship, our religion commands us in ethical principles, of which one of the foremost is *tzedaka* (charity). Again, from the earliest times this commandment was not left solely to the discretion of the individual, but rather it was entrusted to a public organization, with its own treasurer, known as the *gabbai*. This communal organization was so universal that Maimonides (Egypt, 1135–1204), writing in the twelfth century, tells us: "We have never seen, nor heard of, any Jewish community without a charity fund."[2] The Talmud and later writings describe in remarkable detail the proper management of such a fund. As a people, we look back towards four thousand years of history and precedent, but ultimately we are an optimistic and forward-looking people. Studying the Jewish lessons regarding communal funds is not primarily a lesson in history but equally a basis for guiding action today. The lessons of our tradition regarding the administration of communal funds encompass a number of areas: how money is collected; how it is invested; and how it is disbursed. As a guide to investment, this document will consider only the middle category.

Within investment itself, we find a further distinction. Our tradition teaches principles of financial prudence to ensure that public funds are invested in a way that will enable them to fulfill the mandate of their original collection and dedication, alongside principles of ethical investment to ensure that they are invested in a way that promotes the public interest.

Section I: Prudential Investment

Historically, the foremost consideration guiding communal investments was that of prudence. While a private individual investing his own funds is allowed to take any risks he sees fit, communal funds were donated for a specific purpose and the fund administrators must ensure that this purpose is not frustrated by the normal vicissitudes of the market. Preserving the assets of charity funds is in itself an ethical principle, and thus has a certain overlap with what is typically known as *socially responsible investing*.

The Mishnah tells us:

2 Maimonides, *Mishneh Torah, Mattenot Aniyyim* 9:3.

> Rabbi Akiva says, no profit is to be made from Temple funds nor from poor funds.[3]

In other words, money set aside for Temple purchases or for distribution for the poor should not be invested with any eye to profit. The Babylonian Talmud gives the following rationale:

> For Temple funds what is the reason? There is no poverty in a place of wealth. For poor funds what is the reason? Perhaps poor people will appear and there will be nothing to give them.[4]

The first reason is explained as follows: It is unseemly for the holy Temple to be engaged in petty commercial ventures and to haggle over terms. The second reason is very simple. Rabbi Akiva refers to money that was intended for prompt distribution to the poor, but there was fortunately some surplus. If the surplus is invested, even in a very safe vehicle, the problem of liquidity arises; perhaps some needy people will materialize and the funds set aside to help them will be unavailable just as they are needed.

What if the funds were specifically given as a reserve for future needs? Then the immediate-liquidity consideration mentioned by Rabbi Akiva should not apply, yet some standard of prudence is obviously called for. This situation is discussed in the Jerusalem Talmud on this Mishnah:

> However, if he desires that [all] the loss should be his and [half] the profit to the sanctuary, it is permissible. Like the case where some assets of [minor] orphans was deposited by one by the name of Bar Zamina. He consulted with Rabbi Mana, who told him: If you want the loss to be yours and to split the profit, it is permissible. Assets of orphans were deposited by Rabbi Hiyya bar Ada and he did so.[5]

This short passage is of great importance for our question. It provides us with three critical pieces of information:

- In the case where the funds are not needed for immediate use, there is no prohibition on investing the money now.
- Even so, the investment must be such that the principal of the fund must be totally guaranteed, in this case by the personal guarantee of the person accepting the funds for investment.
- The Talmud implicitly likens the investment of public funds to the investment of funds of minor orphans. This is of great significance because there is much more extensive literature, from the Talmud to our own day, on the disposal of orphans' funds than on investment of public funds. (One plausible explanation is that surplus in public funds was relatively unusual; we are familiar today with the situation when many organizations run a deficit. Whereas situations when a father died leaving assets and

3 M *Shekalim* 4:3.
4 BT *Ketubbot* 106b.
5 J *Shekalim* 4:5.

minor children were relatively common, especially in earlier times when life expectancies were so much shorter.)

In light of this parallel, we turn to the following passage from the Babylonian Talmud:

> Rabbah asked Rav Yosef: What do we do with orphans' funds? He said, we deposit them in court, and distribute them little by little. He said, then you exhaust the capital! He said, what then should we do? He said, we investigate a person who has known assets [to collect from in case he should lose the deposit], and deposit their money with him near to profit and far from loss [the active partner splits profits but bears all losses]. . . . That's very well if we find someone who has certain assets, but if we can't find someone who has certain assets shall we let the orphans' funds dissipate? Rather, Rav Ashi stated: We find a person of stable property, reliable, who is obedient to the Torah and is not under a ban, and we deposit it by him in court.[6]

Ideally, we find a fund administrator who can personally guarantee the funds entrusted to him. The Talmud also emphasizes that we choose someone whose assets are known to be his, and not merely a deposit. This is relevant to the situation today when many seemingly wealthy individuals or firms are actually leveraged and their assets are liened. Ultimately, however, the most important thing is to find someone who is stable and reliable, and to make sure there is accountability—that the money is deposited by him in the presence of the court so that all details of the agreement are verifiable.

This flexible standard reminds us somewhat of the evolution of trust investment in common law. Common law holds trust administrators to the "prudent man" rule. Originally, this standard was applied to each investment vehicle in isolation, thus forbidding the investment of trust assets in risky instruments, even when the portfolio as a whole was in fact prudent. Nowadays, this rule is interpreted as the "prudent investor" rule, which evaluates the portfolio as a whole as opposed to any specific asset within it.[7] The principle is that the assets of the fund shouldn't suffer because we can't find a perfect investment that is both profitable and certain.

Thus, when it occasionally became impossible to find business people willing to accept asymmetric conditions—all downside absorbed by the investor yet profits split equally—later authorities allowed a more equitable distribution so that it should not be impossible to invest public assets.

The seventeenth-century Egyptian authority R. Avraham ben Mordechai HaLevi (Cairo, c. 1650–1712) writes:

6 BT Bava Metsi'a 70a.

7 For example, the United States ERISA (Employee Retirement Income Security Act, Part 4, section 1101, (c)(3)(D)) provides that retirement assets be managed "with the care, skill, prudence, and diligence under the circumstances then prevailing that a prudent man acting in a like capacity and familiar with such matters would use in the conduct of an enterprise of a like character and with like aims."

> Those who faithfully deal with sanctified funds and money for the poor, the orphans Torah students and the vulnerable, it is appropriate to waive their obligations and to enable an arrangement which will save them from loss through this, until eventually they are able to pay everything back. And I reach this conclusion for two reasons. One, it is well known the due to our many sins the opportunities for profit have been narrowed and no one knows how to make a profit and these dealers have nearly no benefit from their arrangement, only burdens on their way to returning the amount they obtained from the sanctified funds. It is not right to impose the strict rule on them so that they should come to a loss, and we shouldn't lock the doors before doers of good. Furthermore, if we impose on them in this matter they will find a loophole and an excuse to shake the yoke.[8]

So far we have seen two cases of liquidity needs: In one the money has to be available immediately; in the other, some of the money will not be needed for some time and so it is prudent to invest it. Some funds present an even more extreme case: The principal is meant to remain indefinitely, and charity needs are funded only from profits. For example, R. Asher b. Jehiel (Germany, 1250–1327) discusses a case in which "the donors gave money so that the principal should remain, and they would distribute from the profits to the poor of Jerusalem."[9] In this case, safety is still paramount, because the principal must be preserved, but there is no need at all for the underlying fund to be liquid, since it is never meant to be liquidated.

> One contemporary example which clearly contravenes these guidelines of prudence and liquidity is that of Orange County, California. In the early 1990s, over seven billion dollars in deposits from the county government itself and from almost two hundred local agencies were invested aggressively by County Treasurer Bob Citron in a highly risky strategy that included leverage, derivatives, and unhedged interest rate bets. Eventually the portfolio suffered a huge loss of over $1.5 billion. Furthermore, while the positions were still worth about six billion dollars, they could not be liquidated in time while still providing county services. In 1994 the county had to declare bankruptcy—the largest municipal bankruptcy in U.S. history and in fact one of the very few.
>
> In this case both of the prudential principles were violated: the liquidity limitations meant that even the funds that were solvent were not available for their primary purpose—county services. In addition, the assets were extremely risky and ultimately incurred a huge loss for the county.[10]

An additional concern is for duration matching. Just as in banking, in charity also there is a need for duration matching. Funds that may be needed on short notice must be in short-term or highly liquid assets; conversely, funds that will not be

8 *Responsa* Ginat Veradim Hoshen Mishpat volume 4, 1. Note that his contemporary Perah Shoshan Hoshen Mishpat volume 4, 1 disputes this ruling, but it seems to be mostly a matter of interpretation of the reality.

9 Ruling cited in *Beit Yosef*, Tur, *Yoreh De'ah* 256.

10 See, for example, Floyd Norris, "Orange County's Bankruptcy: The Overview," *New York Times* (December 8 1994); Public Policy Institute of California, "When Government Fails: The Orange County Bankruptcy," retrieved 30/9/2009 at http://www.ppic.org/content/pubs/op/OP_398OP.pdf.

needed for a long time, or assets specifically set aside to be a permanent endowment, need to be invested with a long-term perspective.

Accountability

Above we discussed standards of prudence regarding safety and liquidity. Another standard emphasized in Jewish tradition is accountability. No individual, no matter now prominent, should be trusted implicitly in the investment of even private funds. The Talmud relates the following story:

> Rav Yehuda said in the name of Rav: Anyone who has money and lends it without witnesses, transgresses (Leviticus 19:14) "Don't put a stumbling block before the blind." And Reish Lakish said, he brings a curse on himself, as it is written (Psalms 31) "Silence the lips of falsehood that slander the righteous."[11]

Putting a stumbling block before the blind is the Jewish sages' way of describing tempting someone into wrongdoing. Even a basically honest person may be tempted to misrepresent the terms of a loan when there is no documentation, and while you think you are doing him a favor by not insisting on proof in fact you are doing him a disservice by creating this temptation. Reish Lakish points out an additional problem: If the borrower does deny, the lender suffers a blow not only to his purse but also to his reputation. As it becomes his word against that of the borrower, some observers are certain to question his integrity.

Perhaps we would think that this applies only to an average person; a person of impeccable reputation could be trusted even without accountability. To refute this possibility, the Talmud continues with the following story:

> The students told Rav Ashi: [The great sage] Ravina fulfills all the directives of the rabbis. [Rav Ashi] sent [Ravina] a message late Sabbath eve: "Send me ten zuz, for I have just encountered an opportunity on a small field." He sent back, "Bring witnesses and let us write a deed." [Rav Ashi] sent back, "Even for me?" He sent back, "Especially you, for you are preoccupied with Torah learning and likely to forget, and I would bring a curse on myself."

We see from this that even Rav Ashi, one of the greatest sages in our history, is not to be considered above suspicion when it comes to appropriate accountability. Furthermore, Ravina does not say, "Of course I don't suspect you, but I have to adopt an equitable policy." He insists that in fact no one is immune from requiring the discipline of documentation. Another point is that this is not just considered an idiosyncracy on Ravina's part. The Talmud makes clear that Rav Ashi was testing Ravina to make sure he would indeed conform to the proper standards.

11 BT *Bava Metsi'a* 75b.

Ethical Practices Required by Prudence

A separate section of this guide is devoted to the responsibility of the individual and the community to consider ethical standards when investing money. However, unethical practices are not only wrong; according to our tradition, they are also counterproductive. Thus, it is appropriate to discuss this question in the context of prudential investment as well.

The rabbinic literature gives scores of instances in which we learn that, when business is conducted counter to the guidance of the sages, it "doesn't see signs of blessing." Here is one example relating to ecologically unsound business:

> Those who sell in the alleys, and raise grazing animals and cut down good trees, never see a sign of blessing.[12]

Another danger of unscrupulous practices is that they generally involve us with unscrupulous individuals, who will be as happy to steal from us as they are to steal for us. Here is a passage from tractate *Bava Metsi'a*:

> There are three who cry out [to God] but are not answered [i.e., they have no one to blame but themselves]: One who lends money without witnesses, and one who buys a master for himself, and one whose wife rules over him. What is the case of someone who buys a master for himself? Some say, someone who attributes his funds to a non-Jew [and lends them at interest to Jews]; and some say, one who gives his money to his children in his lifetime, and some say, someone who has it bad in one place yet does not go someplace else.[13]

Someone who attributes his money to a non-Jew is a case of a confederate in wrongdoing. Jews are allowed to borrow money at interest from a non-Jew, so the moneylending Jew tells everyone that the money belongs to a certain gentile, who is evidently in on the deal. But at some stage the putative owner will actually come along and claim the money. The lender imagined that his confederate would cheat for him without cheating from him. The Talmud is telling us that this is an unrealistic expectation; a dishonest person is unreliable for everyone.

Here is a contemporary example illustrating a number of these principles:

> At the end of 2008 it became known that many Jewish charities had substantially all of their funds invested through accounts managed by a single manager—Madoff Securities.[14] While the principal behind this firm, Bernard L. Madoff, was considered by many a reliable and upstanding member of the community, we see from the first story above that it was forbidden to consider even Rav Ashi, one of the greatest rabbis in our history, to be exempt from normal principles of financial prudence, even for a relatively small amount of money. While investors with this individual did have a written deed, which was the appropriate standard of accountability in the time of the Talmud, the firm did not have adequate oversight according to today's financial standards. Investment houses far smaller than

12 *Tosefta Bikkurim* 2:16.

13 BT *Bava Metsi'a* 75a.

14 Others had most of their funds in a "feeder fund" that subsequently invested substantially all its funds with Madoff.

Madoff typically have auditors from very large, reputable, and totally independent accounting firms who send teams of highly trained accountants to check the books. Yet Madoff's firm hired a tiny unknown firm with only a single active accountant, an acquaintance of Madoff's. It is clearly implausible for a single person to vet the books of such a huge operation, and so this could be interpreted to be equivalent to lacking the appropriate documentation and oversight.

Some of the people who invested with Madoff actually did suspect that he was engaging in unscrupulous practices, and hoped to profit from them.[15] These individuals fell into the second trap mentioned above: believing that a crook can be trusted to steal for you but not from you.

The Talmud tells us that even a private individual brings a curse on himself if he doesn't insist on appropriate standards of accountability; so much the more should communal organizations insist on such standards.

The UJA-Federation of New York had a number of safeguards in place, which protected it from exposure to the Madoff debacle:

1. According to its statement,[16] "UJA-Federation does not make any new investment without the manager meeting with, and responding to questions from members of the Investment Committee to give them an understanding of the manager's strategy and execution." Madoff refused to provide this kind of information to UJA-Federation.
2. The statement continues: "In the case of managed accounts (such as we understand Madoff ran), UJA-Federation would insist that securities be held by our independent custodian (JPMorgan)." This would have disclosed Madoff's fraud from the very first month of operation, since the scam depended on sending out forged trading records.

This prudent policy ensured accountability.

Conflict of Interest

The Torah tells us: "Don't curse the deaf, and don't place an obstacle before the blind; fear God, I am the Lord." Addressing this dictum, R. Solomon b. Isaac (Rashi, France 1040–1105 explains:

> Don't place an obstacle before the blind—before someone who is blind to the situation; don't give inappropriate advice. Don't say to him, Sell your field and buy a donkey, when your hidden intention is to buy it from him.[17]

The case described is one of a hidden conflict of interest. The advisor being consulted has an interest in having the asker sell the field, since he is interested in buying it. The problem is that he keeps his intention hidden.

Fundamentally, this law forbids only hidden conflicts of interest. It doesn't prohibit charity funds from allowing conflicts of interest when they are properly

15 As reported in http://finance.yahoo.com/tech-ticker/article/145115/I-Knew-Bernie-Madoff-Was-Cheating--That%27s-Why-I-Invested-with-Him and elsewhere.

16 Originally posted on the Federation website; subsequently reported by various outlets including the Forward: www.forward.com/articles/14757/.

17 Rashi at Leviticus 19:14.

disclosed and discussed. However, it does emphasize the extent to which the sages recognized that conflicts of interest can have an influence on advice.

Following is a contemporary application illustrating considerations of conflict of interest:

> Noted financier and philanthropist Ezra Merkin was the chairman of the investment committee of a prominent Jewish charity. The charity invested millions of dollars in Merkin's Ascot fund; the nominal amount eventually exceeded $100 million. This relationship involved a conflict of interest because Merkin received a fee for managing that investment. Merkin's role and fee were disclosed to that philanthropy.[18] That fund subsequently collapsed in the Ponzi scheme of Madoff.[19] It is noteworthy that Merkin also served on the investment committee of UJA-Federation of NY, but this organization has a strict conflict-of-interest rule forbidding investing Federation money through any member of the investment committee. This was another safeguard that protected it from the Madoff scandal.
>
> The mere existence of a conflict of interest doesn't prove bad advice was given. However,some observers believe that Merkin's personal interest in Ascot may have colored his advice as a member of the investment committee. New York Attorney General Andrew Cuomo filed a complaint against Merkin that alleges:
>
> "Investors in Merkin's Ascot funds paid Merkin an annual management fee, but those who invested with Madoff directly did not. Merkin breached his fiduciary duty to Non-Profit Organization A by accepting its investment in Ascot, and the management fees that came with it, when Merkin and Madoff could easily have arranged for a direct investment with Madoff".[20]

Transparency

Another important issue is transparency. Accountability means that an intermediary is held accountable if there is misconduct, whereas transparency means that the investor is provided with accurate and timely information on the state of his investment.

One very well-known source regarding the importance of transparency is the following mishna, referring to a Temple functionary who enters the vault where coins for Temple use are piled up and collects them together for use:

> The collector may not enter in a loose garment, or with a shoe or sandal, nor with tefillin [phylacteries] nor with a locket. Lest he become poor, and people will say, It is [punishment] because of the sin of the vault; or lest he become wealthy, and people will say, He became wealthy from the vault. For a person has to fulfill the

18 Merkin disclosed that he was managing the money and obtaining a fee. He did not, however, disclose that the same investment could have been made without a fee. This was the complaint of the Attorney General noted below.

19 As reported by Bloomberg on 1/1/2009, retrieved 6/24/2009 from www.bloomberg.com/apps/news?pid=20601170&;refer=home&sid=agi2s78EFGR4.

20 Accessed 7/14/2009 from http://www.charitygovernance.com/files/summons-and-complaint.pdf.

> expectations of his fellow creatures just as he has to fulfill the expectations of the Creator, as it is written: "And you shall be clean towards the Lord and towards Israel" (Numbers 32), and it is written "And he will find favor and good sense in the eyes of God and man" (Proverbs 3).[21]

The mishna recognizes that transparency is needed to avoid not only the substance but also the appearance of impropriety.

We can bring an additional example of the insistence on transparency from the laws of partnerships. The sages of the Talmud recognized the unique level of trust needed in a financial relationship and created an unusual extra layer of accountability in partnership agreements to ensure the highest level of transparency.

In general, Jewish law shuns oaths. While oaths can be a valuable way to convince pious individuals to tell the truth, they have little impact on precisely the dishonest people they are meant to catch. Furthermore, excessive use of oaths can lead to reducing the awe people feel toward them and result in more oaths taken in vain—a transgression so serious it violates one of the Ten Commandments. So, for example, one basic principle to ensure oaths are not overused is that they may be administered only when there is firm evidence that the defendant's claim is false.

However, in a very few cases they saw the need for encouraging openness was so great that they instituted special oaths to be administered by the court. One of the most far-reaching is the "partnership oath." When one person administers the assets of another person on an ongoing basis—for example, business partners or a trustee administering the assets of a household—the rabbis allowed the uninformed party to deWmand an oath from the administrator even when there was no firm evidence of falsehood.

The Talmud's justification for this law is instructive: hen a person has total discretion over someone else's resources, even an honest person feels justified in diverting a little for his own use, as a reward for his care.[22] This is a natural sentiment that can be conquered only by demanding constant accountability.

From a strictly legal point of view, the right to demand the "partnership oath" can be waived, like any other monetary right, and there are also a few exceptions to the rule. So the existence of this legal instrument does not imply that no money manager has the right to keep his strategy secret from investors if they agree. Rather, it is to show how the sages of the Talmud were concerned to legislate a special layer of additional transparency for cases when one person is dealing with the money of another. Evidently such transparency is an important safeguard, and a compelling reason should be required for waiving it.

> An additional claim against Merkin, detailed in the Attorney General's complaint, was that Merkin did not disclose that Ascot's funds were reinvested in accounts managed by Madoff. Merkin claims that he provided adequate

21 M *Shekalim* 3:2.

22 BT *Shevuot* 48b.

disclosure. In any case, some charities that invested in Merkin's funds seem not to have demanded the degree of transparency to which they were entitled.

Let us summarize our overview of Jewish sources on the requirement for prudent investment of charity funds. Communal funds are derived from donors who have the right to know that all of their donations will go to the intended purpose, and they are designated for vital communal functions that need the ability to rely on promised budgets. Therefore, these funds should be invested with a lower risk profile than comparable private funds. The basic principles of prudence include:

- Low risk
- concern for adequate liquidity, including duration matching
- avoiding conflict of interest
- accountability
- transparency

Section II: Principles of Ethical Investment in Judaism

Introduction: JRI—Jewishly Responsible Investment

The last decade has seen an explosion of interest in the area of "socially responsible investment" (SRI)—the principle that an investor should judge investments not only on their risk and return criteria, but also on the belief that the investor bears some responsibility for the actions of the enterprises he or she invests in. It is noteworthy that religious groups have long taken a leading role in this movement; histories of SRI note that one of the most prominent early examples was the eighteenth century prohibition of Quakers to be involved in the slave trade.

Jewish organizations, like those of other affiliations, perceive the benefit of getting a double benefit from investing their endowments: first, using the proceeds to benefit the cause and, second, providing business resources to a firm that also promotes their ideals or at least does not hinder them. It is natural that they would seek guidance from Jewish law and tradition in doing so.

As we examine what principles of Jewish ethics would regulate "Jewishly responsible investment," we need to examine two aspects: investments to avoid and investments to affirm—the analog to negative and positive commandments in the Torah.

First, we will discuss guidance that is applicable to individual investors. Afterwards, we will examine in what cases charitable organizations might be held to a different standard.

Avoiding Improper Investments

Within the aspect of "what do avoid," we have to examine two distinct topics: What is considered improper, and when is the investor considered a participant in what is improper? That is:

- Given that a particular activity is considered forbidden or unseemly, what kind of investment activity would be considered improper involvement or association? What is the "ethical distance" of the investor from the improper activity?
- What particular kinds of business are considered improper in our tradition?

We will discuss these topics separately in the following sections.

The first question we address is that of "ethical distance." Assuming there is some wrongdoing on the part of the vehicle, when is the investor considered complicit in that wrongdoing? There are a number of legal and ethical principles in Judaism that would tend to restrict certain kinds of investments and encourage others. Among these are the following.

Abetting Wrongdoing

The Torah commands (Leviticus 19:14), "Don't place a stumbling block before the blind." Already in the time of the Talmud this verse was given a figurative meaning—namely, not to cause another person to stumble into wrongdoing. The Talmud understands the basic prohibition and later rabbinical extensions to prohibit enabling or even abetting wrongdoing.

Benefiting from Wrongdoing

Another commandment is (Deuteronomy 13:18), "Let not even the smallest amount of what is shunned adhere to your hand." This establishes a unique prohibition against benefiting even indirectly from anything used for pagan worship, which is conceived by the Torah as the progenitor of uncivilized conduct. While its legal import is limited to objects of pagan worship, we find that the rabbis found a figurative meaning to distance ourselves from benefiting from anything despicable.[23]

Condoning Wrongdoing

A number of legal principles relate to condoning or seeming to condone and approve wrongdoing. One of these is the prohibition of flattery; another is the obligation to protest wrongdoing, which is blatantly violated when a person is actually involved or benefiting from what he should be protesting. Another is the mandate, "Don't associate with the wicked."[24]

Let us examine these degrees of complicity one by one.

23 *Responsa Rivash* 171.
24 M *Avot* 1:7.

Abetting Wrongdoing

The most severe problem exists when the investor would be actually involved in the transgression, by enabling or participating in it. This would place the act in the category of the Biblical transgression, "Don't place a stumbling block before the blind," and its rabbinical extensions.

In the mishna, the explicit examples of this prohibition relate to ritual transgressions, such as inducing someone to make a forbidden loan at interest:

> The following transgress a negative commandment: the lender, and the borrower, and the cosigner, and the witnesses. The Sages say, also the scribe. They transgress (Leviticus 25) "Don't give," and (Leviticus 25) "Don't take from him," and (Exodus 22) "Don't be unto him as a creditor" and (Exodus 22) "Don't impose interest on him," and (Leviticus 19) "Don't place stumbling blocks before the blind and fear your God, I am the Lord."[25]

However, from other sources we see that this applies equally to ethical violations in workplace activity:

> If water become mixed in your wine, you may not sell it in a wine-store unless you inform [the buyer]. And it may not be sold to a merchant even if you inform him, for [he buys it] only to mislead.[26]

Rashi explains:

> A storekeeper is equivalent to a merchant, and this storekeeper will sell it in his wine-store as if it is [full-strength] wine, yet there is water mixed into it. And you are the one who sold it to him, thus this involves "before the blind."[27]

The Talmud also applies this to various ethical and educational applications; for example, it states that one who purposely goads someone to anger, or acts in a way likely to induce them to rebel, transgresses this prohibition.

This Biblical prohibition has a widespread rabbinic extension known as "encouraging wrongdoers" (*mechazek yedei ovrei aveira*); this occurs when wrongdoing is not enabled but merely encouraged. (This is sometimes referred to as abetting—*mesayeiya*.) This is stricter because it includes any kind of participation even if it doesn't enable the wrongdoing, but it has a corresponding leniency: We are allowed and even bidden to give the other person the benefit of the doubt, in order to maintain harmonious relations (*darkhei shalom*):

> The house of Shammai state, one may not sell a draft cow in the Sabbatical year [when plowing is forbidden], and the house of Hillel permit it, because he can slaughter it [for meat]. . . . The wife of a sage may lend to the wife of an

25 M *Bava Metsi'a* 5:11.

26 M *Bava Mesi'a* 4:11.

27 Rashi, *Bava Metsi'a* 60a.

> ignoramus a sieve and sift and grind with her, but once water is added [to the dough] she may not touch, for it is forbidden to strengthen the hand of transgressors. And all [of these leniencies] were only made because of the ways of peace.[28]

In the time of the mishna, it was obligatory to knead bread in a state of ritual purity. Even though the wife of the sage was aware that the other woman would ultimately transgress this stricture, it was not forbidden to participate with her until the stage when the actual transgression was imminent—that is, at the time of the kneading.

In the later legal literature, we find these prohibitions extended also to the area of investment, again both in the ritual and ethical wrongdoing.

One Talmudic example of aiding wrongdoers in the ritual sphere is selling items whose only use is for pagan worship. (In the context, it seems to be referring to the cult of the Zurvanite form of Zoroastrianism, which at that time was thought to have persecuted both Jews and Christians.) The early medieval French authorities, the Tosafists, applied the prohibition to investment as well, and ruled on this basis that it was equally forbidden to lend money for the purposes of building a house of pagan worship.

> From this we can learn that it is forbidden to lend money for the purpose of building a place of pagan worship, and so much the more to sell them appurtenances or other items of superstition . . . and one who refrains will succeed.[29]

The unusual expression "and one who refrains will succeed" may indicate that this was viewed as an ethical obligation and not strictly a legal one.

In a later *responsa* of nineteenth-century Iraqi authority Rabbi Ovadiah (Abdallah) Somech (Iraq, 1813–1889) we find the similar principle applied to dishonesty in weights and measures. The case in question was a merchant who had a purchasing agent. The agent, who was not an employee of the questioner but only a factor, used to bribe the overseers of weights and measures in the marketplace in order to make sure they did not give him short weight, but on occasion also in order to give extra weight.[30] Rabbi Somech ruled that the merchant is required to insist that the agent desist in this deceptive practice, insofar as it is done indirectly on his behalf.

A concurring addendum to the responsum was added by the very prominent authority Rabbi Yosef Chaim of Baghdad (Iraq, 1832–1909), who was R. Somech's student and brother-in-law. Rabbi Yosef Chaim explains that there is a general prohibition to do anything forbidden by ordering someone else to do it, whether or not the technical legal definition of agency applies.

One basis for the legal importance of this responsum is that it establishes that the principles of vicarious responsibility for transgression such as abetting transgression should be applied to non-Jews as well as Jews:

28 M, *Sheviit* 5:8–9.

29 Tosafot, *Nedarim* 62b.

30 *Responsa Zivhei Tzedek, Hoshen Mishpat* 2.

> Anything forbidden for a Jew, if he does it by means of a non-Jew, the Sages applied to this the rules of agency, in order to forbid it to the Jew even after the fact. And the reason they decreed this is so that a Jew would not come to do a prohibition by means of a non-Jew and benefit from the transgression [even] after the fact.[31]

Equally important, it establishes that abetting wrongdoing applies even when the wrongdoing will take place in any case, but the participant will result in increasing the extent.

> Let us examine a sample application of this principle.
>
> An individual or organization you don't know well offers to make a large interest-free loan in foreign currency, paid off over a number of years in local currency. Or the donor stipulates that the money be used in a way that obligates you to use a particular vendor. Great care is required. Both of these techniques can be legitimate, but both are commonly used to launder money. Since money is difficult to launder, agreeing to these arrangements when laundering is suspected would often amount to enabling the donor to hide the source of his funds.[32]
>
> If you know that there is some other organization that routinely agrees to make this kind of arrangement with this donor but this time he wants to help you, then you are not enabling the laundering, which would take place in any case. But you are an active participant so you should still refrain.

Condoning Wrongdoing

Whenever we give the impression that we approve of an activity, we encourage others to engage in it. This is particularly relevant to a person or body that has certain ethical influence or standing.

The Talmud tells us:

> Anyone who has the ability to protest the members of his household but doesn't protest, is held liable for the members of his household. For the residents of his city—he is held liable for the residents of his city. For the entire world—he is liable for the entire world.[33]

This passage makes reference to a person who has no involvement whatsoever with the wrongdoing, but even so he is liable if he does not make his objections known.

A key condition in this passage is "has the ability." A person's ability to make an effective protest will depend on his standing; for example, the commentary of R. Shlomo Yitzchaki (Rashi) points out that usually only a national leader would be listened to by "the whole world." But to the extent that a person's opinion matters

31 Addendum to *Responsa Zivhei Tzedek Hoshen Mishpat* 2.

32 The examples were obtained from the guide, "16 Steps for Canadian charities and non-profits to avoid involvement with Terrorism," accessed 30/9/2009 from: http://www.globalphilanthropy.ca/images/uploads/Terrorism_and_Canadian_charities_and_Non_Profit_organizations.pdf.

33 BT *Shabbat* 54b.

to others, he needs to be concerned about seeming to condone wrongdoing by others.

The Talmud in tractate Sotah particularly condemns flattering people of standing when their deeds are wicked.[34] It refers to a group of sages who didn't dare to speak the truth out of fear of offending the King Aggripas.

Default of Duty to Rescue

A contemporary authority who has written extensively on the topic of ethical investing according to Jewish Law is Rabbi Aaron Levine of Yeshiva University. Rabbi Levine's book, *Case Studies in Jewish Business Ethics*, includes an entire section on the topic of ethical investment (p. 366). Rabbi Levine finds a number of legal obstacles to buying stock in a company whose fundamental business involves wrongdoing.

One foundation for Levine's approach is the duty to rescue. In contemporary secular law, the duty to rescue is generally circumscribed; rescue is obligatory for ships at sea, sometimes for motorists, for certain designated rescue workers, and via some limited "Good Samaritan" laws. But in Jewish law, there is a comprehensive duty of rescue. The duty is learned from two Torah verses: "Don't stand idly by the blood of your brother" (Leviticus 19:16), and "Surely return them to your brother" (Deuteronomy 22:1), which refers specifically to returning a lost object but is understood in Jewish tradition to include any effort made to save one's fellow from loss.

Levine states that, insofar as there is a positive commandment to rescue the victims of wrongdoing, seeking to actually benefit from the wrongdoing would seem to contradict this. He uses the example of investing in a fictional tobacco company:

> [B]ecause we are all theoretically obligated to extricate our fellow from the dangers of cigarette smoking, investing in Rawley Tobacco is unthinkable. It would amount to an implicit approval of the company's operations and hence make an outright mockery of the *lo ta'amod* [rescue] obligation (p. 367).

A parallel ethical concern is *chanuppah*, generally translated as *flattery*. This prohibition is inferred from the Biblical verse (Numbers 35:33), "Don't corrupt the land." The word *tachnifu*, translated here as *corrupt*, can refer more specifically to flattery; thus, the verse warns against condoning wrongdoing by failing to oppose it. In Levine's words:

> One could argue that each shareholder, big or small, implicitly communicates to the makers of company policy, "Don't worry, I will not protest your evil. Because I am convinced that society's moral fiber is too weak to stop you, I wish to profit from your evil by investing in your company."

34 BT *Sotah* 41a–42b.

In a similar vein, we find in the Mishna the admonishment, "Don't join with the wicked."[35] Two reasons are prominently mentioned in this connection. Maimonides' (Spain and Egypt, 1135–1204) commentary on this mishna points out that associating with wicked people may lead us to copy their behavior; whereas Rabbi Ovadiah of Bartenura (Italy and Israel, ?–c.1500) suggests that it will reflect badly on us. He gives the metaphor of a person who visits a tannery; even if he does not involve himself with the hides, the stench of the tannery is sure to stick to him even after he leaves.

> Here is a contemporary application of the "benefitting from wrongdoing" principle. Enron was a large and highly profitable energy company. Many were convinced that this company caused blackouts to millions of customers in order to compel local power companies to pay them inflated prices—a suspicion that was later shown to be well-founded.[36] If you had bought stock expecting the company to successfully continue with similar policies, this in no way makes you a participant in their shady conduct. But it does show a willingness to benefit from it. According to Rabbi Levine's criterion this would be wrong.

Shareholder Advocacy

Another point addressed by Levine is shareholder advocacy. Divestment is not the only ethical response to corporate wrongdoing; using the stake obtained to try to rectify the situation is equally called for. "If Rawley tobacco were a Jewish company, a Jew would be duty bound to reprove its policymakers and urge them to make the indicated changes." This would be called for based on the commandment of reproof (Leviticus 19:17), Don't hate your brother in your heart; surely reprove your fellow, and don't bear sin towards him."

The Talmud comments:

> Whence do we learn that if you see something shameful in your fellow that you must reprove him? As it is said, "Surely reprove." If you reproved him and he didn't accept, whence do we learn that he should reprove again? As it is written, "Reprove"—any way. Could it be [obligatory] even if he shows shame? It is written, "Don't bear sin towards him."[37]

Special Considerations Relating to Communal Funds

All the above considerations apply to any investor. However, they may apply somewhat differently in the case of communal funds than they would for an individual investor.

35 Mishnah *Avot* 1:7.

36 Timothy Egan, (February 4, 2005). "Tapes Show Enron Arranged Plant Shutdown". *The New York Times*. http://www.nytimes.com/2005/02/04/national/04energy.html. Retrieved on 06/26/2009.

37 BT *Arkhin* 16b.

In one way, the considerations for communal funds are actually more lenient. In the case of a private investor, the ethical or religious harm from violating any of the above restrictions is weighed against individual benefit, and the ethical and religious considerations dominate. However, in the case of charity funds the benefit redounds to the community, and so in some cases the balance of considerations may be altered.

One example of this is certain rabbinically instituted strictures of the biblical usury prohibition. We pointed out above that orphan's funds should preferably be invested with a condition that the orphans share in the profit without sharing in the loss. This kind of arrangement is normally forbidden since it is dangerously close to the fixed return characteristic of true interest. However, it was made permissible in the case of orphans due to the important public interest served by enabling them to realize a decent return on their assets.[38]

Another example of this is a recent ruling by R. Shmuel Wosner of Israel. While in general a person should ideally show preference to a Jewish workman, even if the cost is higher, R. Wosner ruled that, in the case of a synagogue being built with communal funds, economizing on the use of charity funds is more important.[39]

However, there is reason to claim that in another way a public charity needs to adopt stricter standards, because of their prominence. We can infer this from an instance discussed by R. Chaim Palagi (Turkey 1788–1837). R. Palagi writes that, even in those instances where there is no formal prohibition on indirect involvement with wrongdoing, such conduct is not appropriate for a leading citizen. The context was a prominent citizen who was pressured into renting a courtyard for use as a brothel. He rules that this is forbidden because of the ugliness and prohibition of the use itself, even though the subject of the responsum had no direct involvement in the business.

It is obvious that this is forbidden in itself and unseemly even if it is done by a simple person, so much the more a Torah scholar.

In recommending sanctions, Rabbi Palagi writes:

> There is also an additional distinction: Even though this is a case where the wrongdoing can take place in any case [even without the participation of the accused] . . . even so a prominent individual, from whom others learn, needs to be careful even in this case not to create a stumbling block.[40]

The principle that a prominent individual needs to be held to a higher and less self-interested standard appears dozens of times in the Talmud. Here is a characteristic example: The prominent sage Rav Nachman gave astute legal advice to a relative on how to reclaim a debt that she had ostensibly sold. Afterwards he regretted it:

38 BT *Bava Metsi'a* 70a.

39 *Responsa Shevet ha-Levi* 10:270.

40 *Responsa Hayyim Beyad* 19.

> Rav Nachman said, we have made ourselves like the sharp lawyers. What was he thinking at first [when he offered the advice], and what was he thinking about at the end [when he regretted it]? At first he thought (Isaiah 58:?) "Don't hide yourself from your own flesh" [don't neglect a relative in need], but at the end he thought, a prominent person is different.[41]

Rashi's commentary explains: because others learn from him and will come to do so even for those who are not relatives.

Another example: In the time of the Talmud, powerful individuals in the secular government were often empowered to seize possessions for their own use in a kind of decentralized "eminent domain." For example, a messenger might seize a donkey from one person, ride it until it is tired, then seize some other person's donkey and give him the tired one in return. In theory the tired donkey should be considered stolen property that must be returned, but reconciling themselves to this unfortunate reality the ruling is that it need not be returned. However, a pious individual is expected to return the object.[42]

The idea that others learn from a prominent person seems to stem from two distinct characteristics: because of his prominence, others are *aware* of his conduct, and because of his stature, others *emulate* his conduct.

Both of these aspects would apply to a communal investment fund. A private individual investing in a "vice stock" could excuse it by saying: There is no actual aid to the company, since I buy the stock on the secondary market; and there is no condoning, because no one could ever know I own the stock.

However, a communal investment fund needs to be managed with a high degree of transparency, and the public has a right to know what investments are made. Thus, the problem of condoning misconduct would apply. And this problem would also be subject to the other dimension of a "prominent individual": Others will learn from it. After all, if the community sees fit to invest in certain investment horizons, then a private individual will feel that this is a sanctioned activity.

> Here is an application of this principle:
>
> The board is offered a stake in a company making pornographic films. The company is a reputable and profitable one. Even if the company can easily obtain financing elsewhere, it is unseemly for a public charity to be known as a shareholder in such a morally corrosive endeavor.

Specific Areas of Concern

The variety of screening criteria among so-called Socially Responsible Investment funds is endless. They include animal welfare (testing, trapping), labor practices (working conditions, unionization), environment (forest destruction, pollution),

41 BT *Ketubbot* 86a.

42 Mishneh Torah, *Gezeila* 5:10.

vice (gambling, pornography), as well as political considerations (divestment from companies doing business in Iran, Arab boycott of Israel).

Some of these aims are meaningful to Jews; others are indifferent; still others are objectionable. In the following section we will try to outline the main areas of concern suggested by our tradition. The list is not meant to be exhaustive, but it includes the areas of concern with significant support in our heritage.

Integrity toward the Consumer

Jewish law mandates an entire network of protections for the consumer.

- The seller is not permitted to make misleading statements regarding his product, or even to passively imply them. This prohibition is known as *geneivat da'at*—literally, "stealing judgment." Judgment is "stolen" so that there is a lack of full conformed consent in such a sale.[43]
- Misleading appearances are equally forbidden. This is an application of the Torah prohibition of *ona'ah*, or fraud.[44]
- Overcharging is forbidden when there is a reasonable expectation of getting the market price.[45]
- In terms of product safety and reliability, the Jewish law standard is not caveat emptor but rather a warranty of merchantability; a sale is void if the product doesn't meet normal expectations.[46]

If the fund has well-founded concerns that a firm is deceiving its customers, then it is a bad choice for investment.

> Suggested application: You are offered a stake in a new company selling nutritional supplements to be marketed as a substitute for a popular prescription drug. These supplements are perennial best-sellers, benefiting from vaguely worded statutes that enable them to raise hopes among consumers while evading the strict demands of safety and effectiveness that apply to drugs. It would be inappropriate to profit from this type of subterfuge.

Honoring of Commitments to Workers

Scripture and the rabbinic tradition are replete with admonitions toward the employer to promptly fulfill his obligations to the worker and to free the employment relationship of any degree of servitude or duress. "On the same day pay his wage, don't let the sun set on it" (Deuteronomy 24:15). Willful attempts to deprive workers of benefits due them by mutual agreement or appropriate legislation, or to deprive them of their liberty, should be viewed with gravity.

43 See *Shulhan Arukh Hoshen Mishpat* 228:6.
44 M *Bava Metsi'a* 4:11–12.
45 M *Bava Metsi'a* 4:3–7.
46 See, for example, BT *Bava Kamma* 46a.

Suggested application: You are given the opportunity to invest in a new company in the Far East. You have reliable information that foreign workers in the factory are required to surrender their passports and are held as de facto slave labor. This is an inappropriate investment.

Concern for Public Safety and Well-Being

Relevant laws and regulations dictate the appropriate balance between the needs of industry and the safety and cleanliness of the surrounding community. "The residents of a city are empowered to regulate measures, prices, and wages, and to enforce their rulings."[47] Willful disregard for the demands of public safety and protection of the natural environment, as defined by appropriate binding legal obligations, should be condemned.

Suggested application: ABC corporation is moving its factories to Fredonia because public servants there can be easily bribed to ignore violations of toxic waste dumping regulations. This would be an inappropriate investment.

Concern for Animal Welfare

Jewish law strictly forbids causing animals gratuitous suffering, defined as any suffering that does not advance a legitimate human need or concern. Many of the ritual laws regarding kosher food are reflections of this ethical principal. "Animal suffering is a Torah prohibition."[48] Willful disregard for animal welfare, unaccompanied by any legitimate human consideration, should remove a company from the Jewish investor's screen.

Suggested application: 123 Pharmaceuticals tests eye products on rabbits. New research shows that information obtained from rabbit testing is of insignificant value for human subjects for this particular product. If the original testing program is unchanged then 123 is acting unethically.

Contempt for Law

Respect for the will of the people as embodied in legitimate laws and regulations passed for the public good is itself a Jewish ethical principle. "Shmuel stated, the law of the land is the law."[49]

Suggested application: XYZ corporation is repeatedly cited for regulatory violations. Each time the company pays the fine and continues with its behavior.

47 BT *Bava Batra* 8b.

48 BT *Shabbat* 117b and elsewhere.

49 BT Gittin 10a.

They have concluded that this is cheaper than changing their procedures. This shows a total disregard for the binding nature of legal obligations.

Bribery

The Torah warns us that bribery is a scourge that inevitably colors the judgment of anyone who has to exercise judgment. "Don't take bribes, for bribes blind the wise and distort the judgment of the righteous: (Exodus 23:8.) Later authorities point out that the same logic that imposes a prohibition on judges applies equally to anyone in a position of public trust.[50] Companies that make a habit of obtaining business through bribes should be influenced to change their approach.

Suggested application: Your endowment invests in a small, little-known construction contractor. It becomes known to you that the secret of their success is the special favors they provide to influential individuals in foreign governments. This is an example of wrongdoing.

Protecting the Environment

The Torah commands us (Deuteronomy 20:19), "When you besiege a city a long time, in making war against it to take it, don't destroy the trees thereof by wielding an axe against them. For you may eat of them, don't cut them down; for is the tree of the field man, that you should besiege it?"

While the biblical verse refers specifically to fruit trees, from this the rabbis learned that gratuitous destruction of any other useful resources, whether natural or human, is likewise forbidden.[51]

Suggested application: A company continues with a polluting technology when it could adopt a cleaner one at nominal expense. The minimal cost associated with the upgrade could render its current polluting policy virtually gratuitous.

Positive Aspects of Investment

Ethical investment does not mean just avoiding investments that may do harm; it equally means encouraging investments that do good. With regard to charity funds, the primary good we want to do is to provide for adequate resources for whatever communal purpose the funds were designated for. However, just as we learned above that investments may be ethically inappropriate irrespective of their potential for profit, likewise some investments may be ethically encouraged because of their direct consequences and not only because of their potential to enrich the investor.

50 Rosh and Pilpula Harifta commentaries on *Sanhedrin* 27a.

51 *Mishneh Torah, Melakhim* 6:8–10.

In Jewish law and tradition we find a few categories of ethically encouraged investments.

Investing to Help A Needy or Worthy Person

Typically an entrepreneur does not start a business in order to help society but rather in order to improve his economic situation. The investor may likewise be interested in helping a needy individual financially through a business investment rather than by a charity donation. The Talmud gives precedence to this type of aid.

Rabbi Shimon ben Lakish said, "A loan is greater than a donation, and a business partnership is greater than all of them."[52]

Based on this ruling, Maimonides' states:

> The highest level [of charity], than which there is no higher, is to strengthen the hand of the Israelite who is flagging, and give him a gift, or a loan, or enters into a partnership with him or gives him employment in order to strengthen his hand so that he should not need to request from others.[53]

A variant of this is investing in order to help a worthy person. The sages of the Talmud praised a certain wealthy individual named Todos of Rome because he was accustomed to make business partnerships with Torah scholars. The passage continues, "Anyone who provides inventory to the trade of Torah scholars, will merit to sit in the supernal Academy."[54] As we will show in the next section, this is praised partially because it creates association with Torah scholars, but the commentators add that it is also a way of helping them.[55]

One category of positive SRI screen is not related to the line of business of the company but rather to their internal conduct—for example, if they treat their workers fairly or if they give appropriate opportunities to disadvantaged individuals. There would seem to be a similar precedent for this preference from an ethical point of view from the above examples.

Associating with Worthy Inviduals

One rationale the Talmud gives for engaging in partnership with Torah scholars is not in order to help the scholar but rather to help the investor, by giving him an opportunity to associate with scholars.

> "And you who cleave to the Lord your God, you are alive all of you today." Is it indeed possible to cleave to the divine Presence? Is it not written (Deuteronomy 4) "The Lord your God is a consuming fire!" Rather, anyone who marries his daughter to a Torah scholar, or does business with a Torah scholar, and who uses his possession to benefit Torah scholars, the Scripture considers it as if he cleaves to the divine Presence.[56]

52 BT *Shabbat* 63a.
53 *Mattenot Aniyyim*, op. cit., 10:7.
54 BT *Pesahim* 53b.
55 Novellae *Hatam Sofer* to *Pesahim* 53b.
56 BT *Ketubbot* 111b.

Maimonides includes this law in the section of his Code on right conduct, not in the section on Torah study. In addition, he prefaces it by stating, "It is a commandment to Torah scholars and their students in order to learn from their conduct."[57] This makes it clear that the beneficiary of this conduct is meant to be the investor and not the scholar.

Since investment funds need to have an equitable investment policy and maintain an appropriate arms-length relationship with investment outlets, it does not seem practical to implement this value in the context of an investment fund. The edifying experiences of the fund managers would not in any case benefit the investors.

Promoting Worthy Collective Ends

The most common "positive screen" in the SRI world is to screen for companies whose activities benefit society as a whole—for example, those with policies deemed "sustainable."

In general, Jewish tradition does not grant any particular preference to a particular industry or line of work because of its social benefit. The Mishnah states,

> A person should ever teach his son a clean and easy craft, and pray to Whom all wealth and possessions belong.[58]

The continuation of the mishna is in the same spirit: The main consideration in choosing a profession should be the ability to make an honest living and have time for religious pursuits, and not harm a person's character. The benefit of society is evidently the responsibility of the "Invisible hand"—in this case, the invisible hand of God, not that of the price system as explained by Adam Smith.

However, there is one category of market activity consistently affirmed by the rabbis: developing the land of Israel. The Tosefta states that, even though it is normally forbidden to engage in ordinary business activities on the intermediate days of festivals, it is permissible in order to buy "fields, houses, vineyards" and so on from non-Jews in the land of Israel.[59] Since the leniency of buying on the Sabbath day, which is normally rabbinically forbidden, applies only to the fulfillment of a commandment, we can see that expanding and developing the land of Israel for the Jewish people is the fulfillment of a commandment. Buying a field or a vineyard outside the land of Israel is an ordinary business investment, but inside the land of Israel it has the additional character of a mitzvah.

The noted eighteenth to nineteenth century scholar Rabbi Moshe Sofer suggests that all kinds of economic activity are considered a commandment in the land of Israel:

57 *Mishneh Torah De'ot* 6:2.

58 BT *Kiddushin* 82a.

59 *Tosefta Moed Katan* 1:12.

> And it seems to me that when the people of Israel dwell in their land, it is a mitzvah to gather in the grain, not for his own livelihood . . . but rather because of the mitzvah of the settlement of the land of Israel. . . . And not only agricultural but studying all crafts [as well], because of the settlement and honor of the land of Israel, that they shouldn't say it is impossible to find in all the land of Israel a shoemaker or a builder and so on, and they should have to be brought from distant lands. Therefore, studying a trade is a commandment. And Rabbi Shimon bar Yochai and Rabbi Nehorai [who asserted that one should learn only Torah, not a trade] referred to the situation where we are in exile among the nations, and they have plenty of artisans and they don't need us.[60]

At the simplest level this suggests that Jewish organizations should give preference to companies that help develop the land of Israel. But, from an ethical point of view, it seems to demonstrate a precedent for an investment that is ethically affirmed because it especially promotes some essential element of common good.

Let us summarize our review of "Jewishly responsible investing." Many Jewish charities have strong beliefs about proper and improper conduct—beliefs that are shaped by Jewish ethical principles or by the particular nature of the organization's mandate. Often the principals of the organization will feel it is improper to invest money in a way that fosters behavior the organization discourages. Jewish law provides an instructive framework for gauging the "ethical distance" of the investor from any conduct of the company deemed improper. In addition, Jewish law and tradition have their own standards of right and wrong that should be considered by any Jewish group.

In addition, many charities seek to advance their mandate, not only through spending money, but also through investing it. We find that investing money in a way that helps needy or worthy people, as is investing it in a way that contributes to the security and development of the Jewish people. Such "positive screens" should be considered a legitimate and valuable tool, though not an obligatory one, when they can further the aims of the charitable organization.

Conclusion

Charity and finance have a common denominator: The need for them arises when one person has money yet another person can make better use of it—because of straitened circumstances or because of superior profit opportunities. A community seeking to make the best use of its resources will have advanced institutions for both. These include consideration of prudence, ethical conduct, and appropriate standards of collection and distribution.

60 Torat Moshe commentary at Deuteronomy 20:5.

Communal foundations with money to invest unite these considerations. In this article, we have tried to examine the various legal and ethical guidelines provided by Jewish tradition for each consideration in isolation and particularly when both are combined. This investigation is meant to be of practical contemporary use in guiding the ethical investment of charity funds and the channeling of ordinary investment funds to their most socially productive use.

SELECTED BIBLIOGRAPHY

Eiris (Ethical Investment Research Services). "Investing Responsibly: A Practical Introduction for Charity Trustees." *UK, National Council of Voluntary Organizations* (2005).

Levine, Aaron. *Case Studies in Jewish Business Ethics*. Hoboken, New Jersey: Ktav Publishing House Inc., Yeshiva University Press, 2000, especially 366--92.

CHAPTER 15

THE ART OF MORAL CRITICISM: REBUKE IN THE JEWISH TRADITION AND BEYOND

MOSES L. PAVA

Moral Criticism

Moral criticism, or as the Torah puts it rebuke (*tokhehah*), is a necessary activity for social learning and improvement. In the words of the Torah, "You shall not hate your brother in your heart; you shall surely rebuke your fellow and not bear sin on his account" (Leviticus: 19:17). Moral criticism is part of a give and take among individuals who must necessarily share, at least, a minimal set of core values, including most importantly respect for one another, a common ethical vocabulary, and a basic moral grammar. For moral criticism to take hold and to have any possibility of truly being effective there must *already* exist meaningful channels of communication. As the philosopher Michael Walzer has noted, "We do not have to discover the moral world because we have always lived there. We do not have to invent it because it has already been invented."[1]

Each one of us, simply by virtue of being human, inherits a moral tradition. As we grow and mature we slowly become its spokespersons. We begin to make claims about fairness and justice for ourselves. Next, we begin to feel sympathy for others. We want

1 Michael Walzer, *Interpretation and Social Criticism* (Cambridge, MA: Harvard University Press, 1987), 20.

to live in a world where our own needs and the needs of our close family members are being adequately satisfied. But we also want to be part of a larger community where not only are our own personal needs being met but everyone's essential needs are satisfied. We begin, over time, to choose to take on additional moral responsibilities. As we mature further, it may dawn upon us that we should and do care not only about the members of our own communities, but also about every human being.

As the rabbis of the ancient Talmud put it:

> Anyone for whom it is possible to protest the wrongdoing of a member of his or her household and does not protest, is held accountable for the wrongdoing of the members of his household. So too in relation to the members of his city; so too in relation to the whole world.[2]

As we grow, the circle of moral concern broadens. It need not stop with human beings and we begin to factor in the welfare of all sentient beings, even those yet to be born. As Princeton University philosopher Peter Singer has noted, "in suffering, animals are our equals."[3]

Rebuke or moral criticism is one of the many moral responsibilities that come with advancing maturity and wisdom. It can take on many different forms. It might be as simple as a private conversation between two friends, an email, or a letter to the editor. It might include giving a formal speech, writing an article, engaging in a dialogue, or even writing a book on moral criticism. At its deepest and perhaps most penetrating and useful level, moral criticism may not even look like moral criticism at all. Literature, film, poetry, the visual arts, and even humor—by showing the familiar and everyday in unfamiliar and strange ways—can convey a kind of criticism that direct methods cannot. (See, for example, some of the writings of Richard Rorty.)

Moral criticism, however, can easily backfire. Rather than contributing to a better world, moral criticism can become part of the problem. Is this not the "sin" that the bible itself is warning us about in Leviticus 19:17, "you shall surely rebuke your fellow and not bear sin on his account"? The New Testament famously takes this idea further and notes, "Do not judge so that you will not be judged. For in the way you judge, you will be judged; and by your standard of measure, it will be measured to you. Why, then, do you look at the speck in your brother's eye and pay no attention to the log in your own eye?" (Matthew 7:1–3). Rebuke can make things worse rather than better. I believe that there is a profound truth to James P. Carse's insight that the attempt to eradicate evil completely is itself evil.[4]

Others may see us as competitors, misinformed, old-fashioned, too liberal, too conservative, too post-modern, holier-than-thou, angry, ugly, too religious, not religious enough, jealous, fearful, hypocritical, irreverent, irrelevant, or just plain flat-out wrong. Not only might others not listen to us, worse case, they may seek

2 B *Shabbat* 54b.

3 Peter Singer, *Animal Liberation (London: Pimlico, 1990), p.17.*

4 James P. Carse, *Finite and Infinite Games: A Vision of Life as Play and Possibility* (New York: Random House, 1986).

out revenge and try to hurt us. Thus, moral criticism may end up provoking a negative cycle culminating in violence.

Today, in the age of what some have dubbed "the cheating culture," it seems as if there are fewer and fewer shared core values. Moral vocabulary has thinned. And each one of us possesses a unique moral grammar. Is it still possible to engage in an authentic moral dialogue? Is moral criticism simply an anachronism? Just consider the word *rebuke* for a moment. When was the last time you heard anyone use this word?

Still, I want to suggest that society's health depends upon moral criticism properly pursued. Creativity, imagination, and even genius (on rare occasions) reside in each one of us as individuals. Ralph Waldo Emerson's nineteenth-century teaching, from his famous essay "Self-Reliance," is just as true today as it was when he first wrote it:

> Whoso would be a man must be a nonconformist. He who would gather immortal palms must not be hindered by the name of goodness, but must explore if it be goodness. Nothing is at last sacred but the integrity of your own mind.

It is true that we are products of our own culture and society, but it is also true that culture and society are accountable to the individual no matter how unique or idiosyncratic we may be. Every voice counts and every voice is crucial. In speaking from our own perspectives, inside our own histories and experiences, each of us possesses an irreplaceable and infinitely valuable point of view. You are the only one with your exact set of values, desires, goals, and skills. *You* are the only one that has lived *your* life, experienced *your* experiences, and seen and heard what *you* have seen and heard. As the great philosopher Immanuel Kant noted, you are not only a means to the ends of others, you are an end unto yourself.

But how can one find an appropriate voice in today's fractured and broken world to express moral criticism? A voice that is not too loud nor too soft, a voice that is not too shrill nor too easy, a voice that is neither accusing nor blind to what is going on around you, a voice of both strength and humility. Is not all rebuke by definition harsh and unfair? In criticizing others, are we not always being hypocritical? I do not think that these are easy questions, nor do I think that we have given them sufficient attention.

Rebuke, at its best, according to the ancient rabbis, "leads to love" (*Bereshit Rabba* 54:3). They also noted, however, that "just as it is a *mitzvah* [commandment] to say something which will be listened to, so too is it a *mitzvah* to refrain from saying something which will not be listened to" (B *Yevamot* 65b). So where and how do we draw the line?

I suggest here that the process of moral criticism or rebuke, if it is to be effective at all, must always begin as a form of self-criticism. Before we attempt to encounter the other, we must come face to face with the stranger that is ourselves. Are we indeed "masters of our own house," as Sigmund Freud wondered? The remainder of this chapter outlines a set of open-ended questions as to what this prescription of self-examination entails.

Is my Behavior Consistent with my Rhetoric?

At its simplest and most basic level, self-examination demands that each one of us look critically at our own behavior and actions. Before one criticizes his neighbor one must make sure his own house is in order. Joseph Telushkin, in *A Code of Jewish Ethics*, writes:

> Before rebuking someone for an offense, be sure that you yourself are not guilty of the same wrongdoing. The Talmud tells us that R. Yannai had a tree whose branches extended beyond his private property onto a public road. Another man in the town had a similar tree that interfered with traffic, and some local townspeople, whose passage was obstructed by it, came to R. Yannai to complain. He told them, "Go away now, and come back tomorrow." That night he hired workers to cut down his tree. The next day he ordered the man to have his own tree cut down. The man responded, "But you also have such a tree." R. Yannai replied, "Go and see. If mine is cut down, then cut yours down, and if mine is not cut down, you need not cut yours down."[5]

A careful reading of this story shows that even though R. Yannai's tree "extended beyond his private property," his tree presumably did not interfere with public traffic. Nevertheless, R. Yannai correctly anticipated the response he would elicit if he ordered the man to cut down his tree without cutting down his own tree first.

The near-tragic story of the former Attorney General and Governor of New York, Elliot Spitzer, provides a dramatic and contemporary example of what can go wrong in moral criticism of others if it is completely divorced from self-examination. For years, Spitzer served as a powerful, necessary, and effective critic of corporate greed and excess. He castigated and challenged chief executive officers for their outrageous pay and compensation packages. He took on the largest and most successful investment banks on Wall Street for unfairly inflating their stock prices. Spitzer opposed mutual funds that provided special privileges to selected clients. In the seemingly anything goes world of corporate business practices, Elliot Spitzer was often a lone voice of restraint and common sense.

His inaugural address, after his successful bid for governor with its record margin of victory, provides an eloquent example of moral criticism. With its inspirational message and tone, it is *still* worth quoting at length:

> To return to policies of opportunity and prosperity, we must change the *ethics* of Albany and end the politics of cynicism and division in our state. If ever there was a time that called out for *introspection* by those in government, it is now. Lincoln spoke of listening to "the better angels of our nature." Indeed, those of us who

5 Joseph Telushkin, *A Code of Jewish Law, Volume 1: You Shall Be Holy* (New York: Bell Tower, 2006), 385.

> work in the great building behind me must *hear and heed the serious responsibility* that public service demands and rise to this moment and show the public in words and in deeds that we understand that *our responsibility* is to the people of New York.
>
> The reform we seek is substantial in size and historic in scope. It will require a new brand of politics—a break from the days when progress was measured by the partisan points scored or the opponents defeated. No longer can we afford merely to tinker at the margins of the status quo or play the politics of pitting one group against another. We must replace delay and diversion with energy and purpose in the halls of our capital. What we need now more than ever is *a politics that binds us together*, a politics that looks to the future, a politics that asks not what is in it for me, but always *what is in it for us*. . . . And so, together, we must strive to build One New York through a politics that operates on the principle that we rise or fall as one people and one state.[6]

Unfortunately, I believe for all of us, Spitzer did not heed his own words. While correctly calling for the "introspection" of others, he failed to look inside himself first. Just months before his downfall, he boasted to a reporter, "I'm not great at the self-reflecting type of answers."[7] He failed the first principle of moral criticism, what we might dub the R. Yannai principle: *Cut down your own tree before your order others to cut theirs down.*

Less than fifteen months after Spitzer delivered his inaugural address, he resigned in shame and ignominy as Governor of New York after being taped making arrangements to visit a prostitute who worked for a prostitution ring called the Emperor's Club VIP. Among the saddest sidebars to this story was the report that, inside the New York Stock Exchange, traders spontaneously broke into applause upon hearing the news of Spitzer's speedy and unforeseen resignation. Although it is understandable why those who felt unjustly accused by Spitzer might celebrate his downfall, should we not also pause, if just for a moment, to wonder about what such applause really says about our culture and our future?

What exactly is it that we are celebrating when one of our best and brightest falls so hard? Perhaps it is a momentary relief to know that no one can really live up to the high rhetoric and aspirations of Spitzer's inaugural address. Perhaps there is a strange kind of satisfaction and even a camaraderie to learn that we are all hypocrites (as we most certainly are) of one sort or another.

As we celebrate Elliot Spizter's sudden moral and political collapse, however, at some point it must surely dawn upon us that just as we are applauding *his* downfall we are applauding *our own* downfall, as well. Is it really true that any of us are better off now than we were before Spitzer's fall? To the extent that our moral language has been corrupted and our jointly shared moral capital has been depleted, as it has, I suggest that we are all worse off now than we were before. This is hardly something worth applauding.

6 (Spitzer Inaugural Address, emphasis added, January 1, 2007, as quoted in *The New York Times.*)

7 David Margolick, "The Year of Governing Dangerously," *Vanity Fair* (2008): 52.

What are my Motives?

In addition to asking ourselves about our own behavior and actions—this is really the easy question—we must also ask ourselves about our own motivations. Why do I choose to engage in moral criticism? This is not an easy question to answer. Steven Mitchell is surely correct when he writes:

> Our conscious experience is merely the tip of an immense iceberg of unconscious mental processes that really shape, unbeknownst to us, silently, impenetrably, and inexorably, our motives, our values, our actions.[8]

In engaging in moral criticism, then, we have to ask ourselves questions that go beyond the mere surface reasons we might give to ourselves and to others. Given the fact that moral criticism is such dangerous business (think of even the most successful moral critics in history like Lincoln, Ghandi, and King), why would anyone ever risk it?

The art of moral criticism is like walking a tight rope pulled taught between the poles of self-interest and a regard for others. The first century rabbinic sage, Hillel, put this insight in the form of a question: "If I am not for myself, who will be for me? And, being only for myself, what am I?"

Contemporary would-be moral critics are well-advised to always identify and own up to their own mixed motives. One wonders, for example, whether Elliot Spitzer would have engaged in many of the hard-ball tactics he often used to intimidate (and anger) his opponents if he had understood better his own motives and needs for personal gain and political power.

My point here is *not* to suggest that such motives are always fatal to an effective criticism; rather, to the contrary, such motives are usually necessary to provide sufficient fuel for an ongoing engagement with others (the reason we celebrate Saints so much is that there are so few of them). By better identifying and taking responsibility for such motives, one can consciously examine them and attempt, at least, to balance them with a fair regard for the interests of others. Spitzer, in his inaugural address, correctly spoke about listening to the "better angels of our nature." Perhaps he should have openly noted and acknowledged our baser instincts, as well.

Martin Buber, the great twentieth-century Jewish philosopher, quotes a famous Hasidic Jewish Master, Rabbi Bunam, as follows:

> Everyone must have two pockets, so that he can reach into the one or the other, according to his needs. In his right pocket are to be the words: "For my sake was the world created," and in his left: "I am earth and ashes."

We are a bundle of motives and interests—some high and some low. It is true that the world was created for "my sake," but it is just as true that "I am earth and ashes."

8 Steven Mitchel, *Can Love Last? The Fate of Romance Over Time* (New York: W.W. Norton & Company, 2002), 22.

Mature moral criticism, a kind of rebuke that will effectively improve our world and not tear it apart further, must necessarily be grounded in a realistic assessment of human complexities and contradictions. The opportunity for human improvement is great but not infinitely so. It is bounded by the environment in which we live and by our own natures and limitations. Moral criticism must grow out of a deep respect for such boundaries and not a disregard for them.

For whom am I Speaking? To whom am I Speaking?

> Once, when Rabbi Mordecai was in the great town of Minsk expounding the Torah to a number of men hostile to his way, they laughed at him. "What you say does not explain the verse in the least," they cried. "Do you really think," he replied, "that I was trying to explain the verse in the book? That doesn't need an explanation! I want to explain the verse that is within me." (Quoted by Buber)

Parents and teachers criticize children. Lawyers and doctors criticize clients and patients. Conservatives criticize liberals and liberals criticize conservatives. Americans criticize other nations and other nations criticize Americans. Jews criticize Jews; Christians and Muslims criticize themselves. And everyone criticizes each other.

When we offer moral criticism we speak *out of* a particular role (spouse, parent, teacher, doctor, social worker, etc.). We speak *for a* particular ideology, tribe, or tradition (liberal, conservative, Republican, Democrat, capitalist, socialist, White, African-American, Spanish, Jew, Christian, Muslim, Kantian, utilitarian, secular humanist, gay, straight, man, woman, etc.). We *quote others* but offer the words up as our own.

Authentic moral criticism, however, must go beyond this kind of abstract and theatrical rehearsing. We must learn to speak not only from inside of an inherited ideology and a given point of view, but also as one who can move beyond a fixed ideology and a predetermined set of beliefs. Our own ideology can itself become the object of critical self-reflection.

Effective criticism is concrete and personal. It derives from one's own history and experiences but is always oriented toward the future. It is relevant and in the moment. One must patiently seek and find one's own voice and words and one's own opportunity and appropriate time. In confronting an other with a script in hand, we absent ourselves and substitute our own authentic being for that of an abstract other. We remove ourselves from the space of dialogue and protect ourselves from having to reveal our own self, our own ideas, values, desires, uncertainties, and weaknesses. Moral criticism is useful for a society precisely because it can access and benefit from everyone's point of view. In speaking for a prepackaged ideology, this great benefit is forfeited and the possibility of social advancement is lost.

For whom am I speaking? One should always strive to answer this question in the same spirit that R. Mordecai answers his detractors in the above quote—"I want to explain the verse that is within me." James P. Carse puts this same point as follows:

> To enter a culture is not to do what the others do, but to do whatever one does with the others. This is why every new participant in a culture both enters into an existing context and simultaneously changes that context. Each new speaker of its language both learns the language and alters it. Each new adoption of a tradition makes it a new tradition—just as the family into which a child is born existed prior to that birth, but is nonetheless a new family after the birth.[9]

For sure, we need to fulfill the specific roles that we have taken on or have been assigned as others are counting on us, and certainly we choose ideologies that make sense to us. At our best, however, we learn to infuse these roles with our own personal contributions and meanings. We master an ideology only by emerging from it intact with an ability to value both its strengths and its weaknesses. Responsible moral criticism means that *I* am speaking directly to *you*.

The effectiveness of moral criticism hinges on my ability to articulate my own point of view, to speak for myself, to voice. Equally important, however, is the ability *to listen*: "The heart of dialogue is a simple but profound capacity to listen. Listening requires we not only hear the words, but also embrace, accept, and gradually let go of our own inner clamoring. As we explore it, we discover that listening is an expansive activity."[10] In truth, voicing and listening are two aspects of a single activity.

Moral criticism, if it is merely a monologue, is no moral criticism at all. To be effective, moral criticism must be part of an ongoing dialogue founded upon mutual respect and tolerance. Moral rebuke, when necessary, is not directed to an anonymous other nor is it directed to society in general. At its best, it is an encounter, a turning toward one another, a meeting of equals. Embedded in every authentic critique is an invitation for response and further give and take.

In truth, the other to whom I am speaking is unknowable, a kind of mystery. Just as I am an unfinished product so too he or she is growing and developing over time. Moral criticism must be informed by history, but it is always targeted toward an open and undecided future. Both the content and tone of moral rebuke reflect these inherent uncertainties.

What am I Trying to Accomplish?

Am I speaking merely to hear my own voice or am I trying to better the world? And if it is the latter, precisely how do I intend to accomplish this task? The contemporary Yale University philosopher Seyla Benhabib describes the kind of "communicative ethics" I have been calling for here as follows:

9 Carse, op. cit., p. 71.
10 William Iaacs, *Dialogue and the Art of Thinking Together* (New York: Doubleday,1999), 83.

> When we shift the burden of the moral test in communicative ethics from consensus to the idea of an ongoing moral conversation, we begin to ask not what all would or could agree to as a result of practical discourses to be morally permissible or impermissible, but what would be allowed and perhaps even necessary from the standpoint of continuing and sustaining the practice of moral conversation among us. The emphasis now is less on *rational agreement*, but more on sustaining those normative practices and moral relationships within which reasoned agreement *as a way of life* can flourish and continue.[11]

In other words, by engaging in moral dialogues, we are not necessarily looking for a final agreement, but we are searching together for ways to keep the conversations going. The point of moral criticism is not to force you to change your behavior against your will but to work together with you to establish and maintain "ongoing moral conversation."

James P. Carse distinguishes between two types of games: finite and infinite. "A finite game is played for the purpose of winning, an infinite game for the purpose of continuing the play."[12] Finite games are about borders; infinite games are about horizons. Finite games are displays of power; infinite games demand strength. Finite games are always theatrical; infinite games are always open and dramatic. *Moral criticism can be played as either a finite game or an infinite one.* When it is played as a finite game, there are always winners and losers, the tone is always self-confident and knowing, the purpose is to get you to do what I want you to do. I am stingy with forgiveness both for myself and for you. When it is played as an infinite game, by contrast, there are never winners and losers (if any one of us loses, we all lose); the tone is hesitant, halting, and uncertain. During the course of play, I allow myself room to grow just as I allow you to grow. The point of moral criticism when it is viewed as an infinite game is not to force you into submission, but it is to surrender jointly and playfully to an emergent covenant to which we are both heirs and contributors.

"Whoever plays, plays freely. Whoever *must* play, cannot *play*."[13] If I feel that I *must* rebuke you, I almost certainly *should not* rebuke you. Paradoxically, moral criticism is most appropriate only when I recognize that I have a choice to make and when I am willing to assume responsibility for my own words. I rebuke best not in my role as teacher or father nor as a member of this or that religion. I rebuke, moment to moment, spontaneously, face to face. one person to another.

In the Jewish tradition, there is a deep and abiding tradition that each person is responsible for the other. It is out of this mutual and shared responsibility that moral criticism grows. In the age of terrorism, nuclear capabilities, globalization, and environmental degradation, we must urgently find new and better ways to extend the felt experience of mutuality beyond the members of any one tribe, religion, or nationality. This is a tall order. It represents not just a change in outer

11 Seyla Benhabib, *Situating the Self: Gender, Community and Postmodernism in Contemporary Ethics* (New York: Routledge, 1992), 38, emphasis in original.

12 Carse, op. cit. p. 3.

13 Ibid., 4.

behavior but a deep change in consciousness. It is a movement toward a new kind of this-worldly spirituality.[14]

Is Anyone Listening to me?

The probability of moral criticism actually taking hold is slight. Most moral criticism is only partially heard and usually misunderstood. It is generally viewed as just another self-interested move in a finite game. If it is heard at all, it is probably interpreted in strategic rather than spiritual terms.

In the biblical verse with which this paper began, the Hebrew word for rebuke—*tokheha*—is repeated twice. To the Rabbis this repetition is meaningful: "If one sees his fellow engage in offensive behavior and rebukes him, but his friend does not accept it from him, from where do we learn he must go back and rebuke him again? From our verse in Leviticus 19:17, you shall *surely rebuke*—as many times as necessary" (B *Arakhin* 16b). Moral criticism thus requires patience, a sense of timing, and persistence.

When no one listens, the first instinct is to speak louder. This is almost always counterproductive. If I am using the wrong vocabulary in the first place, what use is there in repeating the same words over again at a higher volume? If we are operating out of two distinct sets of values, how can I hope to convince you that my values are better than yours? In the context of a moral dialogue, it is far better to remain silent and to listen more carefully. There is a rhythm, however slight, to every conversation. To participate in the dialogue you must discover its rhythm.

Moral criticism demands an active kind of listening rather than a passive one. One must learn to listen and accept what cannot be changed. It requires imagination and creativity. Rebuke only works if one has an open mind and is willing to first hear and tolerate the rebuke of others.

Ask yourself, is my behavior consistent with my moral aspirations? What are my motives? For whom am I speaking? To whom am I speaking? And what am I trying to accomplish? In the end, perhaps the best we can do is to become the change we are trying to accomplish in others. The goal in moral criticism is not to control others, but it is to build together a permanent bridge of dialogue as we walk on it.[15] It is a kind of search to find shared values and invent a common moral vocabulary.

Is anyone listening to me? Perhaps this is not the most important question, at all. A self-reflective attitude demands that we finally muster the courage to look deeply into the mirror and question ourselves. Am I listening to myself? For sure, I hear the words I use, but do I really understand them? I form the sentences I write,

14 Sandra Rosenthal and Buchholz Rogene, "The Spiritual Corporation: A Pragmatic Perspective," *Research in Ethical Issues in Organizations* 5 (2004): 55–62.

15 Robert E. Quinn, *Building the Bridge as You Walk On It: A Guide for Leading Change* (San Francisco: Jossey-Bass, 2004).

but do I allow the sentences to re-form me? I polish my rhetoric, but do I really practice it? I listen to you, but do I let it affect me?

Conclusion

The great American philosopher John Dewey stated his ethical postulate at the beginning of his long career as follows:

> In the realization of individuality there is found also the needed realization of some community of persons of which the individual is a member: and, conversely, the agent who duly satisfies the community in which he shares, by that same conduct satisfies himself.[16]

This is a high standard, rarely achieved in practice. I think of this not only as an ethical postulate but as a spiritual achievement, as well. Spirituality, of the sort I am speaking about, is the human experience of blending integrity and integration through acceptance of the past, commitment to the future, reasonable choice, mindful action, and dialogue.

Moral criticism, or rebuke, I suggest is, at times, a necessary part of this kind of spirituality. Nevertheless, *it is an extremely dangerous activity.* It is more likely to go wrong than right. The thesis of this chapter has been that moral criticism, if it is to make any sense at all, must first and foremost be a form of self-criticism. Despite his own personal shortcomings, Elliot Spitzer was surely correct when he stated in his inaugural address, the question is never "what is in it for me, but always *what is in it for us.*"

Effective moral criticism is a rare art. In the Jewish tradition, King David's confidante and advisor, Nathan, provides a precious example of an effective rebuke. It is an example that had an important effect upon David himself, but it has, perhaps even more importantly, through the ages become a permanent part of our moral understanding of what it means to be a fair and just leader.

King David, in an act of amazing hubris, initiates a liaison with Bathsheba, a married woman, and then subsequently and conveniently arranges to have her husband Uriah killed in battle. "Put Uriah in the fiercest part of the battle, and then withdraw from him so that he will fight the enemy alone." After Uriah's death, David marries Bathsheba. Here's how the prophet Natahan rebukes David:

> And Nathan came unto David, and said unto him, There were two men in one city; the one rich, and the other poor. The rich man had exceeding many flocks and herds: But the poor man had nothing, save one little ewe lamb, which he had bought and nourished up: and it grew up together with him, and with his children; it did eat of his own meat, and drank of his own cup, and lay in his bosom, and was unto him as a daughter. And there came a traveller unto the rich man, and he spared to take of his own flock and of his own herd, to dress for the wayfaring man that was come unto him; but took the poor man's lamb, and

16 Quoted in Jim Garrison, "Dewey and the Education of Eros: A Critique of the Ideal of Self-Creation," *Journal of Curriculum Theorizing* 20 (4 2004): 147–61.

> dressed it for the man that was come to him. And David's anger was greatly kindled against the man; and he said to Nathan, As the LORD liveth, the man that hath done this thing shall surely die: And he shall restore the lamb fourfold, because he did this thing, and because he had no pity. And Nathan said to David, Thou art the man. (II Samuel 12:1–7)[17]

This was an artful rebuke that was not designed to eradicate evil or to stop the conversation. It is a rebuke that honors acceptance of the past, commitment to the future, mindfulness, reasonableness, and dialogue. In fact, David did not turn around and challenge Nathan or argue with him but he calmly accepted responsibility for his sin.

To conclude, moral criticism is rare but not extinct. It can be wise and learned as it is in the case of Henry David Thoreau's essay on civil disobedience. It can be short and penetrating as in Abraham Lincoln's second inaugural address delivered in 1865. Moral criticism can be inspiring, healing, and uplifting as in Martin Luther King's "I have a dream" speech. It can represent a life's work as in the case of Rabbi Abraham Joshua Heschel's grand opus.

Or it can be as wordless, nameless, and unforgettable as the Unknown Rebel standing defiantly in front of a line of army tanks in Tianmen Square in 1989. Effective moral criticism (*tokhehah*) is rare but it is as necessary now as ever.

SELECTED BIBLIOGRAPHY

Benhabib, Seyla. *Situating the Self: Gender, Community and Postmodernism in Contemporary Ethics*. New York: Routledge, 1992.

Buber, Martin. *Tales of the Hasidim*. Downloaded on June 12, 2008 from http://members.tripod.com/~chippit/jewish.html.

Carse, James P. *Finite and Infinite Games: A Vision of Life as Play and Possibility*. New York: Random House, 1986.

Iaacs, William. *Dialogue and the Art of Thinking Together*. New York: Doubleday, 19999.

Mitchell, Steven. *Can Love Last? The Fate of Romance Over Time*. New York: W.W. Norton & Company, 2002.

Rosenthal, Sandra., and Rogene Buchholz. "The Spiritual Corporation: A Pragmatic Perspective." *Research in Ethical Issues in Organizations* 5 (2004): 55–62.

Telushkin, Joseph. *A Code of Jewish Law, Volume 1: You Shall Be Holy*. New York: Bell Tower, 2006.

Walzer, Michael. *Interpretation and Social Criticism*. Cambridge, MA: Harvard University Press, 1987.

17 In the Talmudic account of II Samuel 12:1-7, the liaison between King David and Bathsheba is not regarded as being the sin of adultery. This is so because it was common practice for a soldier to hand his wife a divorce before going into battle. The soldier, however, stipulated that the divorce would be effective only if he did not return from the war. In that event the divorce he handed his wife before leaving would become **retroactively** effective from the time the wife received it. Instead of the sin of adultery, the Sages condemn King David's actions to consist of abuse of power and profanation of God's Name. See Rashi *Shabbat* 56a and variant understanding of Tosafot ad locum). The Talmudic account of King David's sin in no way detracts from the point Dr. Pava makes in the text, based on II Samuel 12:1-7 (Editor).

CHAPTER 16

"KNOW BEFORE WHOM YOU STAND": TRUST, THE MARKETPLACE, AND JUDAISM*

JONAS PRAGER

Trust and the Marketplace

Trust is the implicit basis of most economic transactions and hence fundamental to any functioning economic system.[1] We presume that the commodities we purchase are as described, so that the blouse labeled "60% cotton, 40% polyester" is indeed so composed. Similarly, the Oregon apples we buy were truly grown in Oregon, not Mexico, and the 18-carat pair of earrings really are manufactured with 18

*This article is an expansion and refinement of my "Balancing the Scales: *Halakha*, the Firm, and Information Asymmetries" in Aaron Levine and Moses Pava (eds.), *Jewish Business Ethics: The Firm and Its Stakeholders* (Northvale, NJ: Jason Aronson, 1999), pp. 123-146. (For the background of my choice for the title of this paper, see *Berakhot* 28b).

1 "Trust is central to all transactions. . . . It is treated . . . as background environment, present whenever called upon, a sort of every-ready lubricant that permits voluntary participation in production and exchange." Partha Dasgupta, "Trust as a Commodity," in Diego Gambetta, *Trust: Making and Breaking Cooperative Relations* (New York: Blackwell, 1988), 49. Trust is defined by Gambetta as "a particular level of the subjective probability with which an agent assesses that another agent or group of agents will perform a particular action, both *before* he can monitor such action (or independently of his capacity ever to be able to monitor it) *and* in a context in which it affects *his own* action. . . ." (Italics in the original. Gambetta, "Can We Trust Trust?" in ibid., 217). A simpler and no less useful definition comes from Fukuyama: "the expectation that arises within a community of regular, honest, and cooperative behavior, based on commonly shared norms, on the part of other members

carats of gold. Even in large-sum contractual relationships, such as the purchase of major commercial real estate or the merger of two industrial companies, trust permeates the transaction. The attorneys who represent the contracting parties and who draw up the sale or merger contract anticipate that the parties will abide by the terms of the agreement. The legal provisions that deal with breaches of contract are really Plan B—if significant disagreement occurs in the future, the aggrieved party will have recourse to legal redress. But few contracts begin with the supposition that litigation is the first choice. Trust is carried to an extreme in the diamond industry, where million-dollar deals are sealed with a handshake, written contracts are rare, and even verbal commitments are not witnessed.

Hence, when trust is breached, its impact may well extend beyond the local, limited transaction. The breakdown of trust may reverberate throughout the economy both on the microeconomic or individual market level and on the macroeconomic or broad, economy-wide plane. When one can no longer have confidence in the integrity of a single seller, leading to uncertainty about the quality of goods being sold or the service provided, the natural tendency is to seek alternative outlets or to buy less or to expend resources to evaluate the product being offered. When the lack of trust is confined to one or a few vendors, then in a large, competitive market, buyers can easily turn to alternative sources. But if the market is limited or the absence of trustworthiness is pervasive, remedying the problem is neither simple nor inexpensive. Thus, when a securities market is thought to be characterized by manipulation—such as in early twentieth-century U.S. equity markets and frequently, it is believed, in contemporary developing financial markets—the safe course is to avoid trading in such markets. The result from the pure market point of view is an amputated market with fewer trades, each of which carries more risk, provides less liquidity, and is likely to demonstrate greater price volatility. Insofar as equities are an essential component of a diversified portfolio, if a market is characterized by questionable integrity, investor portfolios will be less diversified and almost by definition more risky.[2] Similarly, if one cannot trust sellers of used automobiles to list honestly their products' inadequacies, the market for lemons, in Akerlof's inimitable phrase, dries up.[3]

The Ponzi schemes that made headline news in 2008/9 in the United States and embroiled two financial community luminaries—Bernard Madoff (how appropriate a name for a man who pled guilty to stealing billions of dollars in clients' funds) and

of that community." See Francis Fukuyama, *Trust: The Social Virtues and the Creation of Prosperity* (New York: Free Press, 1995), 26.

Gambetta points out another crucial aspect of trust—namely, that trust must be mutual in order to function effectively in interpersonal (including economic) relationships. "It is important to trust, but it may be equally important *to be trusted*." Op. cit., 221 (italics in the original).

Trust here is viewed as bimodal. Either one has trust or one does not. However, one can posit a trust continuum, with varying degrees of trustworthiness. I might trust someone with my money, but not with my wife. Or vice versa. Such distinctions do not affect the argument here.

2 On the theory of diversified portfolios and risk minimization, see http://en.wikipedia.org/wiki/ Modern_ portfolio _ theory.

3 See George A. Akerlof, "The Market for 'Lemons': Quality Uncertainty and the Market Mechanism," *Quarterly Journal of Economics* 84 (August, 1970), 488–500.

Robert Allen Stanford (alleged to have run a nine-billion-dollar scheme)—are hardly novel. These stalwarts of the financial community (Madoff was at one time chairman of the NASDAQ, the over-the-counter stock trading market; Stanford was knighted by the government of Antigua in 2006) preyed upon the credulity of the individuals and funds who invested with them, many of whom were financially highly sophisticated. These investments are now worthless.[4] But in addition to the losses of individuals and institutions who "invested" with such scoundrels is the unmeasurable loss of confidence in the probity of the financial system and the financial advisers and investment institutions who comprise its legions. Such universal loss of trust may have dire economy-wide consequences.[5] The natural question that must crop up in the minds of individual investors is: If such schemers can dupe even the sophisticated, upon whom can I rely to advise me or invest for me? Such doubts suggest a more risk-averse profile for investors and a decline in the flow of investable funds to primary and secondary securities markets other than for high-quality government bonds. Insofar as investable funds drive the macroeconomy, and certainly finance innovative start-ups that will shape the future progress of any economy, the rise in risk aversion slows the growth of the entire economy.[6]

Confidence-Building Mechanisms and their Flaws

Trust can be instilled internally or fashioned externally. The confidence that members of a family or clan share stems from their family bonds. Such trust may well be imbibed with the mother's milk.[7] It seems natural and does not require an external mechanism to teach the child that she can rely on her parents (for the most part) or

4 The United States does not have a monopoly on Ponzi schemes. Albania, in 1997, shortly after the fall of the Iron Curtain, was subject to one that was national in scope. See Christopher Jarvis, "The Rise and Fall of Albania's Pyramid Schemes," *Finance and Development*, v. 37, no. 1 (March 2000). The Czech Republic's voucher privatization scheme also left a large group of victims. See http://www.telegraph.co.uk/finance/2935803/The-Maverick-The-spectacular- rise- and-fall-of-a-hyperactive-privatiser.html.

5 See for example Cassell Bryan-Low, "Another Wave of Withdrawals Expected to Hit Hedge Funds," *The Wall Street Journal* (March 2, 2009), C1. The journalist writes: "With financial markets in disarray and the alleged fraud by money manager Bernard Madoff casting a pall on the industry, investors have been demanding their money back at a relentless rate in the first weeks of 2009. This is forcing some of the world's best-known hedge-fund managers, who had hoped that massive withdrawals in December would be the worst of it, to brace for another wave." The consequences of such withdrawals are straightforward—the hedge funds are forced to liquidate already depreciated assets in a fragile market, putting further pressure on asset market prices, thereby decreasing the value of their own asset portfolios, leading to further demands for withdrawals from their funds. And the vicious cycle escalates.

6 The relationship between trust and economic growth is explored in Paul J. Zak and Stephen Knack, "Trust and Growth," *The Economic Journal*, v. 111 (April, 2001), 295–321. Also see Fukuyama, op. cit.

7 In a footnote in their article "Trust and Growth," Zak and Knack write: "A case can be made for a genetic basis for honest behavior" (299, n. 4).

her siblings (again, much of the time). Exactly how far this trust will extend is a matter of culture. In a tribal society, which is really the culture of the extended family, trust extends quite far. On the other hand, it would appear that the expression "The Brotherhood of Man" is an exaggeration or at best an ideal rather than a description of reality.[8]

Trust can be earned with experience. One has confidence in another because, in the past, that individual has always proved trustworthy. Indeed, credit history is a key element in the willingness of lenders to lend.[9] The credit profiles of individuals who borrow from banks or who exercise their credit cards and the credit-worthiness of business borrowers who are vetted by credit-rating agencies are fundamentally (though not exclusively) based on the credit experience of borrowers. Hence, the credit ratings of most sovereign governments are stellar because, with few exceptions, default has never occurred and is unimaginable in the future. Large multinationals of outstanding credit reputation normally rank just below governments. And the ratings decline as past credit history points to the perceived uncertainty of likely repayment.

As markets become more complex and personal relationships give way to more impersonal ones, the need to rely upon external confidence-building mechanisms intensifies. The same is true when transactions that were frequent and where personal bonds had developed over time are replaced by occasional, discrete contacts. There is clearly a difference in purchasing from a local appliance store, where the customers interrelate with the owner with whom they have dealt over years, and the branch of a large appliance chain, whose employees have far less incentive to speak candidly with the potential purchaser. And since customers for major appliances are not frequent repeat buyers, the incentive for integrity is weakened even further.[10] Bankers have often claimed the importance of the "customer relationship," but such relationships are far more evident in the local community bank than they are in the branch of a global financial institution.

Customers are forced to rely on a variety of trust-replacing mechanisms to offset the impersonality of the marketplace. Credit-rating agencies are one such mechanism. Investors rely upon the integrity of the rating agencies, whose own reputation is based on their record for unbiased evaluation, when they are unsure of the credit-worthiness of the company in which they are contemplating investing. Ebay's ranking of vendor

8 "The drive to protect one's family is strongest for blood relatives and diminishes as one moves down the family tree. This is known in evolutionary biology as 'Hamilton's rule,' which specifies the level of altruistic behavior among family members . . . that maximizes the survival of ones genes. . . . Transactions among dissimilar agents involve weaker genetic and social ties, so that cheating is more likely. . . ." Ibid., 299.

9 The term *credit* is rooted in the Latin *creditum*, or trust.

10 Game theory, in analyzing the conditions under which mutual trust leads competitors to cooperate, distinguishes between single games and repeated games. The latter recognizes the attractiveness of cooperating; cheating is detrimental. For, if one of the game players deceives the other in one round, his credibility has been damaged, and this will lead to retaliation in the next round. Hence, trust is likely in the repeated games scenario, but it is not a necessary element in the single game. For a simple explanation of this phenomenon, see Jonas Prager, *Applied Microeconomics: An Intermediate Text* (Homewood, IL: Irwin, 1993), Ch. 13. For a more extensive analysis, see Andrew Schotter, *Microeconomics: A Modern Approach* (South-Western, 2009), Ch. 11, especially appendix B.

performance is another such external mechanism. Customers communicate with Ebay and not with the vendors as to their satisfaction or dissatisfaction with their purchases, and the results are posted so that potential purchasers have a sense of the integrity of the vendors. Branding is still another mechanism, as producers hope to convince buyers that their brand name is to be equated with a sterling reputation. Such brand names are frequently backed by warranties and customer service offices to provide dissatisfied users with an address to voice their complaints and often to compensate them in one way or another. Better Business Bureaus provide another venue to enable potential customers to verify past customer dissatisfaction. So, too, are standard-setting functions of professional associations such as the American Medical Association or the American Hospital Association. Their imprimatur testifies to a level of competency of their members. Professionals are being evaluated by their peers—a task beyond the ability of the layman.

Clearly, none of these mechanisms are fail-safe. Credit-rating agencies have been accused of bias based on conflicts of interest, Ebay's mechanism can be gamed, companies do not always respond to customer complaints, and the BBB's information sources are limited. It is also evident that professional societies set minimal standards of competency and do not help the user distinguish among the merely adequate, the good, and the best.

Governments, too, contribute their efforts to limit this imbalanced or asymmetric information especially on the part of sellers.[11] Agency motives are often multifaceted: They wish to maintain fairness in the transactions arena, to enhance the functioning of the market mechanism, and to achieve certain specifically mandated goals. A whole slew of letter agencies in the United States, from the CPSC to the FDA to the SEC, as well as branches of various government departments (Agriculture, Treasury, Federal Reserve System), serve to even out the playing field. Thus, consumer products must be engineered to be safe according to the protocols of the Consumer Product Safety Commission, drug effectiveness must meet standards set by the Food and Drug Administration, new security issuers must adhere to Securities and Exchange Commission regulations, and bankers must comply with various proborrower rules set by national and state banking regulators.

Yet, despite the enforcement powers of government, such regulations are faulty.[12] Loopholes exist and, if not evident at first glance, they are sought, found, and exploited. Moreover, it is hardly surprising that regulations are violated, just as

11 While this chapter focuses on sellers' superior access to information, I do not mean to preclude the possibility of buyers, too, holding the advantage. For example, an expert art buyer may discover a masterpiece in a garage sale, while the seller is totally oblivious to the work's true market value. The discussion of asymmetric information in this chapter should be understood as symmetric.

12 A more fundamental criticism of government regulation may be found among the adherents of the capture theory of government. They argue that the regulatory authorities, having become subservient to the industry they were designed to regulate and thus having perverted the intentions of the legislature, will never be concerned with repairing the imbalance. See, for example, Michael E. Levine and Jennifer L. Forrence, "Regulatory Capture, Public Interest, and the Public Agenda: Toward a Synthesis," *Journal of Law, Economics, and Organization* 6 (1990), 167–98.

laws are violated by some elements in the community. While most people would agree that the presence of such agencies reduces the advantage of the stronger power in a transaction, they would also agree that at best the imbalance is merely reduced, not eliminated.

Incompleteness and implementation failures account for the inability of external constraints such as standards and regulations to fully rectify the asymmetric distribution of power between transactors. No contract and no regulation can cover every conceivable circumstance that might arise and become a source of contention. Loopholes will always exist and stand ready, under appropriate circumstances, to be exploited.[13] But even were such perfect contracts or regulations possible, the enforcement mechanism would likely be imperfect. Just as not all thieves are caught, so, too, will not all violators of standards and regulations be discovered. And even if they were, just as every justice system's limited resources require that priorities be set and cases with low priority be ignored, so, too, must it be with regulators, public or private.

One fundamental reason why external constraints in a market setting cannot work fully is rooted in the incentive structure of markets—namely, the extensive role of the profit motive. Classical economics from the days of Adam Smith found beneficial outcomes in individual pursuits of profit. The Smithian "invisible hand" that drove entrepreneurs to strive for profit also led them to cater to the demands of the public, provide buyers with the goods and services they were willing to pay for, and do so at the lowest possible price. Any single producer who would attempt to exploit his customers in order to increase its profits would understand that other producers stood waiting to meet the buyers' demands at better terms while still achieving their own profitability targets. Indeed, the very understanding that such alternatives could easily be found in the marketplace inhibited unsavory, exploitative actions in the first place.

Classical economic thinking has justified itself over time. The growth of modern economies run on the free enterprise system, with entrepreneurs striving for profits, has seen unimagined increases in product quantity and variety, in technological growth, and ultimately in consumer welfare. Can one question that the average consumer in the twenty-first century is far better off in material goods and services than was the average consumer at the start of the Industrial Revolution at the beginning of the nineteenth century? Equally conspicuous is the improvement in the material welfare of the average citizen—certainly in the developed world, but even in the less-developed regions of the globe—between today and, say, fifty years ago.

But classical economics presumed that the fundamental imbalance in knowledge and hence in power between buyers and sellers was insignificant. If that presumption was ever true, it certainly no longer is. Hence, sellers, motivated by profits, can manipulate the market in such a way that buyers, if they are even aware of it, cannot offset the actions of the sellers.

13 Of course, that's why there is a plan B written into contracts.

Consider a contracting scenario, where a municipality contracts with a private vendor of automotive services to receive regular maintenance of the city's vehicles as well as repair in case of mechanical failures. In the absence of the watchful eye of municipal personnel, the vendor is tempted to shortchange the city by falsifying records, exaggerating costs, using inferior parts, and so on.[14]

The Jewish Religion, Trust, and the Market

Religious faith and law provide an antidote to these issues.[15] Judaism is averse neither to material wealth, nor to the profit motive, nor to the working of the marketplace. The Bible and the Talmud both are replete with references—either explicit or implicit—to wealthy individuals, and see nothing wrong with scholars, merchants, or working people amassing wealth. The life of the self-denying ascetic is not a model encouraged by Jewish law. Similarly, profits are considered part of normal life as buyers and sellers freely transact in the marketplace.[16]

Jewish law, however, sets limits as to how wealth may be amassed and how it should be used; how profits can be earned and when they are judged illicit; and how the marketplace is to be governed even when transactions are freely engaged in by the various parties. Thus, extensive Talmudic discussions are devoted to fairness in the market, not exploiting buyers in circumstances where they are at the mercy of sellers, and limiting the free conduct of buyers and sellers. These discussions were codified as substantive law by numerous Jewish scholars and are binding today as per the sixteenth-century Code of Jewish Law (*Shulhan Arukh*—literally, "The Set Table") as it has been updated to contemporary times by new generations of Halakhists.

14 See Jonas Prager, "Contracting Out: Theory and Policy," *Journal of International Law and Politics* 25,1 (Fall 1992), 73–111; ______, "Contracting Out Government Services," *Public Administration Review* 54,2 (March/April 1994), 176–84; and ______ and Jacob Paroush, "Criteria for Contracting-Out Decisions When Contractors Can Deceive," *Atlantic Economic Journal* (December 1999), 376–83.

Suborning the inspectors remains a real problem, as both the inspectors and the inspected gain financially from this transaction. So, unless the inspectors are monitored, the profit motive leads to further stress in the marketplace.

15 Anthony Pagden, in his "Trust in Eighteenth-century Naples" (in Gambetta, op. cit., 134), writes that, "faith in the certainty of divine sanction may indeed constitute the ultimate guarantee for trust."

We do not directly deal with the argument made by Putnam and evaluated empirically by La Porta and colleagues that "hierarchical religion discourages 'horizontal' ties between people and hence the formation of trust." Their regressions discern "a strong negative association between trust and the dominance of a strong hierarchical religion in a country, most notably Catholicism." See Rafael La Porta, Florencio Lopez-de-Silanes, Andrei Schleifer, and Robert W. Vishny, "Trust in Large Organizations," *American Economic Review, Papers and Proceedings* 87, 2 (May, 1997), 333–38.

16 On this and the next paragraph, see Aaron Levine, *Free Enterprise and Jewish Law: Aspects of Jewish Business Ethics* (New York: Ktav, 1980) and Meir Tamari, *With All Your Possessions: Jewish Ethics and Economic Life* (New York: Free Press, 1987).

Jewish law works through a dual mechanism to achieve its economic goals: an internal belief system and an external enforcement arrangement. To turn to the latter first, Jewish law establishes a court system with rules and regulations to be used not only for narrowly defined religious matters—the broad gamut of G-d–Man relationships—but also for interpersonal relationships, both criminal and civil. Even in the Sinai desert, at the dawn of the Jewish nation and shortly after the exodus from Egypt, Moses set up a dispute-resolution hierarchy, acting upon the advice given by Jethro, Midianite priest, and Moses's father-in-law.[17] Deuteronomy's recording of the Lord's dictum, "You shall appoint magistrates and officials for your tribes . . . and they shall govern the people with due justice,"[18] mandates a judicial system as the capstone of the law enforcement establishment. It is telling that in the early years of Jewish settlement in the land of Canaan the nation was governed by judges, and indeed one of the books of the biblical canon dealing with this period is called "Judges."[19] How telling, too, is the prophet Samuel's brief soliloquy prior to his retirement as the last of the judges, having anointed the first monarch:

> Here I am! Testify against me in the presence of the Lord and in the presence of His anointed one: Whose ox have I taken, or whose ass have I taken? Whom have I defrauded or whom have I robbed? From whom have I taken a bribe to look the other way?[20]

Clearly, the biblical demands for the judicial pursuit of justice and the absolute shunning of bribery[21] in interpersonal dispute resolution found their expression in the behavior of Samuel.

According to Jewish law, the judicial system and its rules can be avoided should the litigants so choose. This informal mechanism is not unlike arbitration insofar as the litigants may select the judge or judges, who need not be legally qualified but who are acceptable to the litigants. The judges then have a free hand in their adjudication procedures—they can permit hearsay testimony that would otherwise be unacceptable in a court of law—and the judges may rule as they see fit even if that decision would violate accepted law or practice.[22] Indeed, concerning this more informal procedure, Maimonides (Rambam, Egypt, 1135–1204) comments: "It is a positive commandment [for the judges] to ask the litigants at the start of the proceedings: 'Do you wish to be judged according to the law or do you prefer a more

17 Exodus 18:13–26.

18 16:18 (translation from Jewish Publication Society's *The Torah* [1962]).

19 Among the judge-leaders was the prophetess Deborah, who "used to sit under the Palm of Deborah . . . and the Israelites would come to her for decisions" (Judges 4:4–5). The prophet Samuel seems to have been an itinerant judge. See I Samuel 7:15–17.

20 I Samuel 12:3 in *The Prophets* (JPS, 1978).

21 "You shall not judge unfairly; you shall show no partiality; you shall not take bribes. . . . Justice, justice shall you pursue. . . ." (Deuteronomy 16:19–20).

22 See Rambam, *Mishne Torah*, *Sanhedrin*, 22:4–5; *Shulhan Arukh* (R. Joseph Caro, Israel, 1488–1575), *Hoshen Mishpat*, 12:2.

informal mechanism [*peshara*]?' "[23] Rambam then comments: "Any court of law that always adjudicates according to *peshara* is to be commended."

However, a judicial system is incomplete if it only employs judges who are charged with interpreting the law and adjudicating disputes. Their decisions need to be implemented, so an enforcement mechanism to carry out their rulings must be in place. The Torah in the verse cited earlier mandates the appointment of "officials," who presumably include court officers who mete out corporal punishment; as the verse states, "If the guilty one is to be flogged, the magistrate shall have him lie down and be given lashes in his presence. . . ."[24] R. Solomon b. Isaac (Rashi, France, 1040–1105) in his gloss to the Babylonian Talmud, tractate *Sotah*, defines "official," albeit in the context of preparations for battle, in an expanded vein: "the one who enforces the command of the judge."[25] A further broadening is to be found in the works of Rambam, the first codifier of the sum of Talmudic law. He begins his Laws of the *Sanhedrin* (i.e., Supreme Jewish Court) with the following description:

> The "officials" are those with staff and strap who stand before the judges. They circulate in the markets, in the streets, and in the stores to realign [misaligned] prices and [inaccurate] weights and to punish all iniquity. All their acts are based on [the orders of the] judges. And whenever they see an injustice, they bring him [i.e., the perpetrator] to court for adjudication.[26]

The Jewish legal system has ample scope for enforcement beyond the technical letter of the law when circumstances so mandate. The Talmud mentions a number of such instances that Rambam generalizes, according the judiciary extralegal rights even so far as to execute an individual who, according to strict legal standards, would not be subject to the death penalty.[27] So, too, may the Jewish monarch override the law when circumstances warrant, again even to execute someone whose life would not be forfeit according to Jewish judicial ruling.[28] This type of flexibility enables the Jewish legal system to cope with changing circumstances and to deter violations of the law that otherwise

23 Modern-day Hebrew translates *peshara* as "compromise," but that clearly is not its meaning in the Talmudic context. "Informal adjudication" or "arbitration" are more consistent with the intent of the term. This citation and the next are found in Rambam, op. cit., 22:4.

24 Deuteronomy 25:2. Note that the prior sentence mentions that this case involves an interpersonal dispute.

25 42a, *s.v. dumya de-shoter* (my translation).

26 Rambam, op. cit., *Sanhedrin* 1:1 (my translation). Rambam's expansion is based on *midrashic* sources. See ad locum, *Lehem Mishne* (R. Abraham b. Moses de Boton, Greece, 1540s–after 1592). But see also BT *Sanhedrin* 46a and BT *Yevamot* 90b.

Professor Shalom Albeck believes that the "officials" were appointees of the individual judges, not of the judicial establishment. He claims this despite his citing a *midrash* in the name of R. Elazar that states: "Once an individual has been found guilty and is obliged to [pay] his fellow litigant, then in the absence of the official to collect the owed sum, once he [i.e., the guilty party] has left the presence of the judges, the judges will be unable to do anything unless they turn him over to the official and he [i.e., the official] will then collect the owed sum." The simple reading of this passage does not compel acceptance of Albeck's view. See his *Batei Ha-Din Be-Yemei Ha-Talmud [Law Courts in Talmudic Times]* (Ramat Gan: Bar Ilan University, 1980), 61.

27 Rambam, op.cit., *Sanhedrin* 34:4–10. He notes that such decisions cannot become normative law but are always viewed as exceptions to standard judicial proceedings. The cases listed all involve violations of either religious or criminal law but would appear to be applicable to civil law as well.

28 Ibid., *Melakhim* 3:10.

would be unenforceable. Although one could "get away with murder" because Jewish criminal law is fenced in with significant procedural protections for murderers, these extralegal provisions allow for the more effective functioning of civil society.[29]

The Jewish legal system did not cease to exist after the destruction of the Second Temple and the subsequent exile. Jewish communities in the Diaspora transported and implemented the same legal system they had practiced in the land of Israel for centuries. Babylonian Jewry prospered under the exilarchs, rabbis, and communal leaders who adapted Torah and rabbinic laws to the new circumstances—a situation that lasted until the early eleventh century. As centralized rabbinic authority waned with the dispersion of the Diaspora, the disparate Jewish communities began to rule themselves, for the most part according to traditional law and practice. That did not and indeed could not mean replicating the system of law in Israel of old. It did mean adhering to its fundamental principles and setting up a judicial establishment that legislated, judged, and enforced laws.[30]

Asymmetric Information and Jewish Law

The preceding discussion presumes that litigants turned to the courts or to arbitrators for adjudication. *Halakha*, however, may intrude in the marketplace even when no civil conflict arises and no litigation lies in the wings. How does *Halakha* deal with enforcing contracts where both parties to the contract voluntarily agree to its terms and yet, in doing so, violate Jewish law? A brief discussion of this question opens the door to the internal belief mechanism mentioned earlier as one, and perhaps the primary, method designed to achieve Judaism's economic goals.

The classic case deals with usury. A borrower and lender agree in a free-market transaction to an interest payment on a loan.[31] This transaction is mutually

29 Although there were few such executions, occasional ones did occur not only during Talmudic times, but also during the Middle Ages in both Spain and Central Europe. See Eric Zimmer, *Harmony and Discord: An Analysis of the Decline of Jewish Self-Government in 15th Century Central Europe* (New York: Yeshiva University Press, 1970), 211, notes 1 and 2, and David M. Shohet, *The Jewish Court in the Middle Ages* (New York, 1931), 136–37.

30 R. Solomon b. Abraham Adret (Rashba, Spain, 1235–1310, cited in the *Bet Yosef* [R. Joseph Caro, Israel, 1488–1575], *Hoshen Mishpat* 2) wrote that "arbitrators [are] permitted to assess monetary penalties or physical punishments as they see fit because it enables the world to survive. Were one to rule according to Torah law . . . the world would be destroyed. . . ." (My translation).

For the practical aspects of Jewish law in the Middle Ages, see, for example, "Communal Enactments," Ch. 19 in Menahem Elon, *Jewish Law: History, Sources, Principles* (Jerusalem: 1994); Shohet, "The Legislative Powers of the Court and of the Communal Organization" (Ch. VI) and "Law Enforcement" (Ch. VII); and Zimmer, "The Community Administration" (Ch. I) and "Law Enforcement" (Ch. IV).

31 In Jewish law, since interest payments are prohibited, there is no distinction between interest payments and usury. This stands in contrast to both Christian and much secular law, where usury is defined as excessive interest. Note that, while Halakha prohibited interest payments, it was familiar with the concept that interest compensates for the lender's opportunity cost—the inability to use funds while they are in others' possession. See BT *Makkot* 3a.

beneficial—the borrower avails himself of the funds; the lender receives payment for providing them. Clearly, this marketplace phenomenon engenders the same positive economic consequences as does any noncoercive agreement that is presumed to be characterized by a win-win outcome. Moreover, interest rates play a critical role in economic theory as an allocator of capital and, in macroeconomics, as a broad-based determinant of investment. And yet, both biblical law and rabbinic law prohibit any payment of interest.[32] In fact, the net is cast quite wide in assigning culpability for an interest-bearing loan. Not only are the borrower and lender guilty of violating the law, but so, too, are the witnesses, the guarantors, and even the scribe who wrote the contract.[33]

Perhaps *Halakha* is suggesting that, in certain areas of Jewish life, economic and financial motives must yield to one's sense of kinship. Lending is one such area; uneven power relationships based on asymmetric information is another.[34]

The key to enforcing this sense of brotherhood is self-restraint, and that is based on one's personal integrity and religious practice. Moral behavior, however, does not arise in a vacuum. Ethical conduct is rooted in both mimetic learning and the formal educational system, both of which have been hallmarks of Jewish society for millennia. Children learn from the teachings and even more so from the behavior and actions of their parents. As Proverbs exhorts the Jewish child: "My son, heed the discipline of your father, and do not forsake the instruction of your mother. For they are a graceful wreath upon your head, a necklace about your throat."[35] Teaching children the proper path upon which they shall embark as they mature and become full-fledged members of the Jewish community is not merely sound advice, but a positive commandment incumbent at least upon the father and according to many Jewish authorities upon the mother as well.[36]

The community, too, bears responsibility for educating Jewish children. At the least, it must provide the appropriate institutions. As Rambam comments:

32 The biblical verses are analyzed at BT *Bava Metsi'a* 75b.

33 BT *Bava Metsi'a* 75b.

34 The motivation for the usury prohibition is variously interpreted, including making symmetrical asymmetric power relationships—the more powerful lender can exploit the less powerful borrower—or to prevent extortion of the poor, who presumably borrow to pay for their meager consumption. Often, it is presumed that money is not productive, and hence does not merit payment for its use. However, there is nothing in the classic halakhic literature, including the Bible, which itself never provides a reason for the prohibition, to support any of these claims. It seems to me that lending money without charge stems from the notion of *gemilat hesed* (i.e., undertaking acts of loving-kindness), the obligation of one Jew to his fellow coreligionist to perform favors without expecting compensation. This sense is almost explicit in the Biblical verses, "You shall not deduct interest from loans to your countryman. . . . You may deduct interest from loans to foreigners. . . ." (Deuteronomy 24:20–21). This seems implicit in *Tur*, a rabbinical diminutive of the work *Arba'a Turim* by R. Jacob b. Asher (Germany and Spain, 1270?–1340), in *Yoreh De'ah* 160, as well as in *Shulhan Arukh*, *Yoreh De'ah*, 160.

35 1:8–9. Instead of the term "discipline" in sentence 9, which the translator of the Jewish Publication Society, *The Writings* (Philadephia, 1982), used, I would prefer substituting "instructions."

36 Aaron Levine, "Aspects of the Lemons Problem as Treated in Jewish Law," *Journal of Law and Religion* XXIII,2 (2007–2008): 409–14. The mother's role vis-à-vis the education of her daughters may well be superior to that of the father. Levine, 411, note 108.

> [It is the community's obligation to] establish teachers of children in every region, satrapy, and city. . . . If [the] city [authorities] fail to establish a school, [the authorities of] that city are to be excommunicated.[37]

The true Jewish believer who accepts and has internalized *Halakha*—G-d's decrees as interpreted by Jewish rabbis over the millennia—behaves accordingly. Hence, if interest payment is anathema, then religious Jews simply do not lend upon interest. Nor do religious Jews offer to pay interest even though it is in their narrow self-interest. In the broad picture that includes not only material well-being but also allegiance to one's religious faith, narrow self-interest can never trump the adherence of the religious personality to one's religious tenets.

Such a high standard, though demanded, may not be realized without an external enforcement apparatus. But, because all the parties are voluntarily complicit in the transaction, the external methods of enforcement mentioned previously are unlikely to prove fruitful. Instead, Judaism turned to a Heavenly enforcement mechanism.

Here is how the Talmud records the sage, Rava (Babylonia, d. 352):

> Why did the Divine Law mention the exodus from Egypt in connection with interest, fringes, and weights? The Holy One, blessed be He, declared: "It is I who distinguished in Egypt between the first-born and one who was not first-born; even so, it is I who will exact vengeance from him who ascribes his money to a Gentile and lends it to an Israelite on interest, or who steeps his weights in salt, or who [attaches to his garments threads dyed with] vegetable blue [i.e., indigo] and maintains that it is real blue [i.e., *tekhelet*, the Torah-sanctioned dye]."[38]

In other words, the authorities may not know, but the All-seeing, All-knowing Divinity cannot be duped. Punishment may not be meted out by the judicial institutions, but it is inevitable.[39]

The two other cases dealt with in Rava's dictum involve asymmetric information and suggest that here, too, the enforcement mechanism partially involves the Divinity. The simpler case is inaccurate weights and measures, which at first glance are hard to spot because external evidence to detect the fraud is lacking. Rava's comment on letting weights absorb salt suggests as much; a more massive weight is simply indiscernible, and its falsity can only be ascertained by weighing it against some standard weight. It is hardly likely that the buyer of potatoes by the kilogram would carry her own weights and insist that they be used instead of

37 *Mishne Torah, Talmud Torah* 2:1. (My free translation.) Rambam notes in *Mishne Torah, De'ot* 4:23 that a scholar is prohibited from living in a community that lacks certain occupations and institutions such as a physician or a bathhouse. A teacher of children is among them.

38 TB *Bava Metsi'a* 61b (Traditional Press edition translation).

39 The phraseology of *Tur, Yoreh De'ah*, 160 is revealing: "The judgment [of someone who circumvents the prohibition against taking interest by an illegal subterfuge] is given over to the Inspector of Hearts, Who will exact payment." (My translation.)

Paying and collecting interest on loans is a complicated issue, with rabbinic prohibitions piled upon biblical ones. This chapter is not the place for reviewing the long history of rabbinic circumventions of rabbinic law in which fixed-payment loans were turned into business transactions with potential losses as well as gains. See the chapters in this volume by J. David Bleich, Daniel Feldman, and Adam Chodorow.

the seller's. As a matter of fact, and as mentioned earlier in a citation from Rambam's code, the authorities did appoint monitors in the marketplace. One of their functions was to establish the integrity of weights and measures used by tradesmen.[40]

Two methods could be used to offset the informational asymmetry. First, the monitors could actually monitor, randomly spot-checking vendor weights and measures against standards that they presumably carried along with them. Second, weights could be branded with an official insignia, and the monitors could eyeball the vendors' weights to determine whether they were officially stamped. Rambam and R. Samuel b. Meir (Rashbam, France, c. 1080-85–c. 1174) seem to focus on the former,[41] while R. Menahem b. Solomon Meiri (France, 1249–1316) and R. Joseph b. Meir HaLevi ibn Migash (Ri Migash, Spain, 1077–1141), in their commentaries to *Bava Batra* 89a, presume that the monitors imprinted and checked weights and measures for an official brand. R. Jeroham b. Meshullam (France and Spain, c. 1290–1350),[42] based on the comments at *Bava Batra* 89b of the Talmudic scholar R. Papa (Babylonia, c. 300–375), points out the restoration of symmetry in this asymmetric relationship. Clearly, buyers, too, will be able to distinguish between stamped and uncertified weights, eliminating the advantage of the sellers. Buyers avoid sellers using unstamped weights. In either case, it was an official body—either Jewish or, in Roman times in Palestine, the Roman authorities—who engaged in preventative monitoring and punishment of those fraudulent traders. (It is fascinating to learn that in the late sixteenth century in Kazimierz, Poland, the Jewish community replicated this ancient practice by appointing monitors of weights and measures. The Jewish community regulations in Nikolsburg, Moravia, that were codified in 1651 specified random checks of vendors' weights and measures.)[43] The authorities'

40 TB *Bava Batra* 89a; R. Samuel b. Meir (Rashbam, France, c. 1080-85–c. 1174), *s.v. agardemin*; *Shulhan Arukh, Hoshen Mishpat* 231:2. (See also Yerushalmi *Bava Batra* 18a.) The monarch, too, may have played a role in policing the marketplace. *Yoma* 9a discusses the term *parhedrin*, which it equates to *pursei*, which Rashi (ad. loc., *s.v. pursei*) defines as "officers of the king." Among others, R. Yom Tov b. Abraham Ishbili (Ritba, Spain, c. 1250–1330) at *Yoma* 8b (*s.v. parhedrin*) interprets the *parhedrin* to be "persons who are appointed [to prevent] price [gouging] and [to insure accurate] weights."

41 *Mishne Torah, Geneva* 8:20; Rashbam, op. cit.

42 *Mesharim*, path 9, section 5, p. 32, col. 3, *s.v. helek hamishi*. This view is cited by both the *Tur* and *Shulhan Arukh, Hoshen Mishpat* 231 and *Shulhan Arukh* (ibid., 231:3) as binding. It is an exception to the prohibition against keeping inaccurate weights and measures in one's household. In communities where the practice is to brand weights and measures, unbranded weights may be preserved, as no fraud is likely to be committed with them. Buyers will not purchase from vendors using unmarked weights.

43 Majer Balaban, *A History of the Jews in Cracow and Kazimierz, 1304–1868* (Jerusalem: Magnes Press, 2002, 2 vols., Hebrew), v. 1, 257. Balaban adds there that the inspectors were charged with "inspecting once monthly whether their use [viz., of the weights and measures] was 'just,' and to punish severely those who counterfeited measures and weights" (my translation). Israel Schepansky in his *Takkanot Ha-Kehillot* (Jerusalem: *Mosad Harav Kook*, 1993, 4 vols., Hebrew) cites the Moravian regulations as follows: "The officials appointed [to regulate weights and measures] should always have a standard *amma* [i.e., a measure of length]. . . . At least four times a year they should come suddenly—whenever they wish—to a trader [or a] shop to inspect the weights and measures to ascertain that each [has accurate weights and measures]" (Vol. 4, 409 –10; my translation).

measures supplemented the reliance upon the religiously motivated integrity of marketplace participants.[44]

The case of fraud in dyeing fringes similarly involves asymmetric information but of an even more extreme type. While Rava refers to a Jew who is trying to mislead by wearing improperly dyed thread, the Talmud in *Menahot* discusses a transaction scenario. The producer/seller of religiously mandated dyed *tsitsit* (the fringes the Torah demands be tied at the corners of a four-corned garment and be dyed *tekhelet*—a shade of blue—extracted from the *hilazon*)[45] could substitute a less-expensive dye without the buyer ever becoming aware of the substitution. Moreover, even if the dye could be tested following the chemical procedure outlined in the Talmud, the Talmud further explains that the *tekhelet* had to be manufactured with the proper religious intention.[46] In such instances, which involve what I have called elsewhere "a pure-credence good"—where the product or service is by its very nature unverifiable even if the production process was observed from the beginning to the end—the buyer is without recourse.[47]

Rava's warning that such deception will be detectable and responded to by the L-rd is clearly germane here as the ultimate deterrent.

Hence, in the first instance, Judaism relies upon a combination of the religious practitioner's faith and his fear of G-d to maintain fairness in the marketplace. Indeed, such constraints within the psyche of the individual may be more powerful than external enforcement mechanisms—the second line of defense. If one cannot avoid temptation in the psychological sense, at least one can refrain from exercising ethically unjustified power. After all, while court officers and judges can be suborned, one's conscience cannot be duped with G-d hovering in the background. For the ethical Jew, acting on unfair advantage because of the power deriving from asymmetric information should never be an issue.

The role of individual integrity in the presence of asymmetric information is perhaps most vividly driven home with respect to the judicial system itself. Jewish law does not have an appeals mechanism. Should one of the litigants feel that a miscarriage of justice has occurred, the only recourse is to convince the judge that

44 The *Nimmukei Yosef* (R. Joseph Habiba, Spain, beginning of the fifteenth century) in his commentary on the *Rif* (R. Isaac b. Jacob Alfasi, Morocco, 1013–1103) (TB *Bava Batra* 89b on p. 45b in the standard *Rif* pagination in the back of the *Bavli, s.v. aval*) comments on the permissibility of maintaining unbranded weights in a community where branding is the practice: "When it [i.e., the weight] is not branded, then he [viz., the owner] will discern it as will the purchasers, and so will not use it to weigh" (My translation).

45 The precise definition of this term has been lost. It is now thought to be a sea snail, *Hexaplex trunculus*. For further information, see the web site of the *Ptil Tekhelet* association, http://www.tekhelet.com.

46 TB *Menahot* 42b–43a. Among the ingredients needed for testing the purity of the dye were liquid alum, fenugreek juice, and the urine of a forty-day-old child. Unfortunately, no proportions are mentioned. A second test involves baking hard leavened barley meal dough into which the test thread had been inserted. Presumably, the civil authorities could have established testing facilities and random inspection to both deter and spot fraudulent sellers. However, such actions would only vitiate one aspect of the asymmetric information issue, without addressing the issue of intention.

47 Prager, "Balancing," op. cit., 125. Analogously, think of a criminal defense attorney—can the defendant be certain that the lawyer has represented him as best she can?

an error has been made.[48] Hence, these judges are producers of pure-credence goods—no one can question their decisions, which did not have to be clarified or recorded[49]—and so judges can easily take advantage of the litigants. To be sure, judges reputed to be biased may see their share of trials be reduced as litigants refuse to appear before them. However, it is one of the characteristics of pure-credence goods that discerning such a bias is virtually impossible.

What then drives judges to judge justly? Their own religious faith that they are serving G-d provides a positive incentive; their understanding that disservice to the L-rd is punishable by Him acts as the negative stimulus. Rambam, having described the character traits of Jewish judges in his second chapter of the Laws of the *Sanhedrin*, devotes his twenty-third chapter to discussing the gravity and the pitfalls of their duties. R. Joseph Caro focuses the opening of the first chapter of his *Shulhan Arukh, Hoshen Mishpat* on the crucial importance of justice and just judges, citing the Torah, the preaching of the prophets, and the practice of the just kings of ancient Israel. The words of Rambam based on *Sanhedrin* 7a-b are worth citing.

> The judge should always visualize himself as if a sword is positioned on his neck and Hell is open beneath him. He should know whom he is judging and before Whom he is judging and Who will punish him in the future should he deviate from the path of truth. . . . Any judge who judges accurately according to the law . . . it is as if he repaired the entire world and caused the Divine presence to rest upon Israel. . . .[50]

It would be naive to presume that all Jewish judges over the ages have achieved these lofty standards. Historical evidence from the early days of the Jewish nation[51] and the prophets[52] testifies to corruption. There is no indication that admonitions and imprecations had a deterrent or remedial effect. Clearly, the people of Israel

48 Although the classical judicial system consisted of different-sized courts—of three judges, twenty-three, and the seventy-one of the *Sanhedrin*—each of these was the court of initial jurisdiction for specific issues or types of cases. Courts with more judges were authoritative in different areas; they were not higher in the sense of being able to reverse a decision of a court of lesser number. Some sporadic exceptions that involved appeals are noted in Simha Assaf, *Batei ha-Din ve-Sidrehem Ahare Hatimat ha-Talmud: homer le-toledot ha-mishpat ha-'Ivri* (74–86 and 137–40) and Elon (op. cit., 647 and 662–64 [Hebrew]). In contrast, the contemporary Israeli religious court system operates with an appeals procedure, a mechanism that preceded the State of Israel and was set up by the Chief Rabbinate of (then) Palestine in 1921. See Elon, 667–68 (Hebrew).

49 See Rambam, op. cit., *Sanhedrin* 22:8; *Shulhan Arukh, Hoshen Mishpat*, 19:2 and 14:4. Although the Talmud (*Sanhedrin* 18b) records that scribes were present at the sittings of the *Sanhedrin* and Rambam records that as binding (ibid., 1:9), it appears that these scribes were for internal purposes only, as is evident from *Sanhedrin* 40a. Moreover, the presence of scribes is not recorded in connection with lesser courts. The litigants were informed of the decision and whether the verdict was split or not, but they were not privy to the reasoning of the judiciary. Since 1943, Israeli religious courts must document their decisions, which Shochetman suggests is related to the appeals mechanism described in the preceding note. His reasoning is straightforward. Without documentation explaining the lower courts' reasoning, no meaningful appeal is possible. Schepansky suggests otherwise, questioning Shochetman's chronology—the vast lag between the institution of the appeals process (1921) and the written documentation requirement (1943). See Schepansky, op. cit., 217–18.

50 23:8–9.

51 See, for example, I Samuel 8:1–3 about Samuel's own sons or the episode in I Kings 21 of Navot the Carmelite, whose property was stolen by King Ahav via a corrupt trial.

52 See, for example, Isaiah 1:21–23; Micah 3:9–12.

suffered to some unknown extent from an injustice system; that justice ultimately will prevail is hardly a solace for the victims. On the other hand, it is equally obvious that the number of upright judges, whose integrity hinged upon their religious convictions or who were deterred by the fear of Divine chastisement, is indeterminate. One must remain agnostic in the absence of comprehensive evidence as to whether jurists operating in the halakhic judicial process actually met its high standards.

The judicial appointment process as found in the Talmud does provide an additional, albeit inadequate, check on the judiciary. Responsibility for knowingly appointing corrupt or incompetent judges redounds on the appointer, who violates a Torah commandment. Indeed, the Talmud equates such an appointment to idolatry.[53] This is a preventative check, designed to assure that the virtually unlimited power of the law is placed only in the hands of the worthy. However, the bottom line is that the halakhic system is not free from the deficiencies characteristic of the secular legal mechanism. There seems to be no fail-safe mechanism for assuring that asymmetric information will not be utilized against the weaker party other than the the stronger party's personal religious belief or the fear of Divine retribution.

Conclusion

In sum, especially in cases of asymmetric information where at least one of the parties to a transaction finds it either difficult or impossible to obtain the necessary knowledge to evaluate options objectively, *Halakha* provides a balancing mechanism to assist the weaker party against the stronger—and in this case, the better informed—party. It begins with the presumption that the imbalance will be self-remedied; the stronger will voluntarily relinquish his advantage. Just as one family member would not exploit his close relative, so, too, should he not take advantage of his coreligionist.

Unfortunately, the belief that individuals will always act with integrity is not borne out by experience. Hence, *Halakha* proceeded a few steps further. Where intentions cannot be fathomed by an outsider and where advantage can be taken with little possibility of discovery, the omniscient G-d will know and act accordingly.[54] This is true whether *Halakha* is dealing with an unjust judge, a scheming seller, or parties to an interest-bearing loan. Finally, in some instances such as the case of debased weights and measures where the individual's limited resources

53 TB *Sanhedrin* 7b and TB *Avoda Zara* 52a; Rambam, op. cit., *Sanhedrin* 3:8; *Shulhan Arukh*, *Hoshen Mishpat*, 8:1.

54 The metaphor of the *Mishna* in *Avot* (known as *Ethics of Our Fathers*) 3:10 is appropriate: "The store is open and the store-keeper gives credit. The ledger is open and the hand writes. Whomsoever wishes to borrow may do so. But the agents circulate daily and collect from the debtor with his knowledge or without it, for they have upon which to rely [i.e., the credit documents]" (My translation).

could not realistically offset the asymmetric information bias, the civil authorities would be expected to redress the imbalance. It is clear, however, that the halakhic system has gaps that can be taken advantage of by the unscrupulous. Ultimately, the halakhic mechanism must fall back on the guiding principle that constitutes the title of this article: *Know Before Whom You Stand!*

SELECTED BIBLIOGRAPHY

Akerlof, George A. "The Market for 'Lemons': Quality Uncertainty and the Market Mechanism." *Quarterly Journal of Economics* 84 (August, 1970), 488-500.

Bible:

Deuteronomy 16:19–20; 24: 20–21; 25:2.

Exodus 16:18; 18:13–26.

Judges chapter 2.

Caro, R. Joseph. *Shulhan Arukh, Hoshen Mishpat* 8:1; 12:2; 14:4; 19:2; 231:2–3.

Elon, R. Menahem. *Jewish Law: History, Sources, Principles* (Jerusalem: 1994).

Fukuyama, Francis. *Trust: The Social Virtues and the Creation of Prosperity* (New York: Free Press, 1995).

Gambetta, Diego. "Can We Trust Trust?" In Diego Gambetta, *Trust: Making and Breaking Cooperative Relations* (New York: Blackwell, 1988), 213-38.

Jacob B. Asher. *Tur, Hoshen Mishpat* 2; 231

Jacob B. Asher. *Tur Shulhan Arukh, Yoreh De'ah* 160.

Levine, Aaron. "Aspects of the Lemons Problem as Treated in Jewish Law." *Journal of Law and Religion* XXIII 2 (2007–2008), 379-424.

Levine, Aaron. *Free Enterprise and Jewish Law: Aspects of Jewish Business Ethics* (New York: Ktav, 1980).

Maimonides (Rambam):

Mishne Torah, Melakhim 3:10.

Mishne Torah, Sanhedrin 1:1; 3:8; 22:4–5, 8; 23, 8:9; 34:4–10.

Mishne Torah, Geneva, 8:20.

Prager, Jonas. "Balancing the Scales: *Halakha*, the Firm, and Information Asymmetries." In Aaron Levine and Moses Pava (eds.), *Jewish Business Ethics: The Firm and Its Stakeholders* (Northvale, NJ: Jason Aronson, 1999, 123-46.

Prager, Jonas. "Contracting Out: Theory and Policy." *Journal of International Law and Politics* 25, 1 (Fall 1992).

Schepansky, Israel. *Takkanot Ha-Kehillot* (Jerusalem: *Mosad Harav Kook*, 1993, 4 vols.).

Shohet, David M. *The Jewish Court in the Middle Ages* (New York, 1931).

Talmud Bavli:

Bava Batra 89a–b.

Bava Metsi'a 61b; 75b.

Menahot 42b–43a.

Sanhedrin 7a–b; 46a.

Tamari, Meir. *With All Your Possessions: Jewish Ethics and Economic Life* (New York: Free Press, 1987).

Zimmer, Eric. *Harmony and Discord: An Analysis of the Decline of Jewish Self-Government in 15th Century Central Europe* (New York: Yeshiva University Press, 1970).

CHAPTER 17

PAYMENT FOR ORGAN DONATION IN JEWISH LAW

FRED ROSNER AND EDWARD REICHMAN

Introduction

In Judaism, a physician's license to heal the sick is considered divinely given. The Talmud[1] derives this from the Biblical phrase, "And he shall surely heal."[2] In fact, according to Maimonides (Rambam, Egypt 1135–1204), a physician is obligated to heal the sick, induce remission of illness, and prolong life.[3] Rambam bases this on the Biblical commandment to restore a lost object to its rightful owner,[4] which he views as including one's lost health. He adds[5] that, if a patient's condition worsens as a result of a physician's refusal to treat them, the physician violates the Biblical interdict against standing idly by the blood of one's fellow man.[6]

Halakhah requires an ill patient to seek medical care. This is derived from several Biblical and Rabbinic admonitions, including "You shall guard yourselves carefully,"[7] and "Beware and watch yourselves very well."[8]

1 BT *Bava Kamma* 85a.
2 Exodus 21:19.
3 Rambam, *Commentary on the Mishnah, Nedarim* 4:4.
4 Deuteronomy 22:2.
5 Rambam, *Mishneh Torah, Retsihah u-Shemirat ha-Nefesh* 1:14.
6 Leviticus 19:16.
7 Deuteronomy 4:15.
8 Deuteronomy 4:9.

Statement of the Problem

Human organ transplantation began nearly half a century ago. Since then, organ donations have been insufficient to meet the needs of patients with diseased organs. Currently, over three thousand people die every year while waiting for a kidney, heart, liver, lung, or other organ.[9] Despite intensive efforts and major initiatives to increase the supply of organs, the number of donations remains the same. Many have proposed solving the shortage by providing some form of financial inducement to donors. Several different structures of compensation have been proposed, as discussed below. There are many Jewish legal considerations involved in financially compensating organ donors. Should donors be encouraged to give only for altruistic reasons? Is it prohibited to pay for organs? Jewish law addresses all of these concerns.

Compensation for organ donation is currently prohibited in the United States, as per the 1984 National Organ Transplantation Act. Although many consider payment for organs anathema, advocates continue to press for some form of financial compensation. Many different suggestions have been offered. The recipient could directly compensate the donor or their estate. They could pay the charity of the donor's or donor's family's choice. Finally, potential owners could be provided with a limited, low-cost life insurance policy redeemable by their family upon donation of their organs.[10]

Proponents of donor compensation argue that altruism alone is insufficient to meet the demand and need for organ donors. They also point to the long-standing practice of payment for blood, blood products, sperm, and human eggs.[11] They claim that it is morally reprehensible to let thousands of patients die while waiting for donor organs.[12] Opponents of payment argue that compensation undermines the altruistic consent process, encourages a black market for organs, and leads to exploitation of the poor. They are also concerned that organs will be bought and sold like any other commodity.[13] Others argue that compensation disassociates the body from the self and treats it like property. But, since the person is no longer alive, can a potential donor or their family be said to own the body? Can they legally profit from its disposition?[14]

Over the past decade, a number of Rabbinic authorities have addressed the halakhic issues involved in compensating organ donors. As many authors focus on limited or selected aspects of compensation, we provide an overview of the major issues. Interested readers can find the expanded legal discussions referred to in the footnotes.

9 See www.unos.org for all current, continually updated statistics on organ transplantation.

10 D. S. Kilter, et al., "Incentives for Organ Donation?" *Lancet* 238 (1991): 1,441–43.

11 A. M. Capron, "Whose Child is This?" *Hastings Center Report* 21 (1991): pp. 37–38.

12 A. L. Caplan, "Sounding Board; Ethical and Policy Issues in the Procurement of Cadaver Organs for Transplantation," *Human Organ Transplantation* 272 (1987): 275.

13 E. D. Pellegrino, "Families' Self Interest and the Cadavers' Organs: What Price Consent?" *The Journal of the American Medical Association* 265 (1991): 1,305–06.

14 D. Joralemon and P. Cox, "Body Values: The Case against Compensating for Transplant Organs," *Hastings Center Report* 33 (January–February 2003): 27–33.

Halakhic Precedents for Selling Body Parts

There is Talmudic precedent for selling body parts, but not organs, and not in a medical or therapeutic context. For example, the Talmud discusses selling one's hair.[15] It seems to be permitted, as the wife of R. Akiva sold her hair to support her family.[16]

While this case bears superficial resemblance to organ donation, there are several distinctions that minimize its relevance to the issue. For one, hair regenerates, unlike kidneys or other organs. Thus, selling a body part that grows back may be permitted, but selling one that does not regenerate may not be allowed. In addition, removing hair requires no incision of the skin and no violation of bodily integrity. There is no potential violation of the prohibition against self-wounding—a major concern in the permissibility of vital organ donation. Finally, donating vital organs constitutes fulfillment of the *mitsvah* to save a life, and this may limit the permissibility of receiving compensation. No such *mitsvah* is associated with donating hair.

In the modern context, R. Moses Feinstein (New York, 1895–1986) addressed the issue of payment for blood donation, which he allowed.[17] His response is premised on a discussion of the laws of self-wounding, which has direct relevance to our discussion. However, his final analysis is particular to blood donation and precludes its application to cases of vital organ donation. R. Feinstein's reasoning is based on the premise that the prohibition of self-wounding is not involved in blood donation, since blood drawing is essentially a painless and harmless procedure that has been practiced for centuries as a therapeutic measure. Hence, blood donation is removed from the category of self-inflicted harm, and there is thus no reason to prohibit a blood donor from asking for and receiving financial compensation.

Prohibition Against Receiving Payment for Performance of a *Mitsvah*

Jewish law forbids receiving financial compensation for fulfilling a *mitsvah* or performing a meritorious act. Physicians, teachers, and judges are all considered to be fulfilling Biblical commandments, and they are enjoined against receiving payment for their services. Jews must emulate God, and just as He heals, teaches, and judges without compensation, so must we. R. Jacob b. Asher (Spain, 1270?–1340)[18]

15 BT *Nedarim* 65b.

16 JT *Shabbat* 6:1.

17 R. Moses Feinstein, *Iggerot Mosheh*, *Hoshen Mishpat* 1:103.

18 *Tur*, *Yoreh De'ah* 336.

and R. Joseph Caro (Ottoman Palestine, 1488–1575)[19] rule that a physician may only receive compensation for his trouble and his loss of time. Modern physicians, teachers, and judges have no other occupations, unlike in Talmudic times. Since they are fully occupied with their professions, they are therefore entitled to receive full compensation for their services.[20]

Is an organ donor or his family permitted to request or accept financial compensation? This may be problematic, as the donation fulfills the commandment of saving a life. One possible solution is to reimburse the donor for time lost and expenses incurred, similar to the physician or teacher. Thus, the donor is technically not receiving payment for the performance of the *mitsvah*. If a physician, who is Biblically mandated to heal the sick, can be compensated in this way, then all the more so an organ donor, who is not required to incur the risks involved in organ donation. This is indeed the conclusion reached by Rabbi Dr. Mordechai Halperin (Israel, contemporary). The compensation does not in any way detract from the fulfillment of the *mitsvah*. The question of what constitutes a reasonable or excessive fee is discussed elsewhere.[21]

Alternatively, some argue that the obligation to perform a *mitsvah* without compensation applies only to obligatory commandments, not optional ones. While the donation of an organ is certainly an extraordinary act of kindness and one fulfills a *mitsvah* thereby, it is clearly not obligatory.[22] This mitigates the concern of receiving payment for the performance of a *mitsvah*. However, some have interpreted R. Ovadiah Yosef (Israel, contemporary) as ruling that kidney donation is indeed obligatory.[23] If so, then payment for kidney donation is just as problematic as payment for any other obligatory *mitsvah*.

The Obligation to Save a Life

The Talmud states a man who sees his neighbor drowning, mauled by beasts, or attacked by robbers is obligated to try to save his life.[24] This Talmudic ruling is codified as normative Jewish law by Rambam.[25] In fact, saving a life takes precedence over all Biblical and Rabbinic laws, with the exception of idolatry, murder, and forbidden sexual relations. Even the Sabbath or Yom Kippur may be desecrated in

19 *Shulhan Arukh, Yoreh De'ah* 336.

20 F. Rosner and J. Widroff, "Physician's Fees in Jewish Law," *Jewish Law Annual* 12 (1997): 115–26.

21 Ibid.

22 A. Steinberg, "Ethical and Halakhic Perspectives in Organ Donation," in S. Raz (ed.), *Kovets ha-Tsiyyonut ha-Datit* (Jerusalem: Histadderut ha-Mizrachi, 2001), 417–41 (Hebrew).

23 R. F. Warburg, "Renal Transplantation: Living Donors and Markets for Body Parts—Halakha in Concert with Halakhic Policy or Public Policy?" *Tradition* 40:2 (2007): 14–48; A. Steinberg, "Ethical and Halakhic Perspectives in Organ Donation," 435.

24 BT *Sanhedrin* 73a.

25 Rambam, *Mishneh Torah, Retsihah u-Shemirat ha-Nefesh* 1:14.

order to save one whose life is at risk. The Talmud emphasizes the significance of this *mitsvah*, stating that one who saves a life is considered to have saved an entire world.[26] The parameters and limitations of this *mitsvah* in relation to selling organs are discussed extensively in the literature. The seminal responsum was written by R. David b. Solomon ibn Abi Zimra (Radbaz, Egypt, 1479–1573), who was asked whether one is required to sacrifice a nonvital limb in order to save another's life. He considers in statistical detail how much risk one is obligated, permitted, or forbidden to incur in order to rescue someone.[27] The interpretation and application of this responsum is extremely relevant to compensation for organ donation.

Ownership Rights Over One's Body

Selling and receiving payment for an item implies rights of ownership. The same should be true for selling organs. But does the body really belong to man? If so, then he is entitled to sell any parts thereof. But if our bodies are viewed as belonging exclusively to God, then perhaps compensation is a moot point.

According to some rabbinic authorities, God owns the body and gives it on loan, charging a person with maintaining it and staying healthy.[28] It follows that a person has no right to wound himself, commit suicide, or otherwise denigrate his body, which does not belong to him. Is it possible to conceive of payment for an organ while still adhering to the notion that we are mere stewards of our bodies? If we restate the nature of the transaction, the answer is yes. The donor is not paid for his organ, but rather for the benefit he confers and the money he loses as a result of donation. R. Shaul Yisraeli (Israel, 1909–1995) maintains that a person has certain rights over his body in partnership with God and is therefore entitled to some form of compensation for donation.[29]

R. Zalman Nehemiah Goldberg (Israel, contemporary) approaches the issue from a different halakhic perspective.[30] He views the ownership of a Canaanite slave as the paradigm for one's rights to their own body. He concludes that the owner of a Canaanite slave cannot remove the slave's limb or organ for his own usage. For example, if he writes a contract on a slave's arm, he cannot detach the

26 BT *Sanhedrin* 37a.

27 *Responsa Radbaz* 3:627. This and other *responsa* of Radbaz are frequently quoted in the halakhic literature on living organ donation. Indeed, Michael Vigoda bases his entire analysis about compensation for organ donation on the *responsa* of Radbaz. See M. Vigoda, "The Sale of Organs," *Shanah be-Shanah* (2000): 119–27 (Hebrew).

28 S. Y. Zevin, "The Case of Shylock," in *Le-Or ha-Halakhah* (Jerusalem: Beit Hillel, 1988), 318–28 and in Moshe Hershler (ed.), *Halakhah u-Refu'ah* 2 (Jerusalem: Regensburg Institute, 1980), 93–100 (Hebrew).

29 S. Yisraeli, *Ha-Torah ve-ha-Medinah* 5–6 (1953–1954), 106–10 and *Amud ha-Yemini* 16, 16 ff. (Hebrew). The essay in *Ha-Torah ve-ha-Medinah* was written in response to R. Zevin's article on the halakhic aspects of Shylock, cited above.

30 Z. N. Goldberg, "Transactions in the Sale of Kidneys," in *Ateret Shelomoh* 2 (1997): 49–55.

arm in order to deliver the contract.[31] R. Goldberg also discusses the case of a Jewish slave, who submits himself to bondage in order to pay off his debts. This might imply permission to sell one's organs to pay off debts, but the precedent is flawed, as a Jewish slave is not permitted to sell himself to a master who may inflict bodily harm upon him. Although the Canaanite and Jewish slave present no acceptable precedent, R. Goldberg marshals support from the position of R. Shneur Zalman of Lyady (Belorussia, 1745–1813) that one has limited rights of ownership to his body. R. Shneur Zalman allows consenting to bodily harm if it is to one's benefit.[32] Thus, R. Goldberg concludes that the sale of an organ is valid, as it is a benefit for the donor to save another's life, and, additionally, the sale could be accomplished through transfer of money.

Prohibitions Against Self-Wounding[33] and Self-Endangerment

Jewish law commands that we diligently watch over ourselves[34] and take good care of our bodies.[35] Based on these and other Biblical precepts, such as the prohibition against wanton destruction, all Rabbinic opinions prohibit self-wounding and self-endangerment. If so, how is a live organ donor permitted to undergo the surgery and anesthesia, subjecting himself to rare postoperative complications and possible side-effects? This issue of *havalah*, or self-wounding, occupies a prominent place in virtually all the contemporary halakhic articles that deal with organ donation.

Although all rabbinic authorities accept the prohibition against self-wounding, as it is stated in the Talmud,[36] they debate its nature and scope.[37] *Tosafot* assert that the prohibition applies even when one incurs benefit, financial or otherwise.[38] This

31 BT *Gittin* 19a. R. Israel Meir Lau also discusses this source in his "Selling Organs for Transplants," *Tehumin* 18 (1988): 125–36, especially 134–35.

32 *Shulhan Arukh ha-Rav*, *Hilkhot Nizkei Guf ve-Nefesh* 4.

33 Deuteronomy 4:15.

34 Deuteronomy 4:9.

35 The prohibition of *havalah* is discussed extensively in the context of cosmetic surgery. See, for example, J. D. Bleich, "Plastic Surgery," *Contemporary Halakhic Problems*, vol. 1 (New York: Ktav, 1977), 119–23; M. Feinstein, "Cosmetic Surgery for a Young Woman to Improve Her Appearance," in *Halakhah u-Refu'ah*, vol. 1 (Jerusalem: Regensberg Institute, 1980), 323–27 (Hebrew); D. B. Ettengoff, "Halachic Implications of Cosmetic Surgery," *Journal of Halacha and Contemporary Society* 15 (1988): 79–93; D. Geisler, "Cosmetic Surgery in Halacha," in *Journal of Halacha and Contemporary Society* 48 (2004): 29–44; C. Eisenstein, "Plastic Surgery for Cosmetic Purposes in Halakhah," *Ateret Shelomoh* 1 (1996): 57–72 (Hebrew); F. Rosner, "Plastic and Cosmetic Surgery in Judaism," in *L'eyla* (December, 1999), 45–48; T. Guttman, "Plastic Surgery in Halakhah," *Ateret Shelomoh* 9 (2004): 171–80.

36 BT *Bava Kamma* 91b.

37 A. Steinberg, "Ethical and Halakhic Perspectives on Organ Donation," 417–41, especially 432–33 (Hebrew).

38 *Tosafot*, BT *Bava Kamma* 91b, s. v., "*ela hai.*"

would seemingly preclude any sale of human organs. However, R. Jacob Joshua b. Tsevi Hirsch Falk (Germany, 1680–1756), based on a Talmudic passage that seems to permit self-wounding, limits *Tosafot*'s opinion to where the benefit is relatively small.[39] Self-wounding is allowed for a relatively great need, however this is to be defined.[40] Indeed, R. Yosef Shalom Elyashiv (Jerusalem, contemporary) accepts this distinction and permits selling a kidney if the donor has great financial need. He adds the additional proviso that the resultant income must actually meet the donor's financial need, and not merely ease his need in a minimal way.[41]

If the donation saves a life, some permit compensation unequivocally.[42] For example, R. Yitshak Zilberstein (Israel, contemporary) states that the great *mitsvah* of saving a life mitigates the prohibition against self-wounding. Furthermore, as the donor is volunteering to donate by his own free will, and there is no obligation to donate, there is no reason he could not request compensation. R. Zilberstein also emphasizes that receiving compensation for the *mitsvah* does not diminish its status or value.[43]

Further reflection reveals a more nuanced analysis. A patient is certainly permitted to pay for an organ in order to save his own life. As we shall see, this is true even when the donor may not be halakhically justified in requesting payment.[44] However, the donor may be prohibited from taking the money. Understanding the distinction requires a careful analysis of the laws of self-wounding. According to R. Feinstein, the prohibition of self-wounding is governed by one's intent. If the wounding is done with a positive intent and purpose, the prohibition does not apply.[45] This widely cited opinion is based on Rambam, who prohibits wounding only when it is done *derekh bizzayon*,[46] in a denigrating manner. However, there is no prohibition when wounding is done for a constructive purpose, and saving a life certainly meets this requirement.

While saving a life excludes organ donation from the prohibition against self-wounding, the nature of the exclusion may impact the permissibility of receiving compensation. Does saving a life eliminate, or supersede, the prohibition against self-wounding and thereby remove its relevance? Or does it merely constitute an exemption to the prohibition, with the prohibition still technically in place? According to the latter approach, one is only exempt if the self-wounding is performed with intent to save a life. However, if it is motivated exclusively by financial gain,

39 R. Jacob Joshua b. Tsevi Hirsch Falk, *Penei Yehoshua*, ad loc.

40 See J. D. Kunin, "The Search for Organs: Halachic Perspectives on Altruistic Giving and the Selling of Organs," in *Journal of Medical Ethics* 31 (2005), 269–72.

41 Ibid, 271.

42 See, for example, A. Sherman, "Donation of Organs for Financial Compensation," in *Tehumin* 20 (2000): 353–62 (Hebrew), and Y. Zilberstein, *Shoshanat ha-Amakim* (Benei Berak: self-publication, 1999), 110–14.

43 Y. Zilberstein, ibid., 110.

44 See, for example, S. Resnicoff, "Supplying Human Body Parts: A Jewish Law Perspective," in *DePaul Law Review* 55 (2005–2006): 851–74, and A. S. Abraham, *Nishmat Avraham*, vol. 4, 2nd expanded ed. (Jerusalem: Schlesinger Institute, 2007), 122–29.

45 *Iggerot Mosheh, Hoshen Mishpat* 1:103.

46 Some versions have the alternate reading of "*nitsayon*." This is the subject of much halakhic discussion.

the exemption does not apply. The self-wounding would revert back to its original prohibited status.[47]

However, according to the former approach, in which saving a life eliminates the prohibition against self-wounding, one's intent is irrelevant. The prohibition against self-wounding is simply nonexistent. Hence, self-wounding is permitted even when one intends for financial gain.

Cadaveric Donation

The majority of the literature on compensating organ donors addresses living donors, in which self-wounding and payment for *mitsvah* performance are key issues. However, in cadaveric donation, these issues are irrelevant. No prohibitions or obligations devolve upon the deceased, who is free from the performance of *mitsvot*. However, just as with live donation, one must still ask to whom the body belongs. Who would theoretically receive compensation for the cadaver's donated organs? It is generally agreed that, while the relatives of the deceased are obligated to care for, guard, and ultimately bury the body, they do not "own" the body in the classical sense. However, as removing organs for transplant requires their consent, they might still be entitled to receive compensation for consenting. Reimbursement for expenses would likely not violate any prohibitions,[48] but profiting from the consent may be problematic. The main issue is the prohibition against deriving benefit from a corpse.[49] R. Solomon Zalman Auerbach (Israel, 1910–1995) prohibits the deceased's relatives from consenting for this very reason. However, Dr. Abraham S. Abraham (Israel, contemporary) constructs a unique case that circumvents the problem, whereby the relatives use the money received to save the life of another person. In this case, *pikkuah nefesh* overrides the prohibition against deriving benefit from the cadaver.[50]

R. Eliezer Judah Waldenberg (Israel, 1912–2006) argues that the relatives may receive money for consenting to donation. Their consent would be required even if no compensation was given. Hence, receiving compensation is considered secondary and cannot be considered a prohibited form of benefit. He compares this to a physician receiving compensation for diagnosing or confirming the death of a patient, which is not considered a proscribed form of benefit from the cadaver.

47 For discussions on the interplay of the prohibitions of *havalah* and *hatsalah*, see S. Resnicoff, "Supplying Human Body Parts"; R. F. Warburg, "Renal Transplantation"; M. Vigoda, "The Sale of Organs."

48 S. Resnicoff, "Supplying Human Body Parts," 871.

49 A. S. Abraham, *Nishmat Avraham*, 126–29. On the general issue of deriving benefit from a corpse, see A. Steinberg, *Encyclopedia of Jewish Medical Ethics*, vol. 1, trans. F. Rosner (Jerusalem: Feldheim Publishers, 2003), 80, 87–88, and J. D. Bleich, "Cadavers on Display," *Tradition* 40,1 (2007): 87–97.

50 For the following, see A. S. Abraham, *Nishmat Avraham*, 126–29.

Despite his permissive approach, R. Waldenberg offers an optional suggestion to mitigate any concern for deriving benefit from the cadaver. If compensation is delayed until after the organ is successfully transplanted, the family technically does not derive any benefit from the dead. The organ is now considered "living" and animated in the recipient's body, and the prohibition against benefiting from the dead does not apply.[51]

R. Zilberstein agrees with the strict position of R. Auerbach that receiving compensation violates the prohibition against benefiting from the deceased. However, he does consider that the recipient of a cadaveric donation should nonetheless offer compensation to the donor's family for the tangible benefit he received. Although technical reasons prevent the donor's family from claiming compensation, this may not absolve the recipient of his obligation to pay.[52]

Compensation for the Organ Broker

A donor must avoid the prohibitions against self-wounding and receiving payment for performing a *mitsvah*, but an organ broker does not have to deal with these concerns. However, is an organ broker allowed to receive compensation for facilitating the *mitsvah* of saving a life? R. Auerbach sees no halakhic or philosophical problem, since he views payment to a broker as compensation for the time and effort involved in coordinating a match between donor and recipient.[53] R. Yisraeli, however, explicitly prohibits any compensation. He claims that a broker fulfills the *mitsvah* of *pikkuah nefesh*, and is thus prohibited from receiving compensation for the performance of a *mitsvah*. However, he could claim reimbursement for expenses incurred.

Donation of Nonvital Organs

Transplanting bone marrow involves similar issues to transplanting vital organs. Bone marrow is technically not a vital organ, but it can save human life. On the other hand, bone marrow can be compared to hair and blood, as it regenerates. Conventional bone marrow harvest requires surgical incision of the bone cortex, so

51 The idea of the prohibition of deriving benefit from the corpse being mitigated by the organ's reanimation after successful transplant was advanced by R. Isser Yehuda Unterman (Israel, 1886–1976) in his *Shevet mi-Yehudah* (Jerusalem, 5715), 313–22.

52 Y. Zilberstein, *Shoshanat ha-Amakim*, 110–11. See also I. M. Lau, "Selling of Organs for Transplantation," 125–36, especially 135, who discusses the obligation of the recipient to compensate the donor.

53 A. S. Abraham, *Nishmat Avraham*, p. 125.

the prohibition against self-wounding must be addressed. However, stem-cell harvesting does not require penetration of the bone. It is similar to blood donation, and, according to R. Feinstein, as quoted earlier, it is exempt from the prohibition against self-wounding. Therefore, bone-marrow donors who undergo this procedure may receive compensation.[54]

Since its inception some fifty years ago, medicine has achieved remarkable success in transplantation of vital organs such as kidneys, livers, and hearts. However, the frontier of nonvital organ transplantation is an entirely recent development. Transplantation of nonvital organs, such as the face, hand, larynx, and uterus, is new and uncharted territory. The uterus can come from a living donor, while the other organs obviously come from cadaveric donation.[55]

For cadaveric donation of nonvital organs, the analysis of Rabbi Shlomo Zalman Auerbach, as mentioned above, would remain unchanged.[56] If one is prohibited from receiving compensation for the cadaveric donation of a vital organ, as it constitutes a proscribed benefit from the dead, surely the same would be true for a nonvital organ donation. However, R. Waldenberg's analysis may differ in this case. His permissive ruling that allows the family to receive money for cadaveric donation is predicated on the fact that the donation would anyway be required and would lead to the saving of a life. The donation of a hand or a larynx would not meet this criterion, and the family would logically not be entitled to compensation in this case.

In the case of living donation of a nonvital organ, donation may be prohibited because of the prohibition of self-wounding. There is no *mitsvah* of *pikkuah nefesh* to mitigate this prohibition. Receiving compensation would also be prohibited, as one is generally enjoined from receiving compensation for a prohibited act.

Sale and transplantation of reproductive tissue, such as sperm, testicular tissue, eggs, and ovaries, merits its own analysis. Male reproductive seed donation involves no self-wounding, and, furthermore, sperm regenerates. However, there is an additional prohibition against *hashhatat zera*, or destruction of male reproductive seed, which is a potential concern. Female egg or ovarian donation does involve self-wounding, and there is no tissue regeneration. Whether donation of reproductive seed constitutes a *mitsvah*, and whether compensation is permissible, are issues that are beyond the scope of this article.

54 For discussions specifically on bone marrow donation in Halakhah, see J. D. Bleich, "May Tissue Donations be Compelled?" in his *Contemporary Halakhic Problems*, vol. 4 (New York: Ktav, 1995), 273–315; idem., "Bone Marrow Transplantation," in his *Be-Netivot ha-Halakhah* (New York: Yeshiva University Press, 1761), 80–84 (Hebrew); N. Bar Ilan, "Bone Marrow Donation," in *Sefer Assia* vol. 9 (Jerusalem: Schlesinger Institute, 2004), 354–66 (Hebrew).

55 On the halakhic aspects of uterus transplantation, see E. Reichman, "Uterine Transplantation and the Case of the Mistaken Question," *Tradition* 37,2 (2003): 20–41.

56 A. S. Abraham, *Nishmat Avraham*, 126–29.

Donation for Research

A corollary to donation of nonvital organs is donation for research purposes. May one donate an organ to a research study that aims to discover life-saving cures? Can one receive compensation for doing so? One might answer in the affirmative for both live and cadaveric donation, based on the principle of *pikkuah nefesh*. However, the prevailing halakhic opinion is that donating organs for research does not constitute *pikkuah nefesh*, as it does not directly lead to the saving of human life.[57] The relationship between the donation and the discovery of a cure is not strong enough. It follows that receiving compensation is prohibited.[58]

In his consideration of the issue, R. Zilberstein notes the Talmud's statement that King David's soldiers had their spleens removed to make them more agile combatants. This is parallel to donating an organ to research, since the organ was not transplanted after its removal. This might suggest that donation to research is permitted. However, the cases are dissimilar, as the soldiers' improved abilities led directly to Jewish lives being saved from the enemy. R. Zilberstein concludes that donation for research has no such justification, since the benefit is not immediate.[59]

Altruism and Organ Donation

One of the accepted secular ethical doctrines of organ donation is the imperative of altruism. This effectively precludes financial compensation, aside from expenses incurred. However, due to an organ shortage and the resultant deaths, this doctrine is currently subject to reevaluation and revision in the ethical literature. Does Jewish law require that organ donations be exclusively altruistic? The most relevant source is the oft-cited position of R. Auerbach that a poor person who would not consider donation without financial inducement may nonetheless be compensated, even at a high price.[60] This decision appears to minimize, if not eliminate, the requirement of altruism in Jewish law. He adds an important caveat that the donor must be aware that his donation saves a fellow Jew and constitutes a *mitsvah*. Hence,

57 A. Steinberg, *Encyclopedia of Jewish Medical Ethics*, vol. 1, trans. Fred Rosner (Jerusalem: Feldheim Publishers, 2003), s.v. "autopsy."

58 See, for example, S. Rabinowitz, "Commerce in Organs," *Assia* 15,1–2 (1998): 58–64, especially 61 (Hebrew). For divergent views on the permissibility of donating one's body to research, see R. Ben-Zion Uzziel (1880–1953), *Mishpetei Uzziel, Yoreh De'ah* 1:28; and R. Jacob Ettlinger (Germany, 1798–1871), *Binyan Tsiyyon* 170. On the status of medical research and whether it constitutes *pikkuah nefesh*, see J. D. Bleich, "Stem Cell Research," *Tradition* 36,2 (2002): 56–83.

59 Y. Zilberstein, *Shoshanat ha-Amakim*, 110.

60 A. S. Abraham, *Nishmat Avraham*, 126–29.

complete altruism is not required, but the organ donor must at least have awareness that he is performing a *mitsvah*. This issue should be understood in the broader context of intent in performance of a *mitsvah*.[61]

Tikkun Olam—Perfecting or Repairing the World

Rabbi Dr. Mordechai Halperin raises an additional point in favor of compensation for organ donation.[62] Some rabbinic authorities allow midwives to receive compensation for services rendered on the Sabbath. Although this would normally be prohibited, those authorities assert that not paying the midwives would cause them to neglect their duties, resulting in danger to patients. Hence, this dispensation is a form of *tikkun olam*. Rabbi Dr. Halperin suggests expanding this principle to all medical activities related to *pikkuah nefesh* where there is concern that the rescuer may not perform his duties.[63] This would allow providing financial inducement for organ donation, motivating people to donate who would otherwise not do so.

A possible additional support for the position of Rabbi Dr. Halperin is that, if financial inducement is permitted for midwives, who are trained and perhaps even obligated to perform their duties, surely such inducement is permitted for people who are neither medically trained nor obligated to perform the service of organ donation. As mentioned above, it would constitute *tikkun olam*. However, based on a particular interpretation of *tikkun olam*, this may not be the case. If *tikkun olam* means "repairing" the world and maintaining proper function of society, it is important that medical professionals provide proper care to society's members. However, society may not have a vested interest in encouraging live organ donation, which is not obligatory and bears some risk. However, if *tikkun olam* is to be understood as "perfecting" the world by improving the moral climate of society, perhaps this would include encouraging its inhabitants, by financial incentives, to engage in organ donation.

61 For a discussion on altruism as it relates to selling organs, see R. B. Grazi and J. B. Wolowelsky, "Non-altruistic Kidney Donations in Contemporary Jewish Law and Ethics," *Transplantation Forum* 75,2 (January 2003), 250–52; J. D. Kunin, "The Search for Organs." For a discussion on altruism in halakhic literature with particular emphasis on altruistic self-sacrifice, including reference to organ donation, see D. Shatz, "'As Thyself': The Limits of Altruism in Jewish Ethics," in J. J. Schacter (ed.), *Reverence, Righteousness and Rahamanut: Essays in Memory of Rabbi Dr. Leo Jung* (New Jersey: Jason Aronson Press, 1992), 251–75.

62 M. Halperin, "Organ Transplantation in Jewish Law," *Sefer Assia* 12,1–2 (1989): 34–61 (Hebrew).

63 For a similar discussion, see S. Rabinowitz, "Commerce in Organs."

Nature of Transaction for Selling an Organ

Some authors dissociate the compensation from the donation and view the compensation as an unrelated monetary transaction between the donor and the recipient. R. Shlomo Goren (Israel, 1917–1994) writes that donation of a kidney in consideration of financial reward does not detract from the positive act of saving the recipient's life.[64] He also claims that there is no legal basis in Jewish law for prohibiting donating a kidney for financial gain, "inasmuch as this reflects an agreement between the donor and the recipient."[65]

Rabbi Dr. Halperin makes an interesting observation that might void such a transaction. A valid transaction requires complete willingness and unmitigated volition on the part of the seller. This can only exist if the seller receives the full value of the sold item. Since compensation for an organ does not constitute full replacement value, and the donor remains without the donated kidney, the transaction may be invalid. Therefore, the transaction should be conducted under guidance of rabbinic authorities experienced in these matters.[66]

Exploitation of the Poor

One of the concerns about commercialization of organ donation is that it will lead to exploitation of the poor. This concern has two dimensions—one philosophical and one legal. The philosophical concern is that it is unjust to devise a system that leads to abuse of the poor, the population most likely to sell their organs. The legal concern relates to the nature of the transaction in the organ sale. Secular ethicists argue that those desperate for money will go to any means to free themselves from poverty, including selling an organ under duress and without giving proper informed consent. The lack of informed consent impugns and possibly invalidates the purchase of an organ from a poor person.

Rabbi Dr. Halperin discusses the halakhic analogues to both dimensions of concern for the exploitation of the poor.[67] Regarding the philosophical concern, he cites the law that one may not remarry his divorced wife and explains its basis in the fear of potential abuse of the poor. While acknowledging a precedent in Jewish law

64 S. Goren, *Torat ha-Refu'ah* (Jerusalem: Ha-Idra Rabbah, 2000), 147 ff. (Hebrew).

65 For a discussion on the contractual aspects of selling organs, see R. F. Warburg, "Renal Transplantation." For a discussion of the nature of the *kinyan* involved in the transaction of selling organs, see Z. N. Goldberg, "Transactions in the Sale of Kidneys," in *Ateret Shlomoh* 2 (1997): 49–55.

66 M. Halperin, "Selling Tissues and Organs," *B'Or ha'Torah* 8 (1993): 45–55.

67 Ibid.

about concern for abuse of the poor, Rabbi Dr. Halperin concludes that these specific concerns do not necessarily preclude commercialization of organ donation.[68] Regarding the legal validity of the transaction, Rabbi Dr. Halperin agrees that the donor's complete consent is halakhically required for organ donation, similar to any other nonlife-saving surgical procedure. Since a desperately poor person may rush into such an arrangement hastily, these transactions must be closely investigated to ascertain that the donor's consent is thorough and complete.

Public Policy

Most of the contemporary halakhic literature reviewed for this essay supports the sale of organs for transplantation. Most authorities consider the public policy ramifications of allowing trade in human body parts as a peripheral issue. The policy discussions, though generally short on specific halakhic references, acknowledge that selling organs may be bad public policy, despite its technically permitted status.[69] However, some authorities have taken steps toward formulating acceptable guidelines for public policy. These include consideration of potential abuse of the poor, regulation of the limits and form of financial compensation, and psychological assessment of the donors. Rabbi Dr. Abraham Steinberg (Israel, contemporary) is one such authority.[70]

Dina De-Malkhuta Dina (The Law of the Kingdom is Law)

Our analysis reveals ample support within Jewish law to allow the sale of vital organs, with certain limitations and restrictions. However, there is an important principle in Jewish law that trumps this permissive approach, known as *dina de-malkhuta dina*, or "the law of the kingdom is law."[71] Even though an act is completely permissible according to Jewish law, the permission is negated if the government prohibits

68 Jewish law illustrates that the concern for social equality mandates limiting the behavior of the rich. In Talmudic times, poor people were embarrassed to bury their dead with simple vestments and coffins. They were so embarrassed by the visible demonstration of poverty that they would often leave their dead and flee. See BT *Mo'ed Katan* 27b. To avert this disgrace to the deceased, the Sages instituted decrees that all Jews, whether rich or poor, must be buried in the simplest garments and coffins. See *Shulhan Arukh, Yoreh De'ah* 352.

69 For discussion of the public policy issues, see Y. Zilberstein, *Shoshanat ha-Amakim*, 110–14; S. Resnicoff, "Supplying Human Body Parts," 869–70; R. F. Warburg, "Renal Transplantation."

70 A. Steinberg, "Ethical and Halakhic Perspectives in Organ Donation."

71 BT *Gittin* 10b.

the act. American law prohibits sale of organs for transplantation, and, hence, American Jews must obey that law. This is in accordance with the view of R. Moses Isserles (Rema, Poland, 1525?–1572)[72] that *dina de-malkhuta dina* applies, with few exceptions, to any civil matters that benefit the government or were enacted for the benefit of its citizens.[73] This view enjoys widespread acceptance among halakhic authorities.[74]

Falling within Rema's ambit is the Jewish courts' responsibility to affirm and enforce government laws pertaining to commercial activity. Historically, European Jewish communities were authorized to operate as autonomous, self-governing entities, even in respect to criminal law. Nowadays, in the absence of self-autonomy, R. Joseph Elijah Henkin (New York, 1880–1973) claims that Jewish communities in democratic countries cede the responsibility of social welfare legislation to various secular governmental bodies.[75] The same principle should govern the prohibition against selling organs.

Further bolstering this conclusion is a ruling by R. Isaac Judah Schmelkes (Poland, 1828–1906). He found no halakhic objection to reissuing a Torah work for commercial gain, but nevertheless prohibited it because it violated *dina de-malkhuta*. R. Schmelkes reasoned that *dina de-malkhuta* prevails over Halakhah, since this only results in a foregone opportunity to earn profit, rather than causing an actual loss.[76] The same principle should operate with regard to selling organs. Since prohibiting the practice merely causes a lost opportunity of financial gain, rather than an actual loss, *dina de-malkhuta* should prevail.

Summary and Conclusions

The value of human life is supreme in Judaism, as saving human life suspends nearly all Biblical and Rabbinic prohibitions. In Halakhah, organ transplantation is a complex topic involving many legal issues. The prohibitions against desecrating, deriving benefit from, and delaying burial of the dead, and other prohibitions are all waived for the overriding consideration of saving the organ recipient's life. Other issues include obtaining consent from the donor or his next of kin and the legal status of a donor buried without all of his organs. These and other issues have been discussed in detailed essays on this subject.

Compensating organ donors or their families to encourage donation involves many halakhic and moral issues. These include the prohibitions against self-wounding and self-endangerment, the prohibition against taking compensation for

72 Rema to *Shulhan Arukh.*, *Hoshen Mishpat* 369:1.

73 Rema to Ibid., 369:11.

74 R. Moses Feinstein, *Iggerot Mosheh*, *Hoshen Mishpat* 2:62.

75 R. Joseph Elijah Henkin, *Teshuvot Ivra*, vol. 2, 176.

76 R. Isaac Schmelkes, *Beit Yitshak*, *Yoreh De'ah* 2:75, part 5.

performing a *mitsvah*, the idea that we do not own our own bodies, and concern for exploitation of the poor. The preponderance of rabbinic opinion is that the value of saving human life overrides all of these concerns.

Therefore, Jewish law permits financial compensation to a live organ donor. Indeed, the Talmud states that, "He who saves one life is as if he saved an entire world."[77] However, the principle of *dina de-malkhuta dina* means that secular law must be taken into account, and presently American law prohibits the sale of organs. Thus, financial compensation would not practically be allowed according to Jewish law. Should the law change, the permissive approach would apply.

SELECTED BIBLIOGRAPHY

Abraham, Abraham S. *Nishmat Avraham*, 2nd expanded ed. Jerusalem: Schlesinger Institute, 2007, 126–29.

Cohen, M. Alfred R. "Sale or Donation of Human Organs." *Journal of Halacha and Contemporary Society* (Fall 2006): 37–64.

Feinstein, R. Moses. *Iggerot Mosheh, Hoshen Mishpat* 1:103.

Halperin, R. Mordechai. "Organ Transplantation in Jewish Law." *Assia* 12 (1989): 34–61 (Hebrew).

———. "Selling Tissues and Organs." *B'Or ha'Torah* 8 (1993): 45–55 (Hebrew).

Lau, R. Israel Meir. "Selling of Organs for Transplantation." *Tehumin* 18 (1988): 125–36 (Hebrew).

Resnicoff, Steven. "Supplying Human Body Parts: A Jewish Law Perspective." *DePaul Law Review* 55 (2005–2006): 851–74.

Rosner, Fred. *Biomedical Ethics and Jewish Law*. Hoboken, NJ: Ktav, 2001, 313–54.

Steinberg, Avraham. *Encyclopedia of Jewish Medical Ethics*, vol. 2. Jerusalem: Schlesinger Institute, 1991, 191–243 (Hebrew).

———. "Ethical and Halakhic Perspectives in Organ Donation." In S. Raz, ed. *Kovets ha-Tsiyyonut ha-Datit*. (Jerusalem: Histadderut ha-Mizrachi, 2001), 417–41 (Hebrew).

Warburg, Ronnie F. "Renal Transplantation: Living Donors and Markets for Body Parts—Halakha in Concert with Halakhic Policy or Public Policy?" *Tradition* 40,2 (2007): 14–48.

77 BT *Sanhedrin* 37a.

CHAPTER 18

THE THEORY OF "EFFICIENT BREACH": A JEWISH LAW PERSPECTIVE

RONALD WARBURG

Efficient Breach

The Law and Economics school of thought has advanced a number of controversial claims in the name of economic efficiency—from promoting trading on inside information to providing markets for the sale of human organs—but none may be as provocative and challenging as the argument of entitlement and economic efficiency underlying the theory of "efficient breach."[1] In its view, there is a positive value in structuring a contractual remedy to permit, if not encourage, contractual breaches that will lead to the maximization of resources (i.e., economic efficiency).[2]

1 Its contemporary relevance is signaled by recent English and American case law addressing this matter. See, for example, *Attorney General v. Blake*, [2001] 1 A.C. 268, (2000) 4 All E.R. (UKHL); *Experience Hendrix LLC v. PPX Enters. Inc.*, 1 All E.R. 830 (Ct. App. 2003); *U.S. Naval Institute v. Charter Communications, Inc.*, 936 F. 2d 692 (2d. Cir. 1991); *EarthInfo, Inc. v. Hydrosphere Res. Consultants, Inc.*, 900 P. 2d 113 (Colorado. 1995); *SEC v. JT Wallenbrock & Assoc.*, 440 F. 3d 1109 (9th Cir. 2006); *U.S.* v. *Snepp*, 444 U.S. 507 (1980). For additional case law, see Melvin Eisenberg, "The Disgorgement Interest in Contract Law," *Michigan Law Rev.* 559, 565 (2006): 105.

2 Robert Birmingham, "Breach of Contract, Damage Measures, and Economic Efficiency," *Rutgers L. Rev.* 273 (1970): 24; John Barton, "The Economic Bases of Damages for Breach of Contract," *J. Legal Studies* 277 (1972): 1; Richard Posner, *Economic Analysis of the Law* (1972), 56–72; Charles Goetz and Robert Scott, "Liquidated Damages, Penalties and the Just Compensation Principle: Some Notes on an Enforcement Model and a Theory of Efficient Breach," *Colum. L. Rev.* 554 (1977): 77; E. Allan Farnsworth, "Your Loss or my Gain? The Dilemma of the Disgorgement Principle in Breach of Contract," *Yale L.J.* 1339 (1985): 94. For a recent survey of the literature, see David Barnes, "The Anatomy of Contract Damages and Efficient Breach Theory," *S. Cal. Interdisc. L. J.* 397 (1997–1998): 6.

This theory can be illustrated by the oft-cited overbidder paradigm (OP1). In this paradigm,[3]

> Seller *S* signs a contract to deliver one hundred thousand custom-ground widgets at one dollar each to buyer B_1 for use in his boiler factory. After *S* has delivered the first ten thousand units, buyer B_2 comes to *S*, explains that he desperately needs twenty-five thousand custom-ground widgets at once since otherwise he will be forced to close his pianola factory at great cost, and offers to *S* two dollars each for twenty-five thousand widgets. *S* sells to B_2 the widgets and therefore does not complete timely delivery to B_1, who sustains one thousand dollars in damages from *S*'s breach. Having obtained an additional profit of twenty-five thousand dollars on the sale to B_2 (twenty-five thousand units multiplied by the difference between two dollars and one dollar), *S* is fifteen thousand dollars economically ahead even after reimbursing B_1 for his loss (the difference between the additional profit of twenty-five thousand dollars and one thousand dollars of damages caused by the breach).

The conventional remedy of damages for breach of contract is the expectation standard, which places the plaintiff (i.e., the first buyer) in the position in which the plaintiff would have been had the contract been performed. According to this theory of efficient breach, the promisor (i.e., the seller) may breach the contract as long as he is prepared to pay the plaintiff his expectation damages.

Notable American economists, jurists, and philosophers have argued that, under such circumstances, said breach is economically, legally, philosophically, or morally uncontestable. Economic proponents of this theory embrace the Kaldor-Hicks Compensation doctrine, which posits that, if the defendant is made better off, even if there is a loss to the contracting party, such breach increases societal gain as long as the benefiting party is able to fully compensate the losing party.[4] In effect, contractual compliance does not necessarily entail actual performance, for the promisor may opt to breach the contract and pay damages. Though, as Richard Craswell noted, "this form of enforcement is rarely considered in the philosophical literature on promising, which usually assumes that promises must either (1) oblige the promisor to perform the promised actions, or (2) have no moral force at all,"[5] economic breach of contract involves an intermediate moral obligation to perform or pay damages. The classic formulation in jurisprudential thought of this position is, of course, Oliver Wendell Holmes' bad man:

> The only universal consequence of a legally binding promise is, that the law makes the promisor pay damages if the promised event does not happen. In every

3 Posner, supra note 2, at 57.

4 Nicholas Kaldor, "Welfare Propositions of Economics and Inter-Personal Comparisons of Utility," Econ. J. 549 (1938): 49; John Hicks, "The Foundations of Welfare Economics," *Econ. J.* 696 (1939): 49. For a discussion of this principle, see Jules Coleman, "Efficiency, Exchange, and Auction: Philosophical Aspects of the Economic Approach to Law," *Calif. L. Rev.* 221 (1980): 68.

5 Richard Craswell, "Two Economic Theories of Enforcing Promises," in *The Theory of Contract Law: New Essays*, 19,27 (Peter Benson ed., Cambridge 2001).

> case, it leaves him free from interference until the time for fulfillment has gone by, and, therefore, free to break his contract if he chooses.[6]

Put slightly differently in a philosophical vein, the notion of a "promise" is to be understood in consequential terms. As Frank Menetrez observed:

> According to a consequentialist, the promisor ought, as always, to do whatever is likely to yield the best consequences overall. That is, the promisor ought to perform if performance is likely to yield better overall consequences, than breach, and otherwise ought to breach. Thus, when the time for performance arrives, the promisor is obligated to perform the promise only if an independent assessment of the consequences recommends performance.[7]

From this perspective, efficiency theorists would argue that economic efficiency, which leads to the maximization of resources by encouraging such actions that benefit some without injuring others, would be the litmus test for determining whether a contractual breach will yield such consequences. Should it yield such beneficial outcome, the breach should be executed rather than performance of the contract.

In effect, adopting this line of argument, one may be accepting a social contract, which, under certain conditions, individuals have chosen or conceived of the notion of wealth maximization as a fundamental moral value. And a utilitarian would advance the claim that a society that aims at wealth maximization will produce an ethically attractive amalgamation of happiness, of rights (to liberty and property), and of sharing with the less fortunate members of society.[8] Alternatively, the adoption of the theory of efficient breach eliminates the moral content from the contractual promise by permitting a breach based on grounds of economic efficiency.

An alternative approach to the morality of agreement compliance is argued by Craswell:

> [I]f there is a general principle that one ought not cause harm to others, that might be enough to justify some sort of rule against [agreement breaking].[9]

For example, promise-keeping may entail benefiting another such as proscribing the manipulation of another and exercising due diligence in guiding others

6 Oliver Holmes, The Common Law, ed. by M. deWolfe Howe 236 (Boston, MA: Little, Brown & Co. 1963). Though the legal literature has attributed this statement to Holmes, it has been demonstrated that Holmes rejected this posture and was "speaking from the bad man's point of view." See Joseph Perillo, "Misreading Oliver Wendell Holmes on Efficient Breach and Tortuous Interference," *Fordham L. Rev.* 1085 (2000): 68.

7 Frank Menetrez, "Consequentialism, Promissory Obligation, and the Theory of Efficient Breach," *UCLA L. Rev.* 863, 874 (1999–2000): 47.

8 Richard Posner, "Utilitarianism, Economics and Legal Theory," *J. Legal Stud.* 103, (1979): 8. For a critique, see Jules Coleman, "Efficiency, Utility, and Wealth Maximization," *Hofstra L. Rev.* 509, 526–539 (1979–1980): 8.

9 Richard Craswell, "Contract Law, Default Rules, and the Philosophy of Promising," *Michigan L. Rev.* 489, 499 (1989): 88.

to form certain expectations.[10] Consequently, promised performance that never transpires or dashed expectations are "harms" caused to the promisee.[11] In this context, the "harm principle" posits that it is proper for the law to interfere with individual liberties since the individual has harmed another person.[12] In short, noncompliance with an agreement undermines the "harm principle." A clear articulation of this posture in general and the relationship between law and morality in particular emerges from the thinking of Joseph Raz. He observed:

> It follows from the harm principle that enforcing voluntary obligations is not itself a proper goal for contract law. To enforce voluntary obligations is to enforce morality through the legal imposition of duties on individuals. In this respect, it does not differ from the legal proscription of pornography.[13]

Complying with a promise may be deemed laudable; however, the failure to do so in and of itself is beyond the province of contract law. The bifurcation of contract law and morality into two separate domains is either because law should not enforce morality or because of their differing goals (i.e., law provides rules for an efficient system of interaction and morality entails the engendering of moral values such as trust in interpersonal relations).

Last, if the enforcement of a promise qua promise means fulfilling an obligation (for example, keeping one's word even when doing so is inefficient or regardless of whether the promise has been relied upon), it follows that this characterization of the nature of this agreement-keeping is diametrically opposed to the aforesaid economic, legal, and philosophical rationales as well as the harm principle underlying the theory of "efficient breach." A most prominent contemporary secular perspective has focused upon the intrinsic value of promises (i.e., freestanding obligation of promise-keeping) rather than its instrumental value such as the avoidance of harm or efficient economic exchange as elaborated upon by Charles Fried, who observed that through agreement-making obligations emerge "just because [they have] promised."[14] Adopting such a stance imbues a promise with moral content and thereby disallows a breach based on grounds of economic efficiency.

10 Thomas Scanlon, *What We Owe to Each Other* (Cambridge, MA, 1998), 296–302.

11 For the problematics in grounding the duty to agreement-keeping in such a harm-based account, see Daniel Markovits, "Making and Keeping Contracts," *Va. L. Rev.* 1325, 1352-1366 (2006): 92.

12 See John Stuart Mill, *On Liberty* (David Spitz ed. 1975), 10–11. More recently, Raz argues, "compensating individuals for harm resulting from reliance on voluntary obligation is . . . a proper goal for the law." See Joseph Raz, "Promises in Morality and Law," *Harvard L. Rev.* 916, 937 (1982): 95.

13 Ibid.

14 Charles Fried, *Contract as Promise: A Theory of Contractual Obligation* (Cambridge, Mass, 1981) 16. See also, James Gordley, "Contract Law in the Aristotelian Tradition," in *The Theory of Contract Law* (Peter Benson ed., 2001), 265.

Jewish Law

Halakhah (i.e., Jewish law; *halakhot* in plural) distinguishes between legal and moral norms. The distinguishing characteristic between them is enforceability.[15] Whereas a halakhic-legal norm is enforceable by a *bet din* (i.e., a court of Jewish law), compliance with a halakhic moral norm is dependent upon individual volition.

There are two components required in the undertaking of an obligation: effectuating a *kinyan* (i.e., symbolic act of acquisition) and *gemirat da'at* (i.e., a concrete articulation of the parties' firm resolve to undertake the obligation).[16] The act of promising reflects the absence of *gemirat da'at* either because a promise entails executing an obligation in the future (e.g., a promise to sell goods) or a promise in respect to transferring title of something that is not yet in existence (e.g., *davar she-lo ba la-'olam*) such as an item that has not been produced or not in his possession (i.e., *eno bi-reshuto*), and therefore such promises are unenforceable in a *bet din*.[17]

Our presentation will address the issue of whether Jewish law explains the halakhic norm of a promissory obligation (i.e., halakhically enforceable agreement) in instrumental terms for which economic efficiency is its identifying characteristic, or is it grounded in, and underwritten by, the halakhic morality of promising? Is the goal of the Jewish law of obligations the enforcement of promises or the righting for—compensation for—harms? And how does the normative sense of the Jewish law of obligations impact upon agreement breaches among fellow-Jews[18] in general and "efficient breaches" in particular?

The efficacy of a promise is codified in the following fashion:

> When one conducts and concludes commercial transactions using words only (the negotiation and agreement not being completed by a formal act of acquisition), that person should stand by his word, even though none of the purchase price has been taken, nor a buyer's mark made on the goods, nor a

15 For the distinction between a halakhic-moral promissory obligation and a halakhic-legal promissory obligation, see Shillem Warhaftig, *The Jewish Law of Contract* (Hebrew)(Jerusalem: 1974), 16–30; Zorach Warhaftig, *Studies in Jewish Law* (Hebrew) (Ramat Gan: 1985), 87–93; R. Zalman Nechemiah Goldberg (Israel, contemporary), *The Halakhic-Legal Validity of a Promise*, (Hebrew) 13 *Tehumin* 371 (5752-5753); Berachyahu Lifshitz, *Why Doesn't Jewish Law Enforce the Fulfillment of a Promise?* (Hebrew) 25 *Mishpatim* 161 (5755), Itamar Warhaftig, *Undertaking in Jewish Law* (Hebrew) 407 (Jerusalem: 2001).

16 There is a scholarly discussion in academic literature regarding the need to avoid presenting invidious comparisons by utilizing modern legal concepts to elucidate Jewish legal categories. For a bibliographical reference regarding this methodological issue in analyzing Jewish law, see Shahar Lifshitz, "Oppressive Contracts: A Jewish Law Perspective," *Journal of Law and Religion* 101, 104, n. 8 (2008): 23. Therefore, throughout this presentation we describe agreement making as undertaking obligations (i.e., *hithayvut*) rather than creating a contract, which is a modern legal concept.

17 For varying approaches toward defining these concepts, see Shalom Albeck, *The Law of Property and Contract in the Talmud*, (Hebrew) (Tel Aviv: 1976); Shillem Warhaftig, n. 15 above; Berachyahu Lifshitz, *Promise: Obligation and Acquisition in Jewish Law*, (Hebrew) (Jerusalem: 1988); Itamar Warhaftig, n. 15 above.

18 See B *Pesahim* 91a; J *Pesahim* 8:6; Maimonides (Rambam, Egypt, 1135–1204) *Responsa* 448; R. Jacob b. Meir Tam (France, 1100–1171) *Responsa* 37 and 39.

> pledge given (for the price): Whoever withdraws from this type of transaction, whether buyer or seller, is deemed a faithless person.
>
> GLOSS: Even though in a transaction that is conducted and concluded by means of words only, where no money is tendered, one can withdraw from such a transaction. . . in any event, a person should stand by his word even though no act of acquisition has been performed, only mere words have passed between the parties. . . .[19]

Where no payment has been made, and the seller articulates an oral commitment to sell realty or personalty to a prospective buyer, and should either party renege on the agreement of sale he is stigmatized as a *mehusar amana* (lit., lacking faith). Given that no act of acquisition (i.e., *kinyan*) has been executed between the parties, technically either party may withdraw from consummating the sale. The noncompliance with the promise is unenforceable. Enforceability depends upon the execution of a *kinyan*.

Because of his reneging on an oral commitment, the community publicly shames him by proclaiming:

> Hear ye, hear ye, this person refuses to keep his word. He has caused displeasure to the scholars and therefore is no longer included among the community of Israel. The remnant of Israel shall not commit sin, nor speak lies (Zephaniah 3:13); for this man is a liar and has made himself a reneger.[20]

In short, the proclamation communicates the Jewish legal position that a promise is binding because of the halakhic need to keep one's word, albeit unenforceable by a *bet din*. Stripped to their essentials, promises create obligations because they are conventionally understood in Jewish law to create religious obligations.

Thus interpreted, the halakhic position regarding promise-keeping stands in bold contrast to the theory of promissory obligation propounded by Charles Fried. Fried's posture is articulated in the following fashion:

> There exists a convention that defines the practice of promising and its entailments. This convention provides a way that a person may create expectations in others. By virtue of the basic Kantian principles of trust and respect, it is wrong to invoke that convention in order to make a promise, then to break it.[21]

The promissory obligation derives not from a religious and moral norm such as natural law, nor even from the reliance of what is promised, but from the

19 R. Joseph Caro (Ottoman Palestine, 1488–1575), *Shulhan Arukh, Hoshen Mishpat* 204:7; R. Moses b. Israel Isserles (Rema, Poland, 1525/30–1572), *Hoshen Mishpat* 204:11. All translations of *Shulhan Arukh* are culled from Stephen Passamaneck, *The Traditional Jewish Law of Sale* (Cincinnati, 1983), 120–21.

20 R. Moses b. Isaac Mintz (Germany, fifteenth century), *Responsa Maharam Mintz*, 1:no.160; R. Shalom Mordechai Shvadron (Maharsham, Poland, 1835–1911), *Mishpat Shalom, Hoshen Mishpat* 204.

21 Fried, n.14 above, 17. For antecedent thinking that fidelity to promises depends on the social convention of keeping agreements, see variant perspectives in David Hume, *A Treatise of Human Nature*, L.A. Selby-Bigge, ed. (Oxford: 1960) at Book III, Pt. II, Ch. V; John Rawls, *A Theory of Justice* (Cambridge, MA: 1971), 344–50; Neil MacCormick, "Voluntary Obligations and Normative Powers I" *Proc. Aristotelian Soc'y* (1972) 46 (Supp. Vol.) 59.

expectation that the promisor will do as he or she promised.[22] In the words of Stephen Smith,

> Fried's argument is that because a promisor has, by intentionally invoking a convention, created a belief that the promisor is under a moral obligation to do the promised thing, the promisor is in fact under such an obligation.[23]

In other words, the social convention of promising would have the effect of creating the obligation.[24] In Searle's nomenclature, Fried's argument for promise-keeping is grounded by deriving "ought" from "is."[25] But whereas Searle concedes that the derivation of "ought" from "is" belies an *institutional* ""ought," Fried's argues that it is a *moral* "ought." In short, such postures differ radically from the halakhic conception of promise-keeping. Avowing a diametrically opposed position, *halakhah* views promise-keeping as aligning oneself with the fulfillment of a religious norm rather than compliance with a norm of natural law, institutional moral norm, or moral norm established by social convention.

In *halakhah*, is there an additional ground for promise-keeping based upon the argument that the promisor caused harm by induced reliance, and that is what creates the binding nature of the promise? A promissory obligation as conventionally understood and induced reliance obligation overlap, but they are not identical. This reliance-based duty is distinguishable from the duty to perform the promise. This duty comes into play only after the promise is not performed. Accordingly, the reliance duty is not to be confused with the duty of promise-keeping, but rather a duty to ensure that one who relies upon another's promise is compensated for being harmed. Is the violation of a reliance-based duty actionable in a *bet din* or is it similar to the contravention of a promissory obligation, a toothless tiger providing no judicial redress?

Responding to our question, the Talmud instructs us:

22 The need to protect the promisee's expectations is a recurring theme in the literature. See Alfred Corbin, Contracts, Sec. 1, at 2 (1952), Charles Goetz and Robert Scott, "Enforcing Promises: An Examination of the Basis of Contract," *Yale L.J.* 1261, 1265-1271 (1980): 89.

On a rudimentary level, one of the bases of this expectation is that the conventional understanding of promise-keeping is that promissors remain obligated even if the human calculus determines that "the best overall" would dictate otherwise. See Joseph Raz, "Promises and Obligations," in *Law, Morality and Society: Essays in Honor of H.L.A. Hart* (P. M. S. Hacker and J. Raz eds., 1977), 210, 221–22.

23 Stephen Smith, "Towards a Theory of Contract," in *Oxford Essays in Jurisprudence: Fourth Series*(Jeremy Horder, ed., 2000), 107, 113.

24 Admittedly, Scanlon concurs with Fried's approach that the social practice of agreement making may create certain expectations. However, the existence of these practices fails to explain why reneging upon agreement is wrong. See Thomas Scanlon, "Promises and Practices," *Philosophy and Public Affairs* 199 (1990): 19. In fact, Fried concedes that the grounds for being morally obligated to fulfill a promise lie elsewhere. See Fried, n. 14 above, 14. In Scanlon's estimation, the moral duty for promise keeping derives from "general principles arising from the interests that others have in being able to rely on expectations about what we are going to do." Thomas M. Scanlon, "Thickness and Theory," *J. Philosophy* 275, 283 (2003): 100. For an elucidation of these moral principles, see Thomas Scanlon, n. 10 above, 295–327.

25 John Searle, "How to Derive 'Ought' from 'Is'," *Philosophical Review* 43 (1964): 73. For the classic critique of Searle's approach, see R. M. Hare, "The Promising Game," *Rev. Internationale de Phil.* 398 (1964): 18.

> If someone gives money to his friend to serve as his agent to go and purchase wine for him during the season while the price was low. And he was negligent and failed to buy it the law is that he has to pay him wine according to the low price. . . .[26]

Here, a promise was made, the promisee relied upon the promisor, and the promisee incurred pecuniary loss. The Talmud concludes that the promisor is liable to compensate for the harm suffered. Should we infer from this ruling that induced reliance affords a judicial remedy in the case of an explicit promise unaccompanied by the execution of a *kinyan*?

The dominant approach is that compensation resulting from a breach of an induced-reliance obligation is because the promisor explicitly agreed at the time the agreement was executed to reimburse the promisee for such loss resulting from failure to consummate the wine purchase. In other words, in the absence of said agreement, any harm suffered from reliance would be unrecoverable. Reliance of the promisee upon the oral commitment of the promisor does not engender monetary liability.[27]

Even pursuant to the minority opinion, however, promissory reliance will only engender monetary liability if it is a halakhically enforceable promise. As R. Aaron b. Joseph ha-Levi (Ra'ah, Spain, c. 1235–1300) notes:

> Here (*Bava Metsi'a* 73b), even though the agent did not contractually agree to assume liability [for failure to fulfill his promise], since the principal gave him money with which to purchase merchandise, and the principal would have either purchased it himself or arranged for another to do so had not the agent promised to do so, and the principal relied upon him and gave him the money based upon the reliance; for that reason the agent is liable to pay the loss caused by the reliance on his promise.[28]

Ra'ah's position contains four propositions. The first is that one does not require an agreement that explicitly stipulates that consequential damages are recoverable. The second proposition is that in the absence of such agreement, by giving money to the agent to effectuate a wine purchase at a location where the selling price was lower than others give, the promisee relied upon the promisor's compliance. The third proposition is that the words of the promisor serve as the act of inducing

26 B *Bava Metsi'a* 73b.

27 R. Solomon b. Abraham Adret (Rashba, Spain, c. 1235–c. 1310), *Hiddushe ha-Rashba*, B *Bava Metsi'a* 73b; R. Asher b. Jehiel (Rosh, Germany & Spain, c. 1250–1327), B *Bava Metsi'a* 5:69; R. Mordecai b. Hillel (Germany, 1240?–1298) B *Bava Kamma* 114:115; R. Joseph Habiba (*Nimmukei Yosef*, Spain, beg. of fifteenth century) B *Bava Metsi'a* 44a; R. Jacob b. Jacob Moses Lorbeerbaum of Lissa (Poland, c. 1760–1832), *Netivot ha-Mishpat* (*Bi'urim*), *Hoshen Mishpat* 176:31, 183:1, 304:2, 306:6, 333:14; R. Avraham Yeshayahu Karelitz (Israel, 1878–1953), *Hazon Ish*, B *Bava Kamma* 22:1; Maharsham, *Mishpat Shalom*, *Hoshen Mishpat* 176:4.

Cf. R. Moses Sofer (Hatam Sofer, Pressburg, 1762–1839), *Responsa Hatam Sofer* no. 168 representation of the dominant position.

28 Though numerous authorities identify the authorship of this view with R. Yom Tov b. Abraham Ishbili (Ritba, Spain, c. 1250–1330), in fact, Ritba is citing the teaching of Ra'ah, his teacher. The text identifies the position with "*moreh ha-rav*" (i.e., his rabbinical teacher). Usage of this appellation refers to Ra'ah. See Issac Brand, "HaNosei Ve'noten Be'devarim: Between Contractual Obligation and Tortuous Reliance," (Hebrew) *Mechkarei Mishpat* 5, notes 107,122–124 (2008): 24.

reliance by the promisee. Moreover, and in the context of Ra'ah's posture more importantly, it is the *be-hahi hana'ah* (i.e., because of the benefit created by the induced reliance that establishes a surety relationship between the two parties) he undertakes the obligation, and therefore the promise becomes halakhically binding upon the promisor and enforceable in case of breach.[29] Similar to an *'arev* (i.e., one who assumes liability because the creditor parted with monies on the strength of his assurance) the individual who was hired to transact business is liable because the investor relied upon him. It is the halakhic-legal norm of suretyship rather than the halakhic-moral norm (i.e., promissory obligation or induced reliance) that endows halakhic-legal validity to the agreement.[30]

To summarize: The undertaking of a promise regardless whether it induces reliance or not mandates the promisor's compliance, albeit a breach of a promise will not be actionable. In other words, in reneging of a promise, the promisee is frequently harmed because he relied on the promise. Concerning compliance with the promise, however, harm is irrelevant. One is halakhically morally obliged to fulfill the promise qua promise (i.e., the religious duty of promise-keeping regardless of whether the promisee has detrimentally relied on the promise or not).[31] In other words, the binding nature of the promise is independent and free-standing, separate from induced-reliance obligation.

Having presented the dichotomy between halakhic-legal norms and halakhic-moral norms in general and a rudimentary definition of a promissory obligation in particular, now we may begin to explore actual cases of breaches of various

29 See generally Baruch Kahane, *Israel: Guarantee* (Hebrew) (Jerusalem: 1991), 78–90, who subscribes to this interpretation of Ra'ah.

30 The underlying premise of Ra'ah's posture is predicated upon the fact that the context of liability is within the framework of *hithayvut* (i.e., undertaking an obligation), rather than being a form of consideration as a vehicle to execute a *kinyan*. See Berachyahu Lifshitz, "Consideration in Jewish Law—A Reconsideration," *The Jewish Law Annual* 115, 122-123 (1989): 8; Berachyahu Lifshitz, *The Promise* (Hebrew) (Jerusalem: 1988), 214. Cf. Kahane, n. 29 above, 6, n. 8.

Others interpret that Ra'ah's position is that an induce-reliance obligation is to be assimilated in the halakhic norms of obligations' natural neighbor—namely, torts. Properly understood, the promisor induces the promisee's reliance triggered by "*ha'na'a*" and, in the wake of a breach, damage ensues and the promisor is obligated to compensate the promisee because of the induced-reliance generated. See Yechiel Kaplan, *Elements of Tort in the Jewish Law of Surety*, (Hebrew) 9–10 *Shenaton ha-Mishpat ha-'Ivri* 359 (5742–5743); Brand, n. 28 above. A breach of a reliance-induced obligation entails a contravention of "the remnant of Israel shall not commit sins or lies." See R. Isaac b. Moses of Vienna (*Or Zaru'ah*, Germany and France, c. 1180-c. 1250) *Responsa Or Zaru'a* 1:748; Rosh, B *Hullin* 3:34, Brand, 28 above, 29, n. 96. In effect, pursuant to Ra'ah's view, a breach of a promissory obligation involves the violation of a "the remnant of Israel shall not commit sins or lies" two times (i.e., once for breach of the promissory obligation and a second time for breach of reliance-induced obligation).

Thus, insofar as the halakhic-moral norm of promissory obligation, promises are given halakhic-moral effect qua promises. However, according to Ra'ah, as far as the halakhic-legal norm of promissory obligation is concerned, promises are given effect qua reliance-inducing acts. It follows that a breach of a promissory obligation occurs when you have induced someone to rely upon you. The person inducing the reliance and subsequently causing a breach must be viewed as an individual who is reneging on a commitment or acting tortuously. Regardless of the halakhic classification of the promisor's breach, judicial redress is contingent upon the integration of the *halakhot* of obligations or torts into the picture.

31 For varying explanations addressing the rationale for nonenforcement of a promissory obligation, see Zorach Warhaftig, n. 15, above 87; Shalom Albeck, *The Nature of Contract in Jewish Law*, (Hebrew) 6 *Iyyunei Mishpat* 517–518 (1978–1979); Lifshitz, n. 15 above, 178–180; I. Warhaftig, n. 15 above, 468–469.

agreements for the purpose of understanding how Jewish law addresses the theory of "efficient breach."

One of the Jewish legal overbidder paradigms (OP2) is codified in the following manner:

> If one is in the process of negotiating to acquire or lease a thing, whether real property or movable property and (during this process) someone else comes and lawfully acquires it, this latter person is deemed wicked (his transaction, however, is valid). This same rule applies when one wishes to hire himself out to an employer (and during the course of negotiations, another person comes and takes the position). . . .
>
> GLOSS: . . . All the above only treats the case in which a price between parties (to a sale) has been mutually agreed upon, and only the act of formal acquisition is lacking (to complete the sale). If, however, no price has yet been agreed upon, the seller wants so and so much, and the buyer wants to pay less, it is permissible for another party (to break into those negotiations). . . .[32]

In rabbinic sources, preempting a sales transaction or an employment agreement is metaphorically compared to an *'ani ha-mehapekh be-harara* (lit., a poor person preparing a cake and another snatching it from him).[33] At what point is an interloper precluded from interfering with negotiations for a deal? According to one opinion, the interdict applies as long as a deal is being brokered; whereas, according to others, a third party may interfere only before the final phase of negotiations prior to the consummation of a *kinyan.*[34]

One who interferes with either the negotiations or the final stage of the brokering of a deal and purchases the item is labeled a "*rasha*"' (i.e., a wicked person).[35] Though the designation serves to stigmatize the offender, nevertheless, the purchase is valid and no formal claim for damages may be leveled against him.

In effect, the interloper's action is viewed morally objectionable in the eyes of Jewish law.[36] Though morally objectionable, nevertheless, his behavior is not actionable in a court of Jewish law.[37] *'Ani ha-mehapekh ba-harara* serves as one of the numerous illustrations of behavior that is morally inappropriate, albeit beyond the halakhic-legal realm of the norms of obligations. Moreover, in stark contrast to OP1, where promoting self-interest and economic welfare is the underlying basis for legal entitlement by the promisor, here the dynamics of OP2 illustrate the

32 *Shulhan Arukh, Hoshen Mishpat* 237:1.

33 B *Kiddushin* 59a.

34 See Aaron Levine, *Free Enterprise in Jewish Law*, (New York: 1980), 124–26.

35 The interloper interdict applies even if the second bidder is unaware of the first agreement. Under such circumstances, once aware of the agreement, the second bidder must withdraw his bid. See R. Moses Feinstein (New York, 1895–1986), *Iggerot Moshe, Hoshen Mishpat* 1:60.

36 This infraction of a halakhic-moral norm either violates "doing what is proper and good in the eyes of God," or entails encroaching upon someone's livelihood. See R. Moses b. Petahiah Isserlein (Germany, 1390–1460) *Terumat ha-Deshen* 340; R. Solomon b. Isaac (Rashi, France, 1040–1105), B *Bava Metsi'a* 71a.

37 However, if the *bet din* is aware that the interloper is momentarily attempting to snatch away another's anticipated gain, a *bet din* may step in and direct the interloper to withdraw his bid. See R. Samuel b. Moses de Medina (Maharashdam, Greece, 1506–1589) *Responsa Maharashdam, Hoshen Mishpat* 259; Maharsham, *Mishpat Shalom, Hoshen Mishpat* 237.

working of a halakhic-moral norm of promissory obligation where we are concerned with the religious propriety, fairness, and appropriateness to hold individuals to promises that they have voluntarily made. Last, the halakhic interloper interdict is more solicitous of a promissory obligation and reliance on preagreement representations than American law traditionally is.[38]

This halakhic-moral dimension of the promissory obligation continues to operate in the workings of another overbidder paradigm (OB3) in the following Talmudic discussion:

> A certain individual told his friend: "If I ever sell this field I will sell it to you for 100 *zuz*." He subsequently went and sold it to another individual for a 120 *zuz*. R. Kahane said: the first one acquired it.
>
> An objection is raised. R. Ya'akov Nehar Pakod objected: "But this individual did not sell him the field voluntarily. Rather, the additional *zuzim* coerced him to sell." The *halakhah* is according to Rabbi Yaakov Pakod.[39]

Similar to other agreements of sales, this one envisions that the parties will comply with the terms of the agreement and that the transfer of ownership ultimately will occur.[40] This agreement, however, is informed by a *tenai* (i.e., condition). When one transfers ownership of either land or movable goods to another, and either the transferor or the transferee has placed conditions on the transaction, which conditions are susceptible of fulfillment: If the conditions are fulfilled, the item, acquisition of which had been formally effected, is deemed purchased; if the conditions are not fulfilled, no sale has occurred. In our scenario, the seller stipulated that if he decides to sell it and he will sell it to him (i.e., the first bidder).

Hence, should the seller agree to sell, R. Kahane argues that the seller must keep his promise and sell it to the first prospective buyer. R. Ya'akov Pakod, however, demurs and argues that the transfer of the extra profit serves as a means of coercing the seller to transfer ownership to the second prospective buyer and, therefore, the sale to him is valid. In these circumstances, the seller was not interested in selling the field but sold it to the prospective second buyer in order to capitalize on a windfall profit. In other words, the windfall profits coerced him to sell to the second person. Given the presence of duress, the fulfillment of the *tenai* never materialized and therefore the seller may break his promise and sell the field to the overbidder.[41] The logical inference that can be drawn from this case is that, had the seller sold it to the second bidder for one hundred *zuzim*, the first bidder would have been entitled to specific performance as a remedy enforceable by *bet*

38 For attempts to reform the state of the law, see Avery Katz, "When Should an Offer Stick? The Economics of Promissory Estoppel in Preliminary Negotiations," *Yale L. J.* 1249 (1996): 105; Richard Craswell, "Offer, Acceptance and Efficient Reliance," Stan. L. Rev. 481 (1996): 48; Lucian Arye Bebchuk and Omri Ben-Shahar, "Precontractual Reliance," J. Legal Stud. 423, 427 (2001): 30.

39 B *Avodah Zara* 72a.

40 The implicit assumption is that the transfer was in actually done "*me-akhshav*," (i.e., from now when he decides to sell it). See Itamar Warhaftig, n. 15 above, 184.

41 Rashi, *Avodah Zara* 72a *s.v. zuzei*; R. Joseph b. Solomon Colon Trabotto (Maharik, Italy, c. 1420–1480), *Responsa Maharik, Shoresh* 20, *Anaf* 8.

din.[42] Moreover, said conclusion that the default remedy for breach of an agreement is specific performance rather than expectation damages dovetails with our representation that the halakhic-legal norm of promissory obligation mandates the fulfillment of a halakhic norm of keeping one's promise and therefore the promisee is entitled to actual performance.[43] The remedy of specific performance is not limited to an agreement to sell immediately realty or personalty (i.e., *hakna'a*—property conveyance),[44] the focal point of this Talmudic discussion, but equally extends to an agreement that obligates the parties now and the transfer of ownership or other obligations will occur in the future (i.e., *hithayvut*).[45]

What happens, however, if the promisor stipulates in advance a sum payable as damages (i.e., liquidated damages) upon breach of the agreement. For example, if *S* obligates himself to sell the field to *B*, and a penalty will be imposed upon *S* for nonperformance, may *S* breach the agreement and pay the liquidated damages, which will serve as compensation to *B*?[46] The answer to this question lies with understanding how *halakhah* wants to address noncompliance of a promise. If the goal of *halakhah* is to compel specific performance, then such a clause ought to be unenforceable.

42 Rosh, *'Avodah Zara* 5:23; *Shulhan Arukh, Hoshen Mishpat* 206:1. Clearly, an agreement for sale must be accompanied by the requisite *kinyan*. See Rashi, *'Avodah Zara* 72a, *s.v. lekha*; Rambam, *Mishneh Torah, Mekhirah* 8:7; R. Jacob b. Asher (Germany and Spain, 1270?–1340), *Arba'ah Turim, Hoshen Mishpat* 195:11.

43 Interestingly enough, though Fried adopts a teleological approach to promise-keeping, emphasizing the moral dimension of the promissory obligation, nevertheless, he argues that a breaking of a promise entitles one to expectation damages rather than specific performance. See Fried, n. 14 above, 16–17. One cannot simultaneously advocate promissory morality and the awarding of expectation damages in cases of a breach.

The endorsement of such a view would give an incentive for promissors to break their promises. The correlation between moral duty to keep a promise and that the law should enforce an agreement is noted by legal scholars. See E. Allan Farnsworth, Contracts, Section 12.1 at 755–56 (3rd ed.: 1999).

44 The assumption is that the passage in B *'Avodah Zara* 72a is dealing with a sale rather than an agreement to sell. See R. Aaron Perahiah ha-Kohen (Greece, seventeenth century); *Responsa Perah Matteh Aharon* 1:7; R. Sasson, *Responsa Torat Emet*, 133. Cf. R. Meir Abulafia (Rama, Spain, 1170?–1244), *Yad Rama*, B *Bava Batra*, 1:26; R. Shabbetai b. Meir ha-Kohen (*Shakh*, Lithuania, 1621–1662), *Hoshen Mishpat* 66:128.

45 Employing a formula of *hithayvuth* coupled with the use of the term "*me-akhshav*" (i.e., from now) will establish the undertaking of an obligation for contemplated actions in the future. See R. Hayyim b. Israel Benveniste (Turkey, 1603–1673) *Kenesset ha-Gedolah, Mahadurah Batra, Hoshen Mishpat* 61, *Hagaha* 10:2. Cf. *Responsa Torat Emet*, 133. Furthermore, whether there is an additional requirement that a person's property serve as a guarantor by the promisor to create a halakhically legal promissory obligation (i.e., *shi'bud nekhasim*) is subject to debate. See *Netivot ha-Mishpat, Hoshen Mishpat* 39:17, 60:7, 203:6; R. Aryeh Leib b. Joseph ha-Kohen Heller (Poland, 1745?–1813) *Ketsot ha-Hoshen, Hoshen Mishpat* 203:2, 206:1. For the grounds for mandating specific performance in case of a breach of an obligation, see B *Bava Batra* 2a; Rashi, B *Bava Batra* 2b, *s.v. ve-ta'amo*; *Tosafot*, (medieval Talmudic glosses, France and Germany, twelfth–fourteenth centuries) B *Bava Batra* 3a, *s.v. ki ratsu*; Rosh, B *Bava Batra* 1:3; *Tosafot, Ketubot* 54b *s.v. af al pi*. For the parameters of specific performance in acquisitions and undertaking obligations, see S. Warhaftig, n. 15 above, 316–33; I. Warhaftig, n. 15 above, 133, 135, 182–85. Though the halakhic promissory obligation implies that an agreement should not be breached and hence should be specifically enforced, nevertheless, an agreement for personal services such as a decree ordering an employee specifically to perform under an employment agreement is construed as involuntary servitude. See Shillem Warhaftig, *Jewish Labor Law* (Hebrew) (Tel Aviv: 1969), 122–29. However, there are legists who contend that a worker or a contractor (i.e., *kabbelan*) who executes a *kinyan* prior to commencing employment cannot rescind his or her agreement for services. See R. Tam cited in *Tosafot*, B *Bava Metsi'a* 48a, *s.v. ve-hu*; *Hiddushe ha-Ritba*, B *Bava Metsi'a* 75b, *s.v. ha-sokher*; R. Jacob b. Joseph Reischer (Czech Republic, c. 1670–1733); *Responsa Shevut Ya'akov*, 2:184; R. Moses b. Joseph Trani (Mabit, Ottoman Palestine, 1500–1580); *Responsa Mabit* 2:132.

46 This question is similar to the situation of a private equity capital commitment, the agreement of which stipulates that if the investor fails to meet his or her capital call there is a remedy for default (e.g., losing his or her entire investment). I thank Leon M. Metzger for this observation.

However, if the telos of the system is to redress the nonperformance by compensating for promissory noncompliance, then such a clause ought to be enforceable. Under such an agreement, the liquidated damages serve as a deterrent, an in terrorem effect to give compensation to the injured party and avoid the expense of litigation in *bet din*. In other words, the payment of liquidated damages does not actually preclude the obligation to perform the agreement. In principle, in cases of promissory noncompliance, a claim for specific performance may be advanced in *bet din*. To avoid the expense of litigation in *bet din*, however, an agreement to pay the liquidated damages may serve as a deterrent to promissory noncompliance.[47] In effect, should the promisor fail to pay liquated damages, the agreement accompanied by a *kinyan* would stipulate that specific performance be in place.[48] In each case, there must be a factual determination whether the crafted provision of the agreement providing for penalty damages is designed to reinforce the act of *kinyan* or is incorporated as a judicial remedy for a potential breach. If the purpose is the former, the promisor must keep his promise; if it is the latter, he may breach his promise and pay damages.[49]

What happens if the promisor breaches the agreement and in the process secures profits from his wrongdoing?[50] Generally, pursuant to *halakhah*, the recoverable damages are calculated based on the expectancy interest (i.e., the difference between the position in which the damaged party would have been had the agreement not been breached and the position in which it is because of the breach). The plaintiff is entitled to be reimbursed and placed in as good a position as he would have been had the defendant performed his obligations.[51] Is the victim of the

47 Rashba, *Responsa Rashba* 3:202-203; *Shulhan Arukh, Hoshen Mishpat* 12:9; R. Elijah b. Solomon Zalman (Gra, Lithuania, 1720–1797), *Bi'ur ha-Gra, Hoshen Mishpat* 12:17. Cf. R. Elijah b. Hayyim (Greece, 1530?–1610?); *Responsa Maharanah*, 1:66, who challenges this position and in the final analysis endorses this position. The impact of the issue of "*asmakhta*" (i.e., the absence of firm resolve of the promissor) is beyond the scope of this presentation.

48 *Tosafot* B *Betsah* 20a *s.v. nazir*; *Bi'ur ha-Gra*, n. 47 above; R. Moses b. Isaac Judah Lima (Lithuania, 1605?–1658) *Helkat Mehokek, Even ha-Ezer* 50:22; *Netivot Ha-Mishpat, Hoshen Mishpat* 12:6 (*Bi'urim*) and 15 (*Hiddushim*). R. Samuel b. David Moses ha-Levi (Poland and Germany, 1625?–1681), *Nahalat Shiv'ah*, 8:10 who notes that this conclusion is unanimously accepted. Cf. R. Joseph Saul Nathanson (1810–1875), *Responsa Sho'el u-Meshiv, Mahadura Tinyana*, 2:81 who argues that the option to choose between performing the agreement or breaching it and paying damages is limited to marital engagements and judicial compromise and is inapplicable to commercial transactions. For the problematics of adopting such a posture, see *Divrei Geonim* 86:1.

49 *Responsa Torat Emet* 64 (end). However, in the case of a breach should the promisee proceed to request recovery of the penalty damages without submitting a claim for specific performance, the promisee loses his right to this remedy. See R. Moses Joshua Judah Leib Diskin (Maharil Diskin, Lithuania and Ottoman Palestine, 1817–1898) *Responsa Maharil Diskin*, vol. 1 (end), *Pesakim* 148.

50 Clearly, proponents of the theory of efficient breach would oppose disgorging such gains. See Sidney DeLong, "The Efficiency of a Disgorgement as a Remedy for Breach of Contract," *Ind. L. Rev.* 737, 742–45 (1989): 22; Farnsworth, n. 2 above, 1380–82.

51 For example, if an employee retracts his offer to work for a company, and the employer can only recruit a replacement at a higher salary and the company incurs additional losses related to the worker's decision to leave, so the company is entitled to recover the differential in the worker's salary from the retracting worker and possibly all other damages. On a halakhic-moral level, *dinei shamayim*, the retracting employee is obligated to compensate for all losses including but not limited to consequential damages. See *Shakh, Hoshen Mishpat* 333:39; *Ketsot ha-Hoshen, Hoshen Mishpat* 333:3; *Hazon Ish, Hoshen Mishpat* 23:25; *Divrei Geonim*, 105:1; *Piskei Din Rabbaniyyim* 15:237 (hereafter:PDR). In other words, the goal of compensation is to reinstate the employer to his financial situation that existed prior to hiring the retracting worker. Cf. David Bass, *Contracts According to Din Torah*, (Hebrew) 17,118 in *Keter*, vol. 1. (Shlomo Ishon and Yitzchok Bazak, eds., 1996).

breach of the agreement entitled to bring an action for tort damages against the perpetrator of this breach (i.e., the expectancy interest)?

Let's address the issue of trade secrets, which is based on the breach of relationally specific duties between the employee and the employer.[52] Clearly, if an employee receives on-the-job training, his employer cannot prevent him from working for himself or a competitor.[53] To qualify as a trade secret, the information, commonly a customer list, business design, or technological process, must confer a competitive edge and it must remain secret.[54] To prevent disclosures of technological developments, business information, and customer-related information, employers may block public access, using passwords and restricting employee access to sensitive locations, and execute confidentiality agreements. In the main, trade secret cases arise when disloyal employees use or disclose their employer's secrets contravening a duty of confidentiality grounded in an employer-employee agreement. As a condition to his employment, the individual had signed a contract in which he obligated himself to refrain from disclosing certain trade secrets due to their market value. But the employee chose to breach the agreement. Can the employer sue him for damages?

In his treatment of the unauthorized opening of a letter and possession of a letter addressed to another, R. Hayyim Shabbetai (Greece, 1556–1647) argued that, though it was unclear whether the victim was entitled to damages, nevertheless, even if the damage was remote (i.e., *gerama*) the offender should be chastised.[55] Although we know all acts entailing remote damages are not actionable in a *bet din*, one remains proscribed from engaging in such tortuous behavior.[56] Should an individual engage in such acts, there are halakhic-moral—to

52 Most agreements will be structured with a provision prohibiting disclosure by an employee who is told a secret in confidence. In other words, we are dealing with an employee who is undertaking an obligation with his employer to refrain from acting in a certain fashion (i.e., disclosure of a trade secret). For the sake of this presentation, we assume that such a construction of an agreement that mandates abstention from an act is valid. See I. Warhaftig, supra n. 15 above, 201–5. Even according to the legists, who invalidate this type of an agreement, should the agreement stipulate that a breach will bring attendant damage, or a penalty will be imposed in the wake of a breach, such an agreement will be valid. See R. Isaac Weiss (Israel, 1902–1989), *Responsa Minhat Yitzhak* 6:170:18. Second, given that tangibility is defined as something that possesses height, width, and depth (see R. Hai Gaon [Babylonia, 939–1038], *Sefer Mekah u-Mimkar*, Vienna ed., *Sha'ar* 2) and therefore a trade secret should be viewed as a "*davar sh'ein bo mamash*" nevertheless, based upon commercial practice (i.e., *minhag ha-soharim*), rabbinic legislation, or its recognition by civil law, it is deemed as something with tangibility. See R. Solomon b. Jehiel Luria (Maharshal, 1510?–1574) *Responsa Maharshal, siman* 36; *Responsa Mabit* 3:225; R. Abraham Zevi Hirsch b. Jacob Eisenstadt (Lithuania, 1813–1868) *Pithei Teshuva, Hoshen Mishpat* 212:1–2; R. Abraham David b. Asher Anschel Wahrmann (Poland, c. 1771–1840), *Kesef ha-Kedoshim*, ad loc.; *Netivot ha-Mishpat, Hoshen Mishpat* 201:1; R. Joseph ibn Lev (Turkey, 1505–1580) *Responsa Mahari ibn Lev* 1:46.

53 I. Warhaftig, n. 15 above, 174–77. Additionally, see *Responsa Hatam Sofer, Hoshen Mishpat* 1:23; *Responsa Minhat Yitzhak*, see n. 52 above. However, for the efficacy of a postemployment agreement not to compete, see Warhaftig, ibid.; Aaron Levine, *Moral Issues of the Marketplace in Jewish Law*, (NY: 2005), 139–74.

54 Roger Milgrim, *Milgrim on Trade Secrets*, Section 5.02 [1], (New York: 2007). Trade secrets are to be distinguished from the information that must be continuously used in the employer's business. Consequently, any knowledge and technical information learnt in the workplace can be appropriated by the employee and used in a future job. See R. Malchiel Tenenbaum (Poland, d. 1910) *Responsa Divrei Malkiel* 3:151; Rabbi Meir Arik (Poland: nineteenth century), *Responsa Imrei Yosher* 3:269.

55 *Responsa Torat Hayyim* 3:47.

56 B *Bava Batra* 22b; *Shulhan Arukh, Hoshen Mishpat* 386:3.

be distinguished from halakhic-legal—consequences to such behavior. A *bet din* has three options: it could grant an injunction demanding that an employee cease and desist from disclosing these documents, regardless whether these are letters or trade secrets; it could invoke a communal ban for the individual to be automatically shunned[57] until he desists or declares his willingness to compensate for any future damages;[58] or actually it can order him he to compensate the victim for any ensuing damages.[59] In short, disclosing professional secrets of one's employer serves as grounds for shunning of the employee, or compensatory tort damages assessed to the employee.

On what grounds does *halakhah* proscribe these nonconsensual takings? A contemporary rabbinic and legal scholar suggests that the protection of trade secrets rests on a privacy argument. Since *halakhah* recognizes some degree of privacy is a necessary condition for reinforcing one's own persona and dignity and a condition for the existence of many of our most meaningful social relationships, people have a right to be free from personal nonconsensual intrusions into their lives, including but not limited to trade secrets.[60] This scholar's line of argument has serious difficulties. First, there is no general obligation to refrain from infringing upon another's privacy.[61] Though there are situations in which the appropriation of information is halakhically improper just because it infringes upon someone else's privacy,[62] the disclosure of trade secrets is not one of them. In other words, privacy is justified

57 Whether the unlawful opening of a letter automatically labels the offender as socially shunned or serves as grounds for invoking a ban is subject to dispute. See Nahum Rakover, *Protection of Privacy in Jewish Law*, (Hebrew) (Jerusalem: 2006), 119–24.

58 *Shulhan Arukh, Hoshen Mishpat* 55:1, *Netivot ha-Mishpat* (*Hiddushim*) ad loc. 3; *Rema, Hoshen Mishpat* 386:3. And, in fact, decisors have invoked injunctions against individuals attempting to divulge professional secrets. See *Responsa Noda bi-Yehudah, Mahadura Tinyana, Hoshen Mishpat* 24; *Responsa Divrei Malkiel* 3:157.

59 Whether the offender must undertake an obligation to pay for ensuing damages by executing a bona fide halakhic agreement is subject to debate. See *Sha'ar ha-Mishpat, Hoshen Mishpat* 26:2.

60 Rakover, n. 57 above, 29–141, 149–52. Prof. Rakover argues that a seventeenth-century legist invokes a privacy argument as grounds for protection of a trade secret. However, upon review of the responsum, one will find that the privacy argument is advanced for other reasons. See R. Mordechai Ha-levi (Egypt: seventeenth century), *Responsa Darkhei No'am, Hoshen Mishpat* 38; Rakover, ad. locum, 150. For a similar perspective on the notion of privacy in *halakhah*, see Emanuel Rackman, "Privacy in Judaism," Midstream 28 (1982): 31; Norman Lamm, "The Fourth Amendment and Its Equivalent in Halakha," Judaism 16 (1967): 53.

61 Whereas a secular legal system offers right-based arguments to legitimate a right to privacy, when we are dealing with a duty-based system, such as the Jewish legal system, one justifies the duty rather than pointing to the right. See this writer's, "May One Destroy a Neighbor's Property In order to Save One's Life," in *Turim: Studies in Jewish History and Literature Presented to Dr. Bernard Lander* (Michael Shmidman, ed., 2007), 331–60. Consequently, we have formulated the privacy argument as a violation of a duty rather than as an assertion of a right.

62 Regarding mandating documentation production in the context of a bet din proceeding, see Rosh, *Responsa Rosh* 68:25; R. Joshua b. Alexander ha-Kohen Falk (Poland, c. 1555–1614) *Sema, Hoshen Mishpat* 17:15; *Netivot ha-Mishpat*, (*Bi'urim*), *Hoshen Mishpat* 17:6. Here again, the requirement illustrates, not a right to privacy, but the parameters of the obligation of rendering testimony. The absence of an obligation to submit documents in a particular case gives rise to a concomitant right of privacy. On one hand, the submission of documentation as testimony is a fulfillment of "*gemilut hesed*," (i.e., an act of kindness). See PDR 5, 132, 139–42; 7:316; Rabbi Zalman Nehemiah Goldberg (Israel, contemporary) *Lev ha-Mishpat*, vol. 1, 13. On the other hand, in a situation that such an act will not be beneficial, one has the right to retain a zone of privacy regarding personal matters. Cf. Itamar Warhaftig, "Clarification of Facts in a Trial by Violating the Privacy of the Individual," (Hebrew) *Mishpete Eretz* 209 (2004): 2 who conceptually follows Rabbis Rackman's, Lamm's, and Rakover's understanding of the role of privacy in *halakhah*. See n. 61 above.

as a means to promote individual autonomy, personhood, and feelings of intimacy.[63] The divulging of trade secrets does not involve the violations of intimate relationships and feelings usually associated with privacy.[64] A cursory review of the rabbinic sources indicates that an infraction of privacy is to be subsumed in a specifically defined halakhic-legal category of trespass and theft, rather than under a general notion of privacy.[65] Therefore, it is not surprising to find that disclosure of trade secrets entails the violation of a specific duty—namely, theft.[66]

May a victim of a breach of an agreement pursue a restitutionary claim to recover profits because of that breach?[67] R. Ezekiel b. Judah Landau (Czech Republic, 1713–1793), author of *Noda' Bi-Yehuda*, addressed the following scenario: A scholar authorized a publisher to print his own commentary at the margin of *Mishnayot*. After completing the printing, the publisher had destroyed the type forms used in the printing, but retained the typeset characters for a future printing of the publisher's own edition of *Mishnah*. By paying the stipulated amount for the printing of his commentary, though the actual characters belonged to the publisher, the scholar understood that any benefit the publisher derived from his work in the arrangement of the characters accrues to the scholar. On the other hand, the publisher claimed that, since he owned the selfsame characters, the scholar was not empowered to dismember the character layout and arrangement.[68]

63 Charles Fried, "Privacy," *Yale L. J.* 475, 477–78 (1968): 77; Richard Wasserstrom, "Privacy: Some Arguments and Assumptions," in *Philosophical Law: Authority, Equality and Personhood*(ed. Richard Bronaugh, 1978), 147, 164.

64 However, in other contexts such as professional responsibility (e.g., rabbinic, mental health, and medical confidentiality) the notion of halakhically protecting feelings is recognized under the rubric of "evil speech" (i.e., *leshon ha-rah*). See J. David Bleich (New York, contemporary), "Survey of Recent Halakhic Periodic Literature, Rabbinic Confidentiality," *Tradition* 33 (Spring 1999), 54; Rakover, n. 57 above, 159–69.

65 J. David Bleich, *Contemporary Halakhic Problems* (NY: 1995), 307. Though from a dogmatic-conceptual perspective *halakhah* differs from American law (see n. 60 above), nonetheless, various eminent commentators equally contend that American law does not recognize a general right to privacy and argue that privacy rights are derivative. See H. J. McCloskey, "Privacy and the Right to Privacy," *Philosophy* 17, 31 (1980): 55; Judith Thomson, "The Right to Privacy," *Philosophy and Public Affairs*, 295, 312 (1975): 4; Richard Epstein, "Privacy, Property Rights and Misrepresentations," *Ga. L. Rev.* 455, 463–65 (1978): 12.

66 R. Chaim Pelagi (Izmir: nineteenth century), *Responsa* Hikekei Lev, 1, Yoreh De'ah 49; *Kesef ha-Kedoshim, Hoshen Mishpat* 183:4; R. Samuel Wosner (Israel, contemporary), *Responsa Shevet ha-Levi* 4:220; PDR 14:289, 292; R. Ya'akov Yeshayahu Bloi (Israel, contemporary), *Pithei Hoshen, Sekhiruth* 7: note 24.

67 In recent years, this issue has been the subject of some discussion regarding insurance law. See Menachem Slae, *Insurance in the Halakha*, (Tel Aviv: 1982), 128–34; J. David Bleich, "Survey of Recent Halakhic Literature," *Tradition* 52, 60 (1997): 31; Nahum Rakover, *Unjust Enrichment in Jewish Law* (Jerusalem: 2000); Itamar Warhaftig, "Insuring Another's Property," (Hebrew) *Shaarei Tzedek* 7 (5767), 99–106. The theory of efficient breach presumes unilateral termination by breach. It is within this context that we pose our question whether *halakhah* protects the disgorgement interest or not. In contrast, should the promisee respect the right of the promisor's right to opt for nonperformance, under such conditions whereby there exists mutual consent for termination there is no halakhic or moral reason to deny the promisor his gains. Under such an arrangement, the promisor knows the actual value the promise assigns for the contracted-for commodity and, by disclosure of this information, the parties can agree on an amount that the promisee will accept in lieu of performance of the agreement. Under such conditions, there would be no requirement to disgorge gains that were made possible by the breach.

68 *Responsa Noda bi-Yehudah, Mahadura Tinyana, Hoshen Mishpat* 24. Earlier treatments of this responsum in secondary literature fail to note the publisher's proprietary right in the typeset. See, for example, Nahum Rakover, *Copyright in Jewish Sources*, (Hebrew) (Jerusalem: 1991), 104; Jonathan Blass, *Unjust Enrichment* (Hebrew) (Jerusalem: 1991), 92; Aaron Levine, *Economic Public Policy and Jewish Law* (NY: 1993), 188. Cf. *Responsa Divrei Malkiel* 3:157, who equally understood that the publisher owned the type forms.

Invoking the Talmudic principle that, if the defendant derives benefit and the plaintiff sustained a loss (i.e., *zeh nehene ve-zeh haser-hayyav*), R. Landau opined that, because the publisher benefited from the scholar's work in the character layout, the publisher must compensate the scholar for the value of the benefit.[69] There exists an implied obligation that the beneficiary did not intend to cause loss to another without providing compensation. In other words, deriving benefit from a person's work mandates compensation.[70] In an employer-employee context, even if the actual working materials belong to the employer, the employee, by dint of investing time and energy, is entitled to compensation for his performance. Despite the publisher's proprietary right,[71] the employer must compensate the employee for his efforts. Failure to provide compensation entails an act of quasi-theft.[72]

The question is whether the misappropriation of a trade secret entitles the employer only to recover the value of the information or additionally requires the employee to disgorge any profits that were accrued by using this information. As we already observed, according to R. Landau, the scholar will be compensated for the value of the layout arrangement of the type forms; the publisher, however, will retain any accrued profits from using the arrangement. In other words, given that the scholar may have sold more copies of his work without the presence of competition by the rival publication, the publisher must compensate him for the loss of this business. The beneficiary, however, is not obligated to share his profits or disgorge them and give them to the owner (i.e., the scholar).[73]

Under what circumstances is the promisor who breached his employment agreement regarding confidentiality of trade secrets obligated to disgorge his profits? The *Mishnah* records a controversy between R. Yosi and other Sages about a person who rents a cow and lends it to a third party. While in the possession of the third party, it dies naturally. The opinion of the Sages is that the third party, who is liable for accidents, is obligated to pay the renter, and that, if the renter swears that it died a natural death, he is not obligated to pay the owner. In effect, the renter profits from a cow that belongs to someone else. R. Yosi demurs and exclaims, "How shall one engage in business with another person's cow? The [value of the cow] must be returned to its owner."[74]

69 Entitlement to the compensation is contingent upon the fact that the scholar lost potential revenue from his own edition due to the issuance of the publisher's newer edition.

70 One commentator on the *Noda bi-Yehudah* argued that Rabbi Landau's avowed position is compensation is due from benefiting from the publisher's property and therefore an untenable view. See *Hagahot ha-Baruch Ta'am, Responsa Noda bi-Yehudah*, 2: 35b. However, as indicated, our read of R. Landau's position is markedly different.

71 The suggestion has been advanced that compensation is derivative of the fact that the scholar has a partial proprietary right in the typeset arrangement. See *Responsa Divrei Malkiel* 3:157. R. Israel Trunk (Poland, 1820–1893), *Responsa Yeshu'ot Malko, Hoshen Mishpat* 22. *Noda bi-Yehudah*'s responsum does not belie such an understanding. Moreover, once the scholar is paid for his work, he relinquishes any ownership right. See Rosh, B *Bava Kamma* 9:14.

72 *Arba'ah Turim, Hoshen Mishpat* 371:10; *Bi'ur ha-Gra, Hoshen Mishpat* 363:14.

73 See also, Rabbi Abraham Samuel, *Responsa Amudei Esh*, 66b; *Responsa Divrei Malkiel*, 3:157.

74 M *Bava Metsi'a* 3:2; B *Bava Metsi'a* 35b. We are assuming that the owner did not authorize the lending of the cow to a third party. See *Sema, Hoshen Mishpat* 307:5; *Shakh, Hoshen Mishpat* 307:2

Though the *halakhah* is in accordance with R. Yosi's view,[75] decisors disagree whether the invoking of his position allows for profit sharing only for the disgorgement of profits.[76] The minority position in this matter is to permit profit sharing. For example, if a person *B* builds a house upon his neighbor *N*'s land and rents it to a third party *T*, in addition to *B*'s paying rent for using the land, any rental income received from *T* must be shared with *N*.[77] Invoking R. Yosi's position, the legist argues that the profit sharing results from the proprietary right of the landowner and the contractor. Similarly, if a tenant pays insurance premiums and the property is subsequently destroyed by fire, a minority of authorities opine that the insurance compensation is divided between the renter and the property owner.[78] The majority opinion, however, understands that invoking R. Yosi's view entails disgorgement of all profits.

In short, the disclosure of a trade secret may entail a breach of an agreement or the violation of a proprietary right. In other words, the resulting consequences of a disgorgement of profits is grounded either in a breach of a written agreement or a violation of a proprietary right. Adopting a property-based conception of trade secrets may lead to different outcomes than propounding an agreement approach.[79] Choosing between a property- and contract-based approach framework would define what information an employee has learned is protected. Under a contractual approach, any valuable information learned on the job would receive protection. In contrast, under a property conception, a trade secret claim will be scrutinized in light of information known in the industry in question, regardless of whether the employer believed it to be secret. A second matter where the clashing approaches could make a difference is regarding the grounds for liability of the former employee. Under the agreement approach, the former employer need not prove the secrecy of the information. Even if the information is readily available in the public domain, it is a breach of an agreement for the former employee to disclose knowledge gained by him in confidence, which is a violation of his fiduciary obligation not to use such information. Last, regarding the scope of liability for a disclosure of a trade secret, under a property-based view, the new employer, which knowingly uses the trade secret of the former employer, would be liable for use of the secret; under an agreement approach, however, the new employer, which has no agreement with the trade secret holder, would not be liable for use of the secret.

75 *Arba'ah Turim, Hoshen Mishpat* 307:5; *Shulhan Arukh, Hoshen Mishpat* 307:5.

76 The impression that one may draw from Professor Levine's presentation of R. Yosi's position is that in every situation the remedy is disgorgement of ill-gotten gains. See Aaron Levine, n. 68 above, 136–38. Our review of the topic suggests otherwise.

77 Rema, Hoshen Mishpat 375:7; Rabbi Akiva Eger (Germany: nineteenth century), *Hiddushe Rabbi Akiva Eger*, Hoshen Mishpat 375:7.

See also, *Hazon Ish, Hoshen Mishpat*, B *Bava Kamma* 22:5; R. Hanokh Agus, (Poland, 1860–1940), *Marheshet* 2:35; Jonathan Blass, n. 68 above, 92–93.

78 See *Pithei Hoshen, Sekhirut* 6:19, n. 44.

79 Conceiving a trade secret as a property right, which includes, most significantly, the right to exclude parties not in contractual privity, may lead to a different outcome than conceptualizing trade secret law as one based on a contractual obligation executed between the parties.

Conclusion

More than forty years ago, Moshe Silberg, a former justice of the Israeli Supreme Court, observed:

> Why should a man pay his debt or fulfill an obligation which he has undertaken? The Roman lawyers, as well as any modern lawyer, would be most surprised by such a question. It is clear, they would say, that the duty of payment of a debt is the correlative of the concept of ownership, and one cannot exist without the other. . . . In Jewish law . . . when a person refuses to pay his debt . . . the concern of the court is not the creditor's debt, his damages, but the duty of the debtor, his religious-moral duty. . . .[80]

Implicitly relying upon a Hofheldian analysis of rights and duties, Silberg argues that a statement about a right entails a statement about a duty and a statement about a duty entails a statement about a right.[81] Conceptually speaking, when dealing with a right-based system, one justifies the duty by pointing to the right; if one requires justification, it is the right that one must justify. When one is dealing with a duty-based system, such as the Jewish legal system, however, one must justify the duty and cannot do so by pointing to the right. Although on a jurisprudential plane there is a conceptual difference between Jewish and other secular legal systems, on a halakhic legal plane, there is no substantive legal difference between Jewish and other legal systems. Clearly, the Jewish legal system, similar to other legal systems, recognizes the notion of property rights. From a halakhic-conceptual perspective, however, we are dealing with two different systems. Jewish law focuses upon duties while others focus upon rights. During the last forty years, contemporary decisors of Jewish law, Jewish historians, law professors, and philosophers alike, have subscribed either wholeheartedly, or with certain reservations, to Silberg's analysis. His conclusion, however, that the Jewish legal system is duty-based has been affirmed by all.[82]

80 Moshe Silberg, "Law and Morals in Jewish Jurisprudence," *Harvard Law Review* 306, 312–13 (1961): 75, reprinted in Moshe Silberg, *Talmudic Law and The Modern State* (New York, 1973), 61, 68–69.

81 For a brief summary of the relevant jurisprudential literature, see Alan White, *Rights* (New York, 1984), 55–73. Compare Feinberg's suggestion that rights are logically prior to duties and serve as grounds for obligations in Joel Feinberg, *Social Philosophy* (NJ: 1973), 58, 62; see also Phillip Montague, "Two Concepts of Rights," Philosophy and Public Affairs 372–73 (1980): 9. Implicit in this understanding of the relationship between rights and duties is the notion that it makes a difference which derivative is from which. See Ronald Dworkin, *Taking Rights Seriously* (London, 1979), 171; Jeremy Waldron, *The Right to Private Property* (London, 1988), 69–73. In our presentation, we are focusing upon the jurisprudential, rather than the practical, differences between the two legal systems regarding duties and rights.

82 J. David Bleich, *Contemporary Halakhic Problems* (New York, 1995), 307; Michael Broyde, "Human Rights and Human Duties in the Jewish Tradition" in *Human Rights in Judaism: Cultural, Religious and Political Perspectives* (Michael Broyde and John Witte eds., 1998), 273–82; Haim Cohn, *Human Rights in Jewish Law* (New York, 1984); Robert M. Cover, "Obligation—A Jewish Jurisprudence of the Social Order," *Journal of Law and Religion* 65-74 (1987): 5; Menachem Elon, *Jewish Law* (Philadelphia, 1994), 117–19; Martin Golding, "The Primacy of Welfare Rights," *Social Philosophy and Policy* 119 (1984): 1; Isaac Herzog, *Main Institutions of Jewish Law*, vol. 1, (London, 1936), 46; Aaron Kirschenbaum, "The Good Samaritan and Jewish Law," *Dine Israel* 7, 15-18 (1976): 7; Berachyahu Lifshitz, "Shetar and Arevut, (Hebrew) in *Memorial Volume to Gad Tedeschi* (Jerusalem, 1995), 35–39; David Novak,

Our study has highlighted the dynamics of the halakhic-moral and halakhic-legal obligation to keep a promise. To wit, *halakhah* as a duty-oriented system mandates that under certain conditions in cases of a breach of an agreement, a promisor must disgorge all of his ill-gotten gains.

SELECTED BIBLIOGRAPHY

Birmingham, Robert. "Breach of Contract, Damage Measures, and Economic Efficiency." *Rutgers L. Rev.* 273 (1970): 24.

Craswell, Richard. Two Economic Theories of Enforcing Promises. In Peter Benson, ed. *The Theory of Contract Law: New Essays.* Cambridge 2001, 19.

Farnsworth, E. Allan. "Your Loss or my Gain? The Dilemma of the Disgorgement Principle in Breach of Contract." *Yale L.J.* 1339 (1985): 94.

Fried, Charles. *Contract As Promise: A Theory of Contractual Obligation.* Cambridge, MA: 1981.

Goldberg, Zalman Nechemiah. "The Halakhic-Legal Validity of a Promise" (Hebrew). *Techumin* 371 (5752–5753): 13.

Lifshitz, Berachyahu. "Why Doesn't Jewish Law Enforce the Fulfillment of a Promise?" (Hebrew). *Mishpatim* 161 (5755): 25.

Posner, Richard. *Economic Analysis of the Law* (Boston: Little, Brown 1972).

Rakover, Nahum. *Unjust Enrichment in Jewish Law* (Jerusalem: The Library of Jewish Law 2000).

Warhaftig, Itamar. *Undertaking in Jewish Law* (Hebrew). (Jerusalem: The Library of Jewish Law 2001).

Warhaftig, Shillem. *The Jewish Law of Contract* (Hebrew). (Jerusalem: Harry Fischel Institute 1974).

Warhaftig, Zorach. *Studies in Jewish Law* (Hebrew). (Ramat Gan: Bar Ilan Universirty Press 1985).

Covenantal Rights: A Study in Jewish Political Tradition (Princeton, 2000), 3–12; Eliav Shochetman, *Ma'asei ha-Ba ba-Avera* (Hebrew) (Jerusalem, 1981), 228–31; Suzanne Last Stone, "In Pursuit of the Counter-Text: The Turn to the Jewish Legal Model in Contemporary American Legal Theory," *Harvard Law Review* 813,865 ff (1990): 59; Ephraim Urbach, *The Sages: Their Concepts and Beliefs* (Hebrew) (Jerusalem, 1975), 337–39; Itamar Warhaftig, *Undertaking in Jewish Law* (Hebrew) (Jerusalem, 2001), 31–35; Ronnie Warburg, "Child Custody: A Comparative Analysis," *Israel Law Review* 480, 490 (1978): 14; Ernest Weinreb, "Rescue and Restitution," *S'vara* 59 (1990): 1.

PART IV

ECONOMIC PUBLIC POLICY AND JEWISH LAW

CHAPTER 19

PUBLIC AND PRIVATE INTERNATIONAL LAW FROM THE PERSPECTIVE OF JEWISH LAW

MICHAEL J. BROYDE

Introduction

Before this article undertakes a systemic analysis of the incorporation of international law into Jewish law, it needs to put forward some global reservations, stemming from the Jewish experience (with emphasis on the past as well as the present) as understood by this writer. Despite wonderful contemporary exceptions such as the United States[1] (and Canada), the Jewish encounter with secular law has been routinely harsh, leading one to question any untempered optimism in an expansive system of world law.[2] International law did not serve as a serious obstacle to the Holocaust in Europe sixty years ago, and even the most casual observer of international law senses that, within the world community, Israel has been a victim of vast discrimination over the last thirty years.

One can suggest that the glaring potential problem of expanded international law is that it might end up being merely another version of legal positivism and

1 For an explanation of why the American experience to date has been unmitigatedly positive, see John Witte, Jr., *Religion and the American Constitutional Experiment* (Boulder, CO: Westview Press, 2005), 143–85.

2 For an example of changes to Jewish law arising from its encounter with the just American system, see Michael J. Broyde, "Informing on Others for Violating American Law: A Jewish Law View," *Journal of Halacha and Contemporary Society* 41 (2002): 5–49.

majoritarian rule, such that the decisions of the many or the powerful become the standards of the group, which are coerced upon all. International law, like national and municipal law in many nations across the globe, would revert to being, to borrow a term from Justice Holmes, a "game according to the rules,"[3] without justice—both procedural and substantive—as its goal. Confident as one can be that the collective decisions of the global community would produce just results, the remembered Jewish experience of being a minority religion in a vast society has hardly been overwhelmingly positive and rarely inspired the Jewish community to believe that one can successfully put one's faith and trust in the just nature of one's neighbors. Although the American Jewish experience of the last fifty years has been just and proper, nothing encountered in the international law community in the last five, ten, or fifty years seems to mitigate such concerns.

When one speaks about international law from the perspective of the Jewish tradition, it is not enough to consider the community now forming and the international treaties that are now developing; it is necessary instead to ponder the procedural and substantive safeguards that need to be put in place to protect the rights of people to be different and unique. For world law to truly succeed, nations and persons must be free to be individual and distinctive, free to preserve their own history and community, free to practice their own religion, and free from unjust pressure to conform to collective standards.

Taken to its logical extreme, international law has the potential to eliminate regional diversity and culture. It could compel adherence to communal norms that have never fit particular regions, religions, or geographical units. There is little text and context in the discussion of international law that presents it as something more than an Athenian democracy, where the sense of the majority is imposed on the minority. It is, in fact, only through minority rights that a real and just world law will be measured.

Jewish Law and the Incorporation of International Law: A Technical Analysis

Notwithstanding the jeremiad in the introduction, the rest of this paper will explore two basic Jewish law questions that reflect on the technical issues related to the applicability of international law proposals within Halakhah. The first question

3 As Judge Learned Hand (*The Spirit of Liberty*, [3rd ed., Chicago: 1960], 306–7) recalled:

> I remember once I was with [Justice Holmes]: it was a Saturday when the Court was to confer. It was before we had a motor car, and we jogged along in an old coupe. When we got down to the Capitol, I wanted to provoke a response, so as he walked off, I said to him: "Well, sir, goodbye. Do justice!" He turned quite sharply and he said: "Come here. Come here." I answered: "Oh, I know, I know." He replied: "That is not my job. My job is to play the game according to the rules."

asks how Jewish law views public international law[4] and whether public international law can be incorporated into the corpus of Jewish law. The second question asks how Jewish law generally incorporates domestic (municipal) law into Jewish law, and if this classical paradigm of integration assists in formulating a Jewish law view of world law. To the best of my knowledge, the first matter is a question of nearly first impression[5] in the Jewish law literature, although one can find specific examples of Aharonim in the last century who applied international law through *dina de-malkhuta dina*—in the area of copyright law, for instance—without any questions or qualms.[6]

Public International Law as Incorporated into Jewish Law

Public international law is—at its core—a system of treaties and agreements and can be readily analyzed within the Jewish law framework for international agreement. The book of Joshua recounts the story of the first treaty that the Jewish nation entered into as follows:

> The people of Gibeon heard what Joshua did to Jericho and to Ai. And they worked with trickery and they made themselves to look like ambassadors. . . . And they went to Joshua at Gilgal and said to him, and to all the people of Israel, "We have come from a far land; make a treaty with us". . . . And they said to Joshua, "We are your servants;" he said to them, "Who are you and where do you come from?" They replied, "From a very far away land. . . ." And Joshua [and the people of Israel] made

4 The law of the United States does not assume that international law or even treaties signed by the United States are binding laws unless there is enabling legislation authorizing the enforcement of such law passed by Congress and signed by the President. (Indeed, even after such legislation is passed, subsequent congressional and presidential action can repeal—as valid law in the United States—any previously enacted international law standard incorporated into American law.) For more on this, see Louis Henkin, et al., *International Law* (3rd ed., St. Paul, MN: West Pub. Co., 1993), 164–66. (This section is entitled "International Law as the 'Law of the Land,'" perhaps reflecting the Jewish law presence in this matter; Louis Henkin is the son of R. Joseph Elijah Henkin, whose work is cited in notes 75, 102, and 107.)

The State of Israel has a similar view, although there are more situations where international law is incorporated into Israeli law implicitly. See Ruth Lapidoth, "International Law within the Israel Legal System," *Israel Law Review* 24 (1990): 451–84.

5 At the Tenth Annual Orthodox Forum of Yeshiva University, March 2004, a draft paper on International Law and Halakhah was presented by R. Jeremy Wieder of Yeshiva University, which this author was privileged to read. The material accompanying notes 61 to 67 benefited significantly from R. Wieder's paper, which has now been published as "International Law and Halakhah" in Lawrence Schiffman and Joel Wolowelsky (eds.), *War and Peace in the Jewish Tradition* (New York: Yeshiva University Press, 2007).

6 For example, R. Isaac Judah Schmelkes (Poland, 1828–1906) in *Responsa Beit Yitshak, Hoshen Mishpat* 30, while discussing a copyright matter, applies what appears to be the Berne Convention of 1886 to the matter through *dina de-malkhuta dina* without any discussion of whether and why such an international law treaty ought to be applied. For more on this, see infra, Copyright Law as a Model, section E, and R. Shemuel Shiloh (Israel, contemporary), *Dina de-Malkhuta Dina* (Jerusalem: Academic Press, 1974), at 421, note 88. (This work is a veritable encyclopedia of *responsa* and analysis on *dina de-malkhuta dina*.)

> peace with them and he signed a treaty with them which was sworn on [ratified by] the presidents of the tribes. And it was at the end of three days after the treaty was signed that [the Jewish nation] heard that [the Gibeonites] were neighbors and lived nearby. The people of Israel traveled and came to their cities on the third day. . . . And the people of Israel did not attack them since the presidents of the tribes had ratified [the treaty]—in the name of God, the God of Israel. The nation [of Israel] complained to the presidents of the tribes. The presidents replied, "We swore [not to attack them] by the name of the God of Israel and thus we cannot touch them."[7]

Though the treaty was entered into under fraudulent pretexts, the Jewish people nonetheless maintained that the treaty was morally binding on them. Indeed, Maimonides (Rambam, Egypt, 1135–1204), in his *Mishneh Torah*, basing himself almost exclusively on this incident in the Bible, codifies the central rule of treaties as follows: "It is prohibited to breach treaties. . . ."[8]

R. David b. Solomon ibn Abi Zimra (Radbaz, Egypt, 1479–1573), in his commentary on Rambam's *Mishneh Torah*, explains that "this is learned from the incident of the *Giv'onim* [the Gibeonites], since breaking one's treaties is a profanation of God's name."[9] According to this rationale, the reason why the Jewish nation felt compelled to honor its treaty with the *Giv'onim*—a treaty that in the very least was entered into under false pretenses—was that others would not have comprehended the entirety of the circumstances under which the treaty was signed, and they would have interpreted the abrogation of the treaty as a sign of moral laxity on the part of the Jewish people. One could argue based on this rationale that, in circumstances when the breach of a treaty would be considered reasonable by others, it would be permissible to abrogate it.

R. Levi b. Gershom (Ralbag, France, 1288–1344) understands the nature of the obligation to observe treaties differently. He claims that the treaty with the *Giv'onim* had to be honored because the Jewish nation "swore" (to God) to observe its obligation, and the nations of the world would have otherwise thought that the Jewish nation does not believe in a God and thus does not take its promises seriously (collectively and individually).[10]

R. David Kimhi (Radak, France, 1160?–1235?) advances an even more radical understanding of the nature of this obligation. Among the possible reasons he suggests to explain why the treaty was honored—even though it was in fact void, as it was entered into based solely on the fraudulent assurances of the *Giv'onim*—is because others would not be aware that the treaty was in fact void and would (incorrectly) identify the Jewish nation as the breaker of the treaty. This fear, that the Jewish nation would be wrongly identified as a treaty breaker, he states, is enough to require that the Jewish nation keep all treaties duly entered into.[11] Views

7 Joshua 9:3–19.

8 Rambam, *Mishneh Torah*, *Melakhim* 6:3.

9 Radbaz, ad loc. Such can also be inferred from Rambam's own comments in *Melakhim* 6:5.

10 Ralbag to Joshua 9:15.

11 Radak to Joshua 9:7. This theory would have relevance to a duly entered into treaty that was breached by one side in a nonpublic manner and that the other side now wishes to abandon based on the private breach of the other side. Radak would state that this is not allowed because most people would think that the second breaker is actually initiating the breach and is not taking the treaty seriously.

similar to each of these three views can be found among many other commentators and decisors.[12]

Each of these theories—whatever the precise parameters of the obligation to honor treaties is based upon—presupposes that treaties are basically binding according to Jewish law.[13] It is only in the case of a visibly obvious breach of the treaty by one party that the second party may decline to honor it. Thus, Halakhah accepts that, when a war is over, the peace that is agreed to is binding. Indeed, even in a situation where there is some unnoticed fraud in its enactment or ratification, such a treaty is still in force.

This broad approach to the binding nature of treaties is fully consistent with the general halakhic conceptualization of universal law for non-Jews (the seven laws of Noah).[14] Jewish law recognizes seven basic frameworks of universal commandments as part of a universal law code.[15] The final commandment is the obligation to create *dinim*—law enforcement or a system of justice. Two different interpretations of this obligation are found among the Rishonim. Rambam rules that the obligation to create laws requires only that the enumerated universal laws be enforced in practice, and that society need not create a more general universal law (although, presumably, it may). He states:

> How are all obligated to create laws? They must create courts and appoint judges in every province to enforce these six commandments . . . for this reason the inhabitants of Shechem [the city] were liable to be killed[16] since Shechem [the person] stole[17] [Dinah], and the inhabitants saw and knew this and did nothing.[18]

According to Rambam, every society bears an obligation to create a system of justice and enforce the first six universal precepts of law that Halakhah believes to be binding upon non-Jews.

12 Compare *Tosafot* (medieval Talmudic glosses, France and Germany, twelfth–fourteenth centuries) to *Gittin* 46a, s.v. "*kinvan*," with Rashba, ad loc., s.v. "*ve-rabbanan*," and R. Yom Tov b. Abraham Ishbili (Ritba, Spain, c. 1250–1330) ad loc., each of whom struggles to resolve certain crucial details. However, each assumes that valid treaties are binding.

It is worth noting that, beyond the short codification of this topic found in Rambam and the occasional explanations of commentators on the Bible, very little has been written on this topic. Thus, for example, the Index (*mafteah*) to Rambam's *Mishneh Torah* found in the Frankel edition shows not a single discussion of this topic among the Aharonim. So, too, R. Yehudah Gershoni's encyclopedic discussion of *Hilkhot Melakhim*, entitled *Mishpat ha-Melukhah* (New York: Safrograph Co., 1949), has not a single reference to this Halakhah.

13 This is also the unstated assumption of BT *Gittin* 45b–46a, which seeks to explain why treaties made in error might still be binding.

14 For more on this, see R. Aharon Lichtenstein, *The Seven Laws of Noah* (2nd ed., New York: Rabbi Jacob Joseph School Press, 1986).

15 The Talmud (BT *Sanhedrin* 56a) recounts seven categories of prohibition: idol worship, taking God's name in vain, murder, prohibited sexual activity, theft, eating flesh from a living animal, and the obligation to enforce laws. As is obvious from this list, these seven commandments are generalities that contain within them many specifications—thus, for example, the single categorical prohibition of sexual promiscuity includes both adultery and the various forms of incest. According to R. Samuel b. Hophni (Babylonia, d. 1013), 30 specific commandments are included; see generally appendix to *Entsiklopedyah Talmudit* 3: 394–96 and supra, note 14.

16 See Genesis 34.

17 As to why Rambam uses the word *gazal* (stole) to describe abduction, see BT *Sanhedrin* 55a and *Hatam Sofer*, *Yoreh De'ah* 19.

18 Rambam, op. cit., *Melakhim* 9:14.

Nahmanides (Ramban, Spain, 1194–1270), argues with this formulation and understands the obligations of *dinim* to be much broader. It encompasses not only the obligations of society to enforce particular regulations of the other six Noahide *mitsvot*, but it also obligates society to create general rules of law governing such cases as fraud, overcharging, repayment of debts, and the like.[19] Within the opinion of Ramban there is a secondary dispute as to what substantive laws Noahides are supposed to adopt. R. Moses b. Israel Isserles (Rema, Poland, 1525/30–1572), writing in a responsum, states that, according to Ramban, in those areas of *dinim* where non-Jews are supposed to create laws, they are obligated to incorporate Jewish law into Noahide law unless it is clear contextually that it is inappropriate.[20] Most authorities reject this interpretation and accept either Rambam's ruling or that according to Ramban those rules created under the rubric of *dinim* need only be generally fair, and need not be identical to Jewish law.[21] This author cannot find even a single Rishon who accepts the ruling of Rema, and one can find many who explicitly disagree.[22]

Rules of War as a Model

World law would, in theory, be a fulfillment of this obligation to create *dinim* according to most Rishonim, both in the view of Rambam as well as most understandings of Ramban. It is clear that Jewish law could well imagine the creation of world law in the field of public international law, grounded in reciprocal treaties, and mandated by society as a fulfillment of the obligation to create an ordered and just society. Treaties to impose international law—if properly entered into and enforced by the many nations of the world—would be fully valid in Jewish law. Halakhah might even smile on a proposal to universalize such justice, if it were properly done.

19 Ramban to Genesis 34:14.

20 *Responsa Rema* 10. His ruling is also accepted by *Hatam Sofer*, *Hoshen Mishpat* 91 (as well as *Likkutim* 14) and R. Jacob Lorbeerbaum of Lissa (Poland, c. 1760–1832), *Nahalat Ya'akov* (*Teshuvot*) 2:3.

21 See R. Isaac Elhanan Spektor (Lithuania, 1817–1896), *Nahal Yitshak*, *Hoshen Mishpat* 91; R. Avraham Yeshayahu Karelitz (Israel, 1878–1953), *Hazon Ish* to *Hilkhot Melakhim* 10:10 and *Bava Kamma* 10:3; R. Isser Zalman Meltzer (Lithuania and Israel, 1870–1953), *Even ha-Azel*, *Hovel u-Mazzik* 8:5; R. Jehiel Michal Epstein (Belarus, 1829–1908), *Arukh ha-Shulhan he-Atid*, *Melakhim* 79:15; R. Naphtali Tsevi Judah Berlin (Lithuania, 1817–1893), *Ha'amek She'eilah* 2:3; R. Abraham Isaac Kook (Lithuania and British Palestine, 1865–1935), *Ets Hadar* 38, 184; R. Tsevi Pesah Frank (Israel, 1873–1960), *Har Tsevi*, *Orah Hayyim* vol. II, *Kunteres Millei di-Berakhot* 2:1; R. Ovadiah Yosef (Israel, contemporary), *Yehavveh Da'at* 4:65; R. Isaac Jacob Weiss (Hungary, England and Israel, 1902–1989), *Minhat Yitshak* 4:52:3. For a more complete analysis of this issue, see Nahum Rakover, "Jewish Law and the Noahide Obligation to Preserve Social Order," *Cardozo Law Review* 12 (1991): 1073, and appendices I and II: 1,098–118.

22 Most authorities do not accept Ramban's opinion; see, for example, Rambam, op. cit., *Melakhim* 10:10; *Responsa Ritba* 14 (quoted in *Beit Yosef*, *Hoshen Mishpat* 66:18); *Tosafot* to *Eruvin* 62a, s.v. "*ben Noah*." The comments of R. Joseph Albo (Spain, fifteenth century) in *Sefer ha-Ikkarim* 1:25 are also worth citing: "One finds that although Torah law and Noahide law differ in the details, the principles used are the same, since they derive from the same source. Moreover, the two systems exist concurrently: while Jews have Torah law, the other peoples abide by the Noahide code."

One model of integrating international law within Halakhah in this way already exists. Most contemporary halakhic decisors rule that international law, rather than Halakhah, governs the rules of war. Although some aver that Halakhah demands a stricter standard, placing more restrictions on the conduct of the Jewish army during war, R. Shaul Yisraeli (Israel, contemporary) demonstrates that the basic framework for the Jewish laws governing war is not found in Halakhah, but instead in secular international law.[23] Understanding why this is so requires a brief foray into the legal theory underlying secular law's role in Halakhah, premised on some basic theological and eschatological assertions.

The Jewish legal tradition wishes neither to proselytize to and convert others nor to be proselytized to and converted. In the grand clash of religious faiths, Judaism desires to be left alone, and to focus on in-reach, the process by which Jews make Jews into better Jews. It does recognize some limited ability to accept proselytes, and thus has a complex mechanism for joining the Jewish faith. But rather than encouraging, Halakhah specifically discourages conversion, and, inversely, there is no right of exit in the Jewish tradition.[24] Jewish law addresses itself predominantly to those born Jewish; its concern with Gentiles is relatively insignificant. Halakhah thus contains parallel, though distinctively sized, tracks of law: a fully fleshed-out system of Jewish law, to constrain and regulate the conduct of Jews; and a skeletal outline of six absolute Noahide rules, with a seventh category, *dinim*, under which rubric non-Jews are to create whatever system of law seems most appropriate to them. This narrow focus of Halakhah is neither universalistic nor particularistic. It does not maintain that only Jews can enter heaven; both Jews and Gentiles can. It does not maintain that Jewish law is binding on all: Jewish law binds Jews; Noahide law binds Gentiles. It does not maintain that all must acknowledge the "Jewish" God; it rather recognizes that monotheism need not be accompanied by recognition of the special role of the Jewish people.[25]

Jewish tradition maintains that even in messianic times there will *and should be* Gentiles—people who are not members of the Jewish faith.[26] The existence of those who are not Jewish is not merely a concession to facts on the ground, but part of the Jewish ideal, wherein all—Jew and Gentile alike—worship the single God differently and distinctly, each in their own mode of worship. Indeed, the Talmud insists that in messianic times conversion into Judaism will not exist: Jews and Gentiles will peacefully coexist.[27]

Several fundamental insights derive from this formulation of the scope of the Jewish tradition. The focus in this context will be on the main topic: the role of

23 R. Shaul Yisraeli, "Military activities of national defense," first published in *Ha-Torah ve-ha-Medinah* 5/6 (19531954): 71–113; reprinted in his *Amud ha-Yemini* (rev. ed., Jerusalem, 1991) as ch. 16., 168–205 (Hebrew).

24 See Michael J. Broyde, "Proselytism and Jewish Law: Inreach, Outreach, and the Jewish Tradition," in John Witte, Jr. and Richard C. Martins (eds.), *Sharing the Book: Religious Perspectives on the Rights and Wrongs of Proselytism* (Mayrknoll, NY: Orbis, 1999), 45–60.

25 Cf., generally, Rambam, op. cit., *Melakhim*, ch. 9 and 10.

26 Ibid., 12:1.

27 BT *Yevamot* 24b.

foreign law, particularly insofar as it regulates war, in the Jewish tradition. Precisely because Jewish tradition does not insist that it be the exclusive source of law governing all of the world's inhabitants, Jewish law has within it doctrines of comity—substantive recognition of the inherent validity of legal rules and systems besides Jewish law—that are encapsulated in the interrelated group of doctrines of *dina de-malkhuta dina*,[28] *dinim*,[29] and *din melekh*.[30,31] In fact, many authorities find some connection between the obligation of Jews to obey *dinim* and the requirement to obey the secular law.[32]

As a direct corollary of not thinking that all people ought to be Jewish, Halakhah does not think that all people ought to obey Jewish law. The rubrics of *dina de-malkhuta dina*, *din melekh*, and *dinim* say to adherents of Halakhah that there will be times and places (almost always outside of ritual law) where Jewish law mandates that Jews obey a legal code besides Jewish law, and that, in certain situations, it can even supplant native Jewish law. The reason these doctrines are so strong in Jewish tradition is obvious: Because we do not think, as a matter of theology, that all people ought to be Jewish, we do not think that all people ought to obey Jewish law. Other legal systems must then be valid, too, and we are called upon to respect and obey these legal systems when they correctly operate in their spheres.

Furthermore, and more to the point here, sometimes those other legal systems will regulate Jews and their conduct. For example, Jewish law maintains that secular courts and secular laws are the proper legal framework for resolving disputes between Jews and Gentiles,[33] and secular criminal law is the proper framework for punishing Jewish or Gentile criminals in the general society.[34] In yet dozens of other such examples Halakhah comfortably and ideally tells its adherents that using secular law as the foundation for one's interactions with the general community is proper.

Of course, ritual law can almost never be affected by these doctrines,[35] and the application of the rules of *dina de-malkhuta dina*, *din melekh*, and *dinim* to cases

28 See infra, The Obligation to Obey the Law of the Land and World Law, section D.

29 See supra, Public International Law as Incorporated into Jewish law.

30 See Rambam, op. cit., *Gezelah va-Avedah*, ch. 5; *Shulhan Arukh*, *Hoshen Mishpat* 225, 369.

31 *Minhag ha-soharim* is a distant cousin of these three doctrines and deals with laws as practiced, a related but different concept. Moreover, *minhag ha-soharim* is essentially contractual in nature, while these three are deeply structural.

32 See, for example, Rashi to *Gittin* 9b. R. Meltzer, *Even ha-Azel*, *Nizkei Mamon* 8:5 freely mixes as near synonyms the terms *dina de-malkhuta dina*, *din melekh*, and *benei Noah metsuvvim al ha-dinim* (Noahides are obligated in *dinim*) in a discussion about why a Jew must return property lost by another when such is required by secular law and not Halakhah.

33 *Shulhan Arukh*, op. cit., 26.

34 Michael J. Broyde, *The Pursuit of Justice and Jewish Law: Halakhic Perspectives on the Legal Profession*, (2nd ed., New York: Yashar Books, 2007), 122–24.

35 One of the very few exceptions is in cases where Jewish law has a number of permissible rituals and one of these secular rubrics seek to curtail one of those options. Some authorities will recognize that as a valid application of *dina de-malkhuta dina* and others will not. Consider for example the question of whether Israeli law can preclude *yibbum* for a Sephardic man living in Israel and insist he only perform *halitsah*. Numerous authorities accept that the state may do so under the rubric of *dina de-malkhuta dina*; R. Ovadiah Yosef (Israel, contemporary) strongly disagrees. For more on this issue, see Elimelech Westreich, "Levirate Marriage in the State of Israel: Ethnic Encounter and the Challenge of a Jewish State," *Israel Law Review* 37, 2–3 (2003–2004): 426–99.

where all parties are Jewish is complex and much more limited.[36] But thinking structurally about Jewish law leads to the obvious conclusion that Jewish law assumes valid legal systems exist independent of Jewish law and that sometimes Jews ought to participate in such legal systems. There might also be cases when the secular legal system is valid as a matter of Jewish law, but still the Talmudic rabbis insisted that Jews ought not participate in the system.[37] More generally, Jewish law is acutely aware of the content of the secular law in any given environment and constantly considers the relationship between Jewish law and secular law.[38]

Our interest is in its application to international law, particularly the laws of war. There is no obvious reason why Halakhah would limit the application of *dina de-malkhuta dina*, *din melekh*, and *dinim* to national, rather than international, law, assuming the international legal system to be both just and impartial. War, in fact, seems almost a perfect case where Halakhah would recognize—assuming war is a legitimate activity[39]—that these legal frameworks would provide the basis for such, as in any activity outside of ritual law, *dina de-malkhuta dina*, *din melekh*, and *dinim* are the touchstones for interactions with the secular world.

Indeed, only a minority of halakhic authorities articulate views wherein the rules governing war derive specifically from Jewish law. R. Elazar Menahem Man Shach (Israel, 1898–2001) is of the view that there are no unique rules of how to fight a war; war is simply the general rules of self-defense writ large.[40] R. Shlomo Goren (Israel, 1917–1994) contends that, though they are covered by layers of dust from generations of disuse, Halakhah in fact does have indigenous rules for waging war that are latent and must be fleshed out.[41] Nevertheless, the vast majority of contemporary authorities agree with R. Shaul Yisraeli that Halakhah has no unique rules of war and that the law of the land determines these matters. Like in many other areas of Halakhah, the rules of war, too, are governed by *dina de-malkhuta dina* writ large.

This majority view is predicated on the famous comments of R. Naphtali Tsevi Judah Berlin (Lithuania, 1817–1893) in his comments in *Ha'amek Davar* regarding Genesis 9:5.[42] Commenting on the verse prohibiting murder to Noahides, R. Berlin writes that a person is only punished for spilling blood "at a time when it is otherwise appropriate to act with brotherhood. But this is not the case during war, when it is a

36 See infra, The Obligation to Obey the Law of the Land and World Law, section D, 12.

37 Thus in the view of R. Feinstein on the prohibition of informing a non-Jewish government of a fellow Jew's violation of the secular law, while the non-Jewish authorities may arrest Jews, Jews are forbidden to assist in the capture or prosecution of nonviolent offenders. See Michael J. Broyde, "Informing on Others," supra, note 2.

38 Such reciprocity would seem to be the very basis of much of Jewish law's exclusionary doctrines in commercial matters. See Michael J. Broyde and Michael Hecht, "The Gentile and Returning Lost Property According to Jewish Law: A Theory of Reciprocity," *Jewish Law Annual* 8 (2000): 31–45.

39 See generally Michael J. Broyde, "Military Ethics in Jewish Law," *Jewish Law Association Studies* 16 (2004): 1–36.

40 R. Elazar Menahem Man Shach, *Be-Zot Ani Boteah* (Benei Berak: Talmidei Maran Shelita, 1969), 10–35.

41 R. Shlomo Goren, "Combat Morality and the Halakhah," *Crossroads* 1 (1987): 211–31; *Responsa Meshiv Milhamah* (3 volumes).

42 See *Tosafot* to *Shevu'ot* 35b, s.v. "*katla had*;" R. Abraham Dov Ber Kahana-Shapiro (Kovno, 1871–1943), *Devar Avraham* 1:11 and *Zera Avraham* 24.

time to hate. Then it is a time to kill and there is no punishment whatsoever for so doing, because this is the way of the world." War has, by its very nature, an element of *hora'at sha'ah* (temporary suspension of law), in which the basic elements of so-called regular Jewish law are suspended. Once killing becomes permitted as a matter of Jewish law, much of the hierarchical values of Jewish law seem to be suspended as well.

Thus, any treaties into which the Jewish state enters fill this legal void and are halakhically binding. So Israel, as a signatory to the Geneva Conventions, for instance, is bound to follow all the dictates thereof. But, to take a contemporary example, there is no doubt that the decision by the government of Israel to ignore the advisory opinion of the International Court of Justice (ICJ) concerning the legality of the separation fence in the West Bank was halakhically permitted. The treaty obligation of Israel to the ICJ requires that Israel only obey decisions of the court in those situations where Israel agrees (at the outset) to accept the judgment of the ICJ on the particular matter.[43] In this case, Israel declined and made no appearance before the International Court of Justice, thus rendering the ICJ opinion without any basis in Halakhah to compel Israel's compliance; indeed, the ICJ recognized Israel's right as a matter of international law to decline to follow this opinion by itself noting that the opinion was advisory.[44] Treaties are limited to their agreed-upon provisions and no more.

Private International Law (*Lex Mercatoria*): Common Commercial Custom

Any analysis of international law through the eyes of Halakhah could not stop at treaties, as treaties would seem to be limited to areas of public international law, where the law is imposed on nations by agreements to which they mutually consent. Most modern proposals go much further than that, in that world law—the expansive term used for international law—aims to bind individuals as well as nations. Jewish law has two distinctly different mechanisms for incorporating private international laws and norms into Jewish law. The first is *minhag ha-soharim*, common commercial custom (lex mercatoria, in Latin), and its application to world law is quite crucial.

Halakhah provides that: (a) any condition that is agreed upon with respect to monetary matters is valid under Jewish law;[45] and (b) customs established among merchants acquire Jewish law validity,[46] provided that the practices stipulated or

43 See *Written Statement of the Government of Israel on Jurisdiction and Propriety* (with cover letter by ambassador and legal advisor Alan Baker) (30 January 2004), at 99–105, available at: www.icj-cij.org.

44 See "*Legal Consequences of the Construction of a Wall . . .*" *(Advisory Opinion)* 2004 I.C.J. 4 (9 July) at 4, noting that this is an advisory opinion, available at: www.icj-cij.org.

45 See, generally, Menachem Elon (Israel, contemporary), *The Principles of Jewish Law* (Jerusalem: Keter, 1973) at columns 880–987.

46 Ibid.

commonly undertaken are not otherwise prohibited by Jewish law.[47] These two principles are arguably interrelated; commercial customs are sometimes said to be binding because business people implicitly agree to abide by them.

The Mishnah pronounces the validity of commercial customs. It states:

> What is the rule concerning one who hires workers and orders them to arrive at work early or to stay late? In a location where the custom is to neither come early nor stay late, the employer is not allowed to compel them [to do so]. . . . All such terms are governed by local custom.[48]

The *Shulhan Arukh*, written by R. Joseph Caro (Ottoman Palestine, 1488–1575), makes it clear that common commercial practices override many default halakhic rules that would otherwise govern a transaction.[49] Moreover, these customs are valid even if the majority of the business people establishing them are not Jewish. In a related responsum, R. Moses Feinstein (New York, 1895–1986) explains:

> It is clear that these rules which depend on custom . . . need not be customs . . . established by Torah scholars or even by Jews. Even if these customs were established by non-Jews, if the non-Jews are a majority of the inhabitants of the city, Jewish law incorporates the custom. It is as if the parties conditioned their agreement in accordance with the custom of the city.[50]

In addition, many authorities rule that such customs are halakhically valid even if they were established because the particular conduct in question was required by secular law, and there is no reason to assume that these *minhagim* (customs) would not be valid if international law gave rise to such practices.[51]

Nevertheless, authorities debate whether commercial custom can (by introducing nonnative concepts) substantively alter Jewish law or merely create alternative methods and mechanisms that resemble existing Halakhah. For example, there are

47 Jewish law prohibits a debtor from offering a "pound of flesh" as collateral for a loan, and, even if the borrower and the lender and the general community of merchants accept such a practice, Jewish law would nonetheless reject such practice as invalid. See R. Solomon Joseph Zevin (Israel, 1885–1978), "*Mishpat Shailok lefi ha-Halakhah* [Shylock in Jewish Law]," *Le-Or ha-Halakhah: Ba'ayot u-Beirurim* (2nd ed., Tel Aviv: Tsiyoni, 1957), 310–36.

48 BT M. *Bava Metsi'a* 7:1.

49 *Shulhan Arukh*, op. cit., 331:1. See also JT *Bava Metsi'a* 7:1(11b) (statement of R. Hoshaya: "*Ha-minhag mevattel et ha-Halakhah*" [Custom supersedes Halakhah]); *Responsa Maharik* 102 and R. Samuel b. Moses de Medina (Maharashdam, Greece, 1506–1589), *Responsa Maharashdam* 108.

50 *Iggerot Mosheh, Hoshen Mishpat* 1:72. See also *Arukh ha-Shulhan, Hoshen Mishpat* 73:20. And see, generally, Steven H. Resnicoff, "Bankruptcy: A Viable Jewish Law Option?" *Journal of Halacha and Contemporary Society* 24 (1992): 10–14, who discusses this issue at great length.

51 See, for example, *Iggerot Mosheh, Hoshen Mishpat* 1:72; R. Hayyim David Hazan (Israel, contemporary), *Responsa Nediv Lev* 12; R. Eliyahu Hazan (Israel, contemporary), *Nediv Lev*, no. 13; R. Isaac Aaron Ettinger (Lemberg, 1827–1891), *Mahariah ha-Levi* 2:111; R. Abraham Dov Ber Kahana-Shapiro, *Devar Avraham* 1:1; R. Israel Abraham Alter Landau (Hungary, 1886–1942), *Responsa Beit Yisrael* 172; R. Jacob Isaiah Bloi (Israel, b. 1929), *Pithei Hoshen, Dinei Halva'ah*, ch. 2, *halakhah* 29, note 82. For example, R. Joseph Iggeret, *Divrei Yosef*, no. 21, states:

> One cannot cast doubt upon the validity of this custom on the basis that it became established through a decree of the King that required people to so act. Since people always act this way, even though they do so only because of the King's decree, we still properly say that everyone who does business without specifying otherwise does business according to the custom.

various conventions as to how to "seal a deal." In some industries, it is said that a handshake is considered binding. These customs are referred to as *sittumta.* It is agreed that *sittumta* can effectuate a *kinyan* (i.e., the transfer of title to property). This is true even though, but for the custom, the particular practice would not otherwise constitute a valid form of transferring title according to Halakhah. Thus, *sittumta* can be used as a substitute for the normal procedures for achieving a *kinyan.* There is a classical controversy among the Rishonim, however, as to whether the mechanism of *sittumta* is capable of effecting actions or outcomes not normally possible according to Halakhah.

R. Asher b. Jehiel (Rosh, Germany and Spain, c. 1250–1327), R. Solomon Luria (Maharshal, Poland, 1510?–1574), and others contend that *sittumta* can accomplish much more than traditional halakhic forms of effecting a deal. For example, even though Halakhah has no native mechanism for transferring ownership of an item that does not now exist in the world (*davar she-lo ba la-olam*), this approach argues that, if the commercial practice of a particular society included a procedure for such transfers, Jewish law in that place would incorporate the practice as valid and enforceable.[52] Again, no basic halakhic form of *kinyan* permits someone to sell *something* that does not yet exist or to sell to *someone* who does not yet exist.[53] Nevertheless, R. Solomon b. Abraham Adret (Rashba, Spain, c. 1235–c. 1310), states:

> Great is the power of the community, which triumphs even without a *kinyan.* . . .
> Even something which is not yet in existence can be sold to someone who does not yet exist [if community practice so provides].[54]

If Rashba is correct and commercial custom can allow transactions to be accomplished that could not otherwise have been achieved under Jewish law, it is possible that world law would create obligations that, though profoundly not found

52 *Responsa Rosh* 13:20; R. Meir b. Baruch of Rothenberg (Maharam of Rothenburg, Germany, c. 1215–1293), cited in *Mordekhai* to *Shabbat* 472; *Maharshal* 36. See also R. Jacob Moses Lorbeerbaum of Lissa, *Netivot ha-Mishpat, Bei'urim al Shulhan Arukh, Hoshen Mishpat* 201:1, who appears to agree, as well as *Arukh ha-Shulhan, Hoshen Mishpat* 212:3.

53 Jewish law distinguishes between different categories of things "that do not yet exist." Perhaps the case about which there is greatest dispute concerns a person's ability to agree to sell property that exists but that he does not possess. The origin of this controversy is found in a difference of opinion between the Hakhamim (Sages) and R. Meir regarding the case of a man who attempts to take all the legal steps necessary to marry a woman at a time before it is legally permissible for them to be wed (BT *Kiddushin* 63a). "Suppose a man says to a woman, 'Be wedded to me after . . . your husband dies.' . . . [Then the woman's husband dies. The Hakhamim rule:] she is not wed. R. Meir rules: she is wed."

According to Jewish law, formation of a Jewish marriage requires a man to acquire "ownership" interests in his intended and the woman to agree to transfer herself to him. Consequently, the Talmud interprets the debate between the Hakhamim and R. Meir as founded on the basic issue as to whether a person has the power to effectuate a transaction involving property not yet in existence or not yet in his possession. The Talmud applies and extends this argument to the sale of a field that the seller has not yet acquired (BT *Bava Metsi'a* 16b), to "what my trap shall ensnare" (ibid.), to "what I shall inherit" (ibid.), and to "the fruit that will grow on a particular tree in the future" (ibid. 33b). In each of these cases, the Hakhamim rule that the agreement is not legally effective or binding.

54 *Responsa Rashba* 1:546.

in Halakhah, could nevertheless be introduced into Halakhah under the rubric of *minhag ha-soharim*.

Other halakhic authorities, however, maintain that Rashba is wrong in attributing expansive powers to nonnative mechanisms. Rosh and others posit that a customary convention functions only as a *substitute* method by which to transfer title and cannot be more effective under Jewish law than the forms of *kinyan* recognized by the Talmud.[55] According to this view, then, the capacity of Jewish law to assimilate world law precepts and private obligations would be somewhat more limited in that it would only be able to incorporate by convention those that could, as a matter of halakhic theory, be accomplished by halakhic mechanisms.[56]

Consider, for example, common commercial standards for the exchange of financial data through an international computer network. While there is no binding legal standard compelling the particular format for the sharing of such data across international borders, standards for such transmission have been developed by those companies involved in this business and have been accepted as industry-wide international standards.[57] One who enters such an international industry is obligated as a matter of Jewish law to determine the relevant standards and adhere to them, as that is the convention among those engaged in this commerce (or announce in a clear and direct way that the custom is not being adhered to). Indeed, courts in the United States have routinely accepted that such common commercial customs can sometimes even trump written legal standards—a result similar to that accepted by Halakhah.[58]

55 R. Jehiel b. Joseph of Paris (France, d. c. 1265) is cited in *Mordekhai* to *Shabbat* 473 and in *Tashbets* (*Katan*) 378. A similar approach can be found in *Responsa Radbaz* 1:278 and is accepted as correct by R. Aryeh Leib ha-Kohen Heller of Stry (Poland, 1745?–1813), *Ketsot ha-Hoshen* to *Shulhan Arukh, Hoshen Mishpat* 201:1.

56 For an excellent application of this dispute, see Michael J. Broyde and Steven H. Resnicoff, "The Corporate Paradigm and Jewish Law," *Wayne State Law Journal* 43 (1997): 1,685–818. (This law review article examines corporations from a Jewish law view, and the previous material is derived from that article.)

57 See, for example, John C. Yates, Electronic Commerce and Electronic Data Interchange, *Practising Law Institute* 471 PLI/Pat 233 (1997).

58 Consider, for instance, the case of *Dixon, Irmaos & Cia, Ltda. v. Chase National Bank*, 144 F.2d 759 (2nd Cir. 1944). In that case, an exporter had contracted to sell cotton to an international purchaser. Chase had issued two letters of credit on behalf of the purchaser. The terms of the credit required Chase to honor drafts accompanied by specified documents, including "a full set of bills of lading." The seller shipped the goods and received two original bills of lading for each shipment, but only one of the two sets of bills of lading was presented to Chase by the due date. In lieu of the other set, the exporter's New York representative, another New York bank, gave Chase an indemnity agreement against loss. Chase dishonored the drafts on the grounds that both full sets of bills of lading had not been presented. The plaintiff introduced evidence that New York banks that financed international sales with letters of credit customarily accepted a guaranty in place of a missing document when the letter of credit required a "full set of bills of lading." The court found that Chase was bound by the custom and had failed to follow it in this instance and was liable, even as formal contract law was consistent with Chase's practice. For more on this issue in American law, see Clayton P. Gillette, "Harmony and Stasis in Trade Usages for International Sales," *Va. J. Int'l L.* 707 (1999): 39. In this writer's opinion, the court here is relying on the correct understanding of the Jerusalem Talmud's statement (JT *Bava Metsi'a* 7:1[11b]) in the name of R. Hoshaya, that custom supersedes Halakhah, which, when properly understood, is limited to cases of financial law where the intent of the parties is the primary adjudicative tool in Jewish law (as well as American law and International law).

All agree, however, that private international law[59] can have the status of common commercial custom in any situation in which it is observed normatively, and, in some fields of commerce, such is the case already.

The Obligation to Obey the Law of the Land and World Law

Halakhah has another framework for understanding and relating to other legal systems, and, though it is usually invoked to assess Jewish law's relationship to national or local law, it should be relevant to a discussion of world law as well. The halakhic doctrine *dina de-malkhuta dina* provides that, in certain circumstances and for particular purposes, secular law is legally effective under Jewish law. A survey of the obligation to obey secular law generally is well beyond the scope of this article.[60] However, a brief review of the relevant theories is required to appreciate how the doctrine of the *dina de-malkhuta dina* would impact on the acceptance of world law in the Jewish tradition.

There are at least five principal perspectives explaining why *dina de-malkhuta dina* is a binding doctrine in Jewish law:

1. R. Samuel b. Meir (Rashbam, France, c. 1080–c. 1174) posits that the ruler of a country governs with the consent of the governed, and law is a form of social contract binding on the community because they all agree to a process that creates law, even if they do not agree with the content of the final law.[61]
2. R. Solomon b. Isaac (Rashi, France, 1040–1105) posits that the ability of society to make law is a fulfillment of the Noahide obligation to legislate, whose results are generally binding even on Jews, except in specific cases (such as divorce).[62]

59 Another use of the term "private international law" or "customary international law" is in the enforcement of public international law, but against private individuals who have violated public international law obligations, such as the prohibition against torture. Consider, for example, *Kadic v. Karadzic*, 70 F.3d 232 (2nd Cir., 1995) concerning a claim for damages against a particular person for torture committed during the Bosnian-Serbian conflict. From the perspective of Halakhah, these types of private international law claims would nearly always be valid, as the underlying conduct would almost always represent either a violation of Jewish law or Noahide law (as only the most severe of violations is permitted to be presented as a matter of international law).

60 R. Shemuel Shiloh's encyclopedic *Dina de-Malkhuta Dina*, supra, note 8, is an excellent resource for this.

61 Rashbam to *Bava Batra* 54b, s.v. "*ve-ha-amar Shemuel dina de-malkhuta dina.*" A similar view is taken by Rambam, op. cit., *Gezelah va-Avedah* 5:18 and many others.

62 Rashi to *Gittin* 9b, s.v. "*kesherin,*" "*huts.*" See also R. Hayyim Hirschenson (Hoboken, NJ, 1857–1935), *Malki ba-Kodesh* 2:2.

3. R. Jacob b. Meir Tam (Rabbeinu Tam, France, 1100–1171) posits that the obligation to obey secular law is grounded in the ability of secular authority to transfer property through eminent domain (*hefker beit din*).[63] A related theory assumes that secular law has the same general power as Jewish kings[64] or Jewish courts.[65]
4. Maharshal posits that the ordered structure of society requires that law exist, and that it cannot be solely defined by religious faith. "If this is not the case, the nation will not stand and will be destroyed." Communities need law, and without it society will collapse into anarchy.[66]
5. R. Nissim b. Reuben Gerondi (Ran, Spain, 1310?–1375?) posits that the people (perhaps only the Jewish people) reside where they do solely by the grace of the king or government that owns that land. Just like one must obey the wishes of one's host when one visits in another person's home, so too one must obey the wishes of one's host nation when one resides in a country.[67]

Each of these theories gives rise to a particular stance concerning robust private world law. A social contract theory like Rashbam has no natural limits on the rule of law, and world law is binding on individuals in the same way as municipal law—it is not the geography that makes the law, but the acceptance. Similarly, law as a fulfillment of the Noahide obligation of *dinim* has no national boundaries, nor is the theory of secular law as *hefker beit din* of Rabbeinu Tam naturally limited to national, rather than international, law. The same can be said for the functional structuralist approach in Jewish law taken by Maharshal. If the foundation of law is order, then world law is just as binding as national law, which is just as binding as local law. Only those who limit law's binding authority to its coercive authority to expel might limit international law, although if world law becomes an accepted legal institution, it will ultimately acquire the coercive authority to be binding in the Jewish tradition in this theory as well.[68]

63 *Responsa Tosafot* 12; this responsum is sometimes cited in the name of R. Jonah b. Abraham Gerondi (Spain, c. 1200–1263).

64 R. Isaac Caro (uncle of R. Joseph Caro), cited in *Avkat Rokhel* 47 and discussed in R. Shemuel Shiloh, *Dina de-Malkhuta Dina*, pp. 77–79.

65 *Devar Avraham* 1:1.

66 *Yam shel Shelomoh, Bava Kamma* 86:14; see also *Yam shel Shlomo, Gittin* 81:22.

67 Ran to *Nedarim* 28a, s.v. "*be-mokhes ha-omed me-elav.*" Similar to Ran is the view of Maharam of Rothenburg, *defus* Prague 1001. The explicit limitation on *dina de-malkhuta* not applying to a Jewish government is first noted by R. Eliezer b. Samuel of Metz (France, c. 1115–c. 1198), quoted by R. Isaac b. Moses (Germany and France, c. 1180–c. 1250), *Or Zarua, Bava Kamma* 447.

68 It is worth noting in writing that one is hard-pressed to find even a single modern halakhic authority who rules that the theory of the Ran is the normative one to be followed, particularly to draw the conclusion that *dina de-malkhuta dina* would not apply in the land or the state of Israel. See R. Ovadia Yosef, *Yehavveh Da'at* 5:64, who demonstrates this. While R. Hershel Schachter (New York, contemporary) notes that the *Hazon Ish* is purported to be of the opinion (unfound in his written work) that, based on the view of Ran, the Israeli government has no right to levy taxes on Jewish residents, R. Schachter goes on to write that this view would have no bearing on other government powers in Israel, such as the ability to mint currency, punish criminals, or set up a general legal system. See R. Hershel Schachter, "'Dina De'malchusa Dina': Secular Law As a Religious Obligation," *Journal of Halacha and Contemporary Society* 1, 1 (1981): 103–32, at note 26.

A more complex conversation among Jewish law authorities concerns the type of legislation that may be implemented through *dina de-malkhuta dina*, be it municipal or world law.

Three theories again predominate.

1. R. Caro rules that secular law is halakhically binding only to the extent that it directly affects the government's financial interests. Thus, secular laws imposing taxes or tolls would be valid under Jewish law,[69] but laws for the general health and safety of society would not.
2. Rema agrees that secular laws directly affecting the government's financial interests are binding, but adds that secular laws that are enacted for the benefit of the people of the community as a whole are also, as a general matter, effective under Jewish law.[70] In this model, all health and safety regulations would also be binding.
3. R. Shabbetai b. Meir ha-Kohen (Lithuania, 1621–1662) disagrees with Rema in one respect. He believes that, even if secular laws are enacted for the benefit of the community, they are not valid under Jewish law if they are specifically contrary to indigenous halakhic precepts.[71] Thus, general health and safety rules would be binding, but—for example—Jewish law has a rule that rooftop railings must be about a meter high,[72] so a secular law setting a lower height would not be accepted as halakhically valid.

There is substantial debate among halakhic authorities as to which approach to follow.[73] Nevertheless, it seems that most modern authorities agree that, at least outside of the State of Israel, Rema's view should be applied, and such is the view of all four of the deans of Halakhah in America in the previous generation: Rabbis Moses Feinstein,[74] Joseph Elijah Henkin (New York, 1880–1973),[75] Joseph B. Soloveitchik (Boston, 1903–1993),[76] and Joel Teitelbaum (New York, 1888–1979).[77] In this view, almost all applications of secular law are valid under

69 *Shulhan Arukh*, op. cit., 369:6, 11.

70 Ibid., 369:11.

71 R. Shabbetai b. Meir ha-Kohen, *Siftei Kohen* (*Shakh*) to *Shulhan Arukh, Hoshen Mishpat* 73:39. Thus, for example, according to *Shakh*, secular law can require that one return lost property in a case that Halakhah permits (but does not mandate that it be returned), but not permit one to keep a lost object that Halakhah requires be returned.

72 *Shulhan Arukh*, op. cit., 427:1.

73 See, for example, R. Yaakov Breish (Zurich, 1895–1976), *Helkat Ya'akov* 3:160 and R. Shemuel Shiloh, *Dina de-Malkhuta Dina*, at pp. 145–60, who list authorities adopting either the approach of *Shakh* or R. Joseph Caro.

74 *Iggerot Mosheh, Hoshen Mishpat* 2:62.

75 *Teshuvot Ivra* 2:176.

76 This is indicated in R. Hershel Shachter, *Nefesh ha-Rav* (Jerusalem: Reshit Yerushalayim, 1994), 267–69, and has been confirmed by many other sources as well.

77 *Responsa Divrei Yoel* 1:147.

Jewish law.[78] Should world law become a legal framework, there is no reason to assume that this same rule would not apply to it—broad doctrines of law would be binding as the law of the land. International law—law of a single sovereign authorized by many nations to create binding law—should be no less binding as a form of *dina de-malkhuta*. This would seem no different than the origins of the federal government in the United States, which derives its authority from a ratified treaty (constitution) of thirteen originally sovereign states. Such a federal authority would seem valid from the view of Halakhah.

Consider, for example, the validity of the rules derived from the North American Free Trade Agreement (NAFTA), ratified by Congress and then signed into law on December 8, 1993. NAFTA sets out rules of economic interaction governing commerce between the United States, Mexico, and Canada, and it directs individual conduct during such commerce (no different from, say, the Uniform Commercial Code).[79] Such a multicountry international agreement—including the provisions depriving American citizens of access to courts of the United States—is a classic example of a situation where Halakhah would classify international law as a valid law of the land, as the United States has decided that certain types of trade shall be governed by international law rather than indigenous American law. The law of the United States may, as a matter of Halakhah, allow or direct its citizens to obey international law.

Of course, just as with respect to commercial custom, there is a question as to precisely what *dina de-malkhuta dina* can accomplish. Some *posekim* clearly rule that, when this doctrine incorporates secular law into Halakhah, the secular law so incorporated can even accomplish things that would have been hitherto impossible under Jewish law.[80]

It is also important to note that the three principal approaches to *dina de-malkhuta dina* described above dealt with the halakhic validity of secular law as

78 See also R. Shemuel Shiloh, *Dina de-Malkhuta Dina*, at 157, who asserts that most halakhic authorities adopt the Rema's view and lists many of these authorities.

A contemporary of his, R. Menasheh Klein (New York, contemporary), in *Mishneh Halakhot* 6:277, questions whether *dina de-malkhuta dina* applies in the United States, and his view would be the same of world law. He states:

> [The applicability of the principle of] *dina de-malkhuta dina* in our times, when there is no king but rather what is called democracy, needs further clarification. As I already explained the position cited in the name of Rivash quoting Rashba, one does not accept *dina de-malkhuta dina* except where the law originates with the king.

Despite R. Klein's views, it is important to note that most authorities have held that *dina de-malkhuta dina* does not apply only to laws issued by a king, as noted by R. Ovadia Yosef in *Yehavveh Da'at* 5:64: "Even in a nation not ruled by a king, but rather by a government chosen by its citizens, the general principle of *dina de-malkhuta dina* applies. . . ." Moreover, a number of preeminent Jewish law authorities have specifically held that *dina de-malkhuta dina* applies within the United States and have not found any problems caused by the democratic form of government. See references to Rabbis Feinstein, Henkin, Soloveitchik, and Teitelbaum above.

79 19 U.S.C. §3311; upheld as constitutional in *Made in the USA Foundation v. U.S.*, 242 F.3d 1300 (11th Cir., 2001).

80 See *Ketsot ha-Hoshen* and *Netivot ha-Mishpat* to *Shulhan Arukh, Hoshen Mishpat* 201:1.

it applies directly to Jews. Jewish law, however, also takes a position as to the validity of secular law in transactions between non-Jews.

As discussed above in the first section, Jewish law provides that non-Jews are bound to observe the seven laws of Noah, referred to as the Noahide Code. In part, the Noahide Code requires non-Jews to establish a system of commercial laws. According to most halakhic authorities, such laws may differ from the rules governing transactions that are only between Jews.[81] Moreover, the majority view is that, in a country governed by non-Jews, the secular law consequences of transactions among non-Jews are valid and can generally be relied upon by Jews.[82] For example, assume that Ahmed and Christopher are not Jewish, and that Ahmed sells Christopher a widget in a transaction that would not be effective under Jewish law but is effective under secular law.[83] Daniel, a Jew, can rely on secular law to establish that Christopher owns the widget and, by purchasing it from him, Daniel becomes its owner under Jewish law. Consequently, it seems reasonable that international law, too, would be a fully effective mechanism between non-Jews and their society, and third-party Jewish participants need not question the efficacy of world law in such contexts.

Even assuming that Halakhah sanctions the application and accepts the results of secular law when applied to Jew-Gentile or Gentile-Gentile transactions, what of transactions between only Jews? Halakhah's response, of course, depends on the nature of the law in question. Broadly, two types of secular laws govern citizens' interactions with one another: civil and criminal. Civil law—like that governing torts, property, contracts, and commerce generally— levels the playing field by creating a consistent framework within which people can interact economically and, inevitably, resolve their disputes impartially. In this broad area, secular law essentially takes the place of contracts, providing default rules. Here, when Jews do business with each other, Halakhah supersedes secular law's default norms and its indigenous laws govern purely Jewish transactions.

But Jewish law often bows to secular law, as in the case of almost all criminal laws. For instance, there is an international convention against having sex with children; Jewish law has no opposition to such conduct after the age of

81 See, for example, *Iggerot Mosheh, Hoshen Mishpat* 2:62. See also Michael Broyde, *The Pursuit of Justice in Jewish Law*, 83–99, as well as the discussion of the view of Ramban above at notes 18 to 22.

82 Secular rules enacted pursuant to the Noahide Code *may* be enforceable by a Jewish litigant against another Jewish litigant, but only if the latter has no substantial connection to Jewish law and would not wish to be governed by Jewish law. Thus, R. Moses Sternbuch (Israel, contemporary), in *Teshuvot ve-Hanhagot*, vol. 1, no. 795 (rev. ed.), suggests the possibility that a litigant who does not generally observe Halakhah and who would not adhere to Jewish financial law when it would be to his detriment *may* not be entitled to insist on Jewish law's rules when they would inure to his benefit. In some areas of law, an apostate has the same status as a non-Jew. R. Sternbuch states that it is not clear whether this rule applies to commercial transactions in which it would operate to the apostate's detriment. For more on this, see Yehudah Amihai, "A Gentile who Summons a Jew to *Beit Din*," *Tehumin* 12 (1991): 259–65. Thus, even authorities who would not ordinarily apply *dina de-malkhuta dina* to enforce secular law against religiously observant Jews enforce secular law against nonobservant Jews.

83 For example, the sale might be void or voidable as violating the Jewish law prohibition against price gouging. See, for example, Aaron Levine, *Free Enterprise and Jewish Law* (New York: Ktav, 1980), 99–110.

maturity, defined as twelve or thirteen, for girls and boys respectively.[84] Nonetheless, Halakhah defers to secular law and forbids otherwise permitted behavior, banning Jews from engaging in sex even with Jewish adolescents.

Copyright Law as a Model

Since Johannes Gutenberg's printing of the Bible in the mid-fifteenth century, the question of authors' (and later, with the advent of recording technology, musicians') rights to their creations has plagued publishers and writers, judges and moralists. The question, on its face, is fairly simple: Can one really own, and thus deserve protection from theft of, a particular arrangement of words or formulation of an idea? The first iteration concerned publishers, rather than writers. If any Tom, Dick, or Harry could come along and reprint any work, the original publisher had no opportunity to recoup his significant investment, much less earn any profit, and so would not go to the trouble of typesetting and printing in the first place. There is a dual concern here both for the actual monetary losses that publishers did or would suffer, and for the promotion of new ideas and inducement of intellectual creativity.

States and nations each struggled with this issue for four hundred some odd years, until 1886, when the Berne Convention for the Protection of Literary and Artistic Works was convened in Berne, Switzerland. There, international copyright standards were set, and within two years Belgium, France, Germany, Italy, Luxembourg, Spain, Switzerland, Tunisia, and the United Kingdom had signed a treaty agreeing to abide by them. Currently, the Berne Convention and four subsequent international copyright treaties have 164 signatory nations, each of which agrees to enforce the provisions of international copyright law. It would hardly be an exaggeration to say that these copyright laws govern the entire world.

Halakhic authorities, too, have grappled with copyright issues. Two broad approaches exist to the problem of extending halakhic copyright protection, though Jewish law has no such concept per se. Both are premised on the assumption that such protections exist with Halakhah; they merely explain why and how. In fact, almost no halakhic authority questions that copyright infringement of some sort is prohibited; the question is to what extent and on what basis. In fact, R. Moshe Feinstein rules unequivocally that copying even a Torah tape is prohibited, simply referring to it as a form of theft.[85]

The first approach seeks to use preexisting concepts from other areas of Jewish law, sometimes stretching or modifying them, to provide copyright protections. Within this broad view, authorities put forward four specific rationales:

84 See Rambam, op. cit., *Ishut* 3:11–12 and 4:7.

85 *Iggerot Mosheh, Orah Hayyim* 4:40.

1. R. Moses Sofer (Hungary, 1762–1839) posits that infringing on a copyright would be a violation of the laws concerning unfair business practices, *hassagat gevul*.[86] Just as fishermen must not trap fish near another fisherman's net that he has labored to set up, publishers may not sell—and readers may not buy—a book that he has copied, benefiting from the efforts of the first publisher.
2. R. Ezekiel Landau (Czech Republic, 1713–1793) posits that copyright infringement would violate the Talmudic rule that, if one benefits from another while causing a loss, he must pay.[87,88]
3. Rema wrote the first approbation, announcing a ban on publishing or purchasing a copied work and threatening excommunication for whoever did so.[89] This became the most common form of copyright protection, with 3,662 approbations from 1499 to 1850.[90,91]
4. R. Zalman Nehemiah Goldberg (Israel, contemporary) posits that, when a producer sells her work, she withholds the right to copy it.[92] When a purchaser in fact copies the work, he commits theft, for the right to copy does not belong to him; he may not simply do whatever he wishes with this work.

The second approach incorporates wholesale secular law's model and provisions of copyright protections. In 1890, R. Isaac Judah Schmelkes (Poland, 1828–1906) wrote that whether Jewish law explicitly awards rights to a creator is irrelevant. Living in Przemysl, Galicia, the laws of his country—specifically the Austrian Copyright Act of 19 October 1846—clearly provided for copyright protections. Through the doctrine of *dina de-malkhuta dina*, then, Jewish law provides authors with the very same protections, forbidding its adherents from infringing upon those rights.[93,94]

Some modern-day authorities find the *dina de-malkhuta dina* approach problematic on theological and philosophical grounds. In their view, Jewish law is all-encompassing and is in no way deficient. Relegating an area of law—in this instance copyright law—completely to secular law's framework implies that Jewish law is in some way lacking; unable to deal in its own terms with the self-evidently moral and proper rights and concepts of copyright law, Halakhah flees the arena, relying on secular law to fill the gaps it cannot address on its own. This contradicts

86 *Shut Hatam Sofer, Hoshen Mishpat* 79.

87 R. Ezekiel Landau, *Noda bi-Yehudah, Hoshen Mishpat* 2:24.

88 BT *Bava Kamma* 20a.

89 *Responsa Rema* 10.

90 Encyclopedia Judaica, Vol. 7, 1,454.

91 See, generally, Nahum Rakover, *Zekhut ha-Yotserim ba-Mekorot ha-Yehudiyim* (Copyright in Jewish Law) Jerusalem, 1991 (Hebrew).

92 R. Zalman Nehemiah Goldberg, "Copying a Cassette without the Owner's Permission," *Tehumin* 6 (1985): 185–207 (Hebrew).

93 *Responsa Beit Yitshak, Yoreh De'ah*, Vol. 2, no. 75.

94 See also R. Ezra Batzri, *Tehumin* 6 (1985), 181–82.

the view of Jewish law as eternal and living, able to tackle all complex situations that life yields, and significantly diminishes its scope and stature.

Yet this is precisely the function of the interrelated doctrines of *dina de-malkhuta dina*, *dinim*, and *din melekh*. This approach's beauty and elegance lies not only in using one neat, simple rule to extend copyright protections, rather than bending or twisting existing halakhic categories to achieve the predetermined legal goal. These doctrines, in fact, protect Jewish law's integrity and provide it with the tools to continue evolving and interacting with surrounding legal systems as they change along with the times. Halakhah does not forbid one from engaging in all that one *should*—in a moral and even theological sense—avoid; nor does it require that one engage in all positive and beneficial—again, both morally and theologically—activities and actions. It recognizes that Gentiles may set up valid and proper systems of law that are distinct and different. Halakhah therefore contains a framework to interact with these legitimate systems and even to incorporate some of their positive, foreign conceptions.

Substantive Fairness as a Limitation to Obey the Law of the Land in the Area of International Law

One of the basic conditions upon which the obligation to observe secular law (as a function of *dina de-malkhuta dina*) is predicated is the fairness or equality of the secular law in question. As R. Shemuel Shiloh (Israel, contemporary) writes, "There is no dispute among the Sages with regard to the principle that the law of the government must apply equally on all members of the community."[95] There is no doubt that if international law (or portions of it) is ever incorporated into Halakhah through *dina de-malkhuta*, international law—just like national law—will be subject to the test of equality and fairness. Jews specifically, and the Jewish state generally, need not show fidelity to a legal system that codifies injustice.

The halakhic test for determining equality and fairness, however, has been subject to a great deal of analysis and discussion. Even though most Rishonim seem to indicate that full equality is a prerequisite for a valid secular law under *dina de-malkhuta*,[96] R. Joseph b. Solomon Colon (Maharik, Italy, c. 1420–1480)

95 R. Shemuel Shiloh, *Dina de-Malkhuta Dina*, 109.

96 The obligation of fairness in secular law was first noted by R. Joseph b. Meir Ha-Levi ibn Migash (Spain, 1077–1141) to *Bava Batra* 54b, and is seconded by Rambam, op. cit., *Gezelah ve-Avedah* 5:14 and *Or Zarua*, *Bava Kamma* 447. Rabbeinu Tam is also quoted as endorsing this principal (see Rosh, *Nedarim* 3:11). It is quite possible that Rosh himself does not fully accept this principle, as he raises a series of questions about Rabbeinu Tam's prooftext.

lays claim to a startling analysis: A secular law can be considered proper in the eyes of Halakhah even if it treats Jews differently as a group from members of other religions or other citizens, at least as a matter of taxation.[97] Indeed, Rema states that this is the proper understanding of the Halakhah. The *Shulhan Arukh* writes:

> When does taxation become like robbery? . . . When the taxation comes from the king with no limitations and precision, but rather the king takes what he wishes; however, a taxation enacted for a finite amount [is valid].[98]

And Rema adds:

> Even if [the government] directs that the Jews pay more than the non-Jews, nonetheless, this is called a finite amount.[99]

Other halakhic authorities—including the R. Caro himself—simply disagree with Rema and posit that in order for any law to be valid as a form of *dina de-malkhuta dina* it must apply equally to all in a given area, and it may not discriminate based on religion.[100]

Many halakhic authorities, however, are open to distinctions in secular law that seem rational, such as distinctions between citizens and noncitizens,[101] wealthy citizens and the impoverished,[102] regulations of one particular profession and not another,[103] or one geographical region and not another,[104] as well as other distinctions that seem consistent with the best interests of the society or community.

This author would like to suggest the possibility that Rema and Maharik might actually recognize this distinction and only permit distinctions based on religion in the area of *dina de-malkhuta dina* when they are consistent with fair government generally and not merely motivated by anti-Semitism. Consider, for example, a general secular law that prohibits surgical procedures outside a hospital and requires that such procedures be supervised by a physician. This writer does not doubt that such regulations are valid as a matter of *dina de-malkhuta dina* according to Rema, and yet also recognizes that an exception to such a regulation allowing circumcision of Jewish children by an authorized *mohel* (circumciser) would be a valid exception to the general application of *dina*

97 *Responsa Maharik* 195 (194 in other editions).

98 *Shulhan Arukh*, op. cit., 369:6.

99 Ibid.

100 See *Shulhan Arukh*, op. cit., 369:6–9 and *Responsa Radbaz* 3:968. For more on this and a full listing of these authorities, see R. Shemuel Shiloh, *Dina de-Malkhuta Dina*, 112.

101 R. Solomon b. Jehiel Luria (Poland, 1510?–1576), *Hokhmat Shelomoh, Hoshen Mishpat* 369:8.

102 R. Joseph Elijah Henkin, "On the Matter of *Dina de-Malkhuta Dina*," *Ha-Pardes* 31 (1957): 54, 3–5.

103 See the view of R. Jacob Israel, cited in *Beit Yosef, Hoshen Mishpat* 369.

104 R. Abraham Hayyim Rodriguez (Livorno, late seventeenth century), *Responsa Orah la-Tsaddik, Hoshen Mishpat* 1.

de-malkhuta dina.[105] Indeed, there are many other situations in which faiths are provided specific exemptions from general laws due to the unique religious needs of their faith, and Rema should be understood as permitting such faith-specific applications of secular law.[106] Thus, even in situations in which the beneficiary of such an exception is not an adherent of Jewish law, and legal discrimination against Jews seems to occur by denying them exemptions, Jewish law would still recognize the validity of such secular laws, such as one that, for instance, exempted Santeria sacrifice rituals from animal cruelty laws.

R. Joseph Elijah Henkin, one of the first *posekim* to ponder the application of *dina de-malkhuta dina* in a just democracy, noted that the proper formulation of the Halakhah is as follows:

> That which the *posekim* stated, which is that a law that does not treat all equally creates no obligation to obey it under *dina de-malkhuta dina*, their intent is when such a law distinguishes between people and groups because of evil motives, such as when a government decrees against the conduct of the Jewish people, Heaven forbid, or simply generally taxing individuals with no just cause, but with malice of the heart.[107]

This standard ought to be equally applicable in the incorporation of international law into everyday life through *dina de-malkhuta dina*.

A brief conclusion is needed to these four technical matters. Halakhah generally recognizes that international law as enacted by treaties agreed to by nations is a valid form of international law in the Jewish tradition, and it becomes binding on all citizens of those nations. Furthermore, Jewish law recognizes that, even when no formal treaty is enacted, international law could become valid through the doctrine of *dina de-malkhuta dina* being a valid source of law, so long as it is substantively fair. Finally, Halakhah notes that, even when there is no law, either national or international, the rubric of common commercial custom (*minhag ha-soharim*), which is fully binding under Jewish law, can form the foundation for global

105 Indeed, many states in the United States have exactly such an exception. Consider, for example, the following statute in Illinois (*Ill. Rev. Stat.* ch. 38, para. 12–32 [1992]):

> A person commits the offense of ritual mutilation, when he mutilates . . . another person as part of a ceremony, rite, initiation, observance, performance or practice, and the victim did not consent or under such circumstances that the defendant knew or should have known that the victim was unable to render effective consent.

***

The offense ritual mutilation does not include the practice of circumcision or a ceremony, rite, initiation, observance, or performance related thereto.

106 Consider, for example, the use of peyote in American Indian religious practice or animal slaughter in Santeria ritual, both of which have sought exemption from secular law. (See *Employment Div., Ore. Dept. of Human Res. v. Smith*, 494 U.S. 872 [1990] and *Church of the Lukumi Babalu Aye, Inc. v. City of Hialeah*, 508 U.S. 520 [1993].) For other examples and an analysis of this issue in American law, see Eugene Volokh, "A Common-Law Model for Religious Exemptions," *UCLA Law Review* 46 (1999): 1,465.

107 R. Joseph Elijah Henkin, supra, note 102 (validating rent control laws).

commercial interactions. World law thus could be a possibility in Jewish law. However, it would have to be a fair and just legal system.

Conclusion

Even if an expansive world law in both public and private spheres could be incorporated into a Jewish law framework, intemperate faith in and an unbridled pursuit of international law solutions might still be a bad idea. Jewish law recognizes that, even when all of the procedural requirements for law have been met, there are situations and cases where governmental action does not rise to the level of law[108]—because such "laws" violate basic rules of substantive fairness. Authority alone does not in the Jewish tradition create law; law must rest on pillars of justice and fairness as well as basic right and wrong. Though the Rishonim tended to point to arbitrary taxation—a procedural violation of due process—as emblematic of unjust regimes,[109] in fact the pursuit of justice entails a much broader obligation: Before law can be truly valid, there must be *both* procedural and substantive fairness in the legal system. Absent that, the Jewish tradition coined a phrase "the theft of the government," which is definitively not the law,[110] and insisted that no person could bear an obligation to obey unjust regimes.

This author suspects that world law will never meet this dual standard, in that it requires the depoliticization of international law, where the wrongs of the mighty are judged by the same standards as the wrongs of the weak and the powerful are held to the same standards of conduct as the powerless—and where the community of nations arrives at these standards without trampling on the rights, freedoms, and beliefs of its minority members. And, of course, those standards must themselves be just in the deepest sense of that holy word.[111]

SELECTED BIBLIOGRAPHY

Bible:

Joshua 9:3–19.

Broyde, Michael J. "Informing on Others for Violating American Law: A Jewish Law View." *Journal of Halacha and Contemporary Society* 41 (2002): 5–49.

108 See "*Dina de-Malkhuta Dina,*" *Entsiklopedyah Talmudit* 7: 295–30.

109 See R. Jacob b. Asher (Spain, 1269–1343), *Tur, Hoshen Mishpat* 128; *Responsa Maharashdam, Hoshen Mishpat* 135, 389; and R. Elijah b. Hayyim (Maharanah, Greece, 1530?–1610?), *Responsa Mayim Amukim*, vol. 2, no. 95.

110 *Hamsanuta de-malketa*; see *Entsiklopedyah Talmudit*, supra, note 108, especially text accompanying note 24.

111 "*Tsedek, tsedek tirdof*" (Justice, justice shall you pursue), Deuteronomy 16:20.

———. "Military Ethics in Jewish Law." *Jewish Law Association Studies* 16 (2004): 1–36.

———. "Proselytism and Jewish Law: Inreach, Outreach, and the Jewish Tradition." In John Witte, Jr. and Richard C. Martins (eds.). *Sharing the Book: Religious Perspectives on the Rights and Wrongs of Proselytism*. Mayrknoll, NY: Orbis, 1999, 45–60.

———. *The Pursuit of Justice and Jewish Law: Halakhic Perspectives on the Legal Profession*, 2nd ed. New York: Yashar Books, 2007, 122–24.

Broyde, Michael J., and Michael Hecht. "The Gentile and Returning Lost Property According to Jewish Law: A Theory of Reciprocity." *Jewish Law Annual* 13 (2000): 31–45.

Broyde, Michael J., and Steven H. Resnicoff. "The Corporate Paradigm and Jewish Law." *Wayne State Law Journal* 43 (1997): 1,685–818.

Caro, R. Joseph. *Shulhan Arukh, Hoshen Mishpat* 331:1; 369:6, 11.

Entsiklopedyah Talmudit. "*Dina de-Malkhuta Dina*." Vol. 7: 295–308 (Hebrew).

Feinstein, R. Moses. *Iggerot Mosheh, Hoshen Mishpat* 1:72.

Ha-Kohen, R., and Shabbetai B. Meir. *Siftei Kohen* (*Shakh*) to *Hoshen Mishpat* 73:39.

Henkin, R. Joseph Elijah. "On the Matter of *Dina de-Malkhuta Dina*." *Ha-Pardes* 31 (1957): 54, 3–5 (Hebrew).

Isserles, R. Moses. *Responsa Rema* 10.

Lichtenstein, Aaron. *The Seven Laws of Noah*, 2nd ed. New York: Rabbi Jacob Joseph School Press, 1986.

Maimonides. *Mishneh Torah, Melakhim* 6:3; 9:14.

Meltzer, R. Isser Zalman. *Even ha-Azel* to *Mishneh Torah, Nizkei Mamon* 8:5.

Nahmanides. Commentary to Genesis 34:14.

Rakover, Nahum. "Jewish Law and the Noahide Obligation to Preserve Social Order." *Cardozo Law Review* 12, 1,073.

Rakover, Nahum. *Zekhut ha-Yotserim ba-Mekorot ha-Yehudiyim* (Copyright in Jewish Law Sources). Jerusalem, 1991 (Hebrew).

Schachter, R. Hershel. "'Dina De'malchusa Dina': Secular Law As a Religious Obligation." *Journal of Halacha and Contemporary Society* 1, 1 (1981): 103–32.

Shiloh, R. Samuel. *Dina de-Malkhuta Dina*. Jerusalem: Academic Press, 1974.

Talmud (Babylonian):

Bava Metsi'a 83a.

Wieder, R. Jeremy. "International Law and Halakhah." In Lawrence Schiffman and Joel Wolowelsky (eds.), *War and Peace in the Jewish Tradition*. New York: Yeshiva University Press, 2007.

Yisraeli, R. Shaul. "Military Activities of National Defense." First published in *Ha-Torah ve-ha-Medinah* 5/6 (1953–1954): 71–113. Reprinted in his *Amud ha-Yemini* (rev. ed., Jerusalem, 1991) as ch. 16, 168–205 (Hebrew).

CHAPTER 20

JEWISH ENVIRONMENTAL ETHICS

YEHUDA L. KLEIN AND JONATHAN WEISER

Introduction

The objective of this chapter is to explore the philosophical foundations of sustainable development. We will discuss the contending worldviews that inform our relationship with the natural world and show how they affect our understanding of the concept of sustainability. In particular, we will review the ethical assumptions that underlie anthropocentric, ecocentric, and theocentric environmentalisms. We will show that each of these perspectives contributes to our understanding of the relationship between Man and Nature and that each informs the debate over how to balance our obligations to our fellow Man, future generations, and other living and blooming creatures.

Sustainable Development

The modern definition of *sustainable development* is traditionally dated to the Brundtland Commission Report, which defined *sustainable development* as "development that meets the needs of the present without compromising the ability of future generations to meet their own needs."[1] Agyeman and Evans characterize sustainable development as the nexus of economic development, social equity, and environmental protection.[2] Sustainable development thus requires that we overcome the conflicts inherent in the pressures that economic development places on natural resources, as well as the demands of social justice (distributional equity) and the needs of future generations (intergenerational equity). The contested terrain of sustainable development is where the demands of growing economies meet a world of limits—both a finite natural resource base and the limited capacity of ecosystems to accept environmental pollutants, the unwanted byproducts of our economy.

The Brundtland formulation of sustainable development clearly presupposed an anthropocentric orientation. The value placed on nature is instrumental (i.e., both environmental preservation and economic development are directed at satisfying human needs). There is an implied tradeoff between social justice and intergenerational equity—providing for the economic needs of developing countries as well as those of less privileged inhabitants of industrialized countries requires that we accelerate the pace of economic development, while concern for the needs of future generations requires that we limit our "environmental footprint," and hence the rate of economic development. The "just sustainability" literature addresses exactly this tradeoff.[3]

This anthropocentric orientation is one of two environmentalisms that dominate current discourse. While anthropocentric environmentalism addresses human needs, and views nature within the context of human needs, ecocentric environmentalism addresses the needs of nature, and views man as a part of nature. "The question of how to best think about our relation to nature is, by definition, a question bigger than we are. To answer such a question, we must appeal to a higher authority than our own. In particular, we might hope for direction from God as communicated by religious tradition. Given our growing power over and danger to nature, it is an appeal to make with increasing urgency."[4]

In the following sections we discuss three approaches to sustainable development: That of neoclassical welfare economics (anthropocentric environmentalism), deep ecology (ecocentric environmentalism), and Jewish environmental ethics (theocentric environmentalism).

1 World Commission on Environment and Development, Our Common Future, Chapter 2: Toward Sustainable Development, last downloaded on 07/10/2009 from UN Documents Cooperation Circles: Gathering a Body of Global Agreements http://www.un-documents.net/ocf-02.htm.

2 Julian Agyeman and Tom Evans, "Toward Just Sustainability in Urban Communities: Building Equity Rights with Sustainable Solutions," The ANNALS of the American Academy of Political and Social Science 590 (November, 2003): 35–53.

3 See Agyeman and Evans, op. cit., and papers cited therein.

4 Andrew J. Hoffman and Lloyd E. Sandelands, "Getting Right with Nature: Anthropocentrism, Ecocentrism, and Theocentrism," Organization and Environment 18 (June, 2005): 145.

The Foundations of Neoclassical Welfare Economics

Welfare economics, the foundation upon which neoclassical environmental economics is built, is "an enormous elaboration of the utilitarian moral philosophy developed by Bentham, Mill, and others in the eighteenth and nineteenth centuries." Modern environmental analysis is a synthesis of classical utilitarian philosophy, in which the goal of individual or collective behavior is to maximize social welfare, and neoclassical utilitarianism, in which the individual is called upon to maximize his own individual utility.[5]

Stiglitz traces the foundations of neoclassical welfare economics back to Adam Smith (1776) and the "Invisible Hand."[6] Smith posited that individuals, motivated only by self-interest, would be led by the "invisible hand" to pursue the society's collective interests. Moreover, he held that the most reliable way to maximize social welfare would be to encourage each individual to pursue his individual self-interest. The history of neoclassical economics has been an effort to establish the conditions under which individual utility-maximizing behavior maximizes social welfare.

Classical utilitarian theory allows us to construct a measure of social welfare, the total welfare of a community, by summing individual welfare measures (utilities) across all the individuals in that community. It is thus possible to construct policies (e.g., environmental policies) that maximize social welfare:

> The problem of maximization of total welfare thus involved the weighing against each other the losses of utility and gains of utility of different individuals. This implies interpersonal comparability of utility, as is seen in the dictum about the marginal utility of a dollar for the poor man and for the rich man. Such implication, however, is open to epistemological criticism on the ground of lack of operational significance.[7]

Neoclassical economics, by rejecting, in principle, the interpersonal comparison of utilities, is forced to fall back on an alternative definition of social welfare maximization. Rather than sum utilities across individuals, neoclassical welfare economics represents social welfare as a vector of individual welfare measures. Although this does not permit us to calculate a scalar measure of social welfare, it is still possible to compare two allocations of resources and determine whether one of them is clearly more desirable.

The standard neoclassical criterion for social welfare maximization, Pareto optimality (or Pareto efficiency), requires that there be no possible reallocation of

5 See Allen V. Kneese and William D. Schulze, "Ethics and Environmental Economics," Chapter 5 in Allen V. Kneese and James L. Sweeney, Handbook of Natural Resource and Energy Economics, vol. I (Amsterdam and New York: North-Holland, 1985), 191–220.

6 Joseph E. Stiglitz, "The Invisible Hand and Modern Welfare Economics," Working Paper No. 3641, National Bureau of Economic Research (Cambridge, MA, 1991).

7 Oskar R. Lange, "The Foundations of Welfare Economics," Econometrica 10 (1942): 215.

resources that could make at least one person better off while making no individual(s) worse off. As a rule, any policy change will have both "winners" and "losers." Hence, the practical criterion for evaluating government policies and programs is that they result in a "potential" Pareto improvement (i.e., that, in principle, the "winners" should be able to compensate the "losers"). Note that this "compensation" principle does not require that compensation actually occur, merely that it could occur.

Of course, the Pareto efficiency criterion does not assure us that any particular outcome will satisfy our criterion for social justice (or distributional equity). Neoclassical welfare economics, however, enables us to address the issue of equity within a market economy:

> The Second Fundamental Theorem of welfare economics has fundamental implications for how we think about economic organization. It says that we can separate out issues of economic efficiency from issues of equity. Economists need not concern themselves with value judgments; whatever the government's distributive objectives, it implements these through initial lump sum taxes and subsidies, and then leaves the market to work for itself.[8]

In practice, however, neoclassical environmental economists have addressed almost exclusively the issue of efficiency. "[D]iscussions of actual compensation have been avoided on the grounds that equity issues are outside the economists' realm."[9]

The basic tool of applied welfare economics, cost-benefit analysis, is an implementation of this Pareto efficiency criterion; if the benefits of a proposed policy change exceed their costs (or alternatively, if the benefit/cost ratio exceeds 1), then it would clearly be possible for the "winners" to compensate the "losers." Cost-benefit analysis, although rooted in neoclassical economics, bears the traces of classical economic assumptions:

> It is neo-classical in that it assumes the maximization of individual utilities rather than the utility of the whole, but it is classical in that in actual quantitative application it must, contrary to the neo-classical tradition, assume both measurable and comparable utility. However, it cannot actually measure utility, and to get around this fact, to exclude considerations of income distribution, and to maintain its logical integrity, it must make some very strong assumptions; for example, that the marginal utility of income is constant and equal for everyone. Under this assumption, in terms of maximizing net total utility, it does not matter who gets a dollar's worth of benefit or who bears a dollar's worth of costs.[10]

The neoclassical welfare economic paradigm is reflected in the formulation of sustainable development in terms of weak sustainability. "The weak sustainability position, held by many mainstream neoclassical economists (such as Solow and Weitzman), is that almost all kinds of natural capital can be substituted by

8 Stiglitz, op. cit., 6–7.

9 Clive L. Spash, "Economics, Ethics and Long-Term Environmental Damages," Environmental Ethics 15 (1993): 131.

10 Kneese and Schulze, op. cit., 206.

man-made capital."[11] To the extent that this assumption can be empirically validated, the Brundtland criterion that we reserve for future generations the same opportunities that we currently enjoy does not preclude either the depletion of exhaustible resources or, for that matter, global climate change. The neoclassical view of sustainability is informed by a faith in the workings of markets coupled with a technological optimism. These premises assure us that, as an exhaustible natural resource is depleted, its price will rise exponentially, and demand will ultimately go to zero. During this inexorable process, we will make transitions to other technologies, and ultimately the use of the exhaustible resource will be displaced by an inexhaustible "backstop" technology.[12]

The ecological economic critique of the neoclassical economic paradigm still operates within the assumptions of anthropocentric environmentalism. The "strong sustainability" criterion for sustainable development rejects the notion that natural and man-made capital are freely substitutable. The strong sustainability criterion requires that we preserve minimum quantities of natural capital stocks and ecosystem services, rather than allowing man-made capital to, over time, displace natural capital stocks.[13] However, the purpose for which nature is to be preserved is the satisfaction of human needs. The value placed on natural capital and ecosystem services is explicitly instrumental—current and future generations of people require them in order to satisfy our basic needs for clean air and water, food, and shelter.

Ecocentric Environmentalism

In contrast to anthropocentric environmentalism, and both the weak and strong forms of sustainability that are built on explicitly anthropocentric foundations, ecocentric environmentalism rejects the premise that human welfare is the primary measure of value. "Since the human species is not necessarily the most important species in the natural environment, priority should not be routinely given to human needs when dealing with environmental issues."[14] Modern

11 Robert U. Ayres, "On the Practical Limits to Substitution," Ecological Economics 61 (February, 2007): 115.

12 See Robert M. Solow, "The Economics of Resources or the Resources of Economics," The American Economic Review 64 (1974), Papers and Proceedings of the Eighty-sixth Annual Meeting of the American Economic Association, The Richard T. Ely Lecture, 1–14.

13 For a full exposition of the ecological economic critique of neoclassical environmental economics, see Herman E. Daly, "Georgescu-Roegen versus Solow/Stiglitz", Ecological Economics 22 (1997): 261–66. See also Robert M. Solow, "Reply: Georgescu-Roegen versus Solow/Stiglitz," ibid., 267–68; Joseph E. Stiglitz, "Reply: Georgescu-Roegen versus Solow/Stiglitz," ibid., 269–70, and Herman E. Daly, "Response to Solow/Stiglitz," ibid., 271–73. For an effort to operationalize the concept of strong sustainability, see Stefan Baumgartner and Martin F. Quaas, "Ecological-economic viability as a criterion of strong sustainability under uncertainty," Ecological Economics 68 (May, 2009): 2008–20.

14 David D. Kemp, Exploring Environmental Issues: An Integrated Approach, (London and New York: Routledge), 21.

ecocentric environmentalism can be traced to the work of Arne Naess, a Danish environmentalist. Deep ecology rejects the instrumental view of nature, as well as the technological optimism that underlies much of mainstream anthropocentric environmentalism. It seeks to restore the balance between man and nature that has been disturbed by both population and economic growth. If man is the problem, then the solution entails a rejection of human welfare as the primary desideratum of environmental policy.[15]

Lynn White goes further, attributing the adverse impacts of the human species on the biosphere to the biblical story of Creation that Christianity inherited from Judaism. White interprets the account found in the Book of Genesis:

> By gradual stages a loving and all-powerful God had created light and darkness, the heavenly bodies, the earth and all its plants, animals, birds, and fishes. Finally God had created Adam and, as an afterthought, Eve to keep man from being lonely. Man named all the animals, thus establishing his dominance over them. God planned all of this explicitly for man's benefit and rule; no item in the physical creation had any purpose save to serve man's purposes."[16]

White attributes our environmental crisis to our privileged position, separate from and superior to the rest of creation. Since the roots of our environmental crisis are primarily cultural or religious, a purely scientific or technological response is insufficient. Rather, we must reexamine our core values.[17]

15 Arne Naess and George Sessions, "Deep Ecology Platform", downloaded on 24 June 2009 from the Foundation for Deep Ecology, http://www.deepecology.org/platform.htm, formulates the governing principles of ecocentric environmentalism:

> 1. The well-being and flourishing of human and nonhuman life on Earth have value in themselves (synonyms: inherent worth; intrinsic value; inherent value). These values are independent of the usefulness of the nonhuman world for human purposes.
>
> 2. Richness and diversity of life forms contribute to the realization of these values and are also values in themselves.
>
> 3. Humans have no right to reduce this richness and diversity except to satisfy vital needs.
>
> 4. Present human interference with the nonhuman world is excessive, and the situation is rapidly worsening.
>
> 5. The flourishing of human life and cultures is compatible with a substantial decrease of the human population. The flourishing of nonhuman life requires such a decrease.
>
> 6. Policies must therefore be changed. The changes in policies affect basic economic, technological structures. The resulting state of affairs will be deeply different from the present.
>
> 7. The ideological change is mainly that of appreciating life quality (dwelling in situations of inherent worth) rather than adhering to an increasingly higher standard of living. There will be a profound awareness of the difference between big and great.
>
> 8. Those who subscribe to the foregoing points have an obligation directly or indirectly to participate in the attempt to implement the necessary changes.

16 Lynn White, "The Historical Roots of our Environmental Crisis," Science 155 (1967): 1, 205.

17 For a detailed examination of White's environmental philosophy, see Ben A. Minteer and Robert E. Manning, "An Appraisal of the Critique of Anthropocentrism and Three Lesser Known Themes" in Lynn White's "The Historical Roots of our Ecologic Crisis," Organization and Environment 18 (June 2005): 163–76.

Theocentric Environmentalism

White's reading of the sources of our "ecological crisis" has provoked a sustained reexamination of the Biblical view of man's relationship with nature. Grula suggests that the ecological crisis that is at the center of White's narrative stems from man's privileged place within Creation. In constructing a more earth-friendly theology, he begins by rejecting the "Judeo-Christian" concept of a Creator in favor of his concept of pantheism: "the doctrine that God is not a personality or transcendent supernatural being but that all laws, forces, manifestations, and so forth of the self-existing natural universe constitute an all-inclusive divine Unity."[18] This understanding of a God within nature has been articulated by Albert Einstein, who traces it to the writings of Spinoza: "I believe in Spinoza's God who reveals himself in the harmony of all that exists, but not in a God who concerns himself with the fate and actions of human beings."[19]

Naess looks for inspiration to nonanthropocentric theologies based on the writings of both Spinoza and the Japanese philosopher Dōgen (1200–1253). "Dōgen lays a non-dualistic, non-anthropocentric grounding common to all beings (sentient and non-sentient) that reveals their interconnectedness."[20]

Tucker frames the debate in terms of the relationship between man and the rest of creation as viewed by the Hebrew Bible. Tucker counterposes two readings of Genesis 1:28 ("And God blessed them, and God said to them, 'Be fruitful and multiply and fill the earth and subdue it, and rule over the fish of the sea and over the fowl of the sky and over all the beasts that tread upon the earth'"). The first construes the exhortation to "subdue" and "rule" as permission to exploit; the second, as giving man the responsibility of stewardship. However, "those two alternatives rest on a common foundation, the assumption that humanity stands over the world."[21]

Williams and Millington clearly delineate the common assumptions shared by neoclassical environmental economics and the traditional Judeo-Christian reading of the Creation narrative. They identify three common elements: "the perception that people are separate from nature; the idea that nature is a 'resource' to be used for the benefit of society or individuals; and the view that we have the right to dominate nature. Taken together, these three strands represent what might be considered a Judeo-Christian conceptualization of the connection between people and nature."[22]

A critique of this attempt to equate anthropocentric and theocentric environmentalisms argues that our ecological crisis stems not from a Biblical perspective

18 John W. Grula, "Pantheism Reconstructed: Ecotheology as a Successor to the Judeo-Christian, Enlightenment, and Postmodernist Paradigms," Zygon 43 (March 2008): 160.

19 John W. Grula, op. cit., 176.

20 Deane Curtin, "Dōgen, Deep Ecology, and the Ecological Self," Environmental Ethics 16 (1994): 197.

21 Gene M. Tucker, "Rain on a Land Where No One Lives: The Hebrew Bible on the Environment," Journal of Biblical Literature 116 (1997): 5.

22 Colin C. Williams and Andrew C. Millington, "The Diverse and Contested Meanings of Sustainable Development," The Geographical Journal 170 (June 2004): 100.

that the world was created for human benefit but rather from post-Enlightenment secularism: "The ecological crisis, wrought by exploitative attitudes toward non-human life (and, in a wider sense, to some human life) and by the careless despoliation of God's world, is surely a manifestation of the broader problems of secularism: a loss of the sense of the sacred and a lack of respect for divine law."[23]

Fisher and van Utt read the Creation narrative as an affirmation of the responsibility of stewardship: "In its biblical context, Genesis 1 serves as an affirmation of the moral or theological context of creation, not as an explanation of how creation happened. As Brueggemann puts it, the world 'belongs to God, is formed and willed by God, is blessed by God with abundance, [and] is to be cared for by the human creatures who are deeply empowered by God, but who are seriously restrained by God.'"[24] This vision of the ethical relationship between man and nature that emerges from the Biblical narrative is strongly contrasted with the pagan Creation myths found in the non-Jewish Middle East:

> In the Enuma Elish, creation emerges from warfare within the pantheon of Babylonian gods, in a tale of duplicity in which the main characters are capricious and give no sense of a larger purpose beyond personal triumph. Genesis 1 transforms the story so as to reflect the Israelite understanding of God as majestic, trustworthy, and purposeful, an understanding that sees creation as revelatory of divine trustworthiness and invites humans to find fulfillment by living in ways that image God's character. The Enuma Elish depicts creation as the result of conflict between competing interests. Genesis insists that creation is the result of a single creative impulse at the heart of all that is, that creation itself is fundamentally good, and that life, spirit, and courage are gifts from that source, gifts to be trusted and lived as creatively and as faithfully as possible.[25]

Friedman and Klein elaborate on the stewardship reading of Genesis 1:28: "God did indeed bless Adam and Eve and say to them: Be fruitful, and multiply, and replenish the earth and subdue it; and have dominion over the fish of the sea, and over the fowl of the air, and over every living thing that creeps upon the earth." The meaning of the phrases "have dominion" and "subdue" does not allow us to harm the environment. Adam and Eve were caretakers and their job was to *protect* the land, not to harm. The *Midrash* (Ecclesiastes *Rabba* 7:13) makes this quite clear: "When God created Adam, He took him and led him round all the trees of the Garden of Eden, and said to him, 'See My works, how beautiful and praiseworthy they are! Now all that I have created, I created for your benefit. Be careful that you do not ruin and destroy my world; for if you destroy it there is no one to repair it after you.'"[26]

With limited exceptions, these approaches begin by reexamining the creation story for clues to a putative Judeo-Christian environmental attitude. This approach

23 Dee Carter, "Unholy Alliances: Religion, Science and Environment," Zygon 36 (June 2001): 359.

24 George W. Fisher and Gretchen van Utt, "Science, Religious Naturalism, and Biblical Theology: Ground for the Emergence of Sustainable Living," Zygon 42 (December 2007): 933.

25 George W. Fisher and Gretchen van Utt, op. cit., 936.

26 Hershey H. Friedman and Yehuda L. Klein, "Respect for God's World: The Biblical and Rabbinic Foundations of Environmentalism," Jewish Law, posted April 25, 2007, downloaded on 29 June 2009 from http://www.jlaw.com/Articles/environmentbible2.pdf, p. 8.

can provide at best a limited, and at worst a misleading, picture of the foundations of a Jewish environmental ethic. While the Bible informs and, arguably, constitutionally underpins Western society and its institutions, it does not do so, directly, on a communal scale. Individuals may cultivate personal relationships with G-d through the revealed word, but religious communities access the Biblical word as mediated through clergy by means of religious scholarship and religious training or instruction.

From a Jewish perspective, it is largely as futile to seek substantive insight into societal worldviews as to derive anew the intricacies of *halakhah* (Jewish law) from a raw, unmediated reading of Biblical accounts and declarations. Societal attitudes form normatively, not by repeated reintroductions to original Biblical texts, but rather through a cadre of recognized and accepted doctrines built upon those texts and effectively canonized as authoritative. The process of discovering the role of the Biblical word as an engine of communal acts requires an examination not only of exegetical Midrashic and Talmudic literature but also of the most standard, classical expositors chiefly of the medieval Jewish academies. In surveying what Judaism has to say about a given subject, the researcher is unfettered in the pursuit of Jewish statements on those subjects. However, in seeking to ascertain what a communally sanctioned Jewish attitude on that same subject might be, it is most sound to focus on those texts that are most universally taught and transmitted to achieve normative curricular objectives.[27]

In this light, statements such as, "Finally God had created Adam and, as an afterthought, Eve to keep man from being lonely. Man named all the animals, thus establishing his dominance over them,"[28] is revealed as being ultra-textual and glib. An approach steeped in the Jewish traditions that have formed the core curriculum of Jewish religious instruction would necessarily eschew the very suggestion of a divine "afterthought." The goal of establishing mankind's "dominance" over the animals is a projection and a presumption to be found nowhere in the text. Moreover, the textual order is reversed; the naming of the animals precedes the formation of Eve, at least in the account that actually discusses the naming of the animals.[29]

As it relates to humanity's relationship to the natural world, this story has not traditionally been interpreted as sanctioning human subjugation and dominance over nature. The creation of Eve does not relate to Adam's "being lonely." It is not good for Adam to be alone, because the state of Adam's singular status in the created world would have led him to the flawed conclusion that he is as much the unchallenged ruler of the earth as G-d is of the heavens. Under this false assumption, Adam would have mistakenly believed the earth to be his own kingdom, uninhibited by

27 Undoubtedly, these have historically included the writings of the likes of R. Solomon b. Isaac (Rashi, France, 1040–1105), Maimonides (Rambam, Egypt, 1135–1204), and Nahmanides (Ramban, Spain, 1194–1270).

28 Lynn White, op. cit.

29 Genesis 2:18–23.

the rule of G-d, a neighboring sovereign.[30] Having once been singular, only Adam, as opposed to other creatures, could be in awe of the unfathomable unity of G-d. Having lost that status, Adam and Eve, as severed parts of a whole, are forced to acknowledge that they are not truly indivisible independent individuals, but are rather incomplete components of the greater whole of creation on which they must rely for survival. The separation of Adam into Adam and Eve was thus pedagogical, not an afterthought.

The naming of the animals is an apparent interlude, separating the narration of finding no suitable mate for Adam among the other creatures from the formation of Eve. Adam observes the nature and needs of each creature. It is more consistent with traditional Jewish thought to state that Adam discovered the name of each creature rather than that he assigned it: "Whatever Adam called each [animal] is [in fact] its name."[31] As such, the naming process instructed Adam of his capacity for reasoning, for understanding through observation the essence of the natural world. It was a step forward in the advent of spoken, rather than silent cognitive, language, which would become necessary once Adam was mandated to partner with another party, Eve, in the propagation of humanity. Most significantly, it is immediately after the naming interlude that Adam is first called Adam without the definite article[32]; in other words, Adam, too, was named in this process.

Adam was the last of all that was created. On the one hand, it was only fitting that this unique being enter a world replete with all of the resources necessary to fill every need.[33] Mankind was the final creation, but the ultimate purpose of creation. In the words of the liturgical poem, *Lekha Dodi*: "Last in creation, first in [G-d's] thought."[34] Nonetheless, should people turn away from G-d, they are to be reminded that the mosquito preceded them in the order of creation.[35] In this sense, man was, dare it be said, a mere afterthought. People may therefore exert dominion over the animals, but only to the degree that they do so with a sense of grave responsibility as ethical agents. This right goes not to the issue only of stewardship,[36] but to the very

30 Rashi, Genesis 2:18; cf. e.g. Genesis 1:24, stating simply that G-d created Adam, "male and female created He them." See R. Aryeh Kaplan (New York, 1935-1982), trans., The Living Torah (Brooklyn, NY: Moznaim Publishing Corp., 1981). Moreover, conventional Jewish tradition accepts an interpretation of this verse that views Adam as having initially been formed as a dual person, essentially a male and a female joined as one, to be separated into two individuals after the recounted incident of naming the animals. Thus, it was not so much that Eve was created as an afterthought as that man and woman would, as the other creatures, exist as separate beings rather than as a combined, self-contained being encompassing both genders.

31 See the commentaries of R. Obadiah b. Jacob Sforno (Italy c. 1470–c. 1550) and Ramban on Genesis 2:19.

32 Genesis 2:20. (i.e., before this point, the Bible refers to Adam as Ha-Adam, the man. Now, for the first time, it uses Adam as a proper name.)

33 B Sanhedrin 38b.

34 "Sof Maase, be-mahashava tehilah." Lekha Dodi was composed by R. Solomon b. Moses ha-Levi Alkabez (c. 1505–1584), a sixteenth-century Kabbalist who lived in Safed, Ottoman Palestine. See Rabbi Nissen Mangel, trans., Siddur Tehillat Hashem, (Brooklyn, NY: Kehot Publication Society, 1978), 132.

35 B Sanhedrin, ibid.

36 An example of the responsibility for stewardship is found in Noah's mandate to care for all of the animals with him in the ark. At one point, Noah grew weary of the task and did not perform it with the requisite enthusiasm. Upon missing the appointed mealtime for the lions, he was mauled by the beast. See Rashi to Genesis 7:23. This story can be understood as an indication that humanity's right to exert dominion over nature is coterminous with an absolute responsibility to care for nature. To the extent that man assumes the role of steward, the obligation to

entitlement not to be dominated by natural forces altogether. When people turn from G-d, they become mere elements of nature, food for predators. Mankind in furtherance of G-d's will may utilize resources for development, but nature is equally entitled to dominate mankind when the latter shirks that duty.[37]

The traditional Jewish view is that the primary objective not only of mankind but also of all Creation is to serve G-d. This understanding reconciles mankind's multiple positions within nature, as subservient to, a part of, and at the pinnacle of Creation. A legitimate critique of ecocentric environmentalism is that it tends highly to anthropomorphize natural elements.[38] As such, this orientation differs little from an anthropocentric viewpoint in that it imposes human desires on nonhuman creatures, presuming these desires to be coterminous. Without delving into the psychology, such as it is, of the nonhuman animate, however, there is no knowing whether human and nonhuman incentives are, in fact, parallel at their cores. Moreover, the ecocentric view centralizes the maximization of all life, the right to live and bloom, as an undisputed normative good, but it is just as tenable to view the preservation of a pristine natural environment as assuming that role. From that perspective, all life is intrusive, parasitic, destructive, and wasteful. If the anthropomorphic tendencies can be extended to the inanimate realm, however, the perspective changes. Theocentric environmentalism, informed by classical Jewish sources, can effectuate this change.

Judaism views all of creation as an affirmation of G-d's ultimate glory and dominion. If humanity, fauna, flora, and the inanimate all share an inherent imperative to serve G-d's will, all must equally acknowledge and accept their respective roles and responsibilities within that complex divine will. Thus, the animal that must be sacrificed exults in the opportunity to do so, but the animal that is wantonly slaughtered is entitled to justice. Concomitantly, the person who sacrifices the

---

do so responsibly is absolute. As a result of any negligence in that undertaking, man is legitimate prey and rightfully succumbs to the power of nature demanding its due. A complementary point can be derived from the understanding that only the blood, housing the soul, of domesticated bovine and ovine cattle can serve to atone for the sullied soul of a sinning person through sacrifice on the altar in the Temple. See Ramban to Leviticus 17:11–12. One component of the complex living soul is its drive for sustenance; the soul of each creature is defined by its unique diet. See Rambam, Shemona Perakim, chapter 1. Thus, as domesticated animals rely on humans for their sustenance, their souls are constituted of a "human element," op. cit., and can serve as a sacrificial surrogate for the human soul. By contrast, upon slaughtering a wild animal for its meat, the butcher is required to cover the blood with dirt, thus, as it were, returning the soul of that animal to the earth, the source of its sustenance. Ramban, ibid.

37 See commentary of R. Hayyim b. Moses ibn Attar (Morocco, 1696–1743), the Or ha-Hayyim, on Genesis 1:28.

38 See Arne Naess, The Shallow and the Deep, reprinted in Mark J. Smith, Thinking Through the Environment: A Reader, (London and New York: Routledge, 1999) 197: "The so-called struggle of life, and survival of the fittest, should be interpreted in the sense of ability to coexist and cooperate in complex relationships, rather than ability to kill, exploit, and suppress. 'Live and let live' is a more powerful ecological principle than 'Either you or me.'" One is left wondering how the proponent of this philosophy would proselytize in favor of it among the nonhuman world. One also wonders why life, per se, becomes the measure of value, equating "seals and whales" with "human tribes and cultures." It is a philosophy that would prove as successful if the planet were to be covered with moss with no other surviving life forms to hinder its growth. The promotion of "life," human, animal, or vegetable, is certainly an invitation to the exploitation of mineral resources, and Naess advances no principled argument to counter the proposition that the simple conservation of resources, and thus the diminishing of aggregate "life," should be a primary objective. Clearly, Naess is projecting human values on the inanimate world.

first animal is rewarded, while the other is punished. The lion's nature is to tear its prey, and the bear's nature is to overwhelm its prey;[39] each is entitled to behave in accordance with its divinely ordained nature, and in that natural cycle, the gazelle must revel in its role as well.

The inanimate, as well, shares the desire to serve the divine will. Lowly rocks are rewarded by unification into a single stone to share in the privilege of nestling the patriarch Jacob's head as he sleeps and dreams of the ladder ascending to heaven, foretelling the future of Israel.[40] Mighty mountains, by contrast, vie for the honor of being the site of Moses' receipt of the Law, but only the lowliest mountain, Sinai, is found worthy of this role, precisely because it could see within itself no topographical superiority.[41] The frogs of the second Egyptian plague jump into ovens in their zeal to fulfill their duty to constitute a plague.[42] Moreover, in bringing the plagues upon the Egyptians, Moses delegates those that would affect Egyptian soil (such as the lice) and Egyptian waters (such as the blood) because he acknowledged acts of kindness that these inanimate geographical elements had bestowed upon him.[43]

Conclusion

Several factors compel the articulation of a theocentrically orientated framework for environmental discourse. First, the tensions that inhere in the respective consequences of adopting either an anthropocentric or an ecocentric foundation for environmental thought would seem of necessity to demand that theoreticians essentially "take sides," espousing one vantage point at the expense of the other. To the extent that the human is apart from the environment in an anthropocentric schema, the environment loses as humans maximize their desiderata. Concomitantly, humans can "win," from an ecocentric perspective, only once they have homogenized those desiderata to where they blend with those of other living and blooming creatures. In this sense, the dichotomy engenders more a dialectic than a dialogue.

39 B Ta'anit 8a. In the end of days, the other animals will challenge the snake for biting and killing people for no useful purpose, such as eating. The snake will retort, "And what is the inherent value of the tongued one [i.e., mankind] anyway?" Humans gossip, hurting others, while themselves receiving no useful benefit. Such mean-spirited behavior forfeits the human entitlement to survive by dominating the natural world and entitles the snake to commit its seemingly gratuitously deadly acts. The difference between humans and snakes, however, is that the snake acts thus by its nature and therefore has the satisfaction of actualizing that ordained nature, whereas the comparable human behavior is an abrogation of human nature as defined through the imposition of divine mandate. See the commentary of R. Samuel Eliezer b. Judah ha-Levi Edels (Maharsha, Poland, 1555–1631) to B Bava Kamma 2b.

40 Rashi, Genesis 28:18.

41 B Megilla 29.

42 B Pesahim 53b.

43 Exodus Rabba, Ch. 10.

A theocentric environmentalist view allows the pursuit of goals common both to humanity as a foil to nature and to nature as a context for humanity. Of course, the introduction of any additional superseding element into a discourse would alter the narrative. Were a meteor to impend the imminent and literal destruction of the entire planet, the question of saving the spotted owls or of storing the nuclear waste would be rendered quickly moot, or its resolution certainly deferred. That the intruding element in theocentric environmentalism is religion, however, means that the courses of conflicting narratives can converge and proceed, rather than abort or surrender. In monotheistic religion, G-d is the focus of ultimate concern and, in being beyond the petty concerns of the mortal and temporal, whether human or not, religion provides fixed and immutable targets toward which to direct practical applications. In Judaism, the cognomen as "*makom*," or "space," is used for G-d, as the *Midrash* expounds, "for G-d is the space in which the World is situated,"[44] and not vice versa. Thus, G-d is the context for all of the potentially conflicting environmental theories, but it is that very fact that impels the attainment of a synthesis among them.

The need for a coherent theocentric environmentalist theory also arises from the imperative purpose that religion tends to inject into any speculative endeavor. "Know G-d in all of your ways," says King Solomon.[45] As Thomas Cahill has observed, the Hebrew Bible introduced the conception of history as linear, as proceeding through tribulation toward an ineluctable culmination.[46] Thus, the theological imperative infuses urgency into discussions that concern all topics of any gravity. For certain, an issue so encompassing as the environment warrants theological explication. The environment is, after all, the medium in which nature, life, and humanity will all find themselves at the end of days. Sensitivity to the needs of the future, implicit in the pursuit of sustainability, is an explicit mandate upon the religious practitioner who is perpetually conscious of existing chiefly as part of a continuum linking a distinctly identifiable past to a certain, if often elusive, future. The Messiah will have to arrive somewhere, and it is the responsibility of the religious adherent if not to tend that place, certainly not to lay waste to it.

Both the anthropocentric and the ecocentric viewpoints fall short of providing sufficient urgency despite exhortations regarding sustainability. Both of these doctrinaire positions largely extrapolate the future from the present. Anthropocentric environmentalist thinkers seek the meeting of present needs "without compromising the ability of future generations to meet their own needs," whatever those might be. The key to this accomplishment would be to utilize only so many resources as are absolutely necessary to achieve a present need—the only imperative, presumably, being the maximization of efficiency. Responsibility for the future, at its core, thus, ends at allowing future generations to use what is left. Ecocentric doctrine

44 Genesis Rabba 68:9.

45 Proverbs 3:6, "In all thy ways acknowledge him, and he shall direct thy paths."

46 Thomas Cahill, The Gifts of the Jews: How a Tribe of Desert Nomads Changed the Way Everyone Thinks and Feels (New York: Nan A. Talese—Doubleday, 1998), 128–32.

focuses squarely on preservation, freezing nature in an Edenic status quo, expending without guilt never a diminishing species nor a dwindling resource. The compulsive and arguably quixotic quest for entirely renewable resources fits this model because of the shared goal, at least conceptually, which prioritizes the attainment of equilibrium, or stability, above development.

A fully articulated theocentric environmentalism, however, would acknowledge future generations as being fully entitled to meet needs by adventitious means, because those generations are neither competitors with the present generation for scarce resources nor mere temporary invaders upon a resentful host. Rather, Mosaic religions view the final, future generation as being the culmination of all preceding endeavors, the climax of the unfolding narrative that history is. From an environmentalist standpoint, meeting the needs of future generations is the current, urgent, imperative duty of each generation in its time.

The last argument militating in favor of theocentric environmentalism that will be mentioned here is that its focus is not so much theological as teleological. It is teleological not just in the sense that it would recognize design, and putatively divine intelligence or purpose, in creation. Rather, such a theory would be teleological in that it strives for a comprehensive explanation rather than a set of convenient technological applications. As religion acknowledges G-d as the metacontext of all contexts, theocentric environmentalism would have to be a fully encompassing theory of the whole of environmental speculation. Thus, no theory that situates any concern other than G-d in a central role, whether anthropocentric, ecocentric, or other-centric, can accomplish that which a theocentric theory can. Only a theocentric perspective can put an end to decisions about which needs must be subordinated to which in order for economic principles to prevail in the environmentalist arena. All needs are equally subordinate to G-d's will and to G-d's demands. Only in that regard can it be earnestly be said that the needs of all are of truly equal value.

The Bible and the *halakhah* that it engenders describe an agrarian society. Jewish history, however, has proven that they do not necessarily prescribe one. The Torah foretells the ideal of a Jewish people living on its land and at one with its land. The nation must behave in a manner that permits it to retain its entitlement to realize that ideal. The people must preserve certain elements of the land without exacting permanent changes.[47] The prophets recount the consequences of that covenant both in its observance and in its breach.

The majority of Jews throughout the millennia of Jewish history have not had the opportunity to live this ostensible ideal. The Jews, driven from their land, have spent centuries in other lands, rarely owning and cultivating property and more often engaged in chiefly commercial, more portable pursuits. Yet, they have at all

47 Examples include the biblical injunction against the destruction of fruit trees. See discussion in Friedman and Klein, n. 27, supra. Another example is the rule that all conveyed lands revert to the heirs of the first grantees of such land at each Jubilee year. Leviticus 25:11; see also Rashi ad loc.

times annually read the Torah in its entirety, studied Talmudic passages relating to farming, and celebrated a cycle of festivals so agriculturally significant as to tie them not only to their land but to land itself.

In administering institutions of learning, a curriculum develops. Once, Jewish children began their studies with the Book of Leviticus, emphasizing purity.[48] In modern times, Jewish schools are more likely to begin from Genesis. Curricular decisions meet the educational objectives demanded by circumstance.[49] Indeed, even since the early days of the Jewish exile, Jewish learning may have been said to have deemphasized speculation into the place of humanity in the natural world.[50]

As humanity today grapples with issues of sustainability, economic and environmental theorists can benefit from a serious exploration of Jewish sources for the philosophical underpinnings of a Judaically informed theocentric model. So, too, Jewish educators can seek opportunities to imbue the curriculum with an awareness of the critical environmental issues that contemporary societies face. Perhaps the eventual synthesis of these converging areas of thought will prove that the most daunting challenges of modernity will find their resolution in the most durable wisdom of antiquity.

SELECTED BIBLIOGRAPHY

Bible:
Genesis 1:24, 28; 2:18-23; 28:18 and commentaries.
Carter, Dee. "Unholy Alliances: Religion, Science and Environment." *Zygon* 36 (June, 2001): 357–72.

48 Leviticus Rabba, Ch. 4.

49 An example of the protean nature of the essential Jewish educational curriculum emerges from an analysis of Tosafot, (medieval Talmudic glosses, France and Germany, twelfth–fourteenth centuries) to B Sota 3a (s.v. rabbi). The Talmud there debates whether a particular act mentioned in the Torah is permissive or mandatory. Tosafot expresses wonder at the very question. Citing B Makkot 23b, Tosafot notes that there are precisely 613 commandments, no more and no fewer. Thus, the question of whether a provision is mandatory or permissive would affect this count; if it is permissive, there would be only 612 commandments. Tosafot does resolve the issue, but the very problem that is presented illustrates several points. First, it is clear that Tosafot does not view the proposition of there being 613 commandments as being common knowledge. Otherwise, no source text would be cited. Moreover, were this proposition presumed to be common knowledge, so, too, would a standard resolution of the Sota dilemma be commonly taught. Arguably, today this Jewish curricular item is more commonly known than its Talmudic source text, and it is so commonly known that few would be as troubled as Tosafot was by the discussion in Sota. It is thought that the codification of lists of commandments was undertaken in reaction to similar activities undertaken by the Karaites, centered chiefly in Iraq during the middle ages, the era of the Tosafot. See Jacob Neusner, Encyclopedia of Judaism: Halakhot Gedolot and Halakhot Pesukot (New York: Continuum Publishing, 2000). As such, the issue would surely have vexed Sephardic educators, seeking to keep Jewish children within the acceptable ambit of traditional, Rabbinic Judaism, than it would educators in the Ashkenazic world of the Tosafot of Germany, England, and France. Indeed, the lists of commandments were compiled chiefly by Sephardic sages during that era.

50 It is noteworthy that the Babylonian Talmud is practically devoid of Amoraic comment on the Mishnaic Order of Zeraim, which is devoted to the agricultural ambit of Halakha.

Fisher, George W., and Gretchen van Utt. "Science, Religious Naturalism, and Biblical Theology: Ground for the Emergence of Sustainable Living." *Zygon* 42 (December 2007): 929–43.

Hoffman, Andrew J., and Lloyd E. Sandelands. "Getting Right with Nature: Anthropocentrism, Ecocentrism, and Theocentrism." *Organization and Environment* 18 (June, 2005): 141–62.

Kneese, Allen V., and William D. Schulze. "Ethics and Environmental Economics." Chapter 5 in Allen V. Kneese and James L. Sweeney, *Handbook of Natural Resource and Energy Economics*, vol. I. Amsterdam and New York: North-Holland, 1985, 191–220.

Lange, Oskar R. "The Foundations of Welfare Economics." *Econometrica* 10 (1942): 215–28.

Levi, Yehudah. "The Problem of Ecology: Living at the Expense of Future Generations." *be-Or ha-Torah* 10 (1997): 31–38.

Naess, Arne., and George Sessions. "Deep Ecology Platform." Last downloaded on 24 June 2009 from the Foundation for Deep Ecology, http://www.deepecology.org/platform.htm.

Solow, Robert M. "The Economics of Resources or the Resources of Economics." *The American Economic Review* 64 (1974), Papers and Proceedings of the Eighty-sixth Annual Meeting of the American Economic Association, The Richard T. Ely Lecture, 1–14.

Tucker, Gene M. "Rain on a Land Where No One Lives: The Hebrew Bible on the Environment." *Journal of Biblical Literature* 116 (1997): 3–17.

Waskow, Arthur., ed. *Torah of the Earth, Exploring 4,000 Years of Ecology in Jewish Thought, Vol.1: Biblical Israel & Rabbinic Judaism, Vol. 2: Zionism & Eco-Judaism.* Woodstock, VT: Jewish Lights Publishing, 2000.

White, Lynn. "The Historical Roots of our Environmental Crisis," *Science* 155 (1967): 1, 203–07.

Williams, Colin C., and Andrew C. Millington. "The Diverse and Contested Meanings of Sustainable Development." *The Geographical Journal* 170 (June, 2004): 99–104.

World Commission on Environment and Development. *Our Common Future.* London and New York: Oxford University Press, 1987.

CHAPTER 21

THE GLOBAL RECESSION OF 2007–2009: THE MORAL FACTOR AND JEWISH LAW

AARON LEVINE

Introduction

In December 2007, the United States economy plunged into the longest and deepest downturn since the Great Depression. The driving force behind the recession was the widespread failure of the subprime mortgage market, the segment of the home mortgage market extending loans to households with impaired credit histories and with little or no documentation of income. The collapse of that sector occurred in a rapid succession of events beginning with the fall of Countrywide Financial in January 2008, followed by the sale of Bear Stearns to JP Morgan Chase, the government takeover of Fannie Mae and Freddie Mac, the bankruptcy of Lehman Brothers, the takeover of Merrill Lynch by Bank of America, and the massive government loans to AIG, which eventually totaled $182.5 billion. The effects of these failures culminated in two massive government bailouts, one by the Bush administration costing taxpayers $700 billion, and another by the Obama administration costing $787 billion.

Jewish law has much to say about the current economic malaise. It can describe the collapse of the subprime market in moral terms and suggest theologically based measures to prevent a recurrence. Moreover, in an economy governed by Jewish law, the subprime market would never grow large and would therefore never reach a level where its collapse could have global ramifications.

The Moral Failure of the Subprime Players

Given the size of the troubled mortgage market, which includes not only the subprime market but also the Alt-A and option ARM segments (defined below), totaling $2.5 trillion dollars in 2008,[1] there is plenty of blame to go around amongst market players.

First, some borrowers were guilty of incurring mortgage debt they knew they could not repay. An example is the 2/28 mortgage, which calls for a fixed rate of interest and very affordable low-installment payments during the first two years, but a variable rate of interest based on current market rates and fully amortized payments for the next twenty-eight years. Accordingly, even if interest rates do not rise, the full amortization means that the installments for the third year can easily amount to more than twice the corresponding payments during the first two years.[2]

Taking on debt obligations that an individual knows he will not, or even may not, meet violates Jewish law's "good faith" imperative, which states that, if an individual makes a commitment, he must intend to fulfill it.[3]

A mortgagor might argue that, although he will not be able to afford the monthly payments after the first two years based on his income, he is still not in violation of the "good faith" imperative because he is relying on an anticipated decline in interest rates or increase in home prices to allow him to meet his obligations. If interest rates drop below the fixed rate he pays during the first two years, he may be able to refinance his mortgage with an affordable monthly installment. Alternatively, if home prices rise, he can either refinance or meet his mortgage obligation by selling his home and renting an apartment to live in.

1 For treatment of Alt-A and option ARM mortgages, see discussion in text accompanying endnotes 3 and 11. In 2008, the subprime and Alt-A markets were $1 trillion each, while the option ARMs market was approximately $500 billion. "A Second Mortgage Disaster on the Horizon?" (CBS News, "60 Minutes," December 14, 2008).

2 Another example of mortgage undertaking that the borrower knows is unaffordable is the negative amortization mortgage loan. In the initial periods, installments are so low that they do not even include interest. The catch is that the unpaid accrued interest is capitalized into the outstanding principal balance. As a result, the loan balance increases by the amount of the unpaid interest on a monthly basis. Negative amortization can continue for a maximum of five years. It also ends when the outstanding balance becomes fifteen percent higher than the principal amount. At that point, called the reset period, the payment increases to a full interest-plus-principal payment. Typically, when the recast kicks in, the debtor will be saddled with a monthly payment three times what it was.

3 BT *Bava Metsi'a* 49a. The duty to ensure that a commitment is made sincerely is referred to as the *hin tsedek* imperative. Abbayei derives the prohibition against making an insincere promise at *Bava Metsi'a* 49a in the following manner: In connection with the Biblical prohibition against false weights and measures, the Torah writes: "Just [*tsedek*] balances, just weights, a just *ephah*, and a just *hin* you shall have" (Leviticus 19:36). Because the *hin* is a measure of smaller capacity than the *ephah*, its mention seems superfluous. If accuracy is required of measures of large capacity, it is certainly required in measures of small capacity. This apparent superfluity leads Abbayei to connect *hin* with the Aramaic word for "yes," *hen*, and he interprets the phrase thus: Be certain that your "yes" is *tsedek* (sincere) and (by extension) be certain that your "no" is *tsedek* (sincere). If an individual makes a commitment or offer, he should fully intend to carry it out.

The Talmudic analogue of an asset-backed loan is God's guarantee to anyone who takes out a loan to finance his Sabbath needs: "Borrow on My account and I will repay [the creditor]." God's guarantee is not a blanket one. Instead, it applies when the borrower does not have cash to repay the loan, but he can repay by liquidating an asset that he owns. Ordinarily, taking out a loan on this basis is prohibited, but, because of the Divine guarantee, making this type of commitment to finance Sabbath needs is not unethical.[4]

Given that the asset-based Sabbath loan is permissible only because of a specific Divine guarantee, it follows that asset-based loans are generally prohibited because the borrower's "good faith" intention to repay is not objectively evident. Selling the asset to repay the debt will likely result in a lower standard of living or a reduced sense of economic security for the borrower, and he may therefore refuse to do so. Moreover, if the asset is thinly traded, liquidating it may fetch a disappointing price, sometimes so low that the proceeds of the sale will prove inadequate to pay off the loan.

Reinforcing the notion that taking on an asset-based loan is unethical is the ruling that a borrower may not incur "unnecessary expenditures" that impair his ability to pay off his outstanding debt. Even charitable giving is considered an "unnecessary expenditure" if it will impair his ability to repay.[5] Such conduct brands the borrower a wicked person.[6] If the law regulates the borrower's *spending* while the debt is outstanding, entering into the loan unable or questionably able to repay surely violates the "good faith" imperative.

In his treatment of the parameters Jewish law sets for ethical borrowing, R. Shimon Malkah (Israel, contemporary) posits that, if the borrower assesses that his income stream is inadequate to pay back the loan, but he sincerely believes that God will orchestrate events to make the payments possible, it is nevertheless unethical for him to commit to make the payments.[7] The underlying basis for his ruling is Jewish law's attitude toward an asset-based loan, as discussed.

Taking on an asset-based debt is unethical even in a scenario where we can infer that the lender (*L*) is fully aware of the risks and proceeds with the loan anyway. One such scenario is where *L* does not require the borrower (*B*) to document his income. *L* thereby indicates that he is fully aware of the risk of default and is relying on the appreciation of home values or the decline of interest rates to protect the value of his investment. *L*'s acceptance of risk is not, however, the equivalent of telling *B* that he will forgive the loan if *B* is unable to repay it, and therefore it does not render *B*'s commitment ethical. *B* still lacks objectively demonstrated "good faith."

Analogous is the law's treatment of a party's waiver to his entitlement in a commercial transaction involving *ona'ah* (price fraud). The law of *ona'ah* prohibits an

4 R. Joshua Boaz b. Simon Barukh (Spain, mid-sixteenth century), *Ein Mishpat* to *Tosafot, Beitsah* 15b.

5 R. Simeon Malkah, *Halva'ah le-Or ha-Halakhah* (Jerusalem: 1997), p. 229.

6 R. Joseph Caro (Israel, 1488–1575), *Shulhan Arukh, Hoshen Mishpat* 97:4, as interpreted by R. Joshua b. Alexander ha-Kohen Falk (Poland, 1555–1614), *Sema* to *Shulhan Arukh*, op. cit., note 5.

7 *Halva'ah le-Or Halakhah*, op. cit., 239–40.

individual from concluding a commercial transaction at a price more favorable to himself than the competitive norm. Depending on how much the price diverges from the competitive norm, the plaintiff may be entitled either to cancel the transaction or to demand a price adjustment.[8] If, however, the buyer (*B*) declares in advance to the seller that, if the transaction is found to involve *ona'ah*, he waives his rights in the matter, *B*'s advance declaration lacks specificity and his *ona'ah* rights are not deemed waived. The specificity condition is satisfied only when *B* quantifies the maximum entitlement he is willing to forgo upon discovery of *ona'ah*.[9]

Based on the specificity condition, unless *L* stipulates in advance a maximum amount he is willing to forgo as a result of *B*'s inability to pay, *L*'s presumed knowledge of the risk he incurs by entering into the loan does not constitute a waiver of any amount due him.

Second, some mortgage brokers misled their clients about the downsides and risks involved in what they were undertaking. Proffering ill-suited advice (*lifnei ivver*)[10] and misleading someone by creating a false impression (*geneivat da'at*)[11] are violations of Jewish business ethics. Moreover, the lender is obligated to disclose in a forthright manner[12] all the flaws[13] of his mortgage product. This means that a mortgage broker must fully explain the meaning and implications of the standard features of subprime loans, such as negative amortization and prepayment penalties.

Since Jewish law places the onus on the mortgage broker to disclose all the risks the mortgage product entails, shifting the responsibility to discover those risks onto the borrower amounts to a "bait and switch" tactic.[14] Moreover, even if the borrower agrees up front to discover the defects on his own and to relieve the mortgage broker of his disclosure duty, the specificity requirement for waivers, discussed above, must be met.

8 For the sources of the *ona'ah* prohibition and the application of this prohibition to the modern marketplace, see Aaron Levine, "*Ona'ah* and the Operation of the Modern Marketplace," *Jewish Law Annual* 14 (2003): 225–58.

9 Maimonides (Rambam, Egypt, 1135–1204), *Mishneh Torah, Mekhirah* 13:3-4; R. Jacob b. Asher (Germany, 1270–1343), *Tur, Hoshen Mishpat* 227; *Shulhan Arukh*, op. cit., 227:21; R. Jehiel Michal Epstein (Belarus, 1829–1908), *Arukh ha-Shulhan, Hoshen Mishpat* 227:22.

10 *Torat Kohanim* at Leviticus 19:14.

11 *Shulhan Arukh*, op. cit., 228:6.

12 For exposition of this principle in general terms, see *Shulhan Arukh*, op. cit., 232:8–9. The seller's duty to disclose the flaws of his product applies even to flaws that are not material in the buyer's decision to buy the product and where the price is "fair" for what the buyer actually gets. The reason is that nondisclosure causes the buyer to feel unwarranted indebtedness to the seller for the bargain he mistakenly thinks he got. A minor exception to this rule obtains in a face-to-face transaction where the defects of the merchandise can be ascertained through visual inspection—for example, if the object of transfer was an animal. The duty of the seller is then only to point out to the buyer the nonobvious defects. The buyer is expected to discover the obvious defects himself. Accordingly, the buyer cannot demand cancellation of the deal based on his discovery of an obvious defect after the transaction is closed. We take his silence at the close of the deal as acceptance of the defect. See *Shulhan Arukh*, op. cit., 228:6, 232:4,6,7; *Arukh ha-Shulhan, Hoshen Mishpat*, op. cit., 232:6–7; R. Judah Itra (Israel, contemporary), *Netiv Yosher* (Jerusalem, 1992), 139–40.

13 For exposition of the principle in general terms, see *Shulhan Arukh*, op. cit., 228:6.

14 The "bait and switch" tactic violates the prohibition against causing someone needless mental anguish (Leviticus 25:17). For a discussion of this case in general terms, see Aaron Levine, *Moral Issues of the Marketplace in Jewish Law* (New York: Yashar Books, 2005), 218–20, 395–96.

Fully elucidating and expounding upon the arcane provisions of the loan contract in no way exhausts the mortgage broker's disclosure duty. The subprime market is a push market in which lenders and mortgage brokers seek out borrowers.[15] The mortgage broker therefore knows that the applicant would be rejected in the prime market based on the standard criterion lenders use to determine creditworthiness—the FICO score. Developed by the Fair Isaac Corporation in 1981, FICO compiles a profile of the applicant's credit history based on the files of the three major national credit bureaus.[16] The profile includes such data as the applicant's outstanding debt, whether the applicant pays his credit accounts on time, whether there are judgments against the applicant, and the percentage of the applicant's credit that he has already used. FICO scores can range from 300 to 850.[17] If the applicant's score is below 620, prime mortgage lenders will reject his application.[18]

A FICO score below 620 informs the mortgage broker that the prime mortgage market has already judged that the applicant cannot afford a mortgage deal on more favorable terms than they have already offered him.[19] Accordingly, when everything is said and done, the mortgage broker must tell the borrower, "Your FICO score indicates that the mortgage deal we're talking about does not fit within your budget." This disclosure should be made especially when the proposed deal involves interest-only and negative amortization mortgages, because the affordable payments in the early period of such a mortgage may well distract the applicant from the fact that the deal is clearly "unaffordable" once the introductory teaser rate period is over.

Third, lenders extended mortgage loans based on borrowers' stated income without requiring verification. This practice was especially common for "Alt-A" loans, which were given to borrowers who presented a good credit score but did not document their stated income.[20]

This practice is illegal according to Jewish law because the borrower's "good faith" imperative effectively imposes an underwriting standard on the lender. The relevant paradigm case is the prohibition against lending money to someone without witnesses.[21] Motivating this law, according to R. Solomon b. Isaac (Rashi, France, 1040–1105), is the concern that an unwitnessed loan tempts the borrower to claim that it never occurred.[22]

15 Elizabeth Renuart, "An Overview of the Predatory Mortgage Lending Process," *Housing Policy Debate* 15,3 (2004): 480.

16 These are Equifax, Experian, and TransUnion LCC.

17 "Understanding Your Credit Score," available at: http://www.bankrate.com/brm/news/credit-management/creditbureau-info.asp.

18 Charles A. Capone, *Research into Mortgage Default and Affordable Housing: A Primer* (Washington, DC: Center for Housing Ownership, 2002), 12.

19 Upon origination, the interest rates of a subprime mortgage are on average two percent higher than those of prime mortgages. See Souphala Chomsisengphet and Anthony Pennington-Cross, "The Evolution of the Subprime Mortgage Market," 88 Fed. Res. Bank St. Louis Rev. 31, 33 fig. (2006).

20 Cf. Alan Zibel, "'Liar Loans' Threaten to Prolong Mortgage Crises," *USA Today*, August 18, 2008 (available by Google-searching title).

21 BT *Bava Metsi'a* 75b.

22 R. Solomon b. Isaac (Rashi, France, 1040–1105) at BT *Bava Metsi'a* 75b.

To understand the relevance of this model to subprime lending, we need only note that, before the emergence of the subprime market in 1992, lenders required borrowers to document their income by providing copies of signed tax returns and pay stubs. "Stated income" and "stated asset" loans did not exist. Finally, the loan-to-value ratio (LTV) was typically eighty percent. When the LTV exceeded eighty percent, lenders required borrowers to obtain private mortgage insurance.[23]

Given the longstanding industry practice of extending mortgage loans only when the borrower convincingly showed he could afford the loan, granting mortgage loans to borrowers with impaired credit histories or without documentation encouraged borrowers to apply for mortgages without a firm commitment to repay the loans.

Empirical evidence powerfully demonstrates that allowing the applicant to state his income without documentation encourages him to lie about his income. A study by the Mortgage Asset Research Institute found that almost sixty percent of the stated incomes it examined were exaggerated by at least sixty percent.[24]

All this might seem to suggest that Jewish law regards the entire subprime market as illegitimate. This is not so. The law permits it, albeit in a different form. Specifically, the consumer base for a subprime market in a society governed by Jewish law consists of applicants who have impaired credit or insufficient income but who commit themselves to change their standard of living so that they can afford the monthly payments. For example, an applicant's commitment to stop buying cigarettes, liquor, and lottery tickets, or to forego vacations and expensive dinners, changes the applicant's lifestyle so significantly that it warrants reassessment of the applicant's ability to meet the monthly payments. The borrower's willingness to commit to change his lifestyle and document his income, and the lender's willingness to take the chance of trusting him, render the risk taking acceptable in Jewish law.

Other candidates for inclusion in the subprime market are those who intend to purchase a home not as a residence but only for investment purposes; households that cannot afford the down payment the prime lender demands; and households with a short credit history.

Fourth, brokers and lenders pressured appraisers to inflate the value of the mortgage property.[25] Because both the lender and the borrower suffer greatly in the event of a default, one might expect that their interests would be sufficiently aligned to ensure that the loan would both be affordable for the borrower and provide an equity cushion in the case of default. However, this alignment of interest never occurred because of securitization, which broke the lending process into its constituent parts. In the first step of securitization, the originator of the loan typically sold the loan to another entity, called a loan aggregator. The loan aggregator, in turn,

23 Alex Nackoul, "Mortgage Brokering: A Short History," *Scotsman Guide*, December 1999 (available by Google-searching title).

24 Mary Kane, "How Fraud Fueled the Mortgage Crisis," *The Washington Independent*, May 1, 2008 (available by Google-searching title).

25 Kenneth R. Harvey, "Appraisers Under Pressure to Inflate Values," *The Washington Post*, February 3, 2007, p. F01.

sold the loans to a securitizer, who sold tranches of the income from the mortgage-backed securities it issued to investors. Since the loan originator had every incentive to ignore quality and concentrate on volume, appraisers naturally felt pressure to inflate home values.

Fifth, securitizers failed to disclose to investors the hidden flaws in their mortgage-backed securities (MBSs). Fundamentally, issuers should have explained the securitization process to investors, thereby making it clear to them that buying the securities involved great risk, because the securitizer had relied on the originator to assess the quality of the loan, but the originator had no incentive to conduct due diligence. Another hidden flaw securitizers failed to disclose was that the value of their investments depended heavily on home prices and interest rates. This disclosure should have been concretized by alerting investors to the various indices[26] that would give them advance warning about the value of MBSs.

The development of MBSs into more complex financial instruments exacerbated the problem of inadequate disclosure. The more complex the financial instrument, the more hidden risk the investor exposes himself to. A case in point is the synthetic Collateralized Debt Obligation (CDO). The securitizer raises cash by issuing different classes of bonds and equity. Instead of using the proceeds to buy assets such as bonds or loans, he buys the right to income streams without ownership rights in any of the assets that generate the income streams—specifically, by using credit default swaps, wherein the CDO receives periodic payments in exchange for agreeing to assume the risk of loss on a specific asset if that asset experiences a default. Like the cash CDO, the risk of loss on the CDO's portfolio is divided into tranches. The senior notes are paid from cash flows before the junior notes and equity securities. Losses are thus borne first by the equity securities, next by the junior notes, and finally by the senior notes. The different tranches offer distinctly different combinations of risk and return, while each reference the same portfolio of debt securities.[27]

Besides incurring the risks of an MBS, the investor in a synthetic CDO incurs the risk of relying on the credit default swap to generate income for him. The credit

26 One index is the S&P/Case-Shiller Home Price Index. Calculated on a monthly basis, it measures the nominal value of the residential real estate market in twenty metropolitan regions in the United States.

Another is the ABX index, which tracks the price of credit default swaps, which are insurance contracts on subprime mortgages. When concerns about mortgage defaults rise, the cost of insuring the risk of default rises and the ABX falls. Long before the subprime financial crisis hit, it was evident that this market was deteriorating because the ABX was falling.

Last, the securitizer should alert investors to follow the ratio between housing values and the rental cost of housing (i.e., the price-to-rent ratio). All things being equal, the higher this ratio, the more attractive rental becomes relative to home ownership. Following this index, in the opinion of Mark Zandi, would have given investors ample warning that the housing market was in a bubble that could burst at any time. Over the last quarter century this ratio has varied from 12.5 to 16.5. When the housing bubble began, which Zandi identifies as July 2003, this ratio stood at 18.5, and, when the bubble burst in April 2006 under the weight of soaring housing prices and tight monetary policy, the ratio was over 24. See Mark Zandi, *Financial Shock* (Upper Saddle River, New Jersey: Pearson Education, Inc., 2009), 161–65.

27 Available at: http://en.wikipedia.org/wiki/Collateralized_debt_obligation.

default swap market is unregulated. As a result, the instrument can be traded to another investor by either of the investors that are party to the transaction without any guarantee that the loss will be made whole in the case of a default.

Sixth, the credit-rating agencies (CRAs) gave a AAA rating to eighty percent of the tranches of the MBSs.[28] Because the mortgage pool consisted of borrowers with impaired credit, the AAA rating suggested that the defect of impaired credit inherent in any one of the mortgages of the pool somehow disappeared when an investor bought a bond that entitled him to a slice of income from the entire pool. Given the duty to disclose hidden flaws, the CRA should have explained why the MBS made the flaw disappear. This would have required the CRA to disclose that the issuer of the bond retained a certain portion of the mortgage pool, typically five percent,[29] and thus took the "first hit" in case the default rate exceeded expectations. In addition, the issuer paid a premium to insure the bond against default.

Explaining the hidden risks of these features would have exposed their delicate underpinnings and would have made even the average investor question the validity of the AAA rating. The profitability of the investment depended entirely on rising housing prices. Any decline in housing values could easily render the "shock absorber" worthless as a protective device. In addition, a decline in housing values would inevitably require the insurer of the MBSs to post more collateral, which, in turn, could cause the insurer to fail. Precisely that circumstance caused the biggest insurer, AIG, to fall apart and require a massive federal bailout. Investors should additionally have been informed that the credit default swaps that served as insurance on MBSs could be traded in the entirely unregulated secondary market.[30]

Given that the issuer of the financial product is the party that pays the CRA for rendering an opinion to the public regarding its credit-worthiness, it is not surprising that the CRAs fell far short of their disclosure duty. R. Moses Sofer (Hungary, 1762–1839) posited that anyone who assumes the role of making public interest judgments is subject to the judicial code of ethics.[31] One aspect of this code of ethics is the Biblical adjuration, "You shall take no gift (*shohad*)" (Exodus 23:8). Exegetical interpretation of this verse prohibits the judge from accepting payment from one of the opposing litigants even with the instruction to acquit the innocent, or to condemn the guilty.[32] Rava's (Babylonia, d. 352) rationalization of this stringency is very telling: "What is the reason for [the prohibition against taking] *shohad*? Because as soon as a man receives a gift from another he becomes so well-disposed toward him that he becomes like his own person, and no man sees himself in the wrong. What [is the meaning of] *shohad? She-hu had*—'he is one with you.'"[33]

28 Zandi, op. cit., 115.

29 Available at: http://www.pascalroussel.net/cdo_cds.htm.

30 This description of the securitization process draws from Kurt Eggert, "Held Up in Due Course: Predatory Lending, Securitization, and the Holder in Due Course Doctrine," *Creighton Law Review* 35 (2002): 534–50.

31 R. Moses Sofer (Hungary, 1762–1839), *Responsa Hatam Sofer, Hoshen Mishpat* 160.

32 TB *Ketubbot* 105b; *Shulhan Arukh, Hoshen Mishpat* 9:1.

33 TB *Ketubbot* 105a.

The bias that the issuer-pays system causes is exacerbated by partial compensation of rating agency executives in stock options. Given that an excellent rating drives up investor demand for the financial product, option-based compensation may bias the process toward overrating.

The CRAs caution the public not to read into their ratings anything more than an opinion regarding the likelihood that the issuer will default and the amount of potential loss upon default. The hierarchy of rating classes, should not, however, be taken as recommendations with a grading system to invest in the issue.[34]

From the standpoint of Jewish law, the CRAs' disclaimer may fall far short of their duty of disclosure. The adequacy of their disclaimer in informing the public that the ratings are not recommendations depends not on the CRAs' intentions, but rather what the typical user of these ratings thinks the ratings convey.[35]

Wrongdoing in the Subprime Market Spiraling into a Financial Meltdown

No amount of wrongdoing by the primary players in the subprime market could have caused a global recession without a mechanism that continuously replenished the capital of mortgage originators. This mechanism is the securitization process described above. For the securitization process to be an effective engine, however, the MBS must be a very attractive investment. A key element in its attractiveness is the immunity investors enjoy against borrowers' claims of fraud and illegal predatory tactics on the part of loan originators and their agents. Investors are protected from these claims by the holder-in-due-course doctrine, under which the party who acquires a negotiable instrument in good faith for value and without notice of certain defects takes the instrument free of claims and defenses.

In his analysis of the securitization process, Kurt Eggert criticizes the holder-in-due-course doctrine and regards it as the culprit that fueled predatory lending in the subprime mortgage market. In Eggert's opinion, the surest solution to the problem of predatory lending is to force the markets that fund subprime lenders to police those lenders, most obviously by making the purchasers of MBSs responsible for the predatory practices of the lenders. The elimination of the holder-in-due-course doctrine for all loans secured by the residences of the borrowers is therefore necessary in order to significantly reduce predatory lending.[36]

34 John Patrick Hunt, "Credit Rating Agencies and the 'Worldwide Credit Crisis:' The Limits of Reputation, the Insufficiency of Reform and a Proposal for Improvement," *Columbia Business Law Review* 109 (2009): 153.

35 Aaron Levine, *Case Studies in Jewish Business Ethics* (New York: Ktav, Yeshiva University Press, 2000), 51–54.

36 Eggert, op. cit., 608–9.

In practice, the CRAs have blocked the passage of legislation designed to abrogate the holder-in-due-course doctrine. A case in point is the Georgia Fair Lending Act (GFLA). The legislation empowered a borrower to sue any party holding his mortgage for violations of the law. Standard & Poor responded to the legislation by informing the public that it would no longer rate mortgage-backed securities containing high-cost loans from Georgia, citing the uncertain breadth of liability under GFLA. Moody quickly joined Standard & Poor in its opposition to GFLA. Faced with the prospect of a crippled home loan mortgage market, the Georgia legislature modified the disputed law by narrowing its definition of a creditor to exclude assignees of a mortgage.[37]

On another front, success was achieved in abrogating the holder-in-due-course doctrine. In 1975, the Federal Trade Commission (FTC) abrogated the holder-in-due-course doctrine for retailer-financed loans. The FTC action was prompted by evidence that unscrupulous retailers were referring customers to a third-party finance company to finance their purchases and then have the customers apply the proceeds to the cost of the retail item. Alternatively, the retailer would enter into a retail installment contract with the consumer directly and then assign the loan at a discount to a third-party finance company. These actions made the buyer's duty to pay independent of the duty of the seller to perform. The FTC's new rule ended this practice by requiring the retailer to notify his customer that whoever held the loan would be responsible for nonperformance.[38]

Jewish law rejects the holder-in-due-course doctrine. Let us illustrate this with the following example: Suppose WaMu, which combined the functions of loan originator and loan aggregator, sells its pool of mortgages to a securitizer, say, Citigroup. Crucial in determining the legal status of this transaction is which party assumes the risk of default. If Citigroup assumes this risk, the transaction is treated as a bona fide sale, with the consequence that Citigroup becomes the new creditor of record[39] for the borrowers. This will hold even if WaMu guarantees the loans

37 Ibid.

38 Siddhartha Venkatesan, "Abrogating the Holder in Due Course Doctrine in Subprime Mortgage Transactions to More Effectively Police Predatory Lending," *Legislature and Public Policy* 7 (2004): 198–200, 211–12.

39 In this scenario, Citigroup merely acquires the right to collect the debt from the pool of borrowers (*B*). Citigroup does not, however, replace WaMu entirely as *B*'s creditor, because, by entering into a loan agreement with WaMu, *B* obligates himself both personally (*shi'abud ha-guf*) and with his property (*shi'abud nekhasim*) to pay back the loan. The sale of the debt can transfer only *B's* property obligation from WaMu to Citigroup. The personal obligation *B* made to WaMu, however, remains intact despite WaMu's sale of the loan to Citigroup. In consequence, if WaMu forgives *B*'s indebtedness, the mortgage is canceled and Citigroup can no longer collect the debt from *B*. This is so because *B*'s property is treated as a guarantor (*arev*) of his personal commitment to make the payments. Once *B*'s personal commitment is waived by WaMu, *B*'s commitment of his property, which is treated as a guarantee of his personal commitment, also ends (see *Shulhan Arukh, Hoshen Mishpat* 66:23, and *Sema* to *Shulhan Arukh*, ad loc., note 55). Notwithstanding its legal efficacy, forgiving the loan is wicked because it causes Citigroup a financial loss. It is therefore prohibited for WaMu to forgive the loan once it has sold the rights of collection to another party. If WaMu forgives the loans after selling them to Citigroup, Citigroup can make a claim against WaMu. For a summary of authorities' views on this matter, see *Pithei Hoshen*, op. cit., 202. Jewish law's treatment of how forgiveness by the loan originator affects the party that bought the loan creates a further complication for investors in MBSs and hence is another factor retarding the securitization process.

against fraud.[40] In contrast, if Citigroup does not assume the risk of default, the law will regard the transaction as a loan: Citigroup's payment is a loan and the income the loan pool generates serves merely as a reference for what WaMu owes Citigroup. However, WaMu remains the creditor of record for the borrowers in the loan pool.[41] In the securitization process, the securitizer assumes the risk of default, albeit not the risk of fraud. Accordingly, if borrowers feel that WaMu defrauded them and therefore refuse to make payment, Citigroup will have to sue the borrowers for nonpayment. In that litigation, the burden of proof of fraud will reside with the borrowers according to the principle of *ha-motsi me-havero alav ha-re'ayah* (i.e., the plaintiff shoulders the burden of proof).[42] If the borrowers win the litigation, the law will regard the prior sale of the pool of loans between WaMu and Citigroup as a *mekah ta'ut* (transaction conducted in error) and will require WaMu to return the purchase price to Citigroup.[43]

The upshot is that the securitization process does not result in the borrower's falling through the cracks and losing his rights. Instead, the securitizer, by accepting the risk of default, becomes the party that the borrower must deal with if he has reason not to pay. Accordingly, the "true sale" that is set up between the loan originator and the securitizer does not immunize the securitizer from the predatory claims of the borrowers. Jewish law hence rejects the holder-in-due-course doctrine.

If investors cannot count on the law to immunize them from class-action lawsuits brought by borrowers claiming predatory practices by lenders, investor enthusiasm for purchasing MBSs will be considerably dampened. Making the holder-in-due-course doctrine illegal hence considerably slows down the securitization process and thus prevents a constant replenishment of the capital of the loan originator.

Jewish law further slows the securitization process through the right of the securitizer to make his purchase of the loan pool contingent on borrowers' demonstration that they had the ability to pay at the time the loan pool was sold.[44] The import of such a clause is to require the loan aggregator to reimburse the securitizer for each default unless the borrower can prove that he had the ability to meet the mortgage debt at the time the loan pool was sold. Insertion of such a clause exposes the loan aggregator to considerably greater liability if his pool of loans is undocumented. To minimize this risk, the loan aggregator would be driven to ensure that all the borrowers in the loan pool were financially positioned to make good on their commitments at the time of loan origination. Insertion of such a clause would at once eliminate the origination of many undocumented loans, which was one of the worst abuses that led to the subprime mortgage crisis.

40 *Shulhan Arukh, Yoreh De'ah* 173:4.

41 R. Mordecai b. Abraham Jaffe (Prague, 1535–1612), *Levush* to *Yoreh De'ah* 173; R. Joshua b. Alexander ha-Kohen Falk, *Perishah* to *Tur, Yoreh De'ah* 173, note 4; R. David b. Samuel ha-Levi (Poland, 1586–1667), *Turei Zahav* to *Shulhan Arukh, Yoreh De'ah* 173, note 3.

42 Cf. BT *Bava Metsi'a* 35a; Ibid. 100a; and BT *Ketubbot* 20a.

43 R. Jacob Isaiah Bloi (Israel, b. 1929), *Pithei Hoshen, Dinei Halva'ah* (Jerusalem: Yeshivat Ohel Mosheh Diskin, 1982/3), 172.

44 R. Abraham Samuel Benjamin Wolf Sofer (Bratislava, 1815–1871), *Ketav Sofer* to *Yoreh De'ah* 85.

Counteracting the Forces that Caused the Global Financial Meltdown

Jewish law has much to say regarding how to counteract the forces underlying the current economic downturn and thereby prevent them from causing another recession. The central relevant moral dictum is the *imitatio Dei* principle, which says that, in our interpersonal conduct, we should emulate the various attributes of mercy and compassion that God displays in His relations with human beings.[45]

The most relevant attribute of Divine mercy to the issue at hand is the weakening of the power of the Evil Inclination that God effects for those who strive for moral betterment. Regarding this dimension of Divine mercy, Reish Lakish (Israel, third century CE) states, "[I]f one wishes to defile himself [with sin], the door is merely opened for him; but if one comes to purify himself, he is assisted."[46]

The seductive power of the Evil Inclination is greatest when man is in an environment that pressures him to sin or finds himself in a setting that gives him the opportunity to engage in veiled misconduct.

To be spared the challenge of a test of piety is regarded in Jewish religious thought as ideal. Witness both the warning of the Sages not to deliberately enter into a situation that will involve a test of piety,[47] and the plea we make to God in our daily prayers not to thrust us into a test of piety.[48]

As private citizens, we are very limited in what we can do to assist our fellow man in his battle against the Evil Inclination. However, *imitatio Dei* is a mandate for government, too,[49] and government can accomplish much in this area. The government's duty is to change the incentive structure of the marketplace to eliminate situations conducive to veiled misconduct and pressures to engage in wrongful conduct.

An Economic Condition Put in Theological Terms

Application of the *imitatio Dei* principle to the subprime market would involve reform of the work environment of market players, equipping it with an incentive system consisting of "sticks" and "carrots" that incline actors toward virtue and away from misconduct.

45 BT *Sotah* 14a; *Sifrei* at Deuteronomy 10:12. In the opinion of R. Naphtali Tsevi Judah Berlin (Russia, 1817–1893), *imitatio Dei* extends beyond a duty to emulate those attributes of God's mercy explicitly enumerated at Exodus 34:6–7. Rather, we are required to emulate God in every manifestation of His mercy. He bases his contention on Joel 3:5 (*Emek ha-Netsiv* to *Sifrei* at Deuteronomy 10:2, *piskah* 13).

46 BT *Yoma* 38b.

47 BT *Sanhedrin* 107a.

48 BT *Berakhot* 60b.

49 Rambam, *Guide of the Perplexed*, trans. S. Pines (Chicago: University of Chicago Press, 1963), ch. 54, 126–27.

Before describing this application in detail, we note that *imitatio Dei* has limitations as a guidepost for private and public policy. *Imitatio Dei* mandates that we emulate the various forms of kindness described in Jewish traditions regarding God's compassion and mercy in His dealing with humankind. But the general rule is that the obligation to engage in acts of kindness, as opposed to the charity duty to the needy,[50] extends only to exertion of toil and effort, not to monetary expenditure.[51] The only exception is that, when the expenditure is trifling, it is improper for someone to rely on this exemption and take no action.[52] There is consequently a difference between kindnesses performed by government and those performed by the private person or business. Specifically, an amount that is substantial for a single household is often trifling when it is shared by the entire federal tax base. Because the United States has a progressive income tax, the cost of an *imitatio Dei* measure can be spread equitably over approximately eighty-three million taxpaying households.[53]

This limitation on the force of *imitatio Dei* as a guidepost for both private and government policy applies only when the proposed measure is designed to promote decision making that is in the public's best interest. If the measure is, however, designed to end prohibited conduct, the fact that compliance with the measure will entail a cost for the would-be violator is not taken into account.[54] In such a circumstance, *imitatio Dei* is a mandate to expand government involvement beyond discovery and prosecution of wrongdoing to preventative measures as well.

We proceed to describe *imitatio Dei* measures intended to prevent future economic crises.

First, requiring borrowers to document their ability to pay puts an end to "liar" (no proof of assets) and "NINJA" (lit., no income, job, or assets) loans. Adopting this simple "stick" immediately raises underwriting standards to acceptable levels.

Federal Reserve rules against abusive lending did not become effective until October 1, 2009. Applying only to new loans, the rules bar lenders from making loans without proof of a borrower's income. They also require lenders to ensure

50 Leviticus 25:35; Deuteronomy 15:7–8, 10. For the extent of the charity duty, see endnote 70.

51 R. Zalman Nehemiah Goldberg (Israel, contemporary), "*Be-Hiyyuvei Gemilut Hesed*" in *Mishneh Torah, REM le-Zekher Eliezer Meir Lipschitz* (Jerusalem, 1975), 97–111.

52 R. Judah in the name of Rav, BT *Bava Metsi'a* 33a, and commentary of R. Joseph Hayyim b. Elijah al-Hakam (Baghdad, 1834–1909), *Ben Yehoyada* ad loc.

53 This statistic is for 2006. See "Fiscal Facts Number of Americans Paying Zero Federal Income Tax Grows to 43.4 Million," Tax Foundation, March 30, 2006 (available by Google-searching title).

54 In Jewish law, obligatory religious duties dichotomize into positive commandments (*mitsvot aseh*) and negative prohibitions (*mitsvot lo ta'aseh*). The extent of financial obligation inherent in each category is a matter of dispute. R. Moses b. Israel Isserles (Rema, Poland, c. 1525–1572) formulates the rule as follows: "To fulfill a *mitsvat aseh*, an individual is required, if necessary, to expend up to one-fifth of his net worth. To avoid violation of a *mitsvat lo ta'aseh*, an individual must lose, if necessary, his entire net worth" (Rema to *Shulhan Arukh, Orah Hayyim* 656:1). See also R. Hayyim Hezekiah b. Raphael Elijah Medini (Russia, 1832–1904), *Sedei Hemed*, vol. 9, 7, 64. Disputing R. Isserles' claim, R. Moses Sofer argues that the stringency for the *lo ta'aseh* category applies only when the negative commandment will be violated in an *active manner* (*kum va-aseh*). To avoid a passive violation (*shev ve-al ta'aseh*), the one-fifth rule applies (R. Moses Sofer, *Responsa Hatam Sofer, Hoshen Mishpat* 177, and his gloss at *Shulhan Arukh, Orah Hayyim* 656:1).

that risky borrowers have money reserved to pay for taxes and insurance. Finally, they place restrictions on prepayment penalties.[55]

Second, in response to the widespread reporting of predatory practices by mortgage brokers, Congress passed legislation in July 2008 that called for the establishment of a nationwide mortgage licensing and registry system. The purpose of the legislation was to oversee and track all loan originations to ensure that they followed educational, ethical, and legal requirements.[56]

One can frame the new legislation in terms of *imitatio Dei*. Specifically, to prevent both the criminal and those ignorant of mortgage law from originating loans, a number of "sticks" were instituted in the form of licensing and registration requirements. However, the *imitatio Dei* principle dictates that regulation must do more. To promote better disclosure and greater transparency, the government should have adopted the proposal that called for loan originators to be bonded.[57] The bonding requirement adds a "stick" by warning loan originators that they might lose their own assets if they are sued for fraud or misrepresentation.

Third, to prevent interference with an appraiser's job, the law should not allow the lender to select a particular appraiser for an assignment. Instead, a lender should be required to hire one of a number of designated professional appraisal organizations, such as the Appraiser Institute. These organizations, in turn, would randomly assign an appraiser for the job from among those of its members in reasonable geographic proximity to the assignment.

Fourth, there can be no doubt that the CRAs played a vital role in making the securitization process a powerful engine for economic expansion. It was the AAA ratings they gave mortgage-backed securities that made these securities attractive investments. But, if the CRAs had fully disclosed to the public how they arrived at their AAA ratings, the average investor would not have given credence to these ratings and the robust demand for these securities would have dissipated long before securitization could have caused an international meltdown of financial institutions.

In the wake of record losses on subprime bonds, the SEC, in July 2008, proposed new rules of operation for CRAs. These proposed new rules, as detailed below, were designed to enhance transparency, reduce conflict of interest, and increase competition in the credit rating industry.

Since 1970, the SEC has outsourced some aspects of its regulatory function to three CRAs: Moody, Standard and Poor, and Fitch Financials. Designating them Nationally Recognized Statistical Rating Organizations (NRSROs), the SEC gave these agencies the authority to decide whether the financial institutions they regulate have sufficient liquidity and investment-grade bonds.[58]

55 "Fed Issues Rules to Stop Abusive Lending Practices," *The Associated Press*, July 15, 2008.

56 Janet Morrissey, "Housing Law Cracks Down on Loan Originators; New Rules Could Boost Industry's Battered Image," *Investment News*, August 4, 2008, 3.

57 "MBA Board of Governors Calls for Broker Accountability," *Mortgage Law Central*, November 19, 2007 (available by Google-searching title).

58 Roger Lowenstein, "Triple-A Failure," *The New York Times*, April 27, 2008 (available by Google-searching title).

That practice changed radically in 2008. Recognizing that the regulatory function it assigned the NRSROs may have played a role in making investors overrate the reliability of their credit ratings, the SEC stripped references to NRSROs from thirty-eight of its rules, including the portion of Rule 2a-7 on money market funds that required such funds to hold debt rated double-A or higher.[59]

Further progress in the reform of rating agencies' operations was achieved when the New York State Attorney General, Andrew Cuomo, reached a tentative agreement with the CRAs to change the way they charge fees. Under present arrangements, a credit rating agency receives its fee when its work is completed. This arrangement allows an investment bank to pit one CRA against another to secure a AAA rating. Under the tentative agreement, the CRAs will charge fees in stages for various analytical tasks and report every three months on transactions they were asked to rate and actually rated.[60]

From the standpoint of Jewish law, as long as the issuer-pays system remains intact, the conflict of interest problem persists. However, a "heavy stick" forcing a CRA to bear the consequences of misjudgment represents a definite improvement.

One such proposal, advanced by John Patrick Hunt, requires the CRA to disclose upfront that its rating is of poor quality. If the CRA opts not to make this upfront admission, it will be required to disgorge the fees it earned from the issuer if it turns out that the issuer performs poorly relative to its assigned rating.[61]

Fifth, a great irony of the subprime crisis is that the ousted CEOs of the companies that sustained the biggest losses left their companies with huge severance packages. For example, E. Stanley O'Neil, CEO of Merrill Lynch, left his company with a $161 million severance package. Similarly, Charles O. Prince III, CEO of Citigroup, left his company with a severance package consisting of a bonus of $10 million, $28 million in invested stock and options, and $1.5 million in annual perquisites.[62]

Had companies linked compensation to performance, the result would have been better decision making, and disaster might have been averted. The manner in which these financial firms approached risk management sharply illustrates this point. In the years leading up to the financial meltdown, the use of a mathematical model called Value at Risk (VaR) was already firmly entrenched in the industry. VaR gave the boundaries of risk for a portfolio over a short duration, assuming normal market conditions. For example, if a portfolio of assets has a VaR of $50 million, it means that, over the course of the next week, there is a ninety-nine probability that the portfolio will not lose more than $50 million dollars.

59 Andrew Ackerman, "SEC Votes to Remove NRSRO From 38 Rules," *The Bond Buyer*, June 26, 2008 (available by Google-searching title).

60 Jenny Anderson and Vikas Bajaj, "Rating Firms Seen Near Legal Deal on Reforms," *The New York Times*, June 4, 2008 (available by Google-searching title).

61 "Credit Rating Agencies and the 'Worldwide Credit Crisis:' The Limits of Reputation, the Insufficiency of Reform and a Proposal For Improvement," op. cit., 193–207.

62 Gretchen Morgenson, "Panel to Review Payouts Given by Troubled Firms," *The New York Times*, March 7, 2008, p. C3.

Though VaR is a powerful risk management tool, it does not take into account all relevant risks and hence uncritical use of it could prove, and did prove, disastrous. For example, the model cannot accurately evaluate the thinly traded, arcane assets in the company's portfolio. The model also does not take into account the risk of a liquidity squeeze. Moreover, as one noted authority, Nassim Nicholas Taleb, points out, the model tells us nothing of what the losses would be in the one percent abnormal condition case when the unthinkable happens in the form of, say, the simultaneous meltdown of all the equity markets. Taleb dubs this unthinkable event a "black swan" event.

A user of VaR must also exercise good judgment. The Goldman Sachs experience of abandoning VaR in the summer of 2007 illustrates this point. In the face of ten straight days of losses in its portfolio and the judgment of its risk management group that the housing market was headed lower, Goldman's management decided to pare down its investments in MBSs and increase its investments in hedging instruments to offset the possible decline in the value of its MBS holdings. By exercising proper caution in the use of VaR and relying on market-experienced people over computer models, Goldman Sachs avoided the multi-billion dollar losses other major financial institutions suffered in the summer of 2007.[63]

From the standpoint of Jewish business ethics, the current compensation system for executives is a moral pitfall. Consider that the basic marketing approach of the securitizer is to inform clients that it not only has a stake in the structured product it is promoting but has shaped the product to reduce risk for the investors. With these representations the securitizer assumes an advisory role, and as such is saddled by Jewish Law with a fiduciary duty. Faithfully executing this responsibility requires that the financial interest of the securitizer be aligned with the financial interest of his clients. Under the present system of compensation, this alignment does not take place. This is so because serving the best interests of his clients requires the securitizer to adopt an investment horizon beyond the current fiscal year. But, since bonuses are calculated on the paper gains or loses of the company's MBSs in the current fiscal year and severance will be unaffected by the performance of the company's share price, the securitizer is geared to a decidedly near-term investment horizon, which is not consistent with the best interest of the clients.

Application of the *imitatio Dei* principle to the structure of executive compensation requires reforms that do no less than change the incentive system the securitizer faces.

In this regard, Paul Krugman proposes an innovative approach to firms' awarding of bonuses. In the boom of the housing bubble, traders leveraged capital with debt and earned huge bonuses based on the unrealized appreciation of the MBSs they bought. However, when the value of these securities declined, shareholders and investors suffered losses while the traders kept the bonuses they had already earned. Linking bonuses to realized gains rather than to paper gains would better match compensation to performance.[64] Minimally, firms should set the unpaid

63 Joe Nocerno, "Risk Mismanagement," *The New York Times Magazine*, January 4, 2009, p. 24.

64 Paul Krugman, "The Madoff Economy," *The New York Times*, December 19, 2008 (available by Google-searching title). See also "Wall Street Profits Were a Mirage, But Huge Bonuses Were Real," *The New York Times*, December 18, 2008, p. A1.

compensation aside in a memorandum account for a minimum number of years, say three, and reduce such notional bonuses by the percentage decline, if any, of the underlying securities (i.e., a clawback).

In the thinking of Richard A. Posner, the aim of reform in executive compensation should be to incentivize executives to look beyond the short run in making investment decisions for the firm. To this end, a substantial share of the compensation of financial executives should be backloaded. This means that a specified percentage of their compensation should be in the form of company stock that they would not be permitted to sell for a specified number of years. In addition, companies should be prohibited from giving their executives severance packages.[65]

Posner's idea prevents the recklessness that was rampant in the housing market by counteracting the lure of possible short-term gain. Instead of getting caught up in the bubble, the executive will be forced to consider that, even if he achieves greater profits by taking on greater risk, there will be nothing in it for him personally, as the bubble may very well burst before he is allowed to cash in his restricted shares.

It was not until 2009 that the Federal government came to grips with the executive compensation issue. Early in the year, the Treasury appointed Kenneth Feinberg to set and review pay for top executives at the largest recipients of federal bailout cash. In July, the house financial service committee approved a bill to give bank regulators the ability to ban "imprudently risky compensation packages" at banks with more than $1 billion of assets. In September, the Federal Reserve made a similar proposal.[66]

Had compensation reform measures been in place, the severity of the financial meltdown might have been considerably mitigated because there would have been less incentive to take risk.

The Housing Bubble and *Imitatio Dei*

The need to implement "carrots" and "sticks" to set right the moral compass of economic actors is considerably reinforced by the circumstance that the current economic malaise developed against the backdrop of a housing bubble. The bubble was fueled by a low-interest-rate environment engineered by the Federal Reserve beginning in 2001, combined with a policy of deregulation in the housing industry. Feeding the euphoria that housing prices would continue to rise was the conviction, espoused by Federal Reserve Chairman Alan Greenspan, that the housing industry would not experience a bubble:

65 Richard A. Posner, *A Failure of Capitalism* (Cambridge, Mass: Harvard University Press, 2009), 299.

66 Damian Palette and Jon Hilsenrath, "Bankers Face Sweeping Curbs on Pay," *The Wall Street Journal*, September 18, 2009, A1–2.

> Housing price bubbles presuppose an ability of market participants to trade properties as they speculate about the future. But upon sale of a house, homeowners must move and live elsewhere. This necessity, as well as large transaction costs, are significant impediments to speculative trading and an important restraint on the development of price bubbles.[67]

In the thinking of the prominent economist Robert Shiller, the low interest rate and rising house prices from 2001 to 2005 fostered no less than a social contagion inviting lenders and financial institutions to loosen their standards and risk default. Similarly, borrowers who took out adjustable-rate mortgages were not deterred by the prospect of an increase in interest rates. If interest rates rose, borrowers expected to be compensated by rapidly increasing home prices. Economic players disregarded their own collected information and put their faith in the boom because they felt that everyone else could not be wrong.[68]

To the extent that the housing bubble distorted judgments about risk-taking, social contagion can be equated with the power of the Evil Inclination to distort judgment, resulting in misconduct. A psychoeconomic phenomenon can therefore be expressed in theological terms.

The Remedy Before the Affliction

Managing the health of the economy requires government to foster economic growth while keeping inflation low. The combination of policies that promotes this goal, called stabilization policy, entails the use of both automatic stabilizers and discretionary monetary and fiscal policies.

Automatic stabilizers are programs that will automatically act as a countervailing force when the economy either goes into a tailspin or becomes overheated. One example of an automatic stabilizer is the progressive income tax, where the tax rate increases as income increases. On the aggregate level, as income rises, government takes a larger fraction of the economy's income in the form of taxes. The progressive tax thus reduces the inflationary pressures otherwise caused by the increased spending that accompanies rising income. If the economy experiences a downturn, government takes a smaller percentage of income in taxes, reducing the decrease in spending that would otherwise occur as a result of the falling income.

67 Remarks by Chairman Alan Greenspan: "The Mortgage Market and Consumer Debt," America's Community Bankers Annual Convention, Washington, D.C., October 19, 2004 (available by Google-searching title). See also *Financial Shock*, op. cit., 162.

68 Robert Shiller, *The Subprime Solution* (Princeton, New Jersey: Princeton University Press, 2008), 29, 39–69.

Another automatic stabilizer is government unemployment benefits. Once in place, they automatically result in increased benefits as a downturn worsens. If the economy is expanding and the ranks of the unemployed are shrinking, the spending emanating from government unemployment benefits drops, moderating inflationary pressures.

Discretionary policies are new government initiatives designed either to stimulate or to slow down the economy, depending on whether the predominant economic condition is recession or inflation. On the fiscal side, if the malaise is inflation, government will legislate an increase in taxes or a reduction in spending. On the monetary side, for these same conditions, the Federal Reserve will engineer either an increase or a decrease in interest rates, as conditions require. More often than not, automatic stabilizers will prove unequal to the task and must be supplemented with discretionary fiscal and monetary policies.

Given the severity of the current downturn, it is not surprising that government discretionary initiatives on both the monetary and fiscal fronts have been massive. What is striking, however, is that none of the regulatory reforms described in this chapter were introduced as preventative measures, before the disastrous consequences of an unregulated market became evident.[69] Because government automatic stabilizers are designed specifically for effecting changes in spending and not for deterring unethical conduct, it is not surprising that the regulatory reforms enacted were reactive and not preventative in nature. Moreover, what prompted some government reforms was the realization in hindsight that certain conduct amounted to "excessive risk taking" and had disastrous consequences for society as a whole. A case in point was the extension of loans to borrowers who were not asked to document their income and/or had poor credit histories. The massive defaults that followed proved disastrous not only to the principals, but to the investing public, because the loans were securitized. In hindsight, commentators characterize these loans as "excessive risk taking." But, because Jewish law focuses on the moral aspects of originating and securitizing subprime loans, it judges that these loans ab initio should not have been undertaken. Based on the *imitatio Dei* principle, preventative measures should have been in place all along.

Implementing the remedy before the affliction is an aspect of *imitatio Dei* conduct.[70] However, policies based on this dictum are subject, as discussed earlier, to a financial constraint. There is, however, theological justification for government to establish preventative measures that are not constrained by the financial restrictions associated with the *imitatio Dei* imperative.

69 See text accompanying endnotes 51, 54–55, 57–59.

70 See BT *Megillah* 17b.

Preventing Poverty and Relieving Poverty

This robust principle can be discovered by analyzing the charity duty as set forth in the Pentateuch. This duty is described twice, once in Leviticus and again in Deuteronomy:

> If your brother near you becomes poor and cannot support himself, you shall maintain him; he shall live with you, even when he is a resident alien.[71]
>
> If one of your brothers is in need in any community of yours within your country which the Lord your God is giving you, you must not harden your heart nor close your hand against your needy brother. Rather, you shall open your hand to him, and you shall grant him enough for his lack which is lacking for him. . . . You shall give him, and let your heart not feel bad when you give him, for because of this matter, Hashem, your God will bless you in all your deeds and in your every undertaking.[72]

The repetition of the charity duty is taken by R. Hayyim Soloveichik (Russia, 1853–1918) to convey its dual aspect. In R. Soloveichik's view, the Deuteronomy passage is directed to the individual, while the Leviticus passage is directed to society as a collective.[73] Within this dual system, the public sector uses its coercive powers to establish social welfare programs.[74]

If the public sector's antipoverty role is rooted in the Leviticus passage, its function goes beyond poverty relief. *Torat Kohanim* interprets the phrase "you shall maintain him," which appears in the Leviticus passage quoted above, to establish that charity in its noblest form consists of aiding a faltering individual from falling into the throes of poverty. The position of such an individual must be stabilized, with his dignity preserved, by conferring him a gift, extending him a loan, entering into a business partnership with him, or creating a job for him.[75]

71 Leviticus 25:35.

72 Deuteronomy 15:7–8, 10.

73 Rabbinic sources differ as to whether the ten percent charity obligation imposed by the Torah on agricultural produce applies to income as well; opinions vary as to whether the income tithe is Biblical or Rabbinic in origin. In his survey of the responsa literature, R. Ezra Batsri (Israel, contemporary), *Dinei Mamonot*, vol. 1, 405, concludes that the majority opinion regards the ten percent level as a definite obligation, albeit by dint of Rabbinical decree. In any case, devoting less than ten percent of one's income to charity is considered to reflect an ungenerous nature. An issue requiring clarification is the extent to which an individual can count government antipoverty measures as part of his ten percent charity duty.

74 R. Joseph B. Soloveitchik in the name of R. Hayyim Soloveichik, quoted by R. Daniel Lander, "*Be-Inyan Dei Mahsoro*," in *Kevod ha-Rav* (New York: Student Organization of Yeshiva, Rabbi Isaac Elchanan Theological Seminary, 1984), 202–6.

In Talmudic times, the public charity duty consisted of weekly collections for the community charity box (*kuppah*) and daily collections for the community charity plate (*tamhui*). In addition, a special charity drive was conducted before the Passover season to enable the poor to purchase *matsah* for the holiday (*ma'ot hittin*). Another dimension of the public subsidy for the poor consisted of a compulsory hospitality scheme, wherein the townspeople were required to take turns providing lodging for guests.

Widespread poverty forced many Jewish communities in the Rishonic period (mid-eleventh to mid-fifteenth centuries) to abandon most of the above elements of public philanthropy in favor of private philanthropy. For discussion and sources for Jewish public charity, see Aaron Levine, *Economics and Jewish Law* (New York: Ktav Publishing House Inc., Yeshiva University Press, 1987), 125–26.

75 *Torat Kohanim* at Leviticus 25:35; *Mishneh Torah*, op. cit., 10:7; *Arukh ha-Shulhan* op. cit., 249:15.

The lesson of *Torat Kohanim* can be generalized to say that prevention of poverty is a greater priority than relief of poverty. By implication, the public sector should vouchsafe the economic well-being of society as a whole by anticipating that certain commercial practices might cause deep and widespread economic misery.[76] For example, once the financial innovation of securitization was created, the public sector should have understood that it would pose a systemic threat to the financial system if borrowers could obtain loans without documenting their ability to pay. Without a documentation requirement, most of the loans in a mortgagor's loan pool, especially if subprime, might be fraudulent. Instead of allowing lenders the freedom to take a risk by not insisting on documentation, the law should have required documentation and audits of loan contracts to ensure compliance. Similarly, once securitization was innovated, the ramifications of a corrupt home value appraisal system should have been understood. Accordingly, instead of allowing the appraisal industry to operate in a nonregulated environment, government should have instituted the various measures and proposals described earlier to ensure the integrity of the process long before the bubble burst in the housing market.

As another example, government should have recognized in advance the bias inherent in a system where an issuer of debt securities pays the CRA for its rating of those securities. Accordingly, the measures the SEC introduced to minimize conflict of interest as well as the innovative ideas that are now coming forward should have been in place long before it became apparent that the CRAs' rating system was of poor quality and was deceiving the public.

The upshot of the above analysis is that *imitatio Dei* as applied to the subprime mortgage market allows greater expenditure than usually because implementations of "carrots" and "sticks" in this sector prevents the economy from falling into an abyss.

Who Watches the Watchdog? The Paramount Importance of Moral Education

The subprime mortgage crisis is essentially the story of broken promises and the widespread failure of people to meet their responsibilities. These abuses continued in increasingly brazen forms because government was either remiss in its oversight

76 We suggest that the stabilization policies the Biblical Joseph implemented represent the first recorded instance of government use of an automatic stabilizer. Joseph predicted that the Egyptian economy would experience a period of seven years of superabundance followed by seven years of famine. As a means of getting through the famine, Joseph imposed a twenty percent tax on the grain that was produced in the years of plenty and stored it in government granaries for future distribution when needed. To ensure an adequate food supply for the years of famine, a much more popular approach would have been to call for the government to purchase and store twenty percent of the crop in each of the years of plenty and sell this surplus during the years of famine. Herein lies Joseph's genius. Buying the grain, instead of taxing it, would have enormously increased the money supply during the years of plenty. This enormous increase in the money supply would wreak additional havoc upon the economy when the long and horrific famine hit, for panic purchasers of grain would come to the marketplace with enormous purchasing power. Compounding the depression, there would be inflation as well.

responsibility or naïve about the likely outcomes. In the face of overwhelming evidence that applicants of home mortgages lie when asked only to state, but not to document, their income and assets,[77] Fannie Mae and Freddie Mac continued to buy and securitize these mortgages and therefore should shoulder much of the blame.

The private sector does not voluntarily implement the necessary "carrots" and "sticks" to incline economic actors toward virtue and away from transgression. A case in point is executive compensation. Linking pay to performance and ending the practice of rewarding failure is no simple matter, because, as Bebchuk and Fried point out, CEOs have a good deal of control over their boards and exert considerable influence over the process by which their own pay is determined.[78]

From the perspective of Jewish law, the most fundamental lesson of the financial meltdown is the need to invigorate the moral fiber of the building blocks of society—namely, parents and the educational system. In a society that condones broken promises and shirked responsibility, parents and schools must be the agents to change this moral climate and inculcate integrity and a rarefied sense of responsibility.

The core of Jewish moral education is training in truth telling and in the ethos of responsibility.

In the thinking of R. Isaiah b. Abraham ha-Levi Horowitz (Poland, 1565?–1630), training in truth telling is the centerpiece of the moral training of youth. The ideal is for the father to spare no effort in emphasizing to his child the importance of truth telling. To this end, in the presence of his child, a father's reaction to a lie should be consternation, and his reaction to truth telling, praise. If the child is caught lying, the father should admonish him harshly, instilling great trepidation in him. This approach will guarantee that the child will always remain honest, even when not under parental supervision. The child will feel forced to tell the truth and will hence always feel compelled to depart from evil and do good.[79]

In designing the educational reforms necessary to inculcate the value of responsibility, the Biblical personalities of Judah and Joseph provide grist for the curriculum.

The very essence of Judah's personality was the assumption and admission of responsibility. Judah rose to the moment in time of crisis by taking charge and proclaiming to his father, Jacob: "Send the lad [Benjamin] with me. Let us get going and travel. Then we will live and will not die [of hunger]. . . . I will guarantee his [safe return]. You can demand him from my hand. If I do not bring him to you, standing [alive] before you, I will have sinned against you forever" (Genesis 43:9–0).

Judah not only assumed responsibility but also owned up to responsibility, notwithstanding the most ignominious consequences, as illustrated in an incident involving his daughter-in-law, Tamar. Convinced that she was guilty of harlotry, Judah gave the order to "Take her out and let her be burned" (Genesis 38:24).

77 The Mortgage Asset Reporting Institute (MARI) first reported on May 24, 2006, how stated income loans increased frauds. See http://www.marisolutions.com/pdfs/mba/MBA8thCaseRpt.pdf. Over the years, the organization has frequently reported to congressional committees. See www.marisolutions.com/reports.

78 Lucian Bebchuk and Jesse Fried, *Pay Without Performance* (Cambridge, MA: Harvard University Press, 2004), 39–41, 54–56, 61–64, 80–86.

79 R. Isaiah b. Abraham ha-Levi Horowitz, *Shenei Luhot ha-Berit, Sha'ar ha-Otiyot* 4.

However, when Tamar reacted to her death sentence by issuing the challenge to Judah, "I am pregnant from the man to whom these belong," Judah confessed: "She is right. She became pregnant from me [justifiably], because I did not give her to my son Shelah" (Genesis 38:26).

Responsibility rises to its most rarefied level when moral failure is personalized as a betrayal of the offender's moral mentors (i.e., parents and educators). The Biblical figure Joseph exemplified such a level. In rejecting the wiles of Lady Potiphar, Joseph tells her, "In this house, there is no one greater than me, and he [your husband] has not withheld anything from me except you, since you are his wife. So how could I do this extremely wicked [act], and sin against God?" (Genesis 39:9). Joseph thus treats a consensual illicit liaison as an act of betrayal of God and Potiphar. Supplying additional detail to the Biblical narrative, the Midrash tells us that Joseph's father, Jacob, appeared to Joseph at this moment and exhorted him not to commit the sin.[80] In the final analysis, Joseph resisted temptation because the thought of submitting to sin gave him the overwhelming feeling that he would be betraying his God, the teachings of his father, and the trust of his master, Potiphar.

The home and school are natural settings for training in truth telling, holding children accountable for their promises, and assigning them responsibilities. When parents and schools hold children accountable to fulfill their promises and not shirk from their responsibilities, the sparkle of Judah and Joseph permeates society. Once the moral building blocks of society—parents and educators—transform the moral climate of society, both government and the private sector will see the need to implement an incentive system in every work environment that inclines economic actors toward virtue and away from sin. Moreover, under a rarefied climate of responsibility, decision makers will be driven to identify all aspects of risk rather than relying blindly on mathematical models; so much so that they will not even suppress the possibility of "black swan" events.

Summary and Conclusion

From the perspective of Jewish law, the key to understanding the current global meltdown is the intrusion of the securitization process into the $2.5-trillion subprime or impaired credit sector of the mortgage market. Securitization is a powerful vehicle for spreading the risk of subprime mortgages on a global level and hence is a powerful engine of economic growth. Yet it creates many settings and temptations for fraudulent and deceptive conduct, improper disclosure, and blatant failure of mortgage originators, borrowers, appraisers, securitizers, and CRAs to perform due diligence. No amount of wrongdoing, however, could have mushroomed into an international meltdown without the holder-in-due-course doctrine, which

80 *Midrash Tanhuma* at Genesis 39:8.

Jewish law rejects. In Jewish Law, the crucial factor in deciding whether a loan purchaser is regarded as the new lender of record is whether the purchaser accepts the risk of default from the loan seller. Since the securitizer accepts the risk of default, Jewish law views the securitizer as the creditor of record for borrowers and therefore the entity the borrowers must deal with directly. The securitizer must sue borrowers who refuse to pay, which reduces the appetite of investors to buy MBSs and encourages honest dealing all along the chain of transactions.

To prevent the recurrence of the current debacle, Jewish law's *imitatio Dei* principle calls for the restructuring of the incentive system confronting economic actors, replacing the current system of perverse incentives with sticks and carrots designed to incline economic actors toward virtue and away from wrongdoing.

Since *imitatio Dei* is no more than a guidepost for the form that acts of kindness should take, it does not mandate policies that entail significant per capita expenditure. But *imitatio Dei* applied to the subprime mortgage market is a much more robust principle because implementation of "carrots" and "sticks" in this sector prevents the economy from falling into an abyss. The *imitatio Dei* program hence fulfills the government's antipoverty mandate, which justifies greater expenditure.

The current economic malaise shows that we live in a society of broken promises. Improving the moral climate of society hence entails reinforcing the values of integrity and taking responsibility seriously. Jewish religious thought places the onus on parents and the educational system to accomplish this.

SELECTED BIBLIOGRAPHY

Bebchuk, Lucian., and Jesse Fried. *Pay Without Performance*. Cambridge, Mass: Harvard University Press, 2004.

Berlin, R., and Naphtali Tsevi Judah. *Emek ha-Netsiv* to *Sifrei* at Deuteronomy 10:2, *piskah* 13.

Bible:

Leviticus 25:35.

Deuteronomy 15:7–8,10.

Bloi, R. Jacob Isaiah. *Pithei Hoshen, Dinei Halva'ah*. Jerusalem: Yeshivat Ohel Mosheh Diskin, 1982/3.

Caro, R. Joseph. *Shulhan Arukh, Hoshen Mishpat* 9:1, 227:21, 228:6, 232:8–9; *Shulhan Arukh, Yoreh De'ah* 173:4.

Eggert, Kurt. "Held Up in Due Course: Predatory Lending, Securitization, and the Holder in Due Course Doctrine." *Creighton Law Review* 35 (2002): 503–640.

Horowitz, R., and Isaiah B. Abraham ha-Levi. *Shenei Luhot ha-Berit, Sha'ar ha-Otiyot* 4.

R. Joseph Hayyim B. Elijah al-Hakam. *Ben Yehoyada* to *Bava Metsi'a* 33a.

Maimonides. *Guide of the Perplexed*. Trans. S. Pines. Chicago: University of Chicago Press, 1963. Ch. 54.

Posner, Richard A. *A Failure of Capitalism*. Cambridge, Mass: Harvard University Press, 2009.

Shiller, Robert. *The Subprime Solution*. Princeton, New Jersey: Princeton University Press, 2008.

Sofer, R. Moses. *Responsa Hatam Sofer, Hoshen Mishpat* 160.

Talmud (Babylonian):

Bava Metsi'a 33a, 35a, 49a, 75b.

Berakhot 60b.

Megillah 17b.

Sanhedrin 107a.

Sotah 14a.

Yoma 38b.

Torat Kohanim at Leviticus 19:14.

Zandi, Mark. *Financial Shock*. Upper Saddle River, New Jersey: Pearson Education, Inc., 2009.

This paper is based, in part, on my article, "The Global Recession and Jewish Law." *The American Economist* 53,1 (Spring, 2009): 6–15. My thanks to Leon M. Metzger for his comments on an earlier draft of this paper.

CHAPTER 22

THE EMPLOYEE FREE CHOICE ACT, UNIONS, AND UNIONIZING IN JEWISH LAW

DANI RAPP

Introduction

Employer–employee relationships are no different from other business interactions, where each party is motivated primarily by self-interest. However, inequities can arise when a small number of employers control a large percentage of the labor market. The law equalizes the imbalance by allowing employees to unionize, putting the negotiating power of employees on par with their employers.[1] By banding together, organized workers gain the ability to strike, neutralizing management's ability to withhold employment.

Labor and business interests have spent the past century trying to influence legislation that limits or expands workers' ability to unionize. A recent development in this ongoing struggle is the Employee Free Choice Act, or "Card Check Act."[2] Currently, the process of forming a union begins when thirty percent of employees request that a union represent them. Next, a secret ballot is held between forty-five and ninety days later. If more than half of the employees vote in favor of the union, the union is certified and the employer must negotiate with them in good faith. The proposed law would

1 National Labor Relations Act, 29 U.S.C. §§ 151–169.
2 H. R. 1409, S. 560.

require that fifty percent of the employees request a union but do away with the secret ballot. Unions claim this change is necessary because management uses the period prior to the secret ballot to intimidate workers from joining the union. However, management argues that removal of the secret ballot will enable unions to intimidate workers and coerce them into submitting their approval.

This chapter aims to examine Jewish law's approach to unions and the process of unionization. It analyzes Halakhah's attempt at creating a fair and equitable bargaining process between employers and employees.

Approach of Jewish Law to Employer–Employee Relations

Jewish law demands equity in all disputes. In Deuteronomy, the Torah states that "you shall not respect persons in judgment. The small and the great alike you shall hear, you shall not be afraid of any man."[3] In Leviticus, we read, "You shall do no unrighteousness in judgment. You shall not respect the poor person nor favor the mighty person. In righteousness shall you judge your neighbor."[4]

Employer–employee relationships are no exception. Each side has rights and obligations, ensuring that the worker receives equitable treatment and the employer receives the full value of the employee's labor. For example, the Torah guarantees a worker's right to be paid in a timely fashion.[5] The Talmud clarifies that one who withholds a worker's pay actually transgresses five negative commandments and one positive commandment.[6] Additionally, the Mishnah states that a worker who disagrees with his employer regarding whether compensation was paid can take an oath and collect his pay.[7] This is an exception to the general halakhic principle that one who wishes to extract money from another faces the burden of proof. It is also unusual that the employer cannot take an oath to exempt himself from payment–an option available in other monetary disputes.[8]

3 Deuteronomy 1:17.

4 Leviticus 19:15.

5 Ibid., 19:13.

6 BT *Bava Metsi'a* 111a.

7 Ibid.

8 BT *Shevu'ot* 44b. Maimonides (Rambam, Egypt, 1135–1204) in *Mishneh Torah, Sekhirut* 11:6 explains that the employer is too busy to remember whom he has or has not paid, but the worker is believed because it is his sustenance. This explanation is also offered by Nahmanides (Ramban, Spain, 1194–1270) and R. Nissim b. Reuben Gerondi (Ran, Spain, c. 1310–c. 1375) to *Bava Metsi'a* 112b.

An employer is enjoined against assigning degrading work, unless the worker specifically agrees to do it at the time of hire.[9] Similarly, some authorities prohibit giving an employee useless "busy work."[10]

The Talmud[11] relates that an employer may be forced to forgo his rights in the case of a needy worker, based on the verse, "That you may walk in the way of good men, and keep the paths of the righteous."[12]

However, a worker has responsibilities as well as rights. He is prohibited against wasting time while on the job.[13] Indeed, the Talmud tells of Abba Hilkiyah, a worker who refrained from greeting a group of prominent rabbis while in the middle of his work.[14] It is noteworthy that they came to meet with him on an urgent matter of national importance. Additionally, a worker is obligated to work with all of his strength. Thus, a day-worker is prohibited from hiring himself out to work at night, as his extra job will tire him out, preventing him from working at full capacity.[15] A worker who does not work to his fullest ability is considered guilty of stealing from his employer. Thus, he must keep himself well nourished[16] in order to ensure proper performance.[17]

R. Moses Isserles (Rema, Poland, 1530–1572) writes that, unless specified otherwise, a worker is obligated to leave his home at dawn and remain working until the stars come out.[18] On the eve of the Sabbath, he may leave early enough only to get home, fill pitchers of water, prepare some food, and light the Sabbath candles. A worker is also limited in his ability to observe religious precepts while on the job. He is allowed to say the *Shema* prayer but may not leave his place of work in order to do so.[19] The Talmud quotes the Academy of Hillel, which allows a worker to interrupt work only for the first, most essential chapter of the *Shema*.[20] *Tosafot*

9 Leviticus 25:39 states, "And if your brother becomes poor and gives himself to you for money, do not make use of him like a servant who is your property." R. Solomon b. Isaac (Rashi, France, 1040–1105) comments that one may not give a slave degrading work that indicates that he is a slave. Rambam (*Mishneh Torah, Avadim* 1:7) limits this prohibition to slaves, who have no choice in what work to accept. The opinion of Rambam is confirmed by later decisors, including R. Abraham ha-Levi Gombiner (Poland, 1637–1683), *Magen Avraham* 169:1, quoting the opinion of R. Isaiah Horowitz (Ottoman Palestine, 1565–1630), *Shelah*, and R. Joshua ha-Kohen Falk (Poland, 1555–1614), *Sema* to *Hoshen Mishpat* 369:18. See, however, R. Moses Schick (Maharam Schick, Hungary, 1807–1879), *Commentary on the 613 Mitsvot* (nos. 345 and 348), who considers the possibility that an employee cannot be forced to do degrading work even if he agreed to it at the time of hire.

10 Rashi, later in his aforementioned comment, prohibits a master from giving his slave useless work. *Torat Kohanim* (*Behar* 6) limits this prohibition to slaves. R. Aaron ha-Levi (Barecelona, 1235–1300), *Sefer ha-Hinnukh* 346, states that, while it is not technically prohibited to assign an employee useless work, it is improper to do so. R. Meir b. Baruch (Maharam of Rothenberg, Germany, 1215–1293), in his *Responsa* (4:85), goes further and states that it is actually prohibited. For a complete discussion, see Aaron Levine, *Case Studies in Jewish Business Ethics* (Hoboken: Ktav, 2000), 242–46.

11 BT *Bava Metsi'a* 83a.

12 Proverbs 2:20.

13 R. Joseph Caro (Ottoman Palestine, 1488–1575), *Shulhan Arukh, Hoshen Mishpat* 337:20.

14 BT *Ta'anit* 23b. For this, BT *Makkot* 24a calls him "the righteous worker."

15 *Tosefta, Bava Metsi'a* 8:2.

16 *Shulhan Arukh, Hoshen Mishpat* 337:19.

17 R. Moses Isserles (Rema, Poland, 1530–1572) to *Shulhan Arukh, Yoreh De'ah* 333:5.

18 *Shulhan Arukh, Hoshen Mishpat* 331:1, based on JT *Bava Metsi'a* 7:1.

19 Mishnah, *Berakhot* 2:4.

20 BT *Berakhot* 16a.

further restrict his rights and maintain that he may interrupt his work only for the first verse.[21] As for the *Shemoneh Esreh* prayer, the worker must pray a shortened version. When he eats, he is exempted from the blessing before the meal, and he recites a shortened version of the grace after meals, known as "the blessing of the worker."[22]

All of these laws were instituted to guarantee employers a full day's work from their employees. Although all of these rules are rendered void when they contradict local custom,[23] local custom may be ignored if a specific condition was made at the time of hiring.[24]

The only real advantage the worker enjoys relates to retracting from a contract. The general rule in Jewish law is that "whoever retracts, he is at a disadvantage."[25] Thus, an employer who backs out of a contract must compensate workers who are unable to find employment at a comparable wage. However, a worker who retracts cannot be forced to complete the job, or to compensate his employer if replacement workers are more expensive. The Talmud derives this from the Torah's verse, "For unto Me [are] the children of Israel servants; they are My servants,"[26] extrapolating that "They are My servants, and not servants of servants."[27] Hence, a worker may retract even halfway through the day.[28] However, this right is limited to hourly workers, and not contract workers. The latter are not bound to work at specific times and therefore never feel that they are treated like slaves.[29]

At first glance, this principle seems to enable workers to use work stoppage to force concessions from employers. However, this is not necessarily the case. A worker does not have the right to retract when it would cause irretrievable loss to the employer.[30] According to R. Joshua ha-Kohen Falk (Poland, 1555–1614), loss of time to the employer is considered to be an irretrievable loss.[31] Rema imposes another caveat, that the right of retraction does not apply when the decision is motivated purely by financial considerations.[32] A worker cannot retract simply because someone is offering him a higher wage. Moreover, R. Solomon Zalman Auerbach (Israel, 1910–1995) rules that, even if the worker has the right to withdraw for a purely financial motive, he does

21 *Tosafot* to ibid., s.v. "*ha.*"

22 BT *Berakhot* 16a.

23 BT *Bava Metsi'a* 87a.

24 *Shulhan Arukh*, *Hoshen Mishpat* 331:1, based on BT *Bava Metsi'a* 83a.

25 Mishnah, *Bava Metsi'a* 6:2.

26 Leviticus 25:55.

27 BT *Bava Metsi'a* 10a; BT *Bava Kamma* 116b; BT *Kiddushin* 22a. *Shulhan Arukh*, *Hoshen Mishpat* 333:4.

28 While the literal rule of midday retraction is practically not applicable in the modern workplace, R. Aaron Levine posits that the underlying logic can be applied to create a "minimal personal communications privilege," which allows employees to make and receive short phone calls during the day, even without having been given specific permission to do so by the employer. See Aaron Levine, *Moral Issues of the Marketplace in Jewish Law* (Brooklyn: Yashar Publishing, 2005), 281–86. See, however, R. Jacob Isaiah Bloi (Israel, contemporary), *Pithei Hoshen* III (7:10), note 24.

29 BT *Bava Metsi'a* 77a with Rashi's commentary.

30 Ibid., 76b.

31 *Sema* to *Hoshen Mishpat* 333:19.

32 *Shulhan Arukh*, *Hoshen Mishpat* 333:4.

not have the right to prevent another from replacing him.[33] R. Auerbach's opinion effectively negates the bargaining power of a work stoppage.

The foregoing implies that an individual worker cannot force an employer to renegotiate terms of employment. However, as will be discussed, workers who band together in guilds or unions may have such abilities.

Sources in Jewish Law for Labor Unions

Trade guilds are mentioned several times in the Talmud. The Talmud discusses the Great Synagogue of Alexandria:

> [People] did not sit randomly, but rather the goldsmiths sat separately, the silversmiths sat separately, the blacksmiths sat separately, the metal workers sat separately, the weavers sat separately; so that when a poor man entered, he would recognize the members of his craft and, on applying to his quarter, obtain a livelihood for himself and the members of his family.[34]

The Talmud also mentions that the *Tarsiyim*, a particular group of craftsmen,[35] had their own synagogue where they would gather to pray.[36] In the fifth century BCE, the prophet Nehemiah mentions organized groups of workers.[37]

Jewish law's earliest discussion of the rights and powers of such groups appears in the *Tosefta*,[38] which states:

> The woodworkers and the dyers are permitted to stipulate that all business that will come to town, they will be partners in. The bakers may agree among themselves that one will work at one time and the other at a different time. The donkey riders are entitled to stipulate that one who loses his donkey should be provided with another donkey.[39]

The powers of these groups are derived from the townspeople,[40] who have the right to establish weights and measures, fix prices and wages, and inflict penalties for infringement of rules.[41] The Talmud alludes to this relationship in discussing the following case:

33 *Responsa Minhat Shelomoh* 87.

34 BT *Sukkah* 51b.

35 *Tosafot* to *Avodah Zarah* 17b (s.v. "*rabban*") state that while "*Tarsiyim*" means "coppersmiths" in tractates BT *Nazir* and BT *Megillah*, in the case mentioned in BT *Avodah Zarah*, it refers to weavers.

36 BT *Megillah* 26a; BT *Nazir* 52a. BT *Avodah Zarah* 17b mentions R. Hanina b. Teradyon as the rabbi of the *Tarsiyim*.

According to the *Arukh*, quoted in *Tosafot* to *Hullin* 57b (s.v. "*matlit*"), not every trade had its own synagogue—as was the case in eighteenth- and nineteenth-century Europe—but, rather, this was unique to the coppersmiths. This was due to the unpleasant smell exuded during the process of smelting copper.

37 Nehemiah 3:8.

38 *Tosefta, Bava Metsi'a* 11:12.

39 From "The donkey riders" and onwards is also quoted in BT *Bava Kamma* 116b.

40 Ramban to *Bava Batra* 9a; *Tosafot* to *Bava Kamma* 116b (s.v. "*u-resha'im*"); R. Asher b. Jehiel (Rosh, Germany, 1250–1327) *Bava Batra* 33; R. Yom Tov b. Abraham Ishbili (Ritba, Spain, 1250–1330) to *Bava Batra* 9a; R. Joseph b. Solomon ibn Habib (Spain, c. 1445–1515), *Nimmukei Yosef* to ibid. (p. 6b in the Rif pagination).

41 BT *Bava Batra* 8b.

> There were [two][42] butchers who agreed that if either slaughtered on the other's day, the hide of his animal should be torn up. One of them slaughtered on the other's day, and the other went and tore up his hide. They came before Rava, who required him [the offending party] to pay. R. Yeimar b. Shalmia challenged Rava's involvement in this matter, since the townspeople themselves are empowered [to] impose penalties for breach of their regulations. Rava did not respond. R. Pappa said that Rava was quite right not to answer him, as townspeople are only empowered when there is no distinguished man in the town. But where there is a distinguished man, they certainly do not have the power to impose penalties.[43]

A detailed analysis of this case is necessary to fully understand the power of unions in Jewish law.

The Powers of the Townspeople

Analyzing right-to-work laws in Halakhah requires looking at cases where a majority can force a dissenting minority to comply with its wishes. One such case relates to services essential for the well-being of the town, where expenditure on such services is binding on all, even when initially proposed only by a minority of the townspeople. Examples of such projects include building a security wall or synagogue, purchasing a Torah scroll,[44] hiring a cantor, and hiring adult males on the High Holidays for the quorum of ten needed for communal prayer.[45]

Certain endeavors, like fixing commercial weights and measures, or setting prices and wages, are not absolutely essential for the material or spiritual well-being of the townspeople.[46] In this case, the degree of consensus needed to make the matter binding is a matter of dispute. R. Samuel b. Moses de Medina (Maharashdam, Salonika, 1506–1589) addresses the issue in the context of a

42 The word "two" is removed by R. Isaac b. Jacob Alfasi (Rif, Algeria, 1013–1103), Rosh, R. Joel Sirkes (*Bah*, Poland, 1561–1640), and R. Samuel b. Joseph Strashun (Rashash, Lithuania, 1794–1872). If one preserves the word "two," it is difficult to understand why a simple agreement between two butchers requires approval. Ramban, as explained by R. Abraham Karelitz (Israel, 1878–1953), *Hazon Ish* (*Bava Batra* 4:8), explains the version that keeps the word as referring to a case where these are the only two butchers in the city. Such an agreement would then effectively eliminate all competition and lead to monopoly pricing, which would raise the price of meat for the entire city. R. Joseph Cologne (Maharik, Italy, 1420–1480), *Responsa* 182:1, uses this text to explain the opinion of R. Isaac b. Abba Mari of Marseilles (France, 1122–1193), the *Ba'al ha-Ittur* (see infra, note 63).

43 BT *Bava Batra* 9a.

44 *Tosefta, Bava Metsi'a* 11:12.

45 *Shulhan Arukh, Orah Hayyim* 55:22.

46 There is a third level of community ordinance, as discussed by R. Solomon b. Abraham Adret (Rashba, Spain, c. 1235–c. 1310), *Responsa* 1:788 and 5:178, where he treats a law that would lead to the double taxation of certain members of the community. If majority rule is implemented in this case, Rashba states that it would be the equivalent of communal robbery. Hence, unanimous approval is required, with the inclusion of those members who stand to lose. However, if the law is passed, it stands even for those people who later move into the community, even if they stand to lose and never agreed to follow the law. R. Hayyim Halberstam (Poland, 1793–1876), *Responsa Divrei Hayyim* 2:59, posits that any ordinance not enacted in order to improve the general welfare of the community requires unanimous approval.

communal ordinance that set a price ceiling on wool purchased from Gentiles.[47] Maharashdam cites the view of R. Jacob b. Meir (Rabbeinu Tam, France, 1100–1171)[48] and others[49] that communal legislation that harms some and benefits others requires unanimous approval to pass. The only exception is legislation designed to protect religious law, where majority sponsorship is sufficient. R. Yom Tov b. Abraham Ishbili (Ritba, Spain, c. 1250–1330) disputes this view. Ritba quotes R. Jonah b. Abraham of Gerona (Spain, 1200–1263), who contends that a majority vote is sufficient to excommunicate a member of the town, and that a unanimous vote is not necessary.[50] Maharashdam concludes that Ritba's view is accepted as normative in Jewish law.[51]

47 *Responsa Maharashdam, Yoreh De'ah* 117.

48 Quoted by Mordecai b. Hillel ha-Kohen (Germany, c. 1240–1298), *Mordekhai* 480.

49 *Responsa Rashi* 247; R. Joseph Bonfils (France, eleventh century), R. Judah b. Kalonymus b. Meir (Germany, d. 1196/1199), and R. M. b. Mordekhai quoted in *Mordekhai* 481; *Responsa Rambam* 329; *Responsa Maharam of Rothenberg* 268, 941, 968; *Mordekhai* 179; R. Jacob Moellin (Maharil, Germany, c. 1360–1427), *Responsa Maharil ha-Hadashot* 153; *Responsa Maharik* 181:2; R. Elijah Mizrahi (Turkey, c. 1450–1526), *Responsa* 14, 57; R. Benjamin b. Mattityahu (Turkey, sixteenth century), *Responsa Binyamin Ze'ev* 290, 296, 299, 300; R. Jehiel Basan (Salonika, 1550–1625), *Responsa Mahari Basan* 98.

50 BT *Avodah Zarah* 36b. R. Joshua Boaz b. Simon Baruch (Italy, sixteenth century), *Shiltei ha-Gibborim* (note 3 to *Mordekhai* 475), presents two proofs from the Bible in support of Ritba's position. First, he asserts that Joseph did not tell Jacob that he was alive during the years that he was in Egypt because of the excommunication that the brothers placed upon whoever revealed to Jacob why he had actually disappeared (*Midrash Tanhuma* at *Va-Yeshev* 2, and *Pirkei de-Rabbi Eliezer* 38). Even though Joseph obviously did not consent to this decree of excommunication, he still considered himself bound by it. Second, I Samuel, ch. 14, tells that Saul proclaimed a fast for the entire army after the battle with the Philistines, and, even though Jonathan did not hear the proclamation, he was still held culpable for violating it. These proofs, however, are not irrefutable. First, the reason Joseph did not inform Jacob of his whereabouts during his stay in Egypt was not necessarily the brothers' excommunication (see Ramban to Genesis 42:9; R. Moses Alshekh [Ottoman Palestine, sixteenth century], *Torat Mosheh* to Genesis 41:5; and R. Naphtali Tsevi Judah Berlin [Netsiv, Lithuania, 1817–1893], *Ha'amek Davar*, ibid.). Second, Ramban (Leviticus 27:29 and *Responsa of Rashba Attributed to Ramban* 288), Rashba (*Responsa* 1:788), and R. Elijah Mizrahi (*Responsa* 14) all point out that Saul, being king, had special powers beyond those of the townspeople (see Joshua 7). R. Hayyim (Eliezer) b. Isaac "Or Zaru'a" (Germany, thirteenth century), *Responsa Hayyim Or Zarua* 222, assumes that Jonathan was bound by Saul's excommunication since, had he been present, he would surely have accepted it. *Responsa Binyamin Ze'ev* 300 assumes that Jonathan was held culpable because he was considered a negligible minority (see supra, note 78).

51 *Responsa Rif* 13; R. Eliezer b. Joel ha-Levi of Bonn (Ravyah, Germany, 1140–1225), quoted in *Mordekhai* 482; R. Meir Abulafia (Spain, 1165–1244), *Yad Ramah, Bava Batra* 1:103; *Din Hermei Tsibbur le-ha-Ramban*, quoted in *Responsa of Rashba Attributed to Ramban* 288; *Responsa Rashba* 1:781, 2:268, 2:279, 3:411, 5:125, 5:126, 5:242, 5:245, 5:270, and *Responsa of Rashba Attributed to Ramban* 65, 280 (see, however, 4:185); Rosh, *Responsa* 5:4, 6:5, 6:7, 7:5; R. Isaac b. Sheshet Perfet (Rivash, Algiers, 1326–1408), *Responsa* 71, 249, 399; R. Simeon b. Tsemah Duran (*Tashbets*, Algiers, 1361–1444), *Responsa* 1:123; R. Levi b. Habib (Maharalbah, Ottoman Palestine, c. 1483–1545), *Responsa* 40; R. Moses b. Joseph Trani (Mabbit, Ottoman Palestine, 1500–1580), *Responsa* 1:84; R. Joseph b. David ibn Lev (Maharival, Turkey, 1505–1580), *Responsa Mahari ben Lev* 2:72; Rema, *Responsa* 73; R. Moses Alshekh, *Responsa* 59; R. Yom Tov Tsahalon (Ottoman Palestine, 1559–1619/20), *Responsa Maharit Tsahalon ha-Hadashot* 199; R. Joshua Hoeschel b. Joseph of Krakow (Poland, 1578–1648), *Responsa Penei Yehoshua, Orah Hayyim* 4; R. Jair Hayyim Bacharach (Germany, 1628–1701), *Responsa Havvot Yair* 81; R. Jacob Emden (Germany, 1697–1776), *She'elot Ya'avets* 78; R. Hayyim Joseph David Azulai (Ottoman Palestine, 1724–1806), *Responsa Hayyim Shaul* 1:30; R. Hayyim Palagi (Turkey, 1788–1869), *Responsa Semikhah le-Hayyim* 15; *Responsa Divrei Hayyim, Hoshen Mishpat* 1:23, 1:24, 1:25, 2:59, 2:62; R. Elijah Gutmacher (Prussia, 1795–1874), *Responsa, Hoshen Mishpat* 6; R. Jehiel Michal Epstein (Russia, 1829–1908), *Arukh ha-Shulhan, Hoshen Mishpat* 231:27; R. Joel Teitelbaum (New York, 1888–1976), *Responsa Divrei Yoel* 2:128; and R. Eliezer Waldenberg (Israel, 1915–2006), *Responsa Tsits Eliezer* 2:23. While, according to all of the above opinions, that majority agreement is sufficient, some may require perfect attendance at the vote. R. Moses Sofer (Bratislava, 1762–1839), *Responsa, Hoshen Mishpat* 116, posits that the perfect attendance requirement is fulfilled by duly publicizing the vote in advance.

The dispute between Rabbeinu Tam and Ritba, as it appears to this writer, turns on the legal underpinning of the community's authority to legislate. Rabbeinu Tam understands that this authority derives from a partnership relationship that community members are entitled to form with one another. Thus, each member of the community has the prerogative not to join the partnership. Ritba, however, views a communal partnership as equal in authority to a monarch, and a king's decree does not require the unanimous consent of his subjects to be binding. Accordingly, a law approved by the majority of the community is binding on all.[52]

However, in an agreement among tradesmen, almost all medieval commentators (Rishonim), including the Ritba himself, agree that unanimous consent is required for the agreement to be binding.[53] This apparent inconsistency is maintained by later halakhic decisors, such as Rema, who rules that townspeople require only a majority to enact an ordinance,[54] while tradesmen need unanimous agreement.[55] R. Asher b. Jehiel (Rosh, Germany, c. 1250–1327) resolves the inconsistency by positing that requiring unanimity for community legislation would enable

52 This concept can be seen in *Responsa Rashba* 1:781 and the *Responsa* of R. Betsalel Ashkenazi (Egypt, 1520–c. 1594), 24. There is a dispute as to whether the power of townspeople is of Biblical or Rabbinic origin. Maharashdam, op. cit., contends that Rosh follows the minority view that the power is of Rabbinic origin. *Shulhan Arukh* (*Yoreh De'ah* 239:4, 6) states the general rule that, when one swears not to obey a Biblical commandment, the oath is not valid. However, when one swears not to obey a Rabbinic decree, the oath is valid, but one is forced to nullify his oath. Therefore, when *Responsa Rashi* (247) declares that an oath not to follow the community's ordinances is invalid, he assumes that the power of the townspeople is of Biblical origin. This opinion can also be found in *Responsa Maharam of Rothenberg* 104; *Responsa Rashba* 3:17, 7:430; R. Moses b. Jacob of Coucy (France, thirteenth century), *Sefer Mitsvot Gadol* (*Semag*), Negative Commandment 238; R. Israel Isserlein (Austria, 1390–1460), *Terumat ha-Deshen* 281; *Responsa Maharashdam, Yoreh De'ah* 97; R. Hayyim Palagi, *Responsa Hikkakei Lev, Hoshen Mishpat* 41; and *Shulhan Arukh Yoreh De'ah* 228:33. R. Elijah b. Solomon Zalman of Vilna (Gera, Lithuania, 1720–1797) in his notes (ibid., 94) disagrees with this point of view, since it is impossible that the Men of the Great Assembly could only make decrees Rabbinic in origin while every town could make decrees Biblical in origin. R. David b. Samuel ha-Levi (Poland, 1586–1667), *Turei Zahav* (ibid., 44), explains this discrepancy by saying that, when an ordinance is made to protect religious law it is Biblical in origin, based on Leviticus 18:30 as interpreted in BT *Yevamot* 21a. Monetary decrees, however, are only Rabbinic in origin. R. Nehemiah Tyler ("Mazkirot ha-Yishuv ve-Hilkhoteha," *Tehumin* 9 [1988]: 103–5) offers a converse opinion, claiming that monetary decrees are Biblical in nature, based on the powers of the king, but decrees to protect religious law are only Rabbinic in nature. Former *Rishon le-Tsiyyon* R. Eliahu Bakshi-Doron (Israel, contemporary), *Responsa Binyan Av* 75, posits that all agree that a decree made by the townspeople is only Rabbinic in nature. The case being discussed, however, is a case where the person swears not to follow *any* of the townspeoples' decrees, and the opinion of Rashi is that the *power* of the townspeople to make decrees is Biblical in origin.

53 *Mishneh Torah, Sekhirut* 14:11; Ramban to *Bava Batra* 9a; *Responsa Rashba* 2:268, 4:185, 5:270, and *Responsa of Rashba Attributed to Ramban* 65; Rosh, *Bava Batra* 1:33; Jacob b. Asher (Spain, 1270–1340), *Tur, Hoshen Mishpat* 231:30; Ritba and Ran to *Bava Batra* 9a; R. Vidal Yom Tov of Tolosa (Spain, c. 1360), *Maggid Mishneh* to *Mishneh Torah*, ibid.; *Responsa Tashbets* 3:45; *Responsa Maharit Tsahalon ha-Hadashot* 199; R. Abraham b. Moses de Boton (Salonika, 1560–1609), *Responsa Lehem Rav* 216; *Responsa Binyamin Ze'ev* 290; *Responsa Semikhah le-Hayyim* 15; *Arukh ha-Shulhan, Hoshen Mishpat* 231:27; R. Isser Zalman Meltzer (Lithuania, 1870–1953), *Even ha-Azel* to *Mishneh Torah, Mekhirah* 14:11. See, however, R. Mordecai Jaffe (Poland, c. 1535–1612), *Levush Ir Shushan* 231:28; R. Isaac Hezekiah Lampronti (Italy, 1679–1756), *Pahad Yitshak*, vol. 2, 31b; R. Moses Feinstein (New York, 1895–1986), *Iggerot Mosheh, Hoshen Mishpat* 1:59; R. Ovadiah Yosef (Israel, b. 1920), *Responsa Yehavveh Da'at* 4:48.

54 *Shulhan Arukh, Hoshen Mishpat* 163:1.

55 Ibid., 231:28.

a dissenting minority to paralyze the whole legislative process.[56] Similarly, Maharashdam says that a community has monarchical power since society cannot function without a means of passing legislation. In sharp contrast, agreements among tradesmen are nothing more than a partnership and hence binding only on those who consent. Tradesmen make agreements for their own benefit rather than that of the community at large, and hence they do not have the kind of power enjoyed by the community.[57]

If indeed an agreement between tradesmen is no different than any other partnership arrangement, why did the rabbis establish a special category for it? The answer seems to be that, theoretically, tradesmen in unanimous agreement can wield the same power as townspeople.[58]

The Powers of Tradesmen

Chapters 19 and 20 of the Book of Judges tell of a civil war between Benjamin and the other tribes of Israel. Upon defeating Benjamin, the tribes swear that "none of us shall give his daughter to Benjamin in marriage."[59] The Talmud derives from the words "of us" that their oath was only binding on that particular generation.[60] The implication is that, without the words "of us," the oath would have been binding on all future generations, even though the other tribes did not explicitly stipulate so. Similarly, communal decrees are binding on future members of the community—both current inhabitants who are not yet come of age as well as those who later move into the community.[61] Thus, tradesmen who agree unanimously upon an ordinance can force future members of the trade to abide by the earlier decree.

56 *Responsa Rosh* 6:7. R. Israel Meir ha-Kohen Kagan (Poland, 1839–1933), in his *Mishnah Berurah* (53:53), implements a similar logic when addressing the topic of the appointment of community leadership positions. Though at one time a unanimous decision from the community could realistically be expected, nowadays rabble-rousers create strife for no valid reason; therefore, unanimity cannot be required.

57 This is not in opposition to the medieval commentators (Rishonim) quoted in note 49, who claim that "just as the townspeople have the right to enact decrees, so do the tradesmen," since Maharashdam (*Yoreh De'ah* 117) explains that this just means that they have similar powers, but not that they necessarily share all special abilities. Another example of a divergence can be seen in *Mishneh Torah, Mekhirah* 14:9–11; Ramban and Ran to *Bava Batra* 9a; *Responsa Rivash* 399; R. Moses b. Isaac Alashkar (Ottoman Palestine, 1466–1542), *Responsa Maharam Alashkar* 49; and *Sema, Hoshen Mishpat* 231:45—all of whom claim that the distinguished man requirement applies only to the tradesmen and not to the townspeople. Another possible explanation for this divergence is suggested by *Arukh ha-Shulhan*, op. cit., who asserts that total agreement is needed only to create a union of individuals. The townspeople are automatically considered a union by dint of the fact that they live in the same town. The tradesmen require unanimous approval only to create a union, but, once the union has been established, only majority approval is required to pass an ordinance.

58 Assuming, according to the opinions listed in note 53, that this is a case where there is no distinguished man.

59 Judges 21:1.

60 BT *Bava Batra* 121a.

61 *Responsa Rivash* 249, 399; *Responsa Eliyahu Mizrahi* 57; *Responsa Maharam Alashkar*, op. cit.; R. Moses Sofer, *Hatam Sofer, Bava Batra* 9a; *Responsa Divrei Hayyim* 2:63; and *Hazon Ish, Bava Batra* 4:14.

There are four different opinions among Rishonim as to what is required to form or dissolve a standard partnership. R. Isaac b. Abba Mari of Marseilles (France, 1122–1190) claims that the partners are bound together by the mutual benefit derived from knowing that each has a share of the other's profits.[62] Therefore, a *kinyan* (a symbolic act to make an agreement binding) is not required. The strength of the partnership is that it cannot be dissolved without the consent of all of the partners.[63]

Maimonides (Rambam, Egypt, 1135–1204) disagrees and posits that an agreement between two parties to divide the profits of a business venture is not legally binding.[64] This is because, at the time the agreement is made, future profits have the status of *davar she-lo ba la-olam* (something not yet in existence), making them outside the realm of binding agreements. Accordingly, even if a *kinyan* is performed, the agreement is unenforceable. Thus, if *A* realized profits subsequent to the agreement, there would be no legal basis for forcing *A* to turn over to *B* his share of the profits.

A third view is offered by R. Abraham b. David (Ra'avad, France, c. 1125–c. 1198) in his glosses on Rambam.[65] Drawing an analogy between a partnership agreement and the contract of an indentured servant (*eved Ivri*) with his master, he claims that a partnership agreement is legally binding. He adds that a *kinyan* is required to make a partnership legally binding, although he does not mention this in his *responsa*.[66] Additionally, his *responsa* consider a partner equivalent to a per diem worker (*po'el*), who is entitled to withdraw from a contract without penalty. This contradicts his glosses, which compare a partner to an indentured servant. R. Joseph Cologne (Maharik, Italy, 1420–1480) reconciles this apparent contradiction by distinguishing between a partnership consummated by a mere verbal agreement and one consummated by a *kinyan*. In the former, each partner has the status of a *po'el* and may withdraw at any moment.[67] However, in the latter case, the *kinyan* confers upon each partner the status of an *eved Ivri*, who can only be released from his obligation by means of the consent his master or, in this case, the other partners.[68]

62 *Sefer ha-Ittur*, letter *shin*—"*Shittuf*," p. 42.

63 This opinion is shared by Rabbeinu Tam and Maharam of Rothenberg, quoted in *Responsa Maharik* 181:2; *Mordekhai* 166 and 663; *Responsa Maharil ha-Hadashot* 144; *Tur*, *Hoshen Mishpat* 176:5; and *Responsa Binyamin Ze'ev* 380. The *Sefer ha-Ittur* reads R. Meir ha-Kohen of Rothenberg (Germany, thirteenth century), *Haggahot Maimoniyot* (*Gezelah va-Avedah* 12:10 and *Sheluhin ve-Shuttafin* 4:1), as agreeing with this opinion, but according to the simple reading it would seem that he agrees with the opinion of Rashba (see infra, note 69). *Responsa Mahari ben Lev* (2:23) claims that the opinion of R. Elijah quoted in *Tosafot* to *Ketubbot* 54b (s.v. "*af*") and in Rosh, *Ketubbot* 5:1, concurs with the opinion of *Sefer ha-Ittur*, but, again, there is no reason to assume that he does not agree with the opinion of Rashba.

64 Rambam, *Mishneh Torah*, *Sheluhin ve-Shuttafin* 4:2. According to Rambam, merchants can create a partnership by buying raw materials together, combining them, and selling the final product.

65 Ibid.

66 R. Abraham b. Isaac of Narbonne (France, 1110–1179), *Responsa Ra'avi ha-Ra'avad ha-Rishon* 127.

67 See supra, note 28.

68 *Responsa Maharik* 181:1. *Hazon Ish* (*Bava Batra* 4:9) explains the opinion of Ra'avad based on Maharik, who says that the verbal agreement creates a lien on the partner's work, while the *kinyan* creates a lien on the partner's body. Several later decisors take issue with the opinion of Maharik for various reasons. One major

The fourth opinion is offered by R. Solomon b. Abraham Adret (Rashba, Spain, c. 1235–c. 1310), who maintains that a verbal agreement is as strong as a *kinyan*.[69] Thus, whether or not a *kinyan* took place, a partner can retract only in regard to future payments.[70]

Despite the divergence of opinions about the binding nature of a standard partnership, all authorities agree that verbal agreement is sufficient for a union of tradesmen to create a binding ordinance. No member may retract without the permission of the majority of the tradesmen.[71]

Like a communal legislative body, tradesmen also have the power to administer penalties for violation of rules.[72] However, the partnership must circumvent certain restrictions. First, the question of *asmakhta* must be addressed.[73] Second, the Mishnah establishes certain requirements, known as *mishpetei ha-tena'im*, for a condition incorporated into a transaction.[74] The Talmud explains that the condition must specify what will happen if the condition is fulfilled, the condition mentioned prior to the outcome, positive before negative;[75] the condition and outcome must be different actions; and it must be possible to accomplish the action through an agent.[76] However, R. Hayyim Palagi (Turkey, 1788–1869)

---

contention is that the "contradiction" is no contradiction, since the notes and *responsa* were written by different people, both named Ra'avad. Nevertheless, this opinion is shared by *Responsa Rosh* 89:2 and R. Jacob Loberbaum of Lissa (Germany, 1760–1832), *Netivot ha-Mishpat* 163:9. The point of divergence between Rambam and Ra'avad is that Rambam sees the *kinyan* as relating to the profits, which are not yet in the world, while Ra'avad sees it as relating to the partners, who are in the world. This point can be seen more clearly in *Mishneh Torah, Mekhirah* 5:14. Ra'avad proves his point using BT *Ketubbot* 58b, which allows a husband to sanctify whatever his wife will produce through her work, since his wife is in the world. (See *Beit Yosef*, op. cit.)

69 *Responsa Rashba* 1:1057, 2:87, and novellae of Rashba to *Bava Batra* 9a.

70 This opinion is shared by Ra'avad, op. cit. (as understood by Ritba to *Bava Batra* 9a; *Beit Yosef*, op. cit.; and *Responsa Maharashdam, Hoshen Mishpat* 168); Ramban to *Bava Batra* 9a (as understood by *Responsa Rivash* 71 and 476, and *Responsa Maharashdam, Hoshen Mishpat* 395); Ritba, op. cit.; Ran, op. cit.; *Responsa Rivash*, op. cit.; *Responsa Maharashdam, Hoshen Mishpat* 274; and R. Shabbetai b. Meir ha-Kohen (Lithuania, 1621–1662), *Siftei Kohen, Hoshen Mishpat* 176:8. *Hazon Ish* (*Bava Batra* 4:8) claims that Ramban subscribes to a fifth opinion—a *kinyan* is necessary for a partnership to go into effect, and a partner can still renege with regard to future dealings. This is also the opinion of R. David b. Solomon ibn Abi Zimra (Radbaz, Egypt, 1479–1589), *Responsa Radbaz* 1:298; *Responsa Mahari ben Lev* (2:23) maintains that this is the opinion of Ra'avad.

71 Ramban to *Bava Batra* 9a; *Mordekhai* 481; *Responsa Rosh* 6:19, 6:21; R. Alexandri Zoislin (Germany, d. 1349), *Sefer ha-Agudah, Bava Batra* 19; *Responsa Tashbets* 1:159, 2:63, 4:15 (see, however, 2:16); R. Solomon b. Simon Duran (Rashbash, Algiers, 1400–1469), *Responsa* 211; *Responsa Maharik* 181:2; *Responsa Eliyahu Mizrahi* 57; *Responsa Radbaz* 1:65; *Beit Yosef, Hoshen Mishpat* 176:4; *Responsa Maharashdam, Hoshen Mishpat* 153, 259, 395; R. Solomon Luria (Lithuania, 1510–1574), *Yam shel Shelomoh, Bava Kamma* 10:43; *Perishah, Hoshen Mishpat* 176:4; *Responsa Lehem Rav* 114; *Responsa Semikhah le-Hayyim* 15. This is also the simple reading of the *Tosefta, Bava Metsi'a* 11:12.

72 BT *Bava Batra* 8b, 9a.

73 *Asmakhta* is an obligation made without *gemirat da'at*—deliberate and perfect intent—and *semikhat da'at*—the generation of reliance on the part of the party to whom the obligation was made. For a more complete discussion of *asmakhta* and ways of circumventing the problem, see Aaron Levine, *Economics and Jewish Law* (New York: Ktav, Yeshiva University Press, 1987), 194–97.

74 Mishnah, *Kiddushin* 3:4.

75 BT *Gittin* 75a.

76 This is according to the opinions of R. Ahai Gaon (Shabha, eighth century), *She'iltot, Parashat Matot* 138; *Sefer ha-Ittur*, letter *Tet*, p. 37b; Rambam, *Mishneh Torah, Zekhiyah u-Mattanah* 3:7-8 and *Ishut* 6:14;

states that these requirements are not compulsory for a union formed by unanimous agreement.[77]

Based on the above sources, only a union started with the approval of the entire[78] workforce[79] has the power of tradesmen. Such a union can force new workers to join, stop members from leaving the union, and pass new rules by a majority. However, if nonunion workers are also part of the workplace, the union is considered no more than a partnership, and, unless the nonmembers approve, the union's rules are not binding on the rest of the workforce.[80] In addition, they may[81] need to perform a *kinyan* to pass a binding agreement on their members,[82] and the union cannot force newcomers to join. However, the union's members *are*

Tosafot to *Gittin* 72a (s.v. "*la-afukei*") and to *Kiddushin* (s.v. "*devarim*"); R. Zerahiah ha-Levi Gerondi (Spain, twelfth century), *Ha-Ma'or ha-Katan*, *Beitsah* 20a; *Mordekhai*, *Sukkah* 758; Rosh, *Bava Batra* 8:58 and *Responsa* 81:1; *Semag*, Positive Commandment 48; and *Tur*, *Hoshen Mishpat* 241:11 and *Even ha-Ezer* 38:12—all of whom agree that the requirements of *mishpetei ha-tena'im* apply to monetary transactions. There is, however, an alternative opinion espoused by *Responsa Rif* 1:31 and 2:107; R. Samuel b. Meir (Rashbam, France, c. 1080–c. 1174), *Bava Batra* 137b; Ra'avad to *Mishneh Torah*, *Zekhiyah u-Mattanah* 3:7-8, and novellae to *Beitsah* 20a; Ramban to *Kiddushin* 61a, *Gittin* 75b, and in *Milhamot ha-Shem* to *Beitsah* 20a and Halakhot, *Nedarim* 3a; Rashba to *Gittin* 75a, *Shevu'ot* 36b, and in *Responsa* 1:1066 and 1:1125; Ritba to *Kiddushin* 50a and 61a, *Gittin* 75a, and *Nedarim* 11a; Ran to *Kiddushin* 50a and 61a, *Nedarim* 11b, and *Shevu'ot* 35b; and *Responsa Rivash* 175. All these contend that monetary transactions are exempt from the requirement of *mishpetei ha-tena'im*.

77 *Responsa Semikhah le-Hayyim*, op. cit. Rambam, *Mishneh Torah*, *Laws of Transactions* 11:6, requires that all agreements include a time constraint. If this requirement is not met, the agreement is not valid, since the contributor was not aware of how much he was obligating himself. *Responsa Lehem Rav* 114 claims that this requirement is waived in the case of the tradesmen. Rashba and Ritba to *Bava Batra* 9a both describe another weakness of a plain partnership: It can obligate a member only to do something actively, but it cannot force him to refrain from an activity. This would effectively kill a nonunanimous union's power to force a strike on its members.

78 While never discussed explicitly, it would seem that there is a dispute as to whether the word "all" must be taken literally or not. *Responsa Lehem Rav* 216 and *Responsa Semikhah le-Hayyim* 15 both imply that "all" must be taken literally, and even one opposing tradesman invalidates the union. On the other hand, *Responsa Maharashdam* (*Hoshen Mishpat* 153) and *Responsa Binyamin Ze'ev* 300 both imply that a negligible minority may be ignored. R. Jacob b. Aaron of Karlin (Lithuania, 1788–1844), *Mishkenot Ya'akov*, *Yoreh De'ah* 17, states that up to ten percent is considered a negligible minority. Thus, once there is an agreement among ninety percent of the tradesmen, the remaining ten percent may be forced to follow the majority since, for all intents and purposes, the agreement is considered unanimous and the overwhelming majority acquires the powers of the tradesmen. *Responsa Semikhah le-Hayyim* would force a dissenting individual to join a new union only when he himself loses by not joining the union. Such a refusal is considered Sodomite in nature, and the "*kofin al middat Sedom*" principle—according to which the authorities force an individual not to behave in a manner considered Sodomite—would be applied.

79 Tradesmen are always referred to in respect to all of the tradesmen in a city. Yet there is no reason to assume that this was done for any reason other than the fact that, up until modern times, each market was represented by the craftsmen present in a particular town. Hence, all autoworkers in Detroit should not have to agree to unionize in order to create a situation of unanimous agreement; rather, each plant should be treated separately.

80 *Responsa Minhat Shelomoh* 87. For an explanation, see supra, note 57.

81 This dispute has carried over to modern times with *Arukh ha-Shulhan* (*Hoshen Mishpat* 176:8) insisting that the majority of opinions agree that no *kinyan* is necessary, at least on work previously completed, while *Hazon Ish* (*Bava Batra* 4:10) claims that the majority of opinions do require a *kinyan*. There does seem to be agreement that we do not follow the opinion of Rambam.

82 A *kinyan* could be either a contract or the handing over of money. *Arukh ha-Shulhan* (ibid., 2) and *Hazon Ish* (ibid., 4:9) both agree that a *kinyan sudar*—a symbolic *kinyan*—would not suffice. *Arukh ha-Shulhan* (ibid., 6) states that a contract must use wording that obligates money; a contract that merely states that a partnership has been created would not be valid. Payment of union dues should be considered a valid *kinyan*.

bound by its agreements. Accordingly, if the union votes to strike, members may not return to work until the union votes to end the strike.[83]

Regulation

It is generally assumed that the "distinguished man's"[84] right of adjudication serves to limit the power of organized tradesmen and prevent them from using monopoly power to raise prices above the fair market level.[85] Since in modern times there are no "distinguished men,"[86] there seems to be no mechanism to regulate union powers. This problem is raised by R. Joseph b. David ibn Lev (Maharival, Turkey, 1505–1580), who points out that this situation always existed in towns that did not have a "distinguished man."[87]

The Talmud relates that officers may be appointed to guard the marketplace from unfair prices.[88] Rambam explains that, while the vendors have the right to set their prices as high as they wish, the courts must patrol the marketplace and force the vendors to keep their prices within one-sixth of the going rate.[89] R. Hayyim Palagi applies this logic to tradesmen and claims that they may pass any ordinance they wish, but, if it is unfair, the townspeople can counter by passing their own ordinances.[90] They may appoint special officers or

83 *Arukh ha-Shulhan* (ibid., 8) states that, after a decision to complete an agreement over a period of time, backing out in the middle of the job is considered reneging even on work completed prior to the time of reneging. (This opinion is most probably based on a disagreement among the Rishonim regarding whether a citizen of a town who leaves the town permanently after a tax is imposed, but before it is collected, is obligated to pay that tax. A minority opinion is expressed by Rabbeinu Tam [quoted in *Mordekhai* and *Haggahot ha-Asheri*, *Bava Batra* 8a] who claims that the individual is exempt from the tax. However, Rema [*Hoshen Mishpat* 163:5] states that we follow the majority opinion, which disagrees. This position is held by Ramban to *Bava Batra* 8a; Ran, ad. loc.; *Nimmukei Yosef*, ad. loc.; Rabbi Isaac of Carcassonne [France, thirteenth century], ad. loc., *Responsa* 2; *Responsa Mabbit* 1:181, 1:316; *Havvot Yair* 157; and *Arukh ha-Shulhan*, *Hoshen Mishpat* 163:5.) Hence, even according to the opinion of Rashba, one would not be able to back out of a strike once it had started. It should follow that, once a union member was part of the union at the time of the vote to strike, he would be bound to the union until the end of the strike.

84 As in the case of the two butchers, above. R. Joseph b. Meir ha-Levi ibn Migash (Spain, 1077–1141), quoted in *Maggid Mishneh* to *Mishneh Torah*, *Mekhirah* 14:11; *Yad Ramah*, BT *Bava Batra* 1:103; Rosh, *Bava Batra* 1:33; *Responsa Tashbets* 4:15; *Responsa Radbaz* 1:65; and *Responsa Semikhah le-Hayyim* 15 all share the accepted opinion that a distinguished man must be both distinguished in his knowledge and appointed by the community. *Mordekhai* 484 is of the opinion that he need only be distinguished in his knowledge. *Responsa Rashba* 4:185 asserts that either distinguished knowledge or appointment creates the status of a distinguished man.

85 This opinion is presented by Ramban to *Bava Batra* 9a. Minority opinions are offered by Ritba, ibid., who relates that the requirement was instituted to give honor to the distinguished man, and *Responsa Eliyahu Mizrahi* (57), which asserts that when an ordinance is passed in the presence of a distinguished man and he is not consulted, there the parties are lacking in *semikhat da'at*.

86 *Iggerot Mosheh*, *Hoshen Mishpat* 1:59.

87 *Responsa Mahari ben Lev* 1:115.

88 *Bava Batra* 89a.

89 *Mishneh Torah*, *Mekhirah* 14:1.

90 *Responsa Semikhah le-Hayyim* 15.

courts[91] to oversee the decisions of the tradesmen and, if necessary, correct them. For example, if a cartel of grocers agrees to raise the price of essential foodstuffs, the courts are obligated to force them to lower prices. If the case involves nonessential goods, the courts may choose to implement a price ceiling.

Dina De-Malkhuta Dina

It is practically unfeasible for Jewish communities outside of Israel to establish the type of regulatory bodies described above. Yet these rules are still relevant. In several places, the Talmud mentions the rule that "the law of the land is the law."[92] It follows that the Torah considers monetary laws promulgated by an honest government in the interests of its subjects as binding on all Jewish citizens. R. Shabbetai b. Meir ha-Kohen (Poland, 1621–1662) comments that such laws are binding even in dealings between two Jews, as the law is considered an implicit condition that all parties are bound to follow.[93]

R. Joseph Elijah Henkin (New York, 1881–1973) posits that, nowadays, without the right of autonomous self-government, Jewish communities in democratic countries cede their obligation to legislate in matters of social welfare to the secular government.[94] Thus, any legislation enacted by Congress would be considered binding under Jewish law and enforceable in any Jewish court (*beit din*).[95]

Conclusion

Under Jewish law, workers do not have any power or rights until they agree to unionize. There are two categories of unions: those that represent the entire[96] labor force in a certain area and those that do not.[97] The former acquires the

91 Former Chief Rabbis of Israel R. Avraham Yitshak ha-Kohen Kook (British Palestine, 1865–1935), in the journal *Netivah* (Nisan 5693), and R. Bentsiyyon Uzziel (Israel, 1887–1953), *Mishpetei Uzziel* 42, both call for the establishment of courts consisting of men who are well-versed in Torah law as well as in the economics of the marketplace, in order to deal with labor disputes.

92 BT *Bava Kamma* 113a; BT *Bava Batra* 54b; BT *Nedarim* 28a; BT *Gittin* 10b.

93 R. Shabbetai b. Meir ha-Kohen, *Shakh* to *Hoshen Mishpat* (73:39). For an overview of this topic, see R. Hershel Schachter, "'Dina De'malchusa Dina': Secular Law As a Religious Obligation," *Journal of Halacha and Contemporary Society* 1,1 (1981): 103–25.

94 *Teshuvot Ivra*, vol. 2, 176.

95 Jewish law mandates that all civil cases between two Jews must be adjudicated by a Jewish court (*Beit Din*) using Jewish law (BT *Gittin* 88b, *Shulhan Arukh, Hoshen Mishpat* [26:1]). Application of secular legislation in situations like this does not pose a problem, as the legislation becomes part of the body of applicable law.

96 See supra, note 78.

97 One further caveat should be mentioned. In United States law, codified in the National Labor Relations Act and amended by the Taft-Hartley Act, 29 U.S.C. Sec. Sec. 141-197, only private employees have the right to

powers of an agreement among tradesmen. They can coerce new laborers to join the union, restrict members from withdrawing, and are not constrained by laws regarding agreements. However, the latter cannot coerce nonunion workers to join,[98] can prevent strikebreaking only among members who originally voted to strike,[99] and are constrained by laws concerning agreements. In both cases, a labor relations board should be established to govern union powers.[100]

Thus, the agreement of a majority of employees would be sufficient to create a union. However, it would not be very powerful, as it could not force nonunion employees to strike. For Halakhah to confer real negotiating power and significant rights upon a union, it would have to be formed by unanimous agreement. Despite the difficulties involved in forming a halakhically valid union, workers are not totally without protection, as the government is entitled to regulate the relationship between labor and management. Any laws they pass are binding and enforceable in Jewish courts.

SELECTED BIBLIOGRAPHY

Auerbach, R. Solomon Zalman. *Responsa Minhat Shelomoh* 87.

Bleich, R. J. David. "Organized Labor" and "Tenure." In *Contemporary Halakhic Problems*, vol. 1. New York: Ktav, Yeshiva University Press, 1977.

Caro, R. Joseph. *Shulhan Arukh, Hoshen Mishpat* 231.

De Medina, R., and Samuel B. Moses. *Responsa Maharashdam, Yoreh De'ah* 117.

Epstein, R. Jehiel Michal. *Arukh ha-Shulhan, Hoshen Mishpat* 231.

Feinstein, R. Moses. *Iggerot Mosheh, Hoshen Mishpat* 1:59.

Isserles, R. Moses. Rema to *Hoshen Mishpat* 231.

---

unionize and strike. States have at times expanded these rights, as is the case with New York's Taylor Law, Article 14 of the New York State Civil Service Law, which gave public employees the right to unionize, but not to strike. *Tosefta, Bava Metsi'a* (11:27) states that workers essential to the public can be prevented from leaving their work. See Aaron Levine, *Free Enterprise and Jewish Law: Aspects of Jewish Business Ethics* (New York: Ktav, 1980), IV, note 72, for a discussion of whether this is the accepted ruling regarding public employees' right to strike.

98 BT *Yevamot* 13b quotes the negative commandment of "*lo titgodedu*"—not to make subdivisions within a city. Rashi, Rosh, Ritba, and Meiri explain that the prohibition seeks to prevent the perception, based on a divergence in how two groups in one town approach certain laws, that there are two versions of the Torah. Rambam (*Mishneh Torah, Avodat Kokhavim* 12:14) explains the commandment as a prohibition against causing conflict. Based on this understanding, *Responsa Rambam* (329) applies this prohibition to community ordinances. While the opinion of Rambam is that the majority cannot force its wishes upon a dissenting minority, still the minority should agree to follow the majority to avoid conflict. Another law that helps nonunanimous unions is that of *marufia* or *hassagat gevul*—tortuous interference with another's business relationship—which *Iggerot Mosheh* (*Hoshen Mishpat* 1:59) applies to stop scabs from taking union jobs during a strike.

99 See supra, note 86.

100 Even though a standard partnership is not bound to the opinion of the distinguished man, still they would be required to listen to the labor relations board, since their power stems from the power of the townspeople, whose decisions must be followed by everyone.

Jakobovits, R. Immanuel. "The Right to Strike." In *Studies in Torah Judaism: Jewish Law Faces Modern Problems*. New York: Yeshiva University Dept. of Special Publications, 1965.

Levine, Aaron. *Free Enterprise and Jewish Law: Aspects of Jewish Business Ethics*. New York: Ktav, 1980.

Maimonides. *Mishneh Torah, Mekhirah* 14:11.

Palagi, R. Hayyim. *Responsa Semikhah le-Hayyim* 15.

Talmud (Babylonian):

Bava Kamma 116b.

Bava Batra 8b–9a.

CHAPTER 23

RABBINIC RESPONSES TO RAPID INFLATION IN ISRAEL, 1973–1985

DANIEL SCHIFFMAN

Introduction

Israel suffered from rapid inflation during the years from 1973 to 1985. Consider that from 1971 to 1972, the annual rate of inflation increased by only one percentage point, from 12% to 13%. But, from 1973 to 1978, the rate jumped to 39%. Inflation skyrocketed to 445% in 1984, before the economy was finally stabilized in 1985. Rapid inflation was accompanied by an expansion of dollarization and indexation arrangements.

This chapter explores the legal opinions of leading rabbis on monetary issues, during and immediately after the inflationary episode of 1973 to 1985. The rabbis were asked to address a variety of questions, including the following: Are loans in United States dollars permissible, or are they considered a form of prohibited interest? Is it permissible to make a loan in domestic currency, indexed to the United States dollar or to the Consumer Price Index? What is the halachic status of government indexation policies? How should free loan societies protect themselves from inflation?

Today, the rabbinic consensus is that dollar and dollar-indexed loans are permissible. However, CPI-linked loans are controversial. I explore the rationale for this distinction and ask whether the experience of rapid inflation led to significant developments in Jewish monetary theory.

This chapter is organized as follows: Following the introduction, the second and third sections are devoted to introducing essential legal precedents from the

Talmudic and post-Talmudic rabbinic literature. The fourth section describes the central economic developments of 1973 to 1985. The fifth and sixth sections, which comprise the core of the chapter, survey the opinions of contemporary rabbis on dollar indexation and CPI indexation. The seventh section concludes.

Essential Talmudic Cases and Concepts

The following Talmudic cases and concepts are essential for understanding the modern halachic literature on money.

A. "Coin" (*Tiva*) versus "Produce" (*Pera*).[1]

In Talmudic law, the physical acceptance of goods (e.g., lifting or pulling toward oneself) by the buyer finalizes a transaction; payment alone does not finalize a transaction. Consider an exchange of coins. Who is the buyer and who is the seller? The Talmud ruled that, when coins of different metals (e.g., gold and silver) are exchanged, the coin that is more widely accepted is considered "coin"—money par excellence—while the other coin is considered "produce"—commodity. The individual who receives "produce" is the buyer; his physical acceptance finalizes the transaction.

The distinction between "coin" and "produce" has another important implication. If prices or exchange rates fluctuate, the fluctuations are attributed entirely to developments in commodity markets and/or changes in the value of "produce" (lesser coins). Since the value of "coin" is fixed, debts denominated in "coin" must be repaid nominalistically, without adjustment for changes in prices or exchange rates.

B. Commodity Loans and Their Repayment Following Price Fluctuations ("*Se'ah Be'seah*").[2]

The Talmud prohibited (interest free) commodity loans because they are likely to lead to ex post interest when evaluated in monetary terms. Consider a loan of wheat for wheat. Should the price of wheat increase, the borrower will end up repaying wheat of a higher monetary value than the original. The commodity loan prohibition is simply an extension of the "coin"/"produce" categorization. Since the value of "coin" is fixed by definition, loans of "coin" are permissible. Commodity values may fluctuate, so commodity loans (including loans of "produce,"—lesser coins) are prohibited.

1 *Bava Metsi'a* 44a–45b.

2 *Bava Metsi'a* 44b, 62b–64b, 72b, 75a.

The Talmud allowed for two exceptions to the aforementioned prohibition: (a) *Yesh lo*—the borrower owns some quantity of the commodity at the time of the loan; and (b) *Yatza hasha'ar*—the commodity has a stable market price that is public knowledge. Thus, the borrower can easily purchase the commodity at that price and repay the loan.

Although commodity loans were prohibited ab initio, the Talmudic rabbis asked how such loans should be repaid post facto. They formulated the following rule: If the price of wheat fell, the borrower must repay the original amount of wheat. If the price of wheat rose, the borrower must repay the original monetary value.

C. Coins That Were Stolen, Then Cracked or Demonetized.[3]

The Mishna ruled that, if a stolen coin cracked (*nisdak*) while in the thief's possession, he must pay its original value. However, if a stolen coin was demonetized (*nifsal*) while in the possession of the thief, he may return it as is. This was the interpretation of the Talmudic sage R. Huna. R. Yehuda disagreed. According to his reading of the Mishna, demonetization is subsumed within the "*nisdak*" category, while "*nifsal*" refers to a coin that was demonetized domestically, but is still accepted abroad.

D. Repayment of a Loan Following Demonetization.[4]

If one made a loan in a particular coin and that coin was subsequently demonetized, Rav required payment in currently acceptable coins. Samuel maintained that the borrower may repay in demonetized coin and tell the lender to "go and spend it in *Meshan*"—a place where the coin is still legal tender. R. Nachman commented that Samuel's position is tenable only if it is feasible for the lender to travel to *Meshan*.

E. Repayment of a Loan Following Reinforcement/ Debasement: the Twenty-Five Percent Rule[5]

A loan was made in a particular coin, and that coin was subsequently reinforced or debased. How should the borrower repay? Theoretically, if the borrower repays in new coin following reinforcement, he will be paying interest (ex post). If the borrower repays in new coin following debasement, the lender will absorb a loss. The Talmudic rabbis formulated the following rule:[6] If produce prices changed due

3 *Bava Kamma* 96b–97b.

4 *Bava Kamma* 97a–97b.

5 *Bava Kamma* 97b–98a.

6 I follow the formulation of Maimonides (Rambam, Egypt, 1135–1204), *Mishne Torah, Malveh Veloveh* 4:11.

to the change in coin weight, the debt should be adjusted fully. If produce prices remained fixed, and the new coin differs from the old coin in weight by more than twenty-five percent, the debt should be adjusted fully. If produce prices did not change, and the new coin differs from the old coin in weight by twenty-five percent or less, the debtor must pay in new coin the exact number of coins that he borrowed, without adjustment.[7]

F. Definition of Interest—Repayment of a Loan Following Exchange Rate Appreciation[8]

A *maah* (one-sixth of a denarius) was lent, and its value was one hundred *perutot* (pennies) at the time of the loan. Subsequently the *maah* appreciated to one hundred twenty *perutot*. The Talmud cited this case as an example of interest.

Post-Talmudic Precedents

The historical evolution of monetary systems generated a vast post-Talmudic rabbinic literature. What follows is a brief survey of some post-Talmudic precedents that were cited by late twentieth-century rabbis.[9]

G. The Compromise Solution

During the sixteenth and seventeenth centuries, the Ottoman Empire experienced frequent currency debasements. This raised the question of how to repay loans that were made in (now) debased currency. In the 1580s, the rabbis of Safed enacted the compromise solution, under which the borrower and the lender share the loss equally.[10]

H. Intrinsic versus Extrinsic Valuation

In the Ottoman Empire, it sometimes happened that a coin appreciated or depreciated against another domestic coin, without any change in the specie content (= weight × purity) of either coin. R. Samuel De Medina (*Maharashdam*, Greece, 1505–1589) advocated adjustment of debts in such cases, in accordance with the

7 For further discussion of the twenty-five percent rule, see Daniel A. Schiffman, "The Valuation of Coins in Medieval Jewish Jurisprudence," *Journal of the History of Economic Thought* 27 (2005): 141–60.

8 *Bava Metsi'a* 60b.

9 This section draws on R. Solomon Daichovsky, "Changes in the Value of the Currency, Past and Present," *Torah Shebeal Peh* 26 (Mossad Harav Kook: 1985): 74–83.

10 Eliav Schochetman, "The Enactment of Safed and the *Responsa* of the Sages of Safed Regarding Changes in the Value of Coins," (in Hebrew) *Sinai* 82 (1978): 109–22.

change in the exchange rate. R. Solomon Hacohen (*Maharschach*, Greece, ca.1520–ca.1601) advocated nominalistic repayment and restricted adjustment of debts to cases in which the specie content had changed.[11] In modern terminology, R. De Medina valued coins according to extrinsic content, while R. Hacohen valued coins according to intrinsic content.

I. Repayment of Debts in Depreciated Banknotes

The advent of banknotes backed by precious metals led to a debate concerning repayment of debts that were made in (now) depreciated banknotes.[12] R. Moses Sofer (*Hatam Sofer*, Austria-Hungary, 1762–1839) advocated nominalistic repayment. He saw banknotes as analogous to demonetized coins (Case D); thus, the borrower may tell the lender to "go spend them in *Meshan*," even though a coin that is accepted only in *Meshan* has little value domestically. R. Mordecai Banet (Austria-Hungary, 1753–1829) rejected R. Sofer's analogy. He argued that, in Talmudic times, the bullion in a demonetized coin was worth twenty-five percent less than the coin's face value. By compelling the lender to accept demonetized coins, the Talmud imposed on him a loss of at most twenty-five percent. Under R. Sofer's ruling, the lender must accept depreciated banknotes, which entails a much greater loss. Based on this logic, R. Banet ruled that the debt must be adjusted, in order to compensate the lender for the depreciation.

J. Official Devaluations

R. Abraham Isaiah Karelitz (*Hazon Ish*, Israel, 1878–1953) discussed the following case: Suppose that a thief stole denarii, at a time when the denarius was worth six *maah*. The king devalued the denarius to five *maah* per denarius, and, as a result, the denarii price of produce increased. According to R. Karelitz, this is analogous to a case in which the king demonetized the first denarius and issued a new, debased denarius. Conceptually, it makes no difference whether the king issued a new coin or debased the current coin. Therefore, the thief's obligation must be adjusted upwards. The same applies to a loan that was made in a specific coin—if the coin was devalued officially, the debt must be adjusted upward.[13]

K. Modern Fiat Money

In the context of a discussion of modern fiat money, R. Karelitz issued the following ruling:[14] "If one borrowed fiat currency notes without any stipulation and they were

11 *Responsa Maharashdam, Choshen Mishpat* 75 and *Responsa Maharschach* 1:62, 2:53.

12 *Responsa Hatam Sofer Choshen Mishpat* 62, 63, 65, 74, *Yoreh De'ah* 134, 289, *Even Haezer*, 126; *Responsa Har Hamor* 37, 38.

13 *Hazon Ish, Yoreh De'ah* 74:8.

14 Ibid., 74:5.

later demonetized, one must repay in currently accepted currency. If the new currency notes depreciated [*nifchat*] because people lost confidence in them (relative to the old notes), this is analogous to debasement. If produce prices increased as a result, the debt must be adjusted upward."

L. *Hetter Iska*

Beginning in the Middle Ages, the rabbis developed a legal device that makes it possible to charge interest on commercial loans. The standard *hetter iska* contract is structured as "half loan, half equity": One-half is an interest free loan, and the other half is an equity investment with a profit-sharing arrangement. Should the borrower claim that he has no profits to share, he is obligated to take an oath. The borrower is expected to decline, because Jewish tradition strongly discourages taking an oath. As a consequence, the borrower must pay the lender his "profit share."[15]

Individuals or institutions may arrange a general *hetter iska*, which automatically covers all future transactions. This document must be signed before a rabbinical court. In contemporary Israel, the government and all major banks operate under a general *hetter iska*.

Economic Developments, 1973–1985[16]

During 1973-1985, Israel experienced the greatest economic crisis in its history. What follows is a description of the main aspects of the crisis. Writing in 1986, Michael Bruno described the crisis as follows:[17]

> The prolonged economic crisis manifested itself in three major areas: stagnation in real growth of output and productivity for almost an entire decade; rising private and public consumption in face of stagnant output leading to a reduction in investment, growing foreign debt, and ever increasing balance-of-payments difficulties which recently bordered on a serious liquidity crisis; and step-wise acceleration of inflation in which each price shock due to external causes or deliberate government action (such as devaluations or other government-induced price hikes) translated into a permanently higher inflation-rate plateau.

Fig 23.1 shows the inflation rate and the rate of devaluation of Israeli currency against the United States dollar.

15 For a detailed explanation, see J. David Bleich, "Heter Iska, the Permissible Venture: A Device to Avoid the Prohibition Against Interest-Bearing Loans," in this volume.

16 This section draws on the following sources: Warren Young and Yakir Plessner, "Economists, Government, and Economic Policymaking in Israel: From 'Crawling Peg' to 'Cold Turkey,'" *History of Political Economy* 37,1 (2005): 292–313; Akiva (Edward) Offenbacher and Roy Stein, "Dollarization and Indexation in Israel's Inflation and Disinflation: There's More Than One Way to Skin a Cat," *Comparative Economic Studies* 45 (September 2003): 278–305; and Michael Bruno, "Sharp Disinflation Strategy: Israel 1985." *Economic Policy* 1,2 (April 1986): 380–407.

17 Michael Bruno, op. cit.

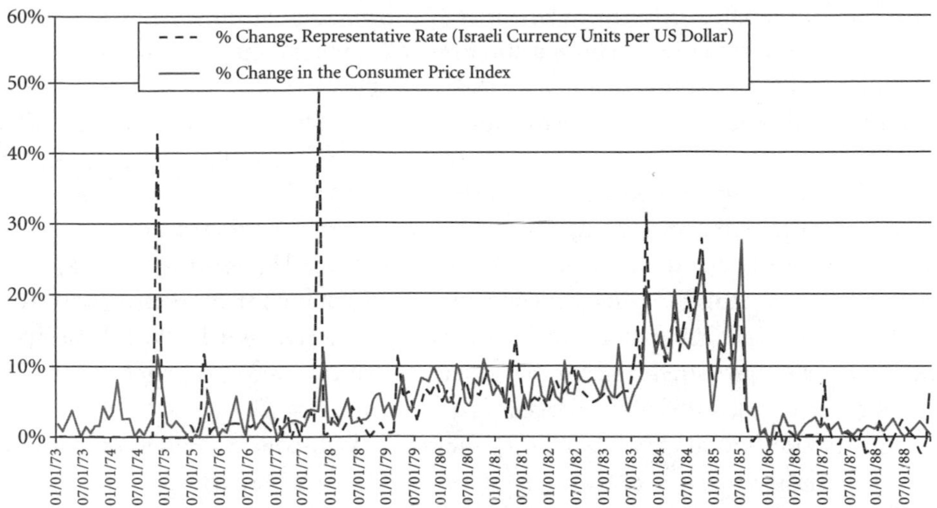

FIGURE 23.1 **Inflation and Devaluation in Israel, 1973–1988 (Monthly)**

It can be seen that inflation and devaluation moved together from 1978 onward. Two sharp devaluations occurred in 1974 and 1977; these devaluations significantly exceeded the rate of inflation.

Annual inflation rose from between twelve and thirteen percent in 1971 and 1972 to thirty-nine percent (average) during 1973 through 1978. There were two major causes: (a) In the aftermath of the Yom Kippur War (October 1973), government expenditures reached seventy-five percent of GDP and stayed at that level until the 1985 stabilization. The budget deficit averaged fifteen percent of GDP; (b) Petroleum prices increased by 360 percent. Since Israel imports all of its petroleum, this created a large current account deficit and generated pressure to devalue the lira (Israeli pound).

Since 1948, the lira's exchange rate was fixed, with periodic devaluations—an "adjustable peg." This exchange rate regime was accompanied by extensive controls on foreign exchange; for example, Israelis were prohibited from holding deposits in foreign banks. This reality changed in the mid-1970s. In November 1974, the lira was devalued by forty-three percent against the United States dollar. In June 1975, the adjustable peg was replaced by the "crawling peg," in which the currency is devalued by a preannounced percentage each month. The crawling peg was officially abolished in October 1977; the lira was devalued by forty-eight percent against the dollar, and most exchange controls were eliminated. The next month, the government shifted to flexible exchange rates officially, but, in practice, the BOI maintained the crawling peg. In April 1979, exchange controls were reimposed,[18]

18 See Oren Sussman, "Financial Liberalization: the Israeli Experience," *Oxford Economic Papers* 44 (1992): 387–402.

and the BOI acknowledged publicly that it was managing the exchange rate. In February 1980, the shekel replaced the lira, at a conversion rate of one shekel = ten lira.

Rapid inflation led to an expansion of indexation and dollarization. Dollar indexation and CPI indexation were widespread, but actual dollars were rarely used in transactions. Dollar indexation was usually based on the "representative rate"—an average of buying and selling rates at the commercial banks. Over 1975 to 1982, taxes and (government) directed credit programs were indexed to the CPI, and dollar-indexed bank deposits were introduced. In the labor market, the Cost of Living Adjustment (COLA) to wages was made more frequently.[19] While business establishments preferred dollar indexation to CPI indexation, the general public overwhelmingly favored CPI-indexed financial assets.

In September and October 1983, the infamous Bank Shares Crisis[20] was resolved by a government bailout of bank shareholders.[21] The public lost confidence in the shekel, and inflation rose to 593 percent (annualized) in the fourth quarter of 1983. After several "package deals" failed to reduce inflation,[22] the government adopted the Stabilization Plan in July 1985. Its key components were: a devaluation of the shekel by seventeen percent, followed immediately by an exchange rate freeze; a freeze of wages, prices, and bank credit; and a drastic cut in the budget deficit. The United States granted emergency aid of $1.5 billion over two years. In September 1985, the New Israeli Shekel (NIS) was introduced, at a conversion rate of one NIS = one thousand old shekels. The stabilization was effective: Inflation decreased sharply, to a range of sixteen to twenty percent during 1986 to 1988.

What caused Israel's inflation? There are two leading theories: the inflation tax theory and the current account theory. The inflation tax theory sees the government budget deficit as the main culprit. The budget deficit was so large that it could not be fully financed by bond issues. Therefore, the government was forced to print money (through the BOI) in order to finance a substantial portion of its budget deficit. This, of course, led to higher inflation. Over time, the government was forced to print money at faster and faster rates, due to the slowdown in GDP growth, the growth in dollar-indexed bank deposits (and other substitutes for domestic currency), and the bank shares bailout.[23]

The current account theory argues that the government devalued the currency constantly, in order to cheapen Israeli exports abroad and make imports more expensive domestically. As a result, exports rose and imports fell, which

19 Jonas Prager, "Wage Indexation and the Israeli Labor Market: The Institutional Imperative," *International Journal of Middle East Studies* 18,3 (August 1986): 259–73.

20 Beginning in the 1970s, the leading banks systematically manipulated their own share prices. The banks withdrew their support abruptly in the Fall of 1983, and share prices collapsed.

21 See Thomas Sargent and Joseph Zeira, "Israel 1983: A Bout of Unpleasant Monetarist Arithmetic," Working Paper, Social Science Research Network, February 2008, http://papers.ssrn.com/sol3/papers.cfm?abstract_id=1106843.

22 The package deals were tripartite agreements between the government, the Industrialists' Association, and the Histadrut labor federation.

23 Sargent and Zeira (ibid).

improved the current account (for our purposes, we may assume that the current account is identical to the trade balance). But this effect was temporary; over time, the domestic currency prices of imports rose, which led to inflation. Higher prices and wages caused domestic production costs to rise, making exports more expensive abroad. The current account worsened, which generated pressure for another devaluation.

Rabbinic Views on Dollarization

As dollarization spread throughout the Israeli economy, rabbis were asked about the permissibility of dollar and dollar-indexed loans. This answer to this question depends on the halachic status of the dollar and of Israeli currency. Is the dollar "coin" or "produce" (Case A)? If it is "produce," does a loan in dollars satisfy the conditions for permissible commodity loans (Case B)? Is Israeli currency still considered "coin," under conditions of rapid inflation?

Writing in December 1974 (under a fixed exchange rate), R. Samuel Wosner[24] ruled that loans in dollars are permissible, even if the dollar is regarded as "produce." The dollar satisfies the conditions for permissible commodity loans. It can be said to have a stable, commonly known market price (*yatza hasha'ar*), because (a) it trades at a definite exchange rate, which is stable on an intraday basis; and (b) it is readily available in organized international markets. R. Wosner interpreted *yesh lo* very liberally, based on two leniencies by R. David Halevi (Poland, ca. 1586–1667): (a) If the borrower has coins of any form, loans of "produce" are permissible; (b) R. Moses Isserles (Poland, ca. 1530–1572) permitted loans of gold coins for gold coins. R. Halevi explained that people often sell movable objects to obtain gold coins. If the borrower owns movable objects, it is as if he owns gold coins, so *yesh lo* is satisfied.[25] R. Wosner also permitted the lender to exchange lira for dollars and lend lira, stipulating repayment in dollars. However, he discouraged such loans if there are rumors of an imminent devaluation.

In 1979, R. Jacob Isaiah Bloi (Israel, b. 1929) wrote that loans that are indexed to the official exchange rate are controversial.[26] On the one hand, such loans should be prohibited based on the premise that the dollar is "produce." On the other hand, there is justification to permit such loans: R. De Medina argued that debts should be adjusted following a change in the exchange rate, if the price of produce increased proportionally (Case H). Perhaps the dollar itself is the "produce" whose price has risen. Alternatively, one may regard the dollar as "coin," due to its international status, and in light of the fact that Israeli prices (including produce prices) are

24 *Responsa Shevet Halevi* 3:109.

25 *Turei Zahav*, *Yoreh De'ah* 162:2, commenting on the gloss of R. Moses Isserles, *Yoreh De'ah* 162:1.

26 *Brit Yehuda*, Ch. 20.

linked to the dollar exchange rate. In addition, the regularity of official devaluations may cause the lira to lose the status of "coin," which means that changes in prices may be attributed to the lira itself, not to developments in commodity markets. At this stage of the analysis, R. Blau offered a caveat: In reality, Israeli prices rise less than proportionately following devaluation. But this is only a short-run effect; in the long run, prices do rise proportionately.

R. Bloi cited two Polish rabbis who permitted dollar-indexed loans during Poland's rapid inflation (1924–1925)[27] and noted that they did not share his reservations with respect to dollar indexation. He concluded that dollar indexation is controversial, and therefore one should arrange a *hetter iska*. *Hetter iska* is critical for ensuring the availability of credit; without *hetter iska*, potential lenders will be concerned that indexation is prohibited and avoid making loans altogether.

For R. Bloi, indexation to the black market exchange rate is prohibited, because the black market dollar is "produce." Presumably, R. Bloi would allow this form of indexation under *hetter iska*.

In February 1980, R. Moses Feinstein (United States, 1895–1986) addressed the following question: How should a charitable organization manage its free loan society under inflationary conditions, in which "the lira loses value each day and has no significance as a coin or as an object"?[28] According to R. Feinstein, a free loan society should not lend unlinked liras unless the borrower qualifies for charity. In Israel, both citizens and the government considered the dollar to be the unit of account, so lira loans are in effect dollar loans. The society should make loans in dollars, to be repaid in dollars. This was permissible because the dollar was "coin" in Israel. Also, (Israeli) individuals may stipulate linkage to the dollar. In summary, R. Feinstein permitted dollar loans by reclassifying the dollar as "coin" and the lira as "produce."

R. Ben Zion Abba Shaul[29] (1924–1998) rejected R. Feinstein's ruling. He explained that R. Feinstein permitted linkage to the dollar's representative rate based on the leniency of R. David Halevi:[30] Since people commonly sell Israeli currency and purchase dollars, if the borrower possesses Israeli currency, it is as if he owns dollars, and *yesh lo* is satisfied.[31]

R. Abba Shaul ruled that dollar loans entail biblically prohibited interest, for several reasons: (a) R. Joseph Caro (Palestine, 1488–1575) disagreed with R. Isserles;[32] (b) the case under analysis is not analogous to R. Isserles' case. The correct

27 *Responsa Havatzelet Hasharon* 87, *Tzur Yaakov* 105.

28 *Responsa Igrot Moshe*, *Yoreh De'ah* 3:37.

29 *Responsa Or Lezion*, v. 1, *Yoreh De'ah* 4.

30 *Turei Zahav*, op. cit.

31 R. Abba Shaul's reading of R. Feinstein is puzzling; R. Feinstein's opinion does not appear to be based on R. Halevi.

32 R. Caro's law code, *Shulchan Aruch* ("Set Table"), is the authoritative code of Jewish law. It is always printed together with the glosses of R. Moses Isserles. When these two authorities disagree, Sephardic Jews (such as R. Abba Shaul) follow R. Caro, while Ashkenazic Jews (such as R. Feinstein) follow R. Isserles.

analogy is to a loan of silver coin for silver coin, to be repaid in silver coin with linkage to gold coin. Such a loan entails interest (Case F); (c) according to secular law, the Israeli shekel was legal tender; i.e. buyers could not compel sellers to accept dollars.[33]

R. Solomon Zalman Auerbach (1910–1995), in an excerpt that predates 1986,[34] argued that the commodity loan prohibition and "coin"/"produce" do not apply to modern fiat monies. If this premise is accepted, then foreign currency loans are permissible without any conditions. R. Auerbach stated that his conclusions were tentative and should not be implemented without further study.

He then proceeded to address practical issues, based on the standard premise that the commodity loan prohibition and "coin/produce" do apply to modern fiat monies. He categorized foreign currency as "produce," which implies that dollar loans are permitted, subject to the conditions for permissible commodity loans. In a footnote, he cited R. David Halevi, and inferred that dollar loans are allowed because the borrower has movable objects and these can always be sold to obtain dollars. However, he was unsure as to whether R. Halevi's leniency extends to foreign currency or is limited to domestic currency only. Again, he stated that his ideas are merely tentative.

In 2002, R. Joseph Shalom Elyashiv[35] was quoted as saying that the United States dollar is very prominent in Israel and should be considered "coin." Therefore, dollar loans are permissible.[36] However, R. Elyashiv prohibited indexation to the dollar's representative rate, unless a *hetter iska* was signed.[37] His rationale was that the representative rate does not reflect the value of an actual currency. It is likely that he held this view during the 1980s.

R. Moses Sternbuch (birth date unknown), writing sometime before 1989, observed that "prices are skyrocketing in a frightening manner, and the value of the shekel is falling drastically every month." He took a mostly stringent position regarding dollar indexation.[38] R. Sternbuch made a critical distinction between two cases: the case of liberalized foreign exchange, in which dollars can be purchased from the banks, and the case of exchange controls, in which dollars cannot be purchased from the banks. It should be noted that exchange controls were in effect until the early 1990s, with the exception of 1977 to 1979.

In the case of liberalized foreign exchange, the *poskim* disagreed regarding the permissibility of dollar-for-dollar loans or dollar-linked sales on credit. Some

33 R. Abba Shaul suggested a special legal device, which facilitates indexation to the dollar's representative rate, without violating any interest prohibition.

34 *Minhat Shlomo* v. 1, 27:3. The first edition was published in 1986; the second edition (2005) also includes footnotes from manuscript.

35 Most of R. Elyashiv's *responsa* remain unpublished.

36 *Meorot Hadaf Hayomi* (*Meorot Hadaf Hayomi*, Bnei Brak, Israel: 2002), v. 5, 232.

37 Y. Leiner, "Guide to Arranging a *Heter Iska*," *Dei'ah Vedibbur* (online newspaper), February 19, 2003, http://chareidi.shemayisrael.com/archives5763/KSS63aheter.htm.

38 *Kitzur Dinei Ribbit*, Ch. 3.

argued that since certain goods, contracted work, and services were priced in dollars, the dollar was "coin" and linkage was permitted. Others argued that, because many purchases were made exclusively in shekels (e.g., grocery stores and public transport), the dollar was "produce." R. Sternbuch cited the Polish rabbis (1924–1925) but did not accept their position. He prohibited dollar or dollar-indexed loans, even if *yesh lo* or *yatza hasha'ar* was satisfied. However, he allowed dollar or dollar-indexed sales on credit, since interest arising from sales on credit never entails a biblical prohibition. R. Sternbuch urged his readers to sign a generalized *hetter iska* (even for sales on credit) in order to avoid halachic problems.

In R. Sternbuch's opinion, those who permitted dollar indexation under liberalized foreign exchange restricted their ruling to simple, symmetric indexation. Under symmetric indexation, the borrower bears the risk that the dollar will strengthen, and the lender bears the risk that the dollar will weaken. Asymmetric indexation, however, is prohibited by all *poskim*. Under asymmetric indexation, the indexation is effective only if the dollar should strengthen; the lender bears no risk, while the borrower bears the risk that the dollar will strengthen. According to R. Sternbuch, most dollar-indexed loans were asymmetric.

Under the case of exchange controls, R. Sternbuch argued that the dollar is "produce." He pointed out that prices were set not in dollars, but in shekels, with linkage to the dollar's representative rate. R. Sternbuch wrote that, for sales (including sales on credit), one must link to the representative rate only. Why? The banks used to sell dollars at the representative rate and charge a fee for the transaction. But, with the imposition of exchange controls, one could no longer purchase dollars at the bank. Dollars were available on the black market, at a premium over the representative rate (this premium was sometimes large). Under these conditions, the dollar must be considered "produce."

In summary, R. Sternbuch prohibited dollar indexation under exchange controls and regarded dollar indexation under exchange rate liberalization as controversial. Because liberalization was in effect for less than three out of the thirteen years in our sample period, we may simplify R. Sternbuch's position somewhat and conclude that he prohibited dollar indexation.

Regarding *yatza hasha'ar*, R. Sternbuch concurred with R. Wosner's lenient interpretation. However, said R. Sternbuch, one may not borrow gold or foreign currency based on the bank exchange rate, even in a place and time where gold or foreign currency can be obtained immediately at the bank. This is because gold and foreign currency are not available at night, when the bank is closed. During the night, the exchange rate and the price of gold always change, because the markets are open in the United States (note: Israel time is seven hours ahead of New York time). This means that the exchange rate/price always changes from the time of the loan until the time that the borrower can purchase foreign currency/gold at his bank (which is the next morning).

R. Sternbuch ruled that, if an unindexed loan was past due, and the shekel was losing value daily, the debt should be linked to the dollar. Since some *poskim* were concerned that this constitutes interest, one should pay the principal, then pay separately for the exchange rate loss.

R. Sternbuch discussed a financial innovation that was introduced under high inflation: a dollar-indexed version of the "half loan, half equity" *hetter iska*.[39] R. Sternbuch described its structure as follows: The "profit" on equity was set at double the profit for the entire transaction, plus double indexation. The rationale for double indexation of equity is that the loan component must be unindexed. As a general rule, the loan component of the *hetter iska* must be interest-free; R. Sternbuch considered indexation to be a form of interest.

R. Sternbuch advanced the following argument: Suppose that a fifteen percent profit rate was applied to the entire transaction. After a year, the shekel was worth only twenty-five percent of its original value (a devaluation of three hundred percent per year). For the sake of argument, assume single (not double) indexation of equity. Under these parameters, what is the minimum profit that the borrower must earn, in order to avoid paying interest on the loan component? The borrower must earn a "profit" of at least thirty percent on the equity component, plus seventy-five percent to pay (single) indexation. A one hundred five percent rate of "profit" was unrealistically high; after accounting for double indexation, the rate of "profit" would have to be even higher. It is obvious that the borrower will end up paying interest on the loan portion, which makes the entire *hetter iska* invalid.

It is difficult to accept R. Sternbuch's argument, because it depends on unrealistic assumptions. In R. Sternbuch's scenario, the rate of devaluation is 300% per year, the *hetter iska* is indexed, yet the borrower's profits are unindexed. No rational person would conduct business without indexation in a high inflation environment, and then compound his error by taking out an indexed loan. The problem raised by R. Sternbuch has a simple solution: The borrower should be required to index all of his transactions to the dollar.

Let us summarize our discussion of dollar indexation. Of the rabbis surveyed here, three permitted dollar indexation (R. Wosner, R. Feinstein, R. Auerbach); three prohibited it (R. Abba Shaul, R. Sternbuch and R. Elyashiv), and one (R. Bloi) was uncertain. R. Elyashiv did permit loans in actual dollars. Of particular interest to economists are the discussions of black market exchange rates, exchange controls and the time difference between Israeli and American currency markets. In the following section, I discuss the question of indexation to the CPI. As we shall see, of the rabbis who debated the question of CPI indexation, most accepted the permissibility of dollar indexation. Furthermore, we shall discover that R. Abba Shaul, who opposed dollar indexation, apparently came to reverse his position. We can therefore conclude that the general consensus was to permit dollar indexation.

39 *Kitzur Dinei Ribbit*, introduction.

Rabbinic Views on CPI Indexation

The CPI was first mentioned in rabbinic literature in the 1970's, when inflation emerged as a major issue in both Israel and the US. In late 1974, R. Ephraim Eliezer Yolles (US, 1897–1989) published a responsum regarding the repayment of old debts in an inflationary environment.[40] May the lender demand compensation for inflation, on the grounds that an earlier repayment would have allowed him to purchase merchandise, which is worth more today? R. Yolles observed that in Israel, the lira had been devalued from four per dollar[41] to six per dollar. This exceeded 25%, so adjustment of the debt was required (Case E). There was no doubt that the loan should be indexed to the dollar, especially at a time when all transactions were based on the dollar's value. R. Yolles cited R. Moses Sofer (Case I), who had ruled that devalued banknotes should be repaid nominalistically. R. Yolles regarded this ruling as a special case, and asserted that in general, R. Sofer agreed with R. Mordecai Banet that the lender should not be forced to take a loss. Based on these arguments, R. Yolles advocated linkage to the dollar in Israel, following any official devaluation that exceeds 25%.

R. Yolles also discussed inflation in the US context. He advocated linkage to the CPI when the purchasing power of fiat money was eroded by inflation. After discussing Case C and its medieval interpretations, he cited R. Abraham Karelitz (Case K) in support of his view.

R. Isaac Jacob Weiss (Israel, 1902-1989) rejected R. Yolles's reasoning.[42] Writing at some point before February 1980, he ruled that, if fiat money is devalued or depreciates, debts must be repaid at their original values; all forms of indexation are prohibited. R. Weiss based his ruling on R. Moses Sofer (Case I), R. Solomon Kluger (Ukraine, 1785–1869), and R. Jechiel Michel Halevi Epstein (Lithuania, 1829–1908). All three rabbis ruled that, if one borrowed banknotes and they were devalued/depreciated, no adjustment should be made. R. Weiss asserted that R. Yolles misinterpreted R. Sofer. R. Weiss cited R. Samuel De Medina (Case H) as a possible proof-text for R. Yolles, but he argued that R. De Medina should be disregarded, since all other *poskim* disagreed with him.

According to R. Weiss, R. Yolles also misinterpreted R. Karelitz. R. Weiss contended that R. Karelitz's words apply to a fiat currency that has been demonetized and replaced by a lower valued fiat currency; they do not apply to a fiat currency that has been devalued but continues to circulate.

In December 1974 to January 1975, a fascinating correspondence took place between R. Ezra Batzri and R. Dov Popovitz.[43] At that point in time, exchange rates

40 R. Ephraim Eliezer Yolles, "A Lender Who Demands that the Borrower Repay an Old Debt According to the Original Exchange Rate," *Hamaor*, Kislev-Tevet 5735 (November–December 1974): 5–6.

41 The actual exchange rate was 4.20. The devaluation took place on November 10, 1974.

42 *Responsa Minhat Yitzchak* 6:161.

43 *Responsa Sha'arei Ezra*, v. 1, 47–50 (Jerusalem: 1978).

were still fixed. R. Batzri prohibited CPI-indexed loans without a *hetter iska*; furthermore, he regarded any agreement to link to the CPI as halachically invalid. R. Popovitz attempted to convince R. Batzri that CPI indexation is permissible, subject to the consent of the parties. Since R. Batzri did permit an exchange rate–linked loan, R. Popovitz claimed that R. Batzri's rulings were inconsistent.

Much of the correspondence centers on the following point: According to R. Popovitz, the borrower of unindexed lira is liable for damages (*mazik*) because his inaction (i.e., failure to pay) causes the lender a loss of potential profits (*mevatel kiso shel chavero*).[44] In the terminology of economics, the borrower causes the lender to incur an opportunity cost. R. Batzri rejected this line of reasoning.[45] The complexities of this discussion are beyond the scope of this chapter; instead, we focus on the monetary aspect of the disagreement between the two rabbis.

R. Batzri maintained a fundamental distinction between devaluation and inflation. He emphasized that the lira was "coin"; thus, all commodity price changes must be attributed to the commodities ("produce"), not to "coin." A devaluation is a "real" alteration in the "body" of the coin. A rise in the CPI reflects a rise in the price of produce, while the currency remains stable. For R. Batzri, a CPI-indexed loan is not a standard commodity loan, so *yesh lo/yatza hasha'ar* cannot be invoked to permit CPI indexation.

R. Batzri objected to CPI indexation on the following grounds: The CPI is an aggregated weighted average of the prices of various commodities. In practice, each lender deals in a different commodity—one deals in real estate while the other deals in wood. Also, lenders have different consumption patterns. Suppose meat prices rise, while bread and sugar prices remain constant. The CPI rises; with a CPI-indexed loan, a lender who purchases bread and sugar would enjoy an increase in his purchasing power, which is effectively an interest payment. To avoid such a scenario, we need to calculate an individualized CPI for each lender. But this is completely impractical; with such an approach, we would never know the true purchasing power of the currency.[46]

R. Batzri posited a fundamental halachic distinction between devaluation and inflation. He made the following points: (a) Devaluation affects tradables prices, but not nontradables prices; (b) inflation leads to wage increases, which in turn affect imports and exports; and (c) the existence of multiple exchange rates introduces additional complications into the analysis. Following this brief foray into economic analysis, R. Batzri argued that halachists should not get involved with the complex economic "problems" that influence the value of currency. Rather, they

44 As R. Popovitz put it, if not for the loan, the lender could have purchased the basket of goods that comprised the CPI, or a CPI-indexed bond.

45 Although the concept of *mevatel kiso shel chavero* is codified in R. Caro's *Shulchan Aruch* (*Choshen Mishpat* 81:32; gloss of R. Moses Isserles, *Choshen Mishpat* 192:7, 386:3) it was not cited in the halachic literature on money before the twentieth century.

46 It is well-known that consumption baskets vary by geographical location, age, and income level. Therefore, the general CPI often does not reflect the actual inflation experienced by an individual.

should simply rule that the value of "coin" does not fluctuate—only the value of "produce" may fluctuate (Case A).

R. Batzri then set out to explain why he permitted linkage to the dollar but not linkage to the CPI. When the parties agree to compensate the lender for devaluation, this is perfectly acceptable. Since certain *poskim* hold that this is required, the borrower says in effect: "I do not know which *poskim* are correct. I wish to compensate you in order to be sure that I have repaid you in accordance with *halacha*." This is a sort of compromise, and as such it is not considered interest. CPI indexation, however, is definitely interest, so CPI indexation payments cannot be viewed as a form of compromise.

R. Popovitz argued that an increase in the CPI reflects an increase in the prices of most goods. R. Batzri disagreed with R. Popovitz's assessment; in reality, a price spike in one or two goods will raise the CPI, even though prices of all other goods are stable.

To support his argument, R. Popovitz offered a description of the relation between inflation and changes in exchange rates. Before reviewing R. Popovitz's description, it is useful to review an economic theory that is known as Relative Purchasing Power Parity (Relative PPP). This theory is highly relevant for Israel, which adhered to ". . . an exchange-rate adjustment policy which roughly followed a purchasing power parity rule."[47]

The theory of Relative PPP may be presented as follows. The real lira/dollar exchange rate is defined as:

> Real lira/dollar exchange rate = (nominal lira/dollar exchange rate * US price level)/Israeli price level

If the real exchange rate (defined in this way) rises, we have a real depreciation; if it falls, we have a real appreciation. This is the standard terminology used by economists, whether the nominal exchange rate is fixed or flexible.

Under Relative PPP, the real lira/dollar exchange rate is constant, which implies that:

> Percentage change of the lira/dollar exchange rate = Israeli inflation – US Inflation
>
> If Relative PPP is violated, the deviation from Relative PPP is:
>
> Deviation from Relative PPP = Percentage change in the real lira/dollar exchange rate = Percentage change of the nominal lira/dollar exchange rate – Israeli inflation + US Inflation

For example, if Israeli inflation is sixteen percent and United States inflation is four percent, Relative PPP predicts that the lira will weaken against the dollar by twelve percent. If the lira/dollar exchange rate remains fixed (a change of zero percent), then the deviation from Relative PPP is negative twelve percent (a real appreciation of twelve percent).

47 Michael Bruno, op. cit.

As we shall see, both R. Popovitz and R. Batzri ignored inflation in the United States. If we set United States inflation to zero, we have the following modified form of Relative PPP:

Percentage change of the lira/dollar exchange rate = Israeli inflation

R. Popovitz reasoned as follows: Even if the CPI increase is caused by an increase in the price of one good, it has major economic consequences that halacha should not ignore. Under flexible exchange rates, an increase in the CPI leads to depreciation. Under fixed exchange rates, an increase in the CPI leads to a rise in the black market exchange rate (R. Popovitz noted that the black market rate is also influenced by other factors). R. Batzri replied that, over November 1973 to November 1974, the inflation rate was much greater than the devaluation rate. In other words, R. Popovitz was overstating the effects of inflation, and his notion of modified Relative PPP failed to hold in reality.

How accurate is R. Batzri's claim? In November 1974, the lira was devalued against the dollar by 42.9 percent. Over November 1973 to November 1974, inflation was 48.4 percent. R. Batzri is correct, although the order of magnitude is somewhat exaggerated. Since both rabbis ignored United States inflation, I repeat the calculation with United States inflation included, in accordance with standard Relative PPP theory. Over November 1973 to November 1974, United States inflation was 12.3 percent. Given a nominal lira devaluation of 42.9 percent and Israeli inflation of 48.4 percent, we can calculate that the real depreciation of the lira was 6.84 percent.

R. Popovitz was willing to accept R. Batzri's statements of fact, if only for the sake of argument. He stated that, even if the devaluation is less than past inflation, halacha should not ignore the phenomenon of CPI inflation. To compare the devaluation of the official exchange rate to CPI inflation was misleading; the official exchange rate differed from the true (= effective) exchange rate, due to the existence of multiple exchange rates and grants (to the export and tourism sectors). This argument failed to convince R. Batzri; both he and R. Popovitz adamantly maintained their original positions.

What were the practical ramifications of R. Batzri's position? Over September 1971 to October 1974, the government maintained the exchange rate peg despite average annual inflation of twenty-four percent. Anyone who made a dollar-indexed loan during this period would have sustained a major loss of purchasing power; this loss would have been prevented, had the loan been indexed to the CPI. Under the crawling peg (June 1975–July 1985), however, there was a fairly tight link between devaluation and inflation; thus, there was little practical distinction between dollar indexation and CPI indexation.

R. Shear Yashuv Cohen permitted indexation to the dollar or to the CPI.[48] In a 1977 essay, he noted that, in the past, the lira was pegged to the dollar, and there were periodic devaluations. But, by 1977, rapid inflation and frequent devaluations

48 R. Shear Yashuv Cohen, "Devaluation and Revaluation of the Currency in Jewish law," *Torah Shebeal Peh* 19 (Jerusalem: Mossad Harav Kook, 1977): 64–76.

had become a cornerstone of government policy, to the point where ". . . no serious businessman, bank or corporation will complete a deal . . . without taking into account in advance . . . the instability of the currency." Indexation to the dollar or CPI was widespread; nonindexed loans were rare, except as acts of charity.

After an extensive review of the halachic literature, R. Cohen reached the following conclusions:

1. Both dollar indexation and CPI indexation are valid. If the parties made a stipulation, the rabbis must recognize it. The CPI represents merchandise or fruit. No interest is involved—the lender is merely protecting the value of his money.
2. If no stipulation was made regarding devaluation, in a situation where the phenomenon of devaluation is universally recognized (as in 1977), no adjustment should be made—the loan should be repaid in devalued lira. However, the judge should encourage (but not coerce) the parties to make a fifty/fifty compromise (Case G).
3. In making transactions, the parties should specify precisely what should happen in the event of devaluation or revaluation. They should link their loan or business deal to a value that is stable and permanent.

Writing in 1979, R. Jacob Isaiah Bloi[49] prohibited CPI indexation in low inflation environments, in accordance with the rule that "coin" should be repaid nominalistically (Case A). R. Bloi discussed the permissibility of indexation to foreign currency, based on the precedent of R. Samuel De Medina (Case H). According to R. Bloi, R. De Medina's ruling (that debts should be adjusted upwards after a devaluation) was subject to an additional condition—that the price of produce increased in proportion to the devaluation. May the CPI be used to measure the increase in produce prices, in order to ascertain whether the condition was in fact satisfied? R. Bloi answered no, for two reasons: (a) The CPI was influenced by factors other than the devaluation. For instance, the rate of produce price inflation was probably below the rate of devaluation, because merchants were selling off old (predevaluation) stock; (b) the prices of necessities did not increase following devaluation, due to government subsidies. Although the consumer did not pay more, producers and importers received a higher domestic currency price. On the other hand, it is essential to recognize that consumers are also taxpayers, which means that they themselves are financing government subsidies. Therefore, it is not clear whether Jewish law should consider the consumer price or the producer price when measuring the inflationary impact of the devaluation. R. Bloi concluded that R. De Medina's precedent is inapplicable in modern times, because it is not clear how to verify whether devaluation is equal to produce price inflation.

R. Solomon Daichovsky permitted CPI indexation under rapid inflation. Early in 1984, R. Daichovsky, R. Jacob Eliezrov, and R. Masoud Elhadad, then of the

49 *Brit Yehuda*, Ch. 20.

Ashdod rabbinical court, adjudicated a case involving indexation of an unpaid electric bill.[50] Each judge authored an individual opinion.[51] R. Daichovsky noted that all government bodies (including utilities) indexed their receivables to the CPI; without indexation, no one could possibly survive in business. He argued that the defendant must make indexation payments for three reasons: (a) He is liable for damages because he caused the lender a loss of potential profits (this is the approach that was rejected by R. Batzri); (b) he derived benefit from another's loss; (c) even if the judges find the defendant not liable according to the letter of the law, they should fine him for late payment. In practice, this fine should be imposed through indexation.

R. Daichovsky presented three views regarding devaluation/depreciation:

First, R. De Medina (Case H): There is implicit agreement between the parties to repay the original purchasing power. Because a change in the value of the coin is considered an uncommon occurrence, an explicit stipulation is unnecessary. Second, those who rejected R. De Medina and regarded compensation for loss of purchasing power as interest. Third, R. Karelitz (Case J): It is as if the original coin was demonetized and replaced by a new coin.

R. Daichovsky proceeded to analyze these three views. Because devaluations occurred frequently in Israel (daily, as of 1984), the precedent of R. De Medina was inapplicable. Indexation was only justified according to R. Karelitz. Since the unpaid electric bill was not an ordinary loan, it was possible to be lenient and utilize R. De Medina as an additional support for indexation. R. Bloi had also ruled likewise: If the debt was not created by means of a loan, and the creditor lost potential profits, it might be argued that the debtor is liable for indexation payments.

R. Daichovsky posed the question: What is the status of the shekel? He answered that, as of 1984, the value of the currency was determined according to the nation's "economic power" and the relationship between its imports and exports. The public had lost confidence in the shekel, and all large or medium transactions were made in dollars. (This was written several months after the Bank Shares Crisis.) Also, the small transactions were indexed in many cases to the dollar. Some great rabbis held that the "coin" in Israel is the dollar, and that the shekel, whose value fluctuated each day, was "produce." Therefore, a shekel loan should not be considered a loan of "coin" but a loan of "produce"—that is, a loan of the purchasing power of the currency at the time—and such a loan should be permitted subject to the conditions for permissible commodity loans.

R. Daichovsky's decision was to order a fifty/fifty compromise, based on R. Moses Sofer, who preferred compromise in cases where the defendant caused the plaintiff to incur an opportunity cost. R. Daichovsky also considered the heavy burden that was placed upon the debtor by indexation. Furthermore, when adjudicating monetary cases, the rabbinical court acts as an arbitrator. In accordance with

50 The state rabbinical courts have jurisdiction over marriage and divorce. Until 2006, rabbinical courts were allowed to arbitrate civil cases, with the consent of the parties.

51 "Indexation of a Debt to the CPI," *Tehumin* 6 (Alon Shevut, Israel: 1985): 208–34.

this principle, the parties agreed in advance that the judges might rule according to the letter of the law or order a compromise, at their discretion.

R. Jacob Eliezrov agreed with the decision but took issue with R. Daichovsky's reading of R. Karelitz. R. Karelitz was speaking of a situation where the king ordered a devaluation. But, in 1984, the currency was losing value due to external causes and a "particular economic situation." The situation was comparable to inflation/deflation (which implied that a nominalistic approach should be taken). Thus, R. Karelitz's view could not be adduced to support CPI indexation.

R. Masoud Elhadad agreed with R. Eliezrov's reading of R. Karelitz; R. Karelitz was speaking only of devaluation. However, he stated (correctly) that the depreciation in 1984 was tantamount to devaluation because it was a deliberate government policy: "In the end, the government recognizes [the depreciation] and agrees to the CPI that is published, which expresses the decline of the currency." If so, the words of R. Karelitz were applicable to the contemporary reality. R. Elhadad consulted with R. Ben Zion Abba Shaul on this point. R. Abba Shaul reasoned that, because the authorities recognized the depreciation after the fact, it was analogous to a royal decree, despite the fact that the government was not pleased with the depreciation. Historically, the monarch sometimes devalued the currency involuntarily, due to the "exigencies of the situation" (this is probably a reference to debasement as a means of emergency war finance). This position contradicts the stringent position that R. Abba Shaul took in his published responsum; it is possible that the responsum was written earlier, and that his views evolved subsequently.

In a case from July 1983, R. Daichovsky[52] revealed an important fact concerning the Orthodox community's adaptation to inflationary conditions. He reported that, even in Bnei Brak (which was at that time the only ultra-Orthodox city), the municipality followed the Interior Ministry's policy of charging interest and indexation on bills in arrears.[53] R. Daichovsky endorsed this practice post facto because: (a) A municipality (or any other public body) is a corporation. Some halachic authorities held that the interest prohibition does not apply to corporations; and (b) indexation and interest are actually a tax, not interest. If a resident causes the municipality to lose revenues, the municipality has every right to impose a tax on him.

R. Moses Sternbuch[54] challenged the very legitimacy of the CPI. He prohibited CPI linked loans or sales on credit, because CPI linkage is tantamount to linkage to the price of "produce." Furthermore, "certainly it is prohibited to link to the CPI, which includes entertainments and luxuries."[55] When indexation was a necessity (e.g., in tort cases), inflation should be measured using necessities only. It is clear that R. Sternbuch assumed that the CPI overestimates inflation in necessities.[56]

52 *Piskei Din Rabaniyim* v. 16, 252–59.

53 This would have required the approval of a leading halachic decisor. I am not aware of any discussion of this issue in the *responsa* literature.

54 *Kitzur Dinei Ribbit*, Ch. 3.

55 R. Moses Feinstein expressed a similar concern in 1971. See *Igrot Moshe*, *Yoreh De'ah* 5:114.

56 R. Sternbuch entertained the possibility of linking to bread prices; see *Ta'am Ribbit*, *Kuntres Acharon* 20.

To summarize, there was a vigorous debate among rabbis regarding the permissibility of CPI indexation; of the rabbis surveyed here, five rabbis permitted it and five rabbis prohibited it. The resistance to the CPI by some rabbis appears to be due to the fact that the CPI is a modern concept, which does not fit neatly into traditional halachic categories. For the economist, the most interesting features of the CPI indexation debate are the criticisms of the CPI by R. Sternbuch and R. Batzri, and R. Popovitz's discussion of the connection between inflation and devaluation.

Conclusion

During the Israeli inflation of 1973 to 1985, the majority of rabbis accepted dollarization as a permissible means of preserving the value of money. However, many rabbis rejected CPI indexation on the grounds that it is a form of interest; some raised fundamental objections to the very concept of the CPI. Other rabbis recognized CPI indexation as a standard business practice and were willing to reinterpret the halachic sources in order to legitimate it.

Did inflationary conditions lead to significant rabbinic innovations in the realm of Jewish monetary doctrine? During 1973 to 1985, Jewish law was applied to the following economic phenomena: black markets in foreign currency, exchange controls, foreign currency trading in globalized markets, the unofficial crawling peg, and the effects of various subsidies on the CPI and on exchange rates. Many of these phenomena had never been discussed in previous rabbinic literature. Furthermore, some rabbis utilized simple economic analysis, especially with regard to the mutual relationship between inflation and devaluation. However, the basic thought categories of Jewish monetary doctrine remained the same. One rabbi seriously considered (but did not adopt) the notion that the Talmudic "coin"/"produce" paradigm was no longer relevant. There was only one doctrinal change that had practical implications. This was the ruling by some rabbis that, under high inflation, debtors who repay late are liable for the opportunity costs that they impose on creditors. For the first time, the Talmudic concept of opportunity cost was applied to problems of monetary instability. In summary, although there were significant changes in the economic subject matter addressed by rabbis, doctrinal innovations were minor.

Several questions remain unanswered. First, it is surprising that so many rabbis rejected CPI indexation. The prohibition against indexation must have imposed substantial losses on lenders, especially in the early 1970s, when dollarization was ineffective in protecting against inflation. There is a longstanding tradition of halachic leniency in situations that involve a large monetary loss; it is not clear why this tradition was not invoked to permit CPI indexation.

Second, we have seen that there were rabbis who strongly criticized the concept of the CPI. It is difficult to understand why these rabbis did not propose an alternative measure of prices. For example, if CPI indexation is unacceptable because the CPI includes luxuries, then the index of food prices could be used instead. Actually, it would be best to use the produce price index, based on the Talmudic convention of using produce prices to measure inflation.[57]

Third, the textual evidence seems to indicate that rabbis relied on their own intuition in matters of economics, rather than consulting with professional economists. The leading decisors of the late twentieth century are known to have consulted with experts in science, technology, and medicine. Unfortunately, little is known about the extent of professional relationships between rabbis and economists.

Regarding the rabbis' disapproval of CPI indexation, I suggest the following explanation: Because the government and the banks always operated under a *hetter iska*, the prohibition against CPI indexation was effectively restricted to intra-Orthodox transactions. The institutionalization of *hetter iska* made it possible for rabbis to oppose indexation as a general (theoretical) rule. At the same time, individuals or (nonbank) institutions who needed to index to the CPI were strongly advised to arrange a *hetter iska*. The practical implementation of *hetter iska*, and its implications for Orthodox Jews and for the Israeli financial system, is an excellent topic for future study.

SELECTED BIBLIOGRAPHY

Abba Shaul, R. Ben Zion. *Responsa Or Lezion*, v. 1, *Yoreh De'ah* 4.

Auerbach, R. Solomon Zalman. *Minhat Shlomo* v. 1, 27:3, 29.

Batzri, Ezra. *Responsa Sha'arei Ezra*, v. 1, 47-50.

Bloi, R. Jacob Isaiah. *Brit Yehuda*, 2nd rev. ed. Jerusalem, 1979.

Bloi, R. Jacob Isaiah. *Brit Yehuda Piskei Dinim* (abridged and updated). Jerusalem, 1999.

Bruno, Michael. "Sharp Disinflation Strategy: Israel 1985." *Economic Policy* 1 (April 1986): 380–407.

Caro, R. Joseph. *Shulhan Arukh Yoreh De'ah* 162, with glosses of R. Moses Issreles and R. David Halevi.

Cohen, R. Shear Yashuv. "Devaluation and Revaluation of the Currency in Jewish law." *Torah Shebeal Peh* 19 (Jerusalem, Mossad Harav Kook: 1977): 64–76.

Daichovsky, R. Solomon. "Changes in the Value of the Currency, Past and Present." *Torah Shebeal Peh* 26 (Mossad Harav Kook: 1985): 74–83.

Daichovsky, R. Solomon, R. Jacob Eliezrov, and R. Masoud Elhadad. "Indexation of a Debt to the CPI." *Tehumin* 6 (Alon Shevut, Israel: 1985): 208–34.

De Medina, R. Samuel. *Responsa Maharashdam, Choshen Mishpat* 75.

Feinstein, R. Moses. *Responsa Igrot Moshe, Yoreh De'ah* 3:37, 5:114.

Heishrik, R. Elijah., and Hershler, R. Moses. *Torat Ribbit*. Jerusalem, 1994.

57 In Israel, two separate price indices, for produce and for other foods, have been available on a monthly basis since 1961.

Levine, Aaron. "Inflation Issues in Jewish Law." *Journal of Halacha and Contemporary Society* 5 (April 1983): 25–45.

Maimonides:

Mishne Torah, Malveh Veloveh 3:10.

Meorot Hadaf Hayomi (*Meorot Hadaf Hayomi*, Bnei Brak, Israel: 2002), v. 5.

Offenbacher, Akiva (Edward)., and Roy Stein. "Dollarization and Indexation in Israel's Inflation and Disinflation: There's More Than One Way to Skin a Cat." *Comparative Economic Studies* 45 (September 2003): 278–305.

Piskei Din Rabaniyim v. 16, 252–59.

Reisman, R. Yisroel. *The Laws of Ribbis: The Laws of Interest and Their Application to Everyday Life and Business*. Brooklyn, NY: Artscroll Mesorah, 1995.

Schiffman, Daniel A. "The Valuation of Coins in Medieval Jewish Jurisprudence." *Journal of the History of Economic Thought* 27 (June 2005): 141–60.

Schiffman, Daniel A. "Rabbinical Perspectives on Money in Seventeenth Century Ottoman Egypt" *European Journal of the History of Economic Thought* 17 (May 2010): 163– 197.

Schochetman, Eliav. "The Enactment of Safed and the *Responsa* of the Sages of Safed Regarding Changes in the Value of Coins." *Sinai* 82 (1978): 109–22.

Sternbuch, R. Moses., and R. Issachar Dov Schreiber. *Kitzur Dinei Ribbit*, 2nd ed. Jerusalem, 2003.

Talmud Bavli:

Bava Kamma 96b–98a.

Bava Metsi'a 44a–45b, 60b, 62b–64b, 72b, 75a.

Weiss, R. Isaac Jacob. *Responsa Minchat Yitzchak* 6:161.

Wosner, R. Samuel. *Responsa Shevet Halevi* 3:109.

Yolles, R. Ephraim Eliezer. "A Lender Who Demands that the Borrower Repay an Old Debt According to the Original Exchange Rate." *Hamaor* Kislev-Tevet 5735 (November-December 1974): 5–6.

Young, Warren, and Yakir Plessner. "Economists, Government, and Economic Policymaking in Israel: From 'Crawling Peg' to 'Cold Turkey.'" *History of Political Economy* 37, Supplement 1 (2005): 292–313.

CHAPTER 24

JEWISH ETHICS, THE STATE, AND ECONOMIC FREEDOM

MEIR TAMARI

INTRODUCTION

THE objective of this chapter is to investigate the balance between private property and economic freedom needed for wealth formation, on the one hand, and morality and communal justice, on the other.

WEALTH FORMATION AND MORALITY AND COMMUNAL JUSTICE

Wealth creation, preservation, and transference to future generations are fundamental necessities of human existence. Fittingly, it has been the focus of religious, political, and philosophical thought, and social movements since the beginning of time. They have all struggled with the fact that, fundamental as it is, the economic need is also the source of greed, envy, crime, violence, bloodshed, and immorality. Some systems have embraced poverty as a solution; others have sought the solution in state or communal planning and control; while others have seen the self-interest of all the players as the keeper of morality in the market place. It should therefore be clear that every economic system, or plan, is not the result of value-free, scientific decisions, but rather of spiritual, religious, or cultural values. Furthermore, all ethical and moral dilemmas have a cost that somebody has to bear; if morality involved no cost, everybody should always act morally and ethically.

Whilst Judaism is not a textbook, it is a value system that can clearly affect, guide, and determine economic behavior. This system draws its normative morality from sources that, although still operative today, are more than 3,500 years old and have covered activity in every country and era in which Jews have lived, under a great variety of economic systems. These sources cover the gamut of economic activity and deal with this aspect of human behavior just as with all the other aspects—spiritual, sexual, shelter, food, clothing, social, and political—of all human activity and life. These are all accepted as legitimate needs and urges for the continuation and development desired by G-d for the world He created—but to be limited, refined, and spiritually ennobling. By providing both legislation and spiritual education, our sources promote a viable economic life based on Judaism's balance between legitimate economic activity and the demands to make even this most materialistic of all human activities part of the sanctification that is the aim of Judaism.

Judaism sees that continuation and development within the following framework:

1. God is neither a stakeholder nor is He a shareholder, but He is the sole source and owner of all wealth and provides therewith for all the needs of all His creatures. This obligates us to earn and use that wealth only in ways consistent with Divine Wisdom and Law.
2. Judaism is a nation-religion; thus, society has obligations and therefore rights in questions of social justice and materialistic righteousness. The public sector thereby becomes a legitimate real economic personality.
3. Sanctification, the source and purpose of ethics and morality, is achieved, primarily through the inculcation of permitted or forbidden actions, and secondarily by an individual's piety or goodness.
4. Humans have free will, which makes them liable for their mistakes but able to enjoy the fruits of their labor.
5. Created in the image of G-d, humans have the ability and the obligation to do those things that are good and straight in His eyes.
6. As the pinnacle of creation, human beings have a guardian relationship to property, both their own and that of others, including all the creatures in nature. Such a relationship militates against damages, waste, and a disregard for the rights of others including those of future generations.

The Legitimacy of Wealth Creation and Private Property

Judaism does not see poverty as spiritual or desirable, nor the creation or increase of private individual wealth as evil or immoral. "The decreasing of wealth is not an act of piety if such wealth is gained in a lawful manner and its further acquisition does not prevent one from occupying himself with Torah learning [a continuous and unlimited obligation of all Jews] and righteous deeds. You are enjoying, as it were, the Lord's hospitality."[1] "One who says, what is mine is yours and what is yours is mine—that is the mark of an ignorant man."[2] Here our sages succinctly saw that the abrogation of private property, while perhaps being the utopian solution to our moral problems, is quite contrary to human nature—not merely a desirable limitation or refinement of the impulses or inclinations. As such it is both undesirable and impossible to abrogate this desire. Judaism does not recognize the validity or necessity for eradicating what G-d has implanted, rather it insists on educating and sanctifying them. Of all these impulses and inclinations, that of money and wealth is the most powerful—one that neither age nor ill health nor even satiety diminish.

There are two causes to the economic immorality and injustice flowing from ownership of property and wealth:

1. Greed: This does not distinguish between needs that are basically limited and wants that are actually unlimited. People are constantly engaged in a pursuit that has no end or limits; more is always better than enough or than less. "One, who has one hundred, desires 200."[3] It is because of the power of this lust, that more than 100 of the 613 commandments, which Jews are obligated to follow, are concerned with restricting and sanctifying that desire.
2. Uncertainty, which is a reality of human life, leads to a constant search for security of wealth and economic assets. Initially, this search is done in ways that are legal and moral such as savings, investments, and insurance. However, often the uncertainty, real or imagined, leads people to illegal and immoral ways to connive, steal, and defraud others to secure wealth for themselves and for their descendants.

Because of Judaism's insistence on the legitimacy of economic activity and the essential reality of private property, both of these two causes of economic immorality require the constraint of enough. Because there can be no morality or ethical economic policies, if the dictum is always "more is better than less," there has to be a philosophy of "the economics of enough," however difficult it may be to define "enough." Thus, in Judaism's faith-based economic system, personal wealth creation and social structure will consistently and consciously abrogate some of the property rights of the individual owner of capital, in all fields of activity. These restrictions come to prevent, or at least to minimize, fraud, exploitation, or damage to the parties in the market place, but equally to fulfill the communal good, to further equity, and to satisfy the social costs. Such a system requires both an enforceable legal framework for economic activity as well a consensus of spiritual, moral, and social values, to be translated into reality.

1 Judah haLevi (Spain, twelft century), *Kuzari* (Jeusalem: Mossad Harav Kook, 1959), 45–50.

2 *Mishnah Avot* 5:10.

3 *Kohelet Rabbah* 1:34.

The Halakhah, the Jewish Legal Framework

A legal framework is essential to any society for regulating the ownership of property and for the conduct of its economy, both because of the conflicting interests of the individuals, and because the economic aims and actions of the individual are not always consistent with the public good. The framework of Judaism is intrinsically different because its Divine origin is meant to make it a way of worshiping God and not merely the ordering of social relations. "The social laws [*mishpatim*] are from Heaven, so they widen and enhance the scope of justice beyond the conception and definitions of human intelligence. Furthermore, such Divine origin predicates that all our actions and thought, even those done in secret and hidden from the eyes of men, are known to God and are rewarded or punished by Him."[4]

This framework of economic matters is part of the *halakhah* (Jewish law) that guides and controls all of Jewish life and is enshrined in all the Codes (e.g., Mishneh Torah, Arba'ah Turim, Shulhan Arukh, Shulhan Arukh ha-Rav, Orakh ha-Shulhan). Throughout the centuries down to the present, the issues arising in this framework were settled by the *Responsa* literature, which recorded the answers of the authoritative scholars to the questions addressed to them. The enactments of the autonomous Jewish communities that existed as independent ministates over the centuries show how the legal framework was translated into everyday reality. In that way, there has always existed an enforceable and normative way of conducting business and an economy that has guided and determined Jewish behavior throughout time down to our own days.

Individuals Vis-à-Vis Individuals

The individual or corporation is required to operate only in a manner permitted by Judaism, and the courts are required to enforce this and adjudicate abuses. This opposes fraud; the oppression of parties to transactions and of minority shareholders; the exploitation of ignorance of harmful goods or services sold; of not making full disclosure of defects in their quality and quantity or of possible conflicts of interest; the use of false weights and measures; harming the property, person, or the aesthetic pleasure of other people; waste of natural resources; abusing trust funds or the role of baileys or of depositors; the mistreatment of wage earners; abusing or not fulfilling fiduciary obligations regarding funds given for investment or safe guarding; and the reneging on contracts or other commercial and financial obligations.[5] It should be noted that all these commercial and economic obligations devolving on Jews are

4 Isaac b. Judah Abrabanel (Spain, 1437–1508), Commentary to Exodus 21.

5 Maimonides (Egypt, 1135–1204), *Mishne Torah, Nizkei Mammon, Kinyan, Loveh u-Malveh.*

binding by Jewish law on Noahides [non-Jews] as well.[6] Furthermore, there are the restrictive policies that apply only to Jews regarding investment, such as those connected to kosher food, the Sabbath and festivals, the Sabbatical and Jubilee Years, and the injunction against borrowing or lending money at interest, irrespective of the rates charged, or of arms sales to rogue governments.

Individuals and the Common Good

"Judaism is not a religion in the accepted form of that word but rather a nation."[7] This is reflected in the economic field by legislation that:

1. Limits or encourages competition, free entry, price control, and profit margins. The primary consideration for deciding restrictive or nonrestrictive policies is the welfare of the majority at that particular time and economic condition.[8]
2. Funds social and welfare costs both through instruments of personal philanthropy and through coerced taxation.[9] There exists a whole halakhic literature regarding tax rates, taxable assets, poll taxes for things that are obligatory on the individual, and taxes on wealth and income.
3. Protects the environment and limits the damages caused either by private property or that of the public. This includes both zoning laws and the prohibition of hazardous industries.

Ethical Consensus

Enforcement of a legal framework, exalted, just essential as it may be, is simply a matter for courts and police; ethical and moral dilemmas, however, only begin where the law ends and their solutions require adherence to a socially accepted consensus. Such a consensus is provided in Judaism by the positive commandments [*mitzvot*] that are as obligatory in the Jewish perspective as those forbidding fraud, damage, and exploitation.

1. Pursuit of justice, economic and judicial, in accordance with the Mosaic demand in Deuteronomy, 16:20, "Justice, Justice, you shall surely pursue."
2. Doing that which is good and straight in the eyes of G-d.

6 Nahmanides (Spain, 1194–1270), Commentary to Genesis 34:13.

7 R. Samson Raphael Hirsch (Germany, 1808–1888), Commentary to Exodus 6:7.

8 R. Joseph Caro (Ottoman Palestine, 1488–1575), *Shulhan Arukh, Hoshen Mishpat*, 227.

9 R. Joseph Caro, op. cit., 153–56.

3. Going beyond the letter of the law, sometimes forgoing even our legal rights.[10]
4. Preserving life and enhancing human partnership with the Creator in the settlement and improvement of the world, as Adam and Eve were commanded in Genesis 2:15.

Actually, all these positive commandments are so intertwined that it is difficult to separate charity [*tzedakah*, more correctly translated as acts of righteousness] from justice [*tzedek*], or human guardianship from settling the world, or all of them from doing that which is good and straight. How are these positive commandments to determine an economic system and life style?

First, mention has already been made of Judaism's injunction against making loans of money against payment of interest—an injunction that over time has been reflected in both Christian and Moslem religious thought. In Judaism, this does not flow from any theory of the barrenness of money but rather from an extension of the concept of charity as may be clearly seen from the equally imperative, even if less known, positive commandment to make interest-free loans. Maimonides and all the codifiers after him classify making such loans, both to poor and to the rich suffering from liquidity shortages, as the highest form of charity. This form includes providing jobs or economic advice to prevent people descending into poverty or to help them break the poverty cycle.[11] Ordinary philanthropy is, at the best, able only to alleviate poverty temporarily but not to enable people to break this cycle. On the other hand, studies in many countries have shown that the creation of new small firms did so. This would help workers made redundant owing to relocation or downsizing, and the working poor, or the large sector of unemployed prevalent today in most of the industrialized world. Not only would they solve their economic problems, but society would solve the social and moral problems of having large underclasses. Corporations and investment funds could make the interest-free loans, to those not served satisfactorily by the normal banking and financial sectors, part of their profit-distribution policies. Corporations could use, at minimal cost, their facilities and business information to retrain dismissed employees to find alternative employment, or to start their own business. Investors could use their financial power to induce them to do so.

Second, people are not merely another one of the species that inhabit this world nor are they to be perceived as being equal to them, but rather as the pinnacle of Creation: "When G-d created the world, all of creation came before Him and complained that now that they had been created they no longer felt bound to Him. So He created Man who would unite the rest of creation with G-d."[12] The positive *mitzvot*[13] come to complete Mankind's fulfillment of their custodian role of natural resources and their role as partners with G-d.

10 R. Samson Raphael Hirsch, Commentary to Deuteronomy, 6:18–19.

11 Maimonides, *Mishne Torah, Mattenot Aniyyim* 10:7.

12 R. Mordechai Yosef Leiner of Izbica, *Sefer HaChassidut*, (Tel Aviv, A. Tzioni, 1955), 126.

13 A positive commandment is in the form of "thou shall," while a negative commandment is in the form of "thou shall not."

The obligation to remove hazardous and despicable materials from the public domain[14] and to prevent natural disasters from causing losses to other people's property or to save that property from such loss[15] are easily translated into investment policies to clean air and water and to prevent or alleviate loss due to such disasters.

Urban sprawl, megacities, and the urge for constant growth often mean haphazard planning, destruction of natural resources and beauty, and the traumatic relocation of people. Investment policies based on the biblical Levitical cities could limit or alleviate these results. These towns were surrounded by a belt devoted to economic activity and by another one that had to remain undeveloped; the townspeople never had the right to change the designation of either belt. This makes for the establishment of small units free of overcrowding and alienation, maintaining an ecological balance, and limiting economic growth in favor of other spiritual and human assets and values.[16]

It must be pointed out limiting economic growth or the economics of "enough" is essential for any viable sustainable ecological policy.

Third, today, the majority of people no longer have any form of job security. The problems of health care have largely been shunted to voluntary insurance and, with prolonged life expectancy and shrinking birth rates, the care of the aged and sick; all these have become universal social and moral problems.

Jewish thinking attaches certain obligations on the employer and the community over and above their contractual ones—to assist employees in their illness, old age, or even in cases where retrenchment is necessary or even simply desirable. Although employers have no moral obligation to provide employment where no such contractual obligation exists, nevertheless, investment policies would have to take rabbinical decisions such as the following into account:

1. Question: "Our cantor has become older and can no longer function as previously. He desires that we employ his son to assist him [tantamount to lightening his work load]. Are we obligated to provide him with this assistance?"
   Answer: "When you decided to employ him, did you think that he would always remain young and capable of the same job? Obviously, you knew that this would not be; therefore, you, consciously or not, agreed to employ him forever. Now you are morally obliged to provide him with this assistance."[17]
2. "The school is obliged to pay severance pay to the dismissed principal [even though no such contractual obligation exists]. A wise man will observe the obligation regarding the Hebrew bondsman (Deut. 15:14) to grant to a worker at the end of his service part of that wealth that G-d has blessed him with."[18]

14 Maimonides, Mishne Torah, *Nizkei Mammon*, 13:22.

15 R. Joseph Caro, op. cit., 426.

16 R. Samson Raphael Hirsch, Commentary to Leviticus 25:34.

17 R. Solomon b. Abraham Adret (Spain, c. 1235–1310), *Responsa* Rashba, 1:300.

18 Rabbinic court decision, Haifa, 1963.

3. "The householders are required to pay the full costs of hospitalization for their domestics for the first two weeks of illness. If a longer period is required, then the costs are shared equally between the employer and the domestic, for another fortnight. The costs of any longer period are to be financed from the charitable funds of the community."[19]

Economics of Enough

A constant spiral of "more is better than less" creates a culture of "wants" translated into "needs," of appeals to egoism and selfishness, and of conspicuous consumption. In such a culture, the defenses of morals and ethics inevitably crumble as each individual struggles to find his place at the ever-receding top of the spiral. This creates jealousy, envy, and hatred that inevitably destroy the social fabric of society. Society needs, therefore, to provide both parameters for acceptable standards of living as well as the education toward a pattern of social living that permits enjoyment of the essential and legitimate private property and economic activity. Judaism provides both the moral literature and the communal norms essential for such parameters of "enough" that must not be confused with philosophies of poverty or egalitarianism.

> The *torah* scholar [Judaism's ethical role model] provides for his family according to his means, yet without excessive devotion to this. His [and their] clothing should be neither that of kings [fashions trendsetters] nor that of the poor, but rather pleasant normal clothing. He should eat his normal meals in his own home [despite the social pressures or the need for ostentation or power] and should not participate in public feasting [which is more expensive and conspicuous] even with scholars, except in association with a religious precept such as the marriage of a scholar to the daughter of a scholar.[20]

Maimonides was only codifying the simplicity of lifestyle that has been an integral part of Jewish living. Communal acceptance and enforcement of such lifestyles is to be seen in the vast literature of enactments of Jewish communities in many countries from the earliest days until our own times, which provide sumptuary laws, voluntary limitations, and even examples of a linkage between tax brackets and permitted consumption.

All these references to the "economics of enough" are an application of the spiritual demand expressed by the prophet Mikhah: "What does the Lord require of you? To do justice, to love righteousness, and to walk modestly with your God" (6:8).

19 *Pinkas HaKesheirim shel Kehilat Cracow*, Enactments of 1595.
20 Maimonides, *Mishne Torah*, De'ot 2:13–14, 5.

Conclusion

The recognition of moral and social responsibilities, both of the individual and of society, requires both moral education and regulation and restrictive legislation to protect weaker members of society.

SELECTED BIBLIOGRAPHY

Caro, R. Joseph. *Shulhan Arukh, Hoshen Mishpat*, 153–156, 227, 426.

Hirsch, R. Samson Raphael. Commentary at Exodus, 6:7, Leviticus, 25:34, Deuteronomy 6:18–19

Maimonides, *Mishne Torah, Nizkei Mammon, Kinyan, Loveh u-Malveh, Mattenot Aniyyim* 10:7, *Nizkei Mammon* 13:22, De'ot 2, 5:13–14.

Nahmanides, Commentary at Genesis 34:13.

PART V

COMPARATIVE LAW STUDIES RELATING TO ECONOMIC ISSUES

CHAPTER 25

ECONOMIC SUBSTANCE AND THE LAWS OF INTEREST: A COMPARISON OF JEWISH AND U.S. FEDERAL TAX LAW

ADAM CHODOROW

Introduction

BOTH Jewish law and U.S. Federal tax law define *interest* broadly as a payment for the use of money.[1] Nonetheless, the two systems diverge widely when determining whether particular transactions involve interest. This chapter compares the different approaches to the laws of interest found in these two systems, in an effort to reveal how underlying goals, practical constraints, and the structure of the legal system affect the development of the law.

The Torah prohibits the charging or paying of interest on loans between Jews. To protect people from inadvertently violating the prohibition, Talmudic authorities extended the ban beyond explicit interest payments on acknowledged loans to cover any transaction that had the economic effect of being a loan and where there was a possibility that a putative lender could receive more than he lent. In contrast, later authorities sought ways to narrow the ban and facilitate credit arrangements. Unable to overturn specific rulings set forth in the Talmud, in many cases they elevated form over substance, permitting parties to enter transactions even where it

1 *See Old Colony Railroad Co. v. Commissioner*, 284 U.S. 552 (1932); *Bava Metsia* 63b and R. Shlomo Yitzhaki (*Rashi*, France, 1040–1105) ad loc.

was clear that the parties intended to circumvent the prohibition against interest. The result is a confusing set of rules, some of which focus on economic substance, while others ignore it entirely.

Federal tax law's concern with interest relates to the desire to tax it appropriately. Parties may have incentives either to disguise payments as interest or to pretend that interest payments are something else. Thus, like Jewish law, it is important that one be able to identify interest. Unlike Jewish jurisprudence on the topic, Federal tax law has generally moved away from formalism in favor of a more substance-based approach to identifying interest. However, as with Jewish law, the approach is not entirely consistent.

Comparing the different ways Jewish law and Federal tax law approach a select number of issues reveals how both systems have struggled to strike the appropriate balance between respecting the form of a transaction and looking to the underlying economic reality.[2] What emerges from this study is not some grand philosophical or principled scheme that explains how and when to respect form or ignore it. Instead, factors such as the ease with which the law can be changed, concerns regarding administrability, and the desired outcome explain the different approaches within each legal system.

The Laws of Interest

The Torah mentions *ribbit* three times.[3] The first occurs in Exodus and states: "When you lend money to My people, to the poor person who is with you, do not act towards him as a creditor; do not lay interest upon him."[4] The second mention is found in Leviticus:

> If your brother becomes impoverished and his means falter in your proximity, you shall strengthen him—proselyte or resident—and let your brother live with you. Do not take from him interest and increase. Do not give him your money for interest, and do not give your food for increase.[5]

2 This article builds on my earlier work comparing Jewish and Federal tax law approaches to various issues. See Adam Chodorow, "Agricultural Tithing and (Flat) Tax Complexity," 68 *U. Pitt. L. Rev.* 267 (2006) (comparing the rules for agricultural tithing to Federal tax rules with an eye toward assessing claims regarding tax reform and eliminating complexity); Adam Chodorow, "Maaser Kesafim and the Development of Tax Law," 8 *Fla. Tax Rev.* 153 (2007) (comparing income definitions developed for nonagricultural tithing and Federal tax purposes); and Adam Chodorow, "Biblical Tax Systems and the Case for Progressive Taxation," 23 *Journal of Law and Religion* 51 (2008) (considering notions of equity implicit in Biblical and Talmudic tax systems and assessing whether they should apply in a secular tax context).

3 The Torah and Talmud use several different terms for interest. The first is *neshech*, from the root "to bite," and refers to the lender biting the borrower by recovering more from the lender than he actually lent. The remaining terms are *ribbit*, *marbit*, and *tarbit*, all of which come from the root "to increase" and refer to the increase that a lender experiences. For ease of reference, I will use the term *ribbit*, regardless of the term used in the Torah, Talmud, or other text.

4 Exodus 22:24. Torah translations are from The Stone Edition of the Tanach, Mesorah Publications, Ltd.

5 Leviticus 25:35–37.

The final mention occurs in Deuteronomy:

> You shall not cause your brother to take interest, interest of money or interest of food, interest of anything that he may take as interest. You may cause a gentile to take interest, but you may not cause your brother to take interest, so that HASHEM, your God, will bless you in your every undertaking on the Land to which you are coming, to possess it.[6]

The first two passages explicitly refer to the poor, while the third does not. Moreover, the Torah explicitly mentions only loans of money and food. Nonetheless, relying on this last verse, Talmudic authorities consistently hold that the ban applies to all loans, regardless whether the borrower is poor, and that it covers more than just loans of money and food. The Torah does not define *ribbit*, but the banned practice is commonly referred to as *agar natar*,[7] which R. Solomon b. Isaac (France, 1040–1105) describes as *sechar hamtana* (a reward for waiting).[8]

Despite the ban's commercial law overtones, it is actually connected to the religious obligations of *tzedakah* (charity/social justice) and *chessed* (kindness), and it is generally included in codes and commentaries covering ritualistic precepts.[9] The double prohibition—against both charging and paying interest—is viewed as a means to reinforce the prohibition;[10] the only way interest can be charged is if both parties to a loan agree to violate the ban. As an additional precaution, the law forbids facilitating a loan at interest by acting as guarantor, witness, or scribe.[11] To underscore the importance of this ban, numerous stories recount how charging interest precludes one from the Resurrection of the Dead, where souls will purportedly reunite with their bodies.[12]

The Torah prohibits only *ribbit ketzuzah*—that is, interest that is prearranged and explicitly called for at the time the loan is made. Nonetheless, to protect people from inadvertently violating the ban, the Talmudic authorities expanded the prohibition to cover virtually all benefits flowing from a borrower to a lender, regardless of how characterized. In addition, they classified as loans a number of other transactions that, while not formally loans, could be seen from an economic perspective

6 Deuteronomy 23:20–21.

7 *Bava Metsi'a* 63b. The phrase is often translated as "renting money."

8 Ad loc. *Rashi.*

9 Consistent with this view, R. Jacob b. Asher (*Tur*, Spain, 1269–1340) and R. Joseph Caro (*Beit Joseph*, Sefat, 1488–1575) include the laws of *ribbit* in their respective codes, the *Arba Turim* and *Shulhan Arukh*, in *Yoreh De'ah*, the section that deals with ritualistic precepts, and not in the sections dealing with civil law.

10 Nahmanides (*Ramban*, Spain, 1194–1270). Deuteronomy 23:20 explains that the ban on borrowers paying was designed as a backstop to the bar against charging interest. See also R. Pinhas ha-Levi of Barcelona (Spain 1235–c. 1290), *Sefer ha-Hinnuch* Vol. III, Leviticus, Part 2 §343 at 431 and Vol. V, Deuteronomy § 572 at 283 (Feldheim Publishers Ltd. New York/Jerusalem, 1978, 3rd rev. ed.).

11 *Bava Metsi'a* 75b; R. Pinhas ha-Levi, *Sefer ha-Hinnuch, supra* note 10, Vol. I, Genesis and Exodus § 68 at 269.

12 In his recent book describing the laws of interest, Israel Reisman cites two tales about those who collected *ribbit*. In one, all souls but one were united with the bodies at the end of time. When asked why, God stated that the excluded soul took *ribbit*. In the other, the owner of a cemetery sought to charge someone who took *ribbit* a significant premium for a plot. R. Akiva Eiger is reported to have said that the cemetery owner acted appropriately, as this man would not be rejoined with his body and would therefore use his plot far longer than others. See R. Israel Reisman, *The Laws of Ribbit* (Mesorah Publications Ltd, 1995) at 17.

as operating like loans. Thus, the authorities developed rules governing credit sales and forward contracts, to name but a few. Rabbinically banned *ribbit* is referred to as *ribbit DeRebanan* (Rabbinic *ribbit*) or *avak ribbit* (the dust of *ribbit*).

By the early middle ages, as Jews were increasingly forced from the land and into the now familiar role of merchant and money lender, the need for credit grew. Late medieval religious authorities could not undo the rulings set forth in the Talmud.[13] However, they could, and did, take a more formalistic approach to the question of identifying loan arrangements and *ribbit*. Unlike their predecessors who focused on economic substance, these later authorities focused instead on a transaction's form to determine whether it violated the ban against *ribbit*.[14] Thus, they permitted credit sales, so long as sellers did not offer two prices based on the time of payment, and no mention was made that the credit price included compensation for the delayed payment. They also sought to and did expand the scope of recognized exceptions to the rules, in some cases to the point where the exceptions swallowed the rules, as was the case in commodity loans.

As a result, current law permits significant commercial activity that may look to secular eyes as entailing interest but that passes religious muster. Because these laws are rabbinic in origin, there is significant variation and debate over their scope, and different authorities adopt different approaches, either strict or lenient, as they decide what is permissible.

The Federal Taxation of Interest

Interest is not banned under the federal tax laws, but it is often treated differently from other types of payments. The Internal Revenue Code (I.R.C., or Code) contains special rules for the deductibility of interest.[15] For example, individuals are permitted to deduct interest incurred in a trade or business or in pursuit of profit, but they are not allowed to deduct "personal interest." Nonetheless, the Code provides for special deductions for home mortgage and student loan interest.[16] Businesses are permitted to deduct interest payments, but they are not permitted to deduct the distribution of profits.

In the context of a sale, any interest paid is not considered part of the purchase price. Thus, interest is excluded when calculating gain or loss to the seller, and it will be taxed at ordinary rates, whereas the gain or loss on the sale of an asset might

13 For a description of Jewish law and its operations, see Menachem Elon, *Jewish Law: History, Sources, Principles* (Bernard Auerbach & Melvin J. Sykes trans., 1994) (1988). See also, Authority, Process and Method: Studies in Jewish Law (Hanina Ben-Menachem & Neil S. Hecht eds., 1998).

14 For a discussion of how economic need spurred rabbinic creativity, see Hillel Gamoran, *Jewish Law in Transition: How Economic Forces Overcame the Prohibition against Lending on Interest* (Hebrew Union College Press, 2008).

15 See, for example, IRC 163.

16 See I.R.C. §§ 163(h)(3) and 221.

be deemed capital in nature and taxed at lower rates. For the buyer, the exclusion of interest affects his basis in the acquired asset (i.e., the measure to be used for determining his gain or loss when he later sells the asset) as well as the amount of depreciation deductions to which he might be entitled. In addition, the buyer may be able to deduct interest paid, whereas other costs of acquisition must be capitalized, thus creating his basis.[17]

The Code does not define interest. However, the Supreme Court defines it as the payment for the use or forbearance of money,[18] effectively adopting the same definition used in Jewish law. Interest is often computed as a percent of the outstanding principle over some period; however, the method of computation does not control.[19] Finally, the labels parties use to describe a payment, either as interest or not as interest, do not control.[20] Instead, tax law generally looks to economic substance to determine whether a payment should be classified as interest. For instance, if Andrew borrows $100 from Barbara and agrees to pay her back $110, the extra $10 will be considered interest, regardless of what the parties call it. Indeed, as described more fully below in the context of credit sales, United States tax law may recharacterize payments as interest even where the parties don't intend interest payments to be made.

Comparing Jewish and U.S. Approaches to Interest

This part considers a select number of issues that arise regarding interest and how Jewish and Federal tax laws address them. A full survey of the laws of interest would require a far more extensive treatment than is possible in a chapter of this length. Accordingly, apart from the first example below, which reveals how similar the approaches can be, I have chosen examples that reveal how the different concerns and indeed the structure of the two legal systems have shaped the law.

This section is broken into two subsections. The first explores acknowledged loans and the questions that arise regarding just what constitutes interest. The second considers transactions that are not structured as loans but that arguably function as loans, thus leading to the possibility of interest.

17 For instance, if purchaser pays $100 for a business asset, but it is determined that $10 is really interest for delayed payment, the purchase price is $90. This amount is not deductible but instead is used for determining gain, loss, and depreciation deductions with respect to the asset. In contrast, the $10 of interest may be deducted currently.

18 See *Old Colony Railroad Co. v. Commissioner*, 284 U.S. 552 (1932).

19 Ibid.

20 See, for example, Rev. Rul. 69–188.

Acknowledged Loans

As mentioned above, where a loan requires the borrower to repay more than he borrowed, both Jewish and Federal tax law will almost certainly classify the excess payment as interest. But what if a borrower gives the lender a gift? How might one distinguish between interest disguised as a gift and a legitimate gift, say for a birthday, completely unrelated to the loan? What if, in addition to repaying the loan, the borrower offers the lender a blessing or praises him to all who will listen? Should nonmonetary benefits be considered a form of interest? Or what if there has been ten percent inflation, such that $110 is equivalent in value to the $100 borrowed the year before? Can a borrower return $110 and claim that there has been no increase? What happens if the value of a borrowed item has gone up during the course of the loan?

This subpart considers three distinct issues addressed under both Jewish and Federal tax law: (a) how to classify gifts and other tangible benefits that flow from borrowers to lenders; (b) whether to classify intangible benefits as interest; and (c) whether loans that include no explicit interest charge can nonetheless be seen as involving interest, even absent other benefits flowing from the borrower to the lender.

Gifts and Other Tangible Benefits

One obvious response to the ban against interest is simply to call it something else. For instance, a lender might write into a loan contract that late fees or gifts, set as a percentage of the loan balance, be paid each year the loan remains outstanding. Despite the labels used, both religious and Federal tax authorities consider such payments to be interest payments.[21] However, what happens if the loan agreement is silent regarding gifts or other benefits, yet the borrower decides to give them anyway? Social norms that do not rise to the level of legal obligation may exist requiring such benefits, creating de facto interest payments. Indeed, the borrower might understand that he would not be permitted to borrow again if benefits of sufficient value were not given.

Both religious and Federal tax authorities have had to struggle with the question of how to treat transfers from borrowers to lenders that fall outside of a loan agreement. While many examples of extracontractual benefits can be found, I focus here on the issues that arise when gifts are given by the borrower to the lender before, during, and after a loan.[22] While the structure of the analysis differs, in both

21 See, for example, *Shulhan Arukh, Yoreh De'ah* 167:16 and Rev. Rul. 69-188.

22 For instance, in the Jewish context, parties could attempt to avoid the ban on *ribbit* by having the borrower grant discounts to a lender or overpay the lender for goods. These practices are forbidden under the same terms that apply to gifts. *Shakh* 160:37 and 173:6. Another issue arises when a borrower selects a lender to be the recipient of a mitzvah. While a loan is outstanding, a borrower may not select his lender to be the recipient of a mitzvah unless he was already in the habit of doing so before the loan was made. *Shulhan Arukh, Yoreh De'ah* 160:7 (relating to *Purim* gifts), 160:10 (relating to tutoring the lender or his son in the Torah). However, where a mitzvah identifies a specific person as the recipient, such as returning lost property to its owner, a borrower may comply, even if the property belongs to his lender. See R. Jacob Isaiah Bloi (Israel, b. 1929), *Berit Yehudah* 10: n2.

cases the systems rely on intent and in some cases the objective manifestation thereof to distinguish between interest payments, on the one hand, and, on the other, unrelated benefits flowing from the borrower to the lender, which should not be construed as interest.

The *Shulhan Arukh* appears to ban all gifts flowing from borrowers to lenders.[23] The difficulty is that loans are often made between friends and family, and an absolute ban on gifts would simply not be workable. Otherwise, if a small child ever gave his parent a birthday present, the parent could never lend the child money. Clearly, some limiting factor or rule must exist to distinguish between permissible and impermissible gifts. The authorities have split into two camps, one focused primarily on objective manifestations of intent and appearances, and the other focused on actual intent.

R. Moses Isserles (*Rema*, Poland, 1520–1572) construed the *Shulhan Arukh* to bar gifts where the giver expresses that the gift is in relation to the loan or where the gift is large.[24] R. Shabbetai b. Meir ha-Kohen (*Shakh*, Poland, 1622–1663) inferred from this ruling that small gifts are acceptable, so long as no mention of the loan is made at the time of the gift.[25] Implicit in these rulings is the presumption that small gifts are not likely to be in payment for a loan and therefore are not prohibited, so long as the borrower/giver does not contradict the presumption by stating that the gift is in payment. R. Shneur Zalman of Lyady (Russia, 1745–1812) introduced the consideration of time, holding that, if sufficient time has passed, even large gifts are permitted, presumably because they would not be related to the loan.[26]

The difficulty with this approach is that it relies too heavily on objective criteria to get at intent. If stating that the gift is given in payment for the loan is the only way to rebut the presumptions created by the objective evidence (i.e., the size of the gift and the time passed), then parties could easily avoid the ban, either by giving small gifts or waiting long enough. Such a rule elevates form over substance but arguably preserves appearances.

In contrast, R. David b. Samuel HaLevi (*Taz*, Poland, c. 1586–1667) argued that the *Shulhan Arukh* followed Maimonides (*Rambam*, Egypt, 1135–1204), who had ruled that intent is the critical factor in determining whether one can give a gift to a lender.[27] Clearly, someone could give a small gift as payment for the loan. Under *Taz's* view, failing to mention the fact should not launder what is clearly meant as interest and turn it into a gift. The benefit of such a rule is that it would permit legitimate gifts, regardless of size or when given. However, it leaves lenders open to temptation and creates the possibility that legitimate gifts might be construed by others as *ribbit*. Such a rule is also difficult to enforce. But, as each person

23 *See Shulhan Arukh, Yoreh De'ah* 160:6.

24 *Rema* 160:6.

25 *Shakh* 160:10. See also *Hokhmat Adam* 131:8–9.

26 Ad loc. 167, quoting *Havvat Da'at*. This, of course, begs the question of what the appropriate time is. Some rabbis have indicated that gifts within three days of a loan are barred, but that gifts before the loan was made or after it is repaid are permitted. *Hokhmat Adam* 131:8.

27 *Taz* 160:3; *Shakh* 160:10.

is responsible to himself for following the law, and as God is the ultimate enforcer, concerns regarding intent-based rules are far less problematic in Jewish law than they are in Federal tax law, where less than omnipotent administrators must consistently and efficiently glean intent from a person's behavior.

Federal tax law also struggles to distinguish between gifts and interest. Gifts are excluded from income,[28] while interest payments are included. Interest payments are often deductible, while gifts never are. Thus, some taxpayers may wish to disguise interest as gifts to avoid tax to the recipient, while others might want to disguise gifts as interest to obtain a deduction and shift income to someone in a lower tax bracket.[29] Tax law uses an intent-based test to determine whether a transfer qualifies as a gift. Taxpayers must demonstrate that the amount given reflects "detached and disinterested generosity."[30] In contrast, interest is payment for the use or forbearance of money. A transfer cannot satisfy both definitions, and the question of whether a transfer should be considered interest therefore resolves into an intent-based test similar to that advocated by *Taz*.

Intent is notoriously hard to determine, and one way tax law approaches the question of intent is through the step-transaction doctrine, under which "a series of formally separate steps may be amalgamated and treated as a single transaction if they are in substance integrated, interdependent, and focused toward a particular end result."[31] This doctrine is embodied in three different tests, including the binding commitment,[32] interdependence,[33] and end result test.[34] As with the *Rema's* approach to identifying intent, each relies on objective factors. The first looks solely to formal obligations linking the steps in question, thus requiring a formal showing of intent. The second gets at intent indirectly by considering whether the steps make sense in isolation. If not, the steps will be collapsed. The third focuses more directly on intent by determining whether the steps form part of a prearranged plan.

In this context, there are two purportedly separate transactions—a loan and a gift in return. The two cannot remain separate if intent linking the two is found under any of the three tests. In other words, the gift will be deemed to be given in return for the loan and classified as interest. Significantly, the reliance here on

28 I.R.C. § 102(a).

29 For example, if Charles earns $100 and wishes to transfer it to David, who is in a lower tax bracket, he could "borrow" money from David and then pay David the $100 as interest. Before 1986, Charles could deduct the interest payment, zeroing out his income, and David would include it. The rules limiting the deductibility of interest on personal loans complicate this ploy, but it can still work if the loan is for business purposes. In contrast, if Charles seeks to borrow money from David but would not be able to deduct the interest because it is personal, he may be inclined to borrow interest-free but make a $100 gift to David, which David could exclude from his income. The rules that now apply to interest-free loans and discussed below may make this gambit largely unproductive.

30 *Commissioner v. Duberstein*, 363 U.S. 278 (1960).

31 *Tandy Corp. v. Commissioner*, 92 T.C. 1165, 1171 (1989).

32 See, for example, *Penrod v. Commissioner*, 88 T.C. 1415, 1429 (1987).

33 See, for example, *Redding v. Commissioner*, 630 F.2d 1169, 1177 (7th Cir. 1980), *cert. den.*, 450 U.S. 913 (1981).

34 See, for example, *Penrod*, supra note 32 at 1429.

objective evidence does not replace intent. Unlike the rule suggested by *Rema* and extended by others, even though no objective evidence is found, if a party is found to have intent, the purported gift will be treated as interest.

Ribbit Devarim

Benefits can take numerous forms, and both Jewish and Federal tax authorities have had to address whether a borrower's provision of intangible benefits, such as expressions of gratitude, should be considered a form of *ribbit*. On the one hand, gratitude has no monetary value, so it hardly seems like interest. On the other hand, it does have psychological value and could be seen as a benefit above and beyond the repayment of the loan. Unlike with gifts, the approach to such benefits in Jewish and United States tax law diverges widely, reflecting the purpose and constraints of the two systems.

Unconcerned with the need to quantify or value interest, Jewish authorities took a broad view and barred expressions of gratitude as a form of *ribbit*, which they termed *ribbit devarim* (*ribbit* of words).[35] The clearest example of an intangible benefit flowing from the borrower to the lender occurs where the borrower praises, compliments, or offers a blessing to the lender. These acts clearly have value, and they are prohibited.[36] However, even a simple "thank you" could be seen as a benefit. The authorities have split on the question of whether to allow borrowers to thank their lenders.[37] Simple greetings could be seen as a form of thank you, but, as with gifts, the problem of a preexisting relationship exists. It would seem incongruous to bar people from greeting one another if they previously did so simply because one had borrowed money from the other. Thus, if the borrower was in the habit of doing so, the authorities permit him to continue. However, he may not greet his lender more warmly than was his custom, as the excess warmth was considered *ribbit*.[38] If the borrower was not in the habit of greeting his lender before the loan, he cannot start doing so.[39]

The issue of intangible benefits arises in the Federal tax context as well when trying to decide what to include in the tax base. At its most abstract, income can be conceived of as a flow of satisfactions.[40] However, early theorists recognized that a real-world definition of income must be capable of calculation. They also recognized that taxes are paid in dollars.[41] Thus, in designing the real-world tax rules,

35 As with the ban on selecting a lender to be the recipient of a mitzvah, see supra note 22, the ban on *ribbit devarim* exists only during the term of the loan.

36 *Shulhan Arukh, Yoreh De'ah* 160:12.

37 See *Beit Yosef* 160, *s.v. v'afelu* and *Igrot Moshe, Yoreh De'ah* 1:80 (precluding thank yous) and S.Z Auerbach (*Minchat Shlomo* 27) (permitting thank yous).

38 *Shulhan Arukh, Yoreh De'ah* 160:11.

39 In contrast, if the lender greets the borrower, the borrower may return the greeting. *Divrei Sofrim* 160:63.

40 *See* Robert M. Haig, "The Concept of Income—Economic and Legal Aspects (1921)," in *Readings in the Economics of Taxation* 54, 55 (R. Musgrave & C. Shoup eds., 1938) ("Modern economic analysis recognizes that fundamentally income is a flow of satisfactions, of intangible psychological experiences").

41 Ibid. at 55–56.

Congress has generally included in the tax base only those things that can be readily valued and that increased a taxpayer's ability to pay taxes. For instance, Congress excludes imputed income from the tax base, despite its clear economic value.[42]

While gratitude is clearly exchanged for the loan and can be conceived of as a payment for the use of money, there is no way to value a blessing or thank you. Moreover, the recipient of a blessing is no more able to pay his taxes than one who has not been blessed. Thus, as with imputed income, Federal tax authorities have not sought to classify gratitude as interest or otherwise include it in the tax base.

"Interest Free" Loans

Presumably, where a lender simply repays what was borrowed, there is no interest. However, under both Jewish and Federal tax law, the possibility of interest exists, though in different instances. In dealing with such cases, Jewish law is motivated by its underlying conception of value and the baselines against which value is to be measured, while Federal tax law is motivated by the desire to stop income shifting and other forms of tax avoidance.

Again, we begin with Jewish law. At the outset, it is necessary to distinguish between loans of a commodity or money, where the lender is only expected to return a like quantity of what was borrowed, and loans of a specific item, such as a tool, where it is expected that the borrower will return the item lent. The former type of loan is covered by the laws of *ribbit*; the latter type of loan is not. Indeed, lenders may charge rental fees for such items.[43] We focus here on the former type of loan.

Talmudic authorities realized that, even where a lender receives back the same quantity of a commodity he lent, the value of the item might have increased in the interim. For instance, the price of wheat can be expected to be low at harvest but high in the dead of winter. Absent some rule to the contrary, a clever person could easily avoid the ban on *ribbit* by lending wheat during the harvest season and seeking repayment in the winter. While he would receive the same amount he lent, he is better off from an economic perspective.

In light of the possibility of this increase in value, early authorities enacted the prohibition of *seah be'seah*,[44] in which they banned the loan of commodities, even where the borrower was required to repay the same amount borrowed. They permitted commodity loans if the value of the commodity was established at the time of the loan, and the borrower agreed to return currency of that value or that value

42 Imputed income is generally defined as "the market-price equivalents of non-market economic activity (such as the value of self-grown crops and the rental value of self-owned assets, and possibly the value of self-performed services)." Joseph M. Dodge, "Accessions to Wealth, Realization of Gross Income, and Dominion and Control: Applying the "Claim of Right Doctrine" to Found Objects, Including Record-Setting Baseballs," 4 *Fla. Tax. Rev.* 685, 705 (2000). Examples include the value received from living in one's own home or of self-provided child care.

43 *Bava Metsi'a* 69b. Some controversy exists whether this is true whenever the same item is expected to be returned or whether the item must also be of the sort that is subject to wear and tear such that it normally declines in value with use. The *Shulhan Arukh* adopts the latter position. *Shulhan Arukh, Yoreh De'ah* 176:2.

44 *Shulhan Arukh, Yoreh De'ah* 162:1. A *seah* is a measure of volume, and the term means a *seah* for a *seah*.

of the commodity when the loan came due.[45] While this could lead to a lender returning more commodity than was borrowed, because the same value was borrowed and returned, there was no *ribbit*.

The need to set a value for commodity loans would have negated one of the main benefits of such loans. Accordingly, authorities quickly developed a number of exceptions. For instance, they exempted loans of small amounts to neighbors, creating a sort of de minimis rule.[46] Other exceptions applied in commercial settings. Commodity loans were allowed where the borrower already had the borrowed commodity (called *yesh lo*).[47] Such loans might occur when the borrower had the goods, but they were locked in a room, and the person with the key was temporarily away. The Mishnah permits such loans on the theory that the transaction is more of a temporary accommodation than a loan.[48]

However, what if the borrower only has a small portion of the commodity in his possession? May he borrow more than he has? The justification for the exception—temporary unavailability—would not seem to apply. Nonetheless, R. Ahai Gaon (Roman Palestine, eighth century) significantly expanded the exception by holding that, if the borrower had *any* quantity of a commodity, he could borrow an unlimited amount of that commodity without running afoul of the ban.[49] Later authorities even allowed lenders to give a small quantity of a commodity to the borrower as a gift, thus permitting the borrower to fall under this exception and effectively rendering the prohibition meaningless.[50]

R. Ahai Gaon also concluded that, even where a borrower had none of the commodity he sought to borrow, if a set market price existed (known as *yatza hashar*),[51] one could borrow commodities and commit to repay the same quantity without violating the laws against *ribbit*.[52] Presumably, the ability to acquire the commodity in the market was sufficient to allow the fiction that the borrower had the goods in stock. These rulings were eventually incorporated into the *Shulhan Arukh*,[53] with the result that, although interest-free loans of commodities were banned in the Talmud, the exceptions, and in particular the extension of those exceptions since the closing of the Talmud, have ultimately swallowed up the general rule.

Implicit in the prohibition of *se'ah be'se'ah* is the notion that some baseline exists against which commodity value is to be measured. That baseline is currency or, to be more specific, gold and silver—the two metals from which currency was made during Biblical and Talmudic times. Even though these currencies can fluctuate in value relative to one another and to goods, authorities treated them as

45 *Havvat Da'at* 165:1; *Berit Yehudah* 17:3.

46 *Rema* 162:1.

47 *Shulhan Arukh, Yoreh De'ah* 162:2.

48 *Bava Metsi'a* 5:9.

49 *She'iltot* 43.

50 *Shulhan Arukh, Yoreh De'ah* 172:2.

51 This translates literally to "the gate is open."

52 *She'iltot* 43.

53 *Shulhan Arukh, Yoreh De'ah* 162:2–3.

having a constant value for purposes of evaluating whether commodity loans could lead to *ribbit*.

If currency is a constant baseline against which to measure commodity loans, it follows that currency should also have a constant value for purposes of evaluating money loans. Thus, the possibility of *ribbit* should not exist when a borrower returns the same quantity of currency he borrowed to the lender. Consistent with this logic, and in contrast to commodity loans, Jewish law permits no-interest currency loans. Nonetheless, issues arise.

Modern currency is no longer on a gold or silver standard, and, as a result, currencies could be seen as another form of commodity. Not only could this lead to a ban on no-interest loans, where the borrower was expected to return the same quantity of currency borrowed, but it could also lead to the claim that interest charges were designed simply to ensure that the borrower received back the same value he had lent, compensating not for the use of money but rather for inflation, as is permissible with other commodity loans.

Rabbi Moshe Feinstein (New York, 1895–1986) addressed the question of inflation and interest in the context of the obligation to tithe.[54] Rabbi Feinstein held that one could take inflation into account for purposes of determining income for tithing purposes. Thus, one can tithe based on economic, as opposed to nominal, gains. However, for purposes of the laws of *ribbit*, he concluded that one must use nominal dollars, regardless of the actual value at the time of the loan and repayment. In other words, local currency is an appropriate baseline against which one measures gain and loss, even though its value is no longer tied to gold or silver.[55]

Federal tax law does not address commodity loans. However, with regard to money loans, it reaches a conclusion directly opposite that reached by religious authorities. Ironically, it is the charitable imperative that underlies the obligation for Jews to lend to one another interest-free—the provision of a benefit to one in need—that leads the Federal tax authorities to impute interest charges and subsequent transfers in interest-free loans even though none are actually made.

The courts figured out early on that an employer allowing an employee to use property, such as a corporate condominium, had value, and they ruled that such value should be included in the employee's income.[56] However, they took the position that interest-free loans did not create income for the borrower, despite the clear benefit conferred.[57] Not surprisingly, taxpayers took advantage of this holding

54 *Iggerot Moshe*, Vol. 5, *Yoreh De'ah* § 2, No. 114. This responsum is partially translated and discussed in Maaser Kesafim, *On Giving a Tenth to Charity*, (4th ed.), (Jerusalem/New York: Feldheim Publishers, 1999) edited by Cyril Domb at 48.

55 In contrast, foreign currency must be treated as a commodity. *See Berit Yehuda* 22:n33. Accordingly, absent an exception such as *yesh lo*, one may not lend foreign currency and ask to be paid back the same amount. There is some debate regarding whether the set market price exception (*yatza hazshar*) should apply. *See Shevet ha-Levi* 3:109 and *Mishnas Ribbit* 6:n12 (quoting R. Y.S. Eliyashev Shlita).

56 See, for example, *Dean v. Commissioner*, 187 F.2d 1019 (3rd Cir. 1951).

57 See, for example, *J. Simpson Dean v. Commissioner*, 35 T.C. 1083 (1961). In part the court reasoned that including the benefit of an interest-free loan in income would be exactly offset by the deduction taxpayers would obtain if they actually paid interest. Congress has since restricted the circumstances under which interest is deductible, see I.R.C. § 163(h), rendering this argument nugatory.

in a number of ways. Family members used interest-free loans to shift income to those in lower tax brackets by lending money to their children tax-free and letting their children earn and be taxed on the interest.[58] Employers used interest-free loans as a form of tax-free compensation.

In response, Congress enacted I.R.C. § 7872 to include in income the benefit imparted to recipients of interest-free loans.[59] But how should that benefit be measured? Interest rates vary depending on the risk undertaken, and the government had to develop a measure for the foregone interest. It picked the "applicable Federal rate," which is based on the risk-free interest rate, generally understood to be that offered on government bonds.[60] To make accounts balance, the borrower is deemed to have paid interest to the lender at the applicable Federal rate. The borrower might be able to deduct the imputed interest payment, depending on his use of the loan proceeds.[61] The lender must include the imputed interest in income. The lender would then be deemed to return the interest payment to the borrower. The borrower must treat the imputed transfer back as a gift, compensation, or dividend, depending on his relationship with the lender. The lender might be able to deduct the imputed transfer back to the borrower, depending on the deemed nature of the transfer.

The divergence in approaches in the case of interest-free loans reflects, on the one hand, the conception of value and the baseline against which it must be measured, and, on the other hand, concerns with taxing benefits conferred and preventing tax avoidance. And the interplay of these two approaches leads to the following conundrum: A Jewish lender subject to American tax laws is damned if he does (charge interest) and damned (or at least subject to tax) if he doesn't.[62]

Identifying Loans And the Interest Implicit In Them

Ribbit cannot exist absent a debtor/creditor relationship. Thus, it is imperative to determine whether a loan exists between parties before attempting to determine whether interest has been paid. Both Jewish and Federal tax authorities recognize that loans may arise through a number of different means, even if they are not formally nominated as such. This subpart considers two situations where this concern arises: credit sales and forward contracts.

58 See Staff of House Comm. on Ways and Means, 98th Cong., 2d Sess., Summary of Comm. Amendment to H.R. 4170, 1373-74 (Comm.Print 1984).

59 Section 7872 distinguishes between gift loans, compensation-related loans, and corporate-shareholder loans, among others. It also distinguishes between demand loans and term loans. For loans that are not gift loans or demand loans, interest is treated under the Original Issue Discount rules set forth in I.R.C. § 1272 et seq. and § 163(e). Describing the mechanics associated with the different types of loans is beyond the scope of this chapter.

60 See I.R.C. § 1274(d).

61 See supra Part o.

62 The argument that interest should not be considered a benefit received because it simply compensates for inflation losses is foreclosed to Federal taxpayers. *See Hellerman v. Comm'r*, 77 T.C. 1361 (1981) (rejecting a claim that the income tax applies to economic, as opposed to nominal, gains). Money has a constant value for both *halachic* and Federal tax purposes.

Credit Sales

Credit sales present a host of *ribbit*/interest issues. Although nominally sales, they can be conceived of as a loan to the buyer, combined with a sale. Under Jewish law, the seller may not charge interest on the loan, as that would clearly violate the ban against *ribbit*. But what if the seller simply charges more for delayed payment than he does for immediate payment? Should the excess cost be considered interest? As described below, in response to its rules banning interest, modern Jewish law tends to take a formalistic approach, ignoring interest implicit in most credit sales. In contrast, Federal tax law looks to economic substance, finding interest even where the parties may not have intended it. These different approaches reflect, on the one hand, the Jewish authorities' desire to facilitate credit in the face of laws banning it that they cannot change, and, on the other hand, the adoption into the law of economic principles and a desire to avoid difficult intent-based tests.

The main concern with credit sales from a *ribbit* perspective is with differential pricing for immediate and credit purchases. In particular, if a seller sets one price for immediate payment and a higher price for later payment, it is clear that the increase in price is *ribbit* (i.e., a charge for borrowing money).[63] Accordingly, sellers may not set two prices for goods, depending on the type of purchase. If a seller does this, the purchaser is allowed to pay the lower price now, but he is prohibited from purchasing on credit because that higher price implicitly includes *ribbit*.[64]

Despite the clear prohibition against charging more for credit sales, religious authorities have found ways to permit merchants to charge for credit. For instance, while charging for credit is not allowed, one may always give a discount. Accordingly, some authorities have held that, if there is a set market price, a vendor may set the market price as the credit price and offer a discount for immediate payment.[65] Other commentators object, noting that it is not possible to distinguish between a discount and a credit charge. Charging more for credit, even if the credit price is the fair market price, amounts to an interest charge.[66] Moreover, given the variability of prices among stores, few goods have a set market price, and it is not clear how often this leniency would apply.

Where items have no set value, a seller who knows that a sale will be on credit may simply state a higher price than he would ordinarily charge, provided he does not state that he is raising the price because of delayed payment and does not simultaneously offer a lower price for immediate payment.[67] However, if the credit price is significantly higher than what the seller would normally charge, the fact that

63 Not all payments in a differential pricing scheme are necessarily interest. For instance, sellers might incur additional costs associated with delayed payment, such as for billing. They may pass those costs along to the buyer, so long as they are separately stated. *Berit Yehudah* 9:n:13. Buyers may also compensate vendors for any out-of-pocket losses associated with late payment, *Berit Yehudah*, based on *Taz* 170:3, but not lost opportunity costs. R. Shlomo ben Adret (Spain, 1235–1310) (Rashba), *Responsa* 3:227.

64 *Shulhan Arukh, Yoreh De'ah* 173:1; *Rema* 173:3.

65 See, for example, R. Avraham Danzig (Vilna, c. 1747–1812), *Hokhmat Adam* 139:5.

66 See *Shulhan Arukh HaRav* § 18.

67 *Shulhan Arukh, Yoreh De'ah* 173:1.

ribbit is being collected cannot be ignored. Thus, any increase must be reasonable, with some authorities setting a twenty percent limit.[68]

This approach could lead to the awkward situation where a seller quotes a price assuming immediate payment, after which the buyer informs him he would like to pay later. The seller may not increase the price, as it would be clear that the increase reflected the cost of delayed payment. However, a seller may withdraw his initial offer and then make a second, higher offer.[69] While such a move makes clear that there is a different price for immediate and credit purchases, the two offers are not outstanding at the same time, and the fiction of one price for all purchases is maintained.

Similarly, a seller can negotiate a sale at the credit price and then, after the sale is final, offer a discount for immediate payment.[70] So long as the original sale document did not contain provisions for a discount for prepayment, this approach will avoid the prohibition against *ribbit*, even if the offer is made just after the sale becomes final. Again, the form trumps economic reality and any tacit understanding regarding the anticipated availability of a post-purchase price reduction is ignored when analyzing the transaction. Instead, appearances are regarded as more important than intent.[71]

The first United States courts to consider the issue of implicit interest in credit sales found none, even where two prices were offered simultaneously. For instance, in *Hogg v. Ruffner*, the Supreme Court considered a claim of usury, where one party agreed to execute notes for $38,000 to forestall collection of a $20,000 debt. When sued to make good on his $38,000 debt, he argued that the debt involved usury and should not be enforced, as the extra $18,000 he agreed to pay was really a payment for the forbearance of money (i.e., interest) and far in excess of the usury limits. The Court rejected this claim noting:

> But it is manifest that if A proposes to sell B a tract of land for $10,000 cash, or for $20,000 payable in ten annual installments, and if B prefers to pay the larger sum to gain time, the contract cannot be called usurious. A vendor may prefer $100 in hand to double sum in expectancy, and purchaser may prefer the greater price with the longer credit, and one who will not distinguish between things that differ, may say, with apparent truth, that B pays a hundred percent, for forbearance, and may assert that such a contract is usurious, but whatever truth there may be in the premises, the conclusion is manifestly erroneous. Such a

68 See, for example, *Shakh* 173:5.

69 See, for example, Rabbi Jacob Lorbeerbaum (Poland, 1760–1832), *Havvat Da'at* 173:2.

70 *Shulhan Arukh, Yoreh De'ah* 173:3; *Rema* 173:3.

71 The approach to credit sales can be viewed as a form of legal fiction, where all the parties know what is going on but pretend otherwise by observing the form of the transaction. As noted by Lon Fuller, legal fictions are often employed where parties need to change the law but cannot or, at the very least, cannot be seen to be doing so. See Lon Fuller, *Legal Fictions* (Stanford University Press, 1967). Relatedly, the approach also raises the question of when norms can or should be taken into accout when determining the legal affect of an agreement. See Alex Raskolnikov, "The Cost of Norms: Tax Effects of Tacit Understandings," 74 *U. Chi. L. Rev.* 601 (2007). I leave the exploration of these issues and the comparison of how Jewish and Federal tax law approach them to another day.

> contract has none of the characteristics of usury; it is not for the loan of money, or forbearance of a debt.[72]

Sixty years later, and in the context of the income tax, the Board of Tax Appeals reached a similar result in *Appeal of Lang*.[73] In this case, a taxpayer was offered two prices for a partnership interest, a lower price, bearing a six percent interest rate, and a higher price, omitting any mention of interest, but to be paid at a later date. The taxpayer attempted to deduct the increase in price as interest. Noting that "the best evidence of [the excess payment's] nature is the contract itself," the Board noted that the excess payment was not designated as interest and indeed was likely in lieu of interest. Accordingly, it denied the claimed deduction.

Over time, tax authorities recognized that setting two prices for a good, a lower price for immediate payment and a higher one for later payment, implicitly involved a loan and interest. However, unlike *halachic* authorities, they were not interested in disguising the fact that interest was being charged and facilitating credit. Instead, they were motivated to identify the interest component of a credit sale and to tax it accordingly, even where only one price was ever offered.

In 1964, Congress enacted I.R.C. § 483 to address the question of interest implicit in credit sales of property (i.e., sales where payments were made beyond one year after the date of the sale).[74] It added § 1274 in 1984, which deals specifically with debt instruments issued in return for property.[75] I.R.C. § 1274 contains many exceptions, and I.R.C. § 483 now acts as something of a backstop for § 1274. Both sections require taxpayers who buy on credit to assess whether the purported purchase price contains implicit interest and set forth the means for doing so.[76] Generally speaking, if the buyer pays the seller interest at or above the applicable Federal rate, described above in the context of interest-free loans, then no recharacterization is necessary, and the stated purchase price is honored as such. However, if insufficient interest is charged, the parties must use the applicable Federal rate to determine the net present value of the payments called for. This value is then treated as the purchase price and used to determine gain, loss, and basis. The difference between the present value and the face value is treated as interest.

I.R.C. § 1274 requires taxpayers who issue debt for property to determine the "issue price" for the debt obligation. This issue price is treated as the purchase price for the property and used to calculate gain or loss and the buyer's basis. If the debt states adequate interest (i.e., interest in excess of the applicable Federal rate), the issue price is the face value of the debt. However, if the obligation does not state sufficient interest, a portion of the face value is recharacterized as interest. In such

72 66 U.S. 115, 118–119 (1861).

73 3 B.T.A. 417 (1926).

74 Pub.L. 88–272, Title II, § 224(a), Feb. 26, 1964, 78 Stat. 77.

75 Pub.L. 98–369, Div. A, Title I, § 41(a), July 18, 1984, 98 Stat. 538.

76 While these sections generally accomplish the same goal of identifying interest implicit in credit sales, they use different terms and different methods. They also have different exceptions and, in some cases, limits. Nonetheless, in most cases, they arrive at the same result. Exploring the precise mechanisms by which these sections operate is not relevant to the analysis here and so is skipped.

cases, the issue price is determined to be the present value of the payments due under the obligation, using the applicable Federal rate as the discount rate. The difference between the "issue price" and face value is treated as interest.

These rules do not apply to "personal use property," defined as property where substantially all of the use is not in connection with a taxpayer's trade or business or a profit-seeking activity under I.R.C. § 212.[77] Thus, for such property, the Jewish and Federal tax treatment is the same. While interest may exist from an economic perspective and may even be intended by the parties, both legal systems turn a blind eye to it. However, where the property is business property, Federal tax law recharacterizes part of the payment as interest and taxes the transaction accordingly. As a result, as occurs with interest-free loans of currency, Jewish purchasers and sellers of goods to be used in business may be deemed to pay or receive interest for Federal tax purposes even though they are not seen as doing so for *halachic* purposes.

Forward Contracts

Forward contracts present a similar issue to that found in credit sales in that buyers prepay for goods, instead of delaying payments. Surprisingly, the approach to such transactions taken by Jewish law and Federal tax law are opposite from what we saw above in the context of credit sales. Jewish law tends to look to the substance of the transaction to determine whether it raises a *ribbit* problem, while Federal tax law tends to respect the form of the transaction and ignores the loan element entirely. The different approaches here may reflect the existence of significant exceptions that permit forward contracts in Jewish law and the lack of tax avoidance associated with forward contracts in Federal tax law.

A forward contract exists when a purchaser pays today for something to be delivered in the future. For instance, Aaron might pay Moshe $100 dollars in January for wheat to be delivered in October, after the harvest. On the one hand, the form and intent underlying this transaction is a purchase and sale agreement, and there is no possibility of interest. On the other, when compared with a sale and immediate delivery, Moshe has use of Aaron's money until he delivers the goods. This is essentially an interest-free loan. Taking the analysis one step further, the transaction can be conceived of as Moshe borrowing money from Aaron, which he later repays with a commodity, raising the possibility of *ribbit* if the commodity is worth more than what was lent. Alternately, if Moshe charges Aaron less for payment in January than he would have in October, it looks as if Moshe is charging one price for immediate payment and a higher price for delayed payment, thus violating the rules associated with credit sales.

As forward contracts are not structured as loans, do not explicitly call for interest, and indeed will only lead to interest if the value of the asset purchased increases before delivery, the Torah does not bar them. Nonetheless, the Talmud does.[78] Despite this general ban, as with pure commodity loans, the Talmud recognizes a number of important exceptions that come close to swallowing the rule.

77 I.R.C. § 1275(b)(1) and (3).
78 *Shulhan Arukh*, *Yoreh De'ah* 173:1.

The first exception is *yesh lo*, which we saw above in the context of commodity loans. If the seller has the goods in stock, the purchase and delivery could have happened simultaneously, but it is as if the buyer simply opted to have the seller hold the goods for later delivery.[79] In such a case, it seems as if the sale took place, and the seller is merely storing the goods for the buyer. Post sale, any increase in price is credited to the buyer, thus precluding *ribbit*. Under this exception, one could purposefully purchase an item at harvest, when the price is low, for delivery in winter, when the price is expected to be high. However, because we assume a sale, the return would be seen as that on an investment and not impermissible *ribbit*. Under the strongest form of this rule, the vendor would need to identify and segregate the goods in question, perhaps even passing title to the buyer. However, the authorities ruled leniently. Not only need vendors not segregate the goods or pass title, they can "sell" the same bushel of wheat to any number of buyers.[80] So long as it was possible to make a sale for immediate delivery, the transaction is treated as a sale.

The second exception arises when the goods purchased are available at a set market price (*yatza hazshar*).[81] The Talmud offers two competing explanations for this exception. First, the vendor could have used the purchase price to acquire the goods at the set market price and delivered them to the buyer, in essence extending *yesh lo* by treating readily available goods as being in the possession of the seller.[82] Second, if there is a set market price, the setting of a guaranteed price for future delivery is of no value to the purchaser because he could go into the market place and buy the goods himself currently.[83] If the fixed price for future delivery is not a benefit, then it is not as if two prices are being offered at once.

These two exceptions may rest on a third explanation. *Davar shelo ba l'olam* is a phrase meaning something that does not exist in the world cannot be sold. Thus, a forward contract for wheat that has yet to grow cannot be considered a sale. Instead, it is a loan until the sale is actually consummated, raising the possibility of *ribbit*. However, if an item is in stock or has a set market price, it is as if it exists, and therefore the fiction of an actual sale may be maintained, even though the vendor may have "sold" the item in stock to earlier customers or does not own the goods in question.

The third exception applies when goods are of such a nature that they have no set market price.[84] Examples include precious stones, used items, and custom-made goods. As the price for such goods cannot be determined by reference to a market, regardless of whether they exist, it is not possible to know whether the price has increased from the time of purchase to the time of delivery. Moreover, it is not

79 This raises the interesting question of what it means to have the goods in stock. The seller must have sufficient goods in his possession to cover the purchase. *Shulhan Arukh, Yoreh De'ah* 175:4. If an item is disassembled, it is deemed in his possession if it can be put together in two or fewer steps. *Shulhan Arukh, Yoreh De'ah* 175:4.

80 *Shulhan Arukh, Yoreh De'ah* 175:4.

81 *Shulhan Arukh, Yoreh De'ah* 175:1.

82 See *Bava Metsi'a* 72b.

83 See *Bava Metsi'a* 63b.

84 See *Berit Yehudah* 24:n6.

possible to determine whether a discount is being offered for immediate payment, leading to the converse (i.e., an interest charge for the delay of payment).

Thus, while authorities recognized that forward contracts were economically equivalent to loans and generally banned them, they ruled leniently and permitted such contracts where it could at least be credibly argued that the substance of the transaction was really a sale.

In contrast, Federal tax law treats all forward contracts as sales, essentially respecting the form of the transaction. Thus, there is no possibility of interest, even where the price of the commodity purchased rises, leading to a gain on the part of the purchaser. Instead, such gain is viewed as if there were a bargain sale, and it will be recognized only if the purchaser resells what he has bought. It is true that the seller has had use of the money until delivery, which could be viewed as an interest-free loan. However, forward sales are not generally used as tax-avoidance devices, where buyers try to provide tax-free benefits to sellers. Accordingly, the need to apply I.R.C. § 7872's interest imputation rule does not arise.

Conclusion

Comparing the Jewish and Federal tax laws of interest reveals how the goals, practical constraints, and legal structures of both systems helped shape the law. Starting with virtually identical conceptions of what constitutes interest—a payment for the use of money—the two systems diverge substantially in their holdings regarding a wide range of transactions.

For instance, unconcerned with the need to measure or tax interest, Jewish authorities were free to include intangible benefits such as greetings and thank yous in their interest definition, while the Federal authorities, who were concerned with measurability, could not. Concerns regarding tax evasion caused Federal tax authorities to impute interest payments for interest-free loans, where doing so in Jewish law would make no sense at all. And the inability of later Jewish authorities to revoke earlier rulings caused them to adopt a formalistic approach to the law in the context of credit sales, through which they were able to set aside intent as the guidepost to identifying interest. In contrast, Federal tax authorities were able to change their approach to credit sales, casting off the form of the transactions in favor of their economic substance, by simply enacting new laws.

These divergent approaches to the question of interest suggest that, even in areas such as finance, the law develops not according to some predetermined pattern, once the starting assumptions are cast. Rather, it is an organic process that is closely tied to and largely driven by cultural factors and circumstances such as the nature and shape of the legal system and the motivations of those charged with developing the law.

SELECTED BIBLIOGRAPHY

Bloi, R. Jacob Isaiah. *Berit Yehudah,* 10:n2, 17:3, 22:n33, 9:n12, and 24:n6.

Caro, R. Joseph., and Shulhan Arukh. *Yoreh De'ah*, 160:6, 7, 11, and 12; 162:1–3; 167:16; 172:2, 173:1 and 3; 175:4 and 176:2.

Danzig, R. Abraham. *Hokhmat Adam*, 131:8–9 and 139:5.

Gamoran, Hillel. *Jewish Law in Transition: How Economic Forces Overcame the Prohibition against Lending on Interest.* Hebrew Union College Press, 2008.

Haig, Robert M. The Concept of Income—Economic and Legal Aspects. 1921 In *Readings in the Economics of Taxation* 54, 55. R. Musgrave & C. Shoup, eds., 1938.

Isserles, R. Moses Isserles. *Rema, She'elot u-teshuvot ha-Rema*, 160:6, 162:1, and 173:3.

Reisman, R. Isreal. *The Laws of Ribbis.* Mesorah Publications Ltd, 1995.

CHAPTER 26

TRANSFER OF OWNERSHIP IN E-COMMERCE TRANSACTIONS FROM THE PERSPECTIVE OF JEWISH LAW: IN LIGHT OF ISRAELI AND AMERICAN LAW

RON S. KLEINMAN AND AMAL JABAREEN

Prologue

Do the practices of electronic commerce in general, and online sales transactions in particular, have halakhic validity,[1] and, if so, how exactly do they derive their legal-halakhic validity?[2]

This chapter attempts to answer the above questions based on critical scrutiny of the writings of contemporary halakhic decisors and scholars who have addressed this issue. These questions will be examined in view of the principles pertaining to modes of acquisition in Jewish law and in light of two other legal regimes—Israeli law and American law.

1 For the purposes of this article, the terms "*halakhah*" and "Jewish law" are identical.

2 This article deals with the purchase of goods—that is, movables—over the Internet. Real estate is generally not purchased over the Internet, and, in any event, should be regarded separately, both from the point of view of Jewish law as well as in modern civil legal systems.

The validity of online sales transactions according to Jewish law depends largely on *local custom* and *civil law*, as will be explained below. To date, the question of this validity, which is the focus of the present article, has been addressed only in Israel. An examination of the writings on this subject requires familiarity with both Jewish law as well as with *Israeli civil law* in this regard.

The Jewish nation has been dispersed among the nations of the world for well over two thousand years. By nature, commercial practices and legal regimes differ from nation to nation and country to country. The position of Jewish law with regard to e-commerce—a position that is based on a country's civil law and local custom—is, thus, also likely to change from place to place.

An examination of the position of Jewish law in each of the countries in which Jews reside is beyond the scope of this chapter. Instead, we have focused on two countries—Israel and the United States. Focusing on Israel is an obvious choice. The decision to focus on the United States is based on the fact that: (a) the United States has a large Jewish population, an important minority of which lives according to the precepts of Jewish law, and (b) the United States is one of the major players in the e-commerce arena today.

This chapter is a comparative study of the similarities and differences between Jewish law and other legal systems, as they relate to e-commerce. However, the analysis of each of the legal systems is intended not only to provide an *external* comparison, but is essential to the *internal* application of the halakhic principles of Jewish law. In other words, the civil law that is in effect in a particular country[3] has great bearing on the application of the principles of Jewish law to e-commerce.

The topic under discussion in this chapter is one of many illustrative examples of the application of the ancient principles of Jewish law to the circumstances of modern civil law and to the dynamic economics and technological developments of the late twentieth and early twenty-first centuries.

A. Introduction

1. Electronic Commerce (E-Commerce): Background and Basic Concepts

Since the mid-1990s, the Internet has served as fertile soil for commercial activity. This activity is termed *electronic commerce* (e-commerce).[4] A large proportion of

3 This article relates to a situation in which a country is governed by civil law. However, the contents of the article are just as relevant when the law in effect is religious law.

4 There is no single definition of electronic commerce. For various definitions, see Paul Todd, *E-Commerce Law* (England: Cavendish Publishing, 2005), 3. In the present article, the term *e-commerce* refers to electronic sales transactions that are conducted over the Internet.

e-commerce involves the purchase of goods. Surveys and studies show that an ever-increasing number of people from around the world, including Israel, view the Internet as a marketplace for the purchase of goods—a kind of post-modern version of the classical marketplace.[5] The exchange process, whereby goods are purchased for money over the Internet, is termed an *online sales transaction*.[6] Its characteristics are different from those of a conventional sales transaction. Because of this difference, policy makers in the different legal systems are faced with adapting current sales laws, the bulk of which were legislated for entirely different circumstances, to online transactions. We will first describe the process of online buying in order to better understand the unique characteristics of this type of sales transaction.

2. Description of the Purchase Process in Online Sales Transactions

For the sake of convenience's, we will refer to the virtual vendor as the *web site*, the *vendor*, or the *seller*. These terms refer to the legal person, whether an individual or a corporation, behind the merchant site.

Robert, the buyer, wishes to buy a digital camera, for example. He visits the web site of the supplier, Paul—the vendor—and begins his shopping trip. Robert browses the product catalog, which is arranged according to different categories. He selects the items that he wishes to buy and adds them to his virtual "shopping cart." At any point, Robert may remove items from the cart or add items to it, as well as review the cart's contents and the amount he must pay for the items he selected. Upon completing the stage of selecting the items for purchase, Robert proceeds to the "checkout" stage. If he is a new customer, he must open a user account and enter his personal data. If he is already registered as a customer, he need only

5 According to a survey conducted in 2006 by the Credit Information Association (CIA), a member of the Gaon Capital Market Group, 2.7 million Israelis surf the Web daily. Some forty percent of them, amounting to 1.1 million Israelis, regularly buy goods and services over the Internet. Consumer transactions on the Web amounted to $1.5 billion in 2005. This was an increase of twenty percent over 2004. See Tal Pamson, "Electronic Commerce in Israel Gathers Momentum" (2006), [Hebrew] www.nrg.co.il/online/16/ART1/053/022.html. This increase in e-commerce among Israeli consumers is part of a worldwide trend. Thus, for example, according to the most recent study conducted by Forrester Research, an international market research company that provides business and technology-based research, analysis, and advice, United States online retail reached $175 billion in 2007 and is projected to grow to $335 billion by 2012. See Sucharita Mulpuru "US eCommerce Forecast: 2008 To 2012," available at http://www.forrester.com/Research/Document/Excerpt/0,7211,41592,00.html.

6 It is customary to divide online sales transactions into three categories: (a) sales transactions that are conducted entirely within the domain of the Internet and are delivered digitally to the buyer, such as computer software, electronic books, or services provided on the Web; (b) transactions to purchase tangible goods, wherein the entire contractual phase is conducted online, but the merchandise is delivered outside the Internet, such as a book or CD purchased over the Internet; (c) an off-line transaction in which the initial connection is made over the Internet, but all other stages, from the negotiations stage onward, are conducted outside the Internet. See J. Barsade, *The Internet and Online Business Law*, 2nd ed. (Tel Aviv: Perlstein-Genosar, 2002), 61, n. 12 [Hebrew]. The present article focuses on transactions belonging to the second category, above.

enter his identity number or any other identifying data in order to open his user account. Robert is then asked to fill out the shipping information for the items, which can be delivered by post or carrier. He is also asked to fill out the method of payment, which may be by credit card or other means. After he has finished entering all of the information, he is shown the order form containing all of the details of the transaction, which he must confirm. Once the order is confirmed, the web site then performs payment clearing and money transmission. After confirmation of payment, the stage of handling the order and shipping the merchandise begins. During the various stages of the transaction, the buyer encounters a list of conditions of use or links to the conditions that the vendor wishes to apply to the interaction between the vendor and the buyer. The conditions of use are available for the perusal of the buyer by clicking on a link, usually located at the bottom of the web site's home page.[7] In some instances, the buyer cannot proceed to the next stage of the transaction without first clicking on a link to confirm that he has read the conditions and agrees to them. In most cases, however, the buyer can proceed to the next stage of the transaction without reading the conditions.

Fig. 26.1, below, describes the acquisition process in an online sales transaction.

3. The Unique Characteristics and Risks of Online Sales Transactions

The previous description, which we will refer to again later, illustrates that the characteristics of an online transaction conducted over an open network are different from those of a conventional sales transaction.[8] This article focuses on one of these characteristics: An online transaction is a distance transaction in which buyer and vendor are separated in time and in space.[9] This is illustrated visually in fig. 26.2.

This separation in time and in space affects both the manner in which the parties meet and conduct the transaction, as well as the manner in which each of the parties fulfills his obligations in the transaction: the vendor's obligation to transfer ownership and the buyer's obligation to pay. In simple sales transactions, in which the vendor and the buyer meet face-to-face, such as in the case of shopping in a supermarket, the parties are able to fulfill their obligations simultaneously: The buyer

7 This link is referred to by different names, such as "Conditions of Use" and "Users Agreement." Thus, for example, eBay's conditions of use are as follows: "Welcome to eBay. By using eBay (including eBay.com and its related sites, services and tools), you agree to the following terms with eBay Inc. and the general principles for the websites of our subsidiaries and international affiliates."

8 For more on the characteristics of online sales transactions, see Amal Jabareen, *The Law and Economics of Consumer Protection in the Internet Era*, Ph.D. Dissertation, (Ramat-Gan, Israel: Bar-Ilan University, 2004), 57 [Hebrew].

9 In the history of consumer markets, there is a relationship between technological developments and the way in which consumers and vendors meet. Thus, for example, the establishment of a postal system made mail-order shopping from catalogs possible; the television created home shopping via the various television shopping channels; telephones facilitated telemarketing. See Choi, Soon-Yong, & Whinston, Andrew B., *The Internet Economy: Technology and Practice* (Austin, TX: Smart Economics Publishing, 2000).

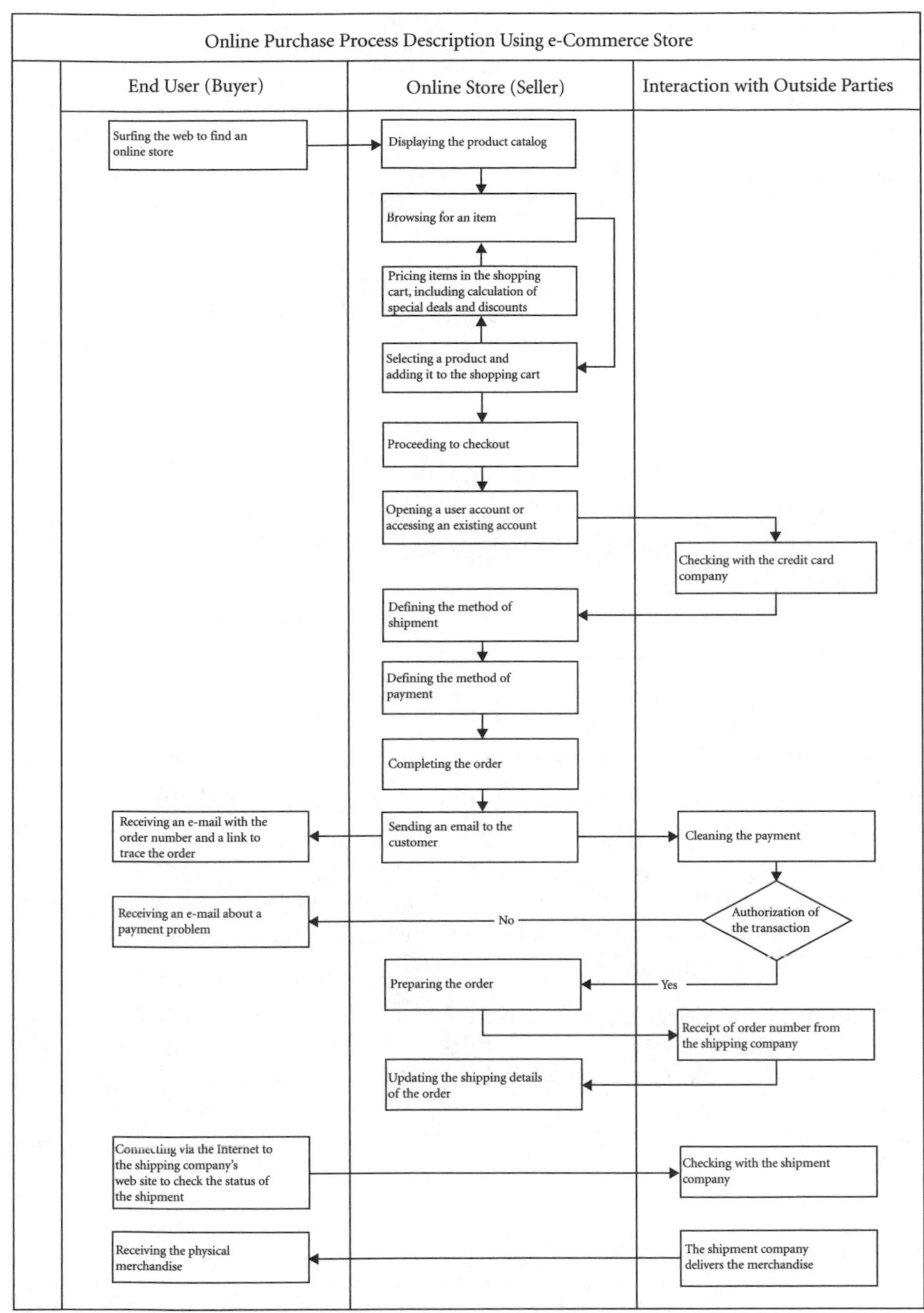

FIGURE 26.1 Online Purchase Process Description Using e-Commerce Store

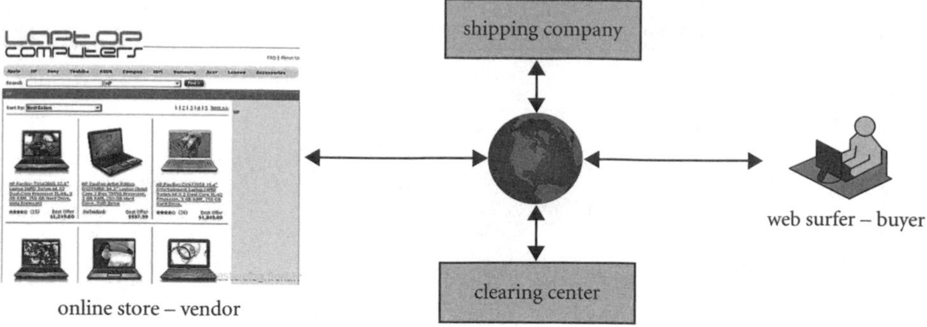

FIGURE 26.2

makes his payment, and, at the same time, the vendor hands him the purchased item. By contrast, the technical separation between the parties to the transaction in an online sales transaction prevents them from meeting face-to-face, thus precluding the simultaneous exchange of goods for payment. In these circumstances, one party to the transaction must fulfill his part in the transaction before the other party does so. Generally, the buyer is the party that is required to fulfill his part of the transaction first—that is, to pay for the goods in advance, before receiving them. Furthermore, because of the distance between the parties, the buyer cannot pay for the goods by the traditional means of payment—money. Instead, he is required to use modern means of payment, the most popular of which is by credit card.[10]

Since an online transaction is a distance transaction whereby the buyer pays for goods—mostly by credit card—before he receives them, he is exposed to various risks that may materialize in the time period between payment for and receipt of the goods. These risks can be divided into three main categories. The *first category* relates to intentional opportunistic behavior on the part of a vendor who is solvent. For example, the vendor might not abide by his obligation to deliver the merchandise at all, or the merchandise might not be that which was agreed upon.[11] The *second category* of risk refers to loss of or damage to the goods after the agreement has been concluded but before the delivery of the goods is effected. The *third category* of risk, which is the one that is relevant to this article, involves a vendor

10 See Jabareen, supra, n. 8, 374; Jane Kaufman Winn, "Clash of the Titans: Regulating the Competition Between Established and Emerging Electronic Payment Systems," *Berkeley Tech. L. J.* 14, (1999): 675, 690–97; John D. Muller, "Selected Developments in The Law of Cyberspace Payments," *Bus. Law* 54, (1999): 403, 407.

11 This phenomenon, known as "item paid for, but not delivered," is common on the Internet. Many unscrupulous individuals set up marketing sites on the Internet that offer all sorts of goods, with the purpose of attracting innocent buyers who pay for goods that they order, while the crooks have no intention of delivering the goods. The Internet is fertile soil for fraud of this kind because the offenders can set up sites at a negligible cost, without any need to display real merchandise or keep any stock. When the buyer eventually discovers the fraud, he has no way of knowing the true identity of the web site owner, who generally does not identify himself on the web site. In most cases, the offender has already managed to perpetrate similar fraudulent deeds, close his web site, and open a new web site under a new name, which makes it difficult to investigate his actions. See John Rothchild, "Protecting the Digital Consumer: The Limits of Cyberspace Utopianism," *Ind. L. J.* 74, (1999): 893, 925; Hebe R. Smythe, "Fighting Telemarketing Scams," *Hastings Comm. & Ent. L. J.* 17, (1995): 347.

who encounters financial difficulties such that he becomes insolvent and cannot supply the goods that were purchased.[12]

4. The Research Question

This chapter focuses on a question that relates to the ownership aspect of online transactions: What constitutes the moment of transfer of ownership for goods purchased in an online transaction?

The above question will be examined from the perspective of Jewish law. However, in property matters, Jewish law relies heavily on local custom and civil law, as we shall see in the next section. Therefore, in order to examine Jewish law in this regard, it is necessary to first understand the way in which the legal regimes of different countries around the world relate to the transfer of ownership in online transactions.

5. The Importance of Establishing the Moment of Transfer of Ownership in an Online Sales Transaction

Ascertaining the precise point in time in which transfer of ownership of goods purchased in an online transaction is effected is important primarily in those cases in which a risk belonging to the third category above materializes—that is, in a case of bankruptcy.[13] In such a case, there is a conflict between the buyer, who has already paid for the merchandise, and third parties who may be affected by the transfer, such as the vendor's creditors.

The following example helps illustrate the problem: Robert (hereinafter: the buyer) visited the web site of TheLight, Inc. (www.Thelight.com) (hereinafter: the vendor), which sells different sorts of electrical appliances. He selects a particular refrigerator, the only one in the warehouse at the time; orders it; and pays for it by credit card. According to the conditions of use, the vendor undertakes to deliver the appliance to the buyer's home within seven days of payment. Let us assume that, in

12 Thus, for example, at the beginning of September, 2005, Nati Sakal, a small company that marketed computers, collapsed. This company had marketed its merchandise on a number of Israel's leading virtual shopping malls, such as P1000, Walla! Shops, NetAction, Sakal On Line, and others. Close to one thousand customers bought computers and other merchandise from this company, paid for them, and received nothing in return.

13 See supra, discussion in text at n. 12. With regard to the first type of risk—opportunistic behavior on the part of the vendor—the buyer has grounds for a complaint against the vendor for breach of contract. Therefore, the moment of transfer of ownership is almost irrelevant. On this matter, see Amal Jabareen, "Virtual Malls as Gatekeepers in Electronic Commerce: An economic perspective," *Bar-Ilan Law Studies* 25 (2009): 735 [Hebrew]. With regard to the second risk category—loss of or damage to the goods—some of the modern legal systems separate the transfer of ownership and transfer of the risk of loss or damage. For example, section 22 to the Israeli Sales Act 1968 (hereinafter: The Sales Act) passes the risk of loss or damage to the goods to the buyer upon his receipt of the goods. The same is provided in Section 2-509 of the American U.C.C. By contrast, in British, French, and German law, the risk of loss of or damage to the goods passes to the buyer along with the transfer of ownership (upon formation of the contract in British and French law, and upon delivery in German law). For more on this subject, see T.B. Smith, *Property Problems in Sale* (London: Sweet & Maxwell et al., 1978), 458.

the period between payment and the vendor's promised date of delivery of the appliance, one of the following scenarios takes place:

Scenario 1 (seizure):[14] Immediately after payment, and before the vendor could deliver the refrigerator to the buyer, a seizure order was issued for all of the goods in the vendor's warehouses, including the refrigerator. The seizure order was issued at the request of Judah, one of the vendor's creditors.

Scenario 2 (bankruptcy): Immediately after payment, and before the vendor could deliver the refrigerator to the buyer, the court made an adjudication of bankruptcy.

In each of the two scenarios, a conflict is created between the buyer and third parties—Judah in the first scenario, and the bankruptcy trustee in the second scenario—over ownership of the refrigerator. The moment in which ownership of the refrigerator is transferred to the buyer is of critical importance for settling the above conflict. Basically, there are three possible points in time in which ownership of the refrigerator can be transferred to the buyer: (a) at the time of ordering the refrigerator—that is, at the time of forming the sales contract; (b) at the time of payment; or (c) at the time of delivery of the refrigerator to the buyer.

If ownership of the refrigerator is transferred to the buyer (a) at the time of forming the contract, or (b) at the time of payment, then in both of the above scenarios the buyer is favored over the third party. In the first scenario, this is because the refrigerator was already in the ownership of the buyer when the seizure order for the vendor's assets was issued, in which case the seizure does not have any bearing on ownership that was effected prior to the court order. In the second scenario, since the refrigerator was already in the possession of the buyer at the time that the vendor began bankruptcy procedures, it is not included in the list of assets to be liquidated.

On the other hand, if transfer of ownership is effected only upon delivery of the refrigerator to the buyer (c), the buyer loses in both scenarios. In the first scenario, it is because the refrigerator is still in the ownership of the vendor at the time that the seizure order was made, and the seizure order therefore prevents the vendor from disposing of the refrigerator, including transferring ownership of it to the buyer. In the second scenario, it is because the refrigerator is still in the possession of the vendor and will therefore be included in the list of assets to be liquidated. These assets will be put up for sale as part of the bankruptcy procedures, and the monies obtained from the sale will be divided among the vendor's various creditors.[15]

14 A seizure order is an order issued by the court at the request of the creditor, which prevents the debtor from selling or disposing of his assets until the seizure order is removed. Seizure does not give the creditor property rights to the debtor's assets.

15 This analysis is based on Israeli bankruptcy laws. Bankruptcy laws are determined according to civil law, even in Jewish law. See R. Moshe Feinstein, *Resp. Igrot Moshe, Hoshen Mishpat*, 2:62. However, others dispute this opinion. See R. Ya'akov Yeshaya Blau, *Pit'hei Hoshen*, 1, *Halva'ah*, (Jerusalem, 2003), 2, n. 63.

B. Jewish Law: Modes of Acquisition and Merchant Customs

1. Modes of Acquisition in Jewish Law: Principles and Concepts

In order for the transfer of ownership and the creation of an obligation to have legal validity according to Jewish law, they generally require—in addition to intention (*gemirut da'at*) on the part of the parties—a physical act, referred to as the *mode of acquisition*[16] (*ma'aseh kinyan* or *derekh kinyan*).[17] Most of the modes of acquisition in Jewish law are listed in the first chapter of *Tractate Kiddushin* in the Mishnah and the Tosefta,[18] and some appear for the first time in the Talmud.[19]

The laws of acquisition in the Mishnah and Talmud are basically formalistic. Each of the modes of acquisition, such as "pulling" (*meshikhah*), "lifting" (*hagbahah*), and "barter" (*halifin*), has a fixed form and must fulfill further conditions. If one of the modes of acquisition was not executed, or was not executed in accordance with the law, the transfer of ownership or the creation of obligation has no validity.

According to Jewish law, monetary laws are essentially given to stipulation.[20] Nonetheless, the prevailing view among the majority of halakhic decisors is that modes of acquisition are not given to stipulation, and the parties may not change them even upon mutual agreement.[21]

New ways of effecting ownership and obligation arose in the post-Talmudic era. These new ways did not exist in mishnaic and talmudic times, and halakhic decisors have been required to determine their legal validity. Thus, for example, decisors have had to decide the validity of practices such as a handshake, an earnest money deposit,[22] drinking a toast, and signing a contract as a means for creating a

16 The Hebrew word *kinyan* has various meanings. These include acquisition (as in *darkei kinyan*—modes of acquisition); ownership, in contrast to obligatory rights; and property (as in *dinei ha-kinyan*—property laws).

17 On this matter and exceptions to it, see "Obligations," *Talmudic Encyclopedia*, v. 11, 245–59 [Hebrew]; Shamma Friedman, "The Concept '*Hana'ah* (Consideration)' in Acts of Acquisition Through Money in Talmudic Law," *Diné Israel* 3 (1972): 115, n. 1 [Hebrew]; R. David Bass, "Contracts According to Din Torah," *Keter* 1 (1996): 60 n. 62 [Hebrew]. On the matter of obligations requiring a "mode of acquisition" (*kinyan*), as does the transfer of ownership, see also Shalom Albeck, "The Different Acquisition Rights in the Talmud," *Sinai*, 68 (1971): 8–31 [Hebrew]; *idem*, *The Law of Property and Contract in the Talmud* (Tel Aviv, 1976), 368–69 [Hebrew]; Itamar Warhaftig, *Undertaking in Jewish Law* (Jerusalem, 2001), 7–8 [Hebrew].

18 Mishnah, *Kiddushin* 1:1–6; Tosefta, Ibid., 1:1–9.

19 For example, acquisition of ownerless objects within a man's four cubits (*kinyan arba amot*), BT *Bava Metzi'a* 10a; JT *Gittin* 8:3, 49c; an acquisition in the presence of three (*ma'amad sheloshtan*), BT *Gittin* 13a.

20 On freedom of contract in monetary matters, see Ron S. Kleinman, *Merchant Customs (Lex Mercatoria) Relating to Methods of Acquisition in Jewish Law: Kinyan Situmta*, Ph.D. Dissertation (Ramat-Gan: Bar-Ilan University, 2000), 131–32 [Hebrew].

21 For more on this subject, see Ibid., 137–44.

22 This refers to making an earnest money deposit in order to finalize a transaction in movables or obligatory rights. In real estate transactions, classical Jewish law regards an earnest money deposit as a mode of acquisition.

contractual obligation, and registering land at the Israel Land Registry as a means for transferring title to land.

For the most part, the attempt to establish the validity of these new practices met with failure, as these practices generally did not fulfill the formalistic demands of the classical modes of acquisition. Instead, halakhic decisors took steps in two other directions.

One method that halakhic decisors have employed to confer validity on new modes of acquisition has been the application of the doctrine "the law of the State is law" (*dina de-malkhuta dina*). In certain circumstances, this doctrine accords halakhic validity to civil laws even when these laws do not conform to Jewish law.[23]

For hundreds of years, the other, main method for conferring halakhic validity on these new practices has been, and still is, a mode of acquisition known in halakhic literature as acquisition by *situmta* (*kinyan situmta*). A *situmta* acquisition is defined as the mode of acquisition in practice in a particular place. By drawing upon the law of *situmta*, halakhic decisors have conferred halakhic validity on prevailing modes of acquisition despite the fact that they are not mentioned in the talmudic literature. The following offers a brief explanation of this law and how it may be applied in the subject under discussion.

2. Acquisition by *Situmta*

The source for a *situmta* acquisition is a short passage in the Babylonian Talmud[24] in which the *amora* Rava establishes that "the *situmta* gives possession" (*hai situmta kanya*). The Aramaic word *situmta* means "seal," and the commonly accepted interpretation of Rava's words was a "seal" or "sign" that the purchaser stamped on the merchandise in order to assert his ownership from that moment.[25] The discussion in the Babylonian Talmud ends with the contention that, where it is customary that *situmta* effects ownership, it does so (with full legal validity).

Rava was most probably referring to a specific mode of acquisition that was familiar to him.[26] However, the law of *situmta* was given a broader halakhic interpretation by both medieval and later rabbis. According to them, acquisition by *situmta* is any method of acquisition that is practiced by the local residents or merchants of a particular locale.[27] Halakhic decisors established that where it is the

23 For more on this doctrine and its limitations, see Shmuel Shilo, *Dina de-Malkhuta Dina* (*The Law of the State is Law*) (Jerusalem: Jerusalem Academic Press, 1974) [Hebrew].

24 BT *Bava Metzi'a* 74a.

25 On the medieval rabbis' (*Rishonim*) different interpretations of the term "*situmta*," see Ron S. Kleinman, "Early Interpretations of the Bible and Talmud as a Reflection of Medieval Legal Realia," *Jewish Law Annual* 16 (2006): 25–50; Berachyahu Lifshitz, "*Situmta*—Between Acquisition and Contract," in M. Corinaldi, M.D. Herr et al. (eds.), *Studies in Memory of Professor Ze'ev Falk* (Jerusalem: Schechter Institution, 2005), 59–69 [Hebrew].

26 On the historical-realia question of how a *situmta* acquisition was implemented, see Ron S. Kleinman, "'*Hai situmta kanya*' (BM 74a): Interpretation of Rava's Statement in Light of Talmudic Realia," *Sidra* 18 (2003): 103–18 [Hebrew]; Lifshitz, *ibid.*

27 It makes no difference whether we are referring to the practice throughout a particular country, a local practice, or the practice of a particular segment of the population.

custom[28] to make an acquisition in a particular way—even if this mode of acquisition is not mentioned in the Mishnah or Talmud—it is valid.

From the twelfth century onwards, decisors have applied the principle of acquisition by *situmta* extensively. This is evidenced by the thousands of *responsa* of medieval and later rabbis and the many rulings of Israel's rabbinic courts and private courts for monetary matters.[29] It would not be an exaggeration to state that in post-Talmudic times it is almost impossible to envisage Jewish property laws without acquisition by *situmta*.

The law of *situmta* has been applied not only to modes of acquisition but also to various forms of obligations, such as an obligation to sell and an obligation to lease. The obligation to execute an act of acquisition, such as an obligation to sell, is termed a "*kinyan e'ten*" (lit. an acquisition of "I will give") in Jewish law, and halakhic decisors were divided over the question of its validity. Most later halakhic authorities, including contemporary halakhic decisors and rabbinical judges, have ruled that, since it is customary nowadays to execute these types of obligations, they have validity by virtue of *situmta*. Thus, the principle of acquisition by *situmta* may be applied not only to effect *transfer of property* rights, but also to confer validity on contractual *obligations*.[30]

We will see below that the majority of halakhic decisors and scholars who have addressed the question of the validity of online sales transactions according to Jewish law have established validity by virtue of the doctrine "the law of the State is law," or the principle of acquisition by *situmta*.[31] In order to draw upon the doctrine "the law of the State is law," it is essential to examine the relevant *civil laws* of the country in which the transaction is executed.[32] In order to apply the law of *situmta*, it is necessary, as mentioned, to ascertain the *custom* in practice in a given locale. Today, monetary customs are generally shaped by civil law, which includes the laws themselves as well as the decisions of the civil courts, since people generally enter into an agreement in accordance with civil law. Thus, the civil laws normally become local custom.

It should be noted, however, that the law of *situmta* is not applied on the basis of the civil law itself, but rather on the degree to which the civil law is reflected in local custom. Therefore, in order to establish the halakhic validity of modern

28 In order for a certain practice to be defined as "local custom," it must be known, clear, and practiced regularly in that place. See Kleinman, supra, n. 20, 9–10.

29 For references to hundreds of *responsa* and rulings that deal with acquisition by *situmta*, see Kleinman, supra, n. 20.

30 This was the ruling, for example, of Hatam Sofer, *Hoshen Mishpat*, 66, s.v. *u'ma shekatav ma'alato de-liknei*; *Resp. Tzemach Tzedek (Shne'orson), Yore De'ah*, 233; *Kesef-Hakodashim, Hoshen Mishpat*, 201:1; *Responsa MaHarshag*, 3:113, s.v. *aval*; R. Isaac Herzog, *Pesakim U'khtavim*, v. 9, *Hoshen Mishpat*, 75–76. See also, Kleinman, ibid., 257–58; Warhaftig (supra, n. 17), 115–88.

31 See infra, text at nn. 63–67.

32 When a transaction takes place in a particular country, it is not difficult to ascertain the local custom. This is far more problematic in international online transactions. In such cases, the rabbinic judges must decide which custom to apply to the transaction, in the same manner that private international law (conflict of laws) determines the law that applies to international transactions. The subject of conflict of laws in Jewish law is beyond the scope of this chapter.

practices by virtue of acquisition by *situmta*, the halakhic decisor must ascertain not only the civil laws of a particular country, but also the extent to which the custom regarding a particular practice is consistent with the civil laws of that country.

In order to verify the "custom" with regard to a particular commercial practice, such as the purchase of goods over the Internet, it is not what the legal experts know that must be taken into account, but, rather, what those who exercise the particular practice—in this case, the online shoppers—think.

The conclusion to be drawn from the above is that, regardless of whether the validity of e-commerce in Jewish law is based on "the law of the State is law" or is based on an acquisition by *situmta*, its validity must first be examined in light of the civil law that applies in a particular country, as well as the custom practiced by online shoppers. Therefore, before we examine the position of Jewish law with regard to the validity of online transactions, we will first present the approach of Israeli law and American law in this regard.

C. Transfer of Ownership in Online Sales Transactions in Israeli and American Law

1. Transfer of Ownership in Online Sales Transactions—the Law in Israel

In Israel, laws that regulate the various aspects of electronic commerce have not yet been legislated.[33] Nevertheless, in recent years, the Knesset has been seeking solutions to certain facets of new technological developments, including the Internet. Thus, for example, the Knesset has legislated the Electronic Signature Act 5761–2001[34] and the Anti-Spam Act.[35]

In the beginning of 2008, the Knesset introduced the Electronic Commerce Bill.[36] This bill is based on a memorandum from 2005— the outcome of a report written by the Shpanitz Committee, which was appointed by the Minister of Justice

33 The absence of a special law that regulates electronic commerce reflects the general absence of specific legislation for the Information Age. Recognizing this need, the Knesset appointed a committee in 1996 to deal with this issue. See the final report of the standing committee on "Preparing Israel for the Information Age," (The Knesset's Economic Affairs Committee, Subcommittee for Computerized Communication and Information, jointly with the National Council for the Development of Computerized Communication and Information Infrastructure (Jerusalem, 1997) (Hebrew), www.knesset.gov.il/docs/heb/infocom/final1_t.htm. The committee established several guidelines for preparing Israel for the Information Age. It recommended, inter alia, adapting the present legislation governing computerized communication and technological developments to legislation formulated by other nations.

34 The Electronic Signature Act, 5761-2001, LSI 210.

35 The Communication Act (Telephony and Broadcasts), 1982, LSI 218.

36 The Electronic Commerce Bill 2008, Bills of the Knesset, 322 (hereinafter: the Bill).

in 2001.[37]According to Sec. 1 of the Bill: "The goal of this law is to regulate various aspects of utilization of electronic documents during the course of commercial activity, and in particular: the fulfillment of any writing requirements, the execution of legal acts by means of electronic documents, the establishment of presumptions concerning the sending and receiving of electronic messages, instructions for limiting the civil liability of the Internet Service Provider with respect to the Internet services provided, and the obligation of the Internet Service Provider to protect the privacy of users."

In every online sales transaction there is an electronic contract between the buyer and the seller. The Electronic Commerce Bill is progressive with regard to certain aspects of electronic contracts, such as the writing requirments that apply to electronic contracts, the execution of legal acts via electronic documents, and the establishment of presumptions concerning the sending and receiving of electronic messages. However, the bill does *not* deal with property matters in general, nor with the transfer of ownership in online sales transactions, in particular.

In the absence of specific legislation to govern online sales transactions, the current legislation applies: the Contracts Act,[38] the Standard Contracts Act,[39] the Contracts Act (Remedies for Breach),[40] the Consumer Protection Act,[41] the Debit Cards Act,[42] and the Sales Act.[43]

As for the transfer of ownership, the applicable provision is sec. 33 of the Sales Act, which provides: "Ownership of the sold object passes to the buyer upon its delivery, unless the parties agreed upon some other time or manner for the transfer of ownership."[44] The first half of the section determines that the time of the transfer of ownership is the time of delivery; however, the second half of the section clarifies that the parties are entitled to set a different time for the transfer of ownership. Thus, according to sec. 33, the physical delivery of the sales item is not a prerequisite for the transfer of ownership; it is merely the default provision. Ownership is transferred upon delivery unless the parties stipulate otherwise.

Hence, in online sales transactions, we must determine whether the parties have stipulated a time for the transfer of ownership. This question requires that we first determine whether a contract was in fact formed between the vendor and the buyer. If so, does this contract include any stipulations regarding the time of transfer of ownership? As a detailed discussion concerning the formation of a contract is beyond the scope of this article, we will treat this question briefly.

37 A partial report of the Committee for the Examination of Legal Issues Associated with Electronic Commerce, published in May 2004: www.justice.gov.il/NR/rdonlyres/989CB3C8-BFEC-49C6-A689-433181BED312/0/electroniccommerce.pdf.

38 The Contracts Act (General Section), 1973, LSI 118 (hereinafter: the Contracts Act).

39 The Standard Contracts Act, 1982, LSI 8.

40 The Contracts Act (Remedies for Breach of Contract), 1970 LSI16.

41 The Consumer Protection Act, 1981, LSI 248.

42 The Debit Card Act, 1986, LSI 187.

43 The Sales Act, 1968, LSI 529.

44 This sections deals with the sale of movables. There is a special law governing the sale of real estate, which provides that transfer of ownership is effected only upon registration in the Land Registry. See sec. 7 of the Lands Act, 1969, LSI 259.

Today, there are essentially two types of standardized electronic agreements: the "click-through agreement" and the "browse-wrap agreement." A click-through agreement is usually presented to the buyer in a conspicuous manner. It is generally located at the bottom of the web site's home page and requires the buyer to click on an acceptance button, which evidences a manifestation of assent to be bound to the terms of the contract.[45] In several recent cases, most legal systems held that, in these kinds of agreements, a contract is indeed formed between the buyer and the web site, because the manner in which the transaction is executed ensures that the consumer is exposed to the terms of the contract and has even had a reasonable opportunity to review them.[46] In the second type of agreement—the browse wrap agreement—the terms are also typically presented at the bottom of the web site's home page; however, mere use of the site constitutes acceptance of these terms, even if the buyer did not read them. The question of whether this kind of agreement constitutes a contract remains an open legal issue. Indeed, different legal systems that have dealt with this question issued contradictory rulings in this matter. Generally speaking, the tendency has been to recognize that this kind of agreement does constitute a contract.[47]

Israeli courts have not yet addressed the formation of electronic contracts,[48] which remains an open legal issue. Our discussion will be based on two possible court rulings: If the court should determine that no contract was formed between the web site and the buyer, then clearly, the parties have also not stipulated a time of transfer of ownership. If, on the other hand, the court should determine that a contract was in fact formed, it must then determine whether the said contract contains a condition that relates to the date of transfer of ownership.

A review of most of the contractual terms in Israel's main merchant sites reveals that they contain various conditions, none of which relate to the date of transfer of ownership.[49] The conclusion to be drawn from this finding is that, according to

45 L. J. Gibbons, "No Regulation, Government Regulation, or Self Regulation: Social Enforcement or Social Contracting for Governance in Cyberspace," *Cornell J. L. & Pub. Pol'y* 6, (1997): 475, 528. In digital markets, the consumer cannot negotiate the terms of the uniform contract, because he has no possibility of speaking to the owner of the web site before visiting the site. In most cases, the consumer cannot obtain answers to the many questions he has regarding the terms of the contract posted on the web site. See also B. Thompson, "The Selling of the Clickerati," *Wash. Post Mag* (Oct. 24, 1999), at W11.

46 Regarding rulings that have recognized the validity of such contracts, see *Forest v. Verizon Comm., Inc.*, 805 A. 2d 1007 (D. C. Cir. 2002); *DeJohn v. The TV Corp.*, 245 F. Supp. 2d 913 (C.D. III. 2003); *Comb v. PayPal, Inc.*, 218 F. Supp. 2d 1165 (N.D. Cal. 2002).

47 For rulings that recognized the validity of these contracts, see *Procd v. Zeldenberg*, 86 F3d, 1447, 1450 (7th Cir. 1996); *Hill v. Gateway*, 105 F. 3d 1147 (7th Cir. 1997); *Hotmail Corp. v. Vans Money Pie Inc.*, 74 U.S. P. Q. 2d (BNA) 1020 (N. D. Cal. 1998); *Caspi v. Microsoft Network L. L. C.*, 732 A 2d 528 (N. J. Super. Cl. App. Div., 1999). For rulings that did not recognize the validity of these contracts, because they lack the fundamentals of formation, see *Ticketmaster Corp. v. Tickets.com, Inc.*, 2000 U. S Dist. Lexis 4553 (C.D. Cal., 2000); *Specht v. Netscape Communications, Inc.*, No. 00 Civ. 4871, 2001 WL 755396 (s.d.n.y., July 5, 2001). The Specht ruling was confirmed on appeal: *Specht v. Netscape*, U. S. 2nd Circuit Court of Appeals, Oct. 1, 2002. The reasoning of the appeals court was that "plaintiffs neither had reasonable notice thereof, nor adequately manifested their assent to be bound thereby."

48 Recently an Israeli court dealt related to this issue, but did not take a stand on it: C.C. 51859/06 (Mag. Tel Aviv) *Attny. Shimon Diskin v. Ha'aretz Newspaper Pub. Ltd*, Tak-shal 2008(4) 3300 (2008).

49 This is also the case on eBay and Amazon, the world's leading merchant sites.

Israeli law (sec. 33 of the Sales Act), ownership of goods in an *online sales transaction is transferred upon delivery*, regardless of whether or not a contract was ever formed (as long as the contract, if formed, did not contain an instruction regarding the date of the transfer of ownership).

Thus, we will now address the question of what constitutes delivery according to sec. 33 of the Sales Act. Generally speaking, there are two approaches among Israeli legal scholars as to what constitutes delivery. The first approach is known as *fictitious delivery*. Under this approach, delivery is executed when the vendor has done all that he is legally obligated to do under the contract of sale and has placed the goods at the disposal of the purchaser in as complete a way as the circumstances of the sale permit. Accordingly, transfer of ownership is affected *when the item is made available to the buyer*, even if it has not yet been delivered to him physically.

The second approach is known as "effective delivery." Under this approach, delivery is executed when the seller physically hands over the item to the buyer. Accordingly, transfer of ownership is effected when the goods are physically transferred to the possession of the buyer.

The accepted scholarly opinion is that sec. 33 refers to the actual physical delivery of the goods (the second approach), as opposed to simply placing them at the buyer's disposal (the first approach).[50] Accordingly, in placing the goods at the buyer's disposal, the vendor fulfills his obligation to deliver, but does not fulfill his obligation to transfer ownership of the goods.[51]

In order to apply the above analysis to the issue of transfer of ownership in online sales transactions, we have to distinguish between the various forms of shipping. Generally speaking, on most web sites the consumer has the option of choosing one of two shipping methods: either by carrier or post, or by self-collection from the vendor's warehouse. We will examine what constitutes delivery for each of these methods.

In the self-collection method, the buyer himself collects the item from the vendor's warehouse by prior appointment. The vendor notifies the buyer that the item is available in his warehouse, and that he may come to collect it. Does the vendor's notification that the merchandise is available at his warehouse constitute delivery that effects transfer of ownership? Based on the above legal analysis, only physical delivery is regarded as delivery. When the vendor designates the merchandise for the buyer by marking it, and allows the buyer to come and take it from the warehouse,

50 See Miguel Deutsch, *Special Contracts Law*, v. 1, (2008), 81 [Hebrew]. For an opposing opinion see C.A.188/84 *Zur Insurance LTD. v. Baruch Hadad*, 40(3) P.D. 1, 8–9 (1986). In this case, the court ruled that placing the merchandise at the buyer's disposal is sufficient for effecting transfer of ownership. See para. 6 of the ruling.

51 In electronic commerce, the sales item is generally not specific, but rather part of a stock of similar items. Thus, for example, a person ordering a digital camera is not ordering a specific camera but is ordering one of several cameras of that type. In such a case, placing the item at the buyer's disposal entails designating one of the items in that stock. This is in accordance with Sec. 8 (b) of the Sales Act, which states: "If the sales item is one of a lot, delivery is fulfilled by doing all that is necessary to designate the item and allow its receipt by the purchaser." In order to designate the item, it is sufficient, for example, for the web site to mark the item, and register the invoice number or the name of the buyer.

the vendor fulfills his contractual obligation to deliver the goods, but this does not constitute delivery that effects transfer of ownership to the buyer. Transfer of ownership is effected only when the buyer comes to the warehouse and physically takes the goods.

In the carrier/post method, the vendor ships the goods by carrier or by post to the buyer. Does this method of shipment constitute "delivery," which effects ownership? Apparently, it does not.

As stated above, transfer of ownership requires physical delivery. Therefore, mere shipment by carrier or by post does not constitute delivery that effects transfer of ownership. Ownership is transferred to the buyer only after the carrier hands him the goods. Furthermore, we may argue that, not only does delivery by shipment not constitute delivery according to the second approach, it does not constitute delivery even according to the first approach. Section 8(c) states: "If it has been agreed that a carrier provide carriage of the object sold, then delivery consists of placing the object sold at the carrier's disposal, provided that the carrier is liable to the buyer under the contract of carriage." Thus, according to sec. 8(c), the vendor satisfies his contractual obligation to deliver only if the carrier is liable to the buyer under the contract of carriage.[52] In an ordinary situation, the carrier is an agent of the vendor, and is liable to him and not to the buyer. Hence, the transfer of the goods from the vendor to the carrier does not effect delivery; delivery is effected only when the carrier actually delivers the goods to the buyer.

2. Transfer of Ownership in Online Sales Transactions—the Law in the United States

American policy concerning electronic commerce was expressed in a policy paper released in 1997 by the Clinton Administration.[53] This policy consists of five principles that serve as the basis for all electronic commerce legislation. The approach underlying these principles is that electronic markets should be allowed to operate freely and without undue restrictions. As a result, most of the legislation that regulates electronic commerce deals only with its technical aspects.

In line with these principles, the National Conference of Commissioners on Uniform State Laws ("NCCUSL") has developed two uniform acts designed to bring legal certainty to electronic transactions. The two uniform acts are the Uniform Computer Information Transaction Act ("UCITA")[54] and the Uniform Electronic Transaction Act ("UETA").[55] The UCITA deals with contracts or transactions in "computer information." A contract involving computer information (for example a software license) may be concluded electronically or may be

52 The ramification of this issue is assuming the risk for loss or damage of the item.

53 See "The White House, *A Framework for Global Electronic Commerce* (July 1, 1997)" at www.ta.doc.gov/digeconomy/framewrk.htm. (hereinafter: White House, Framework).

54 See Electronic Signatures in Global and National Commerce Act, Pub. L. 106-229, 114 Stat. 464, at 15 U. S. C. 7001-7006.

55 See Uniform Electronic Transactions Act, 7 A U. L. A. (Sup. 2000) (hereinafter: UETA).

concluded in person or by other means. The UETA, by contrast, is a statute with broader reach—focusing on all types of electronic transactions.[56]

These uniform acts address mainly contractual rather than proprietary issues. Most importantly, they do not relate to transfer of ownership in online sales transactions. In the absence of specific legislation governing transfer of ownership, the Uniform Commercial Code applies.

The Uniform Commercial Code (UCC, or the Code), first published in 1952, is one of a number of uniform acts that have been promulgated in conjunction with efforts to harmonize the laws of sales and other commercial transactions in all fifty states of the United States of America. The UCC deals with sales, leases, negotiable instruments, bank deposits, fund transfers, letters of credit, bulk transfers and sales, documents of title, investment securities, and secured transactions. These subjects are addressed in separate chapters (referred to as "articles").

Sales transactions are addressed in Article 2, which applies to almost all transactions executed between wholesalers (B2B), between individuals (C2C), or between wholesalers and consumers (B2C).[57] This article also governs online sales transactions.

The issue of transfer of ownership is regulated in Article 2-401(2), which provides:

"Unless otherwise explicitly agreed title passes to the buyer at the time and place at which the seller completes performance with reference to the physical delivery of the goods, despite any reservation of a security interest and even though a document of title is to be delivered at a different time or place; and in particular and despite any reservation of a security interest by the bill of lading.

"(a) if the contract requires or authorizes the seller to send the goods to the buyer but does not require the seller to deliver them at destination, title passes to the buyer at the time and place of shipment; but

"(b) if the contract requires delivery at destination, title passes on tender there."

Hence, in order to determine the moment of transfer of ownership in online sales transactions, we must first inquire as to whether the parties have made any explicit agreement in this regard. A review of the conditions of usage posted on the major American e-commerce web sites reveals that:

1. They contain no conditions pertaining to the transfer of ownership of the sold goods;
2. They provide that the vendor undertakes to ship the goods to a specific destination.[58]

56 These uniform acts are not binding law in a particular state until that state chooses to adopt the act through its legislative process; however, uniform acts authored by NCCUSL are often adopted by all or many states and are generally representative of current and future trends.

57 See Sinai Deutsch, *Laws of Consumer Protection—Foundations and Principals*, Part A, (Tel-Aviv: Israel Bar Association Publishing House, 2001), 323.

58 We are not addressing the question of whether a contract was indeed formed that contains these conditions, as this question was addressed above in the discussion of Israeli law.

Therefore,[59] the conclusion to be drawn from Article 2-401(2)(b) is that ownership is transferred to the buyer only when the goods reach their destination.[60]

D. Online Sales Transactions—The Approach in Jewish Law

1. The Approach of Jewish Law in Israel[61]

As we have seen above,[62] Jewish law recognizes the halakhic validity of new modes of acquisition by drawing upon two different methods. The first is direct recognition of the validity of civil law by virtue of the doctrine "the law of the State is law." The second, more widespread method, is through acquisition by *situmta*, which grants halakhic validity to local custom and, in the present case, to the modes of acquisition in practice in a given place.

In Israel, halakhic decisors and halakhic scholars who have addressed the issue of the transfer of ownership in e-commerce transactions according to Jewish law have indeed based themselves on the two above methods.

In the opinion of some of these experts, e-commerce has validity by virtue of the law of *situmta*.[63] They maintain that the execution of an online sales transaction effects "*kinyan*" (ownership) of the merchandise—that is, the *ownership* of the merchandise is *transferred* to the buyer.[64] One opinion[65] further elaborates that even according to those decisors who hold[66] that an acquisition by *situmta* requires a

59 See Sec. 2-401 of the UCC.

60 If the vendor undertakes to ship the goods to the buyer, but does not undertake to send it to a specific destination, ownership is transferred merely by shipping the goods. See 2-401(2)(b).

61 This section is based on Ron S. Kleinman, "*Kinyan Situmta*—Merchants' Customs Relating to Methods of Acquisition in Jewish Law: Legal Foundations and Implementations in Modern Civil Law," *Bar-Ilan Law Studies* 24 (2008): 277–82 [Hebrew]; *idem*, "Credit Card and E-Commerce Do Not Transfer Ownership (*Kinyan*)", *Techumin* 29 (2009): 21–31 [Hebrew].

62 Supra, Section B1, text at n. 23.

63 R. Yehiel Wasserman, "Online Purchasing," *Techumin* 18 (1998): 248–51 [Hebrew]; R. Shlomo Dichovsky, "The Internet in Jewish Law," *Techumin* 22 (2002): 332–33 [Hebrew]; Shabtai Attelo, "Shopping in the E-Commerce Era," *chiduchei torah*@NDS 1 (2001), Hebrew Section, 8–9; R. Yisrael Glickman, "Insights into Commerce and Acquisition over the Internet," *Hemdat Ha'aretz* 1 (2001): 209–17, and in the Summary, para. 3 [Hebrew]; R. Eliezer Steinberger, "E-commerce—Does it Involve the Prohibition Against Paying Interest?" *Techumin* 23 (2003): 393 [Hebrew]. He suggests (but does not rule): "If it is the custom throughout the world to complete an [online] transaction by entering the credit card number on the website, then this custom makes it a *situmta* acquisition. . . and it then becomes a complete acquisition."

64 R. Glickman, Ibid., 215–16, writes that it is often the case that customers cancel a transaction before the merchandise reaches their home, but are required to pay a cancellation fee. Therefore, he is of the opinion that the transaction is completed only when the item reaches the buyer or, at least, when money is transferred from the credit card company to the vendor. However, it seems to us that this does not reflect the prevailing practice in Israel or Israeli law.

65 R. Wasserman, supra, n. 63.

66 According to the opinion of R. Asher b. Yehiel, *Resp. Rosh* 12:3.

physical act and not merely speech, an e-commerce transaction is, in fact, executed by means of a physical act: clicking on the computer mouse or pressing a key on the keyboard.

Several of these learned individuals arrived at the above conclusion—that the execution of an e-commerce transaction effects ownership—also by virtue of the doctrine "the law of the State is law."[67]

An examination of the above writings of these halakhic experts reveals that they do not regard e-commerce transactions as an *obligatory* agreement, but as a *real* agreement, which effects immediate transfer of ownership to the buyer. That is also the reason why several of them note that, even if online sales transactions have validity by virtue of acquisition by *situmta*, from the perspective of Jewish property law, several problems still remain with regard to the purchasing of the goods. These problems are not unique to e-commerce, but derive from the nature of the sold goods. In modern commerce, sales are often conducted in future goods or intangible goods. With regard to such goods, the principle of immediate transfer does not apply.

Several halakhic experts note that e-commerce transactions give rise to the following problems in terms of Jewish property laws:

1. ***Davar she-lo ba la'olam*** (something which is not yet in existence/future goods) or ***davar she-lo ba lirshuto*** (something not yet in one's ownership): Many of the companies that sell products electronically do not stock them. Instead, they buy the product from the supplier and transfer it to the buyer only after it has been ordered. It may sometimes be the case that the product was not yet manufactured at the time that it was ordered.

   According to Jewish law, transfer of ownership cannot be effected for an item that has not yet been manufactured (*davar she-lo ba la'olam*) or an item that is not yet in the ownership of the vendor (*davar she-lo ba lirshuto*) when the act of acquisition is executed.[68] Therefore, several scholars maintain that the halakhic validity of online sales transactions is problematic because transfer of ownership cannot be effected in future goods.[69]
2. ***Davar she-ein bo mamash*** (something lacking physical properties/intangible goods): In Jewish law, ownership is transferred only with regard to something that is tangible, but ownership in something lacking physical properties—termed *davar she-ein bo mamash*—cannot be transferred. Thus, for example, one cannot effect transfer of an action, such as sitting or walking.[70] An online sales transaction does not deal with the virtual item displayed on a website, but rather with the obligation to supply that item in

67 R. Wasserman, supra, n. 63 (based on *Even Ha-Ezel*); R. Dichovsky, supra, n. 63, 333.

68 Rambam, *Mishne Torah, Purchase* (*Mekhirah*) 22:1, 22:5; *Shulhan Arukh, Hoshen Mishpat*, 209:4–5, 211:1.

69 R. Dichovsky, supra, n. 63, 332–33; Attelo, supra, n. 63, 10–11; R. Glickman, supra, n. 63, 215.

70 Rambam, *Mishne Torah, Purchase* (*Mekhirah*) 22:14–15; *Shulhan Arukh, Hoshen Mishpat*, 203:1, 212:1–2; "Davar she-ein bo mamash," *Encyclopedia Talmudit*, v. 6, 606–12.

the future, and the action of supplying it is defined as *davar she-ein bo mamash*.[71]

According to R. Dichovsky, if the validity of e-commerce transactions is based on "the law of the State is law" or on acquisition by *situmta*, both of the above problems are resolved.[72]

As noted, Israeli halakhic experts who have addressed issues of e-commerce have regarded e-commerce as a *real* agreement (*kinyan*), and that the ordering of the product and the payment for it effect transfer of ownership to the buyer. However, in our opinion, a review of Israeli civil law and local custom leads to a different conclusion.

As mentioned above,[73] according to Israeli law, ownership of merchandise sold in an online sales transaction is transferred to the buyer only when it is handed to him physically, and, until then, the buyer has only a contractual right to receive the product. Therefore, if we base the halakhic validity of e-commerce transactions on Israeli law by virtue of "the law of the State is law," we must conclude that the ordering and paying for the goods constitutes an enforceable contract, but is insufficient for transferring ownership of the goods.

Even if we were to base the halakhic validity of e-commerce transactions on custom, by virtue of the principle of *situmta*, the end result is the same. As mentioned, custom is based on the modes of behavior and the thoughts of the public at large. In order to verify the custom in this case, it is imperative to ascertain what people who execute online sales transactions generally think. In our opinion, the average buyer who purchases a product over the Internet knows that the vendor is obligated to supply the product for which he has paid on the date stipulated in the web site's terms and conditions. But, in most cases, the buyer is totally unaware of the legal issue of the point in time in which ownership of the merchandise is transferred to him. We thus have a situation wherein no clear "custom" exists as to the moment of transfer of ownership.

Since no clear custom exists, the law of *situmta* cannot be applied to the moment of transfer of ownership, and this issue must be decided according to ordinary Jewish property laws. Halakhically, transfer of ownership of movables occurs only upon *physical delivery* of the movables to the buyer, at which point ownership is effected by "pulling" (*meshikhah*) or "lifting" (*hagbahah*).[74] This, therefore, is the moment in which ownership of the item is transferred to the buyer who purchased it over the Internet.[75]

Whether the halakhic validity of an e-commerce transaction derives from "the law of the State is law" or acquisition by *situmta*, based on the above we arrive at

71 This problem in e-commerce (but in a different way from that presented here) was addressed by R. Dichovsky, supra, n. 63, 332; Attelo, supra, n. 63, 10, in the notes. According to some of the medieval rabbis, a *kinyan eten* is regarded as "something lacking physical properties" (*Davar she-ein bo mamash*). See *Encyclopedia Talmudit*, ibid., 610.

72 R. Dichovsky, supra, n. 63, 333.

73 See supra, Section C1.

74 *Shulhan Arukh, Hoshen Mishpat*, 198:1.

75 The conclusion we arrived at in this paragraph is based on R. Asher Weiss (in a conversation with Dr. Kleinman).

one and the same conclusion: In the State of Israel, ownership of merchandise sold in an online sales transaction is effected only at the time that the merchandise is physically delivered to the buyer. As mentioned, the question of whether the transaction constitutes a contractual obligation to sell the product or whether it constitutes transfer of ownership to the buyer has many practical implications, such as, inter alia, in the case of a vendor who goes bankrupt before the merchandise is supplied to the buyer.[76]

Our conclusion that e-commerce creates a contractual obligation only resolves the two above e-commerce problems posed by halakhic decisors. With regard to effecting ownership of "something which is not yet in existence" (*davar she-lo ba la'olam*) or of "something that is not yet in one's ownership" (*davar she-lo ba lirshuto*), the fact that there is no *kinyan*—that is, transfer of ownership—of an item that is not yet in existence or that is not yet in the ownership of the vendor does not preclude the parties' *contractual obligation* to sell that item. Thus, despite the fact that according to Jewish law one cannot *effect ownership* of a nonexistent object or of an object not in one's ownership, there is nevertheless an *obligation* to effect the ownership.[77]

In addition, the fact that in e-commerce we are dealing with an object that will be supplied in the future—which comes under the category of "an object lacking physical properties" (*davar she-ein bo mamash*)—is also not problematic in our opinion. This is because even though, according to Jewish law, selling an action, such as the action of supplying merchandise in the future, does not effect *ownership*—since ownership of an intangible object cannot be transferred, and therefore the transaction does not have halakhic validity—e-commerce nevertheless creates the *obligation* to supply the particular item, when this type of obligation is customary and the accepted practice.[78] Consequently, this obligation to supply the item chosen by the buyer from the models displayed in the web site's catalog gives the transaction halakhic validity.[79]

Thus, based on the approach presented above, we can establish—by virtue of acquisition by *situmta* and "the law of the State is law"—that, even though online sales transactions regularly involve goods that are not owned by the vendor or that do not yet exist, and even though they are supplied in the future, nevertheless, an online sales transaction has halakhic validity as a *contractual obligation*.

Finally, it should be noted that some of the halakhic writings on the subject of e-commerce testify to the writers' lack of familiarity with the details of the relevant Israeli civil laws as well as with the prevailing distinction between the obligatory phase and the proprietary phase of a sales transactions. The application of the principle of acquisition by *situmta* and the doctrine of "the law of the State is law" has led several halakhic sages to conclude that an online sales transaction effects transfer of ownership to the buyer. It is our conclusion, in view of civil law and local custom, that online transactions effect a *contractual obligation* only.

76 See supra, text at nn. 13–15.

77 *Shulhan Arukh, Hoshen Mishpat*, 60:6.

78 By virtue of the law of *situmta*. See supra, at n. 30.

79 R. Shlomo Dichovsky agreed with this conclusion (in a conversation with Dr. Kleinman).

2. The Approach of Jewish Law in the United States

What should be the approach of Jewish law in the United States with regard to e-commerce transactions?

In order to answer this question, we must first understand American law and custom in this regard. As seen above, according to the UCC, ownership of merchandise is transferred to the buyer at the time agreed upon by the parties, in the absence of such agreement, when the vendor fulfills his obligation to deliver the merchandise. Since the parties generally give no thought to the issue of transfer of ownership, and since the conditions listed on the web sites do not generally refer to it, as noted, ownership is transferred at the time of the delivery of the merchandise, as established in the Code.

According to the UCC, the vendor's obligation to deliver the merchandise is contingent upon the method of delivery stipulated in the contract of sale. The conditions of usage of the major American e-commerce web sites provide that the vendor undertakes to ship the merchandise to a specific destination. In such circumstances, the UCC states that ownership is transferred to the buyer only when the merchandise reaches its destination.[80]

We will now relate to the question of how Jewish law in the United States should regard online sales transactions. If the halakhic validity of e-commerce transactions is based on civil law by virtue of "the law of the State is law," the conclusion derives directly from the UCC: Ownership is transferred to the buyer upon the arrival of the merchandise at the agreed-upon destination.

If, however, the validity of e-commerce in Jewish law is based on the principle of acquisition by *situmta*, that is, on "custom," we arrive at a different conclusion. Establishing validity based on the custom practiced by online shoppers leads to one and the same result in Jewish law, be it in Israel or the United States: In each of these countries, the average online shopper gives no thought to the question of the time at which transfer of ownership occurs. Therefore, as stated above, transfer of ownership to the buyer is effected only at the time that the merchandise is physically delivered to the buyer, as in accordance with Jewish law.[81]

E. Summary and Conclusions

This article addresses the issue of whether there is halakhic validity to electronic commerce practices according to Jewish law and focuses on the question: What constitutes the moment of transfer of ownership with regard to goods purchased in an online sales transaction?

80 See supra, section C3 and text at n. 60.

81 See supra, text at nn. 74–75.

Halakhic decisors and halakhic scholars in Israel who, over the past decade, have discussed the validity of e-commerce transactions from the perspective of Jewish law, have based their discussions on civil law and on local custom, in view of the two doctrines mentioned above—"the law of the State is law" and acquisition by *situmta*. Based on these doctrines, most of them have reached the conclusion that the ordering and paying for merchandise over the Internet effects *transfer of ownership* of the merchandise to the buyer.

However, an examination of Israeli civil law as well as the custom in Israel has led us to a different conclusion—that, according to Jewish law, the ordering and paying via Internet creates only a *contractual obligation* on the part of the vendor to supply the merchandise to the buyer. It does not effect transfer of ownership of the merchandise. Ownership of the merchandise is transferred to the buyer only at the time of the physical delivery of the merchandise to him.

As for the United States, the conclusion of the study is that, according to Jewish law, the decision as to what constitutes the moment of transfer of ownership in an online sales transaction there depends on the principle of Jewish law that is applied.

If the validity of e-commerce transactions in Jewish law is based on acquisition by *situmta* and on local custom, we arrive at the identical result for Israel and the United States. In both countries, the average online consumer gives no thought to the question of the moment in which transfer of ownership occurs, and thus there is no "custom" that may be invoked in this regard. In the absence of such custom, the moment of transfer of ownership according to Jewish law must be decided according to classical Jewish property laws. Accordingly, transfer of ownership to the buyer is effected only at the time that the merchandise is physically delivered to him.

On the other hand, if we rely directly on civil law by virtue of "the law of the State is law," the decision arrived at in Jewish law as to the moment of transfer of ownership in the United States derives directly from the UCC.

According to the UCC, the moment of transfer of ownership is contingent upon the method of delivery stipulated in the contract of sale. The conditions of usage of the major American e-commerce web sites provide that the vendor undertakes to ship the merchandise to a specific destination. In such circumstances, the UCC states that ownership is transferred to the buyer only when the merchandise reaches its destination.

SELECTED BIBLIOGRAPHY

Jewish Law

Dichovsky, R. Shlomo. "The Internet in Jewish Law." *Techumin* 22 (2002): 325–33 [Hebrew].

Glickman, R. Yisrael. "Insights into Commerce and Ownership over the Internet." *Hemdat Ha'aretz* 1 (2001); 209–17 [Hebrew].

Kleinman, Ron S. *Merchant Customs (Lex Mercatoria) Relating to Methods of Acquisition in Jewish Law: Kinyan Situmta*. Ph.D. Dissertation, Bar-Ilan University, Ramat-Gan, Israel, 2000 [Hebrew].

Kleinman, Ron S. "*Kinyan Situmta*—Merchants' Customs Relating to Methods of Acquisition in Jewish Law: Legal Foundations and Implementations in Modern Civil Law." *Bar-Ilan Law Studies* 24 (2008): 243–98 [Hebrew].

Kleinman, Ron S. "Credit Card and E-Commerce Do Not Transfer Ownership (*Kinyan*)." *Techumin* 29 (2009): 21–31 [Hebrew].

Wasserman, R. Yehiel. "Online Purchasing." *Techumin* 18 (1998): 248–51 [Hebrew].

Israeli Law

Barsade, Jonathan. *The Internet and Online Business Law*, 2nd ed. Tel Aviv: Perlstein-Genosar, 2002 [Hebrew].

Jabareen, Amal. *The Law and Economics of Consumer Protection in the Internet Era*, Ph.D. Dissertation, Ramat-Gan., Israel: Bar-Ilan University, 2004, [Hebrew].

Jabareen, Amal. "Virtual Malls as Gatekeepers in Electronic Commerce: An economic perspective." *Bar-Ilan Law Studies* 25 (2009): 735 [Hebrew].

Zamir, Eyal. *Sale Law, 1968*. Jerusalem: Hebrew University, 1987 [Hebrew].

American Law

Gibbons, L. J. "No Regulation, Government Regulation, or Self Regulation: Social Enforcement or Social Contracting for Governance in Cyberspace." *Cornell J. L. & Pub. Pol'y* 6, (1997): 475.

Kaufman Winn, Jane. "Clash of the Titans: Regulating the Competition Between Established and Emerging Electronic Payment Systems." *Berkeley Tech. L. J.* 14, (1999): 675.

Muller, John D. "Selected Developments in The Law of Cyberspace Payments." *Bus. Law* 54, (1999): 403.

Rothchild, John. "Protecting the Digital Consumer: The Limits of Cyberspace Utopianism." *Ind. L. J.* 74, (1999): 893.

Soon-Yong, Choi., & Whinston, Andrew B. *The Internet Economy: Technology and Practice*. Austin, TX: Smart Economics Publishing, 2000.

Smith, T. B. *Property Problems in Sale*. London: Sweet & Maxwell et al., 1978.

Todd, Paul. *E-Commerce Law*. England: Cavendish Publishing, 2005.

CHAPTER 27

THE JEWISH GUARANTOR AND SECULAR LAW: STUMBLING BLOCKS AND THEIR REMOVAL

ROGER LISTER

Introduction

Guarantees are an important interdisciplinary meeting point of economics, accounting, and law. A guarantor becomes liable for the debt of a primary debtor if the primary debtor defaults. When is it religiously permissible for a Jew to act as guarantor under an arrangement governed by English law? There is a danger of falling afoul of prohibited usurious or quasiusurious relationships.

The chapter will not provide answers to specific questions in readers' affairs. They must consult their qualified religious advisor.

Disciplinary Context

For the financial economist a financial guarantee is an important contingent claim. A contingent claim is a possible obligation that arises from past events and whose existence will be confirmed only by the occurrence of one or more uncertain future events. The guarantee is part of the package of contingent claims that comprise the value of a business's or an individual's net worth. A business entity is a bundle of contingent claims against the business's uncertain future income stream.

For the accounting profession, guarantees are a significant part of financial reporting. The auditor must establish the answer to a series of questions. Is the guarantee (at one extreme) a proximate claim to be reported in the accounts as a liability? Alternatively, is it so unlikely to crystallize that it can be reported by way of note to the accounts? Or is its consummation so remote that it can simply be ignored?

Like financial economics and accounting, English law is significantly concerned with guarantees—not least with the key determinant of the answer to our question. Andrews and Millet say with respect to English law that, "one of the profound conceptual problems at the heart of the rights of the guarantor against the creditor [is] most notably the question whether the guarantor has any right to compel the creditor to sue the primary debtor."[1]

Economic Value of a Guarantee

A guarantor becomes liable for the debt of the principal debtor if the latter defaults. This makes it fit perfectly into the definition of a contingent claim, being a possible obligation that arises from past events and whose existence will be confirmed only by the occurrence of one or more uncertain future events.

What is the economic value of a guarantee? Merton and his successors analyze guarantees as options.[2] A lender has the option to hand his defaulting debtor's obligation to the guarantor and receive in exchange the full amount of the debtor's obligation. In option language the lender holds a put option by the exercise of which he is saved from the debtor's default. How can this situation be valued?

The first step is to compare two investors. A has purchased a safe bond on the stock market. B has purchased a bond with the same interest and repayment terms but which is risky. He asks a totally reliable guarantor to guarantee the payments in exchange for an economically rational fee. B is now in the same position as A and can stop worrying. If our market is economically rational B's package should, subject to any adjustment for transaction costs, have the same market value as A's bond. In reality, any number of packages can be devised, and a Jewish lender has to be aware of the danger of a package which amounts to an interest-bearing risk-free loan. Formally we can compare values as follows:

1 G. Andrews and R. Millett, *Law of Guarantees*, 3rd ed., (London: FT Law and Tax, 1995), xiii.

2 For example, R. C. Merton, and Z. Bodie, "On the Management of Financial Guarantees," *Financial Management*, Winter (1992): 87–109.

		£		£
Safe bond	=	Risky bond	+	Cost of guarantee
Risky bond	=	Safe bond	–	Cost of guarantee
Cost of guarantee	=	Safe bond	–	Risky bond

What are the parameters of value of a guarantee; that is to say which factors increase the value of a guarantee and which factors harm that value? Taking the case of a guaranteed bond, Merton and his successors answer the question in the idiom of option pricing as shown in table 27.1:

Usury in Judaism

Lending in Judaism is in origin a charitable institution. The Torah is concerned with the poor and the needy.[3] Maimonides (Rambam, Egypt, 1135–1204) begins an account of lenders and borrowers by quoting Exodus 22:24, which instructs that: "When you lend money to any of my people even to the poor with you, you shall not be to him as a creditor; neither shall you lay upon him interest."[4] R. Solomon b. Isaac (Rashi, France, 1040–1105) comments that this is one of only three instances in the Torah where the Hebrew word *im* is to be translated as "when" rather than "if." This indicates such lending to be obligatory, but not only to the poor: The Babylonian Talmud also articulates the merit of lending to a rich person suffering from funds mismatch.[5,6]

When a loan is patently unsafe it is discouraged in favor of a gift or a loan with a pledge or a business partnership. R. Israel Meir Ha-Kohen Kagan (Poland, 1838–1933) explicitly states that it is better to lend with a pledge than to lend without and be compelled to keep dunning the debtor for repayment.[7]

Usury and usury-like transactions are prohibited if they involve Jewish lenders or borrowers. Applications of the usury prohibition appear in the Torah itself, the Talmud, the transactions of the middle ages, the Renaissance, the centuries of evolving mercantilism, and in modern society. In our time, Tamari voices unhappiness about mortgage loans substantially secured by a lien on real estate. Interest on such loans is compensation for the lender's waiting period "and would seem therefore to be a case of biblically proscribed interest . . . since the lender faces no risk."[8] Other vulnerable contemporary contracts include restructuring debt; lease

3 J. H. Hertz, ed., *Pentateuch and Haftorahs*, 2nd ed. (London:Soncino, 1960), Exodus 23; Leviticus 25.

4 Maimonides (Rambam, Egypt, 1135–1204), *Mishneh Torah, Malveh ve-Loveh* 1:1.

5 Babylonian Talmud, published as *Talmud Bavli* by Mesorah Publications, New York, 1994, 2002.

6 B *Bava Metsi'a* 71a.

7 L. Oschry, trans. Hafetz Hayyim, *Ahavat Hesed* (Spring Valley: Feldheim, 1967/1888), 47. R. Israel Meir Ha-Kohen Kagan is the actual name of the author known as the *Hafetz Hayyim*.

8 M. Tamari. *With All Your Possessions* (NY: The Free Press, 1987), 186.

Table 27.1 Influences on the economic value of a guarantee which guarantees the principal of a loan

Influence	Effect on value of guarantee	Reason
1 Increase in bond issuer's assets	Decreases	Lender gains less by exercising the put option (i.e., by invoking the guarantee).
2 Increase in the volatility of bond issuer's assets	Increases	There will be more circumstances in which the lender's option is worth exercising.
3 Increase in the amount due from the bond issuer	Increases	Increase in the potential liability of the guarantor.
4 Extension of loan bond repayment	Increases or decreases	*Increase*: There is more opportunity for the bond issuer's assets to fluctuate i.e. more volatility. *Decrease*: Present value of any amount due from guarantor at bond repayment is less due to its later incidence.
5 Increase in risk of guarantor	Decreases	Risk-adjusted value of guarantee is less.
6 Increase in interest rates	Decreases	Present value of any amount due from guarantor at bond repayment is less due to the effect of higher discounting rate.

agreements; extending an existing period of credit; cash and trade discounts; prepayment; penalty clauses; promissory notes; hedging; futures; sale of debts including assumption of mortgages; bond trading—and guarantees.[9] We will see that the main religious danger faced by a Jewish guarantor is that of falling into a usurious relationship with another Jew.

The Torah essentially forbids a reward for waiting for one's money. R. Nahman (Babylonia, d. 320) states this explicitly and goes on to enumerate commercial deals that can lead to such reward—for example, a surcharge imposed on a buyer who pays late.[10] Plain loan interest fixed in advance is biblically forbidden; other interest-bearing and interest-like transactions are rabbinically forbidden.

Permission to lend at interest to non-Jews has been widely but mistakenly criticized on moral grounds.[11] In fact, the rule facilitates business on equal terms

9 M. Kanner. *A Matter of Interest* (NY: Feldheim, 2002).
S. Wagschal. *Torah Guide for the Businessman* (NY: Feldheim, 1990).
S. Wagschal. *Torah Guide to Money Matters* (NY: Feldheim, 1996).

10 B *Bava Metsi'a* 63b. Other examples appear in B *Bava Metsi'a* at 65a, 68a 69b, 70b, and 104b.

11 J. H. Hertz, ed. *Pentateuch and Haftorahs*, 2nd ed. (London: Soncino, 1960), Deuteronomy 23:21.

with persons who would themselves charge interest to a Jewish debtor and who would certainly not release debts in the Jubilee year. Furthermore, interest can be charged only for mercantile purposes and not when the non-Jew needs funds for subsistence. The usurer is condemned throughout the Talmud. His testimony is unacceptable in a court of law and he is bracketed with thieves and gamblers. The caricatured Shylock should be seen against the backcloth of remarks like Martin Luther's, who said that, "If we prohibit Jews from following trades and other civil occupations we compel them to become usurers."[12] Jews were forbidden to join trade guilds. The massacres of the Crusades forced Jews to seek livelihoods requiring minimal travel.

Guarantees in Judaism

The religious significance of a guarantee has always been considerable. A busy practising solicitor wrote as follows to the author:

> As a solicitor who specialises in property and probate transactions with a high proportion of my clientele being orthodox Jews I can confirm that I have on many occasions been professionally involved either in drawing up of acceptable guarantees or in checking such documents produced by learned Rabbis. I find that the vast majority of my orthodox Jewish clients would only be prepared to enter into legally enforceable loan documents if they are set up in a manner acceptable both to English law and to their religious persuasion.

Is there a biblical basis for the notion of guarantor? R. Huna (Babylonia, c. 216–296) traces the notion of a personal guarantor with secondary liability (*'arev stam*) to Judah's asking his father to let Benjamin go to Egypt, where Joseph awaited them.[13,14] Judah offers to be responsible if Benjamin is not safely restored to his father. Judah says:

> I will be a guarantor (*'arev*) for him—you may seek him from my hand. If I have not brought him to you and set him before you, I will have sinned against you for ever.

However, not all authorities accept that Judah had the status of an ordinary guarantor. R. Hisda (Babylonia, d. c. 309) disagrees and attributes to Judah the more onerous responsibility of a *kabbelan*. A *kabbelan* is deemed to have personally received a loan from a lender and to have conveyed it to the borrower. This makes Judah nearer to a borrower. R. Hisda's grounds for placing Judah in this category are that he asked his father to "give" Benjamin to him.[15] More is said of the *kabbelan* later.

12 Hertz, op. cit., 849.
13 B *Bava Batra* 173b.
14 Hertz, op. cit., Genesis 43:9.
15 B *Bava Batra* 174a.

R. Yom Tov b. Abraham Ishbili (Ritba, Spain, c. 1250–1330) goes further in his commentary on the discussion in the Talmud and says that since Judah asked his father to give Benjamin specifically to him he was entirely a borrower. But he then rescues the definition of guarantor by saying that Judah was in fact offering to guarantee Reuben's earlier request that Jacob give Benjamin to him and his brothers to take to Egypt.[16]

In the face of the above challenges the Gemara finds an alternative biblical source for the institution of guarantor. A lender is exhorted to resort to his guarantor:[17]

> Take [the guarantor's] garment because he became a guarantor for a stranger,
> and on account of an alien take security from him.

R. Samuel b. Meir (Rashbam, France, c. 1080-85–c. 1174) says in his commentary on this Talmudic debate that, since reference is made here to an *'arev stam* and no reference is made to a *kabbelan*, we have a biblical basis for the liability of an *'arev stam*.[18] The Bible tends to disapprove of guarantees, warning us against being "among the guarantors for loans."[19]

Why is the Gemara concerned to find a biblical authority for the liability of a guarantor? The Gemara worries that it appears from the Mishnah, not least because the guarantor seems to receive no benefit or other consideration for acting, that a contract of guarantee does not require the authentication of a *kinyan*—a formal act of acquisition—provided the guarantor became guarantor at the time the loan was made, or later, under special circumstances. The Gemara, however, argues that there is in fact a consideration for the contract in the form of the satisfaction that the guarantor gets from being trusted by the lender.[20]

What are the categories of guarantee under Jewish law? Three categories can be distinguished:[21]

'Arev stam. The lender must exhaust all remedies against the primary debtor before dunning an *'arev stam*.[22] The *'arev stam* may also be dunned if the debtor has died, is violent, is abroad, refuses to appear before the court, or refuses to submit to the judges, or if his property is in another country.

This is the legal treatment of an *'arev stam* as expounded in the Talmud.[23] If the contract says, additionally, that the lender may claim from whom he wishes, he must still claim from the borrower first if the borrower has real assets or other

16 B *Bava Batra* 173, 174.
17 N. Scherman, ed. *Tanach* (1997), Proverbs 6:1–3 and 20: 16.
18 B *Bava Batra* 173, 174.
19 For example, N. Scherman, ed. *Tanach* (1997). Proverbs 22:16.
20 B *Bava Batra* 173b.
21 B *Bava Batra* 173, 174.
Y. Reisman. *The Laws of Ribbis* (NY: Mesorah,1995), 278.
M. Kanner. *A Matter of Interest* (NY: Feldheim, 2002), 32–37.
22 B *Bava Metsi'a* 71b.
R. Joseph Caro (Ottoman Palestine, 1488–1575), *Shulhan Arukh, Yoreh De'ah* 170.
23 B *Bava Batra* 173b.

known assets. This enhanced conditional version of the ordinary guarantee allows the lender some discretion, but remains distinct conceptually and practically from the *kabbelan*. All authorities agree that in the case of the *'arev stam* the lender must exhaust all remedies against the primary debtor before dunning an *'arev stam*. The *kabbelan* distinctively has primary responsibility and may be dunned whether or not the defaulting debtor has assets.

The obligation of the *'arev stam* is coextensive with the principal debtor's obligation, so that, if the latter is void or otherwise ineffective, the guarantor's liability ceases. The Gemara does not accept an alternative possibility—namely that the guarantor's obligation only extends to ensuring the availability of the debtor. Nor does it accept the further concern that when a guarantor agrees to act he may be merely expressing an *asmakhta*, a commitment that he does not expect to have to fulfil, in which case his commitment is not enforceable. The guarantor is deemed to act with full acceptance of the risk. He is deemed willing to act if only out of the sense of gratification already referred to.

'Arev kabbelan. If a guarantor accepts additional responsibility then he is called an *'arev kabbelan* and the lender can at his discretion dun the primary debtor or the guarantor first regardless of the financial condition of the borrower.[24] As the word implies, the *kabbelan* "accepts" the loan from the lender and makes himself in form a primary debtor. R. Simeon b. Gamaliel II (Palestine, first half of second century CE) argues that even in the case of a *kabbelan* the primary debtor must be dunned first if he has assets, but Jewish law does not follow his opinion, the Talmud noting that this is one of the three occasions on which we do not follow R. Simeon b. Gamaliel II.[25]

'Arev shilof dots. An *'arev shilof dots* detaches the debt from the primary debtor and attaches it to the *'arev*. The creditor can only collect from the *'arev*. The borrower is not obliged to pay the lender even if requested.[26] However, if the *'arev shilof dots* cannot repay the lender, the lender can still collect from the borrower under a rule in the Talmud to the effect that that if A owes B and B owes C, then C is allowed to collect from A.[27] The *'arev shilof dots* coincides in practice with the case where a guarantor who actually takes the money in his hand from the lender and gives it to the borrower causes the borrower to be exempt from the lender's claim.[28]

Which expressions determine a guarantee's category? R. Huna discusses how to distinguish the *'arev stam* from the *kabbelan*. To him the term "lend" in a guarantor's request to a lender makes the borrower a primary debtor and the guarantor an ordinary guarantor. Any other requests of the guarantor are subordinated to this rule. Thus, any of the following expressions define the guarantor as an ordinary

24 B *Bava Batra* 174.
25 B *Bava Batra* 173b.
26 B *Yevamot* 109b.
27 B *Kiddushin* 15a.
28 B *Bava Batra* 174.

guarantor: Lend to him and I will be guarantor; lend to him and I will pay; lend to him and I will be liable; lend to him and I will repay.[29]

The term "give" in a guarantor's request to a lender makes the surety a *kabbelan*. The lender is the *kabbelan*'s agent when handing the money to the borrower. Thus, any of the following expressions makes the guarantor a *kabbelan*: Give him and I will be *kabbelan*; give him and I shall repay; give him and I will be liable; give him and I will give.

What if the surety mixes the terms and says, "lend to him and I will be a *kabbelan*" or "give him and I will be guarantor"? In the same debate, R. Yitzhak (Babylonia, fl. c. 280) says that the use of the terms *kabbelan* and *guarantor* determines the meaning of the mixed statement, but R. Hisda counters that all expressions mean *kabbelan* except where both terms indicate ordinary guarantee. This means that "give and I will be guarantor" indicates *kabbelan*, and only "lend and I will be guarantor" amounts to ordinary guarantee. Rava (Babylonia, d. 352), in opposition to R. Hisda, says that all expressions are ordinary guarantees except where both terms indicate *kabbelan*, as in "give to him and I will give." Table 27.2 summarizes the main strands of opinion.

Table 27.2 Significance of expressions in contract

Expression:	R.Huna Lend (vs give) is the determining term. Surety is:	R.Hisda Lend and guarantor both needed for ordinary guarantor Surety is:	R.Yitzhak Guarantor and *kabbelan* are the determining words Surety is:	Rava Give and give both needed for *kabbelan* Surety is:
Lend and I will be guarantor	Ordinary guarantor	Ordinary guarantor		Ordinary guarantor
Lend and I will pay	Ordinary guarantor	*kabbelan*		Ordinary guarantor
Lend and I will be liable	Ordinary guarantor	*kabbelan*		Ordinary guarantor
Lend and I will repay	Ordinary guarantor	*kabbelan*		Ordinary guarantor
Give and I will be *kabbelan*	*kabbelan*	*kabbelan*		Ordinary guarantor
Give and I will repay	*kabbelan*	*kabbelan*		Ordinary guarantor
Give and I will be liable	*kabbelan*	*kabbelan*		Ordinary guarantor
Give and I will give	*kabbelan*	*kabbelan*		*Kabbelan*
Lend and I will be *kabbelan*		*kabbelan*	*kabbelan*	Ordinary guarantor
Give and I will be guarantor		*kabbelan*	Ordinary guarantor	Ordinary guarantor

29 B *Bava Batra* 174a.

Which category of guarantor is religiously permissible? The danger is of a Jew finding himself in a forbidden usurious relationship with a fellow Jew. Yet we read in *Bava Metsi'a*:

> You shall not take from [your fellow-Jew] *neshekh* or *tarbit*. However you may become a guarantor for him.[30]

Guaranteeing an interest-bearing loan between Jews. It is always forbidden for a Jew to act as an *'arev* in an interest-bearing loan between Jews.[31] The *'arev* is one of the parties who transgress "do not impose interest upon him" (i.e., upon the borrower).[32] The *'arev* is one of the five parties to a prohibited loan who commit one or more of six usurious transgressions enumerated by Rambam.[33] Table 27.3 summarizes the various parties' situations.

Guaranteeing an interest-bearing loan between Jew and Non-Jew. While it is always forbidden to act as an *'arev* in an interest-bearing loan between Jews, it is in some circumstances permissible to guarantee a loan from a non-Jew to a Jew and from a Jew to a non-Jew. The danger is that interest will arise between two Jews. If a Jewish borrower from a non-Jewish lender defaults, the *'arev* will pay and then exercise his right[34] to pursue the Jewish party to recover the principal of the debt plus interest accumulated during its term. If a non-Jewish borrower from a Jewish lender defaults the *'arev* will be pursued by the Jewish lender for the principal of the debt plus interest accumulated during its term. If this situation is deemed latent from the time the loan was granted, forbidden interest is accruing between Jews

Table 27.3 Transgressions of the parties to a loan

Transgression:	Don't be as a creditor (Exodus 22:24)	Don't give on interest (Leviticus 25:37)	Don't give food for increase (Leviticus 25:37)	Don't take interest (Leviticus 25:36)	Don't impose interest (Exodus 22:24)	Don't put a stumbling block before the blind (Leviticus 19:14)
Party:						
Lender	/	/	/	/	/	/
Borrower[1]						/
Witness					/	
Guarantor					/	
Scribe					/	

Note: The Gemara tells us that the borrower, in addition to placing a stumbling block, transgresses "You shall not cause your brother to take interest."[1]

[1] Hertz, J. H., Ed. *Pentateuch and Haftorahs*, 2nd ed. London: Soncino, 1960. *Deuteronomy* 23:20, 21.

30 71a, the first sentence being a quotation of Leviticus 25:36 forbidding taking interest.
31 B *Bava Metsi'a* 71b and 75b.
32 Hertz, op. cit., Exodus 22:24.
33 Rambam, *Sefer Ha-Mitzvot, Lo Ta'aseh* 237.
34 B *Bava Batra* 32b.

throughout the loan's term. If, on the other hand, the relationship between the two Jews is deemed to arise only at the end of the term, no interest accrues between them and there is no transgression. Much depends on the category of guarantee as previously defined. In view of this, to what extent is each type of guarantee permissible?

Ordinary guarantees. The Talmud allows a Jew to guarantee a loan from a non-Jew to a Jew if the non-Jew takes upon himself to be governed by the Jewish law applicable to an *'arev stam*, whereby the guarantor has a strictly secondary liability, so that the borrower becomes indebted to the guarantor only when the guarantor repays the debt.[35] At this point a new loan is deemed to arise between the guarantor and the borrower equal to the amount initially lent to the borrower plus interest. This new loan must not itself carry interest.

Without this strictly secondary guarantor (i.e., when we are not dealing with a strict *'arev stam*), potential liability exists, and gathers interest, from the outset between Jewish guarantor and Jewish debtor. It matures when the debtor defaults. Rambam states the case as follows:

> If a heathen lends money to an Israelite it is forbidden for another Israelite to enter as surety. Since under their laws the creditor makes demand for repayment upon the surety first, the surety would be demanding the principal and interest . . . from the Israelite debtor. If, however, the heathen undertook that he should not make demand upon the surety first, it is permissible for the Israelite to enter as a surety.[36]

The danger is of a particularly severe transgression amounting to biblically forbidden interest.[37]

While all authorities allow guarantorship (*'arevut*) in the case of the strict *'arev stam* (ordinary guarantor), Rashi and R. Solomon b. Abraham Adret (Rashba, Spain, c. 1235–c. 1310) disagree with respect to some cases that depart to some degree from the strict case. Rashi states that the contract is prohibited if there is even just a possibility that the lender will claim from the guarantor first.[38] This would be sufficient to create a prohibited liability between guarantor and a borrower from the outset. The *kabbelan* case is accordingly not in order.

Rashba argues that a borrower is someone who will definitely be called upon by the lender to pay a debt, so that a guarantor only assumes the role of creditor of the debtor after he (the guarantor) has paid the lender, at which point a new loan arises. It is sufficient for the lender to have discretion about whom he claims from first for the contract to be in order. The *kabbelan* case is accordingly in order.

The law governing a Jewish guarantor for a Jew's loan to a non-Jew follows from the preceding discussion. R. Joseph Caro (Ottoman Palestine, 1488–1575), in

35 B *Bava Metsi'a* 71b and Rashi's commentary ad loc.

36 Rambam, *Mishneh Torah, Malveh ve-Loveh* 5:5. Translation taken from J. J. Rabinowitz, translator. *The Code of Maimonides [Mishneh Torah]* (Forge Village, MA: Yale University Press, 1949), 94.

37 R. Joseph Caro, *Shulhan Arukh, Yoreh De'ah* 170.

38 To B *Bava Metsi'a* 71b.

his influential legal code *Shulhan Arukh*, states that if a non-Jew borrows from a Jew with interest it is forbidden for a Jew to be an *'arev* unless a stipulation was made that the Jewish lender will dun the borrower first and that the borrower will not deflect the lender to the guarantor as long as he has assets from which payment can be made.[39]

Religious authorities warn about terms in agreements that preclude their being ordinary guarantees:

> Since a bank is not obliged to turn to the borrower first and go through a legal procedure with him, and as immediately—after a few claims—they have the right to claim from the *'arev*, this is like *'arev kabbelan* and is forbidden, and one should only permit this in a case where the bank is obliged to claim from the borrower and claim all his assets first. . . . Even if the bank has a month (or something like that) until it can claim from the *'arev*, nonetheless he has the status of an *'arev kabbelan*, since the bank is not obliged to take the borrower to court and such like. It is worth pointing out that, many times, when the bank sends a letter to the borrower or gives him time to pay before claiming from the *'arev*, this is only because this is the usage and generally they have a legal right to claim immediately from the *'arev*.[40]

A correspondent of the present author recently wrote concerning contracts drafted by English banks:

> Whilst all conditions precedent to the surety's liability must be fulfilled before recourse is made to the guarantor, I have found no authority showing this to mean more than that demand for payment has been made on the debtor which he has failed to comply with within the stipulated or a reasonable time or stating positively that they amount to conditions precedent to the surety's liability.

'Arev kabbelan. The situation for other categories of guarantor (*kabbelan* and *shilof dots*) follows from the discussion of the ordinary guarantor. When the guarantor is a *kabbelan* the creditor can dun the guarantor first even if the primary debtor has real or other known assets. According to Rashi the requirement of secondary liability is not satisfied and a Jew may not act as guarantor. The fact that the lender has the right to dun the guarantor directly makes the guarantor the real borrower. In accordance with this opinion, R. Elazar Menahem Man Shach (Israel, 1898–2001) rules that if a Jew had agreed to act as an *'arev* in such circumstances and was dunned by the lender he should only seek reimbursement of the principal from the borrower. But if he had already received such interest from the borrower he need not return it, as this is rabbinically and not biblically prohibited interest.[41]

Rashba's position has already been mentioned in order to articulate the case of the ordinary guarantor. In sum, he considers the link between guarantor and lender to begin only when the lender approaches the guarantor, so that no interest accumulates between them during the life of the loan. For Rashba, a borrower is

39 R. Joseph Caro, op. cit., 170.

40 For example, R. Yosef Shalom Elyashiv (Israel, b. 1910), *Mishnat Ribbit*, 164: paragraph 4, footnote 3.

41 Commentary on the *Shulhan Arukh*, *Yoreh De'ah* 170:1–2.

someone who will definitely be called upon to pay a debt. The *kabbelan* is not a borrower in his terms. When the debtor is dunned by the *kabbelan* the debtor is compensating the *kabbelan* for a loss. This loss happens to equal the principal and interest that is due from the primary borrower to the lender, but it is of the nature of a loss, not an interest-bearing loan.

Rashba further supports his opinion in his commentary by arguing that his interpretation of the *kabbelan* is the only interpretation that is consistent with *Bava Metsi'a* 75b, where Abbaye (Babylonia, 278–338) says that the *'arev* transgresses only the sin of "neither shall you lay upon him usury."[42] This forbids taking part in a transaction that transgresses the usury prohibition. Rashba maintains that the transgressions committed would be far worse if we were to accept his adversaries' opinion of the wrong committed by a *kabbelan*. Despite this, Jewish law does not follow Rashba and prohibits a Jew from acting as a *kabbelan* for another Jew.[43] However, one of the present writer's patient correspondents points out that Rashba's position can be strongly defended: *kabbelan* cannot be considered a borrower—not least since he never got the money.

'Arev shilof dots. The *'arev shilof dots* is like one who has received the money from the hands of the lender and passed it into the hands of the borrower to whom he becomes a creditor.[44] This plainly amounts to biblically forbidden interest when *shilof dots* and borrower are Jews.

Guarantees Under English Law

A surety can be either the provider of a guarantee or the provider of an indemnity. England has a complex law of principal and surety. Is it permissible under Jewish law for a Jew to be a surety as defined by English law? All depends on whether the surety's position is secondary to an extent that satisfies the requirements of Jewish law. Specifically: Under English law would a Jewish lender have to exhaust all available remedies against the borrower before dunning the guarantor? The first important distinction we meet is between indemnity and guarantee.

Indemnity. Many so-called contracts of guarantees are actually contracts of indemnity. A guarantee imposes secondary liability on the guarantor, but the liability of an indemnifier is primary. The distinction is between saying, in the case of a guarantee, "If he does not pay you, I will," and in the case of an indemnity, "I will see you paid" or "I will save you harmless." This last archaic expression means, "I will keep you from any harm." The indemnifier's liability is independent of any liability of the primary debtor to the creditor. It is not conditional on default by the primary debtor.

42 Hertz, op. cit., Exodus 22:25.

43 Reisman, op. cit., 286.

44 R. Joseph Caro, op. cit., 170.

An indemnifier has an original and independent primary obligation to the lender from the outset. This is a valuable protection for the lender since, for example, an indemnity causes the burden of the primary debtor's insolvency, void contract, or unenforceable contract to fall on the indemnifier. The giver of an indemnity will not necessarily be discharged as a result of performance by the principal debtor of his obligations. All this is not necessarily true in the case of a guarantor.

Hudson states the extent of an indemnity's limited dependence on the obligation of the debtor as follows:

> An indemnity is a promise to make good any loss which the creditor suffers under a transaction whether or not the primary debtor would have been liable to make payment in relation to that loss.[45]

The practical significance of an indemnity is clear from actual cases. Banks' so-called guarantees frequently amount to indemnities or even actual loans to the guarantor, not least when they are lending to unincorporated bodies like religious institutions where they fear difficulty in establishing the personal liability of any particular party. They impose primary liability on the surety.

Gerrard and Doyle's bankers' manual proposes the following form:

> Indemnity. I agree that all sums of money which may not be recoverable from me on the basis of a guarantee by reason of legal limitation disability or incapacity on or of the principal shall nevertheless be recoverable from me as sole or primary debtor.[46]

A bank form supplied to the writer states:

> As a separate and independent stipulation . . . all moneys which cannot be recovered from me on the footing of a guarantee shall, nevertheless, be recoverable from me as sole or primary debtor in respect thereof and I shall repay the same on written demand by the bank.

Guarantee. The guarantor is less vulnerable than the indemnifier but remains distinctly vulnerable. Consider the guarantor envisaged by Andrews and Millett:

> The fact that the obligation of the principal is to pay on demand will not automatically mean that the creditor is obliged to make a demand on the surety as well. The guarantee may contain an express provision requiring such demand to be made on the principal before a demand is made on the surety: it may also contain a provision requiring the creditor to give the surety notice of default by the principal before he takes proceedings against the surety. It is more common, however, for a modern guarantee to contain a provision expressly negating any obligation on the part of the creditor to make a demand on the principal, to notify the surety of his default, or to take any other step before enforcing the guarantee.[47]

45 A. Hudson. *The Law of Finance* (London: Sweet and Maxwell, 2009), 587.

46 A. Gerrard and E. P. Doyle. *Branch Banking Law and Practice*, 2nd ed. (London: Northwick, 1991), Section 16.12 (4).

47 G. Andrews and R. Millett. *Law of Guarantees*, 5th ed. (London: Sweet and Maxwell, 2008), 10.

We are far from a situation in which lender must exhaust all available remedies against the primary debtor before dunning the guarantor. A leading statement of the underlying English law is consonant with the above:

On the default of the primary debtor causing loss to the creditor, the guarantor is, apart from special stipulation, immediately liable to the full extent of his obligation, without being entitled to require either notice of the default, or previous recourse against the principal, or simultaneous recourse against coguarantors.

Unless a demand upon the primary debtor is necessary in order to establish the primary debtor's own liability to the creditor, it is not necessary for the creditor, before proceeding against the guarantor, to request the primary debtor to pay. Nor is it necessary for the creditor to sue the primary debtor, although solvent, or to take arbitration proceedings against him even though the principal contract contains an arbitration clause, unless this is expressly stipulated for in the guarantee.

Nor is it necessary for the creditor to prosecute the primary debtor for any offence he may have committed unless this is rendered essential by the terms of the guarantee or to resort to securities for the guaranteed debt received by the creditor from the primary debtor.[48]

This plainly suggests that a guarantor under English law is not an *'arev stam*. However, the generality has to be qualified in ways that are relevant to our issue.[49]

If a creditor seeks to accelerate payments or if the principal liability is itself a guarantee, a demand must be made to the debtor. But only a demand is necessary, not exhaustion of all available remedies as would be required for permissibility under Jewish law. A guarantor remains liable even when, under a contract that requires the creditor to have availed himself, before resorting to the guarantor, of any bona fide securities belonging to the primary debtor that he holds, it is proved that the creditor neglected to pursue such remedies to the full. Clearly, these cases are unacceptable for a Jewish guarantor.

If, however, the guarantee is limited to sums payable by the primary debtor under a judgment or award, then any arbitration clause or other procedure would have to be acted upon and its outcome obeyed before dunning the guarantor. Subject to specific circumstances this might render a guarantorship permissible under Jewish law.

Andrews and Millett versus *Rowlatt*. Of greater interest and present relevance than the above restricted cases is the explicit conceptual debate among the authorities as to how far the creditor is compelled to exhaust remedies against the principal debtor before having recourse to the guarantor. It is convenient to head this debate *Andrews and Millett*[50] *versus Rowlatt*[51] since these eminent authorities epitomize opposing traditions. They are frequently quoted

48 *Halsbury's Laws of England* (2009). Accessed online May 2009 through LexisNexis service.

49 *Halsbury's Laws of England* (2009). Accessed online May 2009 through LexisNexis service.

50 G. Andrews and R. Millett, *Law of Guarantees*, 3rd ed. (London: FT Law and Tax, 1995). G. Andrews and R. Millett, *Law of Guarantees*, 5th ed. (London: Sweet and Maxwell, 2008).

51 D. Marks and G. Moss, *Rowlatt on Principal and Surety*, 4th ed. (London: Sweet and Maxwell, 1982). G. Moss and D. Marks, *Rowlatt on Principal and Surety*, 5th ed. (London: Sweet and Maxwell, 1999).

by judges in the leading cases. Andrews and Millett essentially argue that the debtor need not be dunned before dunning the guarantor.[52] Support for their position is qualified in leading cases, but the qualifications are insufficient for the purposes of Jewish law.

The decision in *Wright versus Simpson* (1802) concludes that, although immediately upon the default of the primary debtor the liability of the surety becomes a primary liability, it is not a condition precedent of such liability that the creditor should take any steps to enforce his claim against the principal debtor.[53]

But Lord Eldon in this case argues that the creditor should be restrained from first proceeding against the guarantor rather than any confiscated assets in a case where the guarantor could not take advantage of a creditor's rights with respect to these assets. And a creditor must demand from the borrower first but only in limited circumstances—namely, to the extent that demand by the creditor on the principal debtor is essential to complete the creditor's cause of action, as when the principal debtor is himself liable as surety.[54]

A creditor cannot simply contract that the guarantor will be considered as primary debtor. This will succeed only if the wording turns the contract into a contract of indemnity. But we have seen that even if the guarantor's position is secondary under English law it is not sufficiently so for the purpose of Jewish law. So yet again we return to a rather vulnerable guarantor who cannot require the creditor to proceed against the primary debtor before having recourse to the guarantor—the guarantor implied by the majority opinion in *Ewart versus Latta* (1865):

> Every surety is, apart from any term to the contrary, immediately liable to the full extent of his obligation without being entitled to require either notice of default, or previous recourse against the principal, or simultaneous recourse against co-sureties.
> Until (the surety) has discharged himself of his liability, until he has fulfilled his own contract, he has no right to dictate terms, to prescribe any duty or to make any demand upon his creditor.
> The creditor is entirely at liberty to pursue whichever remedies his contract affords him, without having to adopt a course of action at the compulsion of a person who remains his debtor. The guarantor has no right to either notice of default or to previous recourse against the principal or to simultaneous recourse against co-sureties.[55]

The Rowlatt position is more open-minded as to the extent of secondary liability of the guarantor, but their arguments have been persuasively refuted. Rowlatt maintains that the Scottish case of *Ewart versus Latta* (1865) applies in principle under English law. The guarantor cannot require the creditor to take a course of action, including pursuit of the debtor. But Rowlatt contends that there should be an

52 G. Andrews and R. Millett, *Law of Guarantees*, 5th ed. (London: Sweet and Maxwell, 2008). Chapter 11.

53 *Wright v Simpson [1802] 6 Ves. 734.*

54 *Wright v Simpson [1802] 6 Ves* at 1281.

55 *Ewart v Latta [1865] 4 Macq. 983.* at 987 and 989.

exception when there is an accessible solvent debtor or easily realizable securities.[56] The persuasive counterargument is that there are other remedies available to the creditor that provide access to these resources that do not amount to formal pursuit of the debtor as contended by Rowlatt.

Rowlatt's position might appear to be supported by the case of *Ex parte Goodman* (1818) to the effect that sureties have an equitable right requiring the creditor to first prove his debt in the primary debtor's bankruptcy before proceeding against a security given by the sureties.[57] But Andrews and Millett regard the decision as isolated and incorrect and quote authorities to this effect.[58]

The question of surety's equitable right arises where the creditor but not the surety can access relevant resources. This general rule has been debated in the case of *Laing Management versus Aegon Insurance* (1997).[59] The issue was whether a guarantor's status entitles him to call upon creditors to enforce their right of recovery against another party before seeking to enforce the bond. It was stated as a well-established principle of law that a surety could require a creditor to pursue first the remedy for the loss that was open only to him and not to the guarantor; and that, where a creditor has a claim against two funds, one of which the surety cannot make available, resort must be to the latter, available fund first. But it is already clear that *Laing* falls far short of the general requirement of priority of recourse to a debtor that would result in the contract being permissible under Jewish law.

Rowlatt further brings *Cottin versus Blane* (1795) to support his general contention that a guarantor can require a creditor first to sue the principal debtor.[60] The court held that the creditor was compelled to exhaust remedies against the French government, which was detaining a ship, before proceeding against the guarantor.[61] Andrews and Millett counter first that the creditor was not compelled to go against the principal debtor but against an independent fund provided by a third party not as security for the performance of the charter party but as compensation for its nonperformance; second that the fund was personal to the creditor and the surety could never have had recourse to it even by rights of subrogation; and third that the relief was granted only upon the surety paying the debt into court.[62]

Despite the above weight of evidence against them, Rowlatt's editors keep to the position of their predecessors and like-minded colleagues that it remains arguable on the basis of *Wolmershausen versus Gullick* (1891-4)[63] and its authorities that a creditor should be stayed from attempting to place the whole burden of the debt

56 G. Moss and D. Marks, *Rowlatt on Principal and Surety*, 5th ed. (London: Sweet and Maxwell, 1999), 144.

57 *Goodman, Ex parte [1818] 3 Madd. 373.*

58 G. Andrews and R. Millett, *Law of Guarantees*, 3rd ed. (London: FT Law and Tax, 1995), 319.

59 *Laing Management Ltd (formerly Laing Management Contracting Ltd) and another v Aegon Insurance Co (UK) Ltd [1997] 86 B.L.R. 70; 55 Con. L.R. 1, QBD (OR).*

60 G. Moss and D. Marks, *Rowlatt on Principal and Surety*, 5th ed. (London: Sweet and Maxwell, 1999), Chapter 7–03.

61 *Cottin v Blane 1 [1795] Anst. 544.*

62 G. Andrews and R. Millett, *Law of Guarantees*, 3rd ed. (London: FT Law and Tax, 1995), 319.

63 *Wolmershausen v Gullick [1891-4] 2 Ch. 514.*

upon a surety, at least in special circumstances.[64] Rowlatt is attributing to the guarantor an equitable right to compel the creditor to pursue the principal debtor first. This would satisfy the requirements of Jewish law, but the weight of counterargument appears not to permit reliance on Rowlatt's stance.

Andrews and Millett acknowledge that Rowlatt is consonant with Roman civil law and jurisdictions, whose domestic law is based on the Roman civil law.[65]

The decision in *Laing Management versus Aegon Insurance* (1997) summarizes the substantial majority—but still not consensus—of current opinion:

> Nevertheless it was a well-established principle of law that a surety could require a creditor to pursue first the remedy for the loss which was only open to him. . . . The law will intervene at the behest of the surety to require the creditor to pursue first the remedy for the loss which is open only to him. Thus de Colyar *Law of Guarantees* (3rd edn, 1897) p 321 stated (citing *Ex p Kendall* (1811) 17 Ves 514, [1805–13] All ER Rep 295):
>
> The other matter of equitable defence against a claim under the guarantee requiring notice is the surety's right to compel a creditor having a claim upon two funds, one of which the surety cannot make available, to resort to the latter fund first.

Rowlatt on Principal and Surety (4th ed., 1982, p. 133) says:

> The principle appears to have been that the surety had an equity to compel the creditor to recover the debt from the alternative source.

The editors refer to *Cottin v Blane* (1795) 2 Anstr 544, 145 ER 962, as does McGuinness *The Law of Guarantee* (Toronto, 1986, p. 196, fn 17):

> However, where the creditor has a right to recover the debt from a source *to which the surety lacks access*, it appears that the creditor must look to that source before claiming against the surety.

Phillips and O'Donovan, *The Modern Contract of Guarantee* (2nd ed., 1992, p. 461), also refer to *Cottin versus Blane*:

> This was not, therefore, a case of a creditor being compelled to seek compensation from the primary debtor before suing the guarantor but merely a case where the creditor-owner was compelled to claim first against a fund provided by a third party.[66]

Other parameters of the English law of surety. It has been shown that according to authoritative opinion and leading case law the Jewish guarantor in England does not enjoy priority of recourse to the borrower to the extent required by Jewish law.

64 G. Moss and D. Marks, *Rowlatt on Principal and Surety*, 5th ed. (London: Sweet and Maxwell, 1999), Chapter 7–03.

65 G. Andrews and R. Millett, *Law of Guarantees*, 5fth ed. (London: Sweet and Maxwell, 2008), Chapter 11–002.

66 *Laing Management Ltd (formerly Laing Management Contracting Ltd) and another v Aegon Insurance Co (UK) Ltd [1997] 86 B.L.R. 70; 55 Con. L.R. 1, QBD (OR).*

But this is still not the end of the story. Guarantees in English law have further parameters that we have not yet addressed. Do these further parameters generate permissible sets of circumstances or do they merely add to the stumbling blocks that confront a Jewish guarantor? The relevant parameters are coextensiveness, subrogation, and marshalling.

Coextensiveness. Coextensiveness means that the amount, incidence, and conditions of the guarantor's liability are no greater and no less than that of the primary debtor. This distinguishes it from a contract of indemnity. But this general rule can be varied by the court. The measurable impact of any such variation is illustrated in the case of *Moschi versus Lep Air Services Ltd (1973)*, which states that it is the performance of a duty that a guarantor guarantees.[67] This means that immediately this duty is breached the guarantor's liability is effectively equal to the full obligation of the primary debtor without the debtor having been dunned. This will include damages, even if not explicitly stated, since the guarantor is personally liable for the debt, default, or miscarriage in respect of the contract to the same extent as the principal debtor, being liable to pay the creditor a sum of money for the loss thereby sustained. The guarantor's liability is triggered without any proactive action against the primary debtor.

Subrogation. The right of subrogation entitles the guarantor to the same rights against the creditor as the primary debtor. Equity establishes this right to anticipate the unfairness that could befall a guarantor who pays a principal, secured debt if the creditor elects not to avail himself of any securities, priorities, and remedies that were available to the creditor before the principal obligation had been performed. Relevant to our discussion is the word "still" in Andrews and Millett's observation that subrogation operates "to treat the security, which is strictly speaking actually discharged by the payment to the creditor as if it were *still* available to the surety to assist him in recovering the amount he has paid in reduction or extinction of the principal debt."[68] If it is "still" available, this means that this security was deemed to figure in the relationship between the guarantor and the borrower from the outset. This helps to undermine permissibility under Jewish law, as further does the following:

> The surety's right to be subrogated to all the creditor's rights in respect of the guaranteed debt is traditionally said to arise at the moment he has paid in full all that he must pay to the creditor under the guarantee, unless he has waived the right. In fact the strict position is that the rights of the surety to the benefit of a security given by the principal *arise when the guarantee is entered into*, rather than upon payment or performance of the guaranteed obligation.[69]

This means that from the outset the guarantor has a claim against the debtor's pledged asset, which grows as interest accrues—which appears directly to breach the requirement of Jewish law.

67 *Moschi v Lep Air Services Ltd; sub nom Moschi v Rolloswin Investments Ltd; Lep Air Services v Rolloswin Investments [1973 Westzinthus [1833] 5 Ad. & B. 817.*

68 G. Andrews and R. Millett. *Law of Guarantees*, 5th ed. (London: Sweet and Maxwell, 2008), 456.

69 Ibid., 457.

Marshalling compels the creditor before suing the guarantor to look to a security even if it is one of which the guarantor cannot avail himself. Whereas the right of subrogation arises at the time the guarantee is entered into, the equitable right to marshal arises and reduces the guarantor's liability once a demand for payment has been made. The right is available before and after payment. *Re Westzinthus* (1833) makes the guarantor liable even when the creditor has failed to pursue available remedies against the primary debtor.[70] This clearly compounds the religious problem confronting the Jewish guarantor.

Conclusion

The conclusion can be stark and brief. A Jewish surety when contracting with a Jewish borrower or lender under a contract to which the English law of principal and surety applies transgresses, in the absence of special provisions in the contract, the prohibition against usury and usury-like transactions. This transgression will most frequently occur because English law does not require the lender to exhaust all remedies against a borrower before resorting to the guarantor. Furthermore, in practice, lending institutions tend to impose explicitly primary liability on the guarantor.

SELECTED BIBLIOGRAPHY

Andrews, G., and Millett, R. *Law of Guarantees*, 5th ed. London: Sweet and Maxwell, 2008.
Basri, E. *Ethics of Business Finance and Charity*. Jerusalem: Ktav, 1987.
Bible:
Genesis 43:9.
Exodus 22:24.
Leviticus 19:14; 25:36–37.
Deuteronomy 23:20–21.
Proverbs 6:1–3; 20:16.
Bloi, Y. Y. *Berit Yehudah*, 2nd ed. Jerusalem: privately published, 1979.
Bloi, Y. Y. *Berit Yehudah*, abbreviated version. Jerusalem: privately published, 1999.
Caro, R. Joseph. (Ottoman Palestine, 1488–1575). *Shulhan Arukh* (1565), *Yoreh De'ah* 170.
Dishon, Z. H. H. *Mishpat Ha-'Arev*. Jerusalem: Otzar Haposkim, 2000.
Halsbury's Laws of England. 2009. Available online via LexisNexis service.
Hertz, J. H. ed. *Pentateuch and Haftorahs*, 2nd ed, London: Soncino, 1960.
Hirshler, M., and Heishrik, R. H. *Torat Ribbit*. Jerusalem: privately published, 1989.

70 *Westzinthus, re (1833) 5 Ad. And B. 817.*

Hudson, A. *The Law of Finance*. London: Sweet and Maxwell, 2009.
Kanner, M. *A Matter of Interest*. New York: Feldheim, 2002.
Maimonides (Rambam), *Mishneh Torah, Malveh ve-Loveh* 1:1, 5:5.
Moss, G., and Marks, D. *Rowlatt on Principal and Surety*, 5th ed. London: Sweet and Maxwell, 1999.
Reisman, R. Israel. *The Laws of Ribbis*. New York: Mesorah, 1995.
Talmud Bavli:
Bava Batra 173, 174.
Bava Metsi'a 63b, 71, 75.
Wagschal, S. *Torah Guide for the Businessman*. New York: Feldheim, 1990.
Wagschal, S. *Torah Guide to Money Matters*. New York: Feldheim, 1996.

PART VI

JUDAISM AND ECONOMIC HISTORY

CHAPTER 28

BABYLONIAN JEWS AT THE INTERSECTION OF THE IRANIAN ECONOMY AND SASANIAN LAW

YAAKOV ELMAN

The Cultural Background

Our primary evidence for the history of Babylonian Jewry in Late Antiquity (the "talmudic" era) is the Babylonian Talmud (hereafter: the Bavli), which within its minutely detailed description of religious, lifestyle, economic, and social issues presents us with a portrait of the integration of Babylonian Jews within the economic life of the middle classes of the Sasanian Empire. However, since, like all other ancient texts, the Bavli is very short on statistics, the exact degree of integration in various areas is not clear. Thus, though most scholars agree on the importance of farming in the economic life of the Babylonian Jews of Late Antiquity, there has been some dispute over the extent to which Babylonian Jews engaged in commerce, and how that compared to the interest of the Iranians themselves in commerce.[1] While it is undeniable that Zoroastrianism—and thus the formal hierarchy of Sasanian society—placed farmers on a higher plane than artisans, for example, the Sasanian state was well-aware of the importance of commerce and trade for the health of its economy, and it fostered such activities. The summary description of

1 See Moshe Beer, *Amora'ei Bavel: Peraqim be-Hayyei ha-Kalkalah* (Bar Ilan UP, 1974), 156–57.

the role of commerce among Babylonian Jews offered by Moshe Beer in his exhaustive study of the economic role of the Babylonian sages, now more than thirty-five years old, may still serve us:

> In any case, there is no reason to doubt that the Jews in Babylonia took part in commerce within the wide-ranging Persian monarchy. Jews were merchants along with non-Jews, and, needless to say, along with their fellow Jews. However, we have no evidence of their participation in commerce before the third century of the common era. However, the fact of Jewish settlement along the length of the Euphrates, and to some extent along the banks of the Tigris, which were well-known paths of commerce already centuries before the common era, and which joined the land of East and West, and lands of the north and south, understandably influenced the lively participation of the Babylonian Jews in commerce, many generations before the rise of the Sasanian dynasty to power.[2]

The Sasanian state also fostered agriculture by building dams and encouraging the digging of canals, even by private enterprise.[3] Indeed, Mesopotamian agriculture during most of Sasanian times (224–550 CE) reached a level of intensity and productivity that it never had before—and would never reach again.[4] When the decline began, exacerbated in the sixth century by the destructive economic influence of the Black Plague that reached the Middle East in 542 CE,[5] the incessant wars with Rome and others, and possibly the catastrophic effects of a volcanic eruption around 535 that led to a world-wide economic crisis,[6] the talmudic period had already ended. That economic decline forms the backdrop for the many gaonic letters preserved in the Cairo Geniza seeking donations from abroad.

This brings us to the essential difference in the way the two communities were treated by their respective overlords. Unlike the Jews of Roman Palestine, who were considered by the Romans to be an intransigent and troublesome lot, the Babylonian Jews were a significant minority in a vital province; Mesopotamia was both the breadbasket of the Empire and the province most vulnerable to Roman invasion;[7] unlike Christians, who might become a fifth column once Christianity became a tolerated religion in 313, the Jews would support the regime if they were left alone.

2 Ibid., 158–59.

3 See Section II below.

4 See Peter Christensen, *The Decline of Iranshahr: Irrigation and Environments in the History of the Middle East, 500 B.C. to A.D. 1500* (Copenhagen: University of Copenhagen, 1993), 67–70.

5 Ibid, 81–84, and Yaakov Elman, "Marriage and Marital Property in Rabbinic and Sasanian Law," in C. Hezser, ed., *Rabbinic Law in Its Roman and Near Eastern Context*, (Tübingen: Mohr-Siebeck, 2003), 227–76, esp. 273–75.

6 Brian Fagan, *The Long Summer: How Climate Changed Civilization* (NY: Basic Books, 2004), 210, based on David Keys, *Catastrophe: An Investigation into the Making of the Modern World* (London: Century, 1999), 49–50.

7 Neusner is careful not to give a figure for the Jewish population of Mesopotamia, or, indeed, for the Persian Empire as a whole; see Jacob Neusner, *A History of the Jews in Babylonia, I. The Parthian Period* (BJS 62), 3rd printing (Chico, CA: Scholars Press, 1984), 15, "but suggests that the Jews formed minority communities in almost every city of the Euphrates Valley . . . and occupied large tracts of farmland outside of the major cities of Babylonia." Seth Schwartz accepts a figure of 500,000 for the Jews of Palestine in his *Imperialism and Jewish Society, 200 B.C.E. to 640 C.E.* (Princeton and Oxford: Princeton UP, 2001), 11, 41. We must posit a figure several times that for the Jews of Mesopotamia. See also Beer, 22–23, n. 14.

And, generally speaking, they were. As the prominent late-third-century authority R. Huna observed, the Babylonian "exiles" were at ease in Babylonia, as the other exiles—those in the Roman world—were not (B. Men. 110a). And, as noted, the Persian emperor wanted it that way. Indeed, Jews had resided in Mesopotamia, for the most part peacefully from even before Cyrus the Great conquered it in 539 BCE some 750 years before.

Due to the availability of reliable editions of Middle Persian texts—and, in particular, the so-called Sasanian Lawbook, the *Book of a Thousand Decisions*,[8] compiled by Farroxmard ī Wahraman around 620 CE, which allows us to trace the interaction of Persian and rabbinic law in the social and economic life of the Babylonian Jewish community—it is possible to draw a more nuanced portrait of the Babylonian Jewish community than was possible in the past. We can now add more flesh to the bones of the principle that "the law of the land is law."[9] However, most of the sources that can be dated in this work stem from the century and a half before its compilation—that is, to the end of the fourth century; and, while it contains earlier material, we need an independent source to verify that earlier date. Fortunately, the Bavli contains reports of the workings of Persian law for 250 years before that, and perhaps for a century still earlier, to the end of the Parthian period.[10]

Likewise, the Bavli itself is our best source for the acculturation of Babylonian Jews to Middle Persian cultural norms. Indeed, since it is an expression of the thoughts and the doings of the rabbinic elite, we are thus best informed in regard to them. And while in other cases this limits our understanding of Babylonian Jewry, in a paradoxical way in this case it expands our knowledge. Generally speaking, we would expect the rabbis, as the protectors and preservers of Jewish tradition, to have been extremely insular and withdrawn, fiercely protective of Jewish customs in all things, as the *haredim* are in our own time. Instead, we find them speaking (and punning) in Middle Persian, showing familiarity with Middle Persian literary motifs, Zoroastrian religious beliefs, and, along with their nonrabbinic countrymen, adopting Persian dress, food, and Persian customs even in intimate matters.[11] In short, they were thoroughly acculturated and thoroughly familiar with the customs, laws, and *business and agricultural practices* of their day.

Though the Bavli mentions the names of dozens of rabbinic authorities in its 1.8 million words—and while in a general sense it is a collective work, a compilation

8 Beer made as much use as he could of a much older and much less reliable edition, that of S. J. Bulsara, *The Laws of the Ancient Persians*, published in 1936. But that edition is now considered scientifically worthless.

9 See BT *Nedarim* 28a, *Gittin* 10b, *Bava Qamma* 113a, and especially *Bava Batra* 54b.

10 See my "Acculturation of Babylonian Jews at the End of the Parthian Period," presented at "Dynamiken der Religionsgeschichte zwischen Europa und Asien" zum Thema "religiöse Traditionen und Innovationen zwischen Indus und Adria," at the Kollegs für Geisteswissenschaftliche Forschung, Bochum, December 2–4, 2008, which will be published with the proceedings of that conference.

11 See my "Middle Persian Culture and Babylonian Sages: Accomodation and Resistance in the Shaping of Rabbinic Legal Tradition," in Charlotte Elisheva Fonrobert and Martin S. Jaffe, eds., *Cambridge Companion to Rabbinic Literature* (Cambridge UP, 2007), 165–97.

containing the words and deeds of hundreds of authorities of both Roman Palestine and Sasanian Babylonia, along with the odd mention of a Jew who lived elsewhere—its prime movers are some dozen very well-attested Babylonian rabbis whose names appear more than a thousand times each in this massive work, and whose creativity and insight animate it. Two of the best-known, Rava and Abaye, authorities of the second quarter of the fourth century, are mentioned some 3,800 and 2,500 times, respectively; Rav and Samuel, from the first half of the third century, are together mentioned some 3,000 times. The sheer accumulation of data, much of it highlighting the same dozen or so major rabbinic figures, allows us to construct a portrait of the major figures of the Bavli's world along with their times and their interaction with the problems of their world. These portraits confirm the characterization given above of the mainstream of rabbinic figures; Rav, Samuel, R. Yosef, R. Nahman, Rava, R. Papa, R. Ashi, and Ravina were comfortable in their environment, though not unmindful of its challenges. Other major figures, such as R. Yehudah, R. Hisda, Rabbah, and Abaye, continue to elude us, if only because (with the exception of Abaye), we lack the self-reflective comments and observations that allow us to delineate the personalities and cultural proclivities of the first group.

Several limitations must be borne in mind, however. One is that we are best informed about the *urban* rabbinic elite. However, since laws regarding the agricultural commandments constitute a large body of Jewish teaching, the Bavli contains a large body of material touching on agricultural life. Aside from that, questions of land tenure, sale, and the like will always be staples of any legal system. Luckily, the Mishnah legislates on questions bearing on agricultural laborers, share-croppers and tenant farmers, and so on, and the Bavli provides us not only with commentary on those mishnahs, but also enough case histories to give us a sometimes vivid picture of agricultural life. We must also remember that, on the whole, ancient cities were much smaller than modern ones, and, despite the lack of modern communications, the disjunction between city and countryside was much smaller than it is nowadays. As such, urban rabbinic authorities were often called upon to adjudicate cases regarding agricultural land, and they themselves often owned land that share-croppers or tenant-farmers worked for them. Indeed, despite the greater danger of the "evil eyes" of urban passersby on farming land located in the vicinity of a city or town, the advantages of such an arrangement were held to outweigh the disadvantages (BT *Bava Metzia* 107a–b).

Still, as noted above, the Bavli does not provide us with the statistical information necessary for us to gain a true picture of economic activity. How many (or what percentage of) farms were let out to share-croppers? How many to tenant farmers? There is no way of knowing. Nevertheless, with its insistence of following the *minhag ha-medinah*, the "custom of the country," the Bavli will often provide us with an insight into the typical arrangement or arrangements. In this respect, *minhag ha-medinah* is much more important than the rule of *dina de-malkhuta*—that is, governmental law.

We are particularly well-informed about the major community of Mahoza, a suburb of the Persian winter-capital of Ctesiphon, which had been established centuries before on the east bank of the Tigris, south of Baghdad. Ctesiphon was the cultural and religious center of the Empire as well as its political center. Thus, the Jewish community of Mahoza, located directly across the river, was among the most—if not the most—highly acculturated and cosmopolitan in Mesopotamia; it hosted both the exilarch and the bishop of Ctesiphon, heads of their respective communities. In contrast, Pumbedita on the Euphrates and one hundred kilometers from the capital, was much more insular and felt itself more independent of the exilarch.[12] Mahozans were wealthy, cosmopolitan, canny,[13] and skeptical of rabbinic authority; they had the reputation of being perspicacious[14] and delicate (BT *Shabbat* 109a); the women were pampered (BT *Pesahim* 50b) and idle (BT *Shabbat* 23b), and the men pursued still more wealth.[15] In their search for luxuries, they shopped in Ctesiphon, as we shall see.

Having set the stage, let us now examine the rabbinic interaction with Sasanian economic law by examining three cases in which Babylonian Jewish activities impinged on the economic and legal life of the Sasanian Empire. One will refer to commercial life, one to irrigation, and one to the supply of citrons for religious purposes.

Two bridges joined Mahoza, or Be Ardashir, on the west bank of the Tigris with Ctesiphon, the imperial winter capital. Ctesiphon was not only the capital; it was also the metropolis of the Iranian Empire *and* a terminus for the Silk Road out of China. While staples were bought locally, Mahozans seem often to have gone "downtown" for their luxury shopping, presumably for goods such as silk, glass, and the Sasanian silverwork that continues to command interest on the open market. As the Talmud remarks in passing, the merchants of Ctesiphon were familiar with the signatures (*hatimot yada*) of the Mahozans, but the reverse was not the case (BT *Gittin* 6b).

Before proceeding, however, it would be well to clarify the legal point in which this socioeconomic observation is imbedded. The signatures of witnesses on bills of divorce that are executed in one city and presented in another require validation, either because there is reason to suspect that the people in the town in which the divorce decree was executed are not familiar with the intricacies of writing such a document, or in circumstances where it is likely that the signatures or seals are not known. In this connection, R. Hisda, a late third-century and early fourth-century authority, is reported to have required validation even from bills of divorce brought from Ctesiphon to Be Ardashir, but not the reverse. The redactors in BT *Gittin* 6a explain the reason for this is the familiarity of the merchants of Ctesiphon with the signatures or seals of the Mahozans, while the reverse was not so:

12 See my "Acculturation to Elite Persian Norms in the Babylonian Jewish Community of Late Antiquity," in *Neti'ot David*, ed. by E. Halivni, Z. A. Steinfeld, and Y. Elman (Jerusalem: Orhot, 2004), 31–56.

13 See BT *Berakhot* 59b, where Rava explains why the inhabitants of Mahoza are *harifei*.

14 BT *Berakhot* 59b. Rava's characterization of them as *harifei* seems to have been intended as positive.

15 BT *Gittin* 6a (Mahozan's are always on the move), and see BT *Bava Metzia* 59a, where Rava advises the Mahozans on how to become wealthy—by honoring their wives.

> R. Hisda would require [a statement of confirmation by the ones delivering bills of divorce] from Ctesiphon to Weh Ardaxshir, but from Weh Ardaxshir to Ctesiphon he would not require. . . . [The reason was not that the people of the Capital District were not familiar with the requirement that bills of divorce be written specifically for the couple concerned,] but rather, everyone holds [that the reason for the confirmation] is that [such signatures] must be verified, and these [the people of Weh Ardaxshir] go there [to Ctesiphon] to market, and those [the inhabitants of the Ctesiphon] know the signatures of these [the people of Weh Ardaxshir], but these do not know [the signatures] of these. What is the reason? They [the inhabitants of Wed Ardaxshir] are busy with their marketing [in Ctesiphon].

Note that, exceptionally, here Mahoza is referred to by its Persian name, Weh Ardaxshir, a designation used in texts that have an Iranian coloration (BT *Yoma* 19a, BT *Yevamot* 37b, BT *Eruvin* 57b, and here in BT *Gittin* 6a); that is why I have rendered the name in its Middle Persian form. Another point that should be noted is that, though the phrase *hatimot yada*, "signatures," might refer to seals, in BT *Bava Batra* 161a, where the signatures of prominent rabbis are described, it is most likely that signatures are intended. Thus, R. Hisda would sign his name with a large letter S—that is, a *samekh*. In either case, however, it is clear that the transactions mentioned involved documents—a point that will become important when we consider the legal system that governed such sales.

Here the question of what the Mahozans went downtown to buy becomes important. As we know from scattered talmudic references, staples were sold in Mahoza; these included dried figs (BT *Bava Metzia* 22a), *tzahanta*-fish (BT *Avodah Zatah* 40a), and wine (BT *Bava Metzia* 83a, see BT *Avodah Zarah*, 57a–58a)—we know that Mahozans were known as wine drinkers (BT *Ketubot* 65a), as opposed to more plebian beer drinkers. Rams were sold in neighboring Mabkrakta (BT *Eruvin* 47b), and Mahoza produced a particular type of mat (BT *Sukkah* 20b). Thus, there was no point in going downtown for staples that were available in Mahoza. Such an expedition would have involved the purchase of the luxury goods of an empire, including silks from China.

St. John Simpson quotes from a seventh-century Chinese report that lists the following products that were available in Ctesiphon:[16]

> white ivory, lions, ostrich eggs, genuine pearls, mock pearls, glass, coral, amber, ceramic glazes, agate, crystal, emerald [?], gold, silver, zinc ore, diamonds, red beads, steel, iron, bronze, tin, vermilion, mercury, damask brocade, white cotton cloth, felt, woolen rugs, red roebuck hide, as well as frankincense [?], saffron, storax, "dark wood" and other aromatics, black pepper, pippal [pepper], crystallised honey, date palms, monkshoods and wolfbanes, myrobalan, oak galls, "salty green," orpiment and other products (Miller 1959)

16 St. John Simpson, "Mesopotamia in the Sasanian Period: Settlement Patterns, Arts and Crafts," in John Curtis, ed., *Mesopotamia and Iran in the Parthian and Sasanian Periods: Rejection and Revival, c. 238 BC–AD 642*: Proceedings of a Seminar in memory of Vladimir G. Lukonin (London: British Museum Press, 2000), 57–66, see 62–63. See also and from the bibliography: Miller, R. A., *Accounts of Western Nations in the History of the Northern Chou Dynasty* (Berkeley and Los Angeles, 1959).

While Mahozans may have passed on the lions, there are enough products here to tempt the most discerning Mahozan eye. At any rate, whatever, the details of their purchases, the redactional explanation of R. Hisda's decision, which most likely dates to the century *before* the Chinese report, does attest to the Mahozans's shopping habits. And since the merchants of Ctesiphon were familiar with their signatures or seals, we must assume that the Mahozans were "repeat customers." R. Hisda's glancing comment thus gives us a vivid detail regarding the daily interaction of an upscale community with its non-Jewish neighbors. For, on the whole, we must assume that these merchants of Ctesiphon were overwhelmingly non-Jews; there would have been Zoroastrians, Christians of various stripes, Manichaeans, Buddhists, Hindus, perhaps a stray pagan Babylonian or two. All were represented in the glorious multireligious mosaic that was the Sasanian Empire.[17]

Thus, since he mentions *hatimot yada*, "signatures" or perhaps "seals," we may understand that these transactions were facilitated by documents, in accord with Persian law, which allowed ownership of movables to be transferred without *traditio* or *meshikhah*—that is, without being handed over to the buyer, but simply by deed. We cannot assume that the Mahozans kept going over to Ctesiphon to buy real estate over and over again.

It is thus overwhelmingly probable that these merchants were mostly non-Jews, and it is thus significant that R. Nahman, a contemporary of R. Hisda and a Mahozan, allows even an idolator (that is, a non-Jew) to be entrusted with the task of *writing* as religiously sensitive a document as a bill of divorce, even though the non-Jew is disqualified from either *delivering* it or acting as a *witness* (BT *Gittin* 23a).[18] However, other, less religiously sensitive documents *could be witnessed* by non-Jews. Indeed, R. Papa would employ non-Jews to read documents written in Middle Persian and brought to his court for collection:

> When a Persian document drawn up in a non-Jewish court was brought before him, he used to have two non-Jews read it, one without the other, without telling them what it was for (lit., "talking in his simplicity"), and [if they agreed], he would recover [on the strength of] it even from mortgaged property.[19]

Anyone familiar with Pahlavi script will understand R. Papa's problem: Evidently he could understand spoken Middle Persian, and in this he was not atypical of the rabbis, but reading it was another matter! R. Papa's practice of recognizing Persian documents as valid conforms with the redactional comment in BT *Gittin* 10b, appended to M *Gittin* 1:5, which validates such documents, even when *the witnesses themselves were non-Jews*:

> Mishnah: All documents which are accepted in non-Jewish courts, even when they that signed them were non-Jews, are valid [for Jewish courts] except writs of

17 See my "Middle Persian Culture" (n. 11 above), 166–68.

18 My student, Ari Lamm, has examined R. Nahman's positions on these matters in an unpublished paper.

19 BT *Gittin* 19b.

> divorce or emancipation [of slaves]. R. Shimon says: These also are valid; they were only pronounced [to be invalid] when drawn up by unauthorized persons [*hedyotot*].
>
> Gemara: [Our mishnah] lays down a comprehensive rule in which no distinction is made between a sale and a gift. We can understand that the rule should apply to a sale, because the purchaser acquires the object of sale from the moment that he hands over the money in their [the non-Jewish judges'] presence, and the document is a mere corroboration, for if he did not hand over the money in their presence, they would not take the risk of drawing up a document of sale for him. But with a gift [it is different]. Through what [does the recipient] obtain ownership? Through this document, [is it not]? And this document is a mere piece of clay!—Said Samuel: The law of the government is [valid] law [and binding on Jews]. Or if your prefer, I can reply: Instead of "writs of divorce" in the mishnah, read: "[except [documents] similar to writs of divorce [that have religious consequences, or to unofficial documents or documents issued by an unofficial court]."[20]

What then was the purpose of the documents used in Ctesiphon? Two or three possibilities come to mind. They could be sales contracts, or bills of sale, or IOUs. Of course, if a Jew bought on credit, his contract of sale would have to be written with rabbinic strictures in mind, but, since we are assuming that most of the merchants with which the Mahozans dealt were not Jewish, this was not a problem; we will thus leave that issue aside. Since the Mahozans were repeat shoppers, it seems likely that any one of these, or even a combination of such documents, were signed in a single transaction. We may assume that the documents generally related to wholesale deals, as for example the *terasha* documents discussed in BT *Bava Metzia* 65a by R. Nahman, R. Papa, and R. Hamma—all Mahozans, or rabbis who had studied in Mahoza; retail sales were presumably cash-and-carry. In any case, both wholesale and retail transactions could involve the question of safe delivery of the items contracted for, a concern that is evident in both Rabbinic and Sasanian law. It is particularly noteworthy that R. Hamma's *terasha* involved his taking responsibility for the safety of the merchandise until it was sold, at least according to the Rashbam.[21]

However, rabbinic law conceives of *meshikhah* as the prescribed mode of transfer for movables, which were not generally transferred by document or *hazaqah* (*usucapio*), but by *meshikhah* or *halipin*, literally "exchange" or "barter," by which a vessel, or even, in later times, a hankerchief, symbolized the transfer.[22] The latter is described in R. Isaac Herzog's magisterial *Main Institutions of Jewish Law* as follows: "A and B agree to barter a certain article, or articles, the moment A has taken possession of B's article or articles (the subject matter of the agreed barter), B becomes the legal owner of the corresponding article or articles, though still in the

20 So according to Nahmanides, Rashba, Ritva, et al.

21 See *Rashbam*, BT *Bava Metzia* 65a, s.v. *amar R. Hamma*.

22 See mQiddushin 1:5, and Qid 26b, and Ritva Qid 27a, s.v. *Rava*, and see Ramban B.M. 47b, s.v. *devar Torah*. See also Sh.A. H.M. 198.1.

possession of A."[23] What then was the purpose of the *hatimot yada* of Git 6a, the "signatures" by which the Mahozans did business in Ctesiphon? There are two problems with assuming that the transfer of the item was accomplished by deed: First, according to rabbinic law, deeds apply to real property, or to things that are biblically deemed as such (e.g., slaves). Second, the rabbis required *traditio* ("handing over") as a means of transfer because they feared that the seller would not feel obligated to assure the safety of such property in the case of hazard before the purchase actually reached the buyer. If rabbinic law applied to these sales, we have a third problem: According to some opinions, *traditio* did not apply to transactions involving non-Jews. If these transactions were then governed by rabbinic law, R. Hisda must have referred to contracts regarding supply and payment of wholesale goods, but perhaps also IOUs for retail sales. However, if this were so, we may well wonder why the rabbis deprived Jews of the protection afforded by *meshikhah*/*traditio*.

The protection afforded by the enactment of *meshikhah*, that the seller feel responsibility for the safe delivery of the goods sold—which Roman law did not provide—was indeed provided by the Sasanian rule of *drust darišnīh*, a written clause that put such responsibility on the shoulders of the seller.

For convenience, I have translated Macuch's German:

> MHD 6.13–16: If two men together sell one thing to a man, and prepare one deed: "We guarantee [the goods]." Wahrām said: "Then is he [the buyer] permitted to demand the guarantee from whichever [of the two sellers] he wishes.[24]

And see Macuch's note 10 on p. 99:

> That is, the sellers of some goods make themselves responsible to provide a guarantee, *drust dārēm*, "we provide a guarantee." The buyer can demand fulfillment of the contract from either of the designated representatives in the event that the buyer is in dispute with a third party.

This in turn helps us solve another riddle. In three passages in the Bavli (BT *Bava Metzia* 47b–48a, BT *Avodah Zarah* 71a–b, BT *Bekhorot* 13a–b), the question of whether *meshikhah* is valid in transactions with non-Jews is debated. At least two Babylonian sages seem to rule that it is not, and the question naturally arises as to why they would rule in a way that was disadvantageous to Jews in their dealings with non-Jews. Given the integration of the Jewish minority within the much larger non-Jewish economy, these rabbis could hardly be attempting to discourage Jews from dealing with non-Jews, and indeed the great medieval authority, Rabbenu Tam (c. 1100–1171), rules that *traditio* is valid in dealing with non-Jews. One possible solution to this conundrum is that, as the discussion in Bava Metzi'a makes clear, the negative position is based on one interpretation of Lev. 24:14. In Mesopotamia,

23 Isaac Herzog, *The Main Institutions of Jewish Law, Volume One: The Law of Property* (London and New York: Soncino, pb. ed., 1980), 179.

24 Maria Macuch, *Rechtskasuistik und Gerichtspraxis zu Beginn des siebenten Jahrhunderts in Iran: Die Rechtssammlung des Farrohmard i Wahrāmān* (Wiesbaden: Harrassowitz, 1993), text, 88, translation, 93, see n. 11 on 99. References will be accompanied by the usual Iranist acronym, MHD or MHDA, depending on the manuscript.

this stringent position could be put into practice because *minhag he-medinah*, the ordinary course of business practice, would have protected the buyer in any case. There is much more to be said on this issue, but, for now, we may see this as a case of rabbinic attention to the interaction of the two legal systems.[25]

II

The Sasanian regime encouraged private initiative in both commercial and agricultural activities, and the rabbis did their best to enable the Babylonian Jewish community to take advantage of these opportunities. They were also alive to the possibilities that Sasanian law provided in terms of legal concepts or institutions that were lacking in the rabbinic tradition up to their own time. We have already examined a case of commercial interaction involving sale. In the following we will examine interaction between rabbinic and Sasanian law in regard to agriculture, land tenure, and irrigation.[26]

This involves a somewhat gnomic report regarding taking possession of a riverbed. According to the Babylonian Talmud, riverbanks were reserved for certain public uses. For example, porters pulling boats upstream by ropes were to be allowed sufficient space on the banks so as to prevent their falling into the river.[27] Additionally, riverbanks and canal banks were used to unload cargo from waterborne traffic.[28] According to Rashi (1040–1105), this was also a recognized public use of the land.[29] As such, planting was not permitted within four cubits of the river so as not to undermine the riverbank. Furthermore, agricultural land was at a premium in Babylonia, both because of the density of population,[30] and because of the silting up of irrigation canals that had been a problem as far back as Old Babylonian times, two thousand years before.[31] Indeed, the so-called Code of Hammurapi makes maintenance of the riverbank or canal bank the responsibility of the owner of the abutting field.[32]

25 The issue is far more complex than the matter of protection, however, and I have dealt with the details in a paper presented at University College, London, which will be published in the proceedings of that conference.

26 For more details, see my "'Up to the Ears' in Horses' Necks: On Sasanian Agricultural Policy and Private 'Eminent Domain'," *JSIJ* 3 (2004): 95–149.

27 BT *Bava Metzia* 107b; R. Yehuda advises that surveyors allow sufficent space alongside the river; see Rashi ad loc., s.v. *mele kattafei.*

28 BT *Bava Metzia* 23b.

29 BT *Bava Metzia* 108a s.v. *hai man.*

30 See Beer, 50.

31 R. J. Forbes, *Studies in Ancient Technology*, volume I (Leiden: E. J. Brill, 1971), 25. See also the remarks of Joseph Wiesehöfer, *Ancient Persia from 550 BC to 650 AD*, translated by Azizeh Azoudi (London: I. B. Taurus, 2001), 203 s.v. 2. on agriculture, and the literature cited there.

32 See Code of Hammurapi, pars. 53–54; see G. R. Driver and John C. Miles, eds., *The Babylonian Laws* (Oxford: Clarendon Press, 1968), vol. II, 30–31, and the commentary in vol. I, 150–53.

It is in this context that we must understand a report regarding Sasanian rules on land tenure preserved in the Babylonian Talmud. The statement is transmitted in the name of Samuel, a Babylonian Jewish authority (d. 254) who is reported by the Babylonian Talmud to have been on close terms with Shapur I (241–270), a not unreasonable report given what we know of that monarch's religious interests, his protection of Mani, and Samuel's conciliatory policy regarding the new regime.

> Samuel said: That one who took possession of [land on a] riverbank is an impudent person,[33] but we certainly cannot remove him.
>
> But nowadays that the Persian write [in a title], "It [a field on a river] is acquired by you as far as the depth of the water[34] reaching up to the horse's neck, we certainly remove him."[35]

Rabbenu Tam (Rabbi Jacob Tam, c. 1100–1171), Rashi's grandson and arguably the greatest of the Tosafists, suggests that the "impudence" is on the other foot, so to speak. The reason that the interloper is removed, according to Rabbenu Tam, is that "since the king wrote thus to him [that he now owns the margin of the riverbed—Y.E.], he would be impudent to take possession [only] until the water, and therefore we fine him and remove him from the whole [piece of] land [if he does not take possession of the whole parcel including the submerged portion]."[36] According to this interpretation, the interloper was impudent not because he opposed local custom, but because he had not carried out his obligations to the government.

Rabbenu Tam's explanation is particularly apt, since it allows us to understand the later rabbis as working with the government enactment rather than against it. This is not only because of the dictum that "the law of the state is [valid] law," but also because, as we shall see immediately below, in this case government policy was in accord with rabbinic concerns. For it is clear from the parallel to our case in the Sasanian Lawbook that this Persian enactment was intended to encourage the upkeep of irrigation canals and the proper distribution of water; these goals were a constant source of concern to the rabbis as it was to the government. Thus, the rabbis allowed dredging and clearing operations even on the intermediate days of a festival.

The relevant paragraph in the Sasanian Lawbook is found in a chapter concerning the joint construction of a canal by two partners:

> MHD 85:8–11: An irrigation canal that a man makes on his own land or to *hambaragān*-land [land belonging to partners who share in the profits], which he has dug to the depth [lit. "height"] of "an ear," [and] when around it [this land] there is land belonging to others, then those people who are the owners of the

33 MS Florence has *miqari hatzifa*, "is called an impudent one

34 Tosafot ha-Rosh quotes the word as *ba-mayim* "in the water," rather than *maya* "water." The meaning is the same.

35 BT *Bava Metzia* 108a.

36 See Moshe Hershler and Yehoshua Dov Grodetzki, *Tosafot ha-Rosh al Masekhet Bava Metzia* (Jerusalem: Hayyim Gitler, 1959/60), 261a–b.

> land inside the field are not allowed to dig canals on their own land without the agreement [of the partners] [without] payment for that canal, and outside the field they are not allowed to dig another canal except without damaging the land [of those] to whom the canal belongs.[37]

The second part of our talmudic passage and the Sasanian Lawbook relate roughly to the same period of time. Moreover, as problems with supplying water for agricultural purposes existed in both Babylonia and Iran, albeit for different reasons, this chapter of the Sasanian Lawbook may be as applicable to Babylonia as to Iran. If so, the two sources are parallel or overlapping and may thus supplement each other. In this case, the Talmud itself attributes the rule to the "Persians" who "write." Thus, the Iranian phrase "up to the ears" used in the Sasanian Lawbook would refer specifically to *horses'* ears, and the talmudic phrase "up to the neck" refers specifically to the *top* of the neck—that is, to the ears. Each source provides a piece of information lacking in the other. Thus, the owner of the Babylonian riverbank would gain possession of a considerable extent of riverbed, depending on its slope.

As Rabbenu Tam explained, it would seem that a riverbank owner had the responsibility, under Persian law, of improving his river-edge property; this would justify his having taken possession of what had been common land. If he did not, apparently he could be removed, as Rabbenu Tam suggested. The redactional comment thus means: The onus is now on him and, if he does not improve the waterfront property—either by building a quay or planting a taxable crop on it, or on the submerged portion of the land in the river, as in the case of rice cultivation, or, finally, as we have seen from the Sasanian Lawbook, digging a new canal—he can be removed by his neighbors, and the riverbank reverts to its previous common use, for boat haulers and the like.

We must consider the question of the interloper's intentions as well as the Persian authorities' policy regarding economic exploitation of the riverbed. Adams suggests that rice became a commercial crop in Sasanian times; one wonders whether, indeed, rice cultivation could have been possible for some part of these submerged lands. Though such cultivation over the riverbank, rather than in paddies, would seem to be a hazardous enterprise, since a valuable crop will be planted as much as possible, and as rice was one of the crops that was taxed, which suggests it was valuable, it may be that this was one of the uses to which the land was put.

Likewise, if the height of a Sasanian horse's neck runs to around four feet,[38] this is much deeper than the ordinary irrigation channel or ditch in Babylonia, which

37 The text is found in Anahit Perikhanian, *The Book of a Thousand Judgements*, translated by Nina Garsoian (Mazda Publishers in association with Bibliotheca Persica, 1997), 200–2, and in Maria Macuch, *Rechtskasuistik und Gerichtspraxis zu Beginn des siebenten Jahrhunderts in Iran: Die Rechtssammlung des Forrohmard i Wahrāmān* (Wiesbaden: Harrassowitz, 1993, vol. II, 549, 552, and nn. 1–2 on 555–57. Macuch's edition is by far the superior one, and the interested reader is advised to consult it. This translation reflects the helpful comments of Prof. Macuch in a pleasant meeting in Ravenna on October 9, 2003. My thanks to her for her help in this matter and many others; the responsibility for any errors remains mine.

38 See my "'Up to the Ears' in Horses' Necks: On Sasanian Agricultural Policy and Private 'Eminent Domain'," *JSIJ* 3 (2004), 130–31.

seems to have run to about ten handbreadths or less—something less than four feet deep.[39] The land allotted within the riverbed was thus quite a bit deeper. This indicates that the canal opened by the partners was a major project indeed, and one that would seem to have been dug as an entrepreneurial enterprise intended not only to irrigate the partners' field(s) but also to provide water to surrounding fields—at a price. Or, perhaps, taking possession of the underwater property was in preparation for building a quay for wharfage.

This would also account for the use of a measure of depth that would yield variable amounts of riverbed, depending on slope and flood. First of all, the Sasanians could hardly avoid using such a measure, since they could not calculate height above sea level as a more uniform measure.[40] But the consequences were uniform even if the measure was not. Once the builder built his quay or dug his canal to the point of *gōš bālāy at the time of the construction*, the canal or quay was his for *commercial exploitation* and, of course, for *taxation* purposes as well.

Other provisions of this chapter indicate that commercial exploitation was indeed most likely the intent. Moreover, it would seem that the government's policy was to encourage endeavors of this sort. Of course, Zoroastrianism encourages economic endeavors, and agricultural activities in particular.[41] But it was also good economic, political, and social policy, especially for a government continually involved in wars and strapped for cash. Early "oriental despotisms" all over the world arose to manage irrigation systems.

The following sections of the Sasanian Lawbook give the partner who wants to expand operations the right to do so and deprives the more conservative partner of a veto. Thus, MHD 85:11–86:2 rules that:

> Two men dig a canal; until the completion, whenever one digs, the other is not authorized [to refrain from] digging, otherwise he yields his own share [of the income] to the other.

The following sections are variations on this theme. In the next, the conservative partner loses his share in the profits if he does not agree, and the one following that even deprives the conservative partner of his security.

From the foregoing, and much else in the Sasanian Lawbook, it would seem that Sasanian feudalism was, as to be expected, capitalistic in nature; family-based estates established and ran enterprises that in other systems of government would be done by the government. The canal is operated as a profit-making enterprise, and *the partner who wishes to increase the supply of water has the law on his side*; it is government policy to encourage the construction of irrigation systems under private control and to encourage those private entrepreneurs who wish to increase their profits by increasing the water supply.

39 See BT *Bava Qama* 50b.

40 Or, as Ionides reports, the "G.T.S.," the "Great Trigonometric Survey," which relates water gauges to the sea level at Fao; see Ionides, p. 14.

41 See the selection of texts in Beer, 49–52, and see O. Klíma, *Mazdak: Geschichte eine sozialen Bewegung im Sassanidischen Persien* (Prague: Ceskoslovenske Akademie Ved, 1957), 28.

The Iranian jurisconsults were well-aware, as the Babylonian (Jewish?) saying has it, that "the pot of partners is neither hot nor cold"[42]—that partnerships tend to compromise and end up "neither here nor there." Indeed, in one of its uses in the Babylonian Talmud (Eruvin 3a), it is employed by Rava of Parziqiya,[43] an early fifth-century authority, to distinguish between private and public needs. The latter tend to be neglected, in his opinion. It is clear from the provisions of the Sasanian Lawbook that we have examined,[44] and others as well, that public policy was strongly on the side of development or irrigation resources.

It is interesting to note that Rava, the great mid-fourth-century authority of Mahoza, directly across the river from Ctesiphon, the Persian capital, also gave the more active partner the greater rights.

> Rava also said: If two men accept an *ᶜisqa*[45] and make a profit, and one says to the other: "Come, let us divide now" [before the time for winding up]: then if the other objects [saying]: "Let us earn more profits," he can legally restrain him [from closing the transaction]. [For] if he claims, "Give me half the profits," he can reply, "The profit is mortgaged for the principal [in case there are subsequent loses]. If he proposes," Give me half the profits and half of the principal, "he can answer," [The parts of the] *ᶜisqa* are interdependent. "If he proposes," Let us divide the profit and the principal and should you incur a loss I will bear it with you, he can answer, "No. The luck of two is better than that of one."[46]

III

Familiarity with Sasanian law and legal institutions apparently also suggested solutions to pressing problems, solutions that opened new possibilities within rabbinic law itself, as our next example will illustrate.[47] As we shall see, the rabbis did not "borrow" a foreign institution, but they took the concept and applied it to the need of their community, suitably altered to fit the rabbinic system.

The rabbinic interpretation of Lev. 23:40 required the taking of a palm branch, a citron, and two other botanical species that are not usually in short supply.

42 See BT *Eruvin* 3b and BT *Bava Batra* 24b.

43 Probably Bazīqiyā near Mata Mahasya near Sura; see Aharon Oppenheimer, *Babylonia Judaica in the Talmudic Period* (Wiesbaden: Reichert, 1983), 345–47, esp. 346; Obermeyer, 227, who identifies it as near Baghdad, is almost certainly wrong.

44 See "Horses' Necks," 134–40.

45 *Isqa* (lit., "occupation," "business," "merchandise"' as a business arrangement by which one invests money with a trader, who trades with it on the joint behalf of both partners. To avoid the prohibition of usury, the investor took a greater share of the risk than of the profit; for example, he received either half of the profit but bore two-thirds of the loss, or a third of the profit but bore half of the loss (see BT *Bava Metzia* 69).

46 BT *Bava Metzia* 105a.

47 The legal aspects of the following discussion are examined in greater detail in my "Returnable Gifts in Rabbinic and Sasanian Law," *Irano-Judaica* VI (Jerusalem: Makhon Ben Zvi, 2008), 139–184.

However, shortages could occur; according to the Yerushalmi, once, during a sabbatical year, R. Abbahu brought palm branches from Alexandria.[48] Citrons were a greater problem, and shortages could be chronic, since cultivation of citrons (*citrus medica*) is beset with a number of problems that do affect their supply.[49] First of all, though the citron may have been the first citrus fruit to have been introduced to the Mediterranean world, oranges and lemons surpassed it in terms of desirability and ease of cultivation. Generally speaking, once the latter became available, citrons could not compete, making them uneconomical to cultivate, at least in the Roman Empire. In Babylonia, there were other problems.

At any rate, since the citron flowers all year round, it becomes dormant at temperatures above 95°F. These constrictions affected the supply in Mesopotamia with particular severity, and Babylonian Jews could not rely on home-grown citrons when they needed them for ritual purposes, since temperatures in Iraq regularly go above 120°F in July and August—just before the festival. Furthermore, since the citron was considered a royal fruit in Iran, and thus a luxury item, it would have been more expensive for that reason as well.[50] Thus, King Shapur serves his guests a citron in the story in A.Z. 76a–b.

In Palestine, the problem was different: The weather was more favorable, on the one hand, but the citron's need for large amounts of water may have required irrigation in years of sparse rainfall. Again, the fact that citrons did not have a ready non-Jewish market would have militated against a ready non-Jewish supply.

Thus, shortages in the two centers of rabbinic culture had different origins; moreover, we might have thought that the Palestinian problem was less severe than the Babylonian one. However, settlement patterns may have affected the supply, since cultivation of citrons was and is carried out in the coastal plain, and not in the Galilee, where most of the Jewish population of late Roman times was concentrated. Could there have been a problem of organizing supply from the Sharon to the Galilee? The demand in the Galilee may not have been great enough to induce orchard owners of the Sharon to devote much in the way of resources to such a marginal crop—one that was in demand by a relatively small market only once a year. Thus, the shortages would have been caused by lack of demand as much as lack of supply.

The shortage and expense of citrons in Babylonia had legal effects: The Yerushalmi reports, and implicitly accepts, two Babylonian leniencies in regard to the use of citrons. Indeed, JT *Sukkah* 3:10 (54a) not only provides the leniency in the name

48 JT *Eruvin* 3:9 (21c); for the correct text, see Shaul Lieberman, *Al ha-Yerushalmi*, Jerusalem: 1929, 8.

49 The information presented here was gleaned from Herbert John Webber, Leon Dexter Batchelor, *et al.*, eds., *The Citrus Industry* (Berkeley and Los Angeles: University of California, 1945). See also Edward A. Ackerman, "Influences of Climate on the Cultivation of Citrus Fruits," *Geographical Review* 28 (1938): 289–302.

50 I thank Prof. Maria Subtelny of the University of Toronto for this information, which she sent me in an email 3/29/07, following a remark she made in response to a lecture I had given the week before. In the email she referred to the "citron being a Sasanian symbol of sovereignty" and pointed to Shaul Shaked, "From Iran to Islam: On Some Symbols of Royalty," in his collection *From Zoroastrian Iran to Islam: Studies in Religious History and Intercultural Contacts* (Alershot, Hampshire: Variorum, 1995), 83.

of a Babylonian authority, but it also prefaces that leniency with the report that there was a shortage. The Babylonian rabbi was the third-generation authority, R. Nahman b. Yaakov. Again, JT *Sukkah* 3:6 (54d) testifies to yet another leniency that would increase the supply, at least after the first day of the festival, when, according to a rule cited in the name of Samuel, citrons that had been ruled invalid for reasons of *hiddur* (beauty) could be used on the other days of the festival. It is thus striking that the two leniencies that the Yerushalmi records for loosening the supply of citrons are both of Babylonian origin. This unusual fact can be accounted for by examining two factors. One has already been mentioned: climate and the problems of cultivation. The other is a feature of Sasanian law.

Earlier Palestinian sources insist that the ceremony of the taking of the four species be conducted *only* with plants that the celebrant owns *absolutely*. Below I shall present the Galilean toseftan source and its Babylonian parallel. The essential point is that, while the Tosefta requires absolute ownership, the word *gemurah*—absolute—*does not appear in the Bavli's version of this text*, and the Bavli itself uses this story as a proof for the validity of conditional gifts given in order to fulfill the commandment of the four species. However, it should be emphasized that this works only when the text does not include the word "absolute."

> [Tosefta *Sukkah* 2:13] No one can fulfill his obligation with his neighbor's *lulav* on the first day of the festival [of Sukkot], unless [the latter] gives it to him as an *absolute gift*. A story: Rabban Gamaliel and the elders were traveling on a ship and had no *lulav* with them; Rabban Gamaliel bought a *lulav* for a golden dinar. When he had fulfilled his obligation with it, he gave it to his colleague, and his colleague to his colleague, until each of them had fulfilled his obligation with it, and after that they returned it to him.

And here is the Bavli's version of the toseftan text, along with part of its discussion (BT *Sukkah* 41b).

> [BT *Sukkah* 41b] How do we know these things? For the Rabbis taught: "And you shall take"—[this teaches] that should be a "taking" for each one. "For you"—[this teaches that it should be] your own—to exclude the borrowed or stolen [citron].
>
> From here the Sages said: No one can fulfill his obligation with his neighbor's *lulav* on the first day of the festival [of Sukkot], unless [the latter] gives it to him as a *gift*. A story: Rabban Gamaliel and R. Yehoshua and R. Eleazar b. Azariah and R. Akiva who were traveling on a ship and only Rabban Gamaliel had an *etrog*, which he had bought for a thousand *zuz*. Rabban Gamaliel took it and fulfilled his obligation with it and gave it to R. Yehoshua as a gift. R. Yehoshua took it and fulfilled his obligation with it and gave it to R. Eleazar b. Azariah as a gift. R. Eleazar b. Azariah took it and fulfilled his obligation with it and gave it to R. Akiva as a gift. R. Akiva took it and fulfilled his obligation with it and returned it to Rabbah Gamaliel.
>
> Why does it have to state that he returned it to Rabban Gamaliel?
>
> It teaches us something in passing: A gift given on condition of being returned is still considered a gift, as that [case] when Rava said: Here is this etrog on condition that you return it to me, [and then] he took it and fulfilled his

> obligation; [if] he returned it, he has fulfilled his obligation, if he did not return it, he has not fulfilled his obligation.

In the Yerushalmi the story is told of R Nahman, who gave his etrog to his son, and, what is more, it is linked to a shortage of citrons.

> [JT *Sukkah* 3:10 [Vilna 16a]=JT *Gittin* 2:3 [Vilna 12a]] As [in regard to] [the Mishnah's prohibition of giving an unlearned person who is suspected of violating the prohibition of the sabbatical year the wherewithal for two meals], R. Mattaniah explained this [according to the view of both sides of the dispute—R. Eleazar and the Sages] that the citrons were sold at a high price, as in the [case] of those citrons that grew there[51] and R. Nahman b. Yaakov gave the citron to his son. He said to him: When you have acquired the merit of it and its mitzvah, return it to me.

Both talmuds thus attribute this innovation of permitting temporary possession to Babylonian masters, either to R. Nahman according to the Palestinian Talmud, or to R. Nahman and Rava, his disciple, according to the Babylonian Talmud. Note that Rava is a disciple of R. Nahman, and both are Mahozans. And, as I have shown elsewhere, R. Nahman is at once the Bavli's supreme master of Sasanian law[52] and the one most familiar with, and accepting of, Middle Persian culture in general.[53]

Eventually the principle of temporary, conditional gifts was accepted as valid for the four species, and some civil matters, but not for other religious requirement, and not for contracting marriage.[54] On the other hand, temporary gifts and temporary possession are well-established in Sasanian law, and no Sasanian jursiconsult doubts that validity. Cases involving temporary possession and conditional gifts are the object of no fewer than two-dozen cases in the Sasanian Lawbook. It would thus seem that the concept of temporary ownership as valid for religious and secular purposes seems to have been suggested to R. Nahman by its use in Sasanian law and then made its way from Babylonia to Palestine, where it became an accepted method for dealing with the shortage of kosher citrons. Here is one case in the Sasanian Lawbook.

> MHD 50.13: And this was also said: When he says: Let [this property] be held by Zanbud [as *stūr* for ten years], and [during] those ten years offspring is born to Zanbud, then this property comes to the son as possession.[55]

A *stūr* is one who engages in the Zoroastrian equivalent of the biblical levirate marriage. Thus, ordinarily temporary gifts are not *pad xwešīh*—that is, while they go

51 See Pnei Moshe ad loc., who suggests that *metzaftzefin* is equivalent to *retzufim*, "close together," and that citrons were in short supply (*be-dohuq*). Saul Lieberman in *Tosefta Ki-Feshuta*, vol. 4 (New York: JTS, 1962), 866 accepts this interpretation.

52 "Yeshivot Bavliyot ke-Vatei Din," in E. Etkes, ed., *Yeshivot u-Vatei Midrash* (Jerusalem: Makhon Shazar, 2006), 31–55.

53 See "Acculturation" (n. 11, above), 170–75.

54 I trace the process of the reception of this principle in rabbinic law in "Returnable Gifts" (see n. 60 above), 167–75.

55 See Perikhanian, 130–31, and Macuch, *Rechskasuistik*, 309 (text), 326 (translation), and n. 51 on 361; see also Schirazi-Mahmoudian, *Rechtsnormen*, 76.

into the recipient possession, he does not own them; the reason for the difference here is the *stūrīh* whose entire purpose is fulfilled when a son who can inherit his deceased father's estate is born as a result of the *stūrīh*. Here then the possession is not only *dārišn*, "for holding" (Roman *possessio*) but *pad xwešīh*, as an ownership (Roman *dominium*).

This point is an important one in understanding the dynamics of intercultural contacts. For the culture appropriating an element from another will put that element to its own uses; the element will be modified to suit its own needs. Here the religious requirement that the returnable gift be given as an absolute possession trumped the niceties of Sasanian law. And this is just as we might expect: R. Nahman would have felt no need to adhere to the requirements of Sasanian law with a purely religious Jewish context—and he did not.

As James Russell noted in a paper presented at the 1998 Irano-Judaica conference, "influences from one quarter . . . do not preclude promiscuous intermingling with material from another tradition. . .; influences need not be a graft, but can be also a stimulus that brings into prominence a feature that had been present previously, but not important."[56]

CONCLUSION

We have thus seen that the Babylonian rabbis were well aware of what *dina de-malkhuta*—the law of the land—as well as contemporary business practice, *minhag ha-medinah*, entailed, and could apply it, when necessary, to meet the needs of their community. This applied to matters of commercial law, real estate and taxation, and even to internal matters such as the supply of ritual objects.

My thanks to my student David Lasher for his editorial assistance.

SELECTED BIBLIOGRAPHY

Beer, Moshe. *Amora'ei Bavel: Peraqim be-Hayyei ha-Kalkalah*. Bar Ilan UP, 1974

Ben-David, Arye. *Talmudische Ökonomie: Die Wirtschaft des jüdischen Palästina zur Zeit der Mischna und den Talmud*. Hildesheim: Olms, 1974.

Elman, Yaakov. "Acculturation to Elite Persian Norms in the Babylonian Jewish Community of Late Antiquity." In *Neti'ot David*, ed. by E. Halivni, Z. A. Steinfeld, and Y. Elman, Jerusalem: Orhot, 2004 [appeared in 2005], 31–56.

56 James R. Russell, "Ezekiel and Iran," in Shaul Shaked and Amnon Netzer, *Irano-Judaica V* (Jerusalem: Makhon Ben Zvi, 2003), 6.

———. "The Babylonian Talmud in Its Historical Context." For Yeshiva University Museum's *The Printing of the Talmud.* New York, 2005, 19–28.

———. "Marriage and Marital Property in Rabbinic and Sasanian Law." In C. Hezser, ed., *Rabbinic Law in Its Roman and Near Eastern* Context. Tübingen: Mohr-Siebeck, 2003, 227–76.

———. "Middle Persian Culture and Babylonian Sages: Accomodation and Resistance in the Shaping of Rabbinic Legal Tradition." In Charlotte Elisheva Fonrobert and Martin S. Jaffe, eds., *Cambridge Companion to Rabbinic Literature.* Cambridge UP, 2007, 165–97.

———. "Returnable Gifts in Rabbinic and Sasanian Law," *Irano-Judaica* VI, Jerusalem: Makhon Ben Zvi, 2008, 150–95.

———. " 'Up to the Ears' in Horses' Necks: On Sasanian Agricultural Policy and Private 'Eminent Domain'." *Jewish Studies: An Internet Journal* 3 (2004): 95–149.

Krauss, Samuel. *Talmudische Archaeologie*, 3 vols. Leipzig: G. Fock, 1910–1912.

Lukonin, V. G. "Political, Social and Administrative Institutions, Taxes and Trade." In *Cambridge History of Iran* (2)3. Cambridge: Cambridge UP, 1983, 681–746.

Macuch, Maria. *Rechtskasuistik und Gerichtspraxis zu Beginn des siebenten Jahrhunderts in Iran: Die Rechtssammlung des Farrohmard i Wahrāmān*. Wiesbaden: Harrassowitz, 1993.

Neusner, Jacob. A *History of the Jews in Babylonia*, 5 vols. Leiden: E. J. Brill, 1969–1975.

CHAPTER 29

COINS AND MONEY IN JEWISH LAW AND LITERATURE: A BASIC INTRODUCTION AND SELECTIVE SURVEY

LAURENCE J. RABINOVICH

Primitive Money

We live in a world in which coins are still common and useful, although, with the introduction of paper money, credit cards, and, more recently, internet shopping, it is certainly possible to conceive of a commercial system without coins. Even if coins continue to exist, they will make up only a small percentage of the money supply and will be used primarily for small, local purchases. In terms of high finance and international trade, coins are no longer significant.

For over two thousand years, though, following the development of coinage in Asia Minor (seventh century BCE),[1] the association between coinage and a sophisticated international commerce was real. The shortage of coins in Europe after the fall of the western Roman Empire is connected to the severe fall off in trade, and shortages of coins (or, more precisely, specie), periodically reported in both Jewish

1 A. R. Burns, *Money and Monetary Policy in Early Times* (New York: Augustus M. Kelley, 1927) (1965 reprint), 37–44.

and general sources of the High Middle Ages, frustrated merchants and lenders.[2] The rabbis of the Talmud, in an aggadic (i.e., nonlegal) passage, included the circulation of coins as one of the conditions required to ensure society's well-being.[3]

There were, though, great civilizations that knew nothing of coinage. No coins have been discovered in any of the numerous archaeological sites from the Old Kingdom or Middle Kingdom in Ancient Egypt. The first evidence of coins in Egypt dates from the time of the Persian invasion (sixth century BCE), and coinage was not firmly established until the arrival of Alexander the Great.[4] The Assyrian and Old Babylonian Empires were created and maintained without coins.[5] The precoinage system, "primitive" though it might have been, was able to support international trade.

For our purposes, this means that there were no coins in the period of the Patriarchs, or the time of Moses. Nor is there evidence that the Jews of Eretz Israel utilized coins during the First Commonwealth.[6] Jews encountered coins during the Babylonian Exile and we find an apparent reference to gold coins in Ezra 2:69 in the context of the Return to Zion. Only during the Second Temple period do Jews begin to mint coins—in a very limited fashion—and only then do coins begin to be of legal significance.[7]

There are numerous references to exchanges and purchases in the Bible. The traditional understanding from the Talmudic period until modern times was that these transactions involved coins—as suggested earlier, the notion of economic activity without coins was not conceivable once coins became widely used. Thus, Abraham's purchase of the Cave of Makhpelah from Efron the Hittite for four hundred shekels of silver (Genesis 23:15–16) was explained by R. Judah b. Simeon (b. Pazi) (early fourth century CE) as referring to four hundred "Kinterin" (JT *Kiddushin* 1:3), identified by Prof. Daniel Sperber as the Roman centenarius (which was worth 10,000 denarii during the rampant inflation of R. Judah's time).[8] R. Meir (second century CE), expounding on the commandment to Moses (*Exodus* 30:13) to conduct an indirect census by collecting half a shekel of silver from every adult male, imagines God pulling a coin of fire from under His heavenly throne, showing it to Moses, and telling him, "they shall donate (a coin) like this one" (*Pesikta Rabbati*, sec. 16).

The medieval Bible commentators (e.g., R. Solomon b. Isaac, ibn Ezra, R. David Kimhi) also assumed that Abraham had paid Efron in coin—their primary debate was

2 J. LeGoff, *Medieval Civilization 400–1500* (Oxford: Basil Blackwell, 1988) (Translator, Julia Barrow), 23–27; H. Soloveitchik, *Pawnbroking: A Study in the Inter-relationship between Halakhah, Economic Activity and Communal Self-Image* (Hebrew) (Jerusalem: Magnes Press, 1985), 107; E. Hunt and J. Murray, *A History of Business in Medieval Europe 1200–1550* (Cambridge: University Press, 1999), 212.

3 TB Pesahim 54b.

4 Paul Einzig, *Primitive Money: In its Ethnological, Historical and Economic Aspects* (Oxford: Pergamon Press, 1966) (2d. ed.), 196.

5 See, for example, J. N. Postgate, *Early Mesopotamia: Society and Economy at the Dawn of History*, (London: Routledge, 1992) (2003 reprint), 203

6 Ya'akov Meshorer, *Matbe'ot Atikim* (Jerusalem: Keter), 10.

7 Ya'akov Meshorer, *A Treasury of Jewish Coins*, (Nyack: Amphora Books, 2001), a translation of the author's Hebrew master work, sums up the history of the era's Jewish coinage.

8 D. Sperber, "Price of the Cave of Makhpela and the Economic Situation in Eretz Israel in the Mid-Fourth Century," (Hebrew) *Tarbiz* 42 (1972–1973): 55–59.

whether Abraham had been gouged by a greedy Efron, or whether the price was fair.[9] Among the first to notice a difficulty with the assumption was R. Obadiah Sforno (Bologna, c. 1470–1550), who was struck by the Bible's choice of verb in *Genesis* 23:16, "*va-yishkol Avraham le-Efron*"—literally, "and Abraham weighed to (!) Efron." Sforno concluded that the meaning of the word "*va-yishkol*" had shifted from its original meaning and referred to payment. Moses Mendelsohn (Berlin, 1729–1786), in his *Biur*, modified Sforno's interpretation, suggesting that, while the root s-k-l generally refers to weighing, when it is followed by a preposition and an indirect object, the verb assumes an additional meaning—that is, Abraham weighed the silver and paid Efron. S. D. Luzzato (Padua, 1800–1865), in his Commentary to the Pentateuch (Padua, 1871), was perhaps the first Jewish commentator to explicitly reject the assumption that coinage was involved, observing in the context of *Genesis* 23:16 that "their society had no coins."

Most economic historians accept the view that coinage began in the late seventh century BCE, although some believe that the line between primitive money and coinage was crossed at earlier points of Near Eastern History.[10] As Einzig and others have shown, money, in the sense of a unit of account, was established in Mesopotamia not later than the beginning of the second millennium BCE.[11] Goods were valued in silver and were exchanged or bartered in line with those valuations. Some payments were made in grain or in silver, which, as we saw with Abraham, would have been weighed. Those receiving the silver would also have been concerned about the fineness of the silver. It has been suggested that the phrase used alongside the four hundred shekels weighed out and paid by Abraham, "*Kesef 'over la-soher*," with which both commentators and translators have struggled, might refer to a guarantee of fineness of the silver.[12] Scholars have long attempted to identify Near Eastern parallels to the biblical phrase. Avigdor Hurwitz[13] points to Old Assyrian documents from the trading center at Kanish, which describe transactions in which silver (*kaspum*) or some other commodity is to be sent by land (*etēgen*—the Akkadian *ebēru* which is cognate to the Hebrew *'over*—was used only for water transfer, a distinction that does not exist in Hebrew). As in the biblical phrase, the Assyrian verbs in these documents take on an indirect object, which always involves a merchant, often mentioned by name, but in some cases, simply referred to as "merchant" (*tankārun*). The phrases in these documents are more complex than the biblical one, but all have the three basic

9 The rabbis of the Talmud assumed the price was high: For example, *Bereishit Rabbati* (ed. H. Albeck, Jerusalem, 1940), 95, line 12; Babylonian Talmud, *Bava Metsi'a* 87a, and comment of R. Judah b. Simeon cited, supra.

10 As Powell, supra, and others have noted, the people of the Ancient Near East did just fine with their "primitive money." Morris Silver, *Ancient Economies I (Topic III)*, http://sondmor.tripod.com/index-7.html, questions the prevailing view that there were no coins in the Ancient Near East and Ancient Egypt.

11 Einzig, supra, 202–5; see, also, the writings of Marvin Powell including, "A contribution to the History of Money in Mesopotamia Prior to the Invention of Coinage," B. Hrûska and G. Komoróczy (eds.), Festschrift Lubor Matouš II Assyriologia 5, Budapest, 1978, 211–43.

12 For example, David M. Schaps, *The Invention of Coinage and the Monetization of Ancient Greece* (Ann Arbor: University of Michigan, 2004), 91, n. 50. Rashi's grandson, the twelfth-century commentator, R. Samuel b. Meir, also took the phrase to refer to the quality of the silver.

13 V. Hurowitz, *"Kæsæp 'ober lassoher (Genesis 23:16)," Zeitschrift für die alttestamentliche wissenschaft*, 108 (1996), 12–19.

elements found in the biblical phrase—the silver or other product, the verb signifying transport, and the reference to a merchant. Hurwitz argues that the biblical phrase is an abbreviated or evolved form of the term used in these merchant records.

Interestingly, administrative texts from the city of Ugarit (on the main Near Eastern trade route), dating to several hundred years after the time of the Patriarchs, record several real-estate purchases for precisely four hundred shekels of silver. These texts, collected and studied by R. Stieglitz, suggest that then, as now, land prices may vary widely, presumably depending upon the size of the plot, its quality, and its location.[14] Thus, we read that one Rashapabu purchased a plot five *puridum* by three *puridum* (the puridu equaled three cubits) and a house for thirty shekels of silver. *Yakunilu* "freed" (from mortgage) six *iki* of land (each *iku* was about 3,600 square meters) for eighty shekels. Abbanu paid four hundred shekels of silver for two houses and fields. Rashapabu and his wife, Pidda, also paid four hundred shekels for four *iki* of land, which included olive trees. And, Iašinu, son of Addulana, redeemed an estate with its olive trees and vines also for four hundred shekels. Clearly, for certain properties, four hundred shekels was an appropriate price.

As Stieglitz points out, the Ugarit texts do not show basic commodity prices: we would have had a sense of the cost of living if we knew the prices of wheat, barley, oil, and wine, for instance. We are given prices for a sheep (two-thirds shekel to one shekel per head), a young bull (ten shekels), a mare (thirty-five shekels), untreated wool (two to seven shekels per talent), a clay vessel (1/150 of a shekel), and certain other items. The records suggest a 1:4 gold-to-silver ratio.[15]

Abraham's expenditure is not the only, or even the largest, one mentioned in Genesis. The king of Gerar, Abimelekh, chastised by God for kidnapping Sarah, pays Abraham "one thousand shekels of silver" (*Genesis* 20:16). (Although compare ibid., 20:18—perhaps the sheep, cattle, and slaves given to Abraham were valued at one thousand shekels of silver.) Other references to shekels abound. For example, Joseph is sold by his brothers for twenty pieces of silver (presumably twenty shekels) (*Genesis* 37:28). Joseph's brothers pay in silver for the grain they purchase in Egypt, but the silver is returned in their sacks (*Genesis* 42:25, 43:12, 44:1). After Joseph reveals himself, he orders that Benjamin, his full brother, be given a gift of three hundred pieces of (= shekels of) silver.[16]

The nomenclature and structure of the metrological system of Ancient Israel is clearly related to the system of the Near East, although it differed in its details from those systems. Marvin Powell[17] has summarized the Akkad and Old Babylonian weight system as containing (bottom to top) the following steps.

14 R. Stieglitz, "Commodity Prices at Ugarit," *Journal of the American Oriental Society* 99:1 (1979), 15–23.

15 M. Heltzer, "The Goods and Prices in the Ugaritic Trade," Palestinski Sbornik 82 (1969), 7–31. See, also, Heltzer's chapter (10), 423ff. In Wilfred G. E. Watson and Nicholas Wyatt, *Handbook of Ugaritic Studies* (Leiden: Brill, 1999). The documents date from the mid-thirteenth century BCE until c. 1180. There was long-term price stability (M. Powell, "Money in Mesopotamia," *JESHO* 39:3 [1996], 227), but it seems too much to expect that level of stability for six hundred years.

16 There is also the obscure reference in Genesis 33:19 to "one hundred kesitah."

17 "Masse und Gewichte," in D. O. Edzard, ed., *Reallexikon der Assyriologie, Volume 7 (3–4)* (Berlin and New York: Walter de Gruyter, 1988), 510.

Barleycorn (še)	= 1/180 shekel (approx. .046 g)[18]
Little shekel	= 1/60 shekel (approx. .139 g)
Little Mina	= 1/3 shekel (approx. 2.78 g)
šiglu	= 1 shekel (approx. 8.33 g)
Mina	= 60 shekels (approx. 500 g)
Talent (biltu)	= 60 minas (3,600 shekels) (approx. 30 kg)

At some point, the girû (seed of the carob tree) was added to the system and pegged at 1/24 of a shekel or 7.5 barleycorns.

The weight system described (incompletely) in the Bible shares at least some of these terms. Thus, we read (e.g., Exodus 30:13) that the shekel (or, perhaps, only the *shekel ha-kodesh*, the holy shekel—Numbers 18:16) consists of twenty *gerah*.[19] Among modern translators and commentators, Everett Fox renders "*Gerah*" as "grain" and Alter and Hartoum and Cassuto do not translate it. Grain, in any event, seems unlikely. The primary grains of the time, wheat and barley, are generally taken today to weigh roughly .048 and .065 grams, respectively.[20] Twenty of the former would yield a shekel of less than one gram, the latter a shekel of 1.3 grams. That is impossibly small. Some of the rabbis of the Talmud took the *gerah* to be the weight, in silver, of sixteen grains, which works out to .77 grams (if the grain was wheat) or 1.04 grams (if it was barley) per *gerah* and a shekel of 15.4 grams or of 20.8 grams. Ridgeway suggested that the *gerah* was the lupin bean, which at least some cultures equated with eight grains of wheat. If that is correct, the *gerah* weighed about .384 grams and the shekel about 7.68 grams.[21] (This calculation is close to the Syrian or Phoenician shekel of c. 7.8 grams; see Luca Peyronel, "Some remarks on Mesopotamian Metrology during the Old Babylonian Period: The Evidence from Graves LG/23 and LG/45 at Ur," *Iraq*, Vol. 62 [2000] p. 183). The carob seed was traditionally equal to four wheat grains—if we define gerah to be the carob, as Assyriologists have translated, "*giru*," then we get a shekel of less than 4 grams.

18 The authorities are not in complete accord here. W. Ridgeway, *The Origin of Metallic Currency and Weight Standards*, (Cambridge: Cambridge University, 1892), distinguished between the standard for the gold shekel of 130 troy grains (= 130 barley grains) or 8.4 grams, and the standard for the silver shekel, which he pegged at 172 troy grains or 11.2 grams. And see, now, W.B. Hafford, "Mesopotamian Mensuration: Balance Pan Weights from Nippur," in *Journal of the Economic and Social History of the Orient* 45, 3 (2005), 345–87.

19 Gerah is identified with the ma'ah (obol) by the rabbinically sanctioned Aramaic Targum. Maimonides (Rambam, Egypt, 1138–1204) traces the talmudic assumptions about coins in several places (e.g., The Laws of Shekels 1:2–4) and reasons that the ma'ah or gerah equal sixteen "barley" grains. The difficulty about how many gerah are in a shekel—twenty as in the Torah or twenty-four as one was required to conclude under the rabbinic tradition—is attributed by some to a twenty-percent addition to the original weights. See *Sefer Kaftor va-Ferach of* Estori ha-Parhi, (geographer and traveler, c. 1280–1355), Chapter 16, s.v. "*Shekel shel Torah.*" See also the speculations of the Tosafists, Bekhorot 5a, s.v. "*ve-ha-shekel.*"

20 See P. Grierson and L. Travaini, *Medieval European Coinage, Volume 14 (South Italy, Sicily and Sardinia)* (Cambridge: University Press, 1998), 463. As noted above in Powell's chart, the Babylonian še, which is understood by Assyriologists to refer to a barleycorn, works out to a number much closer to the numismatic standard for a wheat grain. This would seem to present a fundamental problem since the terminology across the millennia (and perhaps across the border) is not consistent.

21 Ridgeway, supra, 194, 278.

The *maneh*, sixty shekels in the Babylonian system, is fifty shekels for the Jews.[22] Interestingly, the *maneh* is nowhere mentioned in the Torah, even though there are verses involving large numbers of shekels that could have been expressed in *maneh*. The word appears several times in *Tanakh*, most famously, if ambiguously, at Ezekiel 45:12. The highest weight denomination is the *Kikar* (= talent, i.e., 60 *maneh*); thus, at Exodus 38:24–25 some simple arithmetic confirms that this *kikar* consisted not of 3,600 (as in the Babylonian system) but of 3,000 shekels.[23] It has been observed that the differences between the Jewish and Babylonian (or the Western and Eastern portions of the Near East) are consistently in a 5:6 ratio, which some see as reflecting the contest between the Babylonian base six metrological system, and the competing decimal system later adopted by the Greeks and Romans.

Hundreds of years after Abraham weighed four hundred shekels of silver, King David, who also insisted on paying "the full price" (I Chronicles 21:22), purchased the threshing floor of Aravna the Jebusite for fifty shekels of silver (II Samuel 24:24). (This number is reported, or inverted, in Chronicles as six hundred shekels of gold.)[24] And we find King Omri (c. 882–871 BCE) buying Mount Samaria, where he founded his capital city for 6,000 shekels of silver (two *kikars*) (I Kings 16:24).

We do not know what precise measure is indicated in the Torah by the word "shekel." Nor can we know whether Abraham, Moses, and David used the word shekel to refer to the identical weight. What is reasonably clear, based upon limestone weights dating from the eighth and seventh centuries BCE, is that the shekel in Judea during those centuries was the equivalent of about 11.33 grams.[25] That is significantly higher than the weight of the Assyrian and Babylonian shekels (which were a bit higher or a bit lower than 8 grams). The Judean shekel was also heavier than the basic Egyptian weight, the *qedet* (c. 9.1 grams).[26] It has been suggested, in fact, based on inconsistencies in the inscription system used to mark the different weights, that there was a prior system in place in Judea, which was in line with the Egyptian system, and that around the year 700, perhaps because of changing geo-strategic conditions, the weight of the shekel was raised.[27] This, though plausible, remains conjectural.

Also of interest are the Judean *gerah* weights (1, 2, 3, 4, 5, 6, 7, 8, 9, 10, or 11 *gerahs*) and the fractional shekel weights *beqa* (one-half shekel), piyam (two-thirds shekel), and n-s-f (five-sixths shekel).[28] These clearly show that the shekel was divided into twenty-four *gerah*. Various suggestions have been made to explain how this squares

22 This was typical of the societies west of the Euphrates. *Anchor Bible Dictionary* (New York: Doubleday, 1992), 905.

23 That is, sixty maneh each consisting of fifty shekels. Interestingly, the Talmud suggests a different breakdown of the talent (*Bekhorot* 5a), but we have given the plain meaning of the verse.

24 The contradiction was noted in the Talmud, TB *Zebahim* 116b, and has been addressed by numerous commentators including Gersonides (Provence, 1288–1344), who suggests a distinction between the threshing floor itself, described in Samuel, and the entire mountain-top, the subject in Chronicles.

25 Raz Kletter, *Economic Keystones: The Weight System of the Kingdom of Judah* (London: Sheffield Academic Press, 1988), 131.

26 W.M. Flinders Petrie, *Social Life in Ancient Egypt* (London: Constable & Co., 1923), 156 (145 (Troy) grains = c. 9.4 g); Y. Ronen, "The Enigma of the Shekel Weights of the Judean Kingdom," *The Biblical Archaeologist* 59:2, 123 (June 1996) (9.06g); Kletter, supra, 119 (8.98g).

27 Ronen, supra; cf., Kletter, pp. 120–22.

28 Kletter, 75 & ff.

with the twenty-gerah shekel that is mentioned in the *Torah* (e.g., Exodus 30:13). The other Near Eastern systems divided the shekel into twenty-four gerah. Could the *shekel ha-kodesh* have been smaller than the standard shekel? Or were the twenty-gerah and twenty-four-gerah systems not used simultaneously?[29]

The most famous reference to a fractional shekel unit is the half-shekel that Moses was directed to collect from each adult male Israelite (Exodus 30:11–16) for purposes of taking a census. In later centuries the half-shekel was adopted as the amount of the Temple Tax (although, in Nehemiah 10:33–34, the tax is given as a third of a shekel).[30] The *mishnah* recounts the different coins that were consecutively used to satisfy the yearly obligation during the centuries in which the Second Temple stood (c. 515 BCE through 70 CE):

> When Israel came up from the Exile, they gave *darics* (Persian gold or silver coins—see Ezra 2:69) (for the Temple tax). Later they began to give tetradrachms. Later still, they began to give didrachms. Some sought, later, to give dinars (but this change was not accepted) (*Shekalim* 2:4).

As noted, the weight of the shekel may have been increased during the First Temple period from c. 8 or 9 grams to the 11.3 grams standard seen in the weight stones. As we move to the Second Temple period (515 BCE–70 CE) we begin to deal with coins, as the above-cited *mishnah* teaches. While there has long been a debate in rabbinic sources about just what the shekel standard was, we now have clear numismatic evidence that the shekel, now called the *sela*, was equated no later than the end of the Second Temple period with the Tyrian tetradrachm, which weighed about 14.2 grams (confusingly, shekel was now the term for the "half-shekel," or didrachm).[31]

Coins in the Talmud and Rabbinic Literature

The tannaitic components of the Talmud, which date primarily to the first two centuries CE and which were written and edited in Eretz Israel, reflect the reality of the Roman world, albeit that of an Eastern outpost. The amoraic portions, the bulk of the Talmud, were composed and edited both in Eretz Israel and in the Sasanian Empire during the centuries that followed, and they reflect that dual reality.

29 Ibid., chapter 1 providing a summary of views; Ronen, supra, n. 1.

30 Traditional commentators, such as Nahmanides (Ramban, Spain 1104–1270), who saw a direct connection between the biblical half-shekel and the Temple tax, assume that the third of a shekel at Nehemiah's time was equivalent to half a shekel before (and after) his time. J. Liver, in "The Half-Shekel Offering in Biblical and Post Biblical Literature," *Harvard Theological Review* 56:3 (July 1963), points out the different purposes for the half-shekel donations as described in Exodus 30:11–16 as opposed to the texts describing the Second Temple period, including Nehemiah 10:33–38, the *Mishnah* quoted above, and Josephus.

31 The amora Rava (fourth century, Babylonia, TB *Bekhorot* 50a), representing what appears to have been a minority view, reasoned that the weight of the shekel had been increased at some point by about twenty-one percent. Although his reasoning involves anachronistic elements, he appears to have been correct; in any event, he convinced no less a later authority than Rambam, *Laws of Shekels* 1:2.

A number of scholars have written about the coins (generally bronze coins) minted by Jews during the periods of Hasmonean and Roman rule in Eretz Israel.[32] The Talmud displays no particular interest in Jewish coins per se, its discussions reflecting rather the coins actually in circulation.

The seminal research and analysis of Talmudic era coinage has been done by Sperber and is summed up in his monograph *Roman Palestine 200–400: Money & Prices* (Ramat Gan: Bar Ilan, 1991, 2nd ed.). Sasanian numismatics is far less developed than its Roman counterpart and little has been published on Sasanian coins in the Talmud.[33]

Shortly after 140 BCE, Jews were authorized by Antiochus VII to issue small bronze coins (*Maccabees* 1:15–7), and the coinage system was Syrian-Greek in orientation (six *ma'ah* to the *dinar* based on six *obol* to the drachma).[34] One hundred years later, during the reign of Mattathias Antigonus (40–37 BCE), the system was modified to conform more easily to the Roman system, since Rome now had effective control over the country. There was overlapping of names and Sperber understands that, in order to avoid confusion, Jews invented new names for some of the Roman coins in current use.[35] This, by the way, is crucial background to identifying and quantifying the *pruta*, originally a small bronze coin, which the rabbis identified as the minimum amount for various transactions or exposures.[36]

Among the coins mentioned most frequently in Talmudic sources are the *dinar* and *dinar zahav*. The latter is the Roman gold coin, the *aureus*, minted at forty or forty-two to the pound (each *aureus*, accordingly, weighed about 8 grams in modern terms); the former, the Roman denarius, was minted at eighty-four to the pound by Augustus (c. 4 grams per *denarius*) but ninety-six to the pound after Nero (c. 3.4 grams per *denarius*).[37] (The Roman pound was equivalent to about 325 grams.) With runaway inflation in the third or fourth century CE, the Empire made various attempts to stabilize the economic system as, along with constant tinkering, a variety of new coins were issued, including

32 See Meshorer, supra, whose notes refer to other important works. A listing of older works was assembled in L. A. Meyer, *A Bibliography of Jewish Numismatics*, (Jerusalem: Magnes Press, 1966).

33 Michael Alram is doing much basic research. See, for instance, his "Early Sasanian Coinage," in V. S. Curtis and S. Stewart, *The Sasanian Era: The Idea of Iran, Volume III* (London: I. B. Taurus, 2008), 18–29.

34 Sperber, "Palestinian Currency Systems during the Second Commonwealth," *Jewish Quarterly Review*, New Series, 56:4 (April 1966), 283 & ff.

35 Ibid., see Sperber's chart and comments summarizing his findings in his *Roman Palestine* 27–30.

36 Sperber, "Palestinian Currencies," supra; *Roman Palestine*, 78–79. The pruta or "the value of a pruta" is ubiquitous in rabbinic literature. Thus, for instance, a partial admission of a claim results in exposure if the defendant acknowledges owing at least a pruta (see *Hoshen Mishpat* 88:1), and the fruits produced by a tree in its fourth year, once taken to Jerusalem, are today redeemed for a *pruta* (*Yoreh Deah* 294:1). There have been attempts to estimate the value of the pruta, with references to various coins and weights over the centuries.

37 R. Duncan-Jones, *Money and Government in the Roman Empire* (Cambridge: University Press, 1998), 220–21; F.W. Walbank, "Trade and Industry under the Later Roman Empire in the West, in M. M. Postan et al., ed., *Cambridge Economic History of Europe*, Vol. 2, (Cambridge: University Press, 1987), 97. Rabbinic scholars writing a millennia and more after the aureus and denarius ceased being issued continue to speak of a 25:1 ratio; in fact, by the beginning of the fourth century, as we learn in the *midrash*, the ratio was 800:1 (Sperber, 36–37).

a new (lighter) gold coin, the solidus, first issued by Constantine c. 309, and the *siliqua*, a silver coin 1/24 the value of the solidus. The Talmud treats the dinar as equal to the Persian drachm, called the zuz. The tetradrachm (four drachms), a popular large silver coin, is, as we have seen, referred to in the Talmud as the sela.

During the tannaitic period (i.e., until the early third century) the standard value ratio between the denarius and *aureus* was 25:1 as is clear from several Talmudic sources as well as Roman ones (e.g., Dio Cassius 55:12 and BT *Bava Metsi'a* 44b). At times, the exchange rate changed as the relative value of gold and silver changed (PT *Kiddushin* 1:1 speaks of a 1:24 rate; see Sperber, *Roman Palestine*, pp. 76–77). We must not forget that the various emperors adjusted the gold and silver content of their coins frequently (between 215 and 220 CE, the *aureus* weighed, in turn, 7.2 grams, c. 6.5 grams, c. 6.4 grams, and then again about 7.2 grams) and new coins, such as the (silver) *antoninianus* (one-and-a-half to two dinars), were introduced.[38] The contemporary rabbinic figures would have been familiar with these changes, but the same can not generally be said for those interpreting Talmudic texts decades not to say centuries later.

The 25:1 exchange rate between certain gold and certain silver coins must not be mistaken for the silver-to-gold ratio as R. Tam (R. Yaakov b. Meir, a grandson of R. Solomon b. Isaac, Rashi, c. 1100–1170, France) correctly reasoned.[39] He assumed (also correctly, although the ratio has hovered in the 70–80:1 range in the late twentieth and early twenty-first centuries) that the ratio, which in his time was 12:1, would have been around the same in Roman times and that the 25:1 exchange was the result of the relative weight of the two coins (i.e., the gold dinar must have weighed twice as much as the silver dinar). This is breathtakingly accurate (since he was writing without Roman coins and without historical data) for the initial relationship between the *denarius* and the *aureus* although, as we now know, the Emperors repeatedly fiddled with the weights and fineness of their coins and the silver–gold ratio did not remain constant.

R. Tam is credited with another original piece of economic analysis.[40] There were variant views among medieval scholars on how to value the shekel in contemporary terms, and R. Tam had his own view on that question. He suggested to his student, R. Chaim Cohen, however, that the five shekels of silver a father is obligated to give to a *cohen* (priest) to redeem his firstborn son (Numbers 3:47) could, alternatively, be paid in kind. The Talmud (BT *Ketubbot* 91b) reports that grain was relatively inexpensive in Eretz Israel with four *se'ah* (approximately 25.2 kilograms) selling for a *tetradrachm*. Since the redemption price was five shekels (Numbers 3:47), which the

38 Sperber, *Roman Palestine*, 40.

39 R. Tam's query regarding the gold/silver ratio and his correct solution (which was based entirely on logic—he had no Roman coins or Roman texts), is set out in his *Sefer ha-Yashar* (section of novellae), section 590, and cited in his name in several of the printed Tosafot. R. Tam gives the ratio of his own time at 12:1. In places, R. Tam is quoted as referring to a 10:1 ratio, which is closer to other estimates from the High Middle Ages.

40 R. Tam's view is preserved in several Tosafist sources including R. Isaac of Vienna's *Or Zaruah*, Laws of the First Born, section 523.

mishnah (*Bekhorot* 8:7) equates with five *tetradrachms*, the obligation can be satisfied with twenty *se'ah* of wheat.[41]

Are all coins equal before the law? According to the *mishnah* (*Bava Metsi'a* 4:1), as interpreted over the centuries, the answer is no.[42] The prevailing view was that silver coins (and the reference here was to particular Roman coins such as the denarius) were coins par excellence, and that gold coins, as well as the small value copper coins, were deemed commodities.

The necessary background here is that, under Jewish Law, one does not acquire chattels by paying for them (real estate is subject to separate rules).[43] Rather, one acquires ownership, generally, by physically controlling the object that one has agreed to buy. Common examples involve acquisition by pulling (*meshikhah*)or lifting (*hagba'hah*).[44]

The *mishnah* considers a case in which silver coins and gold coins are "purchased." There was a basis for reading the *mishnah* as dealing with acquisition by barter, but the Talmud and its myriad commentators insist on reading the scenarios set out in the *mishnah* as examples of acquisition by exercise of control. The full *mishnah* consists of rulings on six specific scenarios followed by a general rule that, on the surface, contradicts all six cases. We will look at only the first two cases and then at the rule. The *mishnah*, according to the version set out in the Babylonian Talmud, begins as follows.

> Gold [coins] acquire silver [coins] but silver [coins] do not acquire gold [coins]. Copper [coins] acquire silver [coins] but silver [coins] do not acquire [copper coins].

The Jerusalem Talmud, though, has an alternative opening for the *mishnah*:

41 Z. Safrai, *The Economy of Roman Palestine* (London: Routledge, 1994), 62 estimates a se'ah as 6.3 kg. He also points out that while other prices are mentioned in the Talmud (R. Tam implies this as well), four se'ah to the tetradrachma appears to have been the usual price. Ibid., Appendix, 246.

42 On the two versions of this *mishnah* see S. Lieberman, *Hellenism in Jewish Palestine* (New York: Jewish Theological Seminary, 1994) (reprint of 2nd edition), 88–89. Professor Sperber's treatment of this section, summarized in the text, is particularly detailed and illuminating. *Roman Palestine*, 69ff, 85–88, and 335ff (his supplement constituting a commentary to the passages in the Yerushalmi). Among the economists who have commented on these materials is Ephraim Kleiman, "Bi-Metallism in Rabbi's Time: Two Versions of the Mishna 'Gold Acquires Silver,'" (Hebrew) *Zion* 38 (1–4), 1973, 48–61 (who argues, contra Sperber, that what is being described is the demonetization of gold coins following Caracalla's reform of 215 CE, in a textbook case of Gresham's Law). Both Sperber and Kleiman assume that R. Judah was responding to some current situation, which accounts for his change of heart. A more traditional view would seek a solution unconnected to the specific economic conditions of his time; that is what all of the standard commentators attempt to do. See also, Y. Liebermann, "Elements in Talmudic Monetary Thought," *History of Political Economy* 11:2 (1979), 259–62; D. A. Schiffman, "The Valuation of Coins in Medieval Jewish Jurisprudence," *Journal of the History of Economic Thought* 27:2 (June 2009): 145–48. The legal significance of the material is subjected to a sophisticated analysis in B. Lifshitz, *Promise: Obligation and Acquisition in Jewish Law* (Jerusalem: Magnes Press, 1988) (Hebrew), 288–96.

43 Rambam concludes, in accordance with one of the views set out in the Talmud, that, strictly speaking, a cash purchase should transfer title of a chattel, but that the rabbis voided cash acquisitions and required the buyer to exert control physically by one of several prescribed actions (Laws of Acquisition 3:1).

44 For an introduction in English to the question of acquiring property in Jewish Law see I. Herzog, *The Main Institutions of Jewish Law* (London and New York: The Soncino Press, 1980) (paperback ed.), Vol. 1 ("Property"), 137–200.

> Silver [coins] acquire gold [coins] but gold [coins] do not acquire silver [coins]. Copper [coins] acquire silver [coins] but silver [coins] do not acquire copper [coins].

The Talmud explains the variants as reflecting a change of heart by the editor of the *mishnah*, R. Judah the Prince (c. 135–c. 220 CE). In his youth (which Sperber, p. 71, identifies with the period around 170 CE), R. Judah held that silver coins "acquire" gold coins—that is, the silver coins constitute the produce or commodity. In our scenario, party A has gold coins while party B has silver coins and they wish to execute an exchange. When party A lifts or pulls the silver coins he becomes their owner, and party B has the right to demand payment of the equivalent value in gold coins—that is, lifting the silver coins by A seals the transaction. The lifting of the gold coins by B, however, does not complete the deal, and, for example, until A actually lifts the silver coins, either party can cancel the transaction for any reason or no reason. Title has not yet shifted and the risk of loss remains as it was prior to the transaction. The *mishnah* continues: Just as silver acquires gold, so copper acquires silver since, as the Jerusalem Talmud suggests, "this is the principle: that which is lower in value acquires that which is higher in value."

Later in life, though, R. Judah began to teach, "gold acquires silver"—that is, it is the silver coins, which constitute the currency, and gold, which is produce or commodity. In this version, it is not the valuation that is determinative, since silver is currency both vis-à-vis gold, which is more valuable, and vis-à-vis copper, which is less valuable. The Babylonian Talmud (*Bava Metsi'a* 44a–b) explains that R. Judah underwent a change of heart. He initially thought that currency should be identified with high value but, on reconsideration, concluded that the status of currency depends upon the ease of its circulation.

The debate has received recent scholarly attention. Sperber explains that traditionally the Roman view (like R. Judah's late view) was that gold was a commodity whose price, like that of wheat, is expressed in multiples of the denarius, the key silver coin.[45] Why then would R. Judah have ever viewed the gold coins as currency? Here Sperber found a parallel between the analysis of the fourth-century amora, Rava, and modern scholars, to the effect that after Nero's time the value of the denarius was determined not by its metallic content but by its nominal relationship (25:1) to the gold *aureus*. Even at that, silver was subject to a standard and was coin vis-à-vis copper. Around the year 195 CE, however, silver became far more current and the *aureus* was less available than it had been. That may have led R. Judah to change his mind. Interestingly, the Talmud cites other scholars, including R. Judah's son R. Simeon, who continued to view gold as coin, perhaps influenced by the contemporary debasement of silver coinage.[46]

Even those who read *mishnah* 4:1 in the traditional way set out above (i.e., as involving acquisition of the gold [produce] by party A by exercising control over the gold, which creates a duty for party A to pay party B in cash, i.e., silver) agree that the end of the *mishnah* is focused on a different type of acquisition—acquisition by barter.

45 Sperber, 74, citing A. H. M. Jones, *Economic History Review* (New Series) 5 (1952–1953), 300, and L. C. West and A. C. Johnson, *Currency in Roman and Byzantine Egypt* (Princeton: 1944), 70, 90–93, 181.

46 Sperber, 79.

> (This is the principle.) All chattels acquire one another.[47]

This is understood to refer to an exchange (i.e., barter) of one chattel for another as opposed to the purchase of a commodity by a coin. Thus, we read in Maimonides' summary (Sales 5:1):

> All chattels acquire one another. How? If one exchanges a cow for a donkey, or wine for oil, even if both sides take care to value their merchandise [and are trading with the understanding that the products being exchanged are of roughly equal value] as soon as one party pulls [in the case of the animal] or lifts [in the case of the foodstuff] one product, the other party takes title to the other product regardless of where that product is located, even though the second party has not exerted any control over that product.

In short, an exchange of a gold coin, say, for a silver one is viewed as the purchase of a commodity for money and, just as in any standard commodity purchase, acquisition is made by exercising control over the commodity. But in the basic barter or exchange case, both articles are deemed commodities and the acquisition of one by one party automatically establishes the ownership of the other article by the other party, even if that other object is not present.

There is a second type of acquisition by barter [48] that the Talmud derives, in part, from a verse in Ruth (4:7). This is not really a barter transaction—it involves a sale and, accordingly, it is appropriate to speak of a seller and a buyer, who have agreed on the price of a particular object that need not be at hand. The buyer presents a scarf ("*sudar*"—the mode of acquisition is called *kinyan* [acquisition by] *sudar*) or some other item of nominal value. At the very moment when the seller "acquires" (i.e., lifts) the scarf, the buyer takes title to the purchased item. Because this system is so convenient, it became the most popular mode of acquisition.[49]

The Talmud debates whether coins can acquire or be acquired by means of "acquisition by sudar." The conclusion, according to the majority reading, is that a coin may not be used as the token item lifted by the seller and also that coins may not be acquired by the *sudar* process.[50] The reason is that coins are deemed fundamentally different from produce: Coins are what one buys produce with.[51] But, even then, the matter is not free of doubt— silver coins are excluded, but what of gold coins? Here the early medieval scholars were not in accord. R. Hai Gaon (939–1038, the head of the academy in Pumpedita on the banks of the Euphrates) held that silver coins may not be used for the *kinyan sudar*. In R. Hai's view, however, since the Talmud indicated that gold or copper coins lack the legal status of coins, they could both acquire and be acquired in

47 Several commentators, including R. Yom Tov Lippman Heller (Prague, 1578–1654, in *Tosafot Yom Tov*, ad loc), point out that this phrase makes no sense (i.e., under the traditional interpretation) because it in no way sums up what came before. In fact, it seems to contradict what came before and needs to be explained.

48 I. Herzog, *Main Institutions,* supra, Vol. I, 163, calls this second form, "symbolic barter."

49 Rambam, *Laws of Sales 5:5*.

50 Ibid., 6:1. Coins are thus an exception to the broad rule with which the *mishnah* concludes.

51 Lifshitz, 291–93. The text sets out the explanation offered by R. Hai Gaon. Lifshitz shows that the *geonim* (the leading authorities in the East c. 600–1050) did not accept the cryptic reason for excluding coins proposed by Rav Papa in the Talmud (to the effect that coins are not amenable to acquisition by the exchange

the *sudar* process. The equally influential R. Isaac of Fez (Alfasi, 1013–1103), though, strongly disagreed and insisted that R. Hai had misinterpreted the Talmud. It was only in comparison with silver coins that gold and copper coins were deemed produce. These coins, however, certainly have the status of coins in and of themselves, and the rules against using money for the *kinyan sudar* apply equally to gold and copper coins.[52] It is worth observing that R. Hai, in Bagdad, and R. Alfasi, in North Africa and southern Spain, lived in societies that used both silver and gold coins. Questions relating to gold coins were largely hypothetical in Christian Europe until 1252, when gold coinage was reintroduced.

Additions to or Devaluation of the Currency

Even in an age of primitive money one needed to trust the accuracy of the scale that weighed the metal and to assess the purity of the metal involved. The possibilities for manipulation, by the sovereign or by a dishonest citizen, increase dramatically once we deal with coinage.[53]

We read (BT *Bava Kama* 97a) about a disagreement between the amoraim, Rav and Samuel (early third century CE), with respect to currency modifications:

> We have learned. If one loans a certain sum of coins to another, and, during the term of the loan the coin is replaced [by the sovereign], Rav taught that the loan is paid back in the new coin [i.e., a one-to-one exchange]. Samuel taught that [the borrower] may [pay in the discontinued coin] and say [to the lender] go spend them in Maishan [i.e., Mesene or Charax].[54]

Rava, the fourth-century jurist, cited frequently in the Talmud, posed a similar question to R. Hisda: "What amount is to be paid back if during the term of the loan the sovereign increases the weight [value] of the coin of the realm?" (ibid.). The numerous commentators and decisors who have written about these issues understand that Rav and Samuel were considering a situation in which one coin replaced another but the replacement is of the same weight and fineness. Rava

mechanisms because the party who would be acquiring the coin was relying on the governmental stamp and thus according to Rashi making the coin something less than a "whole" object). Liebermann, supra, 261–62, offers a different understanding of Rav Papa's answer.

52 Folio 26b in Alfasi pages. The Arabs had a bimetallic system. One wonders whether scholars living in a society with gold-standard monometallism (contemporary Byzantium, for instance) would have reacted differently.

53 Numerous sources on this topic were gathered by Shillem Warhaftig in his *Currency in Jewish Law* (Jerusalem: Ariel—Harry Fischel Institute, 1980).

54 The dating of this passage may be significant in light of the conquest by Ardashir I of Mesene, which had been independent, in 224 CE. Thereafter it was a dependent province of the new Sasanian Empire. If the text dates from after the conquest, it suggests that Mesene the Empire was not (yet?) in a position to enforce its monetary position completely in the province.

modifies the fact pattern and wonders if the result changes if the new coin is more valuable than the one being replaced. Interestingly, the Talmud does not deal with the converse scenario, which has been more prevalent historically, of the sovereign reducing the weight or fineness of the coin of the realm. That issue, though, is dealt with in the subsequent literature.[55]

The rules that have emerged for dealing with changes in the monetary system are complex and we can only sketch the outlines. When an existing coin is taken out of circulation, we would expect that the mint would offer to purchase the old coin in exchange for the new at something close to a 1:1 ratio, if no change in value was intended for the new coin. The question that Rav and Samuel debated apparently involved a scenario in which the borrower never spent the money he borrowed, or otherwise ended up with the same type and quantity of coin that he originally borrowed, and he would prefer to pay the loan back in that discontinued coin. The lender insists on being paid back in the new coin. Presumably at issue are the time and trouble involved in taking the coins to the mint for the exchange and payment of whatever amount the mint will charge for the exchange. Rav imposes these obligations upon the borrower, while Samuel, perhaps not disagreeing in principle, suggests that, if this coin is still usable at its former value outside the borders controlled by the sovereign, then the borrower may pay in the discontinued coin since the transaction costs involving the mint can be avoided. The tendency of the literature is to accept Samuel's view when possible: for example, when the lender is a merchant who does business outside the borders of the sovereign, and the coins can be taken out of the country, and so on.

The scenario envisioned by Rava, and its converse involving debasement of the coinage, present a weightier issue. The commentators disagree as to whether the question assumed Rav's basic position that one (always?) pays back in the new coin, or is formulated in line with Samuel's principle, since even according to Samuel there are times one pays back in the new coin.

In either event, if the new coin is heavier than the old one, then, in paying back an equal number of coins, is not the borrower effectively paying interest on the loan? Notwithstanding that consideration, R. Hisda responded to Rava that even under these circumstances one pays back with an equal number of the new coins.

The Talmud immediately conditions R. Hisda's answer—the fact that the coin is heavier does not always mean that it has more purchasing power. Thus, if the new coin purchases the same quantity of produce (presumably because the sovereign controls, or at least supervises, the market and has insisted that prices not be changed when the new coin begins to circulate), then one indeed treats the new coins as the equivalent of the old, and the loan is paid back with an equal number of new coins.

If, though, the introduction of the new coin is accompanied by a change in prices, then it becomes necessary to investigate whether there is a correlation between the changes to the coinage and the price fluctuation.

55 The issues here are related to the problem of "*dina de-malkhuta dina*," the principle, formulated by Samuel, that the law of the land is the law, as Bernard Septimus describes in "Kings, Coinage and Constitutionalism: Notes on a Responsum of Nachmanides," in *Jewish Law Annual* Volume 14 (2003): 295–314.

The Talmud presents this as a problem for R. Hisda's ruling; how can it be that one pays back the same number of coins of the new type—"have not market prices declined?" What this presumably means is that the new, heavier, coin can be exchanged for an increased amount of produce (i.e., greater buying power) raising questions about *ribbit* (usury). Rav Ashi (fifth century, one of the editors of the Talmud) responded that it depends. If, upon investigation, it turns out that prices "fell" (i.e., more produce was exchanged for the new coin than the old one), purely as a result of the change in the coinage, then the borrower must not pay back the loan as stated. Rather, the loan is adjusted so that the value of the old coin is equal to the value of new coins that are paid. If, however, the timing is coincidental and prices fall because of other factors (e.g., supply and demand), then the loan can be repaid in new coin as stated. Whether or not this was R. Hisda's own view, it is the one ultimately accepted.

Interestingly, the Talmud also wonders about the fact that the lender, even if not receiving coins with more purchasing power, is receiving more silver (if one were to weigh the coins) than he lent. Of course, he did not lend silver. Nonetheless, as the commentators explain, if he melts the new coins or breaks them apart, then the extra value that he extracts from the coins might be seen, retroactively, as something that at least looks like usury. The Talmud's conclusion is that, so long as the increase in metal is not more than twenty-five percent, it can be ignored (presumably because of the transaction costs—see R. Asher's commentary to *Bava Kama* 7:12), and the borrower must pay back the full amount in new coins.

What if the sovereign reduces the weight (or the fineness) of the coins? This possibility is not analyzed in the Talmud, perhaps because it does not present an issue of usury. Nonetheless, the scenario is treated identically in Jewish Law. If the purchasing power is reduced, or if the weight is reduced by more than twenty-five percent, then the borrower must make up the difference with additional coins.

The *Ketubbah*

By rabbinic enactment, every bride is presented at her wedding with a document, called a *ketubbah* (the root k-t-b relates to writing) (*kettubot*, when plural) that recites various obligations that the groom has assumed. Among these is the payment of certain sums to the wife in the event of the husband's death or in the event of a divorce.[56]

In the Talmud, which devotes an entire tractate to the *ketubbah*, the standard amount promised to the wife was two hundred *dinars* (or *zuz*). (That is the amount for virgin brides; divorcees or widows who remarried were promised one hundred *zuz*.) The obligation creates a lien on the husband's assets dating to the time of the marriage. (That gives the lien priority over subsequent liens and obligations.)

56 See, for example, D. Piattelli and B. Jackson, in N. Hecht, et al., eds., *An Introduction to the History and Sources of Jewish Law* (Oxford: University Press, 1996), 48–49.

Some commentators and modern scholars view the Talmudic standard of two hundred *zuz* or *dinar* as an amount that would have supported (at the time) the woman for a year, although there is no evidence that in times of inflation the amount was increased.

The Talmud, as noted earlier, treated the *zuz* and *dinar* as equivalent, although those should be seen as approximate equivalences. Thus, the denarius of Augustus weighed about 4 grams, that of Nero was 3.4 grams, and the Sasanian (third century) *drachma* (*zuz*) weighed 3.8 grams.[57] Thus, depending on which coin was being used, the two hundred *zuz* may have ranged from 680 to 800 grams of silver. An alternate formulation using Jewish sources would be as follows: Two hundred *zuz* were equivalent to fifty *tetradrachms*, and tradition equated the *tetradrachm* to 17 to 20 grams (850 grams to 1,000 grams for two hundred *zuz*).[58]

On June 12, 2009, silver for immediate delivery cost $14.31 an ounce in London (Bloomberg). One thousand grams equals about 32 ounces, which in 2009 dollars works out to about $458. The price of silver has fluctuated widely in the early years of the twenty-first century. Even at its current level, though, 1,000 grams of silver are not able to support anyone for very long.

The problem of the declining value of the *ketubbah* settlement was exacerbated in those communities (particularly many Sephardic ones) in which the husband, or his estate, were permitted to satisfy the obligation by paying one-eighth of the amount of silver described above.[59] In medieval Ashkenaz, by the eleventh century, an enactment was in place (its geographic scope has been debated) that required the husband to promise not only the "two hundred *zuz*," the core obligation, but an additional hundred pounds (two hundred marks) of silver.[60] The Talmud had also spoken of "additional *ketubbah* payments" over and above the core obligation, although this was presumably only a fraction of the core obligation. The Ashkenazic approach, to the contrary, was to have the additional payment dwarf the core obligation, which now became, at most, an afterthought.[61]

This was accomplished through a legal fiction that automatically evaluated the bride's dowry at one hundred marks or fifty pounds, even though, in most cases, the dowry was presumably worth quite a bit less than that. The value of the dowry must be returned to the wife as part of the settlement. The husband would then match the dowry and add the matching amount to the settlement. Accordingly, the

57 Sperber, *Roman Palestine*, 145.

58 As noted earlier, the SecondTemple–era *sela* (equated with the biblical shekel under the standard view in the *mishnah*; e.g., *Bekhorot* 8:7) is established by numismatic evidence to be just over 14 grams. The traditionalist view, however, has pegged the shekel at somewhere between 17 grams and 20 grams. See, for example, H. P. Benish, *Middot ve-Shiurei Torah* (Hebrew) (Benei Brak: 1987).

59 See, for instance, Responsum 66 by R. Isaac b. Sheshet (Perfet) (Spain, 1326–1408). R. Samuel de Medina (Salonika c. 1506–1589), in a note to his *responsa* (O.H. 127), expresses surprise when he discovers that the Tosafists (see Bava Kama 36b s.v. "ve-shel") did not accept what he clearly took to be the standard view that the value of the *ketubbah* was one-eighth of two hundred *zuz*.

60 Irving Agus, "The Development of the Money Clause in the Ashkenazic Ketubah," Jewish *Quarterly Review*, Volume 42 (1951), 221–56.

61 Ibid.

ketubbah used by Ashkenazim for the past millennium requires payment of one hundred pounds of silver, an amount far greater than the paltry two hundred *zuz*.

The halakhic literature contains an extensive and ongoing discussion of how to calculate the hundred pounds of silver. In different times and places, the amount was equated with 600 Rhine Gulden, 400 pounds Wiener, and 320, 400, or 500 Polish gulden. Recent rulings equate this with as much as $8,000 to $10,000 based on the value of silver and as much as $50,000 if the standard is a year's worth of living expenses.[62]

In a pair of *responsa* (one directed to his son-in law in 1982 and the other to a grandson in 1980), leading decisor R. Moshe Feinstein contemplated the contemporary value of the *ketubbah* settlement.[63] While the post-World War II period (at least through, say, 1970, and at least in the United States) is generally seen as a period of robust growth, Rabbi Feinstein sees "destruction and scandal." He alludes to the 1944 Bretton Woods agreements (which created international stability by pegging an ounce of gold at $35), and to the 1971 decision by President Nixon that dollars could no longer be exchanged for specie upon demand (which essentially upended the Bretton Woods system).[64] R. Feinstein observed that there had been no halakhic discussions of this fundamental shift from money and coinage with intrinsic value to fiat money.

Rabbi Feinstein's point of departure, based on Talmudic texts, is that the amount of the *ketubbah* payment be high enough that the husband (and wife) not treat the settlement as insignificant. This is rather a different rationale than the notion of providing extensive support following a divorce or death; for him the key factor is that the high cost of divorce keeps the couple together, all else being equal. He was aware from the literature that, in certain places (and times) in Europe, the two hundred marks of silver were equated with four hundred gulden. He recalls that in Minsk, prior to the outbreak of World War I, the custom was to require payment of seventy-five rubles (which he equates with five hundred gulden—fifteen kopecs to the gulden, one hundred kopecs to the ruble) to satisfy the *ketubbah* obligation. R. Feinstein understands that in the Middle Ages ("in the days of our teachers, the '*Rishonim*'") the equivalent of the traditional two hundred *zuz* no longer gave husbands any pause and, accordingly, an enactment was made to require the payment of two hundred marks.[65] The two hundred zuz mentioned in the Talmud and the two hundred marks continue to be listed in contemporary *ketubbot* in spite of the uncertainty involving

62 See Jonathan Reiss and Michael J. Broyde, "Prenuptial Agreements in Talmudic, Medieval, and Modern Jewish Thought," in Michael J. Broyde and Michael Ausubel, *Marriage, Sex and Family in Judaism* (Lanham: Rowman & Littlefield, 2005), 195.

63 *Iggerot Moshe,* Even ha-Ezer (Part 4) numbers 91 (summer 1980) and 92 (summer 1982).

64 Milton Friedman sums up some historical issues relating to convertibility and bimetallism in his *Money Mischief: Episodes in Monetary History* (San Diego: Harcourt Brace, 1994), 128–29.

65 See the discussion of R. Feinstein's view in Reiss and Broyde, supra, 207, n.36. The custom of increasing the *ketubbah* settlement was apparently in force by the ninth century. Edward Fram, *Ideals Face Reality: Jewish Law and Life in Poland 1550–1655* (Cincinnati: Hebrew Union College Press, 1997), 82. Much historical information is preserved alongside the extensive halakhic analysis in chapter 12 of *Nahlat Shiv'a* by R. Samuel b. David ha-Levi (Poland c. 1625–1681), although some recent scholars mistakenly assume that the "zakuk" as in "two hundred zakuks of silver" refers to a coin of some kind. When the amount of the ketubbah was increased, the mark (referred to as a zakuk in Hebrew) was a weight, not a coin.

valuation: One does not lightly change the traditional Jewish texts such as the *ketubbah*. R. Feinstein at one point calls the dollar a "*matbe'ah*" (coin—of course there are dollar coins, but that is not what he means), but one is left wondering what he and other decisors think of the legal status of fiat money.[66]

The Second Tithe and Distributions to the Poor

The amount of two hundred *zuz* recurs elsewhere in halakhic literature. We read in the *mishnah* (Peah 8:8) that one who has two hundred *zuz* may not collect the gleanings left by the harvesters (Leviticus 19:9–10; Deuteronomy 24:19)—a benefit restricted to the poor. One who has fifty *zuz* (Peah 8:9), but uses that amount to buy and sell items and thus support himself, is also forbidden to collect the gleanings.

When the medieval and modern commentators and decisors discuss this law, they continue to use the Talmudic standards, two hundred *zuz* or fifty sela (tetradrachms), even though those coins have not been used for one thousand years and more, and there is no attempt to calculate how much silver was contained in the prescribed number of *zuz*. R. Isaac of Vienna, for instance (thirteenth century), notes that the two hundred *zuz* constitute a year's worth of support (*Or Zarua, Laws of Charity*, section 14) although, citing the Tosafist, R. Samson of Sens (twelfth century), he debates whether the two hundred *zuz* reflects a per-person or per-couple standard.

Tur and *Shulhan Arukh* (*Yoreh De'ah* 253) suggest that the two hundred *zuz* constitute the person's nest egg, which earns sufficient income to support him. This would then refer to one not actively engaged in business. While field gleanings are not the concern of these scholars, they focus rather on the eligibility for collecting charity from the communal network. Thus, the issue was of great practical importance and the Tur, importantly, gives the communal workers a great deal of flexibility in deciding how to allocate the limited funds available for distribution (Ibid., at 253).

Coins have special significance with respect to the laws of the Second Tithe (Deuteronomy 14:22–26) and the similar laws dealing with the fruit of young trees, known as "*kerem (or netah) reva'i*" (Leviticus 19:24). The grains, nuts, fruits, and vegetables subject to the Second Tithe are, during the first, second, fourth, and fifth years of the seven-year agricultural cycle, set aside and carried to Jerusalem where they are eaten by the farmer and his accompanying dependents.

66 R. Moses Sofer (Frankfort, later Pressburg, 1763–1839), for one, thought of paper money as the equivalent of coins (*Responsa, Yoreh De'ah* no. 134).

The Torah recognized that transporting the produce might present technical difficulties, particularly for those living at a significant distance from "the place that G-d will select"; those travelers are accordingly permitted to exchange the produce for an equivalent value of silver and "bundle up the silver in your hand (*ve-tzarta ha-kesef be-yadekha*)." Focusing on these words, the rabbis, operating in a time when coinage was firmly established, interpreted the verse to require exchanging the produce for a coin with a "*tzurah*" (a figure that is a coin that has been minted and properly stamped). This is the view of R. Akiba, as opposed to that of R. Ishmael, who understands the phrase to mean simply to include any items that can be bound in one's hand (see BT, *Bava Metsi'a* 47b).

An asimon, which Sperber identifies as silver (sometimes bronze) bullion, may not be used for exchange with the Second Tithe (in *Ma'aser Sheni* 1:2); only actual coins may be used for the exchange.[67] The *mishnah* also provides that one may not exchange Second Tithe produce for coins that are no longer in circulation or, more precisely, that do not currently circulate in Jerusalem, where the coins are to be spent on food products, thus satisfying biblical direction to eat the produce "Before the Lord" (Deuteronomy 14:23).

Several other texts from Tractate *Ma'aser Sheni*, dealing with the permissibility of secondary exchanges (such as converting the silver coins exchanged for produce into gold coins), or the accidental intermingling of regular money with money exchanged for tithes, are cited by the Talmud in the extended discussions about coins found at the beginning of the fourth chapter of Tractate *Bava Metsi'a* mentioned above.

Summary and Conclusions

We have examined a few of the biblical and talmudic passages that relate to economic history. More significantly, the reading of these passages and others might be improved by the knowledge provided from other scholarly researches: We have seen some examples of that as in the discussion of Rabbi Judah's change of heart on the relative significance of gold and silver coins. But there is a significant challenge here, as well, from the perspective of Jewish Law. Decisors or rabbinic judges tend not to be familiar with or at least tend not to quote such scholarly researches, and there are matters of principle (whether that principle is correct or not) involved in the reluctance to cite foreign sources. Studying the economic significance of

67 Sperber, *Roman Palestine*, 137, 208 n. 12. The Talmud presents differing views on what an *asimon* is. Rav views it as a token such as that used to gain admission into the public baths. (Until relatively recently, in modern Israel, one used a token, called an *asimon*, to dial from a public telephone phone.) The Talmud, though, rejects Rav's explanation and endorses R. Johanan's view that an *asimon* is a folsa (= follis), which, as Sperber argues, referred, toward the end of R. Johanan's life (260–275 CE), to a bag of blank coins. The *mishnah* may have referred simply to unminted silver or bronze.

rabbinic sources provides its own rewards, but it remains unclear if the scholarship produced will work its way back into the system.

SELECTED BIBLIOGRAPHY

Einzig, Paul. *Primitive Money: In its Ethnological, Historical and Economic Aspects*, 2nd ed. Oxford: Pergamon Press, 1966.

Hurowitz, Victor. "Kæsæp 'ober lassoher (Genesis 23:16)," *Zeitschrift für die alttestamentliche wissenschaft*, v. 108 (1996).

Kletter, Raz. *Economic Keystones: The Weight System of the Kingdom of Judah*. London: Sheffield Academic Press, 1988.

Lifshitz, Berachyahu. *Promise: Obligation and Acquisition in Jewish Law*. Jerusalem, Magnes Press, 1988 (Hebrew).

Liver, Jacob. "The Half-Shekel Offering in Biblical and Post Biblical Literature." *Harvard Theological Review* 56, 3 (July 1963).

Meshorer, Ya'akov. *A Treasury of Jewish Coins*. Nyack: Amphora Books, 2001.

Powell, Marvin. "Masse und Gewichte." In D. O. Edzard, ed., *Reallexikon der Assyriologie* 7,3–4 (Berlin and New York: Walter de Gruyter, 1988).

Sperber, Daniel. *Roman Palestine 200–400 Money and Prices*, 2nd ed. Jerusalem: Bar Ilan Press, 1991.

Stieglitz, Robert R. "Commodity Prices at Ugarit." *Journal of the American Oriental Society* 99,1 (1979).

Warhaftig, Shillem. *Currency in Jewish Law*. Jerusalem: Ariel—Harry Fischel Institute, 1980 (Hebrew).

CHAPTER 30

ECONOMICS AND LAW AS REFLECTED IN HEBREW CONTRACTS

YOSEF RIVLIN

Introduction

This chapter discusses economic theories in Jewish law as reflected in contracts written in Hebrew, in most cases deriving from Ashkenazic communities. The contracts originated from followers of R. Solomon b. Isaac (Rashi, France, 1040–1105), his pupils and their pupils, dating back to the thirteenth, fourteenth, and fifteenth centuries. Most of the contracts discussed are in manuscript form and have never been published. The theories will be examined and the contracts compared with corresponding Sephardic contracts.

The contracts include marriage contracts (*ketubbot*), wills and deathbed wills, sales, partnership agreements, and other agreements from all spheres of life. Although in most cases the contracts are general—without identifying the parties, the location, or value of the transaction, and so on—the contracts do reveal fascinating information about legal and economic procedures that were customary in that society. We can assume that the sage or scribe who prepared the contracts prepared those that were common in his time and place.

One of the salient differences between the Sephardic *ketubbah* and its Ashkenazic counterpart is the fixed sum that appears in the Ashkenazic *ketubbah*. What economic theory dictated this practice and made it so common in Ashkenaz? Were women in a position of strength, such that the bridegroom was forced to agree to a large sum? The phenomenon of a husband's absolving his wife from the widow's oath required to receive the sum in her *ketubbah*—an oath that had been required in Jewish society in the Genizah period—was common in Spain. What is the significance of the change, and was it influenced by the sum written in the *ketubbah*?

The bride's father, who gave a dowry, wanted to protect the property he gave to his daughter at her wedding. How could he do this, and what economic theory dictated his actions?

Loan agreements and guarantees were common in collections of contracts. The character of a guarantee is dictated by the place of the loan and the economic situation at the time. What was preferable—a personal guarantee or a lien on property? Was there a difference between goods or property as a security on a loan?

Partnership agreements vary in the collections. An analysis of each variant can reveal important economic factors specific to the place where the agreement was signed. What was included in the partnership? How were the profits divided? Were both partners active, or was the investor a silent partner? Partnership agreements lead us also to discuss the different forms of powers of attorney.

A detailed examination of the phrasing of these agreements reveals information about the economic situation at the time they were written.

The Hebrew Contract

Gulak assumes that the contract was first used by the Jewish people, when the use of writing began to spread.[1] The Bible refers to contracts for divorce and for purchasing,[2] and the Apocrypha mention loans and marriage contracts.[3] We may assume that they used contracts in other circumstances.[4] Contracts written in the Jewish community in Yeb (Elephantine), Egypt, at the beginning of the Second Temple period suggest that there were standard formulae for the various contracts.[5] The discoveries from Qumran include divorce contracts, *ketubbot*, and contracts of gift and sale.[6]

1 A. Gulak, *A Treasury of Contracts Used in Jewish Law* (Jerusalem: Defus ha-Poa'lim, 1925/6; Hebrew), Introduction, 22.

2 Divorce: Deuteronomy 24:1; Purchase: Jeremiah 32:11.

3 Tobias (long version) 5:3; 7:14, Hasefarim Hachitsony'im, ed. Hartoum, Tel-Aviv: Yavne, 1958, 43, 47.

4 For wills, see Y. Rivlin, *Inheritance and Wills in Jewish Law* (Ramat-Gan: Bar-Ilan University Press, 1999) (below: Rivlin, Ha-Yerusha), 137–38.

5 The contracts date back to the fifth century BCE. Many scholars have reservations regarding the consistency of the contracts with Jewish law.

6 *Discoveries in the Judaean Desert,* documents 19–23, 30 include divorce, *ketubbah*, and sale. See Y. Yadin, "Camp 4—The Cave of the Letters" (Hebrew), *Yedi'ot ba-Hakirat Erets Yisrael ve-Atikoteha* 26 (1962): 204–36, particularly 208–21 for a gift. 221–22 have Babata's *Ketubbah*. For bills of sale, see E. Yardeni, *Documents from the Ze'elim River* (Beer Sheba and Jerusalem, 1995). For gifts, see H. M. Kotan, "Shetarot Mattanah min ha-Arkyonim mi-Midbar Yehudah ve-Hok ha-Yerushot," *Erets Yisrael* 25 (1996): 410–15; Y. Yadin and E. Yardeni, "Shetar Mattanah be-Arammit mi-Nahal Hever" (Papyrus Yadin 7), Ibid.: 383–401.

The Mishnah discusses the wording of different contracts—for example, the *ketubbah*, the *get* (divorce contract), and a contract for work on a field.[7] In the Talmudic period, scribes were experts in the laws of contracts, sometimes surpassing the knowledge of the rabbinical judges.[8]

With regard to the post-Talmudic period, we possess a large variety of contracts.[9] It was in the Geonic period that it became customary to prepare books containing examples of contracts. Compilers wanted to satisfy the needs of rabbinical judges and scribes. The books themselves demonstrate the types of use made of contracts.

At the beginning of the tenth century, R. Saadiah b. Joseph Gaon (Rasag, Babylonia, 882–942) prepared a book of contracts. Around the beginning of the eleventh century, R. Hai b. Sherira Gaon (Babylonia, 939–1038) prepared his book of contracts.[10] At approximately the same time, a collection of contracts was prepared in Alisana in Southern Spain.[11] A number of twelfth-century contract collections are extant: that of R. Judah b. Barzillai al-Bargeloni (Spain, late eleventh–early twelfth centuries), R. Isaac b. Abba Mari of Marseilles (France, 1120–1190), and of R. Simhah b. Samuel of Vitry (d. before 1105), a pupil of Rashi.[12] The known thirteenth–century collection is that of R. Meir Abulafia (Rama, Spain, 1170–1244).[13] There is also a collection of contracts used by Jews in England.[14] An important collection was copied in the fourteenth century and reproduced at the end of the München manuscript of the Babylonian Talmud.[15] An additional collection, prepared in the fourteenth century, derived from Spain and was apparently compiled by R. Isaac b. Sheshet Perfet (Rivash, Spain and North Africa, 1326–1408). The collection includes a selection of contracts presented to his court.[16] Similarly, in the last centuries, such collections were prepared, but their academic value as a source is negligible, since they usually rely on previous contracts that are readily available.

7 Mishnah, *Ketubbot* 4:7–8, 10–12; Mishnah, *Gittin* 3:2; Mishnah, *Bava Metsi'a* 9:3.

8 BT *Bava Batra* 136a: "We consulted with the Scribes of Abbayei and they explained."

9 For example: Rabbi Yehuda'i Gaon, *Halakhot Pesukot*, edited by S. Sason (Jerusalem: Makor, 1971), 50, 163; *Halakhot Pesukot (Reu)*, (Jerusalem, 1967), 102, 113, 121.

10 S. Assaf, "R. Hai Gaon's Book of Contracts" (Hebrew), Appendix to *Tarbits*, vol. 1, part 3 (1930) (below: *Shetarot R. Hai*).

11 Y. Rivlin, *Contracts from the Alisana Congregation from the Eleventh Century* (Ramat Gan: Bar-Ilan University Press, 2005; Hebrew) (below: Rivlin, *Alisana)*.

12 *Book of Contracts Belonging to R. Yehudah son of Barzilai of Barcelona*, Halberstam edition, Berlin, 1898; Jerusalem, 1967 (below: *Shetarot R.Y.B.*); R. Isaac b. Abba Mari of Marseilles. *Sefer ha-Ittur*, Meir Yonah edition, 1–2 (Warsaw, Yosef Unterhendler Press, 1883; Hebrew) (below: *Ittur*); R. Simhah b. Samuel of Vitry, *Mahzor Vitry*, edited by Shimon ha-Levi of Horowitz (Nuremberg: Y. Bulka Publishing House, 1929; Hebrew). (below: *Mahzor Vitry*).

13 *Yad Ramah, Bava Batra*, chapter 10, paragraph 89, to BT *Bava Batra* 169a. All the contracts are concerned with collecting debt using Jewish courts.

14 Loewe, H. Starrs and Jewish Contracts, I. Cambridge, 1930, London, 1932. The collection includes contracts reproduced by Davis. See M. D. Davis (ed.), *Hebrew Deeds of English Jews Before 1290* (London: The Jewish Chronicle, 1888).

15 Y. Rivlin, "Examples of Contracts Attached to the Munich Manuscript of the Babylonian Talmud" (Hebrew), *Shenaton ha-Mishpat ha-Ivri* 20 (2005–2007): 281–348.

16 M. Ben-Sasson, "Mekorot le-Toledot Yisrael bi-Sefarad ba-Me'ah ha-14," in A. Mirsky, A. Grossman, and Y. Kaplan (eds.), *Galut ahar Golah: Mehkarim be-Toledot Am Yisrael Muggashim li-Perofesor Hayyim Beinart li-Melot Lo Shiv'im Shanah* (Jerusalem: Hebrew University Press, 1988), 284–336.

The discovery of the Cairo Genizah contributed greatly to the study of Hebrew contracts. The hundreds of thousands of documents from the Genizah provided material for research in a wide variety of fields, including the construction of contracts.

The Sages gave considerable weight to the phrasing of a contract and, in some cases ruled on legal matters on the basis of these contracts. In their *responsa*, the Geonim instruct the scribes, who write contracts, to take care with regard to phrasing and to adapt it to the specific case, rather than relying on a fixed traditional pattern in an exemplar. R. Isaac b. Jacob Alfasi (Rif, North Africa, 1013–1103) was highly critical of people who witnessed a contract without ensuring it was appropriate for the specific case. It is thus sometimes possible to deduce legal rulings from the phrasing of a contract.

Fixed Sums in a Marriage Contract

According to a Talmudic ruling, a widow is required to take an oath when she claims her marriage portion (*ketubbah*) from the heirs. A husband may free his wife from the oath. *Ketubbot* and wills representing the Jewish legal reality in Ashkenaz in the period between the twelfth and fifteenth centuries do not include the formula in which the husband releases his wife from the oath required to receive the monies specified in the *ketubbah*. This formula, which occurs frequently in wills from the Genizah, in contracts from Spain, and in Sephardic legal literature, is almost completely absent in Ashkenaz. Not only that, we do find various forms of compromise agreement between the widow and the late husband's children with regard to the oath. These agreements prove that the husband did not generally release his widow from the oath, and when she came to claim the money from the *ketubbah* after her husband's death, she would have to negotiate with the heirs regarding the oath. Ultimately, the widow would relinquish some of her entitlement in order to be released from the oath. Why is the release from the oath missing from Ashkenazic documents?

The reason seems to be that the value of the *ketubbah* was set at one hundred litres of silver in Askhenaz.[17] In *Mahzor Vitry*, which was compiled by R. Simhah of Vitry, there is an example of a *ketubbah* in which the sum is fixed at one hundred litres.[18] In a responsum written by R. Jacob b. Moses Moellin (Maharil, Germany and Austria, 1360–1427) we find the sum of fifty litres for a widow—one half the

17 Each litre includes twenty *dinars*, and each *dinar* is twelve *peshitas*; thus, one hundred litres is twenty-four thousand *peshitas*. See Y. A. Agus, "Shi'ur ha-Ketubbah be-Tur Kne-Middah le-Emdatam ha-Kalkalit shel ha-Yehudim be-Germanyah bi-Yemei ha-Beinayim," *Horev* 5 (1929): 143–68, 156. The real value of the agreed sum in the *ketubbah* was not uniform throughout Ashkenaz but varied between ten-kilo and fifty-kilo silver (Agus, Ibid., 160–63).

18 *Mahzor Vitry*, ch. 553.

sum for a virgin.[19] The same ruling appears in R. Israel b. Pethahiah Isserlein's (Germany, 1390–1460) *Terumat ha-Deshen*.[20]

The fixed sum of one hundred litres of silver included both the dowry and an addition to the sum of the *ketubbah*. In other words, the bridegroom would value the property that the bride brought with her at fifty litres, without reference to its true value. He himself would undertake to give (upon death or divorce) fifty silver litres in addition to this value. Why was this sum fixed and what did it reflect? According to R. Eliezer b. Nathan of Mainz (*Ra'avan*, Germany, c. 1090–c. 1170), this was a large sum intended to discourage divorce.[21] Agus suggests another reason: The uncertain political situation—pogroms, exiles, and so on—led to frequent loss of the *ketubbah*. The standardized sum meant that the woman could claim her entire entitlement even if she did not have the *ketubbah*.[22] The apparently exorbitant sum in the *ketubbah* is, in Agus's opinion, a compromise between two conflicting demands. On the one hand, the sum is high enough to discourage rash divorces. On the other, it cannot be so high that nothing remains for the children, who will then burden the communal purse. The sum thus reflects the financial situation of the middle class.[23] Freiman rejects Agus's theories.[24] In his opinion, the sum is indeed high and many were unable to pay it.[25] The sum is intended to prevent rash divorces. This is also connected with the Ashkenazic decree not to divorce a woman against her will. In Freiman's opinion the decree was contemporary with the unification of *kiddushin* and *nissu'in* in Ashkenaz, when the *ketubbah* began to be read in order to separate the two ceremonies. The reading aloud of an insignificant sum would embarrass people without resources, and it was thus decided to fix a large amount.[26] Yisrael

19 *Responsa Maharil, Responsa of Rabbi Yaacov Molin—Maharil*, ed. Y. Satz (Jerusalem: Machon Yerushalayim, 1979), ch. 73.

20 *Terumat ha-Deshen*, Part 2, *Pesakim u-Ketavim*, ch. 232. For a list of places that used sums of this magnitude, see Y. A. Dinari, *Hakhmei Ashkenaz be-Shilhei Yemei ha-Beinayim* (Jerusalem: Mosad Bialik, 1984), p. 57, note 5; Y. Y. Yuval, *Hakhamim be-Doram, ha-Manhigut ha-Ruhanit shel Yahadut Germanyah be-Shilhei Yemei ha-Beinayim* (Jerusalem: Hebrew University Press, 1989), p. 368, note 120.

21 Ravan to *Even ha-Ezer* 98:4. [Freiman: *Ravan* 4, 98–99]. See also the *responsa* by R. Meir b. Baruch of Rothenburg (Maharam me-Rothenburg, Germany, c. 1215–1293), ch. 673.

22 Agus, "Shi'ur ha-Ketubbah," 146–47. This may explain the agreed sum but does not provide any basis to claim the monies.

23 Agus, "The development of the Money Clause in the Ashkenazic Ketubbah," *Jewish Quarterly Review* 30 (1949): 221–56; Agus, "The Standard Ketubbah of the German Jews and its Economic Implications," *Jewish Quarterly Review* 42 (1951–1952): 225–32.

24 Freiman, Ibid.

25 The dispute between Agus and Freiman is connected with another dispute between them regarding the date of the decree. In Agus' opinion, it precedes Rashi; he even tries to relate the agreed sum to the *Ketubbah de-Irkasa*, which is ascribed to Rabbeinu Gershom. Most scholars are more convinced by Freiman's approach, which dates the decree to the Ravan period, since he was the first to explain the decree. See E. A. Auerbach, *Ba'alei ha-Tosafot: Toledoteihem, Hibbureihem, ve-Shitatam* (Jerusalem: Mosad Bialik, 1986), 175–76; Y. Y. Yuval, "Ha-Hesderim ha-Kaspiyim shel ha-Nissu'in be-Ashkenaz bi-Yemei ha-Beinayim," in M. Ben-Sasson (ed.), *Dat ve-Kalkalah: Yahasei Gomelin* (Jerusalem: Merkaz Zalman Shazar, 1995), pp. 191–207, at p. 194. In his explanation, Freiman demonstrates that in the original responsum by Rashi (I. Alfenbein, *Responsa of Rashi*, Bnei-Braq, 1980, ch. 173) there is no reference to the fixed sum. I can also suggest two additional sources from two Ashkenazic collections of contracts, which Rashi was certainly acquainted with and in which the sum in the *ketubbah* was not yet fixed: Wein 20; Frankfurt 69 8° (ms. O.H. by Rashi).

26 Freiman, Ibid., p. 373.

Yuval also agrees that one hundred litres was a very large sum.[27] Some scholars believe that the fixed sum is related to the question of inheritance. This is Grossman's opinion, for example.[28] I do not believe that the intention was to ensure an inheritance for the widow. The husband had far more efficient ways to arrange an inheritance. He could have given her the sum in the *ketubbah* as a present and, in that way, she would have been released from the duty of presenting a full report of her late husband's possessions and of her possessions, as well as from the need to swear an oath in order to receive that to which she was entitled. Alternatively, the husband could have released her from the need to swear in order to receive the *ketubbah*. This could have been incorporated either into the *ketubbah* or into his will.

A detailed examination of many bundles of contracts from Ashkenaz that include both *ketubbot* and testaments reveals that this release does not appear. It would seem that the husband intentionally left the burden of the oath on the widow, in order to enable the heirs to negotiate a smaller repayment on the *ketubbah*. It is therefore not surprising that, although such releases are not found, there are many contracts of compromise regarding the *ketubbah* between the widow and the children or their representatives. The heirs release the widow from the oath and she accepts a much smaller sum in payment of the *ketubbah*. Thus, in one example of a compromise between the heirs and the widow, we find the following: "And I wanted to compromise, that I would give up part of my *ketubbah*, my dowry, and he would release me from the oath. . . ."[29] And in another case: "And they released her from the oath."[30]

It was assumed that the high fixed sum would prevent rash divorces, even though the couple must still negotiate the divorce. In this way, the woman started from a stronger position. In the event of the husband's decease, even though the widow must compromise in order to be released from the oath, she would still receive a comfortable sum, by virtue of her strong initial position.[31]

Protecting the Dowry

The *nedunya* (dowry) is the sum of the possessions that a woman brings to her marriage.[32] In many cases, these possessions were very valuable—almost invariably exceeding the sum that the husband brought to the partnership.[33] The aim of

27 Y. Y. Yuval, Ibid.

28 A. Grossman, *Righteous and Rebellious: Jewish Women in Medieval Europe* (Jerusalem: Merkaz Zalman Shazar, 2001; Hebrew) (below: Grossman, *Righteous and Rebellious*), 260.

29 *Asufot* (H. Hirschfeld, Descriptive Catalogue of the Hebrew MSS. of the Montefiore Library, London 1904, no. 134), *Shetar Pesharah le-Yatom*.

30 Ibid., *Shetar Mehilat Ketubbah*.

31 For additional economic aspects, see Y. Rivlin, "Shevu'at ha-Almanah bein Ashkenaz li-Sefarad," *Mehkerei Mishpat* 21 (2005): 705–20; A. Grossman, *Righteous and Rebellious*, 260.

32 Ben-Yehuda *Milon*, vol. 4, 35–36b defines the dowry as the clothes and jewelry that the father gives his daughter before the wedding. The term appears in BT *Bava Metsi'a* 74b; BT *Ketubbot* 54a; and BT *Ta'anit* 24a.

33 Mishnah, *Ketubbot* 6:5 regarded fifty *zuz* as a minimal sum. The father usually gave a large dowry. In the Geonic period, there were cases when a father gave his daughter all his possessions; see *Otsar ha-Ge'onim*,

providing these possessions for the new home was to provide the couple with financial security in their marriage and perhaps to provide the woman with financial security in the event of divorce or of her husband's decease.[34] It became customary for the husband to accept responsibility for the dowry, turning it into a "blue chip" investment for the wife, since it would continue to retain its original value. The value of the property was written into the *ketubbah*, and in the event of divorce the woman was entitled to receive the value of the dowry together with any other payments specified in the *ketubbah*.

Benin Dikhrin (Male Sons)

The Mishnah records an agreement between the families of the bride and bridegroom to ensure that the dowry remains in the bride's family. The agreement results from negotiations between the families and is constructed as an undertaking by the bridegroom. In the *ketubbah*, the bridegroom undertakes that his children from this wife will be entitled to a larger share in his possessions than children from other marriages.[35] The Mishnah improved the agreement and converted it into a decree.

Although the decree had very limited provenance and was enforced for a short period,[36] the weight of the decree coupled with the discussion surrounding it as recorded in the Babylonian Talmud served to substantially contribute to the efforts to protect the dowry. Although we cannot be certain that this was the first such decree enacted, it was certainly the precursor of and precedent permitting all subsequent decrees regarding the dowry.[37]

Decrees Regarding a Barren Wife

The *benin dikhrin* did not deal with the possibility of a woman's dying without issue in her husband's lifetime. Under these circumstances, the husband inherits his wife's *ketubbah* and all her other possessions, and, after his death, these possessions

Ketubbot, responsa, 138–41. There is a similar case in BT *Ketubbot* 53a. For sources about the dowry, see M. A. Friedman, *Jewish Marriage in Palestine, A Cairo Geniza Study* (vol. 1: Tel Aviv: Tel Aviv University Press, 1980; vol. 2: New York: The Jewish Theological Seminary of America, 1981) (below: Friedman, *Nissu'in* 1), 288–311, 399–418; B. Schereschewsky, *Family Law* (Jerusalem: R. Mas, 1984; Hebrew) (below: Schereschewsky, *Family Law*), 116–18; A. Gulak, *Ha-Shetarot ba-Talmud*, 85–98; Z. Falk, *An Introduction to Jewish Law in the Second Temple Period*, 1–2 (Tel Aviv: Tel Aviv University, 1969–1971; Hebrew), 282–84; A. Gulak, *Elements in Jewish Law*, 1–4 (Berlin, Jerusalem, 1923, Tel Aviv, 1967), vol. 3, 44–65; M. Epstein, *The Jewish Marriage Contract: A Study in the Status of the Woman in Jewish Law* (New York: The Jewish Theological Seminary of America, 1927) (below: Epstein, *Ha-Ketubbah*), 89–106.

34 Friedman, *Nissu'in*, p. 391ff.

35 Mishnah, *Ketubbot* 4:10.

36 For a discussion of the *Benin Dikhrin* decree, its development, and disappearance, see S. Assaf, "The Annulling of the Legacy from a Mother's Estate" (Hebrew), *Ha-Tsofeh le-Hokhmat Yisrael* 10 (1926): 18–29 (below: Assaf, *Inheritance*); P. Dickstein, "Legacy from a Mother's Estate" (Hebrew), *Ha-Mishpat ha-Ivri* 3 (1928): 25–82 (below: Dickstein, *Inheritance*), 74–82; Y. Rivlin, "Shetar Hatsi Zakhar" (Hebrew), *Dine Yisrael* 17 (2003–2004): 155–79 (below: Rivlin, *Hatsi Zakhar*), at 158–62.

37 Rivlin, Ha-Yerushah[[see 4]] *and Wills*, 66–68, 96–102.

become the property of his heirs, who have absolutely no connection with his deceased wife or her family. The connection is unclear between the decree of *benin dikhrin* and another decree originating in Palestine intended to preserve the dowry in this situation. The Jerusalem Talmud quotes R. Yosei as saying, "Whoever stipulates that if a wife dies childless, her property returns to her father's house—this is a financial condition and is valid."[38]

The decree regarding the barren woman and that of the *benin dikhrin* were indubitably designed to defend the dowry when the wife predeceased the husband. There were certainly other attempts to defend the dowry in a way that would address all other eventualities. In one case, the father lent the dowry to the husband. The father obviously retained ownership and could repossess them whenever he wished. This situation was probably unusual and is only mentioned once in the *responsa* literature.[39] Another apparently uncommon solution appears in a document from the Genizah. A father gave his daughter parts of his courtyard and of his house as a dowry, to take effect after his death.[40] He stipulated that, if he needed money, he could cancel the gift. In another paper, I quoted this example as possibly the first instance of a complex condition regarding present given by a healthy man.[41] Usually, under Talmudic law, a present given by somebody in good health to take effect after his death was irreversible. The possession was immediately transferred to the recipient, but the donor could enjoy all benefits from it until he died. After his death, the benefits became the property of the recipient. After giving the present and the act of *kinyan* (taking possession), the donor could not reverse the process.[42] At the end of the Geonic period, we witness the introduction of conditions that modify the situation.

Another solution was to give the wife complete ownership of the possessions. The husband was then excluded from his wife's dowry both during her lifetime and after her death. The husband declares: "I have no claims on your possessions or on their products or on their products' products, both during your lifetime and after your death."[43] The Talmud concludes that this statement, made during the engagement period, is valid and binding on the husband.[44] The husband who has renounced any interest in his wife's possessions does not own the products and cannot inherit his wife. The wife is entitled to do whatever she likes with the dowry: to sell it, give it away, will it, and so on.[45] Indeed, we do not find in the Cairo Genizah any examples where a husband used the Mishnah's formula in order to forfeit his wife's

38 JT *Ketubbot* 9:1, 33a. This version, quoted in the name of R. Yosei, is preferable to the version ascribed to R. Yitshak in JT *Bava Batra* 8:6, 16b; see also Friedman, *Nissu'in*, 394–95, note 7.

39 Avraham Eliyahu Harkavy, *Teshuvot ha-Ge'onim* (New York: Menorah, 1959), ch. 197–98, 305–8.

40 Mishnah, *Bava Batra* 8:7.

41 See Y. Rivlin, "Terumat ha-Genizah le-Heker Dinei Yerushah ve-Tsavva'ot" (Hebrew), *Te'udah* 15 (1999): 241–55, especially 251. The document is TS 10J7.6a from the Cairo Genizah.

42 *Tosefta*, *Bava Batra* 8:1.

43 Mishnah, *Ketubbot* 9:1.

44 BT *Ketubbot* 83a.

45 Maimonides (Rambam, Egypt, 1135–1204), *Mishneh Torah*, *Ishut* 23:2,5.

possessions. However, *ketubbot* originating in Palestine, found in the Genizah, occasionally include the clause: "And they are for her and for her son after her."[46]

Takkanot ha-Kehillot (Communal Decrees)

Time passed and communities became institutionalized. As they constructed a framework of decrees, they began to introduce conditions regarding the financial aspects of the *ketubbah* and dowry. These decrees were common to both Ashkenazic and Sephardic communities. A careful reading of the decrees show that they were variously motivated, but in most cases they helped protect the dowry.

The Ashkenazic decrees were less comprehensive. They were apparently influenced by the original decree from Palestine. R. Jacob b. Meir Tam (France, 1100–1171) decreed that, if the wife died in the first year of her marriage, the whole dowry would be returned to her heirs on her father's side.[47] The Tosafists point out that R. Tam reversed his decision,[48] but we find that his decree was adopted by the "Shum" congregations in Germany, who even extended it.[49]

Personal Agreements

The book *Orehot Hayyim* by R. Aaron b. Jacob ha-Kohen of Lunel (France, thirteenth–fourteenth centuries) includes an interesting collection of documents.[50] Together with the well-known contracts are a number of documents not previously encountered. A number of them relate to the dowry, and a minority of them include very strict agreements, signed by both the bride and the bridegroom, concerning the proper use of the dowry and the protection of the value of the *ketubbah*.

In one such contract the bridegroom acknowledges that he has received the dowry in full and that he has no further claims. "I acknowledge . . . that I have received the full sum of the dowry promised me."[51]

The next document concerns the return of the dowry if the wife dies without issue. "I made the following condition, that if my wife should die without bearing me a son or daughter, I will immediately return part of the dowry."[52]

The next contract is highly unusual, and to the best of my knowledge there is no similar contract extant. The bridegroom is required to preserve the dowry, so

46 Wein collection PER H I. See Friedman, *Nissu'in*, 2, 134. The phrase may be found in additional *ketubbot*; see ibid., 184, 229 etc. For a new suggestion regarding this formula, see Rivlin, *Te'udah* 15, ibid.

47 See Y. Cohen, "Takkanot ha-Kahal bi-Yerushat ha-Ba'al et Ishto" (Hebrew), *Shenaton ha-Mishpat ha-Ivri* 6–7 (1979–1980): 133–75.

48 *Tosafot* (medieval Talmudic glosses, France and Germany, twelfth–fourteenth centuries) to *Ketubbot* 47a, s.v. "*katav lah*."

49 Cohen, ibid., 148, note 80; 150.

50 Y. Rivlin, "Tikkun Shetarot le-Ba'al Orehot Hayyim" (Hebrew), *Kovets al Yad* 18 (2005): 223–88 (below: Rivlin, *Orehot Hayyim*). R. Aaron was born in southern France (Provence) in the second half of the thirteenth century and was driven out of France together with the rest of the Jews in 1306. He settled on the island Majorca in the Mediterranean Sea, close to Spain, and apparently wrote his book there.

51 Ibid., 266.

52 Ibid., 267.

that he will be able to pay the *ketubbah* and alimony if necessary. The conditions are strict. The bridegroom must place the dowry in a special chest, closed with two locks. The chest is deposited in the house of a third party. The bridegroom administers the monies together with the third party. The intention is to preserve the value of the dowry or to increase it. The purpose of the two locks is to ensure that the bridegroom will need the other administrator in order to carry out any actions with regard to the dowry. Each administrator has one key. "The dowry is . . . *dinars*, and is security for my wife's *ketubbah*, and it will be deposited in the house of *Peloni* for a certain number of years in one chest with two locks and two keys. I will hold one key and *Peloni* the other."[53]

Among a collection of Ashkenazic contracts appears the following:

> I have reserved the dowry which my wife brought with her, whether it be garments, jewelry, silver or gold or anything else. She shall retain full control to do whatever she wants, to give whatever presents she wishes to whomever she wants, and I have no interest in her dowry and am not permitted to take anything from it.[54]

The purpose of a contract is not always clear. Sometimes the phrasing does not reveal the contract's main purpose. One example is a debt to a daughter. This contract appears in a number of collections connected with Ashkenazic Jewry, where a person declares that he received a sum of money from another person. The money represents a debt and the debtor undertakes to return the money to the creditor's daughter. The daughter is a minor and the debtor is scheduled to return the money at the daughter's marriage. The debtor agrees to work with the money, and the profits are to be given to the daughter. As a security, the debtor mortgages one of his properties to the creditor. After the payment of the debt, the mortgage will be cancelled. This is the text of the contract:

> For the credit of the daughter of *Peloni*, the minor *Pelonit*. We have received monies, to guard them and to make a profit for them on his daughter's behalf, and we accept responsibility for the money in all circumstances. . . . As a security, we have mortgaged land in our possession, located in. . . . When the daughter marries, we will return the money and the mortgage will be cancelled.[55]

One could offer a number of different explanations of this contract. It is possibly intended to protect the dowry. Additional research is required.

We have already seen from Talmudic sources that a large dowry contributes toward the couple's standard of living. The Sages encouraged bargaining to protect the dowry, since this tended to calm the bride's father so that he would be ready to give a substantial dowry.[56] The various financial arrangements and decrees contributed to this end.

53 Ibid., 268.

54 Gift of *Ketubbah*. Oxford, ms. no. 1104.

55 A debt in favor of his daughter, *Asufot*.

56 BT *Ketubbot* 52b.

Loans and Securities

There is one reason for taking a loan: a need for ready cash. Some take a loan in order to invest in a business to make a living. The purpose of the loan will generally dictate the size of the loan. This in turn dictates the types of guarantees that the creditor will require. In the case of a businessman who intends to invest the money, the loan is usually large and the creditor will require corresponding guarantees. There are a number of means to guarantee a loan. The Talmud discusses them in detail, starting with a personal guarantee: guarantor, mortgaging assets, general responsibility, and mortgage.[57] Not only were these precautions of great importance, but the lender was also interested in profits. How could he enjoy some advantage from the use of his money? We must remember that Jewish law did not permit the taking of interest, a circumstance that made it difficult for a person who wanted some advantage from his money. Sages in every generation tried to solve this problem. There are different types of prohibitions regarding interest. One of the key issues is whether the transaction can be regarded as a sale rather than a loan. Thus, if A sells his field to B, B, the new owner, can benefit from the produce from the field, even if A still intends to buy it back. There are only two types of transactions in which the owner of the field can benefit from its produce. If the first transaction between A and B was not the purchase of the field, but rather a loan to A and the transfer of the field to B as security for the debt, then B is not entitled to the produce, since this is considered interest. In both cases, the same money changes hands at the same time, but the first transaction is a sale and permissible, whereas the second is a loan and prohibited.

The possibility of calling a transaction a sale was preferred by many debtors who wished to disguise the loan as a commercial transaction. This was an appropriate solution for a creditor who wanted to benefit from the produce of the field until the loan was repaid. The debtor feared this solution, since, unlike a mortgage, it transferred ownership of the asset to the creditor. The debtor obviously had no interest in giving up his field forever and tried to ensure the return of the field after payment of the debt, using a reversible sale. The structure of such a transaction is: "I sell you my land but buy it back tomorrow."

However, this approach negates the illusion of a sale and reveals the loan beneath. The Sages therefore permitted this transaction only if the return of the asset is not built in. The early rabbinical authorities offered two explanations for the case of a reversible sale found in the Talmud: (a) The buyer, not the seller, initiated the return of the property; (b) the possibility of reversing the sale was not raised at the time of the sale, but afterward. The basis of these two permissible alternatives is the assumption that there is no legal obligation to return the land, and such an intention does not influence the initial sale. The borrower/seller has

57 See Rivlin, *Alisana*, 46ff.

no choice but to rely on the goodwill of the lender/buyer. This was probably the reason that the reversible sale was not common in the Talmud. The mortgage was far more popular.

The Talmud offers a number of possibilities with regard to the mortgage. Some are permissible a priori, others are absolutely prohibited, and some are the subject of heated discussion. The most common and well-known type is the *Mashkanta be Nakyata*. As Ravina says: "This mortgage, where the borrower may pay his debt whenever he wishes, he should only eat of the produce, if the value of the produce is deducted from the debt. . . . R. Kahana and R. Pappa and R. Ashi did not enjoy the produce; Ravina did eat of the produce."[58] The lenient approach is only appropriate where the borrower is not allowed to pay the debt whenever he wants even when the creditor objects. In these circumstances the loan is closer to a sale. However, where the borrower is entitled to pay his debt whenever he likes, the mortgage remains a loan.

The Geonim differed regarding whether to permit the produce as a partial repayment of the loan. R. Sherira b. Hanina Gaon (Babylonia, c. 906–1006) forbade the practice: "We have seen that it is forbidden to eat the produce and to credit the borrower."[59] Similarly R. Hai Gaon in his responsum to *Benei Kiru'ani* writes: "The only sort of mortgage that everybody agrees to permit is *Mashkanta de-Sura*."[60] The author of *Halakhot Gedolot* permitted the *Mashkanta be-Nakyata*: "And these days it is accepted practice that the creditor eats of the produce and credits the borrower."[61] R. Ya'akov Gaon (Babylonia, eighth century) and R. Kohen Tsedek Gaon (Babylonia, tenth century) are of the same opinion.[62] Assaf interprets the situation as a dispute between the *yeshivot* (academies).[63] His approach is confirmed by what we know about the Jewish community in Alisana, which was under the influence of the *yeshivah* in Sura.[64]

The study of Jewish legal sources yields a fascinating picture of the struggle between vision and action, theory and practice. Note that of concern in these cases is not interest per se, but rather with what is called in Jewish sources "the dust of interest" or "pseudo-interest." Thus, while the Sages tended to be strict in theoretical study, practical rulings tended to be more lenient, especially when there was already an established local practice—the guiding principle being that it was preferable to let a Jew to commit a minor sin out of ignorance rather than run the risk that he would rebel against a strict ruling.[65]

In their discussion of the Talmudic source, early rabbinical authorities ruled against Ravina. In other words, they prohibited the creditor from benefiting from

58 BT *Bava Metsi'a* 16b.

59 *Sha'arei Tsedek (Teshuvot HaGeonim, Sha'arei Tsedek*, Jerusalem: Kelal Uperat, 1966), 4, 2, chapter 2, 76.

60 *Sha'arei Tsedek*, 4, 2, chapter 12, 87.

61 *Halakhot Gedolot, Ribbit* (Jerusalem: Mekhon Yerushalayim, 1992), 488.

62 *Ittur*, letter *peh*, *Potiki*, part 1, 65a–b.

63 S. Assaf, *Tekufat ha-Ge'onim ve-Sifrutah* (Jerusalem: Mosad ha-Rav Kuk, 1977), 271–72.

64 Rivlin, *Alisana*, 31–45.

65 Rambam, *Responsa*, responsum 42 (Jerusalem, 1975), 70–71.

the produce of a mortgaged field, even when he deducted the value of the produce from the loan. Rif, R. Hananel b. Hushi'el (North Africa, d. 1055/6), R. Nissim b. Jacob b. Nissim ibn Shahin (North Africa, c. 990–1062), Nahmanides (Ramban, Spain, 1194–1270), R. Isaiah b. Mall di Trani (Rid, Italy, c. 1200–c. 1260), and R. Zechariah b. Judah Aghmati (North Africa, late twelfth–early thirteenth centuries) prohibited the practice.[66] However, R. Solomon b. Abraham Adret's (Rashba, Spain, c. 1235–c. 1310) student presented the dissenting opinions and added: "And there is no need to go into detail, since the practice now is to permit the practice everywhere and with regard to every sort of security, crediting the borrower with the monies, whether it be a house, a field, or a vineyard, whether the borrower can pay off his debt whenever he wants or whether there are restrictions relating to the time when the debt may be repaid."[67] Rif's ruling is worthy of notice. In his legal work he forbade *Mashkanta be-Nakyata*. His *responsa*, however, vary. In some, he forbids the practice. These *responsa* were apparently written when he was in North Africa and were intended for North African Jews, who followed R. Hai Gaon. The *responsa* in which he allowed the mortgage were written in Spain, where the communities followed the rulings of the *yeshivah* in Sura, allowing *Mashkanta be-Nakyata*. Ramban, Rashba, and other authorities adopted the same practice. The *responsa* from Spain reveal that there was a very highly developed system of mortgages there, and the question of the permissibility of the *Mashkanta be-Nakyata* was raised frequently.[68]

The use of *Nakyata* benefits both sides. The borrower receives the loan that he needs; the land that is security for the loan remains his property and is returned to him when he repays. The creditor receives land as a security and his interests are protected. He is allowed to work the land and to eat profit from its produce every year in return for a payment that will be deducted from the loan. It is therefore strange that this arrangement slowly disappears, to be replaced by the reversible sale.

The apparent reason is economic. It would seem that more borrowers were forced to offer their houses as security to their creditors. This situation was caused by a number of factors. First, many Jews had been expelled from their homes and had reached the Balkans and North Africa as paupers. They were so poor that they were barely able to afford a place to live. They had no other possessions to offer a creditor; their house was their only security for a loan. Second, it is very possible that many loans were used in order to buy a house, which was the borrower's only possession of value and thus had to stand as security for the loan. Third, the desire to buy a house was great, since property was scarce and both Jews and non-Jews who owned property charged exorbitant rents. The purchase of a house, even if it

66 See their commentaries to the Talmud.

67 Quoted in *Shitat Kadmonim* to BT *Bava Metsi'a* 56 (New York, 1967), 169.

68 See Rivlin, *Alisana*, 57–59. There are no signs that the importance of the mortgage declined, certainly not in Spain. Compare: S. Lerner, *Elements in the Law of the Security for a Loan in Jewish Law* (Ph.D. dissertation, Hebrew University of Jerusalem, 2000; Hebrew), 39.

had to be mortgaged to a creditor, and even if it was necessary to pay the creditor rent, made economic sense.[69]

The new situation changed the prevailing attitudes toward the *Mashkanta be-Nakyata*. Business was conducted in this way on condition that the creditor profit from the produce and deduct a stipulated sum from the loan in return. However, a mortgage where the borrower remained in the house and paid rent to the creditor was forbidden in the Talmud and in later rulings, and we have not found any attempts in the *responsa* to compromise on such a loan. The economic situation changed the legal conditions, and this combination required a new solution that would be appropriate to the new economic and legal reality: the reversible sale. Only if the property became undisputedly that of the creditor was he allowed to rent it to the borrower.

From the point of view of the seller/borrower, this was the only way to continue living on the property. In other words, from the minute that a person needed to borrow money in order to buy a house of his own or to reduce the rent that he paid, or for any other purpose, and wanted to continue living in his house, the *Mashkanta be-Nakyata* was prohibited, and he had no choice but to sell the house to the creditor in return for the creditor's pledge that he would be willing to return the house on request.

Although the Ashkenazic authorities also permitted the *Mashkanta be-Nakyata*, there are very few *responsa* from Ashkenaz on the subject. Why?

The Ashkenazic contracts and the *responsa* again show that the reversible sale was used considerably less in Ashkenaz. Some scholars attribute this to the severity of the authorities' attitude to substitutes for interest. However, research reveals that this severity was on paper only. In practice, the Ashkenazic rabbinical authorities had a lenient attitude in questions of interest.[70] Others suggest that the utter rejection of interest by Christians was the source of the differences between Sefarad and Ashkenaz.[71] Still others point out that the Ashkenazic *Hetter Iska* rendered the

69 Decrees regarding rights that were enacted in Salonika and Constantinople were the result of the scarcity of accommodation. See Abraham b. Mordecai ha-Levi (Egypt, seventeenth century), *Responsa Ginnat Veradim, Hoshen Mishpat*, principle 6, ch. 2 (Jerusalem, 1992), 228. The first decrees were enacted in the sixteenth century. The scarcity of accommodations continued into the eighteenth century and even later: "Up until the middle of the 19th century, the R. S. of Salonika continued to deal with rights to property as a matter of urgency," M. Molkho, "Takkanat Hezkat Battim, Hatserot, ve-Hanuyot be-Salonike" (Hebrew), *Sinai* 14 (1951), 303. My thanks to Dr. M. Litman who drew my attention to these sources. See also Z. Warhaftig, *Possession in Jewish Law* (Jerusalem: Mosad ha-Rav Kuk, 1924; Hebrew), 246–60; S. Bar-Asher, "Petah Davar," in *Takanot Yehudei Maroko* (Jerusalem: Merkaz Zalman Shazar, 1977; Hebrew), 8–9; A. Namdar, *Hakikat Takkanot ha-Kahal al Pi Hakhmei Salonike ba-Me'ah ha-16* (M.A. thesis, Hebrew University of Jerusalem, 1973), 18–19. Benayahu deals with an act passed in 1730 and he points out that these acts were the subject of litigation in the eighteenth century; see M. Benayahu, "Haskamot Hezkat ha-Hatserot, ha-Battim ve-ha-Hanuyot be-Salonike u-Piskeihem shel R. Yosef Taitachak ve-Hakhmei Doro," *Michael* 9 (1985): 55–146.

70 See H. Soloveitchik, *Halakhah, Kalkalah ve-Dimmui Atsmi: Ha-Mashkona'ut bi-Yemei ha-Beinayim* (Jerusalem: Magnes Press, 1985; Hebrew), 10: "These rulings reflected the adaptation to a new situation"; Y. Katz, *Masoret u-Mashber: Ha-Hevrah ha-Yehudit be-Motsa'ei Yemei ha-Beinayim* (Jerusalem: Mosad Bialik, 1958), 83–87.

71 Research into the economic activity of the Jews in the East and West offers various reasons for the variations in the attitudes to interest, but does not generally ascribe it to the authorities. See, for example, A. Toaff, "Ha-Banka'ut ha-Yehudit be-Merkaz Italyah ba-Me'ot ha-13 ad ha-15," in H. Beinart (ed.), *Yehudim be-Italyah: Mehkarim* (Jerusalem: Magnes Press, 1988), 109–30; D. Karphy, "Le-Toledot ha-Malvim ha-Yehudim be-Montipalchano ba-Me'ah ha-14 ve-Hathalat ha-Me'ah ha-15," in Ibid., 231–74; M. Ben-Sasson, *Tsemihat ha-Kehillah ha-Yehudit be-Artsot ha-Islam: Kiru'an, 800–1057* (Jerusalem: Magnes Press, 1996), 101 (below:

reversible sale superfluous.[72] It is very possible that each of these reasons directly or indirectly contributed to the lack of use of the reversible sale. In my opinion the real cause was economic. The reversible sale developed from the *Mashkanta be-Nakyata*. Therefore, a society that did not use mortgages would not develop the reversible sale. We have already pointed out that the extent of the discussions regarding mortgages is far more limited in Ashkenaz than in Sefarad. This may be ascribed to the expansion of securities, which played a crucial part in the development of credit in Germany.[73] It is possible that the reversible sale did not take root in Germany for the same reasons that securities were preferred over mortgages there. If the reversible sale is, as we have claimed, the result of the influence of Jewish law on the new situation of a housing shortage and consequent incentives to mortgage, then it is clear that, without the initial stage of the mortgage, the reversible sale would not develop.

The *Iska* Partnership

Among business contracts, the "partnership contract" is of special interest. Jewish legal literature discusses two main types of partnership. The first is a regular partnership in which both partners invest and work in the business. In the second type of partnership, one partner provides the money and the second works.[74] In this case of a silent partner, it is assumed the two sides have agreed that half of the money invested is given as a loan, and half is deposited. The difference between the loan and the deposit is the extent of the responsibility of the active partner. In Jewish law, a guardian, even if paid for his services, has limited liability. In cases of force majeure he is not held liable to return the money to its owners.[75] This limited liability has an advantage for the silent partner, or investor: Any profits belong to him. In contrast, the responsibility of the borrower for a loan is absolute, but the creditor cannot

Ben-Sasson, *Kiru'an*); Y. T. Asis, "Ha-Yehudim be-Malkhut Aragonyah u-ve-Azorei Hasutah," in H. Beinart (ed.), *Moreshet Sefarad* (Jerusalem: Magnes Press, 1982), 36–80; Y. Haker, "Yotse'ei Sefarad ba-Imperyah ha-Otmanit ba-Me'ah ha-16: Kehillah ve-Hevrah," Ibid., 460–78; H. Gerber, "Yehudim be-Adiranah ba-Me'ot ha-16 ve-ha-17," *Sefunot* 18 (1985): 35–51; H. Ben-Sasson, *Perakim be-Toledot ha-Yehudim bi-Yemei ha-Beinayim* (Tel Aviv: Am Oved, 1969), 56–72.

72 The *Hetter Iska* is discussed in R. Baruch ha-Levi Epstein (Russia, 1860–1842), *Tosefet Berakhah* (Jerusalem: Moreshet, 1964) to Leviticus 25:36; S. Halevi, *Sefer Nahalat Shiv'ah* (Benei Berak: Frankel, no date; Hebrew), contract 40, 83b–85a. For an economic analysis, see A. Ha-Kohen and Z. Sorotzkin, "Banka'ut le-Lo Ribbit ve-'Hetter Iska' be-'Medinah Yehudit ve-Demokratit'—Halakhah ve-Ein Morin Ken?" in *Sha'arei Mishpat* 2,1 (1999): 77–100. In my opinion, the *Hetter Iska* has a very different purpose from that of the reversible sale. There was no need to connect them and use of one does not preclude use of the other.

73 The reasons and conditions for this development in Ashkenaz are treated in detail by Soloveitchik, *Halakhah, Kalkalah ve-Dimmui Atsmi*; see also M. Elon, *Heirut ha-Perat be-Darkhei Geviyyat Hov ba-Mishpat ha-Ivri* (Jerusalem: Magnes Press, 1964), 134, 153, 262.

74 See Rivlin, *Alisana*, 203–4.

75 Mishnah *Bava Metsi'a* 7:8.

receive more than the capital he lent. We can therefore assume it is in the interests of both sides—the silent and active partners—to split the money in two, part loan and part deposit.[76] The partners are, of course, allowed to make other arrangements—for example, one hundred percent loan or one hundred percent deposit. In every case where part of the capital is defined as a loan, great care is required to avoid interest, as the Talmud points out. If the profits are divided equally, the active partner is paying "the dust of interest." The borrower is, in effect, working for nothing, and this represents an additional payment for use of the capital. The profits must therefore be divided in such a way that the active partner receives more than the silent partner, thereby receiving compensation for his work. The remuneration may also be organized in a different way. The two partners may divide profits equally, with the silent partner undertaking to pay more than half the losses. They can also take equal shares in the profits but allot the active partner a salary from the business.

The Talmud rules that the two partners should not pay expenses equally, to avoid the danger of interest. The *Tosefta* awards the silent partner one third of the profits, while the active partner receives two thirds.[77] The losses are shared equally. In both *Halakhot Pesukot*[78] and *Halakhot Gedolot*[79] there are similar arrangements. The profits are divided equally, but the investor is liable for two thirds of any losses. R. Saadiah Gaon ruled similarly in a case brought before him where the partners had not agreed on the division of losses before setting up the partnership.[80]

There are thus three possible ways to avoid the payment of interest in what is called *Iska* in Hebrew, as summarized by R. Hai Gaon: an unequal division of either the profits or the losses, or the payment of a salary to the active partner. The amount of remuneration, R. Hai rules, should be equal to the salary of an unemployed worker in the same profession. The first priority is to ensure that the investor in this kind of partnership is liable to some element of risk. It is also necessary to ensure that the active partner receives remuneration. If he is not paid, it is as if he works for free for the investor, rewarding him for his investment, which could be interpreted as interest and is therefore prohibited. The best solution is therefore to pay a salary.

However, the silent partner should take some responsibility in the case of a loss. The Geonim (including the authors of *Halakhot Pesukot* and *Halakhot Gedolot*) ruled that, in the event of a loss, the active partner need not return the deposit.[81]

In the *Tosefta*, the active partner's wage was fixed at that of an unemployed worker.[82] A survey of the literature reveals that Rif agrees with R. Hai Gaon that the active partner's wage is fixed at that of an unemployed worker.[83] Maimonides

76 BT *Bava Metsi'a* 104b.

77 *Tosefta, Bava Metsi'a* 4:11.

78 *Halakhot Pesukot*, 49.

79 *Halakhot Gedolot*, 406.

80 *Teshuvot ha-Ge'onim*, ch. 540.

81 Rivlin, *Alisana*, 212–14; H. Gamoran, Jewish Law in Transition (Cincinnati: HUC Press), 2008, 132ff (below: Gamoran).

82 *Tosefta, Bava Metsi'a* 4:11.

83 R. Hai Gaon, *Sha'are Tsedek* 4, 8, 6; Rif to *Bava Metsi'a* idem.

(Rambam, Egypt, 1135–1204) is more stringent and rules that he is entitled to a real wage consonant with the work done. R. Abraham b. David of Posquières (Rabad, France, c. 1125–c. 1198) adopts another approach appearing in the Talmud, ruling that only a symbolic payment is necessary. In his opinion, even one *dinar* is sufficient if the partners had previously agreed on this wage.[84] The early Rabbinical authorities also differed with regard to the allocation of responsibility. Rabad is lenient with regard to the active partner, pointing out that the he is unable to bury the money for safekeeping as is required of a paid guardian, since he needs to work with the money. His responsibility is therefore less, and if the money is lost he is not liable.

Under normal conditions, Rabad tries to place most of the responsibility on the working partner and seems to try to improve the position of the investor. Rabad recommends that the silent partner not sign an agreement with the active partner. Then, if there are profits, he can take half, claiming that in the event of a loss he would have paid two thirds. If there are losses, he pays a wage to the active partner and covers only half of the losses.[85]

In a contract originating in Germany the two sides take equal risks in both profits and losses: "The profits will be divided into two; I, *Peloni*, will take one part, and he will take the other part, and similarly the losses, I one part and he one part." The investor must pay a salary. Since only pseudo-interest is at stake, a symbolic wage is sufficient: "I received 1 *zuz* as compensation for my work."[86]

In the modern period, a new agreement was developed, called the *Hetter Iska*. The main question in such an agreement remains the allocation of responsibility. Two types of requirements were common in the period of the early rabbinical authorities. The first required that the active partner bury the money in the ground. If he did not do so, he would have to return the money. The other type of condition empowered the investor to claim that the active partner was negligent in guarding the money. Only the lay heads of the community, the rabbi, and the *hazzan* (cantor) could overrule the claim.

At a later stage, the question was raised whether the *Hetter Iska* should be used only in the case of money for a business, or whether it could be adapted for other purposes. R. Abraham b. Mordecai ha-Levi (Egypt, seventeenth century), in his book of *responsa Ginnat Veradim*, and R. Abraham Zevi Hirsch Eisenstadt (Poland, c. 1670–1744), in his book *Panim Me'irot*, limit the use of the *Hetter Iska* to business purposes. *Shulhan Arukh ha-Rav* follows their ruling. The general tendency was to be more lenient in the matter. In *responsa Sho'el u-Meshiv*, authored by R. Joseph Saul Nathanson (Ukraine, 1810–1875), it is ruled that if the investor is aware of the purpose of the investment, the *Iska* is definitely permitted. R. Breish (Switzerland, twentieth century) even ruled that the *Iska* may be used in a marriage agreement. This was generally accepted. R. Moses Feinstein (New York, 1895–1986) ruled that it

84 Rabad, *Mishneh Torah, Sheluhin ve-Shuttafin* 6:2.

85 Rambam, ibid., 6:2–5.

86 *Asufot*, Partnership Agreement.

covered the relationship between a client and his bank even when the client was unaware of the existence of the *Hetter Iska*.[87]

Guardianship

There are many wills from the Cairo Genizah in which a guardian is appointed to administer the property of the deceased. In some cases, the guardian has considerable power and is entitled to handle all matters relating to the estate. In other cases, he is responsible for a specific matter. The Sages of the Talmud were of the opinion that the guardian's right to handle (minor) heirs' affairs derives from the Talmudic saying: "One is permitted to benefit a person without his knowledge."[88]

The Mishnah discusses the need for a guardian to take an oath when he completes his task.[89] During the Talmudic and Geonic periods, supervision became more stringent. However, an examination of contracts of appointment of guardians found in the Genizah and the extant contracts from Ashkenaz reveals that the guardian was very often exempted, before beginning the job, from the oath. R. Judah al-Bargeloni writes that a guardian was exempted from the oath because he made it a precondition before agreeing to undertake the task.[90] In every will from the Genizah in which a guardian is appointed, there is a clear attempt to facilitate his work as far as possible. He is freed from all oaths, from all legal claims, and from any other claims against his management; his word is regarded as equal to that of two legal witnesses.[91] The reason is probably that of Abba Shaul: "And if he is obliged to take an oath, then he will not agree to accept the task."[92] Disinclination to take an oath was very strong. The guardian was not paid for his work, apart from the fillip to his reputation. It would seem that the compensation was not sufficient to offset the need to take an oath.[93]

The same occurred in the case of the guardian appointed by the court, who by law was required to take an oath. R. Isaac of Marseilles in his *Sefer ha-Ittur* comments: "And the court may not appoint a guardian without his taking an oath, because one has to be very careful not to harm the heirs."[94] R. Saadiah Gaon provides an example of an appointment of a guardian, which does not include a release from the oath.[95] R. Hai Gaon offers exemption from legal claims and any other

87 Gamoran, ibid.

88 BT *Kiddushin* 42a.

89 BT *Gittin* 5:4.

90 *Shetarot R.Y.B.*, 7.

91 Rivlin, Ha-Yerushah, 230.

92 BT *Gittin* 52b.

93 Regarding the release from an oath given by a husband to his wife, see above, paragraph 3.

94 *Ittur*, letter *peh*, *Potiki*, 67–68.

95 *Shetarot, R. Saadiah Gaon* (S. Assaf, "Sefer Hashetarot shel Rav Se'adya," in: *Sefer Rav Se'adya Gaon*, Jerusalem: Mosad HaRav KUK, 1933), 96. Appointment of a guardian for orphans and their possessions.

claims against his management: "Whatever the guardian does, when the heirs become adults they may not sue him, nor may any other person, whether they are relations or live far away, whether it is an important court or a householder, they are not allowed to appeal his decisions or protest his actions, nor to annul anything that he has done."[96] However, in a contract published by Aptowitzer, an exemption from the oath appears: "We hereby exempt the guardian of these heirs from swearing an oath, from any claims and appeals, and from excommunication and any action of the courts, whether they be Jewish or non-Jewish courts."[97]

Permits (Power of Attorney)

In a collection of contracts from the eleventh century originating in the town Alisana (Spain), I pointed out a number of special permits. One sort of permit is a power of attorney for a representative, who apparently was a sort of lawyer. The owner issued a power of attorney to save inherited goods from the hands of squatters. It would seem that the likelihood of saving the goods through the courts was not high, and the representative was thus offered fifty percent of the value of the goods for his services. The terms are sweeping. The owner of the possessions is not permitted to interfere and has no say in the methods used or in the decisions taken. The owner accepts any decision and any results of the actions taken.[98]

Another form of permit, which is also specific to Alisana, concerns the concealment of payments for services rendered. It would seem that the professional representative received a very high payment and was interested in concealing the fact using the following method. He receives a power of attorney to save property from squatters and together with the power of attorney he also purchases the property. The price paid is low and therefore in the second part of the contract the owner gives up his rights for compensation if the price is found to be lower than the real value.[99]

An examination of contracts from Ashkenaz does not reveal any similar documents. However, there is one contract connected with the repossession of property from squatters: "I appointed a guardian, representative, who has a power of attorney to repossess from any person who is holding goods or books or silver or gold or anything which was the property of my brother *Reb Peloni*, the son of *Peloni* . . . to

96 *Shetarot R. Hai*, p. 50. It appears in Louis Ginzburg's *Ginzei Shechter* in *Teshuvot ha-Ge'onim* (Jerusalem: H. Vagshal, b. 198) with minor changes. See his comments. Compare to R. Hai Gaon's detailed responsum with regard to the guardian in *Teshuvot ha-Ge'onim*, ch. 178, 76–80 (=*Teshuvot Ge'onei Mizrah u-Ma'arav* [New York: Menorah, 1959], ch. 5, 2b–3a; *Otsar ha-Ge'onim, Gittin, responsa*, ch. 275, 106); *Teshuvot ha-Ge'onim*, Marmorstein (Jerusalem, 1967), ch. 6, 21 (=*Otsar ha-Ge'onim*, ibid., ch. 274, 105).

97 V. Aptowitzer, *Mehkarim be-Sifrut ha-Ge'onim* (Jerusalem: Mosad ha-Rav Kuk, 1941), Documents, 29. For the exalted status of the guardian in Kiru'an, see Ben-Sasson, *Kiru'an*, 237–38.

98 Rivlin, *Alisana*, 173–77.

99 Ibid., 195–99.

sue them . . . until he succeeds in retrieving my brother's property."[100] In this case the payment to the representative was not set down.

Summary and Conclusions

This discussion demonstrates that the Hebrew contract is a powerful instrument enabling advanced economic activity. In effect, there is no limit to the range of possible agreements between parties facilitating their economic activity. Family law is also regulated through these agreements. We discussed an example where the husband raised the value of the *ketubbah* but left the final sum open to negotiation between the widow and the heirs. The agreement makes an important contribution to family life. The incentives given to a father to raise the value of the dowry help to set the young couple's married family on a firm financial basis. The incentives are the means used to defend the dowry against loss or erosion.

Personal agreements are obviously of importance when discussing loans. The basic problem in these cases is the prohibition of taking interest. Loaning a businessman money as a return-yielding investment is obviously of service to commerce. We compared the *Mashkanta be-Nakyata* with the reversible sale, examining their advantages and disadvantages. Their use is dictated by the economic situation. Partnership agreements are also based on personal contracts, where the first priority is to escape the prohibition of interest while ensuring that both partners benefit from the agreement.

One of the important instruments used is the power of attorney, regarding which there are once again a variety of contracts, powers, and remunerations.

SELECTED BIBLIOGRAPHY

Assaf, S. "The Annulling of the Legacy from a Mother's Estate" (Hebrew). *Ha-Tsofeh le-Hokhmat Yisrael* 10 (1926): 18–29.

———. "R. Hai Gaon's Book of Contracts" (Hebrew). Appendix to *Tarbits* 1, 3, 1930.

Ben-Sasson, M. *Society and Leadership in Jewish Communities in North Africa in the Medieval Period: Kiruan, 800–1057*. Ph.D. dissertation, Hebrew University of Jerusalem, 1983; Hebrew.

Ben-Sasson, M. "Relics from the Book of the Congregation and the Contracts of Rabbeinu Saadiah Gaon" (Hebrew). *Shenaton ha-Mishpat ha-Ivri* 11–12 (1984–1986): 135–278.

Benoit, P., J. T. Milik., and R. de Vaux. *Discoveries in the Judaean Desert,* vol. 2: *Les Grottes de Murabba'at* (Texts and Plates in separate volumes). Oxford: Clarendon Press, 1961.

100 *Tseidah la-Derekh, Shetar Harsha'ah* (a manuscript, in Hirshfeld catalogue [above] no. 130).

Book of Contracts Belonging to R. Yehudah son of Barzilai of Barcelona, Halberstam edition, Berlin, 1898; Jerusalem, 1967.

Davis, M. D. (ed.). *Hebrew Deeds of English Jews Before 1290*. London: The Jewish Chronicle, 1888.

Dickstein, P. "Legacy from a Mother's Estate" (Hebrew), *Ha-Mishpat ha-Ivri* 3 (1928): 25–82.

Epstein, Louis M. *The Jewish Marriage Contract: A Study in the Status of the Woman in Jewish Law*. New York: Jewish Theological Seminary of America, 1927.

Falk, Z. *An Introduction to Jewish Law in the Second Temple Period*, 1–2. Tel Aviv: Tel Aviv University Press, 1969–1971 (Hebrew).

Friedman, M. A. *Jewish Marriage in Palestine, A Cairo Geniza Study*. Vol. 1: Tel Aviv: Tel Aviv University Press, 1980. Vol. 2: New York: The Jewish Theological Seminary of America, 1981.

Grossman, A. *Righteous Women and Rebellious Women: Jewish Women in Medieval Europe*. Jerusalem: Merkaz Zalman Shazar, 2001 (Hebrew).

Gulak, A. *A Treasury of Contracts Used in Jewish Law*. Jerusalem: Defus ha-Po'alim, 1925/6 (Hebrew).

———. *Elements in Jewish Law*, 1–4. Berlin, Jerusalem, 1923, Tel Aviv: Devir, 1967 (Hebrew).

Halakhot Gedolot. Jerusalem: Halberstam edition, 1967 (Hebrew).

Halevi, S. *Sefer Nahalat Shiv'ah*. Benei Berak: Frankel, no date (Hebrew).

Lerner, S. *Elements in the Law of the Security for a Loan in Jewish Law*. Ph.D. dissertation, Hebrew University of Jerusalem, 2000; Hebrew.

Loewe, H. *Starrs and Jewish Charters Preserved in the British Museum*. Vol. 1: Cambridge: Cambridge University Press, 1930. Vol. 2: London, 1932.

Rabbi Isaac B. Abba Mari of Marseilles. *Sefer ha-Ittur*, Meir Yonah edition, 1–2. Warsaw: Yosef Unterhendler Press, 1883 (Hebrew).

Rabbi Simhah B. Samuel of Vitry. *Mahzor Vitry*, edited by Shimon ha-Levi of Horowitz. Nuremberg: Y. Bulka Publishing House, 1923 (Hebrew).

Rabbi Yehuda'i Gaon. *Halakhot Pesukot*, edited by S. Sason. Jerusalem: Makor, 1971 (Hebrew).

Rivlin, Y. "Tikkun Shetarot le-Ba'al Orehot Hayyim" (Hebrew). *Kovets al Yad* 18 (2005): 223–88.

———. *Contracts from the Alisana Congregation from the Eleventh Century*. Ramat Gan: Bar-Ilan University Press, 2005 (Hebrew).

———. "Shetar Hatsi Zakhar" (Hebrew). *Dine Yisrael* 17 (2003–2004): 155–79.

———. "Examples of Contracts Attached to the Munich Manuscript of the Babylonian Talmud" (Hebrew). *Shenaton ha-Mishpat ha-Ivri* 20 (2005–2007): 281–348.

Schereschewsky, B. *Family Law*. Jerusalem: R. Mas, 1984 (Hebrew).

Warhaftig, Z. *Possession in Jewish Law*. Jerusalem: Mosad ha-Rav Kook, 1964 (Hebrew).

Yadin, Y. "Camp 4—The Cave of the Letters" (Hebrew). *Yedi'ot ba-Hakirat Erets Yisrael ve-Atikoteha* 26 (1962): 204–36.

Yardeni, E. *Documents from the Ze'elim River* (Teudot Nahal Ze'elim). Beer Sheba and Jerusalem, 1995.

CHAPTER 31

TALMUDIC MONETARY THEORY: CURRENCY IN RABBINIC HALAKHAH

LAWRENCE H. SCHIFFMAN

INTRODUCTION

THE Talmudic literary corpus represents the collective exploration of issues of Jewish religious law by the rabbinic leadership of the Jewish people from the last two millennia BCE through the Islamic conquest of the Near East in the seventh century CE. As has been clearly demonstrated since the rise of modern, historical Talmudic scholarship in the nineteenth century, rabbinic literature bears eloquent testimony to the political, social, and economic life of those Jewish communities that followed the rabbis, particularly in Roman Palestine and the Babylonian Diaspora.[1] Among the great accomplishments of recent scholarship has been the ability to chart the interactions between the social, political, and economic circumstances of the lives of the Jewish people at that time and the various theories that lie behind the law.

We should note at the outset that this study seeks to establish the concepts of the Talmudic rabbis in Late Antiquity. For this reason, medieval sources are considered only insofar as they represent exegesis of the ancient texts, and not when they represent new ideas and approaches developed in the context of medieval Jewish society, whether under Christendom or Islam. We shall argue that the Talmudic rabbis had unique and original ideas on the nature and function of currency.

1 For a survey of Jewish history and literature in this period, see L. H. Schiffman, *From Text to Tradition: A History of Second Temple and Rabbinic Tradition* (Hoboken, NJ: Ktav, 1991), 157–239.

Great effort has been put into trying to correlate rabbinic views of money and coinage, particularly regarding gold versus silver, or bimetallic standards, with the historical circumstances. However, given the detailed information about monetary transactions discussed by the rabbis in laying out Jewish law regarding all kinds of commercial and financial transactions, little scholarship has been devoted to asking fundamental questions about the rabbinic understanding of currency—that is, the monetary theory that lies behind the legal rulings in our texts.[2]

This chapter will investigate the monetary theories that lie behind the rabbinic laws found in tractate *Bava Metsi'a*, chapter 4 regarding currency (coinage) and commodities, the trading of one currency against another, or even multiple currencies against one another. The debates recorded in this Talmudic chapter provide perspectives on the views of the ancient rabbis regarding a number of issues of economic theory: nature of currency and commodities, relationship of the value of currency to price fluctuations, inflation, use of precious metals to establish monetary standards, and criteria for valuing currency in an international market. This chapter will examine particular passages in both the Jerusalem and the Babylonian Talmuds in order to elucidate these concepts and show their historical progression.

We must be mindful of the fact that Talmudic rabbis did not mold or even influence the monetary systems of the places in which they lived—the Roman Empire and Sasanian Babylonia. Rather, they sought to assimilate the dominant monetary systems into their understanding of the requirements of Torah law. Accordingly, it is in their legal rulings that we seek to uncover their understanding of how the monetary system under which they lived was constructed as well as their understanding of how currency and commodity were to be conceived.

Barter and Currency

In Jewish law acquisition is accomplished by a variety of legally defined acts known as *kinyanim* ("acts of acquisition").[3] Examination of these procedures clearly indicates that they are founded on the assumption that the original form of acquisition was barter, known in Hebrew as *halifin*. It may appear from the study of Talmudic literature that barter is itself a subset of purchase, but we know from ancient Near Eastern law and from the history of metallic currency that nothing

2 See the important contributions of E. Kleiman, "Ancient and Medieval Rabbinic Economic Thought: Definitions, Methodology and Illustrations," in *Ancient Economic Thought*, ed. B. B. Price (London and New York: Routledge, 1997) 76–96, especially 84–86; Y. Liebermann, "Elements in Talmudic Monetary Thought," *History of Political Economy* 11 (1979): 254–70.

3 These are outlined in M Kiddushin 1:1–4. Cf. C. Albeck, *Shisha Sidre Mishna, Nashim* (Jerusalem and Tel Aviv: Mosad Bialik and Dvir, 1957), 410–12.

could be farther from the truth. In fact, the original system of purchase was barter[4] and it is for this reason that in Jewish law the transfer of money, or other financial instruments, cannot itself effect acquisition of movable property. Rather, taking possession physically in the legally specified manner effects acquisition, and, upon acquisition of a commodity or any object purchased, payment becomes due. Clearly, the commodity has been traded for the payment in what is essentially a barter transaction.

This is not the case with real estate. M *Kiddushin* 1:5 rules that real estate[5] may be acquired by the payment of money to the current owner[6] and that such payment effects transfer of the object to the new owner. Indeed, such a transfer is envisaged in the story of Abraham's purchase of the Cave of *Machpelah* described in Genesis 23:8-20 and in a discussion of the purchase of land in Jeremiah 32:44, where the text states, "fields shall be acquired with money."[7] Actually, however, this possibility only exists on the theoretical level.[8] As part of its ancient Near Eastern heritage, Jewish law required that such transfers of real property be affected by a contract, and such documents were legally required to prove ownership.[9] From all the information that we have, in biblical times, the Second Temple period,[10] and the Talmudic era, such contracts were required.[11]

B *Bava Metsi'a* 47b preserves a debate that is necessary to understand for our purposes. We have mentioned that the rabbinic system for transfer of movable property is essentially the reverse of the normal commercial assumption that the tendering of payment in legal currency effects transfer of ownership with the attendant requirement that the purchased item be delivered by the seller. The advantages of the rabbinic system are in its guaranteeing protection of the property of the buyer. This principle was nonetheless the subject of Talmudic debate in the early amoraic period in the Land of Israel:

4 D. C. Snell, "Methods of Exchange and Coinage in Ancient Western Asia," *Civilizations of the Ancient Near East* (ed. J. M. Sasson et al.; New York: Charles Scribner's Sons, 1995), 3,1487–97; J. H. Kroll, "The Monetary Use of Weighed Bullion in Archaic Greece," *The Monetary Systems of the Greeks and Romans* (ed. W. V. Harris; Oxford: Oxford University Press, 2008), 12–37.

5 Rabbinic literature terms real property "property that is subject to lien," since according to Jewish law, real property may be placed under lien and seized by the court if the owners owe debts for which there exist written, witnessed contracts. Even after sale to another owner, the land may still be placed under lien since the previous owner, while the land was in his possession, had executed loans or other transactions incurring obligations which he did not pay.

6 The *Mishna* also specifies that real property can be acquired by means of a contract, or by taking (physical) possession.

7 Cf. B *Kiddushin* 26a. This verse is understood legally to mean that "fields *may* be acquired by means of an exchange of money."

8 Cf. Maimonides (Rambam, Egypt, 1135–1204), *Commentary to the Mishna* (Hebrew), ed. J. Kafih (Jerusalem: Mossad Harav Kook, 1963), 2.195. Rambam discusses the possibility of purchase of land without a contract; however this seems not to have been the normal practice in ancient times.

9 Cf. C. Albeck, *Nashim*, 411.

10 Jeremiah 32:6–15; The same pattern is reflected in the Elephantine and Samaria Papyri, and in the legal texts from the Bar Kokhba caves. See A. D. Gross, *Continuity and Innovation in the Aramaic Legal Tradition* (Leiden: Brill, 2008), 1–26.

11 Cf. L. H. Schiffman, "Reflections on the Deeds of Sale from the Judaean Desert in Light of Rabbinic Literature," in *Law in the Documents of the Judaean Desert*, eds. Ranon Katzoff and David Schaps (Supplements to the Journal for the Study of Judaism 96; Leiden: Brill, 2005), 185–203.

> Said R. Yohanan: "As a matter of Torah law, coins effect acquisition. But why did they (the rabbis) say, 'dragging effects acquisition?' (It was) a decree lest (the seller) should say to him (the buyer), "Your wheat has been burned in the (storage) attic.'" In the end, however, the one who set the fire will have to pay? Rather, it is a decree lest a fire be set against his (the seller's) will.[12] If you establish it in his property he (the seller) will sacrifice and make an effort to save it. But if not, he will not sacrifice and make an effort to save it.
>
> Resh Lakish said: "Dragging is explicit in the Torah." What is the reasoning of Resh Lakish? The verse says, "When you sell a sold object to your neighbor or when you acquire [an object] from the hand of your neighbor." [This refers to] a thing which is acquired [by handing it] from hand to hand.[13]

One view held that effecting acquisition by "dragging" the item was, indeed, the approach assumed by the Torah, as derived from Leviticus 25:14. The other point of view argued that this was a rabbinic enactment by which the Torah's normal assumption in which transfer of currency effected transfer of ownership was set aside by the rabbis to provide protection to the buyer.

Now we can look at this debate historically in two ways. It is indeed possible that, as is the case with real property in Jewish law, the original form of acquisition for movable property in biblical times was the surrender of money, then in the form of ingots, as is the case regarding real property in the story of Abraham and the Cave of *Machpelah*. Latter on, however, this system was set aside in the case of movable property. It may have been done for the purpose mentioned by the Talmud, or it may have been for some other reason, in which case this later explanation was provided.

However, it is also possible, especially in light of the late development of money in the form of coinage, which actually made the use of currency universal, that the original method of acquisition was, as mentioned, by barter, so that the Talmudic system preserves the original method for acquisition of movable property. The rabbis still had to acknowledge the role of currency for effecting acquisition of land, something eliminated by the requirement of a contract. But in this case the rabbis withheld approval for use of currency to effect acquisition of movable property, both because of tradition and because of the reason they gave—namely, protection of the purchaser.

It may be that the historical debate and the halakhic debate, especially as it developed among the Talmudic commentators, is essentially one and the same. In evaluating the debate between the early amoraim in our chapter, commentators are divided in defining the views. Some have taken the view that the opposing views are as follows: (a) one holds that effecting acquisition of movable property by taking physical possession is found in the Bible along with paying money. Both of these were Torah methods of effecting transfer. However, the rabbis set aside financial payment as a means of acquisition in order to protect the buyer. This view seems to

12 The fire could start simultaneously and so it would be impossible to collect damages.

13 Cf. D. Halivni, *Sources and Traditions: A Source Critical Commentary on the Talmud, Tractate Baba Metzia* (Hebrew) (Jerusalem: Hebrew University Magnes Press, 2003), 168–69.

think that all transactions have two required parts—the transfer of the money and the physical possession. In this view, biblical transfer of ownership was not patterned on barter, but the rabbis called for return to a barter system. (b) The second view holds that the Bible only made possible one means of acquisition—namely the payment of money. Nonetheless, the rabbis set that single means of acquisition aside and substituted a nonbiblical method—physical taking of possession. Accordingly, the latter is not one biblical method of possession, but rather a completely rabbinically ordained approach.

This approach, of course, goes beyond the simple reading of the text. In this reading, one view holds that the Bible originally based its system of acquisition on barter. The other holds that the original system of the Bible was that of payment in money, but that the system was replaced by the rabbinically invented system of physical possession. However, as we have already noted, from a historical point of view there is no question that barter was the original form of exchange before currency was developed.

Nature of Currency

M *Bava Metsi'a* 4:1–2 and the corresponding passages in the *Tosefta*, and in the Jerusalem, and Babylonian Talmuds, deal extensively with the nature of currency and the reasons why it functions as it does.[14] We need to keep in mind that in rabbinic halakhah the object that "acquires" is the commodity and that which is acquired is currency. This concept is parallel to a distinction in Roman law between "merchandise" (also called "wares," equivalent to our term commodity) and "price" (what we term currency).[15] This distinction is attributed to the jurist Paulus who died in 235 CE. After noting that barter was the original form of purchase, he stated that it had been replaced with the development of money and that there was now a distinction between the payment tendered and the merchandise purchased.[16] Clearly, the same concept underlies the rabbinic discussion.

Let us turn to M *Bava Metsi'a* 4:1:

> Gold acquires silver, but silver does not acquire gold.
> Bronze acquires silver, but silver does not acquire bronze.
> Bad coins acquire good, but good [coins] do not acquire bad.
> A slug acquires a coin, but a coin does not acquire a slug.

14 Cf. Liebermann, "Elements," 259–60; D. A. Schiffman, "The Valuation of Coins in Medieval Jewish Jurisprudence," *Journal of the History of Economic Thought* 27 (2005): 145–48.

15 Cf. D. A. Schiffman, "Rabbinical Perspectives on Money in 17th Century Ottoman Egypt," forthcoming in *European Journal of the History of Economic Thought*, available at http://papers.ssrn.com/sol3/papers.cfm?abstract_id=1150335, 10–12. The remainder of his paper deals with these issues as they played out in a much later period.

16 Digest 18.1.1, translated and discussed by T. J. Sargent, F. R. Velde, *The Big Problem of Small Change* (Princeton and Oxford: Princeton University Press, 2002), 93.

> Movable property acquires a coin, but a coin does not acquire movable property.
>
> This is the rule:[17] All movable property acquires other movable property.

Already in this *Mishna*, certain of the definitional issues are put forth. The simple definition—currency is legal tender and commodity is what you buy with it—could not suffice for the rabbinic system. Already in this *Mishna*, we encounter the question of how to decide which is the currency in a transaction in which coins of one metal are traded against coins of another. T *Bava Metsi'a* 3:13 indicates without question that we are speaking about coins—that is, currency, rather than bullion.[18] By implication, this discussion opens up the question of the distinction between currency, termed by the rabbis as "coin," and commodity, termed by the rabbis "fruit." Below, we will regularly substitute the terms "currency" and "commodity" for the original rabbinic terminology.

Another issue raised in the *Mishna* is that of "bad currency" (literally, "bad coins") versus "good currency" (literally, "good coins").[19] Two interpretations are put forth here by the commentators. R. Solomon b. Isaac (Rashi, France, 1040–1105) takes the view that this refers to coins that have been demonetized. Such coins are discussed by the Babylonian amoraim in B *Bava Kamma* 94a:

> It was stated: If a man lends his fellow [something] on condition that it should be repaid in a certain coin, and that coin became obsolete. Rav said that the debtor would have to pay the creditor with the coin that had currency at that time, whereas Samuel said that the debtor could say to the creditor, "Go forth and spend it in Mishan." R. Nahman said that the ruling of Samuel might reasonably be applied where the creditor had occasion to go to Mishan, but if he had no occasion [to go there] it would surely not be so. . . .[20]

Here the coin according to which a loan agreement was entered into has been demonetized. The dispute is over whether or not the debtor may repay the creditor in the demonetized coins. The final ruling of R. Nahman provides that the new currency must be used for repayment, except in cases where the creditor might reasonably be expected to go to the place where the demonetized currency still circulates as legal tender. In this case, we can see that the rabbis were well aware that currency could be demonetized in one area, where it might be considered "bad money," but might be valid elsewhere. This was especially the case in ancient times when boundaries between political entities and even major empires changed often, resulting in changes in the validity of coinage. *Tosafot* (medieval Talmudic glosses, France and Germany, twelfth–fourteenth centuries) understood the dispute in our passage to only apply where a stipulation of the loan was that payment would be made with the standard medium of exchange. Otherwise, in the view of *Tosafot*, it

17 Omitted from the *Mishna* text by R. Isaac b. Jacob Alfasi (Rif, North Africa, 1013–1103) and R. Asher b. Jehiel (Rosh, Germany and Spain, c. 1250–1327).

18 T *Nezikin* (ed. S. Lieberman; New York: Jewish Theological Seminary of America, 1988), 76.

19 Cf. Albeck, *Nezikin*, 422–3.

20 Trans. in A. Levine, "Inflation Issues in Jewish Law," *Journal of Halacha and Contemporary Society* 5 (1983), 29; also available at http://www.jlaw.com/Articles/inflation_issues1.html.

would be permissible at all times to pay back the loan in the currency in which it had been taken, even if that currency had been demonetized everywhere.[21]

Tosafot, however, understands the bad coins of M *Bava Metsi'a* 4:1 to be coins that have deteriorated or have been clipped and are therefore less desirable. While we will deal with the definition of these terms in greater detail below, for now we can note that our text refers to currency of greater or lesser liquidity. Another distinction is that of a minted (that is stamped) coin versus a slug, an unstamped token (that is, an unminted coin).[22] It is apparent, already at this point, that the rabbinic definitions of currency versus commodity will provide us with a hierarchy of levels of liquidity, such that the determination of what is currency and what is commodity will be made based on the relative liquidity of currencies—that is, acceptability in trade—in the case where one currency is being traded for another. We will have to pay careful attention to the difference between bullion and coinage, and we will see that such distinctions are clearly developed by the rabbis.

Relative Values of Currencies

The Jerusalem Talmud (*Bava Metsi'a* 4:1 [9c]), in commenting on the *Mishna*'s discussion of transactions in which currency in one metal is being purchased with another, puts forth a general rule that is of great importance for the rabbinic understanding of currency.[23]

> This is the general rule for (the entire) matter: Anything that is inferior to another acquires the other.[24]

Realizing the importance of this rule, the text labels it as "a general rule for the [entire] matter." The rule is simply that that which is of lesser value (*yarud*) of the two coins is assumed to be the commodity.

It goes without saying that currency is a medium of exchange—one of the classical functions of money as defined by economists. Our Talmudic rule, however, indicates that, among the possible characteristics of money, when compared to a commodity, is that one designation or kind of money may have greater real value than another, even if technically they are of equal nominal value. Another characteristic of money is that it functions as a store of value because it maintains its value over time and, hence, can be reliably exchanged for commodities because of its fixed value. If that is the case, and if the price of an item has been correctly fixed, taking into account its actual value within the

21 Levine, "Inflation Issues," 29–31.

22 So Rashi. R. Jacob b. Meir Tam (France, 1100–1171) takes this as referring to a no longer valid coin (*Tosafot*, B *Bava Metsi'a* 44a).

23 Cf. Liebermann, "Elements," 260–62.

24 E. S. Rosenthal, ed., with S. Lieberman, *Yerushalmi Nezikin* (Jerusalem: Israel Academy of Sciences and Humanities, 1983), 55.

context of the relevant market conditions, then the value of two exchanged items, one the currency and one the commodity, should theoretically be exactly the same. If that is the case, at least for our hypothetical, well-executed transaction, then what can the Jerusalem Talmud possibly mean what it refers to a currency of lesser value? Two possibilities will have to be considered, as we continue our study: (a) It is possible that we are referring here to that currency that is simply preferred, given a number of conditions to be discussed below, including quality of currency, venue of issue, and other such factors; (b) it is also possible that the texts refer here to the relative concentration of value (its efficiency for storing value) of the currency. Thus, to explain in modern terms, we could think of units of gold as having greater value than an amount of iron of equal monetary value. Whether we consider weight or volume, the assumption would be that the more valuable—the currency—is more easily portable because of the smaller size or weight of the currency required to reach the desired value and, hence, it is preferred because of its easy portability. Our passage appears to stem from the tannaitic period, the era of the *Mishna* and *Tosefta*, rather than from the later amoraic age.

The term *yarud*, of lesser value, can better be understood by comparison with a parallel discussion in the BT *Bava Metsi'a* 44a. There, the Talmud is discussing a change in the view of R. Judah ha-Nasi (Roman Palestine, c. 135–220), the editor of the *Mishna*, in which at a younger age he was of the opinion that gold was the currency and silver the commodity, a view he changed as he grew older:[25]

> What did he [R. Judah ha-Nasi] think in his youth, and what did he think in his old age? In his youth he thought that gold that is of greater value [lit. "important"] is the currency; Silver that is not of great value is the commodity, and the commodity acquires the coin. In his old age he thought that silver that is more acceptable in trade [lit. "sharp, strong"] is the currency; Silver which is not [as] acceptable is the commodity, and the commodity acquires the currency.

In this passage, the terms *hashuv*, "important,"[26] and *harif* ("sharp, strong") are introduced as factors in determining which of the two coin metals constitutes the currency and which constitutes the commodity. This introduced the distinction between the actual intrinsic value, or better, its relative value as a currency, and its acceptability in trade. This distinction is introduced into the Talmud by the latest chronological level, the anonymous rabbis who sewed together the discussions of the Babylonian Talmud in the last centuries before the Islamic conquest of the Near East. This last point basically indicates an attempt to understand the meaning of the idea of relative "value" of coins. Two possible definitions compete here. One sees the value of currency as depending on its intrinsic value (*hashuv*) and the other on its acceptability in trade (*harif*).

25 This view is documented in J *Bava Metsi'a* 4:1 9c and in our passage, B *Bava Metsi'a* 44a-b.
26 Aramaic *hashiv*.

METAL STANDARD

The Roman economy was based on an approach of bimetallism, according to which currency is available in two precious metals (gold and silver), the value of each of which is fixed in comparison with the other. This system is distinguished from monometallism, a system in which only one metal is assumed to be valued absolutely. Historically, monometallism has manifested itself in the form of the gold standard, once popular in modern economies and now entirely abandoned and replaced by fiat currency. Talmudic sources require that, in any exchange of coinage of two different metals, one be understood as a currency and one as a commodity. Further, depending on the metals involved, the very same metal may appear in some transactions as a currency and in others as a commodity. Effectively, then, we may speak of rabbinic law as having adopted a situational monometallism. The rabbis recognized the validity of the coinage of three metals—gold, silver, and bronze yet only one in any specific transaction could be seen as currency.

Above, we discussed the changes in R. Judah ha-Nasi's view regarding transactions involving gold and silver coinage. Despite the continued official bimetallism of the Roman Empire, it seems as if R. Judah approached things from a monometallist point of view. Historians have sought to identify the specific circumstances in the history of the Roman economy that led R. Judah to change his view on the relationship of silver and gold. Of the two metals, at an earlier time he saw gold as the currency, but later on he reversed his position and saw silver as a currency. Scholars agree, regardless of the specifics of their point of view, that late in his life a decline in the price of gold led to a situation in which silver maintained a constant value while gold fluctuated.[27] Accordingly, we could say that the gold standard was abandoned by R. Judah ha-Nasi for the silver standard. For our purposes, what is important here is not the exact dating of the change in R. Judah's point of view but rather its underlying assumption. From this point of view, the bimetallism of the empire was effectively not accepted by Jewish law. Rather, Jewish law had to adapt the various changes that took place in the economy of the empire to its basic system of floating monometallism.[28]

It is possible that the fixing of the final texts of M *Bava Metsi'a* 4:1 in the two Talmuds is the result of the prevalent economic conditions in the Roman and Sasanian Empires later in the Talmudic period. According to the Jerusalem Talmud version, silver "acquires," meaning that gold is the currency. This fits well with the prevalence of the gold standard in the Roman Empire. According to the Babylonian

27 E. Kleiman, "Bimetallism in Rabbi's Time: Two Variants of the *Mishna* 'Gold Acquires Silver'" (Hebrew), *Zion* 38 (1972/3), 48–61; D. Sperber, *Roman Palestine 200-400, Money and Prices* (2nd ed.; Ramat Gan: Bar-Ilan University Press, 1991) 69–83.

28 S. Lieberman, *Tosefta ki-Feshutah* Bava Metsi'a (New York: Jewish Theological Seminary of America, 1988) 176 and 177 argues strongly against the significance of these historical parallels since he finds that the text dates this controversy to the time of the houses of Hillel and Shammai, earlier than the supposed changes in the economy of the Roman Empire.

Talmud version, gold "acquires," meaning that silver is the currency. This accords with the practice in the Sasanian Empire.[29] This may be true despite the fact that Roman gold coinage circulated in Sasanian areas, and that the primary currency used in the Roman Empire was virtually always silver.

From the very beginning there is an assumption in rabbinic literature that money is a stamped piece of precious metal and that it functions as "commodity money." From an economic point of view this means that currency is assumed to be pegged to a metal standard. That standard is in turn derived from the economic value of the metal of which the coin is made up (at least theoretically) if it were treated as a commodity. The form in which the metal is packaged by the government, that is, its shape and uniform weight plus its minting (stamping), render it currency, thus further raising its value. The operating assumption is that the metal coins that have the highest value (depending on the approaches to evaluating metal currency discussed above) are assumed to be the standard. Further, a second operative assumption is that currency does not change in value and that all changes in price reflect changes in the value of commodities, usually as a result of supply and demand. Yet the rabbis were well aware of the widespread currency inflation that was taking place around them. It is simply that, for the most part, they saw taking this condition into account in economic transactions as leading to a violation of the prohibitions on the charging of interest, whether on the level of biblical or rabbinic legislation.

Much of the discussion regarding the relative values of coins of different metals can be seen to be about which metal is the actual standard. For this reason, much discussion has revolved around the textual reading of the very first words of M *Bava Metsi'a* 4:1. *Mishna* manuscripts as well as the text of the *Mishna* that served as the basis for the discussion in the Babylonian Talmud read the first line as follows: "Gold [coins] effect acquisition of silver coins." The *Mishna* presented in the Jerusalem Talmud reads instead: "Silver [coins] effect acquisition of gold coins."[30] Given the Talmudic assumption that the root of all trade in movable property is barter, this text means that receipt of a commodity, in this case gold coins, requires the buyer to make payment in currency, in this case silver coins. According to this textual reading, gold coins are seen as a commodity when exchanged for silver coins. This would imply a silver standard, a matter to which we will return below. The other reading would assume a gold standard.

We should note the Talmud's analysis according to which the ease of spending connected with silver coins (of lesser denominations) makes them a more desirable currency than gold coins. However, both the Jerusalem and Babylonian Talmuds testify that the redactor of the *Mishna*, R. Judah ha-Nasi, had earlier in his life formulated the law in the reverse, indicating that, in such a transaction, the gold coins

29 L. Jacobs, "The Economic Conditions of the Jews in Babylon in Talmudic Times Compared with Palestine," *Journal of Semitic Studies* (1957), 355–56 n. 3.

30 Lieberman, *Tosefta ki-Feshutah, Bava Metsi'a*, 176; Halivni, *Bava Metsi'a*, 158 n. 1 who provides further bibliography as well.

constituted the currency and the silver, the commodity.[31] Later stages of Talmudic interpretation in both Talmuds understood the difference in the versions of R. Judah ha-Nasi's opinion over time to depend on whether or not the value of the coin was determined by its intrinsic metallic value—that is, the notion that gold is a more precious metal (*hashuv*) than silver—or rather by its ease of spending (*harif*), for which coins of lesser value such as silver may be more advantageous. We have already noted that modern scholars, however, have sought a completely different kind of interpretation. They have come to the conclusion that changes in the system of currency valuation of the Roman Empire are reflected here. While these are worthy suggestions from a historical point of view, they do not answer the question to which our study is dedicated—namely, that of how the rabbis actually saw the function of currency. These studies consider such issues as monometallic versus bimetallic systems of currency and assume that changes in the Roman Empire generated the response of R. Judah ha-Nasi in this regard. These works contain a wealth of data from various places in the Roman Empire, but their specific conclusions require the assumption that economic conditions in Palestine were the same as in these other places.

What is of greater of interest for our study, however, is a fundamental difference between Talmudic thought and the various monetary theories that existed in ancient times. The dominant ancient systems, certainly in the Roman Empire, assume that the government fixed the monetary standard based on some metal or metals against which it evaluated all other commodities.[32] The rabbis, however, seem to assume a situational standard, in which the circumstances determine which of the two (or three) metals would be the currency.

We will try to summarize their approach: At that time, coins existed in three metals, bronze,[33] silver, and gold (in ascending value). All three metals were recognized by the rabbis as money, meaning that when these coins were traded for commodities, their value was determined by tale and not by weight. This means that, for the rabbis, it was the right of the government to stamp a value on the metal and that value is assumed to be correct unless knowledge was available to the contrary. Coins of any one of the three metals could be used as currency to purchase any commodities, including bullion. Gold or silver coin could virtually always be used to purchase bronze coins, as they were usually assumed to be a commodity when compared to gold or silver coinage. Nevertheless, the possibility was raised and rejected (B *Bava Metsi'a* 44b) in the latest stratum of the anonymous Talmudic discussion that, under certain circumstances, bronze coins could be considered currency when compared to silver coins, since often larger silver denominations would be harder to exchange.

31 For a similarly formulated discussion of R. Judah ha-Nasi's alteration of the *Mishna* text between his youth and old age, see B *'Avoda Zara* 52b.

32 See E. L. Cascio, "The Function of Gold Coinage in the Monetary Economy of the Roman Empire," in Harris, *Monetary Systems*, 160–73.

33 Hebrew *nehoshet* refers usually to bronze, an alloy of copper and tin. See E. J. van der Steen, "Bronze," *New Interpreter's Dictionary of the Bible* 1.504–5. Ancient coins were made of bronze, not pure copper, as the latter was too soft.

> You might have thought to say that these [bronze] *peruta* coins, in a place where they are acceptable, are more acceptable for exchange than silver, [and therefore] I should say that they are currency [and the silver coins for which they are exchanged are the commodity]. So [the *tanna*] comes to teach us [that this is not the case]; since there are places where they are not acceptable, they are considered a commodity.

The notion was rejected because of the fact that bronze coins are not universally acceptable.[34] In the case of bronze, apparently, the fact that in most places bronze coins are considered less desirable than gold and silver renders them always a commodity when compared with gold or silver coinage. In fact, this may have been because of the possible physical deterioration of bronze. This relates to another function of currency: that of its usefulness for the storing of wealth. The point being made here is that, even if a particular currency may appear to be more worthwhile and more desirable for making exchanges, it may, in fact, be inferior because of other purposes served by monetary instruments. Depending on the historical period and the prevailing economic conditions, coins of gold or silver—that is, only one of the two—were considered currency and could purchase coins of the other metal, as well as coins of bronze and various commodities. This means that bronze coins and either silver or gold coins (depending on when) could vacillate between serving as currency or commodity.

In this theory, the determination of the governmental authorities of the system of currency was only one factor in determining how money was to be treated. The inherent factors that we discussed above, as well as the official legal status of the currency, together determine the relation of currency and commodity. As we have noted above, the rabbis worked with a relativistic rather than fixed idea of what constitutes currency, depending on the relationship of the items traded at the time.

The Fixed Value of Currency

We have mentioned above the assumption of the rabbis that currency is by definition always assumed to have a fixed value whereas a commodity ("fruit") is something that is sensitive to price fluctuation. This concept underlies a discussion in M *Bava Metsi'a* 5:9 dealing with the lending of commodities among households:

> A person may not say to his friend, "Lend me a *kor* of wheat and I will give it back to you at the threshing floor." But he may say to him, "lend [it] to me until my son comes" or "until I find the key." But Hillel prohibits it. And Hillel used to say, "A woman may not lend a loaf of bread to a friend unless they fix a price for it, lest it go up in value and they end up [violating the prohibition] against interest.

The Babylonian Talmud terms this type of a loan *se'a be-se'a*, "bushel for bushel."[35] This indicates that the accounting of the exchange is calculated by volume, not by

34 Aramaic *sagyan*, literally "go," that is, are acceptable for spending as legal tender.

35 B *Bava Metsi'a* 15a, 44b, 62a, 63b.

the value of the commodity borrowed and returned. The constant fluctuation of commodity prices led to the possibility that, unless valued in currency, such transactions might be equivalent to lending on interest if the returned commodity assumed a greater value. The majority view, however, was that such transactions were legitimate in cases where the borrower owned some of the same commodity but lacked access to it. If the borrower did not own the commodity, it was considered forbidden for the reasons mentioned here. The fact that the *Mishna* permitted such transactions with no limit in cases where the commodity borrowed was evaluated in terms of the "fixed" currency indicated that the rabbis did not take currency fluctuation into account in transactions between money and commodities. R. Yohanan (B *Bava Metsi'a* 45a) even prohibits *se'ah be-se'a* loans with gold coins, apparently seeing them as commodity.[36]

Closely related is the question of how to value currency in regard to the payment of debts.[37] Should coinage be evaluated according to its real or intrinsic value, or should its nominal value be considered? The problem here is that, if the real value were to be followed, it could lead to the appearance of the taking of interest, which is prohibited according to halakhah. This question is debated in B *Bava Metsi'a* 44b:

> Rav borrowed [gold] *dinarii* from the daughter of R. Hiyya. In the end, they [the *dinarii*] appreciated in value. He came before R. Hiyya. He [R. Hiyya] said to him, "Go pay her back good [*dinarii*] of full weight.[38]

Rav borrowed money and before he paid it back the currency had appreciated. R. Hiyya ruled that he had to pay the debt according to the nominal value in which it was executed. This did not constitute interest despite the appreciation of the value of the gold *dinarius*, because the loan had been made in this currency.

Nonetheless, it would be incorrect to assume that the rabbis were unaware that currency itself fluctuated in value.[39] The following passage in B Bava Kamma 97b deals with this issue:[40]

> Rava asked R. Hisda: What would be the law where a man lent his fellow something [on condition of being repaid with] a certain coin and that coin meanwhile was made heavier? He replied: The payment will have to be with the coins that have currency at that time. Said the other: Even if the new coin be of the size of a sieve?—He replied: Yes. . . But in such circumstances would not the products have become cheaper?—R. Ashi therefore said: We have to look into the matter. If it was through the [increased weight of the] coin that prices [of products] dropped, we would have to deduct [from the payment accordingly], but if it was through the market supplies [increasing] that prices dropped, we would not

36 Cf. Levine, "Inflation Issues," 33–38.

37 Liebermann, "Elements," 264–65.

38 Cf. the parallel in J *Bava Metsi'a* 4:1 (9c).

39 Levine, "Inflation Issues, 26–28." Cf. D. A. Schiffman, "Valuation," 152–58; Y. Z. Kahana, "Change in the Value of Currency in Jewish Law" (Hebrew), in his *Studies in the Responsa Literature* (Jerusalem: Mossad Harav Kook, 1972/3), 330–48.

40 Cf. Lieberman, "Elements," 265–67.

> have to deduct anything. Still would the creditor not derive a benefit from the additional metal? [We must] therefore [act] like R. Papa and R. Huna the son of R. Joshua who gave judgment in an action about coins according to [the information of] an Arabian market commissioner that the debtor should pay for ten old coins [only] eight new ones.[41]

This text deals with a situation in which a certain coin with a specific denomination was demonetized and replaced with another of greater intrinsic worth. R. Hisda took the view that payment of loans had to be made in the coins with the same name and denomination, even when the new coins had greater value resulting from being made of a larger quantity of metal. R. Ashi saw the matter as more complex: If the greater weight of the coin resulted in the lowering of prices, then adjustment would be made in favor of the debtor who would have to repay fewer coins than he had originally agreed to. But if there were a price decrease due to greater supply, it would not affect the debtor's obligation. The conclusion of the passage, however, determines that if as a result of the change in currencies the creditor would derive a benefit that he would not otherwise have derived, adjustments should be made in favor of the debtor, thus lowering the number of new coins that he must pay to discharge his obligation. Medieval authorities took the view that such adjustments were also appropriate when coinage was debased by the governmental authorities.[42]

Money as a Commodity

The Babylonian Talmud also deals with the question of whether it is possible to treat coins as a commodity as part of a barter transaction. Such transactions are known as *halifin*, "exchange," since one item is exchanged for another. The Talmud rules that in such cases acquisition is effected as soon as one of the parties to the transaction physically takes possession, in accord with the legal procedures for doing so, of the object he is acquiring. At that point, the other party automatically takes possession as well. In an amoraic discussion, built on a debate between two third-century teachers, the question is discussed as to whether currency may be acquired in this manner.

> It was said: [there was a dispute between] Rav and Levi. One said: currency can be treated as an object of barter.[43] But the other said: currency cannot be treated as an object of barter. R. Papa said, "What is the reasoning of the one who says that currency cannot be treated as an object of barter? Because his [the receiver's] mind is on the impression [stamped on the coin] and the [validity of the] impression is subject to cancellation [by the government]."[44]

41 Trans. from Levine, "Inflation Issues," 26–27.

42 Medieval decisors set a figure of twenty-five percent for debasement or increase in the value of the metal before such adjustments would be made.

43 Hebrew *halifin*, lit. "exchange."

44 Following Rashi to B *Bava Metsi'a* 45b. Cf. Halivni, *Bava Metsi'a*, 161–63.

Such a transaction would be desirable in a situation in which one wanted to guarantee that the payment in currency would be provided even before the merchandise was delivered. Effectively, such procedure would replace Talmudic law with the system of acquisition prevalent in the societies around the rabbis in both the Roman Empire and Sasanian Babylonia, thus upending the Talmudic system. Essentially, the Talmud was discussing whether its own rulings could be totally avoided by treating the currency as if it were a commodity.

Here we encounter an interesting observation about currency: It is explained that the party who would be tendering currency, supposedly treating it as a commodity, cannot possibly see it as a commodity because of the *tzurta*, the legend on the coin. The fact that this inscription could theoretically be erased, or declared invalid by the government, is taken to show the extent to which the value of the coin has two components—a commodity component, based on the intrinsic worth of the metal, and a fiat component, dependent on government decision. In other words, the Talmud asserts that a person who accepts currency, even in the form of precious metals, to some extent does so because of the government imprimatur. This effectively means that commodity money, forms of currency that are essentially backed by their own intrinsic value along with the authority of the government, cannot be totally separated in this Talmudic view from fiat money, where government authority and not real value is the backing. The decision of the government that this is actually money, taken in the form of stamping its symbols on coins (even when they were pagan images) endows these coins with much of their value. Hence, in this view, it is impossible for a person tendering currency to see it as a commodity.

This view is related to other Talmudic statements that indicate that governmental authorities can declare certain currency to be legal tender in certain areas, whereas other currencies may not be in effect. This, of course, was the case between the Jewish communities of Babylonia and Roman Palestine, since the non-Jewish authorities behind the coins were not only different but usually in a state of hostility with one another. In many circumstances, therefore, the rabbis understood the value of coins to depend on their governmentally sponsored validity. This becomes another factor in determination among coins of two precious metals as to which will be considered currency and which the commodity. It goes without saying that in cases where the government had declared a type of currency demonetized, or where geographic boundaries meant that a specific currency was not in effect, it was relegated automatically to the status of commodity when compared with valid legal tender. This is because it was much harder to spend. In some views, references in rabbinic sources to "good money" and "bad money" are seen as referring to governmentally valid or invalid currencies.[45]

Indeed, after a lengthy discussion and detailed analysis of the language of M *Bava Metsi'a* 4:1, the anonymous final redactional layer of the Talmud concludes (B *Bava Metsi'a* 46a) that the reversal of the Talmudic laws pertaining to currency and

45 Following Rashi to B *Bava Metsi'a* 44a.

commodity cannot be allowed in Jewish law because of the special characteristics of money that we have observed. A long list of authorities is summoned to support this ruling and, yet, there appears another round of argumentation unsuccessfully attempting to set it aside.[46] Here we encounter the notion (46a) that unminted bronze slugs could indeed be acquired by barter.[47] The reason is clear: Such "coinage" does not have government backing nor is it labeled with a denomination.[48] Apparently, in the rabbinic view, minting is a fundamental requirement to turn a slug into a coin—an essential element of currency.[49]

Coin Clipping

Since currency was valued and stamped with its value based on the assumption that the coin contained a certain amount of metal, the rabbis had to concern themselves with the issue of whether or not coins always did in fact contain the official weight of metal.[50] As is well-known, a number of problems contributed to decreases in the amount of metal in coins in premodern times. First was the natural wear and tear on metallic coins produced either from pure metals or from alloys that did not have the stability of modern coins. Second was the practice of coin clipping, in which small amounts of metal were taken off coins by those who sought to profit unscrupulously. Both of these factors led to coins "unofficially" being of lesser value than their designation. But this problem paled when compared to the debasement of the content of coins by governments in an effort to increase revenues—the ancient equivalent of what we call "printing money." This process was highly inflationary, especially in the ancient Roman Empire, since prices responded to the lower value of coinage, even where the designation was maintained.

These issues were dealt with by the rabbis in various ways. M *Bava Metsi'a* 4:5 deals with the issue of coins that do not actually have the designated weights of metal:

> How much can a *sela'* [coin] be missing [less than its full weight] and [its use] still not constitute fraud?[51] R. Meir says: four *issar*,[52] one *issar* per *denarius* [1/24 of

46 The continuation of this discussion in B adds little to the overall conclusion, despite the many interesting laws illuminated along the way.

47 For the definition see 47b and Rashi.

48 Cf. the use of such slugs as tokens for admission to the bath house (B *Bava Metsi'a* 47b). Such usage is similar to the procedure for paying for and then receiving sacrificial animals in the Temple. Money was paid and a token was received. The token was then exchanged for the animal.

49 See *Tosafot*, B *Bava Metsi'a* 44a *s.v. asimon*.

50 Cf. D. A. Schiffman, "Valuation," 149–52.

51 Hebrew *ona'a* in this case refers to a transaction that may be considered fraudulent, even if the party who tendered the payment did not know that the coin was not of full weight. Nonetheless, the transaction is considered to be fraudulent because the rightful payment did not reach the party who was to receive it.

52 Latin *assarius*.

> the total].[53] R. Judah says: four *pundeyon*[54] [in a *sela'*], one for each *denarius* [1/12].[55] R. Simeon says: eight *pundeyon* [in a *sela'*], two *pundeyon* per *denarius* [1/6].[56]

The rabbis generally followed the valuation by tale rather than weight, except where the variation was egregious. This *Mishna* seeks to determine the amount of metal, expressed in terms of currency values, that can be missing from a coin before the use of that coin for payment falls under the category of *ona'a*, an unjust business transaction. Generally, according to Jewish law, transactions regarded as unjust can be resolved in two ways: either by reversal of the transaction at the request of the aggrieved party, or by a demand of adjustment. The question faced by the rabbis here was determination of that amount. What we see here is clearly an attempt to maintain determination of value of currency based on normative rather than real value. This fits well with the rabbis' attempt to see currency as holding stable value and to see commodities as constantly subject to market fluctuation.

Conclusion

In dealing with the circumstances imposed upon them by the Roman and Sasanian empires, the rabbis developed monetary theories that were independent and original. They understood the relationship of currency and commodity to be relative to the specific nature of the things being traded, and instead of accepting either a mono- or bimetallic approach, they approached the three kinds of metallic currency available in their civilization as operating in a flexible interrelationship. Because of the specific Jewish laws prohibiting all interest, they gravitated to the idea that currency did not fluctuate but that, instead, the prices of commodities did. However, they were aware that this was not totally correct and compensated for the possibility that changes in currency could produce changes in prices that resulted from complex interconnected causes.

When Talmudic law faced the challenges of the onset of the more complex medieval and modern economies, these economic theories would have to be modified to make possible the application of Jewish law. Our investigation has shown, however, the sophistication of the approach of the rabbis. It is no surprise, therefore, that these ideas served as the basis for the later development of complex ideas and theories that would make possible the application of Jewish law to new economic circumstances.

53 A *sela'* = four *dinarii* and a *dinarius* = twenty-four *issar*.

54 Latin *dupondium*.

55 A *denarius* = twelve *pundeyon*.

56 One-sixth is the normal amount considered to constitute a fraudulent transaction when either party, the buyer or the seller, is overcharged or underpaid by one-sixth.

SELECTED BIBLIOGRAPHY

Cascio, E. L. "The Function of Gold Coinage in the Monetary Economy of the Roman Empire." In W. V. Harris ed., *The Monetary Systems of the Greeks and Romans.* Oxford: Oxford University Press, 2008, 160–73.

Kleiman, E. "Ancient and Medieval Rabbinic Economic Thought: Definitions, Methodology and Illustrations." In B. B. Price ed., *Ancient Economic Thought*, London and New York: Routledge, 1997, 76–96.

Kleiman, E. "Bimetallism in Rabbi's Time: Two Variants of the *Mishna* 'Gold Acquires Silver'" (Hebrew). *Zion* 38 (1972/3): 48–61.

Kroll, J. H. "The Monetary Use of Weighed Bullion in Archaic Greece." In W. V. Harris ed., *The Monetary Systems of the Greeks and Romans*, Oxford: Oxford University Press, 2008, 12–37.

Jacobs, L. "The Economic Conditions of the Jews in Babylon in Talmudic Times Compared with Palestine," *Journal of Semitic Studies* (1957): 349–59.

Kahana, Y. Z. "Change in the Value of Currency in Jewish Law" (Hebrew), In his *Studies in the Responsa Literature*. Jerusalem: Mossad Harav Kook, 1972/3, 330–48.

Levine, A. "Inflation Issues in Jewish Law." *Journal of Halacha and Contemporary Society* 5 (1983): 25–44; also available at http://www.jlaw.com/Articles/inflation_issues1.html.

Liebermann, Y. "Elements in Talmudic Monetary Thought." *History of Political Economy* 11 (1979): 254–70.

Sargent, T. J., and F. R. Velde. *The Big Problem of Small Change*. Princeton and Oxford: Princeton University Press, 2002, 93.

Schiffman, D. A. "Rabbinical Perspectives on Money in Seventeenth-Century Ottoman Egypt." *European Journal of the History of Economic Thought*, 17, 2 (2010): 163–97.

Schiffman, D. A. "The Valuation of Coins in Medieval Jewish Jurisprudence." *Journal of the History of Economic Thought* 27 (2005): 141–60.

Snell, D. C. "Methods of Exchange and Coinage in Ancient Western Asia." In J. M. Sasson et al. ed., *Civilizations of the Ancient Near East*. New York: Charles Scribner's Sons, 1995, 3, 1487–97.

Sperber, D. *Roman Palestine 200-400, Money and Prices*, 2nd ed. Ramat Gan: Bar-Ilan University Press, 1991.

PART VII

THE ECONOMICS OF JUDAISM

CHAPTER 32

THE ECONOMIC PROGRESS OF AMERICAN JEWRY: FROM EIGHTEENTH-CENTURY MERCHANTS TO TWENTY-FIRST-CENTURY PROFESSIONALS

BARRY R. CHISWICK

Introduction

The American Jewish community has experienced a remarkable economic advancement from the nineteenth century to the present, both in absolute terms and relative to the non-Jewish population of the United States. It is an achievement that is unprecedented in terms of the various racial, ethnic, and religious groups that compromise the American population. It may also be unprecedented in terms of world-wide modern Jewish history.[1]

Most contemporary American Jews are the descendants of the mass migration of Jews who immigrated from Eastern Europe and Russia during the period from 1881 to 1924,[2] when immigration restrictions virtually ended, for several decades,

1 I appreciate the comments on an earlier draft from Carmel U. Chiswick and Evelyn Lehrer.

2 The American Jewish community, which comprises two percent of the US population, currently accounts for of about 41 percent of world Jewry, with another 40 percent living in Israel, and the remaining

migration from Southern and Eastern Europe. At arrival these Jewish immigrants were Yiddish speakers with at best little formal schooling, who worked primarily in craft, operative, and laborer jobs in small establishments in light manufacturing or in retail trade, and were characterized by having low earnings. In contrast, their descendants are now nearly fully integrated into the American economic mainstream, with high levels of proficiency in English, high occupational levels (mainly professionals and mangers), high earnings, and high levels of wealth compared to other Americans.

This chapter will examine the economic progress of American Jews using quantitative data wherever possible. Because of the greater availability of data on occupation than on earnings or wealth, the focus will be on occupational status. A person's occupation is determined by many factors, including educational level, labor market experience, decision-making skills, and efforts to find niches in the economy to minimize the adverse effects of discrimination. Occupational status is also one of the most important determinants of income from the labor market. For most families, both Jewish and non-Jewish, income from labor market activities is the primary source of family or household income and wealth, and hence of their ability to purchase goods and services and to obtain their standard of living.

It is not as easy to study the economic attainment of groups defined by religion, such as Jews, as it is to do so for many other racial and ethnic groups. The decennial Census of the United States, for example, has long been a major source of data to study occupational attainment and, since the 1940 Census, the earnings of minority groups. However, the Census has never asked religion, and responses to the question on ancestry (asked since 1980) that reveal a respondent's religion are masked.[3] The Census Office/Census Bureau did conduct two surveys that permit the identification of Jews that are discussed below. But other indirect techniques, also discussed below, can be used as proxy identifiers of Jews in some Censuses. Other United States government surveys and privately conducted surveys sometimes include a question on religion, but since Jews are a small proportion of the population (at the peak less than four percent of the United States population in 1940, about two percent today) the sample sizes for Jews in these data sets are often too

---

19 percent in other Diaspora countries Sergio DellaPergola, "World Jewish Population," *American Jewish Yearbook*, (New York: American Jewish Committee, 2003, p. 597).

For studies of the economic achievement of Jews in several Diaspora countries, see, for example, Daniel Elazar. with Peter Medding, *Jewish Communities in Frontier Societies: Argentina, Australia and South Africa,* New York: Holmes and Meir,1983; S.J. Prais and Marlena Schmool, "The Social Class Structure of Anglo Jewry, 1961," *Jewish Journal of Sociology*. 16, June 1975: pp. 5–15.; Tikva Darvish, "The Economic Structure of the Jewish Minority in Iraq vis-a-vis the Kuznets Model," *Jewish Social Studies*. 47, no. 3–4 (Summer-Fall, 1985), pp. 255–266.; Moshe Syrquin, "The Economic Structure of Jews in Argentina and Other Latin American Countries," *Jewish Social Studies*. 47, no. 2, Spring, 1985: pp. 115–134; and Nigel Tomes, "Religion and the Rate of Return on Human Capital: Evidence from Canada" *Canadian Journal of Economics*, February 1983, pp. 122–138.

3 See U.S. Bureau of the Census. *200 Years of U.S. Census Taking, Population and Housing Questions, 1790–1990*. (Washington, DC, 1989).

small for meaningful statistical analyses. Yet, where appropriate, analyses of data from these sources are reported.

Jews in the Colonial Period

The American Jewish community has experienced waves of immigration over the past three and a half centuries, since the first Jewish community was established in 1654 in what was the Dutch colony of New Amsterdam (New York City) by a small group of Sephardic Jews fleeing the spread of the Inquisition as Portugal took over the Dutch colony in Racife, Brazil.[4] These first settlers were followed during the American colonial period by small numbers of other Sephardic Jews and German Jews who also settled in east coast seaport cities.[5] Although systematic quantitative data apparently do not exist regarding their economic status, the qualitative material indicates that they became well-established middle class, urban residents.

Many of the Jewish immigrants to Colonial America arrived as indentured servants or were "redeemed" at arrival by their families already in America. They quickly joined the mainstream of the Jewish community. The Jews were typically shopkeepers, merchants, and shippers living in the tidewater seaport cities. Although some were craftsmen (artisans), very few were farmers, laborers, or professionals. Wealthier than the average American, there was a virtual absence of the very poor and the very wealthy. The Jewish merchants engaged in local, interior, coastal, and international (primarily with England and the Caribbean) trade and finance, and, as such, most were self-employed in clerical and managerial occupations. These were relatively skilled occupations at that time as literacy and numeracy were generally required.

The historian Jacob R. Marcus writes that the international trade was facilitated by their "skill, experience, and contacts with Jews in other commercial centers, particularly in the West Indies."[6] Moreover, he notes: "Though a very small percentage of merchants, the Jews *were* merchants, and a progressive and enterprising group of merchants at that" (italics in original).[7] And that: "Then, as today, an upthrusting socioeconomic mobility was characteristic of American Jewish life."[8]

4 For a detailed analysis of Jews in Colonial America, see the three volume study, Jacob R. Marcus, *The Colonial American Jew 1492–1776* (Detroit: Wayne State University Press, 1970). The discussion in this section of the economic status of Colonial American Jews is based on Marcus, 1970, Volume II, Part IV, 518–852; For a brief discussion of Jews in Colonial America, see Jonathan Sarna, *American Judaism: A History* (New Haven: Yale University Press, 2004), Chapter 1.

5 Sarna reports estimates that, by 1776, there were between 1,000 and 2,500 Jews in the United States—that is, 0.4 to 1.0 Jews per thousand population (Sarna, 2004, op. cit., 375). Marcus (1970, op. cit., Volume II, 522) suggests that during the 1700s there were two to three thousand Jews.

6 Marcus, 1970, op. cit., Volume II, 843.

7 Marcus, 1970, op. cit., Volume II, 844, italics in original.

8 Marcus, 1970, op. cit., Volume II, 838.

German Jews

Although a small number of Ashkenazic Jews arrived in the United States before the 1840s, larger numbers started coming in that decade. Changes in Central Europe—in particular, tensions associated with modern political ideas and economic upheavals due to changes in the structure of their economies and recessions in the emerging industrial sectors—and United States economic development and growth brought to the United States an increased number of immigrants from Central Europe, in particular from the German speaking areas, during the 1840s through the 1860s.[9,10]

Picking up the occupations many of them had in Europe, the German Jewish immigrants concentrated in retail trade and, to a lesser degree, wholesale trade. Many became peddlers, as they were in Europe, literally carrying their wares on their backs in the Northeastern, Midwestern, Western, and Southern states. As they prospered, they would acquire a pack animal or horse and wagon. Soon they settled down in cities and towns, large and small, and opened small retail establishments throughout the United States. This was surely an easier life than being on the road most of the time.[11] They were not as geographically concentrated as were the earlier Colonial Jews (Atlantic coast seaport cities) or the later waves of East European/Russian Jews (New York, Chicago, and other major industrial cities in the North and Midwest). Indeed, while German Jews settled as merchants in the Southern states and in small towns across the United States, few East European/Russian Jews moved there.

Some of these German Jewish merchants experienced considerable success and expanded the size and number of their businesses. While most did not become department store magnates, some did, creating such well-known department stores in various parts of the country as Bloomingdales, Gimbels, Saks, Goldwaters, and Nieman-Marcus, among others. Most, however, remained as small operators in major cities, small cities, and towns across the country. Indeed, outside of New York City, the contact that most non-Jewish Americans would have with Jews was in the latter's retail establishments, primarily grocery, dry goods, and small department stores.

9 See Max I. Kohler, "The German-Jewish Migration to America" *Publications of the American Jewish Historical Society*. No.9 (1901): 87–105; Jacob Lestschinsky, "Jewish Migrations, 1840–1956" in Louis Finkelstein, ed. *The Jews: Their History, Culture and Religion. Vol. II.* Third Edition (Philadelphia, PA: Jewish Publication Society of America, 1966), 1,536–96; Lloyd P.Gartner, "Immigration and the Formation of American Jewry, 1840–1925," in Marshall Sklare, ed. *American Jews: A Reader* (New York: Behrman House, 1983), 3–22; Avraham Barkai, "German Jewish Migration in the Nineteenth Century, 1830–1910" in Ira A. Glazier and Luigi DeRosa, eds., *Migration Across Time and Nations: Population Mobility in Historical Contexts* (New York: Holmes and Meier, 1986), 202–19.

10 It is estimated that the Jewish population of the United States increased from about 15,000 (nearly one Jew per thousand population) to 230,000 to 300,000 in 1880 (five to six Jews per thousand of the United States population) (Sarna, 2004, op.cit., 375).

11 See Abram V. Goodman, editor, "A Jewish Peddler's Diary, 1842–1843," *American Jewish Archives* 3 (June 1951):, 81–109.

The earliest systematic quantitative data on the economic status of American Jews appears to be from a survey, "Vital Statistics of Jews in the United States," conducted in 1890.[12] This is better known as the Billings Report, after John Shaw Billings, the head of the project and the author of the report.[13] It is apparently the only survey exclusively of Jews conducted by the Census Office, or its successor, the Census Bureau. Aware of the increasing immigration of Eastern European and Russian Jews in the 1880s and aware that there would be no mechanism for identifying Jews in the 1890 Census, this special survey was undertaken. It was conducted with the assistance of Adolphus Solomons, a prominent member of the Jewish community who was a businessman, philanthropist, community leader, and cofounder with Clara Barton of the American Red Cross.[14] At Solomons' invitation Rabbis and presidents of Jewish congregations provided the names of Jews who were interviewed. The intent was to collect data on the vital statistics (births, deaths, illnesses) of ten thousand Jewish households over the five-year period, 1885 to 1890. The Billings survey included a question on occupation, and the report provides the first systematic quantitative data on the economic status of American Jews.

The law of unintended consequences came into play because only Jews in the United States for at least five years prior to 1890 were to be interviewed. Most Jews in the United States by 1885 were, in fact, German Jews. Although large-scale Eastern European and Russian Jewish immigration began in the early 1880s, it was only later that it turned into a mass immigration. The Billings Report indicates that, of the Jews surveyed, fifty-five percent reported that their mother was born in Germany, while twenty-one percent reported that their mother was born in the United States, eleven percent reported Russia or Poland, and for thirteen percent it was another country or the country was not reported. The younger the respondent the more likely the mother was born in the United States, presumably primarily of German origin.[15]

The data on the 1890 occupational attainment of the Jewish and non-Jewish men are instructive.[16] Fully fifty-seven percent of the Jewish men were in sales, another twenty percent in clerical occupations, twelve percent in craft and operative jobs, with eight percent in professional and managerial jobs, and only three percent in agriculture and laborer jobs. By contrast, among white native-born men in general, as reported in the 1890 Census, only two percent were in sales, six percent in clerical jobs, thirteen percent in craft occupations, twelve percent were operatives, three percent worked in professional occupations, six percent were managers, two percent in service jobs, nine percent as laborers, and forty-six percent

12 See John S. Billings, *Vital Statistics of Jews in the United States*. Census Bulletin, No. 19, (Washington, DC, December 30, 1890).

13 For an analysis of the Billings Report, see Barry R. Chiswick, "The Billings Report and the Occupational Attainment of American Jewry, 1890," *Shofar: An Interdisciplinary Journal of Jewish Studies* 19(2) (Winter 2001), 53–75.

14 Solomons was born in New York City of parents born in England, but of Sephardic origin.

15 See Billings, op. cit., Table II.

16 See Billings, op. cit., Table IV and Chiswick (2001), op. cit., Table 3.

worked in agriculture.[17] Among the Jews in sales, most worked for themselves as peddlers, push-cart operators, or owners of their own small retail outlets. Clearly, the Jewish men in the United States in 1885, predominantly of German Jewish origins, had an occupational distribution distinct from the general population. As will be seen, this occupational pattern is also quite distinct from that of the East European and Russian Jewish immigrants who arrived in the United States in the four decades from the early 1880s until the enactment of the immigration restrictions in the "national origins" quota system in 1921 and 1924.

Occupations of East European Jewish Men: Prior to World War II

Census data cannot be used to identify Jews, or develop proxy identifiers for Jews, until the 1900 Census.[18] Sephardic Jews living in the United States could not be distinguished from others in Census data in the early nineteenth century, nor could the mid-nineteenth century German Jewish immigrants be distinguished from other German immigrants. Although Russian and Russian/Polish places of birth were recorded in the 1890 Census, most of the original records of the first Census that would include many Jews from these origins were destroyed in a fire.[19] Thus, modern data files constructed from decennial Census records for other years cannot be created for the 1890 Census.[20]

As a result, the earliest Census in which Jews can be identified is 1900 by using a Russian or Russian/Polish birthplace or parental birthplace as a crude Jewish identifier.[21]Another Jewish identifier that came into the Census in 1910 and

17 To the extent possible in the analyses that follow Jews are compared to whites, since according to the National Jewish Population Survey and the NORC General Social Survey ninety-eight percent of Jews report that their race is white. The economic advantage of Jews compared to non-Jews would be even greater if they were compared to others regardless of the latter's race. The Jewish share of the population increased from a negligible proportion in 1880 to a peak of less than four percent prior to WWII and has since declined to about two percent. Thus, whether Jews are included or, where possible, excluded from the data on "non-Jewish" comparison groups has little impact on the results. Even in occupations in which Jews are disproportionately represented, they are a *small* minority of members of the occupation.

18 The data on occupational attainment are drawn from Barry R. Chiswick, "The Occupational Attainement and Earnings of American Jewry, 1890 to 1990" *Contemporary Jewry*, 20, 1999, 68–98.

19 See Kellee Blake, "First in the Path of the Fireman: The Fate of the 1890 Population Census," *Prologue* (Spring 1996): 64–81.

20 The 1890 data referred to above on the occupations of the general male population were from a Census Office volume published in 1897 (U.S. Census Office, *Report on Population of the United States at the Eleventh Census: 1890, Part II*, Department of the Interior, Washington, D.C., U.S. Government Printing Office, 1987, 118–19).

21 For analyses of the validity of using the Russian origin method for identifying Jews, see Paul Ritterband, "Counting the Jews of New York, 1900–1991: An Essay in Substance and Method." Department of Sociology, University of Haifa, September 1998; Erich Rosenthal, "The Equivalence of United States Census Data for Persons of Russian Stock or Descent with American Jews." *Demography*. May 1975, 276–90.

remained through the 1970 Census is "mother tongue."[22] Although the exact wording varied from Census to Census, the basic question was identifying a language other than or in addition to English that the respondent spoke at home when the respondent was a child.[23] Yiddish, Hebrew, and Ladino can be used as Jewish identifiers in that those who reported one of these languages have a high probability of being Jewish, and few non-Jews would report these languages.[24] Yet, the limitation of the Jewish mother tongue approach is that many Jews, particularly those from Germany and other parts of Western Europe, and especially those with parents born in the United States, would not report any of these Jewish languages.

Using the Russian–origin technique (which of course includes non-Jews of Russian origin) and the Yiddish mother tongue technique (which, of course, misses many Jews) it is possible to identify Eastern European and Russian Jewish immigrants and their United States–born children from the turn of the century up to World War II. These techniques are of lesser value in the post-WWII period, but some other data sources with direct Jewish identifiers are available.[25]

In 1910, for example, among adult Yiddish mother tongue immigrant men, 9.6 percent were in professional and managerial jobs, 27.1 percent in sales jobs, 31.7 percent in craft employment, and 22.3 percent in operative jobs. Few were in clerical (2.5 percent), service (2.4 percent), or laborer (3.6 percent) jobs, and negligible numbers were in agriculture.

Among foreign-born men who were not Jewish, only 5.6 percent were in professional and managerial jobs, only 6.8 percent in sales, with 25.1 percent in craft, and 17.6 percent in operative jobs. Many worked as laborers (23.5 percent) or in agriculture (13.1 percent). Smaller numbers were in clerical and service jobs (2.1 and 5.8 percent, respectively). The East European Jewish immigrants were in somewhat higher occupational categories than those of other immigrant men, nearly all of whom were also from Europe.[26]

22 For analyses of the validity of the "mother tongue" method of identifying Jews, see Frances E. Korbin, "National Data on American Jewry, 1970–71: A Comparative Evaluation of the Census Yiddish Mother Tongue Sub-population and the National Jewish Population Survey" in U. O. Schmelz, et al., eds., *Papers in Jewish Demography, 1981*, Jerusalem: Hebrew University Institute of Contemporary Jewry, 1983, 129–43, 1983; Ira Rosenwaike, "The Utilization of Census Mother Tongue Data in American Jewish Population Analyses." *Jewish Social Studies* April/July 1971, 141–59.

23 Since the 1980 Census of Population the language question refers to languages *currently* spoken at home.

24 Originally only Yiddish was coded by the Census Bureau, but Hebrew and Ladino were later added to the codes. Ladino is the original language of Sephardic Jews. The last time mother tongue was asked (1970 Census) very few respondents indicated either Hebrew or Ladino.

25 It is estimated that the Jewish population of the United States increased to nearly 1 million in 1900 (about 1.3 percent of the United States population), to nearly 5 million just prior to World War II (a peak of about 3.7 percent of the population), to about 5.3 million in 2000 (just under 2.0 percent of the population) (Sarna, 2004, op. cit., 375). The slow growth of the Jewish population since the passage of immigration restrictions in the 1920s is due to both low immigration and a below-replacement fertility rate.

26 Paul H. Douglas, "Is the New Immigration More Unskilled Than the Old?" *Journal of the American Statistical Association*, (June 1919), 393–403 (393) comments on the higher occupational status of Jewish immigrants as reported at entry into the United States. He notes that ". . . the Jews are the most skilled of the newer races."

The occupational differences by religion in 1910 are even greater when second-generation Jewish men (born in the United States with a Yiddish mother tongue and one or both parents foreign born) are compared with native-born white men. Among the Jewish men identified by mother tongue, 16.1 percent were in professional and managerial jobs (two-thirds of whom were professionals), and many were in clerical jobs (20.3 percent). Sales employment was important (31.5 percent), but the blue collar jobs (service, craft, operative, laborer, and agriculture jobs) became less common (32.2 percent compared to 60.5 percent for the Jewish immigrant men). Among the native-born white men in 1910, 9.9 percent were professionals and mangers, with only 16.3 percent in clerical and sales jobs, nearly half in the non-farm blue collar jobs (44.8 percent), and over a quarter in agriculture (28.7 percent).

Thus, in 1910 the East European Jewish men had occupational distributions very different from those of the primarily German Jews in 1890 (mainly sales and clerical), and they were more urban and higher skilled than non-Jewish men in 1910, whether native or foreign-born. And, among the Jews, those born in the United States compared to those born in Europe were more likely to be in white collar jobs that in general would have required a command of English.

This tendency toward white collar and professional employment is seen vividly in the 1940 Census data. Among the men born in the United States who reported a Yiddish mother tongue, 14.9 percent were in professional and technical occupations, with 22.2 percent as managers. While clerical (14.6 percent) and sales (20.3 percent) jobs were still important, the blue collar jobs were clearly on the wane (27.3 percent). Among native-born white men, only 6.3 percent were professionals, 10.7 percent managers, 13.7 percent in sales and clerical jobs, and fully 69.1 percent were still in blue collar jobs, including agriculture. Thus, by the eve of United States entry into World War II, the United States–born children of Yiddish speaking immigrants had achieved high rates of employment in professional occupations and were well on the road to abandoning the blue collar jobs held by their immigrant parents and grandparents.

Occupations of Jewish Men: Post World War II

Identifying Jews in census data becomes more difficult in the first three Censuses after World War II, and impossible from the 1980 Census onward.[27] Yiddish falls out of use, even among Jewish immigrants, and the question on parental birthplace

27 The data on occupational attainment are drawn from Chiswick (1999) op.cit. and Barry R. Chiswick, "The Occupational Attainment of American Jewry: 1990–2000, " *Contemporary Jewry* 27 (2007), 80–111.

is last asked in 1970. An increasing proportion of Jews are third-generation Americans. For the ancestry question introduced in the 1980 Census, any response that indicates a person's religion is masked.[28] Still, a combination of decennial Census data, and other data, can be used to track Jewish/non-Jewish occupational patterns. In 1990 and 2000/01, the National Jewish Population Survey (NJPS) can be used to identify Jewish occupational attainments.[29]

The Current Population Survey (CPS) has been conducted by the Census Bureau for the Bureau of Labor Statistics every month since 1947. The aim of the survey is to provide data on labor market developments. In March 1957 the CPS for the first and the only time included a direct question on religion. The tables created by the Census Bureau from this survey permit a direct comparison of the occupational attainment of Jews and other white men.[30]

The professionalization of the adult male Jewish labor force continued, reaching 20.3 percent in 1957. Many were still in managerial jobs (35.1 percent); sales was still an important occupation (14.1 percent); while clerical jobs (8.0 percent), craft employment (8.9 percent), and blue collar employment all declined (12.3 percent).

Among other white men, professional employment increased (to 10.3 percent) but not by as much as among Jews. Many fewer were in managerial jobs (13.6 percent) than among Jews. Similar proportions were in clerical jobs (7.1 percent), but a much smaller proportion were in sales (5.6 percent), while nearly two-thirds (63.4 percent) were in blue collar jobs.

While non-Jewish white men experienced an increase in their occupational status from 1940 to 1957, Jews experienced a much sharper increase. Indeed, by 1957 one-in-five Jewish men were in a professional occupation, compared to only one-in-ten non-Jewish white men. Both patterns, improvements for non-Jewish men and greater gains for Jewish men, continued throughout the rest of the twentieth century.

The data on occupational attainment among Jewish men in the 2000/01 National Jewish Population Survey can be compared with that of non-Jewish white men in the 2000 Census of Population. Among Jews, over one-half (53 percent) of the men were in professional occupations, with managerial jobs playing a much smaller role (14.8 percent) than in the past as Jews left managing small businesses. Sales remained important (18.5 percent), but clerical (office) work declined (3.1 percent), while blue collar jobs (including service work) became even rarer among Jews (10.6 percent). Among all white men, professional employment increased, but to only 19.7 percent. Managerial jobs held steady (15.1 percent). Others were employed in sales (10.4 percent) and clerical jobs (6 percent). In spite of the declines

28 In the Census microdata file, any response to the ancestry question indicating a religion (e.g., Jewish, Catholic, Baptist, Mormon) is given the same code. Thus, individual religions cannot be distinguished.

29 The 2010 U.S. Census of Population was limited to only ten demographic questions. Unfortunately, there is no 2010 NJPS, nor are there plans for another National Jewish Population Survey.

30 See U.S. Bureau of the Census. "Religion Reported by the Civilian Population of the United States: March 1957," *Current Population Reports, Population Characteristics*. Series P-20, No. 79, February 2, 1958, Washington, DC; U.S. Bureau of the Census. "Tabulations of Data on the Social and Economic Characteristics of Major Religious Groups, 1957," Washington, DC, no date, mimeo.

in manufacturing and farm employment in the United States economy, nearly half of white men were still employed in blue collar jobs (48.6 percent).

Thus, in the last four decades of the twentieth century non-Jewish white men experienced improvements in their occupational status, but Jewish men both started at a higher level and experienced steeper improvements.

Doctors, Lawyers, and Professors

Given the importance of professional occupations among Jews, it is useful to examine the component occupations. In 1940, among second-generation Yiddish mother tongue men, 14.9 percent were professionals, but of these 2.9 percentage points were in medicine (e.g., doctors and dentists), 3.5 percentage points in law (lawyers and judges), negligible numbers were college and university teachers, and 8.5 percentage points were in other professional occupations.[31] This was a more intense concentration in independent professional practice, medicine, and law than among non-Jewish men. Among male native-born non-Jews, of the 6.3 percent professionals, 0.8 percentage points were in medicine, 0.5 percentage points in law, 0.2 percentage points in college and university teaching, and 4.8 percentage points in other professional jobs.

Using data from the NORC General Social Survey (1972–1987), 43 percent of Jewish men were professionals, with disproportionate numbers in medicine (8.3 percentage points) and law (5.6 percentage points), a peak of 4.9 percentage points as college and university teachers, while 24.2 percentage points (56 percent of the professionals) were in other professional occupations.

By the 2000/01 NJPS patterns have changed even further. While just over half (53 percent) of Jewish men were professionals, the share in independent professional practice had declined (4.8 percentage points in medicine, 5.3 percentage points in law), college and university teaching had declined (1.9 percentage points), and the share in other professions increased (41.0 percentage points). In contrast, among non-Jewish white men in 2000, while 19.7 percent were professionals, there were smaller proportions in medicine, law, and college and university teaching (0.9, 1.1, and 0.9 percentage points, respectively), while most were in other professions (16.8 percentage points).

Prior to World War II professional opportunities for American Jews were limited.[32] Discrimination against Jews in professional jobs was common in most

31 The data on occupational categories among professionals are drawn from Chiswick (1999) op. cit. and Chiswick (2007) op. cit.

32 See Leonard Dinnerstein, *Anti-Semitism in America,* New York: Oxford University Press,1994; Paul Ritterband and H. S. Wechsler *Jewish Learning in American Universities: The First Century,* Bloomington: Indiana University Press, 1994; Armen Alchian and Reuben A. Kessel "Competition, Monopoly, and the Pursuit of Money" in National Bureau of Economics Research, *Aspects of Labor Economics,* Princeton University Press, 1962; Sarna (2004) op.cit., Chapter 5; Barry R. Chiswick, "The Rise and Fall of the American Jewish PhD," *Contemporary Jewry,* 29(1), April 2009, 67–84.

industries, but Jews sought niches in which they could secure professional careers. The problem was compounded by discrimination against Jews in access to the schooling needed to acquire professional credentials. While many young Jews went abroad to study medicine, this was not feasible for law. Jewish hospitals and Jewish law firms were established to provide employment opportunities. But elsewhere, including professional employment in colleges and universities, the opportunities were limited.

With the end of World War II there was a dramatic, yet gradual, change in attitudes toward anti-Semitic employment practices. One of the first sectors in which the barriers were relaxed was in higher education, in terms of both the admission of students and accepting Jews on the faculty. Jews, ever responsive to expanded opportunities, flocked into higher education. With expanded opportunities for employment in college and university jobs and the opening more widely of PhD programs, a greater number of Jews sought the PhD, the de facto "union card" for a position in higher education. Indeed, PhD graduates who had distinctive Jewish surnames increased in the 1960s and early 1970s not only in absolute numbers, but also as a proportion of all PhD's awarded, but thereafter the absolute and relative number declined.[33] So too did the number of Jewish men entering medicine and law. Yet, the total number and share of Jewish men in professional occupations increased. As discrimination declined in other sectors of the economy in the last few decades of the twentieth century, Jews entered these other high-level occupations in larger numbers, thereby reducing their relative numbers in medicine, law, and college and university teaching.

Occupations of Jewish Women

The occupational attainments of women in the early twentieth century are not particularly meaningful since so few married women worked in the labor market, and many women who did work for pay were young and usually not yet married.[34,35] The choice of occupation of those who did work would have been influenced by their anticipating leaving the labor force. By the end of the twentieth century, however, women's labor force participation, even that of married women, had reached high

33 Another proxy identifier for Jews is the Distinctive Jewish Name technique (see H.S. Himmelfarb, R. M. Loar, and S. H. Mott "Sampling by Ethnic Surnames: The Case of American Jews" *Public Opinion Quarterly*, 47, 1983, 247–60; and Ira M. Sheskin, "A Methodology for Examining the Changing Size and Spatial Distribution of a Jewish Population: A Miami Case Study," *Shofar: An Interdisciplinary Journal of Jewish Studies*, 17(1), Fall, 1998, –97–116. Name changes (which were not uncommon at or shortly after immigration to the United States), intermarriage, and religious conversion both in and out of Judaism weaken the effectiveness of this technique. The data on PhDs awarded are drawn from Chiswick (2009) op. cit.

34 The data on the occupational attainment of women are drawn from Chiswick (2007) op. cit.

35 Adult Jewish women who were married with children at home had a lower labor supply than otherwise similar non-Jewish women throughout much of the twentieth century. For the early twentieth century, see Susan A.Glenn, *Daughters of the Shtetl: Life and Labor in the Immigrant Generation*, Ithaca: Cornell University Press, 1990.

levels, although Jewish women were less likely to work when their children were young and more likely to work before children were born or when they are older.[36]

The high occupational status of American Jews is not limited to men, as Jewish women also experienced impressive occupational achievements. Using the data from the 2000/01 NJPS and the 2000 Census, information can be obtained on the occupational attainment of employed women. Among Jewish women, 51.4 percent were in professional jobs, and 15.9 percent were in managerial jobs. Sales occupations were employing 12.9 percent and clerical jobs 12.1 percent, while the remaining 7.4 percent were in blue collar (including service) jobs. Among non-Jewish white women, 28.5 percent were professionals and 11.0 percent managers, 11.1 percent in sales, but a quarter (25.1 percent) were in clerical jobs. The blue collar sector employed nearly a quarter (24.4 percent).

Among Jews, the gender difference in occupations is quite small, especially if sales and clerical jobs are combined into one category, as men are more likely to be in sales and women in clerical positions.[37] The gender differences are more striking among non-Jews, with especially high proportions of white women compared to white men in professional (including public school teaching) and clerical jobs. Yet the differences by religion are greater than the differences by gender. In particular, by the year 2000, over half of employed Jewish men and over half of employed Jewish women were working in professional occupations!

There is a tendency toward "positive assortative mating" in marriage. In simple terms, this means that men and women tend to marry those with similar characteristics, including race, religion, education, and occupation, among other characteristics. This raises the question as to the extent to which high occupational status Jewish men and women marry each other. Using data on employed married couples from the 2000/01 National Jewish Population Survey in which both are Jewish by religion, in fifty-one percent of these couples both spouses are in professional or managerial occupations.[38] The proportion is fifty percent among employed couples in which both are Jewish by religion, ethnicity, or background. The proportion declines to forty-six percent among couples in which one spouse is Jewish by religion, ethnicity, or background and the other spouse is of any religion. This latter decline arises from the lower occupational status of those who are not Jewish. Thus, in about half of all married households in which at least one spouse is Jewish both the husband and the wife have jobs in high level occupations.

36 See Barry R. Chiswick, Barry R. "Labor Supply and Investment in Child Quality: A Study of Jewish and Non-Jewish Women," *Review of Economics and Statistics*, November 1986, 700–3; _____ "Working and Family Life: The Experience of Jewish Women in America" in Sergio Della Pergola and Judith Evans, eds. *Papers in Jewish Demography*, Jerusalem: Hebrew University, Institute of Contemporary Jewry, 1997, 277–87. Jewish women appear to be at home making greater investments in the human capital of their sons and daughters than non-Jewish women.

37 See Moshe Hartman and Harriet Hartman, *Gender Equality and American Jews*, Albany, NY: State University of New York, 1996 and Harriet Hartman and Moshe Hartman, *Gender and American Jews*, (Waltham: Brandeis University Press, 2009).

38 See Carmel U.Chiswick, "Occupation and Gender: American Jews at the Millenium," Paper presented at the Seminar on Creating and Maintaining Jewish Families, (Waltham: Brandeis University, March, 2007).

SELF-EMPLOYMENT

Self-employment is another characteristic of the economic position of a population, although self-employment can range from being a self-employed (own-account) peddler to a self-employed professional to owning a large retail or industrial establishment. The earliest systematic data on self-employment comes from the 1910 Census of Population and extends to the 2000 Census.[39, 40]

In 1910, among the foreign-born Yiddish mother tongue men, 38.4 percent were self-employed, even though there were few farmers among them. Self-employment was much lower (16.1 percent) among the second-generation Yiddish mother tongue men in 1910. Among non-Jewish men, self-employment was lower among the foreign born (22.3 percent), and much higher among the native-born (35.5 percent), many of whom were self-employed farmers.

Self-employment among Jewish men increased by 1940 to 41.4 percent for immigrants and 27.0 percent among the second generation. Among the non-Jewish men there was no change among the immigrants (21.2 percent), but a decline among the native born (to 27.3 percent), reflecting the decline in employment in agriculture.

According to the 1957 Current Population Survey data, with the direct Jewish identifier, nearly one-third of Jewish men were self-employed (31.9 percent), in contrast to half that ratio among the non-Jewish men (15.8 percent). The proportions were roughly the same in the 1970 Census data for white second-generation Americans—31.9 percent for Jews and 14.1 percent for non-Jews.

Self-employment has since declined substantially for Jewish men, falling to 26.8 percent and 23.2 percent in the 1990 NJPS and 2000/01 NJPS, respectively. This is still much higher than the rate of self-employment among non-Jewish white men, which remained steady in recent decades (14.1 percent in 1990, 14.0 percent in 2000).

Women are less likely to be reported as self-employed than men. Even among women, however, self-employment is greater among Jews, but the Jewish female self-employment rate declined from 14.0 percent in 1990 to 11.3 percent in 2000. In contrast, among non-Jewish white women it held steady at 8.6 percent in both years.

Although very few Jews in the United States were in farming, Jews had very high self-employment rates that initially increased in the early twentieth century as workers became owners of small businesses, and then declined sharply in the second half of the twentieth century. The decline was associated with Jews leaving the ownership of small businesses and entering managerial and professional positions in larger firms as salaried workers. That Jews still have a higher propensity for self-employment is, in part, a shift from operating family owned retail and manufacturing firms to self-employed professional employment. The very high self-employment rate among native-born white non-Jewish men in the early twentieth century and the very large decline over

39 See U.S. Bureau of the Census. (1989). op. cit.; Barry R. Chiswick (1999) op. cit; and (2007) op. cit.

40 The published material from the 1890 Billings Report did not include information on self-employment (Billings, 1890, op. cit.).

the course of the twentieth century is largely due to the change in the nature and scope of the agricultural sector.[41]

Earnings of American Jewish Men

Even more scarce than data that can be used for comparing Jewish and non-Jewish occupational status are comparative data on earnings. Yet, over the course of the twentieth century there are a few data sets that permit this comparison.

A question arises as to whether the rapid improvement in the occupational status of turn-of-the-twentieth-century East European and Russian Jewish immigrants reflected a preference for managerial and sales occupations in small businesses over wage and salary employment in other occupations that might have provided higher earnings. Data from the Dillingham Immigration Commission Report published in 1911 can shed light on this issue.[42, 43]

The Dillingham Commission conducted a survey in 1909 of production workers in selected mining and manufacturing industries, with an oversampling of industries with a heavy concentration of immigrants from Southern and Eastern Europe.[44] Jews were treated in the data as a separate race/ethnic group. Jewish immigrant men had, on average, weekly wages ($13.30) that were fifteen percent higher than other Southern and Eastern European immigrants ($11.54), but they were lower by only two percent than those from Northwestern Europe and Canada ($13.56) and lower by five percent than the native-born ($13.98).[45] Controlling statistically for several determinants of earnings (e.g., literacy, marital status, age, duration in the United States, region of United States residence), the Jewish immigrant men earned about fifteen percent more than all other male immigrants (coefficient 0.17, t = 2.70), including more than both other Southern and Eastern European immigrants (coefficient 0.13, t = 2.3) and Northwest European immigrants (coefficient 0.18, t = 1.6).

41 In the 1890 Census, 46.2 percent of native-born non-Jewish white men worked in agriculture as farmers, farm owners, and farm laborers. By 1990 among white men this had fallen to 3.6 percent (Chiswick, 1999, op.cit.).

42 U.S. Immigration Commission. *Reports of the Immigration Commission. Vol. I to 41*. Washington, DC: U.S. Government Printing Office, 1911; and Barry R.Chiswick, "Jewish Immigrant Wages in America in 1909: An Analysis of the Dillingham Commission Data" *Explorations in Economic History* 29(3) (July 1992), 274–89.

43 William P. Dillingham was an anti-immigrant Senator from Vermont who chaired the Commission. Volume one of the forty-one volume report was the policy analysis that took a very dim view of Southern and East European immigrants. The Commission's report was instrumental in the enactment of legislation that resulted in the "national origins" quota system (1921 and 1924) that drastically restricted immigration from Southern and Eastern Europe, including Russia, for four decades, until the 1965 Immigration Amendments.

44 See Chiswick, 1992, op. cit.

45 Ibid. The Dillingham Commission data differentiated between Russian origin and other Jews. There was no difference in earnings between the two groups.

At arrival, Jewish men earned less than the native-born white men, but because their earnings increased sharply with duration in the United States they caught up with the native born at about 4.5 years duration in the United States, beyond which the Jews had higher earnings than their native-born non-Jewish counterparts. Earnings increased more steeply with duration in the United States among the Jewish immigrants than among other immigrants. This implies either greater investments in United States–specific job training, a higher economic return from such training, or both.

The 1940 Census was the first Census to include a question on earnings or income.[46] It asked for wage, salary, and commission income of those with earnings who were not self-employed. Jews could be identified by mother tongue. The average annual earnings among Jewish men was $1,574 and among white non-Jewish men, $1,321 (19.2 percent higher earnings). Other variables the same, however, male Jewish wage and salary workers earned 8.8 percent more than non-Jewish white men ($t = 4.7$). Thus, half of the gross differential is attributable to other variables (e.g., schooling, urban, northern residence) and about half remains unexplained.[47]

The tables constructed from the March 1957 Current Population Survey, which included a question on religion, included data on median annual incomes among men.[48] Jews earned $4,900, considerably more than the $3,728 of white Protestant men (by thirty-one percent) and $3,954 of Roman Catholic men (by twenty-four percent). The differences shrink when the data were limited to employed men living in urban areas and standardized for major occupational group. Then Jews earned 4.8 percent and 5.9 percent higher median income than white Protestant and Roman Catholic men, respectively.[49]

The General Social Survey (GSS) conducted nearly annually since 1972 by the National Opinion Research Center (NORC) includes a question on religion.[50] While each annual survey has too few Jews for statistically meaningful analyses, by aggregating the data across years sufficiently large samples of Jews can be developed. Using the data from 1974 to 1986, Jews are found to have about thirty-eight percent higher earnings ($27,300 for Jewish men compared to $19,800 for other men).[51] When statistical controls are introduced for several variables (including schooling level, urban residence, and marital status), the Jewish earnings advantage declines to sixteen percent, with no obvious trend in the differential over the thirteen-year period.

46 U.S. Bureau of the Census, 1989, op. cit.

47 See Chiswick, 1999, op. cit.

48 U.S. Bureau of the Census, no date, op. cit.

49 For two reasons, the Jewish/non-Jewish earnings differential is smaller in the 1957 Current Population Survey than in the other data on earnings considered elsewhere in this section. When the Census Bureau standardized the data for major occupation group, it essentially held constant another important measure of labor market outcomes—namely, occupational attainment. This narrowed the Jewish/non-Jewish earnings differential. Because of the positive skewness in the distribution of earnings, it is likely that the relative difference in medians is smaller than the relative difference in means.

50 See Barry R. Chiswick, "The Skills and Economic Status of American Jewry" in Robert S. Wistrich, ed. *Terms of Survival: The Jewish World Since 1945*, (London: Routledge, 1995), 115–29.

51 Ibid.

Using the "mother tongue" technique for Yiddish, Hebrew, or Ladino among second-generation Americans in the 1970 Census, a subset of Jews can be distinguished from other second-generation white Americans.[52] Other measured variables the same, Jewish men had a sixteen percent earnings advantage (t = 12.41) over comparable non-Jewish white men with parents born in the British Isles (the benchmark).[53] All of the other parental birthplaces have earnings not significantly different from or significantly lower than those with parents from the British Isles, with one exception—those of Russian parentage who do not report a Jewish language as their mother tongue (coefficient 0.058, t = 4.65). This latter group may include many Jews who are not identified as having a Jewish mother tongue. When major occupational categories are added to the earnings equation, Jewish men earn 10.2 percent more than second-generation white non-Jews (t = 8.0).

The regression analysis using second-generation white Americans in the 1970 Census also revealed two other characteristics of the Jews (defined by mother tongue) under study.[54] One is the larger payoff to education as measured by the coefficient on years of schooling, even when occupational status is held constant. This suggests that Jews are more effective than others in converting schooling into earnings, providing a greater incentive to make these investments. The other is the larger elasticity of annual earnings with respect to weeks worked, suggesting a greater responsiveness of labor market behavior (employment) to economic incentives (wages).

The "New" Russian Jewish Immigrants

The twentieth century began and ended with the immigration to the United States of Jews from the Russian Empire and from its later equivalent, the Former Soviet Union (FSU). The term "Russian Jew" in both periods was applied to those who came from Russia and the territories it occupied, including the Ukraine, the Baltic States, and the Caucuses. While it is not possible to identify American Jews as such in recent Censuses, it is possible to analyze recent Russian Jewish immigrants, as has been done using the 1980 to 2000 Censuses.[55] During the late 1970s and early 1980s and again during the late 1980s through the early 1990s there was a substantial migration of refugees to the

52 See Barry R. Chiswick, "The Earnings and Human Capital of American Jews," *Journal of Human Resources* 18(3) Summer 1983), 313–36.

53 Ibid. The other variables include schooling, labor market experience, marital status, urban residence, residence in a southern state, and parents' country of birth.

54 Ibid.

55 See Barry R. Chiswick, "Soviet Jews in the United States: An Analysis of their Linguistic and Economic Adjustment" *International Migration Review* 27(2) (Summer 1993), 260–86; _____ "Soviet Jews in the United States: Language and Labour Market Adjustments Revisited," in Noah Lewin-Epstein, Yaacov Ro'i and Paul Ritterband, eds., *Russian Jews on Three Continents: Migration and Resettlement*, London: Frank Cass Publishers, 1997, 233–60; and Barry R. Chiswick and Michael Wenz. "The Linguistic and Economic Adjustment of Soviet Jewish Immigrants in the United States: 1980 to 2000", *Research in Labor Economics*, 24, 2006, 179–16.

United States from the Former Soviet Union (FSU), although in the latter period there was a much larger flow from the FSU to Israel. Unlike the Russian Jewish immigrants from 1881 to 1924, who were Yiddish-speaking workers in sales, craft, and operative jobs before migrating, the newer influx spoke Russian and tended to be highly educated individuals who had worked in professional occupations.

For the purpose of analyzing the new influx of Russian Jews, the 2000 Census data were limited to immigrants who came to the United States since 1965, with Jews identified as those born in the Former Soviet Union who were not of Armenian ancestry and did not report that the language that they spoke at home was Armenian or Ukranian.[56]

Other variables being the same, the Russian Jewish immigrants in 2000 had earnings lower than those of other European immigrants, but the earnings differences varied sharply by period of arrival and level of education.[57] Among immigrants in general earnings increased with duration in the United States, but this gradient was much steeper for the Russian Jews. While the earnings of Russian Jews who arrived in the United States between 1965 and 1990 did not differ significantly from other European immigrants, the earnings of Russian Jews were lower among those who arrived more recently.

Analyses for the 1980 and 1990 Censuses also show recent Soviet Jewish arrivals having lower earnings than other European immigrants, with the differences in earnings diminishing and then disappearing with a longer duration. Thus, while recent immigrants from the Former Soviet Union had low earnings in the 1980 and 1990 Censuses, after being in the United States ten years they appear to have attained earnings parity with other European immigrants.

This pattern would be consistent with the refugee nature of the Russian Jews. They were fleeing religious/ethnic discrimination and for most the ability to leave and the timing was generally unexpected, and few planned the move. The greater steepness of the increase in earnings with duration in the United States is consistent with greater investments to increase the transferability of their premigration skills, including language skills, or higher rates of return on postimmigration investments in skill, or both.

It is noteworthy that, in spite of generally lower transferability to the United States labor market of the skills of refugees than of economic migrants, Russian Jews in 2000 received a larger payoff from years of schooling than did other immigrant men (schooling coefficient 0.026 points, or 2.6 percent, higher than the 0.045, or 4.5 percent, for other immigrants). As a result of the greater return from schooling, at the mean level of schooling among Soviet Jews (14.8 years), those in

56 Among the adult male immigrants in the United States in 2000 who immigrated since 1965 from the Former Soviet Union, forty-one percent reported their ancestry as Russian, ten percent gave an ancestry response indicating a religion (specific religion masked by the Census Bureau), eleven percent reported Armenian, and thirty-eight percent gave a variety of other responses. Of the languages spoken at home in the United States, four percent reported only English, seventy-two percent Russian, nine percent Armenian, seven percent Ukranian, and eight percent other languages, of whom only 0.2 percentage points, primarily older men, reported Yiddish (Chiswick and Wenz, op. cit., 2006, Table A-1).

57 Chiswick and Wenz, op. cit., 2006, Table 8.

the United States for ten or more years had achieved earnings parity in 2000 with other European immigrants.

Thus, in spite of their refugee experience that put them at a substantial earnings disadvantage at arrival, compared with other European immigrants the Russian Jews experienced much more rapid improvements in their labor market earnings and greater returns from their schooling. By 2000, those who arrived in the United States in 1990 or earlier with the mean level of schooling for Russian Jews had already attained earnings parity with other, primarily economic, European immigrants. It was the most recent arrivals and those with little schooling who were at the greatest earnings disadvantage.

Wealth

Occupational attainment and earnings reflect the human resources of a person—including schooling, job-related skills, decision-making ability, and other related characteristics of the person, mitigated by the discrimination experienced. Yet, individual and household well-being is also reflected by the nonhuman assets that they own, referred to here as their wealth. Data on the wealth of American households are even more scarce than data on occupation, earnings, or self-employment and do not go back in time. Data on wealth that include a method for identifying Jews, with a sufficiently large number for statistical purposes, are still even more scarce. Moreover, wealth data are plagued by far more measurement issues than are data on the occupation or earnings of an individual. The reporting of wealth is subject to much error, few know the true market value of their owner-occupied house, and even fewer know the asset value of their pension plans. Moreover, family or household composition affects wealth status.

It would be expected that contemporary American Jews would have a high level of financial wealth. The high occupational status and the high earnings would provide the resources for wealth accumulation. The high propensity for non-farm self-employment would also be conducive to wealth accumulation. Furthermore, the low fertility rate implies that the same parental wealth passed on to the next generation would mean a greater inheritance per child, facilitating the intergenerational transmission of wealth among Jews. If, as suggested above, Jews appear to be more responsive to economic opportunities they probably would also be more successful in wealth accumulation.

Keister used the data from the National Longitudinal Survey of Youth (1979 cohort) to study the wealth twenty years later (2000) of respondents by the religion in which they were raised.[58] While she found that the median net worth for all families in these data was $58,000 in 2000, for Jews it was about $221,000. Among the religious groups identified, the next highest wealth holders were the Episcopalians, with a median wealth

58 See Lisa Keister, *Getting Rich: America's New Rich and How They Got That Way.* (New York: Cambridge University Press, 2005), Chapter 6.

of $120,000. Among the groups studied, Jews had the smallest proportion of those with zero or negative net wealth. Jews were more likely than any of the other religion groups identified to: own their own home, own stocks or bonds, have a checking or savings account, and own business assets. Reflecting inheritance patterns, Jews were more likely to have a trust account.

Other determinants of wealth the same, including level of schooling, those who were raised Jewish had a higher level of wealth and were more likely to own stocks.[59] They were more likely to have a trust account and to have inherited assets—measures of intergenerational wealth transfers. In contrast to the simple pattern, when other measured variables are the same, such as schooling, Jews were less likely to own their own home. This may arise from the study not controlling statistically for urban residence, particularly residence in New York City. Home ownership is lower in urban areas in general and in New York City in particular, and Jews are a highly urbanized population. It may also reflect a substitution of investments in financial assets over investments in owner-occupied dwellings among Jews of the same level of schooling as non-Jews. The extent to which American Jews have a higher savings rate or earn a higher return on their investments has not been studied.

The high level of wealth among Jews, perhaps in part due to a greater responsiveness to economic incentives, helps finance the high level of education in the next generation, and hence the high occupational attainment and earnings of their children, as well as their children's financial assets. Thus, there is a greater intergenerational transmission of human and nonhuman resources among Jews compared to those who are not Jewish.

Summary and Conclusion

The occupational patterns of American Jews were influenced by the occupations that they had prior to migration to the United States and the employment opportunities that they experienced once settled in this country. The Jews of Colonial America concentrated in the eastcoast seaport cities and specialized in local, interior, coastal, and international trade and finance. The mid-nineteenth–century German Jewish immigrants spread across the country specializing in clerical and sales jobs in retail trade, often starting as peddlers. Some progressed to owning and managing large and prominent department stores.

The late-nineteenth– and early twentieth–century East European and Russian Jewish immigrants concentrated in New York City and other emerging industrial centers. They started in craft, operative, and laborer jobs, but if not they, then their children, advanced to higher level occupations. By mid-twentieth century many were employed in managerial and professional occupations. At the turn of the

59 Ibid.

twenty-first century over half of Jewish men and women were in professional jobs, compared to only one-in-five among non-Jewish white men and women.

Although few Jews were farmers, throughout their experience in the United States Jews had a high rate of self-employment. However, the nature of the self-employment did change. Among the mid-nineteenth—century German Jews self-employment in the retail sector predominated. Among the East European and Russian Jews in the early twentieth century light manufacturing (e.g., garment industries) and retail trade were the primary industrial sectors for the self-employed. Later self-employment among professionals came to be an important activity.

Although limited, data over the twentieth century permit comparing the earnings of Jews and others in the same data set, thereby assuring comparability of the measures under study within each period. These analyses find substantially higher earnings among Jewish men than other white men overall, and even after controlling for the major determinants of earnings, including years of schooling. The differential appears to be at least sixteen percent, ceteris paribus. When another measure of labor market outcomes, major occupational group, is held constant the differential among men falls to about eight to ten percent. Yet, differentials of these magnitudes are the economic equivalent of about two extra years (or when major occupation group is held constant, one extra year) of schooling. This is in addition to the higher educational attainment of Jewish men and women.

The analyses of earnings suggest that Jews receive a higher economic return from their years of schooling. This may contribute to their obtaining higher levels of schooling. The earnings data also suggest that Jews have a more elastic labor supply curve—that is, that higher wages have a greater impact on increasing employment among Jews. This suggests a greater sensitivity to economic opportunities. Moreover, Jewish immigrants appear to have a steeper increase in earnings with duration in the United States than do other immigrants. Taken together these patterns in earnings suggest that Jews make greater investments in their human capital relevant for the labor market, that they receive greater returns from human capital investments, and that they appear to be more responsive to economic incentives than are others.

Data on wealth are much more limited, and wealth is measured with greater error than is occupation or earnings. Data for adults in the year 2000 suggest that those raised Jewish have a much higher level of wealth (measured by financial assets, business assets, and the value of housing assets) than those raised in another religion. Wealth among Jews is even greater than among the next wealthiest religious group, the Episcopalians. This holds true even when other measured determinants of wealth, including schooling, are held constant. The data suggest a higher rate of accumulation of assets, a higher level of wealth, and a greater intergenerational transmission of wealth. These patterns may be reflecting a greater ability to discern and a greater responsiveness to opportunities for wealth accumulation, a greater willingness to take economic risks, and a higher savings rate.

There are several lessons to be drawn from the economic experience of American Jewry. One is that Jews sought out niches in the labor market in which they would be subject to less discrimination. Some of these niches were in "socially suspect" occupations, such as in entertainment, including the emerging movie industry in the early decades of the twentieth century. When rewarding sectors opened up, Jews entered them.

A second was the application of entrepreneurial and decision-making skills. From the Colonial Jewish merchants and financiers, to the German Jewish shop owners, to the present managers and professionals, Jews demonstrated a capacity for successful entrepreneurial activity. It may be debatable whether the Jews "made" the garment industry or the movie industry or whether these industries "made" the Jews, but there is no debate that the Jews identified and entered emerging economic sectors.

A third is that Jews placed high value on learning the skills necessary for advancement given the time and place. In twentieth-century America that meant schooling, and Jews placed an emphasis on achieving high levels of formal education. For some this meant battling discrimination directly, for some it meant finding ways to avoid the discrimination in the United States (e.g., studying medicine abroad), for some it meant masking or even denying their Jewish religion, heritage, or identity, but for most it meant taking advantage of existing educational and employment opportunities in the United States.

Thus, it appears that American Jews have not achieved a higher occupational status through a sacrifice of earnings, but rather they have achieved both high earnings and high occupational status simultaneously. Moreover, their greater labor market achievements do not appear to have retarded their wealth accumulation, but rather appear to have advanced it. Throughout their 350 year presence in the United States, American Jews have demonstrated extraordinary economic achievements.

SELECTED BIBLIOGRAPHY

Billings, John S. *Vital Statistics of Jews in the United States*. Census Bulletin, No. 19, Washington, DC, December 30, 1890.

Chiswick, Barry R. "The Occupational Attainment and Earnings of American Jewry: 1990–2000" *Contemporary Jewry* 27 (2007): 80–111.

———. "The Billings Report and the Occupational Attainment of American Jewry, 1890." *Shofar: An Interdisciplinary Journal of Jewish Studies* 19(2) (Winter 2001): 53–75.

———. "The Occupational Attainment and Earnings of American Jewry, 1890–1990." *Contemporary Jewry* 20 (1999): 68–98.

———., and Michael Wenz. "The Linguistic and Economic Adjustment of Soviet Jewish Immigrants in the United States: 1980 to 2000." *Research in Labor Economics* 24 (2006): 179–216.

Keister, Lisa. *Getting Rich: America's New Rich and How They Got That Way*. New York: Cambridge University Press, 2005.

Marcus, Jacob Rader. *The Colonial American Jew 1492–1776, Volume II*, Detroit: Wayne State University Press, 1970.

U.S. Bureau of the Census. "Tabulations of Data on the Social and Economic Characteristics of Major Religious Groups, 1957." Washington, DC, mimeo.

CHAPTER 33

HOW ECONOMICS HELPED SHAPE AMERICAN JUDAISM

CARMEL ULLMAN CHISWICK

Introduction

The United States presents an economic environment unlike any other in the millennia-long experience of the Jewish people. As the "Great Experiment" in democracy and religious freedom, America broke with its European roots in ways that greatly reduced the economic penalties imposed by society on Jews per se. American Jews were subject to no special taxes and faced no laws restricting their ability to choose an occupation, to own property, or to enforce contracts. Although anti-Semitism was not completely absent, other minority religious and ethnic/racial groups also faced challenges in America. For European Jews, America was truly a land of opportunity.

In addition to its promise of freedom, the United States participated with the rest of the Western world in a series of technological advances with such dramatic economic and social impacts that they were referred to as an industrial "revolution." New inventions made workers far more productive than they had ever been in the past, mass production greatly reduced the cost of manufactured goods, new modes of transportation supplied city dwellers with inexpensive food, and new technologies in communication connected people in ways that would have been unfathomable in a previous era. The real wages of ordinary workers, conventionally measured as the purchasing power earned by working for one day or one hour, rose to unprecedented levels.

The new technology also placed a high premium on skills, both on the factory floor (blue-collar workers) and in the front office (white-collar workers). The United States was the first country to develop a large-scale system of colleges and universities that were readily accessible to many families. The highly educated graduates of this system would command a substantial wage premium throughout the twentieth century as they facilitated the innovation and adoption of new technologies. Jews, with their traditional emphases on education and on adaptability to new opportunities, participated eagerly and successfully in this process. In a country where real wages were rising for all workers, Jews were acquiring higher education and thus moving toward the higher end of the rising American wage distribution.

This was the economic context in which American Judaism developed its own set of religious practices. Judaism's Great Tradition—Tanach, Talmud, and Rabbinic rulings—would not change, for this is the core that defines Judaism as a religion and Jews as a people. Its European Ashkenazi traditions, however, were not immutable. Religious practices that involved purchasing goods might have been too expensive for Jews in a Russian *shtetl*, but they would be well within the means of even poor Jews in America. In contrast, any practice that required long hours in the synagogue would be far more costly for a high-wage American Jew with many attractive alternatives for leisure as well as work activities. These differences in the relative prices of goods and of time would be instrumental in altering religious practices and hence the shape of Judaism in the United States.

Jewish adaptations in America included the nineteenth-century split into three main synagogue movements (Reform, Conservative, and Orthodox) and the development of a wide variety of communal organizations for social and political as well as charitable purposes. During the twentieth century these synagogue movements and their various offshoots would come to characterize a distinctively American Jewish religious identity. Also during the twentieth century the emergence of Israel as a major cultural, political, and economic center—and a focal point of Jewish life—would have important effects on the cost of being Jewish, and hence religious practices, in the Diaspora.

This chapter explores the economic forces that facilitated and supported these and other changes in American Judaism. It deals first with the immigrant experience and changes in economic incentives associated with upward educational and occupational mobility. It then looks specifically at how this context affected the economics of Jewish religious education in the twentieth century. Within the framework of World Jewry, the relationship among the United States, Europe, and Israel is discussed with regard to the comparative advantage of each community in Jewish education. The economic underpinnings of assimilation in the later decades of the twentieth century is discussed next, viewed mainly as an unintended consequence of economic decisions made by Jewish immigrants and their children during their adjustment to an economic environment in America with virtually no precedent in Jewish experience. In conclusion, these various economic analyses are used to provide a forecast for the future of American Judaism.

The Economics of Immigrant Adjustment

Jews, like nearly everyone else in the United States, originally came to America as immigrants. The earliest Jewish immigrants had to form their own communities, but later immigrants could choose between joining an established Jewish community and forming a new one. In either case, however, an immigrant's primary concern would be to earn a living and adjust to economic circumstances in the new country. The greater the difference between economic life in the old country and the new, the more difficult this adjustment would be and the more likely that economic concerns would heavily influence other aspects of an immigrant's new life.

The earliest American Jewish communities were Sephardic, with members whose occupations in international trade and finance placed them in comfortable economic circumstances.[1] In the mid-nineteenth century, however, they were greatly outnumbered by a wave of Ashkenazi immigrants from German-speaking areas of Central Europe. Many of the German Jewish immigrants were poor, beginning their American experience as itinerant peddlers and eventually working their way up the socioeconomic ladder by expanding their retail operations. The German Jews brought with them Ashkenazi traditions, often modified by changes introduced by the early Reform movement in Germany. In the last decades of the nineteenth century their communities were in turn outnumbered by the massive influx of Yiddish-speaking Jews from Russia and Eastern Europe, ancestors of some ninety-five percent of today's American Jews. The immigrant Russian Jews arrived with few assets and worked mostly as ordinary laborers, operatives, and craftsmen, but as they and their offspring improved their economic circumstances they moved into a variety of occupations, including especially the professions associated with higher education.

The Immigrant Experience

American Jewish history is thus dominated by the story of Jewish immigrants making the transition from the old world to the new, always seeking opportunities to improve their economic condition. In this respect they followed the well-established model of immigrant economic adjustment.[2] Many of the skills they found useful in the old country did not transfer well to the new; their English was poor and they lacked skills with high market value. As a result, they would accept

1 For data on the occupations of American Jews see the chapter by Barry R. Chiswick in this volume.

2 For the economics of immigrant adjustment see Barry R. Chiswick, "The Effect of Americanization on the Earnings of Foreign-Born Men," *Journal of Political Economy*, 86/5 (1978), 897–921. Reprinted in Barry R. Chiswick, *The Economics of Immigration: Selected Papers of Barry R. Chiswick* (Northampton, MA: Edward Elgar, 2005).

low-paying jobs to support themselves while learning such country-specific skills. Perhaps the most important of these skills was the English language, but also important were American customs associated with the job market, such as how to look for and land a good job, how to behave toward supervisors and colleagues, and how to develop efficient networks for finding a job or establishing a business. Also important was knowledge useful in their role as consumers, such as learning the relative prices of goods and services, finding stores with low prices, or where and when to find the good bargains. Although real wages were much higher in the United States than they had been in their countries of origin, new immigrants could not always command the higher wages until they had made these investments in United States-specific skills.

Like many other immigrant groups, Jewish immigrants established synagogue communities in the new country with a minimum of changes. Storefront synagogues, or *shteibls*, were common in the poor Jewish neighborhoods, serving in effect as inexpensive replicas of familiar old-country synagogues. They were places where people with a shared experience and history could meet, where a person could hear and speak a familiar language and fit into a familiar social structure, and could thus serve as an emotional haven in a strange, confusing world. They also served as information exchanges, as a place to learn the ways of the new country, and to network for a better job or for new customers. In this they were the Jewish counterpart of the "immigrant church" that plays an important role in immigrant adjustment during the early years in a new country.[3]

Although the storefront synagogues replicated as much as possible the old-country religious traditions of Russian Jews, there was one very important difference. The opportunity cost of time was very much higher in the United States than it had been in Europe, making every hour of synagogue attendance and home religious observance that much more costly. Even newcomers in low-paying jobs were investing in work related skills that would raise their future earnings, thus raising the opportunity cost of time well above their actual wage rate. People responded to the high value of time by reducing their synagogue attendance and religious ritual activities. For many, the Sabbath and most holiday observances were increasingly confined to the home where they could be comfortably abbreviated, the main exception being the High Holy Days of Rosh Hashanah and Yom Kippur.[4]

The education of Jewish children in the immigrant neighborhoods was also affected by the high opportunity cost of their time. Jewish immigrants understood that an important route to upward socioeconomic mobility in the United States

3 For a fuller development of the role of immigrant churches in the United States See R. Stephen Warner and Judith G. Wittner (eds.), *Gatherings in Diaspora: Religious Communities and the New Immigration* (Philadelphia: Temple University Press, 1998).

4 Jonathan Sarna, "New Paradigms For the Study of American Jewish Life," *Contemporary Jewry* 24 (2004), 157–69.

was through a good secular education, and they were willing to work hard and sacrifice their own consumption levels in order to keep their children in school. The opportunity cost of the child's time, measured as the expected payoff to this educational investment, would have been quite high. In contrast, the expected payoff to an investment in Jewish education was much lower, in part because it would have had little effect on labor market earnings and in part because the immigrants overestimated the extent to which children could learn Judaism by simply living among other Jews. The Jewish religious professions—rabbi, cantor, Hebrew teacher, *shochet*, *mohel*—were low-paying occupations and therefore without much prestige in the immigrant community. An international trading system was developed for these skills: An American Jewish community could send for someone trained in Europe who would work cheaply and consider himself well-paid, although after a few years he might move on to a more lucrative occupation and be replaced by another newcomer.

Americanization and Upward Mobility

Once an immigrant has had a few years to adjust and to learn about the new economic environment, he or she typically chooses a niche in which to build a career and family.[5] Sometimes this involves moving up the job ladder within a firm or industry, sometimes it involves establishing and building a business enterprise, and sometimes it involves acquiring the education needed to enter a profession. This is a period when earlier investments in United States-specific skills are beginning to pay off as the immigrants become more "Americanized." At the same time immigrants in this phase of their economic adjustment invest heavily in their chosen path, acquiring a reputation for hard work and long hours. As they move out of poverty and into the middle class, the opportunity cost of their time is even higher than before.

For immigrants at this stage of assimilation into the American economy, time-intensive religious traditions were increasingly expensive. The newly emergent American lifestyles were becoming less and less complementary with the old-country Jewish observances that had been comfortable for people in very different circumstances. As the German Jews established themselves during the second half of the nineteenth century, they founded new Ashkenazi synagogues with "reformed" practices more compatible with their new economic environment.[6] These reforms were influenced by the classical Reform movement in Germany, which had arisen along with the rapid economic development of that country, but their ready acceptance by American Jews was encouraged by the fact that they reduced the time-intensity of Jewish religious observance.

5 Barry R. Chiswick, op.cit. (1978).

6 For a fascinating description of this process see Jonathan D. Sarna, *American Judaism: A History* (New Haven: Yale University Press, 2004).

Many American Jews stopped observing *kashrut*, especially those living outside of the big-city Jewish enclave neighborhoods. This was only partly because the scarcity of kosher butchers would have made the price of meat very expensive. More importantly, American Jews were participating actively in an open and collegial society in which shared meals played an important social role. The opportunity cost of not joining their non-Jewish neighbors for business lunches or social dining would have been quite high, thus providing a strong economic incentive to accept Reform Judaism's rejection of *kashrut* as an "obsolete" observance.

Reform synagogues adopted other "American" practices, greatly abbreviating the religious service, conducting prayers in English as well as in Hebrew, and introducing mixed seating with men and women together. As these reforms gained momentum, imported clergy trained in European seminaries were less and less prepared to serve in American congregations. As the German Jews continued to prosper in America, they established the Hebrew Union College to train rabbis to serve in Reform synagogues. In the spirit of this new movement, the first graduation ceremony in 1883 was celebrated with the infamous "*Trefa Banquet*," followed shortly thereafter by the formal establishment of Reform Judaism with its even more radical "Pittsburgh Platform."[7]

By the time the Russian Jews moved into middle-class neighborhoods, the American Reform Movement was already established. For many, joining a Reform synagogue was simply another step in their Americanization process. Others, however, were not comfortable with the radical ideology of that movement. They had no difficulty abandoning the storefront synagogues, which they had long ago ceased to attend with any enthusiasm, but their new Conservative synagogues retained the use of Hebrew ritual even as they introduced English for translations and for a sermon. The Conservative Movement did not abandon *kashrut*, nor did it drop the observance of *Shabbat*, although many of its individual members honored these religious laws in the breach.

Orthodox synagogues retained many more of the old-country Ashkenazi religious traditions, but in many respects they were the Jewish counterpart of "immigrant churches."[8] As immigrants became more fluent in English and found an economic niche for themselves, their time became more costly and their need for a "safe haven" less urgent. As an alternative to joining an "American" congregation, however, the immigrant religious community might simply move its old synagogue to the new neighborhood. In such cases, the synagogue service inevitably changed along with changes in the congregants' circumstances. Upward economic mobility made time-intensive practices more costly and donations more feasible, leading to

7 The graduation dinner was a gilded-age affair with many elaborate courses, each one of which violated the laws of *kashrut*. There are many descriptions of this event and its far-reaching consequences. See, for example, Jonathan D. Sarna, *American Judaism: A History* (New Haven: Yale University Press, 2004).

8 The term "immigrant church" is used broadly in the Sociology literature to include any house of worship serving a largely immigrant community, often using the language and customs of their country of origin. Warner and Wittner (eds.), op. cit. (1998) presents detailed descriptions of a number of immigrant churches at the end of the twentieth century.

a systematic tendency toward substituting money for time. Congregants were willing to maintain a building and hire clergy, but their own attendance at services tended to decline. Language study is time-intensive, so English was relied on to make the services "relevant" for congregants with limited Hebrew skills. As religious practices responded to the new incentives, and as the members became more "American" in their lifestyles and sensibilities, synagogue activities were increasingly laced with a heavy dose of nostalgia for traditions that were inevitably disappearing from American Jewish life.

Immigrant churches in general rarely survive more than a generation or two. The immigrants themselves, and some of their children, may continue their attachment to the old-country traditions, but their grandchildren have no direct ties to the old country and are often impatient of the nostalgia enjoyed by their elders. In an upwardly mobile community, the opportunity cost of time is substantially higher for the third generation than for the first- and perhaps even the second-generation immigrants. Some young people left for less time-intensive Conservative or Reform "American" congregations when they moved out of the immigrant neighborhoods, while others remained Orthodox only as long as their parents or grandparents survived. Throughout the first half of the twentieth century, the rising opportunity cost of time in the American Jewish population goes far toward explaining the oft-noted intergenerational progression of many American Jewish families from Orthodox to Conservative to Reform and the declining membership in Orthodox synagogues.

Outside of the synagogues, the upwardly mobile community developed a variety of institutions to address the philanthropic, political, and social needs of American Jewry. Although elsewhere these functions might be the province of the religious communities, this was not the case in the United States, where pluralism generated a different structure in the religious "marketplace."[9] In contrast to the hierarchical religious organizations typical in countries with a state religion, American churches and synagogues were characterized by congregationalism—that is, an organizational structure in which congregations are founded and administered by their lay membership. Without any central authority, these congregations typically form umbrella organizations—organizations in which churches or synagogues per se are members—to serve common religious interests. The Union of American Hebrew Congregations, the United Synagogues of America, and the Orthodox Union were formed in the late-nineteenth century and continue to dominate American Jewish religious life to this day. A congregationalist market structure also leads to the formation of parareligious organizations to serve the nonreligious social and political needs of the religious community. For American Jewry these included not only charities for support to the needy but also organizations that helped the socioeconomic assimilation of Jewish immigrants (e.g., the

9 For an excellent exposition of this phenomenon and its related terminology see R. Stephen Warner, "Work in Progress toward a New Paradigm for the Sociological Study of Religion in the United States," *American Journal of Sociology* 98/5 (1993): 1044–93.

Hebrew Immigrant Aid Society, the Anti-Defamation League), and those that reinforced ties to World Jewry (e.g., Jewish National Fund, the Joint Distribution Committee, Hadassah, and other Zionist organizations).

As noted above, during this demanding phase of their economic adjustment, Jewish immigrants worked long and hard as they invested heavily in their business or profession. The opportunity cost of their time was high, and virtually all of their consumption patterns changed in response. Wherever possible, Jewish immigrants and their children sought to reduce the time-intensity of consumption, and Jewish religious observance was no exception. For some this meant simply reducing their religious observance, but for most it meant religious innovations that would permit substituting money for time. Even as rising wages made time more costly, rising incomes made financial support less difficult. Even as American Jews spent less and less time in the synagogue and in home-based religious observance, they joined and supported new synagogues and gave generously to parareligious charities and communal organizations. Although American Jews were often derided as "nonobservant" and "materialistic," they were also following a long-standing Jewish tradition by adapting their religious practices to a new economic environment.

The Economics of Jewish Education

Education—broadly defined—is the process of investing in human capital. Whether formal or informal, education provides skills useful for consumption as well as production. It is also the means of transmitting the stock of human knowledge from one generation to the next. Jews have always emphasized the importance of education, both secular and religious. A full understanding of how economic incentives affected the shape of American Judaism requires an understanding of how they affected Jewish education.

At the turn of the twentieth century the Yiddish-speaking immigrants from Russia and Eastern Europe were far more preoccupied with acquiring secular skills than they were with Jewish education. The financial payoff to secular skills was very high, and there were many new and exciting cultural, political, and social activities to learn about. In contrast, the early religious institutions that they established were familiar (if not actually perceived as boring) and depended mainly on a set of old-country skills that could be transferred successfully to the new environment. The large difference in rates of return between investments in secular and Jewish human capital led invariably to a strong focus on the former and a marked separation between secular and religious education that would persist for many decades.

Investment in secular human capital was a very high priority for Jewish immigrants. For adult men this usually meant learning English and acquiring job-related or business skills. Jewish women were eager students in settlement houses and learned to use new cookbooks and other "how-to" manuals, many of which were published in Yiddish.[10] Immigrant parents sent their children to the public schools and were willing to make great sacrifices, if necessary, to keep them there as long as possible. Most of these children continued through high school, and many—especially the boys—would continue their education in college. According to a survey of Jewish men taken in the year 2000, more than twenty-five percent of those born before 1940, most of whom would have been the sons of immigrant parents, had not only graduated from college but had also earned some postgraduate professional degree.[11] This is more than double the corresponding figure for non-Jews and is testimony to the very high priority American Jews placed on secular education.

Increases in the level of secular education had far-reaching implications for the economic environment of American Jewry. Schooling provided the skills that qualified men for higher paying occupations, raising both incomes and the opportunity cost of time. By the early post-WWII years nearly sixty percent of all Jewish men were working in high-level occupations, as compared to less than twenty-five percent of the non-Jews. Of the sixty percent, about one-fourth (fourteen percent) were professionals whose occupations would have required an advanced degree. Another two-thirds (forty-five percent) were in managerial occupations—a category that includes owners who manage their own companies but not the owners of small "mom-and-pop" establishments. The proportion in professional occupations would increase steadily for the rest of the century to more than half of the total, and the proportion in management would eventually decline to less than twenty percent, but together these high-level occupations would continue to account for about two-thirds of the American Jewish male labor force. By way of comparison, in the year 2000 less than twenty percent of non-Jewish American men were in the professions, and high-level occupations accounted for only about thirty-five percent of the total.[12]

People in these high-level occupations have skills that place them at the upper end of the United States earnings distribution. Many of these occupations were male-dominated until the later decades of the twentieth century, at which point Jewish women entered them in disproportionately large numbers. Jewish women were much more likely than their non-Jewish counterparts to have attended college, and for every cohort born after World War II more than twenty-five percent of the Jewish women (compared to about ten percent of non-Jewish women) went on to earn an advanced post-college degree.[13]

With the focus on acquiring secular skills that conferred upward economic mobility, Jewish education received much less attention. Families had limited

10 For an interesting description of this and other aspects of Jewish immigrant culture see Jemma Weissman Joselit, *The Wonders of America: Reinventing Jewish Culture 1880-1950* (New York: Hill and Wang, 1994).

11 Carmel U. Chiswick, "Occupation and Gender: American Jews at the Millenium." Paper presented to the *Seminar on Creating and Maintaining Jewish Families* (Brandeis University, 2007). The data are from the National Jewish Population Survey 2000/01.

12 Data on the occupations of Jewish men are from various sources as reported in Barry R. Chiswick, "The Occupational Attainment and Earnings of American Jewry, 1890 to 1990," *Contemporary Jewry* 20 (1994), 68–98, and Barry R. Chiswick, "The Occupational Attainment of American Jewry: 1990 to 2000," *Contemporary Jewry* 27 (2007): 80–111.

13 Carmel U. Chiswick, op. cit. (2007).

money budgets and students had limited time budgets. The rate of return to secular education was large and obvious, while the economic return to a Jewish education was much less so. For many immigrants Judaism was so fundamental to their self-concept that they simply could not imagine that it might be otherwise for their children. Yet, with little attention given to religious studies and not much time spent in home observances, most of the Jewish human capital acquired by second-generation immigrants was what they learned by living in an ethnically Jewish community.[14] Religious human capital acquired in this way was at best perfunctory; although Jewish ethnic characteristics might survive a subsequent move to the non-Jewish suburbs, religious knowledge was often too weak to be imparted to the next generation. The grandchildren of immigrants would grow up to embody the classic American Jewish imbalance, with very high secular skills and very low religious skills. The marginal product of time spent in secular activities would thus be very much higher than in Jewish religious observance, and this in turn would induce a further shift in the time budget from religious to secular activities.[15]

Even as the two types of education compete with each other for resources, the human capital that they create can be mutually complementary. For example, Jews with a strong background in religious studies, especially advanced Talmud study, often excel in secular studies as well. While cause and effect have yet to be well-understood, this is a plausible explanation for the fact that Jews faced a higher rate of return than other groups to investments in secular education, further reinforcing the productivity of investments in schooling.[16] Few American Jews, however, were prepared to carry their religious studies to this point, and a perfunctory Jewish education can have little complementarily with American secular skills.

Gifted Jewish leaders recognized this problem early in the twentieth century and began working on ways to "Americanize" Jewish education. This process had two fronts. On the one hand, taking account of the secular human capital that Jewish students already had permitted Jewish educational methods to become more efficient. On the other hand, changes in American Jewish religious practice meant that the skills required for Jewish observance might differ from those needed in the old country. All three of the major synagogue movements developed new curricula and structures of Jewish education, organizing their schools with graded classrooms and developing English-language texts to complement the study of Hebrew.[17]

14 Jonathan D. Sarna, "New Paradigms for the Study of American Jewish Life," *Contemporary Jewry*, 24 (2004): 157–69.

15 For further development of this point see Carmel U. Chiswick, "The Economics of Jewish Immigrants and Judaism in the United States." *Papers in Jewish Demography 1997* (2001), 331–44. Reprinted in Carmel U. Chiswick, *Economics of American Judaism* (London: Routledge, 2008).

16 See, for example, Barry R. Chiswick, "Differences in Education and Earnings across Racial and Ethnic Groups: Tastes, Discrimination, and Investments in Child Quality," *Quarterly Journal of Economics*, 103 (1988): 571–97.

17 Sarna, *American Judaism: A History* (New Haven: Yale University Press, 2004) and Jack Wertheimer, "Jewish Education in the United States: Recent Trends and Issues," in David Singer (ed.), *American Jewish Year Book 1999* (New York: American Jewish Committee, 1999), 3–115.

Although at first only a minority of the Jewish children acquired this education, by mid-century it was becoming the norm. Most of it took place in after-school programs affiliated with individual synagogues that were in turn affiliated with one of the larger synagogue movements. Typically meeting three days per week, twice on a weekday afternoon and again on Sunday mornings, these after-school programs provided the only Jewish education received by most of the children in Reform and Conservative congregations. Jewish day schools—that is, full-time parochial schools that provided both religious and secular education—were associated mostly with the Orthodox movement. Day schools were most common in cities with a substantial Jewish enclave neighborhood. As the immigrants assimilated and moved to the suburbs, Jewish day schools declined in number and enrollment until well after World War II. The Jewish day school "movement" has expanded dramatically in recent decades, in part because higher incomes have led to an expansion of private schools in general and in part because of an increased concern with Jewish education in particular. Although the proportion of children attending a Jewish day school is far higher among the Orthodox than the other movements, non-Orthodox and community-based Jewish day schools are a relatively new phenomenon with potentially important implications for the future of American Judaism.

American Economics and World Jewry

In 1880 nearly ninety percent of the world's Jewish population was concentrated in the Tsarist Russian Empire, with other communities in the Austro-Hungarian and Ottoman Empires and only two percent in the United States. Between 1880 and the start of World War I, however, a mass migration from Russia and Eastern Europe to the United States significantly altered this distribution. By the early 1930s, on the eve of World War II, nearly thirty percent of the world's Jews lived in the United States, another sixty percent in Europe (including Russia), and the remainder scattered in smaller communities in the rest of the world, including the British Mandate in Palestine. Then the Holocaust effectively destroyed European Jewry, and with the establishment of the State of Israel began a period of mass immigration of refugees from Europe and from Arab lands. As a result, the United States and Israel emerged as the two dominant Jewish communities during the second half of the twentieth century, each of which now accounts for approximately forty percent of world Jewry.[18]

18 These data are from Sergio DellaPergola, "World Jewish Population 2006," *American Jewish Yearbook 2006* (New York: American Jewish Committee), and from unpublished tables compiled by Barry R. Chiswick.

American and European Jewry

As the Jewish community grew and the immigrants established an economic niche for themselves, Americans found themselves innovating new forms of Jewish observance compatible with an economic environment unlike those of the places where most other Jews were living. Throughout the first half of the twentieth century, American Jewish practices, customs, and sensibilities increasingly diverged from those of the rest of the world. No matter how inward-looking Americans might be, however, they remained connected emotionally and traditionally to other Jews and especially to the Ashkenazi Jews of Europe. American Jewish charities included the needs of poor communities elsewhere, and American Jews were intensely concerned with political developments that affected the welfare of Jews in other countries.

International trade is especially profitable when factor prices differ across countries. In the United States, the prices of material goods were generally quite low and the opportunity cost of time was very high, in contrast to most of the rest of the world where the opposite was true. By the turn of the twentieth century American Jewry had developed an implicit system of international trade, exporting goods-intensive commodities (usually in the form of money) to other Jewish communities in exchange for time-intensive services (usually in the form of human capital). For example, American Jews provided financial support for *yeshivas* in Europe and hired their graduates, thus maintaining traditional Jewish institutions while avoiding the high opportunity cost of establishing similar schools in the United States. American Jews also participated in the development of the Jewish community in Israel by contributing money that supported the labor provided by Jewish immigrants to Israel from other countries.

Much as youthful challenge requires a stable authority against which to rebel, American Judaism could be bold in its pursuit of innovation because traditional religious institutions remained relatively strong in Europe.[19] For the same reason, Israeli Jews were also able to concentrate on secular needs and felt free to make their own innovations in Jewish life. This security, reinforced by the possibility of international trade in religious skills, ended with the destruction of European Jewry in the Holocaust. Apart from its emotional and theological impacts, the Holocaust dramatically altered the economic exchange patterns of World Jewry. No longer would Europe be a source of religious human capital and the guarantor of continuity for ancient traditions. If the ancient treasures of Jewish religious culture were to survive at all, they would have to be preserved by the "new" Jewish communities in the United States and Israel.

What followed was a realignment of priorities, in which each of the three main synagogue movements sought to position themselves as preservers of Jewish

19 In fact, the forces of modernity were challenging religious authority in Europe as well. Changes in European Judaism were undoubtedly slowed, however, by the opportunity for dissidents to emigrate. If immigrants to America had a large component of Jews self-selected to be less observant than the average, this would have reinforced their economic incentives to deemphasize Jewish religious education.

tradition in an American setting. The Reform movement became less radically rebellious against religious traditionalism, moving away from its German roots to a less formal, more individualistic synagogue culture accessible to Americans with little Jewish religious education. The Conservative movement increased its emphasis on Zionism, not only as a means of supporting World Jewry but also for Israel's potential to enrich the religious life of American Jews. Orthodox Judaism's declining membership was checked and eventually reversed, in part because of a renewed appreciation of the value of traditional religion and in part because of the stimulus it received when an important remnant of European *yeshiva* life immigrated to the United States. Unlike the case in previous generations when economic considerations were paramount, today's American Jews with their relatively high incomes and secure identities tend to affiliate with the movement that best expresses their own religious temperament.

American Jewry and Israel

With the establishment of Israel as an important Jewish community, American Jewry found new opportunities for religious exchange. At first this was primarily a matter of money, with American Jewish donations to the new State supporting its economic development and refugee settlement. American financial contributions were also important for supporting the educational, medical, and social infrastructure that helped Israel develop rapidly into a strong modern economy. By the 1960s, however, American Jews were beginning to visit Israel in person, where their Judaism was influenced in other ways. When it came to Jewish human capital, Israeli Jews had a comparative advantage relative to American Jews for skills related to the Hebrew language and to biblical history and geography, whereas the Jewish education of Americans focused mainly on synagogue and holiday traditions developed in the Diaspora. By the last decades of the twentieth century modern Hebrew had become an important part of the American Jewish curriculum, sometimes with a semester or two in Israel but more often with an Israeli-trained teacher in America. American synagogues and Hebrew Schools would be influenced by the music, art, and politics of Israeli Jewry, and vice versa.

With the development of Israel into a high-technology modern economy, the economic environment of Israeli Jews has partially converged to that of the United States, and this has induced a corresponding partial convergence of their Jewish practices.[20] There still remain important differences. American Jewry is a tiny minority in a large country, while Israeli Jewry is a large majority in a tiny country.

20 For a fuller discussion of this proposition see Carmel U. Chiswick, "Israel and American Jewry in the Year 2020: An Economic Analysis," in Anat Gonen and Smadar Fogel (eds.), *The Macro Scenarios: Israel and the Jewish People* (Israel 2020: Master Plan for Israel in the Twenty-First Century; Haifa: The Technion, 1996), 257–72 (Hebrew). The original English version is available in Carmel U. Chiswick, *Economics of American Judaism* (London: Routledge, 2008).

The United States is also characterized by religious pluralism with no government support for any specific religious group, whereas Israel is a Jewish state whose government supports several recognized religions. The possibility of capturing state financial support provides an economic incentive for religious groups to organize into political parties, a phenomenon common in Israel but virtually unheard of in the United States.

The entry of religion into the electoral system has other economic implications. Religious affiliation affects political outcomes, and political motives affect religious rhetoric. Israel's electoral system tends to generate many political parties and to favor groups in the extremes of the political spectrum, including the extremes of the religious spectrum. In contrast, American pluralism tends to favor the center in both political and religious spheres. In consequence, the proportion of Jews at either extreme of the religious spectrum, whether ultra-Orthodox or ultra-secular, is very much smaller in the United States than it is in Israel. Interactions between the two communities may erode this distinction, especially among the ultra-Orthodox, where the financial and religious ties are much closer than elsewhere. Despite their growth in recent years, however, the ultra-Orthodox remain a small fraction of American Jewry and are unlikely to reach the importance of their Israeli counterparts. As long as the United States continues its separation of church and state, the large majority of American Jewry is likely to continue to locate itself at the center of the Jewish religious spectrum.

Economics and Assimilation in America

Economic and social assimilation into the American mainstream was an important objective for Jewish immigrants and their children. They pursued it with dedication and intelligence, and they achieved it in a remarkably short time. In Europe, being a Jew was like having an ascribed trait that was difficult, if not impossible, to shed even for those who converted to another religion, married, and raised their children in another faith. Many of the Jewish immigrants to the United States viewed their Judaism as an unwanted old-country artifact that they were prepared to leave behind, and in America they found this to be possible. For most, however, America was a land of economic opportunity regardless of the fact that they were Jews. Even as they strove for economic and social assimilation, few of them expected that American religious pluralism would be in any way a threat to Jewish continuity.

By the end of the twentieth century assimilation was defined differently, as a loss of meaningful Jewish identity, and is now perceived by many to threaten the very survival of American Judaism. As discussed earlier, immigrants invested heavily in their children's secular education without making corresponding investments in Jewish education. When these children grew up and had children of their own, they had little to offer in the way of parental Jewish knowledge. Following values established in the immigrant communities of their youth, many of them viewed Jewish religious ritual as a set of quaint old-country traditions without importance in America. Although rising levels of education, occupations, and earnings soon placed them comfortably in upper-middle-class suburbs, the price of that rapid success was the loss of specifically Jewish human capital.

The immigrants themselves, now grandparents, might provide the family with whatever Jewish tradition they could, but it will be recalled that the immigrants themselves tended to be self-selected for below-average attachment to religious traditionalism. Moreover, children are more likely to turn to their parents as role models rather than their grandparents. Thus, the absence of Jewish education in one generation would be passed on to the next, and each successive generation would have less and less Jewish human capital. Coupled with ever-higher levels of secular human capital, this would induce a reallocation of time away from Jewish observance in favor of secular pursuits, whether work or leisure. Young Jews in later generations would either ignore their Judaism entirely, placing little value on it, or they would feel the need to acquire more Jewish education than their parents, often citing a grandparent as inspiration. By the end of the twentieth century American Jews would effectively split into two groups, those whose Judaism was effectively lost—the fully assimilated Jews—and those whose Judaism was increasing in intensity and thus giving rise to a Jewish "renaissance."[21]

The most visible symptom of religious assimilation is Jewish intermarriage, by which is meant the situation where a Jew marries a non-Jewish spouse. In most of these marriages children are raised either as non-Jews or as Jews in little more than name only. Unlike the situation in most of Jewish history, many non-Jews in America have educational, economic, and social backgrounds quite similar to those of Jews. Further, many of these non-Jews lack the intense anti-Semitic attitudes characteristic of European society and are only loosely attached to their own religions. Most American Jews have many opportunities to meet non-Jewish friends, classmates, and colleagues, readily finding possibilities for a suitable match on characteristics other than religion. The main incentive to select a partner that is Jewish is to improve the efficiency of making a Jewish home, an important component of Jewish religious observance. Even if both of his or her parents were themselves Jewish, a young person raised in a home with little or no Jewish observance or content is unlikely to view this as a high priority. Religious intermarriage at the end of the twentieth century may thus be seen as an unintended consequence of educational and lifestyle choices made earlier in the century.

The number of American Jews effectively "lost" to the community through religious assimilation and intermarriage is substantial, but an important minority remains committed to Judaism and if anything is strengthening Jewish religious

21 The economic theory summarized in this paragraph is developed in C. U. Chiswick, op cit. 1997. For a discussion of the Jewish "renaissance" see Jack Wertheimer, *A People Divided: Judaism in Contemporary America.* (New York: Basic Books, 1993).

culture in the United States. Not every immigrant neglected their children's Jewish education, and even some that did have observed their offspring choosing to "return" to Judaism. Most synagogues and their schools have adapted more or less successfully to the American environment. Developments in Israel fed into American Jewish life in creative ways, and the high comfort level of Jews in American society led to more visibility in Jewish observances. Many colleges and universities have courses and even whole programs in Jewish Studies. The three main synagogue movements of the last century are now joined by a variety of additional (or alternative) movements, including those that style themselves as "postdenominational" and a variety of groups that are characterized in the aggregate as "ultra-Orthodox." This pluralism within the Jewish community is an important part of American Judaism's response to the community's economic success.

An Economic Forcast of the Future

The economic environment of American Jewry during the twentieth century was one of rapid transition. At the beginning most Jews were immigrant blue-collar workers, with little secular schooling and poor English skills. By mid-century they had climbed out of poverty, raised their education levels, and moved into occupations at the forefront of American technological progress. At the end of the century most young adult Jews were third- or fourth-generation Americans, well-educated, raised in upper-middle-class suburban comfort, and fully integrated into American society.

American Jewish institutions were influenced not only by differences between the economic environment of the United States and that of other countries, but also by the rapidly changing economic circumstances of American Jews. To a large extent, Jewish institutions were formed by, and catered to, the needs of an upwardly mobile community, within which there was much inequality as some advanced more rapidly than others. Now that the Jewish community is fairly stable at a high level of economic achievement, and is more homogeneous with respect to income and occupations, the older institutions no longer speak to its current needs. The American Jewish community now finds itself adapting its synagogues and communal institutions to yet another new economic environment and to the new Jewish needs of its members.

In contrast to the upward mobility of the past, the economic environment of today's Jewish community appears to exhibit a large degree of intergenerational stability. Highly educated parents place a high value on the education of their own children and provide them with a family background that advantages them in school. Highly educated parents also work in well-paying professional and managerial occupations that inevitably advantage their children for similar work. People in well-paid occupations also have a high opportunity cost of time, an incentive to substitute in consumption away from time-intensive activities. In particular, they have an incentive to have fewer children and invest heavily in the human capital of each child. Smaller, well-off families tend to invest similarly in both daughters and sons, and young adults tend to marry people with similar age, education, and even occupational characteristics. Most of today's Jewish families are two-career professional couples who expect their own children to grow up into a community with similar economic characteristics.

For the most part, different types of human capital are mutually complementary, in that investment in one type raises the rate of return to investments in others. This means that high levels of secular education increase not only work-related skills but also the incentives to invest in health, in leisure-related activities, in family-related human capital, and in religious skills. American Jews are making all of these investments, and they can be expected to continue doing so. Even though the current Jewish renaissance is important for only a minority of today's young-adult Jews, it is probably a transitional phase, bridging the gap between low levels of Jewish human capital in the past and relatively high levels in the somewhat smaller but more intensely committed American Jewish community of the future. How high these future levels will be, and how many Jews continue to identify strongly with Judaism, depends in large part on how successfully Judaism and Jewish communal institutions can respond to the twenty-first-century American economic environment.

SELECTED BIBLIOGRAPHY

Chiswick, Barry R. "The Occupational Attainment and Earnings of American Jewry, 1890-1990." *Contemporary Jewry* 20 (1999): 68–98.

Chiswick, Carmel U. *Economics of American Judaism*. London: Routledge, 2008.

Lehrer, Evelyn L. *Religion, Economics, and Demography: The Effects of Religion on Education, Work, and the Family*. London: Routledge, 2009.

Warner, R. Stephen. "Work in Progress toward a New Paradigm for the Sociological Study of Religion in the United States." *American Journal of Sociology* 98/5 (1993): 1044–93.

Glossary

AB INITIO. Latin for "from the beginning."

AGGADAH, (ADJ.) AGGADIC. Hebrew designation of a particular genre of rabbinic literature consisting mainly of biblical exegesis of specific books of the Bible.

AHARON, (PL.) AHARONIM. Lit., later rabbinic authorities, in contrast to the *Rishonim*, the earlier authorities. The general consensus is that the period of the *Aharonim* begins with the publication of R. Joseph Caro's *Shulhan Arukh* (first edition, Venice, 1564–1565).

AMICUS CURIA. Latin term meaning "friend of the court." The name for a brief filed with the court by someone who is not a party to the case.

AMORA, (PL.) AMORAIM. Aramaic for "spokesman" or "interpreter." It is the generic term for the rabbis of the post-*Mishnaic* period but prior to the redaction of the *Gemara* (c. 200–500 CE).

AMORTIZATION. Payments that reduce the principal amount of a debt.

'ANI HAMEHAPEKH BAHARARAH. Lit., the poor man casting about (trying to take possession of certain) cake—and another person comes and snatches it away. It refers to the prohibition in Jewish law against interfering with a transaction in progress.

ANTHROPOCENTRISM. A term from environmental political philosophy denoting a human-centered ethical system. The anthropocentric belief is that human beings are the sole bearers of intrinsic value or possess greater intrinsic value than nonhuman nature. It is therefore acceptable to employ the resources of the natural world for only human ends.

ASHKENAZ, (ADJ.) ASHKENAZI. Designation of the first area of settlement of Jews in Northwest Europe, initially on the banks of the Rhine. The term has evolved to take on the broader connotation of a cultural complex that had its beginnings in France and Germany in the second part of the tenth century, spread later to Poland-Lithuania, and in modern times finds adherents all over the world.

ASMAKHTA. An agreement that either lacks the presumption of firm resolve on the part of the obligator or fails to generate a presumption of reliance on the part of the party to whom the commitment is made.

ASYMMETRIC INFORMATION. The unequal knowledge that each party to a transaction has about the other party.

AVAK RIBBIT. Lit., "the dust of interest." Violations of Jewish law's prohibition against interest by virtue of rabbinical, as opposed to Pentateuchal, decree.

BABYLONIAN TALMUD (B, BT). A literary work of monumental proportion (5,894 folio pages in the standard printed edition), consisting of the teachings of the rabbinic authorities from the third to the fifth centuries. The focus of the Talmud is to provide analysis and commentary for both the Mishnah and other rabbinic sources of the same period, called *Baraita* and *Tosefta*. The rabbinic teachings in the Talmud encompass law, ethics, custom, and history. The rabbinic authorities quoted in the Babylonian Talmud are called *Amoraim*. Redacted in the year 500, the Babylonian Talmud provides the basic source material for the practical rulings that appear in the various subsequent Codes.

BET DIN. Jewish court of law.

BIMETALLIC STANDARD. A monetary system in which a government recognizes coins composed of gold or silver as legal tender. The bimetallic standard (or bimetallism) backs a unit of currency to a fixed ratio of gold and/or silver.

CAIRO GENIZAH. An accumulation of almost 280,000 Jewish manuscript fragments that were found in the *genizah*, or storeroom, of the Ben Ezra Synagogue in Fustat, now Old Cairo, Egypt.

CETERIS PARIBUS. Latin for "everything else remaining the same."

COASE THEOREM. The idea that as long as property rights are clearly defined and enforced, bargaining between two parties can produce an efficient outcome without any further government intervention.

CODE OF HAMMURABI (*Codex Hammurabi*). A well-preserved ancient law code created c. 1790 BCE in ancient Babylon. It was enacted by the sixth Babylonian king, Hammurabi.

CONSEQUENTIALISM. Refers to those moral theories that hold that the consequences of a particular action form the basis for any valid moral judgment about that action.

CONSUMER PRICE INDEX (CPI). A measure of inflation based on a market basket of goods and services purchased by urban households.

CREDENCE GOOD. A term used in economics for a good whose utility is difficult or impossible for the consumer to ascertain.

CUM-DIVIDEND. Cum means "with" in Latin. A cum-dividend securities purchase is a purchase of securities transacted before a dividend payment, so that the purchaser is entitled to the next dividend. If restrictions on entitlement to dividends did not exist, people would simply buy shares the day before the dividend was due, collect the dividend, and then sell the shares the day after.

CURRENCY DEPRECIATION. The loss of value of a country's currency with respect to one or more foreign reference currencies, typically in a floating exchange rate system. It is most often used for the unofficial increase of the exchange rate due to market forces.

DARKHEI SHALOM. Lit., "the ways of peace." Refers to the duty to end discord. Toward this end, the use of untruths is, under certain conditions, permitted.

DEVALUATION. An official lowering of the value of a nation's currency relative to those of foreign countries.

DINA DE-MALKHUTA DINA. The *halakhic* rule that for disputes between Jews in civil matters, the law of the country is binding.

DOLLARIZATION. The adoption of the United States dollar as a country's official national currency.

ECOCENTRISM. Term in ecological political philosophy used to denote a nature-centered, as opposed to human-centered, system of values. Ecocentrism denies any existential divisions between human and nonhuman nature sufficient to ground a claim that humans are either the sole bearers of intrinsic value or possess greater intrinsic value than nonhuman nature.

EFFICIENCY. Achieving maximum output value from a given set of inputs, or achieving the desired output with minimum cost of inputs.

ENDOWMENT EFFECT. In behavioral economics, the endowment effect refers to the hypothesis that people value a good or service more once their property right to it has been established. In other words, people place a higher value on objects they own than objects that they do not. In one experiment, people demanded a higher price for a coffee mug that had been given to them but put a lower price on one they did not yet own.

EQUILIBRIUM PRICE. The market price that clears the market. At equilibrium, the number of units suppliers want to offer is equal to the number of units demanders want to buy. Given the stability of supply and demand influences other than the price of the subject product, the market price will tend toward the equilibrium price.

ERETS (ERETZ) ISRAEL. Hebrew name of the Land of Israel. The term *Erets Israel* is biblical, although its meaning varies, designating both the territory actually inhabited by the Israelites (I Samuel 13:19) and the Northern Kingdom (II Kings 5:2). Only from the Second Temple period onward, however, was the term used to denote the Promised Land. It was the official Hebrew designation of the area governed by the British mandate in Palestine after World War I until 1948.

ETROG (*Citrus Medica*). One of the four different plants that the Torah requires the Jew to hold in his hand and wave on the holiday of Sukkot. The obligation is based on Leviticus 23:42; "the fruit of a goodly tree," mentioned in the verse, is identified as the *etrog*.

EX-DIVIDEND PRICE. In a stock market, a share price that does not include entitlement to the forthcoming or accrued dividend.

EX PARTE. A judge's action in conducting a hearing or conference with one party only, without notice to the other party; typically improper, except under the limited circumstance in which a party is seeking a temporary restraining order and alleging that notice to the other party will result in the destruction of evidence or other illegal action.

EXPERIENCE GOOD. A product whose value can be better known after having consumed it.

EXTERNALITY. A side effect of the action of an individual or entity on another individual or entity. Externalities can be positive or negative.

FIAT. Governmental decree.

FIDUCIARY OBLIGATION OR DUTY. Employees' or directors' legal and moral duty to exercise the powers of their office for the benefit of the employer or the firm.

FIRST COMMONWEALTH. The period beginning before the year 1000 BCE under the rule of King Saul, and then King David, and concluding with the destruction of the First Temple by the Babylonians in 586 BCE.

FORCE MAJEURE. Act of God; a natural and unavoidable catastrophe that interrupts the expected course of events.

FRAMING. Presenting an option in a particular manner in order to influence people's decisions. Different presentations of the same option can alter people's decisions with regard to it. Specifically, individuals have a tendency to choose inconsistently depending on whether the choice is framed to emphasize losses or gains.

GAON, (PL.) GEONIM. Formal title of the heads of the academies of Sura and Pumbedita in Babylonia. The *Geonim* were recognized by the Jews as the highest authority of instruction from the end of the sixth century or somewhat later to the middle of the eleventh century.

GEMARA. Aramaic for "completion" or "tradition." This word is popularly applied to the Talmud as a whole, or more particularly to the discussions and elaborations by the *Amoraim* on the Mishnah.

GEMIRAT DA'AT. A firm resolve to conclude an agreement at hand.

GENEIVAT DA'AT. Conduct designed to deceive or to create a false impression.

HALAKHAH, HALAKHA, HALACHAH. Hebrew, from the root *halakh*, "to go." The legal side of Judaism.

HASSAGAT GEVUL. Lit., "removal of boundary." Trespass on economic, commercial, or incorporeal rights.

HETTER ISKA. An elaborate form of the *iska* business partnership wherein conditions are attached with the design of protecting the financier from absorbing a loss on his principal and increasing the probability that he will realize a profit as well. These clauses are structured in such a manner that *ribbit* law is not violated.

HIN TZEDEK. Lit., "a just *hin*" (dry measure). Refers to the duty to make a commitment in good faith.

HOLDER IN DUE COURSE. A person who takes a negotiable instrument, such as a promissory note, without knowledge of any apparent defect in the instrument, nor of any notice of dishonor. Status as a "holder in due course" is an affirmative defense against all legal claims the debtor may have against the original creditor.

HUMAN CAPITAL. The set of skills that an employee acquires on the job, through training and experience, and that increase that employee's value in the marketplace.

IMITATIO DEI. Latin for "imitation of God." Judaism's behavioral imperative consisting of man's duty to emulate God's attributes of mercy in his interpersonal conduct.

INDEXATION. The process of automatically adjusting wages and prices for the effects of inflation.

INFLATION. A continuing rise in the general price level usually attributed to an increase in the volume of money and credit relative to available goods and services.

IN TERROREM. Latin. Conduct designed to produce terror by way of threat and intimidation.

IPO. Initial Public Offering. The first sale of stock by a company to the public. Companies offering an IPO are sometimes new, young companies, and sometimes mature firms that have decided to go public. IPOs are often risky investments, but they often have the potential for significant gains.

ISKA. A form of business partnership consisting of an active partner and a financier, who is a silent partner. In the absence of stipulation, half the capital transfer from the financier to the active partner takes on the legal character of a loan, while the remaining half takes on the character of a pledge. The *iska* arrangement violates *avak ribbit* law and is therefore subject to regulation.

JERUSALEM TALMUD (J, JT, PT). Also called the Palestinian Talmud. A literary work consisting of the teachings of five generations of rabbinic authorities and a few sixth-generation scholars. These teachers are called *Amoraim*. The focus of the *Amoraim* is to provide commentary on the Mishnah and on the other rabbinic sources of the same period, called *Baraita* and *Tosefta*. The rabbinic teachings in the Talmud encompass law, ethics, custom, and history. The Jerusalem Talmud predates its counterpart, the Babylonian Talmud, by about two hundred years.

JUBILEE. A year of emancipation and restoration provided by ancient Hebrew law to be observed every fifty years through the emancipation of Hebrew slaves, restoration of alienated lands to their former owners, and omission of all cultivation of the land.

JURISCONSULT. Latin for "legal adviser," expert in civil law.

KABBELAN. A pieceworker hired to perform a specific task, with no provisions regarding fixed hours.

KALDOR-HICKS COMPENSATION DOCTRINE. The doctrine states that state A is to be preferred to state B if those who gain from the move to A can compensate those who lose and still be better off. This compensation is hypothetical, and the Kaldor-Hicks criterion suggests that A is preferable to B even if compensation does not actually take place.

KANTIANISM. Adherence to the philosophy of Immanuel Kant, which revolves around duty rather than emotional feelings or end goals. Kant invokes the categorical imperative as the criterion for whether a maxim is good or bad. Simply put, the criterion imagines a world where all people act according to the maxim and asks whether the outcome would be satisfactory.

KETUBBAH. Women's marriage contract.

KINYAN. Acquisition of legal rights by means of the performance of a symbolic act.

KINYAN SUDAR. A legal form of acquisition of objects or confirmation of agreements, executed by the handing of a scarf (or any other article) by one of the contracting parties (or one of the witnesses to the agreement) to the other contracting party as a symbol that the object has been transferred or the obligation assumed.

KUPPAH. Communal charity box.

LASHON HA-RA. Hebrew for "evil speech." Talebearing, where A delivers a damaging but truthful report regarding B to C, C being neither the object of B's mischief nor the intended target of his evil design.

LAW OF DIMINISHING RETURNS. A rule stating that, as one factor of production is increased, while others remain constant, the extra output generated by the additional input will eventually fall.

LIFNEI IVER. Lit., "in front of the blind person." Refers to (a) the prohibition against causing those who are morally blind to stumble by giving them the means or preparing the way for them to sin; (b) the prohibition against offering someone ill-suited advice.

LIMITED PARTNERSHIP. A business organization with one or more general partners, who manage the business and assume legal debts and obligations, and one or more limited partners, who are liable only to the extent of their investment. Limited partners also enjoy rights to the partnership's cash, but are not liable for company obligations.

LIQUIDATED DAMAGES. The amount required to satisfy a loss resulting from breach of contract.

LIQUIDITY. Ease with which an investment can be converted into cash for approximately its original cost plus its expected accrued interest.

LULAV. One of the four different plants that the Torah requires the Jew to hold in his hand and wave on the holiday of Sukkot. The obligation is based on Leviticus 23:42; "the branches of the palm tree," mentioned in the verse, is identified as the *lulav*.

MIDDAT SEDOM. The wicked character trait(s) of the people of Biblical Sodom; in particular, denying a fellow a benefit when it costs one nothing.

MIDRASH. Hebrew designation of a particular genre of rabbinic literature consisting mainly of biblical exegesis of specific books of the Bible.

MINHAG. Custom.

MISHNAH. Designates the collection of rabbinic traditions redacted by R. Judah ha-Nasi at the beginning of the third century. The purpose of the Mishnah is to elaborate, systematize and give concreteness to the commandments of the Torah.

MISHPAT IVRI. A term first used around the beginning of the twentieth century to designate that part of the *halakhah* whose subject matter parallels that which normally comprises other legal systems.

MITSVAH, MITZVAH. A religious act or duty.

MORAL HAZARD. A situation in which, as a result of having insurance, an individual becomes more likely to engage in risky behavior.

ONA'AH. Price fraud involving selling above or below the competitive norm.

OPPORTUNITY COST. The value of the best alternative sacrificed when a choice is made.

PARETO OPTIMALITY. A situation in which no reorganization or trade could raise the utility or satisfaction of one individual without lowering the utility or satisfaction of another individual.

PIGOVIAN TAXATION. Tax levied on a market activity associated with negative externalities to correct the market outcome. In the presence of negative externalities the social cost of a market activity is generally more than the private cost of the activity. In such a case, the market outcome is not efficient and the market tends to oversupply the product. A Pigovian tax equal to the negative externality is thought to correct the market outcome to be efficient.

PO'EL. Day-laborer, required to work at fixed hours.

PRIMARY SECURITIES MARKET. Market involving the creation and issuance of new securities. It is the market for initial sales of securities.

PRINCIPAL-AGENT PROBLEM. In political science and economics, the problem of motivating a party to act on behalf of another is known as "the principal-agent problem." The principal-agent problem arises when a principal compensates an agent for performing certain acts that are useful to the principal and costly to the agent, and where there are elements of the performance that are costly to observe.

PUBLIC GOOD. A good that is nonrivalrous and nonexcludable. *Nonrivalrous* means that consumption of the good by one individual does not reduce the availability of the good for consumption by others. *Nonexcludable* means that no one can be effectively excluded from using the good.

PURCHASING POWER PARITY (PPP). The theory that, in the long run, identical products and services should cost the same in different countries. This is based on the belief that exchange rates will adjust to eliminate the arbitrage opportunity of buying a product or service in one country and selling it in another.

QIRAD. A type of contract developed in the medieval Islamic world. This contract is the precursor of the modern limited partnership. The *Qirad* was generally used for financing maritime trade.

RAWLSIAN SOCIAL WELFARE FUNCTION. A social welfare function that uses as its measure of social welfare the utility of the worst-off member of society.

RESPONSA. Exchanges of letters in which one party consults another on a *halakhic* matter.

RIBBIT. In inter-Jewish loan transactions, the prohibition for the lender to charge and for the debtor to agree to make interest payments.

RIBBIT KETZUZAH. Prearranged interest payment.

RISHON, RISHONIM. Hebrew. Lit., the early rabbinic authorities. The period of the *Rishonim* extends from the middle of the eleventh to the middle of the fifteenth centuries.

SASANIAN EMPIRE. The last pre-Islamic Persian Empire in Western Asia and Europe from 224 to 651 CE.

SECOND COMMONWEALTH. The period beginning with the proclamation by Cyrus the Great (c. 538 BCE) permitting the exiled Jews to return to Judea; including eras of political control of Judea by Persians, Greeks, and Romans (with short periods of Jewish autonomy interspersed); and concluding with the destruction of the Second Temple (70 CE).

SECONDARY SECURITIES MARKET. Market involving the transfer of existing securities from previous investors to new investors. It is the market for already issued securities.

SECURITIZATION. A structured finance process in which assets are acquired and pooled. The pool is broken up into a number of parts, referred to as "tranches" (French for "strips"). Each tranche has a different level of credit protection or risk exposure. The different tranches are then offered to investors in the form of a security.

SEMIKHAT DA'AT. Mental reliance. Without the presumption of mental reliance on the part of the principals to a transaction, the agreement lacks legal validity in Jewish law.

SEPHARD, (ADJ.) SEPHARDI. Descendants of Jews who lived in the Iberian Peninsula (Spain and Portugal) before the expulsion in 1492. Jewish communities in Spain can be identified as early as the Visigoth period (fifth century to 711). Under Visigoth rule, Jews were persecuted. With the Arab conquest of Spain in 711, this persecution ended. Muslim rule ushered in a golden era for Spanish Jewry. Early in this period, the Jews in the Iberian Peninsula were in touch with the center of Jewish life in Babylonia/Iraq and carried on the tradition of Babylonian Jewry.

SHI'BUD NEKHASIM. Also *aharayut nekhasim.* A lien on a debtor's real property, which is an effective claim against that property even when it is sold to a third party.

SITUMTA, KINYAN SITUMTA, THE LAW OF SITUMTA. Custom of wine- merchants to mark the barrels that had been purchased. Although this mode of acquisition is not mentioned in the Talmud, *halakhah* recognizes it as a valid *kinyan*, because the purpose of a *kinyan* is to cause the parties to decide to conclude the transaction, and *situmta* has this effect.

SUBROGATION. The legal principle that a person paying a debt on behalf of another may succeed to the rights of that person in order to obtain restitution for that payment of debt. For example, an insurance company that has paid the claim of a third party against one of its clients may, by law, enforce the client's rights against the third party to recover some or all of what it has paid out.

TAKKANAH, (PL.) TAKKANOT. A directive enacted by *halakhic* scholars, or another competent body, enjoying the force of law. *Takkanot* are among the sources of Jewish law.

TAMHUI. Community charity plate.

TANAKH. Hebrew collective term for the Old Testament. The term is composed of the initial letters of the words *Torah* (Pentateuch), *Nevi'im* (Prophets), and *Ketuvim* (Hagiographa).

TANNA, TANNAIM. Aramaic *teni*, "hand down orally." The term designates a teacher dating from Mishnaic times. The *tannaic* period covers five generations of rabbinic authorities, spanning from 20 to 200 CE.

TEKHELET. A blue-green dyestuff for threads and fabrics, mentioned frequently in the Bible. A thread of *tekhelet* had to be included in the fringes, *tzitzit*, of a four-cornered garment (Numbers 15:38).

THEOCENTRISM. As applied to environmental political philosophy, the belief that human beings should look after the world as guardians, in the way in which God wants them to. Humans should be considerate to all, from animals to plants to humans themselves. It maintains that human beings are merely here for a short time and should look after the world for future generations.

THEODOSIAN CODE. Roman legal code, issued in 438 by Theodosius II, emperor of the East. It was at once adopted by Palestinian III, emperor of the West. The code was intended to reduce and systematize the complex mass of law that had been issued since the reign of Constantine I.

TORAH. Hebrew, "teach." The term is used loosely to designate the Bible as a whole.

TORT. A private or civil wrong or injury, not involving a breach of contract.

TOSEFTA. Aramaic for "additional" or "supplementary." Originally, the term was used to describe teachings of the rabbinic authorities who lived in the Mishnaic era that were not quoted by R. Judah ha-Nasi in his Mishnah. Later the term came to denote a particular literary work, "the *Tosefta*," a collection of teachings of Mishnaic-era authorities. This collected work served as a companion volume to the Mishnah.

TRANSACTION COSTS. The time costs and other costs required to carry out market exchange.

UNIFORM COMMERCIAL CODE (UCC). Standardized set of business laws that has been adopted by most states. The Uniform Commercial Code governs a wide range of transactions including borrowing, contracts, and many other everyday business practices. It is useful because it standardizes practices from state to state.

UNJUST ENRICHMENT. Profiting or enriching oneself inequitably at another's expense.

USUCAPTION. A method by which ownership of property can be gained by lapse of time.

UTILITARIANISM. The philosophy that the moral worth of an action is determined solely by its contribution to overall happiness or utility as summed among all people.

WHARFAGE. A fee charged for the use of a wharf or quay.

YESHIVA, (PL.) YESHIVOT. Institutes of Talmudic learning.

List of Abbreviations

ABX. Asset Backed Security Index.
B, BT. Talmud Bavli.
BATNA. best alternative to a negotiated settlement.
BOI. Bank of Israel.
C., Ca. abbreviation for circa, Latin for "in approximation."
CDO. Collateralized Debt Obligation.
COLA. Cost of living adjustment.
CPI. Consumer Price Index.
CRA. Credit Rating Agencies.
IPO. Initial Public Offering.
JESHO. Journal of Economic and Social History.
JSIJ. Jewish Studies, an Internet Journal. (http://www.biu.ac.il/JS/*JSIJ*/jsij1.html).
JT. Jerusalem Talmud.
M. *Mishnah.*
MBS. Mortgage Backed Security.
PT. Palestinisn Talmud. Same as Jerusalem Talmud.
PPP. Purchasing Power Parity.
Shut. Responsa.
Supra. "see above."
T. Tosefta.
UCC. Uniform Commercial Code.

Name Index

Aaron Perahiah ha-Kohen, R., 351
Abba Shaul, R. Ben Zion, 454–455, 457, 464, 466
Abbot, F.F., 122
Abraham b. David of Posqueries, R. (*Ra'avad*), 91, 106, 438, 596, 600
Abraham b. Isaac of Narbonne, R., 438
Abraham b. Mordecai Ha-Levi, R. 597, 600
Abraham, Abraham, 331, 337
Abulafia, R. Meir, 229, 351, 435, 585
Adret, R. Solomon b. Abraham (*Rashba*), 102, 242, 316, 347, 367, 374, 434, 435, 439, 492, 596
Adler, Barry E., 174
Agus, R. Hanokh, 357
Agyeman, Julian, 389
Ahai Gaon, R., 439, 489
Ahavat Hesed, see Kagan, R. Israel Meir ha-Kohen (*Hafez Hayyim*)
Akerlof, George A., 308, 323
Al-Hakham, R. Joseph Hayyim b. Elijah, 416
Alashkar, R. Moses b. Isaac, 437
Albeck, Shalom, 147, 315, 344, 348, 507, 606–607, 610
Albo, R. Joseph, 368
Alchian, Armen A., 634
Alfasi, R. Isaac b. Jacob (*Rif*), 147, 229–230, 235, 320, 434, 576, 587, 610
Alkabez, R. Solomon b. Moses Ha-Levi, 397
Allred, Keith G., 69
Alonso, Andrea M., 177
Alshekh, R. Moses, 435
Ames, R.E, 109
Amudei Esh, see Samuel, R. Abraham
Andreoni, James, 30, 41
Andrews, G., 524, 535–540, 541
Antebi, R. Abraham, 135–138
Arak, R. Meir, 208, 220
Arama, R. Isaac b. Moses, 264–265
Arukh haShulhan, see Epstein, R. Jehiel Michal b. Aaron ha-Levi
Asher b. Jehiel, R. (*Rosh*), 46, 225, 226, 237, 273, 347, 374, 386, 433, 436, 441, 610
Ashkenazi, R. Bezalel, 436
Assaf, S., 321, 586, 590, 595, 601
Auerbach, R. Meir, 234, 237, 249
Auerbach, R. Solomon Zalman, 331–334, 432–433, 443, 455, 457, 466
Aumann, Robert J., xxii, 168, 174
Avigdors, R. Mendel, 198, 203, 209
Avkat Rokhel, see Caro, R. Joseph
Avnei Milluim, see Heller, R. Aryeh Leib
Avraham b. Mordechai HaLevi, R., 272
Ayres, Ian, 174
Ayres, Robert U., 392
Azulai, R. Haim Joseph David, 435

Bacharach, Jair Hayyim b. Moses Samson, 435
Bahya, R. Asher, 80
Baird, Douglas G., 173, 180
Bakshi-Doron, R. Eliyahu, 436
Balaban, Majer, 319
Barkai, Avraham, 628
Barry, Bruce, 69, 71, 73
Baruch, R. Joshua Boaz b. Simon, 406, 435
Basan, R. Jehiel, 435
Batzri, R. Ezra, 382, 458, 466
Baumgartner, Stefan, 392
Baye, M. R., 128, 145
Bebchuk, Lucian Arye, 174, 350, 425, 427
Beer, Moshe, 545–546, 547, 554, 557, 562
Beit Yitshak, see Schmelkes, R. Isaac
Beit Yosef, see Caro, R. Joseph
Ben Yehoyada, see Yosef Chaim of Baghdad, R.
Benveniste, R. Hayyim b. Israel, 351
Berger, A., 122
Berlin, R. Naphtali Zevi Judah (*Netziv*), 368, 371, 415, 417, 435
Bernstein, Richard, 173, 180
Bertinoro, R. Obadiah, 192
Bet Ha-Behira, see Meiri, R. Menahem b. Solomon
Billings, John S., 629, 637
Binyan Tsiyyon, see Ettlinger, R. Jacob
Birkat Avraham, see Erlanger, R. Abraham
Biur HaGra, see Elijah b. Solomon Zalman, R. (*Gra*)
Bivin, David, 183
Blackstone, William, 224
Blackwell, R. D., 127, 307
Blake, Kellee, 630
Blass, Asher, 355, 357
Bleich, J. David, 19, 197, 220, 329, 331, 333–335, 355, 358, 450
Bloi, R. Yaakov Yeshayahu, 252, 256, 259–262, 266, 268, 355, 373, 414, 427, 432, 453, 454, 457, 462–463, 466, 484, 498
Bodie, Z., 524
Bogdanski, John A., 174
Bond, Sandy, 187
Borowski, Oded, 159–160, 163–164

Boton, R. Abraham de, 315
Brit Yehudah, see Bloi, R. Yaakov Yeshayahu
Brown, Keith, 161
Broyde, Michael J, 12, 13, 16, 17, 358, 363, 369, 370, 371, 375, 380, 580

Callen, Jeffrey L., 20, 168, 174
Caro, R. Joseph, 7, 45, 46, 65, 73, 91, 92, 93, 100, 106, 200, 235, 237, 241, 254, 273, 314, 316, 321, 323, 345, 373, 377, 378, 384, 387, 406, 407, 454, 459, 466, 528, 532, 533, 534, 541
Carter, Dee, 395, 402
Carver, T.C., 121
Chiswick, Barry R., 24–25, 625, 629, 630, 632, 634, 635, 637, 638, 640, 641, 645, 650, 654, 655, 656, 658, 660
Chiswick, Carmel Ullman, 25, 625, 636, 654, 655, 658, 660, 662
Chodorow, Adam, 24, 479, 480
Coase, Ronald, 83, 85, 99, 122, 149
Cohen, R. Shear Yashuv, 461, 462, 466
Colon, R. Joseph (*Maharik*), 350

Daichovsky,R. Solomon, 448, 462, 463, 464, 466
David b. Shmuel HaLevi, R. (*Taz*), 227, 237, 414, 436, 453–455, 485
David b. Zimra, R. (*Radbaz*), 439
Denby, H., 110
Derishah, see Falk, R. Joshua b. Alexander ha-Kohen
Devar Avraham, see Kahana-Shapiro, R. Abraham Dov Ber
Dinur, J., 99
Divrei Yosef, see R. Joseph Iggeret,
Divrei Yosher, see Rosenthal, R. Dov
Domb, Yoel, 14, 221
Douglas, Paul H., 631
Doyle, E.P., 535
Driver, G.R., 222, 237, 554
Duff, H., 116
Duran, R. Simon b. Zemach (*Tashbetz*), 137, 435
Duran, R. Solomon b. Simon (*Rashbash*), 439

Edels, R. Samuel Eliezer b. Judah ha-Levi (*Maharsha*), 59, 399
Eiger, R. Akiva, 251, 481
Ein Mishpat, see Baruch, R. Joshua Boaz b. Simon
Eisenstadt, R. Abraham, 353, 600
Elazar, Daniel J., 626
Eldon, Lord, 537
Elhadad, R. Masoud, 462, 464, 466
Elyashiv, R. Yosef Shalom, 330, 455, 457, 533
Eliezer b. Haim Ohr Zarua, R., 435
Eliezer b. Nathan of Mainz, R. (*Ra'avan*), 588
Eliezer b. R. Joel Halevi, R. (*Ravyah*), 435
Eliezrov, R. Jacob, 462, 464
Elijah b. Hayyim, R, 352
Elijah b. Solomon Zalman, R. (*Gra*), 203–204, 206, 220, 352, 436,
Elman, Yaakov, 21, 544, 546, 549
Elon, Menahem, 3, 5, 6, 7, 183, 193, 221, 227, 237, 316, 321, 323, 372, 481, 482
Emden, R. Jacob, 435
Emek Netziv, see Berlin, R. Naphtali Zevi Judah (*Netziv*)
Engel, J. F., 127
Ephraim Solomon of Lunshits, R. (*Keli Yakar*), 80, 244
Epstein, I, 110, 115
Epstein, R. Jehiel Michal ha-Levi, 130, 131, 255, 258, 259, 268, 368, 407, 435, 443, 458,
Epstein, R. Baruch ha-Levi, 202, 598
Epstein, R. Chaim Fishel, 251
Erlanger, R. Abraham, 249
Estori Ha-Parhi, 568
Ets Hadar, see Kook, R. Abraham Isaac
Ettinger, R. Isaac Aaron, 373
Ettlinger, R. Jacob, 334
Evans, Judith, 636
Evans, Tom, 389
Even ha-Ezel, see Meltzer, R. Isser Zalman
Eybeschuetz, R. Jonathan, 249

Faley, Kevin G., 177
Falk, R. Joshua b. Alexander ha-Kohen, 45, 249, 258–259, 330, 354, 406, 414, 431–432, 508, 590, 604
Farmer, Amy, 176
Farnsworth, E. Allan, 340, 351, 352, 359
Feinstein, R. Moshe, 205–207, 214, 220, 235, 237, 252, 255–256, 259–260, 268, 326, 329–330, 333, 338, 339, 349, 371, 373, 378, 379, 381, 387, 436, 443, 454, 457, 464, 466, 490, 506, 580–581, 600
Feldman, Daniel Z., 19, 239
Fennell, Lee Anne, 174
Finkelstein, Louis, 628
Fischel, Daniel R., 174
Fisher, George W., 395, 403
Forrence, Jennifer L., 311
Fossati, A., 107
Frank, R. Tzvi Pesach, 368
Fried, Charles, 343, 345–346, 351, 355, 359, 425, 427
Fried, Jesse M., 174
Friedman, Hershey H., 395, 401
Fukuyama, Francis, 307–309

Gaeth, Gary J, 68, 73
Gambetta, Diego, 307–308, 313, 323
Gartner, Lloyd P., 628
Genesis Rabbah, 43, 57, 59, 66, 69, 73
Gerondi, R. Jonah b. Abraham (Rabbeinu Yonah), 46, 233
Gerrard, P., 535
Gevurat Yitshak al ha-Torah, see Sorotzkin, R. Avrohom Yitzhak
Gibbon, Edward, 224
Ginat Veradim, see Abraham b. Mordecai ha-Levi, R.
Giovanni, Fiorentino, 224, 237
Glazier, Ira A., 628

Glenn, Susan A., 635
Goetze, A., 222
Goldberg, R. Zalman Nehemia, 328, 329, 336, 344, 354, 359
Gombiner, R. Abraham Abele b. Hayyim ha-Levi, 43, 431
Goodman, Abram V., 629
Goren, R. Shlomo, 336, 371
Grazi, Richard, 335
Grosnas, R. Aryeh Leib, 249–251
Grossman, R. Aharon Yehudah, 244
Grula, John W., 394
Guide of the Perplexed, see Maimonides
Gur Aryeh, see Loew b. Betzalel, R. Judah (*Maharal*)
Gustman, R. Israel Zev, 246
Gutmacher, R. Eliyahu, 435

Ha-levi, R. Aaron (*Ra'ah*), 227, 431
Ha-Levi, R. Mordecai, 354
Ha-Ma'or ha-Katan, see Zerahia Halevi, R.
Ha-Mo'adim be-Halakhah, see- Zevin, R. Solomon Joseph
Ha-Torah ve-ha-Mitsvah, see Weisser, R. Meir Loeb b. Jehiel Michel (Malbim)
Ha'amek Davar, see Berlin, R. Naphtali Zevi Judah (*Netziv*)
Ha'amek She'eilah, see Berlin, R. Naphtali Zevi Judah (*Netziv*)
Hacohen, R. Solomon, 449
Hafez Hayyim, see Kagan, R. Israel Meir ha-Kohen (*Hafez Hayyim*)
Haggahot ha-Asheri, see Israel of Krems, R.
Hai Gaon, R., 353, 575, 576, 586, 595–596, 599, 601–602, 603
Halakhot Pesukot, see Yehuda'i Gaon, R.
Halberstam, R. Hayyim, 220, 434
Halperin, Mordechai, 327, 335–337, 339
Hammurabi, 85, 222
Hand, Judge Learned, 198, 290
Har Tsevi, see Frank, R. Tzvi Pesach
Harris, Dr. Ron, 221, 237
Hartman, Harriet, 636
Hartman, Moshe, 636
Havvat Da'at, see Lorbeerbaum, R. Jacob
Hazan, R. Eliyahu, 373
Hazon Ish, see Karlitz, R. Abraham (*Hazon Ish*)
Helkat Mehokek, see Lima, R. Moses b. Isaac Judah
Heller, R. Aryeh Leib, 248, 351, 375,
Heller, R. Yom Tov Lippman, 575
Helwege, Jean, 184
Hemdat Shlomo, see Lipschitz, R. Shlomo Zalman
Henkin, R. Joseph Eliyahu, 338, 378–379, 384–385, 387, 442
Hershler, R. Moshe, 328, 555
Hertz, J.H., 525–527, 531, 534, 541
Herzog, R. Isaac, 358, 509, 552, 573, 575
Hiddushe R. Akiva Eiger, see Eiger, R. Akiva
Himmelfarb, H.S., 635
Hirsch, R. Samson Raphael, 59, 225–226, 237, 472, 473–474, 476
Hirschenson, R. Hayyim, 376
Hirschoff, J., 167
Hizkuni, R. Hizkiyah, 44
Hoffman, Andrew J., 389, 403
Hokhmat Adam, see Danzig, R. Abraham
Hokhmat Shelomoh, see Luria, R. Solomon (*Maharshal*)
Holmes, Oliver Wendel, 341–342
Horowitz, R. Isaiah (*Shlah*), 425, 427, 431,
Hudson, M., 85
Hut Shani, see Karelitz, R. Nissim

Ibbotson, R., 184
Ibn Attar, R. Chaim b. Moses (*Ohr Ha-Hayyim*), 398
Ibn Migash, R. Joseph b. Meir HaLevi, 319, 383, 441
Iggeret, R. Joseph, 373
Iggerot Mosheh, see Feinstein, R. Moses
Imrei Binah, see Auerbach, R. Meir
Innes, Robert, 30, 41
Isaac b. Abba Mari of Marseilles, R., 434, 438, 586, 604
Isaac b. Moses of Vienna, R., 348, 377
Isaac of Carcassonne, R., 441
Ish Le-Rei'eihu, see Kreiser, R. Yitzchak
Ishbili, R. Yom Tov b. Abraham (*Ritva*), 94, 106, 248–249, 319, 347, 367, 433, 435, 527, 552
Isserles, R. Moses (Rema), 229, 257–262, 265, 338, 345, 354, 357, 368, 378, 379, 382, 384–385, 387, 416, 431, 432, 435–436, 440, 441, 443, 453–454, 459, 485–489, 492, 493, 498, 586
Isserlin, R. Israel, 205, 220, 349, 436, 588
Itra, R. Yehudah, 407
Iyyun Ya'akov, see Reicher, R. Jacob b. Joseph

Jabareen, Amal, 21, 499, 502, 504, 505, 522
Jachter, Howard, 15, 255
Jacob b. Asher, R. (Tur), 225, 237, 241, 317, 323, 326, 351, 386, 407, 436, 481
Jacob of Karlin, R., 440
Jaffe, J., 184
Jaffe, R. Mordechai, 414, 436
Jakobovits, Lord R. Immanuel, 444
Johnson, A.C., 122, 575
Jones, A.H.M., 122, 175
Joseph b. David ibn Lev, R., 355, 435, 441
Joseph ibn Habiba, R. (*Nimmukei Yosef*), 433
Josephus, 188, 193, 223, 237, 570
Joshua of Krakow, R. 435
Judah b. Kalonymus, R. 435
Judah b. Samuel He-Hasid, 234, 237

Kaftor va-Ferach, see Estori Ha-Parhi
Kagan, R. Israel Meir ha-Kohen (Hafez Hayyim), 60, 437, 525

Kahana-Shapiro, R. Abraham Dov Ber, 371, 373
Kahneman, Daniel, 68, 73
Kanievsky, R. Israel Jacob, 248
Kanner, M., 526, 528, 542
Kant, Immanuel, 226–227, 238
Kaplow, Louis, 30, 41
Karelitz, R. Abraham (*Hazon Ish*), 147, 247, 254, 347, 368, 434, 449, 458, 463–464
Karelitz, R. Nissim, 233
Karni, E., 137
Kasher, R. Menachem Mendel, 60
Katz, Eliakim, 21, 29
Kehillot Ya'akov, see Kanievsky, R. Israel Jacob
Keister, Lisa, 642, 645
Keli Hemdah, see Plotzki, R. Meir Dan
Keli Yakar, see Ephraim Solomon of Lunshits, R.
Kemp, David D., 392
Kenesset ha-Gedolah, see Benveniste, R. Hayyim b. Israel
Kesef Kedoshim, see Wahrmann, R. Abraham
Kesef Mishnah, see Caro, R. Joseph
Kessel, Reuben A., 634
Ketav Sofer, see Sofer, R. Abraham Samuel Benjamin Wolf
Ketzot haHoshen, see Heller, R. Aryeh Leib
Kimhi, R. David (Radak), 366, 565
Kitzur Dinei Ribbit, see Schreiber, R. Issachar Dov
Kleiman, Ephraim, xxii, 5, 22, 108, 110, 113, 114, 126, 182
Klein, R. Menashe, 379
Klein, Yehuda L., 17, 388, 395, 401
Kleinman, Ron S., 21, 499, 507, 508, 509, 516, 518, 519 522
Kluger, R. Solomon, 215, 220
Kneese, Allan V., 390–391, 403
Kohelet Rabbah, 470
Kohler, Max J., 628
Kolin, R. Samuel b. Nathan Ha-Levi, 43, 73
Kook, R. Abraham Isaac, 368, 442,
Korbin, Frances E., 631
Kreiser, R. Yitzchak, 243
Kuntreisei Shiurim, see Gustman, R. Israel Zev

Lampronti, R. Isaac, 436
Landau, R. Ezekiel, 355–356, 382
Landau, R. Israel Abraham Alter, 373
Lange, Oskar R., 390, 403
Lau, R. Yisrael Maier, 329, 332, 339
Le-Or ha-Halakhah, see Zevin, R. Solomon Joseph
Lehem Mishneh, see Boton, R. Abraham de
Lee, R.W., 225
Lehrer, Evelyn, 625
Lestschinsky, Jacob, 628
Levi b. Gershom, R. (*Ralbag*), 366
Levi ibn Habib, R. (*Maharlbah*), 435
Levin, Irwin P., 68, 73
Levine, Aaron, 42, 66, 108, 112, 126, 130, 144, 168, 169, 174, 181, 257–258, 263, 269, 284, 285, 294, 307, 313, 317, 323, 349, 353, 355, 357, 380, 390, 404, 407, 412, 423, 431–432, 439, 443, 444, 610, 611, 617, 618, 620
Levmore, Saul, 174
Levush, see Jaffe, R. Mordechai
Lewicki, Roy J., 69, 71
Liang, Nellie, 184
Lichtenstein R. Aharon, 367, 387
Liddel, H.G., 117
Liebermann, Yehoshua, xxi, 22, 127–128, 130, 145, 174, 573, 576, 606, 609, 611, 617
Lima, R. Moses b. Isaac Judah, 352
Lipschitz, R. Shlomo Zalman, 260
Lister, Roger, 20, 523
Loar, R.M, 635
Loew b. Betzalel, R. Judah (*Maharal*), 59
Lorbeerbaum, Jacob b.Jacob Moses, 149, 249, 347, 368, 374, 493
Luria, R. Solomon (*Maharshal*), 236, 238, 255, 257, 353, 374, 384, 439
Luzzato, S.D., 566

Macuch, Rudolph, 553, 556, 561,
Magen Avraham, see Gombiner, R. Abraham Abele b. Hayyim ha-Levi
Maggid Mishnah, see Vidal Yom Tov of Tolosa
Mahariah ha-Levi, see Ettinger, R. Isaac Aaron
Maharil Diskin al ha-Torah, see Diskin, R. Moses Joshua Judah Leib
Mahatsit ha-Shekel, see Kolin, R. Samuel b. Nathan ha-Levi
Maimonides (*Rambam*), 29, 41, 44, 64, 91, 106, 130, 131, 129, 131–132, 136, 138, 140, 145, 163, 167, 169, 172, 175, 228–229, 229, 230, 238, 243–244, 246, 246, 249, 254, 270, 291–292, 314–315, 317–319, 321–324, 327, 330, 344, 351, 366–370, 376, 381, 383, 396, 398, 407, 415, 427, 430–431, 435, 438–441, 443, 447, 467, 471, 473–475, 485, 517, 525, 531–532, 542, 568, 570, 573, 575, 591, 599–600, 607
Malik, Arun S., 30
Malkah, R. Shimon, 243, 406
Malki ba-Kodesh, see Hirschenson, R. Hayyim
Mangel, R. Nissen, 397
Manning, Robert E., 393
Marcus, Jacob Rader, 627, 628, 645
Margolies, R. Ephraim Zalman, 209
Marheshet, see Agus, R. Hanokh
Marks, D., 536, 538, 539
Marshal, A., 145
Marshall, A., 120
Marwell, G., 109
Maschler, Michael, 168, 174
Mayshar, J., 81–82, 86
Medding, Peter, 627

Medina, R. Samuel b. Moses de (*Maharashdam*), 134, 234, 238, 328, 349, 369, 373, 389, 434, 443, 448, 449, 453, 458, 462–463, 466
Meir, Asher, 15, 269
Meir b. Barukh, R. (*Maharam* of Rothenberg), 374, 431, 435, 436, 438
Meiri, R. Menahem b. Solomon, 12, 13, 60, 98, 106, 255, 319, 443
Melamed, A.D., 148
Meltzer, R. Isser Zalman, 247, 368, 370, 387, 436
Mendelsohn, I., 222
Menetrez, Frank, 342
Menirav, Joseph, 182
Merton, R.C., 524–525
Mesharim, see Meshullam, R. Jeroham
Meshullam, R. Jeroham, 319
Midrash Lekah Tov, 44, 49, 64
Midrash Tanhuma, 48, 426, 435
Miles, J.C., 222, 238, 554
Milgrom, J., 82
Milhamot ha-Shem, see (Nahmanides)
Mill, J.S., 113–114, 343, 390
Millett, R., 524, 525, 526, 537, 538, 539, 540, 541
Millington, Andrew C., 394, 403
Minhat Asher al Ha-Torah, see Weiss, R. Asher
Minhat Yitshak, see Weiss, R. Isaac Jacob
Minteer, Ben A., 393
Mintz, R. Moses b. Isaac, 345
Mishan, E.J., 112
Mishkenot Ya'akov, see Jacob of Karlin, R.
Mishne Torah, see Maimonides
Mishnah Berurah, see Kagan, R. Israel Meir ha-Kohen (*Hafez Hayyim*)
Mishneh Le-Melekh, see Rosens, R. Yehudah
Mishpat Shalom, see R. Shalom Mordechai Shvadron
Mishpetei Shimon, see Malka, R. Shimon
Mishpetei Uzziel, see, Uziel, R. Bentzion
Mitzvat ha-Hesed, see Rosner, R. Avraham Ze'ev
Mizrahi, R. Elijah, 435, 437, 439, 441
Mo'adim u-Zemanim, see Sterbuch, R. Moses
Moellin, R. Jacob b. Moses, 435, 587
Moorthy, S., 139–140
Moral Issues of the Marketplace in Jewish Law, see Levine, Aaron
Mordecai b. Hillel Ha-Kohen (*Mordekhai*), 347, 435
Morgan, J., 128
Morrison, Michael, 185
Moses of Coucy, R., 436
Moshav Zekanim mi-Baalei ha-Tosafot, 43
Moss, G., 536, 538–539
Mott, S.H., 635
Musgrave, R.A., 112, 126, 487, 498

Naess, Arne, 393–394, 398
Nahal Yitshak, see Spektor, R. Isaac Elhanan
Nahalat Shiv'ah, see Samuel b. David Moses ha-Levi, R.
Nahalat Ya'akov, see Lorbeerbaum, R. Jacob
Nathanson, R. Joseph Saul, 207, 352, 600
Nahmanides, 59, 91, 242–43, 255, 257, 368, 387, 396, 430, 472, 476, 481, 552, 570, 596
Nelson, P., 137–138
Netiv Yosher, see Itra, R. Yehudah
Netivot ha-Mishpat, see Lorbeerbaum, R. Jacob
Nimmukei Yosef, see Joseph ibn Habib, R. (*Nimmukei Yosef*)
Nishmat Avraham, see Abraham, Abraham
Nissim b. Reuben Gerondi, R. (*Ran*), 377, 430
Niv Sefatayim, see Yavruv, R. Nahum
Noda Bi-Yehudah, see Landau, R. Ezekiel
Nougayrol, J., 222

O'Donovan, J., 539
Offenbacher, Akiva (Edward), 450, 467
Or Zaru'ah, see Isaac b. Moses of Vienna, R.
Oschry, L., 525
Oshinsky, R. Isaac, 264

Pahad Yitshak, see Lampronti, R. Isaac
Pakod, R. Yaakov Nehar, 350
Palagi, R. Hayyim, 435, 436, 439, 441, 444
Paroush, Jacob, 313
Pava, Moses L., 295, 306–307, 323
Pecorino, Paul - 176
Perfet, R. Isaac b. Sheshet (*Rivash*), 231, 435, 579, 586
Pergola, Sergio, Della, 626,, 636
Perishah, see Falk, R. Joshua b. Alexander ha-Kohen
Perlow, R. Yerucham Fishel, 243
Pharr, C., 116, 126
Pigou, A.C., 119, 126
Pirkei de-Rabbi Eliezer, 44, 49, 52, 435
Pithe Teshuva, see Eisenstadt, R. Abraham
Pithei Hoshen, see Bloi, R. Yaakov Yeshayahu
Pithei Teshuvah, see R. Abraham Zevi Hirsch b. Jacob Eisenstadt
Plessner, Yakir, 450, 467
Plotzki, R. Meir Dan, 243
Pollak, R. Shimon, 244–245
Polsby, Daniel D., 174
Popovitz, R. Dov, 458–461, 465
Poritz, Deborah T., 181
Posner, Richard, 146, 167, 175, 176, 177, 181, 340, 341–342, 359, 420
Prager, Jonas, 15, 307, 310, 313, 320, 452
Prais, S.J., 626
Price, B.B., 108, 126, 606

Quaas, Martin F., 392

Rabinovich, Laurence J., 24, 564
Rabinowitz, R. Shmuel, 334, 335
Rabinowitz, J.J., 532
Radice, B., 110
Rafael, R. Shiloh, 206, 220
Rakover, Nahum, 368, 382, 387

Rapp, Dani, 17, 429
Raz, Joseph, 343, 346
Reicher, R. Jacob b. Joseph, 58
Reichman, Edward, 15, 324, 333
Reid, J.S., 122
Reischer, R. Jacob b. Joseph, 351
Reisman, R. Yisroel, 252, 254, 481, 498, 528, 534, 542
Resnicoff, Steven. 330–331, 337, 373, 375
Responsa Beit Yisrael, see Landau, R. Israel Abraham Alter
Responsa Binyamin Ze'ev, see R. Benjamin b. Mattityahu
Responsa Binyan Av, see Bakshi-Doron, R. Eliyahu
Responsa Darkhei No'am, see Ha-Levi, R. Mordecai
Responsa Divrei Hayyim, see Halberstam, R. Hayyim
Responsa Divrei Malkiel, see Tenenbaum, R. Malchiel
Responsa Divrei Yoel, see Teitelbaum, R. Joel
Responsa Eliyahu Mizrahi, see Mizrahi, R. Elijah
Responsa Hatam Sofer, see Sofer, R. Moses
Responsa Havvot Yair, see Bacharach, Jair Hayyim b. Moses Samson
Responsa Hayyim Or Zarua, see R. Hayyim (Eliezer) b. Isaac Or Zaru'a
Responsa Hayyim Shaul, see Azulai, R. Haim Joseph David
Responsa Helkat Ya'akov, see Breish, R. Yaakov
Responsa Helkat Yo'av, see R. Yoav Yehoshua Weingarten
Responsa Hikekei Lev, see Palagi, R. Hayyim
Responsa Lehem Rav, see Boton, R. Abraham de
Responsa Lev Aryeh, see Grosnas, R. Aryeh Leib
Responsa Mabit, see Trani, R. Moses b. Joseph (*Mabit*)
Responsa Maharalbah, see Levi ibn Habib, R. (*Maharlbah*)
Responsa Maharam, Meir b. Barukh, R. (*Maharam* of Rothenberg)
Responsa Maharam Alashkar, see Alashkar, R. Moses b. Isaac
Responsa Maharam Mintz, see Mintz, R. Moses b. Isaac
Responsa Maharanah, see R. Elijah b. Hayyim
Responsa Maharashdam, see Medina, R. Samuel b. Moses de (*Maharashdam*)
Responsa Mahari b. Lev, see Joseph b. David ibn Lev, R.
Responsa Mahari Basan, see Basan, R. Jehiel
Responsa Maharik, see Colon, R. Joseph (*Maharik*)
Responsa Maharil Diskin, see Diskin, R. Moses Joshua Judah Leib
Responsa Maharil, see Moellin, R. Jacob b. Moses
Responsa Maharit Tsahalon ha-Hadashot, see Tsahalon, R. Yom Tov
Responsa Maharschakh, see Hacohen, R. Solomon
Responsa Maharshal, see Luria, R. Solomon (*Maharshal*)
Responsa Maharsham, see Shvadron, R. Shalom Mordecai
Responsa Minhat Elazar, see Schapiro, R. Hayyim Elazar
Responsa Minhat Shelomoh, see Auerbach, R. Solomon Zalman
Responsa Nediv Lev, see Hazan, R. Eliyahu
Responsa Noda bi-Yehudah, see Landau, R. Ezekiel
Responsa Orah la-Tsaddik, see Rodriguez, R. Abraham Hayyim
Responsa Penei Yehoshua, see Joshua of Krakow, R.
Responsa Perah Matteh Aharon, see ha-Kohen, R. Aaron Perahiah
Responsa R. Akiva Eiger, see Eiger, R. Akiva
Responsa R. Bezalel Ashkenazi, see Ashkenazi, R. Bezalel
Responsa R. Elijah Gutmacher, see Gutmacher, R. Eliyahu
Responsa R. Moses Alshekh, see Alshekh, R. Moses
Responsa Ra'avi ha-Ra'avad ha-Rishon, see Abraham b. Isaac of Narbonne, R.
Responsa Radbaz, see Zimra, R. David (*Radbaz*)
Responsa Rambam, see Maimonides
Responsa Rashba, see Aderet, R. Solomon b. Abraham
Responsa Rashbash, see Duran, R. Solomon b. Simon
Responsa Rashbets, see Duran, R. Solomon b.Simon
Responsa Rashi, see Solomon b. Isaac, R. (*Rashi*)
Responsa Rema, see Isserles, R. Moses (*Rema*)
Responsa Rif, see Alfasi, R. Isaac b. Jacob (*Rif*)
Responsa Ritva, see Ishbili, R. Yom Tov b. Abraham (*Ritva*)
Responsa Rivash, see Perfet, R. Isaac b. Sheshet (*Rivash*)
Responsa Rosh, see Asher b. Jehiel, R. (*Rosh*)
Responsa Semikhah le-Hayyim, see Azulai, R. Haim Joseph David
Responsa Sha'arei Ezra, see Batzri, R. Ezra
Responsa She'elot Ya'avets, see Emden, R. Jacob
Responsa Shem Mi-Shimon, see Pollak, R. Shimon
Responsa Shevet ha-Levi, see Wosner, R. Samuel
Responsa Shevut Ya'akov, see Reischer, R. Jacob b. Joseph
Responsa Sho'el u-Meshiv, see Nathanson, R. Joseph Saul
Responsa Tashbets, see Duran, R. Simon b. Zemach
Responsa Teshuvah Shleimah, see Epstein, R. Chaim Fishel
Responsa Torat Emet, see Sasson, R. Aaaron b. Joseph

Responsa Tzemach Tzedek, see Shneur Zalman of Lyady, R.
Responsa Tzitz Eliezer, see Waldenberg, R. Eliezer
Ritter, J., 184
Ritterband, Paul, 630, 634, 640
Rivlin, Yosef, 21, 585, 586,, 589, 590, 591, 592, 594, 595, 596, 598, 599, 601, 602, 604
Ro'i, Yaacov, 640
Rock, Edward, 175
Rodriguez, R. Abraham Hayyim, 384
Roll, E., 107
Romereux, R. Yaakov of, 229
Rosenberg, Jacob, xxii, 21, 22, 29, 75, 87, 146, 155
Rosenfeld, Ben-Zion, 182, 193
Rosenthal, Erich, 630, 631
Rosenthal, R. Dov, 243
Rosenwaike, Ira, 632
Rosner, Fred, 324, 327, 329, 331, 334
Rosner, R. Avraham Ze'ev, 243
Russel, James, 562

Safrai, Shmuel 183, 188, 193, 573
Samuel b. David Moses ha-Levi, R., 220, 352, 397
Samuel b. Meir, R. (*Rashbam*), 59, 319, 376–377, 440, 528, 566
Samuel, E, 112
Samuelson, P.A., 109, 114, 126
Sandelands, Lloyd E., 389
Sanders, E.P., 189, 193
Sargent, Thomas, 452, 609
Sarna, Jonathan, 627–628, 631, 634, 649–651, 655
Sasson, R. Aaaron b. Joseph, 351
Saunders, David M., 69, 71
Scanlon, Thomas M., 342, 346
Schapiro, R. Hayyim Elazar, 252
Schepansky, Israel, 319, 321
Schick, R. Moses (*Maharam Schick*), 431
Schiffman, Daniel, 18, 182, 445, 448, 467, 573, 609, 617, 620, 622
Schiffman, Lawrence H., 23, 605, 607
Schleifer, Andrei, 313
Schmelkes, R. Isaac, 338, 365, 382
Schmelz, U.O., 631
Schmool, Marlena, 626
Schochetman, Eliav, 448
Schorr, R. Alexander, 200
Schreiber, R. Issachar Dov, 467
Schulze, William D., 390–391
Schumpeter, J.A., 107
Schwab, Robert M., 30
Schwartz, L., 107, 132
Scott, R.S. 117, 340, 346
Searle, John, 346
Sedei Hemed, see Medini, R. Hayyim Hezekiah
Sefer Agudah, see Zuslin, R.
Sefer ha-Hinnukh, 227, 240, 246, 431, 481
Sefer ha-Ikkarim, see Albo, R. Joseph
Sefer ha-Ittur, see Isaac b. Abba Mari of Marseilles, R.
Sefer ha-Terumot, see HaSardi, R. Shmuel
Sefer Hasidim, 234
Sefer Hemdat Yamim ha-Teimani, 60, 69
Sefer Mekah u-Mimkar, see Hai Gaon, R.
Sefer Mitsvot Gadol (Semag), see Moses of Coucy, R.
Sema, see Falk, R. Joshua b. Alexander ha-Kohen
Serkin, Christopher, 174
Sessions, George, 393
Sforno, R. Obadiah b. Jacob, 397, 566
Sha'ar Mishpat, see Wolf, Israel Isser b. Ze'ev
Sha'arei Hayyim, see Shmuelevitz, R. Hayyim
Sha'arei Tohar, see Volk, R. Shmuel Eliezer
Sha'arei Tziyon, see Sofer, R. Eliyahu Tziyon
Sha'arei Yosher, see Shkop, R. Shimon
Shabbetai b. Meir ha-Kohen, R. (*Shakh*), 147, 255, 259–260, 264, 351–353, 356, 378, 387, 439, 442, 484–485, 493
Shabbetai, R. Hayyim, 353
Shach, R. Elazar Menahem Man, 371, 533
Shakespeare, William, 224
Sharfman, Keith, 23, 168, 169, 173, 174, 175, 176, 178, 180, 181
Shatz, David, 335
Shavell, Steven, 30, 41, 146, 167
She'iltot, see Ahai Gaon, R.
Shell, G. Richard, 66, 67, 73
Shenei Luhot ha-Berit, see Horowitz, R. Isaiah (*Shlah*)
Sheskin, Ira M., 635
Shevet mi-Yehudah, see Unterman, R. Isser Yehuda
Shilo, R. Samuel, 365, 376–379, 383–384, 387
Shiltei ha-Gibborim, see Baruch, R. Joshua Boaz b. Simon
Shittah Mekubetzet, see Ashkenazi, R. Bezalel
Shkop, R. Shimon, 249
Shmuelevitz, R. Hayyim, 246
Shneur Zalman of Lyady, R, 259, 329, 485
Shochetman, Eliav, 359
Shohet, David M., 316, 325
Shoshanat ha-Amakim, see Zilberstein, R. Yitzchak
Shulhan Arukh ha-Rav, see Shneur Zalman of Lyady, R.
Shulhan Arukh, see Caro, R. Joseph
Shvadron, Shalom Mordechai, 207, 220, 345
Sifrei, 415
Siftei Kohen, see Shabbetai b. Meir ha-Kohen, R. (*Shakh*)
Silberg, Moshe, 358
Simpson, St. John, 550
Sirkes, R. Joel (*Bah*), 434
Sklare, Marshall, 628
Smith, Adam, 76, 116, 145, 292, 312, 390
Smith, Stephen, 346
Sofer, R. Abraham Samuel Benjamin Wolf, 414
Sofer, R. Eliyahu Tziyon, 245
Sofer, R. Moses, 200, 215, 220, 291, 292, 347, 353, 367–368, 382, 411, 416, 428, 435, 437, 449, 458, 463, 509, 581

Solomon b. Isaac, R. (*Rashi*), 46, 49–51, 55, 59, 64–66, 73, 91, 94, 97, 100, 102, 105, 117, 131, 183–187, 190, 193, 229, 233–234, 236, 242, 248, 249, 256–258, 261, 268, 276, 281, 287, 306, 315, 319, 349–351, 370, 376, 397, 399, 408, 431–432, 435–436, 443, 479, 481, 525, 532–533, 554–555, 566, 572, 576, 584, 586, 588, 610–611, 618, 619–620
Solomons, Adolphus, 629
Soloveitchik, Haym, 95, 597–598
Soloveitchik, R. Joseph, 378, 423
Solow, Robert M., 391–392
Somech, R. Ovadiah (Abdallah), 282
Sorotzkin, R. Avrohom Yitzhak, 49, 598
Spash, Clive L, 391
Spektor, R. Isaac Elhanan, 368
Srinivasan, K, 139–140
Stein, Roy, 450, 467
Steinberg, Avraham, 327, 329, 331, 334, 337, 339
Sternbuch, R. Moses, 206, 208, 220, 380, 455, 456, 457, 464, 465, 467
Stigler, G. J., 127, 132, 143–144
Stiglitz, Joseph E., 128, 145, 390, 391, 392
Strashun, Samuel b. Joseph (*Rashash*), 434
Sunstein, Cass R., 176
Sussman, Oren, 451
Syrquin, Moshe, 626
Szenberg, Michael, xxi, 23, 182

Talmon, S., 190
Tam, R. Jacob b. Meir (*Rabbeinu Tam*), 229–231, 255, 256, 257, 259, 261, 264, 344, 351, 377, 383, 435, 436, 438, 441, 572–573, 592
Tamari, Meir, xxii, 18, 118, 313, 468, 525
Targum Yerushalmi, 51
Tauber, R. Jehiel, 266–267
Teitelbaum, R. Joel, 378–379, 435
Tenenbaum, R. Malchiel, 353
Terumat ha-Deshen, see Isserlin, R. Moses b. Petahiah
Teshuvot Ivra, see Henkin, R. Joseph Eliyahu
Teshuvot ve-Hanhagot, see Sterbuch, R. Moses
Tevu'ot Shor, see Schorr, R. Alexander
Thaler, Richard, 68, 179
The Laws of Ribbis see Reisman, R. Yisroel
Tinic, Seha, 187
Tomes, Nigel, 626
Torah Shelemah, see Kasher, R. Menachem Mendel
Torah Temimah, see Epstein, R. Baruch ha-Levi
Torat ha-Refu'ah, see Goren, R. Shlomo
Torat Hayyim, see Shabtai, R. Chaim
Torat Kohanim, 407, 423, 424, 428, 431
Torat Moshe, see Sofer, R. Moses
Torat Mosheh, see Alshekh, R. Moses
Tosafot Yom Tov, see Heller, R. Yom Tov Lippman
Tosefet Berakhah, see Epstein, R. Baruch ha-Levi
Tosefta, 97, 105, 108, 112, 117, 118, 126, 150, 161, 167, 200, 275, 292, 431, 433, 441, 433–434, 439, 443, 507, 560, 561, 591, 599, 609, 612, 613, 614
Trani, R. Moses b. Joseph (Mabit), 351, 435, 596
Trump, Donald, 67
Trunk, R. Israel, 356
Tucker, Gene M., 394
Tumim, see Eybeschuetz, R. Jonathan
Tur, see b. Asher, R. Jacob (*Tur*)
Turei Zahav, see David b. Shmuel HaLevi, R. (*Taz*)
Tuv Ta'am va-Da'at, see Kluger, R. Solomon
Tversky, Amos, 68, 73

Unterman, R. Isser Yehuda, 332
Uzziel, R. Bentzion, 334, 442

Van Utt, Gretchen, 395, 403
Ve-Darashta Ve-Hakarta al ha-Torah, see Grossman, R. Aharon Yehudah
Vidal Yom Tov of Tolosa, R., 138, 250, 436
Vigoda, Michael, 328, 331
Vishny, Robert W., 313
Viswanath, P.V., 23, 182, 191, 193
Volk, R. Shmuel Eliezer, 246

Wachter, Michael, 175
Wagschal, S., 526
Wahrmann, R. Abraham, 256, 257, 353
Waldenberg, R. Eliezer, 331–333, 435
Warburg, Ronald, 15–16, 327, 331, 336–337, 339–340, 359
Watson, A., 121,
Watts, M., 82
Wechsler, H.S., 635
Weinfeld, M., 85–86
Weingarten, R. Yoav Yehoshua, 246
Weiser, Jonathan, 17, 388
Weiss, Avi, 22, 75, 87
Weiss, R. Asher, 243, 518
Weiss, R. Isaac Jacob, 215, 220, 368, 458, 467
Weisser, R. Meir Loeb b. Jehiel Michael (*Malbim*), 46, 49, 54
Wenz, Michael, 640–641
White, Lynn, 393, 396
Williams, Colin C., 394
Wistrich, Robert S., 639
Wittman, Donald, 176
Wolf, Israel Isser b. Ze'ev, 225
Wolowelsky, Joel, 335, 387
Wosner, R. Samuel, 267–268, 286, 355, 453, 456–457, 467

Yad Rama, see Abulafia, R. Meir
Yam Shel Shelomo, see Luria, R. Solomon (*Maharshal*)
Yavruv, R. Nahum, 60

Yehavveh Da'at, see Yosef, R. Ovadiah
Yehiel of Paris, R., 375
Yehuda'i Gaon, R., 586
Yeshu'ot Malko, see Trunk, R. Israel
Yisraeli, R. Shaul, 328, 332, 369, 371
Yosef Chaim of Baghdad, R., 282, 416
Yosef, R. Ovadiah, 327, 368, 370, 377, 379, 436
Young, Warren, 450

Zak, Paul J., 309
Zeira, Joseph, 452
Zelder, Martin, 174
Zera Avraham, see Kahana-Shapiro, R. Abraham Dov Ber
Zerahia Halevi, R., 440
Zevin, R. Solomon Joseph, 200, 328, 373
Zilberstein, R. Yitzchak, 330, 332, 334, 337
Zimmer, Eric, 316
Zivhei Tzedek, see Somech, R. Ovadiah (Abdallah)
Zoislin, R. Alexandri, 439
Zuslin, R., 231

Subject Index

Abetting, see *Lifne iver.*
Ability to pay approach, see Taxation.
Accountability, 272–279
Acquisition, see *Kinyan.*
  Administrative costs, 162, 167, 175–178
Agent, see *Shelihut*
Amortization, 217, 405–408
Akhsanya, see also Billeting, 117
allocation of resources, 75–78
'Ani hamehapekh behararah, see also Interloper
  and automobile case, 263–266
  and courtship case, 256
  and discounted item case, 259–260
  and fair competition, 257–258
  and financial means of parties, 261
  and organized marketplace, 258–259
  compounded case, 262–263
  designation as wicked person, 255–256
  dispute between *Rashi* and R. Tam, 256–258
  judicial relief in, 255
  life insurance case, 263
  real estate case of, 265
  recent rabbinical ruling in, 263–268
  seller's preference, 261–262
  stage of negotiations, 258–259
  tutor case, 261
  unintentional intrusion, 260
Anthropocentric, 389–394
Antitrust, see also Monopoly, 75, 180
Anti-Semitism, 384, 634, 646, 660
Acquisition, see *Kinyan*
Agrarian society, 77, 81, 198, 401
Apotrops, 192
Appraisal, 170–181, 417, 424
Appreciated value, 208, 217
Arbitration, 175–176, 213, 314–315, 536
Arev,
  Arev kabbelan, 528–535
  Arev shilof dots, 530, 534
  Arev stam, 528–530, 533, 537
  disciplinary context, 524–525
  economic value, 525–526
  relevant expressions, 531
  under English law, 535–541
Asimon, 582
Asmakhta, 439, 529
Assyrian Code, See Law
Asymmetric information, 316–322
Auction, 179
Avak ribbit, 91–105, 241, 482
  se'ah be'seah, 446–447
  yatza hasha'ar, 446–447, 453–459, 489, 496
  yesh lo, 447, 453–456, 459, 489–490, 496

Banks, 181, 215, 310, 404, 418, 420, 436, 450, 451, 452, 455, 456, 466, 533, 535
Bargaining, 66–71, 176, 430, 433, 594
Barter, 135, 136, 507, 552, 574–576, 606, 607, 608, 609, 614, 618, 620
Benefit principle, see Taxation
Benin Dikhrin, 590–591
Billeting (*akhsanya*), 115–117, 129, 124
Billings Report, 630–631
Bimetallic Standard, see Coins
Blood, donation of, 324, 325, 326, 332, 333
Body, ownership of, 331–332
Bone marrow, donation of, 332–333
Branding, 311, 320
Bretton Woods Conference, 580
Bribery, see *Shohad*

Cadaver, compensation for donation from, 328–329
Cairo *Genizah*, 587, 590, 591, 601, 604
Calendar, Jewish, 188–190
Capital, 95–97, 102, 197, 201, 203–208, 210, 213–214, 217, 243, 272, 299, 317, 391–392, 412, 414, 419, 470, 483, 600, 645, 654, 656, 658, 659, 661, 663
Capital gain, 114–115, 120
Capital Reserves, 181
Care,
  bilateral care, 157–161
  differential care, 163–166
  due care, 149–151
  efficient care, 151–154
  marginal benefit of care, 155
  marginal cost of care, 155
  proper care, 149–151
  unilateral care, 152–160
Categories of damage (*avoth nezikin*), 163
Cave of Makhpela, 566–568
Charade, 200
Charitable Loans, see Loans
Charity, 201, 227–228, 234, 243, 270, 273, 276–279, 286–287, 290–294, 416, 423, 473, 481
  Dei mahsoro, 423
  kuppah, 423
  tamhui, 423

Civil law, 110–111, 148, 240–242, 249–250, 500, 509–510, 516–521, 540
Clean slate, 85–86
Coase Theorem, 109, 111, 148
Co-extensiveness, see Guarantor
Coins, 93, 446–449, 453–457, 565–584, 609–622
  coin clipping, 621–622
  bimetallic standard, 577, 607, 616, 622
Collateral, see Loan
Commenda, 95–97
Commercial practice, see *Minhag ha-soharim*
Commercial transactions, 344–352
Commodity, 567–568, 575–576, 607–622
Commodity loans, see Loans
Communal ban, 354
Communal decrees/legislation/ordinances, 435, 437, 439, 592
Condition, see *Tenai*
Conflict(s) of interest, 178, 276–279, 417–418, 424
Congress, 379, 417, 442, 488, 490, 491, 494
Consecrated property, 171–173, 178–179
Consumer behavior, 127–142
  confidence building mechanism, 309–313
  credence good, 137–138, 320–321
  experience good, 138
  search good, 137, 138
  search for price, 144
  trust-replacing mechanisms, 310
Consumer Price Index, 445–446, 451–466
Contingent claim, 523–525
Contract, 91–105, 169, 170–171, 172, 174–176, 183, 191, 192, 200, 210–212, 215, 218, 244, 267, 308, 312, 313, 316–317, 328–329, 340–348, 352–353, 359, 375–377, 413, 432, 438, 440, 450, 484, 493–496, 501, 505–509, 511–515, 518–521, 537–541, 552–553, 561, 584–604, 607–608
  theory, 99–100, 377
  linear, 96–100, 104
  nonlinear, 100, 104
Copyright, 381–383,
Corporate Debt, see Debt
Cost,
  opportunity cost, 25, 459, 463, 465, 492, 647, 650, 651, 652, 653, 654, 657, 661
  private, 109, 111
  social, 156, 166,
  transactions costs, 128, 133, 140, 175, 178, 182, 421, 525, 578–579
Cost-benefit analysis, 391
Craftsmen, 206, 433, 440
Crawling Peg, 450–451, 461, 465
Creating a false impression, see *Geneivat da'at*
Credence goods, see Consumer behavior
Credit history, 310, 408–409
Credit-rating agencies, 310–311, 411–413, 417–418, 424, 426
Criminal law, 146, 241, 315–316, 338, 370
Culpability, 110, 120–121, 124, 317
Currency,
  and depreciation, 449, 450, 461, 463–464
  and devaluation, 450–466, 577–578
  and exchange controls, 451–452, 455–457
  and exchange rates, 451, 457–461, 466
  as a commodity, 618–620
  dinar, 570–572, 578–579, 587, 588, 593, 600
  dinarius, 617, 621
  drachma, 572, 580
  fixed value, 616–618
  maneh, 192, 569
  metal standard, 613–616
  nature of, 609–611
  primitive money, 565–570
  relative values, 611, 612, 614
  zuz, 185, 192, 572, 579–581
Custom (*minhag*), 547, 548, 555
Customers, 139, 258, 288, 310–312, 413, 496
Customer list, 353
Customer relationship, 310
Customer service, 311

Damages
  consequential damages, 347, 352
  liquidated damages, 170, 351–352
  penalty damages, 253, 352
  remote damages, 353
  tort damages, 168, 353–354
Damage by Fire,
  basic laws, 147–148
  bilateral care, 157–161
  differential care, 163–164
  due care, 149–151
  efficient care, 151–152
  marginal benefit of care, 155
  marginal cost of care, 155
  proper care, 149–151
  R. Shimon's view, 161–162
  tamun rule, 162–166
  unilateral care, 152–156
Darkhei shalom, 57–63, 69, 70, 72, 281–282
Davar shein bo mamash, 517–519
Davar she-lo ba l'olam, 344, 519
Davar she-lo ba lirshuto, 517, 519
Davar she ein ba mamash, 353, 517, 518, 519
Debt/Debtor,
  changes in law, 371–379
  corporate debt, 235–236, 379–382
  developments and changes in retrieval law, 228–232
  enslavement of debtor, 222–223
  ethical underpinnings of Jewish approach, 226–228
  in ancient world, 222–224
  in Jewish law, 225,
  paradigm for changes in retrieval law, 232–235
Default, 216–217, 235, 406, 408–414, 421–422, 427, 524, 529, 531–532, 534–537, 540
Dei mahsoro, see Charity
Democracy, 364, 379, 385, 646
Depreciation, see Currency
Deterrent, 320–321, 352

Devaluation, see Currency
Dillingham Commission Report, 638
Diminishing marginal benefit, 155
Diminshing returns, Law of, 178
Dina de-malkhuta dina, 9, 10, 11, 13, 14, 16, 20, 21, 337–339, 365, 367, 370–371, 376, 377, 378, 379, 380, 382, 383, 384, 385, 387, 388, 442, 508, 562, 577
Dina d'malkhuta dina, see *Dina de-malkhuta dina*
Dinar, see currency,
Dinei Shamayim, 352
Disclosure duty, 54–55, 407–408, 411
Disgorgement, 352, 355, 356, 357, 359
Divine Providence, 52–53, 67
Dollarization, 445, 452–457
Dowry, 579, 588–593, 603
Due diligence, 342, 410, 426
Duress, 288, 350
Duty,
  Reliance based, 346
  Reliance induced, 348

E-Commerce, 499–521
Economic analysis of law, 146, 148,
Economic welfare, 349
Economics of information, 127–128, 144–145
Efficiency, see also Care, Efficient breach,
  and the Jubilee, 74–87
  and the *tamun* rule, 164–166
  behavior, 148–149, 151, 159, 176
  economic exchange, 343
  Kaldor-Hicks compensation principle, 341
  Pareto Optimailty, 390
  system of interaction, 343
  theorists, 342
Efficient Breach, 340–357
Eliezer, 42–72
  agency role, 43–47
  dealmaking, 66–67
  duty to disclose, 54–56
  ethical considerations, 43–47
  test at the well, 47–52
Employee Free Choice Act, 429
Employer-Worker Relations, 353–357, 373, 429–433, 474–475
Employment Agreement, 349–356
Enabling, see *Lifne iver*,
Endowment effect, 179, 180
Enforcement mechanisms, 320
Enforceability, 213, 220, 344–345
Entitlement, 168, 173, 180, 257, 262, 340, 349, 356
Evidence,
  rules of in Jewish law, 29, 171, 175
Environmentalism, 388–402
Equality, 74, 78, 383–386
Equity (fairness), 389, 391, 430
Equity (stock or security representing ownership), 95–96, 101–104, 409, 410, 419, 450, 456, 457, 539, 540
Erekh vows, see Vows
Expectancy interest, 352–353

Experience goods, see Consumer behavior
Expert witnesses, 209
Externalities,
  Negative, 108–112
  Positive, 108–112
  Public goods and regulation, 112–112
  Talmud's view, 110–111

Factors of production, 78
Fair competition, 257
False weights and measures, 47, 405, 471
Fiat money, 449–450
Fiduciary obligation, see Obligation.
Fines, 29–41, 172,
First Commonwealth, 565
First-born, 318
Force majeure (oness), 98, 147
Foreclosure, 215–216
Fraud, 129–144, 210, 212, 215, 318–320, 412–414, 417, 470–472, 621–622

Gemilut Hessed, 354, 481
Gemirat Da'at, 344, 439
Geneivat Da'at, 288, 407
Gezel mi-divrehem, 262–263
Giv'onim, 365–366
Global Recession of 2007–2009, 404–427
Gold, 453–454, 456, 489, 490, 566–577, 606–618
Gold/silver ratio, 568–570, 573
Good Faith imperative, see *Hin Tzedek*.
Government, 78, 110, 124, 273, 287, 298, 309, 311, 337–338, 371–372, 377–379, 383–385, 391, 404, 415–417, 420–427, 442–445, 450–454, 461–467, 491, 539, 553, 556, 558, 614, 615, 616, 618, 619, 620
Guarantee, see *Arev*,
Guarantor, see also *Arev*,
  coextensiveness, 541
  marshalling, 541
  subrogation, 538–541
Guardianship, see *Arev*

Ha'aramah, see *Hetter Iska*
Hair, sale of, 326, 332
Half loan, half deposit, see *Iska*.
Ha-motzi me-chaveiro alov ha-rei'ya, 246
Hasagat gevul, 257–258
Fair competition, see *Hasagat Gevul*
Financial governance, 269–279
Ha'aramah, 198–199
Havalah, 239, 331
Heal, obligation to, 234
Hefker bet din, 377
Hetter iska, 197–220, 253, 450, 454–457, 459, 466, 598–602
Hexaplex Trunculus, see *Tekheilet*
Hin tzedek, 46–47, 405
Hofheldian, 358
Housing bubble, 419–421, 424

Imitatio Dei, 415–422, 427
Immigrants, 627–661
In Terrorem effect, 352
Incentives, 29, 30, 37, 41, 79, 91–105, 123–124, 148, 154, 157, 166, 190, 335, 398, 427, 480, 598, 603, 640, 641, 643, 644–645, 647, 652, 653, 662
Income tax, 416, 421, 491, 494
  interest deduction, 218
Indemnity, 534–535, 540
Indexation, 445–446, 450, 452, 454–457, 458–465, 466
Individual liberties, 343
Induced reliance, 346–348
Inflation, 92–93, 421–424, 445–466, 484, 490–491, 566, 571,
  Israeli inflation crisis, 450–453
Information asymmetry, 132, 138, 182–183, 187–193
Injustice, 383, 470
Institutional moral norm, 346
Interest prohibition-biblical, See *Ribbit ketzuzah.*
Interest prohibition-rabbinic, *Avak ribbit,*
Interloper, see also *'Ani hamehapekh behararah,* 263–265, 349–350, 556–557
Internal Revenue Service, 218
International law, see Law
IPOs, 183, 184
Israeli army, 30
Investment, 76, 79, 96, 100, 197, 201–216, 235–236, 244, 269, 309, 317, 381, 406, 409–420, 450, 471–474, 496, 515, 591, 600–604, 651, 654, 663
  Prudence, 204, 270–275, 279, 293
  Socially responsible, 279–293
  Transparency, 274, 277–279

Jewish education, 648, 651, 654–657, 660–662
Jewish immigration, 625–630, 640–642
Joint venture, 94–96, 100–101, 176, 177, 179, 203, 208–210
Jubilee, 74–86
Judges, 170–192, 232, 290, 314–315, 320–322, 326–327, 367, 381, 463–464, 509, 529, 538, 553, 582, 586, 634
  bias, 179, 321
  compensation, 326–327
  majority rule, 171, 175–177,
  multimember, 175–177
Justice, 74, 119, 120, 148, 295, 312, 314, 320, 321, 322, 364, 367, 368, 370, 372, 386, 387, 389, 391, 398, 468, 470, 472, 473, 475

Kabbelan, 528–535
Kaldor-Hicks Compensation doctrine, see Efficiency
Kantian principles, 345
Ketubbah, 579–581
King, 85, 86, 373, 377, 379, 449, 450, 464, 555
Kinyan, 200, 257, 336, 344–352. 374–375, 438–440, 507–509, 516–519 529, 576, 577, 592
  asmakhta, 439, 529
  situmta, 507–510, 516–522
  sudar, 575, 576, 577

Kuppah, see Charity

Labor Unions, 429–443
Land,
  appraisement of, 192
  price seasonality, 183–190
  productivity of, 187
Law, see also Civil law, Criminal law
  Assyrian Code, 222
  English law, 523–525, 528, 535, 537–542
  Hammurabian, 222
  Hittite, 222
  Natural law, 201, 345–346
  Nuzi, 222
  right-based system, 358
  Roman, 121–123, 224–225, 553, 609
  Sasanian Law, 544, 546, 547, 549, 553, 554, 555, 556, 557, 558, 560, 561, 562, 563
  Sumerian, 85
  Theodosian Code, 116, 126
  world/international, 363–386
Leasehold, 217, 219
Legal fictions, 198, 204, 493
Le-tikkunei shedartikha ve-lo le-ivutei / le-takkonei shaddartikh, 64–65, 74–75
Leverage,
  negative, 67–71
  normative, 67, 72
  positive, 67–68
Levites, 199
Lex Rhodia de Iactu, 121
Lex Mercatoria, 372
Liability, 151–166, 171–172, 176, 205, 210, 235, 347–348, 357, 413–414, 511, 525–542
Liberty, 79–80, 85–86, 229, 288, 342
Lifnei iver, 407
Liquidity, 187, 193, 235, 271–274, 279, 308, 417, 419, 450, 473, 611
Loans, 75, 80, 81, 82, 83, 84, 92–95, 197–220, 221–237, 242–244, 252–253, 445–464, 473, 479–497, 536, 586, 596–597, 604, 618–619,
  charity loans, 226–228, 454, 526–527
  collateral, 80–84, 213, 222–225, 229–230
  commodity loans, 252, 446–447, 453–455, 463, 482, 488–490, 495–496
  mortgage loans, 215–220, 404–427
Lydda, 130–134, 139, 144

Majority rule, 171, 173, 176–177, 434
Managers, 191, 292, 309, 633, 637, 646
Manipulation, 308, 312, 342, 577
Marginalist revolution, 120
Marital Engagements, 352
Mariage Contract, see *Ketubbah*
Marufia, 443
Marshalling, see Guarantor
Mehusar amanah, 345
Mekah ta'ut, 46, 414
Minhag ha-soharim, 370–375, 385–386

Mitzvah, payment for performance of, 326–328
Monopoly/ Monopolies, 75–77, 81, 434, 441
  concentration of factors of production, 76–77, 78, 81, 86
Morality, 235, 242, 253, 342–344, 468–470
  utilitarian moral philosophy, 390
Moral education, 424–425, 476
Mortgage broker, 215, 407–408
Mortgage loans, see Loans
Movable property, 349, 607, 614

Natural law, see Law
Negligence, 151, 159–161, 165, 166
Negotiations, 42–71
Neoclassical welfare economics, 389–392
Noahide, 368–371, 376–377, 380, 387, 472
Non-Jew, 8–14, 199, 200, 215, 275, 282, 283, 292, 367, 368, 369, 371, 373, 380, 384, 526, 327, 450, 531, 532, 533, 546, 551, 552, 553, 559, 586, 588, 590, 602
Noncompliance, 343, 351–352
Nonperformance, 352, 355, 413, 539

Oath, 205–209, 228, 230, 234, 278, 430, 436–437, 450, 585, 587, 589, 601, 602
Obligations, 171–173, 217, 273, 288–290, 331, 343–352, 368, 374–376, 388, 405, 430, 469, 471, 474, 481, 486, 502, 507, 509, 536, 556, 578, 579
Omer Sacrifice, 188
On- the- job training, 353
Ona'ah, 22, 45–46, 65–66, 144–145, 256, 288, 406–407
Opportunity cost, see Cost
Option, 405, 412, 418, 524, 525, 526
Orange County, 273
Organ donation,
  altruism, 334–335
  broker fee, 332
  cadaveric donation, 331–332
  cadaveric donation, 331–332
  compensation for, 326–327
  exploitation of poor, 336–337
  for research, 334
  halakhic precedent, 326
  nature of transaction, 336
  non-vital organs, 332–333
  public policy, 337
  tikkun olam, 335
Overbidder paradigm, 343, 349, 350
Overcharge, see *Ona'ah*

Panels,
  arbitration, 175–176
  multimember, 175–177
  valuation, 171–173, 181
Pardon, 29–41
Pareto Optimality, see Efficiency
Passover, 188–200, 423
Partis Secanto, 224
Pecuniary loss, 347
Periodic profits, 204
Peddlers, 628, 630, 645, 648
Permissible venture, see *Hetter iska*
Peshara, 315
Physician, payment of, 324–327
Po'el, 438
Pornography, 288, 343
Poverty, see also Charity, 233, 271, 336–337, 423–424, 427, 468–469, 473, 475, 650, 661
  Poor tithe, 185
  Preventing, 423–424
Power of Attorney, 603–604
Precautions, 146–167
Preventative Measures, 416, 422
Price
  cum-dividend, 185–186
  dispersion, 127–128, 131–132
  equilibrium, 127, 133, 139, 141–144
  ex-Dividend, 185
  fair, 169
  redemption, 168, 173, 179
Price fraud, see *Ona'ah*
Privacy, 354–355, 511
Profit sharing, 357
Profit and loss allocations, 91–92
Promise, 47, 62, 227, 341–352, 355, 359, 405, 536, 584, 646
Proprietary right, 355–357
Prudence, 45, 204, 270–275, 279, 293
Public Goods, see also Externalities, 107–125
  exclusion principle, 109, 111, 117
Public finance, 111–117
Purchasing Power Parity (PPP), 460

Quasi-theft, 356

Real estate, 46, 114, 171, 178, 216–217, 260, 265, 308, 459, 526, 551, 562, 567, 573, 607
Real property, 171–173, 202, 215, 219, 349, 553, 608–609
Redemption, 79–83, 168–173, 179, 573
Regulation, 75, 111–112, 140, 152, 241–242, 247, 252, 311–312, 337, 417, 441–442, 476, 512,
Reliance duty, 346, 348
Remedy before the affliction, 421–422
Rent, 181, 216–218, 260–262, 264, 357, 385, 598
Rescission remedy, 169, 170
Reward, 30, 278, 336
Ribbit de-rabbanan, see *Avak ribbit*
Ribbit ketzuzah, 93–105, 239–254, 455–464, 480–496, 579
Right-based system, see Law
Risk, 46–53, 68, 71, 72, 100, 91–121, 151, 165, 154–155, 177–178 , 328, 406–427, 456, 491, 502–505, 525–527, 595, 599, 600
  aversion, 91, 99–100, 104, 309
  calculated, 48, 53
  neutral, 31–32, 38
  unnecessary, 46–48, 53

Robbery, 172,

Sabbath, 274, 292, 327, 335, 406, 431, 472, 649
Sasanian Law, see Law
Saving life, 331–335
Search goods, see Consumer behavior
Second Temple, 316, 566, 571, 586, 591, 605, 607
Second Tithe, 171–172, 178, 582–583
Securities market, 208, 308
Self- wounding, see *Havalah.*
Self-employment, 638–639, 643, 645
Self-endangerment, 329–331
Self-interest, 70, 204, 300, 304, 318, 349, 390, 429, 468
Sephardic Jews, 627, 629, 630, 631
Shirking, 91, 99–105
Shi'bud nechasim, 351
Shohad, 411
Situmta, see *Kinyan.*
Slavery, 74–87, 222–226, 230, 233–234,
Social convention, 345, 346
Social welfare, 167, 338, 390, 423, 442
Statute of limitations, 213
Specific performance, 350–352
Stewardship, see *Apotropos*
Subrogation, see Guarantor
Subterfuge, 198–208, 288, 318
Sudar, see *Kinyan*
Surety relationship, see *Arev*
Surety, see *Arev.*
Sustainability, 388–392, 400, 402
Sustainable development, 388–394

Tangibility, 353
Tanning, 111
Tamhui, see Charity
Taxation, 108, 113–114, 119, 121, 198, 384, 472, 480, 487, 557, 562
- allocation of fee for caravan guide, 117–120
- double taxation, 434
- benefit principle, 115, 118, 124
- federal taxation, 482
- financing of town wall, 112–116
- income tax, 416, 421, 491, 494
- Pigovian, 119, 121
- poll, 114, 125
- Temple tax, 125, 571
- window tax, 116

Technological process, 353
Tekheilet, 318, 320
Temple Treasury, 170, 173, 179–181
Tenai, 350
Theft, 29–41
Theodosian Code, see Law
Theory of promissory obligation, 345
Tikkun olam, 335
Title, 199, 200, 216–218, 267, 344, 374–375, 496, 508, 515, 555, 574–576
Tort, 108, 110, 146–147, 168–174, 199, 348, 353–354, 464
Townspeople, powers of, 434–437
Trade secret, 353–357
Tradesmen, powers of, 437–441
Trading volume, 182, 193
Traditio, 554
Transaction costs, see Costs
Transparency, 277–279, 287, 417
Treaty, 365–367, 372, 379, 381, 385
Tribunals, 172
Trust, 205, 234, 269, 272, 278, 290, 307–322, 343, 345, 364, 426
Trust-replacing mechanisms, see Consumer behavior

Ugarit, 222, 568, 584
United States, 311, 325, 365, 375, 379, 385, 445, 461, 483, 500, 520–521, 581, 626–663
Unions, 429–443
Unjust enrichment, 355, 359
Usury, see *Ribbit ketzutah* and *Avak ribbit,*

Valuation, 168–181, 448, 575, 581–582, 616–623
Voluntary obligations, 343–345
Vows, 170–173
- *erekh* vows, 170

War, 290, 367–372, 437, 464
Warranties, 311
Wealth, 50–51, 63–64, 66, 68–69, 113, 115–117, 226, 313, 342, 468–470, 472, 474, 626, 627, 642–645
Wealth distribution, 226
Wealth improvement, 113
Wealth maximization, 342
Windfall profit, 350
Witnesses, 29, 44–45, 162, 205–206, 209–213, 241, 274–275, 281, 317, 408, 550, 552, 601
Worker,
- paid on per hour basis, see *Po'el*
- paid for finished work, see *Kabbelan*

World law, see Law

Zeh nehene ve-zeh haser hayyav, see also Unjust enrichment, 356